FEMINISM IN LITERATURE

A Gale Critical Companion

GALE CRITICAL COMPANION ADVISORY BOARD

FEMINISM IN LITERATURE

A Gale Critical Companion

Volume 1: Antiquity–18th Century, Topics & Authors

Foreword by *Amy Hudock, Ph.D.*
University of South Carolina

Jessica Bomarito, Jeffrey W. Hunter, Project Editors

THOMSON GALE

Detroit • New York • San Francisco • San Diego • New Haven, Conn. • Waterville, Maine • London • Munich

THOMSON
GALE

Feminism in Literature, Vol. 1

Project Editors
Jessica Bomarito, Jeffrey W. Hunter

Editorial
Tom Burns, Jenny Cromie, Kathy D. Darrow, Michelle Kazensky, Jelena O. Krstović, Michael L. LaBlanc, Julie Landelius, Michelle Lee, Allison McClintic Marion, Ellen McGeagh, Joseph Palmisano, Linda Pavlovski, James E. Person Jr., Thomas J. Schoenberg, Marie Toft, Lawrence J. Trudeau, Russel Whitaker

Indexing Services
Synapse, the Knowledge Link Corporation

Permissions
Emma Hull, Lori Hines, Shalice Shah-Caldwell

Imaging and Multimedia
Lezlie Light, Daniel Newell, Kelly A. Quin

Product Design
Michael Logusz, Pamela Galbreath

Composition and Electronic Capture
Carolyn Roney

Manufacturing
Rhonda Williams

Product Manager
Janet Witalec

For more information, contact
Thomson Gale
27500 Drake Rd.
Farmington Hills, MI 48331-3535
Or you can visit our internet site at
http://www.gale.com

LIBRARY OF CONGRESS CATALOGING-IN-PUBLICATION DATA

Feminism in literature : a Gale critical companion / foreword by Amy Hudock ; Jessica Bomarito, project editor, Jeffrey W. Hunter, project editor.
p. cm. -- (Gale critical companion collection)
Includes bibliographical references and index.
ISBN 0-7876-7573-3 (set hardcover : alk. paper) -- ISBN 0-7876-7574-1 (vol 1) -- ISBN 0-7876-7575-X (vol 2) -- ISBN 0-7876-7576-8 (vol 3) -- ISBN 0-7876-9115-1 (vol 4) -- ISBN 0-7876-9116-X (vol 5) -- ISBN 0-7876-9065-1 (vol 6)
1. Literature--Women authors--History and criticism. 2. Women authors--Biography. 3. Women--History. I. Bomarito, Jessica, 1975- II. Hunter, Jeffrey W., 1966- III. Series.
PN471.F43 2005
809'.89287--dc22
2004017989

Printed in the United States of America
10 9 8 7 6 5 4 3 2

CONTENTS

VOLUME 2

VOLUME 3

VOLUME 4

VOLUME 5

VOLUME 6

FOREWORD

When I was a girl, I would go to the library with my class, and all the girls would run to the Nancy Drew books, while the boys would head toward the Hardy Boys books—each group drawn to heroes that resembled themselves. Yet, when I entered formal literary studies in high school and college, I was told that I should not read so much in the girls' section any more, that the boys' section held books that were more literary, more universal, and more valuable. Teachers and professors told me this in such seemingly objective language that I never questioned it. At the time, the literary canon was built on a model of scarcity that claimed that only a few literary works could attain "greatness"—defined according to a supposed objective set of aesthetic criteria that more often than not excluded women authors. New Criticism, a way of reading texts that focuses on a poem, short story, or novel as an autonomous artistic production without connections to the historical and social conditions out of which it came, ruled my classrooms, making the author's gender ostensibly irrelevant. Masculine experience was coded as universal, while women's experience was particular. Overall, I had no reason to question the values I had been taught, until I encountered feminism.

Feminism, sometimes put in the plural *feminisms*, is a loose confederation of social, political, spiritual, and intellectual movements that places women and gender at the center of inquiry with the goal of social justice. When people in the United States speak of feminism, they are often referring to the mainstream liberal feminism that grew out of the relationship between grassroots civil rights movements of the 1960s and 1970s and these movements' entrance into the academy through the creation of Women's Studies as an interdisciplinary program of study in many colleges and universities. Mainstream liberal feminism helped many women achieve more equity in pay and access to a wider range of careers while it also transformed many academic disciplines to reflect women's achievements. However, liberal feminism quickly came under attack as largely a movement of white, heterosexual, university-educated, middle-class women who were simply trying to gain access to the same privileges that white, middle-class men enjoyed, and who assumed their experiences were the norm for a mythical universal "woman." Liberal feminists have also been critiqued for echoing the patriarchal devaluation of traditional women's nurturing work in their efforts to encourage women to pursue traditional men's work, for creating a false opposition between work and home, and for creating the superwoman stereotype that can cause women to believe they have failed if they do not achieve the perfect balance of work and home lives. Other feminisms developed representing other women and other modes of thought: Marxist, psychoanalytic, social/radical, lesbian, trans- and bi-sexual, black womanist, first nations, chicana, nonwestern, postcolonial, and approaches that even question the use of "woman" as a unifying signifier in the first place. As Women's Studies and these many feminims gained power and credibility in the academy, their presence forced the literary establishment to question its methodology, definitions, structures, philosophies, aesthetics, and visions as well at to alter the curriculum to reflect women's achievements.

Once I learned from Women's Studies that women mattered in the academy, I began exploring women in my own field of literary studies. Since male-authored texts were often the only works taught in my classes, I began to explore the images of women as constructed by male authors. Many other women writers also began their critique of women's place in society studying similar sites of representation. Mary Wollstonecraft's *A Vindication of the Rights of Women* (1792), Margaret Fuller's *Woman in the Nineteenth Century* (1845), Simone de Beauvoir's *The Second Sex* (1949), and Kate Millet's *Sexual Politics* (1969) explored how published images of women can serve as a means of social manipulation and control—a type of gender propaganda.

However, I began to find, as did others, that looking at women largely through male eyes did not do enough to reclaim women's voices and did not recognize women's agency in creating images of themselves. In *Sexual/Textual Politics* (1985), Toril Moi further questioned the limited natures of these early critical readings, even when including both male and female authors. She argued that reading literature for the accuracy of images of women led critics into assuming their own sense of reality as universal: "If the women in the book feel real to me, then the book is good." This kind of criticism never develops or changes, she argued, because it looks for the same elements repetitively, just in new texts. Also, she was disturbed by its focus on content rather than on how the text is written—the form, language, and literary elements. Moi and others argued for the development of new feminist critical methods.

However, examination of images of women over time has been fruitful. It has shown us that representation of women changes as historical forces change, that we must examine the historical influences on the creators of literary texts to understand the images they manufacture, and that we cannot assume that these images of women are universal and somehow separate from political and culture forces. These early explorations of woman as image also led to discussions of femininity as image, not biologically but culturally defined, thus allowing analysis of the feminine ideal as separate from real women. This separation of biological sex and socially constructed gender laid the foundation for the later work of Judith Butler in *Gender Trouble: Feminism and the Subversion of Identity* (1990) and Marjorie Garber's *Vested Interests: Cross Dressing and Cultural Anxiety* (1992) in questioning what IS this thing we call "woman." These critics argued that gender is a social construct, a performance that can be learned by people who are biologically male, female, or transgendered, and therefore should not be used as the only essential connecting element in feminist studies. The study of woman and gender as image then has contributed much to feminist literary studies.

Tired of reading almost exclusively texts by men and a small emerging canon of women writers, I wanted to expand my understanding of writing by women. As a new Ph. D. student at the University of South Carolina in 1989, I walked up the stairs into the Women's Studies program and asked the first person I saw one question: were there any nineteenth-century American women writers who are worth reading? I had recently been told there were not, but I was no longer satisfied with this answer. And I found I was right to be skeptical. The woman I met at the top of those stairs handed me a thick book and said, "Go home and read this. Then you tell me if there were any nineteenth-century American women writers who are worth reading." So, I did. The book was the *Norton Anthology of Literature by Women* (1985), and once I had read it, I came back to the office at the top of the stairs and asked, "What more do you have?" My search for literary women began here, and this journey into new terrain parallels the development of the relationship between western feminism and literary studies.

In *A Room of Her Own* (1929), Virginia Woolf asks the same questions. She sits, looking at her bookshelves, thinking about the women writers who are there, and the ones who are not, and she calls for a reclaiming and celebrating of lost women artists. Other writers answered her call. Patricia Meyer Spacks's *The Female Imagination: A Literary and Psychological Investigation of Women's Writing* (1972), Ellen Moers's *Literary Women: The Great Writers* (1976), Elaine Showalter's *A Literature of Their Own: British Women Novelists from Brontë to Lessing* (1977), and Sandra Gilbert and Susan Gubar's *The Madwoman in the Attic* (1979) are a few of the early critical studies that explored the possibility of a tradition in women's literature.

While each of these influential and important books has different goals, methods, and theories, they share the attempt to establish a tradition in women's literature, a vital means through which marginalized groups establish a community identity and move from invisibility to visibility. These literary scholars and others worked to republish and reclaim women authors, expanding the number and types of women-authored texts available to readers, students, and scholars.

Yet, I began to notice that tradition formation presented some problems. As Marjorie Stone pointed out in her essay "The Search for a Lost Atlantis" (2003), the search for women's traditions in language and literature has been envisioned as the quest for a lost continent, a mythical motherland, similar to the lost but hopefully recoverable Atlantis. Such a quest tends to search for similarities among writers to attempt to prove the tradition existed, but this can sometimes obscure the differences among women writers. Looking to establish a tradition can also shape what is actually "found": only texts that fit that tradition. Traditions are defined by what is left in and what is left out, and the grand narratives of tradition formation as constructed in the early phases of feminist literary criticism inadvertently mirrored the exclusionary structures of the canon they were revising.

Some critics began discussing a women's tradition, a lost motherland of language, in not only what was written but also how it was written: in a female language or *ecriture feminine*. Feminist thinkers writing in France such as Héléne Cixous, Julia Kristeva, and Luce Irigaray argued that gender shapes language and that language shapes gender. Basing their ideas on those of psychoanalyst Jacques Lacan, they argued that pre-oedipal language—the original mother language—was lost when the law and language of the fathers asserted itself. While each of these writers explored this language differently, they all rewrote and revisioned how we might talk about literature, thus offering us new models for scholarship. However, as Alicia Ostriker argued in her essay, "Notes on 'Listen'" (2003), for the most part, women teach children language at home and at school. So, she questioned, is language really male and the "the language of the father," or is it the formal discourse of the academy that is male? Ostriker and others question the primacy of the father as the main social/language influence in these discussions. Other critics attacked what came to be known as "French Feminism" for its ahistorical, essentializing approach to finding a women's tradition in language. Despite its problems, it offered much to the general understanding of gender and language and helped us imagine new possible forms for scholarship.

The idea that language might be gendered itself raised questions about how aesthetic judgement, defined in language, might also be gendered. Problems with how to judge what is "good" literature also arose, and feminist literary critics were accused of imposing a limited standard because much of what was being recovered looked the same in form as the traditional male canon, only written by women. Early recovered texts tended to highlight women in opposition to family, holding more modern liberal political views, and living nontraditional lives. If a text was "feminist" enough, it was included. Often times, this approach valued content over form, and the forms that were included did not differ much from the canon they were reacting against. These critics were still using the model of scarcity with a similar set of critical lens through which to judge texts worthy of inclusion. However, because later scholars started creating different critical lenses through which to view texts does not mean we need to perceive difference as inequality. Rather, texts that differ greatly began to be valued equally for different reasons. In order to do this, critics had to forfeit their tendency to place literary forms on a hierarchical model that allows only one at the apex. Instead, they exchanged the structure of value from one pyramid with a few writers at the apex for one with multiple high points, a model which celebrates a diversity of voices, styles, and forms. The model functioning in many past critical dialogues allowed for little diversity, privileging one type of literature—western, male, linear, logical, structured according to an accepted formula—over others—created by women and men who fail to fit the formula, and, thus, are judged not worthy. Creating hierarchies of value which privilege one discourse, predominantly Anglo male, over another, largely female, non-Anglo, and nonwestern undermines the supposed "impartiality" of critical standards. Breaking down the structure of canon formation that looks for the "great men" and "great women" of literature and instead studies what was actually written, then judging it on its own terms, has the potential for less bias. Challenging the existence of the canon itself allows more writers to be read and heard; perhaps we can base our understanding of literature not on a model of scarcity where only a few great ones are allowed at the top of the one peak, but where there are multiple peaks.

Another problem is that the tradition that was being recovered tended to look most like the critics who were establishing it. Barbara Smith's essay "Toward a Black Feminist Criticism" (1977) and bell hooks's *Ain't I a Woman? Black Women and Feminism* (1981) argued that academic feminism focused on the lives, conditions, histories, and texts of white, middle-class, educated women. Such writers revealed how the same methods of canon formation that excluded women were now being used by white feminists to exclude women of color. They also highlighted the silencing of black women by white women through the assumption that white womanhood was the norm. These writers and others changed the quest for one lost Atlantis to a quest for many lost continents as anthologies of African American, Chicana, Native American, Asian, Jewish, lesbian, mothers, and many more women writers grouped together by identity began to emerge. *This Bridge Called My Back: Writings by Radical Women of Color* (1981), edited by Ana Castillo and Cherríe Moraga, is one such collection. Yet, while these and other writers looked for new traditions of women's writing by the identity politics of the 1980s and 1990s, they were still imposing the same structures of tradition formation on new groups of women writers, still looking for the lost Atlantis.

Western feminist critics also began looking for the lost Atlantis on a global scale. Critiques from non-western critics and writers about their exclusion from feminist literary histories that claimed to represent world feminisms is bringing about the same pattern of starting with an exploration of image, moving to recovery of writers and traditions, then a questioning of recovery efforts that we have seen before. Now, however, all these stages are occurring at the once. For example, American feminist critics are still attempting to make global primary texts available in English so they can be studied and included at the same time they are being critiqued for doing so. Chandra Talpade Mohanty in "Under Western Eyes: Feminist Scholarship and Colonial Discourses" (1991) argues that systems of oppression do not affect us all equally, and to isolate gender as the primary source of oppression ignores the differing and complex webs of oppressions non-western women face. Western tendencies to view non-western women as suffering from a totalizing and undifferentiated oppression similar to their own "universal" female oppression cause feminist literary critics to impose structures of meaning onto non-western texts that fail to reflect the actual cultures and experiences of the writers. Therefore, to simply add the women from non-western literary traditions into existing western timelines, categories, and periodizations may not fully reflect the complexity of non-western writing. In fact, critics such as Gayatri Chakravorty Spivak, Ann DuCille, and Teresa Ebert argue post-colonial and transnational critics have created yet another master narrative that must be challenged. Yet, before the westernness of this new, transnational narrative can be addressed, critics need to be able read, discuss, and share the global texts that are now being translated and published before we can do anything else; therefore, this reclaiming and celebration of a global women's tradition is a necessary step in the process of transforming the very foundations of western feminist literary criticism. But it is only an early step in the continual speak, react, revise pattern of feminist scholarship.

Some critics argue that the ultimate goal of feminist literary history should be to move beyond using gender as the central, essential criteria—to give up looking for only a woman's isolated traditions and to examine gender as one of many elements. In that way, we could better examine female-authored texts in relationship with male-authored texts, and, thus, end the tendency to examine texts by women as either in opposition to the dominant discourse or as co-opted by it. As Kathryn R. King argues in her essay "Cowley Among the Women; or, Poetry in the Contact Zone" (2003), women writers, like male writers, did not write in a vacuum or only in relationship to other women writers. King argues for a more complex method of examining literary influence, and she holds up Mary Louise Pratt's discussion of the contact zone in *Imperial Eyes: Travel Writing and Transculturation* (1992) as a potential model for exploring the web of textual relationships that influence women writers. Pratt argues that the relationship between the colonized and the colonizer, though inflected by unequal power, often creates influence that works both ways (the contact zone). Using Pratt's idea of mutual influence and cultural hybridity allows, King argues, women's literary history to be better grounded in social, historical, philosophical, and religious traditions that influenced the texts of women writers.

So, what has feminism taught me about literary studies? That it is not "artistic value" or "universal themes" that keeps authors' works alive. Professors decide which authors and themes are going to "count" by teaching them, writing scholarly books and articles on them, and by making sure they appear in dictionaries of literary biography, bibliographies, and in the grand narratives of literary history. Reviewers decide who gets attention by reviewing them. Editors and publishers decide who gets read by keeping them in print. And librarians decide what books to buy and to keep on the shelves. Like the ancient storytellers who passed on the tribes' history from generation to generation, these groups keep our cultural memory. Therefore, we gatekeepers, who are biased humans living in and shaped by the intellectual, cultural, and aesthetic paradigms of an actual historical period must constantly reassess our methods, theories, and techniques, continually examining how our own ethnicities, classes, genders, nationalities, and sexualities mold our critical judgements.

What has literary studies taught me about feminism? That being gendered is a text that can be read, interpreted, manipulated, and altered. That feminisms themselves are texts written by real people in actual historical situations, and that feminists, too, must always recognize our own biases, and let others recognize them. That feminism is forever growing and changing and reinventing itself in a continual cycle of statement, reaction, and revision. As the definitions and goals of feminisms change before my eyes, I have learned that feminism is a process, its meaning constantly deferred.

—Amy Hudock, Ph.D.
University of South Carolina

The Gale Critical Companion Collection

In response to a growing demand for relevant criticism and interpretation of perennial topics and important literary movements throughout history, the Gale Critical Companion Collection (GCCC) was designed to meet the research needs of upper high school and undergraduate students. Each edition of GCCC focuses on a different literary movement or topic of broad interest to students of literature, history, multicultural studies, humanities, foreign language studies, and other subject areas. Topics covered are based on feedback from a standing advisory board consisting of reference librarians and subject specialists from public, academic, and school library systems.

The GCCC is designed to complement Gale's existing Literary Criticism Series (LCS) , which includes such award-winning and distinguished titles as *Nineteenth-Century Literature Criticism* (*NCLC*), *Twentieth-Century Literary Criticism* (*TCLC*), and *Contemporary Literary Criticism* (*CLC*). Like the LCS titles, the GCCC editions provide selected reprinted essays that offer an inclusive range of critical and scholarly response to authors and topics widely studied in high school and undergraduate classes; however, the GCCC also includes primary source documents, chronologies, sidebars, supplemental photographs, and other material not included in the LCS products. The graphic and supplemental material is designed to extend the usefulness of the critical essays and provide students with historical and cultural context on a topic or author's work. GCCC titles will benefit larger institutions with ongoing subscriptions to Gale's LCS products as well as smaller libraries and school systems with less extensive reference collections. Each edition of the GCCC is created as a stand-alone set providing a wealth of information on the topic or movement. Importantly, the overlap between the GCCC and LCS titles is 15% or less, ensuring that LCS subscribers will not duplicate resources in their collection.

Editions within the GCCC are either single-volume or multi-volume sets, depending on the nature and scope of the topic being covered. Topic entries and author entries are treated separately, with entries on related topics appearing first, followed by author entries in an A-Z arrangement. Each volume is approximately 500 pages in length and includes approximately 50 images and sidebar graphics. These sidebars include summaries of important historical events, newspaper clippings, brief biographies of important figures, complete poems or passages of fiction written by the author, descriptions of events in the related arts (music, visual arts, and dance), and so on.

The reprinted essays in each GCCC edition explicate the major themes and literary techniques of the authors and literary works. It is important to note that approximately 85% of the essays reprinted in GCCC editions are full-text, meaning that they are reprinted in their entirety, including footnotes and lists of abbreviations. Essays are selected based on their coverage of the seminal works and themes of an author, and based on the importance of those essays to an appreciation of the author's contribution to the movement and to literature in general. Gale's editors select those essays of most value to upper high school and undergraduate students, avoiding narrow and highly pedantic interpretations of individual works or of an author's canon.

Scope of Feminism in Literature

Feminism in Literature, the third set in the Gale Critical Companion Collection, consists of six volumes. Each volume includes a detailed table of contents, a foreword on the subject of feminism in literature written by noted scholar Amy Hudock, and a descriptive chronology of key events throughout the history of women's writing. Volume 1 focuses on feminism in literature from antiquity through the 18th century. It consists of three topic entries, including Women and Women's Writings from Classical Antiquity through the Middle Ages, and seven author entries on such women writers from this time period as Christine de Pizan, Sappho, and Mary Wollstonecraft. Volumes 2 and 3 focus on the 19th century. Volume 2 includes such topic entries as United States Women's Suffrage Movement in the 19th Century, as well as author entries on Jane Austen, Charlotte Brontë, and Elizabeth Barrett Browning. Volume 3 contains additional author entries on figures of the 19th century, including such notables as Kate Chopin, Emily Dickinson, and Harriet Beecher Stowe. Volumes 4, 5, and 6 focus on the 20th century to the present day; volume 4 includes coverage of topics relevant to feminism in literature during the 20th century and early 21st century, including the Feminist Movement, and volumes 5 and 6 include author entries on such figures as Margaret Atwood, Charlotte Perkins Gilman, Sylvia Plath, and Virginia Woolf.

Organization of Feminism in Literature

A *Feminism in Literature* topic entry consists of the following elements:

- The **Introduction** defines the subject of the entry and provides social and historical information important to understanding the criticism.
- The list of **Representative Works** identifies writings and works by authors and figures associated with the subject. The list is divided into alphabetical sections by name; works listed under each name appear in chronological order. The genre and publication date of each work is given. Unless otherwise indicated, dramas are dated by first performance, not first publication.
- Entries generally begin with a section of **Primary Sources**, which includes essays, speeches, social history, newspaper accounts and other materials that were produced during the time covered.
- Reprinted **Criticism** in topic entries is arranged thematically. Topic entries commonly begin with general surveys of the subject or essays providing historical or background information, followed by essays that develop particular aspects of the topic. Each section has a separate title heading and is identified with a page number in the table of contents. The critic's name and the date of composition or publication of the critical work are given at the beginning of each piece of criticism. Unsigned criticism is preceded by the title of the source in which it appeared. Footnotes are reprinted at the end of each essay or excerpt. In the case of excerpted criticism, only those footnotes that pertain to the excerpted texts are included.
- A complete **Bibliographical Citation** of the original essay or book precedes each piece of criticism.
- Critical essays are prefaced by brief **Annotations** explicating each piece. Unless the descriptor "excerpt" is used in the annotation, the essay is being reprinted in its entirety.
- An annotated bibliography of **Further Reading** appears at the end of each entry and suggests resources for additional study. In some cases, significant essays for which the editors could not obtain reprint rights are included here.

A *Feminism in Literature* author entry consists of the following elements:

- The **Author Heading** cites the name under which the author most commonly wrote, followed by birth and death dates. Also located here are any name variations under which an author wrote. If the author wrote consistently under a pseudonym, the pseudonym will be listed in the author heading and the author's actual name given in parentheses on the first line of the biographical and critical information. Uncertain birth or death dates are indicated by question marks.
- A **Portrait of the Author** is included when available.
- The **Introduction** contains background infor-

mation that introduces the reader to the author that is the subject of the entry.

- The list of **Principal Works** is ordered chronologically by date of first publication and lists the most important works by the author. The genre and publication date of each work is given. Unless otherwise indicated, dramas are dated by first performance, not first publication.
- Author entries are arranged into three sections: **Primary Sources, General Commentary,** and **Title Commentary.** The Primary Sources section includes letters, poems, short stories, journal entries, novel excerpts, and essays written by the featured author. General Commentary includes overviews of the author's career and general studies; Title Commentary includes in-depth analyses of seminal works by the author. Within the Title Commentary section, the reprinted criticism is further organized by title, then by date of publication. The critic's name and the date of composition or publication of the critical work are given at the beginning of each piece of criticism. Unsigned criticism is preceded by the title of the source in which it appeared. All titles by the author featured in the text are printed in boldface type. However, not all boldfaced titles are included in the author and subject indexes; only substantial discussions of works are indexed. Footnotes are reprinted at the end of each essay or excerpt. In the case of excerpted criticism, only those footnotes that pertain to the excerpted texts are included.
- A complete **Bibliographical Citation** of the original essay or book precedes each piece of criticism.
- Critical essays are prefaced by brief **Annotations** explicating each piece. Unless the descriptor "excerpt" is used in the annotation, the essay is being reprinted in its entirety.
- An annotated bibliography of **Further Reading** appears at the end of each entry and suggests resources for additional study. In some cases, significant essays for which the editors could not obtain reprint rights are included here. A list of **Other Sources from Gale** follows the further reading section and provides references to other biographical and critical sources on the author in series published by Gale.

Indexes

The **Author Index** lists all of the authors featured in the *Feminism in Literature* set, with references to the main author entries in volumes 1, 2, 3, 5, and 6 as well as commentary on the featured author in other author entries and in the topic volumes. Page references to substantial discussions of the authors appear in boldface. The Author Index also includes birth and death dates and cross references between pseudonyms and actual names, and cross references to other Gale series in which the authors have appeared. A complete list of these sources is found facing the first page of the Author Index.

The **Title Index** alphabetically lists the titles of works written by the authors featured in volumes 1 through 6 and provides page numbers or page ranges where commentary on these titles can be found. Page references to substantial discussions of the titles appear in boldface. English translations of foreign titles and variations of titles are cross-referenced to the title under which a work was originally published. Titles of novels, dramas, nonfiction books, films, and poetry, short story, or essay collections are printed in italics, while individual poems, short stories, and essays are printed in roman type within quotation marks.

The **Subject Index** includes the authors and titles that appear in the Author Index and the Title Index as well as the names of other authors and figures that are discussed in the set, including those covered in sidebars. The Subject Index also lists hundreds of literary terms and topics covered in the criticism. The index provides page numbers or page ranges where subjects are discussed and is fully cross referenced.

Citing Feminism in Literature

When writing papers, students who quote directly from the *FL* set may use the following general format to footnote reprinted criticism. The first example pertains to material drawn from periodicals, the second to material reprinted from books.

Bloom, Harold. " Feminism as the Love of Reading," *Raritan* 14, no. 2 (fall 1994): 29-42; reprinted in *Feminism in Literature: A Gale Critical Companion*, vol. 6, eds. Jessica Bomarito and Jeffrey W. Hunter (Farmington Hills, Mich: Thomson Gale, 2004), 29-42.

Coole, Diana H. "The Origin of Western Thought and the Birth of Misogyny," in *Women in Political Theory: From Ancient Misogyny to Contemporary Feminism* (Brighton, Sussex: Wheatsheaf Books, 1988), 10-28; reprinted in *Feminism in Literature: A Gale Critical Companion*, vol. 1, eds. Jessica Bomarito and Jeffrey W. Hunter (Farmington Hills, Mich: Thomson Gale, 2004), 15-25.

Feminism in Literature *Advisory Board*

The members of the *Feminism in Literature* Advisory Board—reference librarians and subject specialists from public, academic, and school library systems—offered a variety of informed perspectives on both the presentation and content of the *Feminism in Literature* set. Advisory board members assessed and defined such quality issues as the relevance, currency, and usefulness of the author coverage, critical content, and topics included in our product; evaluated the layout, presentation, and general quality of our product; provided feedback on the criteria used for selecting authors and topics covered in our product; identified any gaps in our coverage of authors or topics, recommending authors or topics for inclusion; and analyzed the appropriateness of our content and presentation for various user audiences, such as high school students, undergraduates, graduate students, librarians, and educators. We wish to thank the advisors for their advice during the development of *Feminism in Literature.*

Suggestions are Welcome

Readers who wish to suggest new features, topics, or authors to appear in future volumes of the Gale Critical Companion Collection, or who have other suggestions or comments are cordially invited to call, write, or fax the Product Manager.

Product Manager, Gale Critical Companion Collection
Thomson Gale
27500 Drake Road
Farmington Hills, MI 48331-3535
1-800-347-4253 (GALE)
Fax: 248-699-8054

ACKNOWLEDGMENTS

The editors wish to thank the copyright holders of the excerpted criticism included in this volume and the permissions managers of many book and magazine publishing companies for assisting us in securing reproduction rights. We are also grateful to the staffs of the Detroit Public Library, the Library of Congress, the University of Detroit Mercy Library, Wayne State University Purdy/Kresge Library Complex, and the University of Michigan Libraries for making their resources available to us. Following is a list of the copyright holders who have granted us permission to reproduce material in this edition of *Feminism in Literature*. Every effort has been made to trace copyright, but if omissions have been made, please let us know.

Copyrighted material in Feminism in Literature *was reproduced from the following periodicals:*

African American Review, v. 35, winter, 2001 for "'The Porch Couldn't Talk for Looking': Voice and Vision in *Their Eyes Were Watching God*" by Deborah Clarke; v. 36, 2002 for "Phillis Wheatley's Construction of Otherness and the Rhetoric of Performed Ideology" by Mary McAleer Balkun. Copyright © 2001, 2002 by the respective authors. Both reproduced by permission of the respective authors.—***Agora: An Online Graduate Journal,*** v. 1, fall, 2002 for "Virgin Territory: Murasaki Shikibu's Ôigimi Resists the Male" by Valerie Henitiuk. Copyright © 2001-2002 Maximiliaan van Woudenberg. All rights reserved. Reproduced by permission of the author.—***American Literary History,*** v. 1, winter, 1989 for "Bio-Political Resistance in Domestic Ideology and *Uncle Tom's Cabin*" by Lora Romero. Copyright © 1989 by Oxford University Press. Reproduced by permission of the publisher and the author.—***American Literature,*** v. 53, January, 1982. Copyright © 1982, by Duke University Press. Reproduced by permission.—***The American Scholar,*** v. 44, spring, 1975. Copyright © 1975 by the United Chapters of Phi Beta Kappa. Reproduced by permission of Curtis Brown Ltd.—***The Antioch Review,*** v. 32, 1973. Copyright © 1973 by the Antioch Review Inc. Reproduced by permission of the Editors.—***Ariel: A Review of International English Literature,*** v. 21, January, 1990 for "Female Sexuality in Willa Cather's *O Pioneers!* and the Era of Scientific Sexology: A Dialogue between Frontiers" by C. Susan Wiesenthal; v. 22, October, 1991 for "Margaret Atwood's *Cat's Eye*: Re-Viewing Women in a Postmodern World" by Earl G. Ingersoll. Copyright © 1990, 1991 The Board of Governors, The University of Calgary. Both reproduced by permission of the publisher and the author.—***Atlantis: A Women's Studies Journal,*** v. 9, fall, 1983. Copyright © 1983 by *Atlantis*. Reproduced by permission.—***Black American Literature Forum,*** v. 24, summer, 1990 for "Singing the Black Mother: Maya Angelou and Autobiographical Continuity" by Mary Jane Lupton. Copyright © 1990 by the author. Reproduced by permission of the author.—***The Book Collector,*** v. 31, spring, 1982. Reproduced by permission.—***The CEA Critic,*** v. 56, spring/summer, 1994 for "Feminism and Children's Literature: Fitting *Little Women* into the American Literary Canon" by Jill P. May. Copyright © 1994 by the College English Association, Inc. Reproduced by permission of the publisher and the author.—***The Centennial Review,*** v. xxix, spring, 1985 for "'An Order of Constancy': Notes on Brooks and the Feminine" by Hortense J. Spillers. Michigan State University Press. Copyright © 1985 by *The Centennial Review.* Reproduced by permission of the publisher.—***Chaucer Review,*** v. 37, 2003. Copyright © 2003 by The Pennsylvania State University. All rights reserved. Reproduced by permission.—***Christianity and Literature,*** v. 51, spring, 2002. Copyright © 2002 by the Conference on Christianity and Literature. Reproduced by permission.—***CLA Journal,*** v. XXXIX, March, 1996. Copyright © 1966 by The College Language Association. Used by permission of The College Language Association.—***Classical Quarterly,*** v. 31, 1981 for "Spartan Wives: Liberation or Licence?" by Paul Cartledge. Copyright © 1981 The Classical Association. Reproduced by permission of Oxford University Press and the author.—***Colby Library Quarterly,*** v. 21, March, 1986. Reproduced by permission.—***Colby Quarterly,*** v. XXVI, September 1990; v. XXXIV, June, 1998. Both reproduced by permission.—***College English,*** v. 36, March, 1975 for "Who Buried H. D.?: A Poet, Her Critics, and Her Place in 'The Literary Tradition'" by Susan Friedman. Copyright © 1975 by the National Council of Teachers of English. Reproduced by permission of the publisher and the author.—***Connotations,*** v. 5, 1995-96. Copyright © Waxmann Verlag GmbH, Munster/New York 1996. Reproduced by permission.—***Contemporary Literature,*** v. 34, winter, 1993. Copyright © 1993 by University of Wisconsin Press. Reproduced by permission.—***Critical Quarterly,*** v. 14, autumn, 1972; v. 27, spring, 1985. Copyright © 1972, 1985 by Manchester University Press. Both reproduced by permission of Blackwell Publishers.—***Critical Survey,*** v. 14, January, 2002. Copyright © 2002 Berghahn Books, Inc. Reproduced by permission.—***Critique: Studies in Modern Fiction,*** v. XV, 1973. Copyright © by *Critique,* 1973. Copyright © 1973 by Helen Dwight Reid Educational Foundation. Reproduced with permission of the Helen Dwight Reid Educational Foundation, published by Heldref Publications, 1319 18th Street, NW, Washington, DC 20036-1802.—***Cultural Critique,*** v. 32, winter, 1995-96. Copyright © 1996 by *Cultural Critique.* All rights reserved. Reproduced by permission.—***Denver Quarterly,*** v. 18, winter, 1984 for "Becoming Anne Sexton" by Diane Middlebrook. Copyright © 1994 by Diane Middlebrook. Reproduced by permission of Georges Borchardt, Inc. for the author.—***Dissent,*** summer, 1987. Copyright © 1987, by Dissent Publishing Corporation. Reproduced by permission.—***The Eighteenth Century,*** v. 43, spring, 2002. Copyright © 2002 by Texas Tech University Press. Reproduced by permission.—***Eighteenth-Century Fiction,*** v. 3, July, 1991. Copyright © McMaster University 1991. Reproduced by permission.—***Emily Dickinson Journal,*** v. 10, 2000. Copyright © 2000 by The Johns Hopkins University Press for the Emily Dickinson International Society. All rights reserved. Reproduced by permission.—***The Emporia State Research Studies,*** v. 24, winter, 1976. Reproduced by permission.—***Essays and Studies,*** 2002. Copyright © 2002 Boydell & Brewer Inc. Reproduced by permission.—***Essays in Literature,*** v. 12, fall, 1985. Copyright © 1985 Western Illinois University. Reproduced by permission.—***Feminist Studies,*** v. 6, summer, 1980; v. 25, fall, 1999. Copyright © 1980, 1999 by *Feminist Studies.* Both reproduced by permission of Feminist Studies, Inc., Department of Women's Studies, University of Maryland, College Park, MD 20724.—***French Studies,*** v. XLVIII, April, 1994; v. LII, April, 1998. Copyright © 1994, 1998 by The Society for French Studies. Reproduced by permission.—***Frontiers,*** v. IX, 1987; v. XIV, 1994. Copyright © The University of Nebraska Press 1987, 1994. Both reproduced by permission.—***Glamour,*** v. 88, November 1990 for "Only Daughter" by Sandra Cisneros. Copyright © 1996 by Wendy Martin. All rights reserved. Reproduced by permission of Susan Bergholz Literary Services, New York.—***Harper's Magazine,*** for "Women's Work" by Louise Erdrich. Copyright © 1995 by *Harper's Magazine.* All rights reserved. Reproduced from the May edition by special permission.—***History Today,*** v. 50, October, 2000; v. 51, November, 2001. Copyright © 2000, 2001 by The H. W. Wilson Company. All rights reserved. Reproduced by permission.—***The Hudson Review,*** v. XXXVI, summer, 1983. Copyright © 1983 by The Hudson Review, Inc. Reproduced by permission.—***Hypatia,*** v. 5, summer, 1990 for "Is There a Feminist Aesthetic?" by Marilyn French. Copyright by Marilyn French. Reproduced by permission.—***International Fiction Review,*** v. 29, 2002. Copyright © 2002. International Fiction Association. Reproduced by permission.—***Irish Studies Review,*** spring, 1996 from "History, Gender and the Colonial Movement: Castle Rackrent" by Colin Graham. Reproduced by permission of Taylor & Francis and the author.—***Journal of Evolutionary Psychology,*** v. 7, August, 1986. Reproduced by permission.—***Journal of the Midwest Modern Language Association,*** v. 35, 2002 for "The Gospel According to Jane Eyre: The Suttee and the Seraglio" by Maryanne C. Ward. Copyright © 2002 by The Midwest Modern Language Association. Reproduced by permission of the publisher and the author.—***Journal of the Short Story in English,*** autumn, 2002. Copyright © Université d'Angers, 2002. Reproduced by permission.—***Keats-Shelley Journal,*** v. XLVI, 1997. Reproduced by permission.—***Legacy,*** v. 6, fall, 1989. Copyright © The University of Nebraska Press 1989. Reproduced by permission.—***The Massachusetts Review,*** v. 27, summer, 1986. Reproduced from *The Massachusetts Review,* The Massachusetts Review, Inc. by permission.—***Meanjin,*** v. 38, 1979 for "The Liberated Heroine: New Varieties of Defeat?" by Amanda Lohrey. Copyright © 1979 by *Meanjin.* Reproduced by permission of the author.—***MELUS,*** v. 7, fall, 1980; v. 12, fall, 1985; v.18, fall, 1993. Copyright © MELUS: The Society for the Study of Multi-Ethnic Literature of the United States, 1980, 1985, 1993. Reproduced by permission.—***Modern Drama,*** v. 21, September, 1978. Copyright © 1978 by the University of Toronto, Graduate Centre for Study of Drama. Reproduced by permission.—***Modern Language Studies,*** v. 24, spring, 1994 for "Jewett's Unspeakable Unspoken: Retracing the Female Body Through *The Country of the Pointed Firs*" by George Smith. Copyright © Northeast Modern Language Association 1990. Reproduced by permission of the publisher and author.—***Mosaic,*** v. 23, summer, 1990; v. 35, 2002. Copyright © 1990, 2002 by *Mosaic.* All rights reserved. Acknowledgment of previous publication is herewith made.—***Ms.,*** v. II, July, 1973 for "Visionary Anger" by Erica Mann Jong; June 1988 for "Changing My Mind About Andrea Dworkin" by Erica Jong. Copyright © 1973, 1988. Both reproduced by permission of the author.—***New Directions for Women,*** September-October, 1987 for "Dworkin Critiques Relations Between the Sexes" by Joanne Glasgow. Copyright © 1987 New Directions for Women, Inc., 25 West Fairview Ave., Dover, NJ 07801-3417. Reproduced by permission of the author.—***The New Yorker,*** 1978 for "Girl" by Jamaica Kincaid. Copyright © 1979 by Jamaica Kinkaid. All rights reserved. Reproduced by permission of the Wylie Agency; v. 73, February 17, 1997 for "A Society of One: Zora Neal Hurston, American Contrarian" by Claudia Roth Pierpont. Copyright © 1997 by The New Yorker Magazine, Inc. All rights reserved. Reproduced by permission of the author.—***Nineteenth-Century Feminisms,*** v. 2, spring-summer, 2000. Reproduced by permission.—***Nineteenth-Century French Studies,*** v. 25, spring-summer, 1997. Copyright © 1977 by *Nineteenth-Century French Studies.* Reproduced by permission.—***Novel,*** v. 34, spring, 2001. Copyright © NOVEL Corp. 2001. Reproduced with permission.—***Oxford Literary Review,*** v. 13, 1991. Copyright © 1991 the *Oxford Literary Review.* All rights reserved. Reproduced by permission.—***P. N. Review,*** v. 18, January/February, 1992. Reproduced by permission of Carcanet Press Ltd.—***Papers on Language & Literature,*** v. 5, winter, 1969. Copyright © 1969 by The Board of Trustees, Southern Illinois University at Edwardsville. Reproduced by permission.—***Parnassus,*** v. 12, fall-winter, 1985 for "Throwing the Scarecrows from the Garden" by Tess Gallagher; v. 12-13, 1985 for "Adrienne Rich and Lesbian/Feminist Poetry" by Catharine Stimpson. Copyright © 1985, 1986 by Poetry in Review Foundation. Both reproduced by permission of the publisher and the respective authors.—***Philological Papers,*** v. 38, 1992. Copyright © 1992 by *Philological Papers.* Reproduced by permission.—***Philological Quarterly,*** v. 79, winter, 2000. Copyright © 2001 by the University of Iowa. Reproduced by permission.—***Quadrant,*** v. 46, November, 2002 for "The Mirror of Honour and Love: A Woman's View of Chivalry" by Sophie Masson. Copyright © 2002 Quadrant Magazine Company, Inc. Reproduced by permission of the publisher and the author.—***Raritan,*** v. 14, fall, 1994. Copyright © 1994 by *Raritan: A Quarterly Review.* Reproduced by permission.—***Resources for American Literary Study,*** v. 22, 1996. Copyright © 1996 by The Pennsylvania State University. Reproduced by permission of The Pennsylvania State University Press.—***Revista Hispánica Moderna,*** v. 47, June, 1994. Copyright © 1994 by Hispanic Institute, Columbia University. Reproduced by permission.—***Rhetoric Society Quarterly,*** v. 32, winter, 2002. Reproduced by permission of the publisher, conveyed through the Copyright Clearance Center.—***Romanic Review,*** v. 79, 1988. Copyright © 1988 by The Trustees of Columbia University in the City of New York. Reproduced by permission.—***The Russian Review,*** v. 57, April, 1998. Copyright © 1998 *The Russian Review.* Reproduced by permission of Blackwell Publishers.—***San Jose Studies,*** v. VIII, spring, 1982 for "Dea, Awakening: A Reading of H. D.'s *Trilogy*" by Joyce Lorraine Beck. Copyright © 1982 by Trustees of the San Jose State University Foundation. Reproduced by permission of the publisher and the author.—***South Atlantic Review,*** v. 66, winter, 2001. Copyright © 2001 by the South Atlantic Modern Language Association. Reproduced by permission.—***Southern Humanities Review,*** v. xxii, summer, 1988. Copyright © 1988 by Auburn University. Reproduced by permission.—***The Southern Quarterly,*** v. 35, spring, 1997; v. 37, spring-summer, 1999. Copyright © 1997, 1999 by the University of Southern Mississippi. Both reproduced by permission.—***Southern Review,*** v. 18, for "Hilda in Egypt" by Albert Gelpi. Reproduced by permission of the author.—***Soviet Literature,*** v. 6, June, 1989. Reproduced by permission of FTM Agency Ltd.—***Studies in American Fiction,*** v. 9, autumn, 1981. Copyright © 1981 Northeastern University. Reproduced by permission.—***Studies in American Humor,*** v. 3, 1994. Copyright © 1994 American Humor Studies Association. Reproduced by permission.—***Studies in the Humanities,*** v. 19, December, 1992. Copyright © 1992 by Indiana University Press of Pennsylvania. Reproduced by permission.—***Studies in the Novel,*** v. 31, fall 1999; v. 35, spring, 2003. Copyright © 1999, 2003 by North Texas State University. Reproduced by permission.—***Textual Practice,*** v. 13, 1999 for "Speaking Un-likeness: The Double Text in Christina Rossetti's 'After Death' and 'Remember'" by Margaret Reynolds. Copyright © 1999 Routledge. Reproduced by permission of the publisher and the author.—***The Threepenny Review,*** 1990 for "Mother Tongue" by Amy Tan. Reproduced by permission.—***Transactions of the American Philological Association,*** v. 128, 1998. Copyright © 1998 American Philological Association. Reproduced by permission of The Johns Hopkins University Press.—***Tulsa Studies in Women's Literature,*** v. 6, fall, 1987 for "Revolutionary Women" by Betsy Erkkila. Copyright © 1987, The University of Tulsa. All rights reserved. Reproduced by permission of the publisher and the author.—***The Victorian Newsletter,*** v. 82, fall, 1992 for "Revisionist Mythmaking in Christina Rossetti's 'Goblin Market': Eve's Apple and Other Questions" by Sylvia Bailey Shurbutt; v. 92, fall, 1997 for "The Poet and the Bible: Christina Rossetti's Feminist Hermeneutics" by Lynda Palazzo; spring, 1998 for "'No Sorrow I Have Thought More About': The Tragic Failure of George Eliot's St. Theresa" by June Skye Szirotny. All reproduced by permission of The Victorian Newsletter and the author.—***Victorians Institute Journal,*** v. 13, 1985. Copyright © Victorians Institute Journal 1985. Reproduced by permission.—***Women: A Cultural Review,*** v. 10, winter, 1999 from "Consorting with Angels: Anne Sexton and the Art of Confession" by Deryn Rees-Jones. Copyright © 1999, by Taylor & Francis Ltd. Reproduced by permission of the publisher and the author. (http://www.tandf.co.uk/journals).—***Women and Language,*** v. 13, March 31, 1995; v. 19, fall, 1996. Copyright © 1995, 1996 by Communication Department at George Mason University. Reproduced by permission of the publisher.—***Women's Studies: An Interdisciplinary Journal,*** v. 3, 1975; v. 4, 1976; v. 17, 1990; v. 18, 1990; v. 23, September, 1994; v. 30, 2001. Copyright © 1975, 1976, 1990, 1994, 2001 Gordon and Breach Science Publishers S.A. Reproduced by permission.—***Women's Studies in Communication,*** v. 24, spring, 2001. Reproduced by permission.—***Women's Writing,*** v. 3, June, 1996. Reproduced by permission of the publisher; v. 4, 1997 for "(Female) Philosophy in the Bedroom: Mary Wollstonecraft and Female Sexuality" by Gary Kelly. Copyright © Triangle Journals Ltd, 1997. All rights reserved. Reproduced by permission of the publisher and the author.—***World & I,*** v. 18, March, 2003. Copyright © 2003 News World Communications, Inc. Reproduced by permission.—***World Literature Today,*** v. 73, spring, 1999. Copyright © 1999 by the University of Oklahoma Press. Reprinted by permission of the publisher.—***World Literature Written in English,*** v. 15, November, 1976 for "Doris Lessing's Feminist Plays" by Agate Nesaule Krouse. Copyright © 1976 by WLWE. Reproduced by permission of the publisher and the author.

Copyrighted material in Feminism in Literature *was reproduced from the following books:*

Acocella, Joan. From ***Willa Cather and the Politics of Criticism.*** University of Nebraska Press, 2000. Copyright © 2000, by Joan Acocella. All rights reserved. Reproduced by permission.—Aimone, Joseph. From "Millay's Big Book, or the Feminist Formalist as Modern," in ***Unmanning Modernism: Gendered Re-Readings.*** Edited by Elizabeth Jane Harrison and Shirley Peterson. University of Tennessee Press, 1997. Copyright © 1997 by The University of Tennessee Press. All rights reserved. Reproduced by permission of The University of Tennessee Press.—Allende, Isabel. From "Writing as an Act of Hope," in ***Paths of Resistance: The Art and Craft of the Political Novel.*** Edited by William Zinsser. Houghton Mifflin Company, 1989. Copyright © 1989 Isabel Allende. Reproduced by permission of the author.—Angelou, Maya. From ***And Still I Rise.*** Random House, 1978. Copyright © 1978 by Maya Angelou. Reproduced by permission of Random House, Inc. and Time Warner Books UK.—Arenal, Electa. From "The Convent as Catalyst for Autonomy: Two Hispanic Nuns of the Seventeenth Century," in ***Women in Hispanic Literature.*** Edited by Beth Kurti Miller. University of California Press, 1983. Copyright © 1983 by The Regents of the University of California. Reproduced by permission of the publisher and the author.—Arndt, Walter. From "Introduction: I The Akhmatova Phenomenon and II Rendering the Whole Poem," in ***Anna Akhmatova: Selected Poems.*** Edited and translated by Walter Arndt. Ardis, 1976. Reproduced by permission.—Atwood, Margaret. From ***Second Words.*** Anansi Press Limited, 1982. Copyright © 1982, by O. W. Toad Limited. All rights reserved. Reproduced by permission of the author.—Baker, Deborah Lesko. From "Memory, Love, and Inaccessibility in *Hiroshima mon amour,*" in ***Marguerite***

Duras Lives On. Edited by Janine Ricouart. University Press of America, 1998. Copyright © 1998 University Press of America, Inc. All rights reserved. Reproduced by permission.—Barlow, Judith E. From "Into the Foxhole: Feminism, Realism, and Lillian Hellman," in ***Realism and the American Dramatic Tradition.*** Edited by William W. Demastes. University of Alabama Press, 1996. Copyright © 1996, The University of Alabama Press. Reproduced by permission.—Barratt, Alexandra. From ***Women's Writing in Middle English.*** Edited by Alexandra Barratt. Longman Group UK Limited, 1992. Copyright © Longman Group UK Limited 1992. Reproduced by permission.—Barrett Browning, Elizabeth. From "A Letter to Mary Russell Mitford, September 18, 1846," in ***Women of Letters: Selected Letters of Elizabeth Barrett Browning and Mary Russell Mitford.*** Edited by Meredith B. Raymond and Mary Rose Sullivan. Twayne Publishers, 1987. Reproduced by permission of The Gale Group.—Barrett Browning, Elizabeth. From "Glimpses into My Own Life and Literary Character," in ***The Brownings' Correspondence,*** Vol. 1. Edited by Phillip Kelley and Ronald Hudson. Wedgestone Press, 1984. All rights reserved. Reproduced by permission of Eton College.—Bassard, Katherine Clay. From ***Spiritual Interrogations: Culture, Gender, and Community in Early African American Women's Writing.*** Princeton University Press, 1999. Copyright © 1999 by Katherine Clay Bassard. Reproduced by permission of Princeton University Press.—Beauvoir, Simone de. From "The Independent Woman," in ***The Second Sex.*** Translated by H. M. Parshley. Alfred A. Knopf, Inc., 1952. Copyright © 1952, renewed 1980 by Alfred A. Knopf, Inc. All rights reserved. Reproduced by permission of Alfred A. Knopf, Inc., a division of Random House, Inc. and The Random House Group.—Behrendt, Stephen. From "Mary Shelley, Frankenstein, and the Woman Writer's Fate," in ***Romantic Women Writers: Voices and Countervoices.*** Edited by Paula R. Feldman and Theresa M. Kelley. University Press of New England, 1995. Copyright © 1995 by University Press of New England. All rights reserved. Reproduced by permission.—Bell, Barbara Currier and Carol Ohmann. From "Virginia Woolf's Criticism: A Polemical Preface," in ***Feminist Literary Criticism: Explorations in Theory.*** Edited by Josephine Donovan. The University Press of Kentucky, 1989. Copyright © 1975, 1989 by The University Press of Kentucky. Reproduced by permission of The University Press of Kentucky.—Berry, Mary Frances. From ***Why ERA Failed: Politics, Women's Rights, and the Amending Process of the Constitution.*** Indiana University Press, 1986. Copyright © 1986 by Mary Frances Berry. All rights reserved. Reproduced by permission.—Birgitta of Sweden. From ***Life and Selected Revelations.*** Edited with a preface by Marguerite Tjader Harris, translation and notes by Albert Ryle Kezel, introduction by Tore Nyberg from ***The Classics of Western Spirituality.*** Paulist Press, 1990. Copyright © 1990 by the Order of St. Birgitte, Rome. Translation, notes and Foreword copyright © 1990 by Albert Ryle Kezel, New York/Mahwah, NJ. Reproduced by permission of Paulist Press. www.paulistpress.com.—Blundell, Sue. From ***Women in Ancient Greece.*** British Museum Press, 1995. Copyright © 1995 Sue Blundell. Reproduced by permission of the author.—Bogan, Louise. From ***The Blue Estuaries: Poems 1923-1968.*** Farrar, Straus & Giroux, Inc., 1968. Copyright © 1968 by Louise Bogan. Copyright renewed 1996 by Ruth Limmer. All rights reserved. Reproduced by permission of Farrar, Straus and Giroux, LLC.—Booth, Alison. From "Not All Men Are Selfish and Cruel," in ***Greatness Engendered: George Eliot and Virginia Woolf.*** Cornell University Press, 1992. Copyright © 1992 by Cornell University Press. Reproduced by permission of the publisher, Cornell University Press.—Brammer, Leila R. From ***Excluded from Suffrage History: Matilda Joslyn Gage, Nineteenth-Century American Feminist.*** Greenwood Press, 2000. Copyright © by Leila R. Brammer. All rights reserved. Reproduced by permission of Greenwood Publishing Group, Inc., Westport, CT.—Britzolakis, Christina. From ***Sylvia Plath and the Theatre of Mourning.*** Oxford at the Clarendon Press, 1999. Copyright © 1999 by Christina Britzolakis. All rights reserved. Reproduced by permission of Oxford University Press.—Broe, Mary Lynn. From "Bohemia Bumps into Calvin: The Deception of Passivity in Lillian Hellman's Drama," in ***Critical Essays on Lillian Hellman.*** Edited by Mark W. Estrin. G. K. Hall, 1989. Copyright © 1989 by Mark W. Estrin. All rights reserved. Reproduced by permission of The Gale Group.—Brontë, Charlotte. From "Caroline Vernon," in ***Legends of Angria: Compiled from The Early Writings of Charlotte Brontë.*** Edited by Fannie E. Ratchford. Yale University Press, 1933. Copyright © 1933 by Yale University Press. Renewed 1961 by Fannit Ratchford. Reproduced by permission.—Brooks, Gwendolyn. From ***Blacks.*** The David Company, 1987. Copyright © 1945, 1949, 1953, 1960, 1963, 1968, 1969, 1970, 1971, 1975, 1981, 1986 by Gwendolyn Brooks Blakely. All rights reserved. Reproduced by consent of Brooks Permissions.—Brown-Grant, Rosalind. From "Christine de Pizan: Feminist Linguist Avant la Lettre?," in ***Christine de Pizan 2000: Studies on Christine de Pizan in Honour of Angus J. Kennedy.*** Edited by John Campbell and Nadia Margolis. Rodopi, 2000. Copyright © Editions Rodopi B. Reproduced by permission.—Brownmiller,

Susan. From ***In Our Time: Memoir of a Revolution.*** The Dial Press, 1999. Copyright © 1999, by Susan Brownmiller. All rights reserved. Reproduced by permission of The Dial Press/Dell Publishing, a division of Random House, Inc.—Brügmann, Margret. From "Between the Lines: On the Essayistic Experiments of Hélène Cixous in 'The Laugh of the Medusa'," translated by Debbi Long in ***The Politics of the Essay: Feminist Perspectives.*** Edited by Ruth-Ellen Boetcher Joeres and Elizabeth Mittman. Indiana University Press, 1993. Copyright © 1993 by Indiana University Press. All rights reserved. Reproduced by permission.—Bunch, Charlotte. From "Women's Human Rights: The Challenges of Global Feminism and Diversity," in ***Feminist Locations: Global and Local, Theory and Practice.*** Edited by Marianne DeKoven. Rutgers University Press, 2001. Copyright © 2001 by Rutgers, the State University. All rights reserved. Reproduced by permission.—Burke, Sally. From ***American Feminist Playwrights: A Critical History.*** Twayne, 1996. Copyright © 1996 by Twayne Publishers. All rights reserved. Reproduced by permission of The Gale Group.—Butler-Evans, Elliott. From ***Race, Gender, and Desire: Narrative Strategies in the Works of Toni Cade Bambara, Toni Morrison, and Alice Walker.*** Temple University Press, 1989. Copyright © 1989, by Temple University. All rights reserved. Reproduced by permission.—Byerman, Keith. From "Gender and Justice: Alice Walker and the Sexual Politics of Civil Rights," in ***The World is Our Home: Society and Culture in Contemporary Southern Writing.*** Edited by Jeffrey J. Folks and Nancy Summers Folks. The University Press of Kentucky, 2000. Copyright © 2000 by The University Press of Kentucky. Reproduced by permission.—Callaghan, Dympna C. From "The Ideology of Romantic Love," in ***The Weyward Sisters: Shakespeare and Feminist Politics.*** Edited by Dympna C. Callaghan, Lorraine Helms, and Jyotsna Singh. Blackwell Publishers, 1994. Copyright © Dympna C. Callaghan, Lorraine Helms and Jyotsna Singh 1994. Reproduced by permission of Blackwell Publishers.—Carmody, Denise Lardner. From ***Biblical Woman: Contemporary Reflections on Scriptural Texts.*** Crossroad Publishing Company, 1988. Copyright © 1988 by Denise Lardner Carmody. All rights reserved. Reproduced by permission of the author.—Castro, Ginette. From ***American Feminism: A Contemporary History.*** Translated by Elizabeth Loverde-Bagwell. New York University Press, 1990. Copyright © Presses de la Foundation Nationale des Sciences Politiques, Paris, 1990. All rights reserved. Reproduced by permission of New Directions Publishing Corporation and in the UK by Pollinger Limited and the proprietor.—Chadwick, Whitney. From ***Women, Art, and Society.*** Thames and Hudson, 1990. Copyright © 1990 Thames and Hudson Ltd, London. All rights reserved. Reproduced by permission.—Chafe, William H. From "World War II as a Pivotal Experience for American Women," in ***Women and War: The Changing Status of American Women from the 1930s to the 1940s.*** Edited by Maria Diedrich and Dorothea Fischer-Horning. Berg, 1990. Copyright © 1990, by Maria Diedrich and Dorothea Fischer-Hornung. All rights reserved Reproduced by permission.—Chesler, Ellen. From ***Woman of Valor: Margaret Sanger and the Birth Control Movement in America.*** Anchor Books, 1992. Copyright © 1992 by Ellen Chesler. All rights reserved. Reproduced by permission of International Creative Management, Inc.—Cholmeley, Katherine. From ***Margery Kempe, Genius and Mystic.*** Longmans, Green and Co., 1947. Reproduced by permission.—Christian, Barbara T. From an introduction to ***"Everyday Use": Alice Walker.*** Edited by Barbara T. Christian. Rutgers University Press, 1994. Copyright © 1994 by Rutgers, The State University. Reproduced by permission of Rutgers, The State University.—Christine de Pizan. From ***The Writings of Christine de Pizan.*** Translated by Charity Cannon Willard. Persea Books, 1994. Copyright © 1994 by Persea Books, Inc. Reproduced by permission.—Cixous, Hélène. From "The Laugh of the Medusa," in ***New French Feminisms: An Anthology.*** Edited by Elaine Marks and Isabelle de Courtivron. Essay translated by Keith and Paula Cohen. *Signs,* 1975. All rights reserved. Reproduced by permission of University of Chicago Press and the author.—Conley, Verana Andermatt. From ***Hélène Cixous: Writing the Feminine.*** University of Nebraska Press, 1984. Copyright © 1984 by University of Nebraska Press. All rights reserved. Reproduced by permission.—Coole, Diana H. From ***Women in Political Theory: From Ancient Misogyny to Contemporary Feminism.*** Wheatsheaf Books Ltd, 1988. Copyright © Diana Coole, 1988. All rights reserved. Reproduced by permission of the author.—Cooper, Michaela Bruckner. From "Textual Wandering and Anxiety in Margaret Fuller's *Summer on the Lakes,*" in ***Margaret Fuller's Cultural Critique: Her Age and Legacy.*** Edited by Fritz Fleischmann. Peter Lang, 2000. Copyright © 2000 Peter Lang Publishing. All rights reserved. Reproduced by permission.—Cott, Nancy. From "Historical Perspectives: The Equal Rights Amendment Conflict in 1920s," in ***Conflicts in Feminism.*** Edited by Marianne Hirsch and Evelyn Fox Keller. Routledge, 1990. Copyright © 1990 by Routledge, Chapman and Hall, Inc. All rights reserved. Reproduced by permission of Routledge/Taylor & Francis Books and the author.—Cotton, Nancy. From "Women Playwrights in England," in ***Read-***

ings in Renaissance Women's Drama: Criticism, History, and Performance 1594-1998.*** Edited by S. P. Cerasano and Marion Wynee-Davies. Bucknell University Press 1981. Reproduced by permission of Associated University Presses and the author.—Coultrap-McQuin, Susan. From ***Doing Literary Business: American Women Writers in the Nineteenth Century.*** The University of North Carolina Press, 1990. Copyright © 1990 Susan Coultrap-McQuin. All rights reserved. Used by permission of the University of North Carolina Press.—Daly, Brenda. From ***Lavish Self-Divisions: The Novels of Joyce Carol Oates.*** University Press of Mississippi, 1996. Copyright © 1996 by the University Press of Mississippi. All rights reserved. Reproduced by permission.—Davis, Cynthia J. "What 'Speaks in Us': Margaret Fuller, Woman's Rights, and Human Nature," in ***Margaret Fuller's Cultural Critique: Her Age and Legacy.*** Edited by Fritz Fleischmann. Peter Lang, 2000. Copyright © 2000 Peter Lang Publishing. All rights reserved. Reproduced by permission.—de Gouges, Olympe. From "The Rights of Women," in ***Women in Revolutionary Paris 1789-1795: Selected Documents.*** Edited and translated by Daline Gay Levy, Harriet Branson Applewhite, and Mary Durham Johnson. University of Illinois, 1979. Reproduced by permission.—Depla, Annette. From "Women in Ancient Egyptian Wisdom Literature," in ***Women in Ancient Societies: An Illusion of the Night.*** Edited by Léonie J. Archer, Susan Fischler, and Maria Wyke. Macmillan Press Ltd, 1994. Copyright © The Macmillan Press Ltd 1994. Reproduced with permission of Palgrave Macmillan and Routledge/Taylor & Francis Books, Inc.—Deutsch, Sarah Jane. From "From Ballots to Breadlines: 1920-1940," in ***No Small Courage: A History of Women in the United States.*** Edited by Nancy F. Cott. Oxford University Press, 2000. Copyright © 2000, by Sarah Jane Deutsch. All rights reserved. Used by permission of Oxford University Press.—Dever, Carolyn. From "Obstructive Behavior: Dykes in the Mainstream of Feminist Theory," in ***Cross-Purposes: Lesbians, Feminists, and the Limits of Alliance.*** Indiana University Press, 1997. Copyright © 1997, by Indiana University Press. All rights reserved. Reproduced by permission.—Donawerth, Jane. From "Women's Poetry and the Tudor-Stuart System of Gift Exchange," in ***Women, Writing, and the Reproduction of Culture in Tudor and Stuart Britain.*** Edited by Mary E. Burke, Jane Donawerth, Linda L. Dove, and Karen Nelson. Syracuse University Press, 2002. Reproduced by permission.—Doolittle, Hilda. From ***HERmione.*** New Directions Publishing, 1981. Copyright © 1981 by the Estate of Hilda Doolittle. Reproduced by permission of New Directions Publishing Corp.—Douglas, Ann. From ***The Feminization of American Culture.*** Anchor Press/Doubleday, 1988. Copyright © 1977 by Ann Douglas. Used by permission of Alfred A. Knopf, a division of Random House, Inc.—Driver, Dorothy. From "Reconstructing the Past, Shaping the Future: Bessie Head and the Question of Feminism in a New South Africa," in ***Black Women's Writings.*** Edited by Gina Wisker. St. Martin's Press, 1993. Copyright © 1993, by Editorial Board, Lumière (Co-operative) Press Ltd. All rights reserved. Reprinted by permission of Palgrave Macmillan.—DuBois, Ellen Carol. From ***Remembering Seneca Falls: Honoring the Women Who Paved the Way: An Essay.*** Reproduced by permission of the author.—DuBois, Ellen Carol. From "Taking the Law Into Our Own Hands: Bradwell, Minor and Suffrage Militance in the 1870s," in ***One Woman, One Vote: Rediscovering the Woman Suffrage Movement.*** Edited by Marjorie Spruill Wheeler. NewSage Press, 1995. Copyright © 1995 by NewSage Press and Educational Film Company. All rights reserved. Reproduced by permission.—DuBois, Ellen Carol. From the introduction to ***Feminism and Suffrage: The Emergence of An Independent Women's Movement in America.*** Cornell University Press, 1978. Copyright © 1978 by Cornell University. All rights reserved. Used by permission of Cornell University Press.—DuBois, Ellen Carol. From "The Limitations of Sisterhood: Elizabeth Cady Stanton and the Division of the American Suffrage Movement, 1875-1902" in ***Women and the Structure of Society.*** Duke University Press, 1984. Copyright © 1984 by Duke University Press, Durham, NC. All rights reserved. Used by permission.—DuBois, Ellen Carol. From ***Woman Suffrage and Women's Rights.*** New York University Press, 1998. Copyright © 1998 by New York University. All rights reserved. Reproduced by permission of the publisher and the author.—DuBois, Ellen Carol. From "Woman Suffrage Around the World: Three Phases of Suffragist Internationalism," in ***Suffrage and Beyond: International Feminist Perspectives.*** Edited by Caroline Daley and Melanie Nolan. Auckland University Press, 1994. Copyright © by Auckland University Press 1994. All rights reserved. Reproduced by permission of the publisher and the author.—Ducrest, Stéphanie-Félicité. From "The Influence of Women on French Literature," in ***Women Critics: 1660-1820: An Anthology.*** Indiana University Press, 1995. Copyright © 1995 by Indiana University Press. All rights reserved. Reproduced by permission.—Dworkin, Andrea. From ***Letters from a War Zone: Writings 1976-1989.*** E. P. Dutton, 1988. Copyright © 1988 by Andrea Dworkin. Reproduced by permission of Elaine Markson Literary Agency.—Echols, Alice.

From ***The Sixties: From Memory to History.*** Edited by David R. Farber. University of North Carolina Press, 1994. Copyright © 1994 by the University of North Carolina Press. Used by permission of the Publisher.—Ehrenreich, Barbara and Deirdre English. From ***For Her Own Good: 150 Years of the Experts' Advice to Women.*** Anchor Books/Doubleday, 1978. Copyright © 1978 by Barbara Ehrenreich and Deirdre English. All rights reserved. Used by permission of Doubleday, a division of Random House.—Elbert, Sarah. From ***A Hunger for Home: Louisa May Alcott and*** **Little Women.** Temple University Press, 1984. Copyright © 1984 by Temple University. All rights reserved. Reproduced by permission of the author.—Emecheta, Buchi. From "Feminism with a Small 'f'!," in ***Criticism and Ideology: Second African Writers' Conference.*** Edited by Kirsten Holst Petersen. Scandinavian Institute of African Studies, 1988. Copyright © 1988 by Scandinavian Institute of African Studies. All rights reserved. Reproduced by permission of Nordic Africa Institute.—Ensler, Eve. From ***The Vagina Monologues: The V-Day Edition.*** Villard, 2001. Copyright © 1998, 2001 by Eve Ensler. All rights reserved. Reproduced by permission of Villard Books, a division of Random House, Inc.—Enstad, Nan. From ***Ladies of Labor, Girls of Adventure: Working Women, Popular Culture, and Labor Politics at the Turn of the Twentieth Century.*** Columbia University Press, 1999. Copyright © 1999 Columbia University Press, New York. All rights reserved. Republished with permission of the Columbia University Press, 61 W. 62nd St., New York, NY 10023.—Ezell, Margaret J. M. From "Women and Writing," in ***A Companion to Early Modern Women's Writing.*** Edited by Anita Pacheco. Blackwell Publishing Ltd, 2002. Copyright © 2002 by Blackwell Publishers Ltd. Reproduced by permission of Blackwell Publishers.—Fallaize, Elizabeth. From "Resisting Romance: Simone de Beauvoir, *The Woman Destroyed* and the Romance Script," in ***Contemporary French Fiction by Women: Feminist Perspectives.*** Edited by Margaret Atack and Phil Powrie. Manchester University Press, 1990. Reproduced by permission of the author.—Feng, Pin-chia. From ***The Female Bildungsroman*** by Toni Morrison and Maxine Hong Kingston: A Postmodern Reading. Peter Lang, 1998. Copyright © 1988 Peter Lang Publishing, Inc. All rights reserved. Reproduced by permission.—Ferree, Myra Marx and Beth B. Hess. From ***Controversy and Coalition: The New Feminist Movement across Three Decades of Change.*** Twayne Publishers, 1994. Copyright © 1994 by Twayne Publishers. All rights reserved. Reproduced by permission of The Gale Group.—Fishkin, Shelley Fisher. From an interview with Maxine Hong Kingston, in ***Conversations with Maxine Hong Kingston.*** Edited by Paul Skenazy and Tera Martin. University Press of Mississippi, 1998. Copyright © 1998 by University Press of Mississippi. All rights reserved. Reproduced by permission of the author.—Fishkin, Shelley Fisher. From "Reading Gilman in the Twenty-First Century," in ***The Mixed Legacy of Charlotte Perkins Gilman.*** Edited by Catherine J. Golden and Joanna Schneider Zangrando. University of Delaware Press, 2000. Copyright © 2000 by Associated University Press. Reproduced by permission.—Fleischmann, Fritz. From "Margaret Fuller, the Eternal Feminine, and the 'Liberties of the Republic'," in ***Women's Studies and Literature.*** Edited by Fritz Fleischmann and Deborah Lucas Schneider. Palm & Enke, 1987. Reproduced by permission.—Foster, M. Marie Booth. From "Voice, Mind, Self: Mother-Daughter Relationships in Amy Tan's *The Joy Luck Club* and *The Kitchen God's Wife*," in ***Women of Color: Mother-Daughter Relationships in 20th-Century Literature.*** Edited by Elizabeth Brown-Guillory. University of Texas Press, 1996. Copyright © 1996 by the University of Texas Press. All rights reserved. Reproduced by permission.—Fowler, Robert Booth. From ***Carrie Catt: Feminist Politician.*** Northeastern University Press, 1986. Copyright © 1986 by R. B. Fowler. All rights reserved. Reproduced by permission.—Fraiman, Susan. From "The Humiliation of Elizabeth Bennett," in ***Refiguring the Father: New Feminist Readings of Patriarchy.*** Edited by Patricia Yaeger and Beth Kowaleski-Wallace. Southern Illinois University Press, 1989. Copyright © 1989 by the Board of Trustees, Southern Illinois University. All rights reserved. Reproduced by permission.—Francis, Emma. From "Is Emily Brontë a Woman?: Femininity, Feminism, and the Paranoid Critical Subject," in ***Subjectivity and Literature from the Romantics to the Present Day.*** Edited by Philip Shaw and Peter Stockwell. Pinter, 1991. Copyright © Emma Francis. All rights reserved. Reproduced by permission of the author.—Freedman, Estelle B. and Erna Olafson Hellerstein. From an introduction to ***Victorian Women: A Documentary Account of Women's Lives in Nineteenth-Century England, France, and the United States.*** Edited by Erna Olafson Hellerstein, Leslie Parker Hume, and Karen M. Offen. Stanford University Press, 1981. Copyright © 1981 by the Board of Trustees of Leland Stanford Junior University. Reproduced with permission of Stanford University Press, www-.sup.org.—Frenk, Susan. From "The Wandering Text: Situating the Narratives of Isabel Allende," in ***Latin American Women's Writing: Feminist Readings in Theory and Crisis.*** Edited by Anny Brooksbank Jones and Catherine Davies. Oxford at the Clarendon Press, 1996. Copyright © 1996 by Anny Brooksbank Jones and Catherine Davies. All rights reserved. Reproduced by permission of Oxford University Press.—From ***Victorian Women: A Documentary Account of Women's Lives in Nineteenth-Century England, France, and the United States.*** Edited by Erna Olafson Hellerstein, Leslie Parker Hume, and Karen M. Offen. Stanford University Press, 1981. Copyright © 1981 by the Board of Trustees of Leland Stanford Junior University. Reproduced with permission of Stanford University Press, www.sup.org.—Galvin, Mary E. From ***Queer Poetics: Five Modernist Women Writers.*** Praeger, 1999. Copyright © 1999 by Mary E. Galvin. All rights reserved. Reproduced by permission.—Garner, Shirley Nelson. From "Constructing the Mother: Contemporary Psychoanalytic Theorists and Women Autobiographers," in ***Narrating Mother: Theorizing Maternal Subjectivities.*** Edited by Brenda O. Daly and Maureen T. Reddy. University of Tennessee Press, 1991. Copyright © 1991 by The University of Tennessee Press. Reproduced by permission of the publisher.—Ghymn, Esther Mikyung. From an introduction to ***Images of Asian American Women by Asian American Women Writers.*** Peter Lang, 1995. Copyright © 1995, by Esther Mikyung Ghymn. All rights reserved. Reproduced by permission.—Gilbert, Sandra M. and Gubar, Susan. From "Charred Skirts and Deathmask: World War II and the Blitz on Women," in ***No Man's Land: The Place of the Woman Writer in the Twentieth Century, Volume 3: Letters from the Front.*** Yale University Press, 1994. Copyright © 1994, by Sandra M. Gilbert and Susan Gubar. All rights reserved. Reproduced by permission.—Gilbert, Sandra M. and Susan Gubar. From "The Battle of the Sexes: The Men's Case," in ***No Man's Land: The Place of the Woman Writer in the Twentieth Century, Volume 1: The War of the Words.*** Yale University Press, 1988. Copyright © 1988, by Yale University Press, All rights reserved. Reproduced by permission.—Gilbert, Sandra M., and Susan Gubar. From "The Second Coming of Aphrodite: Kate Chopin's Fantasy of Desire," in ***No Man's Land: The Place of the Woman Writer in the Twentieth Century.*** Yale University Press, 1989. Copyright © 1989 by Yale University. Copyright © 1984 by Sandra M. Gilbert and Susan Gubar. All rights reserved. Reproduced by permission.—Gilbert, Susan M., and Susan Gubar. From ***The Madwoman in the Attic: The Woman Writer and the Nineteenth-Century Literary Imagination.*** Yale University Press, 1979. Copyright © 1979 by Yale University. All rights reserved. Reproduced by permission.—Gleadle, Kathryn. From an introduction to ***The Early Feminists: Radical Unitarians and the Emergence of The Women's Rights Movement, 1831-51.*** Macmillan Press Ltd., 1995. Copyright © Kathryn Gleadle 1995. All rights reserved. Reproduced by permission of Palgrave Macmillan.—Golden, Catherine. From "One Hundred Years of Reading 'The Yellow Wallpaper'," in ***The Captive Imagination: A Casebook on "The Yellow Wallpaper."*** Edited by Catherine Golden. The Feminist Press at the City University of New York, 1992. Copyright © 1992 by Catherine Golden. All rights reserved. Reproduced by permission.—Gorsky, Susan Rubinow. From ***Femininity to Feminism: Women and Literature in the Nineteenth Century.*** Twayne Publishers, 1992. Copyright © 1992 by Twayne Publishers. All rights reserved. Reproduced by permission of The Gale Group.—Greer, Germaine. From ***The Madwoman's Underclothes: Essays and Occasional Writings.*** The Atlantic Monthly Press, 1986. Copyright © 1970, 1986, by Germaine Greer. All rights reserved. Reproduced by permission.—Grewal, Gurleen. From ***Circles of Sorrow, Lines of Struggle: The Novels of Toni Morrison.*** Louisiana State University Press, 1998. Copyright © 1998 by Louisiana State University Press. All rights reserved. Reproduced by permission.—Griffin, Alice and Geraldine Thorsten. From ***Understanding Lillian Hellman.*** University of South Carolina Press, 1999. Copyright © 1999 University of South Carolina. Reproduced by permission.—Griffin, Susan E. From "Resistance and Reinvention in Sandra Cisneros' *Woman Hollering Creek*," in ***Ethnicity and the American Short Story.*** Edited by Julie Brown. Garland Publishing, Inc., 1997. Copyright © 1997 by Julie Brown. All rights reserved. Reproduced by permission of the publisher and the author.—Grogan, Susan K. From an introduction to ***French Socialism and Sexual Difference: Women and the New Society, 1803-44.*** St. Martin's Press, 1992. Copyright © Susan K. Grogan 1992. All rights reserved. Reprinted by permission of Palgrave Macmillan.—Grössinger, Christa. From ***Picturing Women in Late Medieval and Renaissance Art.*** Manchester University Press, 1997. Copyright © Christa Grössinger 1997. Reproduced by permission.—Grubbs, Judith Evans. From ***Women and the Law in the Roman Empire: A Sourcebook on Marriage, Divorce and Widowhood.*** Routledge, 2002. Reproduced by permission of the publisher.—Grundy, Isobel. From "(Re)discovering Women's Texts," in ***Women and Literature in Britain 1700-1800.*** Edited by Vivien Jones. Cambridge University Press, 2000. Copyright © 2000 by Cambridge University Press. Reproduced by permission of Cambridge University Press.—Gubar, Susan. From "Feminist Misogyny: Mary Wollstonecraft and the Paradox of 'It Takes One to Know One'," in ***Feminism Beside Itself.*** Edited by Diane Elam and Robyn Wiegman. Routledge, 1995. Copyright © 1995 by Routledge.

All rights reserved. Reproduced by permission of Routledge/Taylor & Francis and the author.—Gubar, Susan. From "Sapphistries," in ***Re-reading Sappho: Reception and Transmission.*** Edited by Ellen Greene. University of California Press, 1996. Copyright © 1996 by The Regents of The University of California. Reproduced by permission of the publisher and the author.—Gunther-Canada, Wendy. From ***Rebel Writer: Mary Wollstonecraft and Enlightenment Politics.*** Northern Illinois University Press, 2001. Copyright © 2001 by Northern Illinois University Press. All rights reserved. Reproduced by permission.—Hagen, Lyman B. From ***Heart of a Woman, Mind of a Writer, and Soul of a Poet: A Critical Analysis of the Writings of Maya Angelou.*** University Press of America, 1997. Copyright © 1997 by University Press of America. All rights reserved. Reproduced by permission.—Hallett, Judith From "The Role of Women in Roman Elegy: Counter-Cultural Feminism," in ***Women in the Ancient World: The Arethusa Papers.*** Edited by John Peradotto and J. Sullivan. State University of New York Press, 1984. Reproduced by permission of the State University of New York Press.—Hansberry, Lorraine. From ***A Raisin in the Sun.*** Modern Library, 1995. Copyright © 1958, 1986 by Robert Nemiroff, as an unpublished work. Copyright © 1959, 1966, 1984, 1987, 1988 by Robert Nemiroff. All rights reserved. Reproduced by permission of Random House, Inc., Jewell Gresham-Nemiroff and Methuen Publishing Ltd.—Harris, Susan K. From "'But is it any good?' Evaluating Nineteenth-Century American Women's Fiction," in ***The (Other) American Traditions: Nineteenth-Century Women Writers.*** Edited by Joyce W. Warren. Rutgers University Press, 1993. Copyright © 1993 by Rutgers University Press. All rights reserved. Reproduced by permission of the author.—Head, Bessie. From "Despite Broken Bondage, Botswana Women Are Still Unloved," in ***A Woman Alone: Autobiographical Writings.*** Selected and edited by Craig MacKenzie. Heinemann, 1990. Copyright © 1990, by The Estate of Bessie Head. Reproduced by permission of Johnson & Alcock.—Head, Bessie. From "The Woman from America," in ***A Woman Alone: Autobiographical Writings.*** Selected and edited by Craig MacKenzie. Heinemann, 1990. Copyright © 1990, by The Estate of Bessie Head. Reproduced by permission of Johnson & Alcock.—Hellerstein, Erna, Leslie Parker Hume and Karen M. Offen from an introduction to ***Victorian Women: A Documentary Account of Women's Lives in Nineteenth-Century England, France, and the United States.*** Edited by Erna Olafson Hellerstein, Leslie Parker Hume, and Karen M. Offen. Stanford University Press, 1981. Copyright © 1981 by the Board of Trustees of the Leland Stanford Junior University. Reproduced with permission of Stanford University Press, www.sup.org.—Henderson, Bruce. From ***Images of the Self as Female: The Achievement of Women Artists in Re-envisioning Feminine Identity.*** Edited by Kathryn N. Benzel and Lauren Pringle De La Vars. The Edwin Mellen Press, 1992. Copyright © 1992 by Kathryn N. Benzel and Lauren Pringle De La Vars. All rights reserved. Reproduced by permission.—Hill, Mary A. From "Charlotte Perkins Gilman: A Feminist's Struggle with Womanhood," in ***Charlotte Perkins Gilman: The Woman and Her Work.*** Edited by Sheryl L. Meyering. UMI Research Press, 1989. Copyright © 1989 by Sheryl L. Meyering. All rights reserved. Reproduced by permission of Boydell & Brewer, Inc.—Hobby, Elaine. From ***Virtue of Necessity: English Women's Writing 1649-88.*** The University of Michigan Press, 1989. Copyright © 1988 by Elaine Hobby. All rights reserved. Reproduced by permission of the author.—Hoffert, Sylvia D. From an introduction to ***When Hens Crow: The Woman's Rights Movement in Antebellum America.*** Indiana University Press, 1995. Copyright © 1995 by Sylvia D. Hoffert. All rights reserved. Reproduced by permission.—Hurston, Zora Neale. From ***Their Eyes Were Watching God.*** Perennial Library, 1990. Copyright © 1937 by Harper & Row, Publishers, Inc. Renewed 1965 by John C. Hurston and Joel Hurston. Reproduced by permission of Time Warner Books UK. In North America by HarperCollins Publishers Inc.—James, Adeola. From "Bessie Head's Perspectives on Women," in ***Black Women Writers across Cultures.*** Edited by Valentine Udoh James, James S. Etim, Melanie Marshall James, and Ambe J. Njoh. International Scholars Publications, 2000. Copyright © 2000, by International Scholars Publications. All rights reserved. Reproduced by permission.—Jardine, Alice A. From an interview with Marguerite Duras, translated by Katherine Ann Jensen, in ***Shifting Scenes: Interviews on Women, Writing, and Politics in Post-68 France.*** Edited by Alice A. Jardine and Anne M. Menke. Columbia University Press, 1991. Copyright © 1991 Columbia University Press, New York. All rights reserved. Reprinted with the permission of the publisher.—Jelinek, Estelle C. From "The Paradox and Success of Elizabeth Cady Stanton," in ***Women's Autobiography: Essays in Criticism.*** Edited by Estelle C. Jelinek. Indiana University Press, 1980. Copyright © Estelle C. Jelinek. Reproduced by permission of the author.—Juhasz, Suzanne. From "Maxine Hong Kingston: Narrative Technique & Female Identity," in ***Contemporary American Women Writers: Narrative Strategies.*** Edited by Catherine Rainwater and William J. Scheik. The University Press of Kentucky, 1985. Copyright © 1985 by The University Press of

Kentucky. Reproduced by permission.—Kaminer, Wendy. From "Feminism's Identity Crisis," in ***Public Women, Public Words: A Documentary History of American Feminism.*** Edited by Dawn Keetley and John Pettegrew. First published in *The Atlantic.* Reproduced by permission of the author.—Kaplan, Cora. From "Pandora's Box: Subjectivity, Class and Sexuality in Socialist Feminist Criticism," in ***Making a Difference: Feminist Literary Criticism.*** Edited by Gayle Greene and Coppélia Kahn. Methuen & Co., 1985. Copyright © 1985 Gayle Greene and Coppélia Kahn. All rights reserved. Reproduced by permission of Routledge and the author.—Keetley, Dawn and John Pettegrew. From "Identities through Adversity," in ***Public Women, Public Words: A Documentary History of American Feminism.*** Edited by Dawn Keetley and John Pettegrew. Madison House Publishers, Inc., 1997. Copyright © 1997 by Madison House Publisher, Inc. All rights reserved. Reproduced by permission.—Kelly, Gary. From ***Revolutionary Feminism: The Mind and Career of Mary Wollstonecraft.*** St. Martin's Press, 1996. Copyright © 1996 by Gary Kelly. All rights reserved. Reproduced by permission of Palgrave Macmillan.—Kempe, Margery. From "Margery Kempe's Visit to Julian of Norwich," in ***The Shewings of Julian Norwich.*** Edited by Georgia Ronan Crampton. Medieval Publishing Institute, 1994. Reproduced by permission.—Kempe, Margery. From ***The Book of Margery Kempe.*** Translated by B. A. Windeatt. Penguin, 1985. Copyright © B. A. Windeatt, 1985. All rights reserved. Reproduced by permission.—Kirkham, Margaret. From ***Jane Austen, Feminism, and Fiction.*** Harvester Press Limited, 1983. Copyright © Margaret Kirkham, 1983. All rights reserved. Reproduced by permission.—Klemans, Patricia A. From "'Being Born a Woman': A New Look at Edna St. Vincent Millay," in ***Critical Essays on Edna St. Vincent Millay.*** Edited by William B. Thesing. G. K. Hall, 1993. Copyright © by 1993 by William B. Thesing. All rights reserved. Reproduced by permission of The Gale Group.—Knapp, Bettina L. From ***Gertrude Stein.*** Continuum, 1990. Copyright © 1990 by Bettina L. Knapp. All rights reserved. Reproduced by permission.—Kolodny, Annette. From "Dancing Through the Minefield: Some Observations on the Theory, Practice, and Politics of a Feminist Literary Criticism," originally published in ***Feminist Studies,*** 1980. Copyright © 1980 by Annette Kolodny. All rights reserved. Reproduced by permission of the author.—Kumin, Maxine. From "How It Was," in ***The Complete Poems: Anne Sexton.*** Houghton Mifflin Company, 1981. Copyright © 1981, by Maxine Kumin. All rights reserved. Reproduced by permission of Houghton Mifflin and The Anderson Literary Agency.—Lamonica, Drew. From ***We Are Three Sisters: Self and Family in the Writing of the Brontës.*** University of Missouri Press, 2003. Copyright © 2003 by The Curators of the University of Missouri. All rights reserved. Reproduced by permission.—Larsen, Jeanne. From "Lowell, Teasdale, Wylie, Millay, and Bogan," in ***The Columbia History of American Poetry.*** Edited by Jay Parini. Columbia University Press, 1993. Copyright © 1993 Columbia University Press, New York. All rights reserved. Reprinted with permission of the publisher.—Lascelles, Mary. From ***Jane Austen and Her Art.*** Oxford University Press, 1939. Reproduced by permission of Oxford University Press.—Lavezzo, Kathy. From "Sobs and Sighs Between Women: The Homoerotics of Compassion in *The Book of Margery Kempe,*" in ***Premodern Sexualities.*** Edited by Louise Fradenburg and Carla Freccero. Routledge, 1996. Copyright © 1996 by Routledge. All rights reserved. Reproduced by permission of Routledge/Taylor & Francis and the author.—Lessing, Doris. From a preface to *The Golden Notebook* in ***A Small Personal Voice.*** Edited by Paul Schleuter. Alfred A. Knopf, Inc., 1974. Copyright © 1974 by Doris Lessing. All rights reserved. Reproduced by permission of Jonathan Clowes, Ltd.—Levertov, Denise. From ***Poems, 1960-67.*** New Directions, 1966. Copyright © 1967, by Denise Levertov. All rights reserved. Reproduced by permission of New Directions Publishing Corporation and in the UK by Pollinger Limited and the proprietor.—Logan, Shirley Wilson. From ***"We are Coming": The Persuasive Discourse of Nineteenth-Century Black Women.*** Southern Illinois University Press, 1999. Copyright © 1999 by the Board of Trustees, Southern Illinois University. All rights reserved. Reproduced by permission of Southern Illinois University Press and the University of South Carolina Press.—Lorde, Audre. From ***The Black Unicorn.*** Norton, 1978. Copyright © 1978, by Audre Lorde. All rights reserved. Reproduced by permission of W. W. Norton & Company and Charlotte Sheedy Literary Agency.—Lumsden, Linda J. From ***Rampant Women: Suffragists and the Right of Assembly.*** The University of Tennessee Press, 1997. Copyright © 1997 by The University of Tennessee Press. Reproduced by permission of The University of Tennessee Press.—Lunardini, Christine A. ***From Equal Suffrage to Equal Rights: Alice Paul and the National Women's Party, 1910-1928.*** New York University Press, 1986. Copyright © 1986 by New York University. All rights reserved. Reproduced by permission of the author.—Madsen, Deborah L. From "Sandra Cisneros," in ***Understanding Contemporary Chicana Literature.*** Edited by Matthew J. Bruccoli. University of South Carolina Press, 2000. Copyright © 2000 by University of South Carolina. Reproduced by permission.—Marder, Herbert. From ***Feminism & Art: A Study of Virginia Woolf.*** University of Chicago Press, 1968. Copyright © 1968 by the University of Chicago. All rights reserved. Reproduced by permission of the publisher and the author.—Marilley, Suzanne M. From ***Woman Suffrage and the Origins of Liberal Feminism in the United States.*** Harvard University Press, 1996. Copyright © 1996 by the President and Fellows of Harvard College. All rights reserved. Reproduced by permission Harvard University Press.—Marsh-Lockett, Carol P. From "What Ever Happened to Jochebed? Motherhood as Marginality in Zora Neale Hurston's *Seraph on the Suwanee,*" in ***Southern Mothers: Facts and Fictions in Southern Women's Writing.*** Edited by Nagueyalti Warren and Sally Wolff. Louisiana State University, 1999. Reproduced by permission.—Mason, Nicholas. From "Class, Gender, and Domesticity in Maria Edgeworth's *Belinda,*" in ***The Eighteenth-Century Novel,*** Vol. 1. Edited by Susan Spencer. AMS Press, 2001. Reproduced by permission.—Massardier-Kenney, Françoise. From ***Gender in the Fiction of George Sand.*** Rodopi, 1985. Copyright © Editions Rodopi B. V. Reproduced by permission.—McCracken, Ellen. From "Sandra Cisneros' *The House on Mango Street*: Community-Oriented Introspection and the Demystification of Patriarchal Violence," in ***Breaking Boundaries: Latina Writing and Critical Readings.*** Edited by Asunción Horno-Delgado, Eliana Ortega, Nina M. Scott, and Nancy Saporta Sternbach. University of Massachusetts Press, 1989. Copyright © 1989 by The University of Massachusetts Press. All rights reserved. Reproduced by permission.—McNamara, Jo Ann. From "Women and Power through the Family Revisited," in ***Gendering the Master Narrative: Women and Power in the Middle Ages.*** Edited by Mary C. Erler and Maryanne Kowaleski. Cornell University Press, 2003. Copyright © 2003 by Cornell University Press. Used by permission of Cornell University Press.—Meisenhelder, Susan. From "Ethnic and Gender Identity in Zora Neale Hurston's *Their Eyes Were Watching God,*" in ***Teaching American Ethnic Literatures: Nineteen Essays.*** Edited by John R. Maitino and David R. Peck. University of New Mexico Press, 1996. Copyright © 1996, by the University of New Mexico Press. All rights reserved. Reproduced by permission.—Mellor, Anne K. From "Possessing Nature: The Female in Frankenstein," in ***Romanticism and Feminism.*** Edited by Anne K. Mellor. Indiana University Press, 1988. Copyright © 1988 by Indiana University Press. All rights reserved. Reproduced by permission.—Mermin, Dorothy. From ***Godiva's Ride: Women of Letters in England, 1830-1880.*** Indiana University Press, 1993. Copyright © 1993 by Dorothy Mermin. All rights reserved. Reproduced by permission.—Millay, Edna St. Vincent. From "Sonnet III of Fatal Interview," in ***Collected Sonnets of Edna St. Vincent Millay.*** HarperCollins, 1952. Copyright © 1931, 1958 by Edna St. Vincent Millay and Norma Millay Ellis. All rights reserved. Reproduced by permission of Elizabeth Barnett, Literary Executor.—Millay, Edna St. Vincent. From "First Fig," in ***Collected Poems of Edna St. Vincent Millay.*** HarperCollins, 1952. Copyright © 1922, 1950 by Edna St. Vincent Millay. Reproduced by permission of Elizabeth Barnett, Literary Executor.—Millay, Edna St. Vincent. From "I, Being Born a Woman and Distressed," in ***Collected Poems of Edna St. Vincent Millay.*** HarperCollins, 1952. Copyright © 1923, 1951 by Edna St.Vincent Millay and Norma Millay Ellis. All rights reserved. Reproduced by permission of Elizabeth Barnett, Literary Executor.—Millett, Kate. From "How Many Lives Are Here...," in ***The Feminist Memoir Project.*** Edited by Rachel DuPlessis and Ann Snitow. Three Rivers Press, 1998. Copyright © 1998 by Rachel DuPlessis and Ann Snitow. All rights reserved. Used by permission of Crown Publishers, a division of Random House, Inc. and Sanford J. Greenburger Associates.—Moi, Toril. From "Who's Afraid of Virginia Woolf? Feminist Readings of Woolf," in ***New Casebooks: 'Mrs. Dalloway' and 'To the Lighthouse.'*** Edited by Su Reid. St. Martin's Press, 1993. Copyright © Su Reid 1993. All rights reserved. Reproduced by permission of Palgrave Macmillan.—Moore, Marianne. From ***The Selected Letters of Marianne Moore.*** Edited by Bonnie Costello. Alfred A. Knopf, 1997. Copyright © 1997 by the Estate of Marianne Moore. Introduction, annotations and additional editorial material copyright 1997 by Bonnie Costello. All rights reserved. Reproduced by permission of Alfred A. Knopf, Inc., a division of Random House, Inc.—Morgan, Winifred. From "Alice Walker: *The Color Purple* as Allegory," in ***Southern Writers at Century's End.*** Edited by Jeffrey J. Folks and James A. Perkins. The University Press of Kentucky, 1997. Copyright © 1997 by The University Press of Kentucky. All rights reserved. Reproduced by permission.—Morrison, Toni. From ***Race-ing Justice, En-Gendering Power.*** Pantheon Books, 1992. Copyright © 1992 by Toni Morrison. All rights reserved. Used by permission International Creative Management, Inc.—Morrison, Toni. From "What the Black Woman Thinks About Women's Lib," in ***Public Women, Public Words: A Documentary History of American Feminism.*** Edited by Dawn Keetley and John Pettegrew. Madison House, 1997. Copyright © 1997 by Toni Morrison. Reproduced by permission of International Creative Management, Inc.—Mortimer, Armine Kotin. From "Male and Female Plots in Staël's *Corinne,*" in ***Correspondences:***

Studies in Literature, History, and the Arts in Nineteenth-Century France: Selected Proceedings of the Sixteenth Colloquium in Nineteenth-Century French Studies, The University of Oklahoma-Norman, October 11th-13th, 1990. Edited by Keith Busby. Rodopi, 1992. Copyright © Editions Rodopi B. V. Reproduced by permission.—Motard-Noar, Martine. From "From Persephone to Demeter: A Feminist Experience in Cixous's Fiction," in ***Images of Persephone: Feminist Readings in Western Literature.*** Edited by Elizabeth T. Hayes. University Press of Florida, 1994. Copyright © 1994 by Board of Regents of the State of Florida. All rights reserved. Reproduced with the permission of the University Press of Florida.—Mukherjee, Bharati. From ***The Middleman and Other Stories.*** Viking, 1988. Copyright © 1988, by Bharati Mukherjee. All rights reserved. Reprinted by permission of Penguin Group Canada and the author.—Mumford, Marilyn R. From "A Feminist Prolegomenon for the Study of Hildegard of Bingen," in ***Gender, Culture, and the Arts: Women, the Arts, and Society.*** Edited by Ronald Dotterer and Susan Bowers. Associated University Presses, 1993. Copyright © 1993 by Associated University Presses.—Oates, Joyce Carol. From ***Where I've Been, and Where I'm Going.*** Plume, 1999. Copyright © The Ontario Review, 1999. All rights reserved. Reproduced by permission of Plume, an imprint of Penguin Putnam Inc. In the United Kingdom by John Hawkins & Associates, Inc.—Okely, Judith. From "Re-reading The Second Sex," in ***Simone de Beauvoir: A Re-Reading.*** Virago, 1986. Reproduced by permission of the author.—Ovid. From "Sappho to Phaon," in ***The Sappho Companion.*** Edited by Margaret Reynolds. Chatto and Windus, 2000. Copyright © Margaret Reynolds 2000. Reproduced by permission of the editor.—Pan Chao. From ***Pan Chao: Foremost Woman Scholar of China.*** Edited by Nancy Lee Swann. University of Michigan Center for Chinese Studies, 1932. Copyright © The East Asian Library and the Gest Collection, Princeton University. Reproduced by permission.—Parks, Sheri. From "In My Mother's House: Black Feminist Aesthetics, Television, and *A Raisin in the Sun,*" in ***Theatre and Feminist Aesthetics.*** Edited by Karen Laughlin and Catherine Schuler. Farleigh Dickinson University Press, 1995. Copyright © 1995 by Associated University Presses. All rights reserved. Reproduced by permission.—Paul, Alice. From ***Party Papers: 1913-1974.*** Microfilming Corporation of America, 1978. Reproduced by permission of Sewall-Belmont House and Museum.—Paz, Octavio. From "The Response," in ***Sor Juana or, The Traps of Faith.*** Translated by Margaret Sayers Peden. Cambridge, Mass.: The Belknap Press of Harvard University Press, 1988. Copyright © 1988 by the President and Fellows of Harvard College. All rights reserved. Reproduced by permission.—Perkins, Annie. From "The Poetry of Gwendolyn Brooks (1970s-1980s)," in ***Women Making Art: Women in the Visual, Literary, and Performing Arts Since 1960.*** Edited by Deborah Johnson and Wendy Oliver. Peter Lang, 2001. Copyright © 2001 Peter Lang Publishing, Inc., New York. Reproduced by permission.—Pierpont, Claudia Roth. From ***Passionate Minds: Women Rewriting the World.*** Alfred A. Knopf, 2000. Copyright © 2000 by Claudia Roth Piepont. All rights reserved. Reproduced by permission of Alfred A. Knopf, Inc., a division of Random House, Inc.—Plath, Sylvia. From ***The Bell Jar.*** Faber & Faber, 1966, Harper & Row, 1971. Copyright © 1971 by Harper & Row, Publishers, Inc. Reproduced by permission Faber & Faber Ltd. In the United States by HarperCollins Publishers Inc.—Pryse, Marjorie. From "Origins of American Literary Regionalism: Gender in Irving, Stowe, and Longstreet," in ***Breaking Boundaries: New Perspectives on Women's Regional Writing.*** Edited by Sherrie A. Inness and Diana Royer. University of Iowa Press, 1997. Copyright © 1997 by the University of Iowa Press. All rights reserved. Reproduced by permission.—Radice, Betty. From an introduction to ***The Letters of Abelard and Heloise.*** Translated by Betty Radice. Penguin Books, 1974. Copyright © Betty Radice, 1974. Reproduced by permission of Penguin Books, a division of Penguin Putnam Inc.—Rendall, Jane. From an introduction to ***The Origins of Modern Feminism: Women in Britain, France and the United States 1780-1860.*** Macmillan, 1985. Copyright © Jane Rendall 1985. All rights reserved. Reproduced by permission of Palgrave Macmillan.—Rich, Adrienne. From "Vesuvius at Home: The Power of Emily Dickinson," in ***On Lies, Secrets, and Silence: Selected Prose 1966-1978.*** W. W. Norton & Company, Inc., 1979. Copyright © 1979 by W. W. Norton & Company, Inc. Reproduced by permission of the author and W. W. Norton & Company, Inc.—Rich, Adrienne. From "When We Dead Awaken: Writing as Re-Vision," in ***Arts of the Possible: Essays and Conversations.*** W. W. Norton & Company, Inc., 2001. Copyright © 2001 by Adrienne Rich. Reproduced by permission of the publisher and the author.—Richmond, M. A. From ***Bid the Vassal Soar: Essays on the Life and Poetry of Phillis Wheatley and George Moses Horton.*** Howard University Press, 1974. All rights reserved. Copyright © 1974 by Merle A. Richmond. Reproduced by permission.—Risjord, Norman K. From ***Representative Americans: The Colonists.*** Second Edition. Rowman & Littlefield Publishers, Inc., 2001. Copyright © 2001 by Rowman & Littlefield Publishers, Inc. All rights reserved. Reproduced by permission.—Robbins,

Ruth. From ***Transitions: Literary Feminisms.*** St. Martin's Press, 2000. Reproduced with permission of Palgrave Macmillan.—Rohrbach, Erika. From H. D. and Sappho: 'A Precious Inch of Palimpsest'," in ***Re-Reading Sappho: Reception and Transmission.*** Edited by Ellen Greene. University of California Press, 1996. Copyright © 1996 by The Regents of the University of California. Reproduced by permission.—Rosenman, Ellen Bayuk. From ***"A Room of One's Own": Women Writers and the Politics of Creativity.*** Twayne, 1995. Copyright © 1995 by Twayne Publishers. All rights reserved. Reproduced by permission of The Gale Group.—Rosslyn, Wendy. From "Don Juan Feminised," in ***Symbolism and After: Essays on Russian Poetry in Honour of Georgette Donchin.*** Edited by Arnold McMillin. Bristol Classical Press, 1992. Copyright © 1992 by Gerald Duckworth & Co. Ltd. All rights reserved. Reproduced by permission of The School of Slavonic Studies in the University of London.—Sanders, Valerie. From "Women, Fiction and the Marketplace," in ***Women and Literature in Britain: 1800-1900.*** Edited by Joanne Shattock. Cambridge University Press, 2001. Copyright © Cambridge University Press 2001. Reproduced by permission of Cambridge University Press.—Sandler, Martin W. From ***Against the Odds: Women Pioneers in the First Hundred Years of Photography.*** Rizzoli International Publications, Inc., 2002. Copyright © 2002, by Martin W. Sandler. All rights reserved. Reproduced by permission of the author.—Saunders, Corinne. From ***Rape and Ravishment in the Literature of Medieval England.*** D. S. Brewer, 2001. Copyright © Corinne J. Saunders 2001. All rights reserved. Reproduced by permission.—Scheick, William J. From ***Authority and Female Authorship in Colonial America.*** The University Press of Kentucky, 1998. Copyright © 1998 by The University Press of Kentucky. Reproduced by permission of The University Press of Kentucky.—Schroeder, Patricia R. From "Remembering the Disremembered: Feminist Realists of the Harlem Renaissance," in ***Realism and the American Dramatic Tradition.*** Edited by William W. Demastes. University of Alabama Press, 1996. Copyright © 1996, by the University of Alabama Press. All rights reserved. Reproduced by permission.—Selous, Trista. From ***The Other Woman: Feminism and Femininity in the Work of Marguerite Duras.*** Yale University Press, 1988. Copyright © 1988 by Yale University. All rights reserved. Reproduced by permission.—Sexton, Anne. From "All God's Children Need Radios," in ***No Evil Star: Selected Essays, Interviews, and Prose of Anne Sexton.*** Edited by Steven E. Colburn. The University of Michigan Press, 1985. Copyright © Anne Sexton. Reproduced by permission of SLL/Sterling Lord Literistic.—Shaw, Harry B. From "*Maud Martha*: The War with Beauty," in ***A Life Distilled: Gwendolyn Brooks, Her Poetry and Fiction.*** Edited by Maria K. Mootry and Gary Smith. University of Illinois Press, 1987. Copyright © 1987 by the Board of Trustees of the University of Illinois. Reproduced by permission.—Shiach, Morag. From an introduction to ***Hélène Cixous: A Politics of Writing.*** Routledge, 1991. Copyright © 1991 by Morag Shiach. All rights reserved. Reproduced by permission of the publisher and the author.—Showalter, Elaine. From ***A Literature of Their Own: British Women Novelists from Brontë to Lessing.*** Princeton University Press, 1977. Copyright © 1977 by Princeton University Press. Renewed 2005 Princeton University Press, 1999 exp. Paperback edition. Reproduced by permission of Princeton University Press.—Showalter, Elaine. From ***Sister's Choice: Tradition and Change in American Women's Writing.*** Oxford at the Clarendon Press, 1991. Copyright © 1991, by Elaine Showalter. All rights reserved. Reproduced by permission of Oxford University Press.—Sigerman, Harriet. From "Laborers for Liberty," in ***No Small Courage: A History of Women in the United States.*** Edited by Nancy F. Cott. Oxford University Press, 2000. Copyright © 2000 by Oxford University Press, Inc. Copyright © 1994, 2000 by Harriet Sigerman. All rights reserved. Used by permission of Oxford University Press.—Signori, Lisa F. From ***The Feminization of Surrealism: The Road to Surreal Silence in Selected Works of Marguerite Duras.*** Peter Lang, 2001. Copyright © 2001 Peter Lang Publishing, Inc., New York. All rights reserved. Reproduced by permission.—Silko, Leslie Marmon. From ***Storyteller.*** Seaver Books, 1981. Copyright © 1981, by Leslie Marmon Silko. All rights reserved. Reproduced by permission.—Simson, Rennie. From "Afro-American Poets of the Nineteenth Century," in ***Nineteenth-Century Women Writers of the English-Speaking World.*** Edited by Rhoda B. Nathan. Greenwood Press, 1986. Copyright © 1986 by Hofstra University. All rights reserved. Reproduced by permission of Greenwood Publishing Group, Inc., Westport, CT.—Sizer, Lyde Cullen. From ***The Political Work of Northern Women Writers and the Civil War, 1850-1872.*** The University of North Carolina Press, 2000. Copyright © 2000 The University of North Carolina Press. All rights reserved. Reproduced by permission.—Smith, Hilda L. From "Introduction: Women, Intellect, and Politics: Their Intersection in Seventeenth-Century England," in ***Women Writers and the Early Modern British Political Tradition.*** Edited by Hilda L. Smith. Cambridge University Press, 1998. Copyright © Cambridge University Press 1998. Reproduced with the permission of Cambridge University Press.—Smith,

Johanna M. From "'Cooped Up': Feminine Domesticity in *Frankenstein,*" in ***Case Studies in Contemporary Criticism: Mary Shelley's* Frankenstein.** Edited by Johanna M. Smith. St. Martin's Press, 1992. Copyright © 1992 by Bedford Books of St. Martin's Press. All rights reserved. Reproduced by permission.—Smith, Sidonie. From "Resisting the Gaze of Embodiment: Women's Autobiography in the Nineteenth Century," in ***American Women's Autobiography: Fea(s)ts of Memory.*** Edited by Margo Culley. University of Wisconsin University Press, 1992. Copyright © 1992 The Board of Regents of the University of Wisconsin System. All rights reserved. Reproduced by permission.—Smith, Sidonie. From ***Where I'm Bound: Patterns of Slavery and Freedom in Black American Autobiography.*** Greenwood Press, 1974. Copyright © 1974 by Sidonie Smith. All rights reserved. Reproduced by permission of Greenwood Publishing Group, Inc., Westport, CT.—Snyder, Jane McIntosh. From ***The Woman and the Lyre: Women Writers in Classical Greece and Rome.*** Southern Illinois University Press, 1989. Copyright © 1989 by the Board of Trustees, Southern Illinois University. All rights reserved. Reproduced by permission.—Sor Juana Ines de la Cruz. From ***The Answer = La respuesta.*** Edited by Electa Arenal and Amanda Powell. The Feminist Press, 1994. Copyright © 1994 by Electa Arenal and Amanda Powell. All rights reserved. Reproduced by permission of The Feminist Press at the City University of New York. www.feministpress.org.—Spender, Dale. From "Introduction: A Vindication of the Writing Woman," in ***Living by the Pen: Early British Women Writers.*** Edited by Dale Spender. Teachers College Press, 1992. Copyright © 1992 by Teachers College. All rights reserved. Reproduced by permission.—Staley, Lynn. From ***Margery Kempe's Dissenting Fictions.*** Pennsylvania State University Press, 1994. Copyright © 1994 The Pennsylvania State University. All rights reserved. Reproduced by permission.—Stehle, Eva. From ***Performance and Gender in Ancient Greece: Nondramatic Poetry in Its Setting.*** Princeton University Press, 1997. Copyright © 1997 by Princeton University Press. All rights reserved. Reproduced by permission of Princeton University Press.—Stein, Gertrude. From "Degeneration in American Women," in ***Sister Brother: Gertrude and Leo Stein.*** Edited by Brenda Wineapple. G. Putnam's Sons, 1996. Copyright © 1996 by Brenda Wineapple. All rights reserved. Used by permission of G. Putnam's Sons, a division of Penguin Group (USA) Inc. and Bloomsbury Publishing Plc.—Stott, Rebecca. From ***Elizabeth Barrett Browning.*** Pearson Education Limited, 2003. Copyright © Pearson Educated Limited 2003. All rights reserved. Reproduced by permission.—Straub, Kristina. From ***Divided Fictions: Fanny Burney and Feminine Strategy.*** University Press of Kentucky, 1987. Copyright © 1987 by the University Press of Kentucky. Reproduced by permission.—Swann, Nancy Lee. From ***Pan Chao: Foremost Woman Scholar of China.*** Russell & Russell, 1968. Copyright © The East Asian Library and the Gest Collection, Princeton University. Reproduced by permission.—Tanner, Laura E. From ***Intimate Violence: Reading Rape and Torture in Twentieth-Century Fiction.*** Indiana University Press, 1994. Copyright © 1994, by Laura E. Tanner. All rights reserved. Reproduced by permission.—Terborg-Penn, Rosalyn. From ***African American Women in the Struggle for the Vote, 1850-1920.*** Indiana University Press, 1998. Reproduced by permission.—Tharp, Julie. From "Women's Community and Survival in the Novels of Louise Erdrich," in ***Communication and Women's Friendships: Parallels and Intersections in Literature and Life.*** Edited by Janet Doubler Ward and JoAnna Stephens Mink. Bowling Green State University Popular Press, 1993. Copyright © 1993 by Bowling Green State University Popular Press. Reproduced by permission of the University of Wisconsin Press.—Trilling, Lionel. From "Emma and the Legend of Jane Austen," in ***Beyond Culture: Essays on Literature and Learning.*** Harcourt Brace Jovanovich, 1965. Copyright © 1965 by Lionel Trilling. All rights reserved. Reproduced by permission of the Wylie Agency, Inc.—Turner, Katherine S. H. From "From Classical to Imperial: Changing Visions of Turkey in the Eighteenth Century," in ***Travel Writing and Empire: Postcolonial Theory in Transit.*** Edited by Steve Clark. Zed Books, 1999. Copyright © Katherine S. H. Turner. Reproduced by permission.—Van Dyke, Annette. From "Of Vision Quests and Spirit Guardians: Female Power in the Novels of Louise Erdrich," in ***The Chippewa Landscape of Louise Erdrich.*** Edited by Allan Chavkin. The University of Alabama Press, 1999. Copyright © 1999, by The University of Alabama Press. Copyright © 1999. All rights reserved. Reproduced by permission.—Waelti-Waters, Jennifer and Steven C. Hause. From an introduction to ***Feminisms of the Belle Époque: A Historical and Literary Anthology.*** Edited by Jennifer Waelti-Waters and Steven C. Hause. University of Nebraska Press, 1994. Copyright © The University of Nebraska Press, 1994. All rights reserved. Reproduced by permission.—Wagner-Martin, Linda. From "Panoramic, Unpredictable, and Human: Joyce Carol Oates' Recent Novels," in ***Traditions, Voices, and Dreams: The American Novel since the 1960s.*** Edited by Melvin J. Friedman and Ben Siegel. University of Delaware Press, 1995. Copyright © 1995 by Associated University Presses, Inc. Reproduced by permission.—Wagner-Martin, Linda. From ***Sylvia Plath: A Literary Life.***

St. Martin's Press, 1999. Copyright © 1999 by Linda Wagner-Martin. All rights reserved. Reproduced by permission of Palgrave Macmillan.—Walker, Alice. From ***Revolutionary Petunias & Other Poems.*** Harcourt Brace Jovanovich, 1971. Copyright © 1970, 1971, 1972, 1973, renewed 1998 by Alice Walker. All right reserved. Reproduced by permission of Harcourt Inc. In the British Commonwealth by David Higham Associates.—Watts, Linda S. From ***Rapture Untold: Gender, Mysticism, and the 'Moment of Recognition' in Works by Gertrude Stein.*** Peter Lang, 1996. Copyright © 1996 Peter Lang Publishing, Inc., New York. All rights reserved. Reproduced by permission.—Weatherford, Doris. From ***A History of the American Suffragist Movement.*** ABC-CLIO, 1998. Copyright © 1998 by The Moschovitis Group, Inc. Reproduced by permission of Moschovitis Group, Inc.—Weeton, Nellie. From "The Trials of an English Governess: Nelly Weeton Stock," originally published in ***Miss Weeton: Journal of a Governess.*** Edited by Edward Hall. Oxford University Press (London), H. Milford, 1936-39. Reproduced by permission of Oxford University Press.—Weston, Ruth D. From "Who Touches This Touches a Woman," in ***Critical Essays on Alice Walker.*** Edited by Ikenna Dieke. Greenwood Press 1999. Reproduced by permission of Greenwood Publishing Group, Inc., Westport, CT.—Wheeler, Marjorie Spruill. From an introduction to ***One Woman, One Vote: Rediscovering the Woman Suffrage Movement.*** Edited by Marjorie Spruill Wheeler. NewSage Press, 1995. Copyright © 1995 by NewSage Press and Educational Film Company. All rights reserved. Reproduced by permission.—Willard, Charity Cannon. From ***Christine de Pizan: Her Life and Works.*** Persea Books, 1984. Copyright © 1984 by Charity Cannon Willard. Reproduced by permission.—Willis, Sharon A. From "Staging Sexual Difference: Reading, Recitation, and Repetition in Duras' *Malady of Death,*" in ***Feminine Focus: The New Women Playwrights.*** Edited by Enoch Brater. Oxford University Press, 1989. Copyright © 1989 by Oxford University Press, Inc. Reproduced by permission of Oxford University Press.—Winter, Kate H. From ***Marietta Holley: Life with "Josiah Allen's Wife."*** Syracuse University Press, 1984. Copyright © 1984 by Syracuse University Press. All rights reserved. Reproduced by permission.—Woolf, Virginia. From "George Eliot," in ***The Common Reader,*** Harcourt, Brace & Company, 1925, L. & V. Woolf, 1925. Copyright 1925 by Harcourt Brace & Company. Renewed 1953 by Leonard Woolf. Reprinted by permission of Harcourt, Brace & Company and The Society of Authors.—Wynne-Davies, Marion. From an introduction to ***Women Poets of the Renaissance.*** Edited by Marion Wynne-Davies. Routledge, 1999. Reprint. Copyright © 1998 by J. M. Dent. All rights reserved. Reproduced by permission of Routledge/Taylor & Francis and the author—Yalom, Marilyn. From "Toward a History of Female Adolescence: The Contribution of George Sand," in ***George Sand: Collected Essays.*** Edited by Janis Glasgow. The Whitson Publishing Company, 1985. Reproduced by permission of the author.—Yu Xuanji. From "Joining Somebody's Mourning and Three Beautiful Sisters, Orphaned Young," in ***The Clouds Float North: The Complete Poems of Yu Xuanji.*** Translated by David Young and Jiann I. Lin. Wesleyan University Press, 1998. Copyright © 1998 by David Young and Jiann I. Lin. All rights reserved. Reproduced by permission.

Photographs and Illustrations in Feminism in Literature *were received from the following sources:*

16th century men and women wearing fashionable clothing, ca. 1565 engraving. Hulton/Archive.—A lay sister preparing medicine as shown on the cover of *The Book of Margery Kempe,* photograph. MS. Royal 15 D 1, British Library, London.—Akhmatova, Anna, photograph. Archive Photos, Inc./Express Newspaper.—Alcott, Louisa May, drawing. The Granger Collection, New York.—Alcott, Louisa May, photograph. Archive Photos, Inc.—Allen, Joan, Joanne Camp, Anne Lange, and Cynthia Nixon, in a scene from the play "The Heidi Chronicles," photograph. Time Life Pictures/Getty Images.—Allende, Isabelle, photograph. Getty Images.—An estimated 5,000 people march outside the Minnesota Capitol Building in protest to the January 22, 1973 Supreme Court ruling on abortion as a result of the "Roe vs. Wade" case, photograph. AP/Wide World Photos.—Angelou, Maya, photograph. AP/Wide World Photos.—Anthony, Susan B., Frances Willard, and other members of the International Council of Women, photograph. Copyright © Corbis.—Atwood, Margaret, photograph by Jerry Bauer. Copyright © Jerry Bauer.—Autographed manuscript of Phillis Weatley's poem "To the University of Cambridge." The Granger Collection, New York.—Beller, Kathleen as Kate in the 1980 film version of Margaret Atwood's novel, *Surfacing,* photograph. Kobal Collection/Surfacing Film.—Blackshear, Thomas, illustrator. From a cover of *The Bluest Eye,* written by Toni Morrison. Plume, 1994. Reproduced by permission of Plume, a division of Penguin USA.—Broadside published by the National American Woman Suffrage Association, featuring "Why Women Want to Vote." The Library of Congress.—Brontë, Anne, Emily and Charlotte, painting by Patrick Branwell Brontë, located at the National Portrait Gallery,

1939, photograph. Copyright © Corbis-Bettmann.—Brontë, Charlotte, painting. Archive Photos.—Brooks, Gwendolyn, holding a copy of *The World of Gwendolyn Brooks,* photograph. AP/Wide World Photos.—Brown, John Mason (right) talking to National Book Award winners Marianne Moore, James Jones, and Rachel Carson, in New York City, NY, 1952, photograph. AP/Wide World Photos.—Brown, Rita Mae, photograph. AP/Wide World Photos.—Browning, Elizabeth Barret, 1848, illustration. Copyright © Corbis-Bettmann.—Burney, Fanny, engraving. Archive Photos, Inc.—Carter, Angela, photograph by Jerry Bauer. Copyright © Jerry Bauer.—Cather, Willa, photograph. AP/Wide World Photos.—Catherine the Great, illustration. Copyright © Archivo Iconografico, S.A./Corbis.—Catt, Carrie Chapman, photograph. The Library of Congress.—Cavendish, Margaret Lucas, engraving. Mary Evans Picture Library.—Child, Lydia Maria, photograph. The Library of Congress.—Childress, Alice, photograph by Jerry Bauer. Copyright © Jerry Bauer.—Chin, Tsai and Tamlyn Tomita in the 1993 film production of Amy Tan's *The Joy Luck Club.* Buena Vista/Hollywood/The Kobal Collection.—Chopin, Kate, photograph. The Library of Congress.—Cisneros, Sandra, 1991, photograph by Dana Tynan. AP/Wide World Photos.—Cixous, Hélène, photograph. Copyright © Bassouls Sophie/Corbis Sygma.—Class on a field trip to Library of Congress, photograph by Frances Benjamin Johnston. Copyright © Corbis.—Cleopatra VII, illustration. The Library of Congress.—Cyanotype by Frances Benjamin Johnson, ca. 1899, of girls and a teacher in a high school cooking class, photograph. Copyright © Corbis.—de la Cruz, Juana Inez, painting. Copyright © Philadelphia Museum of Art/Corbis-Bettmann.—de Pizan, Christine, writing in her study, photograph. MS. Harley 4431, f.4R. British Library, London.—Dickinson, Emily, photograph of a painting. The Library of Congress.—Doolittle, Hilda, 1949, photograph. AP/Wide World Photos.—Duras, Marguerite, photograph. AP/Wide World Photos.—Dworkin, Andrea, 1986, photograph. AP/Wide World Photos.—Edgeworth, Maria, engraving. The Library of Congress.—Eliot, George, photograph. Copyright © The Bettman Archive.—Emecheta, Buchi, photograph by Jerry Bauer. Copyright © Jerry Bauer.—Emily Dickinson Homestead in Amherst, Massachusetts, photograph. Copyright © James Marshall/Corbis.—Erdrich, Louise, photograph by Eric Miller. AP/Wide World Photos.—French, Marilyn, photograph by Jerry Bauer. Copyright © Jerry Bauer.—Friedan, Betty, president of the National Organization for Women, and other feminists march in New York City, photograph. Copyright © JP Laffont/Sygma/Corbis.—Friedan, Betty, with Yoko Ono, photograph. Copyright © Bettmann/Corbis.—Frontpiece and title page from *Poems on Various Subjects, Religious and Moral,* written by Phillis Wheatley. Copyright © The Pierpont Morgan Library/Art Resource, NY.—Fuller, Margaret, painting by John Plumbe. The Library of Congress.—Gandhi, Indira, photograph. Copyright © Corbis-Bettmann.—Garrison, William Lloyd, (bottom right), with the Pennsylvania Abolition Society, photograph. National Portrait Gallery.—Gilman, Charlotte Perkins, cover photograph. Copyright © Corbis.—Gilman, Charlotte P., photograph. Copyright © Corbis-Bettmann.—Godwin, Mary Wollstonecraft, illustration. Copyright © Corbis-Bettmann.—Hansberry, Lorraine, photograph by David Attie. AP/Wide World Photos.—Head, Bessie, photograph. Reproduced by the kind permission of the Estate of Bessie Head.—"Head of Medusa," marble sculpture by Gianlorenzo Bernini. Copyright © Araldo de Luca/Corbis.—Hellman, Lillian, photograph. AP/Wide World Photos.—Hurston, Zora Neale looking at "American Stuff," at the *New York Times* book fair, photograph. The Library of Congress.—Hurston, Zora Neale, photograph by Carl Van Vechten. The Carl Van Vechten Trust.—Hypatia, conte crayon drawing. Copyright © Corbis-Bettmann.—Illustration depicting a woman's body being the subject of political and social conflict, photograph. Barbara Kruger/Mary Boone Gallery.—Jolie, Angelina (right), and unidentified person, in the film *Foxfire,* photograph by Jane O'Neal. The Kobal Collection/O'Neal, Jane.—Karloff, Boris, in movie *Frankenstein*; 1935, photograph. The Kobal Collection.—Kingston, Maxine Hong, photograph by Jerry Bauer. Copyright © Jerry Bauer.—"La Temptation," depicting Adam and Eve in the Garden of Paradise. The Library of Congress.—Lessing, Doris, photograph by Jerry Bauer. Copyright © Jerry Bauer.—Luce, Clare Booth, portrait. Copyright © UPI/Bettmann Archive.—Manuscript page from *The Book of Ladies,* by Christine de Pizan. Bibliotheque Nationale de France.—Manuscript page of *Vieyra Impugnado,* written by Sor Margarita Ignacia and translated to Spanish by Inigo Rosende. Madrid: Antonio Sanz, 1731. The Special Collections Library, University of Michigan.—Martineau, Harriet, engraving. The Library of Congress.—Migrant mother with child huddled on either shoulder, Nipomo, California, 1936, photograph by Dorothea Lange. The Library of Congress.—Millay, Edna St. Vincent, photograph. AP/Wide World Photos.—Montagu, Lady Mary Wortley, engraving. Archive Photos, Inc.—Moore, Marianne, photograph by Jerry Bauer. Copyright © Jerry Bauer.—Morrison, Toni, 1993, photograph. AP/Wide World Photos.—Murasaki, Lady, looking out from the veranda of a monastery, illustration from *Tale of Genji.* Copyright © Asian Art Archaeology, Inc./Corbis.—National League of Women Voters' Headquarters, photograph. Copyright © Corbis-Bettmann.—National Women's Suffrage Association (NWSA), during a political convention in Chicago, Illinois, photograph. Copyright © Bettmann/Corbis.—Naylor, Gloria, photograph. Marion Ettlinger/AP/Wide World Photos.—Oates, Joyce Carol, 1991, photograph. AP/Wide World Photos.—October 15, 1913 publication of the early feminist periodical, *The New Freewoman,* photograph. McFarlin Library, Department of Special Collections, The University of Tulsa.—Paul, Alice (second from right), standing with five other suffragettes, photograph. AP/Wide World Photos.—Pfeiffer, Michelle, and Daniel Day-Lewis, in the film *The Age of Innocence,* 1993, photograph by Phillip Caruso. The Kobal Collection.—Plath, Sylvia, photograph. AP/Wide World Photos.—Poster advertising *Uncle Tom's Cabin,* by Harriet Beecher Stowe, "The Greatest Book of the Age," photograph. Copyright © Bettmann/Corbis.—Rich, Adrienne, holding certificate of poetry award, Chicago, Illinois, 1986, photograph. AP/Wide World Photos.—Rossetti, Christina, 1863, photograph by Lewis Carroll. Copyright © UPI/Bettmann.—Russell, Rosalind and Joan Crawford in the 1939 movie *The Women,* written by Clare Boothe Luce, photograph. MGM/The Kobal Collection.—Salem Witch Trial, lithograph by George H. Walker. Copyright © Bettmann/Corbis.—Sand, George, illustration. Copyright © Leonard de Selva/Corbis.—Sand, George, photograph. The Library of Congress.—Sanger, Margaret, Miss Clara Louise Rowe, and Mrs. Anne Kennedy, arranging the first American Birth Control Conference, photograph. Copyright © Underwood and Underwood/Corbis.—Sappho, bronze sculpture. The Library of Congress.—Sappho, illustration. The Library of Congress.—Sappho performing outdoors, illustration. The Library of Congress.—"Sara in a Green Bonnet," painting by Mary Cassatt, c. 1901. National Museum of American Art, Smithsonian Institution, Washington, DC, U.S.A.—Scene from the film *Mill on the Floss,* by George Eliot, engraving. Hulton Archive/Getty Images.—Segwick, Catherine Maria, slide. Archive Photos, Inc.—Sexton, Anne, photograph. Copyright © Bettmann/Corbis.—Sexton, Anne, with her daughters Joy and Linda, photograph. Time Life Pictures/Getty Images.—Shelley, Mary Wollstonecraft, painting by Samuel John Stump. Copyright © Corbis-Bettmann.—Stael, Madame de, color lithograph. Archive Photos, Inc.—Stanton, Elizabeth Cady, illustration. Copyright © Bettmann/Corbis.—Stanton, Elizabeth Cady, photograph. AP/Wide World Photos.—Stein, Gertrude (left), arriving in New York aboard the S. S. Champlain with her secretary and companion Alice B. Toklas, photograph. AP/Wide World Photos.—Stein, Gertrude, photograph by Carl Van Vechten. The Estate of Carl Van Vechten.—Steinem, Gloria, photograph. AP/Wide World Photos.—Stowe, Harriet Beecher, photograph. Copyright © Bettmann/Corbis.—Suffrage parade in New York, New York, October 15, 1915, photograph. The Library of Congress.—Supporters of the Equal Rights Amendment carry a banner down Pennsylvania Avenue, Washington, DC, photograph. AP/Wide World Photos.—Sur la Falaise aux Petites Dalles, 1873. Painting by Berthe Morisot. Copyright © Francis G. Mayer/Corbis.—Tan, Amy, 1993, photograph. AP/Wide World Photos.—*Time,* cover of Kate Millett, from August 31, 1970. Time Life Pictures/Stringer/Getty Images.—Title page of *A Vindication of the Rights of Woman: With Strictures on Political and Moral Subjects,* written by Mary Wollstonecraft. William L. Clements Library, University of Michigan.—Title page of *Adam Bede,* written by George Eliot. Edinburgh & London: Blackwood, 1859, Volume 1, New York: Harper, 1859. The Graduate Library, University of Michigan.—Title page from *De L'influence des Passions sur le Bonheur des Individus et des Nations,* (A Treatise on the Influence of the Passions upon the Happiness of Individuals and of Nations), written by Stael de Holstein, photograph. The Special Collections Library, University of Michigan.—Title page from *Evelina,* written by Fanny Burney, photograph. The Special Collections Library, University of Michigan.—Title page from *Mansfield Park,* written by Jane Austen. The Special Collections Library, University of Michigan.—Title page of *Mary, A Fiction,* written by Mary Wollstonecraft.—Title page from *Youth and the Bright Medusa,* written by Willa Cather. New York, Alfred A Knopf. The Special Collections Library, University of Michigan.—Title page of *A New-England Tale,* written by Catharine Maria Sedgewick. New York: E. Bliss and E. White, 1822. The Special Collections Library, University of Michigan.—Title page of *Aurora Leigh,* written by Elizabeth Barrett Browning. New York, Boston: C. S. Francis and Co., 1857. The Special Collections Library, University of Michigan.—Title page of *Mrs. Dalloway,* written by Virginia Woolf. London: Hogarth Press, 1925. The Special Collections Library, University of Michigan.—Title page of *The Dial: A Magazine for Literature, Philosophy, and Religion.* Boston. Weeks, Jordan and Company (etc.); London, Wiley and Putnam (etc.). Volume 1. The Special Collections Library, University of Michigan.—Title page of *The House of Mirth,* written by Edith Wharton. New York: C. Scribner's Sons, 1905. The Special Collections Library, University of Michigan.—Title page of *The Little Review,*

March 1916. The Purdy/Kresge Library, Wayne State University.—Title page of *Woman in the Nineteenth Century,* written by Sarah Margaret Fuller. New York, Greeley and McElrath. 1845. The Special Collections Library, University of Michigan.—Title page of *Wuthering Heights,* written by Emily Brontë. New York: Harper and Brothers. 1848. The Special Collections Library, University of Michigan.—Truth, Sojourner, photograph. Archive Photos, Inc.—Tubman, Harriet, photograph. The Library of Congress.—Victoria, Queen of England, illustration. The Library of Congress.—Walker, Alice, 1989, photograph. AP/Wide World Photos.—Welles, Orson, as Edward Rochester, with Joan Fontaine as Jane Eyre, in the film *Jane Eyre,* photograph. The Kobal Collection.—Wharton, Edith, photograph. AP/Wide World Photos.—Wheatley, Phillis, photograph. Copyright © The Bettman Archive.—Winfrey, Oprah, as Celie and Danny Glover as Albert with baby in scene from the film *The Color Purple,* written by Alice Walker, directed by Steven Spielberg, photograph. The Kobal Collection.—Women in French Revolution, invade assembly, demanding death penalty for members of the aristocracy, Woodcut. Copyright © Bettmann/Corbis.—Women workers in a shoe factory in Lynn, Massachusetts, photograph. Copyright © Corbis.—Woodhull, Victoria, reading statement before House Committee, drawing. The Library of Congress.—Woolf, Virginia, photograph. AP/Wide World Photos.—Woolson, Constance Fenimore, engraving. Archive Photos.

● = historical event

■ = literary event

1570 B.C.

● Queen Ahmose Nefertari, sister and principal wife of King Ahmose, rules as "god's wife," in a new position created by a law enacted by the King.

C. 1490 B.C.

● Queen Hatshepsut rules as pharaoh, several years after the death of her husband, King Thutmose II.

C. 1360 B.C.

● Queen Nefertiti rules Egypt alongside her husband, pharaoh Akhenaten.

C. 620 B.C.

● Sappho is born on the Isle of Lesbos, Greece.

C. 600 B.C.

■ Sappho organizes and operates a *thiasos,* an academy for young, unmarried Greek women.

● Spartan women are the most independent women in the world, and are able to own property, pursue an education, and participate in athletics.

C. 550 B.C.

● Sappho dies on the Isle of Lesbos.

C. 100 B.C.

● Roman laws allow a husband: to kill his wife if she is found in the act of adultery, to determine the amount of money his wife is owed in the event of divorce, and to claim his children as property.

69 B.C.

● Cleopatra VII Philopator is born in Egypt.

36 B.C.

● Marriage of Antony and Cleopatra.

C. 30 B.C.

● Cleopatra VII Philopator commits suicide in Egypt.

18

● Emperor Augustus decrees the *Lex Julia,* which penalizes childless Roman citizens, adulterers, and those who marry outside of their social rank or status.

C. 370

- Hypatia is born in Alexandria, Egypt.

415

- Hypatia is murdered in Alexandria, Egypt.

C. 500

- Salians (Germanic Franks living in Gaul) issue a code of laws which prohibit women from inheriting land; the law is used for centuries to prevent women from ruling in France.

592

- Empress Suiko (554-628) becomes the first woman sovereign of Japan.

C. 690

- Wu Zetian (624-705) becomes the only female emperor of Imperial China.

C. 700

- Japanese legal code specifies that in law, ceremony, and practice, Japanese men can be polygamous—having first wives and an unlimited number of "second wives" or concubines—, but women cannot.

877

- Lady Ise, Japanese court lady, is born. She is considered one of the most accomplished poets of her time and her poems are widely anthologized.

935

- Hrotsvitha (also Hrotsvit or Roswitha), considered the first German woman poet, is born.

940

- Lady Ise dies.

950

- Publication of the *Kagero Nikki* (*The Gossamer Years*), a diary written by an anonymous Japanese courtesan. The realism and confessional quality of the work influence the works of later court diarists.

C. 960

- Japanese poet Izumi Shikibu, known for her expression of erotic and Buddhist themes, is born. Her body of work includes more than 1,500 *waka* (31-syllable poems).

C. 1002

- Sei Shonagon, Japanese court lady, writes *Makura no Soshi* (*The Pillow Book*), considered a classic of Japanese literature and the originator of the genre known as *zuihitsu* ("to follow the brush") that employs a stream-of-consciousness literary style.

C. 1008

- Murasaki Shikibu writes *Genji Monogatari* (*The Tale of Genji*), considered a masterpiece of classical prose literature in Japan.

C. 1030

- Izumi Shikibu dies.

1098

- Hildegard von Bingen is born in Bermersheim, Germany.

C. 1100

- Twenty women troubadours—aristocratic poet-composers who write songs dealing with love—write popular love songs in France. About twenty-four of their songs survive, including four written by the famous female troubadour known as the Countess of Dia, or Beatrix.

1122

- Eleanor of Aquitaine is born in Aquitaine, France. Her unconventional life is chronicled for centuries in books and dramatic works.

C. 1150

- Sometime in the twelfth century (some sources say 1122), Marie de France, the earliest known female French writer and author of *lais,* a collection of twelve verse tales written in octosyllabic rhyming couplets, flourished. She is thought to be the originator of the *lay* as a poetic form.

C. 1170

- Marie of Champagne (1145-1198), daughter of King Louis VII of France and Eleanor of Aquitaine, cosponsors "courts of love" to debate points on the proper conduct of knights toward their ladies. Marie encourages Chrétien de Troyes to write *Lancelot,* and Andreas Capellanus to write *The Art of Courtly Love.*

1179

- Hildegard von Bingen dies in Disibodenberg, Germany.

C. 1200

- Women shirabyoshi performances are a part of Japanese court and Buddhist temple festivities. In their songs and dances, women performers dress in white, male attire which includes fans, court caps, and swords. This form of traditional dance plays an important role in the development of classical Japanese noh drama.

1204

- Eleanor of Aquitaine dies on 1 April.

C. 1275

- Japanese poet and court lady Abutsu Ni (1222?-1283) writes her poetic travel diary, *Izayoi Nikki* (*Diary of the Waning Moon*) on the occasion of her travel to Kyoto to seek inheritance rights for herself and her children.

C. 1328

- The French cite the Salic Law, which was promulgated in the early medieval period and prohibits women from inheriting land, as the authority for denying the crown of France to anyone—man or woman—whose descent from a French king can be traced only through the female line.

1346

- Famous mystic St. Birgitta of Sweden (c.1303-1373) founds the Roman Catholic Order of St. Saviour, whose members are called the Brigittines. She authors *Revelations,* an account of her supernatural visions.

1347

- Caterina Benincasa (later St. Catherine of Siena) is born on 25 March in Siena, Italy.

C. 1365

- Christine de Pizan is born in Venice, Italy.

C. 1373

- Margery Kempe is born in King's Lynn (now known as Lynn), in Norfolk, England.

1380

- St. Catherine of Siena dies on 29 April in Rome, Italy.

C. 1393

- Julian of Norwich (1342?-1416?), the most famous of all the medieval recluses in England, writes *Revelations of Divine Love,* expounding on the idea of Christ as mother.

1399

- Christine de Pizan writes the long poem "Letter to the God of Love," which marks the beginning of the *querelle des femmes* (debate on women). This attack on misogyny in medieval literature triggers a lively exchange of letters among the foremost French scholars of the day, and the *querelle* is continued by various European literary scholars for centuries.

1429

- Joan of Arc (1412-1431)—in support of Charles I, who is prevented by the English from assuming his rightful place as King of France—leads liberation forces to victory in Orléans.

1431

- Joan of Arc is burned at the stake as a heretic by the English on 30 May. She is acquitted of heresy by another church court in 1456 and proclaimed a saint in 1920.

C. 1431

- Christine de Pizan dies in France.

C. 1440

- Margery Kempe dies in England.

1451

- Isabella of Castile, future Queen of Spain, is born. She succeeds her brother in 1474 and rules jointly with her husband, Ferdinand of Aragon, from 1479.

1465

- Cassandra Fedele, who becomes the most famous woman scholar in Italy, is born in Venice.

1469

- Laura Cereta, outspoken feminist and humanist scholar, is born in Brescia, Italy.

1485

- Veronica Gambara is born in Italy. Her court becomes an important center of the Italian Renaissance, and Gambara earns distinction as an author of Petrarchan sonnets as well as for her patronage of the artist Corregio.

1486

- *Malleus Maleficarum* (*The Hammer of Witches*), an encyclopedia of contemporary knowledge about witches and methods of investigating the crime of witchcraft, is published in Europe. The volume details numerous justifications for women's greater susceptibility to evil, and contributes to the almost universal European persecution of women as witches that reaches its height between 1580 and 1660 and makes its way to Salem, Massachusetts in 1692.

1492

- Marguerite de Navarre is born on 11 April in France.

1499

- Laura Cereta dies in Brescia, Italy.

C. 1512

- Catherine Parr is born in England.

1515

- Teresa de Alhumadawas (later St. Teresa de Ávila) is born on 28 March in Gotarrendura, Spain.

1524

- Courtesan Gaspara Stampa, widely regarded as the greatest woman poet of the Renaissance, is born in Padua, Italy.

1533

- Queen Elizabeth I is born on 7 September in Greenwich, England, the daughter of King Henry VIII and his second wife, Anne Boleyn.

1536

- King Henry VIII of England beheads his second wife, Anne Boleyn, on 19 May. Boleyn is convicted of infidelity and treason after she fails to produce the desired male heir.

1538

- Vittoria Colonna (1492-1547), an influential woman in Renaissance Italy, achieves distinction as a poet with the publication of her first book of poetry.

1548

- Catherine Parr dies in England.

1549

- Marguerite de Navarre dies in France.

1550

- Veronica Gambara dies in Italy.

1554

- Gaspara Stampa dies on 23 April in Venice, Italy.

1555

- Moderata Fonte (pseudonym of Modesta Pozzo) is born in Venice, Italy.

1558

- Elizabeth I assumes the throne of England and presides over a period of peace and prosperity known as the Elizabethan Age.

- Cassadra Fedele dies in Venice. She is honored with a state funeral.

1559

- Marguerite de Navarre completes her *L'Heptaméron des Nouvelles* (the *Heptameron*), a series of stories primarily concerned with the themes of love and spirituality.

1561

- Mary Sidney, noted English literary patron, is born in England. She is the sister of poet Sir Philip Sidney, whose poems she edits and publishes after his death in 1586, and whose English translation of the Psalms she completes.

1565

- French scholar Marie de Gournay is born on 6 October in Paris. Known as the French "Minerva" (a woman of great wisdom or learning), she is a financial success as a writer of treatises on various subjects, including *Equality of Men and Women* (1622) and *Complaint of Ladies* (1626), which demand better education for women.

1582

- St. Teresa de Avila dies on 4 October in Alba.

1592

- Moderata Fonte (pseudonym of Modesta Pozzo) dies in Venice, Italy.

C. 1600

- Catherine de Vivonne (c. 1588-1665), Madame de Rambouillet, inaugurates and then presides over salon society in Paris, in which hostesses hold receptions in their salons or drawing rooms for the purpose of intellectual conversation. Salon society flourishes in the seventeenth and eighteenth centuries, and stimulates scholarly and literary development in France and England.
- Geisha (female artists and entertainers) and prostitutes are licensed by the Japanese government to work in the pleasure quarters of major cities in Japan.

1603

- Queen Elizabeth I dies on 24 March in Surrey, England.
- Izumo no Okuni is believed to originate kabuki, the combination of dance, drama, and music which dominates Japanese theater throughout the Tokugawa period (1600-1868).

1607

- Madeleine de Scudéry, one of the best-known and most influential writers of romance tales in seventeeth-century Europe, is born on 15 November in Le Havre, France.

C. 1612

- American poet Anne Bradstreet is born in Northampton, England.

1614

- Margaret Askew Fell, who helps establish the Society of Friends, or Quakers, and becomes known as the "mother of Quakerism," is born in Lancashire, England. Quakers give women unusual freedom in religious life. An impassioned advocate of the right of women to preach, Fell publishes the tract *Women's Speaking Justified, Proved and Allowed of by the Scriptures* in 1666.

1621

- Mary Sidney dies in England.

C. 1623

- Margaret Lucas Cavendish, later Duchess of Newcastle, is born in England. She authors fourteen volumes of works, including scientific treatises, poems, and plays, and her autobiography *The True Relation of My Birth, Breeding and Life* (1656).

1631

- Katherine Phillips (1631-1664), who writes poetry under the pseudonym "Orinda," is born. She is the founder of a London literary salon called the Society of Friendship that includes such luminaries as Jeremy Taylor and Henry Vaughn.

C. 1640

- Aphra Behn is born.

C. 1645

- Deborah Moody (c. 1580-c. 1659) becomes the first woman to receive a land grant in colonial America when she is given the title to land in Kings County (now Brooklyn), New York. She is also the first colonial woman to vote.

C. 1646

- Glückel of Hameln, who records her life as a Jewish merchant in Germany in her memoirs, is born in Hamburg.

1651

- Juana Ramírez de Asbaje (later known as Sor Juana Inés de la Cruz) is born on 12 November on a small farm called San Miguel de Nepantla in New Spain (now Mexico).

1670

- Aphra Behn becomes the first professional woman writer in England when her first play *The Forced Marriage; or, The Jealous Bridegroom,* is performed in London.

1672

- Anne Bradstreet dies on 16 September in Andover, Massachusetts.

C. 1673

- Francois Poulain de la Barre publishes *The Equality of the Sexes,* in which he supports the idea that women have intellectual powers equal to those of men. His work stimulates the betterment of women's education in succeeding centuries.

1673

- Margaret Lucas Cavendish, Duchess of Newcastle, dies in England.

1676

- After being captured and then released by Wampanaoag Indians, Puritan settler Mary White Rowlandson (1636-1678) writes what becomes a famous account of her captivity.

1689

- Mary Pierrpont (later Lady Mary Wortley Montagu) is born on 26 May in London, England.
- Aphra Behn dies on 16 April and is buried in the cloisters at Westminster Abbey.

1692

- The Salem, Massachusetts, witch hysteria begins in February, and eventually leads to the execution of eighteen women convicted of witchcraft in the infamous Salem Witchcraft Trials (1692-1693).

C. 1694

- Mary Astell (1666-1731) publishes the treatise *A Serious Proposal to the Ladies* in two volumes (1694-1697). In the work, Astell calls for the establishment of private institutions where single women live together for a time and receive quality education.

1695

- Sor Juana Inés de la Cruz dies on 17 April at the Convent of St. Jerome in Mexico.

1701

- Madeleine de Scudéry dies on 2 June in Paris, France.

C. 1704

- Sarah Kemble Knight (1666-1727), a Puritan author, records her arduous journey from Boston to New York to settle the estate of her cousin.

C. 1713

- Anne Kingsmill Finch (1661-1720) writes many poems dealing with the injustices suffered by women of the aristocratic class to which she belonged. As Countess of Winchilsea, she becomes the center of a literary circle at her husband's estate in Eastwell, England.

1728

- Mercy Otis Warren is born on 14 September in Barnstable, Massachusetts.

1729

- Catherine the Great is born on 2 May in Germany as Sophia Friederica Augusta.

1744

- Abigail Adams is born Abigail Smith on 11 November in Weymouth, Massachusetts.

1748

- Olympe de Gouges, French Revolutionary feminist, is born Olympe Gouze in Montauban, France. She plays an active role in the French Revolution, demanding equal rights for women in the new French Republic.

1752

- Frances "Fanny" Burney is born on 13 June in England.

C. 1753

- Phillis Wheatley is born in Africa.

1759

- Mary Wollstonecraft is born on 27 April in England.

1762

- Lady Mary Wortley Montagu dies on 21 August in London, England.
- Catherine the Great becomes Empress of Russia.

1766

- Germaine Necker (later Madame de Staël) is born on 22 April in Paris, France.

1768

- Maria Edgeworth is born on 1 January at Black Bourton in Oxfordshire, England.

1774

- Clementina Rind (1740-1774) is appointed publisher of the *Virginia Gazette* by the House of Burgesses in Virginia.

1775

- Jane Austen is born on 16 December at Steventon Rectory, Hampshire, England.

1776

- Men and women who hold property worth over 50 pounds are granted suffrage in New Jersey.

C. 1780

- Madame Roland (1754-1793), formerly Marie Philppon, hosts an important salon where revolutionary politicians and thinkers debate during the French Revolution. An outspoken feminist, she presses for women's political and social rights.

1784

- Hannah Adams (1758-1831) becomes the first American woman author to support herself with money earned from writing, with the publication of her first book, *View of Religions* (later *Dictionary of Religions*).
- Phillis Wheatley dies on 5 December in Boston, Massachusetts.

1787

- Catherine Sawbridge Macaulay publishes *Letters on Education,* an appeal for better education of women.
- Mary Wollstonecraft's *Thoughts on the Education of Daughters: With Reflections on Female Conduct, in the More Important Duties of Life* is published by J. Johnson.

1789

- Catharine Maria Sedgwick is born on 28 December in Stockbridge, Massachusetts.
- Olympe de Gouges writes *The Declaration of the Rights of Women and Citizen,* a 17-point document demanding the recognition of women as political, civil, and legal equals of men, and including a sample marriage contract that emphasizes free will and equality in marriage.

1792

- Sarah Moore Grimké is born on 26 November in Charleston, South Carolina.

- Mary Wollstonecraft's *A Vindication of the Rights of Woman, with Strictures on Political and Moral Subjects* is published by J. Johnson.

1793

- Lucretia Coffin Mott is born on 3 January in Nantucket, Massachusetts.
- Olympe de Gouges is executed by guillotine for treason on 3 November.
- Madame Roland is executed in November, ostensibly for treason, but actually because the Jacobins want to suppress feminist elements in the French Revolution.

1796

- Catherine the Great dies following a stroke on 6 November in Russia.

1797

- Mary Wollstonecraft Shelley is born on 30 August, in London, England.
- Mary Wollstonecraft dies on 10 September in London, England, from complications following childbirth.
- Sojourner Truth is born Isabella Bomefree in Ulster County, New York.

1799

- Mary Wollstonecraft's *Maria; or, The Wrongs of Woman: A Posthumous Fragment* is published by James Carey.

1801

- Caroline M. (Stansbury) Kirkland is born on 11 January in New York City.

1802

- Lydia Maria Child is born on 11 February in Medford, Massachusetts.

1804

- George Sand (pseudonym of Armandine Aurore Lucille Dupin) is born on 1 July in Paris, France.
- The Napoleonic Code is established in France under Napoleon I, and makes women legally subordinate to men. The code requires women to be obedient to their husbands, bars women from voting, sitting on juries, serving as legal witnesses, or sitting on chambers of commerce or boards of trade.

1805

- Angelina Emily Grimké is born on 20 February in Charleston, South Carolina.

1806

- Elizabeth Barrett Browning is born on 6 March in Coxhoe Hall, Durham, England.

1807

- Germaine de Staël's *Corinne, ou l'Italie* (*Corinne, or Italy*) is published by Nicolle.
- Suffrage in New Jersey is limited to "white male citizens."

1808

- Caroline Sheridan Norton is born on 22 March in England.

1810

- (Sarah) Margaret Fuller is born on 23 May in Cambridgeport, Massachusetts.
- Elizabeth Cleghorn Gaskell is born on 29 September in London, England.

1811

- Harriet Beecher Stowe is born on 14 June in Litchfield, Connecticut.
- Jane Austen's *Sense and Sensibility* is published by T. Egerton.

1813

- Harriet A. Jacobs is born in North Carolina.
- Jane Austen's *Pride and Prejudice* is published by T. Egerton.

1814

- Mercy Otis Warren dies on 19 October in Plymouth, Massachusetts.

1815

- Elizabeth Cady Stanton is born on 12 November in Johnstown, New York.
- King Louis XVIII of France outlaws divorce.

1816

- Charlotte Brontë is born on 21 April in Thornton, Yorkshire, England.
- Jane Austen's *Emma* is published by M. Carey.

1817

- Madame Germaine de Staël dies on 14 July in Paris, France.
- Jane Austen dies on 18 July in Winchester, Hampshire, England.

1818

- Emily Brontë is born on 30 July in Thornton, Yorkshire, England.
- Lucy Stone is born on 13 August near West Brookfield, Massachusetts.
- Abigail Adams dies on 28 October in Quincy, Massachusetts.
- Jane Austen's *Northanger Abbey and Persuasion* is published by John Murray.
- Educator Emma Hart Willard's *A Plan for Improving Female Education* is published by Middlebury College.
- Mary Wollstonecraft Shelley's *Frankenstein; or, The Modern Prometheus* is published by Lackington, Hughes, Harding, Mavor & Jones.

1819

- Julia Ward Howe is born on 27 May in New York City.
- George Eliot (pseudonym of Mary Ann Evans) is born on 22 November in Arbury, Warwickshire, England.

1820

- Susan B. Anthony is born on 15 February in Adams, Massachusetts.

1821

- Emma Hart Willard establishes the Troy Female Seminary in Troy, New York.

1822

- Frances Power Cobbe is born on 4 December in Dublin, Ireland.

1823

- Charlotte Yonge is born 11 August in Otterbourne, Hampshire, England.

1825

- Frances Ellen Watkins Harper is born on 24 September in Baltimore, Maryland.

1826

- Matilda Joslyn Gage is born on 24 March in Cicero, New York.

1830

- Christina Rossetti is born on 5 December in London, England.
- Emily Dickinson is born on 10 December in Amherst, Massachusetts.
- *Godey's Lady's Book*—the first American women's magazine—is founded by Louis Antoine Godey and edited by Sarah Josepha Hale (1788-1879).

1832

- Louisa May Alcott is born on 29 November in Germantown, Pennsylvania.
- George Sand's *Indiana* is published by Roret et Dupuy.

1833

- Oberlin Collegiate Institute—the first coeducational institution of higher learning— is established in Oberlin, Ohio.

1836

- Marietta Holley is born on 16 July near Adams, New York.

1837

- Mt. Holyoke College—the first college for women—is founded by Mary Lyon in South Hadley, Massachusetts.

- Alexandria Victoria (1819-1901) becomes Queen Victoria at the age of eighteen. Her reign lasts for 63 years, the longest reign of any British monarch.

1838

- Victoria Woodhull is born on 23 September in Homer, Ohio.
- Sarah Moore Grimké's *Letters on the Equality of the Sexes, and the Condition of Woman* is published by I. Knapp.

1840

- Frances "Fanny" Burney dies on 6 January in London, England.
- Ernestine Rose (1810-1892) writes the petition for what will become the Married Woman's Property Law (1848).

C. 1844

- Sarah Winnemucca is born on Paiute land near Humboldt Lake in what is now Nevada.

1845

- Margaret Fuller's *Woman in the Nineteenth Century* is published by Greeley & McElrath.

1847

- Charlotte Brontë's *Jane Eyre* is published by Smith, Elder.
- Emily Brontë's *Wuthering Heights* is published by T. C. Newby.

1848

- The first women's rights convention is called by Lucretia Coffin Mott and Elizabeth Cady Stanton on 19 July and is held in Seneca Falls, New York on 20 July.
- Emily Brontë dies on 19 December in Haworth, Yorkshire, England.
- New York State Legislature passes the Married Woman's Property Law, granting women the right to retain possession of property they owned prior to marriage.

1849

- Maria Edgeworth dies on 22 May in Edgeworthstown, her family's estate in Ireland.
- Sarah Orne Jewett is born on 3 September in South Berwick, Maine.
- Amelia Bloomer publishes the first issue of her Seneca Falls newspaper *The Lily,* which provides a forum for both temperance and women's rights reformers.
- The first state constitution of California extends property rights to women in their own name.

1850

- Margaret Fuller drowns—along with her husband and son—on 19 July in a shipwreck off of Fire Island, New York.
- The first National Woman's Rights Convention, planned by Lucy Stone and Lucretia Mott, is attended by over one thousand women on 23 and 24 October in Worcester, Massachusetts.
- Elizabeth Barrett Browning's *Poems,* containing her *Sonnets from the Portuguese,* is published by Chapman & Hall.
- *The Narrative of Sojourner Truth,* transcribed by Olive Gilbert, is published in the Boston periodical, the *Liberator.*

1851

- Mary Wollstonecraft Shelley dies on 1 February in Bournemouth, England.
- Kate Chopin is born on 8 February in St. Louis, Missouri.
- Sojourner Truth delivers her "A'n't I a Woman?" speech at the Women's Rights Convention on 29 May in Akron, Ohio.

1852

- Harriet Beecher Stowe's *Uncle Tom's Cabin; or, Life among the Lowly* is published by Jewett, Proctor & Worthington.
- Susan B. Anthony founds The Women's Temperance Society, the first temperance organization in the United States.

1853

- Charlotte Brontë's *Villette* is published by Smith, Elder.
- Paulina Kellogg Wright Davis (1813-1876) edits and publishes *Una,* the first newspaper of the women's rights movement.

1854

- Margaret Oliphant's *A Brief Summary in Plain Language of the Most Important Laws Concerning Women,* a pamphlet explaining the unfair laws concerning women and exposing the need for reform, is published in London.

1855

- Charlotte Brontë dies on 31 March in Haworth, Yorkshire, England.
- Elizabeth Cady Stanton, speaking in favor of expanding the Married Woman's Property Law, becomes the first woman to appear before the New York State Legislature.

1856

- Harriot Eaton Stanton Blatch is born on 20 January in Seneca Falls, New York.

1857

- Elizabeth Barrett Browning's *Aurora Leigh* is published by Chapman & Hall.

1858

- Emmeline Pankhurst is born on 4 July in Manchester, England.
- Anna Julia Haywood Cooper is born on 10 August in Raleigh, North Carolina.

1859

- Carrie Chapman Catt is born on 9 January in Ripon, Wisconsin.

1860

- Charlotte Perkins Gilman is born on 3 July in Hartford, Connecticut.
- Jane Addams is born on 6 September in Cedarville, Illinois.

1861

- Victoria Earle Matthews is born on 27 May in Fort Valley, Georgia.
- Elizabeth Barrett Browning dies on 29 June in Florence, Italy.
- Harriet Jacobs's *Incidents in the Life of a Slave Girl, Written by Herself,* edited by Lydia Maria Child, is published in Boston.

1862

- Edith Wharton is born on 24 January in New York City.
- Ida B. Wells-Barnett is born on 16 July in Holly Springs, Mississippi.
- Julia Ward Howe's "The Battle Hymn of the Republic" is published in the *Atlantic Monthly.*

1864

- Caroline M. (Stansbury) Kirkland dies of a stroke on 6 April in New York City.

1865

- Elizabeth Cleghorn Gaskell dies on 12 November in Holybourne, Hampshire, England.

1866

- The American Equal Rights Association—dedicated to winning suffrage for African American men and for women of all colors—is founded by Susan B. Anthony and Elizabeth Cady Stanton on 1 May. Lucretia Coffin Mott is elected as the group's president.
- Elizabeth Cady Stanton runs for Congress as an independent; she receives 24 of 12,000 votes cast.

1867

- Catharine Maria Sedgwick dies on 31 July in Boston, Massachusetts.

1868

- Susan B. Anthony and Elizabeth Cady Stanton found the New York-based weekly newspaper, *The Revolution,* with the motto: "The true republic—men, their rights and nothing more; women, their rights and nothing less," in January.
- Julia Ward Howe founds the New England Woman Suffrage Association and the New England Women's Club.
- Louisa May Alcott's *Little Women; or, Meg, Jo, Beth, and Amy* (2 vols., 1868-69) is published by Roberts Brothers.

1869

- John Stuart Mill's treatise in support of women's suffrage, *The Subjection of Women,* is published in London.

- Emma Goldman is born on 27 June in Kovno, Lithuania.
- Louisa May Alcott's *Hospital Sketches and Camp and Fireside Stories* is published by Roberts Brothers.
- Women are granted full and equal suffrage and are permitted to hold office within the territory of Wyoming.
- The National Woman Suffrage Association is founded by Elizabeth Cady Stanton and Susan B. Anthony in May in New York City.
- The American Woman Suffrage Association is founded by Lucy Stone, Julia Ward Howe, and others in November in Boston, Massachusetts.

1870

- *The Woman's Journal,* edited by Lucy Stone, Henry Blackwell, and Mary Livermore, begins publication on 8 January.
- Victoria Woodhull and Tennessee Claflin publish the first issue of their controversial New York weekly newspaper, *Woodhull and Claflin's Weekly.*

1871

- Women are granted full and equal suffrage in the territory of Utah. Their rights are revoked in 1887 and restored in 1896.
- Victoria Woodhull presents her views on women's rights in a passionate speech to the House Judiciary Committee, marking the first personal appearance before such a high congressional committee by a woman.
- Wives of many prominent U. S. politicians, military officers, and businessmen found the Anti-Suffrage party to fight against women's suffrage.

1872

- Victoria Woodhull, as a member of the Equal Rights Party (or National Radical Reform Party), becomes the first woman candidate for the office of U.S. President. Her running mate is Frederick Douglass.
- Susan B. Anthony and 15 other women attempt to cast their votes in Rochester, New York, in the presidential election. Anthony is arrested and fined $100, which she refuses to pay.
- Sojourner Truth attempts to cast her vote in Grand Rapids, Michigan in the presidential election but is denied a ballot.

1873

- Colette is born on 28 January in Burgundy, France.
- Maria Mitchell (1818-1889), astronomer and faculty member at Vassar College, establishes the Association of the Advancement of Women.
- Willa Cather is born on 7 December in Back Creek Valley, Virginia.
- Sarah Moore Grimké dies on 23 December in Hyde Park, Massachusetts.
- Louisa May Alcott's *Work: A Story of Experience* is published by Roberts Brothers.

1874

- Gertrude Stein is born on 3 February in Allegheny, Pennsylvania.
- Amy Lowell is born on 9 February in Brookline, Massachusetts.

1876

- George Sand dies on 9 June in Nohant, France.
- Susan Glaspell is born on 1 July (some sources say 1882) in Davenport, Iowa.

1877

- Caroline Sheridan Norton dies on 15 June in England.

1878

- Passage of the Matrimonial Causes Act in England enables abused wives to obtain separation orders to keep their husbands away from them.
- The "Susan B. Anthony Amendment," which will extend suffrage to women in the United States, is first proposed in Congress by Senator A. A. Sargent.

1879

- Margaret Sanger is born on 14 September in Corning, New York.
- Angelina Emily Grimké dies on 26 October in Hyde Park, Massachusetts.

1880

- Christabel Pankhurst is born on 22 September in Manchester, England.
- Lydia Maria Child dies on 20 October in Wayland, Massachusetts.
- Lucretia Coffin Mott dies on 11 November in Philadelphia, Pennsylvania.
- George Eliot (pseudonym of Mary Ann Evans) dies on 22 December in London, England.

1881

- Hubertine Auclert founds *La Citoyenne* (*The Citizen*), a newspaper dedicated to female suffrage.
- The first volume of *A History of Woman Suffrage* (Vols. 1-3, 1881-1888; Vol. 4, 1903), edited and compiled by Susan B. Anthony, Elizabeth Cady Stanton, Ida Harper Husted, and Matilda Joslyn Gage, is published by Fowler & Welles.

1882

- Virginia Woolf is born on 25 January in London, England.
- Sylvia Pankhurst is born on 5 May in Manchester, England.
- Aletta Jacobs (1854-1929), the first woman doctor in Holland, opens the first birth control clinic in Europe.

1883

- Sojourner Truth dies on 26 November in Battle Creek, Michigan.
- Olive Schreiner's *The Story of an African Farm* is published by Chapman & Hall.

1884

- Eleanor Roosevelt is born on 11 October in New York City.

1885

- Alice Paul is born on 11 January in Moorestown, New Jersey.
- Isak Dinesen is born Karen Christentze Dinesen on 17 April in Rungsted, Denmark.

1886

- Emily Dickinson dies on 15 May in Amherst, Massachusetts.
- H. D. (Hilda Doolittle) is born on 10 September in Bethlehem, Pennsylvania.

1887

- Marianne Moore is born on 15 November in Kirkwood, Missouri.
- Article five of the Peace Preservation Law in Japan prohibits women and minors from joining political organizations and attending meetings where political speeches are given, and from engaging in academic studies of political subjects.

1888

- Louisa May Alcott dies on 6 March in Boston, Massachusetts, and is buried in Sleepy Hollow Cemetery in Concord, Massachusetts.
- Susan B. Anthony organizes the International Council of Women with representatives from 48 countries.
- Louisa Lawson (1848-1920) founds Australia's first feminist newspaper, *The Dawn.*
- The National Council of Women in the United States is formed to promote the advancement of women in society. The group also serves as a clearinghouse for various women's organizations.

1889

- Anna Akhmatova is born Anna Adreyevna Gorenko on 23 June in Bolshoy Fontan, Russia.

1890

- The National American Woman Suffrage Association (NAWSA) is formed by the merging of the American Woman Suffrage Assocation and the National Woman Suffrage Association. Elizabeth Cady Stanton is the NAWSA's first president; she is succeeded by Susan B. Anthony in 1892.

1891

- Zora Neale Hurston is born on 15 (some sources say 7) January in Nostasulga, Alabama. (Some sources cite birth year as c. 1901 or 1903, and birth place as Eatonville, Florida).

- Sarah Winnemucca dies on 16 October in Monida, Montana.

1892

- Edna St. Vincent Millay is born on 22 February in Rockland, Maine.
- Djuna Barnes is born on 12 June in Cornwall on Hudson, New York.
- Rebecca West (pseudonym of Cicily Isabel Fairfield) is born on 21 December in County Kerry, Ireland.
- Charlotte Perkins Gilman's *The Yellow Wallpaper* is published in *New England Magazine*.
- Frances E. W. Harper's *Iola Leroy; or, Shadows Uplifted* is published by Garrigues Bros.
- Olympia Brown (1835-1926), first woman ordained minister in the United States, founds the Federal Suffrage Association to campaign for women's suffrage.
- Ida Wells-Barnett's *Southern Horrors. Lynch Law in All its Phases* is published by Donohue and Henneberry.

1893

- Lucy Stone dies on 18 October in Dorchester, Massachusetts.
- The National Council of Women of Canada is founded by Lady Aberdeen.
- Suffrage is granted to women in Colorado.
- New Zealand becomes the first nation to grant women the vote.

1894

- Christina Rossetti dies on 29 December in London, England.

1895

- The first volume of Elizabeth Cady Stanton's *The Woman's Bible* (3 vols., 1895-1898) is published by European Publishing Company.

1896

- Harriet Beecher Stowe dies on 1 July in Hartford, Connecticut.
- Idaho grants women the right to vote.
- The National Assocation of Colored Women's Clubs is founded in Washington, D.C.

1897

- Harriet A. Jacobs dies on 7 March in Cambridge, Massachusetts.

1898

- Matilda Joslyn Gage dies on 18 March in Chicago, Illinois.
- Charlotte Perkins Gilman's *Women and Economics* is published by Small Maynard.
- The Meiji Civil Law Code, the law of the Japanese nation state, makes the patriarchal family, rather than the individual, the legally recognized entity.

1899

- Elizabeth Bowen is born on 7 June in Dublin, Ireland.
- Kate Chopin's *The Awakening* is published by Herbert S. Stone.

1900

- Colette's *Claudine a l'ecole* (*Claudine at School,* 1930) is published by Ollendorf.
- Carrie Chapman Catt succeeds Susan B. Anthony as president of the NAWSA.

1901

- Charlotte Yonge dies of bronchitis and pneumonia on 24 March in Elderfield, England.

1902

- Elizabeth Cady Stanton dies on 26 October in New York City.
- Women of European descent gain suffrage in Australia.

1903

- The Women's Social and Political Union, led by suffragists Emmeline and Christabel Pankhurst, stage demonstrations in Hyde Park in London, England.

1904

- Frances Power Cobbe dies on 5 April.
- Kate Chopin dies following a cerebral hemorrhage on 22 August in St. Louis, Missouri.

- Susan B. Anthony establishes the International Woman Suffrage Alliance in Berlin, Germany.

C. 1905

- Lillian Hellman is born on 20 June in New Orleans, Louisiana.

1905

- Austrian activist and novelist Bertha von Suttner (1843-1914) receives the Nobel Peace Prize.

1906

- Susan B. Anthony dies on 13 March in Rochester, New York.
- Finnish women gain suffrage and the right to be elected to public office.

1907

- Victoria Earle Matthews dies of tuberculosis on 10 March in New York City.
- Mary Edwards Walker, M.D.'s pamphlet on women's suffrage, "Crowning Constitutional Argument," is published.
- Harriot Stanton Blatch founds the Equality League of Self-Supporting Women, later called the Women's Political Union.

1908

- Simone de Beauvoir is born on 9 January in Paris, France.
- Julia Ward Howe becomes the first woman to be elected to the American Academy of Arts and Letters.

1909

- Sarah Orne Jewett dies on 24 June in South Berwick, Maine.
- Swedish author Selma Lagerlöf (1858-1940) becomes the first woman to receive the Nobel Prize for Literature.
- "The Uprising of the 20,000" grows from one local to a general strike against several shirtwaist factories in New York City. Over 700 women and girls are arrested, and 19 receive workhouse sentences. The strike is called off on 15 February 1910. Over 300 shops settle with the union, and workers achieve the terms demanded.
- Jeanne-Elisabeth Archer Schmahl (1846-1915) founds the French Union for Woman Suffrage.

1910

- Julia Ward Howe dies of pneumonia on 17 October in Newport, Rhode Island.
- The Women' Political Union holds the first large suffrage parade in New York City.
- Suffrage is granted to women in Washington State.
- Jane Addams's *Twenty Years at Hull House* is published by Macmillan.

1911

- Frances Ellen Watkins Harper dies on 22 February in Philadelphia, Pennsylvania.
- A fire at the Triangle Shirtwaist Factory in New York City on 25 March claims the lives of 146 factory workers, 133 of them women. Public outrage over the fire leads to reforms in labor laws and improvement in working conditions.
- Suffrage is granted to women in California.
- Edith Wharton's *Ethan Frome* is published by Scribner.

1912

- Suffrage is granted to women in Arizona, Kansas, and Oregon.
- A parade in support of women's suffrage is held in New York City and draws 20,000 participants and half a million onlookers.

1913

- Muriel Rukeyser is born on 15 December in New York City.
- Willa Cather's *O Pioneers!* is published by Houghton.
- Ida Wells-Barnett founds the Alpha Suffrage Club in Chicago.
- Suffrage is granted to women in Alaska.
- The Congressional Union is founded by Alice Paul and Lucy Burns.

1914

- Marguerite Duras is born on 4 April in Gia Dinh, Indochina (now Vietnam).
- The National Federation of Women's Clubs, which includes over two million white women and women of color, formally endorses the campaign for women's suffrage.
- Suffrage is granted to women in Montana and Nevada.
- Margaret Sanger begins publication of her controversial monthly newsletter *The Woman Rebel,* which is banned as obscene literature.

1915

- Charlotte Perkins Gilman's *Herland* is published in the journal *Forerunner.*
- *Woman's Work in Municipalities,* by American suffragist and historian Mary Ritter Beard (1876-1958), is published by Appleton.
- Icelandic women who are age 40 or older gain suffrage.
- Members of the NAWSA from across the United States hold a large parade in New York city.
- Most Danish women over age 25 gain suffrage.

1916

- Ardent suffragist and pacifist Jeannette Pickering Rankin (1880-1973) of Montana becomes the first woman elected to the U. S. House of Representatives. She later votes against U. S. involvement in both World Wars.
- The Congressional Union becomes the National Women's Party, led by Alice Paul and Lucy Burns.
- NAWSA president Carrie Chapman Catt unveils her "Winning Plan" for American women's suffrage at a convention held in Atlantic City, New Jersey.
- Suffrage is granted to women in Alberta, Manitoba, and Saskatchewan, Canada.
- Margaret Sanger opens the first U. S. birth-control clinic in Brooklyn, New York. The clinic is shut down 10 days after it opens and Sanger is arrested.
- Margaret Sanger's *What Every Mother Should Know; or, How Six Little Children were Taught the Truth* is published by M. N. Maisel.

1917

- Gwendolyn Brooks is born on 7 June in Topeka, Kansas.
- The National Women's Party becomes the first group in U.S. history to picket in front of the White House. Picketers are arrested and incarcerated; during their incarceration, Alice Paul leads them in a hunger strike. Many of the imprisoned suffragists are brutally force-fed, including Paul. The suffragettes' mistreatment is published in newspapers, the White House bows to public pressure, and they are released.
- White women in Arkansas are granted partial suffrage; they are able to vote in primary, but not general, elections.
- Suffrage is granted to women in New York.
- Suffrage is granted to women in Estonia, Latvia, and Lithuania.
- Women in Ontario and British Columbia, Canada, gain suffrage.
- Suffragists and members of the NAWSA, led by president Carrie Chapman Catt, march in a parade in New York City.
- Margaret Sanger founds and edits *The Birth Control Review,* the first scientific journal devoted to the subject of birth control.

1918

- Willa Cather's *My Antonia* is published by Houghton.
- Suffrage is granted to women in Michigan, Oklahoma, and South Dakota; women in Texas gain suffrage for primary elections only.
- President Woodrow Wilson issues a statement in support of a federal constitutional amendment granting full suffrage to American women.
- A resolution to amend the U.S. constitution to ensure that the voting rights of U.S. citizens cannot "be denied or abridged by the United States or any state on account of sex" passes in the House of Representatives.
- President Wilson urges the Senate to support the 19th amendment, but fails to win the two-thirds majority necessary for passage.
- Women in the United Kingdom who are married, own property, or are college graduates over the age of 30, are granted suffrage.
- Women in Austria, Czechoslovakia, Germany, Luxembourg, and Poland gain suffrage.

- Women in New Brunswick and Nova Scotia, Canada, gain suffrage. Canadian women of British or French heritage gain voting rights in Federal elections.
- Marie Stopes's *Married Love* and *Wise Parenthood* are published by A. C. Fifield.
- Harriot Stanton Blatch's *Mobilizing Woman-Power,* with a foreword by Theodore Roosevelt, is published by The Womans Press.

1919

- Women in the Netherlands, Rhodesia, and Sweden gain suffrage.
- Doris Lessing is born on 22 October in Kermanshah, Persia (now Iran).
- The "Susan B. Anthony Amendment," also known as the 19th Amendment to the U. S. Constitution, after it is defeated twice in the Senate, passes in both houses of Congress. The amendment is sent to states for ratification.

1920

- The 19th Amendment to the U.S. Constitution is ratified by the necessary two-thirds of states and American women are guaranteed suffrage on 26 August when Secretary of State Bainbridge Colby signs the amendment into law.
- The NAWSA is reorganized as the National League of Women Voters and elects Maud Wood Park as its first president.
- Bella Abzug is born on 24 July in New York City.
- Icelandic women gain full suffrage.
- Edith Wharton's *The Age of Innocence* is published by Meredith.
- Colette's *Cheri* is published by Fayard.

1921

- Betty Friedan is born on 4 February in Peoria, Illinois.
- Edith Wharton receives the Pulitzer Prize for fiction for *The Age of Innocence.*
- Margaret Sanger organizes the first American Conference on Birth Control in New York City.

1922

- Irish women gain full suffrage.
- Grace Paley is born on 11 December in New York City.
- Edna St. Vincent Millay's *The Ballad of the Harp-Weaver* is published by F. Shay.

1923

- Edna St. Vincent Millay receives the Pulitzer Prize for Poetry for *The Ballad of the Harp-Weaver.*
- Margaret Sanger opens the Birth Control Clinical Research Bureau in New York to dispense contraceptives to women under the supervision of a licensed physician and to study the effect of contraception upon women's health.
- Margaret Sanger founds the American Birth Control League.
- The Equal Rights Amendment (ERA), written by Alice Paul, is introduced in Congress for the first time in December.

1924

- Phyllis Schlafly is born on 15 August in St. Louis, Missouri.
- Shirley Chisolm is born on 30 November in Brooklyn, New York.

1925

- Amy Lowell dies on 12 May in Brookline, Massachusetts.
- *Collected Poems of H.D.* is published by Boni & Liveright.
- Virginia Woolf's *Mrs. Dalloway* is published by Harcourt.

1926

- Marietta Holley dies on 1 March near Adams, New York.
- Marianne Moore becomes the first woman editor of *The Dial* in New York City, a post she holds until 1929.
- Carrie Chapman Catt and Nettie Rogers Schuler's *Woman Suffrage and Politics; the Inner Story of the Suffrage Movement* is published by Charles Scribner's Sons.
- Grazia Deledda receives the Nobel Prize in Literature.

1927

- Victoria Woodhull dies on 10 June in Norton Park, England.
- Virginia Woolf's *To the Lighthouse* is published by Harcourt.

1928

- Maya Angelou is born Marguerite Johnson on 4 April in St. Louis, Missouri.
- Emmeline Pankhurst dies on 14 June in London, England.
- Anne Sexton is born on 9 November in Newton, Massachusetts.
- Virginia Woolf's *Orlando* is published by Crosby Gaige.
- Women are granted full suffrage in Great Britain.
- Gertrude Stein's *Useful Knowledge* is published by Payson & Clarke.
- Sigrid Undset receives the Nobel Prize in Literature.

1929

- Adrienne Rich is born on 16 May in Baltimore, Maryland.
- Marilyn French is born on 21 November in New York City.
- While Arthur M. Schlesinger Sr. reads her speech for her, Margaret Sanger appears in a gag on a stage in Boston where she has been prevented from speaking.
- Virginia Woolf's *A Room of One's Own* is published by Harcourt.

1930

- Lorraine Hansberry is born on 19 May in Chicago, Illinois.
- Cairine Wilson is appointed the first woman senator in Canada.

1931

- Jane Addams receives the Nobel Peace Prize.
- Toni Morrison is born Chloe Anthony Wofford on 18 February in Lorain, Ohio.
- Ida B. Wells-Barnett dies on 25 March in Chicago, Illinois.

1932

- Sylvia Plath is born on 27 October in Boston, Massachusetts.

1933

- Gertrude Stein's *The Autobiography of Alice B. Toklas* is published by Harcourt.
- Frances Perkins (1882-1965) is appointed Secretary of Labor by President Franklin D. Roosevelt, and becomes the first female cabinet member in the United States.

1934

- Gloria Steinem is born on 25 March in Toledo, Ohio.
- Kate Millett is born on 14 September in St. Paul, Minnesota.
- Lillian Hellman's *The Children's Hour* debuts on 20 November at Maxine Elliot's Theatre in New York City.

1935

- Jane Addams dies of cancer on 21 May in Chicago, Illinois.
- Charlotte Perkins Gilman commits suicide on 17 August in Pasadena, California.
- The National Council of Negro Women is founded by Mary McLeod Bethune (1875-1955).

1936

- First lady Eleanor Roosevelt begins writing a daily syndicated newspaper column, "My Day."
- Margaret Mitchell's *Gone with the Wind* is published by Macmillan.

1937

- Hélène Cixous is born on 5 June in Oran, Algeria.
- Bessie Head is born on 6 July in Pietermaritzburg, South Africa.
- Edith Wharton dies on 11 August in St. Brice-sous-Foret, France.
- Zora Neale Hurston's *Their Eyes Were Watching God* is published by Lippincott.

- Margaret Mitchell (1900-1949) receives the Pulitzer Prize in Letters & Drama for novel for *Gone with the Wind.*
- Anne O'Hare McCormick becomes the first woman to receive the Pulitzer Prize in Journalism, which she is given for distinguished correspondence for her international reporting on the rise of Italian Fascism in the *New York Times*.

1938

- Joyce Carol Oates is born on 16 June in Lockport, New York.
- Pearl Buck receives the Nobel Prize in Literature.

1939

- Germaine Greer is born on 29 January near Melbourne, Australia.
- Lillian Hellman's *The Little Foxes* debuts on 15 February at National Theatre in New York City.
- Margaret Atwood is born on 18 November in Ottawa, Ontario, Canada.
- Paula Gunn Allen is born in Cubero, New Mexico.
- French physician Madeleine Pelletier (1874-1939) is arrested for performing abortions in Paris, France; she dies later the same year. Throughout her medical career, Pelletier advocated women's rights to birth control and abortion, and founded her own journal, *La Suffragist.*

1940

- Emma Goldman dies on 14 May in Toronto, Ontario, Canada.
- Maxine Hong Kingston is born on 27 October in Stockton, California.
- Harriot Eaton Stanton Blatch dies on 20 November in Greenwich, Connecticut.

1941

- Virginia Woolf commits suicide on 28 March in Lewes, Sussex, England.

1942

- Erica Jong is born on 26 March in New York City.
- Isabel Allende is born on 2 August in Lima, Peru.
- Ellen Glasgow (1873-1945) receives the Pulitzer Prize for her novel *In This Our Life.*
- Margaret Walker (1915-1998) becomes the first African American to receive the Yale Series of Young Poets Award for her collection *For My People.*

1944

- Alice Walker is born on 9 February in Eatonton, Georgia.
- Martha Gellhorn (1908-1998) is the only woman journalist to go ashore with Allied troops during the D-Day invasion of Normandy, France in June.
- Buchi Emecheta is born on 21 July in Yaba, Lagos, Nigeria.
- Rita Mae Brown is born on 28 November in Hanover, Pennsylvania.
- Women are granted suffrage in France and Jamaica.

1945

- Eleanor Roosevelt becomes the first person to represent the U. S. at the United Nations. She serves until 1951, is reappointed in 1961, and serves until her death in 1962.
- Gabriela Mistral receives the Nobel Prize in Literature.
- Louise Bogan is named U. S. Poet Laureate.

1946

- Gertrude Stein dies of cancer on 27 July in Neuilly-sur-Seine, France.
- Andrea Dworkin is born on 26 September in Camden, New Jersey.
- Mary Ritter Beard's *Woman as a Force in History: A Study in Traditions and Realities* is published by Macmillan.
- Eleanor Roosevelt becomes chair of the United Nations Human Rights Commission. She remains chair until 1951.

1947

- Carrie Chapman Catt dies on 9 March in New Rochelle, New York.

- Willa Cather dies on 24 April in New York City.
- Dorothy Fuldheim, a newscaster in Cleveland, Ohio, becomes the first female television news anchor at WEWS-TV.

1948

- Susan Glaspell dies on 27 July in Provincetown, Massachusetts.
- Ntozake Shange is born Paulette Linda Williams on 18 October in Trenton, New Jersey.
- Leonie Adams is named U. S. Poet Laureate.

1949

- Simone de Beauvoir's *Le deuxième sexe* (*The Second Sex,* H. M. Parshley, translator: Knopf, 1953) is published by Gallimard.
- Elizabeth Bishop is named U. S. Poet Laureate.
- Gwendolyn Brooks's *Annie Allen* is published by Harper.

1950

- Gloria Naylor is born on 25 January in New York City.
- Edna St. Vincent Millay dies of a heart attack on 19 October at Steepletop, Austerlitz, New York.
- Gwendolyn Brooks receives the Pulitzer Prize for poetry for *Annie Allen.*

1951

- Marianne Moore's *Collected Poems* is published by Macmillan.
- Marguerite Higgins (1920-1960) receives the Pulitzer Prize for Journalism in overseas reporting for her account of the battle at Inchon, Korea in September, 1950.

1952

- Amy Tan is born on 19 February in Oakland, California.
- Rita Dove is born on 28 August in Akron, Ohio.
- bell hooks is born Gloria Jean Watkins on 25 September in Hopkinsville, Kentucky.
- Marianne Moore receives the National Book Critics Circle award for poetry and the Pulitzer Prize for poetry for *Collected Poems.*

1953

- *A Writer's Diary: Being Extracts from the Diary of Virigina Woolf,* edited by Leonard Woolf, is published by Hogarth.
- The International Planned Parenthood Federation is founded by Margaret Sanger, who serves as the organization's first president.
- Women are granted suffrage in Mexico.

1954

- Louise Erdrich is born on 7 June in Little Falls, Minnesota.
- Colette dies on 3 August in Paris, France.
- Sandra Cisneros is born on 20 December in Chicago, Illinois.

1955

- On 1 December American civil rights activist Rosa Parks (1913-) refuses to move from her seat for a white passenger on a Montgomery, Alabama bus and is arrested.

1956

- The Anti-Prostitution Act, written and campaigned for by Kamichika Ichiko, makes prostitution illegal in Japan.

1958

- Christabel Pankhurst dies on 13 February in Los Angeles, California.

1959

- Susan Faludi is born on 18 April in New York City.
- Lorraine Hansberry's *A Raisin in the Sun* debuts in March at the Ethel Barrymore Theatre in New York City.
- Lorraine Hansberry becomes the youngest woman and first black artist to receive a New York Drama Critics Circle Award for best American play for *A Raisin in the Sun.*

1960

- Zora Neale Hurston dies on 28 January in Fort Pierce, Florida.
- Sylvia Pankhurst dies on 27 September in Addis Ababa, Ethiopia.

- The U.S. Food and Drug Administration approves the first oral contraceptive for distribution to consumers in May.
- Harper Lee's *To Kill a Mockingbird* is published by Lippincott.

1961

- H. D. (Hilda Doolittle) dies on 27 September in Zurich, Switzerland.
- Harper Lee receives the Pulitzer Prize for the novel for *To Kill a Mockingbird.*
- President John F. Kennedy establishes the President's Commission on the Status of Women on 14 December and appoints Eleanor Roosevelt as head of the commission.

1962

- Isak Dinesen dies on 7 September in Rungsted Kyst, Denmark.
- Eleanor Roosevelt dies on 7 November in New York City.
- Naomi Wolf is born on 12 November in San Francisco, California.
- Doris Lessing's *The Golden Notebook* is published by Simon & Schuster.

1963

- Betty Friedan's *The Feminine Mystique* is published by Norton and becomes a bestseller.
- Sylvia Plath's *The Bell Jar* is published under the pseudonym Victoria Lucas by Heinemann.
- Sylvia Plath commits suicide on 11 February in London, England.
- Barbara Wertheim Tuchman (1912-1989) becomes the first woman to receive the Pulitzer Prize for general nonfiction for *The Guns of August.*
- The Equal Pay Act is passed by the U.S. Congress on 28 May. It is the first federal law requiring equal compensation for men and women in federal jobs.
- Entitled *American Women,* the report issued by the President's Commission on the Status of Women documents sex discrimination in nearly all corners of American society, and urges the U.S. Supreme Court to clarify legal status of women under the U.S. Constitution.

1964

- Anna Julia Haywood Cooper dies on 27 February in Washington, DC.

1965

- Lorraine Hansberry dies of cancer on 12 January in New York City.
- Women are granted suffrage in Afghanistan.

1966

- Anna Akhmatova dies on 6 March in Russia.
- Margaret Sanger dies on 6 September in Tucson, Arizona.
- National Organization for Women (NOW) is founded on 29 June by Betty Friedan and 27 other founding members. NOW is dedicated to promoting full participation in society for women and advocates for adequate child care for working mothers, reproductive rights, and the Equal Rights Amendment to the U.S. Constitution.
- Anne Sexton's *Live or Die* is published by Houghton.
- Nelly Sachs (1891-1970) receives the Nobel Prize in Literature, which she shares with Shmuel Yosef Agnon.

1967

- Anne Sexton receives the Pulitzer Prize for poetry for *Live or Die.*
- Senator Eugene McCarthy, with 37 cosponsors, introduces the Equal Rights Amendment in the U.S. Senate.

1968

- Audre Lorde's *The First Cities* is published by Poets Press.

1969

- Joyce Carol Oates's *them* is published by Vanguard Press.
- Shirley Chisolm becomes the first African American woman elected to Congress when she takes her seat in the U.S. House of Representatives on 3 January.
- Golda Meir (1898-1978) becomes the fourth Prime Minister of Israel on 17 March.

- California adopts the nation's first "no fault" divorce law, allowing divorce by mutual consent.

1970

- Toni Morrison's *The Bluest Eye* is published by Holt.
- Germaine Greer's *The Female Eunuch* is published by MacGibbon & Kee.
- Maya Angelou's *I Know Why the Caged Bird Sings* is published by Random House.
- Kate Millett's *Sexual Politics* is published by Doubleday and becomes a bestseller.
- Joyce Carol Oates receives the National Book Award for fiction for *them.*
- The Equal Rights Amendment passes in the U.S. House of Representatives by a vote of 350 to 15 on 10 August.
- Bella Abzug is elected to the U.S. House of Representatives on 3 November.
- The Feminist Press is founded at the City University of New York.
- *Off Our Backs: A Women's News Journal* is founded in Washington, D.C.
- *The Women's Rights Law Reporter* is founded in Newark, New Jersey.

1971

- Josephine Jacobsen is named U. S. Poet Laureate.

1972

- Marianne Moore dies on 5 February in New York City.
- *Ms.* magazine is founded; Gloria Steinem serves as editor of *Ms.* until 1987. The 300,000 copy print run of the first issue of *Ms.* magazine sells out within a week of its release in January.
- Shirley Chisolm becomes the first African American woman to seek the presidential nomination of a major political party, although her bid for the Democratic Party nomination is unsuccessful.
- The Equal Rights Amendment is passed by both houses of the U.S. Congress and is signed by President Richard M. Nixon. The amendment expires in 1982, without being ratified by the required two-thirds of the states; it is three states short of full ratification.
- President Nixon signs into law Title IX of the Higher Education Act banning sex bias in athletics and other activities at all educational institutions receiving federal assistance.
- Women's Press is established in Canada.

1973

- The U.S. Supreme Court, in their decision handed down on 21 January in *Roe v. Wade,* decides that in the first trimester of pregnancy women have the right to choose an abortion.
- Elizabeth Bowen dies of lung cancer on 22 February in London, England.
- Rita Mae Brown's *Rubyfruit Jungle* is published by Daughters, Inc.
- Erica Jong's *Fear of Flying* is published by Holt and becomes a bestseller.
- Alice Walker's *In Love and Trouble: Stories of Black Women* is published by Harcourt.
- The Boston Women's Health Book Collective's *Our Bodies, Ourselves: A Book By and For Women* is published by Simon and Schuster.

1974

- Andrea Dworkin's *Women Hating* is published by Dutton.
- Adrienne Rich receives the National Book Award for *Diving into the Wreck: Poems, 1971-1972.*
- Anne Sexton commits suicide on 4 October in Weston, Massachusetts.
- Katharine Graham (1917-2001), publisher of the *Washington Post,* becomes the first woman member of the board of the Associated Press.

1975

- Paula Gunn Allen' essay "The Sacred Hoop: A Contemporary Indian Perspective on American Indian Literature" appears in *Literature of the American Indian: Views and Interpretations,* edited by Abraham Chapman and published by New American Library.
- Hélène Cixous and Catherine Clement's *La Jeune nee* (*The Newly Born Woman,* University of Minnesota Press, 1986) is published by Union Generale.

- Margaret Thatcher is elected leader of the Conservative Party and becomes the first woman to head a major party in Great Britain.
- Susan Brownmiller's *Against our Will: Men, Women, and Rape* is published by Simon and Schuster.

1976

- Andrea Dworkin's *Our Blood: Prophecies and Discourses on Sexual Politics* is published by Harper.
- Maxine Hong Kingston's *The Woman Warrior: Memoirs of a Girlhood among Ghosts* is published by Knopf.
- Maxine Hong Kingston's receives the National Book Critics Circle award for general nonfiction for *The Woman Warrior.*
- Barbara Walters (1931-) becomes the first female network television news anchorwoman when she joins Harry Reasoner as coanchor of the *ABC Evening News.*
- Shere Hite's *The Hite Report: A Nationwide Study of Female Sexuality* is published by Macmillan.

1977

- Alice Paul dies on 9 July in Moorestown, New Jersey.
- Marilyn French's *The Women's Room* is published by Summit.
- Toni Morrison's *Song of Solomon* is published by Knopf.
- Toni Morrison receives the National Book Critics Circle Award for fiction for *Song of Solomon.*
- Labor organizer Barbara Mayer Wertheimer's *We Were There: The Story of Working Women in America* is published by Pantheon.
- Women's Press is established in Great Britain.

1978

- The Pregnancy Discrimination Act bans employment discrimination against pregnant women.
- Tillie Olsen's *Silences* is published by Delcorte Press/Seymour Lawrence.

1979

- Margaret Thatcher becomes the first woman prime minister of Great Britain. She serves until her resignation in 1990, marking the longest term of any twentieth-century prime minister.
- Barbara Wertheim Tuchman becomes the first woman elected president of the American Academy and Institute of Arts and Letters.
- Mother Teresa (1910-1997) receives the Nobel Peace Prize.
- Sandra M. Gilbert and Susan Gubar's *The Madwoman in the Attic: The Woman Writer and the Nineteenth-Century Imagination* is published by Yale University Press.

1980

- Muriel Rukeyser dies on 12 February in New York City.
- Adrienne Rich's essay "Compulsory Heterosexuality and Lesbian Experience" is published in *Signs: Journal of Women in Culture and Society.*

1981

- bell hooks's *Ain't I a Woman: Black Women and Feminism* is published by South End Press.
- Sylvia Plath's *Collected Poems,* edited by Ted Hughes, is published by Harper.
- Sandra Day O'Connor (1930-) becomes the first woman Justice of the U.S. Supreme Court, after being nominated by President Ronald Reagan and sworn in on 25 September.
- Women of Color Press is founded in Albany, New York by Barbara Smith.
- Cleis Press is established in Pittsburgh, Pennsylvania, and San Francisco, California.
- *This Bridge Called My Back: Writings by Radical Women of Color,* edited by Cherríe Moraga and Gloria Anzaldúa, is published by Persephone Press.
- Maxine Kumin is named U. S. Poet Laureate.

1982

- Djuna Barnes dies on 19 June in New York City.
- Sylvia Plath is posthumously awarded the Pulitzer Prize in poetry for *Collected Poems.*
- Alice Walker's *The Color Purple* is published by Harcourt.
- Carol Gilligan's *In a Different Voice: Psychological Theory and Women's Development* is published by Harvard University Press.

1983

- Rebecca West dies on 15 March in London, England.
- Gloria Steinem's *Outrageous Acts and Everyday Rebellions* is published by Holt.

1984

- Sandra Cisneros's *The House on Mango Street* is published by Arte Publico.
- Lillian Hellman dies on 30 June in Martha's Vineyard, Massachusetts.
- Geraldine Ferraro (1935-) becomes the first woman to win the Vice-Presidential nomination and runs unsuccessfully for office with Democratic Presidential candidate Walter Mondale.
- Firebrand Books, publisher of feminist and lesbian literature, is established in Ann Arbor, Michigan.
- bell hooks's *Feminist Theory: From Margin to Center* is published by South End Press.

1985

- Margaret Atwood's *The Handmaid's Tale* is published by McClelland & Stewart.
- Wilma P. Mankiller is sworn in as the first woman tribal chief of the Cherokee nation. She serves until 1994.
- Gwendolyn Brooks is named U. S. Poet Laureate.

1986

- Simone de Beauvoir dies on 14 April in Paris, France.
- Bessie Head dies on 17 April in Botswana.
- Rita Dove's *Thomas and Beulah* is published by Carnegie-Mellon University Press.
- Sylvia Ann Hewlett's *A Lesser Life: The Myth of Women's Liberation in America* is published by Morrow.

1987

- Toni Morrison's *Beloved* is published by Knopf.
- Rita Dove receives the Pulitzer Prize for poetry for *Thomas and Beulah.*

1988

- Toni Morrison receives the Pulitzer Prize for fiction for *Beloved.*
- *The War of the Words,* Volume 1 of Sandra M. Gilbert and Susan Gubar's *No Man's Land: The Place of the Woman Writer in the Twentieth Century,* is published by Yale University Press.

1989

- Amy Tan's *The Joy Luck Club* is published by Putnam.

1990

- Naomi Wolf's *The Beauty Myth: How Images of Beauty Are Used against Women* is published by Chatto & Windus.
- The Norplant contraceptive is approved by the FDA on 10 December.
- Camille Paglia's *Sexual Personae: Art and Decadence from Nefertiti to Emily Dickinson* is published by Yale University Press.
- Wendy Kaminer's *A Fearful Freedom: Women's Flight from Equality* is published by Addison-Wesley.
- Laurel Thatcher Ulrich's *A Midwife's Tale: The Life of Martha Ballard, Based on Her Diary, 1785-1812* is published by Knopf.
- Judith Butler's *Gender Trouble: Feminism and the Subversion of Identity* is published by Routledge.

1991

- Susan Faludi's *Backlash: The Undeclared War Against American Women* is published by Crown.
- Antonia Novello (1944-) is appointed by President George H.W. Bush and becomes the first woman and first person of Hispanic descent to serve as U. S. Surgeon General.
- Bernadine Healy, M.D. (1944-) is appointed by President George H.W. Bush and becomes the first woman to head the National Institutes of Health.
- Suzanne Gordon's *Prisoners of Men's Dreams: Striking Out for a New Feminine Future* is published by Little, Brown.
- Laurel Thatcher Ulrich receives the Pulitzer Prize for history for *A Midwife's Tale: The Life of Martha Ballard, Based on Her Diary, 1785-1812.*

1992

- Carol Elizabeth Moseley Braun (1947-) becomes the first African American woman elected to the U. S. Senate on 3 November.
- Carolyne Larrington's *The Feminist Companion to Mythology* is published by Pandora.
- Marilyn French's *The War against Women* is published by Summit.
- Clarissa Pinkola Estes's *Women Who Run with the Wolves: Myths and Stories of the Wild Woman Archetype* is published by Ballantine.
- Naomi Wolf's *Fire with Fire: The New Female Power and How It Will Change the Twenty-first Century* is published by Random House.
- Mona Van Duyn is named U. S. Poet Laureate.

1993

- Appointed by President Bill Clinton, Janet Reno (1938-) becomes the first woman U.S. Attorney General when she is sworn in on 12 March.
- Toni Morrison receives the Nobel Prize in Literature.
- Toni Morrison receives the Elizabeth Cady Stanton Award from the National Organization for Women.
- Canada's Progressive Conservative party votes on 13 June to make Defense Minister Kim Campbell the nation's first woman prime minister. Canadian voters oust the Conservative party in elections on 25 October as recession continues; Liberal leader Jean Chrétien becomes prime minister.
- On 1 October Rita Dove becomes the youngest person and the first African American to be named U. S. Poet Laureate.
- Faye Myenne Ng's *Bone* is published by Hyperion.

1994

- The Violence Against Women Act tightens federal penalties for sex offenders, funds services for victims of rape and domestic violence, and provides funds for special training for police officers in domestic violence and rape cases.
- Mary Pipher's *Reviving Ophelia: Saving the Selves of Adolescent Girls* is published by Putnam.

1995

- Ireland's electorate votes by a narrow margin in November to end the nation's ban on divorce (no other European country has such a ban), but only after 4 years' legal separation.

1996

- Marguerite Duras dies on 3 March in Paris, France.
- Hillary Rodham Clinton's *It Takes a Village, and Other Lessons Children Teach Us* is published by Simon and Schuster.

1998

- Bella Abzug dies on 31 March in New York City.
- Drucilla Cornell's *At the Heart of Freedom: Feminism, Sex, and Equality* is published by Princeton University Press.

1999

- Susan Brownmiller's *In Our Time: Memoir of a Revolution* is published by Dial Press.
- Gwendolyn Mink's *Welfare's End* is published by Cornell University Press.
- Martha C. Nussbaum's *Sex and Social Justice* is published by Oxford University Press.

2000

- Gwendolyn Brooks dies on 3 December in Chicago, Illinois.
- Patricia Hill Collins's *Black Feminist Thought: Knowledge, Consciousness, and the Politics of Empowerment* is published by Routledge.
- Jennifer Baumgardner and Amy Richards's *Manifesta: Young Women, Feminism, and the Future* is published by Farrar, Straus, and Giroux.

2002

- Estelle B. Freedman's *No Turning Back: The History of Feminism and the Future of Women* is published by Ballantine.
- *Colonize This! Young Women of Color on Today's Feminism,* edited by Daisy Hernandez and Bushra Rehman, is published by Seal Press.

2003

- Iranian feminist and human rights activist Shirin Ebadi (1947-) receives the Nobel Peace Prize.
- Louise Glück is named U. S. Poet Laureate.
- *Catching a Wave: Reclaiming Feminism for the 21st Century,* edited by Rory Cooke Dicker and Alison Piepmeier, is published by Northeastern University Press.

2004

- The FDA approves the contraceptive mifepristone, following a 16-year struggle by reproductive rights activists to have the abortion drug approved. Opponents made repeated efforts to prevent approval and distribution of mifepristone.
- *The Fire This Time: Young Activists and the New Feminism,* edited by Vivien Labaton and Dawn Lundy Martin, is published by Anchor Books.
- *The Future of Women's Rights: Global Visions and Strategies,* edited by Joanna Kerr, Ellen Sprenger, and Alison Symington, is published by ZED Books and Palgrave Macmillan.

WOMEN AND WOMEN'S WRITINGS FROM ANTIQUITY THROUGH THE MIDDLE AGES

Contemporary feminist theory has allowed social and literary critics to observe and reconstruct the past through the lens of the woman, and more specifically, through that of the woman writer. Looking to the premodern eras of antiquity and the Middle Ages, feminist scholars have studied women's roles as artists, leaders, and agents of history. Likewise, they have examined the status of ordinary individuals as the subjects of social and historical change across the millennia. Importantly, most classicists and medievalists who employ the tools of feminist theory in their work have been careful to note that feminism is a decidedly contemporary development, cautioning those who would describe women of the distant past as feminists to be aware of the consequent anachronism. Nevertheless, in their explorations of early literature and past civilizations, these scholars have recognized an emerging consciousness regarding women's issues. While women writers of ancient Greece, Alexandrian Egypt, or feudal Japan can scarcely be labeled feminists by contemporary standards, their unique awareness of themselves and their status in their societies has inspired the endeavor to read and write the history of women in art and literature.

Scholars have unearthed, in the early records of antique civilizations from Bronze Age Greece and Old Kingdom Egypt to ancient China and imperial Rome, suggestions of similar elements within the diversity of women's literature and social roles. Bringing together numerous common themes, such as the conflict between women of influence and the strong patriarchal tendency to marginalize the feminine and codify it symbolically, feminist criticism has offered a new way of looking at the ancient past that seeks to question some of the underlying assumptions of traditional humanist criticism. By examining textual and archeological evidence, critics have endeavored to reassess the society, daily lives, and literary production of women in various cultures of the ancient world. Because women writers of antiquity tended to be individuals with unique talent, their status is generally viewed as highly exceptional. Writers such as the Greek poet Sappho, the Alexandrian mathematician and philosopher Hypatia, and the Chinese scholar Pan Chao (Ban Zhao), in some fashion and for some limited period enjoyed favorable social or familial circumstances that assisted them in their vocations. For feminist critics, their rarity and the treatment they received in society—Hypatia, for instance, was murdered in the streets of Alexandria—suggest a prevalent lack of opportunity and respect for creative and intellectual women in antiquity. Such conclusions have led scholars to probe the origins of misogyny in the patriarchal societies these writers represent and to analyze the system of masculine and feminine semiotics upon which the notion of misogyny rests. Beginning with ancient Greece, commentators have evaluated the gendered distinction between private and public spheres, usually described as a symbolic tension between the feminine *oikos* (household) and masculine *polis* (city-state or society). Thus, women of the Athenian classical period in the fourth and fifth centuries B.C. were expected to attend to their domestic duties without mingling in political affairs. Women's ritual lives were also generally kept separate from those of men, giving rise to the feminine mysteries of ancient Greek religion. Ancient Sparta, in contrast, promoted a more egalitarian view of the sexes, but a woman's primary role remained the bearing of strong future warriors to defend the militaristic city-state. In later times, Roman law placed rather severe restrictions on women, making their legal and social status completely subject to the authority of their fathers and husbands. In a few cases, however, the position of aristocratic women in the ancient world may have been somewhat more favorable. In Ptolemaic Egypt, for example, Queens Nefertiti and Cleopatra appear to have been treated with much the same regard as their male counterparts. Notwithstanding these rare instances, the lives of most antique women were generally circumscribed by limits on education, mobility, and vocation precluding virtually all possibilities that might conflict with either domestic or reproductive responsibilities.

Women's relatively limited social roles are also reflected in the arts and literature of the antique period, from Athenian vase painting to Homeric verse, which suggest that the most common position of ancient woman was in the home, occupied with household duties—cooking, weaving, child rearing,—leaving men to handle political issues, which often meant war. Feminist critics have noted that such representations of women in the ancient period derive from the patriarchal assumptions of premodern societies, which were reflected in the symbolic order of the mythic past. Greco-Roman mythology—embodied for the purposes of literary scholarship here in the Homeric epics the *Iliad* and *Odyssey,* and in Ovid's Latin *Metamorphoses*—encapsulates classical perceptions of the feminine, depicting women as powerful goddesses, vengeful queens, cunning witches, and as the objects or victims of male aggression. Such mythic stereotypes inform an array of world literature and are precisely the sorts of ingrained depictions of women that contemporary feminists wish to discover and understand. Likewise, classical drama, perhaps best typified in the works of Aeschylus, Euripides, Aristophanes, and Sophocles, presents a somewhat divergent view of women, but one that nevertheless betrays antique assumptions about the nature of woman and man that modern feminists seek to question. Literary depictions of women in the Bible, additionally, contributed to a reductive dichotomy that informed the fundamental gender bias of medieval European society and literature. While self-possessed and heroic female figures such as Esther and Judith are present in the Bible, their stories are usually categorized with the Old Testament Apocrypha. For the most part, perceptions of women in biblical contexts became symbolically aligned with one of two poles—the sinning temptress Eve or the flawless Virgin Mary.

Studying continuity from classical and biblical perceptions of women, feminist scholars interested in the Middle Ages have generally focused on the social roles of women depicted in a wide array of texts, in the visual arts of the period, and in the works of a growing pool of female writers. The medieval epoch in Europe and Asia witnessed major developments in women's writings in large part due to the spread of religious education. Consequently, feminist critics have been drawn to the works of female mystic writers, among them Hildegard of Bingen, Julian of Norwich, St. Catherine of Siena, and St. Birgitta of Sweden. Their writings generally include revelatory visions of Christ and the Virgin Mary, religious poetry, and similar works of a spiritual nature. Other medieval European writers, such as Marie de France and Heloise (in her well-known correspondence with Pierre Abelard), offered unique contributions to the romantic and epistolary genres, respectively. In the Far East, the ninth-century Chinese poet Yu Xuanji produced some of the finest lyric poetry in her language, while writers such as Murasaki Shikibu, in her innovative novel *The Tale of Genji,* and Sei Shonagon, in her *Pillow Book,* recorded the flowering and decadence of the imperial court in Heian Japan around the turn of the eleventh century. Despite such literary accomplishments, the essential social and political status of women in the medieval period changed relatively little from that of the antique, and in some respects may even have declined. For the most part, women continued to be valued only for their domestic skills and reproductive role. Those who protested, and thereby failed to acquiesce to the patriarchal social order, were often harshly treated at all levels of society. Among the aristocracy, the example of the twelfth-century Queen Eleanor of Aquitaine demonstrates this point. Scornfully denounced in popular legend as the embodiment of feminine guile and malevolence for requesting a divorce from her husband, Eleanor was unfairly burdened with maintaining the integrity of her family at all costs and regardless of circumstances. Far worse, from the point of view of most men, was that a woman should be guilty of unchaste behavior—an accusation also leveled against the Queen. Critics have observed that this common theme in medieval society and literature was probably best articulated by Geoffrey Chaucer in his *Wife of Bath's Prologue* and *Tale*. Ironically in the view of modern critics, Chaucer, with his compelling description of the Wife of Bath as a self-possessed, outspoken, and boastfully licentious woman, rendered an epitome of the medieval antifeminist tradition, while at the same time sketching a figure in whom many have seen the first inklings of an incipient feminist consciousness.

REPRESENTATIVE WORKS

Abutsu-ni
Izayoi nikki (travel diary) mid 13th century

Aeschylus
Oresteia (dramas) c. 458 B.C.

Aristophanes
Lysistrata (drama) c. 411 B.C.

Ecclesiazusae (drama) c. 393 B.C.

The Bible
Book of Esther (prose) c. 2nd century B.C.

Birgitta of Sweden
Liber celestis revelaciones [*Revelations*] (prose) c. 1377

Catherine of Siena
Libro della divina dottrina [*The Dialogue of the Seraphic Virgin Catherine of Siena*] (prose) c. 1377-80

Geoffrey Chaucer
Troilus and Criseyde (poetry) c. 1385

Wife of Bath's Prologue and *Tale* (poetry) c. 1387

Christine de Pizan
Letter of the God of Love (prose) c. 1399

The Book of the City of Ladies (dialogues) c. 1405

Cynewulf
Elene (poetry) c. 8th-9th century

Elizabeth of Hungary
The Revelations of Saint Elizabeth (prose) c. 1231

Euripides
Medea (drama) c. 431 B.C.

Hadewijch of Antwerp
Visioenen [*Visions*] (prose) mid 13th century

Heloise
Letters of Abelard and Heloise [with Pierre Abelard] (letters) c. 1119-41

Herrad of Landsberg
Hortus Deliciarum [*Garden of Delights*] (prose) c. 1170

Hesiod
Works and Days (poetry) mid 8th century B.C.

Hildegard von Bingen
Liber Scivias (prose) c. 1152

Homer
Iliad (poetry) c. 9th century B.C.

Odyssey (poetry) c. 9th century B.C.

Hrotsvit of Gandersheim
The Martyrdom of the Holy Virgins Fides, Spes, and Karitas (drama) late 10th century

Hypatia
Astronomical Canon (nonfiction) c. 415

On the Conics of Apollonius (nonfiction) c. 415

Izumi Shikibu
The Diary of Izumi Shikibu (diary) c. 1003

Julian of Norwich
Shewings [*Revelations*] (prose) c. 1373-93

Margery Kempe
Book of Margery Kempe (autobiography) c. 1438

Marie de France
Lais (poetry) c. 1170

Murasaki Shikibu
Genji monogatori [*The Tale of Genji*] (novel) early 11th century

Ovid
Metamorphoses (poetry) c. 1

Pan Chao (Ban Zhao)
Nujie [*Lessons for Women*] (nonfiction) 1st century

Han Shu [with others] (history) 1st-2nd centuries

Perpetua

Passio Sanctarum Perpetuae et Felicitatis [*The Passion of Saints Perpetua and Felicity*] (diary) c. 203

Marguerite Porete

Le Mirouer des simples ames [*The Mirror of Simple Souls*] (prose) c.1296-1306

Sappho

Sapphic Fragments (poetry) 6th century B.C.

Sei Shonagon

Makura no soshi [*Pillow Book*] (prose) c. late 10th century

Sophocles

Antigone (drama) 442? B.C.

Trachinian Women (drama) 440-30 B.C.

Electra (drama) 425-10 B.C.

Yu Xuanji

**The Clouds Float North: The Complete Poems of Yu Xuanji* (poetry) 1998

* This title is an edition of Yu Xuanji's collected Chinese poetry translated by David Young and Jiann I. Lin; the poems were composed c. 860-71.

PRIMARY SOURCES

PAN CHAO (POEM DATE C. 1ST CENTURY)

SOURCE: Pan Chao. *Pan Chao: Foremost Woman Scholar of China,* translated by Nancy Lee Swann. Ann Arbor: University of Michigan Center for Chinese Studies, 1932.

The following is an excerpt from the poem "Traveling Eastward," the oldest surviving work composed by the first century A.D. Chinese writer Pan Chao (or Ban Zhao).

It is the seventh year of Yung-ch'u;
I follow my son in his journey eastward.
It is an auspicious day in Spring's first moon;
We choose this good hour, and are about to start.
Now I arise to my feet and ascend my carriage.
At eventide we lodge at Yen-shih:
Already we leave the old and start for the new.
I am uneasy in mind, and sad at heart.
Dawn's first light comes, and yet I sleep not;
My heart hesitates as though it would fail me.
I pour out a cup of wine to relax my thoughts.
Suppressing my feelings, I sigh and blame myself:
I shall not need to dwell in nests, nor (eat) worms from dead trees.
Then how can I not encourage myself to press forward?
And further, am I different from other people?
Let me but hear heaven's command and go its way.
Throughout the journey we follow the great highway.
If we seek short cuts, whom shall we follow?
Pressing forward, we travel on and on;
In abandonment our eyes wander, and our spirits roam. . . .
Secretly I sigh for the Capital City I love, (but)
To cling to one's native place characterizes a small nature,
As the histories have taught us. . . .
When we enter K'uang City I recall far distant events.
I am reminded of Confucius' straitened activities
In that decadent, chaotic age which knew not the Way,
And which bound and awed even him, that Holy Man!
In fact genuine virtue cannot die;
Though the body decay, the name lives on. . . .
I know that man's nature and destiny rests with Heaven,
But by effort we can go forward and draw near to love.
Stretched, head uplifted, we tread onward to the vision. . . .

YU XUANJI (LYRIC DATE C. 9TH CENTURY)

SOURCE: Yu Xuanji. "Joining Somebody's Mourning" and "Three Beautiful Sisters, Orphaned Young." In *The Clouds Float North: The Complete Poems of Yu Xuanji,* translated by David Young and Jiann I. Lin, pp. 52, 54-56. Hanover, N.H.: University Press of New England, 1998.

The following are translations of two lyrics by the ninth-century Chinese poet Yu Xuanji (844-871), a nun who was executed in the latter years of the Tang Dynasty.

Many of [Yu Xuanji's] poems, to be sure, dwell on absence, longing, and loss, as do lyric poems in any culture and period. But their original handling of theme, their inspired sense of detail, their exuberant rightness of tone and form, all counterbalance the painful subject matter with exquisite formal and aesthetic pleasure. Whether this sleight-of-hand fully compensates the poet is not the question: the reader's gift is the distillation of experience, still potent after eleven centuries. In that distillation, the resilience and dignity of the human spirit are held in a kind of suspension. The pain and pleasure mingle, not canceling each other out but simply coexisting. Two truths are told at once—that life is streaked with sorrow and loss, and that existence is a miraculous gift to the responsive spirit.

JOINING SOMEBODY'S MOURNING

You've seen her, bloom of the peach,
posture graceful as jade

breeze through willows and poplars
delicate arch of the eyebrows

pearl hoard in a dragon's cave
that shock of recognition

glimpsed in the mirror at state functions
happy among the chitchat

now changed to a somber dream
lost in mist on a rainy night

hating to hear the story
of bitter times and solitude

hills to the west, sunset
hills to the east, moonrise

and thoughts of loss
that are never going to end.

THREE BEAUTIFUL SISTERS, ORPHANED YOUNG

We used to hear about the south,
its splendid fresh appearance

now it's these eastern neighbors
these sisters three

up in the loft, inspecting their trousseaus
reciting a verse about parrots

sitting by blue-green windows
embroidering phoenix garments

their courtyard filled with colorful petals
like red smoke, billowing unevenly

their cups full of good green wine
tasted one by one

. . . . .

It's dreadful, staring into the mystic pond,
knowing you'll always be female

banished from heaven, stuck in this life,
unable to do what men do

a poet who happens to have some beauty,
ends up being compared

to a gorgeous woman who's silent—
that makes me feel ashamed

me, singing solo love songs
upon this vanishing zither
plucking the four strings softly
murmuring the words

facing my mirror and dressing table
to admire my black silk hair

as if I could rival the moon
by flaunting a white jade hairpin

. . . . .

A little cave among the pines
where dew drips down

the sky above the willows
a great net filled with mist

when you can be like the rain
your heart will have strength to go on

and you won't be afraid to blow the flute
before you've fully mastered it

my mother would get upset
because I talked to flowers

and my lover was from the past
a poet who came to me in dreams

. . . . .

The spirit makes fine, fresh verses
and then is broken

it's like watching a lovely young woman
give up her will to live

these gorgeous young creatures
who knows what they'll come to?

the clouds float north
the clouds float south.

IZUMI SHIKIBU (DIARY DATE C. EARLY 11TH CENTURY)

SOURCE: Izumi Shikibu. "The Diary of Izumi Shikibu." In *Diaries of Court Ladies of Old Japan,* translated by Anne Sheply Omori and Kochi Doi, pp. 147-96. Boston: Houghton Mifflin, 1920.

The following excerpt from the diary of Izumi Shikibu, a Japanese noblewoman of the early eleventh century, describes a clandestine love affair in the imperial court of Heian Japan.

Many months had passed in lamenting the World, more shadowy than a dream. Already the tenth day of the Deutzia month was over. A deeper shade lay under the trees and the grass on the embankment was greener. These changes, unnoticed by any, seemed beautiful to her, and while musing upon them a man stepped lightly along behind the hedge. She was idly curious, but when he came towards her she recognized the page of the late prince. He came at a sorrowful moment, so she said, "Is your coming not long delayed? To talk over the past was inclined." "Would it not have been presuming?—Forgive me—In mountain temples have been worshipping. To be without

ON THE SUBJECT OF...

WOMEN IN CHINESE RELIGION

Buddhism as practiced in Japan and China . . . granted women areas of empowerment while at the same time treating them as subordinates, and portraying them as deceitful in much of the literature. Women went on pilgrimages to Buddhist temples, retreated to nunneries, sometimes gave public lectures, and led temple groups. Chinese Buddhism was at its height during the reign of Wu Zetian, who promoted the religion and even justified her rule by claiming she was a reincarnation of a previous female Buddhist saint. During Wu's reign, and throughout the early to mid Tang period, women enjoyed relatively high status and freedom. Lovely Tang Era paintings and statues depict women on horseback and as administrators, dancers, and musicians. Stories and poems, like those by the female poet Yu Xuanji, also attest to the openness of the period.

In contrast, Confucianism became the most pervasive doctrine to promote a belief in women's "natural place." Confucius himself did not directly denigrate women, although he placed them at the lower end of the patriarchal family structure. Through the ages, however, the belief that men and women had distinct social roles was based on Confucian hierarchical precepts. Prescriptive advice manuals like *Lessons for GMs* reinforced these lessons. Written by the female historian Ban Zhoa (Han Dynasty, ca. 45-120 C.E.), *Lessons* became one of China's most durable sources of advice about female behavior. One nugget tells women to "yield to others; let her put others first, herself last"

Reese, Lyn. "Teaching about Women in China and Japan: A Thematic Approach." *Social Education* 67, no. 1 (January-February 2003): 38-43.

ties is sad, so wishing to take service again I went to Prince Sochi-no-miya."

"Excellent! that Prince is very elegant and is known to me. He cannot be as of yore?" [i.e. unmarried.] So she said, and he replied, "No, but he is very gracious. He asked me whether I ever visit you nowadays—'Yes, I do,' said I; then, breaking off this branch of tachibana flowers, His Highness replied, 'Give this to her, [see] how she will take it'. The Prince had in mind the old poem:

The scent of tachibana flowers in May
Recalls the perfumed sleeves of him who is no longer here.

So I have come—what shall I say to him?"

It was embarrassing to return an oral message through the page, and the Prince had not written; discontented, yet wishing to make some response, she wrote a poem and gave it to the page:

That scent, indeed, brings memories
But rather, to be reminded of that other,
Would hear the cuckoo's voice.

The Prince was on the veranda of his palace, and as the page approached him with important face, he led him into an inner room saying, "What is it?" The page presented the poem.

The Prince read it and wrote this answer:

The cuckoo sings on the same branch
With voice unchanged,
That shall you know.

His Highness gave this to the page and walked away, saying, "Tell it to no one, I might be thought amorous." The page brought the poem to the lady. Lovely it was, but it seemed wiser not to write too often [so did not answer].

On the day following his first letter this poem was sent:

To you I betrayed my heart—
Alas! Confessing
Brings deeper grief,
Lamenting days.

Feeling was rootless, but being unlearned in loneliness, and attracted, she wrote an answer:

If you lament to-day
At this moment your heart
May feel for mine—
For in sorrow
Months and days have worn away.

He wrote often and she answered—sometimes—and felt her loneliness a little assuaged. Again she received a letter. After expressing feelings of great delicacy:

[I would] solace [you] with consoling words
If spoken in vain
No longer could be exchanged.

To talk with you about the departed one; how would it be [for you] to come in the evening unobtrusively?

Her answer:

As I hear of comfort I wish to talk with you, but being an uprooted person there is no hope of my standing upright. I am footless [meaning, I cannot go to you].

Thus she wrote, and His Highness decided to come as a private person.

It was still daylight, and he secretly called his servant Ukon-no-zo, who had usually been the medium by which the letters had reached the Prince, and said, "I am going somewhere." The man understood and made preparations.

His Highness came in an humble palanquin and made his page announce him. It was embarrassing. She did not know what to do; she could not pretend to be absent after having written him an answer that very day. It seemed too heartless to make him go back at once without entering. Thinking, "I will only talk to him," she placed a cushion by the west door on the veranda, and invited the Prince there. Was it because he was so much admired by the world that he seemed to her unusually fascinating? But this only increased her caution. While they were talking the moon shone out and it became uncomfortably bright.

He: "As I have been out of society and living in the shade, I am not used to such a bright place as this"—It was too embarrassing!—"Let me come in where you are sitting; I will not be rude as others are. You are not one to receive me often, are you?" "No indeed! What a strange idea! Only to-night we shall talk together I think; never again!" Thus lightly talking, the night advanced—"Shall we spend the night in this way?" he asked:

The night passes,
We dream no faintest dream—
What shall remain to me of this summer night?

She:

Thinking of the world
Sleeves wet with tears are my bed-fellows.
Calmly to dream sweet dreams—
There is no night for that.

He: "I am not a person who can leave my house easily. You may think me rude, but my feeling for you grows ardent." And he crept into the room. Felt horribly embarrassed, but conversed together and at daybreak he returned.

Next day's letter:

In what way are you thinking about me? I feel anxiety—

To you it may be a commonplace to speak of love,
But my feeling this morning—
To nothing can it be compared!

She answered:

Whether commonplace or not—
Thoughts do not dwell upon it
For the first time [I] am caught in the toils.

O what a person! What has she done! So tenderly the late Prince spoke to her! She felt regret and her mind was not tranquil. Just then the page came. Awaited a letter, but there was none. It disappointed her; how much in love! When the page returned, a letter was given.

The letter:

Were my heart permitted even to feel the pain of waiting!
It may be to wait is lesser pain—
To-night—not even to wait for—

The Prince read it, and felt deep pity, yet there must be reserve [in going out at night]. His affection for his Princess is unusually light, but he may be thinking it would seem odd to leave home every night. Perhaps he will reserve himself until the mourning for the late Prince is over; it is a sign that his love is not deep. An answer came after nightfall.

Had she said she was waiting for me with all her heart,
Without rest towards the house of my beloved
Should I have been impelled!

When I think how lightly you may regard me!

Her answer:

Why should I think lightly of you?

I am a drop of dew
Hanging from a leaf
Yet I am not unrestful
For on this branch I seem to have existed
From before the birth of the world.

Please think of me as like the unstable dew which cannot even remain unless the leaf supports it.

His Highness received this letter. He wanted to come, but days passed without realizing his wish. On the moon-hidden day [last day of month] she wrote:

If to-day passes
Your muffled voice of April, O cuckoo
When can I hear?

She sent this poem, but as the Prince had many callers it could only reach him the next morning. His answer:

The cuckoo's song in spring is full of pain.
Listen and you will hear his song of summer
Full-throated from to-day.

And so he came at last, avoiding public attention. The lady was preparing herself for temple-going, and in the act of religious purification. Thinking that the rare visits of the Prince betrayed his indifference, and supposing that he had come only to show that he was not without sympathy, she continued the night absorbed in religious services, talking little with him.

In the morning the Prince said: "I have passed an extraordinary night"—

New is such feeling for me
We have been near,
Yet the night passed and our souls have not met.

And he added, "I am wretched."

She could feel his distress and was sorry for him; and said:

With endless sorrow my heart is weighted
And night after night is passed
Even without meeting of the eyelids.

For me this is not new.

MARIE DE FRANCE (POEM DATE C. 12TH CENTURY)

SOURCE: Marie de France. "The Nightingale." In *The Honeysuckle and the Hazel Tree: Medieval Stories of Men and Women,* translated by Patricia Terry. Berkeley: University of California Press, 1995.

Below is a translated reprint of Marie de France's twelfth-century lai *titled "The Nightingale."*

The story I shall tell today
Was taken from a Breton *lai*
Called *Laüstic* in Brittany,
Which in proper French would be
Rossignol. They'd call the tale
In English lands *The Nightingale.*

There was near Saint Malo a town
Of some importance and renown.
Two barons, who could well afford
Houses suited to a lord,
Gave the city its good name
By their benevolence and fame.
Only one of them had married.
His wife was beautiful indeed,
And courteous as she was fair:
A lady who was well aware
Of all that custom and rank required.
The younger knight was much admired,
Being, among his peers, foremost
In valor, and a gracious host.
He never refused a tournament,
And what he owned he gladly spent.
He loved his neighbor's wife. She knew
That all she heard of him was true,
And so she was inclined to be
Persuaded when she heard his plea.
Soon she had yielded all her heart,
Because of his merit and, in part,
Because he lived not far away.
Fearful that others might betray
The love that they had come to share,
They always took the greatest care
Not to let anyone detect
Anything that might be suspect.
And it was easy enough to hide:
Their houses were almost side by side,
With nothing between the two at all
Except a single high stone wall.
The baron's wife had only to go
And stand beside her bedroom window
Whenever she wished to see her friend.
They would talk for hours on end
Across the wall; often they threw
Presents to one another too.
They were much happier than before
And would have asked for nothing more—
But lovers can't be satisfied
When love's true pleasure is denied.
The lady was watched too carefully
As soon as her friend was known to be
At home. But still they had the delight[1]
Of seeing each other day or night
And talking to their hearts' content.
The strictest guard could not prevent
The lady from looking out her window;
What she saw there, no one could know.
Nothing came to interfere
With their true love, until one year,
In the season when the summer grows
Green in all the woods and meadows,
When birds to show their pleasure cling
To flower tops and sweetly sing;
Then those who were in love before
Do, in love's service, even more.
The knight, in truth, was all intent
On love; the messages he sent
Across the wall had such replies
From his lady's lips and from her eyes,
He knew that she felt just the same.
Now she very often came
To her window, lighted by the moon,
Leaving her husband's side as soon
As she knew that he was fast asleep.
Wrapped in a cloak, she went to keep
Watch with her lover, sure that he
Would be waiting for her faithfully.
To see each other was, despite
Their endless longing, great delight.
She went so often and remained
So long, her husband soon complained,
Insisting that she must reply
To where she went at night and why.
"I'll tell you, my lord," the lady answered;
"Anyone who has ever heard
The nightingale singing will admit
No joy on earth compares with it.
That's why I've been standing there.
When the sweet music fills the air,
I'm so delighted, I must arise;
I can't sleep, or even close my eyes."
The baron only answered her
With a malicious, raging laughter.
He wrought a plan that could not fail
To overcome the nightingale.
The household servants all were set
To making traps of cord or net;
Then, throughout the orchard, these
Were fixed to hazel and chestnut trees,

And all the branches rimmed with glue
So that the bird could not slip through.
It was not long before they brought
The nightingale; it had been caught
Alive. The baron, well content,
Took the bird to his wife's apartment.
"Where are you, lady? Come talk to me!"
He cried. ""I've something for you to see!
Look! Here is the bird whose song
Has kept you from your sleep so long.
Your nights will be more peaceful when
He can't awaken you again!"
She heard with sorrow and with dread
Everything her husband said,
Then asked him for the bird, and he
Killed it out of cruelty;
Vile as he was, for spite, he wrung
Its neck with his two hands and flung
The body at his wife. The red
Drops of blood ran down and spread
Over the bodice of her dress.
He left her alone with her distress.
Weeping, she held the bird and thought
With bitter rage of those who brought
The nightingale to death, betrayed
By all the hidden traps they laid.
"Alas!" she cried, "They have destroyed
The one great pleasure I enjoyed.
Now I can no longer go
To see my love outside my window
At night, the way I used to do!
One thing certainly is true:
He'll believe I no longer care.
I'll send the nightingale over there,
And a message that will make it clear
Why it is that I don't appear."
She found a piece of samite, gold-
Embroidered, large enough to fold
Around the body of the bird;
There was room for not another word.[2]
Then she called one in her service
Whom she could entrust with this,
And told him exactly what to say
When he brought it to the chevalier.
Her lover came to understand
Everything, just as she planned.
The servant carried the little bird;
And soon enough the knight had heard
All that he so grieved to know.
His courteous answer was not slow.
He ordered made a little case,
Not of iron or any base
Metal but of fine gold, embossed
With jewels—he did not count the cost.
The cover was not too long or wide.
He placed the nightingale inside
And had the casket sealed with care;
He carried it with him everywhere.
Stories like this can't be controlled,
And it was very promptly told.
Breton poets made of the tale
A *lai* they called *The Nightingale.*

Notes

1. Lines 49-51 Some have interpreted this passage to mean that the lady was watched when her husband was at home, but it seems more logical to assume that *cil* refers to the lover when *he* was at home, that is, not at tournaments.
2. Line 138 The cloth was *tut escrit,* which could mean either that it was covered with the gold embroidery or that the message was written or depicted on it. In any case, there was an oral message as well, conveyed by the messenger.

HELOISE (LETTER DATE C. 1163/64)

SOURCE: Heloise. *The Letters of Abelard and Heloise,* translated by Betty Radice. Hammondsworth, England: Penguin Books, 1974.

In the following excerpts from her letters to Pierre Abelard, the twelfth-century nun Heloise (d. 1163/64) proclaims her love for the man who had seduced and secretly married her—a crime for which he was subsequently castrated.

God is my witness that if Augustus, Emperor of the whole world, thought fit to honour me with marriage and conferred all the earth on me to possess for ever, it would be dearer and more honourable to me to be called not his Empress but your whore.

For a man's worth does not depend on his wealth or power; these depend on fortune, but worth on his merits. And a woman should realize that if she marries a rich man more readily than a poor one, and desires her husband more for his possessions than for herself, she is offering herself for sale.

. . . . .

But if I lose you what is left for me to hope for? What reason for continuing on life's pilgrimage, for which I have no support but you, and none in you save the knowledge that you are alive, now that I am forbidden all other pleasures in you and denied even the joy of your presence which from time to time could restore me to myself?

. . . . .

For a long time my pretense deceived you, as it did many, so that you mistook hypocrisy for piety; and therefore you commend yourself to my prayers and ask me what I expect from you. I beg you, do not feel so sure of me that you cease to help me by your own prayers. Do not suppose me healthy and so withdraw the grace of your healing. Do not believe I want for nothing and delay helping me in the hour of my need. Do not think me strong, lest I fall before you can sustain me. . . .

I do not want you to exhort me to virtue and summon me to the fight, saying, "Power comes to its full strength in weakness" and "He cannot win a crown unless he has kept the rules." I do not seek a crown of victory; it is sufficient for me to avoid danger, and this is safer than engaging in war. In whatever corner of heaven God shall place me, I shall be satisfied. No one will envy another there, and what each one has will suffice.

CATHERINE OF SIENA (ESSAY DATE 1370)

SOURCE: Catherine of Siena. *The Dialogue of the Seraphic Virgin Catherine of Siena,* translated by Algar Thorold. Westminster, Md.: The Newman Bookshop, 1943.

In the following excerpted translation of Catherine of Siena's 1370 Dialogue of the Seraphic Virgin, *originally published in 1907, Catherine describes the sufferings and ecstasies of the soul on its path toward blissful union with God.*

How a soul, elevated by desire of the honor of God, and of the salvation of her neighbors, exercising herself in humble prayer, after she had seen the union of the soul, through love, with God, asked of God four requests.

The soul, who is lifted by a very great and yearning desire for the honor of God and the salvation of souls, begins by exercising herself, for a certain space of time, in the ordinary virtues, remaining in the cell of self-knowledge, in order to know better the goodness of God towards her. This she does because knowledge must precede love, and only when she has attained love, can she strive to follow and to clothe herself with the truth. But, in no way, does the creature receive such a taste of the truth, or so brilliant a light therefrom, as by means of humble and continuous prayer, founded on knowledge of herself and of God; because prayer, exercising her in the above way, unites with God the soul that follows the footprints of Christ Crucified, and thus, by desire and affection, and union of love, makes her another Himself. Christ would seem to have meant this, when He said: *To him who will love Me and will observe My commandment, will I manifest Myself; and he shall be one thing with Me and I with him.* In several places we find similar words, by which we can see that it is, indeed, through the effect of love, that the soul becomes another Himself. That this may be seen more clearly, I will mention what I remember having heard from a handmaid of God, namely, that, when she was lifted up in prayer, with great elevation of mind, God was not wont to conceal, from the eye of her intellect, the love which He had for His servants, but rather to manifest it; and, that among other things, He used to say: "Open the eye of your intellect, and gaze into Me, and you shall see the beauty of My rational creature. And look at those creatures who, among the beauties which I have given to the soul, creating her in My image and similitude, are clothed with the nuptial garment (that is, the garment of love), adorned with many virtues, by which they are united with Me through love. And yet I tell you, if you should ask Me, who these are, I should reply" (said the sweet and amorous Word of God) "they are another Myself, inasmuch as they have lost and denied their own will, and are clothed with Mine, are united to Mine, are conformed to Mine." It is therefore true, indeed, that the soul unites herself with God by the affection of love.

So, that soul, wishing to know and follow the truth more manfully, and lifting her desires first for herself—for she considered that a soul could not be of use, whether in doctrine, example, or prayer, to her neighbor, if she did not first profit herself, that is, if she did not acquire virtue in herself—addressed four requests to the Supreme and Eternal Father. The first was for herself; the second for the reformation of the Holy Church; the third a general prayer for the whole world, and in particular for the peace of Christians who rebel, with much lewdness and persecution, against the Holy Church; in the fourth and last, she besought the Divine Providence to provide for things in general, and in particular, for a certain case with which she was concerned.

How the desire of this soul grew when God showed her the neediness of the world.

This desire was great and continuous, but grew much more, when the First Truth showed her the neediness of the world, and in what a tempest of offense against God it lay. And she had understood this the better from a letter, which she had received from the spiritual Father of her soul, in which he explained to her the penalties and intolerable dolor caused by offenses against God, and the loss of souls, and the persecutions of Holy Church.

All this lighted the fire of her holy desire with grief for the offenses, and with the joy of the lively hope, with which she waited for God to provide against such great evils. And, since the soul seems, in such communion, sweetly to bind herself fast within herself and with God, and knows better His truth, inasmuch as the soul is then in God, and God in the soul, as the fish is in the sea, and the sea in the fish, she desired the arrival of the morning (for the morrow was a feast of Mary) in order to hear Mass. And, when the morning came, and the hour of the Mass, she sought with anxious desire her accustomed place; and, with a great knowledge of herself, being ashamed of her own imperfection, appearing to herself to be the cause of all the evil that was happening throughout the world, conceiving a hatred and displeasure against herself, and a feeling of holy justice, with which knowledge, hatred, and justice, she purified the stains which seemed to her to cover her guilty soul, she said: "O Eternal Father, I accuse myself before You, in order that You may punish me for my sins in this finite life, and, inasmuch as my sins are the cause of the sufferings which my neighbor must endure, I implore You, in Your kindness, to punish them in my person."

How finite works are not sufficient for punishment or recompense without the perpetual affection of love.

Then, the Eternal Truth seized and drew more strongly to Himself her desire, doing as He did in the Old Testament, for when the sacrifice was offered to God, a fire descended and drew to Him the sacrifice that was acceptable to Him; so did the sweet Truth to that soul, in sending down the fire of the clemency of the Holy Spirit, seizing the sacrifice of desire that she made of herself, saying: "Do you not know, dear daughter, that all the sufferings, which the soul endures, or can endure, in this life, are insufficient to punish one smallest fault, because the offense, being done to Me, who am the Infinite Good, calls for an infinite satisfaction? However, I wish that you should know, that not all the pains that are given to men in this life are given as punishments, but as corrections, in order to chastise a son when he offends; though it is true that both the guilt and the penalty can be expiated by the desire of the soul, that is, by true contrition, not through the finite pain endured, but through the infinite desire; because God, who is infinite, wishes for infinite love and infinite grief. Infinite grief I wish from My creature in two ways: in one way, through her sorrow for her own sins, which she has committed against Me her Creator; in the other way, through her sorrow for the sins which she sees her neighbors commit against Me. Of such as these, inasmuch as they have infinite desire, that is, are joined to Me by an affection of love, and therefore grieve when they offend Me, or see Me offended, their every pain, whether spiritual or corporeal, from wherever it may come, receives infinite merit, and satisfies for a guilt which deserved an infinite penalty, although their works are finite and done in finite time; but, inasmuch as they possess the virtue of desire, and sustain their suffering with desire, and contrition, and infinite displeasure against their guilt, their pain is held worthy. Paul explained this when he said: *If I had the tongues of angels, and if I knew the things of the future and gave my body to be burned, and have not love, it would be worth nothing to me.* The glorious Apostle thus shows that finite works are not valid, either as punishment or recompense, without the condiment of the affection of love."

ON THE SUBJECT OF...

ST. CATHERINE OF SIENA (1347-1380)

Caterina Benincasa was born in Siena, Italy, in 1347, and had her first vision of Christ smiling at her at the age of six or seven. At age fifteen, she began to actively reject the world and engage in strict self-denial that included little sleep, almost no food or water, binding her hips with an iron chain, and daily self-flagellation. Within a year, she joined the Dominican order in the congregation of the Sisters of Penance, and became well-known as a religious mystic and selfless caregiver to Siena's poor and sick. Her influence soon extended from caretaking to political action in support of the church, and she dictated letters to various political and church officials. Between 1377 and 1378 Catherine composed her well-known mystical work, which she simply called her "Book" but which has come to be known as *Il dialogo della Divina Provvidenza* ("dialogue of Divine Providence," or *The Dialogue*). In this work, she articulated more fully the mystical theology of love and service that was evident in her letters.

When her letters and prayers failed to resolve the Great Schism of the Catholic church (1378-1415), Catherine starved herself to death, hoping that her sacrifice would save the church. She died on April 29, 1380. In 1395, Catherine's confessor, Raymond of Capua, completed his biography of Catherine, *Legenda major* (*The Life of Catherine of Siena,* 1960), which was widely read and copied by others. In 1461, Catherine was declared a saint by Pope Pius II, and she is considered, with Saint Francis of Assisi, a patron saint of Italy. In 1970, Pope Paul VI declared Catherine to be a Doctor of the Church. She and Saint Teresa of Avila are the only women who have been granted this status.

BIRGITTA OF SWEDEN (ESSAY DATE C. 1377)

SOURCE: Birgitta of Sweden. "The Fifth Book of Revelations or Book of Questions" and "The Seventh Book of Questions." In *Life and Selected Revelations,* edited by Marguerite Tjader Harris, translated by Albert Ryle Kezel, pp. 99-156; 157-218. New York: Paulist Press, 1990.

In the following excerpt, originally written in the fourteenth-century, Saint Birgitta of Sweden relates portions of her mystic vision in which Christ and the Virgin Mary appeared before her and spoke. Christ begins on the subject of Birgitta's spiritual conversion, followed by Mary's admonition against priests marrying.

"For your heart was as cold toward my love as steel; and yet, in it there moved a modest spark of love for me, namely, when you thought me worthy of love and honor above all others. But that heart of yours then fell upon the sulpherous mountain when the glory and delight of the world turned against you and when your husband, whom you carnally loved beyond all others, was taken from you by death. . . .

And when at your husband's death your soul was greatly shaken with disturbance, then the spark of my love—which lay, as it were, hidden and enclosed—began to go forth, for, after considering the vanity of the world, you abandoned your whole will to me and and desired me above all things."

. . . . .

"O you to whom it has been given to hear and see spiritually, hear now the things that I want to reveal to you: namely, concerning that archbishop who said that if he were pope, he would give leave for all clerics and priests to contract marriages in the flesh. He thought and believed that this would be more acceptable to God than that clerics live dissolutely, as they now do. For he believed that through such marriage the greater carnal sins might be avoided; and even though he did not rightly understand God's will in this matter, nonetheless that same archbishop was still a friend of God.

But now I will tell you God's will in this matter; for I gave birth to God himself. . . .

For after he [Christ] instituted in the world this new sacrament of the eucharist and ascended into heaven, the ancient law was then still kept: namely, that Christian priests lived in carnal matrimony. And, nonetheless, many of them were still friends of God because they believed with simple purity that this was pleasing to God. . . .

After those earlier Christian priests had observed these practices for a time, God himself, through the infusion of his Holy Spirit, put into the heart of the pope then guiding the Church another law more acceptable and pleasing to him in this matter . . . so that he established a statute in the universal Church that Christian priests, who have so holy and so worthy an office, namely, of consecrating this precious Sacrament, should by no means live in the easily contaminated, carnal delight of marriage."

WOMEN IN THE ANCIENT WORLD

PAUL CARTLEDGE (ESSAY DATE 1981)

SOURCE: Cartledge, Paul. "Spartan Wives: Liberation or Licence?" *Classical Quarterly* 31 n.s., no. 1 (1981): 84-105.

In the following excerpt, Cartledge studies the unique role women held within the militaristic society of ancient Sparta.

[I now begin] tracing the lives of Spartan women in the sixth to fourth centuries B.C. from the cradle to (in some cases) the grave. I use the vague term 'Spartan women' advisedly. The available evidence does not permit inferences of a statistical nature about the experience of a 'typical' Spartan woman, although in some contexts it will be necessary and possible to distinguish that of rich women. Besides, . . . the literary sources who provide the fullest pictures are highly, and consciously, selective, and they are all non-Spartan and male. Their selectivity and bias may, however, be offset to some extent by tapping sources of evidence, in particular inscriptions and material objects, which they themselves did not see fit, or had not devised the techniques, to utilize.

The evidence for the weaning and rearing of Spartan girls is scanty and not worth discussing in detail.[1] But an objection must at least be lodged against an inference drawn from an anecdote in Plutarch's *Lykourgos* (3. 1-6), that all girl-babies in Sparta were normally reared.[2] This would have been extraordinary, I think, in terms of general Greek practice at all periods,[3] quite apart from the evidence suggesting that in Sparta the exposure of neonates was fairly frequent and that women were, if anything, in relatively short supply.[4] But we are not in any case bound to attribute a universal validity to the passage in question nor indeed to accept the construction placed upon it by Lacey and Pomeroy.[5]

It is necessary, however, to dwell rather longer on two cardinal aspects of the childhood and adolescence of Spartan women. First, whereas the Spartan boy left the parental home for good at the age of seven to embark upon the gruelling system of state education known as the *agōgē,* the Spartan girl—like her counterparts in other Greek states (cf. Hesiod, *Op.* 520)—resided with her parents until marriage. Specifically, she continued to reside with her mother, for the matricentral character of a Spartan girl's home-life was heavily accentuated by the fact that her father was expected to spend most of his time living communally and in public with his male peers—indeed, all of his time, should he have become a father before the age of thirty. . . . This may help to explain the incidence of female homosexuality involving an older woman and an adolescent girl reported by Plutarch (*Lyk.* 18. 9).[6]

Secondly, however, unlike girls in all other Greek states, Spartan girls were also given some form of public education. Whether or not we accept the attractive suggestion of Nilsson[7] that they underwent a course of training parallel to the *agōgē,* Spartan girls undoubtedly were educated in a sense other than trained to perform sedentary, and in ancient Greece exclusively feminine, tasks like weaving (Xen. *L.P.* 1. 3 f.; Plato, *Laws* VII. 806A) and baking (Herakl. Lemb. 373. 13).[8] The running races mentioned in Xenophon (*L.P.* 1. 4) and Plutarch (*Lyk.* 14. 3; *Mor.* 227D) and paralleled in other sources (Theokr. 18. 22; Paus. III. 13. 7; Hesych. s.v. *'en Driōnas'*) very likely had a ritual significance,[9] as certainly did the choral dancing in which Spartan maidens participated both in Sparta and at sanctuaries elsewhere in Lakonia and Messenia.[10] But the throwing of the discus and javelin and the trials of strength or wrestling also attested by Xenophon and Plutarch presumably had a mainly secular character. It is, however, a little hard to credit the evidence of Euripides (*Andr.* 597-600) that the girls wrestled naked with the boys.[11] For this looks like a deliberate travesty in line with the view of Euripides—or strictly Peleus, father of Achilles—that it was impossible for a Spartan maiden to be sexually modest (*sōphrōn: Andr.* 595 f.).[12]

Such an accusation, on the other hand, does appear to have some basis in Spartan actuality. For both total nudity in public (at religious processions: Plut. *Lyk.* 14.4-7) and the wearing of a revealingly slit mini-chiton (Pollux VII. 54 f.)[13]—hence the opprobrious epithet 'thigh-showers' first known from Ibykos (fr. 58 Page)[14]—are strikingly confirmed by a series of Spartan bronzes, mostly of the sixth century.[15] These free-standing figurines and mirror-handles portray girls or young women with underdeveloped or de-emphasized secondary sex characteristics. It is not, I think, fanciful to associate this feature with the strongly homosexual orientation of the average Spartan male.[16] But what is most significant is that the nude female figure is not at all frequent in Greek art before the fifth century and then is normally reserved for women of low social status. The shock felt by non-Spartan, and especially perhaps Athenian, males at such uninhibited—indeed, indecent because masculine—exposure may the more readily be comprehended if, as I believe possible, Spartan girls appeared publicly in the nude (or at least scantily clad) after puberty.[17]

According to Xenophon and Plutarch, the Spartan girl's education was confined to physical exertions and designed to serve exclusively eugenic ends, that is, to produce strong mothers of healthy infants and to alleviate the pangs of childbirth (in which, we infer, maternal mortality was not infrequent).[18] No doubt eugenic considerations were important, particularly perhaps after *c.* 500 when, . . . official steps were taken to further procreation. But there is also evidence to suggest that the things of the mind were not entirely neglected.

According to Plato in the *Protagoras* (342D), there were Spartan women who prided themselves on their learning and culture (*paideusis*). He refers specifically to their attainment in speech (*logoi*)—notoriously, Spartan women did have something to say and were reputedly not afraid to say it[19]—and singles out their contribution to quintessentially Spartan brachylogy. But he also mentions their *philosophia* in this passage and, in the *Laws* (VII. 806A; cf. *Rep.* V. 452A), their participation in high culture (*mousikē*). Not much weight can be placed on the testimony of Plato, the philo-Lakonian or at least unorthodox Greek educationist.[20] But Aristophanes (*Lys.* 1237; cf. *Vesp.* 1245-7) apparently refers to a Spartan poetess called Kleitagora;[21] and Iamblichos (*Vita Pyth.* 267) names several female Spartan Pythagoreans. Finally, the epigraphical evidence, though slight and formally ambiguous, at least does not contradict the view that at any rate some Spartan women were basically literate.[22] Basic literacy, after all, was the most that the ordinary Spartan man was expected to acquire.[23]

The real significance of this education, in both its physical and intellectual aspects, is that it reflects an official attempt to maintain some form or degree of parity between the sexes. The chief function of this apparent equality of treatment, however, was not one a modern feminist would necessarily approve, but rather to socialize the non-military half of the citizen population.[24] At all events, it was certainly not designed to promote companionship or partnership in marriage; . . . Aristotle attributed what he took to be the indiscipline of the women, not to the equality of their education, but to the separateness of Spartan married life. On balance, therefore, I incline to think that the introduction or general enforcement of the male *agōgē,* in the course of the seventh and sixth centuries, diminished the status of women in Sparta.[25] Thereafter, much as elsewhere in Greece though in a peculiarly singleminded way, the primary emphasis in their upbringing was on preparing them for their future subordinate role as wives and mothers of warriors.

Notes

1. We do not know whether newborn girls were subjected to the ritualistic and/or hygienic wine-baths endured by their brothers (Plut. *Lyk.* 16. 3). Nor do we know if the Spartan wet-nurses who acquired something of a cachet outside Sparta (Plut. *Alk.* 1. 3, *Lyk.* 16. 5) were of citizen status. The nannies praised by Plutarch (*Lyk.* 16. 4) were perhaps unfree.

2. W. K. Lacey, *The Family in Classical Greece* (London, 1968), p. 197 (hereafter Lacey); Pomeroy, 36. The passage in question also contains a reference to the possibility of abortion (cf. *Mor.* 242C; [Hippokr.], *On the Nature of the Child,* 13. 2); but direct evidence for this (as opposed to infanticide) is non-existent for our period.

3. However, L. R. F. Germain, 'Aspects du droit d'exposition en Grèce', *RD,* 4th ser. 47 (1969), 177-97, at pp. 179 f., doubts whether exposure was frequent in our period.

4. Exposure in Sparta (esp. Plut. *Lyk.* 16. 2): G. Glotz, 'L'exposition des enfants', *Etudes sociales et juridiques sur l'antiquité grecque* (Paris, 1906), pp. 187-27, at pp. 188, 192, and esp. pp. 217-19; P. Roussel, 'L'exposition des enfants à Sparte', *REA* 45 (1943), 5-17. Shortage of women in Sparta: the direct evidence is weak—no spinsters *versus* attested polyandry and only one known instance of bigamy (below)—but see generally Pomeroy, pp. 227 f. Possibly too infant mortality, which was no doubt high in ancient Greece, affected girls more than boys.

5. Such anecdotes may of course legitimately be construed as retrojections of later practice; but it can be rash to generalize from *royal* practice and, secondly, Lykourgos' injunction—that his brother's posthumous offspring, if born female, should be handed over to the women—does not entail that she would then be reared, since she might be born deformed or feeble.

6. D. L. Page, *Alcman. The Partheneion* (Oxford, 1951), pp. 66 f., tentatively attributed this homosexuality to the close association between women and girls in cult and in the gymnasia. C. Calame, *Les choeurs de jeunes filles en Grèce archaïque,* 2 vols. (Rome, 1977), i. 433-6, argues that it had an educative function. K. J. Dover, *Greek Homosexuality* (London, 1978), p. 181, speaks in this connection (following J. Hallett) of 'an overt "subculture", or rather "counter-culture" in which women and girls received from their own sex what segregation and monogamy denied them from men'. However, according to Pomeroy, p. 55, 'the most important factor, both at Sparta and at Lesbos, in fostering female homoerotic attachments was that women in both societies were highly valued'.

7. M. P. Nilsson, 'Die Grundlagen des Spartanischen Lebens', *Klio* 12 (1908), 308-40, reprinted in *Opera Selecta,* 3 vols. (Lund, 1951-60), ii. 826-69, at p. 848. See also below, n. 63.

8. Clothesmaking: P. Herfst, *Le travail de la femme dans la Grèce ancienne* (Paris, 1922), pp. 18-24. Cooking: ibid. pp. 24-32. Exemption of Spartan women: ibid. pp. 112 f. But it was Spartan women who wove the tunic (*chitōn*) for Apollo of Amyklai each year (Paus. III. 16. 2).

9. The sixth-century bronze figurines of girl runners from Sparta (Inv. 3305), Delphi (Inv. 3072), Albania (London, B.M. 208) and Dodona (Athens, N.M. Carapanos 24) are very possibly all of Spartan make. The dress of the third, leaving one breast bare, vividly recalls Paus. V. 16. 3 (race between virgins at Olympia in honour of Hera).

10. Calame, op. cit. (n. 38), esp. i. 350-7, has ingeniously reconstructed a Spartan cycle of female initiation conforming to the model of Van Gennep. Hypothetically, this consisted of a complex series of *rites de passage* designed ultimately to confer on the girls full adult status within the civic community, the primary emphasis being placed on their sexuality, marriage and maternity. However, although his case for the initiatory function of at least some aspects of the cults discussed seems well grounded, the reconstruction as a whole remains far from demonstrated.

11. We do, however, learn from Athenaios (XIII. 566E) of mixed wrestling between adolescents on the island of Chios.

12. This idea may lie behind the *ben trovato* apophthegm (Plut. *Mor.* 232C) purporting to explain why Spartan virgins did not wear veils in public, whereas the wives did. For the topic in general see H. North, *Sophrosyne. Self-knowledge and Self-restraint in Greek Literature* (Ithaca, 1966), esp. pp. 68-84 (Euripides), 95 f. (Kritias), 128 and n. 17 (Xenophon), 197-211 (Aristotle).

13. The dress of the women seems to have been no more inhibiting than that of the girls: Plut. *Mor.* 241B; Teles *ap.* Stob., *Flor.* 108. 83 (*anasyramenē* could be translated colloquially as 'flashing').

14. cf. Eur. *Andr.* 597 f., *Hec.* 933 f.; Soph. fr. 788N; Pollux II. 187, VII. 54 f.; Clement, *Paed.* II. 10. 114. 1. For thighs as an erotogenic feature see Athen. XIII. 602E (though perhaps 'thighs' was a conventional euphemism for a part of the female anatomy which it was literally shameful to reveal). For the way that female clothing has often been deliberately designed to hinder activity see de Beauvoir, p. 190; cf. ibid. pp. 323, 429, 442.

15. The series includes the four items cited above (n. 41), together with Athens, N.M. 15897, 15900; Berlin (Charlottenburg) 10820, 31084; New York, Met. 38. 11. 3, 06. 11. 04; Paris, Louvre; Sparta Mus. 594, 3302; Vienna, Kunsthistorisches Mus. VI 2925, 4979. Th. Karageorgha, *AD* 20. 1 (1965), 96-109, publishes Sparta 3302 with further comparanda; all are discussed in U.

Häfner, 'Das Kunstschaffen Lakoniens in archaischer Zeit' (Diss. Münster, 1965); cf. Cl. Rolley, 'Le problème de l'art laconien', *Ktema* 2 (1977), 125-40, at p. 130. They were almost certainly made by men, some of whom could have been Spartan citizens. But the mirrors at least could have been commissioned and/or dedicated by women; cf. below, n. 54. We may add a unique sixth-century Spartan clay *kylix* (cup) on whose interior are depicted three nude and long-haired girls disporting themselves by a river: C. M. Stibbe, *Lakonische Vasenmaler des sechsten Jahrhunderts v. Chr.* (Amsterdam, 1972), pp. 133, 280, no. 209.

16. The chief sources are Aristoph. fr. 338, *Lys.* 1105, 1148, 1174, with V. Ehrenberg, *The People of Aristophanes* (New York, 1962), p. 180 and n. 7; Xen. *L.P.* 2. 12-14; Plato, *Laws* VIII 836A-C; Plut. *Lyk.* 18. 8 f., *Ages.* 2. 1, *Mor.* 761D; Cic. *de rep.* IV. 4. 4; Hesychius, Suda, Photius *s.v. 'Lakōnikon tropon'*. Dover, op. cit. (n. 38), pp. 185 ff., seems to me somewhat to understate this feature of Spartan society.

17. I suspect, however, that the alleged Spartan practice of stripping virgins in front of foreigners or guest-friends (*xenoi:* Athen. XIII. 566E) is pure invention.

18. . . .

19. On the apophthegms—those attributed to Spartan women are Plut. *Mor.* 240C-242D—see Tigerstedt, op. cit. ii. 16-30. Contrast the conventional male Athenian attitude to free public speech for women: Soph. *Ajax* 293; Eur. *Her.* 476 f., fr. 61; Thuc. II. 45. 2, 46.

20. D. Wender, 'Plato: misogynist, paedophile and feminist', *Arethusa* 6 (1973), 75-90.

21. But see D. M. MacDowell's edition of *Wasps* (Oxford, 1971) ad loc.

22. From the late seventh century onwards we have ex-votos from Sparta inscribed with the name of a dedicatrix. Since the recipient deities were also female and a fair proportion of the uninscribed offerings have feminine associations, many of the dedications were probably offered by women. However, the names of only about a dozen Spartan women are attested epigraphically in our period (the corresponding figure for men is about a hundred), as against about fifty in the literary sources.

23. See my 'Literacy in the Spartan oligarchy', *JHS* 98 (1978), 25-37, where I also discuss brachylogy.

24. The position of Roman women, at least those of the highest social class, seems to me parallel in this respect: cf. D. Daube, *Civil Disobedience in Antiquity* (Edinburgh, 1972), pp. 23 ff.

25. For a succinct exposition of the structure of Spartan society as it had been remodelled by the fifth century see M. I. Finley, 'Sparta', in *The Use and Abuse of History* (London, 1975), pp. 161-77.

DIANA H. COOLE (ESSAY DATE 1988)

SOURCE: Coole, Diana H. "The Origin of Western Thought and the Birth of Misogyny." In *Women in Political Theory: From Ancient Misogyny to Contemporary Feminism,* pp. 10-28. Brighton, Sussex: Wheatsheaf Books, 1988.

In the following excerpt, Coole probes the sources of Western misogyny in the philosophy, literature, and social structure of classical Greece.

Western political philosophy first flourished in Athens, in the fourth century B.C.; it is the names of Plato and Aristotle that are most often associated with these origins. Their concern with arrangements for a just and stable state involved more than constitutional organization, however. Questions regarding the nature of virtue and the good life were meshed with broader inquiries regarding the status of knowledge; birth and death; the order of the universe. Such fundamental questions involved speculations about woman's place in the design of Being and her role in the city-state (*polis*). The answers given would exert a strong influence on more than two millennia of subsequent political theory, offering both assumptions and explicit arguments to its expositors. Over and again we will find the debate between Plato and Aristotle regarding women's nature and role, echoing across the centuries. For their pronouncements on the subject have remained influential well beyond the function they actually ascribed to women in the well-ordered state. Powerful associations between the female and certain qualities viewed as antithetical to politics, even to civilization itself, have also been inherited from these early examples of political thought. Yet Plato and Aristotle were by no means the first to make such allusions. They already wrote within a cultural tradition of misogyny and a social context of women's subjugation. In order to understand the premises underlying their references to woman, it is first necessary, therefore, to look back to the origins of Greek civilization itself.

It is tempting to think that such an excursion into the past might answer that ubiquitous question: how and why did women's oppression begin? The earliest records of Greek life cannot, however, resolve this conundrum; at best they yield a glimpse of the late Bronze Age, when a sexual division of labour and a general pattern of male dominance were already well established. What they do offer us are the earliest literary presentations of women in the West and an opportunity to speculate on the reasons for the generally unfavourable nature of these.

Peoples speaking an early form of Greek began to infiltrate the Attic and Peloponnesian region early in the second millennium B.C. Here they encountered a Near Eastern culture, some of whose elements became integrated into their own. The Greek-speaking Dorians probably arrived as a second wave around 1200 B.C., shortly before the Trojan War. It was about this time that the Mycenean-Minoan civilization that preceded Iron Age Hellenic Greece, mysteriously disappeared. We know very little about this earlier Bronze Age culture apart from the obscure Linear B Tablets. These already record women spinning, weaving, grinding corn, reaping, fetching water and drawing baths.[1] There are great kings who rule yet the priests apparently worship the Great Mother. Subsequently, the art of writing was lost and the first Greek literature appears with the poems of Homer and Hesiod, probably composed around the eighth century B.C.. These were constructed from myths and histories passed verbally across the generations of the Dark Age and were facilitated by the introduction of the alphabet.

Homer's *Iliad* and *Odyssey* tell of the Trojan War and its aftermath, ostensibly depicting something of the older twelfth-century culture, although scholars now locate the social structures described more in the tenth and ninth centuries.[2] Although most commentators find little trace of misogyny in Homer,[3] some of the images that would later degrade women were already present. A misogynous approach is more readily discernible in the work of Hesiod, who recorded events of daily life in Archaic Greece in his *Works and Days* and offered a mythical account of cosmic evolution in his *Theogony.* Over the next three centuries, a clear picture of woman's lesser status and qualities would emerge via equivalent and interlocking accounts offered in myth, drama, science and philosophy. Although these early works were not political tracts, then, they did articulate those ideas pertaining to the sexes that later political writers would adopt.

Homer's depiction of women, in an age he associated with the Heroic past, would be of lasting significance since his poems were still read and recited in Plato's day as an authentic narrative of Greek history, as well as a source of moral exhortation. While the chief females of the *Iliad* and *Odyssey* appear as strong characters and avoid the sort of denigration women would receive in subsequent literature, their subordinate role in the household (*oikos*) remains unquestioned. Indeed, it was the arrangement presented here that Engels would later describe as a manifestation of the new relations imposed after the *'world-historical defeat of the female sex'*.[4]

The heroes of the Homeric epics are the kings who went to fight Sparta in the Trojan Wars, among whom attention focuses on Odysseus and Agamemnon. The heroic virtues they display are manly qualities: courage, physical strength, bravery, prowess. For this was an age when status and duty were defined by one's position in the social structure and virtue was manifested by performing with excellence the virtues ascribed to a given station. The role of the hero is defence of homeland and household.[5] There is no role women can perform that will allow them to excel in this manner, and the term 'hero' has no feminine form.[6] Nevertheless, women's social position does allot them a function and thus an opportunity to display excellence of a different kind. The unity of the household depends upon the loyalty of its members and so the key virtue of the women is fidelity.[7] It is Helen's infidelity that starts the Trojan War to begin with, while Agamemnon's faithless wife Clytemnestra brings political chaos when she takes a new lover. In stark contrast, there is the chaste and honourable Penelope, who maintains Odysseus' kingdom for him during his ten years of wandering. While it is true that fidelity is also demanded of men, it does not in their case have a sexual implication: the husbands are hardly monogamous.

Homer's leading women are powerful agents who use intelligence and cunning to further their ends; they are never passive figures in this virile world. If Penelope cannot become queen in her own right but must choose a new husband who will replace the missing Odysseus as king, and if her son Telemachus is able to silence her and bid her depart to engage in womanly tasks during the proceedings, she is nevertheless successful in deflecting her suitors and in sustaining a public presence that would be denied to women of a later age. And although Penelope and Helen are frequently to be found engaged in domestic pursuits like weaving, no denigration is applied by Homer to such activities.

Nevertheless, the tapestry that underlies the main characters of the Homeric epics tells a rather different tale of women: one where they are viewed merely as pieces of movable property, to be allocated as prizes of war like other booty. The first book of the *Iliad* is illustrative here. Agamemnon has been awarded Khryseis, a beautiful captive, by the army. At first he refuses to return her to her father, swearing he will have her back in Argos 'working my loom and visiting my bed'.[8] He rates her higher than his wife in beauty, womanhood, mind and skill. Learning that Apollo has put a curse on the Greek army while the girl is kept captive, however, Agamemnon agrees to send her home provided the army supplies him with an equivalent prize. This provokes a violent quarrel with Achilles, also recipient of a lovely female captive, whom Agamemnon now seizes. Achilles laments that she is 'my prize, given by the army'[9] and persuades his mother to take his case to Zeus. But Zeus is also having woman trouble: he agrees to help but fears the wrath of his wife Hera, who 'will be at me all day long. Even as matters stand she never rests from badgering me before the gods'. We thus find women depicted in unflattering terms and ones with which they already seem to be stereotyped: the beautiful slave/concubine, unwitting cause of rage and jealousy among men; the nagging and scheming wife (Hera, Clytemnestra) versus her pure and patient antithesis (Penelope).

The background against which these roles were performed was one where society and state had not yet clearly emerged from kinship structures. The household was the unit for the satisfaction of material needs but also the locus of ethical norms and values, obligations and responsibilities, personal and religious relations. When crimes were committed, it was the family which pursued retribution. In so far as public life existed, its main concern was with defence, and its authority relations were understood by analogy with those of kinship roles.

The world of which Homer wrote was therefore one where social relations still centred on *oikos* (household) rather than *polis* (city-state) and where the *oikos* was identified with property rather than with affective bonds. The household did not refer simply to the family but included land, goods, slaves, wives, relatives' wives and children all under the patriarchal authority of the male head. Throughout archaic and classical Greece, emotional bonds between husband and wife would remain weak. Women functioned predominantly as bearers of children and servicers of the household, and their performance was evaluated accordingly.[10] When their husbands took female slaves as sexual partners, no jealousy was expected (although Clytemnestra clearly fails to rise to the occasion when she kills Cassandra, whom Agamemnon brings back from the war as his concubine).

Gods and goddesses perform a significant role in the Homeric poems. Indeed, myth figured strongly in Greek culture as a whole and the line between historical and mythic events or actors is not drawn with any clarity. The function of such myths remains controversial: whether they symbolize real historical events or merely justify a status quo whose origins are unknown; whether they are the playing out of oppositions or emotions underlying all cultures or a primitive attempt to understand and systematize the world. Whatever the answer, it is certain that the male-female antithesis provides a central theme for Greek mythology. And when the conflict is played out between gods and goddesses, it drags in its train a whole series of related oppositions, since the notions of male and female already resonate with a powerful symbolism. Reconciliation is required, but in successful resolutions it is invariably the male principle which triumphs and this result is implied to be necessary if progress is to occur. One account of such a process can be found in Hesiod's *Theogony.*

The *Theogony* became the standard Greek account of creation, although it was composed in a tradition of theogonies (of which Genesis is another example) and probably owed much to Near Eastern models.[11] It tells of the evolution of the gods and of a cosmos personified in deities. Thus Hesiod begins with the Earth, who is mother of all and gives birth parthenogenetically to Sea and Sky. She needs no sexual partner; she is the first and supreme matriarch. However, she subsequently mates with Sky, thereby initiating the line of the gods. In the fourth generation the Olympians, headed by the patriarchal Zeus, appear. While early male gods had played only a hazy role compared with the more significant mothers, it is they who come to the fore once Zeus claims ascendency. The divine hierarchy now moves from female to male dominance and also, with the passing of power from Mother Earth to Sky God, it shifts from material to non-material hegemony.[12] Zeus is himself equated with the law as opposed to an original chaos. The poem thus tells how the earth goddesses, associated with fertility cults and nature, were defeated by the Olympian patriarchs, who represent reason, order and wisdom. It is an account that probably bears some relation to the actual replacement of one religion by another.

The *Theogony* is of symbolic interest *vis-à-vis* its attitudes toward the female in two additional ways: the generation of woman and generation *per se*. First, although its subject is divine creation, it also explains how woman appeared.[13] Angry at Prometheus for stealing the secret of fire, Zeus contrives an 'evil' for all men that will destroy their sojourn in peace and plenty: he bids his co-deities create a 'modest' maiden out of clay and proceeds to parade her for all to see:

> Immortal gods and mortal men / were amazed when they saw this tempting snare / from which men cannot escape. From her comes the fair sex; / yes, wicked womenfolk are her descendants. / They live among mortal men as a nagging burden / and are no good sharers of abject want, but only of wealth. / Men are like swarms of bees clinging to cave roofs / to feed drones that contribute only to malicious deeds; / the bees themselves all day long until sundow / are busy carrying and storing

the white wax, but the drones stay inside in their roofed hives and cram their bellies full of what others harvest. / So, too, Zeus who roars on high made woman / to be an evil for mortal men, help-mates in deed of harshness.[14]

A yet nastier version of this story of Pandora's creation is told by Hesiod in his *Works and Days*. Here the various divinities teach woman her work ('intricate weaving'). They give her 'stinging desire and limb-gnawing passion', 'the mind of a bitch' and a 'thievish nature'. She is made full of 'lies' and 'coaxing words'. She is a 'scourge to toiling men'; with her arrival, 'toilsome hardship' and 'painful illness' appear. For 'the woman with her hands removed the lid of the jar and scattered its contents, bringing grief and cares to men'.[15] It is woman, then, who brings a whole series of misfortunes into the world and whose very existence is but the infliction of punishment. In the *Theogony,* Hesiod says that even he who marries a woman of sound and prudent mind, will spend his life trying to balance the good and bad in her. But he does acknowledge a wife's benefits: she will look after a man in his old age and give him descendants to inherit his property, so her malice must be suffered.[16]

Since the account suggests that men did originally live happily without women, it seems that their birth must have been somehow accomplished without female assistance. Such a possibility is made more explicit in a further passage in the *Theogony,* where Hesiod describes the birth of the goddess Athena. Thus a second level of significance relates to Hesiod's account of generation itself.

Prior to Zeus' rule, there had been a pattern of depositions of male rulers by mothers and sons in alliance. Zeus is warned that the pregnant Metis, goddess of wisdom, will bear him a son and repeat the syndrome. So he swallows her. Eventually, he gives birth, out of his skull, to a fully-armed Athena.[17] A number of benefits accrue to this solution. Zeus ends threats to his sovereignty by giving birth to a female. She has no mother to ally with and is also sufficiently androgynous both to identify with him and to remain impotent. By swallowing Metis he appropriates wisdom, rendering it a male prerogative. And finally, the myth achieves a further erosion of female power by reversing the natural order of generation. It is now the male who gives birth to the female and reproductive capacity is transferred from womb to head, suggesting that the male version is of a superior kind, rooted in reason rather than in the dark recesses of the flesh.

On a more mundane level, Hesiod's *Works and Days,* which gives counsel to tillers of the soil, is sprinkled with misogynous advice. Thus: 'you trust a thief when you trust a woman';[18] 'Five years past puberty makes a woman a suitable bride. Marry a virgin so you can teach her right from wrong';[19] 'Nothing is better for a man than a good wife, and no horror matches a bad one'.[20]

Four major themes pertaining to the female thus appear in Hesiod's poems: the overthrow of the old fertility goddesses by the rational, patriarchal Olympian deities; the explanation of men's woes as a function of woman's creation; the myth of male generation and the more prosaic anecdotes concerning women's generally amoral and unpleasant nature. Such themes reappear in subsequent Greek literature; it is instructive to look at some of the later dramatic presentations of the conflict between male and female principles.

Drama flourished in classical Athens during the fifth century B.C. The three major playwrights, Aeschylus, Sophocles and Euripides, all produced plays which enacted conflicts related to the male-female opposition. In the tradition of the *Theogony,* the male order is associated with reason and the *polis;* with political and legal relations, justice, progress and good organization. The female is correspondingly aligned with the old world of kinship bonds and family honour; with a certain madness that threatens the impersonal relations of justice, with chaos and prejudice. Thus in Sophocles' *Antigone,* the heroine opposes the rational laws of Creon's *polis* in favour of the traditional duties owed to blood relatives. The consequences are tragic. In Euripides' *Bacchae,* failure to reconcile male and female elements ends in disequilibrium and disaster when the irrational forces associated with the women are left to run their course.[21] But it is Aeschylus' *Oresteia* which offers the most resonant account of sexual contradiction across a variety of levels.

The *Oresteia* is a trilogy whose component parts—*Agamemnon, The Choephorae* and *The Eumenides*—tell a continuous story. This draws on Homer's *Odyssey* for its narrative, but its theology is taken from Hesiod. When Clytemnestra murders Agamemnon and takes a new lover, a series of tragic consequences ensues. Orestes slays his mother to avenge his father and thereby re-establishes male authority. But he is in turn pursued by the female Erinyes, who seek retribution on his mother's behalf, for the Erinyes are beings from the Underworld who punish murderers of kin. Orestes turns to Apollo for help, and the god purifies him, insisting that Orestes' crime is a justifiable one, whereupon conflict erupts between the female goddesses and the male Apollo. Crucial to its outcome is the question of whether matricide or homicide is the greater crime and therefore whether blood-bond or bed-bond, kinship or legal relations, mother-right or father-right, takes precedence. Eventually, Orestes flees to Athens, where Athena herself agrees to mediate. She refers the conflict to a tribunal over which she presides. The Erinyes prosecute, Apollo is Orestes' advocate; the tribunal votes inconclusively; Athena intervenes in support of Orestes and the latter wins his case.

What does this victory symbolize? It is not insignificant that Apollo is the son of Zeus, who is identified with law and order. Nor is it incidental that it is a human court that is engaged in judicial procedures and judges the crime, for it represents the *polis* and impersonal justice. The outcome means that marital relations take precedence over those of kinship, and this suggests both control over women's sexuality by the male and the dominance of legal over familial bonds. Furthermore, it is appropriate that the androgynous Athena should be the one to tip the tied vote in Orestes' favour: she argues that she is unable to sympathize with a mother's position, lacking one herself. But most important of all, the outcome is a victory for the new order over the old, since the defeated Erinyes belonged to the ancient pre-Olympian divinities and were regarded as defenders of the natural order of things. Daughters of the Night, they represent primitive incarnations of the female, bloodsucking and oozing poison from every orifice. Thus Clytemnestra exhorts them: 'waft your bloody breath upon him! Dry him up with its vapour, your womb's fire!'[22] And Apollo refers to them as 'gray virgins, ancient maidens, with whom no god or any among men nor any beast has intercourse'.[23] Yet their association with the female, with kinship bonds and Mother Earth, gives the Erinyes power over fertility, and this is not something that can be banished from the new patriarchal order. Only its control is called for. Accordingly, the Erinyes are placated with the offer of a special cult in Athens. If they promise to refrain from causing 'all things that bear fruit not to prosper',[24] they are promised 'sacrifice in thanks for children and the accomplishment of marriage'.[25] Their bargain is homologous with the judgement that marital relations have priority over blood bonds, in so far as women's ancient powers of fertility are retained but controlled within the restraints of a patriarchal legal order. Social advance is won only by the subjugation of the female. Freud and Engels would both see in these events a dramatization of the overthrow of matriarchy.[26]

There is yet a further dimension to this defeat, however. The female's power emanates from her ability to create new life, and this must be defused if male sovereignty and the rationality associated with it, are to be ensured. Thus when the Erinyes ask Apollo how he dares petition for Orestes' acquittal, given that he has spilt his mother's blood ('How else did she nourish you beneath her girdle, murderer?' they ask Orestes. 'Do you disown your mother's blood?'[27]), the god replies that although she might have nourished the embryo, the mother is not strictly a parent:

> She who is called the child's mother is not its begetter, but the nurse of the newly sown conception. The begetter is the male, and she is a stranger for a stranger preserves the offspring[28]

As proof he cites the birth of his sister: 'There can be a father without a mother; near at hand is the witness, the child of Olympian Zeus'. Athena was 'not nurtured in the darkness of the womb, but is such an offspring as no goddess might bear'.[29] The idea of male generation that appears in *The Eumenides* evokes the mythic account given previously by Hesiod.

The belief that the male plays at least the more important role in reproduction, was to remain a popular one throughout Greek thought. It appeared in a rather different form, for example, in Plato's *Symposium*. Here, not only is spiritual love, of which men alone are held to be capable, praised as superior to carnal pleasure, but its outcome is also claimed a superior progeny:

> Men whose bodies are only creative, betake themselves to women and beget children—this is the character of their love; their offspring, as they hope, will preserve their memory and give them the blessedness and immortality which they desire in the future. But creative souls—for there are men who are more creative in their souls than in their bodies—conceive that which is proper for the soul to conceive or retain. And what are these conceptions?—wisdom and virtue in general.[30]

In so far as the purpose of reproduction is immortality, the latter are superior products. The *Republic* will manage . . . even to eliminate women's special relationship with the generation of material beings.

It was in the new scientific theories, however, that the notion of a more important male contribution to reproduction was most literally stated. Although these theories were based on observation and deduction, it is difficult to imagine that they would have taken the form they did had they not arisen within a cultural paradigm already ascribing inferiority to things female. And they, in turn, clearly reinforced the equation. They receive their clearest expression in Aristotle's *Generation of Animals,* but this only represents a more sophisticated version of earlier themes.

For Aristotle, the respective and hierarchical functions of the two sexes are evident: 'the male as possessing the principle of movement and of generation, the female as possessing that of matter'.[31] There emerges a series of opposed terms related to the sexes: soul-body (the 'physical part, the body, comes from the female and the soul from the male'[32]); active-passive (she is the one who 'receives the semen' but is unable to discharge or shape it. Male semen is the 'active and efficient ingredient' which sets and gives form to, the female residue[33]); ability-inability (the colder female body lacks the heat needed to 'concoct' or 'act upon' her own seminal—menstrual—fluid in order to make it fertile: 'the male and female are distinguished by a certain ability and inability'[34]); form-matter ('the contribution which the female makes to generation is the *matter* used therein; semen possesses the "principle" of "form").[35] These equations are all finally ranked as better-worse, superior-inferior. The male is the norm and the female but an 'infertile male'; a 'deformity' identified by an 'inability of a sort':[36]

> And as the proximate motive cause, to which belongs the *logos* and the form, is *better* and more divine in its nature than the matter, it is *better* also that the superior one should be separate from the inferior one. This is why whenever possible and so far as is possible the male is separate from the female, since it is something *better* and more divine in that it is the principle of movement for generated things, while the female serves as their matter.[37]

While the female provides the 'stranger' receptacle that nourishes, it is thus the male who imparts life, soul and reason. Such theories, harking back to the mythical belief in the head as the organ of generation, held that seminal fluid originated in the male's head, flowing down the spine and out through the genitals.

We have already seen how Plato took this idea a stage further, claiming that the soul could actually produce a superior creation—virtue, wisdom—when unadulterated by carnal imperatives. As far as real offspring were concerned, however, Plato evidently believed in an explanation resembling that of Aristotle. Discussing the origin of the universe in the *Timaeus,* he uses the human experience as an analogy, likening the mother to the receptacle and the father to the model. The qualities of the former are that 'it continues to receive all things, and never itself takes a permanent impress from any of the things that enter it; it is a kind of neutral plastic material in which changing impressions are stamped by the things that enter it'.[38]

Finally, these mythic, dramatic and scientific equations between male and female and related oppositions, were reinforced in and by Greek philosophy. Already in the sixth century B.C. the Pythagoreans had seen a universe riven by dualisms. In the table they drew up to classify these, male-female was aligned with light-dark, good-bad, limited-unlimited and so on. Femaleness was linked to that which lacked form; with vagueness, indeterminacy, irregularity. It was the male principle that brought order and rational organization; that gave shape to the indeterminate, in much the same way that Aristotle's male would shape offspring out of the indeterminate female fluids, to suggest a correspondence between embryology and epistemology.

The question remains how and why a whole culture evolved such powerful symbolic associations with the sexes. Clearly, they do not rest upon simply functionalist or empirical arguments about the different physical or emotional capacities related to a sexual division of labour (although they would eventually be used to underpin these).[39] We need to explain why women were seen not merely as different but also as synonymous with a whole host of negative qualities. Our conclusions are important since the equations and deprecations traced thus far reappear in Greek political writing and achieve considerable endurance within the genre.

From the beginning women seem to have been associated with certain natural phenomena, and this is perhaps unsurprising. Their power to create new life was wondered at long before any male contribution was recognized. This power seemed to ally them with the earth and with a nature whose fecundity they shared. The early fertility cults would naturally have been presided over by female goddesses. Plato shows himself still immersed in the equation when he suggests that in conceiving and generating, women imitate the earth, such that there is a correspondence between the milk of motherhood and the grain the earth yields to men.[40] However, women's identification with the earth also seems to have suggested an allegiance with dark powers inimical to the mind (but related to the womb). Most Greek daemons were born of the earth (chthonic) and were female. They threaten their victims with madness. Thus Aeschylus has the Erinyes chant:

> Over our victim / we sing this song, maddening the brain, / carrying away the sense, destroying the mind, / a hymn that comes from the Erinyes, / fettering the mind[41]

By linking woman to darkness via the earth, the Greeks associated her with insanity and also with death. The latter was in turn identified with contamination and women were seen as having an affinity with polluting forces, with which they mediated on men's behalf in religious rituals.[42] At the same time, women's fertility related them to the flesh in a culture that maintained a strict mind-body dualism and hierarchy in its thought. This had important consequences for the theories of knowledge that developed as well as for a political thought which equated the good life with the capacity to subordinate body to soul and a virtuous existence with contemplation and rational discourse.

A variety of explanations has been offered for the misogyny that accompanied this symbolism. From a political perspective it is suggested that the historical overthrow of matriarchal religion and/or matriarchy itself, was sufficiently recent for the new patriarchal order to yet be on the defensive against women's power.[43] It is evident from Homer's account of Heroic Greece that kinship bonds had only recently yielded precedence to the authority of the city-state, and the women associated with familial loyalties are still greeted with suspicion by Plato several centuries later.

City-states first appeared in Greece around the seventh century B.C., bringing with them a decline in tribal and familial authority. Civic republics of a small and intimate nature, they drew no distinction between society and state, fulfilling equally both moral and material needs. They aspired to a harmonious existence; to a community wherein values and destinies were shared, shaped by the rational discourse of virtuous citizens who inhabited the public realm. Citizenship was nevertheless extended only to a minority: women, as well as slaves and foreign residents, were excluded. It brought with it both a sense of membership and a right to participate, in what was perceived as the highest association known to humanity; an association which transcended and bestowed meaning upon lesser groupings such as the family. Since the *polis* defined and facilitated the good life, there was no room for a counter-realm of privacy into which one might retreat. Liberty meant the political autonomy of the republic rather than the rights of individuals within it; justice meant performing the civic role associated with one's station, in order to strengthen the whole. Law meant an escape from arbitrary or customary decrees; an impartial and rational expression of what was objectively right. Against this background, the *oikos* could only represent threats of factionlism, partiality, privacy and avarice.

Engels would associate the Heroic family form with a transition to father-right, engendered by the development of new wealth, private property and a desire by husbands to bequeath that property to legitimate sons, which required rigorous policing of women's sexuality.[44] Certainly, Solon's reforms in the sixth century achieved the latter, while simultaneously freeing individual property from clan control.

As well as the Marxist account, which anchors misogyny in the development of private property, there is a more Hegelian theme implicit in the work of many scholars. This suggests that reason itself could not have emerged in political or philosophical form, without the suppression of all that women had come to represent.[45] Certainly, the Greeks themselves seem to have proffered such a view and it is impossible to conceive whether this type of judgement would even be possible for us, had they not started philosophy off on a course that associated reason with the subjection of a flesh identified with woman.

Genevieve Lloyd develops this theme when she argues that the Greeks associated femaleness with that which reason must leave behind: the vagueness and unboundedness equated with the female were seen as anathema to the clear and ordered thought identified with reason and the male. Although this did not *necessarily* imply that women themselves lacked reason, 'the very nature of knowledge was implicitly associated with the extrusion of what was symbolically associated with the feminine'.[46] With Aristotle the association becomes explicit and it is tempting to discern it, too, in Plato's allegory of the cave. For the cavernous domicile of the uninitiated has a certain affinity with the darkness/earth/womb metaphors equated with woman, while the state of enlightenment is quite literally that: its protagonists escape into the sunlight of knowledge (light/head/sky/male).[47]

A variety of analogous explanations, similarly equating women with phenomena to be transcended in the name of historical progress, has proliferated. Thus it is claimed that the emotion and sexuality linked with the female were perceived as a threat to the *polis;* that their closeness to biological rhythms associated them with the seasons, with birth and death (transitional processes that threatened the desire for permanence, independence and autonomy); that women threatened the clear antimonies (like nature/culture, barbarian/civilization) so dear to the Greek mind.[48] The homosexual practices of the upper classes are also offered as a reason for widespread misogyny,[49] although it is difficult here to disentangle cause from effect. Finally, Simone de Beauvoir suggests that, among other things, men might simply have railed against 'the adversities of married life'.[50]

Perhaps there is some truth in all of these speculations, for as Greek society evolved, so religious, sexual, literary, philosophic, scientific and political attitudes towards women reinforced one another until a coherent dialectical unity, characterized by misogyny, crystallized. The question would then arise as to whether this ideology served some underlying economic purpose, and with this in mind it is salient to look briefly at the socioeconomic conditions under which Greek women lived. Before doing so, however, it should be noted that none of the above accounts of misogyny suggests a simple desire by men to dominate women, although the very fact that the culture described was one devised by men should alert us to women's powerlessness in defining a more positive image of themselves. Women have left virtually no record of their own attitudes and aspirations, apart from the work of a rare poet like the sixth-century Sappho. This is unsurprising since, as we will see below, women in ancient Greece, and especially in the Classical Age, when the arts flourished, had little opportunity for public expression.

Since it was in classical Athens that political thought reached its zenith, it is most useful to concentrate on arrangements here. The position of women can perhaps be understood best if we think of them merely as functionaries of a state conceived as a simply male institution. Their role was to produce legitimate sons who would carry on the family cult and property of the *oikos,* and also to provide the *polis* with new citizens and warriors. They did therefore perform a civic duty, but from within the privacy of the family and with none of the privileges accorded to male citizens. By marrying, women were simply being used as a medium of exchange between men of different households. They were ideally married off at the age of 18, when their father would select a suitable husband and pay him a dowry for his new wife's keep. Divorce was easy for a man provided he returned the dowry, along with his bride, to her father. Husbands might also give their wives to another or fathers might themselves decide to terminate a marriage. Thus women could be transferred to several households during their lives, engendering suspicions among men that their loyalty was suspect.

During this process, women remained under the guardianship of the male to whose *oikos* they currently belonged; they were permanent legal minors. Although they might inherit property, they could not own it. If her father had no sons, then the household property went to the daughter, but only as a means of transmission to another male. For a female heiress, an *epikleros,* was obliged to marry her oldest male relative on her father's side so that the property might remain within the family. Such an arrangement must have had an important economic function in preserving the household property against subdivision.[51]

For the women, one household must have been much like another. Whether young girls or married citizens, they were confined together in the women's quarters, the *gynaeceum.* They were not allowed into the inner courtyard lest they be espied by male relatives; they went out rarely, and then never unescorted. Family festivals offered infrequent opportunities to meet with male kin. There was little education for such persons beyond the learning of skills from older women. These, of course, focused on domestic labours: cooking, cleaning, weaving, childbearing. All of a woman's relationships thus revolved around the home, but these remained strictly limited. There remains no evidence of the sort of relations they might have enjoyed with one another, although the familiar stories of women's love of gossip circulated among the men.[52] In fact, however, it was the men who met for discussion and enjoyed public life. They spent little time at home but visited the market, the assembly, the gymnasium or the symposium, for civic discussion, feasting and drinking. Women were allotted no political responsibilities or privileges; they had no access to the assembly. The only virtue available to Athenian women was *sophrosyne,* meaning modesty, self-restraint, especially over their passions.[53] Strict monogamy was demanded, though rape was seen as an insult to the husband and retribution was settled between the men involved.

This picture of the secluded Athenian woman nevertheless fails to tell the whole story. Female slaves were sent into public places to perform necessary functions (often including sexual availability to the master). Then there were the wives of metics—the foreign residents who worked in Athens—who were obliged to seek employment. Records tell of freewomen in a number of professions: sesame seed-seller; wet-nurse; wool-worker; groceress; harpist; horsetender; pulse vendor; *aulos*-player; honey-seller.[54] Moving down the social scale, the differences between the lives and status of the sexes undoubtedly diminished.[55] There were also large numbers of prostitutes, many of whom worked in state brothels and received wages from the public purse. And there were free courtesans, among them the *hetairas* who might strike up relationships with important men (even with Socrates himself) and who might alone acquire the intellectual skills and personal property that would make them welcome in male company. Athenian men, it follows, were bound by no monogamous restraints. As one fourth-century representative put it, 'we have courtesans for pleasure, concubines to perform our domestic chores, and wives to bear us legitimate children and be the faithful guardians of our homes'.[56] They also had young boys for homosexual relations and older male friends for intellectual discussion. As one author sums up the situation: public life in Athens was a 'men's club'.[57]

The classical situation was far more oppressive than anything portrayed in Homer and had largely resulted from reforms enacted by Solon in the sixth century. It would therefore be wrong to suggest that no alternative was imaginable, and this is especially true since different practices pertained in some of the other Greek city-states. In Sparta, for example, women had much more freedom and public presence. Eugenics rather than legitimacy was the concern of this society with its communal property and military ambition. Thus girls exercised in public to become fit, and clandestine marriages were practised to ensure that a partnership would be a fecund one. Satires like Aristophanes' play the *Ecclesiazusae,* in which the women take over the assembly to institute common property, wives and children, further suggest a familiarity among the theatre-going public with questions of gender relations. There is some evidence to suggest that the woman question was even then in the air.

In conclusion, it is evident that women's social and political position was fully consonant with the misogyny manifest in Greek culture. How far that ideology might have been used to legitimize an arrangement whose true *raison d'être* was an economic one, is hard to say. The greater liberty and esteem accorded to Spartan women in a society that sustained communal property, might be compared with the confinement of Athenian women in a culture favouring private property, to support this view. On the other hand, it is undoubtedly true that male Athenians, *qua* men, reaped benefits from the sexual division. And it would certainly be grossly reductive to suggest that the interlocking facets of Greek culture, with their elaborate images of woman, were but a reflection of economic imperatives. A certain autonomy must surely be granted to the ideas that gave birth to Western thought and that were destined to endure across the millennia, even if they did help to sustain a system of which both men and the institution of private property were beneficiaries.

Notes

1. Sarah Pomeroy, *Goddesses, Whores, Wives, and Slaves: Women in Classical Antiquity* (New York: Schocken Books, 1975), p. 30.
2. M. I. Finley, *The World of Odysseus* (Harmondsworth: Penguin, 1962), p. 48.
3. Pomeroy, *Goddesses,* p. 28; Marilyn Arthur, 'Early Greece: The Origin of the Western Attitude Toward Women' in J. Peradotto and J. P. Sullivan (eds) *Women in the Ancient World: The Arethusa Papers* (Albany, NY: State University of New York Press, 1984). Okin rightly points out, however, that in the *Iliad* at least, women are hardly shown in an elevated light. See Susan Moller Okin, *Women in Western Political Thought* (London: Virago, 1980), p. 16.
4. F. Engels, *The Origin of the Family, Private Property, and the State* (New York: Pathfinder Press, 1972), p. 68.
5. Finley, *World of Odysseus,* p. 28; A. MacIntyre, *After Virtue: A Study in Moral Theory* (London: Duckworth, 1982), ch. 10.
6. Finley, *World of Odysseus,* p. 33.
7. A. MacIntyre, *After Virtue,* p. 116.
8. Homer, *Iliad,* trans. R. Fitzgerald (New York: Anchor Press, 1975), I, lines 1-10.
9. *Ibid.,* lines 310-74.
10. See Finley, *World of Odysseus,* pp. 48-130; Arthur, 'Early Greece'; Mary O'Brien, *The Politics of Reproduction* (London: Routledge & Kegan Paul, 1981); M. I. Finley, *The Ancient Economy* (London: Chatto & Windus, 1973), p. 18; T. Sinclair, *A History of Greek Political Thought* (London: Routledge & Kegan Paul, 1951), ch. 1.
11. A. N. Athanausakis, Introduction to Hesiod, *Theogony, Works and Days, Shield,* trans. A. N. Athanausakis (Baltimore and London: Johns Hopkins University Press, 1983).
12. *Ibid.,* p.7.
13. *Ibid., Theogony,* lines 570-612.
14. *Ibid.,* lines 588-601.

15. *Ibid., Works and Days,* lines 56-105.

16. *Ibid., Theogony,* lines 602-10.

17. *Ibid.,* lines 886-926.

18. *Ibid., Works and Days,* line 375.

19. *Ibid.,* lines 693-9.

20. *Ibid.,* lines 702-3.

21. Regarding *Antigone,* see Hegel's account where he speaks of an antagonism between 'female' law, the law of the ancient gods, and public law. 'This is the supreme opposition in ethics and therefore in tragedy; and it is individualised in the same play in the opposing natures of man and woman'. G. W. F. Hegel, *The Phenomenology of Mind,* trans. J. B. Baillie (New York: Harper & Row, 1967). §166, pp. 114f. Also, see Charles Segal, 'The Menace of Dionysus: Sex Roles and Reversals in Euripides' *Bacchae*' in Peradotto and Sullivan, *Women in the Ancient World.*

22. Aeschylus, *The Eumenides,* trans. H. Lloyd-Jones (London: Duckworth, 1979), lines 137-8.

23. *Ibid.,* lines 68-70.

24. *Ibid.,* line 831.

25. *Ibid.,* lines 835-6.

26. Engels, *Origin* pp. 29f; S. Freud, *Moses and Monotheism* in *The Standard Edition of the Complete Works of Sigmund Freud,* trans. James Strachey (London: Hogarth Press, 1964), vol. 23, pp. 113f. Freud writes that the transition from a matriarchal to a patriarchal culture must have 'involved a revolution in the judicial conditions that had so far prevailed' and 'a victory of intellectuality over sensuality—that is, an advance in civilization, since maternity is proved by the evidence of the senses while paternity is a hypothesis, based on an interference and a premiss'. (p. 114). See additionally Froma Zeitlin, 'The Dynamics of Misogyny in the *Oresteia*' in Peradotto and Sullivan, *Women in the Ancient World.*

27. Aeschylus, *Eumenides,* lines 604-8.

28. *Ibid.,* lines 658-61.

29. *Ibid.,* lines 663-6.

30. Plato, *Symposium,* lines 208-9. All references to Plato's writings are taken, unless otherwise stated, from *The Dialogues of Plato,* B. Jarrett (ed.), 4 vols, 4th edn (Oxford: Clarendon Press, 1953).

31. Aristotle, *De Generatione Animalium,* trans. A. L. Peck (London: Heinemann, 1943), 716a.

32. *Ibid.,* 738b.

33. *Ibid.,* 729a, 729b, 733b, 765b.

34. *Ibid.,* 765b.

35. *Ibid.,* 727b, 765b.

36. *Ibid.,* 728a, 783b, 766a.

37. *Ibid.,* 732a.

38. Plato, *Timaeus,* trans. D. Lee (Harmondsworth: Penguin, 1965), 50, pp. 68f.

39. The later Greeks did move nearer to Aristotle's functionalist view. Xenophon based different sexual functions on differential biological capacities in his fourth century *Oeconomicus,* where he claimed that the gods prepared woman's nature for indoor work while man's body and soul were endowed with the ability to endure extremes of temperature and long journeys. Women were given greater affection because their role was to nourish children. See excerpt in Mary Lefkowitz and Maureen Fant (eds), *Women's Life in Greece and Rome: A Source Book in Translation* (London: Duckworth, 1982), p. 100. The relevant lines are from *Oecomomicus,* lines 7-10.

40. Plato, *Menexenus,* lines 237-8. See also Aristotle, *De Generatione,* 716a, where he relates earth to female and heaven/sun to father.

41. Aeschylus, *Eumenides,* lines 328-32.

42. See Ruth Padel, 'Women: Model for Possession by Greek Daemons' in Averil Cameron and Amelie Kuhrt (eds), *Images of Woman in Antiquity* (London: Croom Helm, 1983).

43. Thus Bachofen, one of Engels' main sources, sees religious change as responsible for the transition to father-right. Both Engels and Freud believed in a prehistoric matriarchy. See also O'Brien, *Politics of Reproduction,* pp. 123-7.

44. Engels, *Origin,* Pt. 2.

45. See, for example, Simone de Beauvoir, *The Second Sex,* trans. H. M. Parshley (Harmondsworth: Penguin, 1972), pp. 106-8.

46. Genevieve Lloyd, *The Man of Reason: 'Male' and 'Female' in Western Philosophy* (London: Methuen, 1984), p. 4.

47. Plato, *Republic,* lines 514-17. All references to the *Republic* are to the F. M. Cornford edition (Oxford: Clarendon Press, 1941).

48. Segal, 'Menace of Dionysus', p. 196.

49. Victor Ehrenberg, *The People of Aristophanes* (Oxford: Blackwell, 1943), pp. 142 f.

50. De Beauvoir, *Second Sex,* p. 123.

51. This function is supported by Aristotle when he criticizes the Spartan constitution for allowing unregulated subdivision of land among the children of large families, reducing many to poverty. Aristotle, *Politics,* trans. Sir Ernest Barker (Oxford: Oxford University Press, 1958), 1270b. For further discussion, see G. E. M. de ste. Croix, *The Class Struggle in the Ancient Greek World: From the Archaic Age to the Arab Conquests* (London: Duckworth, 1981). He argues that Greek wives constituted 'a distinct economic class, in the technical Marxist sense', although he sees in Athenian inheritance a safeguard against concentrations of wealth since women could not be married into wealthy families in order to amass property there, pp. 98-103.

52. See for example Aristophanes' satire *The Ecclesiazusae,* trans. B. Rogers (London: Heinemann, 1931), lines 118-20.

53. R. Flacière, *Daily Life in Greece at the Time of Pericles,* trans. P. Green (London: Weidenfeld & Nicolson, 1965), p. 69. Also MacIntyre, *After Virtue,* p. 128.

54. Lefkowitz and Fant, *Women's Life in Greece and Rome,* p. 29.

55. De ste. Croix, *Class Struggle,* pp. 100f.

56. Pseudo-Demos in *Against Neaera.*

57. Sir Ernest Barker, *Greek Political Theory, Plato and his Predecessors* (London: Methuen, 1918), p. 218.

JENNIFER A. SHERIDAN (ESSAY DATE 1998)

SOURCE: Sheridan, Jennifer A. "Not at a Loss for Words: The Economic Power of Literate Women in Late Antique Egypt." *Transactions of the American Philological Association (1974-)* 128 (1998): 189-203.

In the following excerpt, Sheridan discusses female literacy in Roman Egypt during the early centuries of the common era.

A literate woman was a rarity in the Graeco-Roman world. Only among the upper socio-economic classes could one expect to find any women who could read or write.[1] Ancient men, themselves mostly illiterate, were clearly unsettled by the idea of a literate woman. It is apparent, in a number of sarcastic quips preserved from antiquity, that men understood the power that literacy might bestow on a woman. A fragment of a comic play, for example, reads "The man who teaches a woman letters does not do well; he gives more poison to a frightening asp."[2] In Roman Egypt, schoolboys were taught to write by copying the phrase "Seeing a women being taught letters, he said 'What a sword she is sharpening.'"[3]

Graeco-Roman Egypt provides more information concerning women's literacy than the rest of the ancient world because of the large number of everyday documents, recorded on papyrus, which survived from it.[4] Nevertheless the papyri, plentiful as they are, are still an inadequate source of evidence for women's literacy because they are the products of a world to which women were not privy in large numbers. Women do not appear as frequently in the papyri as men, and when they do, it is very often in a secondary role; women who appear in the documents are often from a select group, the higher socio-economic classes.[5] Women, of course, sent and received letters, but this proves nothing about their literacy, since they could and did employ scribes and readers. Furthermore, since women rarely acted on their own in legal, official, or commercial situations (i.e., the transactions that prompted the creation of papyri), we have less opportunity to see whether they are literate.[6]

Socio-economic forces can also distort our notions of women's literacy. It appears, for example, that there is an increase in the ratio of illiterate women to illiterate men in the papyri during the first and second centuries C.E. Pomeroy argues that this situation is a by-product of the Roman tolerance of woman landholders: it is not that more women are illiterate than at earlier periods, but that more illiterate (normally) women are landholders and accordingly produce documents.[7] Although the papyri can therefore give false impressions, one cannot argue that there was widespread literacy among women, because that is certainly not the case. Still, one must keep in mind that the sources are not telling us all we need to know about this society that excluded women from much of the public sphere.[8]

Rates of female literacy in Egypt seem to have changed over time. In the Ptolemaic era, the education of girls was common, at least in literate Alexandria, where, of course, a number of female authors were well known, who could serve as role models. With the coming of the Romans, however, female literacy rates dropped off, only to increase again in the second and third centuries C.E. Certainly there are a number of factors at play here, including where a woman lived and what social class she belonged to,[9] not to mention other cultural changes in the Empire itself, but—since we are dealing with an imperfect body of data—what appear as changes in the literacy rates of women over time may just be distortions of the facts.

The actual number of literate women known to us from Graeco-Roman Egypt is extremely small. There is no evidence, direct or indirect, for a single literate woman in the countryside, and only a handful from the cities are known. A comprehensive statistical study of women's literacy would yield the same results that a quick impression does: the level of female literacy in Graeco-Roman Egypt was negligible.[10]

The literate women we do know about are statistical abnormalities; that is, they cannot be used in a general argument concerning female literacy rates, since they are such a deviation from the norm. Yet these are the only literate women in antiquity whose lives we can delve into in any depth, because we have actual contact with them through their documents. For this reason, these women from late antique Egypt should be of great interest to scholars of women in the ancient world; and it is that group of scholars to whom this paper is particularly addressed.[11] The women discussed here are not legendary literates like Sappho or Hypatia, but ordinary people whose unselfconscious documents tell us of their histories. From their papyri, we can learn what circumstances in their lives led them to literacy, and what

Cleopatra VII, last of Egypt's Ptolemaic rulers (69-30 B.C.). This illustration depicts Cleopatra experimenting with the effects of poison.

significance literacy had in their lives. Most importantly, we can explore whether these ancient women understood, like their male counterparts, that the ability to read and write endows its holder with power.

. . . . .

This paper will center on one particular literate woman, Aurelia Charite. An extensive papyrus dossier[12] provides us with a great deal of biographical information about her, much of which is relevant to her literacy. As Worp notes in the introduction to that dossier, Charite prospered in the middle Egyptian city of Hermopolis between 320 and 350 C.E. She is mentioned in forty-two documents, five of which are written wholly or partially by Charite herself, and two of which specifically mention her literacy. Hers is one of the few woman's signatures to survive from Graeco-Roman antiquity.

Hermopolis, like other nome capitals, was overlaid with a thick veneer of Hellenism. Its streets were lined with Greek-style buildings interspersed with those in an Egyptian style, and its governmental forms mimicked those of earlier Greek cities. The ruling class of the city, members of the *boule,* also bear many marks of Hellenization, not least of which are their names, many of which are Greek. Because we view this group through their documents in Greek, it is impossible to conclude anything about the actual ethnicity of individuals; many with Greek names may have been Egyptian in origin.

Whether or not it contained an ethnic mix, the bouleutic class was small and exclusive. The *boule* itself comprised approximately one hundred men;[13] the entire class was composed of those men and their female relatives and children. Since the group was heavily intermarried, the total number of bouleutic citizens probably numbered no more than five hundred.[14]

Members of the bouleutic class were the movers and shakers of the city and the entire nome. It was the councillors who held all the important governmental positions in the city. The influence of the bouleutic class was also based on its wealth, i.e., its landholding. Among the councillors would be a small number of the super-rich; the rest, we can assume, were comfortable enough to live on the income from their holdings.[15] Poorer city dwellers and residents of the rest of the nome regularly came into contact with members of the bouleutic class, since councillors were both tax-collectors and landlords; they also owned many of the businesses in the city.

Among groups of landholders it would not be unusual to find a woman. In Roman Egypt, there were no prohibitions against women holding land, and they regularly acquired it through inheritance or as part of their dowry. The overall percentage of landholders who were women is impossible to determine with the information available to us, but approximately thirty-three percent of land at Soknopaiou Nesos was owned by women; forty percent of landholders in a tax roll from Karanis were women,[16] and in a Hermopolite land list fourteen percent of the land was held by women.[17] Thus women had some access to power through wealth; their independent landholding would add to that of their husbands, augmenting the status of the family, and they themselves could act as landlords.[18] But it is rare to see a woman managing her own properties.[19]

Aurelia Charite was born into the affluent, landed upper class of Hermopolis at the end of the third century C.E. Her father, Amazonios, who lived from around 275 until the mid-310s C.E., was a councillor and gymnasiarch. Her mother Demetria, also known as Ammonia, was the daughter of Polydeukes, also a city councillor.[20] Demetria herself was literate.[21]

By the year 314 C.E., Charite had married Aurelios Adelphios, son of Adelphios.[22] Adelphios, also known as Dionysodoros, held the usual offices of a wealthy city dweller—councillor, prytanis (proedros), gymnasiarch, strategos, and logistes.[23] Charite and Adelphios had at least one child who can be identified in the papyri. Their son, Aurelios Asklepiades, was *praepositus pagi* of the fifteenth pagus of the Hermopolite Nome in 340 C.E.; he was also a magistrate and councillor at Hermopolis. Charite may have had other children, but they are not documented.[24] We can assume that when Charite disappears from the papyri, around 350 C.E., she has died. She outlived her husband by about thirty years.

The remainder of Charite's biography concerns her fiscal status and business dealings. Charite was quite wealthy. She belonged to an elite group of metropolitan landholders who not only owned urban properties but also had land in the countryside. Charite's mean property holding in the countryside was 410 or more arouras.[25] The documents do not quantify the property she must have owned in the city of Hermopolis, where she lived.

Although we do not know her absolute wealth, we are able to compare Charite's landholdings with those of her neighbors in the so-called Hermopolite landlists of the mid-fourth century C.E., just before her death. In the landlists,[26] which record the country holdings of residents of the city, Charite is said to own 376 arouras, less than her personal average; but by this late point in her life she may have already distributed some prop-

ON THE SUBJECT OF...

NEFERTITI (C. 1390 B.C.-1360 B.C.)

Nefertiti became one of the most famous women in antiquity with the discovery in 1912 of a limestone bust sculpted and painted in her image by Tutmose during the 18th dynasty. Her name means "The Beautiful One is Come," and Nefertiti is known not only for her great beauty, but for her role as the wife of Akhenaten, the first Egyptian pharaoh to worship only one god. During the early years of Akhenaten's reign, Queen Nefertiti enjoyed significant political importance, evidenced by the large number of carved scenes in which she is shown accompanying Akhenaten during the ceremonial acts he performed. She is depicted taking part in acts quite unlike those relegated to the generally subservient status of previous chief queens, including daily worship and making offerings similar to those of the king. Images of Nefertiti and Akhenaten were erased from Egyptian history after Akhenaten's death, when the succeeding pharaoh denounced monotheism and returned to polytheistic worship.

CLEOPATRA (69 B.C.-C. 30 B.C.)

Cleopatra VII Philopator was the last of the Ptolemaic rulers of Egypt. She was notorious in antiquity and has been romanticized in modern times as the lover of Julius Caesar and Mark Antony. Following the death of her father, Ptolemy XII Auletes, in 51 B.C., the ministers of Cleopatra's brother Ptolemy XIII feared her ambition to rule alone and drove her from Egypt. Cleopatra was determined to use Roman power and when Julius Caesar arrived in Alexandria in 48, she established a union of mutual benefit with him. Caesar helped Cleopatra to reestablish her place on the Egyptian throne and then returned to Rome, followed by Cleopatra in 46. When the emperor was assassinated in 44, Cleopatra returned to Egypt and awaited the outcome of the political struggle in Rome. She soon seduced Mark Antony, who was consolidating his power on the Roman throne. In Rome, however, Octavian was gaining power. Antony later married Cleopatra, but Roman sentiment was against the union. Octavian turned against Antony and defeated a fleet commanded by Antony and Cleopatra in 31 at the Battle of Actium. Antony killed himself. Cleopatra tried, but failed, to captivate another Roman emperor. Rather than suffer humiliation, she also committed suicide, and was buried beside Antony.

erty to her children or grandchildren. Even with 376 arouras, though, she is among the top six percent of landholders in the city, and well above the mean holding of only sixty-three arouras.[27]

The papers in Charite's dossier are those we would expect of a landholder. Twenty-one documents record the payment of taxes on her property. These are typical land taxes for the period, which collect items needed by the army, such as wine, fodder, and barley. Eight documents record Charite's leasing property to others. She let farm land, fodder land, and orchards. A number of her tenants appear repeatedly in the documents and must have had long-term business relationships with her.[28] According to a few documents she also lent money.

Six of Charite's forty-two documents are either written by her or mention her literacy. The number itself is not significant; of the forty-two documents in the dossier, twenty-four are addressed to Charite, eight are lists, one is a letter written by Demetria, Charite's mother, and two are of questionable content. There is only one other document in the dossier that could have been written by Charite (or at least mentioned her literacy) but was not composed by her.[29]

Of the just mentioned "literacy" documents, the only one that contains a definitive date is a receipt for a paid lease, dated 348 C.E. (*PCharite* 8). In the opening lines of the receipt, Charite is referred to as

> Αὐρηλία χαρίτη 'Αμαζουίου ἀπὸ
> Ἑρμοῦ πόλεως τής λαμπροτάτης
> εἰδυεῖα γράμματα χωρὶς κυρίου χρηματίζουςα
> δικαίῳ τὲκνων.
>
> Aurelia Charite, daughter of Amazonios, from splendid Hermopolis, a knower of letters, acting without a guardian and with the *ius liberorum*.

The body of the receipt is written by a scribe, but Charite wrote the subscription:

> Αὐρηλία χαρίτη πεπλή-
> ρωμαι ὡς πρόκειται.
>
> I, Aurelia Charite, was paid in full as set forth above.

Charite is again described as a "knower of letters" (εἰδυεῖα γράμματα) in a money loan dated either 331/2 or 346/7 (*PCharite* 33).[30]

Three additional documents are written either wholly or partially in Charite's hand. These include a four-line order to pay for the value of green fodder written entirely by Charite (*PCharite* 27), a list of deliveries dated circa 322 (*PCharite* 36), and a small two-word fragment that includes her name (*PCharite* 41).[31] Charite also signed an acknowledgment of a receipt (*PCharite* 37).

Charite's claims to literacy appear genuine. Her hand is neat but not elegant, the hand of a literate, not a semi-literate, person. Charite's letters are written with definitive strokes, indicating that she wrote somewhat regularly and without hesitation.[32] She was practiced enough in writing to ligature some letter combinations, such as alpha-iota and epsilon-iota.[33] She uses abbreviations and symbols, which again displays her comfort with writing.[34] Yet she was not the greatest speller, and her documents show some fairly typical misspellings: she regularly confused ει and ι, for example.[35]

. . . . .

We can only conjecture why Charite, or any other literate woman, was taught to write. Charite's mother Demetria was literate and may well have been her daughter's teacher since their hands are strikingly similar.[36] The fact that the family was wealthy may have allowed them the luxury of educating their daughter. If economics alone affected literacy, however, we might expect to encounter many more rich, literate women in the papyri. But this is not the case. . . .

Notes

1. On women's literacy in general in the ancient world, see Cole and Harris 22-24 *et passim*.
2. γυναῖχ' ό διδάςκων γράμματ' οὐ καλῶς ποεῖ / ἀςπίδι δὲ φοβερᾷ προςπορίζει φάρμακον. [Men.] 702 Kock.
3. Ιδών γυναῖκα διδαςκομὲνην γράμματα εἶπεν οἷον ξίφος ἀκονᾶται. *PBouriant.* 1.153 (fourth century C.E.).
4. Literacy in Roman Egypt, of course, refers to the ability to read and write Greek. See Youtie 1975a.
5. Pomeroy 1988: 720.
6. Under the *Lex Julia* of Augustus, women could act without a guardian after they had produced a certain number of children (three in the original law; later fewer children may have been required). One hundred and twenty-three legally independent women are known from Roman Egypt. They are listed in Sheridan.
7. Pomeroy 1988: 718.
8. As Bowman and Woolf so eloquently point out: "Power exercised *over* texts allows power to be exercised *through* texts" (1994b: 8).
9. Pomeroy 1988: 717-19.
10. That literacy rates were small but the percentages themselves were not very significant is true of Egypt in general. See Bowman 1991: 122 and 1994a: 111-12, passages in which he argues that the percentage of literates is not so important as the extent to which the society functioned in a literate mode without many literates.

11. As I am hoping to reach a non-papyrological audience with this essay, I have provided a fairly extensive introduction to literacy and life in late antique Egypt, including information which, while well known to papyrologists, may not be as familiar to other classicists.

12. Worp 1980. There is one further document ("Anhang B") concerning Charite in Worp 1991. The term "archive" is now reserved for papers which were gathered together in antiquity. This is not the case with either of the collections cited in this note.

13. Bowman 1971: 22.

14. I have estimated elsewhere (Sheridan 129) that the maximum size of the female bouleutic population in a city would be one thousand, allowing ten female relatives per bouleutic man. But there probably were fewer, perhaps only a few hundred at any given time, since the women's family roles would overlap, i.e., one man's wife was another's daughter and still another's sister.

15. Rowlandson 115-22, who notes, however, that a small number of members of this class lacked the financial resources needed to bear its burdens, such as liturgies.

16. Hobson 315.

17. Bagnall 1992: 138.

18. Rowlandson 113-15 and 132-35 discusses two very wealthy Oxyrhynchite land-holding women.

19. Rowlandson 284.

20. Worp 1980: 5-7.

21. She writes on behalf of her daughter in *PCharite* 38.

22. Adelphios also left a substantial group of papers, published in Worp 1991. That Adelphios was Charite's husband is virtually, but not absolutely, certain.

23. Worp 1991: 8-10.

24. Worp 1980: 9 points out that Charite is likely to have had a son named Amazonios after her father. Diokles, son of Adelphios, was at one time believed to be Charite's son, but that identification has now been called into question. The fact that Charite had the *ius liberorum,* however, does not necessarily mean that she had three or more children.

25. Worp 1980: 11.

26. *PCharite* 9 = *PHerm. Landl.* I.252-56, II.466-69.

27. Bowman 1985: 146. There was an extremely unequal division of landholding in the Hermopolite Nome. The landlists show that ten percent of the landholders held seventy-eight percent of the land (Bagnall 1992: 142).

28. On Charite as landlord, see Kehoe 123 n. 6.

29. *PCharite* 34, a money loan. Although literate, like most wealthy people Charite regularly used scribes (see Bagnall 1993: 247). This document is fragmentary, so it is possible that she wrote a subscription which is now lost; she signs *PCharite* 37 without first being introduced as literate in its opening (this signature is partially lost, but the restoration is appropriate, since the first four letters of her name, written in her hand, are visible).

30. The word εἰδυεῖα is restored in a lacuna, based on the formula in *PCharite* 8.

31. Worp (1980: 103) identified this fragment as probably coming from the hand of Charite; my examination of the photograph concurs with this identification.

32. Bagnall 1993: 247.

33. Both alpha-iota and epsilon-iota are ligatured in the word χαίρειν in *PCharite* 27.2; the epsilon-iota combination is ligatured in . . . μουειων in *PCharite* 41.2.

34. Αυ for Αὐρηλία in *PCharite* 8.24; ιδικ (*sic*) for ἰνδικτίωνος in *PCharite* 27.3; κν for κνίδιον/α in *PCharite* 36.1, 2, 3, 6, 7. *PCharite* 27.3 preserves the symbol for τάλαντα; the symbol for γίνεται must have preceded it but is lost in a lacuna.

35. There are other errors in *PCharite* 8, 27, and 36.

36. Worp 1980: 2.

Works Cited

Bagnall, R. S. 1992. "Landholding in Late Roman Egypt." *JRS* 82: 128-43.

———. 1993. *Egypt in Late Antiquity.* Princeton.

———. 1995. "Charite's Christianity." *BASP* 32: 37-40.

Bowman, A. K. 1971. *The Town Councils of Roman Egypt.* Toronto.

———. 1985. "Landholding in the Hermopolite Nome in the Fourth Century A.D." *JRS* 75: 137-63.

———. 1991. "Literacy in the Roman Empire: Mass and Mode." In Humphrey 1991. 119-31.

———. 1994a. "The Roman Imperial Army: Letters and Literacy on the Northern Frontier." In Bowman and Woolf 1994c. 109-25.

———, and G. Woolf. 1994b. "Literacy and Power in the Ancient World." In Bowman and Woolf 1994c. 1-16.

———, and G. Woolf, eds. 1994c. *Literacy and Power in the Ancient World.* Cambridge.

Cole, S. G. 1981. "Could Greek Women Read and Write?" In H. Foley, ed., *Reflections of Women in Antiquity.* New York. 219-45.

Harris, W., 1989. *Ancient Literacy.* Cambridge, MA.

Hobson, D. 1983. "Women as Property Owners in Roman Egypt." *TAPA* 113: 311-21.

Kehoe, D. 1992. *Management and Investment on Estates in Roman Egypt during the Early Empire.* Bonn.

Pomeroy, S. B. 1988. "Women in Roman Egypt: A Preliminary Study Based on Papyri." *ANRW* II.10.1: 708-23.

———. 1997. *Families in Classical and Hellenistic Greece.* Oxford.

Rowlandson, J. 1996. *Landowners and Tenants in Roman Egypt.* Oxford.

Sheridan, J. A. 1996. "Women Without Guardians: An Updated List." *BASP* 33: 117-31.

Worp, K. A. 1980. *Das Aurelia Charite Archiv.* Zutphen.

———. 1991. *Die Archive der Aurelii Adelphios und Asklepiades. CPR* XIIA. Vienna.

JUDITH EVANS GRUBBS (ESSAY DATE 2002)

SOURCE: Grubbs, Judith Evans. "The Status of Women in Roman Law." In *Women and the Law in the Roman Empire: A Sourcebook on Marriage, Divorce, and Widowhood,* pp. 16-80. London: Routledge, 2002.

In the following excerpt, Grubbs details the legal status of women in imperial Rome.

Forms of Legal Power: Potestas, Manus *and* Tutela Impuberum

In ancient Rome, virtually all free Roman women were under one of the following three types of legal authority: *patria potestas* ("paternal power"), *manus* (subordination to a husband's legal power), or *tutela* ("guardianship"), for those not under *potestas* or *manus.* (Slavewomen, like slavemen, would be under the control of their master or mistress.) By the reign of Augustus, *manus* had practically disappeared, and Augustus himself weakened *tutela mulierum* by granting freedom from *tutela* to freeborn women with three children and freedwomen with four. *Patria potestas,* however, survived until the end of antiquity, though weakened by late imperial legislation [see Arjava 1998].

A *PATRIA POTESTAS* ("PATERNAL POWER")

Patria potestas was the all-inclusive legal authority of the *paterfamilias,* the male head of the family, over all his children, male and female, and over his sons' children. Male children were as much subject to paternal power as female. The *paterfamilias* was the oldest male ascendant; thus, if a man's sons had children, he would be the *paterfamilias* of his sons and his grandchildren by his sons (his daughters' children would come under the *potestas* of their fathers, the daughters' husbands). A man became a *paterfamilias* himself when all his male ascendants (i.e., paternal grandfather and father) had died. A woman never became a *paterfamilias;* she did not exercise *potestas* over any other person, though if her *paterfamilias* was dead (and if she was not married in a *manus*-marriage, see *Part B* below), she would be *sui iuris,* i.e, legally independent.

The legal authority of the *paterfamilias* over his children was quite extensive. He had the "right of life and death" (*ius vitae necisque*) over them, and theoretically could put even an adult child to death. In fact, there are very few attested cases of a *paterfamilias* executing his adult child, and by the imperial period it seems a *paterfamilias* would utilize his "right of life and death," if at all, only in deciding whether or not to rear a newborn child [Harris 1986; Saller 1994, 114-17].

Far more relevant to Romans of the imperial period than the theoretical *ius vitae necisque* was the father's control over all his children's possessions. Children under *patria potestas* could not own property. Everything given or bequeathed to them legally belonged to their *paterfamilias.* Only when the *paterfamilias* was dead (or had emancipated them; see *Part C* below) could his children, both male and female, own property in their own names. If a *paterfamilias* died without a will, all his children, male and female, were his heirs in equal shares, as was his wife if she had come under his *manus* upon marriage (if he made a will, however, he might apportion his estate less equally). The *paterfamilias'* consent was also required in order for his children's legal transactions, including their marriages, to be valid [Saller 1994, 118-32].

Roman jurists describe *patria potestas* from the point of view of men like themselves—free male citizens:

Gaius, *Institutes* I.48: Concerning the law of persons another division follows. For certain persons are legally independent (*sui iuris*), certain are subject to someone else's law. 49: But again, of those persons, who are subject to someone else's law, some are in power (*potestas*), some in marital subordination (*manus*), some in ownership (*mancipium*) . . . 55: Likewise in our power (*potestas*) are our children whom we have begotten in legitimate marriage (*iustae nuptiae*). This law belongs to Roman citizens; for there are almost no other men, who have such a power over their children as we have.

D.1.6.4 (Ulpian): For of Roman citizens, some are fathers of families (*patres familiarum*), some are sons of families (*filii familiarum*), some are mothers of families (*matres familiarum*[1]), some are daughters of families (*filiae familiarum*). Fathers of families are those who are under their own legal power (*potestas*) whether they have reached puberty or are still below puberty; similarly mothers of families; sons and daughters of families are those who are in someone else's power. For whoever is born from me and my wife is in my power; likewise whoever is born from my son and his wife, that is my grandson and granddaughter, are equally in my power, and my great-grandson and great-granddaughter and so on with the rest.

Women did not have *patria potestas* and could never be *patresfamilias* [see *Part I.B* above]. And though mothers had considerable responsibility and socially approved authority over their children [Dixon 1988], they could never have *potestas* as fathers could, and could not serve as their child's guardian (*tutor*) after their husband's death. Nor could they legally adopt children, since this involved placing the adoptee under the *potestas* of the adopter. However, by the third century C.E., if not earlier, a woman could receive special imperial permission to "adopt" a child (though without acquiring *potestas* over it) if her own children were dead [Cod. Just. 8.47.5 (dated 291); Gardner 1998, 155-65].

B *MANUS* (MARITAL SUBORDINATION)

In early Roman law, most women entered their husband's legal control when they married. This marital power was called *manus* (literally, "hand") rather than *potestas*. While not as extensive as the *paterfamilias'* powers over his children, the husband's authority over a wife under his legal power (*in manu*) were similar. A wife *in manu* could not own property; any possessions she had when she married would henceforth belong to her husband (or to his *paterfamilias,* if he was still alive). She would inherit equally with her husband's children under intestate succession. However, a husband did *not* have the "right of life and death" over his wife.[2]

By the time of Augustus, "*manus*-marriage" had mostly disappeared [Looper-Friedman 1987].[3] Instead, almost all Roman women entered a form of marriage in which the wife remained under her father's *potestas,* though she would leave her family's home and live with her husband. Her children were in the *potestas* of their father (her husband), but she was still under *patria potestas* until her *paterfamilias* died, at which point she became *sui iuris.* The change in marriage form did not mean any more real legal independence for women, except that she might become *sui iuris* sooner, since fathers would probably die before husbands. Marriage without *manus* served the interests of a woman's natal family, because if she remained under her father's power, her property still legally belonged to him (just as his male children's property did).

Because *manus*-marriage had disappeared hundreds of years before the Justinianic legal corpus was compiled, our only description of it in the legal sources is found in the *Institutes* of Gaius, written in the second century:

Gaius, *Institutes* I.109: But indeed, both males and females are accustomed to be in *potestas;* however, only women come into *manus.* 110: Accordingly, in the past they used to come into *manus* in three ways: by *usus, farreum* and *coemptio.* 111: She who remained married for a year continuously would come into *manus* by *usus;* indeed, since she was taken by *usus* by means of yearly possession, she would cross over into her husband's *familia* and would obtain the place of a daughter. Thus by the law of the Twelve Tables it was provided that, if a woman was not willing to come into her husband's *manus* in this way, she was to be away every year for a period of three nights, and in this way would interrupt the *usus* of each year. But this whole law has partly been abolished by legal enactments and partly has fallen into oblivion by its very disuse. 112: They come into *manus* by *farreum* through a certain kind of sacrifice, which is made to Jupiter Farreus; in which bread made of emmer grain (*farreus*) is employed, wherefore it is also called "sharing of emmer bread" (*confarreatio*); many things besides this are done and occur for the purpose of establishing this legal relationship, with certain solemn words and ten witnesses being present. This law is still in use in our own times: for the greater priests, that is, the priests of Jupiter, of Mars, and of Quirinus, and likewise the kings of sacred rites, are not chosen unless they were born from *farreate* marriage: for not even they are able to have their priesthood without *confarreatio.* 113: But they come into *manus* by *coemptio* through mancipation (*mancipatio*), that is, through a kind of imaginary sale. For after summoning not fewer than five Roman (male) citizens and also a scale-holder, the man "buys" the woman, and she comes into his *manus.*[4]

A passage in the Roman historian Tacitus suggests that by the reign of Tiberius (14-37 C.E.), *confarreatio* was considered a cumbersome and undesirable procedure, and that it was difficult to find candidates for the position of flamen Dialis (a priesthood of Jupiter), whose parents were supposed to have been married by *confarreatio:*

Tacitus, *Annales* IV.16 (written early 2nd c.). Around the same time, the emperor (Tiberius) made a pronouncement about choosing a flamen Dialis in place of the late Servus Maluginensis, and at the same time about approving a new law. For (he said), by the ancient custom, three patricians born from parents married by *confarreatio* were nominated together, from whom one would be chosen. But there was not, as there once had been, a plentiful supply (of candidates), because the custom of marriage by *confarreatio* had been abandoned or retained only among a few. He adduced several reasons for this situation, the foremost being the indifference of men and women; added to that the difficulties of the ceremony which were deliberately avoided, and the fact that the man who obtained that priesthood would escape from paternal law and the woman (his wife) would enter the *manus* of the flamen. Thus (the rule) should be amended by a decree of the Senate or a law, just as Augustus had turned certain practices from their uncouth antiquity to present-day usage. Therefore, after deliberating the religious practices, it was decided to depart in no way from the custom of the flamens; but a law was passed by which the flaminica Dialis (would be) in the power (*potestas*) of her husband in regard to religious rites, but otherwise would act by the law common to (other) women. And the son of Maluginensis was appointed in place of his father.

By Gaius' time *manus*-marriage by *usus* was obsolete, and marriage by *confarreatio* was probably entered into by only a few members of the elite, whose families customarily held the high priesthoods at Rome which required priests to be the children of *confarreatio* marriage.[5] All references to *manus*-marriage in the jurists were deleted by the sixth-century editors of the *Digest.*

C *TUTELA IMPUBERUM* (GUARDIANSHIP OF MINORS)

Patria potestas lasted throughout the *paterfamilias'* life. Upon his death, his children, both male and female, would become legally independent (*sui iuris*), and his male children would have *patria potestas* over their own children. Those who had not yet reached puberty (considered to be age fourteen for boys, twelve for girls) when their father died would be placed under *tutela impuberum* ("guardianship of those below puberty"). The guardian, called a tutor, of an underage ward (*pupillus* or *pupilla*) would be appointed by the father in his will, or, if no appointment had been made, guardianship would go to the nearest male relative on the father's side (*agnate*), usually the paternal uncle. In the absence of eligible agnates, application would be made to the authorities, usually by the children's mother, for appointment of a tutor. Under Roman law, a woman could not serve as tutor, though mothers sometimes got around this rule. A tutor did not usually live with his ward, nor was he a substitute parent. Fatherless children generally lived with their mother, but she did not have *potestas* over them or control their property. The original purpose of *tutela impuberum* was to safeguard the child's property in the interests of the agnate relatives until the child was mature enough to manage the property. By the time of Augustus, there was a feeling that guardians should be concerned with their wards' welfare as well as their property, and this belief in the tutor's moral responsibility intensified in the later Empire [Schulz 1951, 162-80, 190-7; Saller 1994, 181-203].

Sometimes a *paterfamilias* "emancipated" his children from *patria potestas* during his lifetime; he would then be in the position of their tutor, though with more authority over them than had other tutors. To judge from the legal sources, by the fourth century it was not uncommon for fathers to emancipate their children from paternal power if they had reached maturity.[6]

When they reached puberty, fatherless male children became, in classical Roman law, free of legal authority. Females over twelve would go from *tutela impuberum* to *tutela mulierum.* But Roman law realized that young people in their teens were still vulnerable to attempts by the unscrupulous to defraud them, and another type of guardianship developed, the *cura minorum* ('"care of minors") for those who had reached puberty but were still under the legal age of twenty-five. A curator's responsibilities were fewer than a tutor's, and in the earlier Empire appointment of a curator was optional (whereas a tutor was required). By the reign of Septimius Severus (193-211), however, curators were common, and by the fourth century they were required for both male and female minors under twenty-five, though those who demonstrated good behavior could request release from guardianship earlier [cf. Cod. Theod. 2.17.1.1 (324)].

Tutela Mulierum *(the Guardianship of Women)*

Under classical Roman law a woman whose *paterfamilias* was dead and who had not entered *manus*-marriage was required to have a "guardian." If she was still below the age of twelve when her father died, she would have a *tutor impuberum,* but aged twelve she would come under *tutela mulierum*—the "guardianship of women." (Vestal Virgins, who were free from *tutela mulierum* were an exception.) A woman would continue to be under *tutela mulierum* after she married, unless she had entered her husband's *manus,* a form of marriage which had become rare by the time of Augustus.

It appears that the original purpose of *tutela mulierum* was to safeguard a woman's paternal inheritance in the interests of her father's relatives, who would be her heirs when she died. Until the first century C.E., a woman's tutor was usually her closest male agnate (relative on her father's side), probably her paternal uncle. Such a tutor was called a *tutor legitimus.* If a woman's *paterfamilias* emancipated her from paternal power, he became a *tutor legitimus* to her. A freedwoman (*liberta*) also had a *tutor legitimus:* her former master (patron) [Dixon 1984; Gardner 1986a, 14-22; 166-8; Schulz 1951, 180-90].

Tutela is usually translated as "guardianship," but a *tutor mulierum* was not a legal guardian of the sort envisioned when we use the word today. He did not live with the woman, nor did he have any real control over her or her property. Certain legal and business activities that she might undertake, such as making a will, selling certain types of property (called *res mancipi;* see *Part A* below at Gaius II.80-5), or manumitting her slaves, required his consent. The tutor's authority was certainly not as extensive as that of a *paterfamilias* (or that of a *tutor impuberum*): he did not own the woman's property, and his consent was not needed for her to enter marriage without *manus* (though it was needed for her to constitute a dowry, which involved property). A tutor was not a personal watchdog, and did not control the woman's private behavior. As the jurist Gaius remarked (*Institutes* I.190, *Part A* below), many women were quite capable of running their affairs without a tutor.

Augustus, as part of his promotion of marriage and procreation, granted women who served the state by child-bearing the *ius (trium) liberorum,* "the right of (three) children." This released freeborn women who had borne three children and freedwomen who had borne four from the need for a tutor. Women with the *ius liberorum* could conduct all their legal and business affairs without a tutor. The emperor Claudius abolished the *tutor legitimus* for most women, which meant they no longer had to have a close agnate relative as tutor, but could have someone with no personal interest in their financial or legal affairs. (The exceptions were emancipated daughters, whose father continued to be *tutor legitimus,* and freedwomen, whose patron was still *tutor legitimus.*) For instance, a woman might have as tutor one of her freedmen, who could be expected to be loyal and obedient. Thus by the mid-first century, *tutela mulierum* did not impose real restrictions on most women's freedom of legal and commercial action. Moreover, at least by Gaius' time, a tutor (except a *tutor legitimus*) could be forced by the urban praetor to authorize a woman's action even if he did not want to, and women could arrange to change tutors.

A Roman husband was not usually his wife's tutor. The emperors Marcus Aurelius and Commodus prohibited a tutor from marrying his ward, but do not seem to have forbidden a husband to act as his wife's tutor after the marriage took place.[7] Roman law frowned on a man being his wife's tutor, for it was believed that this would create a conflict of interest and lead to the corruption of marital affection—though spouses themselves may have felt differently [Arjava 1996, 140-1]. In the eastern provinces, husbands were usually their wives' guardians. . . .

Notes

1. Here *materfamilias* is used as the female equivalent of *paterfamilias* (though with the unmentioned difference, obvious to Romans, that a *materfamilias* never had *potestas* over others). See Saller 1999: 194, and cf. Part I.B above for other meanings of *materfamilias.*
2. Despite the famous statement of Cato the Elder (quoted by Aulus Gellius, *Noctes Atticae* 10.23.2-5) that a husband who caught his wife in adultery could kill her with impunity, there is no evidence that such a right was approved in Roman law. However, husbands who killed wives in flagrante received lenient treatment. See Treggiari 1991a, 268-75.
3. There is evidence for *manus*-marriage in the long inscription known as the *Laudatio Turiae,* . . . dating from the reign of Augustus. "Turia's" father is said to have married his (second?) wife by *coemptio,* by which she would come under his *manus,* and "Turia's" sister also married with *manus.* "Turia" herself may have come under her husband's *manus*: he says that she handed over her property to him to administer, and if she had come under his legal control, her property would have also.. . . The Flavian Municipal Law (*c.*80 C.E.) also refers to *manus.* . . .
4. For another archaic use of *coemptio* ("mock sale") still evidently employed in the second century, see Gaius' account of how a woman could change her *tutor mulierum.* . . .
5. The *senatusconsultum Gaetulicianum,* known only from a papyrus fragment (P.Berol.11753), closed a loophole in the Augustan marriage laws used by childless couples, whereby the wife entered the husband's *manus* and so inherited from him as a daughter when he died (rather than receiving only one-tenth, as under the Augustan law. . . . The date of this decree of the Senate is not known; scholars often put it in the early third century, but David Noy argues for the first century, when other loopholes to the Augustan laws were being closed; see his "The *Senatusconsultum Gaetulicianum: Manus* and Inheritance," *Tijdschrift voor Rechtsgeshiedenis* 56 (1988), 299-304.
6. The extent of emancipation in the third century is debated: Watson 1974a notes the number of rescripts on the subject, but cf. Gardner 1993, 71-2. On emancipation, see Gardner 1998, 6-113 and for late antiquity, Arjava 1998.
7. Whether the tutor forbidden to marry his ward was a *tutor impuberum* or *tutor mulierum,* or both, is debatable. Most scholars assume it was a *tutor mulierum,* or conflate the two. Given the second-century date of the ban on *tutor-pupilla* marriage, when *tutela mulierum* was in decline, the ban was probably aimed at *tutores impuberum,* not *mulierum.*

Bibliography

Arjava, A. (1998) "Paternal Power in Late Antiquity," *JRS* 88, 147-65.

Gardner, J. F. (1993) *Being a Roman Citizen,* London and New York: Routledge.

Noy, D. (1990) "Matchmakers and Marriage-Markets in Antiquity," *EMC/CV* 38, n.s. 9, 375-400.

Saller, R. P. (1999) "*Pater Familias, Mater Familias,* and the Gendered Semantics of the Household," *Classical Philology* 94, 182-97.

Treggiari, S. M. (1991a)*Roman Marriage: Iusti Coniuges from the Time of Cicero to the Time of Ulpian,* Oxford: Clarendon Press.

Watson, A. (1974a) "The Rescripts of the Emperor Probus," *Tulane Law Review* 48, 1122-8.

WOMEN IN THE MEDIEVAL WORLD

JENNIFER WYNNE HELLWARTH (ESSAY DATE JANUARY 2002)

SOURCE: Hellwarth, Jennifer Wynne. "'I Wyl Wright of Women Prevy Sekenes': Imagining Female Literacy and Textual Communities in Medieval and Early Modern Midwifery Manuals." *Critical Survey* 14, no. 1 (January 2002): 44-64.

In the following excerpt, Hellwarth explores the subject of female literacy in the Middle Ages as a threat to patriarchal order, using late medieval midwifery manuals as her textual focus.

Defining the term 'literacy' in medieval and early modern England is not a simple task; it defies the more modern (and relatively uncomplicated) definition of having the ability to read and write. In medieval terminology, a *litteratus* was someone who was learned in Latin, while an *illitteratus* was someone who was not. Eventually, *litteratus* and *illitteratus* came to be associated with the clergy and laity respectively.[1] But these terms were not used for describing literacy in the vernacular, or the various categories and levels of competence in both reading and writing, either in Latin or in the vernacular. Recently, scholars have increasingly been thinking in terms of multiple 'literacies', especially when considering the more elusive female literacy. In her 1998 book, *Gender and Literacy on Stage in Early Modern England,* Eve Sanders asserts that literacy practices following the Reformation played a role in the formation of gender identity, and that 'different levels and forms of literacy' were assigned to each gender.[2] Sanders contributes to what is the project of a growing number of literary scholars, such as Margaret Ferguson and Frances Dolan, who study literacy using gender as a category of examination.[3] By adding gender to the mix, these scholars challenge the more narrow definitions of literacy such as those established by David Cressy's influential *Literacy and the Social Order.*[4] They have sought instead to define literacies by exploring the multiple ways in which the 'products of a culture can be acquired and transmitted.'[5]

By imagining less traditional forms of female literacy, we allow for the possibility of interrogating the cultural currency these broader forms of literacy carried.[6] The examination of medieval and early modern female literacy practices offer us opportunities to continue redefining what it meant to be literate. Evidence suggests that while women across the classes were often denied access to the same kind of education in reading and writing to which their male counterparts had access, some still managed to find ways to learn to read and get access to texts. Though these texts were most often devotional in nature, and therefore more 'acceptable' for use, it appears that women also had access to other kinds of texts and forms of knowledge. Women increasingly became important textual learners, and they were involved in and responsible for the education of their children and families, with or without traditional literacy skills. The means by which women educated their own daughters through communal instruction suggests the existence of a model of female textual communities; it was not uncommon for groups of women to gather around a 'text' with 'literate' women disseminating its contents.[7]

I take the basic notion of a textual community from Brian Stock, who argues that 'what was essential to a textual community was not a written version of a text, although that was sometimes present, but an individual, who, having mastered it, then utilized it for reforming a group's thought and action'.[8] By modifying Stock's notion of textual community, which does not consider gender, we can apply it to women's textual practices in the medieval and early modern periods. These communities could, and did, use their shared 'literacy' to interpret, perpetuate, and rebel against the cultural structures that defined women and their relationship to God, to men, and to mothering. They did this through dissemination of knowledge, through oral transmission (reading aloud, gossiping, teaching), and through private and public reading. Anne Clark Bartlett suggests that reading 'is always a process of negotiation between . . . the culturally activated text and the culturally activated reader, an interaction structured by the material, social, ideological, and institutional relationships in which both texts and readers are inescapably inscribed'.[9] The complexity of the reading process, then, is in part defined by the response of a textual community to its culture through a given text, and in part based on the reader's skills and strategies. In this model there is always circulation, perpetuation, exchange and reconfigurations of the larger culture's ideologies of class, gender, religion, and conduct. Teasing out and identifying some of the mechanisms of this circulation, and the interchange between more and less isolated communities and the larger culture, will have an impact on how we conceive of female textual communities, female literacy as cultural capital, and the negotiation of power between men and women.

One such negotiation that I take up in this essay occurs between the medical patriarchy and female textual and birth communities, and is most evident in midwifery, obstetrical, and gynecological manuals of medieval and early modern Europe. The medieval *Trotula* and 'Sekenesse of Wymmen', the early modern multi-edition *der Swangern frawen und hebammen rosegarten* (*Rose Garden for Pregnant Women and Midwives*), with its essentially English translation *The Byrth of Mankynde,* and Jane Sharp's *The Midwives Book,* all give us ways of thinking about the development of specifically female literacy as capital.[10] These medieval texts draw our attention to the social management of 'women's privy sickness' and childbirth, illustrating the ways that women taught and were taught to manage childbirth. In addition, sixteenth and early-seventeenth century instructional manuals illustrate how men began to take over this field, and these manuals indicate various ways in which men's and women's anxieties about childbirth to some degree fueled this shift. At times these works offer us images of female textual communities and an authoritative social 'voice'; sometimes the voice seeks to participate in or enable the community, sometimes it seeks to infiltrate and disrupt it. While we cannot know whether the descriptions and imaginations of these female textual communities are representative of those who actually acquired and used these texts, they do infer a potential, desired, if not true readership. Thus, these texts give us a sense of a female literacy that is secret yet culturally valuable.

Specifically, midwifery manuals indicate the gendering of literacy in this period and ask us to define a particular 'female medical literacy' that differs from other categories of literacy. In her essay on medieval women's tenuous and limited relationship to 'literate medicine', historian Monica Green suggests the concept of 'medical literacy' as 'a way of acknowledging that not all kinds of texts are read in the same way'.[11] As part of her ongoing inquiry, Green observes that female medical practitioners, prominent in the healing practices, most probably interacted with medical discourse in a number of ways as a result of the relationship between gender and acquisition of literacy. As a historian, Green is interested in defining a documentary relationship between reader and text. My project is interested in the ways this literacy gets imagined. I will argue that the acquisition of such a literacy—often through gossip and other potentially liminal and less formal or conventionally circulated forms of knowledge—was anxiety-producing to the patriarchy in general, and to the medical patriarchy in particular. Further, the cultural negotiations around such texts indicate a textual intercourse between the largely male medical profession and the experiential knowledge and authority of women; paradoxically, they also illustrate a reliance of the patriarchal communities on female textual communities for both their knowledge and their patronage.

Medieval midwifery manuscripts express a mode of empowerment available through the reproductive female body and privy knowledge of that body. Similarly, but with more ambivalence, early modern midwifery and gynecological and obstetrical handbooks emphasize the cultural capital of that power. The consumption and production of the text enables women's literacy practices, yet the text itself represents power over and infiltration into women's childbirth practices. These texts also offer a window into the ideology of the culture since they contain the potential response of men to the text and they imagine, simultaneously, female textual practice. A certain kind of subjection and submission is expected on the part of the female reader, yet the female reader concomitantly exerts a resistance to that force. Bartlett argues that one way resistance might occur is through the literacy skills a woman may or may not have. That is, potential gaps that a woman might have from her particular kind of schooling—full, interrupted, or non-existent-would force her to attempt to create sense out of phrases that might confound her; Bartlett calls these 'reconstructive readings' and shows how they might potentially change a work's meaning in significant ways (20-21). Bartlett argues this in her discussion of devotional texts, but this same hypothesis can be applied to a childbirth community processing information through textual transmission, oral transmission, or both. Reconstructive readings would have created an occasion for anxiety, and we can measure responses to this anxiety by investigating how a text's author addresses his or her 'audience'.

Nowhere is this negotiation better illustrated than in the prefaces and prologues of midwifery manuals—locations where the author, editor, and/or translator asserts his or her purpose and where imagined relationships to the reader and that reader's desired relationship to the text are configured. The prefaces, prologues and 'Notes to the Reader' articulate various relationships between a female and male 'author' and a female audience. The prefaces produced for pregnant women and midwives embody several cultural paradoxes related to the gendering of medical literacy in particular, and female literacy in general. They suggest an ambivalent relationship of the patriarchal medical profession to female literacy, one in which the literate female is both feared and desired. As a form of literacy becomes capital (when it becomes exchangeable), as it does in the case of the specific kind of female literacy practice, the conventional forms of literacy no longer function as viable categories. Thus, paradoxically, once a form of literacy is seen as valuable by the dominant culture, once it is viewed as capital, it becomes both a definable category and more difficult to manage and standardize. . . .[12]

Notes

1. See M. T. Clanchy, *From Memory to Written Record: England 1066-1307,* Second Edition (Oxford UK & Cambridge USA: Blackwell, 1993), Chapter 7, 'Literate and Illiterate', for a more detailed discussion of this issue.

2. Eve Rachele Sanders, *Gender and Literacy on Stage in Early Modern England* (Cambridge: Cambridge University Press, 1998), 2.

3. See Margaret Ferguson, *Dido's Daughters: Literacy, Gender and Empire in Early Modern England and France* (Chicago: University of Chicago Press, forthcoming). See also Frances Dolan, 'Reading, Writing, and other crimes', from *Feminist Readings of Early Modern Culture: Emerging Subjects,* Valerie Traub, M. Lindsay Kaplan and Dympna Callaghan, eds. (Cambridge: Cambridge University Press, 1996), 158.

4. David Cressy, *Literacy and the Social Order: Reading and Writing in Tudor and Stuart England* (Cambridge: Cambridge University Press, 1980).

5. See R. A.Houston, *Literacy in Early Modern Europe* (London: Longman, 1988), 3. Houston suggests that knowledge and information can be disseminated and/or obtained in a number of different ways: through looking at an image, through reading either privately or publicly, by attending that which is read either in small or large, informal or formal groups, and finally, through writing—from a signature to a composition.

6. I am indebted to Margaret Ferguson's concept of literacy as a form of cultural capital from *Dido's Daughters: Literacy, Gender and Empire in Early Modern England and France.*

7. Among others, Michael Van Cleave Alexander argues that medieval and early modern women who learned how to read almost always took care to educate their daughters—he cites Elizabeth Woodville and her daughters, and their daughters in turn. He also offers up family letters that provide 'graphic proof' of the spread of literacy among middle class women. *The Growth of English Education: 1348-1648: A Social and Cultural History* (University Park and London: Pennsylvania State University Press, 1990), 40.

8. Brian Stock is of course most specifically interested in the role the rise of literacy had in the 'formation of heretical and reformist religious groups' (88), and how these groups functioned as textual communities. See his section on 'Textual Communities' from *The Implications of Literacy: Written Language and Models of Interpretation in the Eleventh and Twelfth Centuries* (Princeton: Princeton University Press, 1983), 88-240.

9. See Anne Clark Bartlett, *Male Authors, Female Readers: Representation and Subjectivity in Middle English Devotional Literature* (Ithaca: Cornell University Press, 1995), 2-3.

10. In 1981, Beryl Rowland published the *Medieval Woman's Guide to Health: The First English Gynecological Handbook* (Kent: Kent State University Press, 1981). Rowland's transcription of the *Medieval Woman's Guide* has been particularly useful in drawing attention to some of the actual medieval medical obstetrical and gynecological practices of women, ostensibly from a female practitioners point of view. And while Wendy Arons has published a modern translation of Rosslin's *The Rose Garden,* there is not as yet a published modern edition of England's most significant midwifery treatise of the mid-sixteenth and mid-seventeenth centuries, Raynald's translation of *De Partu Hominis, The Byrth of Mankynde.* See *When Midwifery Became the Male Physician's Province: The Sixteenth Century Handbook: Rose Garden for Pregnant Women and Midwives,* trans. Wendy Arons (Jefferson, N.C.: McFarland & Co., 1994).

11. Monica Green, 'The Possibilities of Literacy and the Limits of Reading: Women and the Gendering of Medical Literacy' in *Women's Healthcare in the Medieval West* (Ashgate Variorum, 2000), 6.

12. Many thanks to Kate Koppelman for contributing her insights here, as well as in many other places.

SOPHIE MASSON (ESSAY DATE NOVEMBER 2002)

SOURCE: Masson, Sophie. "The Mirror of Honour and Love: A Woman's View of Chivalry." *Quadrant* 46, no. 11 (November 2002): 56-59.

In the following essay, Masson stresses the importance of chivalry and its attendant virtues to the lives of European women during the Middle Ages.

Chivalry. Isn't that a bloke's thing? Isn't it to do with being a man-at-arms, with strapping on armour and sallying forth into the wildwood on your horse, your lady's token on your arm, to right wrongs and do great deeds? Isn't the only role of the woman in chivalry to be the inspirer, the muse of a paragon of the knightly virtues? Well, yes—and no. Chivalry was much more than that. And its ideals encompassed both sexes, actively.

As the French-derived term chivalry indicates—it is originally from *chevalerie,* literally meaning horsemanship—it came about as a means of codifying and disciplining a mounted order of military types. Mounted men-at-arms—knights, in the English word, which by the way derives from the same root as knife, referring to weapons—could be a damn nuisance in the early and later Middle Ages. The way they were regarded by many people is perhaps best summed up in the German proverb, *Er will Ritter an mir werden*—he wants to play the knight over me, ride roughshod over me. That is, these mounted men were regarded as tyrannical bullies, delinquents and pests.

That they were pests more often than not is indisputable; a combination of young man's energy, a lack of efficiently centralised civic or moral teaching (the state did not really exist, and the church struggled mightily to tame the warriors for centuries), and the fact that on a horse you could quickly get away from the scene of your crimes, mixed with a kind of carte blanche, a blind eye turned to your high jinks by the man—or woman—who paid your wages when you were at war with their rivals or enemies (but cut you loose when they didn't need you, leaving you to fend for yourself), made for a potent cocktail of public nuisance. The Middle Ages was a young person's period; though many people did live on into old age, the average age of death for a woman was thirty-three; for a man, especially a knight, it was under thirty. The often wild energy, idealism and exaltation that characterises medieval culture comes from that demographic fact. This was real youth culture.

But as time went on, and the disorder of the post-Roman period, the invasions, and the Norman adventures receded, and prosperity and peace descended in Europe, some kind of balance having been precariously achieved, more attention was paid to the fact that the youth had not only to be kept in line, but also to be given a channel for their energies which would make them more productive and more disciplined. Added to that was the change in peacetime culture, particularly in England and France, with women becoming more prominent again, able to provide a guiding hand.

ON THE SUBJECT OF...

ELEANOR OF AQUITAINE (1122-1204)

Eleanor was born in 1122, and became heir to Aquitaine—a vast area in the southwest of what is now France—while still a young girl. Her father had supported troubadours, poets, and storytellers, and through exposure to them and other teachers, Eleanor received a superior education, unusual for a woman of her era. Honoring her father's deathbed wish to unite Aquitaine and France, fifteen-year-old Eleanor married the son of the King of France, and when the king died a few days later, she became the Queen of France, wife of King Louis VII. Their marriage was annulled in 1152, and Eleanor held such power in the south that Louis VII had no choice but to allow her to retain control of Aquitaine. She soon married Henry Plantagenet, who became King of England two years later. Four months after their marriage she gave birth to William, the first of the couple's eight children. Henry had numerous affairs; the most infamous was with Rosamond Clifford, the daughter of a knight. "Fair Rosamond" and her interactions with Eleanor have served as the inspiration for dozens of poems and romances.

Eleanor had considerable impact on the music of her time both as patron of and inspiration for troubadours. In 1168 she returned to rule her subjects in France, and her court became a center of culture. In her "court of love" she and her ladies regularly listened to and judged the poets delivering their verses. When Henry II died in 1189, her third son, Richard I (the Lionheart), became King. While Richard was fighting on a crusade in the Holy Land from 1190 to 1194, Eleanor ruled England herself. Numerous official writs and charters were issued under Eleanor's name, and she (or perhaps Richard) is given credit for publishing a compilation of maritime laws known as the Laws of Oleron. She died in 1204 in the abbey of Fontevrault, where she is buried along with Henry II and Richard the Lionheart.

Modern people all too often view the Middle Ages through distorting mirrors; and one of the most distorting is the idea of medieval women's position. In fact, it is probably true to say that women in the Middle Ages, especially after about the eleventh century and up to the fifteenth, enjoyed a level of relative freedom not equalled until the twentieth. The fall of Rome had also made many of her laws recede into the distance, slowly; Roman statute law was notably more misogynist than the customary law of the tribal groups the empire had conquered. Celtic and Germanic women enjoyed a degree of freedom that scandalised the Romans: perhaps the greatest and most serious of the rebellions against Rome in Britain occurred when an arrogant Roman governor flouted the *realpolitik* of his masters and cut across British customary law by refusing to ratify the awarding of the chieftainship of the Iceni to the widowed Queen Boudicca, or Boadicea.

Now as the Middle Ages advanced and people forgot about Roman law, or cheerfully ignored it, opting instead for a mixture of old and new in their customary law, so the position of women improved. Please don't think I'm talking feminism here. Medieval society, like pre-Roman society, was one of kinship and hierarchy (which is not the same as class, by the way). If you were related to the right people, if you were part of the clan, you had a right to exercise the rights given to you on that basis, no matter what your sex. So women in the Middle Ages, as in the Celtic and Germanic worlds, could openly be chiefs, could command armies, an huge estates, run businesses, inherit and so forth, in a way that women in Roman times and women in the Renaissance—which rediscovered Roman law and reinstated many of the old ways, including the institutionalised repression of women—could not, or could only do through subterfuge. Medieval people recognised custom, and its pre-eminence; kinship, and its inextricable centrality; hierarchy, which meant that everyone had a place but that people could move between places, in case of great personal merit (there were quite a number of serfs who became knights).

What we now think of as chivalry came out of that world. It began, as a codified idea, in the twelfth century, in the courts of two famous and talented and powerful women of the time: the extraordinary Eleanor of Aquitaine, and her daughter, Marie of Champagne. Eleanor was a force of nature, a brilliant figure whose true stature is only slowly being rediscovered. Sole heir to the vast lands of Aquitaine, the teenaged Eleanor married the pious, shy Louis VII of France, who was no match for her wilfulness and talents. She went along with him on Crusade, as an important person in her own right, had several children with him, including Marie, then tiring of him and his font-frog ways, and infatuated with the younger, sexy Henri Plantagenet d'Anjou, (Henry II of England) she concocted an excuse to get rid of Louis. She even managed to persuade the Pope to grant her an annulment on the basis of too-close kinship to her former husband, and so was able to enter into legal marriage with Henry.

She and Henry were a match for each other, but too much so in many ways; though they had six more children, and for a long time had a strong relationship, Henry's roving eye and Eleanor's pride proved the undoing of a partnership that had had all Europe enthralled. During this time, she ran her own court separately in Poitiers, and was the patron of artists, poets, musicians and philosophers.

It was at this court, and at her daughter Marie's in Champagne, that the codes of chivalry and of courtly love were established, in close contact with the great ladies. Eleanor and Marie were aware not only of the delinquent tendencies of knights, but also of the boredom of ladies—and of the many sexual adventures that went on. They would encourage the concept of a new form of chivalry, which would not only emphasise prowess in arms and great deeds, as had been the case in the past, but also the great adventure of love, the way it helped in the journey to self-knowledge and integration. It would mean that women would have a central part in the culture, as muses and inspirers certainly, but also as honourable beings in their own right.

Secular Woman in Romance, and Sacred Woman, the Madonna, dominated medieval culture from the twelfth century, in the process turning a rather rough and ready culture to a most beautiful, subtle and richly patterned one. As well, contact with the East meant that philosophy, astrology and astronomy, and the natural sciences in general, flourished. Indeed, I believe that it would be truer to speak of the twelfth century, rather than the fifteenth, as the Renaissance, for this was the true turning-point in medieval culture. I think too that the new concept of chivalry, whose ideals became deeply ingrained in Western modes of thinking and imagining, represents a major and important divergence between Eastern (particularly Arab, but also Byzantine) and Western cultures at the time.

What were the distinguishing elements of chivalry? I have devised a list of the Seven Qualities of Honour, gleaned from various medieval books, qualities which were firmly to be sought after by both men and women.

Franchise, or Frankness (that is, openness of mind); Pitie, or Compassion; Courage; Courtoisie, or Courtesy; Sagesse, or Wisdom; Largesse, or Generosity; and Temperance, or Moderation. As is obvious, these were not sex-limited characteristics. And though they were ideals, they were often lived up to. From those seven qualities, we can get a sense of the characteristics of post-twelfth-century medieval culture. Hotheadedness was to be restrained; greed and avarice, always pet hates of the times (and major problems) cast into the darkness; ignorant yobbo behaviour firmly rejected.

Respect for others, and for oneself as a growing soul, is intrinsic to the chivalric tradition. It is intended to carry through into all aspects of one's life; at its best it is truly impressive. It is pointless to keep saying, as all too many modern writers do, that the ideal wasn't always lived up to; what ideal ever is? The fact is that this ideal genuinely changed a whole society, and laid the groundwork for many other social developments in the future.

Writers like Chretien de Troyes and Andre le Chapelain—or Andreas Capellanus, as he's often known—wrote books demonstrating and portraying the new ways of being and relating between the sexes: incidentally also changing the face of literature (the romance being the true ancestor not only of the novel in general but of the fantasy novel). As time went on, more and more writers, inspired by the beauty and depth of the ideas embodied within the notions of chivalry, explored it in ever greater depth. Many of these (in the main) male writers saw Woman as Muse: whether spiritually as well as romantically, like Ramon Llull, for instance, or practically and realistically, like Godefroi de Charny (both men wrote books on chivalry which are still in print today). Of course, there were also those who fought hard against it and the implicit validation of women as real human beings worthy of respect, of true love, and even adoration. Such a one was Jean de Meung, writer of the *Romance of the Rose,* an anti-woman diatribe, and the anonymous authors of the scatological *Roman de Renart,* which in many ways functions as an anti-romance.

Between idealism and misogyny, though, there were also those who saw women as equal partners in the great journey of life, and in the quest for honour, and the development of the soul that chivalry represented. At least two of those writers were women: the twelfth-century Marie de France (not the same person as Marie de Champagne) and the early-fifteenth-century Christine de Pisan. Marie wrote lais, narrative poems, romances based on Celtic motifs, full of love, magic, humour and adventure. Christine was a non-fiction writer, who wrote hugely popular and influential books on the achievements and behaviour of women. Some of these were intended as self-help guides; others as witty and fierce ripostes to anti-woman propagandists. One of her books, *The Treasury of the City of Ladies,* talks at length about the ways in which women achieve honour and respect, and the ways in which the chivalric code can be applied to everyday life.

Let's have a look at some of the things the women writers said. Marie, who has a rather salty tongue and sardonic eye and ear for the way people behave, is particularly preoccupied with love and the different ways in which lovers act. She firmly tells her audience that chivalry and courtliness are about real things, that hypocrites and coy flibbertigibbets are without honour:

> The professional beauty will mince
> and preen her feathers, and wince
> at showing she favours a man,
> unless it's all for her gain.
> But a worthy lady of wisdom and valour
> will not be too proud to show her favour
> and enjoy the love of her man
> in every way that she can.
>
> (This quote is from Marie's poem "Guigemar"—the translation is my own; you can find it in my novel centred on Marie, *Forest of Dreams.*)

Marie's outlook is that of an upper-class medieval woman, fluent in several languages, moving easily around Europe, sure of her place and independent within it. She chastises strongly those critics who have said that what she writes about is not serious literature, or that it is immodest, or "untrue", because it has magic in it (I must say that as a writer of fantasy, I felt a great sense of kinship with her there). She is very concerned with female honour, and makes it quite clear that women must show as much courage, courtesy, generosity and the other chivalric virtues as men. She has several examples of female characters who run a love affair from beginning to end, fight, travel, and so on; just as she has a female character, werewolf knight Bisclavret's faithless wife, who is punished severely—not for being a woman but for being faithless. This savage justice is also meted out to men who transgress the code.

Women really did live by this code; there are numerous examples of women left in charge of large estates who faithfully and bravely mounted the defence of those estates against the enemies of their house, and were praised for it by chroniclers of the time. Medieval people had a horror of treachery and cowardice; the two were often felt to go hand in hand. The fact that you were a woman did not absolve you from keeping to the ideals of chivalry, in times of crisis and in your ordinary life. And in her fiction, Marie demonstrates clearly both the complex realities of medieval life, and what was considered honourable for both sexes.

From the twelfth century to the early fifteenth is quite a jump. We come here to the tail-end of the code of chivalry—we have been through the culture-shaking hideousness of the Black Death (which, incidentally, in the latest research is no longer thought to be bubonic plague but a kind of Ebola-like virus), and are close to the shift in thinking represented by humanism and the Reformation. In this climate, propaganda against women was growing, though much of the old chivalric spirit remained and indeed never went away altogether. Women of all backgrounds were still very much in evidence in ordinary life, in all kinds of ways; the cruel Roman-derived statutes, which wiped out many customary rights of inheritance and divorce and so on, had not yet been applied.

Christine de Pisan, a prolific and indefatigable writer who proselytised tirelessly for the recognition of the talents, achievements and potential of women, gave her advice and insights in the form of allegory and exposition. She was enormously influential and popular; her own life story is an inspiration for women desperate to know more about the lives and achievements of women in the past. Left a widow at a young age, with small children to support, Italian-born Christine launched into a professional career as a writer in early fifteenth-century Paris. She was not one to bite her tongue, but took part vigorously in many of the intellectual debates of the day, in which her sharp intelligence, comprehensive education and refusal to be beaten thrilled her fans and infuriated her enemies.

Christine launched into a lively denunciation of the anti-woman *Romance of the Rose,* pointing out tartly the many faults in its logic and its humanity. Her *Book of the City of Ladies* was conceived as a direct riposte to Jean de Meung's jeremiads. She used the device of three allegorical figures—Dame Reason, with her mirror of self-knowledge, the "mirror held up to nature", as she called it; Dame Rectitude, with her rod of peace; and Dame Justice, with her cup from whence she pours out stability and equilibrium—to frame a discourse in which a "City of Ladies" can be constructed which allows women to fully develop their talents and potential. In so doing, she refuted many of the criticisms of women made by contemporary writers, and highlighted the achievements of women in many areas.

Her sequel, *The Treasury of the City of Ladies* (recently republished, in English, as *The Medieval Woman's Mirror of Honour*), was more of a self-help and advice book, tailored not only to aristocratic women but to women of all social backgrounds, from rich merchants to poor cottage women. The thrust of her argument is that, in order to act honourably, women do not need to fight against nature, but to follow selectively and intelligently the dictates of their truest selves.

Real self-knowledge and respect for others, so central to chivalry, are also the centre of Christine's words to her readers, the armour she advises them to put on to sally forth into the great adventure of life. From it grow all those qualities of honour, from courage and generosity to openness of mind and temperance, compassion and courtesy—and the result is true wisdom. For that was the aim of chivalry: a way of reaching one's fullest potential as a human being, but always keeping in view the presence, the needs, and the worth of other people. Chivalry, both male and female, recognised that each of us is, indeed, our brother's or sister's keeper—but also courageously responsible for our own actions. It is an ideal which is of increasing and urgent relevance in the world today.

JO ANN MCNAMARA (ESSAY DATE 2003)

SOURCE: McNamara, Jo Ann. "Women and Power through the Family Revisited." In *Gendering the Master Narrative: Women and Power in the Middle Ages,* edited by Mary C. Erler and Maryanne Kowaleski, pp. 17-30. Ithaca, N.Y.: Cornell University Press, 2003.

In the following excerpt, McNamara investigates the origins and limitations of feminine social and familial power in the medieval period.

The gender system that developed in the second millennium changed the nature of woman's position as part of a couple and advantaged the male, whether celibate or married, by divorcing men from the couple as a functioning social unit and barring women from the exercise of an inherent manliness that earlier theorists had recognized in them.[1] The homosocial bond facilitated male commensurability and relegated women to an ontological femininity that effectively barred them from potency.

Obviously, these changes did not fall like a thunderbolt on the stroke of midnight, 1000. But if the power of women through the family should actually be understood as the power of women as wives and, eventually, as widows, a shift in the nature of the couple would have a major impact on women's power. And this does seem to be the case. Even those women whose aristocratic connections were among their major qualifications to marry a highly placed man were significantly without family support in their public careers. This includes the German empresses, Adelheid and Theophano, and the Merovingian queens, Brunhild and Radegund.

On the other side, the Merovingian period produced some dramatic instances of queens who had made their way up from slavery through personal attraction alone. The Carolingian and post-Carolingian periods provide several dramatic examples of royal widows who appeared to carry a claim to their husband's crown with them into a new marriage.[2] If I were now to create an evolutionary scheme, I would say that women's importance as bearers of familial alliances had little significance until the end of the first millennium. Their importance as counters in aristocratic family strategies apparently emerged only when their personal autonomy was reduced by parental and public control of the passage of wealth and status, in effect, when their masculinity gave way to a heightened concept of femininity.

Now I would propose that manly women did indeed play powerful roles in the early middle ages, and no one was particularly surprised that they could do so successfully. They led armies and defended towns. They sat in judgment and made treaties. They controlled resources and deployed them to gain greater wealth and power. Their female sexuality provided an armory of seductive weapons whereby they attracted and held the most powerful men as their husbands. The virility that a single-gender Aristotelian system conferred on them enabled them to use the position gained by marriage effectively.

As the church slowly imposed the principle of indissoluble monogamy, the corporate couple became ever stronger.[3] Joined as one flesh, their interests were also one. Once formed, the marriage alliance looks like the only one that a beleaguered potentate could trust, especially if his bride had no protector but himself. Clovis could kill all his relatives and then complain that he had no brothers at his side, but his wife was his true partner and confidante. Women like Brunhild and Fredegund, even the sainted Clothild, were ferocious to everyone but their husbands. Fierce Merovingian queens and saintly Ottonian empresses seemed immune from charges of sexual infidelity, perhaps because they acted as alter egos to their husbands.

During marriage, women acted as partners and surrogates for their husbands, and after marriage they often stepped into their roles. The most powerful women were those who took up the government of kingdoms and the leadership of armies after their husbands were dead. The evidence does not even bear out the proposition that widows acted for the sake of their children. Some had no children, and others seem to have had few scruples in dominating their children, shoving them aside for their political interests or even eliminating them from their public lives. Occasionally they went so far as murder. Thus it is the conjugal family that seems to harbor the key to women's power, and it is this thread that I mean to pursue backward in time.

In the partnerships of Germanic kings and queens, a gendered division of labor is often noticeable while the marriage lasts. The king plays the part of the violent warrior, stern judge, and mighty ruler. The queen develops the virtues of sanctity, healing and prayer, intercession for the guilty, and charity for the weak. This is what we might expect from the Ottonians, as shown by Patrick Corbet.[4] But in my own hagiographic studies, I came to realize that the same rule applied to the Merovingians whose kingdoms were not based on any notion of Christian polity.[5] Moreover, unless she elected to spend her widowhood in a convent, a Merovingian queen soon forsook her softer role when taking on the manly powers of her deceased husband.

Was this, as the Romans might have conjectured, a reflection of the barbarity of the northern European peoples, daughters of the Amazons, of Boudicca? Tacitus, more than any other author, created the barbarian woman and linked the partnership of women and men to the uncivilized and wild, to people with no proper sense of boundaries. [Suzanne] Wemple and I began with the idea that despite their personal wealth, women were excluded from the public life of the Roman Empire and gained access to masculine roles only with the collapse of imperial power. But later research has shown that Theodosian empresses played the same game in the Christian Empire of the fourth and fifth centuries that the Ottonian empresses played in the tenth.[6] The sources themselves insist that the model of sainted queenship throughout that ever-lengthening period now known as "late antiquity" was Helena, the mother of Constantine, who played the role of his queen after the execution of his wife.[7]

Tracking the power of women through the conjugal family, therefore, has moved us back into the heyday of the Roman Empire and right through that wall that once divided the master narrative so unshakably into ancient and medieval history. Can we therefore look at Christianity as an instrument of power for women and insist on revising our chronological framework to incorporate the fourth and fifth centuries? To some extent, I think we can. The first ecclesiastical legislation aimed at imposing indissoluble monogamy appears in that period, and missionaries carried the principle with them into the northern forests. It was contested and partial throughout the settlement period until the ecclesiastical revolution of the eleventh century. Only then could we reasonably suggest that there was, at least theoretically, some sort of domestic sphere in Europe to which women could reasonably be assigned.

However, it now seems that Constantine and his immediate successors did little to interfere with the commitment to monogamous partnerships that characterized the pagan society of the empire.[8] Inspired by Stoic writers, Foucault and his followers have situated the Roman turn to couplehood in the early empire.[9] Plutarch and Paul alike preached mutual support and affection between husbands and wives.[10] In the first century, the outcry was very strong against the late Republican aristocratic habits of seeking family power through marriage alliances and frequent divorce. In fact the family power and the activity of women as instruments of family power that I now see as characteristic of dynastic Europe after the turn of the millennium seems to belong also to the Roman Republican period. But the last great Roman who used his daughter in this way was Augustus. From the first century on, Roman sentiment was turned toward respecting the durability of marriage, the bond of the couple to one another, and the consent of the parties involved to seal the validity of the marriage. Christian law as it developed after Constantine put the seal on these sentiments and gave them legal force.

Moreover, if the fourth century seems to sanctify the role of the wife, the real power that empresses had over their husbands and, at least indirectly, their subjects extends much further back. Perhaps it is not entirely coincidental that Tacitus, the chronicler of the terrifying Boudicca, was no less the narrative creator of the frightful Livia. The partnership of husband and wife in wielding power and influence was inherent in the nature of the empire itself and if it is to be a marker in the history of the European gender system, its beginning must be placed in the Augustan age. Thus it would seem that we must look behind the fourth century for the roots of the power that aristocratic women carried into barbarian Europe.[11]

So the power of women as wives, sharers of a common destiny with their mates, did not arise out of the collapse of patriarchal institutions when Rome fell. It was the hallmark of the Roman Empire itself. Of course, the second great pillar of early western civilization developed in the same period. The Christian religion, from the beginning, privileged the couple over the natal family. Moreover, its female martyrs and ascetics, from at least the second century on, enjoyed the adjective "manly" outside the boundaries of the couple. Over the past three decades, this phenomenon has attracted a number of commentators.[12] In the monastic movement, women could be classed within a third gender in which males and females alike enjoyed the higher dominance of self-control envisioned by classical authors.[13] There, women could most effectively utilize the power and wealth of their natal families as abbesses and church administrators (*metropolitanae*), but the real enabling factor was their indissoluble marriage to Christ.

In the light of this new history of women, the family, and gender, I see the "middle ages" dissolving into nothing and the more recent "late antiquity" giving way to a simple division between the first and second millennia. Over the course of the first millennium, the European gender system underwent a series of shifts and changes. Still, there is a certain unity to be found in the dramatic presence of women in the master narrative. The first millennium began with the collapse of a gender system that excluded women firmly, even from the physical precincts of the Senate in Rome. The patriarchy of the Republic may be only a myth created by nostalgic imperial subjects. Its aristocracy was largely destroyed by the civil wars, but as late as the fourth and fifth centuries, we can still see a coterie of die-hard pagan senators clinging to those hoary traditions while their wives, their mothers, and their daughters were diverting their fortunes and obliterating their patrilines.

Thus I envisage European civilization emerging like the Nile out of a tangle of marsh and tributaries around the turn of the first century B.C.E. into the first century C.E. A new master narrative will, I hope, privilege the experiences of women and men over the destinies of institutions and polities. I believe that the relationships between the two sexes within the matrix of a single gender gives coherence to the entire first millennium. It also provides a metaphor for the ongoing development of western civilization. The imperial father and the ecclesiastical bride/mother were sometimes partners, sometimes rivals. The separation of church and state is a product of their dual beginning and like a first millennium marriage, it fluctuated erratically between rivalry and union. Sometimes they played out opposing roles as ruler and nurturer. Sometimes they competed for the same powers: acting out the tensions implicit in the dominant single-gender system. These institutional conflicts penetrated the real world of men and women as well; bishops competed with queens as imperial consorts, for example. This was a society in which women played vital roles in the ongoing history of dynasties. As a consort, the Roman Catholic church—not necessarily the religion that is shared by the Greek and Russian churches or converts spread as far away as China and India—shared and supported the imperial power. And with the death of her first partner, this same church became in some respects his heir, exercising his power by herself in Rome and, to strain my metaphor, carrying it to successive husbands among the Franks and Germans of the north.

Romanization and Christianization are grand terms. They give an intellectual framework to our study of those myriad peoples, slowly accumulating inherited or acquired skills, steadily clearing and populating the Latin West, hardly hampered at all by that event once known as the fall of the Roman Empire. It is a story centered on growth and the opportunities as well as the insecurities that went with it. Above all, it is a master narrative that proposes that in its origins, European civilization was based on the cooperation of men and women whether in the encratic union of a third gender or the intimacy of married consortium. I started once upon a time with a vision of women enjoying power in violent times and losing it to the oppressive security of a more ordered age. I now see that first age as a time of growth and creativity. It was not Arcadia nor even a golden age, but it was a time when the sexes collaborated for good or evil more closely than they did in the millennium that followed. I hope that the feminist movements of our own day may be pointing the way to a newer and better partnership.

Notes

1. I attempted some outline of these twists and turns in "An Unresolved Syllogism: The Search for a Christian Gender System," in *Conflicted Identities and Multiple Masculinities: Men in the Medieval West,* ed. Jacqueline Murray (New York, 1999), 1-24.

2. The Empress Adelheid is an obvious example. This proposition appears to be the only explanation for the scandalous marriage of Charles the Bald's daughter Judith with her stepson, his father's heir to the English crown, and the marriage of Canute with his predecessor's widow, Emma of Normandy.

3. Jo Ann McNamara and Suzanne Wemple, "Marriage and Divorce in the Frankish Kingdom," in *Women in Medieval Society,* ed. Stuard, 95-124.

4. Patrick Corbet, *Les saints ottoniens: Sainteté dynastique, sainteté royale et sainteté féminine autour de l'an Mil* (Sigmaringen, 1986).

5. "The Need to Give: Suffering and Female Sanctity in the Middle Ages," in *Images of Sainthood in Medieval and Renaissance Europe,* ed. Renate Blumenfeld-Kosinski and Timea Szell (Ithaca, 1991), 199-221, and implicitly in the texts compiled in *Sainted Women of the Dark Ages* (with John E. Halborg and Gordon Whatley) (Durham, N.C., 1992).

6. Kenneth Holum, *Theodosian Empresses: Women and Imperial Dominion in Late Antiquity* (Berkeley, 1982).

7. Jo Ann McNamara, "*Imitatio Helenae*: Sainthood as an Attribute of Queenship in the Early Middle Ages," in *Saints,* ed. Sandro Sticca (Binghamton, 1996), 51-80.

8. Judith Evans Grubb, *Law and Family in Late Antiquity: The Emperor Constantine's Marriage Legislation* (Oxford, 1995).

9. Michel Foucault, *The History of Sexuality,* vol. 3, *The Care of the Self,* trans. Robert Hurley (New York, 1988).

10. Jo Ann McNamara, "Gendering Virtue," in Sarah B. Pomeroy, ed., *Plutarch's Advice to the Bride and Groom and a Consolation to His Wife: English Translations, Commentary, Interpretive Essays, and Bibliography* (Oxford, 1999), 151-61.

11. This was the belief I pursued in two early articles on Christian women in the Roman family: "Cornelia's Daughters: Paula and Eustochium," *Women's Studies* 11 (1984): 9-27, and "Wives and Widows in Early Christian Thought," *International Journal of Women's Studies* 2, no. 6 (1979): 575-92.

12. I first grappled with the question of the "manly woman" before there was a developed gender theory to enlighten my efforts, "Sexual Equality and the Cult of Virginity in Early Christian Thought," *Feminist Studies* 3, no. 3/4 (1976): 145-58. Newer thoughts on those

lines have been offered by Gillian Cloke, *"This Female Man of God": Women and Spiritual Power in the Patristic Age (350-450)* (New York, 1995).

13. I develop this idea at greater length in "Chastity as a Third Gender in the Work of Gregory of Tours," in Kathleen Mitchell and Ian Wood, eds., *The World of Gregory of Tours* (Leiden, 2002).

WOMEN IN CLASSICAL ART AND LITERATURE

JUDITH P. HALLETT (ESSAY DATE 1984)

SOURCE: Hallett, Judith P. "The Role of Women in Roman Elegy: Counter-Cultural Feminism." In *Women in the Ancient World: The Arethusa Papers,* edited by John Peradotto and J. P. Sullivan, pp. 241-62. Albany: State University of New York Press, 1984.

In the following excerpt, Hallett investigates the position of women in Roman society as reflected through literature, arguing for an incipient "feminism"—which contradicts Roman women's expected demeanor as subservient and compliant—in Latin love elegies.

Domum servavit. Lanam fecit: "She kept up her household; she made wool." This was the ideal Roman woman—in the eyes and words of what was doubtless a male obituary writer, late second century B.C. vintage.[1] Our information on the role traditionally assigned Roman women—and by *role,* as distinct from social position and rank, I mean the socially prescribed pattern of behavior manifested by females when dealing with people who are not females—suggests that it involved little more than submissiveness, supportiveness, and stability. By the end of the Roman Republic and the beginning of the Empire, the men empowered to determine how women could and could not comport themselves apparently modified certain inconvenient regulations; nevertheless, they remained remarkably faithful to the spirit, if not the letter, of earlier laws reducing women to chattel status. While Roman society undeniably acknowledged the existence of women's physical charms and mental endowments, for the most part it merely "patronized" females, accepting them only when they adhered to rigidly (and externally) delimited norms of conduct. Women were not as a rule admired for their individual qualities, much less permitted to function autonomously or esteemed for so doing.

But very few rules want for exceptions. In Latin love elegy, and the particular upper and upper-middle class social environment in which it flourished, we directly encounter a violation of the general behavioral principles outlined above. The women featured therein managed to attain a singularly exalted stature, to be appreciated as people in their own right. Their admirers, moreover, not only glorified them out of genuine adoration, they were also motivated by a powerful, often mischievously subversive desire to differentiate themselves and their own system of values from existing forms of conduct. Consequently, the amatory elegists do not restrict themselves to venerating their beloved. They even cast her in the active, masterful role customarily played by men. They do not simply conceive of their emotionally-absorbing romantic liaisons as acceptable activities; they consider them, and the poetry emanating from them, no less strenuous and praiseworthy pursuits than conventional Roman careers in business, the military and the law. What is more, they are not satisfied with justifying their behavior; the Augustan elegists even recommend it wholeheartedly to others! By utilizing a new form of art to portray this role-inversion and achieve their sought-after moral conversion, they seem also to characterize themselves as a veritable "counter-culture," a modern term whose applicability to the love elegists deserves further exploration. We should, however, first ascertain the exact role of women in the elegists' Rome so that we can comprehend precisely what they reject and redefine. Then we may redefine. Then we may examine more closely the perversity and proselytism in the elegiac poetry of Catullus, Tibullus, Propertius and Ovid.

I. Mores

We can marshal abundant and varied evidence to substantiate our initial assertion that Roman society relegated women to a subservient, confined role. Tomb inscriptions, for instance, affirm that wifely obedience (the technical Latin term is *obsequi*),[2] domesticity, chastity and fidelity to one man brought their occupants earthly fulfillment and will qualify them for eternal acclaim.[3] Literary works also portray "nice women" as submissive and docile. Capitalizing upon the permissive, "holiday," mood granted comic performances, the playwright Plautus parodies the conventional Roman marriage formula, which consigns the bride to her husband's tutelage (*Cas.* 815-824). There a male slave, masquerading as a blushing bride, receives instruction from a slave woman on a Roman wife's duties and rights. Like everything else in the scene, however, the advice reverses reality: it depicts the *wife* as the dominant, forceful marriage partner.[4] Of equally great interest is the account which the Augustan historian Livy gives of the first protest demonstration over women's rights (or lack thereof), the insurrection against the *Lex Oppia* in 193 B.C. (34.1-8.3). Even the story's most outspoken liberal, the tribune who successfully agitated for the law's repeal, believes that women are by nature passive and retiring. He seasons his complaints over Roman women's lack of privileges and his demands for their equitable treatment with pious homilies on how women prefer dependence on males to emancipation of any sort (34.7.12-13). In this passage, moreover, we may discern the much-touted Augustan attitude toward women, a crucial component of the emperor's moral rearmament programme. This effort (promoted by wool-spinning among the socially invisible women of the imperial household and repeated claims of the empress' virtue) provides further, historical, corroboration for a view of Roman women as quiet, submissive creatures.[5]

But contradictory evidence confronts us as well. Scholars are quick to point out that, by the first century B.C., Roman women enjoyed considerable power and freedom, particularly when one compares them to their counterparts in fifth century Athens and in the early Roman Republic.[6] Marriage no longer required that a husband possess absolute ownership, *manus,* of his wife. Under the conditions of what was called marriage *sine manu,* wedded women could for all intents and purposes control property they had acquired from their male relatives and thereby retain some sort of individual identity; this arrangement also entitled either party to a divorce if he, *or she,* so wished.[7] And upper class Roman women could lead morally relaxed, independent lives without having to resort to *divortium.* One modern scholar notes that they began emulating the conduct of the exotic émigrées, largely Greek freedwomen, who flooded Rome from the eastern cities of her newly-obtained Mediterranean empire.[8] We can probably attribute such consciously loose behavior to a combination of envy and delayed emotional development: married by their fathers at the onset of puberty, Roman women faced the responsibilities of matronhood before they could cope with the romantic and sexual fantasies of adolescence.[9] Whatever the explanation, some *matronae* from illustrious Roman families so completely adopted the freedwoman's dissolute mode of conduct that students of Latin poetry have never been [able] to determine the marital status and social class of the Augustan elegists' mistresses with any certainty.[10]

How, then, can we reconcile these two sets of facts? First, by recognizing that Roman society offered its women only a limited and illusory brand of liberation—visible independence, yes; autonomy, no. Limitations first. For one thing, whatever possibilities for emancipation *did* exist only affected a small minority of Roman women, the wealthy and the rootless. For another, even the most emancipated and self-assertive Roman woman lived in a state of bondage if we compare her to the most retiring Roman male. Historians who deal with first century B.C. Republican Rome are prone to talk about the political sway exercised by the ladies of Rome's leading houses.[11] Women with the right connections—such as Fulvia, wife successively of Clodius, Curio, and Antony, or Brutus' mother Servilia—no doubt constituted a political force in their own right.[12] But to wax enthusiastic over the *total impact women as a group* had on the Roman political scene is in many ways tantamount to marvelling over the extent to which house pets influence their owners' living habits. *Quanta erit infelicitas urbis illius, in qua virorum officia mulieres occupabunt,* Cicero is reported to have said—stating unreservedly that woman's place is *not* in the forum.[13] Forbidden to vote or hold political office, women could not have possibly exerted an influence on political affairs that even vaguely approximated their representation in the general population. We should not, moreover, cling to any false notions about Roman women's freedom to come and go as they liked, or imagine that they cast off all sexual restraints. Before the civil wars women invariably stayed at home while their husbands travelled abroad to fight and engage in provincial administration; even after Augustus formally instituted the practice of taking his wife along on journeys, respectable women practically never left Italy without a male escort.[14] And, as Saara Lilja points out, while husbands had the right to philander as they chose—as long as they respected the chastity of a virgin or of another man's wife—wives were legally bound to uphold *fides marita.*[15]

Moving on to the grand illusions, we must not lose sight of the fact that a woman's social class and social acceptability were determined by the men in her life, her "patrons" as it were. The upper class matron owed her eminence—and probably her blueblooded husband—to the wealth, contacts and maneuverings of her father and other male kinsmen; by the end of the Republic, the very survival of a marriage like hers depended upon her attractiveness as a symbol of success.[16] In addition, she was as strongly compelled to gratify men's whims and yield to their demands as was a freedwoman like Volumnia/Cytheris, an actress whose coquetteries gained her the affections of Rome's leading men (among them Antony and the love elegist Cornelius Gallus). A major historical study of the late first century B.C. relates how some women of the upper classes took selfish advantage of existing social opportunities—involving themselves in politics and the arts, managing their own financial affairs—and paid dearly. Such "uppityness" lost them the ability to attract their male peers. "The emancipation of women had its reaction upon the men, who, instead of a partner from their own class, preferred alliance with a freedwoman, or none at all."[17]

This brings us to the second major *trompe-l'oeil* of Roman women's so-called liberation: the fact that women's new freedoms had really evolved in order to render them more serviceable to men and male political ambitions. As marriage without *manus* deprived a wife of claims to her husband's estate, one scholar on Roman law conjectures that it was originally devised by the prospective bridegrooms' families to obtain for their sons the advantage of a marital alliance without the usual obligations.[18] Easy divorce had similar benefits. It permitted fathers and brothers as well as spouses to discard politically useless in-laws in favor of more useful ones. Furthermore, in this world of constantly changing ententes and enmities, where women functioned as temporary cement, the power-hungry males who selected a kinswoman's marital partners often viewed women as things, not sentient, sensitive human beings. They tended to value women *as* mere political assets and not *for* redeeming personal qualities, evincing no concern for any feelings they might have. Witness Julius Caesar's behavior: how he cold-heartedly broke his daughter's engagement so that he might marry her to Pompey, or how he later contemplated shedding his own loyal wife in order to wed Pompey's daughter.[19] Or how his nephew Augustus forced a match between his daughter Julia and stepson Tiberius, at great emotional pain to them both.[20] Or how their legendary ancestor Aeneas abandons Creusa and Dido, two women who deeply love him, the first basically out of loyalty to male relatives, the second so that he may continue upon a political quest. When Aeneas finally decides to commit himself to a lasting relationship with a woman, he selects as his mate a king's daughter who cares nothing for him; he must also destroy much that is beautiful in primitive Italy to achieve this aim.[21] Hot political properties to be sure, but properties nonetheless, women of the late Republic and early Empire essentially reverted to their acquiescent, 'non-person' status under early Roman law. *Plus ça change, plus c'est la même chose.* No wonder women "over-availed" themselves of what freedoms they did have, indulging in clandestine sex or engaging in challenging activities at the risk of losing male approbation!

But we must reconcile the *ideal* of Roman women's seclusion and obsequiousness with the *fact* that many proper Roman women could and did mingle freely in public and have legally sanctioned carnal knowledge of more than one man. We must also come to grips with the patently licentious behavior of freedwomen and with the openly acknowledged demand for unrestrained, free-wheeling women of their type voiced by the men of the propertied classes. The frequent claims of uxorial rectitude on funeral inscriptions, Augustus' efforts to re-affirm the "old" Roman morality—such insistent self-righteousness suggests that its eulogizers are trying to combat a trend in the other direction, to contrast examples of "what should be" to "what actually is." The *princeps'* moral programme—lest we forget—included not only propaganda and financial rewards for child production. Its architect designed it for the express purpose of replenishing the depleted senatorial and equestrian ranks, Rome's ruling élite; it also featured laws requiring intra-class marriage of upper class males and forbidding adultery.[22] Clearly Augustus, notorious exploiter of the new moral freedom though he was, found the conduct of certain upper class men, and the effect that it had upon the females whose lives they controlled, downright subversive.

Suetonius and Cassius Dio tell us that the "new, moneyed" aristocracy, the equestrian rank, opposed Augustus' marriage and moral legislation.[23] We have, in addition, a far [more] eloquent and extensive protest against the sanctimonious moral assumptions and abusive social conventions of the late Republic and early Empire than ever could have echoed in the halls of the Roman Senate. It is, moreover, readily available and well-known to all students of ancient Roman culture. I refer to Latin love elegy, a form of self-revelation and indirect social criticism created and developed by members of the dissident equestrian class.[24] To be sure, the elegists' personal dissatisfaction with standard *mores* extended far beyond simple disenchantment with women's role—idealized and actual—in contemporary society. Yet Catullus, Tibullus, Propertius and Ovid all reveal discontent with both the traditional Roman view of women as demure, submissive chattels and the current Roman practices which allowed women an ostensible increase in freedom so as to exploit them more fully. They write of a social milieu which pays no heed to common social expectations about female—and, conversely, about male—behavior. The amatory elegists, or at least their literary *personae,*[25] speak on behalf of the people whose iconoclastic actions ultimately struck Augustus as threatening. They constitute what present-day social historians would call a "counter-culture," a movement which seeks to "discover new types of community, new family patterns, new sexual *mores,* new kinds of livelihood, new esthetic forms, new personal identities on the far side of power politics."[26]

I do not employ this current phrase, "counter-culture," simply to sound chic and *au courant.* If the wisdom of the past has anything to teach the present (certainly a belief cherished by all self-aware classicists), then the insights of contemporary man should bear on previous human experience as well. Furthermore, the label I am applying to the Latin love elegists and their coterie could not be more *à propos.* Like the counter-culture which sprang up in the industrialized Western nations during the late 1960's and early 1970's, this particular group was both young and conscious of youth's special privileges,[27] advantaged in terms of social and educational background, and relatively affluent.[28] Their youthful self-assurance, well-placed connections, high degree of intellectual attainment, and financial security enabled them to disdain accepted social practices. While more humble, unschooled and impecunious Romans deemed the "nuclear" family arrangement an economic necessity, the elegists could reject the idea of a subservient, supportive wife who bears multitudinous potentially useful offspring in favor of an exciting, attractive and spiritually inspiring female companion. These same personal advantages also permitted the amatory elegists to display a certain cynicism about politics; Propertius, for example, actually appears to question whether he or *any* individual can influence the governmental processes in what latter-day terminology would call a totalitarian state.[29] Instead, they invested their hopes and energies into maintaining romantic attachments, replacing the loyalty they were expected to pledge their *patria* with undying allegiance to their *puellae.* In addition, the Latin love elegists, like the counter-culturists of today, tried to forge a new, more meaningful set of values, embody them in actions which substituted for conventional social practices, and glorify them through art, the most exalted and effective means of human communication. Their redefinition of female and male roles, our concern here, nicely exemplifies their arch contrariness and wistful inventiveness in all matters; the attractive way in which they generally depict their relationships with women helps recommend their *vitae novae* to others. . . .

Notes

1. *ILS* 8403; cf. also M. I. Finley, "The Silent Women of Rome," collected in his *Aspects of Antiquity* (London 1968) 130-131.
2. See G. Williams, *JRS* 48 (1958) 25, for instances of *obsequi* on the gravestones of Roman women from varied social backgrounds and historical periods.
3. Cf. *CIL* 6. 1527=31670, the so-called *Laudatio Turiae;* cf. also *CE* 81 and 968 and the inscriptions quoted by Williams (above, n.2) 21 n.20.
4. So Williams (above, n.2) 17-18.
5. See R. Syme, *The Roman Revolution* (Oxford 1939) 335, 443-445; cf. also Horace, *Odes* 3.14.5.
6. For example, Syme (above, n.5) 445; G. Luck, *The Latin Love Elegy,* 2nd edition (London 1969) 22-24; S. Lilja, *The Roman Love Elegists' Attitude to Women* (Helsinki 1965) 31-42.
7. On the difference between *manus*-marriage and marriage *sine manu,* see Cicero, *Topica* 3.14 and, *inter alios,* P. E. Corbett, *The Roman Law of Marriage* (Oxford 1930) 68-106, 113.
8. So Luck (above, n.6) 23-24. In dissuading his (male) readers from sexual intrigues with respectable married women, Horace (*Satires* 1.2) implies that adultery, often of a promiscuous variety, on the part of matrons from the best families was a well-acknowledged fact of Roman life in the late first century B.C. Horace condemns such intrigues as dangerous and inconvenient for the men involved—not as immoral in themselves!
9. On the standard age of marriage for Roman women, see J. A. Crook, *Law and Life of Rome* (Ithaca 1967) 100 n.9, who cites M. K. Hopkins, *Population Studies* 1965, 309 ff.
10. See the discussion of Lilja (above, n.6) 37-41, from which one may choose to conclude that the Augustan love elegists deliberately left the social status of their mistresses vague.
11. Cf. Syme (above, n.5) 12, 384 ff., 414.
12. For their political wheeling and dealing, see, *inter alios,* Cicero, *ad Att.* 2.11.2; Velleius Paterculus 74.2.3.
13. The remark is quoted by Lactantius, *Epit.* 33(38)5. See K. Ziegler's fifth Teubner edition of the *De Republica* (1960).
14. See J. P. V. D. Balsdon, *Life and Leisure in Ancient Rome* (New York 1969) 237.
15. See Lilja (above, n.6) 176-177, who in turn cites T. Mommsen, *Römische Staatsrecht* (Leipzig 1899) 22f., 688f. and 691. See also Balsdon, *Roman Women*

(London 1962) 214, who calls attention to the elder Cato's dogged championship of a double standard already codified in law, and Cato's own remarks on the topic given by Aulus Gellius (*Noct. Att.* 10.23.5).

16. See C. L. Babcock, *AJP* 81 (1965) 1-32, on Fulvia, the aforementioned female "politico"; he ascribes her ability to attract three prominent and powerful spouses to her consular stepfather and considerable wealth.

17. Syme (above, n.5) 445.

18. Crook (above, n.9) 104. Marriage without *manus* also enabled the male members of a woman's own family to retain control of her property after her marriage. Admittedly, such an arrangement benefitted women in certain respects. Their husbands no longer held complete sway over them; they could appeal to their fathers against their husbands and vice-versa. But it also permitted and in fact encouraged male relatives to interfere in "personal," conjugal relationships whenever they felt it in their interest.

19. Plutarch, *Caesar* 14.4-5; Suetonius, *Julius* 27.1.

20. Suetonius, *Augustus* 63.2 and 65; *Tiberius* 7.2-3.

21. See K. Rogers, *The Troublesome Helpmate. A History of Misogyny in Literature* (Seattle 1968) 44, who notes Aeneas' imperviousness to female charms, "male chauvinism," and Lavinia's utter vacuity. In all fairness to Vergil's Aeneas. However, it should be said that Creusa's ghost justifies—*ex post facto*—Aeneas' abandonment of her as divinely ordained (*Aen.* 2.776 ff.).

22. Cf. Suetonius, *Augustus* 34.1; Cassius Dio 54.16; Horace, *Carm. Saec.* 17-20; also the review of Balsdon (above, n.14) by T. J. Cadoux, *JRS* 52 (1963) 207.

23. Suetonius, *Augustus* 34.2; Cassius Dio 56.1.2.

24. For a summary of the evidence for the elegists' social standing, see Lilja (above, n.6) 10-16.

25. On the issue of sincerity in the Roman elegists, see A. W. Allen, *CPh* 25 (1950) 145-160. While the elegists' allegedly autobiographical poetry may not be telling the exact truth about their personal lives, it at least presents an internally consistent picture of the "characters" which the elegists assume *gratia artis*. Latin love poetry also must have purposely contained enough general social realism to strike a chord of recognition in readers' hearts; i.e. the Roman literary public must have known other men who acted as Tibullus, Propertius and Ovid claimed to behave. See also Lilja (above, n.6) 23-30.

26. T. Roszak, *The Making of a Counter Culture* (Garden City 1969) 66; cf. also C. Reich's similar descriptions of Consciousness III in *The Greening of America* (New York 1971) 233-285. Counter cultures have blossomed in other historical eras too—recall the medieval Goliards and their revolt against ecclesiastical moral strictures.

27. So Propertius at 2.10.7 ff., Ovid at *Amores* 3.1.26 and 68 label love poetry an art form for young artists.

28. See again the evidence assembled by Lilja (above, n.6) 10-16 about the backgrounds of the Latin love elegists; see Roszak (above, n.26) 26-41 on those of the 1970-style counter-culturists. From what the elegists tell us about their origins and imply about their education and social contacts, we should, I think, infer that the "poverty" of which they speak (e.g. Tibullus 1.1.19-22; Propertius 4.1b. 128-130, 4.5.54-58) is either fictitious or a voluntary form of social protest against the materialistic occupations and preoccupations of the equestrian class.

29. See, for example, his unwillingness to participate in the emperor's military campaigns and the national military spirit in 3.4.15-22. Cf. also two recent studies: J. P. Hallett, *Book IV: Propertius' Recusatio to Augustus and Augustan Ideals* (unpublished dissertation, Harvard 1971) 98-102, on 4.2, which details Vertumnus' futile pleas for continued forum residence in the face of the emperor's projected expansion of the Basilica Julia; J. P. Sullivan, *Arethusa* 5 (1972) 17-25.

DENISE LARDNER CARMODY (ESSAY DATE 1988)

SOURCE: Carmody, Denise Lardner. "Genesis 2:23-24." In *Biblical Woman: Contemporary Reflections on Scriptural Texts*, pp. 9-14. New York: Crossroad Publishing, 1988.

In the following essay, Carmody approaches the book of Genesis from an analytical perspective informed by contemporary feminism.

Then the man said, "This at last is bone of my bones and flesh of my flesh; she shall be called Woman, because she was taken out of Man." Therefore a man leaves his father and his mother and cleaves to his wife, and they become one flesh.

The scholarly consensus is that this text occurs in a stratum of the J, or Yahwist (J from the German *Jahwist*), tradition. J is the oldest of the traditions woven into Genesis, probably having roots as early as the tenth century B.C.E. It is earthy, shrewd, and the source of some of our most memorable Genesis passages. In contrast to the priestly (P) source that opens Genesis and the Bible, J is less interested in questions of cosmic order and more interested in concrete humanity, with its wonders and scars alike.

Our text occurs in a block of J material extending from 2:4b to 3:24. In terms of the full canonical text, this block, concerned with the creation and disobedience of the first human beings, is in part a reprise of the account of the creation of all the things of heaven and earth (see 1:26-29 for the P account of the rise of human beings) and in part a new venture, a much closer look at the creature of most interest to the Bible. Prior to our verses, the J account has narrated the creation of the earth and the heavens and the formation of the man from dust, into which God breaths the spirit of life. Placed in Eden to keep its gardens, the man is commanded not to eat of the tree of the knowledge of good and evil. At this time he is alone, apparently a solitary male, and the full force of both the Lord's creative force and command rest on him. God then seems to observe the solitary state of this man and to decide it will not do. So, to make him a helper, God fashions beasts and birds of every kind. (In the J account, the man is the first creature; in the P account, human beings come at the end of the creative process.) However, none of these beasts or birds is satisfactory. Apparently, the man needs a different sort of helper.

There follows the well-known story of the formation of a woman from the rib of the man, whom God has put into a deep sleep. When God takes the woman to the awakened man, he utters the words of our text, every indication being that he is delighted, if not indeed awed. The etymology of *woman* clearly derives from *man,* and the story of the rib may be a visual way of putting this derivation. A midrash (Jewish interpretational gloss) on this text offers the opinion that humanity originally was bisexual—an undivided whole.[1] How literally we are to take this opinion is uncertain, but it underscores the mysterious affinity between male and female, which is such as to suggest a common source. The second of our two verses seems in the nature of a homily, a short sermon by way of reaction to the man's exclamation. However, it is a homily with an eye to Israelite custom, as well as the well-nigh universal custom of all peoples: when woman and man marry, they leave (emotionally if not physically) what had previously been their strongest emotional ties: those with their parents. Even when one grants that the extended family structures of the ancient Near East make it possible the author meant to include the new family arrangements set between the spouses, who become daughter and son to another set of parents, the basic reference to the implications of heterosexual encounter seems obvious. The two become one flesh, not just because that is how children get born, not just because that is what families arrange so that children get born, but because from the beginning they have been "one flesh" in the sense of allied, so made physically and emotionally that "helping" defines their relationship.

This said, we must also underscore the fairly obvious patriarchalism or male supremacism of the text. This stance seems more unthinking and assumed than deliberately taught, but it shows quite clearly that the J authors thought of male humanity as the primary instance and of female humanity as something secondary, if not derivative. (One should not push images too hard and assume that the woman's coming from the man's rib means the authors thought in terms of direct physical derivation.) In contrast, the creation account in P makes humanity male and female from the outset (1:27). The idea that women exist to be helpers of men, rather than independent agents or species of humanity equally entitled to receive help, buttresses this male-supremacist reading. J takes us into a patriarchal world in which men place themselves at the center of society (indeed, at the center of creation) and in which women (as well as beasts and birds) exist for men's support.

Nonetheless, the tone of the man's exclamation softens this legitimate reading. However much he accepts the notion that he should have a helper, someone to assuage his lonely estate as the overlord of God's work, he is delighted beyond the measure one would expect had he been shown "man's best friend" or a noble steed. Even were these animals to prove themselves exceptional helpers, servants willing and able to labor from dawn to dusk, the man would still be *alone,* the word that dominates Gen. 2:18, where God is musing about the situation of his first creature. The helper the man sees upon awakening from the sleep that allowed the removal of his rib bids fair to dispel his loneliness. Furthermore, we may infer that she seems a work worthy of God, something that can more than redeem the man's loss of part of his bodily substance.

The exclamation thus stresses the unity of the now two examples of humankind. To bone-depth, as something inscribed in the flesh of both, they are together. By cleaving, they make a natural unity, a primordial building block. Indeed, their sexual union will be a reminder of their unified beginnings. Even when the man is made the source of the woman (in an arrogation of birthing symbolism to males that has parallels in other patriarchal societies—woman's primacy in producing new human life is something male-dominated societies everywhere have struggled with), the more important point is the conjunction of their destinies. From the moment the man delights in his womanly helper/companion/coordinated flesh, their story is bound to unfold as one family tale.

If we now step back to take stock of how this text rings in a feminist age, we realize, perhaps fully for the first time, that the Bible is one of feminists' great problems. For centuries, people have been able to go to this text, usually thinking it virtually God's dictated word (both traditional Jews and traditional Christians tended to think this way), and find an anthropology, an understanding of human nature, that makes masculinity primary and femininity secondary, or ancillary. The tip-off to the patriarchal mentality comes in the biological shift that makes the male the producer of the female. This twist so flies in the face of how every mother's son has come into being that we should hear the alarm bells ringing. Patriarchy felt it had to say that, in the beginning, at the crucial first hour, masculinity begot femininity. After that beginning, the fathers perhaps felt, the helper could take over the ongoing reproduction. The male had given the first initiative, had provided the creative impulse (and had been accorded the first honors), so the patriarchal mythology remained intact.

One notes similar tendencies in such parallel creation accounts as the Japanese. There, in the Shinto chronicles, the male, Izanagi, has to speak first, because that is what is fitting. Because Izanami, the female, breaks this fitting pattern, their first child is defective.[2] On the other hand, in many places the Bible is its own debunker of patriarchalism, including in this text. For it is not the first male who really creates, but only the Lord God. Thus any tendency of patriarchal Israelite mythology to snatch the creative power from females and arrogate it to themselves runs into the textual problem of God's creative primacy. At best the first male was the matter from which God fashioned the first female. A certain male primacy remains, in that the myth first considers humanity to be solitary maleness, but this "advantage" is proven inadequate, unworkable, and so any extended claims to male supremacy easily could be debunked ("When you were on your own, you couldn't hack it"). Throughout, God's judgment and creative power are truly significant, and by the end God has made it clear that authentic humanity is a delightful coordination of male and female.

Insofar as present-day culture allows feminists to start from an assumption that men and women are radically equal in their humanity, it places feminists in a dialectical relationship with the biblical text. We shall see that this is a regular occurrence. Here feminists may judge themselves both debtors to the text for a deep insight into the coordination, the shared origin and fate, of men and women, and people called to accuse the text of patriarchal sexual biases. In other words, feminists may find themselves not only recipients of a valuable heritage but people whom honesty forces to challenge, criticize, and even, at places, reject the biblical text. Such a finding implies the heady wine of critical hermeneutics—theory of interpretation that wants both to listen and to respond. We shall see a good deal more of this need for a critical mind, but here we should mark well the maturity that critical interpretation requires. One cannot do it well as an ideologue, an absolutist. Neither unchallenging fidelity to the letter of the scriptural text nor ungracious refusal to recognize the contributions of biblical faith will do the job. If the text manifestly is inadequate to today's feminists' needs, it remains true that the text has helped millions of men and women, however unknowingly, to cherish one another as flesh of one flesh and bone of one bone.

Notes

1. W. Gunter Plaut, ed., *The Torah: A Modern Commentary* (New York: Union of American Hebrew Congregations, 1981), p. 32.
2. Rysyaku Tsunoda, William Theodore DeBary, and Donald Keene, eds., *Sources of Japanese Tradition,* vol. 1 (New York: Columbia University Press, 1964), pp. 25-26. This story is discussed in Denise Lardner Carmody and John Tully Carmody, *The Story of World Religions* (Mountain View, Calif.: Mayfield, 1988), pp. 441-44.

ANNETTE DEPLA (ESSAY DATE 1994)

SOURCE: Depla, Annette. "Women in Ancient Egyptian Wisdom Literature." In *Women in Ancient Societies: An Illusion of the Night,* edited by Léonie J. Archer, Susan Fischler, and Maria Wyke, pp. 24-52. London: Macmillan Press, 1994.

In the following excerpt, Depla focuses on three texts of Old Kingdom Wisdom Literature as they relate to women in ancient Egyptian society.

The Old Kingdom (2628-2134 B.C.) was a period of relative prosperity and stability with 'no obvious challenge to, or major malfunction in, the social order'.[1] Instructions from this period are resolutely upper-class, reflecting the mores and attitudes of the wealthy Egyptian male. Three texts are traditionally assigned to the period, namely, the Instruction to Kagemni, the Instruction of Hordjedef, and the Instruction of Ptah-hotep.[2] Four groups of women can be isolated within these texts: (a) wives, (b) women of other households, (c) mothers and (d) maidservants. The unifying themes in the Instructions are the establishment and maintenance of the household, and living in peace with the community at large. While women are generally portrayed in a positive light, they are also shown to be in need of male protection and support. What does not emerge from the Wisdom Literature of this time is that women could participate fully in some of the most essential and important activities of ancient Egyptian society. They could enjoy the same burial rites as their husbands, and benefit from priestly stipends attached to mortuary chapels.[3]

1 The Instruction of Kagemni

This is an incomplete work of which only the final portion survives. The only reference to a woman is a comparative one. The text is very corrupt at this point, but seems to use the tenderness of a mother to her child as a yardstick against which the 'harsh man's' behaviour is judged.[4] . . . [M]otherhood was the pinnacle of female achievement in the eyes of society. Mothers were regarded as paragons. For someone to be kinder than a mother was to be altogether quite remarkable. Unfortunately, the sentence before this one is too corrupt for translation and so we do not know the context of the statement.

2 The Instruction of Hordjedef

Only the beginning survives of this fragmentary work. It contains the earliest example of a maxim which was a recurring theme in Didactic Literature, namely the establishment of a household:

> If you are an excellent one,
> You should found your household.
> Marry a woman, Mistress of the Heart;
> A son will be born to you.[5]

References in autobiographical texts confirm the importance of this 'landmark'.[6]

There are various interpretations of the phrase 'Mistress of the Heart'. It could mean someone in control of herself (self-control being an attribute greatly admired by the Egyptians), or simply a lovable woman. Other commentators have rendered the phrase as 'a hearty wife' or a 'strong woman'.[7]

3 The Instruction of Ptah-Hotep

This is the longest sapiential text attributed to an Old Kingdom figure. Several of its maxims have been the subject of recent research. The text consists of 37 maxims, of which only two deal exclusively with women, namely numbers 21 and 37. I quote maxim 21 in full:

> If you are excellent, you shall establish your household,
> And love your wife according to her standard;
> Fill her belly, clothe her back,
> Perfume is a prescription for her limbs.
> Make her happy as long as you live!
> She is a field, good for her lord.
> You shall not pass judgement on her.
> Remove her from power, suppress her;
> Her eye when she sees (anything) is her storm wind.
> This is how to make her endure in your house.
> You shall retain her. A female
> Who is in her own hands is like rain:
> She is sought for, and she has flown away.[8]

This is a very complex passage. It appears to have a bipartite form; lines 1-7 relating to a positive attitude on the part of the husband, while lines 8-13 portray a negative attitude towards a wife. Lines 1-7 expand the theme first noted in Hordjedef, namely the founding of a household. The husband is exhorted to love, provide for and protect his wife. The elements food, clothes and oil are later found as the constituents in Maintenance Deeds drawn up by men for their wives after marriage.[9] It has been suggested that line 6, 'She is a field, good for her lord', is a sexual metaphor referring to the procreation of a son, a recurring theme in Wisdom Literature. Other similes for wives found in later Wisdom texts describe them as 'stone surface' (for carving) and a 'stone quarry'.[10] Elsewhere the phrase 'open her with a chisel' is used as a metaphor for intercourse, and figures of speech comparing women to minerals and stones are generally best understood as sexual imagery.[11] The passivity of women inherent in 'stone', is reflected in the imagery of a ploughed field (line 6 of the quotation) and is confirmed by representations of women in ancient Egyptian art, where women are portrayed in static modes in contrast to the vigorous poses of their spouses.[12]

Line 7 'You shall not pass judgement on her' appears to be a concise precursor of an injunction found in Ani not to criticise one's wife, but to observe and admire her skill in managing the house.[13]

The following six lines introduce a different attitude towards women. The wife is portrayed as unpredictable, potentially violent but at the same time of great value. Consequently, she needs to be controlled and kept from wielding power outside the home. These 13 lines encapsulate the dualistic nature of women acknowledged in Egyptian society; what might be termed the conflict between the 'good' and the 'bad' woman.[14] Women who conform to the role demanded of them by society, namely (heroic) mother and loyal wife, were to be highly favoured and were deemed good. Women were not, however, suited to positions of authority outside the home because of their unpredictability and intransigence—the image of the storm wind (line 9) indicates loss of control, an attitude synonymous with *Isft* and unacceptable in a career-minded male. This may be seen as the opposite of Mistress of the Heart who represents the ideal wife, mentioned in Hordjedef.

Both sexes were seen as having dual natures. In men the tension was between natures personified as Horus and Seth (good and evil); in women the conflict is represented as being between Sakhmet and Bast.[15] Sakhmet, the lioness goddess, represented the violent and unpredictable, and Bast, also a lioness goddess but sometimes shown as a cat, was a goddess of pleasure, music, dance and healing.

It seems to me that lines 7-13 can be elucidated by reference to two myths—The Destruction of Mankind,[16] and The Myth of the Sun's Eye.[17] In the tale of The Destruction of Mankind, Re the Sun-God and the King of the gods, instructs his Eye, identified here with Sakhmet, to slay mankind in punishment for plotting against him. It appears that after the initial massacre, Re repents of his decision, but has to resort to a strategy to restrain Sakhmet since it is implied that she could not be recalled by reason. Similarly, in The Myth of the Sun's Eye, Thoth, the god of wisdom and, by extension, reason, is sent to entice the Sun's Eye back to Egypt from whence she had left to the detriment of Re and all Egypt. It is an errand fraught with danger. Thoth encounters the Sun's Eye in her docile form of cat, but her violent form of lioness is never far away. He successfully woos the Sun's Eye back and the wellbeing of Egypt and all her denizens, divine and mortal, is assured. The husband in our text can be paralleled to Re; his wife is then his Eye. Just as Sakhmet had to be controlled by Re, so the husband had to control his wife; and just as the prosperity of Egypt depended upon the return of the Sun's Eye, so the prosperity of a man's house depended on his wife's stability. The value of the wife is underlined by the reference to 'rain'—a very rare and valuable commodity in Egypt, though notoriously difficult to summon or control.

The last maxim of this work, number 37, also concerns advice about the treatment of a wife. The verse contains a number of lexical difficulties. The latest research has produced the following translation:

> If you marry a fat woman
> With a happy disposition and known by her town.
> If she unites these two qualities
> And time with her is pleasant,
> Do not put her aside, but let her eat
> So that she laughs with all her heart
> One will say (then) . . .
> A happy woman controls [her water?][18]

Implicit in this passage are the qualities a man should seek in a wife. Good companionship seems to have been valued higher than good looks: divorce, here referred to as 'to put aside', on the grounds of physical inadequacies, is treated with derision in some texts. Despite this, fatness in women was not a desirable thing. Egyptian art presented the ideal female as thin and svelte. Representations of fat women are extremely rare. Two notable examples are known: (a) the Queen of Nubia shown in a relief in the mortuary temple of Hatshepsut at Deir el-Bahri and (b) fecundity figures from reliefs from the temples of Sahure and Niuserre.[19] Men, on the other hand, with the exception of the king, had two modes of representation on official monuments. Muscular, trim figures were used to symbolise the vigour of youth, while successful and comfortable old age was expressed by rendering the male with a large belly and double chin.[20]

The young man is advised therefore that while his wife may not conform visually to the feminine ideal, a happy disposition and a good reputation were not to be despised. 'Known by her town' was the figure of speech used to denote respectability. . . . [I]n the New Kingdom texts, the stranger, rootless and unknown, was anomalous in Egyptian society and a threat to its stability. This maxim confirms the xenophobic attitude of the Egyptians. . . .

Notes

1. Kitchen (1979), p. 237; Gardiner (1961), pp. 72-106.
2. It is argued by some Egyptologists, such as Lichtheim (1975), pp. 6f., that these works were pseudepigraphical and were attributed to eminent writers and an early date to give them added weight and validity.
3. Fischer (1989), p. 23.
4. Lichtheim (1975), p. 60, n. 8.
5. Posener (1952), p. 113.
6. Lichtheim (1976), p. 12.
7. Lichtheim (1975), p. 58; Simpson (1973), p. 340; Posener (1952), p. 113.
8. Parkinson (1991), p. 55.
9. Pestman (1961), pp. 145ff.
10. See Lichtheim (1976), pp. 176 and (1980) 178; Badawy (1961), p. 144.
11. Manniche (1978), p. 54.
12. Robins (1990), p. 21.
13. See Lichtheim (1976), p. 143.
14. Troy (1984), pp. 77-81; (1986), pp. 7-9 and p. 24.
15. Te Velde (1980), col. 25-7; Troy (1984), p. 78 and n. 8.
16. Lichtheim (1976), pp. 197-9; Troy (1986), p. 24.
17. De Cenival (1988); Smith (1984), col. 1082-7; Boylan (1922); Bleeker (1973).

18. Translation after Cannuyer (1986), pp. 92-103.

19. Naville (1898), plate LXIX, 3rd Register; Baines (1985), pp. 110f.

20. Darby, Ghalioungui and Grivetti (1977), p. 60.

Works Cited

Badawy, A. (1961), 'Miszellen', Zeitschrift für Ägyptische Sprache 86, pp. 144-5.

Baines, J. (1985), *Fecundity Figures. Egyptian personification and the iconography of gender,* Warminster.

Bleeker, C. J. (1973), *Hathor and Thoth,* Leiden (*Studies in the History of Religions: Supplement to Numen* 26).

Boylan, P. (1922), *Thoth the Hermes of Egypt,* London.

Cannuyer, C. (1986), 'L'Obèse de Ptahhotep et de Samuel', *Zeitschrift für Ägyptische Sprache* 113, pp. 92-103.

Darby, W. J., Ghalioungui, P., Grivetti, L. (1977), *Food: The Gift of Osiris, I-II,* London.

De Cenival, F. (1988), *Le mythe de l'oeil du soleil,* Summerhausen (*Demotische Studien* 9).

Fischer, H. G. (1989), 'Women in the Old Kingdom and Heracleopolitan Period', in Lesko (1989a), pp. 5-24.

Gardiner, A. H. (1961), *Egypt of the Pharaohs: An Introduction,* Oxford.

Kitchen, K. A. (1979), 'The basic literary forms and formulations of Ancient Instructional Writings in Egypt', in Hornung, E., Keel, O. (eds), *Studien zu altägyptischen Lebenslehren,* pp. 260-82 (Orbis Biblicus et Orientalis 28).

Lesko, B. (ed.) (1989), *Women's Earliest Records from Ancient Egypt and Western Asia,* Atlanta (Brown Judaic Studies 166).

Lesko, L. H. (1989a), 'The Middle Kingdom,' in Lesko (1989), pp. 31-2.

Lichtheim, M. (1975-80), *Ancient Egyptian Literature I-III,* Berkeley.

Manniche, L. (1978), *Sexual Life in Ancient Egypt,* London.

Naville, E. (1898), *The Temple of Deir el Bahari* 3, London.

Parkinson, R. B. (1991), *Voices of Ancient Egypt. An Anthology of Middle Kingdom Writings,* London.

Pestman, P. W. (1961), *Marriage and Matrimonial Property in Ancient Egypt,* Leiden (Papyrologica Lugduno-Batava 9).

Posener, G. (1952), 'Le debut de l'enseignement de Hardjedef (Recherches Littéraires 4). Compléments aux "Richesses inconnues"', *Revue d'Égyptologie* 9, pp. 109-20.

Robins, G. (1990), 'While the Woman Looks On. Gender Inequality in New Kingdom Egypt', *KMT. A Modern Journal of Ancient Egypt* 1/3, pp. 18-65.

Simpson, W. K. (ed.) (1973), *The Literature of Ancient Egypt,* London.

Smith, M. (1984), 'Sonnenauge, Demotische Mythos vom. A', *Lexikon der Ägyptologie* 5, col. 1082-7.

Te Velde, H. (1980), 'Horus and Seth', *Lexicon der Ägyptologie* 3, col. 25-7.

Troy, L. (1984), 'Good and Bad Women. Maxim 18/284-288 of the Instructions of Ptahhotep', *Gottingen Miszellen* 80, pp. 77-82.

———(1986), *Patterns of Queenship in Ancient Egyptian Myth and History,* Stockholm (Uppsala Studies in Ancient Mediterranean and Near Eastern Civilisation 14).

SUE BLUNDELL (ESSAY DATE 1995)

SOURCE: Blundell, Sue. "Myth: An Introduction." In *Women in Ancient Greece,* pp. 14-19. London: British Museum Press, 1995.

In the following excerpt, Blundell reviews the principal ways in which women are portrayed in Greek myth: typically as powerful goddesses, royal figures, or destructive monsters, but in many cases as liminal or victimized individuals.

Women in Myth: Goddesses, Royals and Monsters

The heading above refers to the three levels of being which women assume in Greek myth. The divine level is dominated by the figures of the six goddesses (Hera, Athena, Artemis, Aphrodite, Demeter, Hestia) who together with six gods (Zeus, Poseidon, Apollo, Hermes, Ares, Hephaestus) form a ruling élite known as the Olympian deities. But there are also many lesser goddesses, the relatives and associates of the Olympians; and a number of divine female collectives, such as the Fates, the Muses and the Graces. On the human level of representation, myth features women from a number of social classes. But it would be true to say that the only ones with starring roles are the queens and princesses of the ruling households, such as Helen or Electra. This is indicative of the fact that the Bronze Age, when many Greeks were still ruled by monarchs, was a crucial time for the creation of myth. Royalty was one of the bits of traditional social baggage that Greek myth carried with it into later ages, but its presence did not mean that the stories were of no relevance to women and men of other classes. When, for example, the tragedian Aeschylus was writing about the queen Clytemnestra in fifth-century Athens, where no royal women existed, his play would not have been dismissed as having no implications for the more egalitarian society of his own day.

On the third level of being there is the female monster, who is part-woman and part-animal. Examples of this type are the Gorgons, three sisters who had golden wings, boars' tusks and snaky hair, and who turned men to stone; and the Sphinx, whose form embraced that of woman, lioness and bird. These creatures speak most obviously of the fear which women inspired in men.

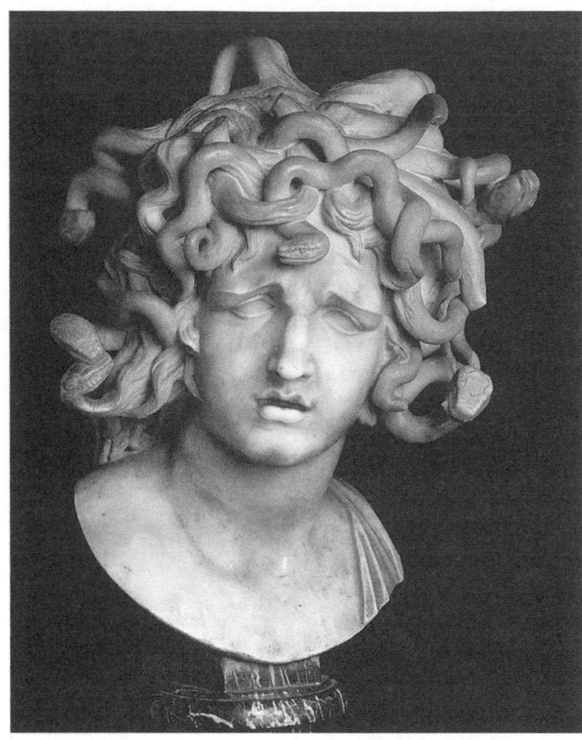

Sculpture by Gianlorenzo Bernini (1630) depicting Medusa, a Greek mythological figure whose gaze turned people to stone.

But it is worth remembering that beings which are terrifying can also be useful, because they help to keep one's enemies at bay. So, while Freud's theory that the Gorgon's head represents the castrating female genitals should certainly not be dismissed out of hand,[1] it should also be borne in mind that antefixes in the form of these heads were commonly used to decorate Greek temples. Similarly the Sphinx, which in myth destroys those hapless passers-by who cannot answer its riddles, often served as a grave-marker in Greek cemeteries of the sixth century B.C. Both these objects doubtless had the function of frightening away evil spirits. This points to the ambiguity of the male response to the female. Even the Furies, the ghastly spirits of vengeance with Gorgon-style snaky hair, who generally seem to be pretty straight-forwardly nasty, turn into kindly beings, or *Eumenides,* at the end of the play of that name by Aeschylus.

The amount of speculation prompted by the Greek goddesses in recent years makes it necessary to provide some additional comment on their history. It is a frequently-noted paradox that the societies which worshipped these prominent female deities were ones in which real women had a very low status. Many commentators have tried to account for this anomaly by resorting to a hypothetical reconstruction of the origins of Greek religion. According to this hypothesis, before the arrival of the Greeks on the Greek mainland, in about 2000 B.C., the native population consisted of settled agriculturalists, who worshipped deities who were primarily female and were associated with the fertility of the earth. The Greeks then brought with them a set of strong male deities more suited to their own way of life, which hitherto had revolved around warfare, pillage and the use of horses. As the native and Greek populations combined, their religions went through a process of fusion whereby the resident females and the incoming males were brought together in a single system. The tensions generated by this development found expression in mythological accounts of friction between females and males, one example being the stormy marriage of Hera and Zeus.[2]

Nowadays it is widely accepted that this reconstruction is a gross oversimplification. The culture of ancient Greece was a complex phenomenon made up of many strands, and its anomalies cannot be explained simply in terms of the racial differences which are the basis of this theory. Archaeological evidence from the Cycladic islands and from Crete, dating from the Early and Middle Bronze Age periods, would certainly seem to indicate that female deities were widely worshipped during that time,[3] and this may go some way towards explaining the prominence of goddesses in later Greek religion. There is, however, very little evidence to support the idea, still commonly encountered, that in the prehistoric era there existed a single unified Mother or Earth Goddess, who was worshipped throughout Europe and the Middle East. It seems much more likely that there were quite a few female deities, with varying functions, in early Greece. The historical process whereby these goddesses were gradually incorporated into a male-dominated pantheon cannot now be recovered, because the evidence simply does not exist. It would undoubtedly have been a complex transformation, involving social, political and cultural changes as well as external influences.

The notion of a prehistoric Mother Goddess has been linked by some people with the idea of matriarchy, or rule by women. The matriarchal era as such is outside the scope of this work, since, if it ever existed, it would have been located in the Stone and Early Bronze Ages. However, since the idea of matriarchy has influenced the interpretation of Greek myths, a brief discussion is necessary. As a theory it relies very heavily on those myths which describe the suppression of women's power. The upholders of matriarchy argue that these contain echoes of the historical transition from matriarchal to patriarchal government. But this reliance on myth makes the theory a very dubious one, since, as we have seen, the myths which we possess were the products of the adaptations worked upon them by later patriarchal societies. For example, it was probably not until the sixth century B.C. that the story of Agamemnon's murder was altered in order to make Clytemnestra the chief perpetrator. In other words, the 'matriarchal' element, the woman's attempt to rule and her violent overthrow, was added at a later stage, at a time when patriarchal domination in Greece was firmly established.

There is no clear evidence to prove that matriarchy ever existed as a historical reality. Many feminist scholars today, while accepting that some prehistoric societies were much more egalitarian than later historical ones, reject the notion of outright female dominance.[4] As a feature of myth, rule by women (which is not in fact all that common) can best be understood, not as a memory of historical events, but as a narrative 'providing justification for a present and perhaps permanent reality by giving an invented "historical" explanation of how this reality was created'.[5] In other words, the myth explains why men and not women rule, and hence helps to validate and reinforce male control. It is the 'justifiable' male take-over which is the crucial factor. So, to take the example of Clytemnestra, as a ruler she is shown to be bloody and tyrannical, and the restoration of male power is seen as something to be welcomed.

A brief survey of the symbolic associations of the mythological female concludes this [essay]. Prominent among these is the identification of women with the wildness of nature—that is, with whatever exists beyond the boundaries of an ordered civilisation. It is generally assumed that it is women's capacity for child-bearing, and hence their alignment with natural forces beyond male control, that prompts these commonly envisaged relationships with trees, plants, springs, birds, and so on.[6] This nature symbolism can often be found to be operating within a 'nature versus culture' model, where men are seen as the representatives of a civilised society which is somehow opposed to the forces of nature. One example occurs in Euripides' play *The Bacchae,* where the king, Pentheus, is associated with ordered life within the walls of the city, while the women worshippers of Dionysus whom he is persecuting are repeatedly linked to the savage world of the mountainside and its wild animals. That the encounter between nature and culture can be seen as leading to the destruction of men is demonstrated in this instance by the appalling fate of Pentheus, who is torn to pieces by the women when he tries to spy on them.[7]

We have already seen, in the discussion of female monsters, that women in myth can be terrifying and destructive. This is equally true of regular mortal women, among whom betrayers, avengers and murderers are legion. Not all of these women are isolated individuals: there are also whole societies of women who murder their husbands, such as the daughters of Danaus or the women of Lemnos. Men in Greek myth can, of course, do their fair share of killing, but this is usually a straightforward manly affair, in the hunt or on the battlefield. Typically, a woman employs trickery and deception in order to dispose of others; and the people disposed of are generally related to her by blood or by marriage. The ultimate negation of the woman who adheres to her proper role in life is the mother who murders her sons, and of these there are several examples. In *The Bacchae,* for instance, Agave is the leader of the band of women worshippers who tear her son Pentheus limb from limb.

Clearly these themes demonstrate a great anxiety about women—one which does not appear to be justified by any of the facts which are known to us. The question of this anxiety will be taken up again. . . . For now, it should be noted that the notion of women's destructiveness can probably be linked in part to their perceived closeness to nature, and hence their perceived remoteness from civilised values. As Gould has written, 'women are not part of, do not belong easily in, the male ordered world of the "civilised" community; they have to be accounted for in other terms, and they threaten continually to overturn its stability or subvert its continuity, to break out of the place assigned to them by their partial incorporation within it. Yet they are essential to it: they are producers and bestowers of wealth and children, the guarantors of due succession . . . Like the earth and once-wild animals, they must be tamed and cultivated by men, but their "wildness" will out.' (1980, p. 57).

Implicit in what Gould is saying here is a notion of women as 'liminal'. This is an anthropological term, meaning 'existing on, or crossing, boundaries'.[8] Women in Greek myth can be seen more often than not to be boundary-crossers: they are represented as anomalous creatures who, while they live in the ordered community and are vital to its continuance, do not really belong there. They are always liable to cross over its boundaries into some disorderly state of being, and for this reason they are seen as highly dangerous.

Perhaps equally as common as the destructive women of myth, though receiving far less attention, are the women who are victims. They are united with their more outgoing sisters in a basic antithesis: mortal women who are active are very often destroyers, while mortal women who are passive are very often destroyed. This is particularly true of the scores of women who are raped or seduced by gods in Greek myth: in the sexual act or in subsequently giving birth they are liable to perish, often in very nasty ways.

Notes

1. See S. Freud (1922). The fact that in visual images the Gorgon has a gaping mouth, and that the Greek word *stoma* denotes both a mouth and either the cervix of the uterus or the lips of the vulva, lends some plausibility to Freud's theory. For Freud, the snaky hair of the Gorgon symbolises both pubic hair and, in a typically Freudian piece of acrobatic thinking, a multiplication of penises.
2. For one version of this theory, see Guthrie (1950), pp. 27-35.
3. For discussions of the evidence, and a résumé of recent references, see Ehrenberg (1989), pp. 66-76, and Goodison (1989), pp. 4-11.
4. For example, see Ehrenberg (1989), pp. 63-6.
5. Bamberger (1974), p. 267.
6. For a much fuller discussion of this symbolisation, see Ortner (1974).
7. I would not want to suggest that in this play Euripides is 'for' civilisation and 'against' nature: the work is far more complex than this. See pp. 174-7.
8. For a useful discussion of liminality, see Friedrich (1978), pp. 132-3.

Bibliography

J. Bamberger (1974) 'The myth of matriarchy: why men rule in primitive society', in Rosaldo and Lamphere (1974), pp 263-80.

M. Ehrenberg (1989) *Women in prehistory* British Museum Press.

S. Freud (1922) *Medusa's head,* reproduced in the *Standard edition of the complete psychological works,* Hogarth Press, 1955, vol. 18, pp 273-4.

P. Friedrich (1978) *The meaning of Aphrodite* University of Chicago Press.

L. Goodison (1989) 'Death, women and the sun: symbolism of regeneration in early Aegean religion' *Bulletin of the Institute of Classical Studies* supplement 53.

J. Gould (1980) 'Law, custom and myth: aspects of the social position of women in Classical Athens' *Journal of Hellenic Studies* 100, pp 38-59.

W. K. C. Guthrie (1950) *The Greeks and their gods* Methuen.

S. B. Ortner (1974) 'Is female to male as nature is to culture?', in Rosaldo and Lamphere (1974), pp 67-87.

M. Z. Rosaldo and L. Lamphere (1974) *Woman, culture and society* Stanford University Press.

WOMEN IN MEDIEVAL ART AND LITERATURE

CHRISTA GRÖSSINGER (ESSAY DATE 1997)

SOURCE: Grössinger, Christa. "The History of Misogyny." In *Picturing Women in Late Medieval and Renaissance Art,* pp. 1-19. Manchester, U.K.: Manchester University Press, 1997.

In the following excerpt, Grössinger examines depictions of women in the visual arts from the fourth to early sixteenth centuries, noting that these portrayals suggest the strong presence of misogynistic thought in the Christian world.

From the beginning, the image of woman was created by man and in the Christian Middle Ages this was the image of Eve. Eve, born from Adam's rib, was tempted by the devil and persuaded Adam to disobey God and eat the forbidden fruit, resulting in the expulsion from paradise, mortality, and life on earth in hardship, tears and sorrow. Since then, female descendants of Eve were held responsible for this loss of paradise and castigated as temptresses and sinners; rebellious and impossible to discipline. Only the Virgin, a woman of absolute purity and humility, born without original sin, was able to redeem humanity, as the second Eve.

The early Church Fathers of the fourth and fifth centuries in particular were responsible for creating the image of woman as temptress, for they fled the world with its temptations and led a life of extreme asceticism in the desert. Evil to them was identified with the flesh. In art, the Temptation of St Anthony[1] best reflected fear of women, showing the holy man in the desert tempted by a worldly woman, beautiful and fashionably dressed, her evil nature often indicated by clawed feet, the snake-like train of her dress or the devilish horns of her headdress, as illustrated in an engraving by Lucas van Leyden. Hieronymus Bosch's triptych of *The Temptation of St Anthony*[2] depicts all the hybrid monsters of hell that afflict the saint, and the woman temptress is right behind him, in the central panel, and also appears to him in the nude from behind a curtain draped around a tree, in the right wing. Only faith in Christ can save the saint, but Christ is barely visible in the background of the central panel, pointing to the Crucifixion. The story of St Anthony's life as a hermit in the desert was originally compiled by St Athanasius and St Jerome, and it was St Jerome (*c.* 342-420), above all, who advocated a life of asceticism and whose negative views on women—expressed in his *Adversus Jovinianum, c.* 393—influenced much of medieval thinking. In his opinion, even to touch a woman was bad, and the very presence of a wife would distract a husband from his prayers, for women's love was insatiable and deprived men of their vigour. In discussing marriage and virginity, St Jerome considered marriage third after virginity and widowhood on the scale of spiritual perfection. However, marriage was superior to lust, for he agreed with St Paul, who in his letter to the Corinthians (I Corinthians 7:8-9) advised the unmarried and widows to marry, saying: 'But if they cannot contain themselves, let them marry; for it is better to marry than to burn.' In his letter to Eustochium, the daughter of his friend Paula, who had taken up a life of virginity, St Jerome advised her on how to beware of carnal temptations by telling her of his own fearsome struggles against fantasies of dancing girls; in spite of castigating his flesh and leading the life of a hermit, intent on contemplation, burning desire would afflict him.[3] Once more, Hieronymus Bosch most vividly depicts St Jerome surrounded by fantastic creatures, plants and idols, among the crumbling ruins of pagan Rome, which to St Jerome represented all the worldly pleasures of a wanton society, for example, *St Jerome,* Venice, Palazzo Ducale. There are, however, no dancing girls in medieval depictions of St Jerome, and even later they rarely appear.

Few are the writers who wrote positively on women. . . . However, another of the early Church Fathers, St Augustine (354-430), in his *The Good of Marriage,* defended women against the extreme opinions held by St Jerome. To him neither the human body nor marriage was all bad, and he saw fidelity as an aid to marriage, which he considered a sacrament. Nevertheless, in his opinion too, woman was the 'weaker' sex, physically subjected to man, although he also says 'In her mind and in her rational intelligence she has a nature the equal of man's.'[4] The source of this view on woman's subjection is Genesis 3:16, where God tells Eve: 'And you shall be subject to your husband, and he shall rule over you.' Although this was said after the Fall, St Augustine commented that, even before her sin, woman had been made to be ruled by her husband and to be submissive and obedient to him.[5] What St Augustine feared most was the force and uncontrollability of sexual arousal, which began with the Fall. Also, he thought that Adam took the apple offered by Eve in order not to make her unhappy, fearing that she might waste away if he refused it, and would die; he therefore accepted it because of his affection for her.[6] St Augustine had met another of the Church Fathers, the Bishop of Milan, St Ambrose (339-97), who had baptised him after his conversion. St Ambrose, too, was much concerned with the nature of women and wrote treatises such as *On Widows* and *On Virgins,* expressing vehement anti-matrimonial opinions. He equated the spiritual with Adam, i.e. the male, and sensibility with Eve, i.e. the female.

All the early Bible commentators, missionaries and Church Fathers had in common a life of single-minded dedication to asceticism which only encouraged their wariness of women. Their ideas of sexuality must have been influenced by their lives in isolation; in their preoccupation with matters spiritual, divorced from the concerns of ordinary people, women would have been a disruptive force. St Augustine was probably influenced by erotic and spiritual experiences, for he had a common-law wife for many years before sending her away after his conversion to Christianity. Much of what these founders of the Church said overlapped, and even if not all of them were anti-matrimonial, they all advocated virginity as the highest goal, and women were most decidedly the 'weaker' sex and temptresses. To Isidore of Seville (d. 636), woman was all body ruled by sexual desires, close to nature and with an undisciplined mind. The only use for women that he could see was procreation.[7] The traditional arguments focusing on woman as Eve were greatly boosted by Pope Gregory VII (1073-85) in his insistence on closer controls on the daily lives of secular priests and a tightening of the rule of celibacy. Women, once more, were seen as disruptive, as a source of disorder, able to lead men astray. Marriage from the turn of the twelfth century was to be monogamous, indissoluble and a sacrament of the Church, and it was from this time onwards that the criticism of women as Eve became ever stronger. In the thirteenth century preachers and moralists, in particular the great theologian Thomas Aquinas (1225-74), based their ideas on Aristotle, whose writings were considered

Illustration depicting Adam and Eve in the Garden of Eden.

'scientific' and therefore authoritative. Here, they had their picture of woman confirmed as being weak, irrational, emotional, governed by passion and always receptive to evil influences. Women were seen as imperfect men with an excess of humidity in their bodies which made them damp and thus limp and unsteady, always changing like the moon. That was why women had to be watched over by men, protected, guarded, led, as the power of rational thinking was by nature stronger in men. In his *Summa Theologiae,* Aquinas asks whether woman should have been created in the first place. He answers this in the affirmative because of Genesis 2:18: 'It is not good for man to be alone; let us make him a help that is like himself.' Although he accepts the reason given in the Bible, he reduces woman's help to one possibility: 'it was absolutely necessary to make woman, for the reason Scripture mentions, as a help for man; not indeed to help him in any other work, as some have maintained, because where most work is concerned man can get help more conveniently from another man than from a woman; but to help him in the work of procreation'.[8] Thomas Aquinas also taught that a married woman could be virtuous as long as she had sexual relationships with her husband for the sole purpose of procreation and kept her mind chaste. He wrote that 'Chastity finds its home in the soul, though its nature lies in the body.'[9]

From these discussions of women in the eleventh, twelfth and thirteenth centuries, Farmer deduces that their position declined, and misogynistic ideas became more vehement.[10] This interlocking of ideas and reality is debatable,[11] but it can be seen that in this period the Virgin Mary became more and more revered and idealised, while woman remained forever Eve, thus widening the gulf between good and bad. The two polarities, of Mary the Virgin and Eve, of good and evil, came to dominate medieval life and thought in images of Life and Death, of the Virtues and Vices, of Body and Soul, of the Fountain of Life and the Fountain of Love, and of the good and bad women from the Old and New Testaments. In writings and visual images, much is made of the antithesis between the Virgin and Eve. The hymn 'Ave Maria Stella' turns 'Eva' into 'Ave', with which the Archangel Gabriel greeted Mary, the new Eve at the Annunciation. St Jerome created the formula: 'Death through Eve, life through Mary';[12] and St Augustine too said: 'through woman, death; through woman life'.[13]

In the Hours of Catherine of Cleves,[14] *c.* 1450, the two opposites Eve and the Virgin with Child are placed on either side of the Tree of Knowledge; they thus represent the two mothers of humanity, Eve and the 'new Eve'. The serpent coiled around the tree hands the fruit to Eve, naked apart from her leaf, while the Virgin and Child are well covered. An angel above the tree holds a scroll with the inscription: 'Eve authoress of sin, Mary authoress of merit'. The idea of the Virgin as Life, and Eve as Death, is illustrated in a miniature of the Missal of the Archbishop of Salzburg,[15] *c.* 1481, for the title-page of the Feast of Corpus Christi. Again, the Virgin clothed and Eve naked stand on either side of the fruit tree, which on the Virgin's side has Christ on the Cross among the foliage, signifying redemption and life, while the skull of Death looks forth on Eve's side. The Virgin crowned as the Queen of Heaven plucks life-giving fruits like hosts to nourish the faithful kneeling at her feet and protected by an angel, while Eve receives the apple from the snake and hands it to her kneeling flock overshadowed by the figure of Death. Adam sits at the foot of the tree. Mary can also be identified with Ecclesia (the Church) and Eve with the Synagogue, and in art they stand on either side of the crucifix, Ecclesia with a banner of triumph, Synagogue with her staff broken. In an illustrated Bible of *c.* 1420, the so-called Zittau Bible,[16] Mary and Eve are pictured on the right and left, respectively, of the Living Cross together with Ecclesia and Synagogue; Mary hands out the true bread to members of the Church, while Eve distributes death's-head fruits to people in Jews' hats.

The close association of death with Eve the temptress becomes quite explicit in a fresco in St Nicholas in Klerant (South Tyrol), *c.* 1475.[17] Here Eve is dressed in a very short yellow shift, tied at the shoulders and buttoned on the hip, and exposing her breasts, thus identifying herself as a prostitute. She reaches for the apple in the tree but what she holds in her hand is a skull. The serpent's head is that of a woman, often thus represented in art because the tempter (devil-serpent) in that manner identifies with Eve; they are mirror-images of each other. In a woodcut by Lucas Cranach, both Eve and the serpent have the same face so that the tempter and the tempted become interchangeable. Thus, in order to gain power over Eve, the devil appeared in her own mirror-image. Eve, therefore, tempted into sin and disobedience, turns temptress herself for the whole of the human race. The image of Death and Temptation has its climax in a painting of Adam and Eve by Hans Baldung Grien from the beginning of the sixteenth century, where the carnality of Eve and her power for evil and death are explored.[18] In this work, as in many of Baldung Grien's works, Eve or woman, always the temptress and seducer, becomes the victim of Death herself. On view in all her sensuality, she furtively hides the apple in her right hand behind her back and glances suggestively towards the serpent, whose coiling tail she touches daintily. But her soft, white flesh is gripped tightly by Death, who doubles as Adam and who plucks an apple, tempted by sexual desire for Eve the temptress. The flesh on his skeletal frame is rotting, hanging off the bones, and blotches of blood spread across his face and skull. While Eve touches the serpent's tail and Death/Adam grabs Eve by the wrist, the serpent sinks its teeth into Death's/Adam's wrist. Thus, they are all interlocked in their doom, Death being the victor. However, what stands out most is the figure of Eve as an object of sexual desire, and this once more makes Eve, representative of all women, responsible for death. Cornelius Agrippa, who wrote on witchcraft and the magic arts with which Baldung Grien was much concerned in his art, stated that it was the excitement that Eve purposefully aroused in Adam, seducing his body and ego with carnal desire, that was the true cause of original sin and the Fall, and not knowledge in general.[19]

The stark contrast between good and evil also found expression in the theme of the Wise and Foolish Virgins (Matthew 25:1-13). The five wise virgins are humble and patient, and their faith in the coming of Christ is unwavering as the light in their lamps is kept burning, while the five foolish virgins extinguish their lamps and enjoy the pleasures of the world. Matthew linked the theme with the Last Judgement, and in medieval art it is often found on and around church doorways, where Last Judgements are usually placed. In thirteenth-century Germany, the Wise and Foolish Virgins were sculpted life-size, most frequently on the Portal of the Virgin (e.g. Magdeburg Cathedral). Usually, they stand on either side of the portal, the wise ones holding their lit lamps aloft, the foolish ones having turned theirs downwards, thus spilling the oil. Generally, the foolish virgins are more fashionably dressed, and their clothes accentuate the shapes of their bodies. In some of the Gothic churches, like Basle and Freiburg Minsters, the foolish virgins are deceived by the beautiful young seducer Satan, who smiles at them and offers them an apple; they fail to notice the evil in him, for it is hidden from their view, in the shape of crawling snakes and toads on his back; in the meantime, the wise virgins walk towards their bridegroom, Christ. Matthew does not mention the seducer, but the close connection with the Last Judgement must have been instrumental in creating this parallel to Satan at the Fall. Ultimate bliss is found in the Paradise Garden to which the wise virgins are welcomed by their bridegroom, and to which all blessed virgins and the Virgin herself withdraw. The Song of Songs (Song of Solomon) is the source for the imagery of the *hortus conclusus,* the enclosed garden, with beautiful flowers and fresh water, in which the Virgin and Child often sit in the company of saints. The *hortus conclusus,* shut off from the outside, earthly world, and surrounded by a wall or trellis of flowers, is symbolic of virginity; all the plants and the fountain of water within the garden refer to the Virgin's purity, her enclosed womb. Well-known flowers associated with the Virgin are the lily and the rose without thorns. In a small, intimate painting of the Paradise Garden, *c.* 1420, from the Rhineland,[20] the Virgin is seated in a flower-strewn enclosed garden, surrounded by saints who repose among the flowers, pick fruit or play with the Child. An engraving attributed to the Master of the Berlin Passion from the Lower Rhine area,[21] 1460s, shows the Virgin and Child with eight female saints in the enclosed garden. The Virgin is making a wreath of roses, taken from a basket held by St Dorothy; and the Child, who has left her lap, is putting a ring on St Catherine's finger. All the saints are identified by their symbols and the angels sing: 'Gloria in excelsis deo et in terra pax hominibus bone volut' (Glory to God in the highest and peace on earth to men of good will). In contrast to the spiritual peace in the gardens of the Virgin, and yet very similar in composition and setting, are Gardens of Love, where the carnal passions rule in contrast to spiritual love, to be discussed later in connection with the evil woman.

Another theme of opposites popular in the late Middle Ages, and particularly in the early Renaissance, was that of famous good and bad women from Scripture and classical antiquity, held up as examples of great heroism or treacherous deeds. Just as the Old Testament preceded the New Testament, so these pagan women were seen as typological parallels to Christian women, capable of good and evil. Examples of good women from the Bible are Judith, Jael, Suzanna, Ruth, Abigail and Esther; examples of bad biblical women are Salome, Delilah, Bathsheba, the daughters of Lot, the wife of Potiphar, and the prostitutes who persuaded Solomon to worship idols. Artists like the Netherlandish Lucas van Leyden and Maerten van Heemskerck did series of printed illustrations, *c.* 1517 and *c.* 1563 respectively.

Both Judith and Jael killed adversaries of the Israelites, i.e. Holofernes and Sisera, and by so doing they saved their people. They acted as instruments of God, and were considered heroic, the more so being women. Taking the example of Judith, the most popular in the arts, she entered Holofernes' camp[22] by seducing him, pretending to come and sleep with him, but instead she got him drunk and cut off his head. The moment most frequently portrayed in the visual arts is that of Judith handing Holofernes' head to her servant girl. This is what happens in an engraving by Israhel van Meckenem, *c.* 1500, where the servant girl holds open a bag to receive the head, and Judith looks the other way; her sword lies by Holofernes' bed and a battle scene is raging round about. Because Judith achieved her aim through trickery, it might seem inappropriate for her to be classed as a 'good' woman; however, as she acted for the good of God's chosen people, she was praised for her deed and seen as a good example. Paintings and prints of this theme became very popular in the workshop of Lucas Cranach the Elder during the Reformation period, because the reformers saw a parallel between Judith's triumph over the enemies of Israel and their own victory, i.e. of the true, reformed Church over the Catholic Church. Lucas Cranach the Elder also depicted the story on two pendant panels: on the left, Judith at the banquet with Holofernes in the camp, and on the right, cutting off his head and putting it into the bag held by the servant girl.[23]

It is 'women's wiles' which characterise the bad women from Scripture, the best-known being Delilah and Salome. Delilah cut off Samson's hair, the seat of his virility and strength, allowing him to be caught by the Philistines. In art, Samson is depicted sleeping in Delilah's lap while she cuts off his hair, often with enormous shears. Salome delighted King Herod with her dancing, and was rewarded with the head of John the Baptist which she had desired. The scene of Salome receiving the head on a platter from the executioner is most frequently represented. Sometimes the different moments of the narrative are combined in one panel, e.g. in *The Beheading of John the Baptist*[24] by the fifteenth-century Netherlandish artists Rogier van der Weyden and Hans Memling, the scenes of the Dance of Salome and the Presentation of the Head of John the Baptist to Herodias (Salome's mother) are in miniature in the background to the main scene of the Beheading of John the Baptist.

With the advent of the Renaissance came a new attitude to the human body and nudity. Throughout the Middle Ages the emphasis on chastity had generated an obsessive fear of the nude, which was equated with shameful nakedness and, therefore, sin. Some of the good women from the Old Testament and antiquity, however, called for representations in the nude, and in the Renaissance artists took advantage of this; also, a renewed interest in the tradition of classical antiquity may have added to the popularity of the theme. North of the Alps, Albrecht Dürer was the first artist who travelled to Italy (1494-5 and 1505-7), who studied theoretical books on proportions and perspective, and who was able to come to grips with the human body. But even he did not always use real-life models, but turned to classical models, his best-known and most influential example being the 1504 engraving *Adam and Eve,* where Adam is modelled on the Apollo Belvedere and Eve on Venus. From the point of view of the meaning of nudity, it is interesting to note that Dürer had originally planned an illustration of Apollo and Diana, as the preliminary drawings show; however, as nudity was associated with sin, a depiction of the Fall was probably deemed more appropriate to the Northern spirit. The artists who, through the influence of Dürer, made the nude one of their main concerns were Lucas van Leyden and Jan Gossaert in the Netherlands, and Lucas Cranach and Hans Baldung Grien in Germany. Classical and mythological themes now became part of the artists' repertoire. Of the good women, Lucretia killing herself with a dagger could be portrayed full-length, half-length, slitting her dress with the dagger, in the nude or in a piece of flimsy drapery. According to Roman legend, she was the wife of Lucius Tarquinius Collatinus who, having been raped by her cousin Sextus Tarquinius, summoned her father and husband to take revenge, stating that, although without sin, she felt that punishment was inevitable, and thus she killed herself with a dagger. Thereupon, not only the culprit but his whole house and the Tarquinians were wiped out and a republic declared in 508 B.C. This illustrates to what extent a woman's honour was essential to the existence of her extended family, and must be guarded at all costs; in this case, Lucretia's suicide was made into an example of the perfect wife, where generally the Church regarded it as a deadly sin. Lucas Cranach and his workshop created many versions of Lucretia, usually standing in the nude, wearing a headdress and a piece of heavy jewellery, her body lithe and of the same erotic type used for other classical beauties such as the Three Graces. In Jan van Scorel's painting[25] Lucretia, nude but for a transparent piece of drapery, looks sideways to the right, while her body is twisted towards the spectator and both her arms are stretched towards the left, to hold the sword that pierces her breast. The Master of the Holy Blood[26] portrays Lucretia in frontal position, three-quarter-length, her dress and bodice open to expose her breast, into which she has plunged her sword; her mouth and eyes are half open, with the glazed look of a pitiful death.

Suzanna in Her Bath is another Old Testament theme, concerning an innocent woman who was wrongfully accused of having had an affair with a young man by two lecherous old men whom she had rebuffed when they surprised her in her bath. Although nudity would be expected for this theme, Suzanna is often well covered up, in particular in Albrecht Altdorfer's example of 1526, although he is one of the young Renaissance artists.[27] She is sitting in a lush garden by a pool of water, her dress pulled up to her knees, and an attendant girl washes her feet in a basin of water, while another combs her long tresses. However, any part of a woman's bare legs or long hair were considered a source of dangerous temptation, as the Knight of La Tour-Landry taught his daughters in his book of advice named after him: a woman should never comb her hair before a man; and even when alone she should not do so for too long, or the devil's bottom might appear in her mirror, as illustrated in a woodcut in the 1493 edition of this book. As a result of this appearance, the book tells, the woman nearly lost her senses and suffered from shock for a long time afterwards.

As for the bad women of antiquity, their seductive nudity best expressed their women's wiles. Lot and His Daughters (Genesis 19) was a good example. Lot's wife, typical of women's nature, had disobeyed God's command, looking back at the burning city they had fled, and turned into a pillar of salt as punishment. As a result of this, Lot and his daughters were the only people to have escaped from Sodom and Gomorrah, and Lot's family line was threatened with extinction. To ensure continuation, the daughters needed to sleep with their father, which they did after plying him with wine, thus diminishing his responsibility. Once more the women were the temptresses, although in the cause of procreation. In many paintings, the scene of one of the daughters sleeping with Lot, while the other is seen handling the wine, takes place in full clothing; in 1537, however, Albrecht Altdorfer shows them as lascivious nudes,[28] the soft skin of the daughter reclining on her father's body contrasting with his darker, leathery skin. The bodies are offset by the lurid background colours of a vibrant green backcloth and the burning red landscape.

Even in mythological themes, like Paris and the Three Graces, where one would think the female nude could not be avoided, some German artists cover the Graces in dresses and exotic headdresses, as in a woodcut in the style of Lucas Cranach the Elder, *c.* 1508.[29] If the Graces were depicted in the nude in the fifteenth century, an inability to deal with the nude in general, and female beauty in particular, became especially apparent. In an engraving by the Master of the Banderolles, *c.* 1470,[30] the three spindly and stiff Graces lack all grace; Paris, in armour, lies at the foot of a fountain and is being roused by Hermes in a long coat. Venus is crowned, and the city in the background across the sea is identified as 'Troja magna'. All the figures have speech scrolls, giving the anonymous Master his name. Lucas Cranach the Elder himself took up mythological themes at the beginning of the sixteenth century, resulting in a large number of paintings of Paris and the Three Graces. The female bodies are serpentine and contorted; they stand on tiptoes, and are seen from different angles; one often looks back at the viewer with alluring eyes, her head twisted at 180 degrees. They all represent the embodiment of sensuous desire, accentuated by a transparent veil that floats over their bodies. As is the norm in German art, Paris is a knight in armour and asleep. He needs wakening by Mercury and often looks at the Graces with a dazed expression. The three Graces are thus a dream vision, and Paris is not fully responsible for giving in to their temptations and for handing the apple to Venus. So again, even with the Renaissance in full swing, there is great timidity in the North about treating themes of love and passion, for the medieval concern with morals remains.

As for the human body, only Dürer and Baldung Grien let it speak, and with very different results: Albrecht Dürer's nudes are harmonious, well proportioned, logically constructed, based on classical sculpture; Hans Baldung Grien transformed them into expressions of human passions, as seen in his paintings of Adam and Eve. But even in the Renaissance, virtue remained associated with a female figure clothed and vice with nudity, as, for example, in Dürer's engraving of *Hercules at the Crossroads,* where the peacefully resting nude woman in the lap of a satyr is surprised by the violent attack by Hercules and clothed Virtue.[31] However, when both good and evil women were dressed, their dresses showed little difference in the late Middle Ages and early Renaissance; especially in works by Lucas Cranach, good and evil women often look very much the same, sometimes differentiated only by their symbols, e.g. Judith and Salome. Albrecht Dürer, in a pen-and-ink drawing of a *Venetian Woman,* 1495, has his subject wear the same low-cut dress as he was later to use for the exotic dress of the *Babylonian Whore* in his woodcut of the *Apocalypse,* 1498, but also for a drawing of *c.* 1500 of *St Catherine.*[32] In the case of the sixteenth-century Netherlandish artist Jan Gossaert, the exaggerated bulging flesh of his mythological nudes is the same as in his portrayals of the Virgin, except that the Virgin is clothed and seems to burst out of her clothes. The female nude had become rounded and weighty by the 1520s and 1530s in the North, but the relationship between flesh and spirit remained problematic, as the medieval tension between content and style remained, e.g. in the late engravings of the *Power of Women* by Lucas van Leyden, where his treatment of erotic nude bodies is aided by gestures and expressions that highlight their evil, sinful nature. The question that remained for Renaissance artists was whether female flesh could be depicted as beautiful, for attractiveness was immediately equated with unchastity; there was always the danger of the triumph of physical beauty over the spirit, of man being tempted into the pleasures of carnal love.

Thus, the visual image of women did not change basically during this period because the mental picture of women in men's minds remained the same. The sharp division between good and bad women stayed in place, and misogynistic depictions proliferated towards the end of the fifteenth and at the beginning of the sixteenth century, increased by the availability of engravings and, in particular, cheap woodcuts. However, the women caricatured in prints were among the weaker, poorer members of society, such as peasants, that became the butt of ribald humour and moralising invective. Choir-stalls are major repositories of satire on women, and in England every large set of choir-stalls has a misericord depicting a woman beating a man, or behaving badly in other ways. Even the universal tool of women in the Middle Ages, the distaff, could symbolise either good or evil, depending on whose hand it was in. In a woodcut by Hans Burgkmair of 1517,[33] *St Elizabeth of Hungary*, crowned and haloed, sits in the midst and above other women and nuns and teaches them to spin. This illustrates the 'spiritual spinner', as in a sermon preached by Geiler von Kaysersberg (Alsace) where cloistered women are addressed and advice is given on spiritual life. In contrast, the ordinary housewife is depicted using her distaff as a weapon with which to beat a man, as in prints by Israhel van Meckenem or on misericords. . . . [T]he spirit of misogyny is strongest in the marginal arts, where woman does not comply with the norms of society created by man, disregards them, rebels and turns the world upside-down.

To sum up, Sebastian Brant best illustrates the opinions of this age in transition in his *Ship of Fools*. There the woodcut of *Hercules at the Crossroads* shows Virtue and Voluptuousness at the top of two mountains: Virtue on the right as an old woman with distaff, well covered up; Voluptuousness in the nude, but for a headdress, pattens and a ribbon of drapery.[34] Hercules, in armour, lies stretched out at the bottom of the mountains, having a vision of these choices before him; the road to Virtue is stony and thistles grow on top, while roses frame Voluptuousness. However, on closer inspection, skeleton Death beckons from behind Voluptuousness, and fire and brimstone burst out of the sky above her, while stars light up the sky above Virtue.

Notes

1. St Anthony, born in Upper Eygpt, *c.* 251-356; founder of monasticism.
2. Lisbon, Museo Antiga.
3. Letter 22: Blamires, 1992, pp. 74-6.
4. *Confessions,* XIII.32: Blamires, 1992, p. 78.
5. *De Genesi ad Litteram,* XI.37: Blamires, 1992, p. 79.
6. *Confessions,* XI.42: Blamires, 1992, p. 81.
7. *Etymologies,* XI: Klapisch-Zuber, C., 1992, p. 43.
8. In his *Summa Theologiae,* Ia, q. 92, a. 1: Blamires, 1992, p. 92.
9. *Summa Theologiae,* II-II, q. 151, a. 1,1: Klapisch-Zuber, 1992, p. 80.
10. Farmer, 1986, pp. 520-1.
11. Rigby, 1995, p. 269.
12. Jerome, PL 22, col. 408: Klapisch-Zuber, 1992, p. 23.
13. PL 38, col. 1108: Klapisch-Zuber, 1992, p. 23.
14. New York, Pierpont Morgan Library, Ms. M. 917, p. 139.
15. Munich, Bayrische Staatsbibliothek, Cod. lat. 15710, fol. 60v. The miniature is by Berthold Furtmeyer.
16. Wroclaw, Cod. M 1006.
17. Vavra, 1986, pp. 283-99, fig. 15.
18. Ottawa, National Gallery.
19. Hieatt, 1983, pp. 298, 299.
20. Frankfurt/Main, Städelsches Institut.
21. Name given by Max Lehrs. The beginning of his activity is thought to be the beginninng of the 1450s. Geisberg thinks that he comes from the Arnhem region, close to Westphalia. His stylistic sources are in Netherlandish art, e. g. Rogier van der Weyden.
22. Holofernes was one of Nebuchadnezzar's generals.
23. Gotha, Schlossmuseum, 1531.
24. In Berlin, Gemäldegalerie, Staatliche Museen Preussischer Kulturbesitz, Berlin-Dahlem, and Bruges, St John's Hospital (Memling Museum).
25. Jan van Sorel (1495-1562), Netherlandish; Berlin, Gemäldegalerie, Staatliche Museen, Preussischer Kulturbesitz.
26. From Bruges, early sixteenth century; Budapest, Szépmüvészeti Museum.
27. German, from Regensburg, *c.* 1480-1538; painting in Munich, Alte Pinakothek.
28. Vienna, Kunsthistorisches Institut.
29. Koepplin, D. and Falk, T. (eds), 1974, vol. I, fig. 116.
30. Koepplin, D. and Falk, T. (eds), 1974, vol. II, fig. 311.
31. The story is related by Xenophon (Strauss, 1972, p. 48) about the young Hercules deciding between Virtue and Pleasure.
32. *Venetian Woman* (lightly coloured) in Vienna, Albertina; *St Catherine* in Berlin, Staatliche Museen, Preussischer Kulturbesitz, Kupferstichkabinett.
33. Stuttgart, Würtembergische Landesbibliothek, Theol. fol. 669.
34. Latin edition, Basle, 1497.

Bibliography

Blamires, A., ed. (1992), *Woman Defamed and Woman Defended: An Anthology of Medieval Texts,* Oxford.

Farmer, S. (1986), 'Persuasive Voices: Clerical Images of Medieval Wives', *Speculum,* 61, pp. 517-43.

Hieatt (1983), 'Hans Baldung Griens Ottowa *Eve* and its Context', Art Bulletin 65, pp. 290-304.

Klapisch-Zuber, C., ed. (1992), *A History of Women in the West, vol. II: Silences of the Middle Ages,* Cambridge, Mass. and London.

Strauss, W., ed. (1972), *The Complete Engravings, Etchings and Drypoints of Albrecht Dürer,* 2 vols, New York.

Vavra, E. (1986), 'Ueberlegungen zum "Bild der Frau" in der mittelalterlichen Ikonographie', in *Frau und Spätmittelalterlicher Alltag,* Vienna, pp. 283-99.

CORINNE SAUNDERS (ESSAY DATE 2001)

SOURCE: Saunders, Corinne. "Introduction: The Contemporary and the Contemporaneous." In *Rape and Ravishment in the Literature of Medieval England,* pp. 1-31. Cambridge: D. S. Brewer, 2001.

In the following excerpt, Saunders details medieval perceptions of gender and the female body as they relate to the subject of rape.

Differences between medieval and contemporary perspectives on rape are . . . rooted in the differences between past and present notions of gender and sexuality. The ideas current in the medieval period were themselves fluid, varying between discourses and often reflecting doubts and uncertainties, but the interplay between ideas and their various developments created a dialogue whose values and perspectives contrast quite dramatically with those of the modern period. Not only does this dialogue provide an essential context for medieval writing on rape and ravishment, but also, in the discourses of natural philosophy and medicine, rape itself is a particularly resonant topic in discussions of differences between male and female, masculinity and femininity, and the relations of these to sexual behaviour.

Judith Butler has argued that individuals may be seen as 'doing' gender: she expands Foucault's ideas regarding the construction of sexual behaviours to suggest that political and cultural intersections produce gender.[1] Theresa de Lauretis employs the phrase 'the technology of gender' to convey the notion of 'gender as the product and the process of a number of social technologies, of techno-social or bio-medical apparati'; the construction of gender occurs precisely in its representation.[2] Gender roles are performative, a set of actions that create the appearance of gender stereotypes:

> . . . the effect of gender is produced through the stylization of the body and, hence, must be understood as the mundane way in which bodily gestures, movements, and styles of various kinds constitute the illusion of an abiding gendered self.[3]

Butler suggests further that the 'regulatory norms of "sex" work in a performative fashion to constitute the materiality of bodies.'[4] She looks back, for example, to Platonic and Aristotelian notions of matter as feminine, and thus of femininity as containing and receptive rather than creative. Such ideas, she posits, underlie our understanding of the very nature of the female body, in that they present its biological and sexual functions in terms of receptivity. A different challenge to essentialism is offered by psychoanalytical critics such as Juliet Mitchell, who reads Freudian theories as constructivist, demonstrating how the patriarchal 'law of the father' operates 'within the life of the individual boy and girl.'[5] Nancy Chodorow and Dorothy Dinnerstein build on the theories of, in particular, Melanie Klein regarding early infancy, to argue that 'the contemporary reproduction of mothering occurs through social structurally induced psychological processes', through 'an unconscious collusion between women and men'.[6] Such theories of gender are liberating in their move away from essentialism such as that of Julia Kristeva or Luce Irigaray, who base their theories on a definition of gender difference rooted in biological determinism. Kristeva indeed relies on Platonic notions of femininity, to the extent that she draws her idea of the *chora,* the fluid female state prior to entrance into the male Symbolic order, from the *Timaeus.*[7] Butler employs a more historical, incremental mode of analysis to point to the changing and performative nature of gender, and to the way that notions of gender form part of Western ideology rather than transcending it.[8]

Butler's terms elucidate the constructed nature of past as well as present notions of gender. In addition, the difference between medieval and modern attitudes to gender offers irrefutable proof of Butler's argument that gender is constructed and performative: whereas gender is today a rather fluid notion that raises questions of nature and nurture, of the complicated network of genetic and social influences that make an individual masculine or feminine, in the Middle Ages the idea of gender as socially constructed would have been incomprehensible despite the existence of differing strands of thought. While there was 'no coherent set of concepts' of gender in the Middle Ages and theories differed widely, certain fundamental philosophical and moral ideas shaped notions of gender.[9] Crucial to all understandings of gender and sexuality was the assumption that there was a fundamental difference between women and men, which extended far beyond that of biology. Different discourses built on this assumption in varying but related ways: natural philosophy and medical treatises tended to address the practical aspects of gender and sexuality, while the Church's focus was on their moral and spiritual significance. These strands of thought formed a complex web of ideas and assumptions; it is only possible here to summarise some of the most influential of these, in order to place the issue of rape in the broader context of past understandings of the human body and its qualities, and of sex difference. Explorations of rape in the various literatures of the medieval period, as we shall see, allowed for engagement with a range of the formative assumptions regarding femininity, masculinity and sexuality.

Aristotle, whose works were widely read after the thirteenth century, provided an influential view of gender, based on the natural good of sex differentiation:

> . . . Aristotelians emphasized the benefits of sexual division of functions and the purpose of those functions, namely, the perpetuation of natural kinds. The final cause of sexual differentiation is reproduction, and the final cause of reproduction is the achievement by the species of what cannot be accomplished by its individuals—immortality.[10]

The Platonic notion discussed by Butler, of primordial matter (*hyle*) as feminine and receptacle-like, was also familiar among, for example, natural philosophers, although Plato's discussion of the differentiation of the sexes in the final section of *Timaeus* was not known. Most influential of all, of course, was the authority of the Bible, which provided an accessible starting-point for questioning the origins of the world, of man, and hence of gender and sexuality. Genesis, the book of beginnings, offered a simple yet enormously significant statement regarding gender: 'Male and female created he them' (Genesis 1:27). The implication was that gender difference was absolute: it did not result from the Fall, but was 'a natural feature of the original human condition'.[11] Christian doctrine corresponded with Aristotle's argument that the purpose of the division of the sexes was the propagation of the species, and it was commonly held by the moral philosophers and theologians that even in Eden some form of sexual intercourse, though one free of the taint of lust, would eventually have occurred.

Biological difference between the sexes, then, was divinely ordained, and in the very act of creation of the two sexes was rooted the essential difference between male and female natures. For according to the second account of the Creation, Genesis 2:21-23, whereas Adam was created when God breathed life into the dust of the ground, Eve was formed from Adam's rib and was identified from the start as his possession, 'this is now bone of my bones, and flesh of my flesh: she shall be called Woman, because she was taken out of Man' (2:23). The woman's origin in human matter and her child-bearing role associated her absolutely with the body, while the man was associated with the rational, the spirit and the soul. In addition, the strength and generative role of the man placed him as biologically superior, and gave him the right of domination. Joan Cadden, in her comprehensive study of the construction of medieval notions of gender and sex difference, traces the use of the terms 'masculinity' and 'femininity', with the sense of 'properties of being male or female', to Latin writers of the late eleventh century.[12] Thinkers such as Hildegard of Bingen, Thomas Aquinas and William of Conches took the notions of masculinity and femininity in different directions. Hildegard's medical treatise, for example, links differentiating physical characteristics with the Creation: because of the man's association with the earth, he is hairier, stronger, more mobile than the woman, who, because she is formed from man, is his inverse and is subject to him.[13]

Whereas in scientific and medical thought the differentiation of the sexes was considered in terms of physical function and effect, theologians tended to focus more on the role played by gender difference in and after the Fall. The obvious disparity in size and strength of the sexes was borne out on a symbolic level by the primary association of the woman with the first sin, 'she took of the fruit thereof, and did eat, and gave also unto her husband with her; and he did eat' (Genesis 3:6). Although there was no doubt of the mutual responsibility of man and woman in this act of disobedience and in the subsequent act of lust, the woman's action gave to her sex both the responsibility for temptation of the man and a reputation for weakness. These traits could easily be associated with the fact that the woman had not been created directly by God but through man, and thus had been singled out as the frailer vessel by Satan, 'Unde et mulierem tentavit, in qua minus quam in viro rationem vigere novit', 'Thus he tempted the woman, in whom he knew reason to flourish less than in the man.'[14] Eve was consequently associated with a series of sins: gluttony, vainglory, avarice. The sin of lust was envisaged as not the cause but the result of the Fall: lust was sexual desire in its fallen state, an effect of the loss of innocence. The original sin itself was identified by Augustine as concupiscence, 'the basic disorder in the human affective dimensions resulting from the refusal to obey the dictates of right reason'; this definition was incorporated into later theological views of original sin as the 'loss of original justice' or of 'ordered harmony'.[15] As a result of Adam and Eve's choice of disorder, the human race came to be predisposed to concupiscence, an effect most physically evident in male sexual desire, in the involuntary movement of the male genitals.[16] One of the most powerful images of the Middle Ages must be that of Origen's response to the involuntary nature of desire in the fallen world, his self-castration. As the title of Payer's study, *The Bridling of Desire,* suggests, the view that fallen human nature was generally predisposed to disorder and required regulation was a pervasive one, and the images of broken reins, corruption and staining recurred in descriptions of human nature. Although such images were not gender-specific, the fact that the woman had sinned first, and then lured the man towards concupiscence and the experience of sexual desire, rendered her a powerful emblem of sexual temptation. Saint Jerome notably condemns the natural provocativeness of women; he writes, for example, in *Adversus Jovinianum* of the woman's great or insatiable capacity for lust, 'uxoris . . . ardentissimam gulam fortuita libido restinguat', 'the casual lust of a woman extinguishes the fiercest appetite.'[17] Saint Paul's epistles repeatedly warn against women as frail, tempting, and inferior, the 'second sex'.

Views of femininity were most of all defined by the notion of the bodiliness of women, the consequence of their origin in the physical matter of Adam's rib. This notion led to a set of very common generalisations: women were more physical, sexual and emotional than men, governed not by rationality but by nature, by instinct rather than intellect; their potential threat to men was such that their temptations needed to be kept strictly under control: they were 'luxurieuses, lubriques', 'lecherous and lustful'.[18] While such assumptions are clearly misogynistic from a modern perspective, it is notable that they in fact correspond to a number of residual gender stereotypes: women tease men sexually; women invite seduction; women mean yes even when they say no; men are the victims of feminine wiles.

These doctrinally rooted notions of the female nature were supported by medical theories. While Aristotle had argued for the good of sex differentiation, he had not implied equality of the sexes. According to his theory of conception, women provided only the material and not the spiritual elements; the female seed, though necessary, was of little formative importance and female children could be viewed as defective males.[19] Although medical opinion varied regarding the role of the female seed, the definition of women 'by deprivation' rather than difference to men was a powerful one, and created a pervasive set of binary gender oppositions that complemented the notion of female bodiliness.[20] That women were believed to lack rationality while possessing abundant sexuality meant that they were viewed not only as weaker, but also as predominantly physical, defined most by natural functions, and particularly by sexuality and motherhood. Virginia Woolf identifies just such gender stereotypes in *Three Guineas,* 'Nature, the priests said, in her infinite wisdom, had laid down the unalterable law that man is the creator. He enjoys; she only passively endures.'[21] The enduring nature of these gender associations is made evident in, for instance, Hélène Cixous's powerful formulation of the Male/Female opposition:

> Activity/passivity,
> Sun/Moon,
> Culture/Nature,
> Day/Night,
> Father/Mother,
> Head/heart,
> Intelligible/sensitive,
> Logos/Pathos.
>
> Form, convex, step, advance, seed, progress.
> Matter, concave, ground—which supports the step, receptacle.
>
> *Man*
> Woman[22]

Such a construction of the nature of women underlies the essentialist theories of Freud and Lacan, but also of some of their feminist interpreters; indeed, for Kristeva and Irigaray, for example, the distinctiveness of the woman's voice is directly related to notions of lack, absence, otherness, the body and the maternal. This view of women should, however, not be seen as unquestioned in the medieval period: Christine de Pisan, writing in the fifteenth century, is able very directly to state the falseness of such physiological theory. In the *Book of the City of Ladies,* translated into English by Brian Anslay and printed in 1521, she criticises the natural philosophy of the work known as the *Secreta Mulierum,* claiming that its ascription to Aristotle must be wrong; 'it is drawne all of lesynges*' (*lies; I, ix).[23] She addresses directly the view that the female body is weaker than the male, a poor imitation of masculine perfection:

> Madame I am remembred that amonge these other thynges he hath sayd when he hath spoken ynoughe of the impotence imperfeccyon & feblenes which is cause of mysshappynge of womans body in the wombe of the moder that nature is ashamed / when she sawe that she had fourmed suche a body as a thynge imperfyte.
>
> (I, ix)

For Christine, the virtue, excellence and nobility of women are proven beyond dispute by God's creation of Eve in His chosen manner, by the perfection of the soul which is in God's image, and most of all by the birth of Christ through woman ('he hathe goten more hyghe degre by oure lady Mary than he lost by Eue', I, ix). Her argument reveals the widespread existence of misogynist stereotypes but also the possibility of dispute and refutation.

The assumptions made in medieval medical thought and natural philosophy regarding the nature of women were in many ways focused in the situation of rape. Rape became a kind of touchstone for medical thinkers, an instance of female weakness as well as an example of the way that the reproductive processes worked. One widely circulated medical theory, based on the ideas of Galen, held that women as well as men emitted seed, and therefore that only when such an emission was made, through orgasm, could conception occur: 'Failure of either partner to achieve orgasm rendered intercourse nonprocreative. . . .'[24] While some theories of conception developed Aristotle's notions of gender to argue that there was only one, male, seed, the woman's pleasure seems generally to have been viewed as playing a significant role: Hildegard of Bingen, for example, argued that the woman, through desire, received the seed and drew the uterus around it or that the cold uterus rejoiced in receiving the warm seed.[25] In fact, there were strict guidelines in medical texts on how to enhance the woman's enjoyment, as well as how to avoid movements that might jeopardise the seed.[26] According to the Galenic theory of conception, for pregnancy to occur as a result of rape was impossible: pregnancy would therefore prove that the woman had taken pleasure in the sexual act, even if she had not consented.[27] William of Conches and Vincent of Beauvais both give the example of conception in rape as proof of female pleasure: William of Conches writes, 'Etsi raptis, in principio opus displiceat, in fine tamen, ex carnis fragilitate, placet' ('And if at the start the act of rape is displeasing, in the end as a result of the weakness of the flesh, it becomes pleasing');[28] this view seems to have been fairly common and is repeated, for example, in the English medical text known as *The Prose Salernitan Questions* (c.1200).[29] The notion of female susceptibility to pleasure would have offered a convenient explanation for any instances of folk experience of rape that seemed to militate against the theory that conception was impossible without desire. A counter-argument regarding conception was proposed by the Aristotelian thinkers, who emphasised the formative importance of the male seed: for them, the raped woman who conceived proved that the female seed was less important than the male.[30] The first argument seems, however, to have been the favoured one: as we shall see, it appears in legal discourse as well as in the writings of influential thinkers such as William of Conches and Vincent of Beauvais, whereas the Aristotelian counter-argument seems to be limited to a number of specialised medical and scholastic texts.[31] Indeed, the idea that pleasure was required for procreation endured until the scientific advances of the eighteenth century.[32] Christine de Pisan's writing suggests the familiarity of the assumption that women experience pleasure in rape:

> . . . yet it greueth me of that that many men say that women wolde be rauysshed / and that it dyspleaseth them not though they saye the contrary with theyr mouthe. But it were a grete thynge to make me to byleue it that it were agreable to theym.
>
> (II, xliiii)

Once again, Christine firmly refutes the misogyny of the natural philosophers and patristic thinkers, this time by instancing the noble and virtuous examples of women such as Lucretia. Her treatise makes very clear the weight of literary evidence against any assumption that women were universally viewed as enjoying rape, but illuminates too a powerful strand of patriarchal thought.

Medical theory and natural philosophy intersected with the ideas of theologians regarding gender, sexuality, and the frailty and bodiliness of women to form a powerful and insidious set of cultural assumptions; the example of rape could provide the means of focusing such assumptions. Yet as Christine's writing so clearly demonstrates, this perspective on rape represents only one strand within a much more complex and varied dialogue. Although medical and philosophical discourses were not entirely sympathetic to the raped woman, the issues raised by rape ensured that she retained an immense importance in various strands of cultural discourse—secular law, canon law, theology, moral philosophy. The notions of gender and sexuality discussed above inform all these discourses, yet despite and sometimes as a result of the often misogynistic attitudes of the medieval period, the act of rape maintains a profound personal and public significance and becomes a topos with its own complex cultural and literary history, interwoven with larger notions of ravishment. Writers such as Chaucer in fourteenth-century England and Christine de Pisan in fifteenth-century France react strongly against some commonly held ideas, while these ideas are explored repeatedly, less overtly but with memorable resonance, in literary genres as diverse as hagiography and romance. The topic of rape can initiate further exploration and questioning of the unsettling subjects of gender and sexuality, both directly and indirectly, and literary narratives of ravishment of various kinds can address the question of female will in ways more empowering to women than the recurring gender stereotypes and generalisations would suggest.

Notes

1. Judith Butler, *Gender Trouble: Feminism and the Subversion of Identity,* Thinking Gender Series (New York and London: Routledge, 1990), see especially 140-41. Butler's ideas are rooted in Michel Foucault, *The History of Sexuality,* 3 vols (I: *Introduction*; II: *The Use of Pleasure*; III: *The Care of the Self*), trans. Robert Hurley (French edn 1976, 1984; English trans. 1978, 1985, 1986; Harmondsworth: Penguin Books, 1990, 1992).
2. Theresa de Lauretis, 'The Technology of Gender', *Technologies of Gender: Essays on Theory, Film and Fiction,* Theories of Representation and Difference (Bloomington and Indianapolis: Indiana University Press, 1987), 1-30: 3.
3. Butler, *Gender Trouble,* 140.
4. Judith Butler, *Bodies that Matter: On the Discursive Limits of 'Sex'* (New York and London: Routledge, 1993), 2.
5. Juliet Mitchell, *Psychoanalysis and Feminism* (Harmondsworth: Penguin, 1974), xvi, and see especially 'The Holy Family', 359-416.
6. Nancy Chodorow, *The Reproduction of Mothering: Psychoanalysis and the Sociology of Gender* (Berkeley: University of California Press, 1978), 7; Vivien Bar, Introduction to Dorothy Dinnerstein, *The Rocking of the Cradle and the Ruling of the World* (1976; London: The Women's Press, 1987), viii. For Melanie Klein, see in particular 'Envy and Gratitude' (1957), in *Envy and Gratitude and Other Works, 1946-1963,* ed. Hanna Segal (1975; London: Virago, 1988), 176-235. See also Estela V. Welldon, *Mother, Madonna, Whore: The Idealization and Denigration of Motherhood* (New York and London: The Guilford Press, 1988).
7. Kristeva's association of woman with receptivity, the body and maternality is especially evident in her essay 'Stabat Mater', which is in part a lyrical essay on the birth of her son and in part a study of the Virgin Mary. See Julia Kristeva, 'Stabat Mater', trans. Arthur Goldhammer, in *The Female Body in Western Culture: Contemporary Perspectives,* ed. Susan Rubin Suleiman (Cambridge, Mass. and London: Harvard University Press, 1985-86), 99-118; the essay was first published as 'Héréthique de l'amour', *Tel Quel* 74 (1977), and reprinted as 'Stabat Mater' in Kristeva, *Histoires d'amour* (Paris: Denöel, 1983).
8. Butler's interest is primarily in the present, so that she does not, for example, take account of the dissemination of texts.
9. Joan Cadden, *Meanings of Sex Difference in the Middle Ages: Medicine, Science, and Culture,* Cambridge History of Medicine (Cambridge: Cambridge University Press, 1993), 2. See also Thomas Laqueur, *Making Sex: Body and Gender from the Greeks to Freud* (Cambridge, Mass. and London: Harvard University Press, 1990, pbk 1992).
10. Cadden, 189.
11. Pierre J. Payer, *The Bridling of Desire: Views of Sex in the Later Middle Ages* (Toronto, Buffalo, London: University of Toronto Press, 1993), 21.
12. Cadden, 8.
13. See also Aquinas's account of the different roles and duties of man and woman, *Summa Theologiae,* I.92, discussed by Cadden, 192-93.
14. Peter Lombard, *Sententiae in 4 Libris Distinctae,* Spicilegium Bonaventurianum 4 and 5, 3rd edn, 2 vols (Rome: Collegii S. Bonaventurae ad claras aquas, 1971 and 1981), vol. 1, II, xxi, cap. 1.2, p. 433; instanced by Payer, *The Bridling of Desire,* 42; for a lucid and scholarly discussion of temptation and the original sin of concupiscence, see Payer, *The Bridling of Desire,* 42-50.
15. Payer, *The Bridling of Desire,* 48.
16. Albertus Magnus, for example, discusses this effect, '. . . dicimus enim non voluntarie saepius moveri cor et genitalia . . .', *Liber de principiis motus processivi,* in *Opera Omnia* 12, ed. Bernard Geyer (Aschendorff: Monasterii Westfalorum, 1955), II, cap. 9, pp. 68-69; his argument is cited by Payer, *The Bridling of Desire,* 48.
17. Jerome, *Adversus Jovinianum,* in *Opera Omnia,* ed. J. P. Migne, *Patrologia Latina 23,* 1st series (Paris: Vrayet, 1845), cols. 213-338, Bk I, xxxvi, col. 260, no. 295c.
18. Georges Duby, *Le Chevalier, la femme et le prêtre: Le mariage dans la France féodale,* Collection Pluriel (Paris: Hachette, 1981), 72; trans. Barbara Bray; intro. Natalie Zemon Davis, *The Knight, the Lady and the Priest: The Making of Modern Marriage in Medieval France* (1983; London: Allen Lane, 1984), 66. See also the essentialising description of Donald Weinstein and Rudolph M. Bell, *Saints and Society: The Two Worlds of Western Christendom, 1000-1700* (Chicago and London: University of Chicago Press, 1982): 'Women were sexually charged and morally lax, ready agents for the devil's work. Celibate males were fair and delectable game, not only for prostitutes and outwardly lewd women, but even for normally respectable matrons. Any woman might suddenly become inflamed by a man's looks, or even by his aura of innocence, and scheme to encounter him alone so she could seduce him', 81. Payer, *The Bridling of Desire,* and Elaine Pagels, *Adam, Eve and the Serpent* (1988; Harmondsworth: Penguin Books, 1990), characterise attitudes to women in similar terms.
19. See Cadden for a detailed consideration of views of the male and female seeds, and the determination of gender, 117-34; 195-201.
20. Elizabeth Robertson, *Early English Devotional Prose and the Female Audience* (Knoxville: University of Tennessee Press, 1990), 34.
21. Woolf, 160.
22. Hélène Cixous, *Sorties,* trans. Ann Liddle, in Elaine Marks and Isabelle de Courtivron, eds, *New French Feminisms: An Anthology* (1980; Brighton: Harvester Press, 1981), 90-98: 90; Robertson uses a very similar set of binary oppositions to describe medieval notions

of the female nature, *Early English Devotional Prose*, 34; Robertson cites Ian Maclean, *The Renaissance Notion of Woman: A Study in the Fortunes of Scholasticism and Medical Science in European Intellectual Life* (Cambridge: Cambridge University Press, 1980), 8, but both surely derive their oppositions from Cixous.

23. I have chosen to quote from this early English translation of Christine's treatise, *The Boke of the Cyte of Ladyes*, trans. Brian Anslay (Henry Pepwell, 1521), circulated so soon after many of the works discussed in the following pages. A facsimile of the treatise has been published in *Distaves and Dames: Renaissance Treatises for and about Women*, intro. Diane Bornstein (Delmar, N.Y.: Scholars' Facsimiles and Reprints, 1978). I have silently expanded all abbreviations; all subsequent references will be from this edition and cited by book and chapter. There is in fact still no published edition of the original French; a full modern English translation may, however, be found in Christine de Pizan, *The Book of the City of Ladies*, trans. Earl Jeffrey Richards (New York: Persea Books, 1982).

24. James A. Brundage, *Law, Sex, and Christian Society in Medieval Europe* (Chicago and London: University of Chicago Press, 1987), 450.

25. Cadden, 79, 98.

26. See Brundage, *Law, Sex, and Christian Society*, 451.

27. See esp. Cadden, 93-100.

28. William of Conches, *Dialogus de substantiis physicis: ante annos ducentos confectus, à Vuilhelmo Aneponymo philosopho* (Frankfurt/Main: Minerva GMBH, 1967, reprinted from 1567 ed.), Bk. VI, 241. See also Vincent of Beauvais, *Speculum Naturale*, in *Speculum Quadruplex sive Speculum Maius: Naturale/Doctrinale/Morale/Historiale*, vol. 1 (1624; Graz: Akademische Druck, 1964), Bk. 31, ch. xxvi, p. 2313. Vincent cites William of Conches.

29. See 'Queritur quare quedam sine omni semine ac delectatione concipiunt?' ('We enquire by what means certain women conceive without both seed and pleasure?', in *The Prose Salernitan Questions*, ed. Brian Lawn, Auctores Britannici Medii Aevi. V (London: Oxford University Press, for The British Academy, 1979), B 11, p. 6.

30. These various theories of conception are discussed by Danielle Jacquart and Claude Thomasset, *Sexuality and Medicine in the Middle Ages*, trans. Matthew Adamson (Princeton: Princeton University Press, 1988; first published Paris: Presses Universitaires de France, 1985), 61-70.

31. See Cadden, 97.

32. See Angus Maclaren's discussion, 'The pleasures of procreation: traditional and biomedical theories of conception', in *William Hunter and the Eighteenth-Century Medical World*, ed. W. F. Bynum and Roy Porter (Cambridge: Cambridge University Press, 1985), 323-41.

DAVID SALTER (ESSAY DATE 2002)

SOURCE: Salter, David. "'Born to Thraldom and Penance': Wives and Mothers in Middle English Romance." *Essays and Studies* (2002): 41-59.

In the following excerpt, Salter discusses misogyny, the depiction of gender, and the marginalization of women in medieval romance.

Wommen are born to thraldom and penance,
And to been under mannes governance.
Geoffrey Chaucer, *The Man of Law's Tale* (286-7)

Romance: A Feminine Genre?

Near the beginning of Book II of Chaucer's *Troilus and Criseyde*, during the first encounter that we witness between Criseyde and her uncle, Pandarus, there is a brief but characteristically witty exchange between the two characters that offers us a tantalising glimpse of contemporary responses to romance, and the ways in which those responses were bound up with, and shaped by, prevailing attitudes towards women. Chaucer tells us that Pandarus searching for his niece finds her with two female companions listening to a maid reading from the story (or 'geste') of the siege of Thebes. Criseyde informs her uncle that 'This romaunce is of Thebes that we rede' (100),[1] and she then proceeds to tell him of the death of King Layus at the hands of his son, Edippus, as well as of the last incident that had been read to them—the descent into hell of the 'bisshop' Amphiorax. Pandarus responds to his niece's brief rendering of the story by claiming to know it himself. But whereas Criseyde refers quite explicitly to 'this romance', and describes a series of episodes unique to the vernacular, romance versions of the story, Pandarus cites as his source the 'bookes twelve' (108) of Statius's first-century Latin epic, the *Thebaid*, the classical account from which the medieval *Roman de Thebes* is derived.[2]

Although this episode is both brief and somewhat incidental to the main action of the scene—the attempt by Pandarus to persuade Criseyde to accept Troilus as her lover—it can, if carefully interpreted, tell us much about contemporary attitudes towards romance. As Paul Clogan notes, by alluding to the *Thebaid*, Pandarus is able to demonstrate his knowledge of a more authoritative and culturally prestigious version of the story than the one known to Criseyde.[3] Pandarus's allusion to the *Thebaid* can thus be seen as an assertion of the dominance of the ancient over the contemporary, of Latin over the vernacular, and of the genre of epic over that of romance. So Pandarus would seem to be engaged in a game of point scoring with his niece, but one that—as Susan Crane reminds us—is as much about gender as it is about genre.[4] For those authoritative, cultural forms with which Pandarus aligns himself were regarded as masculine in nature, while Chaucer presents the vernacular realm of romance as both literally and metaphorically an exclusively female domain (a suggestion seemingly confirmed by the Nun's Priest's famously dismissive descrip-

ON THE SUBJECT OF...

MARIE DE FRANCE (FL. 12TH CENTURY)

The earliest known female French writer, Marie de France is considered one of the finest poets of her century. She is best known for her *Lais,* a collection of twelve verse tales written in octosyllabic rhyming couplets. Historians speculate that Marie may have been the originator of the form, but they concede that the absence of extant Breton lays, upon which Marie claimed to have based her *lais,* makes it difficult to determine the extent of her originality. Very little is known for certain of Marie's life, and much of the information cited by biographers is conjectural. Biographers generally agree that Marie was born in France in the last half of the twelfth century and that she lived for many years in England. Many critics have held that her vocabulary, style, end knowledge of Latin, French, and English indicate that Marie belonged to an aristocratic, perhaps even noble, family.

Marie's *lais* are undoubtedly romances and share certain elements with the traditional love tales of her day. Yet they differ from the prevailing forms of medieval romance, especially the chivalric tales of courtly love, in that Marie informs her work with an unprecedented feminine sensibility and writes about women as significant characters, not just as objects of devotion. Contemporary critics describe Marie as a storyteller of great charm and imagination, who wrote with wit, intelligence, and economy. In her narratives Marie conveys not only style of dress and manner of speech, but also the behavioral codes and societal attitudes of the late twelfth century. Her vivid portrait of life in the medieval Anglo-Norman court, as well as her insightful and vigorous treatment of love and human relationships, have earned her both critical attention and acclaim.

tion of 'the book of Launcelot de lake' as a text 'that wommen holde in ful greet reverance'). Whatever the actual gender composition of the romance audience, then, it would seem that, as Crane has claimed, the genre itself was perceived to be quintessentially feminine.[5] Moreover, it could be argued that the comparatively low cultural status that Pandarus ascribes to romance was determined, at least in part, by the prevailing anti-feminism of the time.

But, if we accept that romance is indeed a feminine genre, we are nonetheless presented with something of a paradox, for what seems to confront us when we examine romance is a feminine genre with virtually no female heroines. The massive preponderance (particularly in Middle English romance) of male heroes can be attested simply by turning to any anthology or bibliography of the genre, and listing a selection of the titles that we find there: Sir Gawain and the Green Knight, Sir Orfeo, Sir Isumbras, Sir Gowther, Amis and Amiloun, King Horn, Kyng Alisaunder, Torrent of Portyngale, Sir Tristrem, Ywain and Gawain, Sir Percyvell of Gales, Sir Degare, and so on. That the title of each of these romances is derived from the name of its hero (or heroes) is a reflection of the strongly masculine bias or orientation of the genre as a whole. With just a few notable exceptions—the tales of Constance and Griselda, and their various analogues—Middle English romance is a genre that deals almost exclusively with male concerns, and that puts male experience at the centre of its universe.

Of course, this is not to say that women do not figure at all in Middle English romance. Rather, it is to note that they almost always play a secondary or supporting role, and one that is both defined and determined by the central male figure. So women tend to be presented not so much as protagonists in their own right, but as the mothers, wives, sisters, and lovers of the protagonist. And the precise nature of the parts played by women in romance comes into still sharper focus when we consider the kind of narratives with which we are concerned. Of the sample of twelve reasonably representative romances listed above, all but two—Sir Orfeo and Sir Isumbras—deal with the growth and development of young men, and their emergence from a state of dependence on authoritative, parental figures, into a life of autonomy and independence. As Derek Brewer remarks, romances are typically 'stories that are about being young and growing up'—a rite of passage that is given a distinctly gendered inflexion in Middle English romance.[6] For in this genre, the hero's journey from childhood to the adult world almost always involves a transfer of love and loyalty from one woman to another, as he loosens the intense emotional bond that ties him to his mother (or to some other maternal figure), and establishes in its place a new relationship with the woman, who, in the fullness of time, will become his wife.

While to a great extent Middle English romance does tend to marginalise female experience, it nonetheless acknowledges the centrality of women in moulding and developing the identity of the male hero. And it is particularly through their roles as wives and mothers that women in romance are able to accomplish this shaping of male identity. Of course, in the world of romance, just as in that of day-to-day experience, the roles of wife and mother cannot always be neatly separated, and the combination of marriage and motherhood frequently leads to conflicts of interest. For the mother of the romance hero, when married, often finds that the conjugal obligations she owes her husband clash with the love and loyalty she bears her son.

Because marriage and motherhood are the two aspects of women's lives that are given by far the most prominence in Middle English romance, I shall explore . . . some of the different ways in which wives and mothers are represented in the genre. Of course, the criteria employed by romance for evaluating the actions of wives and mothers are not gender neutral; women tend to be judged on whether they are good wives and mothers to their respective husbands and sons. So we find that in romance, even those very restricted roles and identities that are available to women tend to be governed by masculine codes and concerns.

Rather than exploring the representation of marriage and motherhood across a range of romance narratives, my analysis will concentrate in detail on just two texts that offer radically different visions of these two female roles. The first of these, the anonymous fourteenth-century Middle English romance, *Octavian,* is in many ways unexceptional, both in terms of its overall narrative structure, and more particularly in its treatment of women within its highly conventional narrative form.[7] And it is precisely because it is so representative—because it provides such a typical portrayal of female virtue and nobility—that I have decided to use it. However, in stark contrast to the conventional, and extremely laudatory image of female virtue and nobility that is presented in *Octavian,* the second of the two texts to which I shall turn, which tells of the miraculous conception of Alexander the Great, takes a much less sympathetic, more openly misogynistic line in its treatment of women. In terms of the sheer scale of his achievements, and the almost superhuman nature of his ambition, the biography of Alexander the Great (356-323 B.C.) has much in common with a romance narrative, and it was principally through a massively popular but highly fictitious romance that Alexander's life and deeds came to be known in the Middle Ages.[8] Throughout his adult life, the historical Alexander had an extremely intense and emotionally troubled relationship with his mother, Olympias, which gave rise to his well-known remark, reported by the Greek historian, Arrian, that 'she was charging him a high price for his nine months' lodging in her womb'.[9] Just as Olympias elicited ambivalent feelings in Alexander himself, as well as in the Greek and Roman historians who wrote about his life, so the medieval romances of Alexander find her a deeply troubling presence. The romance version of Alexander's miraculous conception and birth, which tells of Olympias's adulterous union with an Egyptian pharaoh who disguises himself as a dragon, and which is reported with a mixture of prurient horror and erotic fascination, provides a strikingly alternative vision of femininity to the comparatively anodyne account of wifely and maternal constancy that we find in *Octavian*. . . .

Notes

1. Geoffrey Chaucer, *Troilus and Criseyde,* Book II, Line 83, in Larry D. Benson et al, ed., *The Riverside Chaucer* (Oxford: Oxford University Press, 1987). All subsequent quotations from Chaucer's work will be from this edition.

2. For an edition of the twelfth-century Old French *Roman de Thebes* (the earliest known version of the story in the vernacular), see Raynaud de Lage, ed., *Le Roman de Thebes,* 2 vols (Paris, 1966-7). An excellent translation of the *Thebaid* has recently been published by the Clarendon Press. See Statius, *The Thebaid,* trans. A. D. Melville (Oxford, 1992). This episode from *Troilus and Criseyde* has been subject to a detailed analysis by Paul Clogan in his study 'Criseyde's Book of the Romance of Thebes', *Hebrew University Studies in Literature and the Arts* 13 (1985), 18-28.

3. Clogan, 'Criseyde's Book of the Romance of Thebes', pp. 26-7.

4. Susan Crane, *Gender and Romance in Chaucer's Canterbury Tales* (Princeton: Princeton University Press, 1994), p. 10.

5. Crane, *Gender and Romance in Chaucer's Canterbury Tales,* p. 10.

6. Derek Brewer, *Symbolic Stories: Traditional Narrative and the Family Drama in English Literature* (Cambridge: D. S. Brewer, 1980), p. 74.

7. See below. . . .

8. See below. . . .

9. Arrian, *The Campaigns of Alexander*, trans. Aubrey de Selincourt (Harmondsworth: Penguin, 1971), Book 7, p. 368.

SUSAN CARTER (ESSAY DATE 2003)

SOURCE: Carter, Susan. "Coupling the Beastly Bride and the Hunter Hunted: What Lies behind Chaucer's *Wife of Bath's Tale*?" *Chaucer Review* 37, no. 4 (2003): 329-45.

In the following excerpt, Carter elucidates the critical feminine subjectivity of Chaucer's "loathly lady," the Wife of Bath, as seen in her tale of King Arthur's court in The Canterbury Tales.

We do not know where Chaucer found the loathly lady motif. Whatever source he encountered, whatever transmutation to it had occurred, he evidently appreciated the more immediate destabilization of gender roles that springs from the loathly lady seen as a personification of the kingdom. Jill Mann pinpoints exactly what is so powerful in the *Wife of Bath's Tale* when she notes that "[t]he 'anti-feminist' elements . . . constitute the force behind the tale's challenge to male domination. When the knight surrenders to female 'maistrye', he surrenders not to the romanticized woman projected by male desire, but to the woman conceived in the pessimistic terms of anti-feminism."[1] To her observation I add that the loathly lady contributes pagan weight to this task of turning misogyny back upon itself. Acceptance of what is repulsive about women is inherent in the motif. Chaucer's loathly lady directly relates to the Wife of Bath's obsession with the dynamics of heterosexual commerce: the manipulation of power ratios by desire, pleasure, and frustration. Moreover, vestiges of the earlier tales' framework brings the anagogic force inherent in the Irish tales into the courtly English work. The sense of a deep truth, a truest truth, such as that underlying the testing of the true king, is poetically imprinted in these vestiges and brought into the Wife's field of interest in the background details of Chaucer's tale.[2]

Before the hag appears at the forest side, manifesting herself as a dance of ladies to lure her venial knight into her clutches, the Wife sets the scene of her tale by establishing "Kyng Arthour" in apposition with a fairy queen who once danced upon "many a grene mede" (III 861), a nostalgic reminder of fairy influence over natural space.[3] "Greet honour" is reportedly attributed to Arthur, but the fairy queen dances "with hir joly compaignye," so that high esteem for the male is countered by something more communal, lively, and attractive for the female. The subtle privileging of the fairy queen over Arthur—syntactically, with just a little more word space and more movement—accurately establishes the appositional pattern that the hag will develop fully. Just as the Irish Sovranty Hag takes her authority from the land of which she is a personification, so the fairy aspect of the loathly lady takes strength from outdoor space.[4] The opening emphasis on the female at home in the green meadow sets up a paradigm that the hag will fully realize.

Despite the acknowledgment of Arthur's reputation for honor, his court is flagrantly subverted by the Wife of Bath's subjective narration.[5] Once the Wife has set the stage in "th'olde dayes of the Kyng Arthour" (III 857), that specifically British king, she does not valorize the knights of the Round Table. Chaucer precedes Malory with a redaction that is conspicuously more sophisticated in licensing a wry female perspective. Malory's knights are often bunglers of the adventure God gives them, such as when Sir Gawain returns from his first episode with a maiden's head, having botched the principle of mercy, but Malory expresses straight-faced regret for such misadventure with a tone of authorial respect: living by the sword simply has a bit of a downside. In contrast, the Wife presents the house of Arthur as unquestionably the source of sexual "oppressioun" (III 889). The male lead is a young knight who belongs to Arthur—"And so bifel that this kyng Arthour / Hadde in his hous a lusty bacheler" (III 882-83)—and who launches the tale by raping a maiden.

This event contrasts startlingly with the Irish tales and most other loathly lady tales—for example the *Wedding of Sir Gawain and Dame Ragnell* and the ballad *King Henry*—which begin with a knight hunting, engrossed in that aristocratic masculine pastime.[6] Like the forest, the hunt is a topos grounded upon actuality, but with a literary life of its own. Marcelle Thiebaux likens the hunt to "the familiar narrative framework of the Journey."[7] This observation makes sense of the *Bildungsroman* quality of many of the loathly lady tales (arguably, Chaucer's included) in which the male protagonist makes a journey through conflict and harrying to self-realization. In the *Wife of Bath's Tale* the motif is suppressed, although when we first meet the knight he may be riding from the river, as Christine Ryan Hilary suggests, because he is hawking for waterfowl.[8] Anne Rooney notes that "The noble hunt in England was especially limited in its scope," and that "hunting manuals paid no attention to the utilitarian trapping of animals . . . for food."[9] Perhaps hawking for waterfowl is also unworthy of mention, being at a remove from the hunter, as well as less dramatic than the killing of larger animals, and thus Hilary's assumption is in keeping with literary convention. But I suspect that it is based on her sensitivity to the formula by which, in the earliest versions, the male is out hunting when he encounters the hag.

Although the audience may be meant to presume that any knight by a river is hunting fowl, as Hilary proposes, Chaucer's tale slips away from the hunt—with its resonance of fate, magic, and the testing of prowess—to displace the contestation onto the female person: the maid whom the knight rapes. The knight's hunt is transposed to the rape of the "mayde walkynge him beforn" (III 886)—like a stalker he approaches from behind—in keeping with Chaucer's more significant relocation: the placing of sovereignty within the personal power politics of marriage rather than in the kingship which the word *sovereignty* literally signifies. Since the knight is a sexual predator rather than an aristocratic sportsman, the turning of the power ratio to make him a sexual victim is acutely appropriate. The rape, so inappropriate for a true hero, signals that Chaucer's tale is more interested in gender power imbalance than in the qualities that make a good king.

The Wife's subjective voice is also authenticated by her sharply critical view of the reality of knights and maidens. The Wife sees that maidens are grist for the mill in the chivalric scheme—objects with the limited option of being either rescued or raped—and her response is to rewrite the script, allowing the hag to oppress and reeducate the errant knight. Her cynicism goes so far as to displace the males from the central position and to promote instead the women of the court.[10] The reaction to the rape is "swich clamour / And swich pursute unto the kyng Arthour" (III 889-90) that the knight is condemned to death through "cours of lawe" (III 892). In theory, Arthur is the ultimate adjudicator, pressed by the people to punish his own, a reminder that his knights provide an elite-military system of justice. However, the last we see of Arthur is when he concedes jurisdiction over the knight to the queen, who has prayed for his "grace" in this matter for "[s]o longe," along with "other ladyes mo" (III 894-95). The sense of a full court surrounding the king and queen is thus achieved only by the inclusion of these ladies, who beg the king for control with a persistence that seems to match the earlier clamor for his punishment. Although Arthur is named and Guinevere is not, and although his household looses the "lusty bacheler" into the countryside, it is women who people the Arthurian court interior.

The feminization of Arthur's court, and of justice, is compounded when the knight returns to either answer the riddle correctly or submit his neckbone to iron. "Whan they be comen to the court" (III 1023) to judge the knight's response, "they" are made up entirely of women: "Ful many a noble wyf, and many a mayde, / And many a wydwe" (III 1026-27) assemble. Although Gower's and Chaucer's unknown source is likely to have come through a French filtration, the sense that Chaucer's hag is related to the Celtic triple moon goddess tales is reinforced in the three stages of womanhood assembled with life-or-death power over the knight.

The head to this feminine body politic is the queen, "hirself sittynge as a justise" (III 1028). When Arthur relinquishes the matter to his queen, his surrender is complete, and she is authorized to take over the king's power as ultimate judge. Malory's Guinevere is isolated from feminine company, never given legitimate power, and resented as a breaker of male bonds; she is a single representation in the court of the dangerous sexuality of the female species. The Wife, in contrast, places Guinevere in the seat of judgment, surrounded by a court of curious women, who "Assembled been, his answere for to heere" (III 1029). This feminine jury will help her to decide the knight's fate. The Wife thus briskly usurps the male prerogative of justice, redistributes it to the women of the court, and puts the knights of the court in the shadows off the edge of the narrative, the spot usually reserved for the ladies.

Even in the closure of the tale, patriarchy is not restored to the court, despite the fact that the loathly lady offers her groom ultimate jurisdiction over her person, declaring somewhat excessively, "Dooth with my lyf and deth right as yow lest" (III 1248). Her problematic concession of will is made in a narrow world peopled by two who share "parfit joye" (III 1258), thus in the context of consensual sex. Is it too essentialist to assume that what is said in intimate play may not be a definitive statement on power relations, but an indulgence, equivalent to Mars allowing his lover to wear his armor during dalliance? The unequal power balance between the hag who can change shape and the knight who remains nameless is well-established by this stage; the bride hands over phallic power to a man she has selected, won, and is bedding in a private moment of pleasure, presumably so that her own pleasure will be enhanced by his empowerment. For the purposes of this tale, the court is represented by what women want; the bedchamber in which a husband is rendered as subservient as a lover subsumes the usual representation of the court, its hall, and Round Table, as the seat of masculine power. As well as creating a sense of authentic feminine subjectivity in the Wife's assessment of the Arthurian court, her regendering is sympathetic to the Sovranty Hag's ultimate jurisdiction over the male court. . . .[11]

Notes

1. Jill Mann, *Geoffrey Chaucer* (New York, 1991), 92.

2. The *Wife of Bath's Tale* is a *lai* in the romance genre. Louise O. Fradenburg considers whether this makes it a "regressive fantasy" and finds that, conversely, it makes the Wife seem "progressive or modern" ("The Wife of Bath's Passing Fancy," *Studies in the Age of Chaucer* 8 [1986]: 31-58, at 34-35). Fradenberg observes that "The very escapism of romance thus points, paradoxically, to the genre's potential as an instrument for change" (41). Sarah Disbrow conversely finds the Wife's genre to be an "antiquated fairy tale" and proposes that the Wife is intended to be "an allegorical figure representing human carnality much like her male counterpart, January" ("The Wife of Bath's Old Wives' Tale," *Studies in the Age of Chaucer* 8 [1986]: 59-71, at 59-60). Disbrow speculates that, by giving this tale to the Wife, Chaucer "hoped to discredit Arthurian romance" (61). However, Chaucer is building up a convincing feminine perspective when he allows the Wife to deconstruct Arthurian romance, and, since I agree with Mann's summation of the Wife as finally likeable (as January is not), I am not convinced by Disbrow's argument.

3. Angela Jane Weisl briefly notes the spatial significance of this outdoors dance, proposing that "by moving the outside inside, the friars have chased away those who lived in the natural world" (*Conquering the Reign of Femeny: Gender and Genre in Chaucer's Romance* [Cambridge, Eng., 1995], 90), although she is more interested in the temporal comparison that the Wife sets up than in the implications inherent in the interior and exterior spaces.

4. This contrasts with the mortal women in medieval literature, who are typically confined to the domestic interiors of narrative settings and are vulnerable to danger when they are found outdoors, as are, for example, Dame Herodis of *Sir Orfeo* and Guinevere (kidnapped while out on a May picnic) of Malory's "The Knight and the Cart" episode.

5. Weisl declares that *WBT* is "an essentially court-based one," since all within it speak the "language of courtly romance" (*Conquering the Reign,* 91). Granting this, the court within the poem is no ordinary one, being insistently feminized.

6. In the "Lughaidh Mal" the seven sons of Daire are all called Lughaidh, "In hopes the prophecy in them would be fulfilled" (["Appendix A to The Genealogy of Corca Laide," *Miscellany of the Celtic Society,* Dublin, 1849] 69). Daire's deer is immediately introduced as though bound into the prophecy: "Daire had a magical fawn as a familiar / In the shape of a yearling deer" (69). Four of the sons meet the deer, who "passed on swiftly, / Until he reached the stream" where "the fawn was slain / By the four noble and very comely youth" (71). Iteration of the youth's nobility and comeliness counters the possibility that the slaying of a father's familiar is loutish behavior. In "Lughaidh Laidhe" king-making begins with Lughaidh's capture of a golden fawn. Niall, too, in the *Adventures of the Sons of Eochaid,* is a hunter out in the forest with his brothers when he encounters the hag.

7. Marcelle Thiebaux, *The Stag of Love: The Chase in Medieval Literature* (Ithaca, N.Y., 1974) 21.

8. Gloss to *ryver, Riverside Chaucer,* ed. Larry D. Benson (Boston, 1987) 117.

9. Anne Rooney, *Hunting, in Middle English Literature* (Suffolk, 1993) 3.

10. Susanna Fein notes that in the "faery realm" of *WBT,* "[a] maternal presence supersedes the laws fixed by the king" and that "maternal justice . . . takes a more flexible view of women's bodies" ("Other Thought-worlds," [*A Campanion to Chaucer,* ed. Peter Brown Oxford, 2000] 337): "woman with her permeable body is the archetypal shape-shifter" (340). My consideration of the Irish Sovranty Hag's contribution endorses Fein's interpretation of the effects of "the full force of mystical 'femenye'" (341) on the rapist knight.

11. Fein notes that "It is almost as if, figuratively, the realm of feminine faery surrounds, womb-like, the masculine world of Arthur and his virile knights" ("Other Thought-worlds," 340), without underscoring the Irish Sovranty figure's control of the king as the model for this dynamic.

CLASSICAL AND MEDIEVAL WOMEN WRITERS

NANCY LEE SWANN (ESSAY DATE 1932)

SOURCE: Swann, Nancy Lee. "The Moralist." In *Pan Chao: Foremost Woman Scholar of China,* pp. 133-39. New York: Russell & Russell, 1968.

In the following excerpt, originally published in 1932, Swann examines the moral precepts of Pan Chao's first-century A.D. treatise Lessons for Women, *the oldest known work of its kind.*

Pan Chao holds a unique place in the history of Chinese philosophy, as the first thinker to formulate a single complete statement of feminine ethics. Despite its brevity, her "Lessons for Women" not only contains an elucidation of the science of the perfecting of womanly character—a system of theoretical moral principles,—but also lays down rules for the practical application of these principles. Although the basis of this science is an unchanging moral code, which is affirmed in the most absolute manner, many of its rules are such as could easily be restated in new terms to meet the conditions of a new age, so that the work may be considered as involving in some degree the concept of relative ethics.

According to the *Mémoires concernant les Chinois,* followed by S. Wells Williams in his article, "Education of Woman in China," Pan Chao composed the "Lessons" in her position as instructress to the young consort of the emperor Ho (89-105 A.D.), intending them also, however, "for the improvement of her sex at large."[1] Perhaps there is, or was, a Chinese written source for these statements; but Pan Chao's own explanation, given in her introduction, is that the book was intended for "unmarried girls," whom she asked to make, each for herself, a copy for personal use.[2] The term *chu nü* could never be interpreted to include the empress. That she wrote primarily for the girls in her own family seems to be clear from the fact that a reference to her son is followed by the reflection that "a man is able to plan his own life . . . but I do grieve that girls just at the age of marriage have not at this time training and advice." In writing the treatise she may well have had in view also "the improvement of her sex at large;" but she does not say so in any definite statement. However the work was handed, as soon as it was completed, to Ma Rung, who so highly approved of its contents that he "ordered the wives and daughters (of his family) to practise it."

Indisputably the "Lessons" were designed to meet the needs of the women of the period, as Pan Chao saw them. By the use of the phrase *chih mien êrh,*[3] "I know how to escape (from my fears or my faults)," she suggested her desire that her daughters, and no doubt young women in general, should be spared the terrors which she had herself experienced as a young bride in a strange house. Although the Classical Writings which she knew and loved are filled with moral teachings illustrated by precept and example, there existed then no treatise[4] especially devoted to the practical everyday life of woman in the home. It was from her own studies and experiences that Pan Chao evolved her ethical system with its homely rules for training girls in personal deportment and right appreciation of family relationships.

In this system the cardinal virtue of the ideal young woman is precisely that humility which is now so strongly condemned by modern Chinese youth. Pan Chao made no attempt to raise the question of the equality of the sexes. She assumed the superiority of man over woman as a matter of course, just as she did that of the old over the young, whether man or woman. Through her interpretation of the symbolic customs of the ancients at the time of the birth of a girl she inculcated humility, and formulated practical rules of conduct implying that the young woman must claim nothing for herself. While strength was the chief glory of man, the beauty of woman's character lay in gentleness, and the most important lesson for woman to learn was that of respectful acquiescence. In the home, however, woman should fill her place as perfectly as man fills his in the larger and perhaps more important world of affairs. "That which must be done, let her finish completely, tidily, and systematically." Probably implying that she must bear sons for this purpose, Pan Chao assigned to the woman the duty of ensuring the continuance of worship in the home, as well as the tasks of preparation for the rites. She went so far as to say that boys and girls are equally important, and though it must be the woman who should seek to win[5] her husband's heart, she "need not use flattery, coaxing words, and cheap methods of intimacy." It was the modest and obedient gentlewoman who would become illustrious in her district and win honor and fame for herself and her parents.

The conduct of such a woman would be dictated by her own respect for her husband. In the high place accorded to her as his consort in the family line of ancestors and descendants, she should take upon herself as a sacred duty the preparation of the offerings of food and wine for worship. The routine tasks which ensure cleanliness in person, food, and household must be carefully and systematically performed, with no waste of time in gossip and silly laughter. In quietness of spirit, attending to her own affairs, thinking before speaking, the wife should follow the correct way in thought, action, and speech. With full control of self, and with mind at peace, she must be content.

The gentlewoman should be industrious. "Late to bed, but early to rise" meant long hours, with many tasks, some easy, some difficult. Always ready and willing to serve others, orderly and neat in her work, giving her whole heart to the duties of the household, she would have neither leisure nor inclination to stand in the gateway or to gossip in the courtyard. She would find her joy in the womanly vocations of sewing and weaving, sanctified by her illustrious predecessors in the homes of her forbears.

Tucked away in chapter two of Pan Chao's treatise is her remarkable plea for the education of girls, a plea which would of itself be sufficient to ensure its author a place of first importance in the history of the advancement of women not only in China but in the world. She was just as convinced that girls needed education in order to fulfill their duties in the home as she was that boys needed it in order to perform the tasks of their own sphere of life. She wished to apply to girls as well as to boys the ancient rule that children should be occupied from the age of eight to fifteen in what may be termed primary studies as distinguished from the higher or cultural instruction after that age. For this later period Pan Chao proposed no changes in the customary procedure of her time regarding young women. Some idea of this procedure may be obtained from passages in the *Li Chi,*[6] which may be taken as a fair indication of the ideals if not the practices of the Han age. It is there stated that a girl at fifteen years of age "assumed the hair-pin; at twenty she was married, or, if there were occasion (for the delay) at twenty-three." "Three months before the marriage of a young lady, . . . she was taught in . . . the public hall (of the members of her surname) . . . the virtue, the speech, the carriage, and the work of a wife."

It is significant that Pan Chao's stand for equal education up to fifteen was taken at a time when boys were already receiving a classical education with a view to official employment. There was no question in the minds of the cultured men of the period that boys ought to be taught, but about girls they had no such conviction. To Pan Chao this neglect to instruct girls meant a disregard of an essential requirement for the proper relationship between men and women. Her appeal for the education of girls in the primary studies was based on the argument that it was necessary for the correct relationship between the married woman and the family into which she married. Had her appeal been listened to by her own generation, it is possible that later moralists might have incorporated this reform in their teachings, and Chinese women might have been spared the eighteen centuries of illiteracy and the long ages of footbinding to which they have been subjected.

But the doctrine that the early education of boys and girls should be the same was too radical not only for Pan Chao's contemporaries but for all the moralists who succeeded her. It was not until the eighteenth century that the appeal was renewed. In 1738 a work entitled "Women's Culture"[7] by a Fukienese, Lan Lu-chou, was published in two volumes. Its author accepted the principle that education is fundamentally necessary for training girls in morals. "Their dispositions incline contrary ways," he wrote in his preface, "and if it is wished to form them alike, there is nothing like education."[8] "A Chinese Declaration of Rights of Women" was made in no uncertain terms by Li Ju-chên in his novel, "Flowers in the Mirror,"[9] which was published about 1825. This man spoke out frankly not only for the moral training of girls according to the four womanly qualifications of Pan Chao's ideal, but also for political as well as educational rights for women as members of society. He advocated the opening of the then prevailing system of examinations for political office to women, which would of course have necessitated the classical education prerequisite to such examinations. This bold advocate of women's education and political rights is a worthy forerunner of the hundreds of young men and women in China who to-day are striving for the equality of the sexes in education and politics as well as in the home.

The relationship of wife to husband is easily the most important of those with which Pan Chao dealt, and she devoted to it three out of the seven chapters of her "Lessons." Her belief in the superiority of man over woman involves no idea of any degradation of womanhood. Rather she took for granted a differentiation of functions in two entirely distinct spheres of life. In their relation to others the husband and wife had but one purpose; in their relation to one another the man controlled the woman, the wife served her husband. The two constituted a single link in the chain of the life of the family, but the functions of that link were divided; the man's share was without, the woman's within the home. For the man remarriage was authorized by the "Rites," but for the woman no such canonical sanction existed. Her will must be the will of her husband, whether he were alive or dead, and throughout her life her endeavor must be to learn the lessons of respect and obedience, of devotion and tenderness, and of contentment with her lot.

The "Lessons" were addressed to women only, and they portray the model woman as one who by her attitude of respect and acquiescence has succeeded in accomplishing the adaptability necessary for wedded life. Yet throughout the delineation of the model woman's conduct there surely runs the thought that respect and caution were also necessary on the part of the husband towards the wife; that the need in fact was mutual. The method inculcated for the practical application of the moral principles involved is that of constant self-examination and self-restraint. Since for the woman the marriage agreement was final, and the power of the husband over his wife absolute, she affirmed the need of a lasting devotion by wife to husband, and of correct behavior on the part of the woman in order to gain and to hold the affection of the man.

Further, the daughter-in-law must obey the parents-in-law.[10] Although the man had authority over the woman, the old, whether man or woman, was superior to the young. Thus there should always be supreme respect for old age. In all the affairs of the home the mother-in-law was supreme; the daughter-in-law was bound to obey the parents-in-law. "If a daughter-in-law," quoted Pan Chao, "is like an echo and a shadow, how could she not be praised?" If her views differed, the daughter-in-law must sacrifice her personal opinions. There could be no question of right and wrong; it was hers only to obey.

Pan Chao maintained that the wife could live in cordial relationship with her husband's brothers and sisters. This was best assured by the young woman's yielding to the wishes of her husband's family instead of exalting her own. It is true, said Pan Chao, that a young girl going into a strange home will inevitably make mistakes, but if like Yen Tzû she never repeat an error, then she will win the love of her husband's family and they will stand by her. The concrete picture of the model young woman which Pan Chao drew in this connection is certainly applicable only to the family system of the Orient, but the underlying principle upon which it is based is true in East and West alike.

Pan Chao did not, unfortunately, formulate any general principle to summarize the detailed precepts which she laid down. Her treatise is severely practical, and follows a definite plan. Having accepted the two beliefs of her age that man was superior to woman and that the old were superior to the young, she set out to present the picture of a model young bride in three relationships, namely, in relation (1) to her husband, (2) to her parents-in-law, and (3) to her brothers- and sisters-in-law. The humility required in all three of these relationships must be taught to her from birth. For the maintenance of the right relationship with the husband, Pan Chao pleaded that the girl should be educated in the same subjects as the boy up to the period of cultural training. After that, the special cultural training of the girl along the lines of the four "womanly qualifications" of "virtue, suitable language, good bearing, and industry" would fit her to win and hold her husband's affection by "whole-hearted devotion" and correct manners. At the same time the entire educational process—the lessons in humility, the primary studies of childhood, the cultural training—should, when aided by lasting attachment for her husband, in no wise hinder the young bride from rendering the proper obedience to her parents-in-law, and should likewise make her more able to adapt herself in her new home to the wishes of her brothers- and sisters-in-law. Thus she would become an example to the world, the model young bride in her husband's home.

It is regrettable that the form of Pan Chao's instructions gives to permanent truths so impermanent an application. The feminine virtues are immutable, and what is required by modern conditions is a restatement rather than a rejection of Pan Chao's instructions. Twentieth century China can more easily repudiate the rules of the *Li Chi* for the "Inner Apartments,"[11] or the pious platitudes of Pan Chao's successors in the field of morality, than the profound psychological truths which underly the "Lessons." Perhaps it is because Pan Chao understood and valued the position of women in an age of culture and refinement such as the Han period, that her interpretation of the ideals of the ancients has so much value even for the present time. Modern Chinese womanhood needs a leader who, like Pan Chao, can interpret anew for a new age the permanent truths of the functions and relations of the sexes in human society.

Notes

1. III, 367: *Chinese Recorder,* XI (1880), 50.

2. [Chinese characters deleted.]

3. [Chinese characters deleted.]

4. The *Nü Hsien* or "Pattern for Women" is twice quoted by Pan Chao, but no further information concerning the contents of this lost book has been discovered.

   It may be that the manners and customs in the homes of the women of the Eastern Han period, as well as the responsibilities for the duties involved in them, will be revealed from further study of the Han relics discovered in Han tombs in Korea, see Harada: *Lo-Lang.*

5. The Chinese marriage agreement is still generally made for the couple by their families. It is customary for the bride and groom not to meet before the wedding ceremony. Any such courting as may take place in these circumstances is done as man and wife.

6. Legge: *Li Ki, SBE,* XXVII, 479, XXVIII, 432. Cf. pp. 84-87.

7. *Nü Hsüeh.*

8. Trans. from *Chinese Repository,* IX (1840), 542. The object of education he thus conceived to be uniformity. Lan Ting-yüan, (1680-1733), district magistrate of P'u-ning. The *Nü Hsüeh* in six *chüan* consists of extracts from classical and historical writings. It is divided into four parts devoted respectively to the illustration of the virtues, sayings, conduct, and works of renowned women of past times, see Wylie: *Notes,*

pp. 37 and 88; Giles: *Biog.,* no. 1083. Without following Pan Chao's order, it quotes her entire treatise.

9. For "Flowers in the Mirror," see Hu Shih, "A Chinese Declaration of Rights of Women," *Chinese Soc. and Polit. Review* (1924), VIII, no. 1, 100-109. Preface by Hu Shih.

10. For the reaction in contemporary China against the frequently intolerable despotism of the mother-in-law, see an article by Ku Chieh-kang. *The Renaissance, chüan* 2, vol. 4, May, 1920.

11. Legge: *Li Ki, SBE,* XXVII, 449-479.

BETTY RADICE (ESSAY DATE 1974)

SOURCE: Radice, Betty. Introduction to *The Letters of Abelard and Heloise,* translated by Betty Radice, pp. 9-55. Harmondsworth, Middlesex: Penguin Books, 1974.

In the following excerpt from her introduction to the collected letters of the twelfth-century lovers Heloise and Abelard, Radice outlines the principal events of their forbidden passion.

Nothing at all is known of Heloise's parentage, though much has been conjectured.[1] She is thought to have been about seventeen at this time and born in 1100 or 1101. Fulbert's possessiveness has suggested to some that she was really his daughter, but taken with his brutal treatment of Abelard it would seem to have a strong sexual element, probably subconscious. Every credit is due to the nuns at Argenteuil for her early education, and to Fulbert for his encouragement of her remarkable gifts at a time when women were rarely educated at all. During the short time she was studying with Abelard they probably worked on philosophy; it was certainly a trained logical mind which argued so cogently against the marriage he proposed.

Heloise saw clearly, as Abelard would not, that a *secret* marriage was not going to satisfy Fulbert for a public scandal and, indeed, 'that no satisfaction could ever appease her uncle'. She therefore opposed any form of marriage, first because of the risk to Abelard, secondly because it would disgrace them both. Both have a low view of marriage, derived from St Paul and St Jerome; they see it from the Christian monastic standpoint as no more than legalization of the weakness of the flesh. As a scholar Abelard was a clerk (*clericus*), and as *magister scholarum* of Notre Dame he would be a member of the Chapter and a canon. Neither was a legal bar to marriage; though a married *magister* might be unusual, one feels that his personality could have made the situation acceptable. It is not known whether he was a priest in orders at this time: probably not. In any case, the Church forbade marriage only to the higher orders of the clergy. It is important to remember that there was no career open to an educated man at this time except in the Church, and that Abelard was prepared to sacrifice his ambitions for high office in order to secure Heloise for himself. He admits in a later letter (p. 149) that 'I desired to keep you whom I loved beyond measure for myself alone.' Any marriage, open or secret, would be an effective bar. An open marriage would damage his reputation but might, just possibly, appease Fulbert, though Heloise who knew him well thought not. A secret marriage would not be damaging but would be dangerous in its effects on Fulbert.

All the authorities are now agreed that the question of reputation is crucial to Heloise's arguments and refers to something much deeper than self-interest on Abelard's part. If her arguments are read closely it is clear that she was much less concerned with the possible loss of Abelard's services to the Church than with the betrayal of the ideal which they both admired, that of the philosopher as a man who is set apart and above human ties. She argues from a classical rather than a Christian viewpoint, and she takes her illustrations from Theophrastus, Cicero, Seneca, and Socrates as recorded by St Jerome. 'The great philosophers of the past have despised the world, not renouncing it so much as escaping from it, and have denied themselves every pleasure so as to find peace in the arms of philosophy alone.' (p. 72) She points out the distractions and petty hindrances of domestic life which are inimical to philosophic contemplation, and compares the philosophers with 'those who truly deserve the name of monks', that is, the dedicated solitaries such as John the Baptist or the ascetic sects of Jewish history. She concludes (Abelard says) that 'the name of mistress instead of wife would be dearer to her and more honourable for me', because then they would both be free from a permanent legal tie and Abelard would not incur the disgrace of renouncing the realization of his true self as a philosopher. They should be bound only by *gratia*—love freely given; marriage can add nothing of significance to an ideal relationship which is also classical in concept: that described in Cicero's *De amicitia,* a work they both knew, which sets the standard for true friendship in 'disinterested love' where physical love would be sublimated.

Heloise amplifies this point in her first letter (p. 114), in the well-known passage where she says that if the Emperor Augustus offered marriage she would still choose to be Abelard's whore; she says this in the context of preferring 'love to wedlock and freedom to chains'. She has loved Abelard only for himself, not for anything he could give her, and indeed, in her view, marriage for what either party could get from the other was no better than prostitution. By contrast, a lasting relationship should rest on the complete devotion of two persons; this is true disinterested love, based on what she calls 'chastity of spirit'. To such an ideal union a legal marriage could add nothing, and the presence or absence of an erotic element is, in a sense, irrelevant. The intention towards the ideal relationship is all-important. This is the 'ethic of pure intention' in which both Abelard and Heloise believed and to which she often returns. 'Wholly guilty though I am, I am also, as you know, wholly innocent. It is not the deed but the intention of the doer which makes the crime, and justice should weigh not what was done but the spirit in which it is done. What my intention towards you has always been, you alone who have known it can judge.' (p. 115-16).

For Heloise the issue was clear and unequivocal, however difficult it is for us to follow her. Conventional morality would speak of a young woman who is willing to 'live in sin' with a man, so as not to stand in his path, as sacrificing herself, but for her living wholly for Abelard is self-realization. Abelard was torn by an impossible conflict between his desire for Heloise and all the jealous possessiveness which went with it, and his belief that his duty was to realize himself as a philosopher and to preserve his intention towards that ideal. It has been pointed out[2] that the quotations used by Heloise all appear in a work of his own (Book II of his *Theologia Christiana*) written after they parted but several years before the *Historia.* It certainly seems likely that he filled in the outlines of her arguments with references to chapter and verse when he wrote his account for circulation. But there is no suggestion that he did not accept their validity; he simply refused to be persuaded. Perhaps it was too much to expect of an ardent lover and a proud and hypersensitive man. 'But at last she saw that her attempts to persuade or dissuade me were making no impression on my foolish obstinacy, and she could not bear to offend me; so amidst deep sighs and tears she ended in these words: "We shall both be destroyed. All that is left us is suffering as great as our love has been." In this, as the whole world knows, she showed herself a true prophet.' (p. 74)

Heloise never reproaches Abelard for the *secrecy* of the marriage, which to her must have seemed an act of hypocrisy and another betrayal of the ideal. She was even ready to lie on Abelard's behalf and deny it when Fulbert broke his promise and spread the news. Years later, however, in a bitter moment she pointed out the irony of the fact that they had been spared when guilty of fornication but punished 'through a marriage which you believed had made amends for all previous wrongdoing' (p. 130). There were furtive meetings followed by scenes with Fulbert, which made Abelard decide to remove her from her uncle's house. The convent at Argenteuil where she had spent her childhood was the obvious place to take her, and it was near enough Paris for further meetings to be fairly easy. We know that Abelard could not keep away; he argues in one of his letters (p. 146) that they were more justly punished for their conduct when married than for anything they did before, because of their sacrilege in making love in a corner of the convent refectory, the only place where they could snatch a moment together alone. What he had in mind when he made her wear a postulant's habit no one can know, unless it was to give greater protection from Fulbert, but it was a disastrous thing to do. She could have stayed indefinitely with the nuns without it, and Fulbert very naturally assumed that Abelard was trying to get rid of her by making her a nun. This was the immediate cause of his horrible revenge: his servants broke into Abelard's room at night and castrated him.

Long afterwards Abelard could write of this to Heloise with hindsight as an act of God's mercy which rid him of his personal dilemma along with the torments of the flesh. But in the *Historia* what he vividly recalls is the pain and horror, his urge to escape and hide from the noisy sympathy of the crowds outside and the outcry of his pupils pushing into his room, his feelings of humiliation and disgust at being a eunuch, the unclean beast of Jewish law. He admits that 'it was shame and confusion in my remorse and misery rather than any devout wish for conversion which brought me to seek shelter in a monastery cloister' (p. 76).

Notes

1. McLeod, Enid, *Héloïse,* 2nd edn, Chatto and Windus, London, 1971, p. 8 ff. and notes.
2. J. T. Muckle, *Mediaeval Studies,* Vol. XII, pp. 173-4.

JANE MCINTOSH SNYDER (ESSAY DATE 1989)

SOURCE: Snyder, Jane McIntosh. "Women Philosophers of the Hellenistic and Roman Worlds." In *The Woman and the Lyre: Women Writers in Classical Greece and Rome,* pp. 99-121. Carbondale: Southern Illinois University Press, 1989.

In the following excerpt, Snyder recounts the life of the martyred Alexandrian mathematician and philosopher Hypatia.

Of all the women discussed [here] none—with the possible exception of Sappho—has enjoyed more enduring fame than Hypatia, the philosopher-mathematician who was murdered in Alexandria, Egypt, by a mob of antipagan Christians in 415 A.D. In the nineteenth century the figure of Hypatia was romanticized in Charles Kingsley's lengthy novel, *Hypatia, or New Foes with an Old Face*. Kingsley offers what no doubt tells us more about his own peculiar views of a woman scholar than about the real Hypatia. Here is the Kingsley Hypatia—literally quivering with emotion after delivering a lecture to her students on Book 6 of Homer's *Iliad*:

> And the speaker stopped suddenly, her eyes glistening with tears, her whole figure trembling and dilating with rapture. She remained for a moment motionless, gazing earnestly at her audience, as if in hopes of exciting in them some kindred glow; and then recovering herself, added in a more tender tone, not quite unmixed with sadness—
>
> "Go now, my pupils, Hypatia has no more for you today. Go now, and spare her at least—woman as she is after all—the shame of finding that she has given you too much, and lifted the veil of Isis before eyes which are not enough purified to behold the glory of the goddess.—Farewell."[1]

Far from being represented as a figure of authority imparting information to her students, this Hypatia is a curious mixture of helplessness, pretentiousness, and titillation.

Hypatia seems to have fared somewhat better in the present century. She has been mentioned in recent popularizing accounts of the history of science such as Carl Sagan's television series, "Cosmos," and she (along with Sappho) has a place setting among the women honored in the artist Judy Chicago's "Dinner Party." She has also been written about in journals of the history of mathematics, and her name appears routinely in recent biographical dictionaries of women in science. As Alic notes, she is often the only woman cited in contemporary histories of astronomy and mathematics.[2] Moreover, an American journal founded in 1983 as a forum for research in feminist philosophy was appropriately [titled] *Hypatia.*

Although not a word of anything that can be definitely attributed to Hypatia remains to us today, a rough idea of the circumstances of her life and death and a reasonably complete sketch of her interests in mathematics, astronomy, Platonic philosophy, and what might be termed engineering can be reconstructed through the accounts of the fifth-century A.D. ecclesiastical historian, Sokrates, and especially through several letters of her student Synesios of Cyrene. The correspondence of Synesios (who was elected Bishop of Ptolemais in Libya) with and about Hypatia represents the closest we can come to Hypatia's own thinking. Further details of more dubious accuracy can be supplied from late sources such as the *Suda* or the ninth-century scholar Photius, whose hostile comment nevertheless shows Hypatia's continuing reputation in the Byzantine period: "Isidore (of Seville) was much different from Hypatia, not only as a man differs from a woman, but also as a real philosopher differs from a woman who knows geometry."[3]

Before we examine what can be deduced about Hypatia's written contributions to scholarship, let us first review briefly the main facts of her life and death insofar as they can be gleaned from the ancient sources. The task of presenting a coherent sketch of her biography is complicated by inconsistencies among these sources and even within the same source; the unusually long encyclopedia entry on Hypatia in the *Suda,* for example, is quite obviously a patchwork of at least two variant sources, for it begins with a very brief description of her family, works, and death, claiming that she was the wife of Isidore, and then begins over again with the phrase "Concerning Hypatia the philosopher"; in the second (much lengthier) account, she is described not as anyone's wife but as a beautiful virgin.[4]

The ancient sources do agree that Hypatia was the daughter of the Alexandrian geometrician and philosopher Theon, who may have been connected with the research institute known as the Museum in Alexandria, where Hypatia was raised and educated. She herself is described as a geometrician, mathematician, astronomer, and exponent of Platonic and Aristotelian philosophy—interests that are borne out by the known titles of her works. The sources also generally agree on the period of her activity; she was born in 370 A.D. and was murdered at the age of forty-five in 415.

As has been recently noted, the "spectacularly brutal murder . . ." as well as its subtle political and religious overtones encouraged both friends and enemies to remember her. Not surprisingly, all of the reports place more emphasis on the social impact of her life than on her contributions to science and mathematics.[5] The first section in the *Suda* provides only the barest outline: "She was torn to pieces by the Alexandrians, and her body was shamefully treated and parts of it scattered all over the city. She suffered such treatment on account of envy and because of her superior wisdom, especially in the area of astronomy; some say the envy was on the part of Cyril [Bishop of Alexandria], while others claim that these events took place on account of the innate rashness and proclivity towards sedition among the Alexandrians."[6] For a more detailed report, we must turn to the contemporary account provided by the ecclesiastical historian, Sokrates:

> There was in Alexandria a certain woman named Hypatia, daughter of Theon the philosopher. She had achieved such heights of erudition that she surpassed all the philosophers of her time, succeeded to the Platonic school derived from Plotinus, and delivered all the philosophy lectures to those who wished to listen. Accordingly, everyone who wanted to study philosophy flocked to her from all directions. On account of the majestic outspokenness at her command as the result of her education, she came face to face even with the magistrates without losing her composure, and felt no shame at being in the presence of men. Everyone revered her for her outstanding composure, and at the same time found her a source of amazement. It was at that time that envy arose against this woman. She happened to spend a great deal of time with Orestes [Prefect of Egypt], and that stirred up slander against her among the people of the Church, as if she were the one who prevented Orestes from entering into friendship with the Bishop [Cyril]. Indeed, a number of men who heatedly reached the same conclusion, whom a certain Peter (who was employed as a reader) led, kept watch for the woman as she was returning home from somewhere. They threw her out of her carriage and dragged her to the church called Caesareum. They stripped off her clothes and then killed her with seashells. When they had torn her body apart limb from limb, they took it to a place called Cinaron and burned it. This deed brought no small blame to Cyril and to the Alexandrian Church. For murder and fighting and other such things are completely alien to those who profess Christianity. These deeds were done in the fourth year of Cyril's bishopric, in the tenth consulship of Honorius and the sixth of Theodosius, in the month of March during Lent.[7]

Ironically, Hypatia's unfortunate end seems to have led Sokrates, as a Christian historian, to regard her as a kind of pagan martyr whose Christian murderers should be condemned for their violent act. It is worth remarking that both in the *Suda* and in Sokrates' contemporary account, although the exact reasons behind the plot to assassinate Hypatia are not clear, the exceptional character of her position as an outstanding woman scholar is noted as a source of hostility toward her. As Lefkowitz remarks, "We may well ask whether her death was to some extent caused by her being a woman."[8] Whether or not we agree with Gibbon, who argued that Cyril "prompted, or accepted, the sacrifice of a virgin," it is clear that Hypatia's fame as a learned woman made her a vulnerable target for the antipagan factions in Alexandria.[9] In the ancient biographies, at least, she takes on the mythical proportions of an Antigone figure—a female whose extraordinary nature and deeds are the source of her downfall at the hands of male authority.

Hypatia of Alexandria (c.370-415)

Turning from Hypatia's life and death to the question of her writing, we must again note that our only sources of information about her scientific and philosophical interests are the titles of her works (insofar as they have been preserved), and a collection of eleven letters of her pupil, Synesios, in which she is either the addressee or the subject of a passing reference. According to the *Suda,* Hypatia wrote three major works: a commentary on Diophantos (an Alexandrian author of a treatise on algebra), a treatise entitled *Astronomical Canon* (presumably on the movements of the planets), and a commentary entitled *On the Conics of Apollonius,* in which she treated the subject of conic sections previously expounded upon in the third century B.C. by Apollonius, yet another scholar from Alexandria.[10] But for one book, Apollonius' treatise survives to this day (either in the Greek original or in Arabic translation), but not a word of Hypatia's study is extant. (Ironically, several works by her less famous father, Theon, do survive.) These three titles suggest a focus on mathematics and astronomy, but the ancient biographical notices and

ON THE SUBJECT OF...

HYPATIA (C. 370-415)

Widely regarded as the first female mathematician, Hypatia was born and spent most of her life in Alexandria, a center—with Athens—of late fourth-century Greek intellectual activity. She was greatly influenced by her father, Theon, a noteworthy mathematician, astronomer, and teacher who supervised her early education. As a young woman, she began instructing a privileged circle of students in private classes at her home, and later added public lectures as her fame increased. She was reputed to be a woman of intelligence, modesty, dignity, and beauty. Despite the widespread respect she enjoyed in Alexandria—or perhaps because of it—Hypatia apparently became the object of factional hatred in a city troubled by conflicts between Christians, Jews, and pagans. In 415 she was attacked by a mob in the streets of Alexandria and brutally murdered.

The letters of Synesius of Gyrene (c. 370-413), a philosopher and churchman who studied with Hypatia for many years and was devoted to her, refer to Hypatia's mechanical abilities and credit her with several inventions, including astronomical instruments and an apparatus that measured the density of liquids. Socrates Scholasticus (c. 379-450) documented Hypatia's life in his *Ecclesiastical History* and reported that she attracted students from throughout Egypt and beyond, exerting considerable influence in Alexandria's political and social life. The *Suda,* an anonymous tenth-century historical and literary collection, indicates that Hypatia was awarded an official appointment as public lecturer in philosophy, drawing audiences from the highest ranks of society as well as from the academy. Three major works are commonly attributed to Hypatia: a commentary on the *Arithmetica,* Diophantus's great treatise on algebra; an edition, with commentary, of the geometrician Apollonius of Perga's *Conic Sections,* and the *Astronomical Canon.*

the letters of Synesios imply that Hypatia's intellectual interests ranged from Plato and Aristotle to Homer to technological inventions as well.

Since we do not have even fragments of Hypatia's work, the nearest we can come to some sense of her as a thinker and a writer—rather than as a martyr—are the letters of her student, Synesios, who, despite his interest in Neoplatonism, was a Christian who held office as Bishop of Ptolemais. Three of these letters are translated here as representative samples of this one-sided correspondence between master and pupil. The first is interesting for its allusion to Synesios' hope for regular correspondence from his former teacher, whom he depicts as flourishing in a group of like-minded individuals:

> To the philosopher Hypatia:
>
> Blessed lady, I send greetings both to you yourself and, through you, to your most fortunate companions. For a long time I would have been eager to accuse myself of not being worthy of your letters; but now that I know that I have merely been overlooked by all of you—in this case, while I have done no wrong, I have encountered a good deal of ill luck, as much ill luck as a man could encounter. But if indeed I were able to receive letters from you, and to learn how you are spending your time (certainly you are in good company and are experiencing good fortune), I would fare only half so badly, and in all of you I would find my own good fortune. But as it is, this is only one of the difficulties that have overtaken me. I am deprived both of my children and of my friends, and of goodwill from everyone; and most of all, of your divine spirit, which alone I had hoped would remain with me as a force stronger than this heaven-sent ill fortune and the fluctuations of fate.[11]

. . . . .

After Hypatia's death in 415 A.D., the philosophical school of thought that she represented—the blend of Platonic, Aristotelian, Pythagorean, and Stoic elements conveniently known as Neoplatonism—continued as a dominant intellectual force through the end of the ancient world and even on into the medieval and Renaissance periods. Other Neoplatonist philosophers (such as Hierocles and Hermeias) succeeded to the leadership of Neoplatonic teaching in Alexandria, but none seems to have captured the imagination of later writers in the way that Hypatia did.[12] One of the Greek epigrammatists, Palladas (fifth or sixth century A.D.), honors her place as philosopher, astronomer, and teacher in the following poem:

> Whenever I look upon you and your words, I
> pay reverence,
> As I look upon the heavenly home of the virgin.
> For your concerns are directed at the heavens,

Revered Hypatia, you who are yourself the
beauty of reasoning,
The immaculate star of wise learning.[13]

Some scholars have argued that the second line of the poem refers to the constellation Virgo, but it may be that the "virgin" ("parthenon") is Hypatia herself and that her home is "heavenly" because of its occupant's astronomical concerns (as explained in the next line).[14] The metaphor is extended through the last line of the poem, in which the addressee herself, in her role as teacher, becomes a star.

Notes

1. Charles Kingsley, *Hypatia, or New Foes with an Old Face* (New York: Thomas Crowell, 1897), 127.
2. Margaret Alic, *Hypatia's Heritage: A History of Women in Science from Antiquity through the Nineteenth Century* (Boston: Beacon Press, 1986), 41.
3. Photius, *Biblioteca* 24-2.38 in *Photius: Bibliothèque,* ed. and trans. R. Henry, 3 vols. (Paris: Société d'édition "Les belles lettres," 1959-62).
4. See Karl Praechter, "Hypatia," *Real-Encylcopädie der Klassischen Altertumswissenschaft.*
5. Marilyn Bailey Ogilvie, *Women in Science: Antiquity through the Nineteenth Century* (Cambridge: MIT Press, 1986), 104.
6. "Hypatia," in *Suidae Lexicon.*
7. Sokrates, *Historia Ecclesiastica* 7.15, in *Patrologiae, Patrum Graecorum Traditio Catholica,* ed. J.-P. Migne (Paris: 1864).
8. Mary R. Lefkowitz, *Women in Greek Myth* London: Duckworth, 1986), 107.
9. For an excellent discussion of Gibbon's account in particular and of Hypatia's philosophical interests in general, see J. M. Rist, "Hypatia," *Phoenix* 19 (1965): 214-25. A very detailed study of the ancient and Byzantine sources may be found in R. Hoche, "Hypatia, die Tochter Theons," *Philogus* 15 (1860): 435-74.
10. "Hypatia," in *Suidae Lexicon.*
11. Synesios, epistle 10, in *Epistolographi Graeci,* ed. R. Hercher (Paris: Didot, 1871), 638-739. For Synesios' letters in the context of early Christianity and the classical background, see Stanley K. Stowers, *Letter Writing in Greco-Roman Antiquity* (Philadelphia: Westminster Press, 1986).
12. On the succession, see R. T. Wallis *Neoplatonism* (London: Duckworth, 1972), 138-78.
13. Palladas, *Anthologia Palatina* 9. 400, in *The Greek Anthology,* ed. and trans. W. R. Paton, 5 vols. (London: Heinemann, 1948).
14. Georg Luck, "Palladas—Christian or Pagan?," *Harvard Studies in Classical Philology* 63 (1958): 455-71. Points out that "oikos" in line 2 cannot mean "constellation." He argues, however, that Palladas is not the author of the poem and that the Hypatia referred to is not our Hypatia.

ALEXANDRA BARRATT (ESSAY DATE 1992)

SOURCE: Barratt, Alexandra. "The Fourteenth Century and Earlier." In *Women's Writing in Middle English,* edited by Alexandra Barratt, pp. 27-136. Essex: Longman, 1992.

In the following excerpt from her collection of medieval women's writing, Barratt briefly summarizes the lives and careers of Marguerita Porete, Elizabeth of Hungary, Birgitta of Sweden, and Julian of Norwich. The critic also provides concise commentary on the major works of these writers that have appeared in Middle English.

Marguerite Porete

Marguerite Porete was a late thirteenth century béguine from Hainault in Flanders (béguines were laywomen vowed to chastity who were self-supporting and led a disciplined life, either at home, in convents or in béguinages, i.e. settlements or special areas within a town). Some time between 1296 and 1306 she wrote a lengthy and obscure mystical treatise in Old French, *Le Mirouer des Simples Ames,* a dialogue between Lady Love, Lady Reason and the Free Soul, which was condemned by the local bishop as heretical and publicly burnt. The bishop considered that Marguerite's book was associated with the heresy of the Free Spirit, a loosely organised Continental movement whose adherents (many of them women) taught that Free Spirits, i.e. advanced and favoured souls whose wills were united with the Divine, no longer needed to observe the moral law or avail themselves of the Church and the sacraments (see Lerner 1972). In spite of this condemnation, Marguerite Porete continued to circulate copies of *Le Mirouer* and seek approval from theologians of its orthodoxy. She was therefore arrested by the Inquisition, brought to Paris and imprisoned. In 1309 fifteen suspect articles extracted from *Le Mirouer* were examined and condemned by twenty-one prominent Paris theologians. In 1310 she was condemned by the Inquisition as a relapsed heretic and burnt at the stake, having refused to speak in her own defence (see Verdeyen 1986: 47-94).

Of the French original only one late and somewhat corrupt manuscript survives, from the late fifteenth or early sixteenth century. Four manuscripts, three from the fourteenth century, survive of the Latin translation, which may have been made by the Inquisition as part of their investigation, and translations were made into Italian as well as into Middle English. None of the surviving manuscripts of the original or of the translations identifies the author or indicates that the text had been condemned as heretical. It was not until 1965 that an Italian scholar, R. Guarnieri, linked the historical Marguerite Porete, of whose trial and condemnation there are full historical records which do not, however, name her heretical book, with the French, Latin and English versions of *Le Mirouer.* Since then there has been much discussion of whether Porete was indeed a heretic, and much favourable comment on the literary value of her writings, which combine the conventions and language of courtly love with a passionate and exalted mysticism (see Dronke 1984: 217-28).

The Mirror of Simple Souls is a late fourteenth- or fifteenth-century Middle English translation of *Le Mirouer,* probably made by a Carthusian, a member of a strict and austere contemplative order of monks who led the lives of hermits within their monasteries. We do not know his name, only his initials, 'M.N.', with which he signed various editorial comments inserted to explain passages in his translation that he feared might be misunderstood. He tells us that his original version had indeed been poorly received and misinterpreted.

Although the Carthusians avoided all contact with women, they took a great interest in women's mystical texts and we owe to them the preservation of both the Short Version of Julian of Norwich's *A Revelation of Love* and *The Book of Margery Kempe*. But it is interesting that this translator clearly had no suspicion that his original was composed by a woman who had been condemned as a heretic (see Colledge and Guarnieri 1968). In medieval England, therefore, *The Mirror of Simple Souls* was not perceived as a woman's text, but this very fact is significant for it indicates the difficulty of assigning gender to texts in the absence of external evidence.

Comment: Generally, *The Mirror of Simple Souls* is a difficult and challenging text; as the translator puts it, it is written 'full mistily'. His translation is literal and consequently does not always make obvious sense, nor does it read elegantly; it also contains a number of mistranslations which may be due as much to the corruption of the original as to the translator's shortcomings. And his own translation is further corrupted in the three surviving manuscripts. (Most notably, they all have the garbled phrase 'Far night' for what must have been the translator's original rendering of Marguerite's term for God, OF *loing-pres,* as 'Far-nigh'.) But fortunately these factors still cannot obscure the intellectual daring, spiritual passion and profound originality of Marguerite Porete.

The dialogue form is not in itself unusual in visionary and mystical writings, which often consist largely of exchanges between the visionary and God or the Virgin (cf. *The Revelations of St Elizabeth*). In medieval didactic literature, from Boethius's *Consolation of Philosophy* to Christine de Pisan's *Book of the City of Ladies,* dialogues between the narrator and various abstract personifications are also common. But Marguerite's use of the form, with its three female protagonists, is distinctive. Reason when personified in medieval literature is invariably female because L. *ratio* and OF *raison* are grammatically feminine nouns. 'Lady Reason' is usually a direct descendant of Boethius's Lady Philosophy; she is prominent in the great thirteenth-century French allegorical dream poem *Le Roman de la Rose,* and also appears in Christine's *Book of the City of Ladies.* But Marguerite's Lady Reason is very different: she is seen as earth-bound and must die before the soul can progress. The figure of Lady Love is also unusual. L. *amor* is masculine, though its OF derivative is usually a feminine noun and Love is more usually personified as a male figure, especially as the God of Love, in medieval literature. However, Marguerite's near-contemporary, Mechtild of Hackeborn, also personifies Divine Love as a female figure. Finally, the soul too, as always in Christian tradition, is female.

The first passage, from the dialogue between Lady Love and Lady Reason, comes from the early part of the text and contains those daringly paradoxical and extravagant statements about the freedom of the 'free', 'surmounted' (i.e. sublime) soul which led ultimately to Porete's condemnation. The second passage comes from very near the end of the book, after the death of the invincibly ignorant and incorrigible Lady Reason, and records a crucial but agonising stage in the soul's progress towards perfection and complete union with the Divine, when she is faced with the need completely to annihilate her own will in order to mature spiritually and finally enter the Country of Freedom. The extreme passivity which this requires, though cultivated by male as well as female mystics, can be seen in part as a logical extension of the role forced on women in the Middle Ages. . . .

. . . . .

Elizabeth of Hungary

Two Middle English translations of *The Revelations of Saint Elizabeth* are extant. One (like most of the manuscripts of the Latin) attributes the original to the Elizabeth of Hungary who died in

1231, i.e. to Elizabeth of Thuringia (b. 1207). Elizabeth, who was the widow of the Count of Thuringia and the mother of his three children, was devoted to poverty and to the care of the sick. She never became a nun but was a Franciscan tertiary (i.e. a member of the Third Order of St Francis, lay people who led a disciplined and dedicated life in the world), and there is no authentic early tradition that she was a visionary. Although St Elizabeth of Schönau, a twelfth-century German Benedictine nun and mystic, has been suggested as a more likely candidate for the authorship of the *Revelations,* a better case can be made for Elizabeth of Toess (*c.* 1294-1336), the great-niece of Elizabeth of Thuringia and also, like her, daughter of a king of Hungary. This Elizabeth was a Dominican nun in the Swiss convent of Toess whose life, together with those of her sisters in religion, was written in Middle High German by Elsbeth Stagel, the close friend and spiritual daughter of the great Rhineland mystic Henry Suso.

As an account of her spiritual experiences, the *Revelations* must have originated with Elizabeth. But she apparently communicated them orally to another person, presumably a fellow nun (probably Elsbeth Stagel), who was responsible for the literary form of the work. The Middle English versions were translated from a Latin text, but the original text of the *Revelations* may not have been in that language. There are two, rather different, Latin versions extant and both may be translations from a now vanished original, possibly composed in Middle High German (see Barratt 1992). In the Middle Ages the *Revelations* also circulated in Italian, French, Spanish and Catalan translations.

The Book of Margery Kempe almost certainly refers to this text when it speaks of 'Saint Elizabeth in her treatise', whose tears were like Margery's. There are many references in the *Revelations* to Elizabeth's noisy and boisterous weeping and other points of contact make it clear that either Margery herself or her scribe knew this text well, in a Latin or Middle English version (see Ellis 1990: 164-8).

Comment: As nine out of the thirteen individual visions consist of dialogues with the Virgin, she is a central figure in Elizabeth's *Revelations*. Generally she both models and validates the visionary's own ecstatic, affective (i.e. emotional) and unrestrained spirituality. In the first passage, which opens the *Revelations,* the Virgin is also presented as a multivalent figure of supreme power: as 'lady' with all its feudal overtones, as mother and as 'maystresse'. (L. *magistra,* like 'mistress', can specifically mean 'teacher' as well as, more generally, 'woman in a position of authority'.) Elizabeth swears allegiance to her with the traditional gesture of feudal submission which establishes a contractual relationship between them. The written charter, which the notably silent St John the Evangelist is later commanded to provide, acts merely as a record. . . .

. . . . .

Bridget of Sweden

Bridget of Sweden (1302 or 1303-1373) was a devout noblewoman who, before she was widowed, spent much time at the Swedish court attempting to influence King Magnus and his French wife Blanche by her own example and her constant exhortations to moral reformation. A mother of eight, after her husband's death in 1344 she started to experience visions which led her to found a religious order dedicated to the Virgin, whose apotheosis Bridget took to new heights. The Order of the Most Holy Saviour was a double order for nuns and monks, ruled by an abbess; Bridget's own daughter Katherine presided over both the men and women in the mother house at Vadstena in Sweden.

Although Bridget was the first woman in the Western Church to found a religious order, she never herself became a nun. She travelled to Rome to seek papal approval for her new order and stayed to press for the return of the pope from Avignon in France where, for political reasons, all the popes had lived with their courts since 1304. As a result of her efforts Pope Urban V did indeed return in 1367 but, finding conditions intolerable, left again in 1370, only to die a month later. It was left to another woman visionary, Catherine of Siena, to help bring about the permanent resettlement of the papacy in Rome and to accidentally precipitate the election of a rival pope, leading to the crisis known as the Great Schism.

Bridget died in 1373 and, renowned for her holiness, her works of charity and her miracles, was canonised in 1391. But she was as well known for her numerous visions, many of which denounced the corruption of the Church in general and of certain individuals in particular, and stressed apocalyptic themes of the judgemental wrath of God. Other visions were vivid recreations of events in the lives of Christ and the Virgin, which had a strong influence on the representation of the Nativity and the Crucifixion in the later Middle Ages.

Bridget was a very popular saint in fifteenth-century England and in 1415 Henry V founded Syon, the only English Bridgettine house, at Twickenham in Middlesex (it later moved to Isleworth). Until its closure in 1539 it continued to enjoy close ties with the Lancastrians and their descendants, including Lady Margaret Beaufort (see Keiser 1987b: 11-13). It was renowned for its austerity, its influence at court and its learning. Bridget, who had learnt Latin late in life, encouraged scholarship as much as asceticism among her nuns; her Rule, which otherwise stressed personal poverty, allowed them as many books as they needed for reading. Syon continued its corporate existence abroad after the Reformation and, having returned in the nineteenth century, is the only religious community in England that can claim an unbroken existence since the Middle Ages.

Bridget's revelations, too, were widely known. Indeed, of all the continental women mystics included in this anthology whose writings were translated into English, she is the only one to have achieved real popularity and widespread circulation among layfolk as well as religious. . . . [A] first set of passages . . . derives from the *Liber Celestis,* the vast collection of Bridget's visions originally dictated by her in Old Swedish, translated and recorded in Latin by her spiritual directors, and then checked by her. The visions were later translated into Middle English in several versions; there are two translations of the complete text and in addition numerous extracts and selections (see Ellis 1982). The passages . . . come from a collection which has extracted and rearranged individual revelations to construct a life of the Virgin, as told by her to Bridget; this forms an interesting parallel with the preference of so many medieval women visionaries for hagio-autobiography.

[Another] set of extracts comes from *The Rule of St Saviour,* the Middle English translation of the Latin Rule that was dictated by Christ himself, Bridget claimed. The translation was one of the official legislative documents of the Bridgettine monastery at Syon and was presumably made for the benefit of the nuns, who could not read the original Latin.

Comment: . . . Bridget's best-known revelation [is] a vivid and emotional vision of the Nativity which had an immediate and continuing influence on its representation in art (Butkovich 1972: 31-4). It stresses the supernatural, if not anti-natural, aspects of Christ's birth, with a passion for ingenious detail that clearly derives from the visionary's own experience of childbirth (contrast the very different treatment of the subject by the lifelong nun Mechtild). Thus it emphasises the status of the Virgin as the Mother of Christ in a way that could not have occurred to male commentators.

. . . [A] second passage shows Bridget's passion for detail extending to a curiosity that goes beyond what would now be considered the bounds of good taste. It also asserts the Virgin's supremacy as head of the apostles after Christ's Ascension, a position used in the final extract to justify the unusual power structure of the Bridgettine order within which the abbess, elected by the sisters alone, had absolute authority over all the temporal affairs of the monastery.

. . . [A] third passage shows the same concern for detail finding a practical outlet in prescribing the distinctive, not to say eccentric, habit of the Bridgettine nuns. The good sense of their winter outfit, with its sheepskin cloak, boots and stockings, reminds us that Bridget was not only the first woman but also the first Northern European to draft a religious rule. . . .

. . . . .

Julian of Norwich

Very little is known about Julian of Norwich, not even her baptismal name. She was born in 1342. On 8 or 13 May 1373, when aged thirty, she experienced a series of visions as she lay dying, followed by a miraculous recovery. She wrote two accounts of this experience, one almost at once and another up to twenty years later. Before 1413 she became an anchoress at St Julian's Church, Norwich, from which she may have taken her name in religion. She was still alive in 1416, when a will of that year left her a bequest, but was dead by 1426 when another will refers to the male recluse at St Julian's.

Julian was not a nun or an anchoress at the time of her revelations. She mentions that her mother, the parish priest and a small boy were present at her sick-bed, which would have been impossible if she were an enclosed religious. She had probably been married, for unmarried laywomen of thirty were virtually unknown in medieval England, but as there is no mention of her husband we may deduce that she was a widow (like Bridget of Sweden, Christine de Pisan, Eleanor Hull and Lady Margaret Beaufort) and that, if she had borne children, they too were dead by 1373.

Julian has been the object of much ill-informed adulation and dubious interpretation.

She was a profound thinker, a difficult writer and an original theologian, not at all the simple, homely and cheerful woman of popular perception. Although one manuscript asserts that 'she did not know a letter', i.e. was illiterate or at least without Latin, and Julian describes herself as 'lewd' (i.e. uneducated), she was clearly literate in English and in the Latin of the Vulgate at least; how much further her learning extended is, like so much about her, a subject of dispute. . . . A passage in the Short Version of *A Revelation of Love* apologising for her temerity in writing as a 'woman, lewd, feeble and frail' has been removed from the later Long Version. She was also unlike other women visionaries in her tendency to engage in theological speculations on the most intractable of topics, such as the reality of sin and the constitution of the Trinity, rather than in affective, emotional recreations of events from the life of Christ. Her probing, analytical mind is most like that of her near-contemporary Catherine of Siena.

Comment: . . . [T]wo passages are from the Short (Carthusian) Version of *A Revelation of Love*. The first, which provides the context for Julian's visionary experiences, makes it clear that Julian was originally a medieval pious woman of a not uncommon type who, like many others, desired personal religious experience to enhance her faith based on the authority of the Church. Her longing for a more intense realisation, a 'bodily vision', of Christ's Passion, as if she had herself been present at the Crucifixion, is similar to that of Margery Kempe or Bridget of Sweden. What is slightly unusual, however, is her choice of St Cecilia as a role model; a combative early Christian martyr who converted her husband and his brother, she was popular in the Middle Ages (her legend is told by, among others, Chaucer in his *Second Nun's Tale*) but she represented a type of heroic, apostolic spirituality out of sympathy with late medieval piety. She was a preacher and teacher, a role Julian too ultimately adopted.

. . . [A] second passage is one of six revelations concerned with Christ's Passion, granted Julian in response to her request for her first 'grace'. The vision is painfully vivid, though not morbid or grotesque as late medieval devotion can so often be: the physical description of the suffering Christ is balanced and ultimately obliterated by her perception that even such physical pain is less than the spiritual pain of Christ's thirst for souls or the anguish of despair. Above all, Christ's love is stronger than his pain, and finally the suffering of Christ, of the visionary and of the whole of creation is transformed into joy.

. . . [A] third passage, from the Long (Benedictine) Version of the text, is part of Julian's radical attempt to reconstruct the traditional model of the Trinity on a Father-Mother rather than Father-Son basis. The latter part of the argument, in which Julian describes Christ's motherhood as an aspect of the humility of the Incarnation, his Passion as the travail of childbirth, and the Eucharist as his feeding his children with his body and blood as a mother does with her milk, is clear enough. So is her moving description of how Christ deals with the individual soul as a mother relates to her growing child, providing nurture, support and an education in which mistakes and setbacks (i.e. sins) actually play a positive role. No experience is wasted, for sin is not so much something from which we must dissociate ourselves as a part of ourselves through which we grow but which we eventually outgrow. The model is developmental, a very modern idea of fulfilling one's potential, through God's grace, and becoming the ideal, complete person whom God has eternally in mind.

But it would misrepresent the complexity of Julian's thought to omit the earlier part of the passage, difficult and obscure though it is. For the motherhood of God is a truth which operates on more than one level and springs ultimately from a conception of the Trinity as primarily a Father-Mother relationship, and of Christ—who as the Second Person of the Trinity was traditionally both the masculine *logos* or cosmic Reason and the feminine Wisdom or divine creative activity—as God our Mother in relation to God our Father. One cannot consider Julian's teaching on the motherhood of God without remembering that it is complementary to her concept of God's fatherhood, nor can it be fully understood without some knowledge of medieval theories about the biological roles of father and mother. Some medieval physiologists, following Aristotle, gave the mother a subordinate role in reproduction; she retained and nourished the father's seed and in due course produced it, but did not contribute anything herself to the initial conception (Rousselle 1988: 27-32).

. . . [A] final passage illuminates the compositional history of the texts. In this moving conclusion Julian draws a careful distinction between the visions and their meaning. For all their complexity, she finally sees that their meaning is single: 'Love was Our Lord's meaning.' All that ever can be drawn out of the revelations can neither exceed, nor exhaust, that parameter. . . .

Bibliography

Butkovich, A. (1972), *Revelations: Saint Birgitta of Sweden,* Los Angeles.

Colledge, E. and Guarnieri, R. (1968), 'The Glosses by M.N. and Richard Methley to "The Mirror of Simple Souls"', *AISP,* Vol. v, pp. 357-82.

Dronke, P. (1984), *Women Writers of the Middle Ages,* Cambridge.

Eccles, A. (1982), *Obstetrics and Gynaecology in Tudor and Stuart England,* Kent, Ohio.

Ellis, R. (1982), '"Flores ad fabricandum . . . coronam": An Investigation into the Uses of the Revelations of St Bridget of Sweden in Fifteenth-century England', *Medium Aevum,* Vol. li, pp. 163-86.

———(1990), 'Margery Kempe's Scribe and the Miraculous Books' in H. Phillips (ed.), *Langland, the Mystics and the Medieval English Religious Tradition,* Woodbridge, Suffolk, pp. 161-75.

Keiser, G. (1987b), 'Lady Margaret Beaufort and the Economics of Devotionalism' in M. Glasscoe (ed.), *The Medieval Mystical Tradition in England: Exeter Symposium IV,* Cambridge, pp. 9-26.

Lerner, R. E. (1972), *The Heresy of the Free Spirit in the Later Middle Ages,* Berkeley, Los Angeles and London.

Rousselle, A. (1988), *Porneia: On Desire and the Body in Antiquity,* trans. by F. Pheasant, Oxford.

Verdeyen, P. (1986), 'Le procès d'inquisition contre Marguerite Porete et Guiard de Cressonessart', *Revue d'histoire ecclésiastique,* Vol. lxxxi, pp. 47-94.

MARILYN R. MUMFORD (ESSAY DATE 1993)

SOURCE: Mumford, Marilyn R. "A Feminist Prolegomenon for the Study of Hildegard of Bingen." In *Gender, Culture, and the Arts: Women, the Arts, and Society,* edited by Ronald Dotterer and Susan Bowers, pp. 44-53. Cranbury, N.J.: Associated University Presses, 1993.

In the following excerpt, Mumford focuses on the contemporary feminist rediscovery of Hildegard of Bingen as the embodiment of the "modern women's spiritual quest."

The past decade has seen a great surge of interest in the works of Hildegard of Bingen, abbess and visionary who lived from 1098 to 1179. One of the first persons to call attention to Hildegard in the 1980s was the feminist artist Judy Chicago, who invited her to the magical "Dinner Party" that has since appeared in twelve major museums in the United States and Canada.[1]

More recently, Hildegard's theology, music, poetry, and images have engaged the interest of both academic scholars and New Age seekers after spiritual truth. One critic claims, in his unrestrained enthusiasm for her work, that "records of her music are outselling pop stars; her opera is being performed on various continents; most of her books now exist in critical German and Latin editions and are being translated into English; her mystical writings are being studied, prayed, and danced to; plays are being written of her work and life. . . ."[2]

Barbara Newman, whose *Sister Wisdom: St. Hildegard's Theology of the Feminine* is the most illuminating scholarly analysis of Hildegard's work to date, acknowledges that "[the day is past] when St. Hildegard's theological enterprise could be dismissed as a curiosity in church history, and she herself patronized as a token woman and thereby marginalized. . . . Within the past decade, this exceptional woman of God has won considerable recognition in the English-speaking world."[3] Newman laments the fact that Hildegard has been taken up as a kind of "New Age mystic" by "gurus of creation-centered spirituality" like Matthew Fox, partly because, as she justly observes, the translations of Hildegard's work on which Fox bases his analysis are "not to be trusted" (250).

The legendary "Sibyl of the Rhine" inspiring passionate interest in three such radically different groups—feminist artists, academic scholars, and New Age mystics—was a German visionary, poet, abbess, and founder of Benedictine communities who lived in what has been called "an age of great abbesses." As Bonnie Anderson and Judith Zinnser observe in the first volume of their fine new history of women, ". . . the world of the great abbesses was disappearing. By the end of the next [13th] century, the circumstance and attitudes that had favored learned establishment and had allowed holy women like Hildegard intellectual achievement and spiritual power had gone forever."[4]

As a direct result of the church's derogation and suppression of women's creative and intellectual activity in all spheres of life, both in community and in secular contexts, the involvement of women in the formation of Christian theology was cut off at the root by an increasingly deliberate policy on the part of the church fathers of excluding women from the life of the mind. Millions of women died at the stake, on the rack, and in other ghastly torments as a result of this vicious suppression of the feminine. More than 800 years after the death of Hildegard, women are still suffering some of the effects of ecclesiastical and clerical fear and hatred of women. It is particularly important, given these circumstances, to go back to the work of Hildegard of Bingen to comprehend the magnitude of what has been lost. The extraordinary spiritual and intellectual power vested in Hildegard and many other women of the early and high Middle Ages, as Anderson and Zinnser have amply demonstrated, attests to the importance, for feminist teachers, of re-membering and reclaiming the distant past.

Hildegard's achievement, then, can be located in the context of the high Middle Ages, on the threshold of a new dark age for women. But in many ways she epitomizes the concept of the Renaissance woman long before the concept of the Renaissance man came into being. In addition to her powerful work as theologian and visionary, Hildegard was a poet, playwright, composer of innovative music, preacher, scientist, healer, correspondent, and spiritual biographer whose images of the inner life are often astonishing in their artistic power and authenticity. In the midst of a long and busy life as founder or administrator of three communities of Benedictine women, she wrote, among other things, seventy-seven songs and a morality play set to music; three great works of theology accompanied by illuminations of her mystical visions; treatises on medicine, physiology, and pharmacology; and hundreds of letters to the great, the near great, and the humble, in which she chastised the great for their spiritual corruption or offered wise counsel to those who sought her advice.

This essay attempts to suggest something of Hildegard's sense of herself not only as a child of God and as a Christian but also of herself as a woman, a woman whose insights into the nature of her spiritual life are sometimes expressed in startling images of unconscious feminine archetypal material.

In doing this work it would be tempting to define oneself as a "romantic feminist" in Barbara Newman's sense of the word, a label based on the distinction between liberal and romantic feminism in Rosemary Radford Ruether's *Sexism and God-Talk: Toward a Feminist Theology* (1976). A "romantic radical feminist" accepts an "absolute distinction between male and female modes of being in the world," (268) and rejects "the Christian tradition altogether in order to celebrate the feminine divine as Goddess . . ." (269). In the academy, romantic feminists are likely to be scorned as essentialist in their assumptions about female nature. Newman defines liberal feminists, on the other hand, as the "overwhelming majority of American and European feminists," who ". . . (veto) the notion that gender is a metaphysical category" (267). Feminists in this group believe that "gender-related differences are culturally conditioned rather than innate" (267) . . . in other words, they accept a deconstructionist or social constructivist point of view, although not all who embrace that critical stance would describe themselves as liberal.

I suspect that Newman's position on the feminist spectrum and my own position are not so far apart as would first appear. She speaks in terms of the "traditional framework of Christian symbolics . . . the great feminine paradigms of Eve, Mary, and Ecclesia, or Mother Church" (xvii). Obviously these are the literal terms in which Hildegard herself expressed her conceptions of the feminine. These paradigms, however, sound very like archetypes of the feminine divine perhaps unconsciously reflected in Hildegard's poems and illuminations. Newman observes that ". . . at the heart of [Hildegard's] world there stands the numinous figure she called Sapientia or Caritas; holy Wisdom and Love divine, a visionary form who transcends allegory and attains the stature of theophany" (xvii-xviii). This seems an apt description of a goddess archetype, except for holy Wisdom's transcendent separation from an earthly female body, and Hildegard supplied that missing aspect, as we shall see, in certain of her illuminations.

Newman's brilliant analysis of the intersection of gender and the feminine divine in Hildegard's theology must be the foundation for any feminist examination of archetypal material in the illuminations and songs. Basing her own work on the pioneering studies of Hildegard by Peter Dronke and of gender in twelfth-century religious life by Caroline Bynum, Newman rightly observes that ". . . as [Hildegard] pursued her highly 'unfeminine' career as writer, reformer, and preacher, she naturally encountered opposition, both from her enemies and from within her own psyche. As a result, she developed an unusual degree of self-awareness about her gender and its social and spiritual implications" (xviii). Furthermore, Newman agrees with romantic radical feminists that "We may boldly claim Hildegard as the first Christian thinker to deal seriously and positively with the feminine as such, not merely with the challenges posed by and for women in a male-dominated world" (xvii).

Newman is reluctant to see the works of Hildegard in the context of modern women's spiritual quest or in the context of women's writing, categories she feels are "too broad to give us a suitable context for Hildegard" (xvi). My own work suggests that Hildegard's spiritual autobiography reveals significant connections with the stages of women's spiritual quest identified by Carol Christ in the works of such modern writers as Kate Chopin, Margaret Atwood, Doris Lessing, Adrienne Rich, and Ntozake Shange. Although such comparisons between Hildegard and modern women writers are ahistorical and thus in danger of universalizing women's experience, I am going to take what Diana Fuss, quoting Stephen Heath, calls the "risk of essence" to suggest the possibility of a spiritual connection between Hildegard and *some* modern women, myself included, who have seen in Hildegard's words and illuminations radical images of their own spiritual experience.[5] Although Christ's description of these stages of "women's" spiritual quest is expressed in essentialist terms, it is possible to qualify the conception by suggesting that these stages can be said to refer only to the experience of *some* modern British and American women writers:

> Women's spiritual quest takes a distinctive form in the fiction and poetry of women writers. It begins with an *experience of nothingness.* Such women experience emptiness in their own lives—in self-hatred, in self-negation, and in being a victim; . . . in the values that have shaped their lives. . . . The experience of nothingness often precedes an *awakening,* similar to a conversion experience, in which the powers of being are revealed. A woman's awakening to great powers grounds her in a new sense of self and a new orientation in the world . . .
>
> Awakening often occurs through mystical *identification,* which women's traditional attunement to the body and mothering processes have prepared them for. Women's mystical experiences often occur . . . in community with other women.
>
> Awakening is followed by a new naming of self and reality that articulates the new orientation to self and world achieved through experiencing the powers of being. Women's new naming of self and world often reflects wholeness, a movement toward overcoming dualisms of self and world, body and soul, nature and spirit, rational and emotional, which have plagued Western consciousness. Women's new naming of self and world suggests directions for social change and looks forward to the realization of spiritual insight in social reality—the integration of spiritual and social quests.[6]

Many of these psychological epiphanies can be recognized in Hildegard's spiritual autobiography, from her description of herself as "a poor little figure of a woman" (2) and as "wretched and more than wretched in the name of woman" (8) to the great mystical visions of the later years, when she envisioned the creation as the consequence of male and female aspects of divinity working through the cosmos. . . .

Notes

1. Judy Chicago, "From the Creation to the Fall: A Discussion of the Birth Project, *Power Play,* and *The Holocaust Project*" (keynote address, Woman, The Arts, and Society, Susquehanna University, 5 November 1988).
2. Matthew Fox, ed. *The Illuminations of Hildegard of Bingen* (Santa Fe: Bear Press, 1985), 13.
3. Barbara Newman, *Sister of Wisdom: Hildegard's Theology of the Feminine* (Berkeley: University of California Press, 1987), xv. Subsequent page references to this text are given parenthetically in the text.
4. Bonnie S. Anderson and Judith P. Zinnser, *A History of Their Own: Women in Europe from Prehistory to the Present,* vol. I (New York: Harper & Row, 1988), 190.
5. Diana Fuss, *Essentially Speaking: Feminism, Nature, and Difference* (New York: Routledge, 1989), 18.
6. Carol Christ, *Diving Deep and Surfacing: Women Writers on Spiritual Quest* (Boston: Beacon Press, 1980), 13-14.

VALERIE HENITIUK (ESSAY DATE FALL 2002)

SOURCE: Henitiuk, Valerie. "Virgin Territory: Murasaki Shikibu's Ôigimi Resists the Male." *Agora: An Online Graduate Journal* 1, no. 3 (fall 2002) http://www.humanities.ualberta.ca/agora/articles.cfm? ArticleNo=150 (accessed 21 October 2003).

In the following excerpt, Henitiuk offers a feminist reading of gendered space and female circumscription in Murasaki Shikibu's The Tale of Genji.

> *We must not look at goblin men,*
> *We must not buy their fruits:*
> *Who knows upon what soil they fed*
> *Their hungry, thirsty roots.*
>
> —Christina Rossetti

The controversial Japanese critic, author, and translator Setouchi Jakuchō has characterized the early 11th-century *Genji monogatari* (*The Tale of Genji*) as a sex education manual designed at least in part to guide Empress Akiko, who was brought to Court as a young child, through the complex maze of male/female relations.[1] In this context, the Ôigimi story is highly instructive regarding author Murasaki Shikibu's attitude toward love and sexuality, dealing as it does with the ultimately fatal anorexia of a woman who feels an overpowering need to escape being wedded and bedded. Many episodes found in Japanese literature of the Heian period (8th through 12th century) show how, despite varying degrees of initial reluctance, women are married off. Michitsuna no Haha, author of the biographical *Kagerô nikki* written in the mid- to late-10th century, accepts Kaneie's suit and, in the *Genji monogatari,* the young Murasaki, the Akashi Lady, Tamakazura, and countless others do in the end become brides, to name but a few examples. Thus, while Heian heroines are frequently portrayed as offering a posture of resistance to the sexual demands made by men, most do at one time or another yield more or less willingly to such demands. In the darker Uji chapters that form the final third of the *Genji,* however, a unique female character appears, one who clings to her decision to resist marriage and all that it entails, even unto death. When viewed microscopically, the actions of this *ie no onna* (literally, "house woman," i.e., one not serving at the imperial court) may well appear paranoid and irrational (or, in Freudian terms, frigid), but macroscopically, taking into account the women's stories that have come before, they are all too justifiable. Through a discussion of the tactics she uses to resist her suitor, and especially of the rationale behind such resistance, this article will argue that Ôigimi's behaviour actually demonstrates a powerfully subversive response to male invasion and attempted appropriation of the self.

In the interests of readability, references to Murasaki Shikibu's text will be drawn primarily from Edward Seidensticker's 1976 English version (1989 Knopf edition), with Japanese terms and phrases introduced only where specifically relevant. While use of a translation rather than the original is necessarily problematic, this strategy has the not inconsiderable benefit of rendering my argument accessible to an audience beyond that versed in the Classical Japanese language.[2] Critical works written in both English and Japanese (in the latter case, translations are my own) will, of course, be employed throughout.

Similarly, while examples drawn from elsewhere in Japanese literature will be used to illustrate the various points, I have also chosen to engage with certain textual references more familiar to a Western reader. Given that both Comparative Literature and feminist research are largely interdisciplinary in scope, they expose the falsity of many purportedly common-sensical divisions, revealing that certain artificial barriers may have "obstructed a complete view of women's situations and the social structures that perpetuated gender inequalities" (Hesse-Biber 1) and suggesting that there is an inherent value to bringing disparate elements together, to moving beyond the bounds of national literatures. In a recent report on the status of the discipline, Charles Bernheimer argues convincingly that

> comparative literature illuminates the artistic and cultural patterns of sameness and difference which exist both within and between societies, and it

ON THE SUBJECT OF...

HILDEGARD VON BINGEN (1098-1179)

Born into a noble family, Hildegard was entered at the age of eight by her parents into a hermitage attached to a Benedictine monastery, where she demonstrated a talent for leadership and theology. In 1136, when the abbess died, the nuns unanimously elected Hildegard as her successor. Although Hildegard possessed a gift for prophetic visions from an early age, it was not until she was in her forties that she revealed her visionary gifts to others. During this time, Hildegard worked toward the completion of the *Scivias* (c. 1151; *Scito vias Domini; or Know the Ways of the Lord*)—a documentation of the images and messages she received directly from God—while her fame as a prophet, healer, and visionary grew. Hildegard established her own convent at Rupertsberg, near Bingen, in 1150. Throughout the next decade, the convent flourished and Hildegard began to write works on medicine and natural philosophy, along with another visionary treatise, the *Liber vitae meritorum* (c. 1163; *The Book of Life's Rewards*).

Between 1158 and 1161 she embarked upon a series of preaching tours, and in 1163 she began the last of her visionary writings, the *Liber divinorum operum* (c. 1170; *Book of the Divine Works*). Often regarded by several scholars as Germany's first woman doctor and scientist, Hildegard's *Liber subtilitatum diversarum naturarum creaturarum libri novum* (c. 1158; *Nine Books on the Subtleties of Different Kinds of Creatures*), which is comprised of two parts—*Physica* and *Causae et curae*—is a pharmacopoeia and an encyclopedia denoting the characteristic medicinal properties of various plants, animals, and minerals, and contains discussion of the origin and treatment of disease. The later years of Hildegard's life were marked by her controversial yet successful defiance of church decrees when they were contrary to her own impulses and beliefs. This defiance has been the focus of much of the contemporary feminist criticism and analysis of Hildegard's life and works.

Lady Murasaki (c. 973-c. 1020).

> thereby gives us a precious contrastive portrait of societies' values and beliefs, as well as their aesthetic and literary traditions.
>
> (81)

New ways of seeing and theorizing the condition of women may well be revealed when the point of departure is located elsewhere than in Europe and North America. Ultimately, by focussing attention on a work of pre-modern Japanese literature, I am making an argument for a decentring move, questioning and destabilizing assumptions as to how our world can be understood and thus potentially leading to a re-thinking of certain feminist projects that have previously been rooted in the West.

Reading a 1000-year-old Japanese text from an early 21st-century Canadian perspective does inevitably run the serious risk of appropriation of voice. As Toril Moi rightly cautions, "it is not an unproblematic project to try to speak *for* the other woman, since this is precisely what the ventriloquism of patriarchy has always done: men have constantly spoken *for* women, or in the name of women" (67-8). Any analysis of a culture other than one's own needs to remain aware of the danger of daring to speak for the Other, of appropriating and (mis) interpreting what those from utterly different centuries and circumstances have said. While one could assert that every attempt to interpret a cultural artefact means a *de facto* act of speaking for its creator, whether sympathetically or not, it is a fact that the cross-cultural researcher must always remain especially conscious of the need to respect another's separate identity and experience if s/he is to avoid the pitfalls of misrepresentation and ahistoricism. One has also to be wary of anachronistic terminology such as "medieval feminist" and unjustified exploitation of early texts for supporting an unrelated, foreign perspective. Terms and phrases such as "patriarchal oppression" and "violation of personal space" certainly were not part of the vocabulary (be it Japanese or English) until very recent times indeed. Regardless, the ideas and emotions behind this modern-day wording are hardly new or geographically specific. Despite obvious and significant differences of culture and language, therefore, an examination of similar literary strategies can fruitfully exemplify and shed light on many of the concepts and arguments that have fascinated readers in both past and present, east and west.

Turning now to our main topic, we note that the reader is given a multitude of reasons for the elder Uji princess' rejection of Kaoru's advances. Her most often stated rationale is the desire to honour her father's wishes and protect the family name from ridicule (*hitowarae*). As Haruo Shirane explains at some length in *The Bridge of Dreams,* while her high rank requires Ôigimi to marry within an elite group or suffer social opprobrium, the family's status has diminished to the point where she has little hope of marrying well, if at all.[3] The aristocratic Kaoru's offer should, therefore, logically be received as a welcome one. As for the purported parental disapproval, Hachi no Miya (the Eighth Prince) clearly had never intended his stricture against marrying to apply in this case; on the contrary, he entertained the fond hope that one of the daughters would indeed wed his trustworthy and admirable pupil. The Prince makes several rather vague comments about the nature of the relationship either Ôigimi or Nakanokimi might eventually enter into with Kaoru, such as "his thoughts have turned to you because I once chanced to hint at a hope that he would watch over you after my death" (Seidensticker 1989: 792). Nonetheless, other statements become much more explicit: "I have done what I could to bring you together. You have years ahead of you and I must leave the rest to you" (805), and especially: "Kaoru was exactly what he hoped a son-in-law might be" (801). Should a proposal be made, therefore, it would scarcely fall into the category of "unsuitable marriages" (807) against which he warns the sisters, and one is hard pressed to misinterpret the father's actual wishes in this matter.

So why does Ôigimi adamantly refuse the suitor? A far more convincing factor behind her decision not to accept this husband is a fear of what intimacy with men will entail. While allowing males to have access to her person would provide the support (*ushiromi*) Ôigimi needs to make her way in society, accepting such support would place her completely at the mercy of a patriarchy that is more than a little misogynous. Consequently, the resistance she manifests can be viewed as a conscious attempt to retain her autonomy and sense of self. Ironically, in this case, self-preservation is possible only through self-annihilation, and the reader bears witness to Ôigimi's inexorable progress toward death.

While the isolated domestic space of Uji initially offers a stable place of refuge for the princesses, loss of the father-protector exposes them to Kaoru's and Niou's claims to right of access. Despite her initial protestations that she prefers to spend the rest of her life alone with her sister, Nakanokimi soon succumbs to what is considered a normal woman's fate and marries Niou. The elder sister, however, is unable to conceive of wedlock as a desirable or even imaginable option, and repeatedly rejects Kaoru's overtures. Unwilling or unable to accept this quite unparalleled resistance as genuine, the hero nonetheless continues to badger her. Given that external flight is not a viable option, Ôigimi's fear of the Phallus (and the threat it represents) necessitates ever further retreat within the inner sphere. Eventually, her desperate efforts to maintain spatial integrity lead her to reject any trespass of bodily boundaries, including via the act of eating. By starving herself to death, she gradually succeeds in eliminating her own physicality, which has served to attract the unwanted and insistent suitor. To Ôigimi's mind, intimacy with the male can be achieved only by sacrificing autonomy and identity, and is thus a destiny to be avoided at all costs.

Although born in Heian-kyô, Ôigimi and Nakanokimi have spent many years of their lives in the Uji villa, isolated from the capital and the glories of civilization it has to offer. Poetic allusions in *The Tale of Genji* and elsewhere play repeatedly on the association of the place name Uji with *ushi,* an adjective meaning gloomy, wearisome, distasteful, or miserable. Indeed, the Eighth Prince moved his family to this location only as a last resort, when their principal residence in the city burned down. He is aware of the hardship such a rusticated life may pose for his young daughters, but has no viable alternative. This environment is described in quite forbidding terms:

> Mountain upon mountain separated his [the Prince's] dwelling from the larger world. Rough people of the lower classes, woodcutters and the like, sometimes came by to do chores for him. There were no other callers. The gloom continued day after day, as stubborn and clinging as 'the morning mist on the peaks'.
>
> (779-80)

Not only is the villa remote from the city and human companionship, it is constantly enshrouded in oppressive mist and surrounded by dense undergrowth:

> As he [Kaoru] came into the mountains the mist was so heavy and the underbrush so thick that he could hardly make out the path; and as he pushed his way through thickets the rough wind would throw showers of dew upon him from a turmoil of falling leaves.
>
> (783)

The modern reader cannot help but be reminded of *Sleeping Beauty,* where the hero must fight his way through an almost impenetrable forest to rescue a virginal and insensible heroine. Nevertheless, as we will see below, in this case the acutely sensible beauty considers the wilderness an asylum and, to the consternation of her would-be champion, declines to be delivered from her unwed status in the traditional manner.

As Rachel Brownstein points out, this cult of the chaste maiden is an important and recurring motif in Western literature: "A beautiful virgin walled off from an imperfect world is the central figure in romance" (35). During Japan's Heian period as well, high-born women were very much "walled off," in that they remained jealously guarded behind several layers of both moveable and immoveable barriers. Clearly defined separate spheres for the sexes were fundamental to the elaborate etiquette of the time: "Good manners maintained proper distance, which amounted to upholding the accepted social order. [. . .] Domestic space, divided by screens, curtains, blinds, and so on [. . .] upheld distance and inviolate dignity" (Tyler xix). It is important to note that women in this society normally lived apart from their husbands in property owned by themselves, and thus could, at least in theory, limit intrusions to a significant degree. Direct access by even closely related adult males was not socially acceptable, with the result that the interior is portrayed as an almost exclusively female-gendered space. As a recent Japanese critical study on the architectural setting of the *Genji* (Yasuhara Morihiko, *Genji monogatari: Kûkan dokkai,* 2000) points out, female ownership of real estate meant that the woman's ability to decide what went on in her home was widely recognized, including even where a male visitor was allowed to sit.[4]

Ironically, however, most Heian architecture is revealed to be insubstantial, in that physical, visual, and aural penetration is within the reach of any moderately resourceful voyeur. Indeed, the entire tragedy of Ôigimi begins to unfold with Kaoru catching a hint of music wafting from the sisters' quarters. In this initially accidental, although not unqualifiedly innocent[5], aural violation of their privacy, the young man becomes tantalized by the faint strains of the lovely and melancholy duet that Ôigimi and Nakanokimi are playing on koto and biwa. Once he learns that the Prince, whom he has intended to visit, is away on a spiritual retreat (and that the two young women are thus alone and unprotected), the titillating possibility of a chance at *kaimami* (literally, "peering through a gap in the fence," but more generally this literature's omnipresent peeping tom motif) proves irresistible. With the connivance of a guardsman employed by the princesses, he hides behind a fence and, by the light of the moon shining out from behind a cloud, is able to peer at the two unsuspecting women under their raised blinds. The reader participates in this surreptitious violation of their privacy and Kaoru's resulting arousal, which fact is made clear in countless illustrations (such as the emaki, or picture scrolls) of this and similar scenes. As Joshua Mostow comments:

> The female narrator and her illustrator have internalized the masculine gaze and have been colonized by it: the narrator and viewer both merge with Kaoru and become complicit in his voyeurism. Essential to the voyeur's pleasure is the obliviousness of his object: the one he views must be totally absorbed in her own actions and unaware of the presence of a viewer.
>
> (467)

Ôigimi and her sister certainly have no reason to suspect the presence of a peeping tom, although they do subsequently blame themselves for being oblivious to Kaoru's distinctive aroma, which had been carried to them on the breeze. After all, they are described here as *uchi naru hito* (Abe 16: 131)—literally, "the people inside"—thus hardly sitting out in the open, or even on the verandah as two of their ladies-in-waiting do. It is only reasonable for the princesses to assume that they were sheltered from prying eyes there in their private quarters, behind gates and fences, surrounded by serving women and protected by guardsmen outside, as had been the case until this fateful day.

In these chapters, nature and geography appear to offer additional barriers to violation and protect Ôigimi and Nakanokimi from unwanted intrusions. The Uji palace is presented as both a religious and secular sanctuary, the tortuous route from the capital serving to discourage most gallants and thus keeping its occupants safe from harm. Seidensticker rightly comments on the significance of the "gothic mists and waters of Uji" (1983: 203), and one is tempted to see the Uji River as a moat-like additional defense against invaders. Of course, being on the far side of the Eighth Prince's property, it does not pose a physical barrier to access. Nevertheless, the river is repeatedly described in terms that make of it an omnipresent symbol of nature's power, serving as a warning to those from outside but somehow a source of comfort to the female inmates. I have already pointed out that prospective suitors must struggle through almost impassible thickets and underbrush, their passage made more difficult by the ever-present fog. Until Kaoru thoughtlessly discloses their existence to the licentious Niou, the sisters enjoy an almost uterine security in what is in effect a secure, woman-centred world. Let us not forget that this is a society where homes are principally inherited on a matrilineal basis, and thus female characters are intimately associated with their residences.

Given that Ôigimi lost her mother at a tender age, this locale can even, to a certain extent, be taken as a mother figure—an abstraction of the feminine principle. It is worth noting in this connection that, as a would-be priest who, despite pressure from members of his household, declines to remarry following his wife's death, the Eighth Prince is presented as a de-sexed or not-male character. Norma Field underscores the effeminate nature of the princesses' father by positing a homoerotic attraction between Kaoru and his spiritual tutor. Along these lines, Ôigimi's anorexia can be interpreted as a rejection of her own sexuality or femaleness in imitation of her sole parental role model: a final desire to regress to childhood, to undifferentiation, even if this regression means death. Such a reading would then significantly parallel the failed attempt by the Third Princess (another motherless child in the *Genji*) to cling to the prepubescent space that she views as her one refuge from the menacing Phallus.[6] Kaoru's violation would accordingly take on even more ominous overtones as an attack on not only Ôigimi herself, but also Child or Woman in general.

Bearing all these connotations associated with Uji in mind helps make more readily comprehensible Ôigimi's inward-looking obsession and consistent reluctance to leave. The security of her home is not something an intelligent woman throws away lightly, and the princesses have no hope of effective support elsewhere. As Brownstein points out, heroines of romance, symbolized by a rooted flower fated passively to await the male, must stand guard over their spatial and corporeal boundaries:

> Everything that can happen to the Rose while the lover struggles to reach her happens inside. She cannot but be self-preoccupied (which is not to say self-aware); unlike the Lover, she has no Rose outside of herself to draw her out or up. Her life must be passed in staring at the bare insides of garden walls. Eternal vigilance is her lot; if she lets herself be distracted it may be dangerous.
>
> (36)

The interior is clearly identified as her predestined space, and allowing any male to have access is a step fraught with danger. This lesson seems to have been instinctively learned by women in the Heian period: "So the last veil had been stripped away, thought Ôigimi. One thing was clear: theirs was a world in which not a single unguarded moment was possible" (835). The fatal conclusion of her story proves just how dangerous distraction can be.

Space is unambiguously presented as a locus of power relationships. While Ôigimi has long been marginal to society at large and the class into which she was born, she conversely enjoys a pivotal position in the domestic haven at Uji. Her role as mistress of the house, companion to her father, and mother-substitute to Nakanokimi has been relatively autonomous. She thus resists Kaoru's intention to displace her from her house to his, where she would clearly become more subject to another's whims. This situation is strikingly analogous to that of the Akashi Lady from earlier in *The Tale of Genji,* who has benefited from a childhood and youth where the world revolved around herself, and who sees no personal advantage—indeed considerable disadvantage—in being transported to Genji's household. As Charlotte Perkins Gilman once wrote:

> The life of the female savage is freedom itself . . . compared with the increasing constriction of custom closing in upon the woman, as civilization advances, like the iron torture chamber of romance.
>
> (65)

To these intellectually astute women who have come of age in the hinterlands of Uji or Akashi, which offer (relatively speaking) a certain amount of personal freedom, Heian-kyô and the patriarchal society there enshrined do symbolize such an iron chamber waiting to close in on them. In their view, far from the pinnacle of joy and security that it represents to the waiting women and others in their entourage, the capital is a site of dependence and potential humiliation. Ôigimi's preference for the independence she has known, in spite of its obscure and peripheral nature, is thus understandable and leads her to resist being brought to a central position (i.e., to an estate within the city limits) that will inevitably be a weaker one. What makes the situation of this Uji princess even more untenable than most is the fact that, in his concern for the well-being of his daughters, the Eighth Prince has to a certain degree dispossessed her by making both sisters *de facto* wards of another man. (This other man is, of course, Kaoru, the stubbornly persistent suitor.) Although she does inherit the property that has been her home for many years and thus gains increased nominal autonomy, Ôigimi finds herself even more reliant on Kaoru's good will than ever before as, in his role as protector sanctioned by her late father, he presses her with unwelcome attentions that she now finds extremely awkward and risky to rebuff.

Ôigimi's dilemma is a metaphor for woman's ambiguous position within and without the dominant male culture of Heian Japan and elsewhere, where the appropriation of space signifies appropriation of the body. A paralyzing fear of, or at least pronounced distaste for, intimacy with men offers little mystery in a society where women can achieve sexual union only at the cost of totally sacrificing independence and self. It has been said that, "conceiving of herself as the creature of her relationships with others, and bound by her woman's fate to a life of relationships, the conscious heroine longs for solitude and separateness" (Brownstein 288-9). . . .

Notes

1. "Akiko wa jûni-sai de kôkyû ni hairaretan dakedo, nenne de, ren'ai mo sekusu mo wakaranai. O-ningyô mitaina hito deshô. Tsumari, 'Genji' wa isshu no seikyôiku hon datta no yo." ("Akiko was twelve years

old when she entered the Court, and knew nothing of either love or sex. She was like a little doll. In short, 'Genji' was a sort of sex education manual.") Tawara Machi. "Ima mo mukashi mo ai koso jinsei no gendôryoku." Interview with Setouchi Jakuchô. (Tokyo: Shûkan Asahi, August 21-8, 1998) 45.

2. Readers wishing to delve into the question of translation accuracy with regard to women's writing in Heian Japan may find my article entitled "Translating Woman: Reading the Female through the Male" to be of interest.

3. Haruo Shirane, *The Bridge of Dreams: A Poetics of 'The Tale of Genji'* (Stanford: Stanford University Press, 1987). See especially pp. 140-41. As a frequently cited footnote in Abe *et al.* (15:23 n. 25) makes clear, the vast majority (85%) of princesses of the blood remained single during the first two centuries of the Heian period, primarily owing to the scarcity of appropriately ranked marriage partners.

4. Further, the exact location within the home to which she accords him access is of great import, implying minute differentiations of degrees of intimacy. As Yasuhara (201) puts it, *Kono onna no kûkan ni oite wa onna ga otoko no suwaru ichi o kimeta. Misu de au ka, hisashi de au ka no sa wa ôkii.* ("In this woman's space, it was the woman who decided the place where a man would sit. There was a vast difference in whether she met him at the bamboo blind or closer to the eaves.")

5. In having Kaoru travel to Uji through darkness and rain, dressed inconspicuously and accompanied by a reduced number of retainers, the narrator accords him all the trappings of a lover on his way to a secret tryst. Indeed, our hero, unfamiliar with such intrigues, seems to derive a certain level of sexual exhilaration from the escapade, even before the women appear on the scene: "This was not the sort of journey he was accustomed to. It was sobering and at the same time exciting" (783).

6. For an in-depth discussion of this heroine's use of temporal suspension, see my forthcoming article entitled "Seeking Refuge in Prepubescent Space: The Strategy of Resistance Employed by *The Tale of Genji*'s Third Princess."

Works Cited

Abe Akio, Akiyama Ken, and Imai Gen'e, eds. *Genji monogatari.* Nihon Koten Bungaku Zenshû vols. 12-17, 1970-1976.

Bernheimer, Charles, ed. *Comparative Literature in the Age of Multiculturalism.* Baltimore and London: The Johns Hopkins University Press, 1995.

Bronfen, Elisabeth. *Over Her Dead Body: Death, Femininity and the Aesthetic.* Manchester: Manchester University Press, 1992.

Brownstein, Rachel. *Becoming a Heroine: Reading about Women in Novels.* New York: Columbia University Press, 1994.

Field, Norma. *The Splendor of Longing in the Tale of Genji.* Princeton: Princeton University Press, 1987.

Gilman, Charlotte Perkins. *Women and Economics.* Ed. Carl N. Degler. New York: Harper and Row, 1966.

Henitiuk, Valerie. "Seeking Refuge in Prepubescent Space: The Strategy of Resistance Employed by The Tale of Genji's Third Princess." *Canadian Review of Comparative Literature/Revue Canadienne de Littérature Comparée.* Forthcoming.

———. "Translating Woman: Reading the Female through the Male," *Meta* 44.3 (September 1999): 469-84.

Hesse-Biber, Sharlene, et al., ed. *Feminist Approaches to Theory and Methodology: An Interdisciplinary Reader.* New York and Oxford: Oxford University Press, 1999.

Imai Hisayo. "*Migushi no koborekakaritaru o kakiyaritsutsu mitamaeba:* Otoko to onna no hazama ni wa. Ôigimi to Kaoru no koimonogatari." Genji monogatari tekusuto tsua-, v. *Kokubungaku* 45:9 (July 2000) 172-77.

Keene, Donald, trans. *Essays in Idleness: The Tsurezuregusa of Kenkô.* New York: Columbia University Press, 1967.

Komashaku Kimi. *Murasaki Shikibu no messêji.* Tokyo: Asahi, 1991.

Miller, Nancy K. *The Heroine's Text: Readings in the French and English Novel, 1722-1782.* New York: Columbia University Press, 1980.

Moi, Toril. *Sexual/Textual Politics: Feminist Literary Theory.* London and New York: Routledge, 1985.

Mostow, Joshua S. "'Just Like a Picture': Metaphors of Beauty, Romance, and the Feminine Regard." *ICLA '91: Tokyo: The Force of Vision I: Dramas of Desire, Visions of Beauty.* 1995. 463-69.

Nakamoto Takako. "The Female Bell-Cricket." Trans. Yukiko Tanaka. *To Live and To Write.* Yukiko Tanaka, ed. Seattle: The Seal Press, 1987. 135-44.

Ôba, Minako. "Special Address: Without Beginning, Without End". Trans. Paul Gordon Schalow. *The Woman's Hand.* Ed. Paul Gordon Schalow and Janet A. Walker. Stanford: Stanford University Press, 1996. 19-40.

Orbaugh, Sharalyn. "The Body in Contemporary Japanese Women's Fiction." *The Woman's Hand.* Ed. Paul Gordon Schalow and Janet A. Walker. Stanford: Stanford University Press, 1996. 119-164.

Rossetti, Christina. "Goblin Market." *The Norton Anthology of English Literature.* Ed. M. H. Abrams. New York: W.W. Norton & Company, 1979. 1523-35.

Seidensticker, Edward. *Genji Days.* New York: Kodansha International, 1983.

———. trans. *The Tale of Genji.* New York: Alfred A. Knopf, 1989.

Shirane, Haruo. *The Bridge of Dreams: A Poetics of 'The Tale of Genji'.* Stanford: Stanford University Press, 1987.

Tawara Machi. "Ima mo mukashi mo ai koso jinsei no gendôryoku." Interview with Setouchi Jakuchô. *Shûkan Asahi* August 21-8, 1998. 41-45.

Tyler, Royall. "Introduction." *The Tale of Genji.* By Murasaki Shikibu. Trans. Royall Tyler. New York: Viking, 2001. xi-xxix.

Yasuhara Morihiko. *Genji monogatari: Kûkan dokkai.* Tokyo: Kashima Shuppankai, 2000.

FURTHER READING

Criticism

Antonopoulos, Anna. "The Double Meaning of Hestia: Gender, Spirituality, and Signification in Antiquity." *Women and Language* 16, no. 1 (spring 1993): 1-6.

Semiotic study of the Greek goddess of the hearth, Hestia, which suggests she may represent an "omphalos" (navel) symbol that stands in opposition to the phallus.

Arens, Katherine. "Between Hypatia and Beauvoir: Philosophy as Discourse." *Hypatia* 10, no. 4 (fall 1995): 46-75.

Compares literary interpretations of two female philosophers, one modern, Simone de Beauvoir, and the other classical, Hypatia, in order to explore the constraints placed upon feminine philosophical discourse.

Bar On, Bat-Ami, ed. *Engendering Origins: Critical Feminist Readings in Plato and Aristotle.* Albany: State University of New York Press, 1994, 248 p.

Collection of twelve essays by various contributors featuring feminist approaches to the writings of Plato and Aristotle on the subjects of women and philosophy.

Black, Nancy B. "Woman as Savior: The Virgin Mary and Empress of Rome in Gautier de Coinci's *Miracles.*" *Romanic Review* 88, no. 4 (November 1997): 503-17.

Considers thirteenth-century Benedictine monk Gautier de Coinci's depiction of the empress of Rome as a saintly spiritual figure akin to the Virgin Mary in his collection Miracles de Nostre Dame.

Blamires, Alcuin. Introduction to *Woman Defamed and Woman Defended: An Anthology of Medieval Texts,* edited by Alcuin Blamires, pp. 1–16. Oxford: Oxford University Press, 1992.

Presents an overview of the sources and themes of antifeminism in the literature of the Middle Ages.

Bremmer, Jan N. "Gender." In *Greek Religion,* pp. 69-83. Oxford: Oxford University Press, 1994.

Details the daily and ritual life of women in ancient Greece, considering in particular a number of religious festivals reserved exclusively for women.

Brosius, Maria. *Women in Ancient Persia, 559-331* B.C. Oxford: Oxford University Press, 1996, 258 p.

Studies Greek perceptions of Persian women in Achaemenid Persia (559-331 B.C.), examining social customs and rituals, especially among the aristocracy.

Cameron, Alan, and Jacqueline Long. "Hypatia." In *Barbarians and Politics at the Court of Arcardius,* pp. 39-62. Berkeley: University of California Press, 1993.

Chronicles the life and teachings of the Alexandrian philosopher and mathematician Hypatia, observing her active role in the public life of fourth-century Roman Egypt.

Cartwright, Jane. "Dead Virgins: Feminine Sanctity in Medieval Wales." *Medium Aevum* 71, no. 1 (spring 2002): 1-28.

Compiles biographical and historical evidence concerning female Welsh saints of the fifth, sixth, and seventh centuries, noting that their stories typically focus on humane acts and efforts to maintain their own chastity.

Castelli, Elizabeth A. "Gender, Theory, and the Rise of Christianity: A Response to Rodney Stark." *Journal of Early Christian Studies* 6, no. 2 (1998): 227-57.

Illuminates the role of women in the spread of Roman Christianity during the early centuries of the modern era, claiming that evidence of the social benefits of Christianity for women during this period is relatively thin.

Chadwick, Whitney. "The Middle Ages." In *Women, Art, and Society,* pp. 37-58. London: Thames and Hudson, 1990.

Surveys the role of women as artists and scholars in the Middle Ages, with particular emphasis on Herrad of Landsberg's encyclopedic Hortus Deliciarum *and Hildegard of Bingen's visionary manuscript, the* Scivias.

Chamberlain, David. "Marie de France's Arthurian *lai*: Subtle and Political." In *Culture and the King: The Social Implications of the Arthurian Legend,* edited by Martin B. Shichtman and James P. Carley, pp. 15-34. Albany: State University of New York Press, 1994.

Analyzes Marie de France's Arthurian "Lai de Lanval" in the context of twelfth-century social and political themes.

Chance, Jane, ed. *Gender and Text in the Later Middle Ages.* Gainesville: University Press of Florida, 1996, 342 p.

Features essays on such topics as feminine mysticism, misogyny, and female self-representation in works by Julian of Norwich, Birgitta of Sweden, Margery Kempe, Hadewijch, Marie de France, Christine de Pisan, and others.

Cherewatuk, Karen, and Ulrike Wiethaus, eds. *Dear Sister: Medieval Women and the Epistolary Genre.* Philadelphia: University of Philadelphia Press, 1993, 215 p.

Collection of essays that survey women's contributions to the literary tradition of letter-writing from the sixth to the sixteenth centuries.

Cowell, Andrew. "Deadly Letters: 'Deus amanz,' Marie's 'Prologue' to the *Lais,* and the Dangerous Nature of the Gloss." *Romanic Review* 88, no. 3 (May 1997): 337-56.

Evaluates Marie de France's efforts to appropriate traditionally male forms of legitimizing narrative authority in her prologue to the Lais.

Duby, Georges. *Women of the Twelfth Century, Volume Three: Eve and the Church,* translated by Jean Birrell. Chicago: University of Chicago Press, 1998, 122 p.

Discusses the twelfth-century recognition by leaders within the Christian Church of the unique spiritual and social expectations of women in the Middle Ages.

Evans, Ruth, and Lesley Johnson, eds. *Feminist Readings in Middle English Literature: The Wife of Bath and All Her Sect.* London: Routledge, 1994, 257 p.

Consists of nine essays that approach Chaucer's Wife of Bath and other figures—both historical and literary—of the medieval period generally associated with a protofeminist critique of patriarchal society.

Faraone, Christopher A. "Salvation and Female Heroics in the Parodos of Aristophanes' *Lysistrata.*" *Journal of Hellenic Studies* 117 (1997): 38-59.

Comments on the theatrical reenactment of what would have been to classical Greek audiences a recognizable ritual celebration of salvation by women in Aristophanes's drama Lysistrata.

Foley, Helene P. "The 'Female Intruder' Reconsidered: Women in Aristophanes' *Lysistrata* and *Ecclesiazusae.*" *Classical Philology* 77, no. 1 (January 1982): 1-21.

Problematizes the tension between oikos *and* polis *(household and city-state), generally depicted in terms of a binary opposition between feminine and masculine spheres, by drawing counterexamples from classical Greek drama.*

———. *Female Acts in Greek Tragedy.* Princeton, N.J.: Princeton University Press, 2001, 410 p.

In-depth study of the gendered conflict between private and public concerns depicted in the tragic drama of Sophocles, Euripides, and Aeschylus.

Fulkerson, Laurel. "Epic Ways of Killing a Woman: Gender and Transgression in *Odyssey* 22.465-72." *Classical Journal* 97, no. 4 (April-May 2002): 335-50.

Treats the theme of infidelity in Homer's Odyssey *by contrasting the unfaithfulness of twelve serving maids, later hanged by Telemachus, with Penelope's lifelong constancy to Odysseus.*

Garber, Rebecca L. R. *Feminine Figurae: Representations of Gender in Religious Texts by Medieval German Women Writers 1100-1375.* London: Routledge, 2003, 295 p.

Book-length study of gender and genre focused on the three literary forms associated with medieval women writers: the vision cycle, sister-book, and personal revelation.

Gold, Barbara K., Paul Allen Miller, and Charles Platter, eds. *Sex and Gender in Medieval and Renaissance Texts: The Latin Tradition.* Albany: State University of New York Press, 1997, 322 p.

Investigates representations of women and of the female body in a number of Latin texts of the medieval and early Renaissance periods, including works by Hrotsvit, St. Augustine, and Petrarch.

Greer, Germaine. "The Cloister." In *The Obstacle Race: The Fortunes of Women Painters and Their Work,* pp. 151-68. New York: Farrar, Straus, and Giroux, 1979.

Evaluates the unique social position of the convent in medieval Europe, exploring the link between monasticism and the creation of illuminated manuscripts by women.

Harris, Kevin. "The Place of Women." In *Sex, Ideology, and Religion: The Representation of Women in the Bible,* pp. 30-78. Brighton, Sussex: Wheatsheaf Books, 1984.

Highlights the relative absence of women as significant or active figures in the Bible in contrast to biblical men.

Havelock, Christine Mitchell. "Mourners on Greek Vases: Remarks on the Social History of Women." In *Feminism and Art History: Questioning the Litany,* edited by Norma Broude and Mary D. Garrard, pp. 45-61. New York: Harper & Row, 1982.

Focuses on antique vase paintings as they offer insight into the status and emotional life of women in classical Greece.

Head, Pauline. "Who Is the Nun from Heidenheim? A Study of Hugeburc's *Vita Willibaldi.*" *Medium Aevum* 71, no. 1 (spring 2002): 29-46.

Probes Hugeburc's eighth-century biographies of Willibald and Wynnebald, describing narrative tensions between hagiographic convention, the author's feminine subjectivity, and her male literary subjects.

Hedreen, Guy. "Image, Text, and Story in the Recovery of Helen." *Classical Antiquity* 15, no. 1 (April 1996): 152-84.

Analyzes Athenian vase-paintings depicting Helen of Troy and her husband Menelaos as they suggest social relationships between men and women in Bronze-Age Greece.

Hurtig, Dollian Margaret. "'I Do, I Do': Medieval Models of Marriage and Choice of Partners in Marie de France's 'Le Fraisne.'" *Romanic Review* 92, no. 4 (November 2001): 363-79.

Suggests that Marie de France's twelfth-century lai *"Le Fraisne" introduces a notion of the bond between marriage and love that at the time may have been quite revolutionary.*

Janan, Micaela. "'There beneath the Roman Ruin where the Purple Flowers Grow': Ovid's Minyeides and the Feminine Imagination." *American Journal of Philology* 115 (1994): 427-48.

Focuses on Ovid's evocation of feminine desire in the stories of his Metamorphoses *involving the Minyeides, viewing it as a force disruptive to all social and institutional constraints.*

Jensen, Anne. *God's Self-Confident Daughters: Early Christianity and the Liberation of Women,* translated by O. C. Dean, Jr. Louisville, Ky.: Westminster John Knox Press, 1996, 347 p.

Endeavors to construct a feminist history of women and the church in late antiquity, with sections on the education, marginalization, martyrdom, and the spiritual teachings of women in the early Christian period.

Klein, Stacy S. "Reading Queenship in Cynewulf's *Elene.*" *Journal of Medieval and Early Modern Studies* 33, no. 1 (2003): 47-89.

Explains the influence of Cynewulf's poem Elene *in defining the nature of queenship in Anglo-Saxon England.*

Koloski-Ostrow, Ann Olga, and Claire L. Lyons, eds. *Naked Truths: Women, Sexuality, and Gender in Classical Art and Archaeology.* London: Routledge, 1997, 315 p.

Collection of essays oriented toward the redefinition of classical art history from the perspective of contemporary feminism (featuring selections on antique representations of such figures as Sappho and Clytemnestra), as well as on classical renderings of the feminine form in the visual arts.

Lesko, Barbara S. *The Great Goddesses of Egypt.* Norman: University of Oklahoma Press, 1999, 321 p.

Detailed study of the seven goddesses of the ancient Egyptian pantheon and of the temples and cults devoted to them.

Lewis, Sian. *The Athenian Woman: An Iconographic Handbook.* London: Routledge, 2002, 261 p.

Documents and analyzes representations of Athenian women in Greek painting and sculpture of the fifth and sixth centuries B.C., encapsulating what can be known of their social and personal life from these sources.

McLaren, Anne, and Chen Qinjian. "The Oral and Ritual Culture of Chinese Women: Bridal Lamentations of Nanhui." *Asian Folklore Studies* 59 (2000): 205-38.

Interprets the bridal lamentation ritual performed by women of the Yangtze River delta region in imperial China—one of only a few available insights into the spiritual and personal life of generally secluded and socially marginalized Chinese women during this period.

Pomeroy, Sarah B. "Women in the Bronze Age and Homeric Epic." In *Goddesses, Whores, Wives, and Slaves: Women in Classical Antiquity,* pp. 16-31. New York: Schocken Books, 1975.

Surveys the position of women in Bronze-Age Greece as portrayed in Homeric epics the Iliad *and the* Odyssey, *noting that despite the patriarchal bent of this early civilization, Homer's works remain relatively free of misogyny.*

———. *Spartan Women.* Oxford: Oxford University Press, 2002, 198 p.

Full-length history of women in ancient Sparta that features sections on education, marriage, motherhood, the aristocracy, and religion in Spartan society.

Richmond, Colleen D. "Hrotsvit's Sapientia: Rhetorical Power and Women of Wisdom." *Renascence: Essays on Values in Literature* 55, no. 2 (winter 2003): 133-45.

Argues that in her play The Martyrdom of the Holy Virgins Fides, Spes, and Karitas, *the tenth-century Saxon canoness Hrotsvit offers an empowering reassessment of women that breaks with many of the patriarchal stereotypes found in classical Roman drama.*

Rigby, S. H. "The Wife of Bath, Christine de Pizan, and the Medieval Case for Women." *Chaucer Review* 35, no. 2 (2000): 133-65.

Adapts Christine de Pizan's rhetorical strategies in defense of women to the critical debate surrounding Geoffrey Chaucer's Wife of Bath as either an outspoken champion of feminist rights or the embodiment of negative and patriarchal stereotypes regarding women.

Rose, Christine M. "What Every Goodwoman Wants: The Parameters of Desire in *Le Menagier de Paris/The Goodman of Paris.*" *Studia Anglica Posnaniensia: International Review of English Studies* 38 (mid-summer 2002): 393-410.

Assesses the ways in which women may have been manipulated by popular medieval conduct and advice books written by men, using the example of the fourteenth-century Le menagier de Paris, *a housekeeping book written by a 60-year-old French official for his 15-year-old wife.*

Rossi, Mary Ann. "The Passion of Perpetua: Everywoman of Late Antiquity." In *Pagan and Christian Anxiety: A Response to E. R. Dodds,* edited by Robert C. Smith and John Lounibos, pp. 53-85. Lanham, Md.: University Press of America, 1985.

Analyzes the text of the Passio Perpetuae, *highlighting insights the diary provides regarding Perpetua's status as a female Christian convert within the patriarchal society of imperial Rome.*

Salisbury, Joyce E. *Encyclopedia of Women in the Ancient World.* Santa Barbara, Calif.: ABC-CLIO, 2001, 385 p.

Presents brief entries on literary and historical women of antiquity and topics of related interest.

Shaw, Brent D. "The Passion of Perpetua." *Past & Present,* no. 139 (May 1993): 3-45.

Studies the document known as the Passio Sanctarum Perpetuae et Felicitatis, *which includes Perpetua's account of her arrest and imprisonment prior to her execution in early-third-century* A.D. *Rome. The critic stresses Perpetua's clear and direct literary mode of self-expression and also examines the additions of a male editor to the text of her diary.*

Shaw, Michael. "The Female Intruder: Women in Fifth-Century Drama." *Classical Philology* 70, no. 4 (October 1975): 255-66.

Evaluates distinctions between masculine and feminine social roles portrayed in classical Greek drama.

Sikorska, Liliana. "Internal Exile: Dorothea of Montau's Inward Journey." *Studia Anglica Posnaniensia: International Review of English Studies* 38 (mid-summer 2002): 433-44.

Documents the solitary pilgrimage and writings of fourteenth-century saint and mystic Dorothea of Montau.

Thompson, Patricia J. "Dismantling the Master's House: A Hestian/Hermean Deconstruction of Classic Texts." *Hypatia* 9, no. 4 (fall 1994): 38-56.

Concentrates on the gendered tension between domestic and public spheres in ancient Greece (usually typified in the symbolic opposition between oikos *and* polis*) in terms of the gods Hestia and Hermes as respective guardians of private and public space.*

Walcot, Peter. "Greek Attitudes towards Women: The Mythological Evidence." In *Women in Antiquity,* edited by Ian McAuslan and Peter Walcot, pp. 91–102. Oxford: Oxford University Press, 1996.

Claims that the Greek representation of women in mythic literature suggests that male perceptions of the opposite sex were conditioned by a fear of female sexuality. This essay was originally published in 1984.

Walters, Barbara R. "Women Religious *Virtuosae* from the Middle Ages: A Case Pattern and Analytic Model of Types." *Sociology of Religion* 63, no. 1 (2002): 69-89.

Comparative analysis of five female religious models of the thirteenth century (including Hadewijch of Antwerp, Marguerite Porete, and Gertrude of Helfta) that endeavors to rework Max Weber's sociological theory of medieval mysticism.

White, Rachel Evelyn. "Women in Ptolemaic Egypt." *Journal of Hellenic Studies* 18 (1898): 238-66.

Compiles evidence relating to royal mothers, sisters, and wives in Ptolemaic Egypt, and includes brief descriptions of the queens who bore the name Cleopatra.

Wren, James A. "Salty Seaweed, Absent Women, and Song: Authorizing the Female as Poet in the *Izayoi nikki.*" *Criticism: A Quarterly for Literature and the Arts* 39, no. 2 (spring 1997): 185-204.

Discusses the travel diary of the twelfth-century Japanese nun Abutsu as it presents a literary challenge to the patriarchal culture of feudal Japan.

Zeitlin, Froma I. "The Dynamics of Misogyny: Myth and Mythmaking in the *Oresteia.*" *Arethusa* 2 (1978): 149-81.

Argues that Aeschylus's dramas enact the conflict between female and male principles in a patriarchal society.

WOMEN IN THE 16TH, 17TH, AND 18TH CENTURIES: AN OVERVIEW

Women in the sixteenth, seventeenth, and eighteenth centuries were challenged with expressing themselves in a patriarchal system that generally refused to grant merit to women's views. Cultural and political events during these centuries increased attention to women's issues such as education reform, and by the end of the eighteenth century, women were increasingly able to speak out against injustices. Though modern feminism was nonexistent, many women expressed themselves and exposed the conditions that they faced, albeit often indirectly, using a variety of subversive and creative methods.

The social structure of sixteenth century Europe allowed women limited opportunities for involvement; they served largely as managers of their households. Women were expected to focus on practical domestic pursuits and activities that encouraged the betterment of their families, and more particularly, their husbands. In most cases education for women was not advocated—it was thought to be detrimental to the traditional female virtues of innocence and morality. Women who spoke out against the patriarchal system of gender roles, or any injustice, ran the risk of being exiled from their communities, or worse; vocal unmarried women in particular were the targets of witch-hunts. Anne Hutchinson, who challenged the authority of Puritan clergy, was excommunicated for her outspoken views and controversial actions. Anne Askew, a well-educated, outspoken English Protestant, was tried for heresy in 1545; her denial of transubstantiation was grounds for her imprisonment. She was eventually burned at the stake for her refusal to incriminate other Protestant court ladies. Elizabeth I ascended to the throne in 1558, a woman who contradicted many of the gender roles of the age. She was well educated, having studied a variety of subjects including mathematics, foreign language, politics, and history. Elizabeth was an outspoken but widely respected leader, known for her oratory skills as well as her patronage of the arts. Despite the advent of the age of print, the literacy rate during this period remained low, though the Bible became more readily available to the lower classes. Religious study, though restricted to "personal introspection," was considered an acceptable pursuit for women, and provided them with another context within which they could communicate their individual ideas and sentiments. In addition to religious material, women of this period often expressed themselves through the ostensibly private forms of letters and autobiographies.

The seventeenth century was not an era of drastic changes in the status or conditions of women. Women continued to play a significant, though not acknowledged, role in economic and political structures through their primarily domestic activities. They often acted as counselors in the home, "tempering" their husbands' words and actions. Though not directly involved in politics, women's roles within the family and local community allowed them to influence the political system. Women were discouraged from directly expressing political views counter to their husbands' or to broadly condemn established systems; nevertheless, many women were able to make public their private views through the veil of personal, religious writings. Again, women who challenged societal norms and prejudices risked their lives—Mary Dyer was hanged for repeatedly challenging the Massachusetts law that banished Quakers from the colony. Though their influence was often denigrated, women participated in various community activities. For example, women were full members of English guilds; guild records include references to "brethern and sistern" and "freemen and freewomen." During the seventeenth century, women's writings continued to focus on largely religious concerns, but increasingly, women found a creative and intellectual outlet in private journal- and letter-writing. Mary Rowlandson's captivity narrative, published in 1682, is a famous narrative written ostensibly for personal use that was made public and became a popular success.

The eighteenth century brought the beginning of the British cultural revolution. With the increasing power of the middle class and an expansion in consumerism, women's roles began to evolve. The economic changes brought by the new middle class provided women with the opportunity to be more directly involved in commerce. Lower- to middle-class women often assisted their husbands in work outside the home. It was still thought unseemly for a lady to be knowledgeable of business so, though some class distinctions were blurring, the upper class was able to distinguish themselves from the rest of society. The rise in consumerism allowed the gentry to place a greater emphasis on changing fashion and "display," further distancing them from the middleclass. With the advent of changes in rules of fashion and acceptable mores within society, some women established a literary niche writing etiquette guides. Also due to the cultural revolution, mounting literacy rates among the lower classes caused an increase in publishing, including the rise of the periodical. Men and women of all classes found new means to express ideas in the wider publishing community. Though women's writing during this period continued largely to be an extension of domesticity, and focused mainly on pragmatic, practical issues, women found a wider market for publication. The act of professional writing, however, was still considered "vulgar" among the aristocracy. Significant colonial expansion during this period provided would-be writers with unique subject matter—letters written by women abroad discussed foreign issues and culture, and offered a detailed view of far-off lands. These letters were often circulated among members of an extended family, as well as in the larger community. In defiance of social strictures, women such as Mary Wollstonecraft began to speak out publicly on women's rights, including education and marriage laws. Though women had better access to education, the goal of women's education was to attain an ideal "womanhood"—a "proper education" was viewed as one that supported domestic and social activities but disregarded more academic pursuits. Women such as Wollstonecraft advocated access to education for women that was equal to that of their male counterparts. Marriage laws, which overwhelmingly favored men, also spurred public debate, though little was accomplished to reform laws during this period.

Throughout the world, women took action to advance their political and social rights. Catherine the Great of Russia devised a coup d'etat to take the throne in 1762, an aggressive act to prevent her son's disinheritance. Catherine continued to rule in an unconventional, independent manner, withdrawing from the men who made her ascension possible and remaining unmarried to ensure her power. Catherine was a shrewd politician, and used wide public support to enact laws that significantly altered the Russian political system. In France, Olympe de Gouges demanded equal rights for women in the new French Republic, and was eventually executed by guillotine in 1793. Madame Roland, who also met an untimely death in 1793, influenced revolutionary politicians and thinkers during the French Revolution through her famous salon. She, too, was an activist for women's social and political rights and was executed for treason, largely due to her outspoken feminist ideas. Phillis Wheatley, an African-American slave, examined slavery and British imperialism in her poetry, and became a notable figure among abolitionists in America and abroad. Increasingly, women rebuked traditional roles and spoke out against the social and political inequalities they faced. The century closed with the deaths of visionaries such as Mary Wollstonecraft and Catherine the Great, and the births of a new breed of female writers and scholars. The political and social changes that took place in the eighteenth century paved the way for these future writers and activists to advance the cause of women's rights.

REPRESENTATIVE WORKS

Marie Jean Antoine

On the Admission of Women to the Rights of Citizenship (essay) 1790

Elizabeth Ashbridge

Some Account of the Fore-Part of the Life of Elizabeth Ashbridge (autobiography) 1774

St. Teresa de Avila

El libro de su vida [*The Life of the Mother Teresa of Jesus*] 1562

El libra de las fundaciones de Santa Teresa de Jesús [*The Book of the Foundations*] 1576

El castillo interior, o las moradas [*The Interior Castle; or, The Mansions*] 1577

Mary Astell

A Serious Proposal to the Ladies for the Advancement of Their True and Greatest Interest. By a Lover of Her Sex (essay) 1694

A Serious Proposal to the Ladies, Part II. Wherin a Method is Offer'd for the Improvement of Their Minds (essay) 1697

Aphra Behn

Oroonoko; Or, The Royal Slave. A True History (novel) 1688

The Lady's Looking-Glass, to dress herself by; or, The Whole Art of Charming (novel) 1697

Anne Bradstreet

The Tenth Muse (poetry) 1650

Margaret Cavendish

CCXI Sociable Letters (correspondence) 1664

Daniel Defoe

"On the Education of Women" (essay) 1719

Elizabeth I

The Public Speaking of Queen Elizabeth: Selections from Her Official Addresses (addresses) 1951

Mary Evelyn

Mundus Muliebris: Or, the Ladies Dressing-Room Unlock'd, and her Toilette Spread (prose poem) 1690

Cassandra Fedele

Letters and Orations [edited and translated by Diana Robin] (letters and speeches) 2000

James Fordyce

Sermons to a Young Woman (handbook) 1766

Mary Hays

Letters and Essays, Moral and Miscellaneous [with Elizabeth Hays] (letters and essays) 1793

Memoirs of Emma Courtney 2 vols. (novel) 1796

Appeal to the Men of Great Britain on the Behalf of the Ladies (essay) 1798

Female Biography: or Memoirs of Illustrious and Celebrated Women, of All Ages and Countries (biographies) 1803

Eliza Haywood

The Female Spectator. 4 vols. (periodical) 1744-46

Charlotte Lennox

The Female Quixote; or, The Adventures of Arabella. 2 vols. (novel) 1752

The Lady's Museum [editor] (essays, prose, poetry) 1760-61

Bathusa Makin

An Essay to Revive the Antient Education of Gentlewomen (essay) 1673

Lady Mary Wortley Montagu

**Letters of the Right Honorable Lady M—y W—y M—e: Written, during her Travels in Europe, Asia and Africa, To Persons of Distinction, Men of Letters, & c. in Different Parts of Europe.* 3 vols. (letters) 1763

Marguerite de Navarre

L'Heptaméron des Nouvelles [*Heptameron*] (novellas) 1559

Modesta Pozzo (Moderata Fonte)

Il Merito delle donne (novel) 1600; translated as *The Worth of Women,* 1997

Anne Radcliffe

The Female Advocate; or, An Attempt to Recover the Rights of Women from Male Usurpation (essay) 1799

Jean-Jacques Rousseau

Lettres de deux amans, habitans d'une petite ville au pied des Alpes. 6 vols.; also published as *La Nouvelle Héloïse* (novel) 1761

Du contrat social [*The Social Contract*] (essay) 1762

Émile, ou l'education. 4 vols. (novel) 1762

Mary Rowlandson

The Soveraignty & Goodness of God, Together with the Faithfulness of His Promises Displayed; Being a Narrative of the Captivity and Restauration of Mrs. Mary Rowlandson, Commended by her to all that Desire to Know the Lord's Doings to, and Dealings with Her. Especially to her Dear Children and Relations. [republished as *A True History of the Captivity & Restoration of Mrs. Mary Rowlandson, A Minister's Wife in New-England: Wherein is set forth, The Cruel and Inhumane Usage she underwent amongst the Heathens for Eleven Weeks time: And her Deliverance from them. Written by her own Hand, for her Private Use: and now made public at the earnest Desire of some Friends, for the Benefit of the Afflicted,* 1682] (autobiography) 1682

George Savile, Marquis of Halifax

The Lady's New Year's Gift; or, Advice to a Daughter (handbook) 1688

William Shakespeare

Comedy of Errors (play) 1592-94

Romeo and Juliet (play) 1595-96

Twelfth Night (play) 1601-02

Anne Wheathill

A Handfull of Holesome (though Homelie) Hearbs (devotions) 1584

Phillis Wheatley

Poems on Various Subjects, Religious and Moral (poetry) 1773

Mary Wollstonecraft

Thoughts on the Education of Daughters: With Reflections on Female Conduct, in the More Important Duties of Life (essay) 1787

The Female Reader; or, Miscellaneous-Pieces, in Prose and Verse, Selected from the Best Writers, and Disposed Under Proper Heads; for the Improvement of Young Women [editor] (poetry and essays) 1789

A Vindication of the Rights of Men, in a Letter to the Right Honourable Edmund Burke; Occasioned by His Reflections on the Revolution in France (essay) 1790

A Vindication of the Rights of Woman: with Strictures on Political and Moral Subjects (essay) 1792

Maria; or, The Wrongs of Woman: A Posthumous Fragment (unfinished novel) 1799

* This work is commonly referred to as *Turkish Embassy Letters.*

PRIMARY SOURCES

ANNE WHEATHILL (ESSAY DATE 1584)

SOURCE: Wheathill, Anne. "*A Handfull of Holesome (though Homelie) Hearbs.*" In *Lay by Your Needles Ladies, Take the Pen: Writing Women in England, 1500-1700,* edited by Suzanne Trill, Kate Chedgzoy, and Melanie Osborne, pp. 50-56. London: Arnold, 1997.

In the following excerpt from her 1584 work, Wheathill offers a collection of prayers.

To all Ladies, Gentlewomen, and others, which love true religion and vertue, and be devoutlie disposed; Grace mercie, and peace, in Christ Jesus

For a testimonall to the world, how I have and doo (I praise God) bestowe the pretious treasure of time, even now in the state of my virginitie or maidenhood; lo heare I dedicate to all good Ladies, Gentlewomen, and others, who have a desire to invocate and call upon the name of the Lord, a small handfull of grose hearbs; which I have presumed to gather out of the garden of Gods most holie word. Not that there is anie unpurenes therein, but that (peradventure) my rudenes[1] may be found to have plucked them up unreverentlie, and without zeale.

Whereupon of the learned I may be judged grose[2] and unwise; in presuming, without the counsell or helpe of anie, to take such an enterprise in hand: nevertheles, as God dooth know, I have doone it with a good zeale, according to the weakenes of my knowledge and capacitie. And although they be not so pleasant in taste, as they can find out, to whom God hath given the spirit of learning: yet doo I trust, this small handfull of grose hearbs, holesome in operation and workeing, shall be no lesse acceptable before the majestie of almightie God than the fragrant floures of others, gathered with more understanding.

But without presumption I may boldly saie, they have not sought them with a more willing hart and fervent mind; nor more to the advancement of Gods glorie, and the desire of acceptation, than I have doon. Which if I may obtaine, with the good judgement and liking of all my brethren and sisters in the Lord, I shall thinke my time most happilie bestowed: for that thereby I did avoid idlenes, to the pleasing of almightie God; and have gained those, whom I know not, as well strangers to me, as my acquaintance, to be my freends, that shall taste these grose hearbs with me.

The Lord Jesus Christ, who moisteneth all his elect[3] with his most pretious blood, give us all a sweete taste in him: whome I humblie beseech, from the bottome of my hart, to give unto those that are vertuouslie bent, a desire to increase therein; and those, which have not yet reached thereunto, I praie the holie Ghost to inspire their hearts from above, that they and we may be worthie to meete together, in the blessed kingdome of our heavenlie father, which his deare sonne our saviour Jesus Christ did purchase for us; whose blessed name, with the living father, and the holie Ghost, be praised and magnified now and for ever, Amen, Amen.

Yours in Christ,

Anne Wheathill,

Gent

1. A Praier for the Morning

O Mightie maker and preserver of all things, God omnipotent, which like a diligent watchman, alwaies attendest upon thy faithfull people, so that whether they sleepe or wake, live or die, thy providence never forsaketh them: looke favourablie upon me, O Lord, thy poore and sinfull servant, which am not woorthie, but through thy great mercies offered to me in Christ, once to lift up mine eies unto thy mercie seat.

Wherefore in the name of thy deere sonne my Lord and Saviour, I offer unto thee, through him, the sacrifice of praise and thanks giving; that thou hast preserved me both this night, and all the time and daies of my life hitherto, untill this present houre. I beseech thee of thy great mercie to illuminate my understanding, that I may lead and frame my life as thou hast taught me in thy holie word, that my light may so shine here on earth, that my heavenlie father may be glorified in me, through Jesus Christ our Lord and redeemer; for whose sake heare me deare father, and send thy holie Ghost to direct me in all my dooings. To thee O glorious and blessed Trinitie, the Father, the Sonne, and the holie Ghost, be given all honor and praise, now and for ever more, Amen.

4. An Evening Praier

O Everlasting light, whose brightnesse is never darkned; looke favourablie upon me thy poore and sinfull servant, who hath not onelie this daie, but all the daies and time of my life hitherto, untill this present houre, offended thy divine Majestie, in thought, word, and deed; wherby I have most justlie provoked thy wrath and indignation against me. And now I bow the knees of my hart unto thee most mercifull and heavenlie father, beseeching thee for Jesus Christ his sake, to forgive me all my sinnes, negligences and ignorances. For I confesse how wickedlie I have mispent the talent that thou gavest me, abusing thy gifts of grace manie waies, burieng the same in obscure darknesse, woorse than the servant that hid his maisters treasure, not putting it to anie increase; for he delivered the principall againe [Matt. 25: 14-30].

But I most miserable creature, can shew unto thy majestie no part of that which thou gavest me, to use to thine honor and glorie: for the which I am most hartilie sorie, and doo unfeinedlie repent, having no meane to helpe myselfe, but onelie to lift up the eies of my faith unto thy deare sonne Jesus Christ, beseeching him most instantlie to make perfect my wants, and to renue whatsoever is lacking in me. For I commit my bodie and soule, this night and evermore, into his most holie hands; hoping, O Christ, thou wilt make me an acceptable sacrifice unto thy father.

I have no place to flie unto, but to shrowd me under the wings of thine almightie power, who wast so loving unto us, that thou wast contented to shed thy most pretious bloud, for the sinnes of the whole world; for the which I most humblie and hartilie yeeld unto thee thanks, honor, praise and glorie.

O lambe of God, sonne of the father, heare thou me, thou that saiedst; I am thy health and salvation, I am thy peace and life; cleave fast unto me, and thou shalt live. O Lord I am the woonded man, and thou art the good Samaritane: powre oile into my wounds, and bind them up [Luke 10: 25-37]. Lord heale thou me, and I shall be whole: for thou art my God and Saviour.

Heare thou therefore my supplications from heaven, and have mercie. Take from me all my sinnes and wickednesse, and give me thy grace and holie spirit. Lighten mine eies, that I sleepe not in death: so shall I joiefullie, after this sluggish sleepe of sinne, rise againe, living in thy feare all the daies of my life. Which grant me to doo, O Father, Sonne, and holie Ghost, three persons and one true God, world without end, Amen.

21. A praier of the creation of mankind, of the true Samaritane, and for strength against temptation

O Father of heaven, of power almightie, which with thine onlie word diddest create and make all the whole world, and all for the profit and service of man, whom thou diddest create of all other a most noble and perfect creature, giving him power upon earth, the waters, and all the fowles and birds of the aire; thou madest him also after thine own similitude and likenes, induing him with a reasonable soule, and all the powers thereof, thou also diddest put him in the pleasant garden of paradise, excepting nothing from him, but the eating of the onelie tree of knowledge of good and evill: and further, for his helpe, comfort, and companie, of a ribbe of his side thou madest for him a woman, and gavest hir to him to be his wife [Gen. 1-3].

There had they instructions given them, and the lawe of life for an heritage. Before them was laid both life and death, good and evill, with a freewill given them to take which liked them best. But their frailtie was such, that they, through a small intisement, chose the evill, and left the good: they left life, and chose death. Thus Lord, through sin and breaking of thy commandements, man lost the freewill that was given him in his creation, and purchased death to all his posteritie.

In the waie as he went to Jerusalem and Jericho, he fell in the hands of theeves, who hurting and wounding him sore, departed, leaving him halfe dead; so that he could have helpe of none, but only the good Samaritan, who, as he passed by the same waie, powred wine and oile into his wounds, and tooke the cure of him.

This onelie Samaritan was thy deare Sonne Christ, which tooke upon him all the iniquities of mankind, and laid them on his backe by his death, purging and clensing him, not onelie from the originall sin of our father *Adam,* but also from all our sins which we commit from time to time, by the vertue of his passion, and the sacrament of baptisme upon our repentance. For as by *Adam,* death came to mankind, so by Jesus Christ was mankind restored to life.[4]

For this great and high benefit of thy sonnes blessed passion for our redemption, we thy poore creatures praise and thanke thee, most humblie acknowledging his inestimable love towards us, in that thou vouchsafedst to die for us, being then sinners, and thy mortall enimies. Neverthelesse, most mercifull father, we are of our selves not able to do any thing that good is, no not so much as to thinke a good thought, without thine aid and assistance. We wander here miserablie, in the lowe parts of the vile earth; our strength will not serve us to clime to the high of the hilles, where thou dwellest in thy mount Sion, a place prepared for thine elect, a chosen inheritance of thy faithfull servant *Abraham,* and his seed.

Wherefore since we, being burthened with the affects of worldlie pleasures, and also with other cares and troubles, can by no meanes ascend to thee, that art on the top of so high a mountaine, (so manie legions of angels attending on thy Majestie) we have no remedie, but with the prophet *David* now to lift the eies of our harts and minds towards thee, and to crie for helpe to come down from thee to us thy poore and wretched servants.[5]

We wander here below as lost sheepe, having no shepheard; we are assailed on every side with manifold enimies; the divell ravening and hungering, seeketh whom he may devoure; the world allureth us also to hir deceitfull vanities; our flesh also, which we carrie about us, is our enimie readie and prone to drawe us unto all vices and pleasures. From this can we by no meanes be defended, but by thee Lord.

Send us therfore thy helpe and holie angell, to assist and strengthen us: for of thee most mercifull Father floweth all bountie and goodnes. Thou O Lord God madest heaven and earth for thine honour, and mans commoditie; establish therefore good Lord the chosen works of thy hand with thy eternall helpe: from heaven send us downe the welspring of thy grace, and thy strong angell to aide us by his helpe, that no assault of our spirituall enimies doo prevaile against us: but from all evils by thy word defend us, Lord, both touching the bodie, and also the soule, that no temptation prevaile against us.

Thou hast beene our protectour, even from our mothers wombe [Ps. 22: 9]; and our trust is that thou wilt so continue all the daies of our life, and speciallie at the houre of our death, that we may ascend to the heavenlie Jerusalem, where we shall reast in the bosome of our father *Abraham,* the father of all faithfull beleevers, there to praise thee, and thy loving Sonne, and the holie Ghost, world without end, Amen.

31. A praier that we may heare the word of God and keepe it

I am thy servant, Lord, give me understanding, that I may learne thy lawe and decrees: incline my soule to the words of thy mouth, bicause thy talke floweth like unto dew. The Israelites said unto *Moses*; Speake thou unto us, and we will heare thee, but let not the Lord speake, least we die [Exod. 20: 19]. Howbeit, I praie not so, O Lord, but rather with the prophet *Samuel* I doo humblie and earnestlie beseech thee thus; Speake on Lord, for thy servant dooth hearken [1 Sam. 3: 9, 10], for thou art the giver and inspirer of life, who art able without anie to instruct me.

Thy Ministers speake for thee thy secreats, but thou unlockest the understanding of the things pronounced; they rehearse to us thy commandements, but it is thy aid and helpe that giveth strength to walke over the same, and givest light unto the minds. Wherefore, bicause thou art the everlasting truth, speake thou Lord my God unto me, least I die, and be made unfruitfull: for thou hast the words of everlasting life. Speake therefore that thing, which may bring both comfort unto my soule, and amendment unto my life, and also may cause glorie and immortall honor unto thee. For man dooth perish, but thy truth indureth, O God, for ever.

Blessed are they therefore, whom thou instructest and givest knowledge unto O Lord, and doost teach thy lawe, that thou maist helpe them in time of trouble, that they perish not. Looke favourablie upon me, O God, and graunt (I praie thee) that thy truth may teach me, keepe me, and bring me unto a happie end. Let the same deliver me from all wicked lusts, and from inordinate love. Thou hast infinit means, and all creatures are at thy commandement; therefore good Lord shewe some signe, whereby I shall be delivered, and send thine holie angell before me, to keepe me in thy waie, and to bring me to the place which thou hast provided for me, that I may live with thee everlastinglie, world without end, Amen.

39. A praier of lamentation, wherein the sinner lamenteth his miserable estate, and crieth for mercie

My God, when I do earnestlie behold mine owne state, whereunto I am brought through sinne, not onelie being naked and bare of all goodnes, but also to be overwhelmed in the depth of all iniquitie; I cannot but lament, moorne, and crie for helpe, as dooth a woman, whose time draweth neere to be delivered of hir child; for she can take no rest, till she be discharged of hir burthen.

No more can I, Lord, as long as I feele my selfe loden with my heavie burthen of sinne, the weight wherof draweth me downe to the deepe bottome of all miserie; from whence I can by none be delivered, but onelie by thee, that art the guide and the eie to those that are blind through ignorance, the succor of the oppressed, the comfort of the weake, the life of those that are dead; so that they repent and turne unto thee.

It is not the long distance of us from thy highnesse, which keepeth our praiers from thee; thine eares are readie in the hearts of all that are willing to crie for the help of thy grace. Who so is made farre from thee, through sinne, by repentance is made neere unto thee. He that is in the bottom of the sea of miserie, if he beginne to call for thy helpe, he shall not be suffered to sinke. From all deepe dangers most mercifull God deliver me.

I crie and call pitiouslie unto thee, which art onelie able to helpe me. Heare therefore, I most hartilie praie thee, my sorowfull praier, and let my poore petition pearse the eares of thy Godhed. And since thy sonne Christ died for to release us of sinne, let not my sinnes be a staie, whereby my praiers should not be heard, but wipe them cleane awaie, that they never more appeere. For I miserable sinner doo flie to the gentlenes, of thy favourable mercie, whose nature and propertie is to have pitie and compassion.

From thee floweth all mercie and grace, which was so great unto us, that it mooved thee to send thine onlie Sonne to die for our redemption; whereby thy justice was satisfied, and thy mercie found that it sought. O how fervent was this thy noble charitie to us vile wretches! It tooke root and beginning in thy mightie deitie, and from thence it was derived to mankind; being an example that we thy christian people should, like loving brethren, beare one anothers burthen.

Wherefore I am most willinglie contented, to remit all injuries doon to me; as it hath pleased thy goodnes to forgive me much greater offenses comitted against thee. And whensoever it shall please thee to scourge and punish me, I will gladlie receive thy chastisement, for that I knowe it proceedeth of love for my wealth and suretie; trusting that after my long abiding and suffering in this life, I shall surelie obteine thy reward, by thy promise, that is; If we suffer with Christ, we shall also reigne with him [Rom. 8: 17].

Such sure hope have I ever had in thee Lord, and by the same hope I trust to have thy favour, and live for ever. For blessed are they that trust in thee, most mercifull Father; and cursed are they that trust in man. Of thy grace and mercie onelie commeth all goodnes; thy mercie forgiveth onelie our sinnes dailie and hourelie, and the painfull death of thy sonne Christ delivereth us from all the paines due for our sinnes. Thou boughtest us not with gold and silver, but with the pretious bloud of that lambe without spot, thy blessed Sonne, whose death had beene sufficient for thousands of worlds.

The greatnes of thy love caused the plentifull paiment of the price of our redemption. The charitie of our Lord Jesus Christ hath burnt up, and consumed, by his death, all our iniquities. Wherefore the faithfull, being thus delivered from all dangers, by thine onlie goodnesse, may now give thanks unto thy mightie Majestie, resting in hope to have, after this life, everlasting joie and felicitie; through Jesus Christ our mercifull Lord and redeemer; to whom with thee O deare Father, and the holie Ghost, be given all honor, glorie, and praise, now and for ever, Amen.

GEORGE SAVILE, MARQUIS OF HALIFAX (ESSAY DATE 1688)

SOURCE: Halifax, George Savile, Marquis of. "Advice to a Daughter." In, *The Lady's New Years Gift, or, Advice to a Daughter* pp. 24-38. London: Gillyflower and Partridge, 1688.

In the following excerpt, Savile, the Marquis of Halifax, gives suggestions to his daughter concerning marriage.

Husband

That which challengeth the next place in your thoughts is how to live with a husband. And though that is so large a word that few rules can be fixed to it which are unchangeable, the methods being as various as the several tempers of men to which they must be suited, yet I cannot omit some general observations, which, with the help of your own, may the better direct you in the part of your life upon which your happiness most dependeth.

It is one of the disadvantages belonging to your sex that young women are seldom permitted to make their own choice; their friends' care and experience are thought safer guides to them than their own fancies, and their modesty often forbiddeth them to refuse when their parents recommend, though their inward consent may not entirely go along with it. In this case there remaineth nothing for them to do but to endeavour to make that easy which falleth to their lot, and by a wise use of everything they may dislike in a husband turn that by degrees to be very supportable which, if neglected, might in time beget an aversion.

You must first lay it down for a foundation in general, that there is inequality in the sexes, and that for the better economy of the world the men, who were to be the lawgivers, had the larger share of reason bestowed upon them; by which means your sex is the better prepared for the compliance that is necessary for the better performance of those duties which seem to be most properly assigned to it. This looks a little uncourtly at the first appearance, but upon examination it will be found that nature is so far from being unjust to you that she is partial on your side. She hath made you such large amends by other advantages for the seeming injustice of the first distribution that the right of complaining is come over to our sex. You have it in your power not only to free yourselves but to subdue your masters, and without violence throw both their natural and legal authority at your feet. We are made of differing tempers, that out defects may the better be mutually supplied: your sex wanteth our reason for your conduct, and our strength for your protection; ours wanteth your gentleness to soften and to entertain us. The first part of our life is a good deal subjected to you in the nursery, where you reign without competition, and by that means have the advantage of giving the first impressions. Afterwards you have stronger influences, which, well managed, have more force in your behalf than all our privileges and jurisdictions can pretend to have against you. You have more strength in your looks than we have in our laws, and more power by your tears than we have by our arguments.

It is true that the laws of marriage run in a harsher style towards your sex. Obey is an ungenteel word, and less easy to be digested by making such an unkind distinction in the words of the contract, and so very unsuitable to the excess of good manners which generally goes before it. Besides, the universality of the rule seemeth to be a grievance, and it appeareth reasonable that there might be an exemption for extraordinary women from ordinary rules, to take away the just exception that lieth against the false measure of general equality.

It may be alleged by the counsel retained by your sex, that as there is in all other laws an appeal from the letter to the equity, in cases that require it, it is as reasonable that some court of a larger jurisdiction might be erected, where some wives might resort and plead specially, and in such instances where Nature is so kind as to raise them above the level of their own sex they might have relief, and obtain a mitigation in their own particular of a sentence which was given generally against womankind. The causes of separation are now so very coarse that few are confident enough to buy their liberty at the price of having their modesty so exposed. And for disparity of minds, which above all other things requireth a remedy, the laws have made no provision, so little refined are numbers of men by whom they are compiled. This and a great deal more might be said to give a colour to the complaint.

But the answer to it in short is, that the institution of marriage is too sacred to admit a liberty of objecting to it; that the supposition of yours being the weaker sex having without all doubt a good foundation maketh it reasonable to subject it to the masculine dominion; that no rule can be so perfect as not to admit some exceptions, but the law presumeth there would be so few found in this case who would have a sufficient right to such a privilege that it is safer some injustice should be connived at in a very few instances than to break into an establishment upon which the order of human society doth so much depend.

You are therefore to make your best of what is settled by law and custom, and not vainly imagine that it will be changed for your sake. But that you may not be discouraged, as if you lay under the weight of an incurable grievance; you are to know that by a wise and dexterous conduct it will be in your power to relieve yourself from anything that looketh like a disadvantage in it. For your better direction I will give a hint of the most ordinary causes of dissatisfaction between man and wife, that you may be able by such a warning to live so upon your guard that when you shall be married you may know how to cure your husband's mistakes and to prevent your own.

First then, you are to consider you live in a time which hath rendered some kind of frailties so habitual that they lay claim to large grains of allowance. The world in this is somewhat unequal, and our sex seemeth to play the tyrant in distinguishing partially for ourselves, by making that in the utmost degree criminal in the woman which in a man passeth under a much gentler censure. The root and the excuse of this injustice is the preservation of families from any mixture which may bring a blemish to them; and whilst the point of honour continues to be so placed, it seems unavoidable to give your sex the greater share of the penalty. But if in this it lieth under any disadvantage, you are more than recompensed by having the honour of families in your keeping. The consideration so great a trust must give you maketh full amends, and this power the world hath lodged in you can hardly fail to restrain the severity of an ill husband and to improve the kindness and esteem of a good one. This being so, remember that next to the danger of committing the fault yourself the greatest is that of seeing it in your husband. Do not seem to look or hear that way: if he is a man of sense he will reclaim himself, the folly of it is of itself sufficient to cure him; if he is not so, he will be provoked but not reformed. To expostulate in these cases looketh like declaring war, and preparing reprisals, which to a thinking husband would be a dangerous reflexion. Besides, it is so coarse a reason which will be assigned for a lady's too great warmth upon such an occasion that modesty no less than prudence ought to restrain her, since such an indecent complaint makes a wife more ridiculous that the injury that provoketh her to it. But it is yet worse, and more unskilful, to blaze it in the world, expecting it should rise up in arms to take her part; whereas she will find it can have no other effect than that she will be served up in all companies as the reigning jest at that time; and will continue to be the common entertainment till she is rescued by some newer folly that cometh upon the stage, and driveth her away from it. The impertinence of such methods is so plain that it doth not deserve the pains of being laid open. Be assured that in these cases your discretion and silence will be the most prevailing reproof. An affected ignorance, which is seldom a virtue, is a great one here; and when your husband seeth how unwilling you are to be uneasy there is no stronger argument to persuade him not to be unjust to you. Besides, it will naturally make him more yielding in other things; and whether it be to cover or redeem his offence, you may have the good effects of it whilst it lasteth, and all that while have the most reasonable ground that can be of presuming such a behaviour will at last entirely convert him. There is nothing so glorious to a wife as a victory so gained; a man so reclaimed is for ever after subjected to her virtue, and her bearing for a time is more than rewarded by a triumph that will continue as long as her life.

DANIEL DEFOE (ESSAY DATE 1719)

SOURCE: Defoe, Daniel. "(On) The Education of Women." In *English Essays from Sir Philip Sidney to Macaulay*, pp. 1-16. New York: Collier, 1910.

In the following essay from 1719, Defoe praises women's natural abilities and argues for their education.

I have often thought of it as one of the most barbarous customs in the world, considering us as a civilized and a Christian country, that we deny the advantages of learning to women. We reproach the sex every day with folly and impertinence; while I am confident, had they the advantages of education equal to us, they would be guilty of less than ourselves.

ON THE SUBJECT OF...

LAURA CERETA (1469-1499)

Laura Cereta of Brescia, Italy, was one of the first female humanists. Widowed while still in her teens, Cereta devoted herself to writing essays in the form of letters to male scholars and leaders of the church and the state. Her works expressed ideas very unusual for the time. She rejected traditional views of men's and women's roles, argued that housework imposed limits on women's intellectual growth, and portrayed marriage as a kind of slavery. Cereta's bold writings had a strong influence on later feminists of the Renaissance and the centuries that followed.

MODERATA FONTE (1555-1592)

And when it's said that women must be subject to men, the phrase should be understood in the same sense as when we say that we are subject to natural disasters, diseases, and all the other accidents of this life: it's not a case of being subject in the sense of obeying, but rather of suffering an imposition; not a case of serving them fearfully, but rather of tolerating them in a spirit of Christian charity, since they have been given to us by God as a spiritual trial. But they take the phrase in the contrary sense and set themselves up as tyrants over us, arrogantly usurping that dominion over women that they claim is their right, but which is more properly ours.

Fonte, Moderata (Modesta Pozzo). "First Day." In *The Worth of Women, Wherein Is Clearly Revealed Their Nobility and Their Superiority to Men,* ed. and trans. Virginia Cox (University of Chicago Press), p. 59. 1997. Originally published as *Il Merito delle donne* (1600).

Moderata Fonte is the pseudonym of Modesta Pozzo, author of *Il Merito delle donne* (1600; *The Worth of Women,* 1997), in which seven noblewomen debate the unequal treatment of women in Venetian society, presenting what was, at the time, a revolutionary indictment of patriarchy and misogyny and defense of women's rights by a woman writer. Fonte died during childbirth at the age of thirty-seven, only a day after completing *The Worth of Women.* The work was published eight years after Fonte's death, by her daughter, Cecelia de' Zorzi.

One would wonder, indeed, how it should happen that women are conversible at all; since they are only beholden to natural parts, for all their knowledge. Their youth is spent to teach them to stitch and sew or make baubles. They are taught to read, indeed, and perhaps to write their names, or so; and that is the height of a woman's education. And I would but ask any who slight the sex for their understanding, what is a man (a gentleman, I mean) good for, that is taught no more? I need not give instances, or examine the character of a gentleman, with a good estate, or a good family, and with tolerable parts; and examine what figure he makes for want of education.

The soul is placed in the body like a rough diamond; and must be polished, or the lustre of it will never appear. And 'tis manifest, that as the rational soul distinguishes us from brutes; so education carries on the distinction, and makes some less brutish than others. This is too evident to need any demonstration. But why then should women be denied the benefit of instruction? If knowledge and understanding had been useless additions to the sex, God Almighty would never have given them capacities; for he made nothing needless. Besides, I would ask such, What they can see in ignorance, that they should think it a necessary ornament to a woman? or how much worse is a wise woman than a fool? or what has the woman done to forfeit the privilege of being taught? Does she plague us with her pride and impertinence? Why did we not let her learn, that she might have had more wit? Shall we upbraid women with folly, when 'tis only the error of this inhuman custom, that hindered them from being made wiser?

The capacities of women are supposed to be greater, and their senses quicker than those of the men; and what they might be capable of being bred to, is plain from some instances of female wit, which this age is not without. Which upbraids us with Injustice, and looks as if we denied women the advantages of education, for fear they should vie with the men in their improvements. . . .

[They] should be taught all sorts of breeding suitable both to their genius and quality. And in particular, Music and Dancing; which it would be cruelty to bar the sex of, because they are their darlings. But besides this, they should be taught languages, as particularly French and Italian: and I would venture the injury of giving a woman more tongues than one. They should, as a particular study, be taught all the graces of speech, and all the necessary air of conversation; which our common education is so defective in, that I need not expose it. They should be brought to read books, and especially history; and so to read as to make them understand the world, and be able to know and judge of things when they hear of them.

To such whose genius would lead them to it, I would deny no sort of learning; but the chief thing, in general, is to cultivate the understandings of the sex, that they may be capable of all sorts of conversation; that their parts and judgements being improved, they may be as profitable in their conversation as they are pleasant.

Women, in my observation, have little or no difference in them, but as they are or are not distinguished by education. Tempers, indeed, may in some degree influence them, but the main distinguishing part is their Breeding.

The whole sex are generally quick and sharp. I believe, I may be allowed to say, generally so: for you rarely see them lumpish and heavy, when they are children; as boys will often be. If a woman be well bred, and taught the proper management of her natural wit, she proves generally very sensible and retentive.

And, without partiality, a woman of sense and manners is the finest and most delicate part of God's Creation, the glory of Her Maker, and the great instance of His singular regard to man, His darling creature: to whom He gave the best gift either God could bestow or man receive. And 'tis the sordidest piece of folly and ingratitude in the world, to withhold from the sex the due lustre which the advantages of education gives to the natural beauty of their minds.

A woman well bred and well taught, furnished with the additional accomplishments of knowledge and behaviour, is a creature without comparison. Her society is the emblem of sublimer enjoyments, her person is angelic, and her conversation heavenly. She is all softness and sweetness, peace, love, wit, and delight. She is every way suitable to the sublimest wish, and the man that has such a one to his portion, has nothing to do but to rejoice in her, and be thankful.

On the other hand, Suppose her to be the very same woman, and rob her of the benefit of education, and it follows—

> If her temper be good, want of education makes her soft and easy.
>
> Her wit, for want of teaching, makes her impertinent and talkative.
>
> Her knowledge, for want of judgement and experience, makes her fanciful and whimsical.
>
> If her temper be bad, want of breeding makes her worse; and she grows haughty, insolent, and loud.
>
> If she be passionate, want of manners makes her a termagant and a scold, which is much at one with Lunatic.
>
> If she be proud, want of discretion (which still is breeding) makes her conceited, fantastic, and ridiculous.
>
> And from these she degenerates to be turbulent, clamorous, noisy, nasty, the devil! . . .

The great distinguishing difference, which is seen in the world between men and women, is in their education; and this is manifested by comparing it with the difference between one man or woman, and another.

And herein it is that I take upon me to make such a bold assertion, That all the world are mistaken in their practice about women. For I cannot think that God Almighty ever made them so delicate, so glorious creatures; and furnished them with such charms, so agreeable and so delightful to mankind; with souls capable of the same accomplishments with men: and all, to be only Stewards of our Houses, Cooks, and Slaves.

Not that I am for exalting the female government in the least: but, in short, I would have men take women for companions, and educate them to be fit for it. A woman of sense and breeding will scorn as much to encroach upon the prerogative of man, as a man of sense will scorn to oppress the weakness of the woman. But if the women's souls were refined and improved by teaching, that word would be lost. To say, the weakness of the sex, as to judgment, would be nonsense; for ignorance and folly would be no more to be found among women than men.

I remember a passage, which I heard from a very fine woman. She had wit and capacity enough, an extraordinary shape and face, and a great fortune: but had been cloistered up all her time; and for fear of being stolen, had not had the liberty of being taught the common necessary knowledge of women's affairs. And when she came to converse in the world, her natural wit made her so sensible of the want of education, that she gave this short reflection on herself: "I am ashamed to talk with my very maids," says she, "for I don't know when they do right or wrong. I had more need go to school, than be married."

I need not enlarge on the loss the defect of education is to the sex; nor argue the benefit of the contrary practice. 'Tis a thing will be more easily granted than remedied. This chapter is but an Essay at the thing: and I refer the Practice to those Happy Days (if ever they shall be) when men shall be wise enough to mend it.

OVERVIEWS

DALE SPENDER (ESSAY DATE 1992)

SOURCE: Spender, Dale. "Introduction: A Vindication of the Writing Woman." In *Living by the Pen: Early British Women Writers,* edited by Dale Spender, pp. 1-35. New York: Teachers College Press, 1992.

In the following excerpt, Spender surveys outstanding eighteenth-century women writers and discusses their motivations, situations, and accomplishments.

While many changes took place in the eighteenth century, two are of primary concern here; they are:

the emergence of the novel, and

the establishment of the professional woman writer.

But these two major developments of the eighteenth century are not in themselves the sole concern. That the two occurrences are not normally linked together, that the possible correlations between the success of women *and* the genre have not been a focal point in literary history, is also a matter which calls for attention. In drawing together these two great events—the birth of the novel and the growth of the professional woman writer—and in looking at some of the reasons behind their apparent separation and suppression, new issues are raised and new connections are made.

The following questions help to suggest the scope of this fascinating literary area:

Who were these eighteenth-century women writers,

what did they write, and

what was their relationship to the novel?

Why did they write,

what did they write about, and

what was the response to their writing?

What were the conditions under which they wrote,

what was their creative and professional achievement and

Why is their emergence and contribution not part of the readily acknowledged cultural heritage?

Although it is not possible in this introduction to address all these questions at length, it is possible to give some idea of the extent and diversity of this heritage and to posit some of the research priorities of the future.

Because of the increasing interest being shown in early British women writers, the picture is constantly changing. Already these questions have lost some of the shock-force they had when asked in 1985; that was the year the University of London Institute of Education planned a summer school at which the course Early British Women Writers was to be offered. When taught in 1987, the course not only proved to be very popular (with many of the participants providing contributions for this volume), but it also prompted a particular line of discussion: How could it be that there were so many early women writers, that they had overcome so many obstacles and written so many books, when in contemporary times so few of them were in print, so few of them were known, there were so few courses (were there any others?), so few publications on them. (One exception was Fidelis Morgan's excellent publication on the women playwrights, *The Female Wits: Women Playwrights of the Restoration,* 1981.) There are questions here about the nature of knowledge as well as those about the women and their work. (Many of these issues are discussed in Cheris Kramarae and Dale Spender, in press.)

Since 1985 some of the more pressing problems have been remedied. For example, many of these early British women writers are now much better known thanks to the availability of such excellent publications as *Fetter'd or Free? British Women Novelists 1670-1815,* edited by Mary Anne Schofield and Cecilia Macheski (1986); *The Rise of the Woman Novelist; From Aphra Behn to Jane Austen* by Jane Spencer (1986); and the considerable contributions of Janet Todd—*Sensibility; An Introduction* (1986) and *A Dictionary of British and American Women Writers 1660-1800* (1987); to name but a few.

Some of these early women writers have been brought back into print, partly because of the efforts of women's publishing houses and presses (see particularly *Mothers of the Novel Reprint Series* [a list of reprint titles is included at the end of this article] and Virago Classics). Internationally, in English departments and Women's Studies courses, more interest is being shown—perhaps even as a product of feminist interest and pressure—in the contributions of these women writers in both their own times and in contemporary terms. But still, many issues remain unresolved and many questions unanswered: issues about professional women writers and about the transmission of knowledge from one generation to the next.

Then too, the area is so vast that it is difficult to survey and itemize all that it contains. It is located so far in the past (and has been so shamefully neglected) that much of the material and many of the records have been lost, buried, or mislaid, so that it is a demanding task to find all the women and their publications, let alone to read and assess them. Currently, the information which has become available has done little else than whet the appetite.

A door may have been opened and a rich resource glimpsed, but impatience to explore and document the find is not the only response; there is a measure of frustration as well. Why was the door ever closed? Why does it seem so difficult now to keep it open? And is this concealment of women's creativity but an unfortunate accident of the past, or does it have contemporary implications? What is the position of the woman writer, the place of her work, past, present, and future?

These are some of the topics that are the substance of this collection. Not that any claim is being made for comprehensiveness; quite the contrary. As might be expected with a relatively recently unearthed research area, the gaps in knowledge are extensive. But in opening the door just a little further, in noting what *is* there, as well as what remains to be examined, this book plays a part in recovering and reconstituting women's participation in the literary heritage.

Because the articles in this collection cannot attempt to cover the many concerns that emerge, this overview is provided. Once the broad outlines have been sketched, it can be much easier to place in context the individual writers and works, as well as their collective achievement and the response it gave rise to. Where possible, further reading will be referenced, and where practicable, future research directions will be recommended.

Who Were the Eighteenth-Century Women Writers and What Did They Write?

The number of women writers of the period and the range of their publications are readily demonstrated by the list of entries in *A Dictionary of British and American Women Writers 1669-1800.* And while the table now requires modification (with more entries added and some of the existing ones clarified), the inventory which is published in *Mothers of the Novel* (Dale Spender, 1986: pp 119-137) and which includes 106 writers and their 568 novels, serves to emphasize the astonishing extent of the achievement. Not that women's literary output was confined to novels, of course.

Women wrote across every existing genre and played an innovative role in the evolution of new forms as well. The following summary provides some of the basic information in terms of who these women were and what they wrote.

ON THE SUBJECT OF...

ST. TERESA DE AVILA (1515-1582)

One of the most significant figures in the sixteenth-century Spanish mystic movement, St. Teresa de Avila (also known as St. Teresa de Jesus) is also highly regarded as an accomplished prose writer. Her autobiography *El libro de su vida* (1562; *The Life of the Mother Teresa of Jesus*) is one of the most widely read books in Spain. Teresa was born in Avila, and in 1536 she entered the convent of Encarnación de Avila as a novice in the Carmelite order. Two years later, Teresa suffered a severe bout of illness, during which she read a number of religious works and began to question her own beliefs about the nature of religious devotion. In 1555 she underwent a conversion experience, and convinced that she had been granted a mystical union with God as a result of her intense meditation and prayer, she began to advocate a more contemplative, ascetic life for the Carmelites in reformed, or Discalced convents, which she established throughout Spain between 1563 and 1576.

Teresa authored several books, including *El libra de las fundaciones de Santa Teresa de Jesús* (1576; *The Book of the Foundations*), a continuation of her autobiography with an account of the Carmelite reform, and *El castillo interior, o las moradas* (1577; *The Interior Castle; or, The Mansions*), an allegory of the process of spiritual maturation. Long revered for her importance as a writer of spiritual and devotional works, Teresa has received much critical attention as a literary figure during the twentieth century. Numerous scholars have praised her wit and entertaining prose style while recognizing her skill in clarifying enigmatic theories. In recent years studies of Teresa's works have focused on the influence of gender in her autobiography, the psychological implications of her writings and her mystic visions, and the rhetorical goals of her works.

LETTERS AND JOURNALS

The primary source of women's writing was letters and journals. As so many female critics have suggested, Virginia Woolf among them, letter writing has been one of the literary forms actively encouraged in women. It has also been suggested that it is a mark of women's creative achievement that they should have been able to transform this genre into the epistolary novel and, in the process, provide themselves with a profession (see Perry, 1980, for further discussion).

This was the pattern that evolved: allowed to excel at the art of letter writing, women expanded the form to meet some of their own needs for information, self-realization, and wider communication. They created for themselves a public voice and the potential to influence values, views, events, not just among their own sex but throughout the whole society. Women made a crucial contribution to the transition of the private letter into the public/published epistolary novel and the development of fiction.

What has to be noted is that in the seventeenth and eighteenth centuries, the only communication, apart from direct contact, had to be through letters; with the establishment of the Post Office in 1660 and the introduction of the "penny post" twenty years later, letter writing really came into vogue during this period—And not just letters which maintained family relationships and for which women could be expected to assume responsibility. Letters then were very different from the displaced form they have generally become today:

> Educated people were expected to know how to write graceful letters, how to compose their thoughts on paper. Schools trained this skill—letter writing was a standard composition assignment and students read and copied from classical examples. Londoners must have been accustomed to writing them, for THE SPECTATOR reports a steady stream of letters addressed to the editor; "I have Complaints from Lovers, Schemes for Projectors, Scandal from Ladies, Congratulations, Compliments and Advice in Abundance"[1]—testimony to the readiness with which readers took pen in hand to scribble off their reactions to even so impersonal a target as that popular daily.
>
> (Ruth Perry, 1980 p. 64)

Women, however, were not likely to have enjoyed such a range of letter writing opportunities; not normally "educated," nor encouraged to go "public," their choices were considerably curtailed. (At a time when newspapers did not usually find their way into many homes but were confined to coffee houses and such places on the grounds that their content was inappropriate for females, women probably comprised very few of the writers to the editor or writers of travel reports, dispatches, business letters, etc.) But the letter certainly became a significant form of communication (and self-expression) in the seventeenth and eighteenth centuries, and the boundaries of women's literary possibilities were extended as a result.

As Ruth Perry (1980) has commented, "Letters were the one sort of writing women were supposed to be able to do well" (p. 68) and in the expansive climate of the time, it is not surprising that women should have extended their horizons beyond the members of their own family and the intimate communications of the private sphere. That extraordinary and prolific writer, Margaret Cavendish, Duchess of Newcastle (1623-73)—whose literary contribution cries out for critical evaluation—published her *Sociable Letters* in 1664, and it is clear from their contents that they were never intended as personal correspondence with a friend but as advice and counsel to a much wider circle. One of the early women writers who sought professional status for her sex, Margaret Cavendish's efforts afford a good example of Ruth Perry's assessment that letter writing "was the mode of expression appropriated by women writers *en route,* so to speak, to professional authorship" (p. 68).

This was Virginia Woolf's thesis as well. In *A Room of One's Own* and "Women and Fiction," where she accounts for the emergence of the professional woman writer, Virginia Woolf also starts with the remarkable contribution of Margaret Cavendish and then moves on to the oft-quoted and illuminating letters which Dorothy Osborne (1627-1695) wrote to her lover, William Temple:

> "Had she been born in 1827, Dorothy Osborne would have written novels;" says Woolf, "had she been born in 1527 she would never have written at all. But she was born in 1627, and at that date though writing books was 'ridiculous for a women' [as Dorothy Osborne said of the Duchess of Newcastle when she dared to write and publish her *CCXI Sociable Letters*] there was nothing unseemly in writing a letter."[2]
>
> Furthermore, letter writing could be made to fit in with the scope and expectations of a woman's life. "It was an art that could be carried on at odd moments, by a father's sick-bed among a thousand interruptions, without exciting comments, anonymously as it were, and often with the pretense that it served some useful purpose"[3]
>
> (Ruth Perry, 1980 pp. 68-69)

No doubt there were times when letter writing was an onerous obligation, but there would have been times too when for women, letter writing (and journal keeping) were eagerly embraced activities. Given the isolated circumstances which were the limits of many women's lives, a letter could be one of the few means of communicating with the world outside, and a journal entry one of the few means for creating a friend or confidante (see Fanny Burney, in Joyce Hemlow, 1958: p. 26; and the introduction to *The Diary of Elizabeth Pepys* for further discussion on the role of journals).

Men had much more freedom of movement; the mobility of women was restricted, either because they belonged to a class which could not *afford* travel, or else to a class which would not *allow* women to move about independently. In this context, the letter could be a vital link to experience beyond the "here and now."

Apart from providing access to information and experience outside one's own four walls, the letter was also a primary means of maintaining relationships. "Correspondence became the medium for weaving the social fabric of family and friendships in letters of invitation, acceptance, news, condolence and congratulations," comments Ruth Perry (p. 69).

Then too there was the opportunity that the letter provided for the author to create a "self," and one which was positive, exciting, entertaining—worthy of esteem. "Letters were the perfect vehicle for women's highly developed art of pleasing, for in writing letters it is possible to tailor a self on paper to suit the expectations and desires of the audience" (Ruth Perry, 1980, p. 69).

The capacity of letters to forge and foster relationships and to provide a forum for the self-actualization of the author became even more significant during the period of British expansion, when letters to and from the farflung colonies were the only fragile life lines among families and friends. And when from strange continents women wrote home, aware that their audience could be the entire assembled family who waited on every word, it is not difficult to detect yet another influence working to transform the letter into the epistolary novel. Rare was the women who wanted to worry those back home, so some of the most serious and stressful experiences were recorded between the lines or commented on only AFTER the danger or despair had passed. More common was the woman correspondent who composed the entertaining episode—in virtually serial form—in which she figured as the "heroine" confronting challenges in an exotic climate. For example, Rachel Henning wrote some of the most entertaining "stories" about Australia between 1853 and 1882 and without any background information, it simply would not be possible to determine whether her letters were indeed real or works of fiction. (For further discussion of this aspect of Australian women writers, see Dale Spender, 1988.)

That women used letters (and diaries) to explore and explain so many aspects of their personal lives was another contributory factor in the development of the epistolary novel, according to Perry: "Because so many private relationships came to be conducted in letters, especially for home-bound women, these exchanges came to be understood as the repository for emotions usually enclosed by convention, the place to look for records of a person's secret doings" (p. 70). Not surprisingly, there was a growing market for such disclosures. During the eighteenth century, the literary distinction between public and private became blurred when real private letters were sometimes seized for publication (though even here, as in the case of Delariviere Manley's and Katherine Philips' poems, there is some debate as to whether the material was truly seized or whether it was a ruse), and where fictional letters were sometimes presented as the real thing (as with some of Aphra Behn's publications). What can be said with confidence is that the boundaries between letters and fiction collapsed, and that women played a critical role in the process.

But if letters were at the center of literary innovation in the seventeenth and eighteenth centuries, they have no such significance today. Many are those who regret their passing; although the concern that biographers might be deprived of sources with the displacement of the letter by the telephone is not now quite so serious given the appearance of the fax machine. Another matter for regret, however, is that this literary form of the past, with all its strengths, complexities, and nuances, is so little studied. Far from being a "popular" or prestigious research area (a status well warranted), women's letters are rarely included in the valued literary tradition; and this can have no correlation with the quantity—or quality—of the contribution (see Dorothy van Doren, 1929, for some indication of the art of the area). There have been so many women letter writers whose accounts provide a fascinating documentation of self-examination, of interpersonal networks and friendships, as well as an illuminating record of their time *and* a satisfying example of literary skill and accomplishment. The suggestion that it is because they are the work of women that women's letters have not become part of the legitimated "world of letters" is one which deserves serious attention.

Lady Mary Wortley Montagu (1689-1762) is one woman writer whose letters have enjoyed a measure of public acclaim; but still more could be known—and more could gainfully know—of her witty *Embassy Letters* (written in Turkey in 1716) which are a remarkable "anthropological" study of period and place. An inveterate traveler and letter writer (who recorded her own part in the popularization of smallpox vaccination, for example), Lady Mary's letters inform, entertain, and present much of the inner life of a perceptive woman and her relationships with daughter, granddaughter, with love, marriage, and women's education!

Apart from the correspondence of individuals such as the remarkable Elizabeth Montagu (1720-1800), older sister of the equally remarkable novelist, Sarah Scott (1723-1795), there are the many letters of groups of women, such as the Bluestockings. To be able to study the extensive correspondence between Elizabeth Carter (1717-1806) and Catherine Talbot (1721-1770)—not to mention that of Hester Thrale Piozzi (1741-1821) and Mary Delaney (1700-1788)—with all their contemporary references to literary women and their influences, would be an exciting, even inspirational prospect. The letters of so many "literary ladies" (particularly those written to each other) could be another source of enormous interest, and because of the position they occupied at the center of literary innovations, their correspondence could cast further light on the shift from personal letters to public ones.

There are letters between women and letters between women and men; Mary Hays's love letters (literally used as part of the text in *The Memoirs of Emma Courtney,* 1796-1987) and Mary Wollstonecraft's Letters to Gilbert Imlay (1798), as well as her travel *Letters Written During a Short Residence in Sweden, Norway and Denmark* (1796), can only begin to suggest the range of women's epistolary writing during the seventeenth and eighteenth centuries.

And of course, diaries and journals began to come into their own during this period; dependent upon a notion of individual identity and worth, the seventeenth and eighteenth centuries witnessed women's move away from the devotional record (such as that of Lady Margaret Hoby's *Diary,* 1599-1605) to the focus on self-examination and character development—all very consistent with the evolution of fiction. And very useful too as a form of literary apprenticeship, as Fanny Burney's diary demonstrates.

AUTOBIOGRAPHIES AND BIOGRAPHIES

Margaret Cavendish—again—was a pioneer in the area of autobiography and biography; "A True Relation of My Birth, Breeding and Life" (which occurred at the end of *Nature's Pictures Drawn By Fancy's Pencil to the Life,* 1656) is, in the words of Nancy Cotton (1987), "the first autobiography published by a woman in England," and *The Life of the Thrice Noble, High and Puissant Prince, William Cavendish, Duke, Marquess and Earl of Newcastle*" (1667) "is considered the first biography of a husband to be published by an Englishwoman" (p. 232)

Charlotte Charke (1713-1760), novelist, playwright *and* autobiographer, wrote a scintillating account of her life with an ulterior motive, that of "persuading" her father to leave her a legacy (which he did not), and published in serial form in the *Gentleman's Magazine* in 1755. Laetita Pilkington (1712-1750) published her three volumes of *Memoirs* (the first in 1748) in the attempt to realize her self and define her life. There was no literary area into which women did not venture in the seventeenth and eighteenth centuries and no form on which they did not leave their mark.

In relation to biographies, it was not uncommon for women to write "testimonials" for their husbands; Lucy Hutchinson (1620-?) wanted to record her husband's part in the Civil War (*The Memoirs of Colonel Hutchinson*—not published until 1806) and Anne Fanshawe (1625-1680) wrote an account of her husband's life, after his death, so that their son would be aware of his father's qualities and worth.

In taking these pioneering literary steps, in providing an account of one person's life, in telling a story, and developing a character, these women were also making a contribution to the novel in its present form. Currently there is a revival of interest in biography as the bridge between "fact" and "fiction" (with many suggestions that the increasing popularity of the genre with women writers and readers is precisely because of the way in which it can reveal the private life behind the public figure). To return to the origin of contemporary biography and the contribution of women is to construct an enriching continuity. Though not for long did women confine themselves to biographies of husbands;

Hester Thrale Piozzi's account of Samuel Johnson (*Anecdotes of the Late Samuel Johnson,* 1786) extended the scope of women's literary efforts and revealed the way the figure of a great man can appear very different when portrayed through the eyes of a gifted women.

POETRY

The seventeenth and eighteenth centuries marked the transition from the high-culture poetry, written by aristocratic women (such as Katherine Philips, 1631-1664) to the published poems of milkmaids; and while many privileged women might have continued to write classical poetry for their own private purposes and many milkmaids might not have turned to verse, the published efforts of women poets during this period are quite extraordinary. Anne Finch, Countess of Winchilsea (1661-1720) deserves sustained critical study, and there are so many more whose contributions should be represented in the literary heritage (see Germaine Greer, Jeslyn Hedoff, Melinda Sansone, Susan Hastings, 1988, for an indication of the range, diversity, and excellence of women's achievements during this period).

That no poets per se have been included in this volume is a matter for regret; for with the contributions of such women as Elizabeth Rowe, Mary Robinson, Helen Maria Williams, Anna Seward, not to mention that of Charlotte Smith, there is sufficient justification for numerous volumes on early women poets alone. In such a context, the contribution of women working class poets could also be explored. Ann Yearsley (1752-1806), who was referred to as *Lactilla,* the poetical milkwoman, was assisted in her efforts by another celebrated woman writer, Hannah More, and published *Poems on Several Occasions* in 1784. Janet Little (1759-1813) was the author of *Poetical Works of Janet Little, The Scotch Milkmaid* (in 1792), and Elizabeth Bentley, (1767-1839), the daughter of a cordwainer, published *Genuine Poetical Compositions on Various Subjects* in 1791.

PLAYS

Apart from the contribution of Fidelis Morgan (*The Female Wits*) and that of Kendall (*Love and Thunder; Plays by Women in the Age of Queen Anne*), very little attention has been given to the outstanding achievement of women playwrights during this period. Indeed, despite the overwhelming evidence to the contrary, (now *and* then) the assertion that women have not excelled as dramatists can still persist.

Many of the early women writers wrote plays, and many of them were marvelous successes. During the Restoration era, it is likely that women of the caliber of Aphra Behn, Catherine Trotter, Delarivière Manley, Mary Pix, and Susanna Centilivre, were in the ascendancy, and much more research could be undertaken on them and their individual and collective contributions to the theatre. More too should be known about some of the popular playwrights such as Anna Wharton, Jane Wiseman, Mary Davys, and Sophia Lee, as well as of the highly influential playwright, poet, and religious writer, Hannah More (1745-1833). In the eighteenth century there was Frances Boothby, Elizabeth Powhele, Elizabeth Cooper, Catherine Clive, Frances Brooke, and Elizabeth Griffith who all deserve attention in their own right, not to mention playwright and novelist Frances Sheridan (1724-1766), whose satirical *The Discovery* (staged in 1763) and *The Dupe* (also 1763) were highly successful. Frances Sheridan's *A Journey to Bath* (published but not staged) contains a colorful character, Mrs. Tryfort, "the prototype for Mrs. Malaprop in her son's play, *The Rivals*" (David Meredith, 1987: p. 283).

Eliza Haywood wrote plays, as did Fanny Burney, and Elizabeth Inchbald not only acted and authored numerous plays, she also wrote the critical prefaces to Longman's 25-volume *British Theatre*—thereby becoming one of the first drama critics in the English language.

Joanna Baillie, whose contribution is treated briefly in this collection, was another whose achievement should have permanently laid to rest the myth that women could not be dramatists; poet and playwright, she made a classic contribution to the development of drama, and she was acclaimed as *the* woman playwright of her day.

And still, there were more. These are only the broad outlines of women's part in the drama; it is clear that the whole area of the history of women and theater needs more detailed attention and evaluation.

CRITICISM

During this period, women also started to write as literary critics. With the shift from aristocratic patronage and a commitment to high culture, to more popular forms (a shift which Alexander Pope of course deplored and decreed to be the end of the world of letters), women were not so disadvantaged by their exclusion from formal education and were more confident about their ability to appraise the literary output of the period. So Elizabeth Inchbald became the drama critic and Anna Laetitia Barbauld (1743-1825) edited *The British Novelists* (1810) in fifty volumes.

Novelist and critic Clara Reeve (1729-1807) wrote *The Progress of Romance* (1785), one of the first evaluations of fiction (in which a distinction is made between novels and romance, a distinction which is discussed in this volume in Ros Ballaster's provocative article "Romancing the Novel; Gender and Genre in Early Theories of Narrative" p. 188) Maria Edgeworth was another who "defended" fiction and its form; *Letters for Literary Ladies* (1795; reprinted in part in Dale Spender & Janet Todd, 1989, pp. 355-371) is a critical text in any appreciation of the role that literature has played in women's lives.

There is no accessible history of women's literary criticism but such a compilation would not only make exciting reading, it could change fundamentally some of the received wisdom about the literary tradition and the process of its construction.

GUIDEBOOKS

During the seventeenth and eighteenth centuries, there was a great demand for books on the education of young women. Not necessarily interested in expanding intellectual horizons, the bulk of these publications was concerned with the cultivation of good manners and refinement, and the conduct books were turned out by male and female authors alike. Perhaps because—as Mary Wollstonecraft was to assert so authoritatively—it was that women were made, not born, it was necessary to produce so much material on the desirability of gracious dependence and the necessity of meek subservience. Many of the women who earned their living by their pens wrote such guide books, often from the paradoxical position of trying to persuade their readers to follow the path NOT "of what I do, but of what I say."

POLITICS

Then there were the political treatises; *A Serious Proposal to the Ladies* (1694) and *Some Reflections on Marriage* (1700) made clear the position of Mary Astell (1666-1731). Her critique of women's education and channeling for the self-denial of marriage is still relevant today, as is the protest of Mary Wollstonecraft (*Vindication of the Rights of Woman*). Mary Hays (1760-1843) wrote *Appeal to the Men of Great Britain in Behalf of Women* (1798), as well as *Female Biography: or Memoirs of Illustrious and Celebrated Women, of All Ages and Countries,* 1802, and she was in good company with other Rights' philosophers such as Mary Anne Radcliffe (1745?-1810?, who wrote *The Female Advocate; or, An Attempt to Recover the Rights of Women from Male Usurpation,* 1799). As Janet Todd has said, "Almost every female author [of this time] considered the state of her sex, and, however conservative, in some way disturbed patriarchal assumptions—necessarily so since her very existence as a writing subject challenged the prevailing ideology of female marginality" (1987, p. 23).

TRAVEL, HISTORY, AND TRANSLATION

Lady Mary Wortley Montagu (as has been mentioned) wrote of Turkey; Mary Wollstonecraft wrote of Scandinavia; and many were the women who "went abroad" (including Celia Fiennes [1662-1741] who wrote *Through England on a Side Saddle in the Time of William and Mary,* 1881) and wrote "letters" and other accounts of their travels. Helen Maria Williams not only reported on Switzerland in turmoil, she chronicled the course of the French Revolution, while Catherine Macaulay (1731-1791) wrote her six volume *History of England from the Accession of James I to that of the Brunswick Line* (published between 1762-1783).

When it came to translations, women's work was ubiquitous. Despite the educational disadvantages, there were women who translated from the classic (Sarah Fielding and Elizabeth Carter among them); more common, however, were translations from contemporary European sources with Mary Wollstonecraft for example, teaching herself German from a dictionary in order to work as a paid translator.

MAGAZINES

While women's magazines then were not as popular as they have become today, some of the seeds of the contemporary product were planted in the eighteenth century. Eliza Haywood, who was not only the author of plays, novels, and conduct books but of translations as well, also played a pioneering role on women's magazine publications; from 1744 to 1747 she brought out *The Female Spectator.* And there is some suggestion that this was not her first venture; an earlier publication, *The Parrot* (1728), was edited by one, Mrs. Penelope Prattle, often taken to be Eliza Haywood.

The Female Spectator was also preceded by *The Female Tatler* (1709), under the editorship of Mrs. Crackenthorpe, widely assumed to be Delarivière Manley—if not indeed the editor, there is some evidence that Delarivière Manley wrote for *The Female Tatler* (see Janet Todd, 1987, p. 211).

While these publications had their share of scandal sheets (and advice columns!), they also contained political items, pleas for education, and some short fiction (which requires further examination, particularly in relation to the first short story writers, Harriet and Sophia Lee (see Dale Spender, in press). But *The Female Tatler* and *The Female Spectator* did not reach the same standard as Charlotte Lennox's monthly periodical, *The Lady's Museum* (which was also one of the first publications to include serialized fiction, in this case Charlotte Lennox's own novel, *Sophia*).

Then too there was Lady Mary Wortley Montagu's political periodical, *The Nonsense of Commonsense* (published every Tuesday, it ran to nine issues from December 16, 1737 and was intended to refute the Whig opposition paper, *Commonsense*). And Frances Moore Brooke (1724-1789) published *The Old Maid* under the pseudonym of "Mary Singleton, Spinster"; this periodical ran from November 15, 1755 until April 10, 1756, and while the title remains something of a mystery (Frances Moore became the wife of John Brooke in 1756), there can be no doubt about its contents. Frances Brooke wrote "with lively wit on subjects ranging from courtship to current events, from religion to theater," comments Leo Manglaviti (1987, p. 61).

Conclusion

While this survey suggests some of the major innovations, lists some of the outstanding writers, and gives some idea of the dynamism of the time, it cannot begin to document in detail the number of women writers and the individual significance of their works. That specific articles on Mary Wollstonecraft, Ann Radcliffe (1764-1823), Sarah Scott and Harriet and Sophia Lee are not included in this collection is a regrettable omission; while many attempts were made to find people who could comment on the achievements of these writers, they were, unfortunately, not successful. (For further discussion of Mary Wollstonecraft and Ann Radcliffe, see Dale Spender, 1986. There is also an illuminating introduction by Jane Spencer to Sara Scott [1723-1795] and her friend, Lady Barbara Montagu, in the Virago edition of *Millenium Hall* [1762 and 1986], an account of an utopian female community. Harriet [1757-1851] and Sophia [1750-1824] Lee also call for further examination; Harriet for her contribution to the short story [see *Canterbury Tales,* 1799-1805]; and Sophia for her rewriting of women's history in fictional form in *The Recess* [1783-85]—where the heroines are the twin daughters of Mary, Queen of Scots, and it is their version of history the reader is provided with. The information is supposed to have come from an old manuscript, and in summarizing the author's intention, Jane Spencer [1986] says that Sophia Lee promises to disinter some of the buried truths of women's history, "through the story of these two sisters, revealed in their own writings, which were preserved for posterity by being entrusted to a female friend" [p. 195]. Such a significant novel deserves a collection concerned with its own contribution to the genre and the tradition of women's writing.)

Perhaps the most important point that can be made in relation to all these early women writers and their contributions is that this was a critical period in women's history; it marks the beginning of the development of women's literary culture, which, with all its associated characteristics, continues to this day and nourishes concepts of education, self-realization, and women's rights.

Deprived of formal education, denied professional occupation, and increasingly confined to the domestic sphere in the seventeenth and eighteenth centuries, many females sought knowledge of the world and intellectual stimulation—and they frequently taught themselves to read and write. Then they turned their talents towards communicating with others; and so a literary community came into being. This was an age when there was a dramatic increase in the size of the female reading public and in the number of female writers. The two were closely interrelated. The more women readers there were, the more women writers were required; the more women writers who emerged, the more women readers they won. Each helped to mold and shape the other, and both created an environment conducive to the development of a literary culture and the success of the novel.

What Was Women's Relationship to the Novel?

Any discussion of women's relationship to the novel must encompass some of the issues involved in the difference between the novel and the romance!

Basically, romances were a known genre at the beginning of this period; the term customarily referred to the "romance literature" of the classical or courtly love tradition (particularly of France; see Madeleine de Scudery for example). A romance consisted of fantastical acts performed by fantasy figures in far away and idyllic pastures, in different times. And the new form, the novel, was distinguished from this rarified plane by its social and domestic realism. "Romances" happened to princely people in distant places, but novels could be about ordinary people leading ordinary lives in the place next door. Clara Reeve (1785) made this distinction in her critical work when she declared that "The Romance is a heroic fable which treats of fabulous persons and things—The Novel is a picture of real life and manners and of the times in which it was written" (*The Progress of Romance, I,* 1785, p. 111).

Which is all very neat and orderly, and it would have been convenient if fiction writers and literary critics had continued to preserve this distinction; but, unfortunately, most of them didn't.

Romance and novel, as Ros Ballaster makes clear in this volume, became a gender distinction as well; and almost invariably, women are associated with romances, and men with novels. And this may have little or nothing to do with the content of their contribution. While on the one hand there is ample evidence—now and then—that women could be just as concerned with social and domestic realism, on the other hand they were (and still are) likely to be branded with the pejorative term romance.

Eliza Haywood, for example, made an explicit and courageously creative comment about her commitment to realism in the introduction to *The Disguised Prince, or the Beautiful Parisian*:

> Those who undertake to write Romances are always careful to give a high Extraction to their *Heroes* and *Heroines*; because it is certain we are apt to take a greater Interest in the Destiny of a Prince than a *private person*. We frequently find, however, among those of a middle State, some, who have Souls as elevated, and Sentiments equally noble with those of the most illustrious Birth; Nor do I see any reason to the Contrary; *Nature* confines her blessings not to the *Great* alone. . . . As the following Sheets, therefore, contain only real Matters of Fact, and have, indeed, something so very surprising in themselves, that they stand not in need of any Embellishments from Fiction: I shall take my *Heroine* just as I find her, and believe the reader will easily pass by the Meanness of her Birth, in favour of a thousand other good Qualities she was possessed of.
>
> (1728, pp. 1-2)

But no matter her protestations about an ordinary heroine and "Matters of Fact," Eliza Haywood is labeled as a romantic writer. In one sense, this is not surprising; virtually *all* women novelists from Jane Austen to Mary Gordon, from Elizabeth Gaskell to Margaret Drabble, Alice Walker—*and Barbara Cartland*—are broadly categorized as writers of romance in contemporary literary circles. Which says more about the nature of literary judgments than the nature of women's writing (see Dale Spender, 1989, for clarification).

In the circumstances it is tempting to suggest that—one woman's realism is another man's romance.

This is certainly consistent with some of the conventional evaluations of women's writing. As Candida Lacey (1986) pointed out in her perceptive appraisal of proletarian writers of the thirties, in the United States, when women writers introduced the added—*and realistic dimensions*—of the conflict between working for the union or becoming a wife, the verdict was invariably that these novels were flawed. Rather than recognize that for women it can be common place to have to choose between career and marriage—between being the union organizer and being the *wife* of the union organizer—female proletarian writers were criticized and condemned for their inclusion of "romantic interests" which distracted from the centrality of the class struggle.

(Interestingly, however, the same standard does not seem to apply in general to male writers who include—or even concentrate on—relationships in their fiction. D. H. Lawrence, for example, is not ordinarily devalued as a writer of romances, and the question arises as to whether *his* treatment of relationships is qualitatively different from that of the women who are consigned to the category. It could be revealing to undertake "blind" studies of some of his work; if placed between the typical covers of a popular romantic press's publication, would his novels pass as romance?)

Of course, one of the characteristics of most women's novels is that they focus on relationships, frequently on relationships between the sexes. And it could be that this is the salient feature which attracts the derogatory label—*romance.*

The primary reason that relationships are central to women's fiction is that they are central to women's lives; whether this fascination with human relationships is born of necessity (because women are so frequently on the receiving end in male-dominated society and must know which way the wind blows, managing their lives indirectly by managing relationships) or whether it is born of desire (the proper and most profitable study of humankind, *is* humankind) is impossible to determine. Certainly the combination of women, novels, and relationships is a complex and enduring one. It was at the heart of women's literary culture when it came into existence, and it still characterizes the reality of many literate women today. That the area is so under-researched, under-reported and under-recognized, however, is more an indication of traditional literary priorities than of women's realities.

Why women read novels, what they read, what they get from them, who they share their experiences with, what communities and networks they create from this common cultural exposure, how they are changed by the process—*and why women write novels for other women to read*—are among some of the most elementary and enlightening issues which could be addressed, particularly in contemporary times, when the very existence of the book and the novel is being questioned. The study of women's relationship to the novel in every century since the seventeenth and including the twenty-first, has much to recommend it in the interest of establishing the scope and nature of women's literary traditions and contemporary community.

What began as a trickle of women's novels at the beginning of the eighteenth century became a proverbial flood by the end, with women writers such as Fanny Burney, Maria Edgeworth, and Ann Radcliffe commanding respect as the leading literary figures of their day. While, as has been indicated, women still wrote in every other genre, it was the novel which was recognized as "women's form."

Perhaps this was because—as Virginia Woolf suggested—it was that the novel was *the* new form and was, therefore, sufficiently malleable to be bent to women's purposes. But perhaps the novel now has its recognizable form precisely because it was shaped by women and reflects the reality of their lives. Either way, it can be stated with conviction that in the eighteenth century women became avid writers and readers of the novel and to this form they brought the experiences of their own particular circumstances.

As it was within women's experience to write letters, the shift to the epistolary novel was accomplished relatively easily. As it was within women's experience to construct and maintain relationships—which meant that women were required to be sensitive to responses—writing the replies as well as the original letters was no great departure into the unknown. As Ruth Perry (1980) has commented, the epistolary novel called for "two or more people, separated by an obstruction which can take a number of forms, (who) are forced to maintain their relationship through letters" (p. 93). Such a format did not even demand an imaginative leap on the part of many women writers.

And once women realized the opportunity to write *in* the familiar style which they cultivated in their letters and to write *about* the domestic realities of women's lives, there was no stopping them. Women wrote about their own position, about relationships, about love and marriage, and, even in the eighteenth century, they wrote novels about ideas, politics, and the nature of reality (see Helen Thomson's fine article on Charlotte Lennox in this volume, pp. 113-125), although this did not prevent their novels from being labeled and belittled as romances.

Women's relationship to the novel as writer, reader, and critic is a story yet to be told in full; some of the contributions in this volume provide the outline for what promises to be a stimulating and fascinating narrative of the future.

Why Did Women Write?

Women wrote for business, and women wrote for pleasure; women wrote for many of the reasons that men wrote—because they needed occupation, and remuneration, and writing was something they were able to do, and which provided them with certain satisfactions. And the women who are included for discussion in this volume typify women's reasons for writing.

If Aphra Behn had not been paid for her writing, she surely would have spent more than one short period in debtors' prison. For Eliza Haywood, who left her husband, the choice was simple; she needed to earn her living and she preferred to sell her literary labors than to sell her self. Delarivière Manley also appears to have had a choice between working at the oldest profession for women or the newest; for all these women who had neither privilege nor patron the way was clear—if they didn't write, they didn't eat.

Sarah Fielding welcomed every penny she earned (although she was never wholly financially independent, and it probably isn't a coincidence that she was concerned with the construction of utopian societies and the principles of sharing). And while Elizabeth Inchbald was known for her parsimonious practices, the fact that she spent some time as a penniless actress (reduced even to stealing and eating raw turnips in a field) no doubt helped her to seek decent payment for her work and to protect her financial interests.

Charlotte Smith wrote desperately to keep the wolf at bay and to support her many children, as well as her granddaughter! And Charlotte Lennox's adult life seems to have been one long battle with poverty—which she lost, dying destitute; like Charlotte Smith, she too left her husband who was a terrible financial burden.

Fanny Burney's *first* novel, *Evelina* (1778), may have been written for pleasure, but *Camilla* (1796) was written to support husband and family.

Joanna Baillie earned her living by her pen, and of the women discussed in this anthology, it was probably only Maria Edgeworth and Mary Brunton who were supported by men and who wrote more for the pleasure than the profit. So much for the old allegation that women were dilettante writers, who had no need to earn their bread. As Jane Spencer has wryly commented: "Well born or not, most women novelists needed the money" (1986: p. 7).

Women also wrote because the opportunity to write was available; "Writing for publication, especially fiction," comments Janet Todd (1987), "was one of the few growth industries at a time when more traditional female occupations from millinery to midwifery were being appropriated by men" (p. 1).

But these are just the basic reasons for women seeking employment; why women should turn to writing as their particular profession has its psychological and aesthetic rationales as well.

Women wrote because they needed to find a form of self-expression, because they needed to consciously construct their reality, realize their potential, and define their own lives. Women wrote too because they needed a voice; they needed to feel that they had agency, that they were participants on the human stage and could affect some of the events of their domestic circumstances and their own society. Sometimes they even wrote to vindicate themselves and their writing.

And women wrote because they needed to make contact with other women and to create a community, a sense of solidarity; so a clergyman's daughter in one country town (Jane Austen) could communicate with a clergyman's daughter in another country town (Charlotte Brontë). So Maria Edgeworth subscribed to Jane Austen's novels and offered the highest praise to Elizabeth Inchbald in relation to *A Simple Story:* "I never read *any* novel—I except *none*—I never read any novel that affected me so strongly, or that so completely possessed me with the belief in the real existence of all the persons it represents" (in Anne Elwood, 1843, p. 325). So Jane Austen was intimidated by Mary Brunton's *Self Control,* and then included reference to so many of her sister writers in *Northanger Abbey;* by such means is a community created, isolation overcome, and a cultural milieu generated.

When Delarivière Manley published her novels, Lady Mary Wortley Montagu protested in her letters that she couldn't obtain a copy of the "key" to work out who the scandalous representations applied to; when Fanny Burney published *Evelina,* conversations, letters, and diaries of the day concentrated on speculations about the author and her heroine and whether either should or should not have indulged in certain activities.

And instead of being condemned to routine and monotonous lives, women readers became privy to a wide range of marvelous characters and witness to any number of exciting events—which is why there is no mystery about their enthusiasm for the novel and the demand for women writers.

These conversations, which can bring characters alive, continue to this day; whether they are about Evelina, Emma, Mrs. Ramsay, or the likely eventuality of *The Handmaid's Tale,* members of this literary community have a shared experience which can cross national boundaries and which addresses some of the central issues of women's lives.

Many of the early women writers were aware of the contribution they were making to this "conversation" (though it is unlikely that they knew how long it would continue or how extensive it might become); and many of them took their role very seriously. In the absence of an educational curriculum for women, women's novels frequently served as women readers' connection with the wider world. It was from novels such as *Evelina or Adeline Mowbray* or *Emmeline* or even *Emma* that women readers could become acquainted with the pitfalls that threatened innocent women in society and with the tragic consequences of "going wrong."

Discussions as to whether Adeline Mowbray was noble or a fool when she went to live with her lover were no mere titillations; they represented the genuine moral dilemmas of the day (and indeed, in this case, were meant to reflect the realities of Mary Wollstonecraft's life; see Dale Spender, 1986, p. 318-323). The questions of whether a woman should marry, or marry for love, or money, whether she should follow the dictates of her heart or elect to provide security for her mother and brother (as is the case in Frances Sheridan's *The Memoirs of Miss Sidney Bidulph*), were not self-indulgent speculations but real conflicts of interest in many women's lives. And deprived of direct experience of the world, of education, and tutoring in the exercise of moral judgment, novels were the best means available for trying to determine why people behave as they do and whether there are other viable options.

Few are the issues that novels did not raise or the lessons they did not teach. It is no exaggeration to suggest that novels can (and have) covered the gamut of human experience that can be articulated; even today, it would be possible to use women's novels as a basis for an excellent education. To construct such a curriculum would be a rewarding challenge and a refreshing experience.

What Did They Write About?

Heroines, in the main, were the subject of early women's writing. But to choose to write convincingly about ordinary women's lives was not without its difficulties—And not just because the events of ordinary women's lives may not have been the best raw material for the making of an exciting or edifying narrative, but because to provide a woman with adventures was to make her unfit to be a heroine of her time. "In the eighteenth century," comments Jane Spencer (1986) wryly, "the very word *adventure* in connection with a woman implies a loss of virtue. . . . (The) ideal woman in eighteenth century society is the woman about whom there is nothing to say. . . . Any woman whose life is eventful enough to be the subject of romance has compromised feminine virtue" (Spencer, 1986, p. 190). No properly brought up or supervised young lady would ever be in a dramatic or discreditable predicament (hence the abundance of orphans in early fiction writing), and no respectable, responsible married woman would do anything which attracted attention to her person. So certain "devices" had to be developed which allowed authors to create heroines who clearly retained their virtue, but who also had their share of risk taking in their lives. And as Katharine Rogers has revealed in this volume, Elizabeth Inchbald excelled in her efforts to overcome this contradiction.

Motherless daughters afforded considerable potential; like Evelina, their lack of information about the world could leave them open to a number of dramatic possibilities without necessarily calling their virtue into question. Then too, there were the daughters of inadequate mothers (a category into which Amelia Opie's heroine, Adeline Mowbray, falls) which presented similar authorial opportunities; these heroines were given poor or improper advice by their mothers and could not be blamed completely for their ignorance or mistakes (as Jane Spencer explains, this volume, pp. 201-211).

Both the motherless daughter and the inadequately reared one allowed the authors to show their heroines engaged in a learning process, involved in self-examination and personal insight, and this also conveniently provided a context in which a case could be made for better education for women and for a more just and equitable society.

Eliza Haywood exploited a new vein when she presented a reformed heroine in the shape of Betsy Thoughtless—a poor but honest heroine—and made it very difficult for her audience to condemn such a likable young woman who, admittedly, behaved very foolishly (though not at all wickedly) and who soon saw the "error of her ways." And limitless were the opportunities for adventure that such a format provided. The heroine could get into all manner of scrapes—some very dangerous, some very comic—but while even she recognized that she had done the wrong thing and was prepared to make amends (even if only in the last chapter), she could pass as an acceptable leading lady.

The reformed heroine was also put in the position of being a "learner"; she too could lament her own inadequate preparation for the world (including the absence of an education), and she too could call for the end of a sexual double standard. By the end of the eighteenth century, the young women who had "learned" from being exposed to temptation were quite popular characters in women's novels. In some respects the association of *didacticism* with women's fiction has its origins in this particular configuration. But if the heroine learned a lesson, the writers learned as well; there was more than one way for women to know something of the world and to preserve their good name and standing.

For many reasons Charlotte Smith created an entirely different sort of heroine; no flighty young woman who is sobered and matured by the lessons of the world provides the focus of her fiction. Rather, she starts with the women who have tasted some of the bitter fruits of experience, who have suffered the fate of "women's lot." As Pat Elliott points out in her appraisal of Charlotte Smith (see page 91), many of the author's characters reflect the circumstances and conclusions of her own life. And as Charlotte Smith herself was a victim of marriage, husband, and an unjust society, so too do some of her "heroines" deal with debt, dissolute husbands, and the desire for a better life. While it may have presented the author with many more problems to write a captivating account of these trials (and to arrive at a happy ending), there can be no doubt of Charlotte Smith's ability to hold her audience's attention, even if it was to issue a warning or to remind readers of the awful penalties that could be paid for an error of judgment. Dire consequences could await the woman who chose "the wrong man."

That the choice of a husband should be a primary concern in the novel is perfectly understandable, given that this was often the biggest event in a woman's life. And it was a choice on which so much rested; the happiness of the heroine, the happiness of her husband. Should a woman marry to obey her father or please her mother? Or should she too treat marriage as a career and look for promotion and the best financial prospects? Or was this a marriage market to which she had vehement objections?

(That women writers of the time might have been most concerned with this issue in fiction and in life is a point made by Janet Todd, [1987]: "Writing women, especially professional ones, no doubt represented a higher incidence of failed marriages than the population as a whole; otherwise marriage could almost be said to have broken down" [p. 7].)

How *not* to choose a man is part of the moral of Charlotte Lennox's amazing tale, *The Female Quixote: the Adventures of Arabella*; in this satire the author introduces a heroine who has no proper parental guidance (her mother is dead, and her father keeps her isolated). Arabella has been reared on a diet of romance literature to the extent that she believes the world works on the principles of courtly love and high sentiment—and of course the author makes the point that only by keeping the heroine from the real world could such a false construction of reality have been possible. The novel, which is extremely entertaining as well as intellectually provocative, is structured around many of Arabella's misapprehensions; given her romance-reality, she sees the gardener as a young nobleman in disguise (and after her hand), a gentleman out riding as someone trying to abduct her, and the Thames as a refuge, inviting her into its welcoming depths when she believes she is being pursued by ravishers. Always center stage and convinced of her great courtly powers and capacity to command, Arabella calmly contemplates the death of the suitors she rejects, and orders Glanville (later her husband) to go, to stay, and when ill, to survive!

It's all very heady, and highly amusing stuff. We are confronted with a heroine who holds power. But of course, the power is only an "illusion." This is a point which Charlotte Lennox makes with persuasive clarity. For Arabella to let go of romance and join the world of mere mortals is for her to give up power; it is for her to give up her adventures:

> To retain her virtue, Arabella must relinquish her adventures; but as we can see from the subtitle of the novel, *The Adventures of Arabella,* this means giving up the story of her life and her identity as heroine.
>
> (Jane Spencer, 1986, p. 190)

While Arabella persists in thinking she is a romantic heroine who holds power over men, she is not a virtuous woman and cannot become Glanville's wife; but to become the virtuous woman, to recognize the realities of everyday life, is to abandon her concept of self and the romantic society. It's not much of a choice.

Charlotte Lennox has written a novel which works at many levels, and—as Helen Thomson argues—should stand at the starting point of any appreciation of women and fiction. It is a novel about the nature of romance and reality, of emotion and reason, of subjectivity and objectivity, and as Glanville tries to lead Arabella from feminine "error" to masculine "truth," (Jane Spencer, 1986, p. 189), the echoes of gender division are again loud and clear.

What does emerge from *The Female Quixote* is that the focus on romance, courtship, and marriage is not necessarily a narrow one. Rather, it can serve as a microcosm for the discussion of the range of human values. Issues of truth, objectivity, the nature of knowledge and reality—all issues of profound importance in this postmodern world—are treated perceptively by Charlotte Lennox and many other women writers as well. Indeed, some of the fundamental philosophical questions of why human beings behave as they do and whether they can behave differently provide the framework for much of women's fiction.

Do women (and men) behave as they do as a result of nature or nurture? Will they behave differently given a decent education? What is the proper form of expression for female power and influence? And would society have to be structured differently if women were to realize their full potential? All of these issues are consistent with the discussion of love and marriage and the role these institutions play in women's lives.

Early women writers wrote about the world, but they did so from women's perspective; the objects and events of the world pass through a different filter when women are in charge of the reality, which is why there are different priorities, perceptions, protests in the work of women. So, for example, while men may have been critical of their own educational provision, they were not obliged to question whether or not education was a good thing. But for women—who were excluded, for whom educational opportunities were actually limited after Henry VIII's dissolution of the religious houses, and who were routinely informed that, for women, education could be physically and psychologically damaging—the entire educational debate assumes very different dimensions (including those of: "Who says that women's uteruses would burst and their brains atrophy if exposed to education?").

Early women writers used fiction to explore their own world and to remedy some of the deficiencies of their exclusion and isolation:

> When asked why she does not read history, Catherine Morland, [the heroine of Jane Austen's novel, *Northanger Abbey*] replies, "history, real, solemn history, I never could be interested in . . . the men all so good for nothing, and hardly any women at all."
>
> (Jane Austen, 1969, p. 108)

But Catherine Morland reads novels, particularly Gothic novels where women are at the center of the action and where women's view of the world prevails:

> [Catherine Morland's] reason for preferring Gothic fiction is the same as Arabella's for preferring the versions of history that she gets in the French romances: women are acknowledged there as they are not in history books. Women's fiction has always been concerned with redressing the balance and restoring women to the record. . . .
>
> (Jane Spencer, 1986, p. 192)

This is one of the main reasons that women have written fiction.

What Was the Response to Their Writing?

Readers, reviewers, and critics in the eighteenth century knew something not always widely known in the twentieth; namely, that the novel was "the woman's form." It was the genre which bore their imprint, and men could learn much from paying attention to the creative efforts of the woman writer. So accepted was the premise that this was the area where women predominated, that there were males who adopted female pseudonyms in order to increase their ratings as authors.

"Among other literary frauds it has long been common for authors to affect the stile [sic] and character of Ladies," wrote a reviewer in the *Gentleman's Magazine* (June 1770, p. 273), and readers were assured that every attempt would be made to detect these great deceivers of the reading public. The *Critical Review* also contributed to reader awareness and exposed any likely false practices. "We suspect," wrote their reviewer in April 1778, "that Madame la Comtesse may be found in some British garret, without breeches, perhaps, but not yet in petticoats."

So on the one hand the response was positive; women were acknowledged as *the* writers of the novel. But on the other hand, the novel did not enjoy the highest status as a literary genre.

There could have been many reasons for this; the first, that it was primarily because women were associated with it that the novel was not accorded high status (see Spender, 1989, for a discussion of gender and status in the world of letters). Or an explanation could have been that the novel was a new—and lesser—form, and that, unlike poetry and drama, (it was argued) its production did not demand a classical education or understanding on the part of the author.

Alternatively, it could have been because it was popular that the novel was devalued. Popularity and prestige have not always been compatible within the literary canon, and while there was no doubt about the *quantity* of women's output in the eighteenth century (with F. G. Black, 1940, estimating that women wrote between two-thirds and three-quarters of the novels in the period 1760-1790), their very success could have been used to challenge their *quality*. (Such popularity could also have been a factor in the gender-based division of fiction into men's novel and women's romance.)

This would help to account for a literary heritage in which it is exclusively male authors who are held up as the originators of the novel, while so many of the works of female writers have been consigned to virtual oblivion; why all women's fiction can be classified as romance and treated as an inferior achievement.

If, however, there was a double standard in relation to the novel, it was not confined to the differential status of the sexes. There was a whole set of different expectations which related to female and male authors and which played an influential role in determining the critical response to individual women writers.

It might have been all right for a man to write bawdy, to present a tale about the sexual exploits of a hero; but it was a very different matter for a woman to write bawdy, to write about a young man's amorous adventures and escapades (young women, of course, not being allowed to have them). The response to the woman writer would be outrage; for her to know such things was to be condemned as a woman and, hence, as a writer.

Some of the women even took this issue up in their writing, Aphra Behn among them. Many of her prologues and prefaces contain protests about the unfair treatment of women writers who wanted to write—realistically—about the world outside the narrow sphere a woman was supposed to be confined to. (One reason that has since been given for Aphra Behn's "fade from fame," is that she was such an indecent writer; it has to be said that men who wrote bawdy do not seem to have suffered a similar fate, but rather, have been relished for their colorful and robust contributions to the literary heritage.)

A woman writer was supposed to be virtuous; she was enjoined to write about the virtuous and to recommend the blameless life. Which meant that many female authors were obliged to extol the virtues of an existence that was very much at odds with the way they lived their own lives. Admonishing young women to do their duty, to be subservient, obedient, and deferential, was not all that consistent with the survival strategies employed by many of the early women writers. Jane Spencer (1986) comments on the contradictions and the pressure this placed on women writers, and she provides an illustration with the life and work of Frances Brooke. In *The Excursion* (1779) Frances Brooke "produced an impeccably 'moral' work by criticizing the kind of independent and ambitious behaviour she showed in her own life," Jane Spencer states dryly (p. 20).

Trying to appear virtuous and trying to write about the virtuous, in a gripping and memorable style, were additional obstacles which confronted the woman writer. And if there were penalties for failure, there were also penalties for success.

Eliza Haywood was one of the most prolific and popular of the early women writers. She was also the target of some of the worst verbal attacks of the day. It was precisely because she was so successful that Alexander Pope, for example, tried so hard to discredit her; and because she was a woman, his attack centered on her sexuality. So he offers her sexual favors as a prize in a urinating competition between two publishers and portrays her in the most appalling, sexist terms.[4] And while Pope's attack on popular writers who were "lowering the standards" was not confined to females, in "his attack on Haywood he could draw on an existing stereotype of the woman writer, according to which she was unclean, untidy, disgustingly sexual and a whore" (Jane Spencer, 1986, p. 5).

Today we could label Pope's actions as sexual harassment. There is considerable contemporary literature available on the way in which some men use sexual harassment as a device for keeping women out of territory they have defined as their own particular preserve (see MacKinnon, 1979). And certainly in the eighteenth century many men had defined the world of letters as their world and were prepared to go to great lengths to keep women out. (The extent to which authorship is seen as a male prerogative is discussed at length in Gilbert and Gubar, 1980.)

There is also some evidence that this strategy worked. For many years after the attack on her in *The Dunciad,* Eliza Haywood did not publish (at least, not under her own name). Whether this was because she was intimidated, or whether it was because publishers were influenced by Pope's treatment of her (and did not want to publish her work) is a matter for conjecture. Either way, it can be stated that when women did well, there were men who tried to prevent them from continuing to work in the area; women writers could be damned if they did well and damned if they did not. To some extent this is the salient feature of the reponse to women's writing.

What Were the Conditions Under Which They Wrote?

The more general conditions under which women wrote were those of a society moving towards industrialization, where the economic position of women was deteriorating.[5] In defiance of the traditional historical theory of "steady progress," women found their opportunities persistently eroded during this period. "The disappearance of the convents at the time of the Reformation had deprived girls not only of convenient local places of learning, but also of a pool of women teachers in the shape of the nuns themselves," states Antonia Fraser (1984, pp. 123-124). And with men's appropriation of some of women's traditional occupations (such as midwifery), along with the adoption of the increasingly fashionable concept of bourgeois femininity (which had as its ideal the seclusion of women and the servicing of men) the result was "that by the eighteenth century women had been forced to withdraw from many public activities" (Spencer, 1986: p. 14).

But paradoxically, the very forces that were pushing women out of paid work and public influence were the same ones that were helping to make possible the emergence of the novel and women's expanded opportunities for authorship.

At the simplest level there had to be some sense of isolation and privacy before the realistic novel—in the domestic setting—could have a rationale for existence. It's probably not an accident that "novels" have not developed in small communities where little distinction is made between PUBLIC and PRIVATE and where the members of the community are reasonably familiar with the details of each other's lives. This changed with industrialization and urbanization, and the entrenchment of the private sphere; a curiosity began to surface as to what was happening behind other people's closed doors. It was the desire to know the intimate details of other people's lives (as well as the emergence of concepts of INDIVIDUAL and CHOICE) which established the context for the novel.

But before the novel could become the popular medium, certain conditions had to be fulfilled; there had to be the technological means of producing and distributing the books, and there had to be sufficient literate members of the population with time to read, and money to purchase the works of fiction.

To deal with the finances first. Of course the fact that men purchased more novels—and figured more prominently on subscription lists—cannot necessarily be taken as an indication of their commitment to literature, or as a mark of their reading habits; it is more a measure of their relative purchasing power and their ability to decide how money should be spent. Perhaps women readers did not have access to the same number of titles until the advent of the circulating library, which provided novels (in abundance) to those who could not afford to buy them. But book sales and library circulation constituted a huge demand (and an audience of both sexes) and generated at one level a positive climate for the development of the woman writer.

This was a period in which the reading public expanded (though there is something of the chicken-and-egg debate in trying to determine whether such expansion facilitated the growth of the novel, or whether it was a response to it, or both). During the seventeenth and eighteenth centuries writing and reading ceased to be the prerogative of the aristocracy (or the product of patronage) and became much more part of the repertoire of the urban middle classes. Tradesmen, "shopkeepers, clerks and their families—and also to some extent servants" were all members of this new community, which was ripe for the evolution of fiction (Jane Spencer, 1986, pp. 6-7).

That writing and reading were theoretically the only skills that women required to be the writers and readers was particularly fortunate; for at this time (in contrast to contemporary wisdom), it was considered quite normal for girls who had the opportunity in terms of books, light, and leisure, to teach themselves these skills. While there were privileged females who had access to some tuition—through parents, governesses, or brothers' tutors, etc.—if school attendance had been a necessary condition of authorship, there would have been many women writers who were disqualified.

So many women taught themselves to read and write, and took to it with such a vengeance; and so many made the "art" of both seem so effortless that many are the dismissive comments that have been made about women's facility for writing (and reading!) fiction. (This has been true even in the twentieth century; the Australian novelist, Vance Palmer, trying to illustrate how easy it was for women to write novels, in contrast to the creative struggle it meant for men, stated that "Writing a novel seems as easy to almost any literate woman as making a dress," (*Bulletin 3,* July 29, 1926).

So popular did writing and reading become with women (which supports the thesis of the creation of a continuing literary community) that grave fears were expressed that soon every woman would be doing it, even the servants. And with what disruptive consequences:

> . . . the number of *Authoresses* hath of late so considerably increased, that we are somewhat apprehensive lest our very Cook-wenches should be infected with *Cacoethes Scribendi,* and think themselves above the vulgar employment of mixing a pudding, or rolling a pye-crust.
>
> (*Monthly Review, 27,* 1762: p. 472)

Of course it wasn't just the writing that was questioned; in the eighteenth century and into the nineteenth grave fears were also expressed about the dangers of fiction for young women. (The fact that reading novels might have provided women with a world of their own, one that men did not directly have access to, and that it also made them "unavailable" to attend to men, could also have had something to do with the objections to women's novel reading. My discussions with women readers reveal that many men can still find it threatening when women are engrossed in novels, and they can even report that men will use disruptive strategies to prevent women from reading and to obtain their attention. This is apart from the fact that women can "get ideas" and become "awkward" as a result of reading.)

But while novel reading was often viewed with disapprobation, it was writing and the power of agency that it afforded which was reserved for the greatest condemnation.

> When a farmer's daughter sits down to *read* a novel, she certainly mispends [sic] her time, because she may employ it in such a manner as to be of real service to her family; when she sits down to *write* one, her friends can have no hope of her.
>
> (*Critical Review, 33* 1772, p. 327)

Women's efforts were rarely welcomed by the literary establishment. It wasn't just that women were considered to be without artistic merit, that they had their works rendered apolitical and "trivial" by being labeled as romance, but their very presence in the literary marketplace was deplored by many men as a "lowering of standards";

> So long as our British Ladies continue to encourage our hackney Scribblers, by reading every Romance that appears, we need not wonder that the Press should swarm with such poor insignificant productions.
>
> (*Monthly Review, 28* 1760, p. 523)

And there are contemporary echoes (see Spender, 1989).

The resistance to the idea that women's writing and reading represent skill still persists (even among women themselves, unfortunately).[6] And this climate of devaluation characterizes the conditions under which women have routinely written. Mary Wollstonecraft insisted that one of the last male bastions to fall would be that which appropriated for men intellectuality and creativity. While enormous material and legal gains have been made in the two hundred years since she presented her case in *Vindication of the Rights of Woman* (1792), it could be argued that when it comes to the accreditation of women's authority as intellectual and creative beings, few, if any, changes have been made.

Women became writers in the seventeenth and eighteenth centuries for the very good reason that it was not possible to prevent them from doing so. They were, of course, often discouraged; denied education, informed that they were inferior, ridiculed at times for their literary efforts, and cautioned against the corrupting influence of novels. It took enormous faith and confidence for women to declare that they possessed—and could use well—creative and intellectual faculties.

What they did not normally do in this period, however, was assert that they wrote because they were ambitious and sought artistic fulfillment, financial independence, or VISIBILITY AND RECOGNITION OF THEIR WORK. While the pretexts for venturing into the literary work place are discussed at more length in the final chapter, what must be stated here in relation to the writing woman's working conditions, is that she had to collude in the making of the myth that women were NOT autonomous beings who could occupy space in the public sphere and have a political agenda:

> . . . Let a woman write to amuse her leisure hours, to instruct her sex, to provide blameless reading for the young, or to boil the pot; moral zeal was an accepted justification and poverty an accepted excuse; but there was one motive which could be neither justified nor excused—ambition, the "boast" of conscious power, craving to perform its task and receive its reward. The proper attitude for a female talent was diffidence; the proper field for its exercise, the narrow circle of her intimate friends; and if for any of the permitted reasons she stepped outside the circle, let her at least sedulously avoid the disgraceful imputation of assurance.
>
> (J. M. S. Tompkins, 1969, p. 116)

It was an offense for women to be confident, visible.

Many women wrote in the seventeenth and eighteenth centuries in psychological circumstances that would not now be considered conducive to writing; many women wrote without "a room of their own" or "five hundred pounds a year," the very basics advocated by Virginia Woolf as the conditions for the writing of fiction. Despite these "limitations," they played a crucial part in shaping and extending and securing the viability of a literary community, and their contribution deserves to be much better appreciated and more widely known.

What Were the Creative and Professional Achievements of These Writing Women?

The professional achievement of women is treated in more detail in the concluding chapter, and the underlying purpose of this overview has been to establish the extent of the early women writers' creative achievement. While they wrote across every genre and could be studied for their contribution to everything from drama to letters, from history to poetry, the part they played in the development of the novel is remarkable, and the full implications of their achievements will only be realized when even further research is undertaken on their lives, their work, and the traditions they helped to forge. And this is where the final question is relevant; *why is it that these women have not been at the center of the valued literary tradition which resources the views and values of the entire culture and which is transmitted from one generation to another?*

Why women are NOT at the center of the literary tradition—why they are not equally represented in the production of legitimated literary culture—is a question which invites numerous alternative explanations. If the full range of possibilities is to be canvassed, then one which must be entertained is that women have no central presence in the heritage for the very simple reason that their writing is not up to standard; that what they write, and how they write does not warrant praise, prestige, accreditation, or emulation. The identification of such a deficiency would then serve to account for women's relative absence from the canon and exclusion from the curriculum and their relative invisibility in the cultural and educational heritage (for further discussion, see Dale Spender, 1989, and Joanna Russ, 1983).

But to discount the contribution of women in this manner is not to put an end to the problematic matter of women's lack of representation. On the contrary, to devalue women writers on the basis of their gender is to raise yet more awkward questions—not the least of which would be that there is no study within literary criticism which establishes the inferior nature of women's authorship. Despite the implicit assumptions and explicit assertions that women's writing is not as good as men's, there is no evidence which would support such a thesis.

However, the absence of a definitive study on the deficiencies of the writing woman has not always pre-empted the devaluation of her contribution; in some respects the history of literary criticism is the history of the dismissal of women's achievement, as so much of feminist literary criticism makes clear. But if women have been—and still are—being judged as inferior when there is no conclusive evidence about the *standard* of their contribution, then this in itself becomes the overriding issue; *who decides*? Who is determining that women's writing is not of the same order as men's and not worthy of equal representation in the literary tradition?

Literary criticism is not immune from some of the epistemological questions which have challenged many of the disciplines in the social sciences and humanities:

- who are the knowledge makers?
- what is the nature of the knowledge they generate?
- whose interests are served by such knowledge construction? and
- how are the benefits of vested interests justified/rationalized?

Although issues about authority, validity—and vested interest—may not have been addressed in any systematic way in the past, they are, nonetheless, proper areas of investigation within the literary criticism paradigm. And they can give rise to some disturbing considerations.

The striking fact is that it has been literally the "men of letters" who have been primarily the knowledge makers; it has been mainly men—and a PARTICULAR group of white, educated, privileged (able-bodied, and heterosexual) MEN—who have determined that the work of white, middle-class men is the best that can be written and deserves pride of place in the canon.

Such a value judgment and coincidence does not necessarily imply any insidious or conspiratorial strategy on the part of male literary critics of past generations. Rather, their preferences are understandable; for the very same reasons that women readers—and critics—may find the work of women more meaningful, relevant, more enriched with detail, nuance, and delineation, and hence *a greater artistic achievement,* so too may men place greater value on the offerings of their own sex. It is not male preference *per se* which has been responsible for women's eclipse (for women writers may have been the choice of women readers and critics, but this in itself has not resulted in the disappearance of the work of the men); it is that the preferences of men have prevailed. Men have been in a position to insist on the rightness (and the impartiality!) of their own assessments.

It is not difficult to establish that when it comes to the construction of the literary heritage and to the classification of good and great writers and their inclusion in a tradition which is transmitted from one generation to the next, it is men who almost exclusively have been the knowledge makers. They have constructed a tradition which has favored the contributions of their own sex (and class and ethnicity); they have provided a rationale which serves their own interests; and they have made their own case for their own supremacy in the area. The history of the novel constitutes a critical example.

As is argued in *Mothers of the Novel; 100 Good Women Writers Before Jane Austen* (Spender, 1986), the men of letters have rewritten literary history so that the greater contributions of women—in terms of number of titles, number of sales, payment for manuscripts, innovative and artistic developments—have been denied in favor of achievements of five males who are deemed to have been the originators of the novel.

Since the seventeenth and eighteenth centuries, women have written; some would go so far as to suggest that they may have even written more fiction than men. So it has been no mean feat to exclude this mammoth amount of work from the literary heritage. In the case of the fiction, extraordinary "revisions" were necessary to remove "the majority of eighteenth century novels" from the heritage. As Joanna Russ has indicated, extraordinary denials of women's achievements were required for these revisions to be rationalized:

> She didn't write it.
> She wrote it, but she shouldn't have.
> She wrote it, but look what she wrote about.
> She wrote it, but "she" isn't really an artist and "it" isn't really serious, of the right "genre"—i.e. really art.
> She wrote it, but she wrote only one of it.
> She wrote it, but it's only interesting/included in the canon for one, limited reason.
> She wrote it, but there are very few of her.
> (Joanna Russ, 1983, p. 76)

Such a challenge to the conventions of literary judgment is indicative of the increasing emphasis in feminist criticism on the sexual double standard and the role it has played in the exclusion of women. And the criticism has been leveled not so much at past social arrangements which accorded privileges to males so that they occupied the position of literary critics, nor at their preference for the writing of their own sex; for, while not excusable, such patterns of the past are understandable. What is of concern in the contemporary climate is the reluctance of the literary establishment to put its own house in order and to "revise its revisions"; it is the failure of many institutions and individuals to treat the nature of critical judgment as a serious issue and to seek to remedy some of the past omissions by reinstating women as equal representatives as writers and critics. What is of concern is the *continued* practice of the exclusion of women and the refusal of too many agencies—from course programmers to schools of criticism, from anthology compilers to research supervisors—to make the process of canon construction and value judgments (including those related to class and ethnicity) the subject of constant scrutiny and assessment. At the center of literary evaluation should be the premise that it is not just the study of those who are good and great (if these are to be the desired categories) but *who says so,* which is the range of reference for the discipline. Then questions of *why women have been*—and continue to be—*excluded* would become fundamental rather than marginalized issues.

Currently women are far from being equally represented in the tradition that is transmitted to the next generation in English speaking communities; while there is some difficulty in obtaining figures, the consensus seems to be that in college English courses fewer than seven percent of the writers studied are women.[7] And despite the perceived gains of the last decades, this could actually constitute a decrease in women's representation.

And it is not the case that the work of women has been systematically studied, that quantitative and qualitative analyses have been undertaken and have revealed women's writing to be below standard. Quite the reverse; it is not that women have been given a fair hearing and found wanting, but that women are found wanting, and are not given a fair hearing (and this is the thesis of *The Writing or the Sex? or, why you don't have to read women's writing to know it's no good*).

Prejudice against the writing woman still persists, and it works against women in a variety of ways. Just as in the seventeenth and eighteenth centuries it was not possible to prevent women from taking up their pens and enjoying considerable success in print, so too it has not been possible to prevent women writers from enjoying enormous success over the last decades. And yet just as the early women writers were kept out of the mainstream, so too are many contemporary writers precluded from representation in the establishment. For while the last twenty-five years have witnessed a virtual explosion in the publication of women's books, the reality is that *there has been no significant change in the canon or the curriculum.* When less than seven percent of the writers taught are women, it is obvious that female authors, past and present, continue to be silenced, suppressed, excluded.

In the seventeenth and eighteenth centuries, when women were denied access to formal education, women's novels were a welcome substitute; they were a means of communication which gave shape and substance to women's lives, which promoted an exchange of information and the encouragement of growth and learning. Perhaps in the current context they continue to provide a comparable service. For it is not uncommon to find the bookshop on the college campus stocked with a vast range of women's books which will sell widely to students—but which are not taken up and set as texts in the halls of learning. So women continue to write for each other and to generate an informal but shared literary culture. Which, while it may have its advantages, places the continuity of women's contribution in jeopardy. It's not just that women's writing from the past has not been incorporated into the cultural heritage; it is also that women's writing in the present could suffer a similar fate.

Living by the Pen; Early British Women Writers is both an attempt to reclaim a heritage and to ensure that it becomes a permanent and prized part of the literary repository for future generations. And while the women who have worked to contribute to these pages have made a significant start, much more remains to be done before women are assured of their rightful place and there is a Vindication of the Writing Woman.

Notes

1. See *The Spectator, 581,* August 16, 1714.
2. From *The Second Common Readers,* 1984, p. 151.
3. p. 52
4. Charlotte Brontë was subjected to the same double standard; with the publication of *Jane Eyre* (under the pseudonym of Curer Bell), the critical response was that if written by a man it was excellent but if by woman it was scandalous (see Spender, 1989, for further discussion).
5. There are quite a few informative surveys of women's economic status in the seventeenth and eighteenth centuries, including Alice Clark, (1919 1982), Antonia Fraser (1984), and Ruth Perry (1980, pp 27-62).
6. Eva Cox's current research on the assessment of women's skills, reveals how reluctant women are to perceive themselves as skilled; they can be gifted, but are often very resistant to the idea of having a range of skills (private communication, 1990, on ongoing research).
7. Such a figure does not include Women's Studies courses where women writers are included; see Dale Spender, 1989, for further clarification.

References

Adburgham, Alison. (1972). *Women in print: Writing women and women's magazines from the Restoration to the accession of Victoria.* London: Allen & Unwin.

Austen, Jane (1969). Northanger Abbey. In Robert William Chapman (Ed.), *The novels of Jane Austen, Volume V.* Oxford: Oxford University Press.

Black, F. G. (1940). *The epistolary novel in the late eighteenth century: A descriptive and bibliographical study.* Eugene, OR: University of Oregon. *Bulletin.* (1926, July 29). *3,* 3.

Chapman, Robert William, Ed. (1969). *The novels of Jane Austen.* Oxford: Oxford University Press.

Clark, Alice. (1919/1982). *Working life of women in the seventeenth century.* London: Routledge and Kegan Paul.

Critical Review. (1772). *33,* 327.

Cotton, Nancy. (1987). In Janet Todd (Ed.), *A dictionary of British and American women writers 1660-1800.* London: Methuen.

Dorr, Priscilla. (1988). Joanna Baillie. In Paul Schlueter and June Schlueter (Eds.), *An encyclopedia of British women writers.* New York: Garland Publishing.

Elwood, Anne. (1843). *Memoirs of the literary ladies of England.* 2 Volumes. London: Henry Colburn.

Fraser, Antonia. (1984). *The Weaker Vessel: Woman's lot in seventeenth century England.* London: Weidenfeld & Nicolson.

Gilbert, Sandra M. and Gubar, Susan. (1980). *The madwoman in the attic; The woman writer and the nineteenth century literary imagination.* New Haven: Yale University Press.

Greer, Germaine; Medoff, Jeslyn; Sansone, Melinda; and Hastings, Susan (Eds.). (1988). *Kissing the rod: An anthology of seventeenth century women's verse.* London: Virago.

Haywood, Eliza. (1728). *The disguised prince, or the beautiful Parisian.* Ln. Publ.

Hemlow, Joyce. (1958). *The history of Fanny Burney.* Oxford: Clarendon Press.

Henning, Rachel. (1985) *The letters of Rachel Henning.* Melbourne: Penguin.

Kramarae, Cheris and Spender, Dale (Eds.). (in press). *The knowledge explosion: Generations of feminist scholarship.* Elmsford, NY: Pergamon Press.

Kendall, (Ed.). (1988). *Love and thunder: Plays by women in the age of Queen Anne.* London: Methuen.

Lacey, Candida. (1986). Striking fictions: women writers and the making of a proletarian realism.

Women's Studies International Forum, 9(4), 373-384. In Candida Lacey (Ed.), *Political Fiction.*

MacKinnon, Catharine, A. (1979). *Sexual harassment of working women.* New Haven: Yale University Press.

Meads, Dorothy M. (1930). *The diary of Lady Margaret Hoby, 1599-1605.* London: Routledge.

Meredith, David W. (1987). In Janet Todd (Ed.), *A dictionary of British and American women writers 1660-1800.* London: Methuen.

Monthly Review. (1760). *28,* 523.

Monthly Review. (1762). *27,* 472.

Morgan, Fidelis. (1981). *The female wits: Women playwrights of the Restoration.* London: Virago.

Morgan, Fidelis. (1986). *A woman of no character: An autobiography of Mrs. Manley.* London: Faber & Faber.

Perry, Ruth. (1980). *Women, letters and the novel.* New York: AMS Press.

Piozzi, Hester Thrale. (1786). *Anecdotes of the late Samuel Johnson.*

Reeve, Clara. (1785). *The progress of romance.* 2 Volumes. Colchester: W. Keyymer. (Reprinted in 1970 by Garland Publishing, New York.)

Russ, Joanna. (1983). *How to suppress women's writing.* London: The Women's Press.

Russell, Rosalind. (1987). The "immortal" who fell from literary grace. *Scotsman,* February 2, 1987.

Schnorrenberg, Barbara Brandon. (1984). Joanna Baillie. In Janet Todd (Ed.) *A dictionary of British and American women writers.* London: Methuen.

Schofield, Mary Anne. (1990). *Masking and unmasking the female mind: disguising romances in feminine fiction 1713-1799.* New Jersey: Associated University Presses.

Schofield, Mary Anne and Macheski, Cecilia, (Eds.). (1986). *Fetter'd or free? British women novelists, 1670-1815.* Athens, OH: Ohio University Press.

Spencer, Jane. (1986). *The rise of the woman novelist: From Aphra Behn to Jane Austen.* Oxford: Basil Blackwell Ltd.

Spender, Dale. (1986). *Mothers of the novel: 100 good women writers before Jane Austen.* London: Pandora Press.

Spender, Dale. (1988). *Writing a new world: Two centuries of Australian women writers.* London: Pandora Press.

Spender, Dale. (1989) *The writing or the sex? or why you don't have to read women's writing to know it's no good.* Elmsford, NY: Pergamon Press.

Spender, Dale. (Ed.). (in press). *The diary of Elizabeth Pepys.* London: Grafton Books.

Spender, Dale. (Ed.). (in press). *Anthology of women's short stories.* London: Pandora Press.

Spender, Dale and Todd, Janet (Eds.). (1989). *Anthology of British women writers.* London: Pandora Press.

Todd, Janet (Ed.). (1987). *A dictionary of British and American women writers 1660-1800.* London: Methuen.

Todd, Janet. (1986). *Sensibility: An introduction.* London: Methuen.

Tompkins, J. M. S. (1932, 1969). *The popular novel in England 1770-1800.* London: Methuen.

van Doren, Dorothy. (1929). *The lost art: Letters of seven famous women.* New York: Coward-McCann.

White, Cynthia. (1970). *Women's magazines 1693-1968.* London: Michael Joseph.

Wollstonecraft, Mary. (1792). *Vindication of the rights of woman.* London: Joseph Johnson.

Woolf, Virginia. (1928, 1974). *A room of one's own.* Harmondsworth: Penguin.

Woolf, Virginia. (1984). *The common reader.* London: Hogarth Press.

SOCIETY

GARY KELLY (ESSAY DATE 1996)

SOURCE: Kelly, Gary. "Gender, Class and Cultural Revolution." In *Revolutionary Feminism: The Mind and Career of Mary Wollstonecraft,* pp. 1-22. New York: St. Martin's Press, 1996.

In the following essay, Kelly discusses the influence of women on the British middle-class cultural revolution of the 1790s.

Mary Wollstonecraft was a Revolutionary feminist—an advocate of the rights or claims of women in a specific revolutionary situation. There were two related aspects of that situation: the French Revolution and the cultural revolution that founded the modern state in Britain.[1] Many cultural revolutionaries in Britain saw the Revolution in France, at least in its early stages, as an example of what they themselves could achieve. But the British cultural revolution was itself a field of struggle in which the fortunes of various contestants, including Revolutionary feminism, were influenced by the changing course of the French Revolution. Paradoxically, the Revolution soon turned against feminists in France, yet it was also used as a reason to reject feminism, along with other forms of 'innovation' or 'French principles', in Britain.

The British debate on the French Revolution was part of the struggle for power within the British cultural revolution and it was conducted through writing, one of the cultural revolution's main instruments. Thus it was necessarily through writing, or print, that Wollstonecraft aimed to intervene in both the French Revolution debate and the cultural revolution in her own country, to turn them in the direction of a feminism for the Revolutionary decade. She did so not only by advancing feminist arguments in writing, but by challenging the entire male-dominated institution of writing in her time. She used the available resources of style, genre and discourse to show that the limited education, experience and professional opportunities assigned to women in both the pre-Revolutionary order and the British cultural revolution could lead not to subordination but to feminist consciousness, and the emancipation of women. Wollstonecraft's Revolutionary feminism was a writing revolution, exemplified and conducted in writing.

'Feminism' and 'revolution' are of course problematic terms. As Philippa Levine points out, 'The definition of feminism in the historical context is . . . fraught with difficulties.'[2] 'Feminism' in the usual modern sense—advocacy

Woodcut depicting women invading the assembly during the French Revolution.

of the rights or claims of women—did not come into the English language until the campaign for women's electoral rights in the 1890s, but it can be argued that there were feminisms in Britain before then, such as Renaissance feminism, seventeenth-century court and anti-court feminism, mid-eighteenth century Bluestocking feminism, and feminisms within cultural movements such as Sensibility and Evangelicalism.[3] After 1800 there was a Romantic nationalist feminism and, later still, socialist feminism, mid-nineteenth century movements for women's legal and educational rights and the later campaign for women's suffrage, giving rise to the modern use of the word 'feminism'. Each of these feminisms was conditioned by different social and historical circumstances, different horizons of possibility.

'Revolution' usually means a sudden or violent transformation in the established order and Wollstonecraft lived in an age of such revolutions, but some revolutions are less sudden. The Revolutionary feminists of the 1790s advocated the rights and claims of women within an intense debate over a sudden and violent revolution, and within the longer revolution that founded the modern state in Britain. This cultural revolution was not sudden or massively violent, but it transformed the culture, society and political structure of Britain, and naturalized this order for individuals in daily life and experience. Within this cultural revolution gender difference was a major issue, deeply implicated in other major revolutionary issues and in the struggle to define and lead the classes by and for whom the cultural revolution was being carried out.[4]

Social class may be taken as a particular historical phenomenon rather than a transhistorical social reality, a manifestation of social conflict rather than the cause of it, as different social groups come to see themselves having common interests, identity and opponents.[5] The cultural revolution of the late eighteenth century was carried out by and for the bourgeoisie or middle classes—the 'middle ranks' or 'middling sort', as they were then called—led by the professional class. Their revolution aimed to remake society in their own image and interests by imposing their culture, or forms of it, on other classes. But their cultural revolution was conditioned by their own changing experience of social conflict and the politics of culture. In the middle decades of the eighteenth century, bourgeois social critics, along with others, attacked court government and culture as well as emulation of court culture by the gentry and middle classes. Toward the end of the century, and especially in the 1790s, they also attacked the lower classes, both urban and rural, whom they saw as either subordinated to court culture or challenging for political power, if not for social and cultural domination in their own right. Yet the professional cultural revolution owed much to these different class rivals.

The professional bourgeoisie were especially marked by relations with their 'betters'—the landed classes. Historically, the professionals had been closely associated with these classes and dependent on them.[6] The aristocracy and gentry placed second and third sons in the professions—careers often controlled by the landed classes through patronage. But the professions also offered upward social mobility to the commercial and mercantile middle classes. The gentry married first daughters off within their own class to secure family alliances and thus build a broader base of power through patronage; second and third daughters could be married off to useful and promising professional men or sons of well-to-do commercial or manufacturing families. Heiresses of the commercial and manufacturing classes raised their families' status by marrying into the gentry and brought new money for agrarian capitalism and the conspicuous consumption that affirmed the gentry's power and prestige.

The professional bourgeoisie were an increasingly distinct group within the middle classes from the seventeenth century on, but their increasing power and prestige in the eighteenth century were due to the pre-eminence of the landed classes. The latter had established their power with the Glorious Revolution of 1688 and used it to enhance their prosperity through capitalist land management, improved production and technological advance. Some of the new prosperity went into the traditional gentry culture of conspicuous consumption, which in turn increased the numbers, wealth and status of the professionals who provided administrative, cultural and personal services.[7] Economic expansion also led to the growth of towns, where most professionals lived and which they came to dominate; in fact, they were often called 'the town gentry'.[8] These developments enabled professional people to develop distinctive identity, interests, culture and values. Increasing distinctness accompanied increasing sense of distinction, or social importance and dignity. Other differences reinforced these distinctions, as with the religious Dissenters who had been legally and socially excluded from most patronage and power since the seventeenth century.[9]

Yet in the last three decades of the century there was an increasing sense of class conflict. Increased social distinction and economic opportunities led to increased social frustration for those professional people not in élite professions or well-connected to the gentry-dominated system of patronage that still controlled economy and state.[10] Because of this domination, membership in the gentry continued to be the aim of socially ambitious individuals and groups, and those who could not quite make it into the gentry emulated them socially and culturally or challenged their domination. While social and cultural changes were enhancing the status and power of the professional class, they also increased distinctions within the middle classes. Middle-class emulation of their 'betters' and desire for upward social mobility led to increasing disdain for the 'lower orders' and sharper distinctions between the professions, the commercial and manufacturing bourgeoisie and mere 'tradespeople'. The increasing numbers and wealth of the professionals also widened gaps between 'learned' professions such as law and the clergy, 'gentlemanly' professions such as the military, and professions still associated with crafts or trades. Even in the law there was a strong distinction between the élite barristers and the mere attorneys.

There was increased hostility between the lower classes and the others, arising from the shift to a wage economy, accelerated enclosure of common lands, abandonment of customary doles, suppression of popular sports, pastimes and festivals, exclusion of the 'vulgar' from public spaces in towns, and the development of 'standard' forms of language and culture from which the lower classes were excluded.[11] Furthermore, economic development and improved communication between the regions of Britain made their social, historical, cultural and religious differences more noticeable. The growing towns were very different from one another. People of all classes retained strong local loyalty and regional identity, which could cut across an emergent sense of national solidarity and common interest within a particular social class. Many events gave prominence to these social divisions, including the Jacobite rebellions, unrest in Ireland, antiquarian and folklore movements, the rise of local presses, the rise of the 'reading public', the feminization of literature and culture, the Gordon Riots and other disturbances.

Then events of the 1790s, such as the debate on the French Revolution, political unrest in Scotland and open rebellion in Ireland, formation of organized lower-class opposition to government, the association of religious Dissent with sympathy for the Revolution, and the debate on women's rights, revealed dangerous regional and social divisions in Britain and within the professional and middle classes.[12] Meanwhile, events in France showed how a professional middle-class revolution could go wrong. Nevertheless, in the 1780s and 1790s some middle-class and professional people were ready to form a coalition with the literate, politicized artisan classes in order to carry out a middle-class revolution: overthrow of the court system, the patronage system and the hegemony of the upper classes. Such circumstances sharpened both the struggle for leadership within the professional and middle classes and these classes' competition with other classes.

In this conflict of loyalties, identities and distinctions, gender difference was increasingly important and complex.[13] The extent to which women identified with or distinguished themselves from the men of 'their' class or social group was and is a difficult question. R. S. Neale argues that 'while men might have the illusion of freedom, women never could', for 'all family relationships, marriage, love and morality were determined by, and the servants of, property; they were facets of total alienation'. Thus 'the value stance expected of women may be encapsulated in the word propriety—one might say that among the landed classes propriety was to women as property was to men'.[14] This may have been even more the case for women of the professional class, whose capital and property were, in the first instance, intellectual and moral—of the 'mind'—the basis of 'propriety' as conduct.

Within the professional middle class gender differences also parallelled and reinforced class differences. Wives of merchants and tradesmen could participate in their husbands' businesses but wives of professional men could not.[15] The leisured and cultivated 'lady' of the landed classes was distinguished from the mere 'woman' because she possessed a class-based culture that exhibited the status and wealth of the men and families of her class. Therefore she was emulated by middle-class women, and many socially ambitious middle-class men wished their women to become 'ladies'. Yet the sacrifice of women to mere family interest and ambition—that is, the interest and ambition of men—was widely deplored in all classes. The courtly lady who used or was used in sexual intrigue for political ends—the so-called 'mistress system' of court politics and patronage—was widely condemned, and the upper-class or would-be upper-class coquette symbolized the decadence and injustice of the court system.

It is true that women subordinated within the upper classes could seem parallel to a bourgeoisie that felt itself subordinated by the upper classes. On the other hand, since women were subordinated in all classes they would seem to have good reason to betray family or class in order to marry up the social scale or to be seduced by a more powerful and (therefore) attractive social superior. Both quasi-feminist sympathy for women and anti-feminist resentments and fears are represented in plays, novels, newspaper scandals and trials for adultery and 'crim. con.' during the century. 'Woman' could either symbolize a class's own sense of its weakness or embody its ideal image of itself. The ideal was developed as 'domestic woman', representing the values and practices of the professional middle class in particular, as distinct from what was seen as the merely public and social sphere dominated by the upper classes.[16] 'Domestic woman' was a figure embodying social and cultural values, but it affected women because of their role in everyday domestic life, social customs and relations, habits and patterns of consumption, and the class-based exercise of choices and distinctions.

In living out such distinctions cultural consumption was increasingly important, for economic and technological change were creating another revolution: the commercialization of culture which made possible or necessary a greater range of consumer goods and services, a larger field for exercise of the social distinctions and conflicts just described.[17] New modes of manufacture and marketing were intertwined even before the Industrial Revolution, and were dependent on social emulation, the fashion system, a culture of novelty and patterns of consumption stemming from the dominant landed gentry, aristocracy and court class. A wide range of products and services, including professional ones, flourished on historic patterns of emulation, but the commercialization of culture made cultural revolution more obvious, more comprehensive and more powerful.

Like the cultural revolution, the consumer revolution was a field of struggle. The landed class's culture of conspicuous consumption was related to court culture of display and magnificence. Bourgeois social critics saw such display as an instrument of power, dazzling the common people and blinding them to the corruption and decadence of court government. Display was also politically dangerous for the gentry and middle classes because it conflicted with rational use of capital and forced its victims into the court patronage system, to recoup over-expenditure on display or 'luxury' by means of sinecures, 'places', offices of state, monopolies and commercial privileges. Together, 'luxury' and the patronage system were thought to undermine both the merit system and the market system, be it a market in goods, services or talent. The 'men of merit', that is, the professional men, dependent on intellectual capital, had the greatest stake in the critique of display, 'luxury' and 'fashion', but upper-class losers in the patronage system also joined this critique in a temporary coalition with bourgeois cultural revolutionaries.

Members of the middle classes who succumbed to 'luxury' or 'fashion' were in double jeopardy. They lacked the public credit and base of family financial support available to members of the landed classes, and had to manage their capital carefully or risk falling into the ungenteel lower middle classes or even lower. Moreover, commercialized consumption reproduced and disseminated upper-class culture by providing consumers in other classes with cheaper versions of the novelties being consumed by their 'betters'. These novelties covered a great range of material culture and 'manners', including clothing, dinnerware, health products and services, arts and architecture, travel, 'correct' pronunciation, education, courtship practices and so on. Thus criticism of fashion, luxury and display addressed both upper-class culture and emulation of that culture by the middle classes and, later, the lower classes. Women were thought to play an important role in fashion, luxury and display, partly because of their role in court culture. Numerous eighteenth-century satires depict a woman ruining her husband or family through extravagant emulation of her 'betters'. The fashionable woman symbolized the middle classes' emulation of their 'betters' through cultural consumption; but she also represented the consumer revolution's commodification of women, making them into objects as well as agents of conspicuous consumption for competing men and social classes.

A major form of cultural consumption was print. Yet print culture was historically associated with the professional middle class and in the eighteenth century became a major way of disseminating their cultural revolution. The 'rise of the reading public', much commented on at the time, was facilitated by increasing numbers of circulating libraries, publishers and booksellers, newspapers and magazines.[18] Well-appointed circulating libraries, exclusive book clubs and stylish but inexpensive reprints also enabled middle-class people to participate in book culture as a genteel avocation.[19] Literary culture, as distinct from merely professional writing, was both an aspect of the consumer revolution and a way of disseminating it, for miscellany magazines and 'books of the day'—especially novels—purveyed information on manners, fashion, high society, public issues, the arts, 'proper' language and so on to readers who would otherwise find it unobtainable. Even when this fashion system was being condemned in some magazine or novel, readers were learning how the system worked, and bourgeois social critics often saw 'books of the day' as disseminators of ideology and culture hostile to their own interests. Print could be seen to both foster and disable the sense of common interest and nation-wide identity among the 'reading public'—the professional and other middle classes.

Since Renaissance Humanism at least, these classes had participated with the upper classes in literature as a broad, classically based culture.[20] But in the eighteenth century literary culture moved from domination by aristocratic coteries and patronage to domination by the market-place and the 'reading public'. 'Literature' ceased to mean predominantly 'the extant writing on a particular subject' and came to have its modern sense of 'written verbal art'. Yet 'literature' was increasingly commercialized, specialized and professionalized, while maintaining a façade of genteel belletrism. The professional class had a vested interest in literature in both main senses. Many professionals specialized in the interpretation and production of literature in the older sense, from Holy Scripture to official documents, contracts, legislation, technology, plans and projects, and scholarly or scientific research of various kinds. But many professionals needed literature in the new sense for the social aspects of their work, associating with cultivated patrons, employers and colleagues through a broad, shared literary culture. More importantly, literature in

Engraving (c. 1565) depicting contemporary fashion in the sixteenth century. From left to right, typical nobleman's attire, military dress, middle-class dress, noblewomen's attire, and merchant's dress are shown.

both senses made up a discursive order that enabled the professional bourgeoisie, who were widely scattered through Britain, to communicate among themselves according to a shared set of assumptions and conventions, thereby reproducing themselves daily, in the act of reading, as members of a national class.

A sense of common identity, transcending local ties and limits, could readily be conveyed through print. Ephemeral periodicals such as newspapers and magazines repeatedly made a common culture available—daily, weekly or monthly—to widely scattered professional and middle-class readers, through their nature as much as through their contents. Print culture seemed superior to both the oral, communal culture of the lower classes and the social culture of the landed classes. Lower-class culture had to be reinforced by frequent contact in everyday life; upper-class culture depended on social contacts in country and town houses, and at seasonal social, political, judicial and administrative gatherings. The rise of what Benedict Anderson calls 'print capitalism' gave the professionals and their followers greater potential to become a national class than their social rivals—unless those rivals also participated in the new print culture.[21] But if they did so, it would be on the terms of the professional people who increasingly commanded print culture as the 'reading public'.

Literature in the new sense addressed a wider readship than narrowly professional writing. Writing as verbal art supplemented and validated writing on a particular, usually professional subject, ennobling it by association. Yet 'written verbal art' was also in some ways writing as an end in itself, distinct from and transcending mere professional writing. Literature as *belles-lettres,* a genteel avocation, especially in the older, aristocratic literary culture, seemed to relegate professional writing to a merely utilitarian, vulgarly middle-class sphere. But in the latter half of the eighteenth century literature as verbal art was becoming professionalized, while remaining distinct from other professional writing, and validating the entire domain of writing as professional craft and art.[22]

In Mary Wollstonecraft's lifetime both print culture and literature became the class property of the professional bourgeoisie, used as instruments in a class-based cultural revolution. But print culture and literature were also divided by gender distinctions. The learned discourses and noble genres were conventionally reserved for men, both as practitioners and readers, and included theoretical and abstract writing such as philosophy, science, political economy, aesthetics and rhetoric; scholarly writing such as natural science, technology, topography, encyclopaedias, historiography, classical studies, biblical studies, textual criticism and editing, and literary and other criticism in the arts; controversial writing such as political polemics or theological disputations; and the noble or sublime genres such as tragedy and epic. By contrast, most women writers kept to kinds of writing that could be seen as extensions of women's domestic range of education and experience: useful and practical subjects, and lighter, entertaining, desultory, occasional and personal forms of *belles-lettres*. These included educational writing and books for children; conduct books for girls and young women; devotional verse and prose; comedy; verse narrative; poems of domestic or quotidian life and subjective experience; and of course prose fiction, seen in the later eighteenth century as *the* women's genre. The gendering of writing reinforced and was reinforced by the domestication of women of the middle and upper classes. 'Books of the day' or ephemeral, entertaining, 'polite' kinds of literature were especially associated with women, strengthening the association of women with the fashion system. The gendering of writing left women in a paradoxical relationship to it—at once merely domestic and merely 'fashionable'.

Though print and literary culture were class property, divided by gender, highly commercialized and implicated in social emulation, they were also major disseminators of the professional middle-class cultural revolution. In this cultural work women writers played an important if undervalued role, partly because the genres left to women popularized the professional cultural revolution and made it available to a wide range of 'the reading public'. Writing was also highly suited for representing central themes and practices of the cultural revolution, particularly the subjective self, the 'domestic affections' and domesticity and the 'national' community. These themes were appropriated from other social classes but made to embody the values, self-image and interests of the professional middle classes and their followers. These themes were subjects of controversy and conflict in the cultural revolution, but before 1800, at least, they were often expressed through a particular construction of the figure 'woman', in which women writers could reasonably claim interest and expertise.

Practices of subjectivity, or what Michel Foucault calls 'technologies of the self', can be found even in early historic cultures, and such practices may in fact have been made possible by writing.[23] But in the middle third of the eighteenth century there was rapid development of subjectivity as complex, autonomous, authentic and pre-social or extra-social.[24] This idea of the self was appropriated from late Renaissance and seventeenth-century court culture, or rather from oppositional and marginal culture within court society.[25] By the early eighteenth century much courtly literature depicted subjectivity as true personal merit in the face of the merely public, social, political rank of court personages, a refuge from and a critique of mere courtliness. Significantly, court literature often embodied this subjectivity in a heroine. For a woman could represent anyone, man or woman, subject to domination, courtship or seduction by another—usually more powerful and male. Such a model of subjectivity could also appeal to the non-courtly classes, whether gentry or bourgeoisie, lower down the chain of court patronage or frustrated in attempts to infiltrate other patronage systems.

Subjectivity was a social practice paradoxically pretending to be extra-social; but writing seemed to solve the paradox. Writing and reading are solitary practices but they are also cultural and social practices available to anyone who is literate. The 'rise of the reading public' coincided with a rapid and diverse development in the writing of subjectivity, from Lockean 'mental philosophy' to religious devotional literature, from personal lyric poetry to Rousseauist autobiography, from Sentimental novels to political theories of the 'rights of man' based on the 'natural' inviolability of the personal self. As appropriated by the professional class, subjectivity was equated with the kind of moral discipline and intellectual training necessary to professional men who had to make their way in a hostile, competitive, seductive and uncongenial social world. This moral and intellectual discipline was represented as 'virtue' and 'reason'—words that recur often in eighteenth-century philosophy and social criticism, including the writings of Mary Wollstonecraft.

This culture of subjectivity realized through writing distinguished and defended the middle-class individual from both upper and lower classes. The 'lower orders' were depicted as lacking in developed, complex subjectivity; their 'merely' social and communal culture was seen as parallel to the 'merely' social, courtly, fashionable society of the upper classes. Thus subjectivity was used by the bourgeois cultural revolution to counter a social, public and political domain thought to be occupied by the dominant but 'merely' social courtly upper classes on one hand and by the un-individualized, communal and subordinated lower classes on the other.

The bourgeois cultural revolution used the 'domestic affections' and domesticity in a related way, to provide authentic social relations for the subjective self, in contrast to what were seen as the vitiated, self interested, exploitative social relations of a courtly society. The domestic affections subsumed friendship as well as family relations, for ideas of 'family' and 'friend' were themselves altered by the cultural revolution.[26] The upper-class family was seen as an unofficial joint stock company based on the landed estate, the lower-class family as a collective and communal production unit. The cultural revolution refashioned both as the family based on conjugal, parental and filial relations, excluding servants and more distant relations and excluding obvious economic production from the home. This kind of family was based on neither landed property nor communal production, but was to 'produce'—or reproduce—the moral and intellectual individual suited for middle-class and especially professional life.[27] Nevertheless, this reproduction was to be different for males and females: the former were to be trained for professional and public life while the latter were to be trained as companions for such men and as sustainers of the authentic domestic realm. 'Friend' ceased to mean someone sharing or assisting in a material, social or political interest, and came to mean someone with mutual moral, intellectual and emotional interests. In these new senses family and friends were appropriated from upper-class and lower-class culture by being domesticated and feminized.

Domesticity was the daily culture of family and friends in the new sense. It included the idea of home as a refuge from a hostile and competitive social world. It included the constitution of the quotidian, local and particular as 'real' life in contrast to the courtly and cosmopolitan, which were represented as artificial, fantastic and a mystification of 'reality'. It included 'domestic education', or the development of the moral and intellectual self necessary to master a competitive, seductive social world. Domesticity included the cult of the cottage or bourgeois pastoral, the separation of home from place of work, and the rise of the suburb. It led to domestication of the arts—parlour music rather than concert or ceremonial music; drawing and watercolour rather than formal painting; genre painting rather than history painting; engravings rather than paintings; private theatricals and closet drama rather than the public theatres; privatization of formerly public spaces; gardening that could be carried out by the individual without large income and gardening staff; family reading; needlework; and a host of other activities.[28] This domesticity may have originated in various aristocratic and bourgeois practices, but it contrasted with courtly social relations—the mistress system, 'gallantry', libertinism, mingled sexual and political intrigue and notorious intra-family rivalries, such as the hostility between George III and his son the Prince of Wales. The literature of domesticity developed with the rise of the professionals in the 1730s and 1740s and became a flood in the second half of the century, from the novels of Samuel Richardson through Rousseau's *La nouvelle Héloïse* to the 'conversation poems' of Coleridge.

Subjectivity, the domestic affections and domesticity together formed the basis for new ideas of national identity, community and culture.[29] Older forms of national identity, as loyalty to a ruling dynasty, had given way in Britain to national identity as a complex of social, economic, political and regional 'interests'. These 'interests' were dominated by the ruling class as a network of interrelated families based on large landed estates. 'Patriotism' in the eighteenth century often meant opposition of the landed interest to a court faction supposedly leading king and country to domestic ruin and to defeat by external enemies, trading competitors and imperial rivals. In the latter part of the century, however, national identity and culture were represented as residing in 'the people' and rooted in domestic affections and social sympathies of particular kinds.

Great Britain was a complex state whose disparate regional cultures seemed to find expression in antiquarianism, local natural history, 'popular antiquities' or folklore, literary 'fakelore' or forgeries such as Macpherson's 'Ossian' and Chatterton's poems, and collecting and imitating popular ballads. In fact, these activities assimilated the local and regional to a national culture of writing commanded by the professional bourgeoisie. Writing transformed local and regional class cultures into apparently classless ones by transposing them from speech communities to the national community of print. Transcribing the oral culture of the common people transformed it into a culture subject to the interests and expertise of the professional middle class.[30] The 'imagined community' of the nation that could only be experienced in print was an alternative to the 'political nation' of large landed families who controlled national politics and local administration. It was also an alternative to the 'nation' as the common people, especially during the Revolutionary decade of the 1790s.

Women, or rather 'woman', had a central place in these major themes of the professional middle-class cultural revolution. 'Woman' was a figure or persuasive device in the rhetoric of cultural transformation rather than the actual women of any class or all classes.[31] 'Woman' linked the major themes of the bourgeois cultural revolution and was therefore central to the rhetoric of revolution. Some women, especially in the professional and other middle classes, saw themselves in this figure of 'woman', participated in it or helped construct it in writing. Other women, including Mary Wollstonecraft, argued that 'woman' oppressed women and betrayed the middle-class cultural revolution. 'Woman', like other themes and figures, was both an instrument of the cultural revolution and a field of struggle within it.

For one thing, 'woman' was a major figure for the new subjectivity. In courtly literature woman is often represented as a vessel of feeling. Excluded from the public, political and martial spheres and subordinate in the ceremonial of court life (except by dynastic accident), women were associated with the private, personal, aesthetic and amorous domains. Because love was seen as a personal and aesthetic experience, not a public or political one, courtly amorous culture was often depicted as presided over by women. Professional middle-class culture of the eighteenth century appropriated woman in this role, but dropped the associations with sexual-political intrigue and modified courtly love to romantic love as a personal, subjective absolute.[32] Yet elements of courtly 'gallantry' remained, and it was these that Revolutionary feminism attacked.

Woman as emblem for both romantic and courtly love was an ambiguous figure—both subject and object in an upper middle-class culture that was ambivalent about the courtly culture it was appropriating and refashioning. In professional culture, and increasingly in the culture of the commercial and manufacturing bourgeoisie and the master artisans, women were excluded from the public domain and restricted to the domestic sphere. Yet this restriction was thought to exaggerate their emotional, affective, subjective development. The ambiguous character of woman as emblem of subjectivity and romantic love also shows that woman represents more than femaleness or femininity. Woman was subject *par excellence,* to be courted yet denied independence, equality and power, and thus could stand for the bourgeois subject regardless of sex and for the bourgeoisie in general, especially if subjectivity were equated with desiring inwardness in any individual or the social class as a whole.

Such desiring inwardness is the seducible element, open to ideological penetration and subjection by the social other. In professional middle-class culture woman as subject was a counter to the public, social, political domains seen to be dominated by the social other. But woman was also a figure for class anxiety and uncertainty, cast as erotic desires and relations, amorous seductions and betrayals. For this reason 'woman' became a central topic of concern in the various Enlightenments—movements of social and cultural criticism emphasizing 'reason' as an objective and transcendent criterion against 'unenlightened' culture of both court and common people. In the Enlightenments' gendering of intellectual and cultural values, woman as desiring subject often represented 'unreason'.[33]

For this reason woman was redefined as domestic in order to appropriate the positive values she represented for the Enlightenments as social critiques of the Old Regime.[34] The culture of Sensibility, or Sentimentalism, which was based on Enlightenment rationalism and materialism, developed the two themes of subjectivity and domesticity in a wide-ranging feminization of culture in the 1770s and 1780s, to some extent in opposition to the masculinist values of the Enlightenments.[35] Woman is defined as domestic in order to confine her there, in contrast to negative figures of femininity: the too public, too political, independently desiring woman of the courtly upper classes; the too social, 'managing' woman of the commercial and trading bourgeoisie; and the labouring, sexually available woman of the servant and other lower classes.[36]

'Woman' constructed for a particular class interest and culture was then made to stand for women of all classes. Nature as biology was invoked, not for the first or last time, to extend woman's physical roles as mother and wife to the moral and social domain of the domestic affections. As friendship came to be seen as less a business or social relationship and more a personal, affective one, woman was made responsible for the home as a place fostering the extra-domestic friendships of husband and other family members. Yet female friendships outside the family caused anxiety to many social critics. Domestic woman became a female version of the professional man, distinguished from woman as partner in a family-owned business and woman as ornament in courtly upper-class life. She was to be a non-labouring worker, overseeing the household, the management and early education of children, and encouraging various class-based cultural values and practices. Woman of the professional bourgeoisie was to provide a moral-intellectual service, ostensibly without remuneration. In this too she was a female version of the male professional, requiring the same kind of self-discipline and method ('virtue' and 'reason'), but not the same intellectual training, and working in a distinct, parallel sphere.

To fulfil this role, however, domestic woman required a proper education. A decorative and aesthetic role was retained for her in emulation of upper-class woman. Education in the decorative and entertaining arts, or 'accomplishments', was to make domestic woman a proper companion for the professional man after the rigours of his professional work and after his trying experiences in a hostile and competitive public social world. This function was parallel to that of woman in court culture, but domestic woman was also to have a form of the moral and intellectual training required by professional men. This would guard her from excessive courtliness, from questioning her lot, from temptation to a more glamorous social life and from personal or domestic extravagance damaging to the family interest. The exact nature of domestic woman's training was debated, but its general aim was to distinguish her from both courtly upper-class woman and vulgarly middle-class or lower-class woman, yet to exclude her from the public sphere and assign her a subaltern role in the professional middle-class family. She was assigned a diminutive or domestic version of the intellectual and artistic culture of men. Because of her restricted sphere of experience and observation, domestic woman was supposed to be a specialist in 'real life', local observation, the detail of quotidian life, domestic heroism and the 'trivial sublime', or intimations of grandeur and transcendence in common life. In short, domestic woman was a figure for distinguishing traits of professional middle-class culture; but by being domestic she was also distinguished and firmly subordinated within that culture.

This domestication of culture and social relations was important for the reconstruction of the national identity, culture and destiny in the interests of the professional bourgeoisie. The site of the essential, authentic national identity was shifted from the public and political sphere to the domestic and personal, in order to wrest the power to define the national interest from the courtly and landed classes. This process was important for the cultural revolution's ability to respond to events outside Britain, especially the French Revolution. Even before the 1790s woman's role in the 'national' culture was seen as an extension of her central role in domesticity, and Britain's vicissitudes abroad were represented by their effects on domestic relations and affections, and on woman as wife, mother, sister and daughter. During the 1790s and the Revolutionary aftermath of Romantic nationalism woman was also made the repository of national 'folk' culture, as the essence and unifying element in a society that Revolutionary threat, domestic political upheaval, feminist protest, regional revolt and international crisis revealed to be dangerously divided by class, region and gender.

Prescriptions for the construction of domestic woman can be found everywhere in writing of the period. Yet the plentifulness of such prescriptions suggests that woman was also emblem of the professional middle class's ideological, social and cultural vulnerability and sense of powerlessness, and therefore that women were seen as a problem in those classes. These prescriptions took the form of conduct books—instructions for the construction of woman for the bourgeois cultural revolution. The conduct books in turn merely gave systematic statement to themes widely diffused in literature of all kinds, including philosophy, history, essays, plays and especially novels.[37]

One of the most reprinted conduct books was *The Lady's New Year's Gift; or, Advice to a Daughter* by George Savile, Marquis of Halifax, first published in 1688, the year of the Glorious Revolution. Just over a century later, in another revolutionary year, Wollstonecraft published an extract from it in her anthology *The Female Reader.* Halifax, like most conduct-book writers, recommends religion to allay the dangerous passions, personal and social, to which women were supposed to be subject. Passion is what rebels against difference as oppression and desires the social other through a mingled erotic and social drive. As Halifax puts it, 'A devout mind hath the privilege of being free from passions, as some climates are free from all venomous kinds of creatures.' Poison or venom was a common figure for the silent, invisible, perverting or fatal operation of alien ideology. Behind Halifax's platitude is a sophisticated understanding of the social and personal function of religion for the subjugated and divided, be they a class, a race or a sex.[38] Halifax then prescribes a domestic role for women, rooted in nature and divine will, and advises against excessive socializing, gaudy dress and self-display—attributes of courtly society. In order to fulfil their domestic role, women are told to 'get understanding, and practise virtue', but Halifax is less specific on how this should be done than later conduct writers would be. 'Reason' and 'virtue' commonly represent the intellectual and moral training used to subject women within professional middle-class culture and to secure them against seduction from above or contamination from below.

Halifax's views continued to appeal to the professional middle classes, but they were modified and even challenged. In 1696 Mary Astell, in *An Essay in Defence of the Female Sex,* declared that 'souls are equal'. Mind should therefore be developed in women as well as men if women were to gain salvation and also play their role in emergent professional middle-class culture. Similar views were widely disseminated in the early eighteenth century through such advocates of fusing genteel and professional cultures as *The Spectator.* In 1739 'Sophia, a Person of Quality' argued in *Woman Not Inferior to Man* that the difference between the sexes was due to education, custom and circumstances. Relying on a Lockean materialist epistemology, she (if she was a she) argues that women have more delicate senses than men and, since all knowledge is acquired through the senses, women should 'at least keep pace' with men in learning and should be debarred from no profession, including the military. Like the Revolutionary feminists half a century later, she condemns the appropriation of courtly subjection of women by the professional middle class.

By mid-century 'domestic woman' had been constructed for the professional middle-class revolution, not only in Britain but also in France and elsewhere on the Continent.[39] This movement coincided with the emergence of the professional middle class as a major social and cultural force, but the ambivalence in middle-class patriarchy between courtly woman and domestic woman remained.[40] For example, the Scottish Enlightenment philosopher David Hume asserted the importance of women to national culture, but did so by appropriating aspects of courtly woman and courtly gallantry. In his essay 'Of the Rise and Progress of the Arts and Sciences' (1742) he argues that the modern age had superior 'politeness', or intellectual culture, because 'modern notions of *gallantry,* the natural produce of courts and monarchies', enabled 'the company of virtuous women' to modify the natural harshness of the male character. Hume opposes confining women to the domestic sphere because their polishing influence on men would be lost. This Enlightenment sociology of 'progress' in the arts and sciences is an *embourgeoisement* of court culture, fusing courtly and bourgeois values and practices in a feminization of culture.

The most influential appropriation of courtly woman for the bourgeois cultural revolution, even in Britain, was that of Jean-Jacques Rousseau. He was the leading writer of the intellectual and cultural movement known as Sensibility, related to and overlapping the Enlightenment.[41] In his novel *La nouvelle Héloïse* (1761) and his educational quasi-novel *Émile* (1762) Rousseau idealizes domestic woman and the domestic affections and contrasts them with the corrupt courtly mistress system and gender relations based on coquetry and gallantry which filtered down through the rest of society by the process of social emulation. In his influential essay on political theory, *Du contrat social* (1762), he takes the family based on domestic affections as the model for the state. Rousseau follows the Enlightenment and Protestant Nonconformist view of woman as an equal soul and mind with man; but he also asserts that woman has a different moral and intellectual character. Whereas man thinks, reasons and abstracts, woman feels, sympathizes and puts into practice. Therefore woman should obey man; but lest man become a tyrant, woman may use coquetry to achieve a balance of power. Within the family and state man should have ultimate authority, modified by woman's kind of knowledge, not through reasoning, for that is man's domain, but by woman controlling her erotic desire in order to govern man's and thereby influence his judgement. In this way Rousseau appropriates the courtly mistress system of political and amorous intrigue to bourgeois domesticity.

Rousseau's influence on the construction of domestic woman in Britain was reinforced by Dr James Fordyce's *Sermons to Young Women* (1766). Fordyce was a man of the Scottish Enlightenment and a popular preacher, and his combination of familiar conductbook precepts with Rousseau's domestication of courtly woman took *Sermons* through at least twenty editions by 1800. Following Hume, he envisages woman gentrifying man through a bourgeois form of courtly love called 'honourable love': 'that great preservative of purity, that powerful softener of the fiercest spirit, that mighty improver of the rudest carriage, that all-subduing, yet all exalting principle of the human breast, which humbles the proud, and bends the stubborn, yet fills with lofty conceptions, and animates with a fortitude that nothing can conquer'. Such love is contrasted to 'that false and vicious gallantry which gains ground amongst us every day' and which is 'effeminate' rather than feminized. Fordyce goes on to link the influence of woman through 'honourable love' to the national destiny, particularly in the face of the historic enemy, France, which Britons equated with court government and court culture.[42] The themes, arguments and even the words and rhythms of Fordyce's 'honourable love' passage would be echoed in Edmund Burke's paean to 'antient chivalry' in *Reflections on the Revolution in France,* thereby making this appropriation of courtly woman central to the counter-Revolution. Not surprisingly, Rousseau, Fordyce and Burke were all objects of Mary Wollstonecraft's feminist polemic in the 1790s.

Thus 'woman' was a central figure in the rhetoric of the cultural revolution—so important that the cultural revolution could be seen as a feminization of culture, advancing the claims and position of women, permitting women to participate in the cultural revolution, and even taking the form of feminist movements such as Bluestocking feminism, Enlightenment feminism, Sentimental feminism, Evangelical feminism and Revolutionary feminism, each of which proposed a somewhat different figure of 'woman' and her attendant 'rights' as part of the bourgeois cultural revolution. But men of the revolutionary classes could also see themselves in these figures. 'Woman' could signify differently to men and women in the cultural revolution, yet both could read themselves in that figure, and in this way were brought together in the revolution. In fact the cultural revolution was not only class-based but gender-biased. 'Woman' of the cultural revolution oppressed middle-class women in ways not found in the classes which the revolution attacked, and as Margaret Walters writes, 'during the eighteenth century, when some women were beginning to articulate their rights, the distinction between the sexes was in fact becoming harder and sharper', and middle-class women 'more firmly excluded from public affairs and the world of work'.[43] For this reason 'woman' was not only a powerful figure in the rhetoric of cultural revolution but a field of struggle, fought over by factions contending for leadership and definition of that revolution.

Mary Wollstonecraft attempted the most thorough feminist transformation of the cultural revolution in her time, though her career and her feminism were made possible by that revolution. She was constructed as a self-divided being by the interlocked class and gender distinctions of her society, but this very division enabled her to recognize that culture, language, discourse and identity were not free spaces for the natural play of individuality but structured by power relations of several kinds in order to shape personal and social identity in the interests of dominant social groups, be these groups defined by class or gender, or both.[44] Accordingly, she constructed an identity and career as social critic in order to cope with her self-division and attack the social and cultural causes of it. Inevitably, this identity was paradoxical in terms of her culture—a woman of 'mind', 'a woman who has thinking powers', a 'female philosopher'.

The cultural revolution made possible Wollstonecraft's identity as social critic, as a woman of 'mind'; she then turned her 'mind' to one of the few professional careers available to women—that of professional writer. The French Revolution then provided the occasion for turning her 'mind' and career to Revolutionary feminism. As Virginia Woolf puts it,

> The Revolution . . . was not merely an event that had happened outside her; it was an active agent in her own blood. She had been in revolt all her life—against tyranny, against law, against convention. . . . The outbreak of the Revolution in France expressed some of her deepest theories and convictions.

Or as Toril Moi puts it, Wollstonecraft's 'essay on the rights of woman was made possible by the emancipatory if bourgeois-patriarchal ideas of *liberté, égalité* and *fraternité*'.[45]

'Mind' is a key word in Wollstonecraft's life and writings, and by it she meant the moral-intellectual being required by professional men. As she defined it, 'mind' included reason and imagination, feeling and critical thought, according to the full definition in Johnson's *Dictionary.* She accepted that most women's careers would be domestic—nurturing professional culture, reproducing it in the next generation and disseminating a diminutive version of it to the lower ranks who came within women's domestic sphere. But she argued that women needed 'mind' themselves if they were to fulfil the career prescribed by the cultural revolution's ideal of 'woman'. Wollstonecraft also argued that some women should be allowed to enter professions outside the home, and she even suggested that, to further their civism and patriotism, women should have electoral rights. But the central argument of her Revolutionary feminism was the need for distinct but parallel careers of 'mind' for (middle-class) men and women, if the professional middle class were to revolutionize society in their own image and interests, especially in a time of Revolutionary crisis.

Ultimately, Revolutionary feminism became a casualty of that crisis. It exposed contradictions in the cultural revolution in Britain, as far as women were concerned and involved. But at a time of sharply increased competition within the cultural revolution for leadership and power, such exposing of contradictions could seem dangerous to the revolution itself. The 1790s saw increased resistance not only to feminism but to the feminization of culture within the British cultural revolution, just as the French Revolution of 1793 to 1795 aimed to reverse the supposed feminization of culture and politics in the Revolution of 1789 to 1792. The failure of the first phase of the French Revolution, which corresponded to the character and aims of the bourgeois cultural revolution in Britain, led to a withdrawal from Revolutionary feminism in Britain along with withdrawal from coalition with 'progressive' elements of the upper and lower classes. In the 1790s most British cultural revolutionaries turned to 'femininism' or even anti-feminism; Revolutionary feminism and its immediate heirs were marginalized, suppressed or adopted by rival revolutionary programmes.

Notes

1. On cultural revolution and state formation, see Philip Corrigan and Derek Sayer, *The Great Arch: English State Formation as Cultural Revolution* (Oxford and New York: Basil Blackwell, 1985); on revolutionary élites and state formation, see Theda Skocpol, *States and Social Revolutions: A Comparative Analysis of France, Russia, and China* (Cambridge: Cambridge University Press, 1979); on culture, domination, and resistance, see Joan Cocks, *The Oppositional Imagination: Feminism, Critique and Political Theory* (London and New York: Routledge, 1989) chs 1-3.

2. Philippa Levine, *Victorian Feminism, 1850-1900* (London: Hutchinson, 1987) p. 14.

3. See, for example, Anne M. Haselkorn and Betty Travitsky (eds), *The Renaissance Englishwoman in Print: Counterbalancing the Canon* (Amherst, Mass.: University of Massachusetts Press, 1990); Elaine Hobby, *Virtue of Necessity: English Women's Writing, 1649-88* (London: Virago Press, 1988); Katharine M. Rogers, *Feminism in Eighteenth-Century England* (Brighton, Sussex: Harvester Press; Urbana, Ill.: University of Illinois Press, 1982); Alice Browne, *The Eighteenth-Century Feminist Mind* (Detroit, Mich.: Wayne State University Press, 1987).

4. Mary Poovey, *The Proper Lady and the Woman Writer: Ideology as Style in the Works of Mary Wollstonecraft, Mary Shelley, and Jane Austen* (Chicago, Ill. and London: University of Chicago Press, 1984) ch. 1.

5. For a review of the problems of definition and a survey of accounts of class in this period, see R. J. Morris, *Class and Class Consciousness in the Industrial Revolution, 1780-1850* (London: Macmillan, 1979); for a broader treatment, see R. S. Neale, *Class in English History, 1680-1850* (Oxford: Basil Blackwell, 1981).

6. Gordon E. Mingay, *The Gentry: The Rise and Fall of a Ruling Class* (London and New York: Longman, 1976); Lawrence Stone and Jeanne C. Fawtier Stone, *An Open Elite? England, 1540-1880,* abridged edn (Oxford and New York: Oxford University Press, 1986).

7. Geoffrey Holmes, *Augustan England: Professions, State and Society, 1680-1730* (London and Boston, Mass.: George Allen and Unwin, 1983); Harold Perkin, *The Origins of Modern English Society, 1780-1880* (London: Routledge and Kegan Paul; Toronto and Buffalo: University of Toronto Press, 1969) pp. 213-17, 428-9. On the triumph of the professional bourgeoisie in the present century, see Harold Perkin, *The Rise of Professional Society: England since 1880* (London and New York: Routledge, 1989), which argues that 'the professional society' superseded a society based on class.

8. Penelope J. Corfield, *The Impact of English Towns, 1700-1800* (Oxford: Oxford University Press, 1982).

9. Alan D. Gilbert, *Religion and Society in Industrial England: Church, Chapel and Social Change, 1740-1914* (London and New York: Longman, 1976).

10. For an account of the process in Scotland, see Charles Camic, *Experience and Enlightenment: Socialization for Cultural Change in Eighteenth-Century Scotland* (Chicago, Ill.: University of Chicago Press, 1983). See also Wilfred Prest (ed.), *The Professions in Early Modern England* (London: Croom Helm, 1987).

11. Edward P. Thompson, 'The Moral Economy of the English Crowd in the Eighteenth Century', *Past and Present,* vol. 50 (Feb. 1971) pp. 76-136; Robert W. Malcolmson, *Popular Recreations in English Society, 1700-1850* (Cambridge: Cambridge University Press, 1973); Bob Bushaway, *By Rite: Custom, Ceremony and Community in England, 1700-1880* (London: Junction Books, 1982).

12. On the 1790s, see Carl B. Cone, *The English Jacobins: Reformers in Late 18th Century England* (New York: Charles Scribner's Sons, 1968); Albert Goodwin, *The Friends of Liberty: The English Democratic Movement in the Age of the French Revolution* (London: Hutchinson, 1979).

13. For a brief survey of the social position of women, see Roy Porter, *English Society in the Eighteenth Century,* rev. edn (London: Penguin Books, 1990) pp. 21-34.

14. Neale, *Class in English History,* pp. 199-200. See also Joan Kelly, *Women, History, and Theory* (Chicago, Ill. and London: Chicago University Press, 1984) pp. 1-18; Christine Delphy, *Close to Home: A Materialist Analysis of Women's Oppression,* trans. Diana Leonard (London: Hutchinson, with The Explorations in Feminism Col-

lective, 1984) pp. 71-6; Pamela Abbott and Roger Sapsford, *Women and Social Class* (London and New York: Tavistock Publications, 1987).

15. Ivy Pinchbeck, *Women Workers and the Industrial Revolution, 1750-1850* (1930; London: Virago, 1969).

16. See Nancy Armstrong, 'The Rise of Domestic Woman', in *The Ideology of Conduct: Essays in Literature and the History of Sexuality*, ed. Nancy Armstrong and Leonard Tennenhouse (New York and London: Methuen, 1987) pp. 96-141.

17. Neil McKendrick, John Brewer and J. H. Plumb, *The Birth of a Consumer Society: The Commercialization of Eighteenth-Century England* (London: Hutchinson, 1982); Maxine Berg, *The Age of Manufactures: Industry, Innovation and Work in Britain, 1700-1820* (London: Fontana, 1985); Colin Campbell, *The Romantic Ethic and the Spirit of Modern Consumerism* (Oxford and New York: Basil Blackwell, 1987).

18. John Feather, *A History of British Publishing* (London and New York: Routledge, 1988) Part 2.

19. Devendra P. Varma, *The Evergreen Tree of Diabolical Knowledge* (Washington, D.C.: Consortium Press, 1972).

20. Anthony Grafton and Lisa Jardine, *From Humanism to the Humanities: Education and the Liberal Arts in Fifteenth- and Sixteenth-Century Europe* (London: Duckworth, 1986).

21. Benedict Anderson, *Imagined Communities: Reflections on the Origin and Spread of Nationalism* (London: Verso, 1983).

22. See J. W. Saunders, *The Profession of English Letters* (London: Routledge and Kegan Paul; Toronto: University of Toronto Press, 1964) ch. 7.

23. See Walter J. Ong, *Orality and Literacy: The Technologizing of the Word* (London and New York: Methuen, 1982) pp. 178-9; François Furet and Jacques Ozouf, *Reading and Writing: Literacy in France from Calvin to Jules Ferry*, English trans. (Cambridge: Cambridge University Press; Paris: Éditions de la Maison des Sciences de l'Homme, 1982) p. 310; and Luther H. Martin, Huck Gutman, and Patrick H. Hutton (eds), *Technologies of the Self: A Seminar with Michel Foucault* (Amherst, Mass.: University of Massachusetts Press, 1988).

24. Stephen D. Cox, *'The Stranger Within Thee': Concepts of the Self in Late Eighteenth-Century Literature* (Pittsburgh, Pa: University of Pittsburgh Press, 1980).

25. On court culture, see Norbert Elias, *The Court Society*, trans. Edmund Jephcott (Oxford: Basil Blackwell, 1983).

26. See Raymond Williams, *Keywords: A Vocabulary of Culture and Society* (Glasgow: Fontana/Croom Helm, 1976).

27. Eli Zaretsky, *Capitalism, The Family, and Personal Life*, rev. edn (New York: Harper and Row, 1986); Lawrence Stone, *The Family, Sex and Marriage in England, 1500-1800*, abridged edn (Harmondsworth, Middx: Penguin Books, 1979); Randolph Trumbach, *The Rise of the Egalitarian Family: Aristocratic Kinship and Domestic Relations in Eighteenth-Century England* (New York: Academic Press, 1978); Leonore Davidoff and Catherine Hall, *Family Fortunes: Men and Women of the English Middle Class, 1780-1850* (London: Hutchinson, 1987); Philippe Ariès and Georges Duby (eds), *A History of Private Life*, vol. 3, *Passions of the Renaissance*, trans. Arthur Goldhammer (Cambridge, Mass., and London: Harvard University Press, 1989).

28. On the place of needlework in the construction of femininity, see Rozsika Parker, *The Subversive Stitch: Embroidery and the Making of the Feminine* (New York: Routledge, 1984) ch. 6.

29. Gerald Newman, *The Rise of English Nationalism: A Cultural History, 1740-1830* (New York: St Martin's Press, 1987).

30. Anderson, *Imagined Communities*, pp. 39-40.

31. 'Woman' is now thought to indicate an essentialist view of women, in contrast to a 'materialist' view that treats women and the gender category 'woman' as socially and historically specific. See Annette Kuhn and AnnMarie Wolpe (eds), *Feminism and Materialism: Women and Modes of Production* (London and New York: Routledge and Kegan Paul, 1978); Denise Riley, *'Am I That Name?': Feminism and the Category of 'Women' in History* (Minneapolis: University of Minnesota, 1988) ch. 1. I use 'woman' throughout, often with quotation marks, to refer to the cultural and rhetorical figure of the late eighteenth century, and 'a woman' or 'women', though usually without quotation marks, to refer to people who would have been considered women at that time.

32. See John Mullan, *Sentiment and Sociability: The Language of Feeling in the Eighteenth Century* (Oxford: Clarendon Press, 1988) ch. 2.

33. See Jane Rendall, *The Origins of Modern Feminism: Women in Britain, France and the United States, 1780-1860* (London: Macmillan, 1985) ch. 1; and Genevieve Lloyd, *The Man of Reason: 'Male' and 'Female' in Western Philosophy* (London: Methuen, 1984).

34. See Jean Bethke Elshtain, *Public Man, Private Woman: Women in Social and Political Thought* (Princeton, N.J.: Princeton University Press, 1981) ch. 3.

35. See Campbell, *The Romantic Ethic and the Spirit of Modern Consumerism*, ch. 7; Jean Bethke Elshtain, *Meditations on Modern Political Thought: Masculine/Feminine Themes from Luther to Arendt* (New York: Praeger, 1986) pp. 46-7.

36. Lawrence Stone, *The Family, Sex and Marriage in England, 1500-1800*, abridged edn (Harmondsworth, Middx: Penguin Books, 1979) p. 404.

37. Nancy Armstrong, 'The Rise of Domestic Woman', in *The Ideology of Conduct: Essays in Literature and the History of Sexuality*, ed. Nancy Armstrong and Leonard Tennenhouse (New York and London: Methuen, 1987) pp. 96-141; Joyce Hemlow, 'Fanny Burney and the Courtesy Books', *Publications of the Modern Language Association of America*, vol. 65 (1950) pp. 732-61.

38. See Peter Berger, *The Social Reality of Religion* (1967; Harmondsworth, Middx: Penguin Books, 1973).

39. Paul Hoffmann, *La Femme dans la pensée des lumières* (Paris: Ophrys, 1977); *French Women and the Age of the Enlightenment*, ed. Samia I. Spencer (Bloomington, Ind.: Indiana University Press, 1984) Part 5.

40. Nancy Armstrong, *Desire and Domestic Fiction: A Political History of the Novel* (New York and Oxford: Oxford University Press, 1987).

41. For 'an attempt at definition' of Sensibility, see R. F. Brissenden, *Virtue in Distress: Studies in the Novel of Sentiment from Richardson to Sade* (London: Macmillan, 1974) pp. 11-55, and the works cited there.

42. James Fordyce, *Sermons to Young Women* (1766), 8th edn, corrected and enlarged (Dublin, 1796) pp. 11, 18.

43. Margaret Walters, 'The Rights and Wrongs of Women: Mary Wollstonecraft, Harriet Martineau, Simone de Beauvoir', in *The Rights and Wrongs of Women,* ed. Juliet Mitchell and Ann Oakley (Harmondsworth, Middx: Penguin Books, 1976) p. 305.

44. On discourse and power, see Diane Macdonell, *Theories of Discourse: An Introduction* (Oxford and New York: Basil Blackwell, 1986). For a different way of envisaging language and culture as a field of struggle, relying on a Lacanian model of the construction of the subject, see Margaret Homans, *Bearing the Word: Language and Female Experience in Nineteenth-Century Women's Writing* (Chicago, Ill., and London: University of Chicago Press, 1986).

45. Virginia Woolf, *Women and Writing,* ed. Michèle Barrett (London: Women's Press, 1979) p. 98; Toril Moi, *Sexual/Textual Politics: Feminist Literary Theory* (London and New York: Methuen, 1985) p. 64.

DAWN KEETLEY AND JOHN PETTEGREW (ESSAY DATE 1997)

SOURCE: Keetley, Dawn and John Pettegrew. "Introduction: Part I: Identities through Adversity." In *Public Women, Public Words: A Documentary History of American Feminism,* edited by Dawn Keetley and John Pettegrew, pp. 3-7. Madison, Wis.: Madison House Publishers, 1997.

In the following essay, Keetley and Pettegrew discuss the challenges that women colonial dissenters faced.

The first European settlers in New England brought with them family structure that vested authority unambiguously in the hands of the father. Woman's place in this "patriarchal" institution was clearly delimited; less autonomous individuals than wives and mothers, women throughout the North American colonies were subject to an intricately organized hierarchy that placed them below father, husband, brothers, and even adult sons. Unable to inherit either the land or the offices of their fathers, women became virtually invisible in the public life of the thirteen colonies. With its strict gender stratification and divisions of labor, the patriarchal family served as a model for and basis of social and political relations and institutions. In the 1637 trial of Anne Hutchinson for dissent from the Puritan church, for instance, the issue of Hutchinson's revolt against the subordinate status of women was inextricable from her religious rebellion. As one of her accusers proclaimed: "You have rather bine a Husband than a Wife and a preacher than a Hearer; and a Magistrate than a subject"—thus drawing a direct line between Hutchinson's religious unruliness and her perceived political and sexual disorder.

Patriarchal power in the colonies was not absolute, however. Due to the centrality of the household in an agrarian, primarily subsistence economy, women did create important economic and social roles for themselves. The case of Margaret Brent illustrates both how women could gain some power in the political sphere of colonial life, and also how the law inevitably circumscribed that power. In 1648, Brent petitioned the Maryland Assembly for the right to vote, an unprecedented act that was nevertheless in keeping with Brent's active legal and political career. She never married and frequently served as her brothers' business advisor and legal representative. A major landowner in her own right, Brent also represented herself in court cases, and for her acumen she was named the executrix of Maryland's governor—a close friend—when he died in 1657. It was on the grounds of her legal right to protect the former governor's interests that Brent sought the vote. Although her request was denied, the record shows that Brent "protested."

Aside from the economic and legal actions of a handful of prominent, land-owning women, the first stirrings of feminism in the colonies were the individual acts of rebellion against one institution—the Puritan church. Dissenting women, however, necessarily challenged those other institutions from which religion was inseparable, notably family and gender. Paradoxically, these early feminists drew their power to challenge established religion and the sexual hierarchies it instituted from Puritanism itself. Religious dissenters in New England carried the Puritan idea of the "aloneness" of believers in their relation with God so far that even the ministry became an obstacle to faith. "Grace," which was located within the self, accrued liberating possibilities in that it potentially challenged the hegemony of the clergy—the powerful elite of both church and state. The radical potential of the individual and its corollary—the spiritual equality of each individual regardless of sex—caused tensions in a society based on female subordination and finally created an avenue for women to question that subordination. The assertion of one's inner feeling of God's grace, of a distinctly personal revelation, could be used to justify rebellion against any and all of the authoritarian structures in which the individual was situated. Conversely, any woman who questioned the church was also perceived to be disavowing her place in secular and family life, of transgressing even her sex. In subsequent centuries it was this "wayward" and radically individualistic Puritan *woman* who would become an icon of the feminist individual, challenging a culture that on the one hand celebrates individualism and on the other hand limits, by gender and race, its realization.

One major strand of dissent was the Antinomian heresy, in which Anne Hutchinson played a central part. Antinomianism placed the private experience of religion above the formal rules of orthodox Puritanism, stressing that questions of salvation were decided between an individual and God, without the intervention of ministers. Hutchinson came under attack from the Puritan clergy of the Massachusetts Bay Colony precisely because of her defiance of their authority; she held meetings in her home every Sunday to discuss the day's sermon, even as rumors began to circulate that both the religious and political leadership were being criticized. Ordered to appear before a convocation of ministers, Hutchinson was ultimately excommunicated and banished; she and five of her six children were killed by Indians five years later on Long Island.

Another strand of religious dissent in colonial North America was Quakerism. Like the Antinomians, the Quakers believed in the "Inner Light"—rather than the authoritarian, institutional structures of the church—as a means to truth and salvation. The Society of Friends empowered women through their belief in spiritual equality and also in the development of co-equal status in church organization, including encouraging women to preach. The women's movement of the nineteenth-century was in part made possible by the legacy of Quaker women in the seventeenth and eighteenth centuries; indeed, a large number of the first nationally-known women's rights advocates were Quakers, including Sarah and Angelina Grimké, Lucretia Mott, and Susan B. Anthony.

One of the most prominent of early Quaker women was Mary Dyer, who exemplified the Quaker belief in religious freedom and also nonviolence, two values that would persist and flourish within the women's movement. Like Hutchinson, Dyer was tried and convicted in Massachusetts for religious dissent; she became the only woman executed for defying the Puritan authorities. Dyer protested, specifically, the 1658 Massachusetts law that banished all Quakers from the colony on pain of death. She had come to Boston after the passage of the law in order to support two friends who were imprisoned; after being banished twice by the authorities, Dyer returned to Boston, refusing to leave peacefully after the magistrates executed her friends and fellow Quakers. Accusing the magistrates of "disobedience," Dyer warned them in a letter of 1659 of the dire consequences of their sins. She paid for her challenge to Puritan authority and for her convictions about the freedom of conscience with her life.

When trying dissenters, Massachusetts courts inevitably delivered a sentence of banishment, forcing "heretics" into areas beyond the bounds of the Puritan theocracy such as Rhode Island and Pennsylvania. In a sense, this banishment functions as a metaphor for a second legacy that early American rebellious women bequeathed to subsequent generations of feminists: an oppositional or "liminal" impulse—an unruly existence, in other words, beyond the pale of established structures. Whether by choice (as in the case of the religious dissenters) or not (as in the case of Mary Rowlandson, forcibly removed from her town by Indians), some colonial women lived outside the confines of patriarchal society. While they spoke from beyond the literal and institutional borders of their culture, however, these women shaped and changed that culture, contributing in part to the loosening of oppressive hierarchies.

Perhaps the epitome of the liminal woman—of her social marginality, of her occupation of the borders of society—is the figure of the witch. Accusations of witchcraft reflect the anxiety of a culture that anticipates its own dissolution and thus demonizes and expels that which it fears is the cause of incipient social breakdown. Often that "culprit" in colonial New England was the independent, unmarried woman, more frequently the victim of witch-hunting than any other group. Carol Karlsen has added that "witches" were often women without brothers or sons—women, that is, who "stood in the way of the orderly transmission of property from one generation of males to another."[1] Clearly having gained enough power to provoke such deep-seated fears in the first place, the "witch" was at the same time a victim of those social processes that she defied.

Both Susannah Martin and Martha Carrier were victims of the Salem witchcraft "hysteria," which began in 1692 when a group of adolescent girls claimed to be possessed and began naming several of their neighbors as having consorted with the devil. Out of the 200 people (mostly women) who were accused of witchcraft in Salem during the course of the summer of 1692, thirteen women and six men were finally executed.

Lithograph by George H. Walker depicting the Salem Witch Trials.

Some of the women executed as witches at Salem were clearly nontraditional women who did not conform to ideals of Puritan womanhood. A contemporary, Thomas Maule, for instance, estimated that two-thirds of the accused in the Salem witchcraft trials had either rebelled against their parents or committed adultery. Certainly, women accused of witchcraft were often on the margins of society, frequently unmarried and sometimes with a history of outspokenness. Susannah Martin had been involved in altercations with her neighbors; she expressed anger toward her accusers at her trial, using her own reading of the Bible to try to discredit them. Martha Carrier, charged with at least thirteen murders, had argued with neighbors over land and threatened a male antagonist with physical violence; in her examination, she charged the magistrate as the only "black [i.e., satanic] man" she had seen and insisted that she be believed over a group of hysterical girls. Like Mary Dyer, Martin and Carrier died because of their integrity; the public legacy of all three women helped to ensure that the execution of "deviant" women in New England would not last.

That women began to develop a distinct identity and voice in colonial America was a prerequisite for the subsequent emergence of a collective and public feminist movement. Only as women began to define and represent themselves could they start to transcend gender roles imposed from without by the state, the church, the law, and other social and cultural forms. Women in America first found a public voice and identity through religion, again discovering, paradoxically, a certain amount of freedom in the system that also oppressed them. Puritanism incorporated an emphasis on self-scrutiny, often in the form of written conversion narratives and spiritual autobiographies, in which one would detail personal struggles on the path to salvation. At a time when women had virtually no social or institutional frameworks within which to express themselves, written or spoken words of religious introspection and nascent subjectivity became the first step to subverting patriarchal discourse and power.

Two of the earliest autobiographies by women in America were those of Mary Rowlandson and Elizabeth Ashbridge, both of which began to shape women's distinct consciousness and individuality. Published in Boston in 1682, Mary Rowlandson's narrative tells the story of her three-month long captivity by the Naragansett tribe of Native Americans. Rowlandson's account of her experience with the Naragansetts is one of the earliest of the captivity narratives, regarded by some as the first distinctively "American" literary genre. In her account, Rowlandson is clearly directed by the Puritan belief in the providential nature of the colonists' encounter with the Indians; she interprets each event as part of God's divine plan to test his "chosen people" through their encounter with the "evil" natives. Placed in exigent circumstances, however, Rowlandson's individuality—separate from the Puritan orthodoxy—starts to emerge; she finds her own food, makes things to trade with her captors, and even shifts her opinion about Indians, refusing to recognize them as simply evil.

Elizabeth Ashbridge quite literally creates herself anew in her autobiography of 1774; there is virtually no record of her other than that which her own hand transcribes. Evidence suggests that Ashbridge was authorized by her local Quaker meeting at Goshen, Pennsylvania, to travel and to preach and that it was generally acknowledged that she spoke with an increasingly authoritative voice. Ashbridge's text is a spiritual autobiography—the story of her struggle to achieve grace and a divine life, a story given symbolic expression in the dream she has of a woman bearing a lamp. As a Quaker, Ashbridge's "lamp" is, of course, the Quaker "Inner Light" that Mary Dyer died for over a century earlier; it is also the light of personal faith for which Anne Hutchinson was excommunicated. Like both Dyer and Hutchinson, Ashbridge's story is not just a quest for *spiritual* freedom though; her text, makes explicit her challenge to patriarchal institutional authority in secular areas of life such as the family, a challenge that was more covert in the religious struggles of Hutchinson and Dyer. Ashbridge's search for her personal truth is undertaken not just in the face of male-dominated religion but also in the face of tyrannical social and sexual relations, and her trials include, an exploitative master and a coercive, abusive husband. Finally, Ashbridge does achieve not only freedom of conscience but also a relatively autonomous identity.

Another literary genre at which women excelled in the colonial period was poetry, which was originally a distinctly masculine discourse in Puritan New England. Women poets not only stepped into the public sphere themselves, giving future women writers intellectual forebears, but they also carried on women's cultural work of defining their own subjectivity, making their own preoccupations part of the store of public knowledge. Anne Bradstreet first encroached on that terrain in 1650 when her book of poems, *The Tenth Muse,* was published in London, the first book of original poetry written in America. Publicly challenging the preconception that poetry was a masculine endeavor, Bradstreet asserts in "The Prologue" that "I am obnoxious to each carping tongue / Who says my hand a needle better fits." In both "The Prologue" and "The Author to Her Book," Bradstreet reflects on and defends her own role as a woman poet. Like proponents of women's education in the late-eighteenth century, Bradstreet insists that her intellectual work is not incompatible with domestic duties and childrearing.

About a century after Bradstreet issued her volume of poetry, Phillis Wheatley became the first African-American to publish a poetic work, her *Poems on Various Subjects, Religious and Moral* (1773). Wheatley's poetry was a distinct assertion of subjectivity at a time when most Anglo-Americans believed that African-Americans had none; there was even a "hearing" shortly after publication to determine if Wheatley was in fact the writer of the poems, since intellectual output from a black woman and a slave at that time was considered scarcely credible. Wheatley's writing, then, began to replace the patriarchal constructions of women—especially African-American women—with their own authentic self-constructions. Wheatley's poetry, however, contributed to political issues other than the subjectivity of women and slaves. "On Being Brought from Africa to America" expresses a spiritual vision that necessitates an equality between the races inimicable to the institution of slavery. And "The Right Honourable William, Earl of Dartmouth" reflects Wheatley's interest in the politics of the pre-Revolutionary ferment. Her poetry represents, albeit somewhat obliquely, the first entry of an African-American woman into the political issues of slavery and British imperialism.

To write about "feminism" in the colonial period is to commit somewhat of an anachronism; and those few historians who have even broached the topic of feminism in early America do so tentatively. The "disorder" of colonial women was not, after all, directed self-consciously against the collective situation of women *as* women. Anne Hutchinson is probably closest to such an ideal, as she did specifically argue for the right of women to exercise religious freedom and as she drew a crowd of largely female followers. (A contemporary of Hutchinson wrote that "'the weaker sex' set her up as 'a Priest' and 'thronged' after her.")[2] But these early rebels and intellectuals laid the groundwork for future feminist action—daring to transgress their allotted place, daring to oppose patriarchal authority within the institutions of the church and the family, and daring to move into masculine literary territories. Colonial women developed, in great adversity, an individuality that they expressed publicly.

Notes

1. Carol F. Karlsen, *The Devil in the Shape of a Woman: Witchcraft in Colonial New England* (New York: Norton, 1987), 116, 213.

2. Lyle Koehler, "The Case of the American Jezebels: Anne Hutchinson and Female Agitation During the Years of Antinomian Turmoil, 1636-1640," *William and Mary Quarterly* 31 (1974): 61.

JANE DONAWERTH (ESSAY DATE 2000)

SOURCE: Donawerth, Jane. "Women's Poetry and the Tudor-Stuart System of Gift Exchange." In *Women, Writing, and the Reproduction of Culture in Tudor and Stuart Britain,* edited by Mary E. Burke, Jane Donawerth, Linda L. Dove, and Karen Nelson, pp. 3-18. Syracuse, N.Y.: Syracuse University Press, 2000.

In the following essay, Donawerth details how women of Tudor and Stuart times circulated their writings through gift exchanges.

If women were constrained by early modern English culture to be "chaste, silent, and obedient," and if "silent" extended to writing, how did so many women come to circulate their writings in manuscript or print?[1] Drawing on early modern letters and documents, as well as on anthropological theory, I suggest that many women gained authority to write by envisioning their poems as part of the Tudor-Stuart gift-exchange system, which helped to weave the social fabric of court, community, and extended family.

Letters by sixteenth- and early-seventeenth-century English women show that women participated in and even managed a precapitalist gift-exchange system that was still a fundamental basis of English social life and economy. Centered on the family but extending across all classes to the family's political affiliations, the system circulated food, cloth and clothing, jewelry, animals, medicines, cash, prayers, relics, and favors.[2] For example, in the 1530s in France, the Lisle letters record exchanges between family members of money, cloth, clothing, and jewelry. In addition, gifts circulated between the Lisle family and the de Riou household, where the girls lived and learned French: the girls requested or the parents sent a "mastiff," "birds," "a needlecase," "a couple of lanners [falcons]," a "horn," "shoes and hosen," and "an English greyhound";[3] Mme. de Riou was not paid, for teaching French was also a gift.[4] The cover illustration is taken from an accouchement set—bowl and platter—that was designed to be a gift to the mother at a christening after childbirth; it depicts the bustling happy scene of attending on a new baby and mother. The exchanges recorded in the Lisle letters established the "reciprocal dependence" of gift exchange rather than the "reciprocal independence" of barter systems (to use the terms of anthropologist C. A. Gregory). The major purpose of exchanging gifts rather than payments was to establish social bonds.[5]

In a further exchange in the Lisle letters, Anthoinette de Saveuses, a nun who was cousin to Mme. de Riou, convinced Lady Lisle to offer her husband's intercession with the French king to restrain Mme. de Riou's husband from gambling away his wife's fortune; in gratitude the nun returned prayers, medicine, and a religious relic (Byrne, *Lisle Letters* [abridged], 121-24 [no. 99]). And in 1537, gifts of quails to the pregnant English queen, Jane Seymour, prompted her to invite one of the Lisles' daughters to live as a lady-in-waiting at court, giving the daughter an opportunity to make an aristocratic marriage (*Lisle Letters,* abridged, 205-7 [nos. 176-79]). Personal attention and signs of affection were part of the recognized value of a gift, which, as anthropologists Caroline Humphrey and Stephen Hugh-Jones explain, is a mode of "non-monetary exchange which derive[s] from, and create[s] relationships" (18).

In his classic treatise on gift exchange, Marcel Mauss analyzes the three principles of such a system of nonmarket exchange of goods and services: one must give gifts, one must receive gifts, and one must reciprocate (13, 39-42). A sixteenth-century humanist reader could have read these rules in Seneca's *De Beneficiis* (esp. sigs. Ai^r, $Aiii^r$, Bi^r, Eiv^v, and $Gi^{r\text{-}v}$). We can see the principle of reciprocity at work in Mary Stuart's 1587 letter to her brother-in-law Henry III of France: facing execution, she asks him to recompense her servants and to pay for masses for her soul, and obligates him with a gift of medicine—"two stones, rare for the health" (Travitsky, ed., *Paradise of Women,* 206-7). In an elaborate exchange recorded in a letter by Elizabeth More, Lady Wolley, to her father on 16 September 1595, Sir Robert Cecil gave Queen Elizabeth three partridges, and she gave them to Lady Wolley, "wth expresse charge that [she] should send them" to her sick father. But Lady Wolley instead returned them to Cecil at Cecil's request, writing her father

ON THE SUBJECT OF...

CASSANDRA FEDELE (1465-1558)

Cassandra Fedele was the first Italian woman writer to engage, publicly and independently, in scholarly discussions of morality, philosophy, education, literature, and politics, and was a steadfast and vocal proponent of the education of women. Fedele was born in Venice, Italy, and as a child was tutored—by her humanist father and others—in a variety of subjects, including Latin, Greek, classical literature, and rhetoric. By the age of sixteen, Fedele had established herself as a humanist and liberal arts prodigy, and was invited frequently to speak before various audiences of learned men.

In 1487, Fedele's cousin graduated with honors from the University of Padua—the center of learning for Venetian scholars—and Fedele presented a public oration on Latin, which was subsequently printed at Modena, Venice, and Nurenberg. The widespread publication and popularity of her oration led to Fedele's correspondence with numerous scholars, religious leaders, and educators worldwide, including the king of France, Pope Alexander VI, and Spain's Queen Isabella and King Ferdinand, who invited her to join their court. Although Fedele entertained the Spanish monarchs' invitation, the Venetian senate prevented the twenty-two-year-old Fedele from accepting it, claiming that the state could not afford to lose her. Fedele presented a public oration in praise of literary scholarship before the Doge and senators of Venice, and her last oration, in 1556, was delivered in honor of the visiting Queen of Poland. When she died in 1558, Fedele was honored with a state funeral. The majority of Fedele's letters and her three public orations are collected in *Letters and Orations* (2000), edited and translated by Diana Robin.

to send thanks to the queen: in this case, the gift had gone through the hands of four people and, in a matter of minutes, returned to the original giver. Such a cycle is not unusual according to Mauss.[6] Lady Wolley managed this gift exchange for her family, standing in for her sick father and maintaining her family's political connections by giving the partridges back to one of Elizabeth's chief advisors. She follows both the requirement of receiving the gift by having her father pretend to receive the partridges and the principle of required giving by returning the partridges to Cecil. The episode further shows that gifts were not given once and consumed but were *circulated,* gathering value by the hands they had been through and establishing the bonds of community.[7]

In 1603, Arbella Stuart, cousin to King James, wrote Mary Talbot, Countess of Shrewsbury, that she would give the queen "2. paire of silk stockins lined with plush and 2. paire of gloves lined" and the king "a purse" "I am making" for New Year's presents. The letter demonstrates the English custom of gift giving on New Year's Day. It further illustrates that the value of a gift was linked to personal concern rather than cash equivalent, for Arbella criticizes the queen, who "neither liked gowne, nor peticoate so well, as somm little bunch of Rubies to hang in hir eare, or somm such dafte toy"—that is, who preferred jewelry to clothing embroidered by the woman who gave it. The letter also suggests that embroidery on New Year's gifts was done by the women who gave them, even among the aristocracy.[8] Many lists of the monarch's New Year's gifts are extant, demonstrating "the affirmation of peaceful solidarity and the establishment of rank" ("Beyond the Market," 70) that Natalie Zemon Davis assigns as the primary cause of early modern gift giving.[9] Queen Elizabeth's New Year's donors, for example, are listed in hierarchical and gendered order: earls and viscounts; marquesses, duchesses, and countesses; bishops; lords; baronesses; ladies; knights; gentlewomen; and (nonknighted) gentlemen.[10] Indeed, Mauss argues that holiday gift exchanges are ceremonies of recognition of identity, competitions for esteem (8 and 40). "The ritual exchange of gifts," maintains Lisa Klein about Elizabeth's court, "fostered allegiances and affirmed hierarchical relationships" (461).

The New Year's lists suggest that the gifts themselves were stratified and gendered. To Elizabeth in 1598, all the earls gave gold coins except for the earl of Northumberland, who gave a gown of pink taffeta; many of the marquesses and countesses gave gold, but others gave pendants (of gold, diamonds, and pearls), kirtles, petticoats, handkerchiefs, and "loose gowns"; the bishops all gave gold coins; many lords gave gold, but others gave gowns, pendants, mantles, and jewels; a few baronesses gave gold, but others gave waistcoats, taffeta cloaks, loose gowns, embroidered accessories, and, in one case, a painted wooden gilt stool with "stawberries in silkewoman's worke"; only two ladies gave gold, and the rest gave bracelets, mantles, ruffs, kirtles, pendants, pettyrobes, smocks, cloth, and "attire for the head"; only four knights gave gold, whereas the rest gave kirtles, pendants, and pettyrobes; no gentlewomen gave gold, but instead pendants, bracelets, handkerchiefs, gloves, smocks, ruffs, mantles, lawn (a kind of cloth), and a stool; nonknighted gentlemen gave gilt cups, a lump of silver, gloves, ruffs, ginger and other spices, and a book of arms.

Thus, it was more appropriate for lords and ladies to give gold coins and for gentlefolk to give spices or gloves or kirtles, but it was also more appropriate for men to give coins or gowns and for women to give feminine crafts—embroidered smocks or petticoats, looking glasses, worked combcases, and ruffs.[11] Indeed, in the lists of gifts from women, the most frequently recurring phrase is "embroidered all over" (Nichols, *Progresses,* 2:68). For example, in 1577-78, the current countess of Pembroke, Mary Sidney Herbert, gave the queen "A dublet of lawne embrowdred al ouer with gold, siluer, and sylke of divers collors, and lyned with yelow taphata." The ability to give gold was a good indication of status in sixteenth-century England: in the same class, women who gave gold usually gave smaller amounts than did their menfolk, and the value of the gold went down as one descended the hierarchy by class, until gentlemen and gentlewomen could not afford it. In the lists I found, only men gave books, and only women gave smocks. But some women did give books, since Elizabeth gave her translation of Marguerite de Navarre's "The Mirror, or Glass, of the Sinful Soul" as a New Year's gift to Catherine Parr in 1544-45.[12] Gifts were given to the monarch in the morning, and the monarch reciprocated in the afternoon (Fumerton, 219-20 n. 41) by giving silver plate, the Tudor equivalent of savings bonds. As Arthur Marotti points out, New Year's was also an occasion for giving poems ("Transmission of Lyric Poetry" 22-24).

Thus, women of Tudor and Stuart times participated in this gift-exchange system and often even managed it. In this system, women who were subordinates could garner influence and trade power,[13] and despite the hierarchy, class boundaries could be crossed more freely than in the mainly masculine patronage system, where the purpose was to establish loyalty to a faction rather than more general social bonds.[14] Unlike market exchanges, this gift-exchange system figured into the value of the gifts the marks of caring, of personal concern, and of previous owners attached to them—Golding's translation of Seneca's *De Beneficiis* calls it the "goodwill" of the giver. As a result, the prayers and needlework of women were as important as cash or jewelled "toyes"; even if money circulated, it was not in itself the standard of value.[15] Indeed, the letters recording these exchanges need to be considered part of the gifts. Arbella Stuart, for example, wished the countess of Shrewsbury to refrain from sending letters to others at court, for her letters were "a favour I desire onely may be reserved still for my selfe" (no. 35, 194).

This gift-exchange system also included other writings as gifts. The earliest poem by a woman in English that I know of is enclosed in a Valentine's Day letter from Margery Brews to John Paston III in 1477: Margery assures her fiancé in doggerel verse

An yf ye commande me to kepe me true
 whereever I go,
I wyse I will do all my myght yowe to love and
 never no mo.
And yf my freendys say that I do amys, thei
 schal no me let so for to do,
Myn hearte me byddys ever more to love yowe.
(Norman Davis, 1:106, no. 76)

As anthropologists argue about gifts in general, this poem as gift obligates the recipient by sending with it part of the donor's self (Mauss, 12). Because marriage negotiations between father and prospective son-in-law were foundering on the issue of money, this gift may also be a political move by the would-be bride to offer some of herself in order to lower the bridegroom's demands. Constance Aston Fowler's early-seventeenth-century commonplace book seems also to be a record of literary gift exchange, housing poems sent her by friends and especially by her brother: "'Send me some verses,'" she writes in a letter to him, "'I want some good ones to put in my booke.'"[16]

Much of English Renaissance poetry by women may fit into this system. Elizabeth Cary notes in her dedicatory poem that *The Tragedy of Mariam* (1603?)—presumably a manuscript book now lost—was a gift for her sister-in-law Elizabeth, which had been preceded by another play (also now lost) given to her brother-in-law (*Tragedy of Mariam,* 66). In Lady Mary Wroth's *Urania,* Pamphilia gives her poems to her cousin Amphilanthus before he goes off to battle, a reference to the sonnet sequence "Pamphilia to Amphilanthus" that closes the 1621 printed *Urania* and that perhaps was also a dedication and gift by Lady Mary Wroth to William Herbert, who was her lover (*Poems,* 24-27). In the rest of this essay, then, I read sixteenth-century poems by English-women—Anne Lok, Isabella Whitney, and Mary Sidney—as gifts, asking what difference this context makes.

Anne Vaughan Lok, from the London merchant class, hosted and corresponded with John Knox, and spent several years with her children in exile in Geneva during the reign of Queen Mary.[17] Home in 1560, she published a translation, *Sermons of John Calvin, Vpon the Songe that Ezechias made after he had bene sicke,* with a sonnet sequence meditation on Psalm 51 to fill up the end pages of the book.[18] The book is dedicated as a New Year's gift to Catherine Willoughby Bertie, duchess of Suffolk, who had also been an exile in Geneva: "I wishe your grace continuall health of life and soule for your preseruation, not onely for this newe yeare, but also for the tyme that shall excede all extent of yeares, besechinge you to accepte bothe my worke and prayer" (sigs. A7ᵛ-A8ʳ).[19] Thus, the first sonnet sequence in English, as Thomas Roche has pointed out, by a woman,[20] was also presented as a New Year's gift to another woman and so was part of the Tudor gift-exchange system.[21]

Designed to wish good health of body and soul to the duchess for the New Year, the book is presented by Anne Lok as both a prayer and a medicine, gifts regularly exchanged by women as we have seen in their letters. Lok distributes the making of the gift among a spiritual community: "This receipte God the heavenly Physitian hath taught, his most excellent Apothecaire Master John Calvine hath compounded, and I, your grace's most bounden and humble, have put into an Englishe box and do present unto you" (sig. A3ʳ⁻ᵛ). The book is a cure for the diseased mind, and just as we feel gratitude to a physician for curing our body, we must feel gratitude to God for curing our souls and to Calvin for making the medicine available to us. Anne Lok requires no thanks from the duchess because of the enormous duty she owes her; Calvin takes as recompense, Lok assures us, any Christian's profit from his medicine; and the duchess is a model of thankfulness to God, expressed through her "profession of his worde" and her "godly conuersation" (sig. A3ᵛ). The epistle thus characterizes Lok's book as a medicine, a prayer, and a gift—"This medicine is in this litle boke brought from the plentifull shop & storehouse of Gods holye testament" (sig. A6ʳ). Lok invokes both the rule that a gift must be returned (the gratitude owed to God and Calvin) and the resulting community—not only God, Calvin, Lok, and the duchess, but also all "trewe beleiuyng Christians" (sig. A4ʳ).[22]

Extending the medicinal metaphor to the poetry, Lok uses the sonnet sequence as a meditation aimed at restoring spiritual health:

> With swete Hysope besprinkle thou my sprite:
> Not such hysope, nor so besprinkle me,
> As law unperfect shade of perfect lyght
> Did vse as an apointed signe to be
> Foreshewing figure of thy grace behight.
> With death and bloodshed of thine only sonne,
> The sweet hysope, cleanse me defyled wyght.
> Sprinkle my sould.

The fourteen-line sonnet in iambic pentameter from which I quote is written in plain style. It offers a meditation on verse 7 of Psalm 51, quoted in the poem's margin as "Sprinkle me, Lorde, with hisope and I shalbe cleane: washe me and I shalbe whiter then snow." Anne Lok's psalm meditations were published in the same year as the Geneva Bible and typeset in similar but reversed fashion—biblical verse on the side, commentary in the middle. Indeed, the two works may be linked, although Lok does not quote from the Geneva translation; in the Geneva gloss to Isaiah 38, Hezekiah's penitential song, which is the text of the sermon by Calvin that Lok translated, the commentators recommend considering these two biblical poems together: "He left this song of his lamentacion and thankesgiuing to all posteritie, as a monument of his owne infirmitie & thankeful heart for Gods benefits, as Dauid did, Psal 51."[23]

Throughout her sonnet sequence Lok has heightened the metaphors of sickness of the soul and medicinal cleansing. The hyssop used to treat leprosy represents here the grace that cures sin.[24] Anachronistically placing Christ at the center of this psalm, Lok also provides an extremely reformed reading of David's lament: in the quoted poem she stresses Christ's mercy over the "law unperfect shade of perfect lyght," or faith over works fulfilling the law.[25] Throughout the sequence she emphasizes the healing powers of faith: translating the Geneva Bible's "God of my saluacion" as "God of my helth" and praying "my broosed bones . . . / Shall leape for ioy." Thus, this poem as a gift is also conceived as a medicine, something women in this culture made and exchanged among themselves.

Lok also uses the metaphor of a recipe for herbal medicine to link her own meditation on David's Psalm 51 to the sermons by Calvin on Isaiah 38 that she translates: Hezekiah's song, the subject of Calvin's sermons, ends with a recipe that heals him to show God's mercy (Isaiah 38:21). Several of Lok's wordings in her meditative elaboration of David's psalm recall Hezekiah's song: her Sonnet 6 (first line), like Isaiah 38:18-19, argues that the Lord needs to save the speaker so that s/he can praise him, telling of his mercy; Lok's Sonnet 10, like Isaiah 38:13, emphasizes God's ability to break the speaker's bones; and Lok's Sonnet 16, like Isaiah 38:20, sees the singing of songs—by extension, the writing of poems—as an expression of gratitude for God's salvation. Lok thus places herself among poets who include Hezekiah and David, and she signs her poem with puns on her name—"look," "lock," and "bul-lock" (especially in Sonnet 11).

Dedicated to the duchess of Suffolk, Lok's book may be seen as a gift with political designs on its audiences, meant to build community, religious and social. The duchess was connected to many reformers in the new religion: Hugh Latimer dedicated a book of sermons to her and served as her chaplain; her sons studied with Martin Bucer at Oxford; and she supported both John Foxe and Miles Coverdale in her household (Hogrefe, *Women of Action,* 91-102). She was a popularizer of the word, supporting sermons, martyrology, and translations of the Bible and of continental reform treatises. At New Year's in 1560, she must have just returned from Geneva, and January 1 was also the anniversary of her exile from England in 1555 (Hogrefe, *Women of Action,* 86-103). As a gift to the duchess of Suffolk, Lok's book would further bind the duchess into the English Protestant community and would obligate her to help build the New Jerusalem.

Especially in the final four sonnets, Lok's meditations on David's psalm restate a principle of the reformed community: faith not works. Sonnet 18 suggests that a Christian must not count on an exchange of "cattel slayne and burnt . . . / On altars broylde" (5-8) but must instead rely on "thy swete sonne alone" (9), God's gift of grace. In return for God's gift ("The praise of that I yeld for sacrifice" [14]), one gives one's self, one's prayers, even a poem, all of which are more appropriate than going to mass. The true gift that God requires of his people is a "trobled sprite," a "broken and an humbled hart" (Sonnet 19, margin and 3-4, 11-12, and 14). In Sonnet 20 Lok suggests that, having given a gift, the speaker can then ask God to reciprocate with his grace for the New Jerusalem—"Defend thy chirch" (9). In Sonnet 21, I thus read "in thy walled towne" as London: reformed Christians in this new London under Elizabeth will offer God a new gift—"Many a yelden host of humbled hart" (6). Quoting from scripture in the margin of Sonnet 21, Lok lays her own name among the "bul-lockes" as a gift for God on the altar of her heart, asking other English Christians to do the same.

Isabella Whitney, a London poet of the gentry working class who left service because of illness, similarly uses the metaphor of herbal medicine to describe her poetry as gift. *A Sweet Nosgay of pleasant posye* (1573),[26] Whitney's second collection of poems, self-consciously employs gift exchange as a structural metaphor for a life well lived and well ended.[27] Echoing the diversity of popular miscellanies, the text organizes prose, verse, moral maxims or "flowers," a collection of verse letters to family members, and the "Auctors Testament" or will around the theme of the author's life-threatening illness. Demonstrating how to live and leave the good life through the unifying conceit of the exchange of gifts, these writings transform deathbed advice from sad to joyous. In her dedication to George Mainwaring, Whitney puts her writings in the context of gift exchange. Her poems are flowers, picked from Plat (a pun on the name of the author she used as source for her proverbs), made into a nosegay to prevent pestilence, and given to her friend as recompense for past benefits. "The Auctor to the Reader" figures the reader as recipient, too: "the Flowers are good, / Which I on thee bestow" (sig. A8^{r}).

Whitney begins and ends this section of maxims in *Nosgay* by presenting her poems as herbal medicine, the kind of gift frequently made and exchanged by women. In "The Auctor to the Reader," the speaker advises,

> But in a bundle as they bee,
> (good reader them accept:)
> It is the gever: not the guift,
> thou oughtest to respect,
> And for thy health, not for thy eye,
> did I this Posye frame:
> Because my selfe dyd safety finde,
> by smelling to the same.
>
> (sigs. A5-A6)

"Smelling" refers to the bouquets of herbs that Londoners smelled to ward off plague and other airborne diseases. This section concludes with "a soueraigne receypt": using the "Iuce of all these Flowers," the poet explains, make a "conserue" to "preserue" your health (sig. C5^{r}). Whitney's poems are thus a series of intertwined secular moral maxims—such sentences were often called "flowers"—put together for the moral health of her readers. As gifts, they are meant to create a bond of "respect" to the donor. Hovering behind these moral maxims drawn from the ancients are the many forms of Christian charity, here recast as obligations in the gift-exchange cycle. Advocating friendship, charity, and "the contented mind," and discouraging the dis-eases of love, Whitney's versified maxims also sketch the virtues expected of those involved in gift exchange: the requirement to give (no. 6, sig. B2^{v}), especially to friends (no. 58, sig. B7^{v}), the contented mind that doesn't "gape" after gifts (no. 81, sig. C2^{r}), charity to neighbors (no. 97, sig. C3^{v}), and the capacity to reward those who ask least (no. 99, sig. C4^{r}).

Whitney extends this metaphor into the epistles to her siblings that are gathered after the "Nosgay." In "To Her Sister Misteris A. B.," for example, she reciprocates a gift already given from her sister: if she didn't write, her older sister might think she had "vainely . . . bestowed expence" on the younger. We see again the linking of family and binding of community through reciprocal exchange of letters and gifts: "for nature dyd you bynde: / To doo mee good: and to requight, / hath nature mee inclynde" (sigs. D1^{r}-D2^{r}). As her epistle to her two younger sisters shows, as well as later letters in the sequence from family members consoling her during her illness, moral advice counts as a gift, as well as material goods. The section of letters to the speaker's family thus defines charity as the family's provision of spiritual and material support; it depicts the family as an institution for facilitating gift exchange even when its members are separated from each other.

The benefit of family is linked to the *ars moriendi* theme of the next section in Whitney's sequence. The letters from and to family in this section constitute a conversation about the poet's ill health, her desire to die, and the proper attitude of a Christian humanist toward suffering—all within a supporting network of extended family. The letters are an enactment of an exchange of love expressed as advice, but this very human exchange of gifts is not enough. This section adds the divine—the speaker praying for God's gift of patience: "Wherfore (my God) geue me that gyfte, / As bedyd IOB vntyll: / That I may take with quietnesse, / What soeuer is his wyll" (sig. D6^{r}).

The fictional "I" of this set of poems does not recover but ends her sequence with her last will and testament, her last act in a joyous cycle of gift exchange that affirms her life and the leaving of it. In this last section, the speaker leaves to Londoners all the gifts of the streets of London.[28] Much like the New Year gift lists, Whitney's poem details the wealth that circulates in the gift-exchange cycle: "Linnen," "silke," "Juels," "Plate," "Siluer," "Golde," "Hoods, Bungraces ['bongrace,' veil or hat to protect from the sun], Hats or Caps," "French Ruffes," "Lawne," and "Purse or kniues . . . combe or Glasse" (sig. E4^{r}). Her death is not an ending because the abundance of gifts that constitute material life on earth continues—the giving and enjoyment go on without her. She uses her goods and moves on, leaving those goods to others—with joy.

Whitney's sequence of prose and verse writings is thus a joyful *ars moriendi*: the gift cycle works effectively as a symbol of preparing for death—through nourishing moral health and education, through establishing a community of kin and friends to support oneself in despair, through acknowledging the joy of the life one leaves to others—because the gift represents not only the humanist Christian's solace (God who freely gave his son), but also the thingness, the joyful materiality, of life.

Mary Sidney, countess of Pembroke, was a patron and poet, sister to the poets Sir Philip Sidney and Robert Sidney, whose mother had been lady-in-waiting and advisor to Queen Elizabeth.[29] The manuscript book of the Sidney translation of the *Psalms* includes Mary Sidney's dedicatory poem to Elizabeth (1599), "Even now that Care," in which she uses not the metaphor of herbal medicine, but the metaphor of cloth to describe the gift (24) that she and her brother have made:

> but hee did warpe, I weau'd this webb to end;
> the stuffe not ours, our worke no curious thing,
>
> . . . . .
>
> And I the Cloth in both our names present,
> A liuerie robe to bee bestowed by thee.
>
> (27-36)

As editors have shown, Sir Philip Sidney translated the first 43 psalms, but the countess translated the remaining 106 and revised her brother's work (*Psalms,* xi and xxv-xxvi). Mary Sidney presents his beginning and her ending the project as warp and woof of a piece of cloth, which they have made into a "liuerie robe" that Elizabeth may bestow on another: the poetry is like a piece of cloth in the gift-exchange system. But the poet also imagines the psalms as wearing this English translation as a livery. As in traditional gift-exchange cycles, the recipient has already given what is returned: Mary and Philip return to Elizabeth the English language that she already owns.

In this dedicatory poem Mary Sidney changes the tenor of the metaphor of cloth yet a third time, presenting David's prayers in the psalms as "holy garments" that "all sort to none but thee" (63-64)—clothing once worn by King David, put on in meditative exercises by every Christian, but fitting exactly only a similar holy monarch and poet, Queen Elizabeth. Mary Sidney also offers her translation of the psalms as a gift personally fitted to Elizabeth, and the personal concern is presented as part of that gift. As often happens in the gift-exchange system, then, this gift also represents an obligation: that Queen Elizabeth be like David, the king who originally wore these clothes, the king whom Protestants used to figure a militant Protestant intervention in European affairs.[30] The poem to Queen Elizabeth by Mary Sidney after her brother's death, like many of her brother's works before his death, thus attempts to garner influence over the queen's religious policies. Here the gift becomes explicitly political. As Margaret Hannay points out, "by reminding the Queen of Philip's death in the first half of the dedication, Mary Sidney was continuing the family tradition of seeking to influence Elizabeth toward a more radical Protestant stance. By comparing her to the Psalmist in the second half of the dedication, she was continuing the tradition of admonitory flattery, which was a standard element in the dedication of Scripture to sovereigns in both England and France" (*Philip's Phoenix,* 91). In the end, according to this poem, servant and monarch give each other the best gifts when they simply act the roles God gave them: the poet must "Sing what God doth," and the monarch must "doo What men may sing" (95).

Many women writers offered their poetry as a gift within the gift-exchange system. Seeing poetry as part of this system in which they had operated all their lives must have made it easier for them to write and to publish. Poetry, like herbal medicines and needlework, was a gift made by women in the household to give to family and friends, and to be judged not only by the cash value or craftsmanship but also by the affectionate care intended. As Klein suggests, such gifts show "women as active participants in cultural exchange, using their material objects to forge alliances" (462). As a gift, however, poetry still might be a means to establish a larger political support community and even to influence political decisions. Also, like many gifts, once given, it could be given again.

In an essay that includes a pun in French, "Des marchandise entre elles"—the merchandise among themselves, among *her*selves—Luce Irigaray asks,

> *But what if the "goods" refused to go to market?* What if they maintained among themselves "another" kind of trade? Exchange without identifiable terms of trade, without accounts, without end. . . . Where use and exchange would mingle. . . . Utopia? Perhaps. Unless this mode of exchange has always undermined the order of trade and simply has not been recognized . . . [and we have been] forbidden a certain economy of abundance. (110)

In the Tudor-Stuart gift-exchange system, was it possible for the goods to get together among themselves—for women who were legally propertyless, who were sometimes themselves counted as merchandise—to circulate gifts? Certainly, in this system women could own and give many things: the nun's prayers, medicines, and relics mentioned in the *Lisle Letters*; the black velvet dress passed to Mary Sidney from her mother; recipes, medicines, spices, and embroidered "work" from women's hands on dresses, petticoats, and purses; and poems. The poems I have discussed were written by women and given to other women. Poems, especially, may circulate in an "economy of abundance," for they do not require much in the way of raw materials, and because given, they still are not spent.

Notes

1. Many scholars have analyzed the early modern English ideal of the "chaste, silent, and obedient" woman: see Pearl Hogrefe, *Tudor Women,* 3-9; Suzanne W. Hull, *Chaste, Silent, and Obedient*; Lisa Jardine, *Still Harping on Daughters,* 103-40; Catherine Belsey, *The Subject of Tragedy,* 149-91; Peter Stallybrass, "Patriarchal Territories"; and Margaret W. Ferguson, "A Room Not Their Own." On women's publication despite the cultural prescription to be silent, see Margaret Hannay, introduction to *Silent But for the Word,* 1-14; Margaret Ezell, *Patriarch's Wife,* 62-100; Elaine Hobby, *Virtue of Necessity,* 1-23; Ann Rosalind Jones, *Currency of Eros,* 11-35; Mary Ellen Lamb, *Gender and Authorship,* 3-19; Betty Travitsky, introduction to *Renaissance Englishwoman in Print,* 19-20, 25-28; Wendy Wall, "Isabella Whitney"; and Tina Krontiris, *Oppositional Voices,* 1-23.
2. See Davis, "Beyond the Market," 69-88, who emphasizes the communal interchange; and Lisa Klein, "You Humble Handmaid," 459-93, who emphasizes the power and class politics of gift exchange. See also, Ronald Sharp, "Gift Exchange," 250-53; and Mark Burnett, "Giving and Receiving," 288-89, and 299-301.
3. See *Lisle Letters* (abridged) edited by Muriel St. Clare Byrne, 113 (no. 84), 115 (no. 88), 119 (no. 96), and 120 (no. 97).
4. See Fumerton, 36-43, who suggests that children, too, were circulated in the Tudor-Stuart gift-exchange system.
5. Gregory, 42. See also introduction to Humphrey and Hugh-Jones, 12. For the quotations from Marcel Mauss's classic treatise, see 5, 59, and 80. On gift exchange, see also, Pierre Bourdieu, "Selections from *The Logic of Practice,*" 190-230, and "Marginalia," 231-41, in Schrift.

6. Elizabeth More, Lady Wolley, no. 130 in Kempe, 317-18. Elizabeth McCutcheon pointed out these letters at a 1990 conference; for a summary of her workshop, see Travitsky and Seeff, 103-5. Mauss discusses circular gift exchange or returning to the giver, 30.

7. In the Shakespeare Birthday Lecture at the Folger Shakespeare Library in 1993, Peter Stallybrass discussed the "magic" of cloth and clothing that had been circulated as gifts in Elizabethan England as appropriated for theatrical performance.

8. Letter no. 35, to Mary Talbot, countess of Shrewsbury, in Stuart, edited Sara Jayne Steen, 194-95. I learned of this letter at a 1990 conference; for a summary of Sara Jayne Steen's workshop, see Travitsky and Seeff, 103-5.

9. My thanks to Karen Robertson for the references to the lists of New Year's gifts. Her responses to my paper on gift exchange at the Patristic, Medieval, and Renaissance Conference at Villanova University, 1 October 1993, as well as those by Carole Levin, Margaret Jaster, and Lori Newcomb, have helped me greatly. I have looked at the following New Year's gift rolls: the 1556 list of gifts to Mary, in Nichols, *Illustrations,* no page numbering; the lists of gifts to Elizabeth I in John Nichols, *Progresses,* in vol. 1: 1561/2, 1571/2, 1572/3, 1573/4 (and the 1574 list of gifts from Elizabeth's progress); and in vol. 2: 1576/7, 1577/8, 1578/9, 1588/9, and 1599/1600. I have also looked at two gift rolls in vellum manuscript (my thanks to the Folger Shakespeare Library in Washington, D.C.): Great Britain, Sovereigns (Elizabeth), *Lists of New Year Gifts,* 1584/5 and Great Britain, Sovereigns, Elizabeth, *List of New Year Gifts,* 1598-99. For lists of other extant New Year's rolls, see A. Jefferies Collins, 247-53.

10. Based on the Folger manuscript lists under Great Britain, Sovereigns. In the Folger manuscript for 1584/5, listing Elizabeth's gifts, there are no members of the royal family, twenty-one earls and viscounts, eighteen marquesses and countesses, eighteen bishops, fourteen lords, twenty baronesses, nineteen ladies, fifteen knights, thirty-four gentlewomen, and thirty-four nonknighted gentlemen. In several of the lists recorded by Nichols, gifts from members of the immediate royal family precede all others; in the list in Nichols's *Illustrations* of Mary's New Year's gifts, bishops preceded all but earls and viscounts—perhaps a difference in Mary's and Elizabeth's placing of the church in the hierarchy.

11. In the list of gifts given to Mary in 1556, all the earls and viscounts gave gold coins, except for one, who gave a gilt cup; all the bishops gave gold coins (smaller amounts), except for one, who gave "Christophersen, a book written, couered with crymson vellat"; many of the duchesses, marquesses, and countesses gave gold coins, but others gave "a cushen-cloth, frenged and tasselled with golde," gilt salt and pepper sets, and "a smoke [smock], wrought all ou' with silke, and color [collar] and ruffes of damaske golde, purle, and siluer"; the viscountesses gave gold coins and handkerchiefs; most of the lords gave gold coins, but one gave crystal cruets and another embroidered handkerchiefs; many of the ladies gave gold coins, and the rest gave clothing, embroidered works, toiletries, and condiments—smocks, gloves, handkerchiefs, ruffs, waistcoats, cushion-cloths, a sacrament cloth, purses, combcases, "a faire christall glase [mirror]," and figs, orange water, and sugar loaves; most of the knights gave gold coins, and others gave a spice box, handkerchiefs, waistcoats, hose, a lute, a map of England, "a booke of Spanish, couered with blake vellat," and "a prymer, couerid with purple vellat"; the chaplains gave gold coins or religious items—a psalter, a book of prayers, a "table" embroidered with the passion; a few gentlewomen gave gold coins, but others gave partlets, ruffs, kerchiefs, smocks, silk bags, handkerchiefs, gloves, combcases, a picture of the Trinity, a gilt holy water sprinkler, a walnut stool, gilt spoons, turkey hens, geese, capons, swans, oranges, lemons, and pippins; some of the nonknighted gentlemen gave coins, while others gave cushions, handkerchiefs, fans, pots of conserves, oxen, cups, pomegranates, a cloak, a crossbow, rosewater, sugar loaves, ginger, nutmeg, a painting of "the Maundy," "a book in Laten, entitelid '*Vita Christ,*'" "an Exhortacion to younge men," and a book in French (Nichols, *Illustrations,* no page numbering).

12. On Elizabeth's translation of Marguerite de Navarre's "The Mirror or Glass of a Sinful Soul" for Catherine Parr as a New Year's gift, see Travitsky, *Paradise of Women,* 76-77; and Lisa Klein, 476-81. On women giving books as gifts, see also Georgianna Ziegler's essay in this volume, "'More Than Feminine Boldness': the Gift Books of Esther Inglis."

13. See Barbara Harris, "Women and Politics," esp. 260 and 268, on the conflation of private and public in women's political actions; 265-67, on gift exchange; and 271 and 275 on New Year's gifts.

14. I am following the anthropologists in distinguishing between gift exchange, with its goal of unified community, and patronage, with its goal of political faction. See S. N. Eisenstadt and Louis Roniger, "Patron-Client Relations," 42-77, who argue that patronage differs from gift exchange in three ways—patronage is voluntary not obligatory, it is always hierarchical, and it establishes solidarity around the faction of the patron rather than solidarity with the more general society or community. See also Lewis Hyde on the differences between "commodity exchange" and gift exchange, *Gift,* 4. Frequently historians and literary critics of the early modern period do not distinguish between these different uses of gifts: see, for example, Robert Evans, *Ben Jonson,* 23-30, who subsumes all these relationships under the category of patriarchal, hierarchical patronage; or Krontiris, *Oppositional Voices,* 14, who writes, "Like the position of the courtier, that of the lady-in-waiting was part of the larger system of patronage, which was based on an exchange of favours." Clearly, gift exchange and patronage overlap, but it is useful in my essay to start with the distinction inasmuch as all women participated in gift exchange, but fewer women than men participated in the patronage systems in Tudor and Stuart Britain.

15. In gift exchange, money may be circulated but cannot be the standard to determine value of other gifts (Strathern, 175). See Ralph Waldo Emerson, "Gifts," in Schrift, 26, on the value of a gift as resulting from giving part of oneself.

16. On Constance Fowler, see Ezell, *The Patriarch's Wife,* 72.

17. See Patrick Collinson, "The Role of Women," 258-72; my thanks to Virginia Beauchamp for remembering this essay from reading it fifteen years earlier! My thanks, too, to Carole Levin, for pointing out to me the letters by John Knox "To His Loving Sister, Mistres Anne Locke": see *The Works of John Knox,* Vol. 4, no. xxxii and xxxiii, 237-41.

18. The endpages containing the sonnet sequence are not paginated the way the other pages are. My thanks to

Linda Dove, who introduced me to Anne Lok by bringing me a reference to Thomas Roche, *Petrarch and the English Sonnet Sequences,* 155. Because we have continued our discoveries about Anne Lok in conversation with each other, I will never properly sort out my great debt to her reading of Lok's poems, especially to her unpublished essay, "Anne Lok's 'poore basket of stones': Building a Reformed Church in Tudor England." On the question of the authorship of Lok's sonnets, see Hannay, "'Wisdome the Wordes,'" 79, n. 4; and Susan Felch.

19. See Collinson, 265; on the duchess of Suffolk, see Hogrefe, *Women of Action,* 86-103.

20. Roche, 155. As Davis notes, "printed books could be part of systems of gift and obligation in the sixteenth century, passing beyond the transactions of buying and selling ("Beyond the Market," 69); and "the world of gifts expanded as an alternative to the market and market values. . . . Books were dedicated or given for broad social purposes that went beyond strict reciprocity" (87).

21. In contrast, the second translation with accompanying poetry published by Anne Lok (now Anne Vaughan Lok Dering Prowse), *Of the Markes of the Children of God,* a sermon translated from Jean Taffin, seems much more in line with anthropologists' definitions of patronage systems than with the gift-exchange system. Prowse dedicates the work to the countess of Warwick, "a professour, but also a louer of the treueth" (sig. A3v), apparently aiming to build a radical Protestant faction around the Sidney family and former Marian exiles, addressing an audience of English Protestants (sig. A3r-v).

22. According to Lok's preface, however, this true-believing community cannot include papists (sig. A3v), because they provide poisonous medicine, "the pangs wherof when the deceiued sick man feleth, he to late spieth the falshod of the murtherous phuysician" (sig. A4r).

23. Thus Lok links herself as a poet to these two great biblical models, Hezekiah and David. Linda Dove first noticed this connection between these songs in the Geneva Bible.

24. See Hannay, "'Wisdome the Wordes,'" 65-82, esp. 72 on hyssop as treatment for leprosy. Hannay argues that Lok interprets negatively, as painful, in her translation of Psalm 51, the process of grace that the countess of Pembroke interprets positively, as gift, in her translation. I would suggest, instead, that Lok interprets as comfort the necessary, healing pain, whereas Sidney interprets as comforting God's erasure of pain—neither pictures a God who delights in punishment. See also Susanne Woods's more optimistic reading of Lok's poetry in "The Body Penitent," 137-40.

25. Contrast the verse translation by Mary Stuart, Queen of Scotland, of part of Psalm 51, *"L'ire de Dieu par le sang ne s'appaise,"* which stresses works, in Travitsky, 260, and 200-201.

26. All quotations are from Isabella Whitney, *A Sweet Nosgay* (1573) from *Floures of Philosophie (1572) by Hugh Plat and a Sweet Nosgay (1573) . . . by Isabella Whitney.* On the few facts and speculations available on Whitney's life, see Travitsky, *Paradise of Women,* 117-18, and Jones, *Currency of Eros,* 37. My fellow editors tell me that the giving of "spiritual bouquets" is still practiced. Mary Burke's mother made them for her mother as a child, and Karen Nelson received one from the Phillipines as a wedding gift in 1990.

27. In *Currency of Eros* Jones suggests that *Nosgay* centers on the moral maxims, the epistles illustrating the Senecan themes of the maxims (37-43). In "Writing Public Poetry," 252-53, and 256-57, Elaine Beilin views Whitney as humanist who adapts the classical genre of the epistle to the purpose of social satire. In "Isabella Whitney and the Female Legacy" (35-58) Wall reads *Nosgay* in the tradition of the female legacy or mother's advice manual, and argues strongly that we must read all the writings together as a patterned whole; Wall also briefly places Whitney's work in the context of gift exchange: "By including letters sent between family members and friends and by referring to the text's place in a gift/patronage cycle, Whitney sets up a textual exchange system within the work" (47). See also Wendy Wall, *Imprint of Gender,* 297-98.

28. "When she carefully details the streets of London," argues Wendy Wall, "describing the teeming activity and bounty they offer, Whitney casts this world as the object of her own generous bequeathing. She thus creates a myth of ownership to which she asks her reader to bear witness." ("Isabella Whitney," 50); see also Wall, *Imprint,* 301. I would argue, instead, that Whitney is creating a myth of community, where since gifts circulate abundantly, individual ownership is transient and unimportant.

29. On Mary Sidney's life, see Hogrefe, *Women of Action,* 105-27; Gary F. Waller, *Mary Sidney;* and Hannay, *Philip's Phoenix.*

30. On the Protestant politics of the Sidney Psalm translations, see Waller, "'This Matching,'" 22-31; Hannay, "'This Moses,'" 217-26, and "'Princes you as men must dy,'" 22-41.

Works Cited

Belsey, Catherine. "Constructing the Subject: Deconstructing the Text." In *Feminist Criticism and Social Change: Sex, Class, and Race in Literature and Culture,* edited by Judith Newton and Deborah Rosenfelt, 45-64. New York: Methuen, 1985.

———. *The Subject of Tragedy: Identity and Difference in Renaissance Drama.* London: Methuen, 1985.

Burnett, Mark Thornton. "Giving and Receiving: *Love's Labour's Lost* and the Politics of Exchange." *English Literary Renaissance* 23.2 (1993): 287-313.

Byrne, Muriel St. Clare, ed. *The Lisle Letters.* 6 vols. Chicago: Univ. of Chicago Press, 1981.

———. *The Lisle Letters: An Abridgement.* Selected and arranged by Bridget Boland. Chicago: Univ. of Chicago Press, 1983.

Collins, A. Jeffries, ed. *Jewels and Plate of Queen Elizabeth I: The Inventory of 1574.* London: Cambridge Univ. Press for Trustees of the British Museum, 1955.

Collinson, Patrick. *The Elizabethan Puritan Movement,* 1967. Reprint. Oxford: Oxford Univ. Press, 1991.

———. "The Role of Women in the English Reformation Illustrated by the Life and Friendships of Anne Locke." *Studies in Church History* 2 (1965): 258-72.

Davis, Natalie Zemon. "Beyond the Market: Books as Gifts in Sixteenth-Century France." *Transactions of the Royal Historical Society,* 5th ser., 33 (1983): 69-88.

Eisenstadt, S. N., and Louis Roniger. "Patron-Client Relations as a Model of Structuring Social Exchange." *Comparative Studies in Society and History* 22, no. 1 (1980): 42-77.

Evans, Robert C. *Ben Jonson and the Poetics of Patronage.* Lewisburg, Pa.: Bucknell Univ. Press, 1989.

Ezell, Margaret. *The Patriarch's Wife: Literary Evidence and the History of the Family.* Chapel Hill: Univ. of North Carolina Press, 1987.

Felch, Susan. Introduction to *The Collected Works of Anne Vaughan Lock.* Binghamton, N.Y.: Medieval and Renaissance Text Society, 1999.

Ferguson, Margaret W. "A Room Not Their Own: Renaissance Women as Readers and Writers." In *The Comparative Perspective on Literature: Approaches to Theory and Practice,* edited by Clayton Koelb and Susan Noakes, 93-116. Ithaca: Cornell Univ. Press, 1988.

Fumerton, Patricia. *Cultural Aesthetics: Renaissance Literature and the Practice of Social Ornament.* Chicago: Univ. of Chicago Press, 1991.

Gregory, C. A. *Gifts and Commodities.* London: Academic, 1982.

Hannay, Margaret. "'House-confined maids': The Presentation of Woman's Role in the *Psalmes* of the Countess of Pembroke." *English Literary Renaissance* 24, no. 1 (1994): 44-71.

———. Introduction to *Silent But for the Word: Tudor Women as Patrons, Translators, and Writers of Religious Works,* edited by Margaret Hannay, 1-14. Kent, Ohio: Kent State Univ. Press, 1985.

———. *Philip's Phoenix: Mary Sidney, Countess of Pembroke.* New York: Oxford Univ. Press, 1990.

———. "'Princes you as men must dy': Genevan Advice to Monarchs in the *Psalmes* of Mary Sidney." *English Literary Renaissance* 19, no. 1 (Dec. 1989): 22-41.

———. "'This Moses and This Miriam': The Countess of Pembroke's Role in the Legend of Sir Philip Sidney." In *Sir Philip Sidney's Achievements,* edited by M. J. B. Allen, Dominic Baker-Smith, and Arthur F. Kinney, with Margaret M. Sullivan, 217-26. New York: AMS, 1990.

———. "'When riches growes': Class Perspective in Pembroke's Psalms." *Sidney Newsletter* 13 (1994-95): 9-19.

———. "'Wisdome the Wordes': Psalm Translation and Elizabethan Women's Spirituality." *Religion and Literature* 23, no. 3 (1991): 65-82.

Harris, Barbara J. "Women and Politics in Early Tudor England." *Historical Journal* 33, no. 2 (1990): 259-82.

Hobby, Elaine. "'Discourse so unsavoury': Women's Published Writings in the 1650s." In *Women, Writing, History 1640-1740,* edited by Isobel Grundy and Susan Wiseman, 16-32. Athens: Univ. of Georgia Press, 1992.

———. *Virtue of Necessity: English Women's Writing 1649-1688.* London: Virago, 1988.

Hogrefe, Pearl. *Tudor Women: Commoners and Queens.* Ames: Iowa State Univ. Press, 1975.

———. *Women of Action in Tudor England.* Ames: Iowa State Univ. Press, 1977.

Hull, Suzanne W. *Chaste, Silent, and Obedient: English Books for Women 1475-1640.* San Marino, Calif.: Huntington Library, 1982.

Humphrey, Caroline, and Stephen Hugh-Jones, eds. *Barter, Exchange and Value: An Anthropological Approach.* Cambridge: Cambridge Univ. Press, 1992.

Jardine, Lisa. *Still Harping on Daughters: Women and Drama in the Age of Shakespeare.* Totowa, N.J.: Barnes and Noble Books, 1983.

Jones, Ann Rosalind. *The Currency of Eros: Women's Love Lyric in Europe, 1540-1620.* Bloomington: Indiana Univ. Press, 1990.

Kempe, Alfred John, ed. *The Loseley Manuscripts.* London: John Murray, 1836.

Klein, Lisa M. "Your Humble Handmaid: Elizabethan Gifts of Needlework." *Renaissance Quarterly* 50 (1997): 459-93.

Knox, John. *First Blast of the Trumpet Against the Monstrous Regiment of Women.* Geneva, 1558.

———. "To His Loving Sister, Mistres Anne Locke." In *The Works of John Knox.* Vol. 4, edited by David Laing, 237-41. Edinburgh: James Thin, 1895.

———. *The Works of John Knox,* edited by David Laing. 6 vols. Edinburgh: James Thin, 1895.

Krontiris, Tina. *Oppositional Voices: Women as Writers and Translators of Literature in the English Renaissance.* London and New York: Routledge, 1992.

Lamb, Mary Ellen. "The Agency of the Split Subject: Lady Anne Clifford and the Uses of Agency." *English Literary Renaissance* 22, no. 3 (1992): 347-68.

———. *Gender and Authorship in the Sidney Circle.* Madison: Univ. of Wisconsin Press, 1990.

Nichols, John. *Illustrations of the Manners and Expences of Antient Times in England, in the Fifteenth, Sixteenth, and Seventeenth Centuries, Deduced from the Accompts of Churchwardens, and Other Authentic Documents.* London, 1797.

———. *The Progresses and Public Processions of Queen Elizabeth.* 3 vols. London, 1823.

Roche, Thomas P. *Petrarch and the English Sonnet Sequences.* New York: AMS, 1989.

Schrift, Alan D., ed. *The Logic of the Gift: Toward an Ethic of Generosity.* New York: Routledge, 1997.

Sharp, Ronald A. "Gift Exchange and the Economics of Spirit in *The Merchant of Venice.*" *Modern Philology 83, no. 3 (1986): 250-65.*

Stallybrass, Peter. "Patriarchal Territories: The Body Enclosed." In *Rewriting the Renaissance: The Discourses of Sexual Difference in Early Modern Europe,* edited by Margaret W. Ferguson, Maureen Quilligan, and Nancy J. Vickers, 123-42. Chicago: Univ. of Chicago Press, 1986.

Stuart, Arbella. *The Letters of Lady Arbella Stuart,* edited by Sara Jayne Steen. New York: Oxford Univ. Press, 1994.

Travitsky, Betty S. "Placing Women in the English Renaissance." Introduction to *The Renaissance Englishwoman in Print: Counterbalancing the Canon,* edited by Betty S. Travitsky and Anne M. Haselkorn, 3-41. Amherst: Univ. of Massachusetts Press, 1990.

———, ed. *The Paradise of Women: Writings of Englishwomen of the Renaissance.* Westport, Conn.: Greenwood, 1981. Reprinted New York: Columbia Univ. Press, 1989.

Travitsky, Betty S., and Anne M. Haselkorn, eds. *The Renaissance Englishwoman in Print: Counterbalancing the Canon.* Amherst: Univ. of Massachusetts Press, 1990.

Travitsky, Betty S., and Adele F. Seeff, eds. *Attending to Women in Early Modern England.* Newark: Univ. of Delaware Press, 1994.

Wall, Wendy. *The Imprint of Gender: Authorship and Publication in the English Renaissance.* Ithaca: Cornell Univ. Press, 1993.

———. "Isabella Whitney and the Female Legacy." *ELH: English Literary History* 58, no. 1 (1991): 35-62.

Waller, Gary F. *Mary Sidney, Countess of Pembroke: A Critical Study of Her Writings and Literary Milieu.* Salzburg Studies in English Literature: English and Renaissance Studies, no. 87. Salzburg: Institute for English and American Studies, Univ. of Salzburg, 1979.

———. "'This Matching of Contraries': Calvinism and Courtly Philosophy in the Sidney Psalms." *English Studies* 55 (1974): 22-31.

Whitney, Isabella. *The Copy of a Letter, Lately Written in Meeter, by a yonge Gentilwoman: to her unconstant Louer. With an Admonition to al yong Gentilwomen, and to all other Mayds in general to beware of mennes flattery.* London, 1567.

———. *The Floures of Philosphie (1572) by Hugh Plat and a Sweet Nosgay (1573) and The Copy of a Letter (1567) by Isabella Whitney.* Introduction by Richard J. Panofsky. Delmar, N.Y.: Scholars' Facsimilies and Reprints, 1982.

———. *A sweet Nosgay, or pleasant posye, contayning a hundred and ten Phylosophicall Flowers.* London, 1573.

Woods, Susanne. "Aemilia Lanyer and Ben Jonson: Patronage, Authority, and Gender." *Ben Jonson Journal* 1 (1994): 15-30.

———. "The Body Pentitent: A 1560 Calvinist Sonnet Sequence." *ANQ: American Notes and Queries* 5, nos. 2-3 (1992): 137-40.

Ziegler, Georgianna. "Hand-Ma[i]de Books: The Manuscripts of Esther Inglis, Early-Modern Precursors of the Artists' Book." *English Manuscript Studies* (forthcoming).

EVE RACHELE SANDERS AND MARGARET W. FERGUSON (ESSAY DATE JANUARY 2002)

SOURCE: Sanders, Eve Rachele and Margaret W. Ferguson. "Literacies in Early Modern England." *Critical Survey* 14, no. 1 (January 2002): 1-8.

In the following essay, Sanders and Ferguson discuss the wide range of levels of literacy that existed in sixteenth-century England.

Literacy, in the sixteenth century, was construed as multiple, variable, subject to redefinition by edict from above and by practices from below. The importance of regulating changes in skills and behaviors, in particular, increased reading of the Bible, was hotly debated as the Reformation got underway. In England, the Tudor state intervened erratically, first encouraging the reading of the English Bible for all, then forbidding its reading to all but a privileged few. In 1538, every parish church was required by a royal injunction to purchase an English Bible and place it in the choir.[1] The Great Bible, published in 1540 with a new preface by the Archbishop of Canterbury, stressed the ideal of an England peopled by 'all manner' of readers of Scripture in the vernacular: 'Here may all manner of persons, men, women, young, old, learned, unlearned, rich, poor, priests, laymen, lords, ladies, officers, tenants, and mean men, virgins, wives, widows, lawyers, merchants, artificers, husbandmen, and all manner of persons, of what estate or condition soever they be, may in this book learn all things'.[2] Only three years later, however, in 1543, the self-vauntingly named Act for the Advancement of True Religion and for the Abolishment of the Contrary attempted to undo that opening of the floodgates by lowering them again to allow for only a trickle of elite readers to have access to Scripture. Reading the Bible in English was prohibited outright for women, artificers, journeymen, serving-men of the rank of yeoman and under, husbandmen and laborers; noblewomen and gentlewomen could read the Bible silently; only noblemen, gentlemen, and merchants were permitted to read it aloud to others.[3]

The contradictions of that early effort to police reading and writing, the contentitiousness of it signaled by backtracking on earlier initiatives, provide a window onto the topic of this special issue of *Critical Survey* and its theme of literacies in early modern England. The interjecting of social categories into the debate over scriptural literacy indicates the breadth and complexity of concerns stimulated by greater access to books by a greater portion of the population. In the emerging brave new world of cheap print and increasingly widespread skills in decoding vernacular texts, who would be allowed to read what? And to whom? How would various social rubrics—sex, marital status, age, occupation, wealth and class—determine who would have entry to institutions in which books were read in more or less formally determined ways? The list of no less than twenty-two different categories of potential Bible readers (men and women, young and old, learned and unlearned, etc.) invoked by Archbishop Thomas Cranmer illustrates by its exhaustiveness the mixed and uneven nature of the skills and approaches that reading designated at that time. In the hands of 'priests' or 'lawyers', in those of 'tenants and mean persons', or of 'virgins, wives, and widows', the Bible—or any other book—would have been read with different levels of fluidity, different accents, different purposes, assumptions, pleasures.

This volume presents a collaborative effort to investigate the implications of literacies (in the plural) for early modern culture. We speak here of 'literacies' because the phenomenon under scrutiny in these essays resists reduction to the kind of mono-lingual three R's (two R's if numeracy is excluded) often taken for granted today as a quantifiable standard for use in economic development programs, a standard for measuring uniform 'basic skills'. In early modern England, as the work of a growing number of scholars has shown, acquiring the ability to decipher, sound, and reproduce the letter of the emergent, not-yet-standardized national language was far more variegated, both in its procedures and in its results, than previously understood or acknowledged. Reading and writing took place in two stages, the second of which never arrived for the majority of young learners, those who would have had to abandon schooling for economic or ideological reasons about when they turned seven, the approximate age at which instruction in writing and the rudiments of Latin grammar began for the privileged rest (poorer children were expected to dedicate their labor to their families at that age; girls of all classes faced the additional hurdle of prescriptions discouraging female writing).[4]

Different type fonts and forms of script shaped different experiences of literacy. Letters learned by beginners were printed in Gothic type. Roman type, for them, was near-unreadable code. So, too, were various forms of handwriting, including the most common, italic and secretary, scripts more advanced writers alternated between or combined into a 'mixed hand'.[5] Factors such as these—varieties of script forms and type fonts, kinds of language instruction ranging from English-only to classical Latin and Greek, variable access to kinds of books and tiers of educational institutions—all helped the emergence of multiple literacies in this period: reading-only literacy, scribal-literacy, English-only literacy, vernacular foreign-language literacy, Latin-literacy, scriptural literacy, heraldic literacy, legal literacy, etc. Moreover, the relatively standardized English of the printing press, which helped serve the Protestant nationalist agenda of the Tudor state, still had to vie with rival languages, Irish and Welsh, and with its own regional variants. To illustrate that point, the printer William Caxton recounted the story of an English merchant who was rebuffed when he found

ON THE SUBJECT OF...

MARGUERITE DE NAVARRE (1492-1549)

An important figure in the transition between medieval and Renaissance literature, Marguerite de Navarre was one of the first women in Europe to write fiction. She is best known for *L'Heptaméron des Nouvelles* (1559; the *Heptameron*), a series of stories, or "novellas," primarily concerned with the themes of love and spirituality. Marguerite received a classical education and became particularly interested in literature. She moved to court when her brother became the King of France in 1515, and immersed herself not only in the social pleasures of court life but in diplomatic responsibilities and intellectual opportunities as well. Marguerite moved with her second husband, the King of Navarre, in 1527, to Navarre, an independent kingdom located between France and Spain. She continued her political activity, engaged in charitable work, and became a patron of the arts.

The stories in the *Heptameron* are framed by a narrative in which ten travellers—five men and five women of various ages and social roles—are stranded in an abbey in Navarre after a bridge is washed out, and entertain themselves for a week by storytelling. Both comedic and tragic, the stories concern love, marriage, adultery, and human weakness; they offer glimpses of aristocratic, monastic, and common life in the sixteenth century, and suggest a critical perspective on the inequities that emerge from differences in class, gender, and political power. The *Heptameron* has been praised primarily for its psychological realism and complex narrative structure. Recent scholarship focuses on the disruption of social expectations through the transgression of proscribed gender and class roles, depicted in many of the stories, as well as Marguerite's own position as an female author in the Renaissance.

himself in a different region of England and tried to purchase 'eggys' from a local household.[6] The word meant nothing to the farmwife who answered the merchant by saying she didn't speak French (in her dialect the word was 'eyren'). As this anecdote conveys, a transaction as simple as the purchase of eggs between residents of different English shires could be frustrated by lack of a common vocabulary. English itself was multiple, a designation for a host of regional dialects that emerged as a national language only gradually through concerted efforts at standardization, uniform curricula, state supervision. Moreover, as Cranmer's crisscrossing categories—sex, marital status, age, occupation, wealth and class—of potential Bible readers indicates, the varied literacies of different social groups applied in overlapping ways to the same individuals. Early moderns found themselves at the interstices of competing languages, symbolic systems for writing and deciphering them, social, institutional and professional settings requiring particularized textual and linguistic competencies.

The work of our colleagues and our work in this area contributes to a still-forming field. Literacy studies, along with the related fields of the history of reading and the history of the book, center on a set of connected topics: acquisition of reading and writing, variable practices of those skills, books and documents as material artifacts. This domain is capacious enough to accommodate the work of scholars in many disciplines, both in the social sciences and in the humanities, and to foster as well an unusual degree of information sharing and collaboration between disciplines. From our particular vantage points within that larger field, literacy studies matter outside of the contribution they make to our knowledge about reading and writing as central cultural practices in the history of much of the world (nearly all of it if we include post-Colonial history). From where we stand, from our positions as teachers in departments of English, we believe that literacy studies matter also because of the new perspectives they bring to our understanding of familiar subjects (writers, readers) and objects (books, manuscripts) of literary studies. Materials and approaches made available through literacy studies are enabling crucial reconceptualizations of received literary tradition. As a growing body of research shows, works that literary scholars have always studied—poems, plays, prose romances, sermons, letters, diaries—take on new dimensions and meanings in the context of broader changes in language and society that shaped the writing, acquisition, circulation, and reading of such texts.

This questioning of literature via literacy has sparked disagreements and debate; it has also furthered among a number of scholars a consensus about several points. First, 'literacy' is in need of redefinition. The term requires updated explanation if it is to refer usefully to the specific configuration of practical skills, in potentially multiple languages, differentially valued, that reading and writing present in a given society. Second, literacy, if we use the singular to denote the phenomenon in a general sense, was in the early modern period a domain of social contest. Most of the population of Europe between the fourth and the eighteenth centuries was unable to read or write in any language; literacy conveyed status in sixteenth and early seventeenth-century England precisely because the majority lacked advanced instruction (schooling beyond the elementary level) at a time when ordinary dealings increasingly required it (selling livestock, answering legal charges, participating in local government, etc.).[7] Finally, for all of the disparities it helped to consolidate, particularly with respect to those who lacked writing, literacy was also a source of unanticipated agency for readers. The market for books, partly responsive to the purchasing preferences of readers, gave book buyers some influence over titles and content; moreover, the uses to which readers put what they read were unpredictable, often contrary to expectations, implicit or explicit, on the part of authors or censors.

The essays in this volume present a diversity of perspectives on early modern literacies. Together, they illustrate the work of redefining literacy currently ongoing in the field. Mary Ellen Lamb's analysis of the play *The Old Wives Tale* challenges the notion that literacy and its social distribution can be understood in binary terms: literacy versus illiteracy, men versus women. She argues that that representation of literacy as a polarized phenomenon did not reflect a social reality but rather a social agenda. The very coinage 'old wives' tales' reflects a bias to promote Latinate classroom culture over and against the culture of oral narrative. In her view, literacy was a multiple phenomenon rather than a single one conceptually defined against 'illiteracy', not only because there were gradations of difference between more or less educated individuals, which were not keyed invariably to sex, but also because even the Latin-based grammar school was not impervious to oral culture, ballads and old wives tales, narratives linked with illiteracy and the illiterate. Works by writers ranging from George Peele to Philip Sidney and William Shakespeare testify to the lasting traces of orally-transmitted narratives even on minds schooled in humanist classrooms. Similarly, Janet Starner-Wright and Susan Fitzmaurice challenge the notion of a hard and fast divide between print and oral cultures. In their discussion of *The History of Edward II,* published in 1680 and believed by many modern critics to have been written by Elizabeth Cary, the authors argue that Cary, like other history writers of her day, draws upon conventions of print publishing interchangeably with those of traditional storytelling, mixing Latin phrases with proverbial sayings.

This destabilization of existing social and cultural categories by writers and readers shows why literacy was a site of contest. In her study of Roman capital letters, Bianca F.-C. Calabresi argues that uppercase letters, which evoke classical tradition and royal decrees, had the effect of bestowing dignity and high status on those who learned to form them (uppercase letters were considered an advanced skill that could be acquired only after mastering that of writing lowercase ones). To take the example of the forged letter that appears in *Twelfth Night,* Maria's use of Roman capitals in inscribing that document displays her social aspirations and, indeed, achieves them in part. As Elizabeth Rivlin also reminds us in her reading of *The Comedy of Errors,* the fact that literacy was perceived as a marker of hierarchy made it also an instrument for upsetting hierarchy. The drama, then, highlights the conflictual dimensions of literacy by heightening our sense of how ambiguous writing can be as a marker of position, hence how indeterminate or superficial also the nature of social standing itself. Judith Rose explains that among Quakers requiring women to write down their prophecies constituted a means of restricting their expression: 'once women's prophecies were written down, they could be censored, witheld, or circulated only in manuscript; they were therefore more manageable, less incendiary'. Following the Restoration, however, what had been a source of restriction during the Civil War era turned into a force for enabling women's expression when Quaker schools, unlike other educational establishments, included writing on the curriculum for girls. Ironically, innovations introduced as instruments for the containment of one generation provided another with tools for social mobility and intellectual training.

The shift in perspective that brings into clearer focus the activities of Quaker prophets, old wives and man servants, also brings to our attention the behaviors of readers, another previously underexamined category of participants in literate culture. Previously, only the author or the text (after the proverbial 'death of the author') was ascribed proprietary rights over meaning or play of meaning; more recently, due to the painstaking work of many scholars, the reader now is understood to have played a crucial role as well in working out the meanings texts accrued. Readers were not (and are not) passive recipients of content; they argued with the texts they read; they emended and corrected them, cut from the pages elements they found valuable or objectionable; they added to them their own owner marks, marginal comments, insignia, poems, unrelated notes and scribblings.[8] Often, readers formed associations and at times larger social networks through their reading. In the roles of consumers, they exerted influence as well over textual production. As Jennifer Hellwarth demonstrates, early modern midwifery manuals give clear indication that their authors, male medical practitioners, though dismissive of midwives, nevertheless were reliant on a female readership for information and financial support. This point about the agency of the reader arises in a more figurative context in Rivlin's essay. She notes that one of the servants in Shakespeare's *Comedy of Errors* is shown at first to be a passive recipient of blows that inscribe his body as a text, as 'if the skin were parchment and the blows . . . were ink' (3.1.13); however, the servant then asserts his own explanation of those marks—his own bodily text—and emerges as an independent reader-interpreter. The humor of the scene depends not only on the mercurial qualities of the identities of the two pairs of identical masters and identical servants but also on those of writing itself, at once indelible in its mark and unstable in its meaning.

'Reading, viewing and listening', Roger Chartier has commented, 'are, in fact, so many intellectual attitudes which, far from subjecting consumers to the omnipotence of the ideological or aesthetic message that supposedly conditions them, make possible reappropriation, redirection, defiance, or resistance'.[9] The present collection of essays adds to our understanding of the subjective and social dimensions of literate practices, their availability to personal and communal adaptation and innovation. Scholars, as readers themselves, interpret newly texts that have been read differently before; in so doing, they redefine meanings and concepts in ways that may go against doxical or ideological definitions. The definitions of literacy emerging from current discussion among scholars in this field are multiple, provisional, and often counter-intuitive. They are opening conceptual territory for newly important types of evidence (the marked copy of a book rather than the clean copy, the margin along with the central text, the 'paratext' or prefatory materials preceding the 'main' text) and newly shared questions: is it possible to measure literacy with any precision if we define it to be multiple and compound? In early modern England, how did literate practices participate in the formation of the self? (And, in this age of computer literacy, how do they continue to do so to this day?) What is the relation between literacy and literature? These questions continue to be the work of many volumes and many scholars. They point the way to some larger implications of the multiple literacies documented here.

Notes

1. Joan Simon, *Education and Society in Tudor England* (Cambridge: Cambridge University Press, 1966), 175.
2. C. H. Williams, ed., *English Historical Documents 1485-1558* (New York: Oxford University Press, 1967), 827.
3. H. S. Bennett, *English Books and Readers: 1475 to 1557* (Cambridge: Cambridge University Press, 1970), 27.
4. W. J. Frank Davies, *Teaching Reading in Early England,* 1973; rpt. New York: Barnes & Noble, 1974.
5. Keith Thomas, 'The Meaning of Literacy in Early Modern England,' in *The Written Word: Literacy in Transition,* ed. Gerd Baumann (Oxford: Clarendon Press, 1986), 97-131.
6. Margaret Ferguson discusses the anecdote and its implications for the linguistic diversity of English in her book, *Dido's Daughters: Literacy, Gender and Empire in Early Modern England* (Chicago: University of Chicago Press, 2002). Caxton tells the story in the preface to his translation of Virgil's *Aeneid* (*Eneydos,* as Caxton's title has it) published in 1490.
7. Keith Thomas points out that in early modern England, 'It . . . became increasingly common to require that holders of local offices should be literate and to discharge them if they were not.' Moreover, literacy was an asset in commercial transactions as well, since 'anyone involved in business ran the risk of being cheated if he could not read a document or a set of accounts' ('The Meaning of Literacy in Early Modern England,' in *The Written Word: Literacy in Transition,* ed. Gerd Baumann [Oxford: Clarendon Press, 1986], 110).
8. In his 1473 English translation of a French collection of philosophers' sayings, *The Dictes and Sayeings of the Philosophers,* Caxton acknowledges the proprietary attitudes of contemporary readers toward their books when he recommends that any reader offended by certain misogynistic maxims of Socrates (omitted by the translator and reinserted by Caxton) simply remove that passage, 'wyth a penne race it out or ellys rente the leef oute of the booke'; for the reader's convenience, Caxton printed the passage as a detachable appendix at the back of the book (cited by Susan Schibanoff, 'Taking the Gold Out of Egypt: The Art of Reading as a Woman,' in *Gender and Reading: Essays on Readers, Texts, and Contexts,* eds. Elizabeth A. Flynn and Patrocinio P. Schweickart [Baltimore: The Johns Hopkins University Press, 1986], 85). Stephen Orgel provides the example of an owner of Holinshed's *Chronicles* who added to his copy heraldic shields of families figured in the narrative; a subsequent owner of the volume cut out some of the shields ('Records of Culture,' in *Books and Readers in Early Modern England.* Eds. Jennifer Andersen and Elizabeth Sauer [Philadelphia: University of Pennsylvania Press, 2002], 282-9).
9. Roger Chartier, *Cultural History: Between Practices and Representations,* trans. Lydia G. Cochrane (Ithaca, New York: Cornell University Press, 1988), 41.

POLITICS

HILDA L. SMITH (ESSAY DATE 1998)

SOURCE: Smith, Hilda L. "Introduction: Women, Intellect, and Politics: Their Intersection in Seventeenth-Century England." In *Women Writers and the Early Modern British Political Tradition,* edited by Hilda L. Smith, pp. 1-14. Cambridge, England: Cambridge University Press, 1998.

In the following essay, Smith notes difficulties in trying to determine seventeenth-century women's understanding of politics and their roles in the political arena.

Relating women's intellectual history to British political thought in the early modern era leaves one in a perpetual state of schizophrenia. With rare exceptions, scholars working in these distinct areas do not pursue the same primary texts, or trust the judgments of the same set of contemporary scholars. Women's intellectual contribution to the era has been studied mostly through biography, or through a focus on individual authors, with a very few—Aphra Behn; Mary Astell; Margaret Cavendish, duchess of Newcastle; and Margaret Fell Fox—garnering the overwhelming attention. Otherwise, women have fallen within categories formed by broader alliances: sectarian women, Leveller women, sympathizers for royalist or revolutionary causes. Or, they have been tied to their genres, as writers of meditations, poets, tractarians, playwrights, and authors of domestic advice.[1]

There has been, and perhaps this is wise, little attempt to characterize women's writings generally, and virtually no attempt to do so for those of non-fiction authors whose primary interest was politics. In contemplating disparate approaches to seventeenth-century women's political writings, a number of questions arise in this volume based on traditional assumptions concerning women and politics. How can women write about what they cannot do? or about what is considered outside, and, by some, antithetical to their nature? or about which they have been kept essentially ignorant? All of these realities covertly and overtly confronted women when they wrote about political topics in the early modern period. How could they presume to give advice across such a large divide? And, when an individual woman did offer such advice, what was her inspiration, what empowered her to speak?

In other words, what did politics mean for the women included in this volume, and early modern women more broadly? To what extent and in what proportions was it composed of office holding (either by a female monarch or by lesser officials), of attendance at court, of involvement in parliamentary elections, of jury service, or of broadly defined duties and obligations of property holders and burghers in their locale? Certainly, as with others of their era, they would have thought more about obligations, less about privileges, and little about rights when discussing politics.

In offering analyses that begin to deal with these broader questions, while presenting a range of women authors not often known outside of feminist scholarly circles, this volume addresses a dual purpose. The first is to analyze and place in context the works of a range of women writing on politics from the fourteenth through the eighteenth century. The second is to provide an analysis of the political and intellectual structures in which these, and other, women operated. This volume will treat women's significant contributions to peace theory, to political thought, to revolutionary debates, to religious disputes, and to the operation of government more widely. But it will also discuss how their societies defined the political and where that definition intersected with views of women's nature and appropriate roles.

Women intellectuals faced a myriad of institutional and scholarly resistance to their writing and their ideas. Central to this resistance was the identification in the minds of their readers, and among later scholarly commentators, of learning with a few academic institutions and professional societies which excluded women. Intellectual histories for the period focus almost wholly on the writings of a few great male thinkers, and institutional histories focus overwhelmingly on Oxford, Cambridge, and the Royal Society in England, the University of Paris and the French Academy in France, and Lutheran theologians in the Imperial German states. Even with the great growth of popular political and legal publications by the mid-seventeenth century, there was still an acceptance of traditional institutions as offering not simply the atmosphere most conducive to scholarly creativity, but also its validation. The court was a competing institution for intellectual and cultural productivity in both France and England, and women fared better there than among more strictly academic institutions. Yet in both linguistic and visual imagery a scholar, an author, a learned or wise "person" was clearly situated within university and professional circles and embodied a male figure.

Reflecting their existence outside the boundaries of institutionalized learning, women were not expected to produce scholarly treatments on a range of topics. Rather, the types of writings expected from them were circumscribed. If they chose to write on religious subjects, most appropriate were works of private meditation or stories of personal faith, but not theological treatises or anything verging upon a sermon. Nor were they to critique ecclesiastical structure, as a number of Puritan and Quaker women did. And, if women wished to write works of advice, they should be directed to other women (or children if the authors were mothers). There was probably no category of acceptable political writings on the part of women, but, again, personal memoirs or pleading for the views or needs of male political allies was most apt to be tolerated. A female author was to avoid wide-ranging analyses and criticisms of the political system, or of a single political leader. And few women authors, at least during the seventeenth century, dealt with political topics unfiltered through a religious lens. During times of crises, Leveller and Quaker women used arguments that blended a need for immediate action or redress, biblical and historical injunctions to act, and the contention that they were as responsible for the well-being of society as their male colleagues. But they did not demand their own political rights—only, at points, a political voice.[2]

Why not? I should like to throw out a couple of suggestions: one, that these seventeenth-century women considered women's exclusion from all public and political roles less certain than we've come to believe today; thus they did not have to offer an explicit demand for such status when at least some women held it. And, women during the seventeenth century had at once a broader and more inclusive understanding of politics than we possess today. They considered local office holding, political obligations of families among the governing class, as well as voting and political rights, as constituting politics, while we would be more apt to equate the term only with the latter. Thus it was necessary for women writers to deal with broader issues of women's situation in seventeenth-century England, than simply a demand for political rights.

Margaret Cavendish, duchess of Newcastle's *Sociable Letters* (1664) offers one of the best examples of a seventeenth-century author grappling with the integrated realities that circumscribed women's political standing. Cavendish was both a royalist and a feminist who raised some of the most profound questions about the intersection of women's place in government, the common law, marriage, and motherhood during the 1600s. In her oft-quoted, evolving understanding of women's place in the state, she started with women's ignorance: "and, as for the matter of governments, we women understand them not." But Cavendish did not stop there. She next contended that women were almost not a part of government, then pointed out their not swearing either to loyalty or supremacy, and finally concluded with women's separation from the state: "If we be not citizens in the Commonwealth, I know no reason we should be subjects to the Commonwealth." It is not easy to decipher the duchess of Newcastle's intent, but I should like to stress her argument that women cannot be forced to serve two masters, a husband and the state. She was inclined to believe that women were not subjects at all, but, she concluded, if they were, "it is to our husbands." Ignoring the political standing of single women, Cavendish based her arguments on the married state.

Yet she was hardly alone in lumping all women under the disabilities of the wife. The most famous example was likely from the 1632 treatise, *Lawes Resolutions of Womens Rights* which noted that all women were understood "either as married or to be married." While women were not tied to the universalizing principles of individualism that were emerging for men during the century, they were defined by a particularist set of qualities denoting their essential and proper state as one of dependence, not individuality.[3]

For seventeenth-century women, it was likely more difficult than for men writing about politics, to ignore familial constraints while investing the state with power and authority, and the citizen with independence and judgment. Thomas Hobbes, for example, acknowledged little conflict between empowering women as mothers in the state of nature when he claimed in *De Cive* that "every woman that bears children, becomes both a *Mother,* and a *Lord*" and his definition of the family within civil society that not only empowered the father, but treated the mother as non existent. "A *Father,* with his *sonnes* and *servants* growne into a civill Person by vertue of his paternall jurisdiction is called a FAMILY."[4]

Women who wrote about politics, and did it from a consciously woman-centered perspective, embraced both the realities of some women's power and the need to define the state more broadly so that the family's reflection and engendering of political status would be recognized. But historians of political thought have, for the most part, ignored gender conflicts in earlier texts or in their own work. For them, politics have only occurred in a public arena, within established modes of governing, and among definable institutions. While feminist political theorists, along with women's historians, have raised questions about the issues of women's exclusion from such a realm, they have done less to redefine the realm altogether. Questions have been raised in two areas: first, the feminist contention that the personal is political and thus what happens in the home, the school, the office, etc. is clearly based on power relationships, sets of strategies, and covert and overt agreements about the parameters of discourse and action. And, second, a myriad set of arguments contend that masculine and feminine qualities and spheres must be taken into account in defining the political, so that supposedly non-gendered terms such as public, reason, objective, and (on the negative side) less nurturing, empathetic, emotional, and sensitive are termed masculine, while the feminine is posited in opposition to positive male qualities and embodies those considered lacking in men.[5]

Such thinking is seen as anachronistic when applied to early modern political thought and political realities. And this criticism does not seem off the mark. As many social historians have contended, the distinction between private and public is to a great extent a product of the nineteenth century and the growth of bourgeois culture—but already under construction with the growing importance of sensibility during the eighteenth century. In the seventeenth century when the household functioned more clearly as a unit of the state in which the father established public order and enforced accepted moral and religious values for his various dependents, the distinctions between public and private, political and nonpolitical, were less clear. And, when dynastic politics and a court system meant socializing, plotting marriage and kinship strategies, and included a patronage system that used the standing and contacts of both male and female members of the governing class, then what was masculine and feminine, private and public, political and nonpolitical was blurred.[6]

Yet, the broadly gendered nature of early modern politics and citizenship has received little attention. Gender constructions are employed without their significance for actual men and women being clarified. Examples are numerous, but one example appears in John Guy's essay in *The Varieties of British Political Thought, 1500-1800,* where he delineated the importance of counsel to a prince in Tudor political thought. Generally a discussion of the role of gender is simply absent, but, when noted, it is usually as an unanalyzed aside such as in Guy's essay where he states: "In this mode *imperium* was represented as male and *consilium* as female: their relationship was conjugal. (A married woman shared in the administration of her husband's household and mitigated his *imperium* just as equity tempered the rigour of the common law.)"[7] Leaving this gendered terminology, he concludes that "good counsel" negotiates the difference between "order and chaos," and that advising rulers away from tyranny and toward "the ways of virtue and honesty" constituted "the touchstone of government." As with others, Guy does not mention women's absence as counselors or as authors of any of the classic humanist texts on the subject, nor assess what this gendered quality might mean for the men offering counsel and the men (and some women) who received it. Later in the same volume William Lamont, after presenting a long list of early and mid-seventeenth-century thinkers, without a single female voice, states that scholars are "not listen[ing] attentively enough to what the seventeenth-century source is saying"; and follows with, "if what he or she is saying seems actually contradictory" one must expand the set of contextual works. Although relevant writings by women clearly existed for Lamont's topic, the Puritan revolution, they appear only in this feminine pronoun.[8]

Also, two of the essays in *Varieties of British Political Thought* discuss Henry Parker's early arguments for parliamentary supremacy by undercutting Charles I's authority as built upon patriarchal authority within the family. Yet neither mentions Parker's clearly gendered argument about both the place of independent men in the state and the role of the wife in the household. The husband, he contends in *Observations upon some of his Majesties late Answers and Expresses* (1642), wields greater authority than the king because "the wife is inferior in nature, and was created for the assistance of man"; but, he continues, "it is otherwise in the State between man and man, for *that* civill difference which is for civill ends, and those ends are, that wrong and violence be repressed by one, for the good of all, not that servility and drudgery may be imposed upon all for the pompe of one." Yet, as is typical of other histories of political thought, such references to gender-based justifications in disputes over the legitimacy and sovereignty of a ruler are not explored.[9]

As we reassess the history of British political thought through the lens of gender, how would we come to see it differently? I think up to this point we do not have sufficient knowledge or a sufficiently integrated perspective to answer this question. Feminist scholars have contended the following: the writings of political theorists are masculine and thus have no relevance for women; or certain constructs such as the social contract were not intended for or do not work for women; or the canonical works of political thought are studied and thought of in a manner not afforded works by women; or such works, when in the rare instances they speak about women, do so outside their systematic analysis of the state; or, it is all pretty irrelevant for real women interested in politics because the canonical texts, and their later analyses, are mostly not about women, but about the supposedly "feminine," and its symbolic expressions. While each of these points of view may hold merit, it is difficult to bring them together to offer an integrated critique of political theory. We need, therefore, to think more clearly about how we apply gender when speaking of political writings and political actions in the past.

In considering early modern England, two propositions might prove useful: (1) that women had a clear, widespread, and real presence in political and economic structure and (2) that language was so constructed as to deny both the reality and the significance of their standing. Certainly the reality of women's standing is intertwined with how contemporaries and later scholars have defined it. In dealing first with the second point, it seems hard to grasp when language is meant to be gender inclusive or exclusive. Are there any principles or clues that can guide us here? One such pattern has struck me: that when an author wants to highlight the universal significance of a phenomenon or quality, he is most apt to ignore women, and the only sure, but not the only, indication of inclusion is a precise reference. For example, in Tudor politician Thomas Starkey's proposed council of fourteen to govern for parliament when not in session, his language was purposely inclusive, yet so framed that women were not directly represented. His council was "to represent the whole body of the people . . . to see unto the liberty of the whole body of the rea[l]m, and to resist all tyranny which by any manner may grow upon the whole commonalty." Made up of clergy, judges and four "of the most wise citizens of London," its composition and representation surely did not incorporate women. But Thomas More, who was upset over anti-clerical sentiments being written in English, lamented that the work's author "would have the lay people both men and women look on them." Obviously "lay people" would have sufficed, but More wanted to emphasize that he meant to include women among those who could not normally read Latin. To what extent, then, are we to believe thinkers meant to include women only when they specifically referred to them?[10]

In studying the gendered nature of early modern English guilds, I was struck by the large amount of evidence, in statutes, in aldermanic records, and in apprenticeship rolls, to support the view that women were full members of guilds, that they wore livery, and that members of guilds were consistently called "brethern and sistern" or "freemen and freewomen," but that later historians utilized terms such as brothers, brotherhood, or members, that obscured the reality of women's standing. Earlier documents might use generic nouns such as members, but that term would be followed by a descriptor that noted it referred to both sexes. An example comes from Henry VIII's charter to establish a separate guild for London cloth workers in which he stated that the master and wardens should "make and have among the Citizens of the same City, being then Brethren and Sisters of the same Fraternity of Cloathworkers and the most sufficient thereunto, one livery or Robe." Later accounts, however, ignored the defining clause and employed only the inclusive noun, leading others to think that only men were intended. And many property-owning women shared with their male counterparts an amalgam of office holding, appointing others to office and voting. Perhaps what is needed is more serious attention to the underlying gender distinctions in terms, even when we assume that we know their meanings; and to wonder whether we are asking the right questions about women's political standing in the seventeenth century, or the early modern period more broadly.[11]

If we focus too narrowly on issues of rights, and voting, as constituting political standing, are we imposing a more recent understanding of politics than seventeenth-century authors would have employed? We need to ask more directly just what realities did early modern women take as a given about the standing of women from the governing classes; did they assume a greater role for women than we have seen or acknowledged based on our current-day lens and lack of a detailed or integrated picture of women's political actions on the local level, or even at court?[12]

Finally, it is important to give more attention to the gendered nature of male citizenship, and especially its tie to a system of male maturation in which men prepared to be independent adults, head families, own property, do politics, and be active economic actors. Much has been written on the growth of modern individualism, but less has been done about its gendered nature. Such investigations should lead to a revision of the accepted public/private divide. As men prepared for their independence in forms that ranged from apprenticeship to the Grand Tour, there evolved institutions both to support them and to provide ideological, professional, and emotional support. They included grammar schools and universities, guild structures, professional societies, local county societies, and even life at court. These institutions allowed men to take their private world with them into the public. Thus the nurturing, supportive function ascribed to the family which has enabled men to do productive work outside the home existed for them outside of the home as well. This support included payment in kind: high table and housing offered by universities; funeral arrangements, banquets, social honors by guilds; and recognition and camaraderie among a range of political, professional, and social groupings.

For example, when lawyers and judges were required to go on assize rounds, they could count upon the bar mess to provide them with all the comforts of home. In an account of the eighteenth-century bar, Daniel Duman (while failing to indicate its gender implications) notes that the bar mess was mostly involved with eating, entertainment, and drinking, but "in addition the messes acted as guardians of the professional conduct of the members and fostered a feeling of professional brotherhood and communal spirit among the barristers." Such ties between the socialization of adult males and their economic status blurred the distinction between personal and public life and created a system which taught and conferred a particular status and then reinscribed its nature and significance continually through the symbols and institutions that supported it. And there were so many institutions that continually aided men, inscribed their status, and supported their public and individual successes, that it is hard to argue that men embodied a distinctly public world, separate from the private world of the home. Surely this ability to integrate the support of the private into the world of the public was essential in distinguishing between men and women, even though individual women, usually single or widowed, did quite comparable things to their brothers.[13]

How can we, then, relate the reality of women's active political and economic roles to these institutions that validated and supported men's public standing? Women's public economic activities were broadly accepted, but when economic effort was used to buttress public standing or become the basis for citizenship, authorities resisted such a connection for women. Yet guild membership and urban citizenship empowered men in their political efforts in England both during the Civil War and in the 1680s. While often performing the same functions as men, or similar ones, women seemed most excluded from the validation of public recognition and symbolic expressions of economic independence and the qualities of citizenship.[14]

Such confused realities are connected to women's failure to employ universalizing symbols, tying the public and political role of their group to discussions of what constituted political standing and national identity more broadly, as did men. For example, John Wildman, when defending in 1650 the free election of city officers by a cross-section of London freemen, unhampered by the dominant power of the mayor and council of aldermen, claimed that the privileges of London citizens, "in their elections of their chief officers," were tied to "those very foundations of Common Right which the parliament have declared to us." Such privileges were based on the principle "that the original of all just power under God proceeds from the People." In opposing aldermanic self-perpetuation, he does not include the interests of independent women, but does threaten the mayor and aldermen thus: "take some speedy course that the blood of the Fatherless and the Widow may not stick to these walls."[15]

In this rhetorical claim, as in so many others, women are characterized in a restricted way: as the whore of Babylon, as silly women open to the lure of competing religions, as the needy exemplified as widows, as the unlearned who are taken in by superficial arguments, or, on the positive side, as the naturally pious, or good, or caring, or peaceful. But it is difficult to imagine when women might say: "we as midwives, as rearers of children, as seamstresses, etc." represent that group tied to "those very foundations of Common Right which the parliament have declared to us." They may be included at some points, but it seems they can virtually never link their identity as a group of women, or women in a certain role, to the central qualities of the nation, or of humanity. To function effectively in politics, and as political thinkers, is it necessary for women to be able to incorporate such universal symbols of human nature and aspirations in their goals or vision of themselves? What is the power, then, of Wildman's call to the rights granted all the people, during an internal dispute with the mayor and aldermen of London? And how much has men's continual use of such imagery, and later scholars' failure to deconstruct such use on grounds of gender, contributed to the identification of men with the political realm? And, on the other side, how much has women's rare (and even more rarely successful) use of such universal symbols contributed to their absence (and supposed absence) from that realm?

To answer these questions, we need to complicate our understanding of gender values in early modern political thought. Not merely will we gain clues from listening to women who have been omitted from the canon, but we will gain from seeing male theorists' views of the relationship of gender to the state in more complex terms. Both Hobbes and Locke held internally inconsistent, or at the least, evolving opinions about the nature of men and women, their relationship, their roles within the family, and their connection to the state. Hobbes shifts from his independent, powerful mother within the state of nature to a powerless/nonexistent wife under the state, and Locke shifts from equal honor due both parents in his *First Treatise* to a state formed by male property owners to protect their individual interests in the *Second*. Yet examining Hobbes's language in his discussion of the nature of dominion offers some clues as to conflicted views about sex difference and its relevance to the state.

He notes:

> Among children the Males carry the preheminence, in the begining perhaps, because for the most part (although not always) they are fitter for the administration of greater matters, but specially

> of wars; but afterwards, when it was grown a custome, because that custome was not contradicted; and therefore the will of the *Father,* unlesse some other custome or signe doe clearly repugne it, is to be interpreted in favour of them.[16]

One possible reading of this passage, and one that I lean toward, is that of a man hedging his bets and displaying discomfort with an easy acceptance of male superiority or male rule. Hobbes, for whom logic and reason were paramount, finally finds justification for any sexual difference in power and ability only on grounds of custom. Before he reaches the refuge of a customary explanation for male preeminence, he includes four phrases which question or limit the nature of male superiority: "in the beginning perhaps," "for the most part," "although not alwayes," and "specially of wars." And, even after reaching the point where male superiority "was grown a custome," he still does not seem home free and continues to write hesitantly in support of language concerning custom-bestowed ability and authority. The legitimacy of custom is acceptable only "because that custome was not contradicted," and remained subject to the following limitation: "unless some other custome or signe doe clearly repugne it." And his final positive phrase is hardly an outright acceptance of patriarchal authority "[it] is to be interpreted in favour of them."[17]

Analyzing such language more carefully can aid a reassessment of the operation of gender in early modern politics. We can clearly learn much both through reading the political writings of women and through analyzing the gender assumptions embedded within the intellectual and political structures of the period. This volume is intended as a step in that direction.

Notes

1. Treatments of women's writings during the seventeenth century, among more recent works, include my *Reason's Disciples: Seventeenth-Century English Feminists* (Urbana: University of Illinois Press, 1982), Sara Heller Mendelson's *The Mental World of Stuart Women: Three Studies* (Amherst: University of Massachusetts Press, 1987), and, among those studies treating women's religious works, Phyllis Mack's *Visionary Women: Ecstatic Prophecy in Seventeenth-Century England* (Berkeley: University of California Press, 1992), Patricia Crawford's *Women and Religion in England, 1500-1720* (London: Routledge, 1993), and Hilary Hinds's *God's Englishwomen: Seventeenth-Century Radical Sectarian Writing and Feminist Criticism* (Manchester: Manchester University Press, 1996). Recent studies and editions of an individual writer's publications include: Margaret Cavendish, *The Blazing World and Other Writings,* ed. Kate Lilley (London: Penguin Books, 1994) and *The Sociable Letters,* ed. James Fitzmaurice (New York: Garland Publishing, 1997); Mary Astell, *The First English Feminist: Reflections upon Marriage and Other Writings,* ed. Bridget Hill (New York: St. Martin's Press, 1986), and most recently, *Astell, Political Writings,* ed. Patricia Springborg (Cambridge: Cambridge University Press, 1996), as well as a biography by Ruth Perry, *The Celebrated Mary Astell* (Chicago: University of Chicago Press, 1986). Annotative bibliographies and commentaries on seventeenth-century women's writings include Elaine Hobby's *Virtue of Necessity: English Women's Writing, 1646-1688* (Ann Arbor: University of Michigan Press, 1988) and Hilda L. Smith and Susan Cardinale's *Women and the Literature of the Seventeenth Century: An Annotated Bibliography Based on Wing's Short-Title Catalogue* (Westport, Conn.: Greenwood Press, 1990). For the eighteenth century, there are no broad studies of women's non-fiction writing, but there is a collection of women's writings compiled by Bridget Hill (London: Allen and Unwin, 1984) and studies, biographies, and editions of the work of individual writers including *The Republican Virago: The Life and Times of Catharine Macaulay, Historian* by Bridget Hill (Oxford: Clarendon Press, 1992), Virginia Sapiro's *A Vindication of Political Virtue: The Political Theory of Mary Wollstonecraft* (Chicago: University of Chicago Press, 1992), *The Works of Mary Wollstonecraft* in seven volumes, edited by Janet Todd and Marilyn Butler (London: Pickering, 1989) and Janet Todd's edition of *Mary Wollstonecraft: Political Writings* (Toronto: University of Toronto Press, 1993), as well as biographies of Wollstonecraft by Eleanor Flexner (New York: Coward, McCann and Geohegan, 1972), Jennifer Lorch (New York: Berg, 1990), and Claire Tomalin (London: Weidenfeld and Nicolson, 1974). The vast majority of scholarship on women's writings during the 1700s has been on their works of fiction, especially as early novelists.
2. There has been a great deal of scholarship on the nature of women's writings. Perhaps most useful for an assessment of their religious and political views, and the prescriptions for such views for the period 1640-60, appears in *Pamphlet Wars: Prose in the English Revolution,* ed. James Holstun (London: Cass, 1992). The nature of women's religious writings and efforts is drawn most fully in Phyllis Mack's *Visionary Women.* Of the 637 works published by women from 1641 to 1700, 55 percent were on religious topics, and of these, 171 titles were from Quaker women (Smith and Cardinale, *Women and the Literature of the Seventeenth Century,* xii-xiii). A recent treatment of women Levellers by Ann Hughes, "Gender and Politics in Leveller Literature", appears in *Political Culture and Cultural Politics in Early Modern England,* eds. Susan Ammusen and Mark Kishlansky (Manchester: Manchester University Press, 1995). Greatest attention to women's personal censorship is presented in Elaine Hobby's *Virtue of Necessity,* and a recent and broad overview of the prescriptions for, and the nature of, women's writings (while tilted toward literary works) can be found in *Women and Literature in Britain, 1500-1700,* ed. Helen Wilcox (Cambridge: Cambridge University Press, 1996).
3. Margaret Cavendish, *Sociable Letters,* 25-26; *The Lawes Resolutions of Womens Rights: Or, The Lawes Provision for Woemen* (London: Printed by the Assignes of John More, 1632), 7.
4. Thomas Hobbes, *De Cive,* the English Version, ed. Howard Warrender (Oxford: Clarendon Press, 1983), 122-26. In addition to this assessment of women's authority within the state of nature, and their ultimate exclusion from the family in its relationship to the

state, Hobbes similarly discussed women's standing in chapter 20 of *The Leviathan,* which includes the following:

> there be always two that are equally parents: the dominion therefore over the child, should belong equally to both; . . . which is impossible; for no man can obey two masters. And whereas some have attributed the dominion to the man only, as being of the more excellent sex; they misreckon in it . . . If there be no contract, the dominion is in the mother.
>
> (*Leviathan, Or the Matter, Forme and Power of a Commonwealth, Ecclesiastical and Civil,* ed. Michael Oakshott, Oxford: Blackwell, 1947, 130-31)

5. While works on traditional political thought and works in feminist political theory differ fundamentally in approach and subject matter, they are similar in one respect. Both consistently omit treatment of women's political writing. Two important collections which have recently appeared on early modern political thought, *Political Discourse in Early Modern Britain,* eds. Nicholas Phillipson and Quentin Skinner (Cambridge: Cambridge University Press, 1993) and *The Varieties of British Political Thought, 1500-1800,* ed. J. G. A. Pocock (Cambridge: Cambridge University Press, 1993) continue the pattern of omitting women authors—although there is a mention of one or two in the Pocock volume—and not treating women as political actors. Of feminist approaches to political thought, an older work such as Susan Okin's *Women in Western Political Thought* (Princeton: Princeton University Press, 1979) does offer historical grounding for conceptions of women by political theorists, but the work moves from Plato to Aristotle to Rousseau to Mill, and only mentions Mary Wollstonecraft once. More recent treatments, such as the collection *Feminists Theorize the Political,* eds. Judith Butler and Joan Scott (New York: Routledge, 1992), include mention of some women writers (here, George Sand and Hannah Arendt), but seldom placed within their intellectual context and rather studied as a lesson for current feminist theorizing. Other works such as Wendy Brown's *Manhood and Politics: A Feminist Reading in Political Theory* (Totowa, N.Y.: Rowman and Littlefield, 1988) and Christine di Stefano's *Configurations of Masculinity: A Feminist Perspective on Modern Political Theory* (Ithaca, N.Y.: Cornell University Press, 1991), conceptualize political theory and politics as a masculine arena; while offering useful critiques of the often unstated equation of male with political, still one effect of these works is to deny the existence of women's political writings, or to remove such writings from the intellectual and political debates they helped shape.

6. There are numerous treatments of the role of the family and gender in the construction of local communities and national politics in early modern England, as well as women's role at court. For discussion of these topics see Susan D. Amussen, *An Ordered Society: Gender and Class in Early Modern England, 1560-1720* (New York: Columbia University Press, 1988), Keith Wrightson, *English Society, 1580-1680* (London: Routledge, 1993), and an article by Barbara Harris on women's role in the Tudor court (*Historical Journal* 33(2) [1990]: 259-81), Linda Levy Peck's discussion of women's role in "Benefits, Brokers and Beneficiaries: The Culture of Exchange in Seventeenth-Century England," *Court, Country and Culture: Essays on Early Modern British History in Honor of Perez Zagorin* (Rochester: University of Rochester Press, 1992), 109-28, and on the importance of the duchess of Portsmouth in access to power and policy formation during the reign of Charles II in Nancy Klein Maguire, "The Duchess of Portsmouth: English Royal Consort and French Politician, 1670-85," *The Stuart Court and Europe: Essays in Politics and Political Culture* (Cambridge: Cambridge University Press, 1996), 247-73. For the best discussion of the developing ideology of sex differences that underlay the separate spheres ideology of the nineteenth century, see G. J. Barker-Benfield, *The Culture of Sensibility: Sex and Society in Eighteenth-Century Britain* (Chicago: University of Chicago Press, 1992).

7. John Guy, "The Henrician Age," in Pocock, *The Varieties of British Political Thought,* 16; *Political Discourse in Early Modern Britain* includes a range of less prominent political writers, but still omits any women authors, or any analysis on the place of women or the role of gender in politics except in mentioning individual queens.

8. William Lamont, "The Puritan Revolution: A Historiographical Essay," in *The Varieties of British Political Thought,* ed. Pocock, 19.

9. *The Varieties of British Political Thought,* 132-33, 152-56.

10. Ibid., 19; Thomas More, *Selected Letters,* ed. Elizabeth Frances Rogers (New Haven: Yale University Press, 1961), 95-105.

11. The Charter of the Company of Clothworkers of London (London, 1648), 1-4; *The Ordinances of the Clothworkers' Company together with . . . fullers & Shearmen of the city of London,* transcribed from the Originals (London: Clothworkers Company, 1881), 13-22.

12. The most comprehensive study of women's early political standing remains C. C. Stopes, *British Freewomen: Their Historical Privilege* (London: S. Sonnenschein, 1894).

13. Daniel Duman, *The Judicial Bench in England, 1727-1875* (London: Royal Historical Society, 1982).

14. See Natalie Davis's essay on the gendered nature of the crafts in sixteenth-century Lyon in her *Society and Culture in Early-Modern France* (Stanford, Calif.: Stanford University Press, 1975) and Merry E. Wiesner's discussion of women as skilled artisans in *Working Women in Renaissance Germany* (New Brunswick, N.J.: Rutgers University Press, 1986).

15. *London's Liberties, Or a Learned Argument of Law & Reason, upon Saturday, December 14, 1650* (London: Printed by Ja. Cottrel for James Calver, 1651), preface, 4-5.

16. Hobbes, *De Cive,* 128.

17. For alternative interpretations of Hobbes's treatment of questions relating to gender and women's family and political status see Christine Di Stefano, "Masculinity as Ideology in Political Theory: Hobbesian Man Considered," *Women's Studies International Forum* 6 (1983): 633-44, Carole Pateman, "'God Hath Ordained to Man a Helper': Hobbes, Patriarchy and Conjugal Right," *British Journal of Political Science* 19 (1989): 445-64, and Gabriella Slomp, 'Hobbes and the Equality of Women," *Political Studies* 42 (1994): 441-52. Di Stefano emphasizes the masculinist quality of Hobbes's competitive vision of man; Pateman accepts his equal state for women in the state of nature while focusing

on his empowering the husband within civil society in such a way that the wife loses political standing, and Slomp is more favorable to Hobbes's contention of sexual equality. However, she interprets the passage quoted here as restricting his acceptance of women's equality. In addition, Hobbes's emphasis on women's equal standing is often considered something found primarily in his early writings—it was presented most fully in the *De Cive*—but, he continued to insert gender into his writings quite late in life and in a manner that differed from his contemporaries. In defending himself against the charge of atheism, he includes the following passage in a work written in 1680, *Considerations upon the Reputation, Loyalty, Manners, & Religion, of Thomas Hobbes of Malmesbury,* where he states his opponents are offended by: "his Attributing to the Civil Soverign all Power Sacredotal. But this perhaps may seem hard, when the Sovereignty is in a Queen: But it is because you are not subtle enough to perceive, that though Man may be male and female, Authority is not" (*Considerations . . . Written by himself,* By way of Letter to a Learned Person. London: Printed for William Crooke, 1680, 40).

ISABEL DE MADARIAGA (ESSAY DATE NOVEMBER 2001)

SOURCE: de Madariaga, Isabel. "Catherine the Great: A Personal View." *History Today* 51, no. 11 (November 2001): 45-51.

In the following essay, de Madariaga explores the life, accomplishments, and political writings of Catherine the Great.

Since I first took Catherine seriously as a ruler, some forty years ago, I have grown to like her very much. This is not therefore going to be an exercise in debunking, it is a personal portrait of someone who has become a close friend.

For nearly two hundred years the Empress Catherine II of Russia (1762-96), or Catherine the Great, as she is known, has had a very bad press as a German usurper from a minor ducal family, without any claim to the Russian throne. Women on the throne were an anomaly and it was expected that they would rule through favourites or husbands. But Catherine had blotted her copy book in a more serious way: she had mounted the throne as the result of a military *coup d'etat* in June 1762, over the body of her murdered husband, Peter III, the grandson of Peter the Great. From Catherine's point of view at the time it was a question of 'who whom', as Lenin later put it. Peter was supposed to have been about to repudiate her, disinherit her son and marry his mistress. Catherine's many friends in the army joined in a plot to de-throne Peter and seized power with her full approval and participation. She circumvented the men who helped her to seize the throne in 1762 and was wise enough never to enter into a publicly recognised marriage. She shocked opinion even further by having many publicly acknowledged lovers at a time when virtue was still demanded of a woman. By modern standards, Catherine was not really promiscuous. She had only twelve well-documented lovers in some forty-four years. But neither Victorian England nor Victorian Russia approved. Alexander Herzen (1812-70), the great Russian revolutionary, who later sought asylum in England, exclaimed in the mid-nineteenth century that 'the history of Catherine the Great cannot be read aloud in the presence of ladies'.

The prejudice was so great that for a long time it prevented an objective study of the events of Catherine's reign, and fostered the assumption that she had achieved nothing. Nineteenth-century historians, often populists or Marxists viewed her proclamation of the tenets of the French enlightenment as hypocrisy—as did the poet Alexander Pushkin in his young days—because she did nothing to free the serfs. With the coming of the Bolsheviks, the publication of Catherine's official papers ceased almost entirely and study of the class war superseded study of the action of individuals. It is only since the fall of Communism that Russian historians have been freed to undertake fresh documentary research, and to approach their past in an objective spirit. Historians have thus rescued their most impressive and intellectually distinguished ruler from the undeserved neglect she has suffered in the country she ruled over so successfully for thirty-four years.

Sophia of Anhalt-Zerbst, the name of the girl baptised Catherine on her conversion from Lutheranism to the Orthodox religion, arrived in Russia in 1744, aged fourteen, and was married at sixteen to a seventeen-year-old who failed to consummate the marriage for some years. The reigning Empress Elizabeth, Peter the Great's daughter, was so perturbed at the lack of an heir to the throne that she conveyed a message to Catherine urging her to produce one, if not by her husband, then by someone else, which Catherine duly did, and her son Paul, probably fathered by a courtier known as 'handsome Serge' Saltykov, was born in 1754.

The Empress Elizabeth died in 1762, and Catherine's husband became emperor. He soon showed himself as unsatisfactory as a ruler as he had proved as a husband. It was not so much what he did, but the way in which he did it. His gracelessness and his lack of judgement alienated all the powerful social groups, including his wife for whom he had ceased to have any regard: 'she will squeeze you like a lemon', he had said 'and then she will throw you away'. But Catherine through her lover, the guards officer Grigory Orlov and his four dashing brothers, won over the army to her cause, and by sheer force of personality, many of the high officials as well, even those close to Peter III. Her supporters proclaimed her not as regent for her son Paul, as some had hoped, but as ruler in her own right, as Empress regnant.

What sort of woman was she? By the time she came to power, she had spent eighteen years steering her way through the many pitfalls of the Russian court. During this time she had given birth to one son by a lover, to a daughter, who died, by another lover, Stanislas Poniatowski, and to a second son by her lover Grigory Orlov, born in secret only four months before her *coup,* who was not recognised by Peter III. She had had to manoeuvre between the many factions in the Russian court, her friends had been removed, some disgraced and sent into exile, leaving her at times in considerable solitude. And yet always she had had to share a bed with a totally uncongenial man, who for instance court martialled a rat caught in her bedchamber and executed it. She took refuge from boredom in reading, mainly history, politics, and philosophy, a great deal of French literature and a life of Henri IV of France, who became her model of a king. In this way Catherine accumulated a considerable fund of knowledge of the theory of government, and of comparative politics. She was greatly influenced by Montesquieu's *Esprit des Lois* which became for a while her bedside book and profoundly affected her legislation; she read Voltaire, of course, with whom she began a regular correspondence. When Diderot met with obstacles over the publication of the *Great Encyclopedia* in France, Catherine offered to publish it in Russia. A translation fund she established published works by Voltaire, Rousseau, Mably, *Gulliver's Travels,* Robertson's *History of America,* and in 1778 a translation of Sir William Blackstone's *Commentaries on the Laws of England* (from the French) which exercised a great influence on her political and legal thinking until her death.

Brought up a Lutheran, religion sat very lightly on her. She fulfilled all her Orthodox religious duties punctiliously, was courteous to the Russian hierarchy but gave the Church no access to political institutions, and confiscated its lands. She turned a blind eye to the presence and activities of the Old Believers, wound down Orthodox missionary activity among Muslims and pagans and allowed 'reputable' religions to build churches, run their own schools and practise their religion freely though under state inspection of their organisation and finances. In theory, religion was no obstacle to participating in elective local government posts—even for Jews whose number within the borders of Russia increased considerably after the first partition of Poland in 1772. Who knows what she believed in? She would attend all-night services in church but sat at a little table out of sight where she could pass the time with a pack of cards, playing patience.

Catherine was also extremely hardworking. She rose early, read or wrote, copied out her drafts, and discussed them with her advisers. Thousands of sheets of paper covered in her handwriting have survived, and her writings, both political and *belles lettres,* occupy twelve substantial volumes. The most outstanding of them was her *Great Instruction,* published in 1767 in order to lay before an assembly of elected representatives of the nobles, the townspeople, cossacks, tribesmen and state peasants (not the serfs) the general principles on which laws should be codified by this assembly. The *Instruction,* comprising some 650 articles in all, defined the functions of social estates and laid down the means of establishing the rule of law and the welfare of the citizens. Catherine drew on a number of important German and French thinkers of the time, and there is even a suggestion that she may have known about the work of Adam Smith. She was very proud of her compilation, which was published in over twenty-five languages, including English. It was so radical that it was condemned by the Sorbonne in Paris.

From the Italian jurist Cesare Beccaria, Catherine drew her condemnation of torture in judicial proceedings in her *Great Instruction*:

> The innocent ought not to be tortured; and in the eye of the law every person is innocent whose crime is not yet proved.

This axiom, which sounds so familiar to an English ear, was completely novel in eighteenth-century Russia. One cannot say that the Empress succeeded in eliminating torture entirely from Russian legal procedure, but she did succeed in reducing its sphere of operation. It is not unfair to Catherine's predecessors to state that she was the first ruler of Russia to have any sense of legality, of what the rule of law meant. Indeed, there was no university in Russia until 1755, no teaching of jurisprudence except by Germans who taught in Latin. The first professor of Russian law (trained in Glasgow) teaching in Russian was appointed by Catherine II in 1773. As a result Russian officials were prone to override the decisions of judges in

Catherine the Great (1729-1796).

favour of what they might regard to be common sense, convenient, or politically desirable.

In a document intended to teach her subjects how to draft laws, Catherine spent some time in defining how laws should be written: in the vernacular, in simple, concise language, bearing in mind that they were written for people of moderate capacities; they should be published as a small book which could be bought as cheaply as the catechism, and which should be used in schools to teach children to read. Napoleon had the same idea.

What is striking about Catherine's *Instruction* is that it formed part of a plan to shake up the political culture of Russia in a dramatic way. It was a pedagogical instrument designed to instruct public opinion in the assembly which was to draft her new code. It was read through in public every month from cover to cover from August 1767 until the Assembly was disbanded in autumn 1768 on the outbreak of war with Turkey. The deputies were thus subjected to a flood of unheard of ideas in what amounted to a speech from the throne.

It is worth pausing for a moment to consider this aspect of Catherine as a ruler. She had a profound understanding of the nature and importance of public opinion, and of the need to mould it. Her correspondence with Voltaire, Diderot, Falconet, Grimm and others, served to promote her interests and to portray her personality and ideas in the most attractive light. Thus the proceedings of the Assembly were public, and accounts of its activities were published in the Moscow and St Petersburg gazettes. No such gathering had been held in Russia since the seventeenth century, nor was one to meet again until after the revolution of 1905. It is a tribute to Catherine's political courage, that a mere five years after seizing the throne, she did not fear that such a gathering might provide a focus for opposition to her rule. Indeed, the sluices were opened for a freedom of speech unheard of in Russia and rendered possible by the fact that the deputies needed only to start their contributions with the words: 'As the Empress says in para xyz of her *Instruction*'.

Much of Catherine's future programme of legislation is to be found in embryo in her *Great Instruction,* and in the documents collected by the Assembly, which provided her with a vast amount of information about the state of her realm. What of the serfs who were not represented? There was of course much information about them available in the form of the murder of landowners and local risings on private estates which had to be put down by troops. Catherine herself was opposed to serfdom and she took some steps to introduce non-servile tenures on imperial estates which proved highly unpopular with the serfs. Chapter XI of her *Instruction* dealt with serfdom and slavery. She showed it to some of her advisers who cut out vast portions. The leading Russian dramatist of the period, A. P. Sumarokov, complained that the nobles would have neither coachman nor cook nor lackey, for they would all run away to better paid jobs, whereas at present the nobles all lived quietly on their estates. Catherine did not agree; she noted in the margin of Sumarokov's comments: 'and have their throats cut from time to time'.

It was only in 1907 that the suppressed portions of Chapter XI were brought to light, so that the Empress's real views were simply unknown to the general public for more than a century. She had, for instance, suggested that serfs should be entitled to purchase their freedom, or that servitude should be limited to a period of six years. Subsequently she stopped up many holes which enabled people to be enserfed, but she did not pursue total emancipation. Historians have also criticised her for giving away thousands of 'free' peasants to her favourites and public servants, thus enserfing them. Stated bluntly like that of course it sounds terrible, and what actually happened is probably not much better. For, in fact, three-quarters of the peasants she gave away were already serfs on estates acquired in the partitions of Poland. This has been known by historians since 1878, but . . . shall we say forgotten?

What marks Catherine's approach is the careful planning of a programme of interrelated measures, steadily pursued over a number of years. Local government and the judiciary were remodelled in 1775, with elected participation by nobles, townspeople and state peasants and separation of the new network of courts based on social rank from the administration. Local responsibility for certain welfare functions such as schools, hospitals and almshouses was also established, and a national network of primary and secondary schools, free and co-educational, which even serf children could attend with the permission of their owners. The civil rights of nobles and townspeople were set out in terms which reflect English legal thought in charters issued in 1785. Some of Catherine's work survived until 1864, some until the Bolsheviks in 1917.

Thus far the ruler. What of the woman? After Sergey Saltykov, Catherine found another lover, Count Stanislas Poniatowski, a Polish noble, who came to St Petersburg in the suite of the English ambassador, Sir Charles Hanbury Williams, and may well have introduced Catherine to the pleasures of collecting. Poniatowski was handsome, well bred, cultured, and fell genuinely in love with Catherine, who in turn found a soul mate and an intellectual companion for the first time in her life. In dangerous and sometimes farcical circumstances Catherine conducted her affair and gave birth to their daughter. But a political crisis in 1758 cut short their relationship, and Poniatowski returned to Poland. Love for a handsome guards officer, Grigory Orlov, as well as concern for her own safety led Catherine into a new affair, in which she proved remarkably faithful since it lasted twelve years.

In 1772, kind friends warned Catherine about her lover's infidelities and she dismissed him. Emotionally vulnerable and at a loss, Catherine was also faced with a political crisis: by the winter of 1773, the Pugachev revolt was in full swing, the war against the Ottoman Porte marked time, and her son Paul attained his majority, which might threaten her hold on the throne. At this point her whole emotional life changed gear for good. She summoned to her side Grigory Potemkin, ten years her junior, a man who had reached the rank of Lt General on the battlefields, whom she knew since he had played a minor part in her *coup d'etat,* and who had the authority to impose himself on the armed forces, the imagina-

ON THE SUBJECT OF...

CATHERINE THE GREAT (1729-1796)

Born a German princess, Catherine was schooled under a French governess, who taught her French and introduced her to the neoclassical plays of such dramatists as Racine, Moliére, and Corneille. She converted to the Russian Orthodox faith, took the name Ekaterina Alekseevna, and married her cousin, Peter Fedorovich, in 1745. She escaped the unhappy marriage by travelling the kingdom, engaging in intellectual pursuits, and involving herself in several scandalous sexual relationships. When his mother died in 1761, Peter Fedorovich took the throne; he reigned for six months while Catherine was in seclusion, pregnant with the son of one of her lovers. Shortly after giving birth, Catherine took the throne from Peter in a coup of 1762, and within a week her supporters had murdered Peter.

Catherine worked hard to demonstrate her competence and to advocate a cultural program designed to bring Russia into the Enlightenment that had already swept across most of Europe. She was a great patron of the arts, encouraging the works of playwrights and poets, and corresponding with major Enlightenment figures. Her first publication, the *Bol'shoi nakaz* (1767; *Great Instruction*) reflected Catherine's interest in constitutional law and social reform. She also sponsored a journal, the translation of foreign classics, and attempted serious intellectual endeavors in the fields of Russian language and history. Possessed of a powerful personality and acquainted with some of the leading intellectuals of the modern age, Catherine produced letters and memoirs—containing a detailed and quite lively view of her relationships with Voltaire, Diderot, and others, as well as her observations about court life, political developments, and philosophy—that have remained of great interest to readers and scholars throughout the centuries.

tion and the political acumen to make his way to the top of the political tree, and the energy to sweep all rivals aside. He also offered her total devotion, both as a woman and as his liege lady. (I use this archaic phrase deliberately because it represents how he thought of her to his dying day.) He was a handsome man (though he had lost an eye), imposing, witty and well-educated. Their meeting was explosive, and led to a stormy, passionate and well-documented love affair. Potemkin was conscious that his position was insecure and was very jealous of Catherine's past lovers. He sulked and made scenes, but so great was Catherine's trust in him that it is generally accepted now that she went through a religious ceremony of marriage with him, thus giving him, as her husband, the security he needed. For after barely two years, the passion between them wore out, though the love remained. Catherine needed him as her partner in government, particularly in military affairs, and he loved her and served her unconditionally. They found a way out of their dilemma by separating sex from love: Catherine chose a series of lovers, one after the other, and he chose his mistresses, starting with three of his nieces who became protégées of the Empress and much loved by her. To the surprise of Catherine's public servants and courtiers, Potemkin continued in greater favour than ever, and remained by the Empress as unacknowledged prince consort until his death fifteen years later in 1791.

But there were occasional difficulties with Catherine's lovers. She seems to have been easily bored, and broke with several of them, sending them away to travel abroad or to live in Moscow, well endowed. Some of them deserted her. We cannot tell how important the sexual aspect of this relationship was to her, but what is clear from her letters to others is that there was a strong dose of maternal feeling for them. She valued them as participants in her intellectual and artistic occupations.

As a woman, Catherine was generous, considerate and humane and not at all vindictive. There are endless examples of her servants' love for her. An early riser, she would make up her fire herself in order not to rouse her stoker. My favourite example of her thought for others occurred one day when she entered a room in the Winter Palace where a young soldier, supposedly on guard, was sitting reading at a table. Horrified at being caught off guard, he sprang to his feet. The empress asked him what he was reading and talked for a while with him. A few days later she gave orders to set aside a room and to establish a library for the palace staff. Her easy manners and lack of social pretensions were commented on by all who attended court. When she travelled to the Crimea in 1787, she stopped in many towns on her way to attend receptions and emerged from the crush with her cheeks covered with rouge from kissing the highly made-up bourgeois ladies. Her simplicity of manner is what made working for her pleasurable. She chose her senior advisers—her ministers—well and kept them on for years. Prince A. A. Vyazemsky, to all intents and purposes her Home Secretary and Finance Minister, worked for her from 1764 to 1792, and when he became too ill to continue, her minister of commerce from 1772 to 1792. When she received the news of the death of Potemkin in 1791 she had to be bled, wept for days, and was never the same again. None of her senior public servants was ever exiled or sent to Siberia, so that high office became a safe occupation. She spoke freely to her advisers and welcomed frank speaking to her; she did not dismiss her staff for making mistakes, not even for losing battles, she merely encouraged them to do better next time. This contributed greatly to the stability of the regime and the sense of security and continuity in government.

Catherine loved the theatre and wrote for it herself. 'I cannot see a sheet of blank paper without wanting to write on it.' She wrote short pieces for a satirical journal, and quite a number of plays, 'because I enjoy it'. She was among the first to take an interest in Shakespeare, whose plays she read in German translation. She commented:

> . . . imitations of Shakespeare are very convenient, for since they are neither comedies nor tragedies and have no other rules but tact, but a feeling for what the spectator can bear, I think we can do anything with them.

She tried to imitate Shakespeare in a play called *How to have both the linen and the basket,* based on the *Merry Wives of Windsor,* and also wrote historical plays like 'From the life of Ryurik, an imitation of Shakespeare without the dramatic unities' in which there are many echoes of *Henry IV* parts I and II. She wrote fairy tales for her grandchildren, treatises on conduct, education and bringing up children (I should perhaps mention that children in the Foundling Homes she established were given muesli for breakfast). She issued an *ukaz* recommending the cultivation of potatoes with instructions on how to cook them and potatoes were even served in the palace. She even devised a special garment for babies which could be easily pulled off with one tug of a tape, and sent the pattern to the King of Sweden for his wife.

So far I have shown the side of Catherine that won her many admirers. I must now try to find a few faults. First of all she was vain, vain of her achievements, but also of her role as a woman on the throne who outshone many men as a successful modern and reforming ruler, as a correspondent of leading minds in Paris and Germany, as an art collector. She was proud of the victories of her armies, and determined to assert the equality of Russia—a newcomer—with the other great powers in Europe. She was delighted at the successful dispatch of several Russian Baltic fleets to the Mediterranean in 1769-74. It did indeed astound most European countries, and could not have been achieved without the help of Britain. But her letter to her ambassador in London notifying him of her intention reads almost like that of a gleeful little girl:

> We have aroused the sleeping cat, and the cat is going to attack the mice and you will see what you will see, and people will talk about us and nobody expected us to make such a rumpus . . .

As she grew older her vanity took on a Russian nationalist flavour with an unpleasant tendency to browbeat her enemies. Her strong nerves enabled her to overcome the anxieties of indecisive campaigns, but during the Ochakov crisis in 1791 she had to be bullied into climbing down by the pressure of Potemkin, more aware than she of the military danger of a Prussian attack on land and of a possible British naval attack in the Baltic, but she was saved from total surrender by the collapse of Pitt's policy in England. There is one aspect of her increasingly brash attitude to other powers which I personally find unforgiveable and that is her treatment of her ex-lover Stanislas Poniatowski as a man, and of Poland as a nation. The destruction of Poland was carried out with a ruthlessness and an undercurrent of raillery which is extremely unpleasant and Catherine's bullying of Stanislas himself was downright cruel. For she could be ruthless in defence of her own position, and the existing political and social structure.

Yet she had an original and creative political mind, and the disciplined temperament of a statesman. To the end of her life she continued to ponder over possible ways of associating elected representatives of the Russian nobility, townspeople and peasantry with a decision-making body in the government of Russia, drawing often on English models. Her attitude to government can be summed up in a remark attributed to her by Potemkin's one-time secretary, V. S. Popov. When he expressed his surprise to her at the blind obedience with which her every order was treated:

> She condescended to reply: It is not as easy as you think. In the first place my orders would not be carried out unless they were the kind of orders which could be carried out. You know with what prudence . . . I act in the promulgation of my laws. I examine the circumstances, I take advice, I consult the enlightened part of the people and this way I find out what sort of effect my law will have. And then when I am already convinced in advance of general approval, then I issue my orders, and have the pleasure of observing what you call blind obedience. And that is the foundation of unlimited power.

Further Reading

Catherine II, *The Correspondence with Voltaire and the Instruction of 1767 in the English Text of 1768.* Edited under the title *Documents of Catherine the Great* by W. F. Reddaway (Cambridge University Press, 1931); Carol S. Leonard, *Reform and Regicide: the Reign of Peter III of Russia* (Indiana University Press, 1992); Isabel de Madariaga, *Russia in the Age of Catherine the Great* (reprint forthcoming, Phoenix Press, January 2002); Isabel de Madariaga, *Catherine the Great: A Short History* (Yale University Press, 1991); Isabel de Madariaga, *Politics and Culture in Eighteenth Century Russia* (Longmans, 1998); T. Alexander, *Catherine the Great—Life and Legend* (Oxford University Press, 1989); Simon Sebag Montefiore, *Prince of Princes, The Life of Potemkin* (Weidenfeld and Nicolson, 2001).

WOMEN IN LITERATURE

DYMPNA C. CALLAGHAN (ESSAY DATE 1994)

SOURCE: Callaghan, Dympna C. "The Ideology of Romantic Love." In *The Weyward Sisters: Shakespeare and Feminist Politics,* edited by Dympna C. Callaghan, Lorraine Helms, and Jyotsna Singh, pp. 59-101. Cambridge, Mass.: Blackwell Publishers, 1994.

In the following excerpt, Callaghan examines Romeo and Juliet *to determine its influence on society's notions of desire.*

"To this end . . . is this tragicall matter written, to describe unto thee a couple of unfortunate lovers, thralling themselves to unhonest desire, neglecting the authority and advice of parents and friends . . ." (Evans, 1057). Thus Arthur Brooke defines the ideological project of his poem, *The Tragicall History of Romeous and Juliet* (1562), which was to become Shakespeare's primary source for *Romeo and Juliet.* The lovers' "unhonest desire" was always a compelling feature of the story, but in Shakespeare's version the fate of that desire is presented as profound injustice as much as proper punishment.[1] For Brooke's rendition of the story bears a moral aversion to what Shakespeare's tragedy accomplishes in producing for posterity the lovers' desire as at once transgressive ("unhonest") and as a new orthodoxy (tragically legitimated). It is precisely this ambivalence that is at the heart of the play's appeal as one of the preeminent cultural documents of love in the West.

Romeo and Juliet was written at the historical moment when the ideologies and institutions of desire—romantic love and the family, which are now for us completely naturalized—were being negotiated. Indeed, the play consolidates a certain formation of desiring subjectivity attendant upon Protestant and especially Puritan ideologies of marriage and the family required by, or least very conducive to the emergent economic formation of, capitalism.[2] The goal of this chapter is to examine the role of *Romeo and Juliet* in the cultural construction of desire. Desire—variously generated, suppressed, unleashed, and constrained—is particularly significant for feminist cultural studies because in its most common formulation as transhistorical romantic love it is one of the most efficient and irresistible interpellations of the female subject, securing her complicity in apparently unchangeable structures of oppression, particularly compulsory heterosexuality and bourgeois marriage.

It would be wrong to suggest that romantic love is devoid of positive and even liberatory dimensions. As Denis de Rougement has shown in *Love in the Western World,* its advent in the twelfth century represents something of an improvement on earlier organizations of desire. It seems likely, however, that the extra-marital love that flourished among the feudal aristocracy was considerably less restrictive for women (though not actively empowering) than was the marital version that emerged with early capitalism. Feudal romantic love was generally constructed as the unrequited passion of a male subject leading ultimately to his own spiritual self-transcendence, as opposed to the emergent construction of romantic love as mutual heterosexual desire leading to a consummation in marriage, a union of both body and spirit. One of its crucial features, a signal of its effectiveness, is that the ideology of romantic love centers from the Renaissance onward on women's subjective experience. Yet this focus serves to control and delimit intimate experience rather than to allow the fullest possible expression of female desire. It is also true that when we are in its throes, romantic love is a classic instance of false consciousness. Among its oppressive effects, the dominant ideology of (heterosexual, monogamous) romantic love relegates homosexuality to the sphere of deviance, secures women's submission to the asymmetrical distribution of power between men and women, and bolsters individualism by positing sexual love as the expression of authentic identity. Men are not, of course, immune to these effects, but they are more likely than women to derive benefit from them. My analysis of this phenomenon proceeds first by examining the ideological function of *Romeo and Juliet* in the Renaissance and in the present, and then moves on to critique the discourses (those of psychoanalysis and history) which should enable the historicization of desire in Renaissance studies, but which in certain key respects actually impede it. Here, my approach is necessarily and deliberately synoptic because I endeavor to place desire in terms of the determinate, global conceptual categories of Marxism. The final sections of the chapter address the complex operations of desire within the play itself.

Reproducing the Ideology of Romantic Love

Shakespeare's text has been used to perpetuate the dominant ideology of romantic love, and its initial ideological function has intensified since its first performance. The play enacts an ideological propensity to posit desire as transhistorical. For what is extraordinary about the version of familial and personal relations—of desire and identity and their relation to power—endorsed by *Romeo and Juliet* is that they are in our own time so fully naturalized as to seem universal. Feminist psychoanalytic critic Julia Kristeva writes: "Young people throughout the entire world, whatever their race, religion, or social status, identify with the adolescents of Verona . . ." (210). According to Kristeva and countless Shakespeareans, the play constitutes a universal legend of love representing elemental psychic forces of desire and frustration purportedly characteristic of the human condition in every age and culture.[3]

The iteration of a particular configuration of desire does not end, therefore, in 1595 when the first performance puts it in place, but rather is a phenomenon that has been perpetuated, indeed universalized, by subsequent critical and theatrical reproductions of the play.[4] As Joseph Porter points out, *Romeo and Juliet* "has become far more canonical a story of heterosexual love than it was when it came to Shakespeare's hand" (141). Consider, for example, that in its Elizabethan production,

Romeo and Juliet were portrayed not by an actor and actress but by a suitably feminine-featured male performer and a slightly more rugged youth, and that the erotic homology produced by this situation was compounded by the presence of the profoundly homoerotic Mercutio. The play's initial ideological project—the valorization of romantic love between the young couple—thus becomes consolidated and intensified with subsequent re-narrations. Indeed, the affective power of the story and of romantic love itself—its "dateless passion" (Evans et al., 1057)—occurs not in spite of its repetition but rather depends precisely on reiteration.

The narrative mechanisms of the text itself tend towards self-replication. Shakespeare's play perpetuates an already well-known tale, and Act V produces "closure" on desire only by opening up the possibility of endless retellings of the story—displacing the lovers' desire onto a perpetual narrative of love (see Whittier, 41; Jones).[5] The lovers' story is recapitulated by the prologue, by the lovers, and by the Friar. The Prince offers the concluding incitement to "more talk": "never was a story of more woe / Than this of Juliet and her Romeo" (V. iii. 307; 309-10). The play's ending thus constitutes a means of monumentalizing (quite literally in the golden statues of the lovers) and thereby reproducing *ad infinitum,* "whiles Verona by that name is known" (V. iii. 300), the ideological imperatives of the lovers' most poignant erotic moments. Crucially, then, the social effectivity of the ideology of romantic love is characterized fundamentally by its capacity for self-replication. Thus, the narrative imperative of *Romeo and Juliet* to propagate the desire with which it is inscribed constitutes a resistance to historicization that has been extended by criticism's production of the play as universal love story. In this respect, the mimetic dynamic curiously mirrors the capitalist mode of production, whose goal is not immediate use but accumulated and multiplied future production (see Kamenka and Neale, 18). The play's inclination towards replication and multiplication is a maneuver that propagates a version of erotic love which is consonant with the needs of an emergent social order.

Romeo and Juliet, then, marks the inauguration of a particular form of sexual desire produced in accordance with the specific historical requirements of patriarchy's shifting modality. As Eli Zaretsky argues in his pathbreaking study *Capitalism, the Family, and Personal Life,* "courtly love anticipated ideals of love and individualism that the bourgeois located within the family and that were generalized and transformed in the course of capitalist development" (38). In the early modern teleology of desire, the family, newly emphasized as the focus of political, social, legal, and economic organization becomes the social destination of desire.[6] Thus, *Romeo and Juliet* both instantiates the ideology of romantic love as universal, timeless and unchanging and yet is marked by its own historical specificity. The degree to which *Romeo and Juliet* appears to constitute the transcription of the universal features of the experience of love indicates its profoundly "ideological" nature; that is to say, the play's ideological project has become the dominant ideology of desire. In this way, the text both positions itself within and reproduces the hegemonic. *Romeo and Juliet* consolidates the ideology of romantic love and the correlative crystalization of the modern nuclear family.

Disciplining Desire: Psychoanalysis and History

The tendency to posit desire as transhistorical, as we shall see, is not confined to Shakespeare's text. Freud himself conflated psychic, social, and historical processes, most notoriously perhaps in his account of the origins of patriarchy in *Totem and Taboo.* Here, the primal father is overthrown and eaten by his sons, who in their guilt, after a considerable period of time, reinstate the father's strictures, which by now they have all too thoroughly and literally ingested: "Each single one of the brothers who had banded together for the purposes of killing their father was inspired by a wish to become like him and had given expression to it by incorporating parts of their father's surrogate in the totem meal" (505). Posited as a fact of prehistory, this is a far more literal manifestation of the rivalry between father and son inherent in the Oedipus complex.[7] Freud also argued that we all carry a philogenetic memory of this "real" event, a claim he repeated in his last work, *Moses and Monotheism.*[8] The point here is not to add weight to the already heavy indictment against Freud; rather, what is critical is that he posited a real event as the origin of the human family, a site of the individual psychic scenario, and was himself (particularly in these texts which are examples of his speculative, as opposed to his strictly psychoanalytic writings) grappling with, or conversely evading, the problem of "real history."[9]

In contemporary critical analyses, the understanding of desire as transhistorical is similarly produced by the way psychoanalysis (the dominant critical apparatus of desire) is positioned in relation to questions of historical specificity.[10] Feminism, far from resolving this conflicted relationship, is in fact heavily invested in it. This is because, on the one hand, constructions of gender and sexuality are seen to be historically specific and, on the other, fundamental aspects of patriarchy are stubbornly tenacious—well nigh universal. The law of the father has been an apparently immutable force in psychic and social organization and is enacted in and structured by the Oedipus complex,[11] and the desire which is a necessary condition of human subjectivity comes into being under the "Law of the Father." There are always "two parents of the opposite sex and their relationship to each other and their offspring, and its to them" (Mitchell, *Woman's Estate,* 169; see also Coward, 15, and Weeks, 159). Juliet Mitchell argues, "this pattern is as inherent in our culture as it is in our biology . . . and we must remember there always *is* a father and it is the *idea* of him that Freud was commenting on" (*Woman's Estate,* 169-70). He *is* the history into which the (proto) subject is inserted. Mitchell contends: "He [Freud] examined the 'eternal' structures of patriarchy in what is for us their most essential particularity: the bourgeois, patriarchal family . . . The Oedipus complex is universal while the particular form used to redescribe it is specific" (*Psychoanalysis and Feminism,* 380-1; see Kaplan, 167).[12] The danger here for feminism is that the way psychoanalysis describes the structure of patriarchy may actually corroborate its oppressive order, in that the family in which human beings advene desire is posited as unchanging and unchangeable. That is, the oedipal situation becomes coterminous with the patriarchal family. Crucially, this conceptualization of the family—culturally constructed at the level of both the psychic and the social as the organizing principle of desire—is the mechanism that produces desire as transhistorical.

Psychoanalysis, then, does not theorize the way in which the family itself is socially determined, but rather attempts to explain the family in terms of itself, projecting the family of developed capitalist society onto all periods of history. This does not make psychoanalytic interpretation irrelevant to a materialist history of desire; it is the most compelling narrative of the psychic structuring of desire we possess and one that forestalls a purely functionalist understanding of its operations. Rather, psychoanalysis is relevant only insofar as it can be seen to undermine certain of its own assumptions—that is, when it can help to uncover the production of desire in patriarchal structures that are shifting and heterogeneous rather than static, monolithic, and universal.

While the "universalism" of psychoanalysis cannot be equated unproblematically with the universalizing of the liberal humanist tradition because the former disrupts rather than secures the coherent subject of the latter, it remains ironically true that in their dominant disciplinary formations psychoanalysis and history, despite their alleged antithesis, can be seen to rely upon strikingly similar notions of the patriarchal family. In Renaissance studies psychoanalysis is largely viewed as causally belated if not downright anachronistic, on the grounds that it erases temporal specificity by proposing a universal psychic scenario embedded in its foundational procedures and assumptions. History, in contrast, is typically understood as the common sense of our area of inquiry. Yet the history referred to is still what Jameson calls "the common garden-variety empirical history," that constitutes "bourgeois historiography" rather than "a genuine philosophy of history" (132; see also Cressy, 124). The result of this theoretical and ideological blind spot in the otherwise deservedly influential work of many social historians of the early modern era, such as Alan Macfarlane, David Cressy, and Keith Wrightson, is a prevailing tendency toward ahistoricism about desire and the nuclear family.

The ahistorical treatment of desire in early modern social history is especially apparent in the debate about the degree of continuity between Puritan ideals of love with those of prior and succeeding centuries.[13] It is now generally accepted that the conventional notion of the extended feudal family is misleading (Sharpe, 59-60). Even Lawrence Stone, much indicted for his insistence on change, does not deny a basic continuity: "most of the features of the modern family appeared before industrialization and among social groups unaffected by it and . . . even those exposed to it responded in different ways" (*The Family, Sex and Marriage,* 665).[14] This fact does not, however, obviate the need to account for the increasing pervasiveness of the ideology of nuclear familialism in early modern England, which required, produced, and interpellated female subjectivities of a *different* (though not necessarily "improved") order from those of preceding centuries (Newman, 20; Davies, 59). The permutations of the ideology of the family are significant for feminism because, as we have noted, that ideology constitutes a central structure in the psychic and social dimensions of women's oppression (Barrett, 251; Swindells and Jardine, 69). With the advent of capitalism, and the notion of private property, there is a new conception of the family as an independent economic unit within a market economy (Zaretsky, 32). The problem is that when social historians critique the naïve model of the shift from feudal clan to nuclear family and the now obsolete theory that Protestantism invariably offered conditions for women much improved from those of an allegedly benighted pre-Reformation Catholicism, they tend to collapse historical distinctions altogether and to relegate the ideological to the realm of ideas of a purely cognitive kind (Houlbrooke, 36). Further, the stress on the slow, almost imperceptible, evolution in the internal constitution of the household from the "extended" to the "nuclear" family is, as Eli Zaretsky points out, whether consciously or not, ideologically motivated: "Viewed in this way, the seeming inertia of the family has been in marked contrast to the continuous upheaval of political and economic history, a contrast that lends plausibility to the view that 'history' is the realm of politics and economics while the family is confined to 'nature'" (32).

In a recent essay, David Cressy indicts literary scholars for their allegedly naïve notions about the radical discontinuity in the history of the family attendant upon the advent of Protestantism, and especially their recourse to Lawrence Stone's *The Family, Sex and Marriage*:[15]

> This is not just a professional squabble among historians, nor is it a technical dispute about sources. The disagreement goes to the heart of how we do history, about how we make sense of the past. Should we choose material to support pre-drawn conclusions, or should our argument be distilled from the sources? Is the past baffling and contradictory, or can we reduce it to patterns? . . . Nor are we dealing with a simple matter of taste, synchronic versus diachronic styles, or a predisposition toward watersheds and rifts rather than slow glacial flows. It comes down to evidence versus agenda.
>
> (130)

Clearly, it is important to move away from the reductive notion of history as straight-arrow teleology, but Cressy then returns us to an empiricist history which is essentially inscrutable, "baffling and contradictory." This is paradoxical since at the same time sources are seen as more or less transparent documents that will speak to the objective, "more cautious . . . more reliable" (130) historian who has laid all predrawn conclusions aside. Stone is not, of course, beyond the reach of criticism: he makes generalizations on the evidence of aristocratic families alone, for instance. For all that, what is at issue here is not simply the merits of Stone's book, but the politics of historiography. Cressy does not see that what constitutes "evidence" is itself the product of an "agenda" whether it be an explicitly political one concerned with struggle, conflict, and change, or merely a condition of bafflement.

Similarly, Keith Wrightson, whose book *English Society 1580-1680,* tries to account for both continuity and change, defines his conceptual hold upon the period in question as simply the product of "a *personal attempt* to bring together, to come to terms with and make sense of what has been revealed both of the nature of English society and of the course of social change within the century" (12, my emphasis). For Wrightson, change is never a matter of changes in state and economic structure; it is always a matter of "local diversity" (222):

> Within the flexible structure of the neighbourhood there already flourished a cultural emphasis on the interests of the individual nuclear family which was a powerful enough incentive to override traditional social obligations where there was gain to be made. Such attitudes needed only the opportunity to express themselves more fully, and in the fiercely competitive climate of the late sixteenth and seventeenth centuries they found it.
>
> (223)

The family becomes naturalized, as does change itself—a "climate" which permits already existing conditions to flourish. Once again, the critique of Stone is instructive and indicative of a particular way of reading history:

> [T]here is little reason to follow Professor Stone in regarding the rise of the companionate marriage as a new phenomenon of the later seventeenth and eighteenth centuries. It seems to have been already well established . . . It may well be that these are less evolutionary stages of familial progress, than the poles of an enduring continuum in marital relations in a society which accepted both the primacy of male authority and the ideal of marriage as a practical and emotional partnership.
>
> (Wrightson, 103-4)

In *Marriage and Love in England 1300-1840,* Alan Macfarlane (incidentally, Stone's best-known detractor) concedes like most other historians that while "the strengthening of the husband-wife bond is part of . . . emotional and economic nucleation" (174), which is regarded as one of the preconditions of modernity, and a distinctive feature of western families—"it is not the pivot of social structure in the majority of societies" (174)—he proceeds to go back and forth across centuries and genres to show that things were always the same from Anglo-Saxon England to the nineteenth century:

> As far back as we can easily go, there is evidence of the same insistence. If we leap back to the early thirteenth century we find in the encyclopedia by Bartholomaeus Anglicus a similar emphasis on love, "fellowship", affection, consideration . . . [T]he revolution to conjugality and companionate marriage, which is both unusual and so influential, had occurred at least by the time of Chaucer in England, if not long before.
>
> (183)

In fact "continuity"—a perfectly valid if not entirely accurate postulate—has been erased by the complete collapse of historical difference. It would undoubtedly be futile to argue that human beings have not felt genuine emotional intimacy and overwhelming desire through the ages, but the form, figure, and meaning of these phenomena are historically specific. Macfarlane's text is symptomatic of a prevailing tendency toward ahistoricism among early modern social historians about the social construction of desire institutionalized as marriage and the nuclear family. He devotes a chapter on romantic love almost entirely to literary "evidence." The argument for the ubiquity of a uniform romantic love is not adequately supported by the great list of literary quotations Macfarlane offers by way of historical verification. I am not arguing here that literary texts are irrelevant to history: my own text takes Shakespeare's play as a cultural document of a particular historical circumstance. But I find it impossible to agree with Macfarlane that *Romeo and Juliet* figures as the acme of and the evidence for timeless love:

> The passion of love in its myriad manifestations is brought into conflict with a thousand obstacles, and the resolution of these difficulties keeps audiences in the past and today in a state of suspense and enchantment . . . reaching exquisite perfection in *Romeo and Juliet.*
>
> (184)

Romantic love is here completely divorced from social considerations so that it becomes a transhistorical "emotion." In short, desire is placed resolutely outside history, untouched by temporal and other differences.[16]

Paradoxically, then, historians arrive at a view of the family which bears an uncanny resemblance to its situation in psychoanalysis. The family, it turns out, is for social historians, as much as it is for a psychoanalytic theorist like Juliet Mitchell, "a *relatively* constant unit in relation to the entire course of social history. As such, it has a certain autonomy and inflexibility, whatever the stage of economic development of the society as a whole" (*Woman's Estate,* 159).[17] The point here is not that such an assertion, whether enunciated by psychoanalytic critics or social historians, is ludicrously retrograde; it is rather that both psychoanalysis and history are epistemological configurations whose ostensible antipathy has obscured their shared participation in the cultural processes whereby the family is peculiarly insulated from historical change, and thus desire, produced within the family and circulated among families, is excluded from the process of historicization.

A final example from the debate about Stone will perhaps make clear why, despite its shortcomings, the overall conception of his book remains useful. For Stone, the modern family of capitalist development is presented as a more significant site of sexual and emotional satisfaction than its early modern precursor. He has been attacked for the proposition that there could have been little emotional investment in families in former times because of arranged marriages and high rates of infant mortality; people surely loved one another and grieved for one another in the past as now. However, when social historians critical of Stone take up this point, they use this issue as a way of asserting the universality of emotional investment in family life. That "affection, co-operation and mutual give-and-take" may have existed in early modern domestic arrangements, or even "passionate attachment" (Sharpe, 69, 62) is not, therefore, identical with the *ideology* through which these relations are constituted. The conceptual tools of social historians simply do not allow for a distinction between sexual passions and the ideology of romantic love with which we are concerned. As a result, they are blind to the distinct, historically mutable *material effects* of ideology. Of course, neither does Stone have a theory of ideology, and so it is only a Marxist-feminist reading of Stone that can account for social change in the social institutions which structure and regulate human intimacy.

Notes

1. There is in Shakespeare's play only a dim residue of this earlier moralism in the Friar's caveat that "these violent delights have violent ends" (II. vi. 9); see Bullough.

   All references to the play are to the Riverside edition, edited Evans et al.

2. For a useful guide to the literature on the debate about the transition from feudalism to capitalism, see Taylor. See also: Anderson (1979; 1983); Baechler; Baechler et al.; Brenner; Hirst; Katz; Kamenka and Neale; Medick; Mooers; Wallerstein.

3. For example, Arthur Kirsch who uses a Christian/Freudian approach comments: "Central to my understanding of the treatment of love in Shakespeare has been the assumption that the plays represent elemental truths of our emotional and spiritual life, that these truths help account for Shakespeare's enduring vitality . . ." (ix). In such criticism, Freud merely discovered a different way of expressing what Shakespeare had already said. History becomes the changing stage scenery of a continuum—the costumes may change, but the essence remains unchanged (6).

4. Even when the text was staged in a version thought more suited to the times, the result was the enhancement of its message for a post-Puritan world wherein the ideals it presented required a certain modification. See Barnet on the theatre history of the text. The Restoration saw the popularity of a happy ending (Evans et al., 1802).

5. For Kristeva, however, such repetition is born not of ideological necessity but of a psycho-linguistic one. Commenting on the centrality of night imagery in the play, she argues: "it is not nothingness, lack of meaning, absurdity. In the polite display of its black tenderness there is an intense longing that is positive with respect to meaning . . . Let me emphasize the nocturnal motion of metaphor and *amor mortis*: it bears on the irrational aspect of signs and loving subjects, on the nonrepresentable feature on which the renewal of representation depends" (214, ellipsis in the original).

6. As Susan Amussen puts it, in nascent modernity "[b]oth economic realities and political and social thought, then, draw us to the family as a central institution" (2). Further, Sharpe points to the irrefutable arrival of one new family type: "the legitimate family of clergymen" (61).

   For debates on the family see also: Chaytor; Houlbrooke; Outhwaite; Stone.

7. "The fact, too, that in this situation he regards his father as a disturbing rival and would like to get rid of him and take his place is a straightforward consequence of the actual state of affairs" ("Some psychical consequences," 672).

8. Freud's insistence on this point leads Rosalind Coward to argue that we cannot defend the ahistoricism of Freud's theories by arguing that they are applicable to a specific, if inordinately lengthy, period of time, namely the patriarchal era (189; see also Weeks, 158-9).

9. There is a sense too in which the processes of psychoanalysis and those of conventional historiography are analogous. Freud saw himself as something of an archeologist of the psyche: "the analyst's final reconstruction of the repressed psychic life of the analysand was the objective historical truth about repressed psychic reality" (Novick, 558).

10. Even Deleuze and Guattari, who reject the oedipal construct, merely replace its universality with the fragmentation of desire, a displacement which ignores gender categories and is in danger of ignoring choice, reason, and history along with them. See Weeks, 173-6, for an excellent critique of *Anti-Oedipus*.

    For Valerie Traub, whose goal is to articulate the historical specificity of women's homoerotic desire, it is imperative "to tease out the mutually implicated but distinct relation between gender and eroticism . . . Such a project involves specifying erotic discourses and practices; describing institutional delimitations on erotic practice; detailing the resistance of subjects to the ideological and material constraints upon their erotic lives; and tracing the play of erotic discourses and practices throughout history" ("Desire and the difference it makes," 90). For this reason it is important to understand the binarism "desire and history" as ideologically constructed rather than as natural and self-evident. Jeffrey Weeks points out:

    > "Desire" dances on the precipice between determinism and disruption. After Freud, it cannot be reduced to primeval biological urges, beyond human control, nor can it be seen as the product of conscious willing and planning. It is somewhere ambiguously, elusively, in between, omnipotent but tangible, powerful but goal-less. Because of this it can lay claim to universality, to being out of time and beyond identity, infiltrating the diverse spaces of our social lives, casting out delicate strands which embrace or entrap, isolate or unify. But it also has a history. The flux of desire is hooked, trapped and defined by historical processes which far from being beyond understanding, need to be understood.
    >
    > (157)

11. The principal objections to the use of psychoanalysis in conjunction with materialist criticism have been, as one Renaissance critic put it, that it is "ahistorical, Europocentric, and sexist . . ." (Brown, 71). (On phallocentricity see also Michael Ryan, 104-11). As a result, psychoanalysis has a complex history within the women's movement; for that matter, it has also acquired something of a troublesome geography given its very different place in British, American, and French feminist struggles. This, of course, omits Australia, another western nation which has taken Lacan to its bosom (see, for example, Grosz). There is vehement (and justifiable) antipathy to psychoanalysis among feminist activists in the American tradition of Kate Millett, which is the response to the repressive, normalizing elements of psychoanalysis as well as to the practices of clinical psychology (which does not adhere to the fundamental—and most radical—principles of psychoanalysis as Freud formulated them). Yet there is also a strong Francophone tradition in the US represented by, for example, Shoshana Felman, Jane Gallop, and Alice Jardine. In France, there has been opposition to Freud and Lacan (the forms of psychological theory which can properly be labelled as psychoanalytic), but it has been within the intellectual perimeters of psychoanalysis rather than a repudiation of psychoanalysis as such (Irigaray, Montrelay, Kristeva, etc.). These feminist proponents/opponents of psychoanalysis while they are vigorously political (more obviously so than their American Francophone counterparts) can hardly be described as materialists. In Britain, on the other hand, where there

is a strong tradition of intellectual Marxism, psychoanalysis has been seen as less antithetical to materialism than elsewhere, a tendency reinforced early on in the women's movement by Juliet Mitchell's pathbreaking defence of the radical potential of psychoanalysis, *Psychoanalysis and Feminism.* However, even in Britain one can think of examples of materialist feminists who are quite opposed to psychoanalysis, for example Michèle Barrett, whose widely influential book, *Women's Oppression Today,* offers a riposte to Mitchell, and more recently Chris Weedon's *Feminism and Poststructuralism* which repeatedly delineates the shortcomings of psychoanalysis for feminism. Jane Moore and Catherine Belsey have lately argued, in a position representative of the British compromise on feminism and psychoanalysis, that psychoanalysis *versus* feminism is a reductive binarism in which "for" or "against" are the only possible positions. This is itself, they contend, a failure to historicize the role of this discussion within feminism where different questions have been asked at different historical moments. Thus, for example, ". . . Millett is concerned with the way patriarchy victimizes women, while Mitchell and Rose are concerned with evidence that victims of patriarchy are in a position to strike back" (7).

There is, then, a pervasive sense that materialism and psychoanalysis are incompatible and yet a Marxist tradition from Trotsky, which is quite the reverse, with perhaps its most recent manifestation in Terry Eagleton's declaration that "psychoanalysis is nothing less than a materialist theory of the making of the human subject" (163). That tradition of critical engagement with the most radical aspects of psychoanalytic theory in Marxist criticism includes, for example, Louis Althusser's "Ideology and ideological state apparatuses" and "Freud and Lacan" (in *Lenin and Philosophy*) and Fredric Jameson's, *The Political Unconscious: Narrative as a Socially Symbolic Act.* It also includes, of course, famous attacks on psychoanalysis such as Gilles Deleuze and Félix Guattari, *Anti-Oedipus: Capitalism and Schizophrenia.* Colonial and post-colonial criticism has also engaged with psychoanalysis since it was Freud who first drew the analogy between the operations of colonialism and psychic repression (Brown, 71), and which has been taken up most powerfully by Nigerian writer, Franz Fanon in *Black Skin, White Masks.* Fanon is concerned with the political constructions of identity, and the way in which in our very psychic interiority we take up race and national identities within ideology and in the service of the hegemonic order. Similarly, Cora Kaplan has argued that this is equally true of gender and class: "Our identities are still constructed through social hierarchy and cultural differentiation, as well as those processes of division and fragmentation, described in psychoanalytic theory" (175).

To return to the specifics of the feminist tradition, there is a tension on the one hand between the desire to register the fact that constructions of gender and sexuality are historically specific (Newton and Rosenfelt, xvi) and, on the other, that certain fundamental aspects of patriarchy are stubbornly tenacious, and that they are enacted and structured even at the level of consciousness itself. Further, although gendered identities are constructed as stable, they are profoundly unstable and subject to a resistance which is at the heart of psychic life (Newton and Rosenfelt, xviii).

One of the sources of this tension, I contend, is in the desire to critique liberal humanist understandings of the subject, particularly its emphasis on the individual in the notion of an autonomous psychic interiority, which thus transcends history. Yet psychoanalysis, perhaps more than any other contemporary discourse, has effected a Copernican revolution in the sphere of the subject. The autonomous, unified coherent self of liberal humanism has been replaced by a fragmented subjectivity constituted in language rather than in some otherworldly realm of souls. Nonetheless, psychoanalysis and the "universalism" allegedly present there is unreasonably, in my view, equated with the universalizing of the liberal humanist tradition.

For a useful overview of this issues from a humanist perspective, see Gardiner.

An example of the dilemma from the perspective of feminist Renaissance studies is Valerie Traub's essay on the repressed maternal body of the history plays. She writes, "The salient difference between the Henriad and psychoanalysis . . . is less ideological than sytlistic" ("Prince Hal's Falstaff," 458). Thus Traub emphasizes the historical continuity of the phallocentric repression of the mother as a significant actor in the oedipal drama.

12. Elsewhere in the book, however, Mitchell comments, "The degree of specificity and universality has, I think, still to be worked out" (363). Addressing the argument that Freud's theories can only be applied to the nineteenth-century Vienna in which he formulated them she writes: "Certainly, then, psychoanalysis, as any other system of thought, was formed within a particular time and place; that does not invalidate its claims to universal laws, it only means that these laws have to be extracted from their specific problematic—the particular material conditions of their formation" (xviii).

13. For a summary of this debate, see Houlbrooke, chs 1 and 2.

14. For Stone's comments on developments in academic historiography, see Novick, 620.

15. The use of Foucault, let alone Freud or Lacan, is viewed as "an exercise in anachronism and dislocation" (Cressy, 125). Similarly, Cressy charges that literary scholars engage in a naïve use of the work of Lawrence Stone. However, he does not cite Mary Beth Rose's critique of Stone, which addresses the limitations but also suggests why he is useful for literary scholars who are more attuned to concepts of ideology than empiricist historians (Rose, 2-3).

    In a somewhat lengthy meditation on the age of marriage in early modern England, Peter Laslett worries the question of Juliet's age (fourteen) and that of her mother (twenty-eight):

    > The more the point is laboured, the less credible the view that there was anything realistic whatever in the literary intentions of the play in these respects.
    >
    > If we ask ourselves what those intentions were, we might suppose that Shakespeare was playing upon the rather hazy information of the bulk of his audience about the maturational differences between aristocrats and the mass of people . . . Much more

> plausible is the view that he was deliberately writing a play about love and marriage amongst boys and girls without any recognition of the facts about the age of women at their weddings or at sexual maturity.
>
> (*The World We Have Lost,* 85)

The reason for this, Laslett concludes, is that writers of literature have a penchant for the unusual, the out of the ordinary. He concludes that, as a result, literary evidence is almost systematically unreliable.

16. It is significant that Macfarlane ("The cradle of capitalism") is not entirely convinced of the fact that there was a transition from feudalism to capitalism. Because he can find capital in the feudal era, he questions the "supposed transition" from one mode of production to another. Macfarlane here ignores one of Marx's most fundamental definitions of capitalism. That is, "capital" always exists, but it only functions as such within specific sets of economic and social relations, just as gold has value only within particular relations.

17. Interestingly enough, it is in Lawrence Stone's *The Past and the Present* that we find the sort of unambivalent pronouncement about the (antithetical) relation between psychoanalysis and history that we would expect from a historian:

> Nothing in the historical record disproves Freud's theory about how at different stages of infantile development different erogenous zones become the foci of sexual stimulation, thus providing a logical explanation of the later relationship between oral, anal, and genital pleasure. Nor does the historical record do anything to belittle the importance of sublimation, or of the unconscious operating with a secret dynamic of its own. What it does do, however, is to cast very great doubt upon the assumption that particular kinds of infantile traumas upon which Freud laid so much stress have been suffered by the whole of the human race at all times and in all places. It is now fairly clear that four of the main traumas Freud looked for and found among his patients, and therefore assumed to be universal, are dependent on particular experiences which did not happen to the vast majority of people in most of the recorded past, but which were peculiar to middle-class urban culture of late Victorian Europe.
>
> (216-17)

Works Cited

Althusser, Louis, *Lenin and Philosophy and Other Essays,* trans. Ben Brewster (New York, Monthly Review Press, 1971).

Amussen, Susan Dwyer, *An Ordered Society: Gender and Class in Early Modern England* (Oxford, Basil Blackwell, 1988).

Anderson, Perry, *Lineages of the Absolutist State* (London, Verso, 1979).

———, *In the Tracks of Historical Materialism* (London, Verso, 1983).

Baechler, Jean, *The Origins of Capitalism,* trans. Barry Cooper (Oxford, Basil Blackwell, 1975).

Baechler, Jean, Hall, John, and Mann, Michael, *Europe and the Rise of Capitalism* (Oxford, Basil Blackwell, 1988).

Barnet, Sylvan, "*Romeo and Juliet* on stage and screen," in J. A. Bryant (ed.), *The Tragedy of Romeo and Juliet,* The Signet Classic Shakespeare (New York, Penguin, 1986), 227-38.

Barrett, Michèle, *Women's Oppression Today* (London, Verso, 1980).

Barrett, Michèle and McIntosh, Mary, *The Anti-Social Family* (London, Verso, 1982).

Belsey, Catherine and Moore, Jane (eds), *The Feminist Reader: Essays in Gender and the Politics of Literary Criticism* (Cambridge, MA, Basil Blackwell, 1989).

Brenner, Robert, "The Origins of capitalist development: a critique of neo-Smithian Marxism," *New Left Review,* 104 (1977), 25-92.

Brown, Paul, "'This thing of darkness I acknowledge mine': *The Tempest* and the discourse of colonialism," in Jonathan Dollimore and Alan Sinfield (eds), *Political Shakespeare: New Essays in Cultural Materialism* (Ithaca, Cornell University Press, 1985), 48-71.

Bullough, Geoffrey (ed.), *Narrative and Dramatic Sources of Shakespeare,* vol. 1 (New York, Columbia University Press, 1957).

Chaytor, Miranda, "Household and kinship: Ryton in the late sixteenth and early seventeenth centuries," *History Workshop Journal,* 10 (1980), 25-60.

Coward, Rosalind, *Patriarchal Precedents: Sexuality and Social Relations* (Boston, Routledge & Kegan Paul, 1983).

Cressy, David, "Foucault, Stone, Shakespeare, and social history," *English Literary Renaissance,* 21(2) (1991), 121-33.

Davies, Kathleen M., "Continuity and change in literary advice on marriage," in R. B. Outhwaite (ed.), *Marriage and Society: Studies in the Social History of Marriage* (New York, St Mantiu's Press, 1981).

Deleuze, Gilles and Guattari, Félix, *Anti-Oedipus: Capitalism and Schizophrenia,* trans. Robert Hurley et al. (Minneapolis, University of Minnesota Press, 1983).

Eagleton, Terry, *Literary Theory; An Introduction* (Oxford, Basil Blackwell, 1983).

Evans, G. Blakemore et al. (ed.), *The Riverside Shakespeare* (Boston, Houghton Mifflin, 1974).

Fanon, Franz, *Black Skins, White Masks,* trans. Charles Lam Markmann (New York, Grove Press, 1967).

Freud, Sigmund, *Moses and Monotheism* (1939), trans. Katherine Jones (New York, Vintage, 1962).

———, *Totem and Taboo: Resemblances between the Psychic Lives of Savages and Neurotics,* in Peter Gay (ed.), *The Freud Reader* (New York, Norton, 1989), 481-513.

———, "Some psychical consequences of the anatomical distinction between the sexes," in Peter Gay (ed.), *The Freud Reader* (New York, Norton, 1989), 670-7.

Gardiner, Judith Kegan, "Psychoanalysis and feminism: an American humanist's view," *Signs,* 17 (winter 1992), 437-54.

Gibbons, Brian (ed.), *Romeo and Juliet,* the Arden Shakespeare (London, Methuen, 1980).

Greenblatt, Stephen, *Renaissance Self-Fashioning from More to Shakespeare* (Chicago, University of Chicago Press, 1980).

———, "Psychoanalysis and Renaissance culture," in Patricia Parker and David Quint (eds), *Literary Theory/ Renaissance Texts* (Baltimore, Johns Hopkins, 1986), 210-24.

Grosz, Elizabeth, *Jacques Lacan: A Feminist Introduction* (New York, Routledge, 1990).

Hirst, Paul Q., *Marxism and Historical Writing* (London, Routledge, 1985).

Houlbrooke, Ralph A., *The English Family, 1450-1700* (New York, Longman, 1988).

Howard, Jean, "The New Historicism in Renaissance studies," *English Literary Renaissance,* 16(1) (winter, 1986), 13-43.

Jameson, Frederic, *The Ideologies of Theory: Essays 1971-1986,* vol. 1 (Minneapolis, University of Minnesota Press, 1981).

———, *The Political Unconscious: Narrative as a Socially Symbolic Act* (Ithaca, Cornell University Press, 1985).

Jardine, Alice, *Gynesis: Configurations of Woman and Modernity* (Ithaca, Cornell University Press, 1985).

Jones, Barry, "Romeo and Juliet: the genesis of a classic," in Eric Haywood and Cormac Ó Cuilleanáin (eds), *Italian Storytellers: Essays on Italian Narrative Literature* (Dublin, Irish Academic Press, 1989), 150-81.

Kahn, Coppélia, *Man's Estate: Masculine Identity in Shakespeare* (Berkeley, University of California Press, 1981).

Kamenka, Eugene and Neale, R. S., *Feudalism, Capitalism and Beyond* (London, Edward Arnold, 1975).

Kaplan, Cora, *Sea Changes: Culture and Feminism* (London, Verso, 1986).

Katz, Claudio J., *From Feudalism to Capitalism: Marxian Theories of Class Struggle and Social Change* (New York, Greenwood Press, 1989).

Kirsch, Arthur, *Shakespeare and the Experience of Love* (New York, Cambridge University Press, 1981).

Kristeva, Julia, *Tales of Love,* trans. Leon S. Roudiez (New York, Columbia University Press, 1987).

Laslett, Peter, *The World We Have Lost Further Explored* (London, Methuen, 1965, 1983).

———, "The European family and early Industrialization," in Jean Baechler et al. (eds), 234-41.

Macfarlane, Alan, Review of Lawrence Stone's *The Family, Sex and Marriage in England, History and Theory,* 18 (1979), 103-26.

———, *Marriage and Love in England: Modes of Reproduction 1300-1840* (Oxford, Basil Blackwell, 1986).

———, "The cradle of capitalism: the case of England," in Jean Baechler et al. (eds), 185-203.

Marx, Karl and Engels, Friedrich, *The Marx-Engels Reader,* ed. Robert C. Tucker (New York, Norton, 1978).

Medick, Hans. "The transition from feudalism to capitalism: renewal of the debate," in Raphael Samuel (ed.) *People's History and Socialist Theory* (London, Routledge & Kegan Paul, 1981).

Mitchell, Juliet, *Woman's Estate* (New York, Vintage, 1973).

———, *Psychoanalysis and Feminism: Freud, Reich, Laing and Women* (New York, Vintage, 1975).

Mitchell, Juliet and Rose, Jacqueline, *Feminine Sexuality: Feminine Sexuality and the ecole freudienne,* trans. Jacqueline Rose (London, Macmillan, 1982).

Montrose, Louis, "Renaissance literary studies and the subject of history," *English Literary Renaissance,* 16(1) (1986), 5-12.

Mooers, Colin, *The Making of Bourgeois Europe: Absolutism, Revolution, and the Rise of Capitalism in England, France, and Germany* (New York, Verso, 1991).

Mooney, Michael, "Text and performance: *Romeo and Juliet,* Quartos 1 and 2," *Colby Quarterly,* XXVI (2) (June 1990), 122-32.

Newman, Karen, *Fashioning Femininity and English Renaissance Drama* (Chicago, University of Chicago Press, 1991).

Newton, Judith and Rosenfelt, Deborah (eds), *Feminist Literary Criticism and Social Change* (New York, Routledge, 1986).

Novick, Peter, *That Noble Dream: "The Objectivity Question" and the American Historical Profession* (Cambridge, Cambridge University Press, 1988).

Novy, Marianne, *Love's Argument: Gender Relations in Shakespeare* (Chapel Hill, University of North Carolina Press, 1984).

Outhwaite, R. B. (ed.), *Marriage and Society: Studies in the Social History of Marriage* (New York, St Martin's Press, 1981).

Porter, Joseph, "Marlowe, Shakespeare, and the canonization of heterosexuality," *South Atlantic Quarterly,* 88(1) (1989), 127-47.

Rose, Mary Beth, *The Expense of Spirit: Love and Sexuality in English Renaissance Drama* (Ithaca, Cornell University Press, 1988).

Rougement, Denis de, *Love in the Western World,* trans. Montgomery Belgion (Princeton, NJ: Princeton University Press, 1983).

Ryan, Kiernan, "*Romeo and Juliet*: the language of tragedy," in Willie van Peer (ed.), *Taming the Text* (New York, Routledge, 1988), 106-21.

Ryan, Michael, *Marxism and Deconstruction* (Baltimore, Johns Hopkins, 1982).

Sharpe, J. A., *Early Modern England: A Social History 1550-1760* (London, Edward Arnold, 1987).

Sinfield, Alan, *Literature in Protestant England, 1560-1660* (Towota, NJ, Barnes & Noble, 1983).

Smith, Bruce R., *Homosexual Desire in Shakespeare's England: A Cultural Poetics* (Chicago, University of Chicago Press, 1991).

Stockholder, Kay, *Dreamworks: Lovers and Families in Shakespeare's Plays* (Toronto, University of Toronto Press, 1987).

Stone, Lawrence, *The Family, Sex and Marriage in England 1500-1800* (New York, Harper & Row, 1977).

———, *The Past and the Present* (Boston, Routledge & Kegan Paul, 1980).

Swindells, Julia and Jardine, Lisa, *What's Left? Women in Culture and the Labour Movement* (New York, Routledge, 1990).

Taylor, Barry, *Society and Economy in Early Modern Europe: A Bibliography of Post-War Research* (New York, Manchester University Press, 1989).

Traub, Valerie, "Kay Stockholder. *Dream works: lovers and families in Shakespeare's plays,*" *Shakespeare Quarterly,* 40(1) (spring 1989), 100-2.

———, "Prince Hal's Falstaff: positioning psychoanalysis and the female reproductive Body," *Shakespeare Quarterly,* 40(4) (1989), 456-74.

———, "Desire and the difference it makes," in Valerie Wayne (ed.), *The Matter of Difference: Materialist Feminist Criticism of Shakespeare* (Ithaca, Cornell, 1991), 81-114.

Veeser, Aram H. (ed.), *The New Historicism* (New York, Routledge, 1989).

Wallerstein, Immanuel, *Historical Capitalism* (London, Verso, 1983).

Wayne, Don E., "New historicism," in Martin Coyle, Peter Garside, Malcolm Kelsall, and John Peck (eds), *Encyclopedia of Literature and Criticism* (London, Routledge, 1990).

Weedon, Chris, *Feminism and Poststructuralism* (London, Routledge, 1989).

Weeks, Jeffrey, *Sexuality and its Discontents: Meanings, Myths, and Modern Sexualities* (London, Routledge, 1985).

Whittier, Gayle, "The sonnet's body and the body sonnetized in *Romeo and Juliet,*" *Shakespeare Quarterly,* 40(1) (spring 1989), 27-41.

Wrightson, Keith, *English Society 1580-1680* (New Brunswick, NJ, Rutgers University Press, 1982).

Zaretsky, Eli, *Capitalism, the Family and Personal Life* (London, Pluto, 1976).

LEAH MARCUS (ESSAY DATE OCTOBER 2000)

SOURCE: Marcus, Leah. "Elizabeth the Writer." *History Today* 50, no. 10 (October 2000): 36-38.

In the following essay, Marcus praises Queen Elizabeth's oratory strengths.

In July 1597, a dashing young Polish ambassador made his debut at the Elizabethan court. The English welcomed him with pageantry that was more splendid than usual and prepared to celebrate a 'great day.' But the young ambassador's formal Latin oration of greeting froze the cordial environment, offering the aging Queen Elizabeth a series of rebukes rather than the diplomatic platitudes that had been expected. What happened next was predictable to those who had seen the Queen in action before, but astonishing to those less acquainted with her oratorical skills. Sir Robert Cecil marvelled in a letter to the Earl of Essex, 'to this, I swear by the living God that her majesty made one of the best answers *extempore* in Latin that ever I heard, being much moved to be so challenged in public, especially so much against her expectation.' Her reply to the Polish ambassador expressed her astonishment at 'so great and insolent a boldness in open Presence' and tartly corrected his 'ignorant' misapprehension of 'the law of nature' and 'of nations,' and 'what is convenient between kings.' She closed with a suggestion that he 'repose himself' or 'be silent,' depending on how much indignity one wishes to infuse into the translation of Elizabeth's Latin.

The learning and rhetorical skill displayed in this public rebuke were characteristic of Elizabeth I. Typically, her public speeches were not penned in advance, but delivered more or less impromptu. She was at her best when she was most spontaneous, both as a speaker and as a writer, and she was much admired by her contemporaries for both talents. No doubt, those who admired her literary skills saw them through the usual haze of flattery that surrounds a reigning monarch's every gesture. And we moderns have been hesitant to acknowledge the power of many of Elizabeth's writings out of fear that we will be suspected of a similar uncritical adulation. Nevertheless, as we begin a new century, her work is of increasing interest to historians and literary scholars. Her reputation as a writer is arguably higher now than it has been at any time since her own era.

For all their acknowledged brilliance in delivery, Elizabeth's speeches are elusive, precisely because they did not exist in advance copies. Lacking modern recording devices, contemporaries who wanted to preserve her utterances were required either to take down the queen's words in rudimentary shorthand as she spoke them or, more likely, record them from memory as soon as possible after the end of the speech. Frequently, they record their frustration at not having captured her performance adequately. In 1601, for example, Sir Roger Wilbraham, the Queen's solicitor general for Ireland, complained as he attempted to record her speech of December 19th, besides the fact that 'I could not well hear all she spake, the grace of pronunciation and of her apt and refined words, so learnedly composed, did ravish the sense of the hearers with such admiration as every new sentence made me half forget the precedents'.

Because they were written down after the fact, different manuscript versions of Elizabeth's speeches often display strikingly different wording. In the first of her impromptu 1586 replies to

ON THE SUBJECT OF...

QUEEN ELIZABETH I (1533-1603)

Elizabeth I was the reigning monarch of England from 1558 to 1603. She preserved the English nation against internal as well as external threats, and during her forty-five-year reign the island kingdom emerged as a world power. It is because of her influence that the latter half of the sixteenth century in England is known as the Elizabethan Age.

Elizabeth was the daughter of King Henry VIII and his second wife, Anne Boleyn. Because Henry VIII had defied the Pope and married Boleyn in the hope of producing a male heir to the throne, he was bitterly disappointed in the birth of a second daughter. Before Elizabeth was three, the king had her mother beheaded and their marriage declared invalid. Although now considered an illegitimate child, Elizabeth was still third in line to the throne (after her half brother Edward and half sister Mary). She received tutoring from leading Renaissance scholars who noted her intellect and seriousness, and became fluent in Greek, Latin, French, and Italian. On 17 November 1558 Elizabeth became queen of England, and quickly surrounded herself with experienced and loyal advisers.

The remarkable literary flowering that took place during Elizabeth's rule, when William Shakespeare, Edmund Spenser, Sir Philip Sidney, and Christopher Marlowe were all writing, has kept alive the idea that Elizabethan England enjoyed a golden age. Elizabeth was successful at maintaining peace at home and abroad and also at establishing her own image as a loving and able ruler. Although her own writings—speeches, poetry, and devotional works—do not begin to equal the greatest of her age, they were nevertheless important in creating and sustaining that age.

a parliamentary delegation urging the queen to consent to the execution of Mary, Queen of Scots, for example, one manuscript has Elizabeth complaining about 'pettifoggers of the law, who look more on the outside of their books than study them within.' The version Robert Cecil printed shortly after the speech's delivery is more polite: 'you lawyers are so nice in sifting and scanning every word and letter that many times you stand more upon form than matter, upon syllables than sense of the law.' In this case, the difference in wording may be a result of the Queen's own revision, for we possess in her own hand corrections made to the speech in preparation for its publication. But to make her corrections, she had to rely on someone else's written copy made from memory after her delivery of the speech. We can judge pretty closely what she wanted her public to read, since her written corrections correlate fairly closely with the speech as printed. But how does that version compare with the speech as she actually delivered it? We can make educated guesses, but we will never know certainly.

The Queen's most famous speech before Parliament was undoubtedly her 'Golden Speech' of November 1601, delivered in answer to the Commons' complaint about her toleration for monopolies that restricted trade and impoverished her subjects. Here, as usual, contemporaries bemoaned the fact that their written recollections of the speech preserved it so imperfectly. One copyist recorded, 'Many things through want of memory I have omitted, without setting down many her majesty's gestures of honour and princely demeanor used by her. As when the speaker spake any effectual or moving speech from the Commons to her majesty, she rose up and bowed herself. As also in her own speech, when the Commons, apprehending any extraordinary words of favour from her, did any reverence to her majesty, she likewise rose up and bowed herself.' In the case of the Golden Speech, however, the version published immediately after the event is even less reliable than usual as a guide to the speech in delivery as we have it recorded by MPs present at the occasion. The official printed version is a disappointingly short abstract that omits most of the 'golden' language for which the speech became famous. The uncertainty of contemporary evidence is surely one reason why it has taken us so long fully to acknowledge Elizabeth's formidable skills as an orator.

Roger Wilbraham's adulatory remarks are typical of auditors' responses to speeches at the end of Elizabeth's reign, when the Cult of Elizabeth was in full swing and her oratorical powers had become the stuff of legend. Four decades earlier, she was probably just as eloquent but aroused a rather different reaction from MPs. Most of her addresses from the first years of her reign were designed to deflect parliamentary petitions urging her to marry and declare a succession. She ended her very first speech before Parliament (February 1559) by deftly parrying their demands and declaring, 'And in the end this shall be for me sufficient: that a marble stone shall declare that a queen, having reigned such a time, lived and died a virgin.' Later speeches on the same general topic are less pacific towards those who would coerce her into procreation. In a 1562 conversation with the Scottish ambassador, she complained that to declare a succession would be like holding up her own winding sheet before her eyes. In November 1566, incensed that parliamentarians were tying their grant of funds to run her government to her promise to marry and declare a succession. Elizabeth lashed out against their presumption: 'When I call to mind how far from dutiful care, yea, rather how nigh a traitorous trick this tumbling cast did spring, I muse how men of wit can so hardly use that gift they hold. I marvel not much that bridleless colts do not know their rider's hand, whom bit of kingly rein did never snaffle yet.'

After 1567, Elizabeth spoke less frequently before Parliament. We have only one full-length speech from the 1570s, and only the speeches on the execution of Mary, Queen of Scots, from the 1580s. One of her most arresting productions was her famous 'Armada Speech', delivered before the troops at Tilbury who were awaiting Spanish invasion in 1588. As we would expect, this stirring address exists in several versions which display intriguing differences. The earliest known published version of the speech dates from 1654, and is, according to the compiler of the volume in which it appears, based on the recollection of Lionel Sharp, an adherent of the Earl of Leicester who was present at the speech's delivery. This version has the Queen protesting her fearlessness to appear in public, despite threats of assassination: 'And therefore I am come amongst you, as you see at this time, not for my recreation and disport, but being resolved in the midst and heat of the battle to live or die amongst you all.' A manuscript that can be dated closer to the time of the speech's actual delivery has Elizabeth promising, 'Wherefore I am come among you at this time but for my recreation and pleasure, being resolved in the midst and heat of the battle to live and die amongst you all.' In this version, death in battle becomes her highest pleasure, a blood-feast of daring and sacrifice. We cannot be certain whether the published version is a later tidying clarification of the Queen's highminded *sprezzatura* in the face of the Spanish threat, or whether it is closer to what she actually said than the surviving manuscript. As usual, the early evidence allows us to come close to recapturing what she uttered, but leaves us at a tantalising distance from certainty.

Elizabeth's speeches are arguably her most glorious literary production, even though, in the forms we have, they are imperfect records of performance. But she also produced poems, prayers, and hundreds of letters. The Armada threat of 1588 inspired her to intense literary activity. Beyond the Armada Speech itself, we possess two public prayers of thanksgiving for the Armada victory, one of which shows the Queen in high, vatic mode as a priestess of her people, thanking God for creating the four elements by which, acting in concert, the Spanish fleet was destroyed:

> Everlasting and omnipotent Creator, Redeemer, and Conserver, when it seemed most fit time to Thy worthy providence to bestow the workmanship of this world or globe, with Thy rare judgment Thou didst divide into four singular parts the form of all this world, which aftertime hath termed elements, they all serving to continue in orderly government the whole of all the mass: which all, when of Thy most singular bounty and never-earst-seen care Thou hast this year made serve for instruments both to daunt our foes and to confound their malice.

Elizabeth's enigmatic French verses, which record a mystical rise into otherworldly constancy and spiritual equilibrium, may have been inspired by the Armada victory, as was a little-known 'Song' that was, according to the heading of the single known copy, 'made by her majesty and sung before her at her coming from Whitehall to Paul's through Fleet Street' in public celebration of the scattering of the Spanish ships. In this highly psalmic poem, she offers herself as a sacrifice in thanksgiving for the victory:

> Look and bow down Thine ear, O Lord.
> From Thy bright sphere behold and see
> Thy handmaid and Thy handiwork,
> Amongst Thy priests, offering to Thee
> Zeal for incense, reaching the skies;
> Myself and sceptre, sacrifice.

Given the importance of its occasion, it is astonishing that the Queen's 'Song' has until now been so little known.

The most famous of Elizabeth's political verses is 'The doubt of future foes', written in 1570-71 in response to the Northern Rebellion and the abortive plot to place the Duke of Norfolk and Mary,

Queen of Scots, on the throne of England. Her contemporaries admired this poem greatly for its extended 'dark conceit', a threat of death, half submerged in allegory, against Mary, the 'daughter of debate,' and Elizabeth's rebellious subjects. The poem begins:

> The doubt of future foes
> Exiles my present joy
> And with me warns to shun such snares
> As threatens mine annoy

and ends with the promise to prune her 'foes' with an instrument of war:

> My rusty sword through rest
> Shall first his edge employ
> To poll their tops who seek such change
> Or gape for future joy.

Like her speeches, this poem is securely attributed to Elizabeth and exists in a number of manuscript copies, all of them different in their precise wording. But her less obviously political poems are more elusive, and many of them may be lost for good. Most of them were composed as verse conversations with courtiers like Sir Thomas Heneage and Sir Walter Ralegh, and were carefully kept from circulation. To the extent that they have survived, it is often because of the fortuitous durability of the surface on which they were composed or copied. Two of Elizabeth's lyrics survive only as marginalia in religious books, and the verse exchange between Ralegh and Elizabeth was printed decades later, shorn of its personal references and the names of its authors, as a broadside ballad entitled 'The Lover's Complaint for the Loss of His Love' and 'The Lady's Comfortable and Pleasant Answer.' Even when Elizabeth's lyrics were copied, their attribution to the Queen was frequently recorded in the manuscript, and then cancelled out—a clear marker of the ambivalence her subjects felt about daring to preserve her verses.

Luckily, with Elizabeth's numerous letters, we are on firmer ground, because they are, like the speeches, always acknowledged as hers. To read her correspondence from the first awkward girlish production addressed to her father 'the most illustrious and most mighty King Henry the Eighth' through to the instructions to Charles Blount, Lord Mountjoy, for the submission of the Earl of Tyrone at the very end of her reign, is to survey the major events of the Elizabethan age through the perceptions of its major actor. Elizabeth's letters are fascinating for their diversity and stylistic range: pleas for her life during her 'troubles' under the reign of her sister Mary, love letters (or so, at least, she wanted them to appear) to the Duke of Alencon, advice about rule in numerous impatient harangues to James VI of Scotland and Henry IV of France, condolences, pleasantries and intimate advice to her courtiers. As usual, Elizabeth's writing is at its best when she is in her mode of high indignation, as in a characteristic opening to James, 'I rue my sight that views the evident spectacle of a seduced king, abusing Council, and wry-guided kingdom'. Elizabeth usually gets high marks for her diplomatic skills, but we have not fully acknowledged how much of her success can be traced to her brilliance with language.

FURTHER READING

Alexander, Meena. "Introduction: Mapping a Female Romanticism." In *Women in Romanticism: Mary Wollstonecraft, Dorothy Wordsworth and Mary Shelley,* pp. 1-17. Savage, Md.: Barnes & Noble Books, 1989.

Examines how women authors faced the "anxiety of authorship" and social constraints.

Berry, Philippa. *Of Chastity and Power: Elizabethan Literature and the Unmarried Queen.* London: Routledge, 1989, 193 p.

Considers literary representations of Elizabeth I.

Burroughs, Catherine B. "English Romantic Women Writers and Theatre Theory: Joanna Baillie's Prefaces to the 'Plays on the Passions'." In *Re-Visioning Romanticism: British Women Writers, 1776-1837,* edited by Carol Shiner Wilson and Joel Haefner, pp. 274-96. Philadelphia: University of Pennsylvania Press, 1994.

Discusses Baillie's closet theatre theory in the context of the tradition of women writing about the stage.

Dixon, Annette. "Women Who Ruled: Queens, Goddesses, Amazons 1500-1650: A Thematic Overview." In *Women Who Ruled: Queens, Goddesses, Amazons in Renaissance and Baroque Art,* edited by Annette Dixon, pp. 119-179. London: Merrell Publishers Limited, 2002.

Features dozens of plates of art depicting the power of female rulers.

Garrard, Mary D. "Artemisia and Susanna." In *Feminism and Art History: Questioning the Litany,* edited by Norma Broude and Mary D. Garrard, pp. 146-71. New York: Harper & Row, Publishers, 1982.

Analyzes the paintings of Artemisia Gentileschi that portray Susanna of the Apocrypha.

Glenn, Cheryl. "Inscribed in the Margins: Renaissance Women and Rhetorical Culture." In *Rhetoric Retold: Regendering the Tradition from Antiquity through the Renaissance,* pp. 118-72. Carbondale: Southern Illinois University Press, 1997.

Explores Renaissance rhetoric and the contributions made by Margaret More Roper, Anne Askew, and Elizabeth I.

Gutwirth, Madelyn. "Gendered Rococo as Political Provocation." In *The Twilight of the Goddesses: Women and Representation in the French Revolutionary Era,* pp. 3-22. New Brunswick, N.J.: Rutgers University Press, 1992.

Examines some of the underlying issues of rococo art.

Hellwarth, Jennifer Wynne. "'I wyl wright of women prevy sekenes': Imagining Female Literacy and Textual Communities in Medieval and Early Modern Midwifery Manuals." *Critical Survey* 14, no. 1 (January 2002): 44-63.

Considers the cultural implications of the prefaces to medieval midwifery manuals.

Hull, Suzanne W. *Women According to Men: The World of Tudor-Stuart Women.* Walnut Creek, Calif.: AltaMira Press, 1996, 240 p.

Describes the world of English women from 1525 to 1675 using the written words of contemporary men.

Kelly, Joan. "Did Women Have a Renaissance?" In *Feminism and Renaissance Studies,* edited by Lorna Hutson, pp. 21-47. Oxford, England: Oxford University Press, 1999.

Contends that during the Renaissance women experienced a diminishment of public and personal power.

Miller, Nancy K. "Men's Reading, Women's Writing: Gender and the Rise of the Novel." *Yale French Studies,* no. 75 (1988): 40-55.

Criticizes past attempts at writing a history of women's involvement in the development of the eighteenth-century novel.

Rose, Judith. "Prophesying Daughters: Testimony, Censorship, and Literacy Among Early Quaker Women." *Critical Survey* 14, no. 1 (January 2002): 93-110.

Contends that attempts to contain literacy among Quaker women actually led to greater self-empowerment.

Schor, Naomi. "The Portrait of a Gentleman: Representing Men in (French) Women's Writing." *Representations,* no. 20 (autumn 1987): 113-33.

Analyzes descriptions of men by Mme. de Lafayette, Mme. de Staël, and George Sand.

Smith, Hilda L. "Humanist Education and the Renaissance Concept of Woman." In *Women and Literature in Britain, 1500-1700,* edited by Helen Wilcox, pp. 9-29. Cambridge, England: Cambridge University Press, 1996.

Examines the definition of the concept of "woman" during the Renaissance, particularly for humanist writers.

Spongberg, Mary. "'Above Their Sex'? Women's History 'before' Feminism." In *Writing Women's History since the Renaissance,* pp. 63-85. Hampshire, England: Palgrave MacMillan, 2002.

Documents female historical writers from the Renaissance to the French Revolution.

Sturkenboom, Dorothée. "Historicizing the Gender of Emotions: Changing Perceptions in Dutch Enlightenment Thought." *Journal of Social History* 34, no. 1 (2000): 55-75.

Uses eighteenth century Dutch periodicals to investigate prevailing ideas on the genderedness of emotions.

Summit, Jennifer. "The Reformation of the Woman Writer." In *Lost Property: The Woman Writer and English Literary History 1380-1589,* pp. 109-61. Chicago: University of Chicago Press, 2000.

Discusses the political significance of religious women's writing.

Turner, Cheryl. *Living by the Pen: Women Writers in the Eighteenth Century.* London: Routledge, 1994, 261 p.

Studies the rise of women's fiction and the beginnings of the professional woman writer.

Walker, Kim. "'Busie in my Clositt': Letters, Diaries, and Autobiographical Writing." In *Women Writers of the English Renaissance,* pp. 26-46. New York: Twayne Publishers, 1996.

Explores how literate Renaissance women pushed the boundary between private and public writing.

Wall, Wendy. "Dancing in a Net: The Problems of Female Authorship." In *The Imprint of Gender: Authorship and Publication in the English Renaissance,* pp. 279-340. Ithaca, N.Y.: Cornell University Press, 1996.

Explores the different reactions of Isabella Whitney, Mary Sidney, Amelia Lanyer, and Mary Wroth in response to the inhibiting factors affecting their writing.

Wiesner-Hanks, Merry E. *My Gracious Silence: Women in the Mirror of 16th Century Printing in Western Europe,* edited by Axel Erdmann. Luzern, Switzerland: Gilhofer & Ranschburg, 1999, 319 p.

Examines women writers' responses to societal admonitions that they remain silent.

WOMEN'S LITERATURE IN THE 16TH, 17TH, AND 18TH CENTURIES

With the advent of print in Europe in the mid 1400s, literature began to garner a much larger audience. The most famous early book was the *Gutenberg Bible* of 1456, and twenty years later, William Caxton effectively originated print in England when he set up his press at Westminster. The trend toward literacy and the wider distribution of texts throughout the sixteenth, seventeenth and eighteenth centuries significantly altered not only the intellectual landscape of Europe, but the role of women writers—as print made literature more widely available to the middle class and to middle-class women, the focus of literature changed significantly. Despite often being denied the educational opportunities afforded to men, far more women were able to express themselves in writing than before this period.

Much early writing, including that of female authors, was devotional in nature. Many women wrote prayers, translations of religious works originally in Latin, and other texts primarily centered on spirituality. Notable, and often autobiographical, religious works by authors such as Margery Kempe, were especially popular. The increasing availability of print gradually allowed literature to focus on more secular themes, and many women contributed to the body of literature by writing journals, essays, and letters. Initially a private genre, letters evolved from a basic form of communication into a significant public literary style. Epistolary writing by such authors as Margaret Cavendish and Mary Wortley Montagu elevated the style, contributing to the creation of the epistolary novel genre and to the development of fiction itself. These and other letters by women are currently studied not only for their social and historical commentary, but for their literary merits as well.

Nancy Cotton has traced the contributions of women playwrights to the fourteenth century, noting that the first known woman playwright in England, Katherine of Sutton, rewrote traditional liturgical plays between 1363 and 1376. Cotton credits the Countess of Pembroke, with her *Antonie* printed in 1592, as the first woman in England to publish a play. Angela J. Smallwood examines eighteenth-century British theater, and notes that the second half of the century was a "heyday of genteel comedy for female as well as male writers." A playwright as well as a novelist, Aphra Behn is known as the first woman to earn her living entirely from writing. Her novels, especially *Oroonoko* (1688) are widely studied to this day, as are the romantic works of Madeleine de Scudéry, and both authors were highly influential in the further development of literature. Women also participated heavily in the poetry of the era. As poetry writing changed from an act practiced by the aristocracy to one available to women of all classes, working-class women such as Ann Yearsley and Hannah More joined noblewomen such as Anne Finch, Countess of Winchilsea, as published poets. Women made significant contributions to a wide variety of literature and literary periods, from the rise of the periodical in the sixteenth century to the rise of literary criticism.

Modern analyses of women's literature from 1500 to 1800 investigate the effects of social, economic, and political conditions under which women lived, in addition to studying the literary merits of their works. For instance, Marion Wynne-Davies demonstrates how women's very lack of status and financial independence served as an important impetus to publish, since they recognized their literary skills as a means to earn money. Elaine Hobby contends that women were more suited than men to write religious meditations, due to the "specifically female advantages of abandoning the world," and its "concerns of state." Margaret J. M. Ezell explains that women's literature was historically neglected by scholars, except in the area of nineteenth-century novels, but that literary historians, particularly since the 1970s, have recovered many previously unknown texts and manuscripts. Isobel Grundy analyzes the many elements involved in recovering a particular text and explores why a text might have been suppressed in the past. The recovery of such texts enables the study of early female writers, and the critical study and popular appeal of these authors continues to grow.

REPRESENTATIVE WORKS

Abigail Adams

Letters of Mrs. Adams, The Wife of John Adams (letters) 1840

Elizabeth Ashbridge

Some Account of the Fore-Part of the Life of Elizabeth Ashbridge (autobiography) 1774

Anne Askew

The first examinacyon of the worthy servant of God, Mistresse Anne Askewe . . . lately martyred in Smith-fielde, by the Romish Antichristian Broode . . . with the elucydation of Johan Bale (personal narrative) 1546

The lattre examinacyon of the worthye servaunt of God mastres Anne Askewe (personal narrative) 1547

St. Teresa de Avila

El libro de su vida [*The Life of the Mother Teresa of Jesus*] 1562

El libra de las fundaciones de Santa Teresa de Jesús [*The Book of the Foundations*] 1576

El castillo interior, o las moradas [*The Interior Castle; or, The Mansions*] 1577

Mary Astell

A Serious Proposal to the Ladies for the Advancement of Their True and Greatest Interest. By a Lover of Her Sex (essay) 1694

A Serious Proposal to the Ladies, Part II. Wherin a Method is Offer'd for the Improvement of Their Minds (essay) 1697

Aphra Behn

Oroonoko; Or, The Royal Slave. A True History (novel) 1688

The Lady's Looking-Glass, to dress herself by; or, The Whole Art of Charming (novel) 1697

Anne Bradstreet

The Tenth Muse (poetry) 1650

Margaret Cavendish

CCXI Sociable Letters (correspondence) 1664

Anne Finch

Miscellany Poems, on Several Occasions (poems) 1713

Anne Killigrew

Poems By Mrs. Anne Killigrew (poetry) 1686

Sarah Kemble Knight

The Journals of Madam Knight, and Rev. Mr. Buckingham. From the Original Manuscripts Written in 1704 & 1710 (journals) 1825

Charlotte Lennox

The Female Quixote; or, The Adventures of Arabella. 2 vols. (novel) 1752

The Lady's Museum [editor] (essays, prose, poetry) 1760-61

Elizabeth Major

Honey on the Rod: Or a comfortable Contemplation for one in Affliction (devotions) 1656

Bathusa Makin

An Essay to Revive the Antient Education of Gentlewomen (essay) 1673

Catherine Parr

Prayers or Meditations, Wherin the Mynde is Styrred Paciently to Suffre all Afflictions Here [editor] (meditations) 1545

The Lamentation of a Sinner, Made by ye Most Vertuous Ladie, Quene Caterine, Bewayling the Ignorance of Her Blind Life (autobiography) 1547

Eliza Lucas Pinckney

Journal and Letters of Eliza Lucas, Now First Printed (journal, letters) 1850

Mary Rowlandson

The Soveraignty & Goodness of God, Together with the Faithfulness of His Promises Displayed; Being a Narrative of the Captivity and Restauration of Mrs. Mary Rowlandson, Commended by her to all that Desire to Know the Lord's Doings to, and Dealings with Her. Especially to her Dear Children and Relations. [republished as *A True History of the Captivity & Restoration of Mrs. Mary Rowlandson, A Minister's Wife in New-England: Wherein is set forth, The Cruel and Inhumane Usage she underwent amongst the Heathens for Eleven Weeks time: And her Deliverance from them. Written by her own Hand, for her Private Use: and now made public at the earnest Desire of some Friends, for the Benefit of the Afflicted,* 1682] (autobiography) 1682

Mercy Otis Warren

History of the Rise, Progress, and Termination of the American Revolution: Interspersed with Biographical and Moral Observations (history) 1805

Phillis Wheatley

Poems on Various Subjects, Religious and Moral (poetry) 1773

Isabella Whitney

The Copy of a Letter, Lately Written in Meeter, by a Youge Gentilwoman: To Her Vnconstant Louer [as Is. W.] (prose poetry) 1567

A Sweet Nosgay, or Pleasant Posye: Contayning a Hundred and Ten Phylosophicall Flowers [as Is. W.] (prose poetry) 1573

Hannah Wolley

The Gentlewomans Companion; or, A Guide to the Female Sex, (essay) 1675

Mary Wollstonecraft

Thoughts on the Education of Daughters: With Reflections on Female Conduct, in the More Important Duties of Life (essay) 1787

The Female Reader; or, Miscellaneous-Pieces, in Prose and Verse, Selected from the Best Writers, and Disposed Under Proper Heads; for the Improvement of Young Women [editor] (poetry and essays) 1789

A Vindication of the Rights of Men, in a Letter to the Right Honourable Edmund Burke; Occasioned by His Reflections on the Revolution in France (essay) 1790

A Vindication of the Rights of Woman: with Strictures on Political and Moral Subjects (essay) 1792

Maria; or, The Wrongs of Woman: A Posthumous Fragment (unfinished novel) 1799

Lady Mary Wroth

The Countesse of Mountgomeries Urania (novel) 1621

Pamphilia to Amphilanthus by Lady Mary Wroth (poetry) 1977

PRIMARY SOURCES

MARY ROWLANDSON (ESSAY DATE 1682)

SOURCE: Rowlandson, Mary. "Captivity, Sufferings, and Removes (1682)." In *Public Women, Public Words: A Documentary History of American Feminism,* edited by Dawn Keetley and John Pettegrew, pp. 21-26. Madison, Wis.: Madison House, 1997.

In the following excerpt from her 1682 book, Rowlandson relates her time spent as a captive of American Indians.

On the 10th of February, 1675, the Indians, in great numbers, came upon Lancaster. Their first coming was about sun-rising; hearing the noise of some guns, we looked out; several houses were burning, and the smoke ascending to heaven. There were five persons taken in one house, the father, the mother, and a sucking child they knocked on the head; the other two they took and carried away alive.—There were two others, who being out of the garrison upon occasion, were set upon; one was knocked on the head, the other escaped: another there was, who running along, was shot and wounded, and fell down; he begged of them his life, promising them money, (as they told me) but they would not hearken to him, knocked him on the head, stripped him naked, and ripped open his bowels. Another, seeing many of the Indians about his barn, ventured out, but was quickly shot down. There were three others belonging to the same garrison, who were killed; the Indians getting up on the roof of the barn, had advantage to shoot down upon them over their fortification. Thus these murderous wretches went on burning and destroying all before them.

At length they came and beset our own house, and quickly it was the dolefulest day that ever mine eyes saw. . . . Now is the dreadful hour come, that I have often heard of (in the time of the war, as was the case with others) but now mine eyes see it. Some in our house were fighting for their lives, others wallowing in their blood, the house on fire over our heads, and the bloody heathen ready to knock us on the head if we stirred out. Now might we hear mothers and children crying out for themselves and one another, *Lord what shall we do*! Then I took my children (and one of my sisters her's) to go forth and leave the house: but as soon as we came to the door, and appeared, the Indians shot so thick, that the bullets rattled against the house, as if one had taken an handful of stones and threw them, so that we were forced to give back. We had six stout dogs belonging to our garrison, but none of them would stir, tho at another time, if an Indian had come to the door, they were ready to fly upon him and tear him down. The Lord hereby would make us the more to acknowledge his hand, and to see that our help is always in him.—But out we must go, the fire increasing, and coming along behind us, roaring, and the Indians gaping before us with their guns, spears, and hatchets, to devour us. No sooner were we out of the house, but my brother-in-law (being before wounded, in defending the house, in or near the throat) fell down dead, whereat the Indians scornfully shouted, and hallooed, and were presently upon him, stripping off his cloaths. The bullets flying thick, one went thro my side, and the same (as it would seem), thro the bowels and hand of my poor child in my arms. One of my elder sister's children (named William) had then his leg broken, which the Indians perceiving, they knocked him on the head. Thus were we butchered by those merciless heathens, standing amazed, with the blood running down to our heels. My elder sister being yet in the house, and seeing those woeful sights, the infidels hauling mothers one way, and children another, and some wallowing in their blood: and her eldest son telling her that her son William was dead, and myself wounded, she said, *Lord, let me die with them.*—which was no sooner said than she was struck with a bullet, and fell down dead over the threshold. I hope she is reaping the fruit of her good labours, being faithful to the service of God in her place. In her younger years she lay under much trouble upon spiritual accounts, till it pleased God to make that precious scripture take hold of her heart, 2 Cor. xii. 9. And he said unto me, My Grace is sufficient for thee. More than twenty years after, I have heard her tell how sweet and comfortable that place was to her. But to return; the Indians laid hold on us, pulling me one way, and the children another, and said, Come, go along with us: I told them they would kill me; they answered, If I were willing to go along with them, they would not hurt me.

Oh! the doleful sight that now was to behold at this house! Come behold the works of the Lord, what desolations he has made in the earth. Of thirty seven persons who were in this one house, none escaped either present death, or a bitter captivity, save only one, who might say as in Job 1. xv. And I only am escaped alone to tell the news. There were twelve killed, some shot, some stabbed with their spears, some knocked down with their hatchets. When we are in prosperity, ho, the little that we think of such dreadful sights, to see our dear friends and relations lie bleeding out their hearts blood upon the ground.—There was one who was chopped into the head with a hatchet and stripped naked, and yet was crawling up and down. It is a solemn sight to see so many christians lying in their blood, some here and some there, like a company of sheep torn by wolves. All of them stripped naked by a company of hell hounds, roaring, singing, ranting and insulting, as if they would have torn our very hearts out; yet the Lord, by his almighty power, preserved a number of us from death, for there were twenty four of us taken alive and carried captive.

I had often before this said, that if the Indians should come, I should choose rather to be killed by them, than taken alive: but when it came to the trial, my mind changed; their glittering weapons so daunted my spirits, that I chose rather to go along with those (as I may say) ravenous bears, than that moment to end my days. And that I may the better declare what happened to me during that grievous captivity, I shall particularly speak of the several Removes we had up and down the wilderness.

The First Remove

Now away we must go with those barbarous creatures, with our bodies wounded and bleeding, and our hearts no less than our bodies. About a mile we went that night, up upon a hill within sight of the town, where they intended to lodge. There was hard by a vacant house, (deserted by the English before, for fear of the Indians) I asked them whether I might not lodge in the house that night to which they answered, What, will you love Englishmen still. This was the dolefulest night that ever my eyes saw. Oh, the roaring, and singing, dancing, and yelling of those black creatures in the night, which made the place a lively resemblance of hell: and as miserable was the waste that was there made, of horses, cattle, sheep, swine, calves, lambs, roasting pigs, and fowls, (which they had plundered in the town) some roasting, some lying and burning, and some boiling, to feed our merciless enemies, who were joyful enough, though we were disconsolate. To add to the dolefulness of the former day, and the dismalness of the present night, my thoughts ran upon my losses, and sad bereaved condition. All was gone, my husband gone, (at least separated from me, he being in the bay; and to add to my grief, the Indians told me they would kill him as he came homeward) my children gone, my relations and friends gone, our house and home, and all our comforts within door and without, all were gone, (except my life) and I knew not but the next moment that might go too.

There remained nothing to me but one poor wounded babe, and it seemed at present worse than death, that it was in such a pitiful condition, bespeaking compassion, and I had no refreshing for it, nor suitable things to revive it. Little do many think, what is the savageness and bruitishness of this barbarous enemy . . .

The Third Remove

The morning being come, they prepared to go on their way: one of the Indians got up on a horse, and they set me up behind him, with my poor sick babe in my lap. A very wearisome and tedious day I had of it; what with my own wound, and my child being so exceedingly sick, and in a lamentable condition with her wound, it may easily be judged what a poor feeble condition we were in, there being not the least crumb of refreshment that came within either of our mouths from Wednesday night to Saturday night, except only a little cold water. This day in the afternoon, about an hour by sun, we came to the place where they intended, viz. an Indian town called Wenimesset, northward of Quabang. When we were come, Oh the number of pagans (our merciless enemies) that there came about me! I might say as David, Psal. xxvii 13. *I had fainted, unless I had believed, &c.* The next day was the sabbath: I then remembered how careless I had been of God's holy time; how many Sabbaths I had lost and misspent, and how evilly I had walked in God's sight; which lay so closely upon my spirit that it was easy for me to see how righteous it was with God to cut off the thread of my life, and cast me out of his presence forever. Yet the Lord still shewed mercy to me, and helped me; and as he wounded me with one hand, so he healed me with the other. This day there came to me one Robert Pepper, (a man belonging to Roxbury) who was taken at Capt. Beers's fight; and had been now a considerable time with the Indians, and up with them almost as far as Albany, to see King Philip, as he told me, and was now very lately come with them into these parts. Hearing that I was in this Indian town, he obtained leave to come and see me. He told me he himself was wounded in the leg at Capt. Beers's fight; and was not able for some time to go, but as they carried him, and that he took oak leaves and laid on his wound, and by the blessing of God, he was able to travel again. Then I took oak leaves and laid on my side, and with the blessing of God, it cured me also; yet before the cure was wrought, I might say as it is in Psai. xxxviii 5, 6, *My wounds stink and are corrupt, I am troubled, I am bowed down greatly, I go mourning all the day long.*—I sat much alone with my poor wounded child in my lap, which moaned night and day, having nothing to revive the body, or cheer thee spirits of her; but instead of that, one Indian would come and tell me one hour, your master will knock your child on the head; and then a second, and then a third, your master will quickly knock your child on the head. . . .

The Seventh Remove

After a restless and hungry night there, we had a wearisome time of it the next day. The swamp, by which we lay, was as it were a deep dungeon, and a very high and steep hill before it. Before I got to the top of the hill, I thought that my heart, legs, and all would have broken, and failed me. What through faintness and soreness of body, it was a grievous day of travel to me. As we went along, I saw a place where English cattle had been; that was comfort to me, such as it was. Quickly after that, we came to an English path, which so took with me, that I thought I could there have freely lain down and died. That day, a little after noon, we came to Squauheag, where the Indians quickly spread themselves over the deserted English fields, gleaning, what they could find: some picked up ears of wheat, that were crickled down; some found ears of Indian corn; some found groundnuts, and others sheaves of wheat, that were frozen together in the shock, and went to threshing them out. I got two ears of Indian corn, and whilst I did but turn my back, one of them was stolen from me, which much troubled me. There came an Indian to them at that time, with a basket of horse-liver; I asked him to give me a piece. What, (says he) can you eat horse-liver? I told him I would try, if he would give me a piece, which he did; and I laid it on the coals to roast; but before it was half ready, they got half of it away from me; so that I was forced to take the rest and eat it as it was, with the blood about my mouth, and yet a savoury bit it was to me, for to the hungry soul every bitter thing is sweet.—A solemn sight I thought it was, to see whole fields of wheat and Indian corn forsaken and spoiled, and the remainders of them to be food for our merciless enemies. That night we had a mess of wheat for our supper.

The Eighth Remove

On the morrow morning we must go over Connecticut river to meet with king Philip; two canoes full they had carried over; the next turn I was to go; but as my foot was upon the canoe to step in, there was a sudden out-cry among them, and I must step back; and instead of going up the river, I must go four or five miles farther northward. Some of the Indians ran one way, and some another. The cause of this rout was, as I thought, their espying some English scouts, who were thereabouts. In this travel, about noon the company made a stop, and sat down, some to eat and others to rest them. As I sat amongst them, musing on things past, my son Joseph unexpectedly came to me: we asked of each other's welfare, bemoaning our doleful condition, and the change that had come upon us; we had had husband, and father, children, and sisters, friends, and relations, house and home, and many comforts of this life; but now might we say with Job, *Naked came I out of my mother's womb, and naked shall I return: The Lord gave, and the Lord hath taken away, blessed be the name of the Lord*. . . .

But to return: We travelled on till night, and in the morning we must go over the river to Philip's crew. When I was in the canoe, I could not but be amazed at the numerous crew of pagans that were on the bank on the other side. When I came ashore, they gathered all about me, I sitting alone in the midst; I observed they asked one another questions, and laughed, and rejoiced over their gains and victories. Then my heart began to fail, and I fell a weeping; which was the first time, to my remembrance, that I wept before them; although I had met with so much affliction and my heart was many times ready to break, yet could I not shed one tear in their sight, but rather had been all this while in a maze, and like one astonished; but now I may say as Psal. cxxxii. 1. *By the River of Babylon, there we sat down, yea, we wept when we remembered Zion*. There one of them asked me, why I wept? I could hardly tell what to say; yet I answered, they would kill me. No, said he, none will hurt you.—Then came one of them, and gave me two spoonfuls of meal, to comfort me; and another gave me half a pint of peas, which was more worth than many bushels at another time. Then I went to see King Philip; he bade me come in, and sit down; and asked me whether I would smoke it? (an usual compliment now-a-days, among saints and sinners): But this no way suited me. For though I had formerly used tobacco, yet I had left it ever since I was first taken. It seems to be a bait the devil lays, to make men lose their precious time. I remember with shame, how formerly, when I had taken two or three pipes, I was presently ready for another; such a bewitching thing it is: but I thank God, he has now give me power over it; surely there are many who may be better employed, than to sit sucking a stinking tobacco pipe. . . .

During my abode in this place, Philip spake to me to make a shirt for his boy, which I did; for which he gave me a shilling; I offered the money to my master, but he bade me keep it, and with it I bought a piece of horse flesh. Afterward he asked me to make a cap for his boy, for which he invited me to dinner: I went, and he gave me a pancake, about as big as two fingers; it was made of parched wheat, beaten, and fried in bear's grease, but I thought I never tasted pleasanter food in my life. There was a squaw who spake to me to make a shirt for her sannup; for which she gave me a piece of bear. Another asked me to knit a pair of stockings, for which she gave me a quart of peas. I boiled my peas and bear together, and invited my master and mistress to dinner; but the proud gossip, because I served them both in one dish, would eat nothing, except one bit that he gave her upon the point of his knife. . . .

The Ninth Remove

But instead of going either to Albany or homeward, we must go five miles up the river, and then go over it. Here we abode a while. Here lived a sorry Indian, who spake to me to make him a shirt; when I had done it, he would pay me nothing for it. But he lived by the river side, where I often went to fetch water; I would often be putting him in mind, and calling for my pay; at last he told me, if I would make another shirt for a papoos not yet born, he would give me a knife, which he did, when I had done it. I carried the knife in, and my master asked me to give it to him, and I was not a little glad that I had any thing that they would accept of, and be pleased with. . . .

My son being now about a mile from me, I asked liberty to go and see him; they bade me go, and away I went; but quickly lost myself, travelling over hills and thro swamps, and could not find the way to him. And I cannot but admire at the wonderful power and goodness of God to me in that tho I was gone from home, and met with all sorts of Indians, and those I had no knowledge of, and there being no Christian soul near me, yet not one of them offered the least imaginable miscarriage to me. I turned homeward again, and met my master, and he shewed me the way to my son. When I came to him I found him not well; and withal he had a boil on his side, which much troubled him: we bemoaned one another a while, as the Lord helped us, and then I returned again. When I was returned, I found myself as unsatisfied as I was before. I went up and down mourning and lamenting, and my spirit was ready to sink with the thoughts of my poor children. My son was ill, and I could not but think of his mournful looks, having no Christian friend near him, to do any office of love for him, either for soul or body. And my poor girl, I knew not where she was, nor whether she was sick or well, alive or dead. I repaired under these thoughts to my bible, (my great comforter in that time) and that scripture came to my hand, *Cast thy burden upon the Lord, and he shall sustain thee.* Psal. lv. 22.

But I was fain to go and look after something to satisfy my hunger; and going among the wigwams, I went into one, and there found a squaw who shewed herself very kind to me, and gave me a piece of bear, I put it into my pocket, and came home; but could not find an opportunity to broil it, for fear they should get it from me; and there it lay all that day and night in my stinking pocket. In the morning I went again to the same squaw, who had a kettle of groundnuts boiling: I asked her to let me boil my piece of bear in the kettle, which she did, and gave me some ground-nuts to eat with it, and I cannot but think how pleasant it was to me. I have sometimes seen bear baked handsomely among the English, and some liked it; but the thoughts that it was bear, made me tremble: But now that was savoury to me that one would think was enough to turn the stomach of a brute creature.

One bitter cold day, I could find no room to sit down before the fire: I went out, and could not tell what to do, but I went into another wigwam, where they were all sitting around the fire; but the squaw laid a skin for me and bade me sit down, and gave me some ground-nuts, and bade me come again; and told me they would buy me, if they were able; and yet these were strangers to me that I never knew before. . . .

[Rowlandson, along with her son and daughter, were finally redeemed from the Indians and allowed to return home.]

Our family being now gathered together, the south church in Boston hired an house for us; Then we removed from Mr. Shepard's (those cordial friends) and went to Boston, where we continued about three quarters of a year. Still the Lord went along with us, and provided graciously for us. I thought it somewhat strange to set up house-keeping with bare walls; but, as Solomon says, *Money answers all things*: And that we had, thro the benevolence of christian friends, some in this town, and some in that, and others; and some from England, so that in a little time we might look and see the house furnished with love. The Lord hath been exceedingly good to us in our low estate, in that, when we had neither house nor home, nor other necessaries, the Lord so moved the hearts of these and those towards us, that we wanted neither food nor raiment for ourselves nor ours. Prov. xv.ii. 24. *There is a friend that sticketh closer than a brother.* And how many such friends have we found, and now live among! . . .

OLYMPE DE GOUGES (ESSAY DATE 1791)

SOURCE: de Gouges, Olympe. "The Rights of Women." In *Women in Revolutionary Paris 1789-1795: Selected Documents,* edited and translated by Daline Gay Levy, Harriet Branson Applewhite, and Mary Durham Johnson, pp. 87-96. Urbana: University of Illinois, 1979.

In the following excerpt from her 1791 pamphlet addressed to the Queen, Marie Antoinette, de Gouges offers a declaration of women's rights.

Man, are you capable of being just? It is a woman who poses the question; you will not deprive her of that right at least. Tell me, what gives you sovereign empire to oppress my sex? Your strength? Your talents? Observe the Creator in his wisdom; survey in all her grandeur that nature with whom you seem to want to be in harmony, and give me, if you dare, an example of this tyrannical empire. Go back to animals, consult the elements, study plants, finally glance at all the modifications of organic matter, and surrender to the evidence when I offer you the means; search, probe, and distinguish, if you can,

ON THE SUBJECT OF...

MADELEINE DE SCUDÉRY (1607-1701)

Although Madeleine de Scudéry was one of the best-known and most influential writers of romance tales in seventeeth-century Europe, many critics suggest that neither her talent nor the extent of her influence was recognized until the twentieth century. In part, her gender was to blame for her undeserved poor reputation: in Scudéry's time, writing for pay was considered an unworthy occupation for either sex, and in the case of women writers, often led to accusations of immorality and sexual licentiousness. It was perhaps for that reason that Scudéry published under the name of her brother, Georges, until his death, even though it was widely known that she was largely responsible for such romantic novels as *Ibrahim; ou, L'illustre Bassa* (1641; *Ibrahim; or, The Illustrious Bassa*), *Artamène; ou, Le grand Cyrus* (1649-53; *Artamenes; or, The Grand Cyrus*), and *Clélie: Histoire romaine* (1654-60; *Clelia*).

Scudéry received an unusual honor as the only woman in the seventeenth century to be acknowledged by the Academie Français, for her essay *Discours sur la gloire* (1671; *An Essay upon Glory*). Scudéry's work was greatly influenced by, and did much to popularize, *préciosité,* the exquisite politeness and delicate manners of the world of the Paris salons she frequented. Although such authors as Molière and Nicholas Boileau satirized the exaggerated posturings of these overly zealous précieux in their works, they respected Scudéry, and critics now believe it likely that Molière was impressed and influenced by Scudéry's feminist ideas. Some critics have demonstrated that Scudéry's work was familiar to Samuel Richardson, who is considered one of the foremost creators of the English novel. Her revisions of the romance genre, focusing on the inner life of her characters and drawing material from contemporary society, are considered among the key early contributions to the development of the novel.

the sexes in the administration of nature. Everywhere you will find them mingled; everywhere they cooperate in harmonious togetherness in this immortal masterpiece.

Man alone has raised his exceptional circumstances to a principle. Bizarre, blind, bloated with science and degenerated—in a century of enlightenment and wisdom—into the crassest ignorance, he wants to command as a despot a sex which is in full possession of its intellectual faculties; he pretends to enjoy the Revolution and to claim his rights to equality in order to say nothing more about it.

Declaration of the Rights of Woman and the Female Citizen

Mothers, daughters, sisters [and] representatives of the nation demand to be constituted into a national assembly. Believing that ignorance, omission, or scorn for the rights of woman are the only causes of public misfortunes and of the corruption of governments, [the women] have resolved to set forth in a solemn declaration the natural, inalienable, and sacred rights of woman in order that this declaration, constantly exposed before all the members of the society, will ceaselessly remind them of their rights and duties; in order that the authoritative acts of women and the authoritative acts of men may be at any moment compared with and respectful of the purpose of all political institutions; and in order that citizens' demands, henceforth based on simple and incontestable principles, will always support the constitution, good morals, and the happiness of all.

Consequently, the sex that is as superior in beauty as it is in courage during the suffering of maternity recognized and declares in the presence and under the auspices of the Supreme Being, the following Rights of Woman and of Female Citizens.

ARTICLE 1

Woman is born free and lives equal to man in her rights. Social distinctions can be based only on the common utility.

ARTICLE 2

The purpose of any political association is the conservation of the natural and imprescriptible rights of woman and man; these rights are liberty, property, security, and especially resistance to oppression.

ARTICLE 3

The principle of all sovereignty rests essentially with the nation, which is nothing but the union of woman and man; no body and no individual can exercise any authority which does not come expressly from it [the nation].

ARTICLE 4

Liberty and justice consist of restoring all that belongs to others; thus, the only limits on the exercise of the natural rights of woman are perpetual male tyranny; these limits are to be reformed by the laws of nature and reason.

ARTICLE 5

Laws of nature and reason proscribe all acts harmful to society; everything which is not prohibited by these wise and divine laws cannot be prevented, and no one can be constrained to do what they do not command.

ARTICLE 6

The laws must be the expression of the general will; all female and male citizens must contribute either personally or through their representatives to its formation; it must be the same for all: male and female citizens, being equal in the eyes of the law, must be equally admitted to all honors, positions, and public employment according to their capacity and without other distinctions besides those of their virtues and talents.

ARTICLE 7

No woman is an exception: she is accused, arrested, and detained in cases determined by law. Women, like men, obey this rigorous law.

ARTICLE 8

The law must establish only those penalties that are strictly and obviously necessary, and no one can be punished except by virtue of a law established and promulgated prior to the crime and legally applicable to women.

ARTICLE 9

Once any woman is declared guilty, complete rigor is [to be] exercised by the law.

ARTICLE 10

No one is to be disquieted for his very basic opinions; woman has the right to mount the scaffold; she must equally have the right to mount the rostrum, provided that her demonstrations do not disturb the legally established public order.

ARTICLE 11

The free communication of thoughts and opinions is one of the most precious rights of woman, since the liberty assures the recognition of children by their fathers. Any female citizen thus may say freely, I am the mother of a child which belongs to you, without being forced by a barbarous prejudice to hide the truth; [an exception may be made] to respond to the abuse of this liberty in cases determined by the law.

ARTICLE 12

The guarantee of the rights of woman and the female citizen implies a major benefit; this guarantee must be instituted for the advantage of all, and not for the particular benefit of those to whom it is entrusted.

ARTICLE 13

For the support of the public force and the expenses of administration, the contributions of woman and man are equal; she share all the duties [corvees] and all the painful tasks; therefore, she must have the same share in the distribution of positions, employments, offices, honors and jobs [industrie].

ARTICLE 14

Female and male citizens have the right to verify, either by themselves or through their representatives, the necessity of the public contribution. This can only apply to women if they are granted an equal share, not only of wealth, but also of public administration, and in the determination of the proportion, the base, the collection, and the duration of the tax.

ARTICLE 15

The collectivity of women, joined for tax purposed to the aggregate of men, has the right to demand an accounting of his administration from any public agent.

ARTICLE 16

No society has a constitution without the guarantee of the rights and the separation of powers; the constitution is null if the majority of individuals comprising the nation have not cooperated in drafting it.

ARTICLE 17

Property belongs to both sexes whether united or separate; for each it is an inviolable and sacred right; no one can be deprived of it, since it is the true patrimony of nature, unless the legally determined public need obviously dictates it, and then only with a just and prior indemnity.

OVERVIEWS

NANCY COTTON (ESSAY DATE 1998)

SOURCE: Cotton, Nancy. "Women Playwrights in England: Renaissance Noblewomen." In *Readings in Renaissance Women's Drama: Criticism, History, and Performance 1594-1998,* edited by S. P. Cerasano and Marion Wynne-Davies, pp. 32-46. London: Routledge, 1998.

In the following essay, Cotton provides a history of England's early women playwrights.

The first recorded woman playwright in England was Katherine of Sutton, abbess of Barking nunnery in the fourteenth century. Between 1363 and 1376 the abbess rewrote the Easter dramatic offices because the people attending the paschal services were becoming increasingly cool in their devotions (*'deuocione frigessere'*). Wishing to excite devotion at such a crowded, important festival (*'desiderans . . . fidelium deuocionem ad tam celebrem celebracionem magis excitare'*), Lady Katherine produced unusually lively adaptations of the traditional liturgical plays.[1] Particularly interesting is her *elevatio crucis,* one of the few surviving liturgical plays that contains a representation of the harrowing of hell. In the *visitatio sepulchri* that follows, the three Marys are acted not by male clerics, which was customary, but by nuns.[2] The Barking plays are not unique, however, in showing the participation of nuns. In religious houses on the continent women sometimes acted in church dramas, and Hrotsvitha of Gandersheim and Hildegard of Bingen wrote Latin religious plays. Although the destruction of liturgical texts in England at the Reformation makes certainty impossible, it is likely, in view of the uniformity of medieval European culture and the considerable authority of women who headed the medieval nunneries, that other English abbesses contributed to the slow, anonymous, communal growth of the medieval religious drama.

Katherine of Sutton was a baroness in her own right by virtue of her position as abbess of Barking.[3] Only women of similar rank wrote drama in England until the Restoration. Virginia Woolf in her fable of Shakespeare's sister in *A Room of One's Own* (New York, 1929) was of course right in her statement that no middle-class woman, however talented, could have written for the Elizabethan public theaters. But Renaissance noblewomen, although they shared some of the disabilities of middle-class women, nonetheless wrote closet dramas, masques, and pastoral entertainments.

The English Renaissance fostered rigorous classical training for ladies, who, like male humanists, translated the ancients. The earliest extant English translation of a Greek play was the work of Lady Jane Fitzalan Lumley (*c.*1537-77), who made a free and abridged prose version of Euripides' *Iphigeneia in Aulis.*[4] Lady Lumley probably translated Euripides shortly after her marriage at the age of 12. This precocious marvel worked directly from the Greek at a time when secondhand translation from Latin was much more usual. The Latin tragedies of Seneca of course found many translators. Even Queen Elizabeth, during the early years of her reign, sometime around 1561, translated the chorus of Act II of *Hercules Oetaeus.*[5]

Imitations of Senecan tragedy were popular in aristocratic and academic circles. An influential figure in this tradition was Mary Sidney Herbert, Countess of Pembroke (1561-1621).[6] Mary Sidney studied at home with private tutors and attained proficiency in French, Italian, probably Latin, and perhaps Hebrew. At the queen's request, she lived for a time at court, which served her as a finishing school. When she was 16, her parents married her to Henry Herbert, Earl of Pembroke, a match economically and politically advantageous, even though the earl was nearly thirty years older than Mary. After her marriage Mary Herbert lived at Wilton House, the earl's home in Wiltshire, where she had four children, collected a notable library, and became famous as a translator, patron of literature, and editor of the *Arcadia.* The countess's dramatic activity grew out of her close relationship with her brother, Sir Philip Sidney (1554-86). In his *Defence of Poesie* Philip attacked English romantic drama, advocating instead the classical drama of Seneca. He admired a play 'full of stately speeches, and wel sounding phrases, clyming to the height of Seneca his style, and as full of notable morallitie, which it dooth most delightfully teach'.[7]

After Philip's death Mary translated the *Marc-Antoine* of Robert Garnier (1534-90), the most assured French Senecan dramatist, whose eight tragedies were notable for their vigorous but polished style. Written in 1590, the countess's *Antonie* transforms rhymed French alexandrines into pedestrian blank verse. Rather better are the choral lyrics, written in a variety of meters and rhymes. Here, for example, is the opening of the chorus to Act III:

Alas, with what tormenting fire
Us martireth this blinde desire
  To staie our life from flieng!
How ceasleslie our minds doth rack,
How heavie lies upon our back
  This dastard feare of dieng!
Death rather healthfull succor gives,

Death rather all mishapps relieves
    That life upon us throweth:
And ever to us doth unclose
The doore, wherby from curelesse woes
    Our wearie soule out goeth.[8]

The Countess of Pembroke had *Antonie* printed in 1592 and thus became the first woman in England to publish a play. *Antonie* was reprinted in 1595, 1600, 1606, and 1607;[9] although unacted, it was widely influential. Swayed by example, or coerced by friendship or patronage, members of the countess's circle turned out numerous Senecan imitations. Among the earliest, oddly enough, was a translation of Garnier's *Cornelie* made in 1594 by Thomas Kyd, who, as author of *The Spanish Tragedy* (1587), was the chief exponent at the time of the blood-and-thunder action drama. Presumably hoping for patronage, Kyd promised a translation of *Porcie*, but this never appeared. Samuel Daniel, long a protégé of the countess, wrote *Cleopatra* (1593) and *Philotas* (1604), the best of the plays on the Pembroke model. Samuel Brandon in 1598 published *The Virtuous Octavia*. Fulke Greville, Lord Brooke, Philip Sidney's friend and later biographer, wrote *Mustapha* and *Alaham* in the late 1590s, and in the next decade William Alexander, Earl of Stirling, published *Darius, Croesus,* and *The Alexandraean Tragedy.*

The countess also published a dramatic dialogue, which she wrote for the royal entertainment about 1592, when she was expecting a visit from the queen. A pastoral containing ten six-line stanzas, *Thenot and Piers in Praise of Astraea* was published in 1602 in the anthology *A Poetical Rhapsody,* which went through four editions by 1621. In each of the ten stanzas, Thenot's praise of Astraea (goddess of justice, a poetical name for Queen Elizabeth) is criticized by his fellow shepherd Piers. The last stanza, in a graceful turn of compliment, discloses why Piers is dissatisfied at praise of the queen:

THENOT.
    Then Piers, of friendship tell me why,
    My meaning true, my words should ly,
        And strive in vaine to raise her.

PIERS.
    Words from conceit do only rise,
    Above conceit her honour flies;
        But silence, nought can praise her.[10]

This is the first original dramatic verse written by a woman to appear in print.

Before the Countess of Pembroke died, and probably because of her example, an Englishwoman for the first time wrote and published a full-length original play. This was Elizabeth Tanfield Cary, later Viscountess Falkland (1586-1639). More is known about Elizabeth Cary than about most figures of the period because one of her daughters wrote a detailed biography of her mother.[11] Lady Falkland was the only child and heiress of a wealthy Oxford lawyer, Lawrence Tanfield, later Sir Lawrence and Lord Chief Baron of the Exchequer. She was startlingly precocious, teaching herself French, Spanish, Italian, Latin, Hebrew, and 'Transylvanian' (*Life,* p. 5). She loved to read so much that she sat up all night. When her parents refused her candles, she bribed the maids to smuggle them in; by the age of 12 she had run up a debt to them of a hundred pounds 'with two hundred more for the like bargains and promises' (*Life,* p. 7), a considerable sum in those days even for an heiress. As a child she made translations from Latin and French and at 12 found internal contradictions in Calvin's *Institutes of Religion*—upsetting behavior for a child of good Protestants.

About the age of 15 or 16 Elizabeth Tanfield was married to a knight's son named Henry Cary. After the marriage had secured the Tanfield fortune, Henry followed the custom of the times and left his bride with her parents while he finished his military service abroad. During this period, sometime between 1602 and 1605, Elizabeth Cary, who, according to her daughter, loved plays 'extremely' (*Life,* p. 54), wrote two closet dramas. Cary's first play was set in Sicily and dedicated to her husband; the title is unknown and the play is lost. Her second play, dedicated to her sister-in-law, was *Mariam, the Fair Queen of Jewry.*

A Senecan tragedy based on Josephus's *Antiquities, Mariam* is carefully researched and constructed. The play is attentive to historical details but also is sensitive to dramatic effectiveness. As the play opens, rumor has just reached Jerusalem that Caesar has executed Herod at Rome. The first half of the play shows the effects of this news. Queen Mariam is torn between grief for her husband and joy. She rejoices at Herod's death because he had killed her brother and grandfather and because he had left orders for her own death in case he did not return. Pheroras, now happily freed from his brother's authority, immediately makes a love marriage with his maid Graphina. Herod's cast-off first wife Doris now hopes to unseat Mariam's children as heirs and install her own son Antipater on the throne. Only Salome regrets the loss of Herod, but her sorrow is self-interested. She wishes to marry her Arabian lover Silleus. If Herod were alive, she could accuse her husband Constabarus of treason for protecting the two sons of Baba. Salome also hates Mariam, but sees no way to remove her haughty sister-in-law. While these events are underway, constant pointers remind us that the characters believe the rumor of Herod's death because they wish to.

The reversal comes in 3.2 with the news that Herod is alive and will arrive immediately. Herod's delight as he returns in Act 4 is short-lived. Salome now has the upper hand and her machinations lead to the catastrophe. She offers to protect Pheroras and his bride if he will accuse Constabarus of treason. She tricks Herod into believing that Mariam has been unfaithful in his absence. Herod, a man of impulse, orders the executions of Constabarus, Baba's sons, and his own beloved queen. In Act 5 a nuntius recounts to Herod the noble death of Mariam. He also reports that Salome's agent in the plot against Mariam has confessed and committed suicide. Herod now realizes the magnitude of his loss and becomes frantic with grief.

The play is a sophisticated performance for a largely self-educated person of 17. Cary is careful with details, and the absence of anachronisms is unusual in the period. Stylistically and dramaturgically, the play is competently though conventionally Senecan. Action is discussed rather than dramatized, and the gory details of the execution are properly left to a nuntius. Cary uses literarily varied prosody instead of the dramatically supple blank verse of her theatrical contemporaries. *Mariam* is written in rhymed quatrains, with occasional couplets and sonnets inserted. Cary has, however, infused this dramatically awkward mixture of verse forms with emotional intensity at key points.

Salome, for example, is most convincing when she meditates an unorthodox method of removing Constabarus so that she can marry Silleus:

> He loves, I love; what then can be the cause,
> Keepes me f[rom] being the Arabians wife?
> It is the principles of Moses lawes,
> For Con[s]tabarus still remaines in life,
> If he to me did beare as Earnest hate,
> As I to him, for him there were an ease,
> A separating bill might free his fate:
> From such a yoke that did so much displease.
> Why should such priviledge to man be given?
> Or given to them, why bard from women then?
> Are men then we in greater grace with Heaven?
> Or cannot women hate as well as men?
> Ile be the custome-breaker: an beginne
> To shew my Sexe the way to freedomes doore.
>
> (sig. B3r)

In the Renaissance this was of course villainess talk, but villainess or not, Salome was ahead of her time in her attitude toward equitable divorce laws.

The active and lustful Salome makes a provocative contrast with the passive and chaste Mariam, who initiates no action whatever, not even to save her own life. As she is facing death, she decides that her fault was a sullenness of temper that prevented her from defending herself. She feels guilty because she had placed her full reliance on her chastity of body without giving her husband her chastity of spirit; she had, then, been guilty of a certain infidelity of mind. This seems a harsh self-accusation for a woman whose husband had murdered two of her close relatives, but her conclusion is nonetheless reinforced by the chorus's strong statement of the duties of wives:

> When to their Husbands they themselves doe bind,
> Doe they not wholy give themselves away?
> Or give they but their body not their mind,
> Reserving that though best, for others pray?
> No sure, their thoughts no more can be their owne,
> And therefore should to none but one be knowne.
>
> Then she usurpes upon anothers right,
> That seekes to be by publike language grac't:
> And though her thoughts reflect with purest light,
> Her mind if not peculiar is not chast.
> For in a wife it is no worse to finde,
> A common body, then a common minde.
>
> (sig. E4r)

These are hard beliefs for a woman who wished to be a writer.

The vividness of Cary's treatment of Mariam and Salome suggests that she had the range of emotional experience and the imaginative power to appreciate both attitudes toward experience. Cary apparently entered marriage with an impossible idealization of wifely behavior, which she expresses through Mariam, and with an even more impossible ideal of an independent, even rebellious, intellectual life, embodied in Salome. These deeply ambivalent attitudes shaped the remainder of her life. An intellectual heiress of Catholic leanings joined with a careerist courtier in a Protestant court, Cary lived with her husband twenty years, during which she bore eleven children and was nearly always either pregnant or nursing. Her intellectual and artistic talents found their only outlet in religion. During her marriage she continued to read theology and discussed religious doctrines with distinguished prelates. At the same time, she acted out her ideals of wifely behavior. She taught her children to love their father better than their mother. She acceded to her husband's wishes that she become a fashionable dresser and an accomplished horsewoman, despite her indifference to clothes and terror of horses. She mortgaged her jointure to advance her husband's career, whereupon her father disinherited her in favor of her oldest son, Lucius Cary, who also inherited his mother's literary talent. It is not surprising that she had periods of depression severe to the point of mental illness. Meanwhile, Henry Cary achieved a seat on the Privy Council, the rank of viscount, and the Lord Chief Deputyship of Ireland.

In 1626 Lady Falkland rebelled. She converted to Catholicism, nearly ruining her husband's career. He repaid her by abandoning her, taking custody of her children, and stripping her house of the bare necessities of life. Lady Falkland's poverty and suffering were severe; for long periods she lived in semistarvation. She appealed to the court for help (Queen Henrietta Maria was a French Catholic) and finally in 1627 the Privy Council ordered Lord Falkland to support his wife, although seven months later he still had not complied with the order. Lady Falkland turned again to writing, producing a life of Edward II, poems to the Virgin, and lives of saints. She translated Catholic polemics; her translation of Cardinal Perron's reply to King James was publicly burned. Lady Falkland kept her rebellious spirit to the end. In her last years she kidnapped two of her sons and, defying the Star Chamber, smuggled them to the continent to become Catholics.

Given the outward docility of Elizabeth Cary's married life until 1626, it is strange that *Mariam* was ever published. None of her other creative works were printed, and *Mariam* was not entered for publication until 1612, ten years after it was written, and did not actually appear until 1613. Her daughter claims, 'She writ many things for her private recreation . . . one of them was after stolen out of that sister-in-law's (her friend's) chamber, and printed, but by her own procurement was called in' (*Life,* p. 9). This explanation is suspect for a number of reasons, not the least of which is that the Stationers' Register shows that there was nothing surreptitious about the publication of the play.[12] Moreover, Lady Falkland's daughter makes the standard excuse of the period for an aristocrat who stoops to publication. Cary herself scorns such excuses in the introduction to her translation of Cardinal Perron: 'I will not make use of that worn form of saying I printed it against my will, moved by the importunity of friends.'[13]

A more likely explanation is that the publication of *Mariam* was inspired by the Countess of Pembroke. Both Mary Herbert and Elizabeth Cary were well acquainted with John Davies of Hereford, the famous master of calligraphy. Davies was a protégé and intimate of the Pembroke circle; he made a beautiful manuscript of Philip Sidney and Mary Herbert's translation of the psalms. He was also Elizabeth Cary's writing master. Davies must have spoken to his brilliant young pupil about his distinguished patroness and her activities. Indeed, the immediate cause that prompted Cary to publish her play may have been a poem by Davies. In 1612 he prefaced his 'Muse's Sacrifice, or Divine Meditations' with a poetical dedicatory letter to the Countess of Pembroke, the Countess of Bedford, and Elizabeth Cary. Davies compliments the Countess of Pembroke for her psalms and then praises 'Cary, of whom Minerva stands in feare':

> Thou mak'st Melpomen proud, and my Heart great
> of such a Pupill, who, in Buskin fine,
> With Feete of State, dost make thy Muse to mete
> the scenes of Syracuse and Palestine.
>
> . . . . .
>
> Such nervy Limbes of Art, and Straines of Wit
> Times past ne'er knew the weaker Sexe to have;
> And Times to come, will hardly credit it,
> if thus thou give thy Workes both Birth and Grave.[14]

Davies then chides all three ladies because they 'presse the Presse with little' they have written. Could the woman who wrote Salome's speech resist the appeal for publication on behalf of her sex's honor? *Mariam* was entered for publication in December of the same year as the appearance of Davies's poem. However *Mariam* came to be printed, and so preserved, it was never intended for acting. Neither the Countess of Pembroke nor Viscountess Falkland wrote their plays for the stage; *Antonie* and *Mariam* were written as closet drama. To write for the public stage was déclassé. It was a queen who broke down this barrier of caste and helped break down also the barriers against actresses.

Queen Henrietta Maria (1609-69) arrived in England at the age of 16 as the bride of Charles I.[15] In 1626, during her first year in her new country, the young queen acted at court in a pastoral play and masque that she herself wrote and directed. The play, which has been lost, was written in French and performed by the French ladies who attended the queen. Letters of Englishmen commenting on the occasion show the dismay produced even in an audience carefully handpicked:

> On Shrovetuisday the Quene and her women had a maske or pastorall play at Somerset House, wherin herself acted a part, and some of the rest were disguised like men with beards. I have knowne the time when this wold have seemed a straunge sight, to see a Quene act in a play but *tempora mutantur et nos.*

'I heare not much honor of the Quene's maske, for, if they were not all, soome were in men's apparell.' Ambassadors from continental courts were more sophisticated. The Venetian ambassador admired the 'rich scenery and dresses' and the 'remarkable acting' of the queen. 'The king and court enjoyed it, those present being picked and selected, but it did not give complete satisfaction, because the English objected to the first part being declaimed by the queen.' The ambassador from Florence was equally complimentary:

> She acted in a beautiful pastoral of her own composition, assisted by twelve of her ladies whom she had trained since Christmas. The pastoral succeeded admirably; not only in the decorations and changes of scenery, but also in the acting and recitation of the ladies—Her Majesty surpassing all the others. The performance was conducted as privately as possible, inasmuch as it is an unusual thing in this country to see the Queen upon a stage; the audience consequently was limited to a few of the nobility, expressly invited, no others being admitted.[16]

The English disapproval of the queen's performing a role on stage must have come as a surprise to Henrietta Maria. She had been reared in a court where nobility and even royalty acted in masques and plays. Her brother Louis XIII as a child led his brothers and sisters in amateur theatricals.

Although she has been suggested as the author of the anonymous lost pastoral *Florimene,* presented by the queen's ladies at court in December 1635, Henrietta Maria apparently wrote no more plays, but her incorrigible love of acting liberalized aristocratic attitudes towards actresses. After the disapproval of her 1626 court performance, she continued to have amateur theatricals in her private apartments and to dance in court masques. In 1633 she took the chief part in another play, *The Shepherd's Paradise,* written by the courtier Walter Montague for her and her ladies. Again there was a furor. Puritan William Prynne had the bad luck to publish *Histriomastix,* his attack on the stage, within a few days of the queen's performance. Prynne inopportunely denounced 'Women-Actors, notorious whores': 'And dare then any Christian woman be so more then whorishly impudent, as to act, to speak publicly on a Stage (perchance in man's apparel, and cut hair, here proved sinful and abominable) in the presence of sundry men and women?'[17] Prynne was condemned to have his ears cut off, the queen continued to act, amateur theatricals became common in polite circles, and by 1660 the profession of acting on the public stage was open to women. The admission of actresses to the stage was important for women playwrights because as actresses women for the first time obtained practical theatrical apprenticeship. By the eighteenth century there would be a number of actress-playwrights.

Henrietta Maria helped transform aristocratic attitudes not only toward actresses but also toward the commercial stage. She was the first English queen to attend plays at public theaters. Her considerable power over her husband caused Charles I to do what no English king had done before—he looked over scripts and even suggested plots for several plays written by others. The queen introduced from France the cults of *préciosité* and Platonic love and persuaded courtiers like Cartwright and Carlell to write plays illustrating her pet theories; thus the gentleman playwright came into existence. By the Restoration persons of the highest social rank in England were writing for the public stage.

This upper-class interest in playwrighting is seen in Lady Jane Cavendish (1621-69) and her sister Lady Elizabeth Brackley (*c.* 1623-63).[18] The Cavendish sisters, daughters of William Cavendish, Duke of Newcastle, were, by both upbringing and marriage, part of the world of aristocratic theatricals. Before the war their father was a patron of the playwrights Brome, Shirley, and Jonson. In 1633 and 1634 Jonson wrote entertainments for the king's visits to the Newcastle estates; perhaps Jane and Elizabeth were present. About 1640 *The Country Captain,* publicly attributed to Newcastle but largely written by James Shirley, was performed at the Blackfriars Theatre. Lord Brackley, Elizabeth's future husband, in 1634 appeared with the king in Thomas Carew's masque *Coelum Britannicum.* The same year Brackley acted in Milton's *Comus* at Ludlow Castle; his sister and brother were also principal performers, their parents the chief spectators. With this background, it is not surprising that the Cavendish sisters should themselves write plays. Sometime between 1644 and 1646, the young women, both in their early twenties, collaborated on two plays. *A Pastoral* remains in manuscript, but *The Concealed Fansyes* was published in 1931. The authors here had promising raw material but were unable to construct a coherent plot. The story line, clumsily handled, shows a sound and simple comedic pattern: two sisters, Lucenay and Tattiney, are wooed by Courtly and Presumption. The men plan to tame their wives after marriage, but the women turn the tables and tame their husbands. The dialogue reflects the concerns of the authors as heiresses. Lucenay and Tattiney repeatedly and bluntly discuss marriage as the buying and selling of heiresses for dowries and estates. Lucenay dreads marriage: 'My distruction is that when I marry Courtly I shall bee condemn'd to looke upon my Nose, whenever I walke and when I sitt at meate confin'd by his grave winke to looke upon the Salt, and if it bee but the paireing of his Nales to admire him' (p. 815). After her marriage she describes how she escaped this servility. By refusing to keep her place, she throws her husband into a

> conflict, betwixt Anger and mallencholly not knoweinge whether my behaivour proceeded from neglect or ignorance, then hee declared himselfe by allygory and praysed a Lady, obedyent ffoole in towne, and swore hir Husband was the happyest man in the world. I replyed shee was a Very good Lady, and I accounted him happy that was hir Husband, that hee could content hinmselfe with such a Meachanick wife. I wishe sayd hee shee might bee your Example, and you have noe reason to sleight hir, for shee is of a noble family. I knowe that sayd I, and doe the more admire why shee will contract hir family, Noblenes and Birth, to the servitude of hir husband, as if hee had bought hir his slave, and I'm sure hir Father bought him for hir, for hee gave a good Portion, and now in sense who should obey?
>
> (pp. 834-5)

The conversational patterns are convincing; the use of indirect conversation suggests a writing skill born of epistolary, rather than dramatic, cultivation.

After collaborating with her sister in *The Concealed Fansyes,* Lady Jane Cavendish was present during the military action when the Parliamentarians captured and recaptured her home, Welbeck Abbey. She saved the art treasures of Bolsover Castle, another of the Newcastle estates. She raised money for her exiled father by selling her jewels and plate and sent him a thousand pounds of her private fortune. She refused to marry until the age of 33 because she refused anyone but a royalist, and at the time most royalists were in exile. After her marriage, she bore three children and continued to write, producing several volumes of verse. Nothing further is known of Lady Brackley.

The Cavendish sisters' young stepmother, Margaret Cavendish, Duchess of Newcastle (1623-73), was the first woman in England to publish collections of plays and England's first feminist playwright.[19] Her career as a prolific writer is surprising in view of her secluded upbringing and poor education. She was born Margaret Lucas, youngest of the eight children of a wealthy country gentleman who died before she was 2, leaving the family affairs in the strong hands of his wife. The family was exceptionally close-knit and exclusive, drawing the sons- and daughters-in-law into the family orbit. Margaret, as the youngest, grew up painfully shy of strangers. As a child she was indulged in her habit of wearing clothes of her own flamboyant design, one of the trademarks of the 'eccentricity' for which she was later notorious among her contemporaries. Her education was undisciplined. After the death of Queen Elizabeth, a reaction had set in against rigorous studies for gentlewomen. Margaret describes an education almost negative:

> As for tutors, although we had for all sorts of virtues, as singing, dancing, playing on music, reading, writing, working, and the like, yet we were not kept strictly thereto, they were rather for formality than benefit; for my mother cared not so much for our dancing and fiddling, singing and prating of several languages, as that we should be bred virtuously, modestly, civilly, honorably, and on honest principles.[20]

Her lack of education marred all her writing; she never absorbed some elementary principles of grammar, and the idea of revision was unknown to her. Later in life, Margaret felt keenly her lack of learning and spoke strongly for education for women.

At the age of 20, the bashful Margaret Lucas astonished her family (and her biographers) by attending the distressed Queen Henrietta Maria as a maid of honor and then following the queen into exile in France. The explanation of her puzzling behavior is that Margaret was a female cavalier, whose romantic gesture for a lost cause was in the spirit of the age. In France she met and married the exiled Marquis, later Duke, of Newcastle, thirty years her senior, whom she adored with fervent hero worship. Her marriage was an ideal one for a seventeenth-century woman writer. William Cavendish was himself an amateur poet and playwright, and a generous patron of writers, philosophers, and artists. He encouraged and assisted his young, beautiful, childless wife in her writing, her 'chiefest delight and greatest pastime' (*Plays Never Before Printed,* 1668). She describes their relationship in a letter to the duke in her *Philosophical and Physical Opinions* (1663):

> Though I am as Industrious and Carefull to serve Your Lordship in such imployments, which belong to a Wife, as Household affairs, as ever I can . . . yet I cannot for my Life be so good a Huswife, as to quit Writing. . . . you are pleased to Peruse my Works, and Approve of them so well, as to give me Leave to Publish them, which is a Favour, few Husbands would grant their Wives; But Your Lordship is an Extraordinary Husband, which is the Happiness of Your Lordships Honest Wife and Humble Servent Margaret Newcastle.

After her marriage, she began, out of ambition, to write with a view to publication: 'I am very ambitious, yet 'tis neither for beauty, wit, titles, wealth, or power, but as they are steps to raise me to Fame's tower, which is to live by remembrance in afterages.'[21] This desire for fame is the key to her personality.[22] She saw literature as the only avenue to renown for a woman:

> I confess my Ambition is restless, and not ordinary; because it would have an extraordinary fame: And since all heroick Actions, publick Imployments, powerfull Governments, and eloquent Pleadings are denyed our Sex in this age, or at least would be condemned for want of custome, is the cause I write so much.
>
> (An Epistle to my Readers, *Natures Pictures,* 1656)

The first Englishwoman to publish extensively, the duchess produced a dozen books, including poetry, fiction, scientific and philosophical speculations, letters, and declamations. She was the first woman in England to publish her autobiography, the first to publish a biography of her husband, the first to write about science.

In 1662 the duchess published *Plays,* a collection of closet dramas written while she was abroad. The volume includes fourteen plays, several in two parts. In 1668 she brought out a smaller collection, *Plays Never Before Printed,* which includes five plays and various dramatic fragments. In these volumes are some of the most ardently feminist plays ever written. In Part II of *Loves Adventures,* for example, Lady Orphan, disguised as the page Affectionata, wins great fame as a soldier; the Venetian States make her Lieutenant-General of the army and a member of the Council of War. The Pope invites Affectionata to Rome and offers to make her a cardinal.

Another military woman, Lady Victoria, appears in *Bell in Campo.* Refusing to be left at home when her husband goes to war, Lady Victoria raises a female army and accompanies the men to battle. Victoria points out to her troops that masculine contempt for female ability ultimately rests on the physical weakness of women, but urges that right education could make women good soldiers, 'for Time and Custome is the Father and Mother of Strength and Knowledge' (*Plays,* p. 588). She urges:

> Now or never is the time to prove the courage of our Sex, to get liberty and freedome from the Female Slavery, and to make our selves equal with men: for shall Men only sit in Honours chair, and the Women stand as waiters by? shall only Men in Triumphant Chariots ride, and Women run as Captives by? shall only men be Conquerors, and women Slaves? shall only men live by Fame, and women dy in Oblivion?
>
> (*Plays,* p. 609)

Encouraged by Victoria, the woman army achieves heroic exploits, rescuing the men from military disaster. They are rewarded after the war with special privileges. Lady Victoria herself is given a public triumph, a suit of gold armor, and a sword with a diamond hilt; her statue is set up in the center of the city.

In *Youth's Glory and Death's Banquet* Sir Thomas Father Love, over the objections of Lady Mother Love, is rearing their daughter, Lady Sanspareille, with an education masculine and intellectual:

> MOTHER LOVE. What? would you have women bred up to swear, swagger, gaming, drinking, whoring, as most men are?
>
> FATHER LOVE. No, Wife, I would have them bred in learned Schools, to noble Arts and Sciences, as wise men are.
>
> MOTHER LOVE. What Arts? to ride Horses, and fight Dewels.
>
> FATHER LOVE. Yes, if it be to defend their Honour, Countrey, Religion; For noble Arts makes not base Vices, nor is the cause of lewd actions, nor is unseemly for any Sex.
>
> (*Plays,* p. 124)

Lady Sanspareille is melancholy because of her desire for fame, which she describes in words like those that Margaret used about herself:

> Know it is fame I covet, for which were the ambitions of Alexander and Caesar joyned into one mind, mine doth exceed them . . . my mind being restless to get to the highest place in Fames high Tower; and I had rather fall in the adventure, than never try to climb.

She despairs that she may not have 'a sufficient stock of merit, or if I had, yet no waies to advance it' (*Plays,* p. 130). She resolves, with her father's consent, never to marry, but to devote herself to poetry:

> for that time which will be lost in a married condition, I will study and work with my own thoughts,

> and what new inventions they can find out, or what probabilityes they conceive, or phancies they create, I will publish to the world in print . . . but if I marry, although I should have time for my thoughts and contemplations, yet perchance my Husband will not approve of my works, were they never so worthy, and by no perswasion, or reason allow of there publishing; as if it were unlawfull, or against nature, for Women to have wit. . . . some men are so inconsiderately wise, gravely foolish and lowly base, as they had rather be thought Cuckolds, than their wives should be thought wits, for fear the world should think their wife the wiser of the two.
>
> (*Plays*, p. 131)

In Part II Lady Sanspareille fulfills her ambitions, addressing assemblies of amazed savants on learned and literary topics. After her untimely death, her memory is preserved by statues set up in all the colleges and public places in the city.[23]

While interesting for their early feminist heroines, the Duchess of Newcastle's plays are the poorest of her works. Her plays, like those of her stepdaughters, are structurally incoherent. She produces original and arresting raw materials for plots that are never constructed; actions are discussed rather than dramatized. Her usual method of organization is to take three unrelated story lines and alternate scenes among them mechanically. Often the individual scenes have no beginning, middle, or end; one scene simply stops abruptly and an unrelated scene follows. The most common type of scene is a dialogue or trialogue in which one character orates, harangues, or lectures to the other(s). Occasionally there is a real conversation, but generally there is no interaction among characters. The characters are personified abstractions, such as The Lord Fatherly, The Lord Singularity, The Lady Ignorant; and development of such characters rarely occurs.

The duchess was aware of these obvious flaws: 'Some of my Scenes have no acquaintance or relation to the rest of the Scenes; although in one and the same Play, which is the reason so many of my Playes will not end as other Playes do' (To the Reader, *Plays*). She offered this poem as 'A General Prologue to all my Playes':

> But Noble Readers, do not think my Playes,
> Are such as have been writ in former daies;
> As Johnson, Shakespear, Beaumont, Fletcher writ;
> Mine want their Learning, Reading, Language,
> wit:
> The Latin phrases I could never tell,
> But Johnson could, which made him write so
> well,
> Greek, Latin Poets, I could never read,
> Nor their Historians, but our English Speed;
> I could not steal their Wit, nor Plots out take;
> All my Playes Plots, my own poor brain did
> make
> From Plutarchs story I ne'r took a Plot,
> Nor from Romances, nor from Don Quixot,
> As others have, for to assist their Wit,
> But I upon my own Foundation writ.

There is another reason for the peculiar structure of her plays. In the 1662 collection she says that she wrote her plays from her husband's example, and, indeed, the duchess's plays follow the pattern of the duke's unaided efforts. An example of his unretouched work survives, *A Pleasante & Merrye Humor of A Roge*,[24] an unstructured dramatic sketch. Professional playwrights like Dryden, Shirley, and Shadwell turned the duke's sketches into professional plays which were then performed in the London theaters. The duchess, looking up to her husband, assumed that this was the way plays were written: 'I have heard that such Poets that write Playes, seldome or never join or sow the several Scenes together; they are two several Professions.' She explains that, as her plays were written while she was in exile, she was 'forced to do all my self . . . without any help or direction' (To the Readers, *Plays*).

Structurally incoherent as they are, the plays of the Duchess of Newcastle are historically significant as early feminist statements. They made a statement to her contemporaries partly by their physical appearance. The two volumes of plays, like all the duchess's works, were large, handsome books with sumptuous engravings of the author's portrait. Her title pages carried the resounding ascription 'Written by the Thrice Noble, Illustrious, and Excellent Princess, the Duchess of Newcastle.' With princely arrogance, she sent copies to friends, protégés, and even to the libraries of the universities. And no matter how much she was ridiculed, she was too rich and powerful to be ignored. Her books, although often empty of artistic worth, existed, and the medium—handsome folios written by a woman—was the message.

Contrary to general contemporary belief, none of her plays was performed. Pepys, on 30 March 1667, recorded, 'Did by coach go to see the silly play of my Lady Newcastle's called "The Humourous Lovers".' A month later Pepys was still unaware that the play was a professional version of one of the duke's sketches. In April he wrote that the duchess 'was the other day at her own play, *The Humourous Lovers*.'[25] The same play was attributed to the duchess by others. In May 1667, Gervase Jaquis wrote to the Earl of Huntington, 'Upon monday last the Duchess of Newcastls play was Acted in the theater in Lincolns Inne field the

King and the Grandees of the Court being present and soe was her grace and the Duke her husband.'[26]

Notes

1. Katherine of Sutton's plays are preserved in the Barking ordinarium. Sibille Felton, abbess of Barking from 1394 to 1419, caused this to be written and presented it to the convent in 1404. Karl Young was the first to publish the Barking plays, in 'The Harrowing of Hell in Liturgical Drama,' *Transactions of the Wisconsin Academy of Sciences, Arts, and Letters* 16 (1910): 888-947. Young later included the plays in his *Drama of the Medieval Church,* 2 vols (Oxford: Clarendon Press, 1933), 1: 164-6, 381-4. Meanwhile, the entire ordinale had been edited by J. B. L. Tolhurst and printed in two volumes of the Henry Bradshaw Society Publications in 1927-8. The Latin quotations are from Young, *Drama,* 1: 165.

2. Although English women did not act on the public stage until almost exactly three hundred years later, they participated more widely in English medieval drama than is generally realized. Women belonged to religious gilds responsible for plays—for example, the York Pater Noster Gild and the Norwich St Luke's Gild—and participated to some extent in the trade gilds. See Karl Young, 'The Records of the York Play of the *Pater Noster,' Speculum* 7 (1932): 544; Lucy Toulmin Smith (ed.) *York Plays* (Oxford: Clarendon Press, 1885), pp. xxviii-xxxix; Harold C. Gardiner, *Mysteries' End,* Yale Studies in English, 103 (New Haven, CT: Yale University Press, 1946), p. 42; Eileen Power, *Medieval Women* (Cambridge: Cambridge University Press, 1975), pp. 55-69. At Chester the 'wurshipffull wyffys' of the town bound themselves to bring forth the pageant of the Assumption of the Virgin. This pageant was a regular part of the Chester cycle until it was excised at the Reformation. The wives acted their play separately in 1488 before Lord Strange and again in 1515. See W. W. Greg (ed.) *The Trial and Flagellation with Other Studies in the Chester Cycle,* Malone Society Studies (Oxford: Oxford University Press, 1935), pp. 137, 170-1; F. M. Salter, *Mediaeval Drama in Chester* (Toronto: University of Toronto Press, 1955), pp. 50, 70-1. Women also participated in church *ludi.* There are records of an Abbess of Fools or Girl Abbess elected from the novices on Holy Innocents' Day at the nunneries of Godstow and Barking in the thirteenth century. See Eileen Power, *Medieval English Nunneries c. 1275-1535* (Cambridge: Cambridge University Press, 1922), p. 312.

3. Barking was an abbey holding of the king in chief; as tenant in chief, Katherine of Sutton was a baroness in her own right. She was almost certainly a noblewoman by birth also. In the later Middle Ages Barking accepted novitiates only from the aristocracy and the wealthiest bourgeois class; moreover, the nun of highest social rank usually became abbess. See Power, *Medieval English Nunneries,* pp. 4-13, 42.

4. Information about Lady Lumley is taken from the introduction to *Iphigeneia at Aulis,* edited by Harold H. Child for the Malone Society Reprints (London: Chiswick Press, 1909). Myra Reynolds, *The Learned Lady in England 1650-1760* (Boston, MA: Houghton Mifflin, 1920), pp. 13-14, also discusses Lady Lumley.

5. In *The Poems of Elizabeth I,* ed. Leicester Bradner (Providence, RI: Brown University Press, 1964).

6. Biographical information is taken from Frances Berkeley Young, *Mary Sidney Countess of Pembroke* (London: David Nutt, 1912) and Mona Wilson, *Sir Philip Sidney* (London: Duckworth, 1931). *Antonie* has been edited by Alice Luce (Weimer: E. Felber, 1897) and by Geoffrey Bullough in *Narrative and Dramatic Sources of Shakespeare,* 8 vols. (New York: Columbia University Press, 1957-75), 5: 358-406. The translation of the psalms by the Countess of Pembroke and Sir Philip Sidney has been edited by J. C. A. Rathmell (Garden City, NY: Doubleday, 1963). This volume is supplemented by G. F. Waller, *'The Triumph of Death' and Other Unpublished Poems by Mary Sidney, Countess of Pembroke* (Salzburg: Institut für Englische Sprache und Literatur, 1977). The Pembroke circle of Senecan writers is discussed by John W. Cunliffe, *The Influence of Seneca on Elizabethan Tragedy* (London: Macmillan, 1893); Joan Rees, *Samuel Daniel* (Liverpool: Liverpool University Press, 1964); Cecil Seronsy, *Samuel Daniel* (New York: Twayne, 1967). T. S. Eliot discusses the influence of the Pembroke circle in 'Apology for the Countess of Pembroke,' *The Use of Poetry and the Use of Criticism* (London: Faber and Faber, 1933). Mary Herbert is memorialized beautifully but stereotypically in 'On the Countesse Dowager of Pembroke,' long ascribed to Ben Jonson but written by William Browne of Tavistock, in *Ben Jonson,* ed. C. H. Herford and Percy and Evelyn Simpson (Oxford: Clarendon Press, 1925-52), 8: 433.

7. *The Complete Works of Sir Philip Sidney,* ed. Albert Feuillerat (Cambridge: Cambridge University Press, 1912-26), 3: 38.

8. *The Countess of Pembroke's 'Antonie',* ed. Luce, p. 97.

9. A. W. Pollard and G. R. Redgrave, *A Short-Title Catalogue of Books Printed in England, Scotland, and Ireland 1475-1640* (London: The Bibliographical Society, 1926), pp. 255, 412.

10. *A Poetical Rhapsody,* ed. Hyder Rollins (Cambridge, MA: Harvard University Press, 1931), 1: 17.

11. This was edited and published in 1861 by Richard Simpson as *The Lady Falkland: Her Life* (London: Catholic Publishing Company). In-text citations refer to this volume. Two biographies based on the *Life* are Lady Georgiana Fullerton, *The Life of Elisabeth Lady Falkland* (London: Burns and Oates, 1883) and Kenneth B. Murdock, *The Sun at Noon* (New York: Macmillan, 1939), pp. 6-38. Both are concerned with Cary as a Catholic convert; neither is aware of her unique position in the history of English drama. *Mariam* was edited for the Malone Society Reprints by A. C. Dunstan and W. W. Greg (Oxford: Oxford University Press, 1914). In-text citations refer to this edition; I have modernized the u/v and i/j conventions and discarded nonfunctional italics. *Mariam* is discussed at length by A. C. Dunstan in *Examination of Two English Dramas* (Königsberg: Hartungsche Buchdruckerei, 1908). Dunstan also discusses Cary's use of source material in the introduction to the Malone Society edition of the play. *Mariam* is briefly discussed by Alexander Witherspoon, *The Influence of Robert Garnier on Elizabethan Drama* (New Haven, CT: Yale University Press, 1924), pp. 150-5, and Maurice J. Valency, *The Tragedies of Herod and Mariamne* (New York: Columbia University Press, 1940), pp. 87-91. Valency points out that Cary's *Mariam* is the first of many English plays written about Herod and Mariamne. Donald A. Stauffer, 'A Deep and Sad Passion,' *The Parrott Presentation Volume,* ed. Har-

din Craig (1935; reprinted, New York: Russell and Russell, 1967), pp. 289-314, shows that Elizabeth Cary wrote *The History of Edward II,* formerly ascribed to Henry Cary.

12. Introduction to the Malone Society edition, p. ix.
13. Quoted by Fullerton, *Life of Lady Falkland,* p. 120.
14. *The Complete Works of John Davies of Hereford,* ed. Alexander Grosart (Edinburgh: Edinburgh University Press, 1878), 2: 4-5.
15. Biographical information is taken from Carola Oman, *Henrietta Maria* (London: Hodder and Stoughton, 1936). Henrietta Maria's pervasive influence on theatrical history is discussed in detail by Alfred Harbage, *Cavalier Drama* (1936; reprinted, New York: Russell and Russell, 1964), which suggests the queen as the author of *Florimene;* and by Kathleen M. Lynch, *The Social Mode of Restoration Comedy* (New York: Macmillan, 1926).
16. Quotations are from Gerald Eades Bentley, *The Jacobean and Caroline Stage* (Oxford: Clarendon Press, 1941-68), 4: 548-9.
17. Quoted by Harbage, *Cavalier Drama,* pp. 14-15.
18. Except for my inferences about the effect of Newcastle's dramatic activities on his daughters, biographical information on the Cavendish sisters is taken from the DNB and from Nathan Comfort Starr's introduction to his edition of *The Concealed Fansyes* in *Proceedings of the Modern Languages Association* 46 (1931): 802-38. Page references in the text refer to Starr's edition. Harbage, *Cavalier Drama,* pp. 228-9, describes the plays of the Cavendish sisters.
19. I have drawn on a number of sources for biographical information. Standard and useful are Douglas Grant, *Margaret the First* (Toronto: University of Toronto Press, 1957) and Henry Ten Eyck Perry, *The First Duchess of Newcastle and Her Husband as Figures in Literary History* (Boston, MA: Ginn, 1918). Of the numerous biographical essays, the finest is Virginia Woolf's in *The Common Reader* (New York: Harcourt, Brace, 1925), pp. 101-12. The best source of biographical material is the duchess herself, particularly in the introductions, dedications, and letters in her various works. Her autobiography, 'A True Relation of my Birth, Breeding, and Life,' originally the last section of *Natures Pictures* (1656), is included by C. H. Firth in his edition of the duchess's *Life of William Cavendish, Duke of Newcastle* (London: John C. Nimmo, 1886). These two works of the duchess are available in several editions. Firth also prints the duchess's letter 'To the Two Most Famous Universities of England,' a moving appeal for education for women.
20. 'A True Relation,' ed. Firth, pp. 157-8.
21. Ibid., p. 177.
22. My interpretation draws upon Jean Gagen, 'Honor and Fame in the Works of the Duchess of Newcastle,' *Studies in Philology* 56 (1959): 519-38.
23. Jean Gagen focuses on this type of character, which she calls 'the oratorical lady,' in her excellent discussion of the duchess's plays in 'A Champion of the Learned Lady,' ch. 2 in *The New Women: Her Emergence in English Drama 1600-1730* (New York: Twayne, 1954). Gagen's discussion led me to examine the pervasive feminism in the duchess's plays.
24. Francis Needham (ed.) *Welbeck Miscellany,* 1 (1933) from a fair copy in the duke's handwriting.
25. *Pepys on the Restoration Stage,* ed. Helen McAfee (New Haven, CT: Yale University Press, 1916), pp. 171-2.
26. *The London Stage, 1600-1700,* ed. William Van Lennep (Carbondale, IL: Southern Illinois University Press, 1965), p. 108. Harbage, *Cavalier Drama,* pp. 232-3, suggests that the duchess wrote at least the first draft of *Lady Alimony,* performed at the Cockpit in 1659. While the play is structurally odd and schematic enough to be hers, its anonymity is conclusive proof against her authorship.

MARION WYNNE-DAVIES (ESSAY DATE 1998)

SOURCE: Wynne-Davies, Marion. Introduction to *Women Poets of the Renaissance,* edited by Marion Wynne-Davies, pp. xix-xxix. New York: Routledge, 1999.

In the following essay, originally published in 1998, Wynne-Davies provides an overview of female Renaissance poets, discusses their social positions, and examines their literary concerns.

And in oblivion bury me
And never more me name.

These words are taken from Isabella Whitney's *The Manner of Her Will . . . to London* (lines 267-8), where she asks the city to bury her without show or ostentation. They could apply as succinctly to the body of her work as to her own mortal remains, for, after the first publication of her poem in 1573, the text was buried in oblivion until the late twentieth century, and Whitney's 'name' ceased to be recorded in the annals of English poetry. Nor is such obscurity confined to Whitney (the first poet in this anthology), for, with the exception of Queen Elizabeth I, none of the women represented here is well-known or widely published. Even Elizabeth is recognized more as an icon and a symbol of English heritage than as an author in her own right. This lack of contextual and interpretative information raises some basic questions. To begin, we need to ask: 'Who were these women poets and what were they writing about?'

It has often been assumed that in the early modern period it was only noblewomen, having greater access to education, space and economic security, who were able to venture into the realms of creative writing or scholarly translation. It is unsurprising that several of the poets anthologized here fall into this category: Elizabeth I, Anne Cecil de Vere, Mary Sidney, Mary Wroth, and Jane and Elizabeth Cavendish all had academic and material support, which ensured that they had the time and encouragement to write poetry. Yet three of these women, perhaps fearing the censure resultant upon female authorship, chose primarily to translate rather than originate material (Elizabeth I, Anne Cecil de Vere and Mary Sidney). What is particularly unexpected is that the remaining writers could not have relied upon such provision. Instead they must be allocated to two lower rank or class groups: the gentry and the bourgeoisie. Those in the first group, Anne Dowriche, Aemilia Lanyer and Diana Primrose, were all in some way attached to the court, but remained distinctly on the margins, more in need of patronage than in a position to offer it. The remaining women, Isabella Whitney, Rachel Speght, Alice Sutcliffe and Anne Bradstreet, seem to have had more or less adequate financial resources, but from what little we know of them—and this in itself is an indicator of status—they belonged to the bourgeoisie and were mostly involved in some sort of domestic employment. In these two latter groups Whitney specifically complains of penury: 'I whole in body and in mind, / But very weak in purse' (*The Manner of Her Will . . . to London,* lines 1-2), while Lanyer regrets the passing of a secure period of patronage in 'The Description of Cooke-Ham', where she writes:

> Farewell (sweet place) where virtue then did rest,
> And all delights did harbour in her breast,
> Never shall my sad eyes again behold
> Those pleasures which my thoughts did then
>   unfold.
>
> (lines 7-10)

Both poets stress their lack of material security and use their texts expressly to enhance their position: Whitney through the remuneration ensuing from publication, and Lanyer in the hope that Margaret Clifford, the Countess of Cumberland, will renew her assistance. Rather than being an obstacle to their literary activity, their lack of status and wealth appears to have been an important impetus, suggesting that Renaissance women poets, like their male counterparts, increasingly regarded their literary skills as a saleable commodity. Thus, although it is undoubtedly true that women writers of the early modern period did not have the same opportunities as men, they did not always form a separate and distinct group on the basis of their sex. Instead, they correspond quite closely to the same economic and rank divisions as male authors, and the resemblances are clearly apparent in each category, nobility, gentry and bourgeoisie. For every Mary Sidney there is a Philip Sidney; for every Aemilia Lanyer there is an Edmund Spenser; and for every Isabella Whitney there is a Thomas Dekker. Two conclusions may thus be drawn from this initial enquiry: firstly, class was an essential factor in determining the female poetic subject during the English Renaissance, and, rather than privileging the nobility, it allowed a fairly broad cross-section of women to become poets. Secondly, male and female poets cannot be treated as disconnected groups, since they were clearly both integral parts of the same social and economic system.

While rank and money were key factors influencing literary productivity in the early modern period, location and familial associations were equally important for women writers. In Lanyer's poem 'The Description of Cooke-Ham' the country house from which she has been exiled is as important to her security as the support of the Countess of Cumberland, although both are of course inextricably linked. Lanyer's vision of a pastoral idyll in which poet and patron co-exist in perfect harmony is quite possibly the first example of a country-house poem in English (the other contender being Ben Jonson's 'To Penshurst'), but she is not alone amongst the women represented here in focusing upon her environment. For example, the 'Penshurst' lauded by Jonson is also a key site for the two Sidney women included in this anthology: Mary Sidney and Mary Wroth both refer to the estate, and particularly to the flooding of the River Medway, which runs through Penshurst's lower meadows. In *Pamphilia to Amphilanthus* Wroth's poetic second-self, Pamphilia, uses the image of the river to compare fickleness with steadfastness in romantic love, 'you do well, lest staying here might breed / Dangerous floods, your sweetest banks t'o'er-run' (P51, lines 5-6). By contrast, Mary Sidney uses the flooding river as a metaphor for the instability of human existence:

> Rivers, yea, though rivers roar,
>   Roaring though sea-billows rise
> Vex the deep, and break the shore
>
> (Psalm 93, lines 10-12)

which she rejects in favour of the truth and constancy of God: 'Stronger art thou, Lord of skies. / Firm and true thy promise lies' (lines 13-14). These themes of mutability and firmness, which are related to secular and spiritual love respectively, commonly recur in early modern poetry, but the specific locational imagery is particular to the Sidney family; indeed, Philip Sidney, Robert Sidney and William Herbert all use exactly the same trope drawn from the Medway's propensity to flood. Yet women poets are not confined to a pastoral vision of their environment: Whitney's vision of London in 'The Manner of Her Will . . . to London' is acutely satiric; Jane and Elizabeth Cavendish acknowledge in their play *The Con-*

cealed *Fancies* that their home, Welbeck Abbey, has become a prison during the Civil War; and Anne Bradstreet draws a dramatic vision of the hardships of life in the New World when her house burned down ('Verses upon the Burning of Our House'). In each instance the home of the female poet is a site of security and stability, but, tellingly, in each instance that protection has been destabilized through betrayal, death, poverty, war or destruction.

In her justly famous account of a Renaissance woman dramatist, 'Judith Shakespeare', in *A Room of One's Own,* Virginia Woolf pointed out that women writers need economic and locational security in order to write; however, for the early modern period she could well have added 'familial support'. Almost all the poets collected here benefited from the support of their families in the pursuance of their literary careers. The most famous family groups are the Sidneys (Mary, Philip and Robert Sidney, together with Mary Wroth and William Herbert) and the Cavendishes (Jane, Elizabeth, William and Margaret Cavendish), but Anne Cecil de Vere belonged to the illustrious Cooke family (all four of her aunts were authors), and Elizabeth I benefited from a programme of humanist education condoned by her father, Henry VIII, and actively encouraged by her stepmother, Catherine Parr. These groups are, however, all aristocratic to a certain extent, and so close familial bonding might well be expected. What is particularly interesting is that the gentry and bourgeoisie produced similar literary families. Isabella Whitney had a brother, Geoffrey Whitney, who published a book of emblems; Anne Dowriche's husband wrote at least one extant work, to which she added decicatory verses; Rachel Speght had a number of literary connections, including her father and husband; the most likely candidate for identification as Diana Primrose's father also published his own work; Anne Bradstreet's family produced other writers; and even Aemilia Lanyer belongs to the scholarly Clifford group through her childhood associations. Of all the poets in this anthology, only Alice Sutcliffe appears to have had no relatives who were writing and publishing their own works, and this might well be explained by the fact that we know so little about her life. Moreover, an analysis of a similar group of male poets would not reach the same conclusion, although the function of literary, non-blood kinship was arguably as important for men as actual familial ties were for women. Nevertheless, while class and money were equally important elements in male as well as female

ON THE SUBJECT OF...

ANNE BRADSTREET (1612?-1672)

Bradstreet was America's first published poet and the first woman to produce a lasting volume of poetry in the English language. Her work is considered particularly significant for its expression of passion, anger, and uncertainty within the rigid social and religious atmosphere of Puritan New England, and for the insight it provides into the lives of women from that period. Bradstreet was born in England to a Puritan family. Her father, Thomas Dudley, was steward to the Earl of Lincoln, a leading nonconformist in the religious strife of England. Because of her father's high position and the availability of the Earl's extensive library, Bradstreet's education was unusually comprehensive for a woman of her time. In 1630 she moved with her husband and her parents to the Massachusetts Bay Colony.

In 1647 her brother-in-law returned to England, taking with him the manuscript of Bradstreet's poems. He published them without her knowledge, under the title *The Tenth Muse, Lately sprung up in America* (1650). The volume met with immediate success in London. Surprised by the work's reception, though unhappy with its unpolished state, Bradstreet revised the poems, some of which were lost in a fire that destroyed the Bradstreet home in 1666. In 1678, six years after Bradstreet's death, the revisions and some new poems were published under the title *Several Poems Compiled with great variety of Wit and Learning, full of Delight.* Her prose meditations and later poems did not appear in print until 1867. Most of Bradstreet's works may be placed into one of two distinct periods. The "public" poems that appeared in *The Tenth Muse* are structurally and thematically formal, written in the style of Renaissance poetry. Bradstreet's later poems—described by most scholars as her "private" poems—are less stylized in form and more personal in content.

creativity during the early modern period, women were more inclined to focus upon environmental security and were uniquely reliant upon family support.

In the above analysis of the personal context of the poets in this anthology, there is a tacit acceptance of the autobiographical nature of their writings. This affiliation between women writers and autobiography has been thoroughly excavated since the advent of feminist criticism in the 1970s, so it is no surprise that women Renaissance poets drew upon personal experience rather than scholarly authority. For example, one of Elizabeth I's Woodstock poems derives from her imprisonment by her sister, Mary I, on the grounds of her possible implication in a plot to overthrow the queen:

> Much suspected by me,
> Nothing proved can be;
> Quoth Elizabeth prisoner.
> ('Woodstock: the Window Poem')

Similarly, Whitney in her assertion of penury, Lanyer in her account of her youth at Cooke-Ham, the Cavendish sisters in their account of the Civil War, and Bradstreet with her evocations of the New World, all refer to their individual circumstances at the time of writing. However, there are two particular genres that seem to reveal more about the private self of the women poets than any others: love poetry and elegies.

The elegies are perhaps the most poignant of all the poems in this collection. Mary Sidney continued the Psalm translations begun by her dead brother Philip and prefaced them with a dedicatory poem clearly depicting her grief:

> To which these dearest offerings of my heart
> (Dissolved to ink, while pen's impressions move
> The bleeding veins of never-dying love)
> I render here: these wounding lines of smart,
> Sad characters indeed of simple love
> (Not art nor skill which abler wits do prove)
> Of my full soul receive the meanest part.
> ('To the Angel Spirit . . .', lines 79-85)

Jane Cavendish offers a similar eulogy to her sister, Elizabeth, with whom she was involved in literary collaborations in a manner not dissimilar to that of Mary and Philip Sidney:

> And when Death's heavy hand had closed her eyes,
> Me-thought the world gave up its ghost in cries.
> ('On the Death of My Dear Sister', lines 7-8)

These expressions of sibling closeness are, however, rivalled by the grief of mothers and grandmothers at the death of children: Anne Cecil de Vere's four epitaphs upon her dead son repeat her grief continually: 'With my son, my gold, my nightingale, and rose, / Is gone,' (Epitaph 2, lines 5-6); while Anne Bradstreet recounts sadly of her grandson, Simon, 'No sooner came, but gone, and fall'n asleep' ('On . . . Simon Bradstreet', line 1). These personal statements are the most overtly autobiographical of all the poetry collected here and show that, while familial relationships might have enabled women to write, they were regarded as far more than an advantageous encouragement to literary productivity.

Perhaps the most personally revealing examples of love poetry come from Mary Wroth's sonnet sequence *Pamphilia to Amphilanthus,* in which she adopts the persona of Pamphilia (all-loving) and endows her cousin and lover William Herbert with the character of Amphilanthus (lover-of-two). Much of this sonnet sequence may be read as a close familial allegory which recounts the narrative of Wroth's love affair with Herbert, but at the same time the poems participate fully in the courtly-love discourse of the period and could easily be interpreted as general rather than particular in their allusions. Exactly the same may be said for Elizabeth I's poem 'An Answer', which was directed to Walter Ralegh; its specific references are easily balanced by the focus upon more comprehensive themes such as the fickleness of fortune. Even Elizabeth Cavendish's personal avowal of love, 'I love thee, ever have, and still shall do' ('Spoken Upon Receiving . . . a Heart', line 5), and Anne Bradstreet's address to her absent husband, 'My head, my heart, mine eyes, my life, nay, more' ('A Letter to Her Husband', line 1), are couched in the language and metaphors of courtly love. Unlike the elegies, which are intensely personal, the love poems are more open to a general interpretation, perhaps echoing the dominance of the latter genre in early modern poetry. What is unexpected, however, is the distinct lack of love poetry in this collection. It was not a genre generally adopted by Renaissance women poets; although their writing is strongly autobiographical, this is more often expressed in conjunction with their political and religious beliefs rather than the private concerns of love.

In discussing elegies and love poetry we have gradually been moving away from the question, 'Who were they?' to the interrogation 'What did they write?', and, in recognizing the widespread absence of intensely private material, we have also shifted from the personal to the public sphere. Yet, with a sharp sense of introspection, the most recurrent political topic utilized by women poets of the time is the life and reign of one of their own number: Elizabeth I. Perhaps her popularity as subject-matter rested on the fact that, in issues of government and national policy, Elizabeth offered the unique combination of absolute power and female gender. Allusions to the queen often take the form of brief references found in a number of poems: for example, Anne Dowriche praises the queen as the upholder of England's religious and political security ('Lord, long preserve and keep / That noble queen, Elizabeth, chief pastor of thy sheep', *The French History,* lines 2247-8); Mary Sidney combines panegyric with tacit Protestant advice in '[To Queen Elizabeth]'; and Aemilia Lanyer refers to 'great Eliza' (*Salve Deus Rex Judaeorum,* 'To the Queen's Most Excellent Majesty', line 110). Two texts, however, focus solely on Elizabeth I: Diana Primrose's *A Chain of Pearl* takes the queen as an exemplar of moral virtue, beginning in eulogistic style:

> Thou English goddess, empress of our sex,
> O thou whose name still reigns in all our hearts,
> To whom are due our ever-vow'd respects;
> ('The Induction', lines 13-15)

while Ann Bradstreet's 'In Honour of that High and Mighty Princess Queen Elizabeth of Happy Memory' similarly presents Elizabeth as divine:

> So great's thy glory and thine excellence,
> The sound thereof raps every human sense,
> That men account it no impiety,
> To say thou were a fleshly deity.
> (lines 5-8)

In all these instances the references to Elizabeth do not initially appear to be gender-specific; indeed, the numerous panegyrics written to Elizabeth during her own lifetime, together with the nostalgic allusions to her after her death, are as frequent with male as they are female poets. Her political significance was also manipulated by both men and women; the Protestant ideology of Dowriche and Mary Sidney is easily identified in their male counterparts such as Spenser and Philip Sidney; while the romanticizing of the Elizabethan age in order to criticize the Stuart monarchy was as present in the works of authors such as Primrose and Bradstreet as it was in the writings of Jonson and Ralegh. For women writers, however, Elizabeth's gender was important, and several of the poets mentioned above combine a comment upon the idealized power of the queen with a resolute defence of their common sex. Before returning to this self-conscious identifying of gendered subjectivity, however, it is important to acknowledge that the political framework of the verse in this collection extended beyond such singularity towards a broader treatment of national and religious concerns.

The political poetry which treats non-gendered subject-matter deals with material as diverse as Dowriche's historical narrative of the persecution of the Protestants in France, or Bradstreet's account of English history in several poems, including that addressed to Elizabeth I. While not an overtly stated concern, Mary Sidney in her Psalm translations, and the Cavendish sisters in their Civil War writings (especially their play *The Concealed Fancies*), notably display an interest in politics of their time, from the externalized threat of Catholicism to the internal schisms of the English Civil War. There is, however, one overriding factor—religion. Radical English Protestantism is one of the most powerful unifying forces evinced by the poets in this collection: Dowriche, Sidney, Speght, Primrose, and Bradstreet are all forceful in their defence of their Church and virulently anti-Catholic. For example, Dowriche introduces Satan as one of the characters who advises the Catholic forces in her poem *The French History.* The majority of the remaining poets, Isabella Whitney, Elizabeth I, Anne Cecil de Vere, Lanyer, Wroth and the Cavendish sisters, are non-committal in the verses included here, but their Protestant affiliations are quite clear from other texts and their biographies. This leaves only Alice Sutcliffe, whose poetry suggests a possible Catholic sympathy, although such a religious link was still dangerous enough in 1634 for the text to be ambiguous about any specific faith. There can be no doubt that the women writers of the early modern period felt that their literary activities, even the publication of their works, was completely justified by the dominant concerns of their faith. If patriarchal authority on earth prohibited female expression then the greater authority of God could be invoked to counteract such an earthly prohibition.

The behaviour of early modern women was carefully policed by the dominant male hierarchy of their age: the ideal woman was chaste, silent and obedient. The act of writing was clearly an impingement upon 'silence', since the written word was a material validation of female articulacy, but to go further and publish their works also laid women open to charges of immoral behaviour in that, by allowing all men to see/hear their words, they came to be regarded as unchaste. These condemnations explain why many women of the period chose to allow their works to exist only in manuscript form and to be read privately

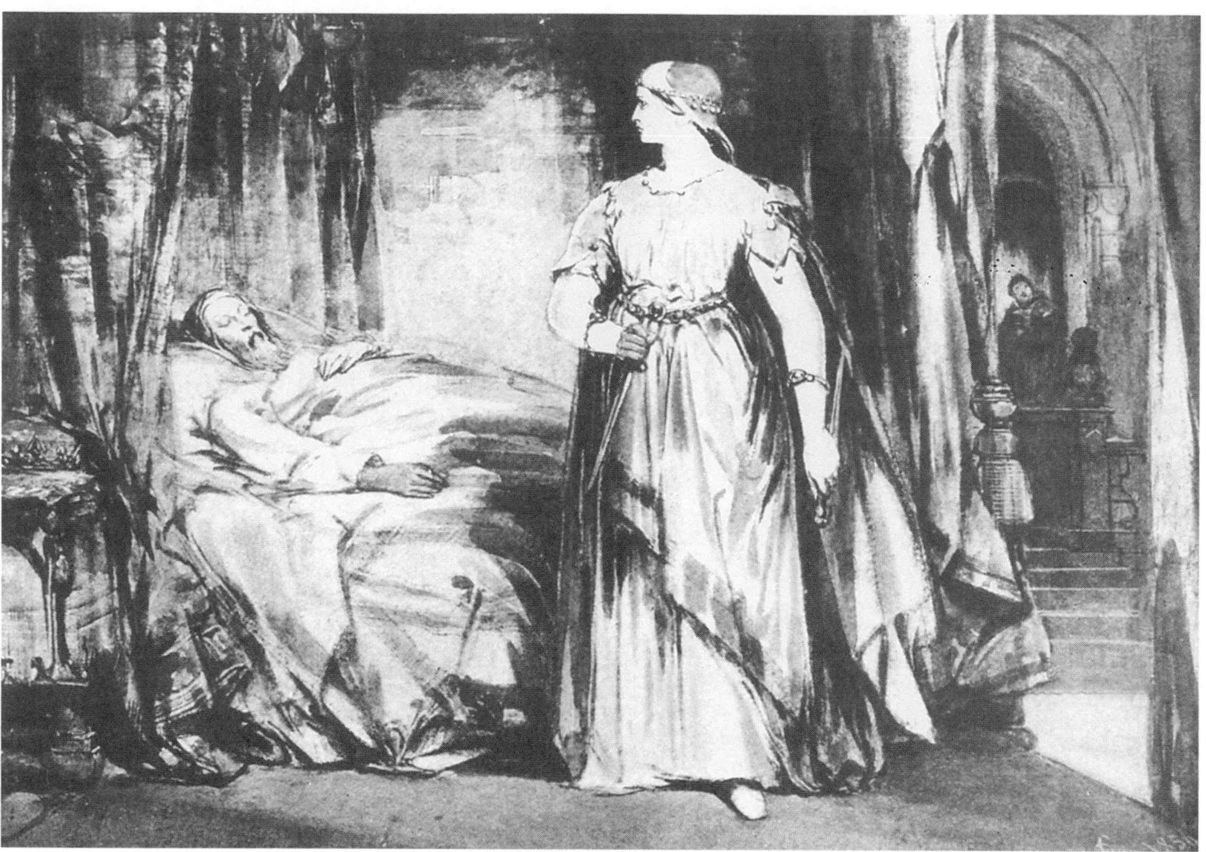

After Macbeth fails to kill Duncan, Lady Macbeth seeks to finish the deed in Act II, scene ii of *Macbeth.*

by their own families—certainly not to be displayed in printed form for the general public. Beyond the breaches of female self-containment offered by writing and publishing lay the still worse transgression of writing and/or publishing material to be acted. Quiet reading of a female-authored text at least retained the 'words' within the boundaries of private contemplation, but any work which contained or facilitated dramatic structures inevitably drew the female voice into the public arena, even if the works were never intended for public performance. It is important to note that in England no early modern woman had her plays performed on the stage, although evidence from manuscripts suggests that private readings or performances took place. It is clear from the extant plays written by women of the period that they had envisaged such productions. Consequently, plays written by Renaissance women writers should be considered as part of their public voice rather than the private discourses of love poetry and elegies. There are two poetic extracts from plays in this anthology: Mary Sidney's *The Tragedy of Antonie* and Jane and Elizabeth Cavendish's *The Concealed Fancies.* The former work is considered to be a closet drama, written to be read aloud by a small family group or cultural coterie, and certainly not to be acted in one of the large London theatres. The speeches chosen, however, have more in common with the powerful language and acute characterization of plays by Shakespeare and Marlowe than with the formal style of Mary Sidney's French original. Antonius' speech might easily have been written by a male tragedian of the period:

> Since cruel heaven's against me obstinate;
> Since all mishaps of the round engine do
> Conspire my harm; since men, since powers
> divine,
> Air, earth, and sea, are all injurious;
> And that my queen herself, in whom I lived,
> The idol of my heart, doth me pursue:
> It's meet I die.
>
> (I.1-7)

The Cavendish drama is very different in tone. Aside from being a light romantic comedy, it is uniquely situated between the courtly discourse of Ben Jonson's masques and the witty interchanges of Restoration theatre. However, since much of the comic material is found, as might be expected, in the prose speeches of the play, the poetic extracts included here have more in common with the nostalgia of Primrose than with the sharp dramas of Aphra Behn. While these are the only two plays I have included, the dramatic form adopted by Anne Dowriche in her poetry signifies that her writing must be considered as accessing the public voice of literary performance. The speech given by Catherine de Medici in *The French History* is the most interesting and bears comparison with some of the well-known parts given to villainesses, such as Lady Macbeth, in male-authored plays of the period. The introduction immediately makes us aware of the text's dramatic potential:

> But here the prologue ends, and here begins the play,
> For bloody minds resolved quite to use no more delay.
> The Mother Queen appears now first upon the stage,
> Where like a devilish sorceress with words demure and sage . . .

and Catherine goes on to plot the massacre of the Protestants on St Bartholomew's Day:

> What though ye do forswear? What though ye break your faith?
> What though ye promise life, and yet repay it with their death?
> Is this so great a fault? Nay, nay, no fault at all,
> For this we learn we ought to do, if such occasions fall. . . .
> What shame is this that I (a woman by my kind)
> Need thus to speak, or pass you men in valour of the mind?
> For here I do protest, if I had been a man,
> I had myself before this time this murder long began.
>
> (lines 1393-6, 1421-4, 1433-6)

This combination of a self-aware use of dramatic discourses, and a focus upon a strong female character, makes Dowriche's poem an important example of how women adopted a public voice during the early modern period, and it is particularly fitting that the formal aspects of the text exactly mirror its political content.

The speech quoted above is notable not only for the early use by a woman of a semi-dramatic form, but also in its comment upon gender roles, specifically a female character's powerful assertion of equality. Dowriche is not alone in this self-aware construction of a gendered authorial subjectivity: each of the women writers anthologized here makes specific reference to her sex. The most radical choose to invert traditional patriarchal expectations: for example, in *Salve Deus Rex Judaeorum,* Lanyer completely overturns Biblical convention and the orthodoxies of the Church, when she claims that the fall from grace was man's fault and not woman's: 'Her fault, though great, yet he was most to blame' (line 778). Similarly, Rachel Speght and Anne Bradstreet confound those who would detract from women's achievements. In *Mortality's Memorandum* Speght makes a direct allusion to the controversial debate about women, and attacks Joseph Swetnam (who wrote the misogynistic *The Arraignment of Women*) as a 'monster or a devil [who] on Eve's sex . . . foamed filthy froth' (lines 242-3); while in 'In Honour of That High and Mighty Princess Queen Elizabeth of Happy Memory' Bradstreet notes:

> Now say, have women worth? or have they none?
> Or had they some, but with our Queen is't gone?
> Nay masculines, you have thus taxed us long,
> But she, though dead, will vindicate our wrong;
> Let such as say our sex is void of reason,
> Know 'tis a slander now, but once was treason.
>
> (lines 95-100)

In parallel, Primrose, Wroth and the Cavendish sisters all choose to invert the accepted dialectic of virgin/whore by demonstrating that women could be honourable in love and that men were not always the innocent victims of feminine wiles. Thus, Diana Primrose in *A Chain of Pearl* challenges the usual representation of women as leading men astray with sexual allurements by referring to 'men's siren-blandishments, / Which are attended with so foul events' ('Temperance', lines 5-6). Similarly, Mary Wroth's sonnet sequence *Pamphilia to Amphilanthus* presents women as constant and men as fickle in love, and Jane and Elizabeth Cavendish point out that male lovers 'profane' women by suggesting that they are 'wantonly fair' (*The Concealed Fancies,* lines 2-3). Although not overtly defending the female sex, Elizabeth I's lyrics, Anne Cecil de Vere's elegies and Mary Sidney's introductory poems all positively and openly acknowledge women's virtues. This leaves only Whitney's satiric mocking of her own sex by referring to women as 'foolish' ('A Communication', line 7) and Alice Sutcliffe's more conventional surprised tone when suggesting that 'Ought good [may be] expressed by our sex's act' (*Meditations of Man's Mortality,* 'An Acrostic upon the . . . Earl of Pembroke', line 13). From the above evidence it seems that women writers of the early modern period felt compelled to confront the issue of their sex in some manner and that the majority of them did this in a positive manner, many actively working to overturn the conventional gender identities of their day. It is, therefore, all the more ironic that the voices of these women have been silenced over the centuries, brought once more into the oblivion they strove so hard to evade in their own lifetimes.

This Introduction began with a bleak recognition of the oblivion that awaited so many women writers not only of the early modern period, but of all prior generations. Inevitably, therefore, the critical and editorial work undertaken on these female authors must provide the basic materials for, and undertake the initial excavations necessary to, the pursuance of more complex and extended scholarship. This edition of Renaissance women poets participates in the common project to make the works of female poets readily available to students and the general reader. The extracts chosen are all intended to make previously obscure texts understandable and enjoyable to a new readership. It is to be hoped that this will encourage further editions of individual writers, and new critical investigations into the authors and themes I have addressed. Indeed, even though over the past two decades research into early modern women writers has become increasingly common, providing us with excellent editions and criticisms (many of which are referred to in the Select Bibliography), there is still an enormous amount of work to be done. Therefore, in conclusion, I should like to turn to the last poet in this collection, Anne Bradstreet, and rehearse her lines, with their invocation not to forget the names and works of early modern women poets, but to respond to them with the articulation of our own critical and editorial 'sighs':

> And if chance to thine eyes shall bring this verse,
> With some sad sighs honour my absent hearse.
> ('Before the Birth of One of Her Children', lines 25-6)

ISOBEL GRUNDY (ESSAY DATE 2000)

SOURCE: Grundy, Isobel. "(Re)discovering Women's Texts." In *Women and Literature in Britain 1700-1800,* edited by Vivien Jones, pp. 179-96. Cambridge, England: Cambridge University Press, 2000.

In the following essay, Grundy discusses the process of recovering women's texts and by what standards the works should be judged.

Discovery has a bad name in the late twentieth century. The old idea that Columbus 'discovered' America is now recognised to be Eurocentric. America was there already, full of human societies whose rich experience had not included the knowledge of Europe. Electricity, too, was pulsing through the air and through the human brain before anybody discovered it. Early texts by women have most of them served the purpose for which they were written; but a text which is not now in the hands of readers is in some sense nonexistent.

Still, it is worth pausing over what we mean by (re)discovery and why we need it, before proceeding to what has been done and what needs doing. 'Undiscovered' may mean unknown, or lost, or merely neglected. No one at all seems to have read or even heard of the little autobiographies of Martha Moulsworth and Mary More between the time of their composition in the mid seventeenth century, and that time in the 1980s and 1990s when Robert C. Evans and Barbara Wiedemann, and Margaret Ezell, came on them in the course of research. Neither of these early modern women offered her work to the public. But within a decade of their 'discovery' each has had hundreds of readers. Moulsworth has had the text of her poem published with elaborate apparatus; Mary More occupies a central chapter in a monograph by Ezell which includes the text of her prose account.[1] These works were unknown for so long because, it seems, their authors wrote—although with great artistry and polish—purely for their own satisfaction.

A similar fate can overtake works written for fame or for cash. Sarah Gardner's comedy *The Advertisement* was staged for her benefit in 1777. The cast turned in a disgraceful performance, though the audience was fairly positive. The play was never put on again. Of course the censorship office retained a manuscript copy; but no one had cause to look at it. Gardner's manuscript, *and* her angry narrative of how the play was killed, lay for 180 years in a cupboard or recess in Colyton in Devon, until a Sunday morning when the householder decided to strip some wallpaper. The play is still unpublished and unprinted, but it has been written about; it is available.[2]

Rediscovery has proved necessary for others not half so well hidden as Gardner. After the inimitable Laetitia Pilkington at last received a serious scholarly edition, Margaret Doody marvelled at the way in which, for so long, scholars of Jonathan Swift have managed to make use of Pilkington without attending to her, and have blithely ignored the need to examine or elucidate the various problems and issues raised by her work.[3] Because she wrote about Swift, she has had her footnote in literary history; but in that footnote she has not figured as a writer—neither as biographer, autobiographer, humorist, satirist, or poet—but solely as a member of Swift's entourage, or as an amusingly scandalous little divorcée.

Aphra Behn (1640?-c. 1689).

Further up the scale of visibility than Pilkington, Aphra Behn and Frances Burney have never been lost; but they have been unacceptable and therefore unavailable. Behn has been seen (like Pilkington) as sexy and scandalous, Burney as virtuous and boring. They experienced two rather different individual unveiling processes. Behn became available in anthologies for classroom use well before scholarly editors got to grips with her works, while Joyce Hemlow's rigorous and expensive edition of Burney's journals and letters (but only the later ones) helped to create the taste which made paperbacks of her longer novels finally feasible.[4] Now Behn and Burney have scholarly biographies, scholarly editions, and stage productions, besides a whole clutch of different paperback texts and critical analyses.

Behn and Burney have achieved both the markers which measure full accessibility (which in turn equates to full canonical status). One is cheap availability, which means chiefly paperbacks, though it may come more and more to mean other and probably electronic forms. The other is scholarly or research availability, which is harder to measure. Cheap availability depends on the market, on publishing and bookselling practices (which just recently have been acting strongly in favour of early women's writing); research availability depends on the state of knowledge. In one sense any extant writing which is in the public domain (not hidden from it as Moulsworth and More and Gardner have been) needs only to be mentioned (whether in a periodical article or in the English Short Title Catalogue)[5] to become available to scholars. Even if a work survives only in a unique copy, once the catalogue knows or suspects it was written by a woman, any student of women's writing is free to travel to the location of that text, or to order herself a copy, by microfilm if necessary.

But the word 'free' is ironical: this freedom costs a lot. For a generation now, any student wanting to work on Lady Mary Wortley Montagu's letters has had a scholarly text available;[6] work on Elizabeth Montagu's letters still demands an extended visit to the Huntington Library in California. A student of Behn's works or Burney's plays can now order up Janet Todd's or Peter Sabor's edition, and can trust the printed text on issues of transcribing, dating, attribution, and the elucidation of puzzling points. A few years ago such a student would have needed either to travel to the New York Public Library (in the case of Burney) or to round up copies of many obscure seventeenth-century texts (in the case of Behn, since she could not wholly trust Montague Summers's edition). Now Behn and Burney are once again in play; people are reading them, responding to them, arguing over them.

I hope these specific examples will communicate the romantic aspect of rediscovery. The manuscripts in the papered-over cupboard, the printed words lying unrecognised and ignored, conjure up an idea of their authors not unlike Virginia Woolf's image in 'Lives of the Obscure': of the stranded ghost waiting in the darkness for us, the scholarly search-party, to advance with lights 'across the waste of years to the rescue'.[7] But this remains a metaphor or a fantasy. In practice discovery is usually non-heroic. One stage of it is more like noticing something which was there all the time, in full view but nevertheless overlooked. The next stage is more like a work of renovation: scraping off accretions, dismantling, reconstructing, making good.

Rediscovery is not an event; it is a process. And despite the glamour of the individual find, the individual reprint, the really significant point is the rediscovery of women's writing as a whole. The really significant issue just now is the state of that overall historical process.

When I studied English at Oxford, at the end of the 1950s, Jane Austen was the earliest woman we read. We all (of both sexes) had perfect confidence that no criterion of choice had been used but that of selecting the best. The former omission of the Metaphysical poets had been rectified; all was right with the canon. Women's writing was largely undiscovered by it. We supposed this to be some kind of norm, a timeless or ahistorical condition, and not the product of our particular point in history. The same misconception was presumably shared by, for instance, the selectors of titles for Everyman's Library or the Penguin Classics, who at that date had hardly heard of women writers either. Even (dare one say it?) Woolf herself had not treated her rescued 'obscure' women authors (Laetitia Pilkington and Ann Taylor, later Gilbert) as if they were real writers at all, and she did not mention Ann's sister Jane. Now Jane, it seems to me, has exactly that power of extracting poetry from the commonplace that one might expect Woolf to admire; and one might also expect her to feel some kinship with Ann's writing of an overdue review, 'As to "Miss Edgeworth," I feel in despair, for I cannot seclude myself, and nurse up my mind as I have always found necessary to composition.'[8] Ann Gilbert's life-writings seem to me to offer many of the pleasures of Woolf's own (an engagement with daily life, with experience felt on the pulses), but Woolf treats her as quaint.

Women were absent from university curricula in those days; but not until many years later did I notice that here and there small, emphatic reinforcements of their exclusion were being enacted. In what was to become my own period, the eighteenth century, established scholars apparently thought it an aspect of their duty to make sure that women's stock did not rise. Harold Williams, editing Swift's letters, wrote this footnote on Mary Barber: 'Swift's infatuation with Mrs Barber led him into an unjustified estimate of her gifts.'[9] R. W. Chapman, editing Samuel Johnson's letters, wrote this footnote on Charlotte Lennox's *Shakespear Illustrated*: 'J. contributed a dedication. He was perhaps too busy to pay much attention to the text, which I am assured is full of absurdities. Like some scholars of our own time, but with better excuse, J. was ever lenient to the work of learned ladies, especially if they had the claim of poverty.'[10] Such gestures of abhorrence would not have been used for minor male contemporaries. Swift's protégé William Dunkin, or Johnson's dedications for Charles Burney or proposals for the Revd William Shaw, could pass without ritual exorcism. Johnson's praise of Lennox is so shocking to Chapman that he both flaunts his willingness to pronounce on a book without reading it, and rushes off the point to insult his female contemporaries. Women writers were not only without status themselves; it seems that without careful management they might also damage the status of their great male contemporaries.

The exclusion of women from university syllabuses in English Literature becomes less surprising in the light of these footnotes. The growth of English as an academic subject had coincided with a period (the late nineteenth and early twentieth centuries) which was strong both in current women's writing and in rediscovery of earlier women's writing. But the shapers of the syllabus were backward-looking. English studies had to earn a reputation for rigour and value comparable to that of classical studies. Philology and textual scholarship were at a premium. Texts were prized for their difficulty; but a history of difficulty in *reception,* such as attends many women's texts, looked less attractive. Woolf's obscure memoir-writers, Pilkington and Gilbert, were strictly recreational reading.

This was, nevertheless (a couple of generations before Williams and Chapman and their footnotes), a time when (re)discovery of women writers was gathering steam in the academy as elsewhere. The first decade of the twentieth century produced works like Myra Reynolds's edition of Anne Finch's poems and the biography of Lady Mary Wortley Montagu by 'George Paston'.[11] But these works of scholarship occupied a minority or marginal position: there was no expectation that their subjects would claim a place in the canon, or that it was incumbent on a specialist in Pope, for instance, to have read them.

A similar status was occupied by Joyce Tompkins's monographs of the 1930s. They dealt explicitly with uncanonical eighteenth-century fiction, therefore predominantly with women authors; they were books for specialists or for the curious, not for the general run of students. Mary Lascelles, at the same period, wrote about such novels as a background to the study of Jane Austen, so her work gained wider currency.[12] But much scholarly discovery of women writers has heretofore shared with its subject-matter a propensity to become lost, and has turned out sooner or later to need rediscovery itself.

The twentieth century was not the first period either of intensive rediscovery or of admirable scholarly work associated with it. Women of the late eighteenth century waded with enthusiasm into the task of collecting and preserving earlier women's writing and getting it published. Mary Berry, sorting and cataloguing letters for the Duke of Devonshire in 1815, became 'an enthusiast for [the] character' of Lady Rachel Russell, turned herself into a fair amateur scholar, and published a biography with a selection of Russell's letters in 1819.[13] When memoirs by Lucy Hutchinson and by Ann, Lady Fanshawe, first appeared in print (in 1806 and 1829 respectively, well over a century after their composition),[14] this crowned the searching and conserving efforts of a whole series of writing women, including Catharine Macaulay the historian, Eleanor Butler and Sarah Ponsonby (the 'Ladies of Llangollen'), and Catherine Fanshawe.

We can now more clearly see the historical causes of the attitudes which shaped my student reading. Syllabuses without women authors were constructed in the shadow of the classics; they persisted in the afterglow of English and of European dominance. The absence of women from syllabuses in England was closely related to the premium which other syllabuses (scorned by Oxbridge undergraduates of the 1950s) placed upon Great Books of the World. Devotion to Great Books is of course a political attitude; and today an interest in women's writing as such looks just as political as does a prejudice against it. Such an interest tends to be allied with more general interest in multiple and minority viewpoints, in literature as a site of struggle and debate (rather than as a repository of enduring truths), in voices which sound in discord with dominant ideology.

However eagerly one may wish (as I do myself) to champion women's writing chiefly on account of its literary qualities, this is not the best foundation to support the project of rediscovery. True, many early women are a delight to read: they are passionate or cheeky, moving or incisive. They weave verbal fabrics of intriguing and satisfying complexity. With some of them gender produces instant rapport: to many women today it seems that these early writers' views, their tone, even their jokes, would be quite at home in this morning's email. The phrases, characters, or arguments of early women writers have become part of the furniture of my own mind, and seem to me well worth house-room in other people's.

We stand to benefit, I believe, from adopting a more inclusive, less exclusive idea of literary quality, or from learning to apply standards of judgement to the past in a manner rather closer to the way we apply them to our contemporaries. Half a dozen novels are short-listed for the Booker Prize each year, and even those who quibble about the selection do so on the basis that other, more worthy novels have been unjustly passed over. It is assumed that half a dozen good novels every year is a reasonable expectation. But it's hard to win assent to the proposition that half a dozen eighteenth-century novels per year might be actually worth reading today. There is a curious reluctance to accept that both talent and achievement might have been thickly sown in the past.

But even if the short-list principle is accepted, it remains hard to draw up the list. The argument from literary quality is doomed to get bogged down in the incompatibility of subjective judgements. When I wrote that Eliza Fenwick's *Secresy* was one of the finest novels of the 1790s, Terry Castle replied that she finds it bad beyond belief.[15] Debate on this kind of topic is not viable in print, but only around a dinner-table or over a drink. The case for rediscovery must be made on other grounds as well. So when one has praised some author's sensibility and range, and noted (as Woolf notes about her imaginary Mary Carmichael) that she takes her fences like a bird,[16] one still needs *further* arguments for rediscovering her. The argument from literary quality needs reinforcement from the argument for the value of knowledge.

If as students we wish to know, and if as teachers we wish our students to know, something about the workings of gender in society, then we need those early women's voices. They alone can teach us something of how it felt to live as a woman in a culture (so different from our own, yet sharing so much with it) in which the inferiority and subordination of women was utterly taken for granted. They can teach us something important, too, about the impulse to literature—the sources of poems, stories, and so on—something of how to read the work of those who broke into literature from the outside, who in taking up the pen were claiming a privilege which in general was denied to them.

As necessarily present-oriented fields of enquiry, feminism and women's studies are liable to, and are not infrequently weakened by, assertions made in ignorance about the past. The remedies for this include the historian's approach: the application to the past of clear and rigorous twentieth-century conceptual thinking. But even the finest historical research can never convey the nuances of the historical subject's experience as can her own voice. Of course such voices are often unavailable. For some periods and some situations (especially as regards the lower ranks of society) there is indeed a scarcity of women's voices. But in many areas historical generalisations are still being made which ignore, or deny, or misrepresent, the evidence which exists, still unrecovered or disregarded, in those women's own writings.

It is sometimes argued that women who wrote were by definition exceptional, and that therefore their accounts are of limited relevance to understanding the norm. While recognising the value of statistical, norm-directed historical enquiry, I would argue that the concept of a norm is slippery at best, misleading at worst. Feminist scholarly interest focuses particularly on how women interacted with their situation, how they came to terms with or resisted the paths mapped out for them by society. If women's writing over-represents resistance rather than under-representing it, that makes it of more and not less value to feminist historians.

To summarise, therefore, early women's writing needs rediscovering because much of it is still forgotten, because it can prove a delight to read, because without it our notions of literature become misleadingly one-sided, and because it offers insights into the historical condition of women (and therefore obliquely into our own situation) which are unavailable from other sources.

In the process of recovery we have come a long way. The later-medieval writers Julian of Norwich and Margery Kempe, for example, are now readily available. The latter, who was first published only in 1940, has now been modernised in two separate, competing paperback texts. The Renaissance has been equally well served.[17] Not only Aemilia Lanyer (who left a single, manageable published volume of poetry) but also the Countess of Pembroke and Lady Mary Wroth, whose works are more voluminous, are available in wonderfully informed scholarly editions[18] and well represented in anthologies for teaching.

It is instructive to look at the problems these Renaissance women present to their editors. Margery Kempe's simple disappearance has nothing on them. Lanyer, with her one-volume output, is the least problematic, yet she suffered the indignity of being reprinted by A. L. Rowse in 1978 under the title *The Poems of Shakespeare's Dark Lady.* Rowse was a seasoned scholar who, starting from scratch, successfully unearthed many of the facts of Lanyer's life. But his conviction that she was the dark lady of Shakespeare's sonnets rested on almost nothing but the desire that it should be so—since from his viewpoint this alone could give his discovery of her some interest. Now that Susanne Woods has rescued Lanyer from Rowse,[19] it is easy to feel superior to him, but more salutary to reflect that all scholars have an investment in the newsworthiness of their results, and are therefore liable to equivalent temptations. The eighteenth-century equivalent is perhaps a woman like Mary Robinson, whose obvious gossip-column value actively competes with her reputation as a writer.[20]

For Wroth the problem has been one of length and accessibility. Josephine Roberts's sequence of scholarly editions (*Poems* 1983; the *Urania,* as published in 1621, 1995) was tragically interrupted at her death; but the unpublished sequel to the *Urania* has now been edited. For Pembroke the issue has been the long and slow unravelling of her authorship from that of her more famous brother, Sir Philip Sidney. Pembroke's literary career presents an exaggerated version of woman performing her traditional role as helpmeet and enabler of man. On her brother's untimely death she set herself the mission of publishing his completed works and finishing his uncompleted ones. It is now recognised that the 'New Arcadia' is substantially her work and that 107 of the 150 metrical psalms are solely by her—though the critical history of those works (like the praise accorded the psalms by John Ruskin in 1877) attached them not to her name but to Sir Philip's.[21] Neither Sarah Fielding nor Hester Thrale has ever been so overwhelmed as this by the reputation of her more famous literary brother or friend; but the same principle has been at work.

It is worth noting here that presumably not all Lanyer's or Wroth's works have been, or ever will be, rediscovered. Each of them published: an unusual but not exceptional step for a gentlewoman of that time to take. But each of them published as a highly accomplished poet (and fiction-writer, in the case of Wroth), and neither could have reached that level of skill without a long apprenticeship. Their early works are lost, unless some library or some cupboard is holding them in trust for the future.

In Elizabeth Cary, Lady Falkland, several of these problems are compounded. Her *Tragedy of Mariam* (a youthful work, published as by E. C., for Elizabeth Cary) was reprinted by the Malone Society as early as 1914 and now exists in no fewer than five fine scholarly editions.[22] An edition of some of her more mature works, written as Lady Falkland, is in process, begun by the late Jeremy Maule. But many of the 'innumerable slight things in verse' mentioned by her biographer-daughter, many saints' lives and hymns to the Virgin—

works which would have altered today's critical perspective on her, and would not have made it easier—are almost certainly gone beyond recall. Her *Edward II* has been edited by Diane Purkiss with *Mariam* under the title *Plays,* although agreement that Falkland did indeed write it is not yet quite universal. To class this generic experiment as a play has the merit of linking it with *Mariam* (which is far and away its author's best-known work). But at the same time it separates it from other, less-known aspects of Falkland's broader *oeuvre,* and it blurs a fine example of the way women writers so often look like square pegs in the round generic categories which were developed without reference to their work.[23]

Generic issues surface again in the case of Lady Anne Clifford, a lifelong diarist and family historian. She inherited from her mother a family history compiled not on any literary motive but for the express, practical purpose of proving inheritance rights. This she worked at and reworked. Clifford is a significant figure: Woolf used her to stand for the Common Reader, since her early diary, written at Knole, records and comments on her purely literary (that is, purely recreational) reading. That early diary—the two-and-a-half-years'-worth of it which survives—has recently received the benefit of up-to-date editing. (This not only establishes an accurate text and identifies people named in it, but is open, though tentative, on such matters as the likelihood that Lady Anne's first husband had a homosexual relationship which she was not happy about.)[24] But Clifford's early diary, though incomplete and cryptic in style, is at least continuous and survives in a single version. Her later writings (transcribed by herself and others in longer and shorter versions) are far more difficult to deal with, and demand involvement with *Proceedings of the Archaeological Institute at York,* 1846, and a Roxburghe Club edition of 1916. Clifford stands in rather the position that Cary occupied early in this century.

Clearly the more closely a writer approximates to modern concepts of the literary, the more attractive a proposition she is to scholars, and thus the more likely she is to receive help in her transition into availability. Those women who stuck to short poems or the novel (once they had invented it) have a lead in the race for canonicity. Fine work is being done in these fields, and the accepted outline of literary history transformed, by new editions of women's novels or poetry volumes, like Ann Messenger's and Richard Greene's forthcoming edition of Mary Leapor. Leapor opens a particular gateway: she is perhaps the most complex and rewarding of all the women labouring-class poets of the eighteenth centurv, and the first to achieve a scholarly edition in (just) the twentieth. (Mary Collier's major work, *The Woman's Labour,* has appeared both as an austere Augustan Reprint (1985) and as an elegant little volume with drawings, edited by E. P. Thompson; but her other poems have not yet been reprinted.)[25]

Collier and Leapor were both great subverters of genres, but they did this mainly within the broadly familiar category of Augustan poetry. Much valuable writing by women falls outside any familiar generic boundary. We must be thankful for the Brown Women Writers Project, for making available in print such texts as Anne Askew's *Examinations* and Jane Sharp's *Midwives Book* (as well as for their longer list of electronic texts).[26] Still availability finds it hard to climb out of the rut of expectations. Why, when Bathsua Makin (one of many women writers whose life-story has recently been rewritten almost unrecognisably, so inaccurate was the now-discredited former version) is now well known for *An Essay to Revive the Antient Education of Gentlewomen* (published 1673, reissued as an Augustan Reprint in 1980), is Hannah Wolley still so little heard of?

Makin's reputation is thoroughly earned. She complains in a rousing feminist preface that a learned woman is seen as a comet (something flamboyant and abnormal, boding no good). After an early life connected with the court, she published the book which made her reputation at an advanced age, while running her own school. She proposes a solid and demanding academic syllabus for upper-class girls, which will benefit the status of women in general through a trickle-down effect. Wolley works in a related field. She concerns herself with the education of ladies, gentlewomen, and other women in need of learning; but her concern is less with reading and the classics than with training in the managerial and practical arts of running a complex seventeenth-century household. She began publishing with *The Ladies Directory,* 1661, and issued seven more titles, of which several were reprinted in her lifetime. She is claimed by Elaine Hobby as the first woman to earn her living by her pen, a decade before the incomparably more famous Aphra Behn.[27]

It is easy to see how Makin conforms more closely than Wolley to the object of a modern feminist's desire. The former may be read as suggesting that women's sphere lies in the academy, the latter as suggesting that it lies in the home. But to accept these suggestions would be to overlook the differences between late twentieth-century and late seventeenth-century female experience. Wolley reminds us of difference; it may be that we prefer to be reminded of similarities. Also, where Makin offers a single text (her two earlier publications are heavily specialised and little known), Wolley offers a whole *oeuvre,* none of which any serious scholar of her can afford to ignore. This makes serious study of her less common. Furthermore, what might appear to be her most rewarding work (*The Gentlewomans Companion; or, A Guide to the Female Sex,* 1675, which incorporates a defence of women's abilities and status which clearly responds to Makin as well as to ongoing antifeminist debates) turns out to have been wholly spurious, put together by the male hack Dorman Newman. Wolley's actual texts can be read as making a 'feminist' statement, but they do so by indirection. The overall view she offers of women's lives is arguably more various and fuller of opportunities than Makin's view. But her books cannot be as widely read and discussed as they deserve, until they are there for the reading.

It sometimes seems as if the problems cluster more thickly in the early part of the long eighteenth century, when the generic choices made by so many women were distinctively un-modern. During the Georgian period many women became not only writers but primarily novelists, or else poets and playwrights. This makes them a more attractive proposition for editors. So we have Oxford editions of all Frances Burney's novels, as well as Peter Sabor's splendid edition of her plays. Burney, however, is the good news. Though we have *almost* complete availability of Sarah Fielding's works, the editorial standard varies somewhat; and for any such magisterial undertaking as the ongoing Wesleyan edition of Henry Fielding (or the successive complete editions of Henry which preceded it) we shall no doubt look in vain. The early novelists have fared relatively well: the major though not the complete works of Jane Barker are available from Oxford, New York, and in autumn 1999 the major though not the complete works of Mary Davys are due to join them from Kentucky. Editions of works by Eliza Haywood have been burgeoning like flowers in spring, though the extent and versatility of Haywood's *oeuvre* makes it impossible to hope for completeness, except possibly in electronic form.[28] The hankering for a uniform, scholarly edition which seems so natural in the case of Sarah Fielding seems less so for Haywood, who was all her life an opportunist and a chameleon; women writers can perhaps do without the kind of scholarship industry which once made it a viable proposition to gather into a collected edition all the bagatelles flung into the world by Swift.

But let us consider, just for argument, the case of Phebe Gibbes. Her very first novel, *The Life and Adventures of Mr Francis Clive,* 1764, had a Garland facsimile in 1975. Her *Friendship in a Nunnery, or the American Fugitive,* 1778, was quickly followed by two more eighteenth-century editions (with some variation in title)—which suggests that its controversial handling of American political issues brought it attention from the outset, as it has continued to do in the twentieth century. It has not, however, been reprinted. Her *Hartly House, Calcutta,* 1789, had a paperback reprint in the year of its two-hundredth anniversary, published by Pluto Press in London and in Winchester, Maryland: from a Calcutta edition of 1908. Unfortunately the paperback appeared with 'Anonymous' on its cover; Gibbes's authorship (which is firmly established both by Robert Dodsley's correspondence and the Royal Literary Fund archives) was not then known.

Gibbes is creeping into critical notice, but she is not likely to be rediscovered in the foreseeable future except by those with access to a very good research library indeed. Serious work on her will need to engage with her truly villainous handwriting in the RLF archives, to identify the various untraced works which she there illegibly claims to have written. But, meanwhile, of the half-dozen novels which can be confidently attributed to her, only two have modern reprints and those are unsatisfactory. In this situation she is not likely to cross the threshold of a classroom, and that is a pity. She is perhaps an extreme case, both for the interest of her writing and for the difficulty of getting hold of it; but there are many cases which are similar if not quite so acute.

For scholars setting out to make texts available, various issues jostle for priority. In all the modern editions mentioned above, in the novel series by World's Classics (Oxford University Press), Broadview Press, University of Kentucky Press, and other publishers, and in many other scholarly texts, the authors' work is presented to the reader with a full apparatus of information and explanation. An editor of such a work must identify the copy-text to be reproduced, must reproduce it faithfully, note any points at which it is problematic (such as divergences from other contemporary texts), and provide certain kinds of explanation or contextualisation. This last involves notes on words or passages in the text which readers may not understand, and some account of the author's life, of the place of this work in it, and of issues raised in the text. Some information about the current political situation is absolutely essential for readers of Mary Wollstonecraft's two *Vindications,* as information about the educational situation is for Makin or Wolley, or information about the hair-raising materialities and ideologies of childbirth is for Jane Sharp. Many editions contain much more: chronologies, bibliographies, excerpts from contemporary documents which may throw light on the text in question. For any kind of life-writing a good index is vital to the reader's use and pleasure; fiction *à clef* like that of Delarivier Manley and Eliza Haywood requires a key and an index; travel-writing requires maps, as in Christopher Morris's editions of the journeys of Celia Fiennes.[29] A simple facsimile reproduction has something to recommend it in the period flavour it conveys; but the long 's' and unfamiliar formatting may be obstacles to many readers. Augustan Reprints in this style, of short texts with helpful introductions, can be wholeheartedly recommended. The Garland novel reprints of the 1970s, published with minimal introduction and no annotation, were most welcome at the time (and remain so where no better text has followed), but are less than satisfactory.

Now the traditional editorial methods have been joined by a new option: electronic text, which may be consulted on line or printed out by the user. Electronic publication cannot entirely escape the marketplace economics which make conventional publishers look askance at reprints; but it can to some extent circumvent them. It cannot help readers who lack a computer or access to the World-Wide Web; but access of this kind is rapidly growing easier to attain. Electronic publishing of early material cannot escape, either, the need for high-class editorial input. In the early days of the Web there arose the Gutenberg Project and one or two similar endeavours, which have circulated very seriously deficient texts: a late-Victorian reprint of Lady Mary Wortley Montagu's letters, for instance, in which, through no fault of anyone living at the time of reprinting, many date-and-place headings to letters are purely fictional. The leader in the online field for the early period is the Brown Women Writers Project, whose standards of editorial rigour and accuracy are high.

However strongly a scholar may feel the potential appeal of early women writers to an intelligent general readership, the readership they will actually get will be mostly students: readers under advice and instruction. The relation be-

ON THE SUBJECT OF...

APHRA BEHN (1640-1689)

Behn is best remembered as the first woman to earn her living solely by writing, and she is credited with influencing the development of the English novel toward realism. Behn competed professionally with the prominent "wits" of Restoration England, including George Etherege, William Wycherley, John Dryden, and William Congreve. Similar to the literary endeavors of her male contemporaries, Behn's writings catered to the libertine tastes of King Charles II and his supporters. Her works, especially her dramas, are usually coarse, witty farces which focus upon the amatory adventures of her characters. Occasionally they excel as humorous satires recording the political and social events of the era. After nearly 300 years, however, Behn's most enduring work is the novel *Oroonoko; or, The Royal Slave* (1688). This work is considered one of the earliest novels to use a realistic technique, and the title character is often regarded as the first portrait of the "noble savage" in English literature.

Behn is acknowledged for her revolutionary influence on the novel form and as a pioneering example for other professional women writers. She was a controversial and vital figure during her lifetime, contributing to Restoration literature and boldly attempting to overcome the barriers of seventeenth-century prejudices. Behn dared to expose the hypocrisy of the era by advocating, through both her literary works and her manner of living, individual freedom for women in matters of love, marriage, and sexual expression. Although her works never equaled the polished, sophisticated writings of her more prominent contemporaries, such as Dryden or Congreve, they provided Restoration audiences and readers with the kind of farcical entertainment they enjoyed. Today her dramas and novels offer the modern reader an interesting and perceptive account of the colorful period in which she wrote.

tween such readers and pre-Romantic women writers is something of a paradox. On the one hand, the writers exert a fascination which editors of texts need to respond to and even exploit. Early modern women writers have a burning concern with gender roles which is matched only by our own moment in history. Many of their texts question the attitudes of their age, and students of both sexes find them (despite the difficulties they present) more accessible than the work of their male contemporaries.

On the other hand, the fascination they exert must not be allowed to gloss over their difficulty or their difference. Even intelligently feminist students, even with the best of scholarly and pedagogic help, will not find early modern women's texts instantly accessible or readily relevant on account of their gender. The common ground between the dawn of the twenty-first century and the early modern period is tenuous to say the least. Early women's texts share to the full in that jolting and tantalising remoteness from ourselves which seems to me a chief reason for reading early literature. They think differently; they stretch *our* minds. To read them, to listen to them carefully, we need to feel our own ignorance and to address it. Women have known this since the late eighteenth century, when they invented the historical novel, and the early nineteenth century, when they did scholarly work on foremothers' texts.

Editors therefore need not to minimise but to highlight the way their texts are of their time, not ours: enmeshed in problems which look soluble to us, or passionately involved in issues which look dead, or deeply committed to religious views which look alien.

So how successful have we been in bringing these texts back to light, in making relevance perceptible across barriers of difference? Optimists will answer one way, pessimists another. I have hinted now and then in this piece the temptations that exist to quick and dirty publishing, to texts inadequately or misleadingly presented. It is true that male writers mostly appeared in definitive editions at a time when beautiful scholarly books were, relatively, cheap—while for buyers of female writers today it sometimes seems as if the choice lies between sticking with paperback or taking out a bank loan.

The good news can be summed up as the creation from scratch of a level of awareness of, and openness to, the fact that early women may be worth reading and worth studying. Such an awareness is now commonplace at both popular and academic levels. Forty years ago Joyce Hemlow, a young Canadian, was publishing *The History of Fanny Burney.* Robert Halsband, a young American, had just published *The Life of Lady Mary Wortley Montagu.* Each one was opening a fertile furrow.

During the last half-century a sizeable audience for early women's writing has been reared and recruited almost from scratch. Montagu and Burney, Manley and Lennox, are both on syllabuses and in bookshops, clocking up more readers than ever before. Working at this essay in April 1998, I heard Isabella Whitney's 'Wyll and Testament' being read on Radio 4: not in any self-consciously literary or intellectual context, but as the voice of an interesting Londoner.

We cannot read the minds of our foremothers, and we ought not to try. But it is a good guess that Whitney would have enjoyed being on Radio 4 more than being taught in a classroom. These women wrote not for us but for themselves; we need to read them for themselves. It is more appropriate to see rediscovery in terms of treasure-hunting than of rescue. No scholar today, at whatever level, is likely to share Chapman's attitudes, but none of us is exempt from the temptation to take someone else's word for what the inside of a book is like. Rediscovery, the bringing of lost books to new readers, has made huge strides in our lifetimes, and has done so as part of a broadening of the readership for books of other periods, other cultures. The canon has become broader, more flexible, and more accessible, and at the same time harder to cover in its entirety; complacency among its guardians has become a more difficult attitude to sustain. Rediscovery of early women writers has contributed generously to the excitingly various and non-monolithic intellectual life of our time.

Notes

1. Martha Moulsworth, *'My Name was Martha': a Renaissance Woman's Autobiographical Poem,* ed. Robert C. Evans and Barbara Wiedemann (West Cornwall, CT: Locust Hill Press, 1993); Margaret J. M. Ezell, *The Patriarch's Wife: Literary Evidence and the History of the Family* (Chapel Hill and London: University of North Carolina Press, 1987).

2. Larpent MS 387, Huntington Library, San Marino, California; Isobel Grundy, 'Sarah Gardner: "Such Trumpery" or "A Lustre to Her Sex"', *Tulsa Studies in Women's Literature,* 7 (1988), 7-25.

3. Laetitia Pilkington, *Memoirs* (1748-54), ed. A. C. Elias, Jr (Athens and London: University of Georgia Press, 1997); Margaret Anne Doody in *London Review of Books,* 20 January 1988.

4. *The Works of Aphra Behn,* ed. Janet Todd, 7 vols. (London: William Pickering, 1992-6); *The Journals and Letters of Fanny Burney,* ed. Joyce Hemlow, et al., 12 vols. (Oxford: Clarendon Press, 1972-84); *The Early Journals and Letters of Fanny Burney,* ed. Lars Troide, et al. (Oxford: Clarendon Press, 1988-); Frances Burney, *Complete Plays,* ed. Peter Sabor with Geoffrey M. Sill and Stewart J. Cooke, 2 vols. (London: William Pickering, 1995).

5. Formerly titled the Eighteenth-Century Short Title Catalogue, this massive bibliography (available online) has already listed holdings of major libraries in Britain and North America, and aims to extend its coverage to every extant work published in English before 1800.

6. Lady Mary Wortley Montagu, *Complete Letters,* ed. Robert Halsband, 3 vols. (Oxford: Clarendon Press, 1965-7).

7. 'Lives of the Obscure ii. Laetitia Pilkington' in *The Essays of Virginia Woolf,* ed. Andrew McNeillie (London: Hogarth Press, 1986-), IV (1994), 119.

8. Ann Taylor Gilbert, *Autobiography and Other Memorials,* ed. Josiah Gilbert (London: H. S. King, 1874), I, 295.

9. *The Correspondence of Jonathan Swift,* ed. Harold Williams, 5 vols. (Oxford: Clarendon Press, 1963-5), IV, 192n. Swift's praise of Barber was in fact quite muted.

10. *The Letters of Samuel Johnson, with Mrs Thrale's Genuine Letters to him,* ed. R. W. Chapman, 3 vols. (Oxford: Clarendon Press, 1952), I, 44.

11. Anne Finch, Countess of Winchilsea, *Poems,* ed. Myra Reynolds (Chicago: University of Illinois Press, 1903); 'George Paston' [Emily Morse Symonds], *Lady Mary Wortley Montagu and Her Times* (London: Methuen, 1907).

12. J. M. S. Tompkins, *The Popular Novel in England 1770-1800* (1932; rpt. London: Methuen, 1961), *The Polite Marriage . . . eighteenth-century essays* (London: Cambridge University Press, 1938); Mary Lascelles, *Jane Austen and her Art* (Oxford University Press, 1939).

13. [Mary Berry], *Some Account of the Life of Rachael Wriothesley Lady Russell . . .* (London: Longman, et al., 1819). Berry edited Lady Russell's love-letters to her husband, which now hold a place in the history of the intimate familiar letter. An earlier publication had selected letters of political interest, i.e. those bearing more on the fame of Lord Russell than of his wife.

14. *Memoirs of Lady Fanshawe . . . written by herself,* ed. Sir N. H. Nicholas (London: Colburn, 1829); Lucy Hutchinson, *Memoirs of the Life of Colonel Hutchinson, Governor of Nottingham Castle and Town,* ed. Revd Julius Hutchinson (London: Longman, et al., 1806).

15. Eliza Fenwick, *Secresy, or The Ruin on the Rock* (1795), ed. Isobel Grundy (Peterborough, ON: Broadview Press, 1994; rev. edn 1998); Terry Castle in *London Review of Books,* 23 February 1995.

16. Virginia Woolf, *A Room of One's Own* (1928; London: Penguin Books, n.d.), 92-3.

17. *The Book of Margery Kempe,* ed. Sanford Brown Meech and H. E. Allen (London: Early English Text Society, 1940); *The Book of Margery Kempe,* trans. by B. A. Windeatt (Harmondsworth: Penguin Books, 1985); Tony D. Triggs, *The Book of Margery Kempe: a New Translation* (Tunbridge Wells: Burns & Oates, 1995). For further discussion of women writers in the Medieval and Renaissance periods, see Carol M. Meale (ed.), *Women and Literature in Britain, 1150-1500* (Cambridge University Press, 1993) and Helen Wilcox (ed.), *Women and Literature in Britain, 1500-1700* (Cambridge University Press, 1996).

18. *The Poems of Aemilia Lanyer: Salve Deus Rex Judaeorum,* ed. Susanne Woods (New York: Oxford University Press, 1993); *The Psalms of Sir Philip Sidney & the Countess of Pembroke,* ed. J. C. A. Rathmell (New York University Press, 1963); *The Triumph of Death & other unpublished & uncollected poems by Mary Sidney, Countess of Pembroke (1561-1621),* ed. G. F. Waller, Salzburg Studies in English Literature 65 (University of Salzburg, 1977); *The Poems of Lady Mary Wroth* (Baton Rouge and London: Louisiana State University Press, 1983); *The First Part of the Countesse of Montgomery's Urania by Lady Mary Wroth,* ed. Josephine A. Roberts, Medieval & Renaissance Texts and Studies 140 and Renaissance English Text Society, 7th ser., 17 (Binghamton, NY, 1995); second part, ed. Josephine A. Roberts, Suzanne Gossett, and Janel Mueller (University of Chicago Press, 1999). The Countess of Pembroke's versions of the Psalms and Petrarch's 'Triumph of Death' are now also available in *The Collected Works of Mary Sidney Herbert, Countess of Pembroke. Volume I: Poems, Translations, and Correspondence. Volume II: The Psalmes of David,* ed. Margaret P. Hannay, Noel J. Kinnamon, and Michael G. Brennan (Oxford: Clarendon Press, 1998).

19. A. L. Rowse (ed.), *The Poems of Shakespeare's Dark Lady: Salve Deus Rex Judaeorum* (London: Cape, 1978). He perpetrated a real howler in reading the word 'brave' as 'brown', and thus creating 'evidence' about Lanyer's complexion. See Suzanne Woods, *Aemilia Lanyer: a Renaissance Woman Poet* (New York: Oxford University Press, 1999).

20. On Mary Robinson, see: M. J. Levy's introduction to her *Memoirs* (London: Peter Owen, 1994), and Clare Brant in ch. 13, below pp. 290-2.

21. Rathmell in Pembroke, *Psalms,* pp. xxiv-xxv. Ruskin published a selection as *Broken Pieces of Sir Philip Sidney's Psalter. Laid up in Store for English Homes*: the second volume of his anthology *Bibliotheca Pastorum* (London and Orpington: Ellis & White, and George Allen, 1877).

22. *The Tragedy of Mariam*: with *The Lady Falkland: Her Life by One of Her Daughters,* ed. Barry Weller and Margaret Ferguson (Berkeley: University of California Press, 1993); in *Renaissance Drama by Women: Texts and Documents,* ed. S. P. Cerasano and Marion Wynne-Davies (London: Routledge, 1996); ed. Stephanie Wright (Keele University Press, 1996); in *Major Women Writers of Seventeenth-Century England,* ed. James Fitzmaurice, et al. (Ann Arbor: University of Michigan Press, 1996); and in *Renaissance Women: the Plays of Elizabeth Cary; the Poems of Aemilia Lanyer,* ed. Diane Purkiss (London: William Pickering, 1994).

23. For further discussion of genre in relation to women's writing, see ch. 9, pp. 198-201 and especially Clare Brant's discussion of miscellaneity, ch. 13, pp. 285-9.

24. Brenda R. Silver (ed.), '"Anon" and "The Reader": Virginia Woolf's Last Essays', *Twentieth-Century Literature,* 25 (1979), 356-441; Katherine Acheson (ed.), *The Diary of Anne Clifford, 1616-1619: a Critical Edition* (New York: Garland, 1996).

25. *The Works of Mary Leapor,* ed. Richard Greene and Ann Messenger (Oxford University Press, 1999); *'The Thresher's Labour' by Stephen Duck and 'The Woman's Labour' by Mary Collier: Two Eighteenth Century Poems,* ed. E. P. Thompson and Marian Sugden (London: Merlin Press, 1989). On Mary Leapor see also Margaret Anne Doody, ch. 10, below pp. 224-7.

26. *The Examinations of Anne Askew,* ed. Elaine V. Beilin (New York and Oxford: Oxford University Press, 1996); Jane Sharp, *The Midwives Book; or, The Whole Art of Midwifery* (1671), ed. Elaine Hobby (New York and Oxford: Oxford University Press, 1999).

27. Elaine Hobby, 'A Woman's Best Setting Out is Silence: the Writings of Hannah Wolley' in Gerald Maclean (ed.), *Culture and Society in the Stuart Restoration: Literature, Drama, History* (Cambridge University Press, 1995), pp. 179-200.

28. On Jane Barker, see Margaret Anne Doody, ch. 10, below p. 221; on Eliza Haywood, see Ros Ballaster, ch. 9, pp. 203, 208-10.

29. Christopher Morris (ed.), *The Journeys of Celia Fiennes* (London: Cresset Press, 1947), and *The Illustrated Journeys of Celia Fiennes* (London: Macdonald & Co., 1982). Fiennes's travel writings remained unpublished during her lifetime (1662-1741).

MARGARET J. M. EZELL (ESSAY DATE 2002)

SOURCE: Ezell, Margaret J. M. "Women and Writing." In *A Companion to Early Modern Women's Writing,* edited by Anita Pacheco, pp. 77-94. Oxford, England: Blackwell Publishing, 2002.

In the following essay, Ezell discusses the circumstances and motivations of numerous women writers.

But, why not women write, I pray?

Sarah Jinner, 'To the Reader', *An Almanack or Prognostication of Women (1658)*

If this essay were being composed in the 1920s or 1930s the task would have been at once harder and simpler. It would have been harder in that the topic of early modern women writers had not been defined as an area suitable for intellectual enquiry beyond obscure antiquarian or genealogical interests. During that period, too, the dominant metaphor for literary history was of the literary past as a landscape and the historian's job was to provide a map or tour guide through its major points of attraction, defined by genre or monumental figures. The literary critic's task was to point out both the particular and the characteristic beauties of a region and also to warn the reader away from any deceptive shifting sands or literary fens.

In this version of literary history the territory occupied by writing women was largely populated by nineteenth-century novelists. Earlier female authors could be pointed out as interesting examples of rare creatures; typically mentioned in passing were Katherine Philips and Anne Finch, who dwelt in the realm of feminine sentimental or melancholy verse, or Margaret Cavendish, who occupied the isolated mansion of aristocratic, eccentric scribblers. Those readers game for a more robust tour of the literary past might encounter the bawdy Restoration dramatist Aphra Behn but none of her female contemporaries, respectable or not.

This topographical understanding of literary history, however, also made the task easier. The numbers of individuals to be discussed was small and the regions, or genres, in which to search for them clearly defined, either poetry or fiction. Using this approach, the critical questions to be answered about early modern women writers would have been why did not more women write and why were there no great women writers to rival their male contemporaries, apart from a handful of later women novelists.

While a recent literary historian will start with the same premise that a 1920s or 1930s one would, that early modern women writers existed within a conventionally patriarchal and hierarchical social structure, the oft-cited injunction that women should be chaste, silent and obedient and confine their creative work to needles and threads rather than pen and paper can no longer be taken as an accurate delineation of women's participation in early modern literary culture. Likewise, the traditional assumption that one reason why so few women wrote was because so very few were literate has also come under fire during the last few decades. As Margaret W. Ferguson has observed in her article examining Renaissance concepts of the 'woman writer', it is important to recognize still that we 'know little about how many women might have merited the label "writer" in any of that term's various senses', and that the 'concept of the "woman writer" in the early modern period signifies a shifting mix of illusion and empowerment; the consequences of women's emergence as writers were equally complex' (Ferguson 1991: 149, 163). What has changed between the 1920s and recent modes of thinking about women writers is not only the ways in which literacy is assessed but also the development of an appreciation of what is encompassed by the term 'authorship', the layers of issues involved in assessing connections between early modern women who wrote and women who read in terms of how texts were created, reproduced, circulated and preserved.

Since the 1970s, literary historians have recovered significant numbers of women's texts in both manuscript and print form. In addition to making rare individual items more widely available through the ESTC microfilm project, other groups such as the Brown University Women Writers Project, the Renaissance Women Writers Online, and the Perdita Project have worked to include such texts in electronic databases. Simultaneously, the last twenty years have seen an explosion of printed anthologies and editions, from Angeline Goreau's early collection *The Whole Duty of a Woman: Female Writers in Seventeenth-Century England* (1985), Germaine Greer et al.'s *Kissing the Rod: An Anthology of 17th Century Women's Verse* (1988), Roger Lonsdale's *Oxford Book of Eighteenth-Century Women Poets* (1989), to the most recent *Oxford Book of Early Modern Women Poets* (2001), edited by Jane Stevenson and Peter Davidson. Along with such anthologies, facsimile reprint series such as the Ashgate Library of Essential Writings by Early Modern English Women headed by Betty Travitsky and Patrick Cullen continue to call attention to the wide range of texts by early modern women which were in circulation among their contemporary readers.

Helen Wilcox has noted the paradox about early modern women that 'the centuries in question were thrilling ones in terms of new achievements by women writers . . . [however, their accomplishments] have always to be set against the backdrop of women's severely constrained social and legal position. In law, women had no status whatsoever but were only daughters, wives or widows of men' (Wilcox 1991: 4). Clearly, our earlier assumptions (shaped in part by Virginia Woolf's fictitious Judith Shakespeare in *A Room of One's Own*) that these conditions absolutely prevented women from writing, were misleading. Indeed, Jane Stevenson states that in the preparation of *The Oxford Book of Early Modern Women Poets* the editors determined that 'there were in the region of fifty English and Scottish women who wrote some kind of verse before 1600 which still survives in some form or other (and also a number of women composing in Welsh, Scottish Gaelic, or Irish, whose work falls outside this discussion). Of these fifty, about half printed at least some of what they wrote' (Stevenson 2000: 1). To explore more fully these rediscovered texts by women who lived and wrote within such social and legal constraints, we need to consider several issues in a larger context of literary culture and the dynamics of textual production and circulation. We need to think about not only women who wrote and published and got paid for doing so, but also about women who wrote and circulated texts socially, women who compiled volumes and managed the preservation and transmission of texts by themselves and by others, women who patronized and supported other writers through their writings, and even those early modern women who owned books and who interwove their own writing into others' texts.

Sites of Writing, Scenarios of Authorship

> I turned it into English in a roome where my children practiz'd the severall qualities they were taught, with their Tutors, & I numbred the syl lables of my translation by the threds of the canvas I wrought in & sett them downe with a pen & inke that stood by me.
>
> (Lucy Hutchinson, dedication of her translation of Lucretitus' *De rerum natura*)

Traditionally, when thinking about women and writing, the first question asked has been *what* a woman wrote, in terms of genre: did she write poetry? Fiction? Drama? A diary? Perhaps a more revealing way of rethinking the literary culture of early modern women might be to ask *where* did she write and *why*. Virginia Woolf imagined the early modern woman writing secretively, hiding her activity, yet her ultimate goal was to achieve public recognition and money. For Woolf, one essential requirement for being an author was the possession of private physical space for writing, a room of one's own, with a lock on the door, enabling the woman writer to close out the distractions of everyday domestic life as well as her society's definitions and expectations of her as a woman. Given the recovery of a much wider range of early modern women's texts than Woolf had access to in shaping her story of women and writing, what other scenarios can we imagine for an early modern woman writing? What types of questions can we raise for exploration of her writing and her reading as part of a larger picture of literary culture? Did some have a 'room of her own', some female domestic space, or was this, indeed, even viewed as a necessary prerequisite for authorship in early modern literary culture?

Let us begin with familiar images of women writing. Certainly, during the early modern period there were women writing in solitude and isolation as Woolf imagined them. Most, however, sought no immediate readership other than themselves and their God, and they wrote not for the financial reward which Woolf felt validated the act of writing for women, but for personal profits. Elizabeth Burnet (1661-1709), who wrote extensively and published her *Method of Devotion* (1708), observed that for the purpose of serious meditation a crowded household should still be able to provide 'little rooms or closets' in which to retreat. Sometimes used as a dismissive adjective of women's writing, such 'closet writing' needs to be reconsidered. The importance of the closet as a feminine site of authorship is combined with the fact that it also served multiple social functions in the household in addition to private devotional ones, from the preparation of medicinal concoctions to a place of private reflection and storage of books and writing materials.

It was in this type of domestic space, for example, that Anne, Lady Halkett (1623-99) retired to both read and write. At her death she left behind 21 folio and quarto manuscript volumes, composed between 1644 and the late 1690s, which are now housed in the National Library of Scotland, in addition to what her contemporary biographer described as 'about thirty stitched Books, some in Folio, some in 4tc. Most of them of 10 or 12 sheets, all containing occasional Meditations' ('S.C.', *Life*: 64). Her biographer 'S.C.' explained that Halkett regularly set aside five hours a day for devotion, 'from 5 to 7 in the Morning, from one in the afternoon to two, from 6 to 7, and from 9 to 10, together with nine [hours] for Business', and 'ten for necessary refreshment' (ibid.: 55). Clearly, for Anne Halkett, the act of writing down her meditations on the texts she read, her analysis of her dreams, her hopes for her children, and her autobiography were a vital part of her daily domestic devotions. As she herself observed in one of the volumes begun in 1676, 'It is naturall for all persons to please themselves in pursuing what is most suitable to there inclination. & to aime att an eminency in what ever profession there Genius lead them to, from wch many have arived to Great Knowledge in Severall Arts and Sciences' (National Library of Scotland MS 6494, f.1). Anne Halkett, as did other early modern women, wrote extensively and wrote for pleasure, but it was for her spiritual, not worldly, profit.

Examples of domestic devotional writing by women throughout the seventeenth and eighteenth centuries span numerous social classes and settings, from mothers recording spiritual advice for children (Dorothy Leigh, *The Mother's Blessing: Or the Godly Counsaile of a Gentlewoman not long since deceased, left behind for her children,* 1616; Elizabeth Clinton, Countess of Lincoln, *The Countess of Lincoln's Nurser,* 1622; Elizabeth Richardson, *A Ladies Legacie to her Daughters,* 1645), to women recording private prayers and meditations and keeping diaries or journals. Many of the volumes of this type of women's writing were published as historical records during the nineteenth and early twentieth centuries, but many still remain in manuscript copies. A brief survey of only a representative few suggests the appeal of diary and journal writing for early modern women of a variety of social backgrounds, religious persuasions and political positions: Lady Elizabeth Brackley, Countess of Bridgewater (1626-63), who wrote pastorals, occasional verse, and masques with her sister Lady Jane Cavendish, which will be discussed later, left behind a manuscript collection of *Meditations on the Several Chapters of the Holy Bible*; a maid of honour in Catharine Braganza's court, Elizabeth Livingstone Delaval (1649-1717), created an elaborate memoir intertwining pious devotions and prayers with her romantic misadventures; the businesswoman Alice Thornton (1626-1707) wrote down her prayers as well as her fears over childbirth and poverty in her *Diaries*; Elizabeth, Vicountess Mordaunt (1632/3-79) carefully recorded wasting her time reading plays as well as the arrest of her husband for treason against the commonwealth in 1658; the parliamentarian paymaster's wife Mary Carey (1609/12-80) shared the pages of her meditations and verses with those of her second husband, George Payler, as they moved from town to town with the army.

Elizabeth Bury (1644-1720) offers an extended example of this type of women's writing. Born into a comfortable but not aristocratic family, Bury devoted her life to study, 'of almost every Thing . . . taking continual Pleasure in Reading and Conversation' (5). Her husband had portions of her diary printed after her death, noting that during her life, she had maintained an extensive correspondence on philosophical, historical, and spiritual subjects: 'in Writing of Letters, she had a great Aptness and Felicity of Expression; and was always so close and pertinent, and full to the Purpose; and withal, so Serious, Spiritual, and Pungent, that her Correspondence was greatly valued, by some of the brightest Minds, even in very distant Countries' (ibid.). This same talent for expression, Mr Bury maintains, shines through her diaries, begun when she was between 18 and 20 years of age and kept continuously until the end of her life; he was only able to publish the portions written after 1690, when she changed from recording her thoughts in shorthand with 'many peculiar Characters and Abbreviations of her own' (ibid.: 11). In her diaries, in which she wrote both in the morning and evening, 'with a very great Liberty and happy Variety of Expression', she recorded daily events, including providential acts of God towards herself and her family, 'the solemn transactions betwixt GOD and her own Soul, in her Closet, in her Family, in the Assembly, and in her daily Walk and Conversation with others; the Substance of what she had Read or Heard' (ibid.: 11-12). In short, Elizabeth Bury used writing to record, interpret and create a spiritual narrative of the events of the everyday life of a clergyman's wife in late seventeenth-century Suffolk.

For Englishwomen living abroad as part of religious houses, writing, too, was an integral part of their religious avocation and the convent house. Such separate devotional communities, including the Anglican community of Little Gidding, have remained a very little appreciated site of female participation in the creation, preservation and circulation of texts, as a site of communal authorship and vital supporting roles in maintaining a literary culture. The English nuns residing at the Benedictine community at Cambrai, founded in 1623 by Dame Gertrude More, produced meditations and prayers as part of their daily spiritual practice. Heather Wolfe stresses the importance of both reading and writing in these women's lives, pointing out that 'there was a particular emphasis on reading during Lent' in this community and that 'death notices' or biographies of fellow nuns were important texts as 'an example to posteritie' (Wolfe 2000: 206). At a nun's death, Wolfe notes, her 'loose papers' frequently were placed in the convent's library, bound together in a titled volume, such as 'a little book of Dame Mary Watsons Collections' or 'Eight Collection Bookes of . . . Mothere Clementia Cary'. Wolfe argues that the *Life of Lady Falkland* is an example of such convent-created texts. Other texts by the nuns, including the prayers and meditations of Gertrude More, for example, were occasionally published later for a general readership.

There are scenarios of women writing in solitude to consider other than religious retreat; some women had solitude imposed on their practice of writing because of their particular personal circumstances. Elaine Hobby has called such writers women who were 'making a virtue of necessity'. Hobby discusses at length the examples of Elizabeth Major and An Collins as 'celebration[s] of women's writings' where an authorial voice is created out of bodily distress and spiritual trials (Hobby 1989: 61-6). Elizabeth Major tells her readers that after having led a secular life wedded to 'earthen pleasures', 'God was pleased to visit me with lameness. . . . Then I was forc't to repair home to my Father again'. As part of her repentance, Major created *Honey on the Rod: Or a comfortable Contemplation for one in Affliction* (1656), detailing in prose and verse how her illness, 'I / In prime arrested, here I in prison lie', forced her to analyse the narrative of her past life as part of seeking future salvation and to organize and communicate her findings poetically (Greer et al. 1988: 183, 184).

Likewise An Collins, who published her *Divine Songs and Meditacions* (1653), was kept housebound by her illnesses and offers her poetry as 'the offspring of my mind' since her body will not have children. For Collins, her apparently sickly childhood created a scenario of authorship as a means of overcoming those 'Clouds of Melancholy over-cast / My heart' and writing formed part of her recreation: 'I became affected to Poetry, insomuch that I proceeded to practise the same; and though the helps I had therein were small, yet the thing it self appeared unto me so amiable, as that it enflamed my faculties, to put forth themselves, in a practise so pleasing' (Collins 1653: Sig. A1). Through writing, Collins continues in 'The Preface', 'sorrow serv'd but as springing raine / To ripen fruits, indowments of the minde, / Who thereby did abillitie attaine / To send forth flowers' and, although her circumstances dictate solitude while writing, she is determined to 'publish . . . those Truths' and to 'tell what God still for my Soule hath wrought'.

Thus far we have looked at scenarios of women writing which are not far removed from our modern expectations of the requirements of authorship: solitude, leisure and private domestic space. What other scenarios are revealed when one examines texts by early modern women writers? *Lady Falkland: Her Life* (1645), written (as Heather Wolfe has convincingly argued) by her daughter Lucy while a member of the convent at Cambrai, offers glimpses of some unexpected circumstances under which an early modern woman might conduct her reading and writing. We are told that as a child Elizabeth Cary, Lady Falkland (1586-1639) 'spent her whole time in reading; to which she gave herself so much that she frequently read all night; so as her mother was fain to forbid her servants to let her have candles' (Weller and Ferguson 1994: 187). Married at age 15 to Sir Henry Cary, the young bride fell out with her mother-in-law who 'used her very hardly, so far, as at last, to confine her to her chamber; which seeing she little cared for, but entertained herself with reading'; when her mother-in-law had all the books removed from Elizabeth Cary's room, 'then she set herself to make verses' (ibid.: 189). Life improved with the return of her husband and

> he grew better acquainted with her and esteemed her more. From this time she writ many things for her private reaction, on several subjects, and occasions, all in verse (out of which she scarce ever writ anything that was not translations). One of them was after stolen out of that sister-in-law's (her friend's) chamber and printed, but by her own procurement was called in. Of all she then writ, that which was said to be the best was the life of Tamberline in verse.
>
> (Ibid.: 189-90)

In addition to the solitude imposed on her by her mother-in-law, Elizabeth Cary supposedly was able to compose under rather more distracting circumstances: she cared little about her appearance except to satisfy her husband's wishes and 'her women were fain to walk round the room after her (which was her custom) while she was seriously thinking on some other business, and pin on her things and braid her hair; and while she writ or read, curl her hair and dress her head' (ibid.: 194).

Throughout her subsequent conversion to Catholicism and her estrangement from most of her family and friends, Elizabeth Cary continued to write. Her environment was drastically changed, but her literary output continued even in conditions represented as being far removed from the comfort of her previous life. During this period of her life, waiting ladies did not follow her from room to room as she wrote, but instead she was reduced to living with a single servant, her room only furnished with a bed on the ground and 'an old hamper which served her for a table, and a wooden stool'; according to her daughter, here is where she composed in verse the lives of 'St Mary Magdalene, St Agnes Martyr, and St Elizabeth of Portingall . . . and of many other saints' (ibid.: 213-14).

Elizabeth Cary might seem to be an anomalous example of an early modern woman writing in extreme situations, but a closer look at the elements which characterize her sites of writing—her writing spaces, her scenarios of authorship, and her readers and the nature of the production of her texts—suggests further possibilities for exploring the literary activities of other women. Clearly, for Elizabeth Cary, the possession of a special space for writing was not central to her endeavours as an author. Nor do we see the scenario of the writer as the self-imposed social exile because of her literary pursuits, nor the woman hiding her identity as an author. As Margaret W. Ferguson points out in the preface to Cary's translation of *The Reply to the Most Illustrious Cardinall of Perron* (1630), 'she not only used her own name but explicitly mentioned her refusal to "make use of the worne-out forme of saying I printed it against my will, moved by the importunitie of Friends"' (Weller and Ferguson 1994: 158).

The close connection between Elizabeth Cary's reading and writing habits is a key element in Barbara Kiefer Lewalski's assessment of the literary activities of other aristocratic women writing during the Jacobean period. Lewalski examines the accumulated writings of Lady Anne Clifford (1590-1676), including her histories of her parents as well as her own. Writing about her mother, Margaret Clifford, Anne noted that 'for though she had no language but her own, yet was there few books of worth translated into English but she read them, whereby that excellent mind of hers was much enriched' (Lewalski 1993: 134). In addition to her habit of studious reading, Margaret Clifford was also 'a lover of the study and practice of alchemy, by which she found out excellent medicines that did much good to many', which she, like many early modern women, recorded in a manuscript volume. Lewalski notes that in the 'Great Picture' of the Clifford family Margaret is painted with all the elements of her reading and writing practices defining the nature of her domestic space, 'holding the Psalms of David; the Bible, and English translation of Seneca, and (her own) handwritten book of alchemical distillations and medicines are on a shelf over her head' (ibid.: 373, n. 43).

Cary's example also invites a reconsideration of how and why women were writing. The scenario of Cary surrounded by her waiting women as she both read and wrote, for example, is one which Louise Schleiner has called a 'reading formation', a social situation consisting of aristocratic women and their waiting ladies, 'circles of women encompassing two or three social classes liv[ing] in daily association, reading and often making music together' (Schleiner 1994: 3). The practice of reading as part of a female circle, Schleiner maintains, 'might inspire various urges to write, up and down its encompassed social spectrum' and, she argues, is mirrored in the way in which women poets such as Aemilia Lanyer and Isabella Whitney use paratexts to celebrate the relationship between the waiting woman and her aristocratic female reader or, as in Whitney's situation, to lament its loss (ibid.: 4, 23, 25). Examples such as these cause us to ponder the scenario of a woman writing for an audience of women readers, perhaps even doing such writing in their company: in this scenario, rather than the isolated individual writing in solitude and not daring to seek an audience, we have instead the performance of reading and writing among women as part of their domestic life and an accepted elite social practice.

The female reading circles discussed by Schleiner and those women loosely associated with Queen Anne's court between 1605 and 1609 at Hampton Court and Somerset (Denmark) House, the Countess of Bedford, Cecily Bulstrode, Lady Ann Southwell (more of whom later in this essay) and Lady Mary Wroth also suggest that we can look for women writing as part of intricate social interactions as well as for moral or medicinal improvement. Leeds Barroll places Anne of Denmark at the centre of a 'rich and hospitable climate' for the arts, surrounding herself with literate and literary women and female patrons of contemporary male writers (Barroll 1998: 55). Mary Ellen Lamb likewise points to the importance of 'poetic numbers' for early modern women writers: for Lady Mary Wroth in particular, the numerous women writers in the Sidney family as well as the Vere family provided a '"safe house" in which women could write' ambitious literary projects (Lamb 1990: 150). On a more casual level, as Jane Stevenson has observed, surviving textual evidence suggests that 'a number of women of the rank of gentlewoman or above participated in the writing of ephemeral poetry as a social activity' (Stevenson 2000: 4). Lewalski (1993) notes that some of the prose 'inventions' by Bulstrode and Southwell ended up being included in Sir Thomas Overbury's collection of miscellaneous pieces, *Sir Thomas Overbury His Wife* (1611), and Stevenson points to George Gascoigne's even earlier *Hundred Sundrie Flowers* (1573) containing several examples of witty exchanges of verses between gentlewomen and their male admirers (Stevenson 2000: 5-7).

Later in the seventeenth and early eighteenth century, the titles of women's poems found in published volumes often reveal both the connection between a woman's reading and her writing and the social or coterie origins of her verse. Writing at the end of the seventeenth century, the poet, novelist and medicinal writer Jane Barker (1652-*c*.1727) participated in a number of literary exchanges throughout her life. Kathryn R. King describes Barker's first appearance in print, *Poetical Recreations* (1688), as an example of a 'sociable text'; 51 of the 109 poems are by Barker and the rest are by 'Gentlemen of the Universities, and Others' (King 1994: 552). The titles of the poems reflect the occasions of their composition and their function as a type of social performance. This same pattern of linked verses where one poet writes in response to another's verse, typically written to record social occasions from weddings and deaths to broken friendships and flirtations, is not infrequently found in posthumous collections of poetry by women writers, such as Anne Killigrew's *Poems* (1686) and Mary Monck's *Marinda* (1716). Such posthumous volumes serve as a type of blueprint of the patterns of social verse exchange among women and their friends, both male and female: Killigrew's volume includes, for example, 'To My Lord Colrane, In Answer to his Complemental Verses sent me under the Name of Cleanor', while Mary Monck's volume includes 11 poems addressed to her as 'Marinda', as well as one entitled 'Upon an Impromptu of Marinda's, in answer to a Copy of Verses'.

This practice of the exchange of verses as part of a social pastime is clearly continued throughout the seventeenth and eighteenth centuries, and was not restricted to highly placed courtiers and aristocrats. At some times, too, the composition, compilation and preservation of manuscript volumes by women also act as a means of confirming religious or political loyalties within the woman's literary circle. Constance Aston Fowler organized her family and friends to contribute verses to her compilations in the 1630s and 1640s, and her correspondence contains several references to her compilations and to her family's lively literary life (Ezell 1999: 25-8). Fowler's manuscript miscellany reveals both her reading and writing practices: in addition to collecting poems by her father, her brother Herbert Aston (whose wife later assembled a separate manuscript volume of his verse), her brother-in-law Sir William Pershall, her sister-in-law Katherine Thimelby, her friend Lady Dorothy Shirley, and possibly herself, Constance Fowler also included verses by Ben Jonson, John Donne, Richard Fanshawe and Aurelian Townshend. Victoria Burke has described this as 'a clearly definable literary network', tying together a diverse group bound by their 'embattled Catholic faith', ranging from 'her blood relatives, to her relatives by marriage, to her friends in the Catholic faith, to diplomatic friends of her father's, to the people who were the means by which popular poetry circulating in manuscript reached her' (Burke 1997: 139).

The same practice of literary compilation and collaboration among family members rather than

Engraving by Diepenbeke depicting Margaret Cavendish, Duchess of Newcastle (1623-1673).

the scenario of the isolated artist is found in the manuscript volumes compiled by Lady Jane Cavendish (1621-69) and Lady Elizabeth Brackley (1626-63), the daughters of the Duke of Newcastle by his first wife. As with the Aston family circle, the manuscript volume, *Poems Songs and a Pastoral,* also reveals how literary exchanges were used to cement social bonds during times of duress. The two sisters were at Welbeck when it was besieged by parliamentary troops, and several of the verses reflect the women's concerns for their absent relatives fighting for the king in the Civil War, while the play *The Concealed Fansyes* features scenes of witches overturning natural order and harmony to create civil strife. As preserved miscellanies and family papers show us, the Duke of Newcastle encouraged his children from an early age to write and to compose little social verses; their surviving manuscript volumes embody their continuing literary activities as young women, wives and mothers (Ezell 1998: 256-7).

The social aspect of women's writing can also be seen in the practice of writers sharing space on the page itself. The Cavendish sisters, for example, intermingled their poems, not dividing them into separate author sections. Manuscript volumes often reflect multiple generations of women readers and writers at work, and such volumes often display their multiple functions within the family and household. Anna Cromwell Williams assembled *A Books of Several Devotions collected from good men* (1656, 1660), whose inscription declares it to have been a gift between sisters. Williams also embellished the good men's devotions with her own verses; in the same volume other hands recorded poems on family events, such as the death of Bettina Cromwell (British Library Harl. Ms. 2311).

The shared commonplace book of Lady Anne Southwell (1573-1636) and her second husband, Captain Henry Sibthorpe, likewise displays multiple hands, voices, agendas and genres of writing. Lady Anne's original verses are mingled with copies of her letters, one to Cicely MacWilliams on the superiority of verse to prose, and one to Elizabeth Cary's husband on his return to England. The same volume also contains the hand of her father-in-law, John Sibthorpe, prosaically recording his account of receipts for moneys spent during the Dutch war, as well as Ann Johnson and Mary Phillips signing receipts for rents. As Jean Klene notes, this remarkable collection also includes Henry Sibthorpe's tribute to his departed wife, 'the pattern of conjugall love and obedience', and Klene views the preservation of manuscript text with all its hands and purposes as a husband's monument to his remarkable spouse (Klene 1998: 165).

Still other women joined together to write collaboratively for pressing political reasons. By far the largest single group of women publishing their writings during the Restoration period were Quakers, who wrote not only to record their individual spiritual journeys for the assistance of their fellow travellers, but who also turned out accounts of persecutions, trials and incarceration where the authorship of a single document is the work of several hands, carrying several signatures. They sent petitions and appeals with over 100 women's signatures attached to plead their causes. Such use of the press to present a public appeal can be seen as a continuation of the practices of other women petitioners during the 1640s and during the Civil War years. In 1642 the 'Gentlemen and Tradesmens Wives, In and About the City of London' petitioned parliament to protect its citizens against the dangers of papistry and false prelates (Archbishop Laud), citing as their precedent for writing Esther's petition to King Ahasuerus on behalf of the church. During the war years women associated with the Leveller movement petitioned for the release of John Lilburne in 1649, and in 1653 a group of some 6,000 women petitioned parliament to stop his trial. The Quaker Mary Forster (*c.* 1620-87) explained 'To the Reader' in a petition presented in May 1659 arguing against tithes that the 7,000 women who attached their names to the petition do so in order to be the 'weak means to bring to pass his mighty work'.

Better known than such examples of multiple women writers combining to create a single female public voice are individual women such as Katherine Chidley (believed to have participated in the Leveller group petitions), who used pamphlet writing to explain her political opposition to a national church and to argue for the right of women to preach. Other women turned to printed pamphlets and broadsides to map out their visions of England's future: Mary Cary (*c.* 1621-53) wrote petitions explaining to parliament the plans to build God's kingdom on earth, *A New and Exact Mappe or Description of New Jerusalems* (1651), and in *Twelve Humble Proposals* (1653) she, like Chidley and the 1659 women petitioners, recommended the abolition of tithes as a first step. In the 1680s and 1690s Elinor James (fl. 1675-1715), in contrast, used broadsides to support the established church and the Stuart monarchy, the titles of her broadsides clearly displaying her loyalties; for example, 'Mrs. James's Defence of the Church of England in a short answer to the canting Address: with a word or two concerning a Quakers good advice to the Church of England' (1687) and 'Mrs. James's letter of thanks to the Q———n and both houses of Parliament for the deliverance of Dr. Sacheverell' (1710).

We also find individual women making their private writing public in response to legal cases involving their families. During the war years individual women such as Elizabeth Lilliburne petitioned on behalf of their imprisoned husbands. During the Restoration women such as Mary Love approached parliament with numerous petitions to spare the life of her husband Christopher; the unsuccessful petitions were subsequently published, along with letters between the husband and wife in a volume called *Love's Name Lives* (1663). Rachel, Lady Russell (1636-1723) took the notes at her husband's trial for high treason that were used as part of his defence; like Mary Love, she unsuccessfully pleaded for his life and as with the letters of Love, Lady Russell's letters to her husband and to her spiritual advisers were subsequently published.

Still another group of women whose writings begin appearing as printed volumes during the period following the Restoration were motivated by a desire to improve the status of the female sex as a whole and to respond to male writers' representation of women's roles and natures. Polemical writers such as Judith Drake (fl. 1696), Bathsua Makin (*c.* 1600-?) and Mary Astell (1666-1731) argued strenuously for the education of middle- and upper-class women as rational rather than ornamental creatures. Others such as Sarah Fyge Egerton (1669-1722) turned to satire, publishing *The Female Advocate* (1686) to rebut Robert Gould's attack; Mary, Lady Chudleigh (1656-1710) was sufficiently provoked by the Revd John Sprint's advice to brides to reply with *The Ladies Defense* (1701). All of these women share the view that while men had rejected the notion of absolutism in national politics, they had strenuously preserved it in the domestic realm. For these women, writing and reading were the keys to middle-class women's improvement of their lives, and they argued for a system of education for women which paralleled that offered to men of that station.

Finally, the scenario of authorship most familiar to us, the commercial, professional woman writer, also begins to be performed more frequently during the latter part of the seventeenth century. As Janet Todd has observed, 'the Restoration and early eighteenth century is the first period when women as a group began writing for money clearly and openly' (Todd 1989: 37). With the reopening of the theatres, the expansion of commercial publishing, as well as the development of new types of literary genres such as periodicals, earning money by writing became more of a possibility for middle-class women in search of an income. The theatres were hungry for new materials to present, and women dramatists such as Aphra Behn (*c.* 1640-89), Delarivier Manley (*c.* 1663-1724), Catherine Trotter (1679-1749), Eliza Haywood (1693-1756) and Mary Pix (1666-1729) provided comedies and tragedies for the new theatre companies at a considerable rate. Jacqueline Pearson's study of women dramatists of the period credits Behn with over 20 plays, Manley 6, Pix 13 and Susanna Centlivre (?-1723) with 19 (Pearson 1988: 288-91). While Trotter produced fewer dramas, only five, she was widely known for her attempts to write for a 'reformed' stage, although she, along with Pix and Manley, was satirized in *The Female Wits* (1696). As unpleasant as the caricatures of these women dramatists are, it does suggest that women commercial writers as a group posed a sufficient, visible competition to provoke defensive measures from concerned professional rivals.

Although professional women writers drew attacks from male professionals, it is also clear that women writers were frequently supportive of the literary activities of their peers. Todd notes that during the later part of the seventeenth century 'there was . . . a sense of a female writing community, which in many ways looked towards the Bluestocking groupings of the last half of the eighteenth century' (Todd 1989: 40). Sometimes the public, printed endorsement of another woman's writing was simply a continuation of a literary relationship begun as part of a social literary exchange: Elizabeth Thomas wrote enthusiastic letters and poems to Mary Chudleigh which she later published; Chudleigh and Mary Astell knew and endorsed each other's works and opinions in verse as well as prose; and Chudleigh introduced Thomas to Astell's circle. Women dramatists provided prefaces and commendatory verses for other women's plays. Aphra Behn included verses by other women, such as 'Mrs. Taylor', in her verse miscellanies. In *Nine Muses, or Poems written by as many Ladies Upon the Death of the Late Famous John Dryden Esq* (1700) Manley assembled poems by herself and her female acquaintances, including Egerton, Trotter, Pix, and Trotter's patron, Lady Sarah Piers.

The self-representations of this generation of women writers we see in their printed texts are remarkably similar to the various masks of authorship assumed by their male contemporaries. Elizabeth Singer Rowe (1674-1737) jauntily rejected the advice of a friend 'Who Persuades me to leave the Muses' on the grounds that her literary pursuits harm no one:

> Forego the charming Muses! No, in spite
> Of your ill-natur'd prophecy I'll write;
> And for the future paint my thoughts at large,
> I waste no paper at the hundred's charge:
> I rob no neighbouring geese of quills, nor slink
> For a collection, to the church for ink:
>
> Yet I'm so naturally inclined to rhyming,
> That undesigned, my thoughts burst out a chiming;
> My active genius will by no means sleep,
> Pray let it then its proper channel keep.
> I've told you, and you may believe me too,
> That I must this, or greater mischief do:
> And let the world think me inspired, or mad,
> I'll surely write whilst paper's to be had.
> *Poems on Several Occasions, Written by Philomena,* 1696
>
> (Goreau 1985: 291-2)

In her poem 'The Liberty' Sarah Fyge Egerton voiced even more strongly her commitment to her pen in her role as the defender of the female sex. She rejects the model of a woman's writing as being confined to 'lofty Themes of useful Houswifery, / Transcribing old Receipts of Cookery': for Egerton, 'My daring Pen, will bolder Sallies make / And like myself, an uncheck'd freedom take' (Greer et al. 1988: 347). Elizabeth Tipper (fl. 1690s), on the other hand, considers and rejects the role of satirist for herself: 'Where's then my Muse? Does my Poetick Vein! / Want Skill or Courage for this useful strain? / . . . / I find no Moment where I need explore / The Faults of others, but my own deplore' ('The Pilgrim's Viaticum', 1698; ibid.: 71-2).

Although, as we have seen, the genres of women's texts varied widely and most wrote in more than one, there are some recurrent metaphors used by women for writing which transcend both period and geographical location. While the metaphor of a poem or a book as the author's child is a common one for both male and female writers during the early modern period, it seems important to look at the particulars when considering how early modern women viewed their writing. While male authors such as Dudley, 4th Lord North, tended to dwell upon the image of poetic creation as involving labour and birth pains—'a burden of perplexed thoughts, the very being delivered (a terme well known to you Ladyes)' (Ezell 1999: 35)—the use of the image by women more typically focuses on the pleasure of the creation and the subsequent fond pride in the literary 'offspring'. This characterization of writing by women as giving birth and the writers' affection for their productions crosses the social classes of those women who wrote about writing. Margaret Cavendish, Duchess of Newcastle (1623-73), in 'An excuse for so much write upon my Verses', pleads: 'Condemme me not for making such a coyle / About my Book, alas it is my Childe' (*Poems, and Fancies,* 1653, Sig. A8v). A year before her volume appeared, 'Eliza' published *Eliza's Babes: or The Virgin's Offspring* (1652), describing, as did An Collins, the pleasure of writing; her poems, 'my Babes . . . were obtained by vertue, borne with ease and pleasure' through divine inspiration (Sig. A3). In a more exasperated use of the metaphor, in the American colonies, Anne Bradstreet (1612-72) described her collection of verses as 'my rambling brat' when she remarked on their publication in England under the title *The Tenth Muse*: 'Thou ill-form'd offspring of my feeble brain, / Who after birth didst'st by my side remain, / Till snatcht from thence by friends, less wise then true' ('The Author to her Book', *Several Poems,* 1678). For such women, writing was a natural process of generation from the woman's self and a process over which nature, not the individual will, had the final say about production.

Early modern women also shared with contemporary male writers reasons to write other than God's command or the urging of friends. In her 'Preface' to her *Miscellany Poems* (1713) Anne Finch, Countess of Winchilsea (1661-1720) quotes from Beaumont's verse to Fletcher: 'no more can he, whose mind / Joys in the Muses, hold from that delight / When nature, and his full thoughts, bid him write'; adding 'I not only find true by my own experience, but have also to many witnesses of it against me, under my own hand in the following poems'. She concludes, sounding rather like her friend Alexander Pope, that it was 'an irresistible impulse' which is her primary reason for writing. Occasional dramatist, coffee-house keeper, and novelist Mary Davys (1674-1732) used the preface to her *Works* (1725) to assure her readers that 'idleness has so long been an excuse for writing, that I am almost ashamed to tell the world it was that, and that only, which produced the following sheets'. She concludes by hoping that 'my pen is at the service of the public, and if it can but make some impression upon the young unthinking minds of some of my own sex, I shall bless my labour and reap an unspeakable satisfaction'. Writing for women was variously presented as childbirth, as an irresistible compulsion, a divine channelling, and an amusing pastime, and the wide variety of metaphors employed suggests to us the wide variety of scenarios of authorship.

Conclusion: Why Write?

Surveying the different materials written by early modern women as a whole, we find that by the end of the seventeenth century into the early part of the eighteenth, we are looking at a collage of various overlapping sites and scenarios of women writing rather than a map giving us individual landmarks and clearly defined territories. For example, the practice of keeping diaries and journals for private spiritual improvement feeds into the developing forms of fiction for profit; the mother writing for her children seems related to the woman writing for the improvement of her sex; the woman sitting with her waiting ladies or sending her poems to her friends in letters seems reflected in the links between the growing numbers of professional women writers praising and contributing to each other's works.

How did early women themselves describe their desires to write? As we have seen, many felt compelled to share with others their experiences of God and salvation, pain and hope. Tudor women, Margaret P. Hannay suggests, found a means to 'find their own voices through their proclamations of the Word of God' as translators and devotional writers (Hannay 1985: 14). During the Civil War years and Restoration period, women prophets from diverse social backgrounds such as the Quaker Ester Biddle (*c.*1629-96) and aristocratic Lady Eleanor Douglas (1590-1652) felt compelled to publish their warnings and prophecies for the good of England. Other women were clearly motivated by a compelling combination of contemporary politics and profit. As Paula McDowell has suggested in her study of the women writers, printers and booksellers occupying Grub Street during the years after the Restoration, 'religious and religio-political works' formed the 'largest category of women's (and men's) writings' (McDowell 1998: 18), but these are markedly different from the books of private devotions or solitary prophecy from the start of the century. The period following the Civil Wars, as she notes, was remarkable for the simultaneous 'birth of the modern literary marketplace . . . concurrent with women's emergence in significant numbers as publishing authors' (ibid.: 5). We are most familiar with women's participation in commercial literary culture as authors, but, in the same way that we have tended to overlook women's participation in the production and dissemination of manuscript texts, McDowell draws our attention to the activities of women 'working in *all* aspects of material literary production, and doing so for pay' (ibid.).

Where were early modern women writing and why? As their surviving manuscripts and volumes reveal, writing for women and men was a social activity as well as a means of private consolation. Once we leave behind the notion of authorship as an act defined by solitary alienation and the text as an isolated literary landmark, we start to see a much livelier literary landscape for early modern women. While looking at the diversity of texts they created and which have recently been recovered, we now can see them more clearly at their writing—alone, in groups, in the closet, in the courtroom—and for whom they wrote—for themselves, God, their friends, their children, parliament and for future readers. For many early modern women, writing was an essential part of their devotional life, as much a part of daily domestic life as prayer; while historians are right to remind us about the separation of the teaching of reading and writing skills, it is well to remember the role that reading played in inspiring many such women to write their own thoughts in response to what they read. For other women, writing was a means to reinforce family and social ties, often in manuscript volumes compiled by women and passed through generations of family readers and contributors. Writing women also created collections and compilations of others' works and added their annotations to printed books in their libraries. Separately printed broadsides and pamphlets permitted individual women such as Anna Trapnel, Lady Eleanor Douglas and Jane Lead to share their prophetic visions of God's wishes for England, while petitions gave groups of women a means of making written statements on political events which they were legally barred from participating in directly.

For early modern women, writing could be both a private pleasure and a means of public performance. Writing could be a response to a particular life crisis or a sustained life-long practice. When we imagine scenarios of authorship for these women, we need to remember that writing could function as an act of creation, a bid for fame, an affirmation of allegiances, and a part of a prayer, and that a woman who wrote probably did so in a variety of genres for a variety of audiences. In this expanded sense of the literary stage for early modern women—in her closet, in the children's schoolroom, in the sickroom, in the kitchen, in the great hall, in the courtroom, in prison and in the parlour—wherever one looks, the possibility is there that one will find women writing and that, indeed, there are more early modern women writers still waiting for us to see them.

Works Cited

Barroll, Leeds (1998). 'The arts at the English court of Anna of Denmark.' In S. P. Cerasano and Marion Wynne-Davies (eds), *Readings in Renaissance Women's Drama: Criticism, History and Performance 1594-1998* (pp. 47-59). London: Routledge.

Beilin, Elaine V. (1987). *Redeeming Eve: Women Writers of the English Renaissance.* Princeton, NJ: Princeton University Press.

Blaine, Virginia, Grundy, Isobel and Clements, Patricia (eds) (1990). *The Feminist Companion to Literature in English.* New Haven, CT: Yale University Press.

Burke, Victoria (1997). 'Women and early seventeenth-century manuscript culture: four Miscellanies.' *The Seventeenth Century,* 12, 135-50.

Collins, An (1653). *Divine Songs and Meditacions.* London.

Ezell, Margaret J. M. (1998). '"To be your daughter in your pen": the social functions of literature in the writings of Lady Elizabeth Brackley and Lady Jane Cavendish.' In S. P. Cerasano and Marion Wynne-Davies (eds), *Readings in Renaissance Women's Drama: Criticism, History and Performance 1594-1998* (pp. 246-58). London: Routledge.

———(1999). *Social Authorship and the Advent of Print.* Baltimore, MD: Johns Hopkins University Press.

Ferguson, Margaret W. (1991). 'Renaissance concepts of the "woman writer".' In Helen Wilcox (ed.), *Women and Literature in Britain 1500-1700* (pp. 143-68). Cambridge: Cambridge University Press.

Goreau, Angeline (1985). *The Whole Duty of a Woman: Female Writers in Seventeenth-Century England.* Garden City, NY: Dial Press.

Greer, Germaine, Medoff, Jeslyn, Sansone, Melinda and Hastings, Susan (eds) (1988). *Kissing the Rod: An Anthology of 17th Century Women's Verse.* London: Virago Press.

Hannay, Margaret P. (1985). 'Introduction.' In M. P. Hannay (ed.), *Silent But for the Word: Tudor Women as Patrons, Translators, and Writers of Religious Works* (pp. 1-14). Kent, OH: Kent State University Press.

Hobby, Elaine (1989). *Virtue of Necessity: English Women's Writing 1649-88.* Ann Arbor: University of Michigan Press.

King, Kathryn R. (1994). 'Jane Barker, *Poetical Creations,* and the social text.' *English Literary History,* 61, 551-70.

Klene, Jean (1998). 'Introduction.' In J. Klene (ed.), *The Southwell-Sibthorpe Commonplace Book, Folger MS V.b. 198* (pp. xi-xliii). Tempe, AZ: Medieval and Renaissance Texts and Studies.

———(2000). '"Monument of an Endless affection": Folger MS V.b. 198 and Lady Anne Southwell.' In Peter Beal and Margaret J. M. Ezell (eds), *English Manuscript Studies 1100-1700,* vol. 9 (pp. 165-86). London: British Library.

Lamb, Mary Ellen (1990). *Gender and Authorship in the Sidney Circle.* Madison: University of Wisconsin Press.

Lewalski, Barbara K. (1993). *Writing Women in Jacobean England.* Cambridge, MA: Harvard University Press.

McDowell, Paula (1998). *The Women of Grub Street: Press, Politics, and Gender in the London Literary Marketplace, 1678-1730.* Oxford: Clarendon Press.

Pearson, Jacqueline (1988). *The Prostituted Muse: Images of Women and Women Dramatists 1642-1737.* New York: St Martin's Press.

Prior, Mary (ed.) (1985). *Women in English Society, 1500-1800.* London: Methuen.

'S.C.' (1701). *The Life of Lady Halkett.* Edinburgh.

Schleiner, Louise (1994). *Tudor and Stuart Women Writers.* Bloomington: University of Indiana Press.

Stevenson, Jane (2000). 'Women, writing and scribal publication in the sixteenth century.' In Peter Beal and Margaret J. M. Ezell (eds), *English Manuscript Studies 1100-1700,* vol. 9 (pp. 1-32). London: British Library.

Todd, Janet (1989). *The Sign of Angellica: Women, Writing and Fiction, 1660-1800.* London: Virago Press.

Weller, Barry and Ferguson, Margaret W. (eds) (1994). Elizabeth Cary. *The Tragedy of Mariam The Fair Queen of Jewry with The Lady Falkland Her Life.* Los Angeles: University of California Press.

Wilcox, Helen (1991). 'Introduction.' In Helen Wilcox (ed.), *Women and Literature in Britain 1500-1700* (pp. 1-6). Cambridge: Cambridge University Press.

Wolfe, Heather (2000). 'The scribal hands and dating of *Lady Falkland Her Life*.' In Peter Beal and Margaret J. M. Ezell (eds), *English Manuscript Studies 1100-1700*, vol. 9 (pp. 187-217). London: British Library.

WOMEN'S LITERATURE IN THE 16TH, 17TH, AND 18TH CENTURIES

FAYE VOWELL (ESSAY DATE WINTER 1976)

SOURCE: Vowell, Faye. "A Commentary on 'The Journal of Sarah Kemble Knight'." *The Emporia State Research Studies* 24, no. 3 (winter 1976): 44-52.

In the following essay, Vowell praises Knight's narrative as "fresh," "delightful," and "humorous."

The Journal of Sarah Kemble Knight is one of those delightful, almost forgotten, pieces of American literature which one occasionally encounters. The journal itself recounts a trip made by horseback between Boston and New York, with an intermediate stop in New Haven, in the year 1704. But the account is lifted out of the ordinary by the fact that the journey was made by a thirty-eight year old woman. A middle class American woman capable and assertive in her own right, Sarah Kemble Knight contradicts the stereotypes of the delicate female, and the shy, sheltered housewife. She is not only a successful businesswoman, but also the mediator in settling her niece's estate, on the pretext of which she makes her journey. Brave, despite her assertions to the contrary, Knight is a truly remarkable woman whose sometime pose of helpless female is belied by her adventurous actions. Madame Knight uses her awareness of the power of words effectively to make a statement about life in colonial New England. Besides its use as an historical document, *The Journal* lays claim to further consideration by its skillful use of personae, its humor, and its vivid backwoods dialect.

Previous critics have given *The Journal,* at best, only a passing reference,[1] and most begin their studies of American humor and its accompanying distinctive idiom with A. B. Longstreet and other Southwestern humorists. Yet an examination of Madame Knight's journal will reveal it to be a closer progenitor of Southwestern humor than Byrd's *Histories of the Dividing Line,* to which it is sometimes compared. In fact, Madame Knight's journal occupies an intermediate point between the works of Byrd and Longstreet in terms of its

ON THE SUBJECT OF...

MERCY OTIS WARREN (1728-1814)

Warren was a foremost patriot during the revolutionary period and one of the United States' first women of letters. A prominent pamphleteer and historian, she is remembered for her anti-Loyalist dramas, which helped to stir patriotic fervor at a crucial time in American history. Critics value her *History of the Rise, Progress, and Termination of the American Revolution: Interspersed with Biographical and Moral Observations* (1805), one of the first accounts of the revolutionary war, as an astute analysis and vivid firsthand description of the era. Critics also assert that her *History* stands as a testimonial to its author, who ventured with confidence and success into areas outside the proscribed realm of women of her time. In the 1950s and 1960s, commentary on the *History* focused on such issues as Warren's application of morality to history and the philosophical background of her works, and there has been a particular emphasis on the latent feminist philosophy expressed in the *History* in criticism published since the 1970s.

Through the *History,* and her other works, which included the essay *Observations on the New Constitution and on the Federal Convention by a Columbian Patriot, Sic Transit Gloria Americana* (1788), Warren was an outspoken champion of independence and Republican democracy at a time when few women were involved in politics. Many of the nation's leaders, including John Adams, Alexander Hamilton, George Washington, and Thomas Jefferson, were personal friends who respected her opinions and sought her advice, and Warren is counted among them as one of the most eloquent and independent thinkers in the early history of the United States. Her correspondence with John Adams was published in the 1878 collection *The Correspondence of John Adams and Mercy Warren.*

use of persona, language, and kind of humor. Though Byrd and Knight were contemporary, Byrd is very much the aristocrat striving to impress an absent English audience. Even the audience of his peers, to whom the *Secret History* was directed, operates under these basic assumptions. Thus, Byrd's persona describes the incompetence of the North Carolina surveyors and lazy North Carolina colonials from a superior moral vantage point. The final form of the *History* detaches the persona almost totally from the action, and the entire story is told in his words, without the intrusion of the "vulgar common speech." In *Georgia Scenes,* Longstreet also uses the framing device of a gentleman narrator, yet he consciously allows his other characters to speak in the vernacular. In addition, the attitude of his narrator toward the lower class is not as derogatory as that of Byrd.

Knight's *Journal* falls somewhere in between and even points the way to later developments. Though the narrator feels definitely superior to many of the people she encounters, she is not at all detached from the action. Neither is she of the nobility. In fact, she is refreshingly middle-class, as revealed in her language and that of the other characters. *The Journal* itself chronicles a journey made to conclude a business deal, and Knight subscribes to the American business ethic in several places. However, she does have certain literary pretensions in common with the upper class, and at times breaks out in passable occasional verse, as well as less literary rhyme. Though her journal reveals a certain English influence, its debt is less than that of Byrd. Rather, the liveliness of her humor and language, with its sprinkling of anecdotes, is clearly related to later American humorists. The most distinguishing facet of her language is perhaps that its humor is not used to make palatable sadism and violence, as Kenneth Lynn suggests is the purpose of Southwestern humorists in *Mark Twain and Southwestern Humor.* Knight's humor is more in the comedy of manners tradition, directed against herself and others, toward some universal human failing. However, to understand the humor and language of Madame Knight's work, one must look at the journal as a whole and at the different personae she creates.

The historical Madame Knight was known as a teacher, recorder of public documents, and a successful businesswoman. Yet when her journal was first published in 1825, the editor assumed it to be fiction.[2] The journal itself shows evidence of careful rewriting, obviously from the daily diary, which Knight mentions frequently. There is also a definite indication that the journal was written for an audience, through such "casual" statements as that of an invitation to dine with Governor Winthrop: "I stayed a day here Longer than I intended by the Commands of the Honerable Governor Winthrop to stay and take a supper with him whose wonderful civility I may not omitt."[3] Functioning in some ways as a guidebook, the journal also contains such diverse elements as detailed descriptions of the towns of New York and New Haven and points in between, a thumbnail sketch of people and customs in both the towns and the country, a recounting of the horrors of travels, and successful business deals. What better way to express these various subjects than through several personae, or one persona with different voices for use at different times? This is what Knight has done, using four main roles or voices for her persona: the frightened female traveller, the curious recorder of facts, the acute businesswoman, and the superior, and at times sarcastic, commentator.

Knight refers to herself occasionally as a "fearful female travailler" and in the first part of the journal dwells on her fears of the dark night and crossing swift rivers:

> The Canoo was very small and shallow, so that when we were in she seem'd redy to take in water, which greatly terrified mee, and caused me to be very circumspect, sitting with my hands fast on each side, my eyes stedy, not daring so much as to lodg my tongue a hair's breadth more on the side of my mouth than tother, nor so much as think on Lott's wife. . . .
>
> (p. 10)

> Sometimes seing my self drowning, otherwhile drowned, and at the best like a holy Sister Just come out of a Spiritual Bath in dripping garments.
>
> (p. 11)

She pretends to be repeatedly frightened by her guide with stories of coming dangers, yet her fear is almost always undercut with humorous allusion, as well as by the confident tone in other places. For instance, Madame Knight, though thirty-eight years old in an age when life expectancy was not much greater, sets off on a journey on October 2 at three in the afternoon, hardly a time of the year or the day to expect easy travelling. She chooses to journey on after dark to reach a self-appointed goal. Subsequent timorousness on her part seems a bow to convention, especially when far greater danger of being lost in a snowstorm later confronts her and she betrays no fear at all. She simultaneously assumes the pose of gentlewoman accepted by society, and deflates it through the vigor of her actions. She is no helpless, sheltered lady; rather she is a new breed of American woman, equally capable of caring for himself and of posing as a "fearful female" when it furthers her purpose.

This conventional guise also gives her the opportunity to compose some verses to "Fair Cynthia" and to speak in rather elevated language that seems out of place when contrasted with the other voices. "Now was the Glorious Luminary, with his swift Coursers arrived at his Stage, leaving poor me with the rest of this part of the lower world in darkness . . ." (p. 11). But here, again, Knight is only manipulating an accepted poetic pose, while her actions burlesque it. When at the end of her journey she desires "sincearly to adore [her] Great Benefactor for thus graciously carrying forth and returning in safety his unworthy handmaid" (p. 72), the reader again senses an acquiescence to literary tradition in the style and imagery. Thus, the guise of "fearful female travailler," with equal emphasis on the *fearful* and the *female,* is useful when Knight is being consciously literary and is quite undercut when contrasted with the other voices.

The voice to which it is most directly antithetical is the many-faceted one of the businesswoman or woman of affairs. Knight chooses what time and with whom she will travel, bargaining with her guide for a good price. Further, though she has gone to settle the inheritance of a relation, she snaps up a chance to make a profit on a quick deal herself:

> Mr. Burroughs went with me to Vendue where I bought about 100 Rheem of paper w[ch] was retaken in a flyboat from Holland and sold very Reasonably here—some ten some Eight shillings per Rheem by the Lott w[ch] was ten Rheem in a Lott.
> (p. 52)

At times, Knight foreshadows the modern American business ethic in her standard of morality: correct conduct in business matters overrides other concerns, even religion. In a comment about the people of New York she says, "They are not strict in keeping the Sabbath as in Boston and other places where I had bin, But seem to deal with great exactness as farr as I see or Deall with" (p. 54). And like a good business woman she refuses to be deflected from her purpose, no matter what the inconvenience (p. 67). This sense of purpose and dispatch becomes more noticeable toward the latter part of the journal. Days become condensed and less attention is given to humorous detail. It is as if, nearing the end of her business, Knight wishes to wrap things up and get them out of the way.

Knight's third guise as the curious recorder of facts is quite compatible with that of the businesswoman; in each she takes a practical view of the world around her, carefully observing and recording all relevant details. The persona of recorder of facts is most dominant after the arrival in New Haven, since from this point the focus of the journal seems to change. Heretofore, the narrative has focused on the hardships of the journey and the oddities of the rural people encountered; now, more attention is given to manners and customs in an urban setting, the first evidence of which is Knight's description of New Haven. Anxious that neither she nor the reader misses a detail, she discusses law, religion, customs such as Lecture days—Election Day, Training Day, marriage customs, food, the Indian question, and merchant practices. Moreover, like a good logician, she states first the good points, then the bad. The tone throughout is informative and casual. At no time does the reader wonder about Knight's opinion of these things, for she repeatedly interjects her comments with humorous asides and anecdotes.

This thorough, opinionated inquisitiveness is apparent in her description of New York. There, she even notes the architectural details of the houses in comparison with those in Boston. On the return trip from New York, she comments on many of the small villages, which she had ignored before. No vestige of the "fearful female travailler" remains as she assesses the scene before her. "This is a very pretty place, well compact, and good handsome houses, Clean, good and passable Rodes, and situated on a Navigable River, abundance of land well fined and Cleerd all along as wee passed" (p. 59). Thus, the latter part of the journal becomes a very factual travel book or guide book to that part of the country, though it is still leavened with humor.

The final, probably most delightful, voice is that of a superior, sarcastic commentator who comments on and participates in the action. The most pervasive and, thus, most fully developed, this voice binds the others together with the characteristic humor and viewpoint of a sophisticated city woman, passing judgment on country bumpkins. An instance of this observation is seen from the very beginning when she characterizes some tavern drinkers as "being tyed by the Lipps to a pewter engine" and slyly describes the figure of the guide as "a Globe on a Gate post." Perhaps it is Knight's very human annoyance with apparent stupidity that so appeals to the reader. For example, she expresses this annoyance in pithy terms when a dull-witted country wench is slow to give her food and lodging at a tavern:

> Miss star'd awhile, drew a chair, bid me sitt, And then run upstairs and putts on two or three Rings, (or else I had not seen them before,) and returning, sett herself just before me, showing the way to Reding, that I might see her Ornaments, perhaps to gain the more respect. But her Granam's new Rung sow, had it appeared, would have affected me as much.
>
> (p. 7)

In language at once vivid and concrete, Knight deflates the girl's attempt to impress her; her use of the "sow" comparison is especially insulting because it is directed from one woman to another. But to fully understand the effect of this voice one must also examine the type of humor and the idiom used to create it. This passage demonstrates one of the ways humor surfaces in the *Journal* and agrees with Kenneth Lynn's description of frontier humor, "the humor [is] the vernacular and the vernacular [is] the humor."[4] In using this persona to tell numerous anecdotes and relate the incidents of the journey, the author reveals her awareness of the power of words and her ability to manipulate them.

Knight's vivid description of the way merchants do business in Connecticut makes the reader feel he is present at the scene. Her language is graphic, if not too flattering, and the words the country bumpkins speak reinforce and complete the picture. Yet one is also aware of the regional tension in her portrayal, critical of both classes of people from Connecticut:

> Being at a merchants house, in comes a tall country fellow, with his alfogeos full of tobacco; for they seldom Loose their Cudd, but keeping Chewing and Spitting as long as they'r eyes are open, . . . At last, like the creature Balaam Rode on, he opened his mouth and said: have You any Ribenin for Hatbads to sell I pray? . . . Bumpkin Simpers, cryes its confounded Gay I vow.
>
> (p. 42)

The bumpkin's female counterpart does not fare much better. Knight's tendency to make names descriptive is apparent in the characterization of "Jone Tawdry" who "curtsees" fifty times before she speaks and then speaks in an awed, ignorant tone: "Law you . . . its right Gent, do You, take it, tis dreadful pretty" (p. 43). These portraits, together with those of the other rustic Knight encounters, create the figure of the typical New England bumpkin, the ancestor of the archetypal Yankee.[5] Yet Knight is also quick to point out that they only lack education, "for these people have as Large a portion of mother witt, and sometimes a Larger, than those who have bin brought up in citties" (p. 43). Cohen and Dillingham's description of Southwestern humor well applies to this situation:

> When the narrator abandoned his gentlemanly pose and made the characters themselves speak, he was laying the foundation for a new style in American writing. Rich in similes, metaphors, and in exaggerations, this backwoods language is characterized by concreteness, freshness and color.[6]

Knight's narrator, rather than her characters, most forcefully exhibits this kind of concrete, fresh language. In addition, she clearly points the way to this treatment of humor through her manipulation of dialect, long before Longstreet, who is more popularly seen as the originator.

Along with the creation of comic stereotypes and usage of common speech, Knight uses certain words and images which comment on the prejudices and concerns of her time. Religion is often a tool used to produce the mocking, humorous tone so pervasive in the journal. The Quakers are twice an object of derision. Once, describing a locquacious hostess, Knight says, "I began to fear I was got among the Quaking tribe, beleeving not a Limber tong'd sister among them could out do Madm. Hostes" (p. 3). She speaks of the hostess "catechis'ing" John for going with her, and doubts the truth of her "Call" to fulfill this mission.

In her later description of the towns, Knight invariably comments on the church and on how the inhabitants keep the Sabbath. The villagers of Fairfield receive her special attention. She notes they are "litigious" and do not agree with their minister. "They have aboundance of sheep, whose very Dung brings them great gain, with part of which they pay their Parsons sallery. And they Grudg that, prefering their Dung before their minister" (p. 63). As a kind of divine retribution, she notes they get their comeuppance; they were "once Bitt by a sharper who had them a night and sheared them all before morning." Here, the stereotype of the thrifty Yankee who makes use of everything rises to the surface, as Knight illustrates the popular moral that scoundrels tend to get what they deserve.

Knight is also quite free in her allusions to the devil, who is not the same object of awe and terror as early Pilgrims imagined him. In an extended rather labored metaphor, she compares a bad innkeeper to Satan, thus rendering them both ridiculous. "I questioned whether we ought to go to the Devil to be helpt out of affliction. However, like the rest of Deluded souls that post to ye

Infernal dinn, Wee made all posible speed to this Devil's Habitation" (p. 20). In these casual references to religion and her uses of religious metaphor, Knight typifies the attitude of the common New Englander, of whose carelessness or laxness one is not too aware when reading only the religious treatises of the time.

Another interesting detail revealed through Knight's use of language is the New Englander's prejudice toward the English, the Negro, and the Indian. Understandably perhaps, all connected with the Indian is deplorable to her, and the very word *Indian* becomes pejorative. Poor food is described as "Indian fare," a poverty stricken back woodsman is described as "an Indian-like animal [who] . . . makes an Awkerd Scratch with his Indian shoo" (p. 25). Indian customs are disparaged and the English censured for emulating them in their practice of divorce. The Black also comes in for his share of indictment, and, again, the English are tainted by an association with them.

> . . . too Indulgent (especially ye farmers) to their slaves: sufering too great familiarity from them, permitting y[m] to set at Table and eat with them (as they say to save time,) and into the dish goes the black hoof as freely as the white hand.

This intolerant attitude toward those who differ from her in class or race is probably a clue to an understanding of one of the several anecdotes Knight tells:

> A negro Slave belonging to a man in y[e] Town, stole a hogs head from his master, and gave or sold it to an Indian, native of the place. The Indian sold it in the neighbourhood, and so the theft was found out. Thereupon the Heathen was seized, and carried to the Justices House to be Examined. But his worship (it seems) was gone into the feild, with a Brother in office, to gather in his Pompions. Whither the malefactor is hurried, And Complaint made, and satisfaction in the name of Justice demanded. Their Worships cann't proceed in form without a Bench: whereupon they Order one to be Imediately erected, which, for want of fitter materials, they made with pompions—which being finished, down setts their Worships, and the Malefactor call'd, and by the Senior Justice Interrogated after the following manner. You Indian why did You steal from this Man? You sho'dn't do so—it's a Grandy wicked thing to steal. Hol't Hol't cryes Justice Junr Brother, You speak negro to him. I'le ask him. You sirrah, why did You steal this man's Hoggshead? Hoggshead? (replys the Indian,) me no stomany. No? says his Worship; and pulling off his hatt, Patted his own head with his hands, sais, Tatapa—You Tatapa—you; all one this. Hoggshead all one this. Hah! says Netop, now me stomany that. Whereupon the Company fell into a great fitt of Laughter, even to Roreing. Silence is comanded, but to no effect: for they continued perfectly Shouting. Nay, sais his worship, in an angry tone, if it be so, *take mee off the Bench.*
>
> (pp. 34-36)

This anecdote is interesting for several reasons. On the surface, it is a naive and rather crude joke, yet with closer scrutiny, it becomes something else. It reveals prejudice against the Indian and Black, but also a refreshing ridicule of authority. The participants are an Indian, a Negro, and two white Judges. The Negro and Indian are the stock dishonest, sly characters. Surprisingly, they are presented in a better light than the judges and could even be said to triumph in this joke. The two judges are out in the field gathering pumpkins when they are called upon to render a decision. Yet, like the two generals in *Catch-22* who know they have no authority without their badge of office, they build a bench of pumpkins. Like typical lawyers, each has his own idea of how to proceed, and each only succeeds in making himself a laughingstock. In comparison with the lowest members of society, these justices are made to seem even more ridiculous.

The effect of this joke is totally dependent on word play, emphasizing, again, Knight's manipulation of language. The Indian does not know the meaning of "Hoggshead," and the pantomime of the judge make him believe that the judge is referring to his own head as a Hoggshead (perhaps the first pig joke in our history). Yet there is a nice discrimination between types of language, also. The first judge is interrogating the Indian incorrectly because he is "speaking Negro" to him, "it's a Grandy wicked thing to steal." The junior judge thinks he will succeed by speaking what he considers to be Indian to him. Since he has to pantomime part of the action, his opinion of the Indian's mentality is quite low. "Tatapa—You, Tatapa—you; all one this. Hoggshead all one this." The justice reacts the way one would to a foreigner and tries to make him understand by loudly repeating the words, which in this case sound like bad TV Indian dialogue. Perhaps this comic stereotype is also older than heretofore imagined.

Thus, humor for Sarah Kemble Knight becomes a vehicle to express her view of reality. Language is the medium to convey the humor, and she effectively experiments with language, with the use of the vernacular, to portray her view of life in colonial New England. Unconsciously or consciously, she reveals an attitude toward religion and toward business which is closer to that of Ben Franklin than that of the Mathers; her language reveals the sectionalism already surfacing in New England, especially in her criticism of the Connecticut colony. Furthermore, in her use of anecdote and concrete language she lays a foundation for the stereotypical Yankee and creates a persona with four distinct voices.

The Journal of Sarah Kemble Knight is not great literature, yet it is worthy of more consideration than it has been given in American literary history. Its social considerations are just as important as its historical ones. *The Journal* gives an insight into the life of a colonial woman who defies stereotype. She is cultured enough to be aware of society's genteel expectations of woman and of English poetic traditions, while she is practical and American enough to reject them when they do not suit her. She also reveals of independence of women in America, both in the realm of finance and of adventure. She is, indeed, a representative of the "liberated woman," in a time and place where we expect no liberation.

Notes

1. Walter Blair, *Native American Humor* (San Francisco: Chandler Publishing Co., 1960), p. 4, states, "By contrast two rare frivolous souls of colonial times, Sara Kemble Knight and William Byrd, in their treatment of typical details, foreshadowed American humor." See also Willard Thorp, *American Humorists* (Minneapolis: University of Minnesota Press, 1964), p. 5.
2. A very good article for bibliographical information is Alan Margolies, "The Editing and Publication of 'The Journal of Madame Knight,'" *Bibliographical Society of America Papers,* 58 (1964), 25-32.
3. George Parker Winship, *The Journal of Madame Knight* (New York: Peter Smith, 1935), p. 68. All subsequent references will be to this text.
4. Kenneth S. Lynn. *Mark Twain and Southwestern Humor* (Boston, Toronto: Little, Brown & Co., 1959), p. 31.
5. For discussions of the Yankee figure in early American literature see Constance Rourke, *American Humor: A Study of National Character* (New York: Harcourt, Brace & Co., 1931), pp. 12, 14; Jennette Tandy, *Crackerbox Philosophers in American Humor and Satire* (New York: Columbia University Press, 1925), p. 2; and Walter Blair, pp. 8, 9.
6. Hennig Cohen and William B. Dillingham, *Humor of the Old Southwest* (Boston: Houghton, Mifflin Co., 1964), p. xvii.

ELAINE HOBBY (ESSAY DATE 1989)

SOURCE: Hobby, Elaine. "Religious Poetry, Meditations and Conversion Narratives." In *Virtue of Necessity: English Women's Writing 1649-88,* pp. 54-75. Ann Arbor: The University of Michigan Press, 1989.

In the following essay, Hobby examines the writings of several women who described their experiences of religious conversion.

While radical sectaries were out in the streets pamphleteering, proclaiming the social implications of the belief that each person had an individual relationship with God, other women were engaged in its more private anatomising, analysing and recording the development of their spiritual well-being. Such texts fall into two main groups. First, there are three books of poetry and meditations, the authors of which are clearly well to the right of Quakers and Baptists. Second, there is a series of spiritual autobiographies composed by members of Independent congregations, mostly in London. What all these writings have in common is the fact that their authors faithfully promote highly restrictive ideologies about women's duties and necessary passivity, while at the same time finding ways to justify their own unfeminine activities.

> My bounded spirits, bounded be in thee,
> For bounded by no other can they be.
>
> (*Eliza's Babes,* p. 36)

For a woman to write for publication at all in the seventeenth century was to challenge the limits of acceptable feminine behaviour. Between 1652 and 1656, three women published books of religious poetry and meditations, all of them finding ways within their work of making such activity possible. In their texts they construct models of a writing, female Christian who is supposed to be acceptable to the reading public. The ideal female author who appears in these texts is able to enter the public world free from male prefaces, but nonetheless is restricted by the characteristics of this ideal. All these texts, to a lesser or greater extent, are didactic, creating for writer and reader an image of desirable femininity which can embrace the identity of poet.

Much of *Eliza's Babes,* 1652, was produced abroad, possibly at the court of Elizabeth of Bohemia, after the anonymous author had fled England during the 1640s. Her references to the civil war ('To the King, writ, 1644', p. 23) make it clear that she was a royalist who had hoped for some compromise between king and parliament in the mid-1640s. Once in exile, however, she rejoiced in the unexpected delights found in forced exclusion from her country, and in 'To the Queen of Bohemia' celebrates the fact that her exile had made it possible for her 'To see that queen, so much admir'd' (p. 23).

Many of the defeated royalists, of course, had to find some way of making failure and withdrawal from the world palatable. In *Eliza's Babes,* however, we also find an exploration of the specifically female advantages of abandoning the world. The Eliza persona that the poems create demonstrates the freedoms available for women who retire from the public domain and immerse themselves in religious devotions. Not only can women dismiss concerns of state; they can also, to some extent, retire from the family structures which compose it.

The title page of *Eliza's Babes* announces that the author 'only desires to advance the glory of God, and not her own'. This reiterates the point that Eliza makes several times in introductory remarks: the normally reprehensible act of publishing her works is acceptable, even necessary, because of her duty to God. Publishing is a Christian act, she argues, because Christ died a 'public death', compelling her 'to return him public thanks, for such infinite and public favours' (sig. A3). This action should be emulated by all true believers, and not criticised in her.

> And if any shall say 'Others may be as thankful as thee, though they talk not so much of it'; let them know that if they did rightly apprehend the infinite mercies of God to them, they could not be silent: and if they do not think the mercies of God worth public thanks, I do.
>
> (sig. A3)

Like her more radical sectary sisters, she uses the idea that women should be the most lowly of creatures to argue that, therefore, they are least able to resist being used by God to his greater glory.

> And now I dare not say 'I am an ignorant woman, and unfit to write', for if thou will declare thy goodness and thy mercy by weak and contemptible means, who can resist thy will.
>
> (p. 75)

Although inhabiting this passive role restricts her subject matter—in one of her poems she exhorts 'Lord let no line be writ by me, / That excludes, or includes not, thee'—it also frees her from fear of human disapproval. Her opening poem exults in this licence.

> I glory in the word of God,
> To praise it I accord.
> With joy I will declare abroad,
> The goodness of the Lord.
>
> All you that goodness do disdain,
> Go; read not here:
> And if you do; I tell you plain,
> I do not care.
>
> For why? above your reach my soul is placed,
> And your odd words shall not my mind distaste.
>
> (p. 1)

Eliza has committed herself to Christ—'He is my spouse', she assures God (p. 21)—and her description of herself as Christ's wife is a highly developed image, drawing on the language and concepts of courtly love poetry. In 'The Flight', for instance, she reworks the conventional notion of a lover dying from grief at his (usually) beloved's death.

> Eliza for, ask now not here,
> She's gone to heaven, to meet her peer.
> For since her Lord, on earth was dead,
> What tarry here? she'd not, she said.
> And to the heavens, she took her flight,
> That she might be still in his sight;
> And so to us she bid adieu,
> But proved herself a lover true.
>
> (p. 11)

As 'a lover true' she delights in praising her beloved, 'his fair sweet lovely face' and 'his pleasing eyes [that] do dart / Their arrows which do pierce my heart' (pp. 24-5).

When it comes to earthly love, however, she asks God to harden her heart 'as hard as steel' (p. 2): 'Great God, thou only worth desiring art, / And none but thee, then must possess my heart' (p. 12). The comparison between earthly love and divine affection, made repeatedly in the poems' use of love poetry conventions, is clear and consistent. As God's spouse she has peace and freedom. Repeatedly and wittily she dismissed the claims of men to possess her as a limitation, even a slavery.

> Since you me ask, why born was I?
> I'll tell you; 'twas to heaven to fly,
> Not here to live a slavish life,
> By being to the world a wife.
>
> (p. 31)

If we turn to her poem 'What I Love', we find that what might at first glance be anticipated as a heartfelt declaration of love for some man, in fact mocks the very idea of her deigning to feel affection for any man.

> Give me a soul, give me a spirit,
> That flies from earth, heaven to inherit.
> But those that grovel here below,
> What! I love them? I'll not do so.
>
> (p. 36)

The product of this marriage with God is her book of poems, her 'babes'. Her first use of the term 'babes' to describe her work serves to emphasise her purported passivity in its production. Addressing other women as 'my sisters', she urges them

> Look on these babes as none of mine,
> For they were but brought forth by me;
> But look on them, as they are divine,
> Proceeding from Divinity.
>
> (sig. A^{v})

Publishing her writings, even though she claims divine sanction, was as great a risk to her modest reputation as sexual irregularities would have been. Defining herself on the title page as a 'virgin', and stressing the modesty of her entry into the public domain with these 'babes', she adds: 'I am not ashamed of their birth; for before I knew it, the Prince of eternal glory had affianced me to himself; and that is my glory' (sig. A2). These offspring, the result of an 'irregular union' with God, are a blessing to their 'mother' which makes them far preferable to children of flesh and blood born in wedlock, since 'they immortalise the name' (p. 42; children of the flesh, of course, would only immortalise a husband's name). Addressing 'a Lady that bragged of her children', Eliza delights in the joy and holiness of her own 'babes'.

> If thou hast cause to joy in thine,
> I have cause too to joy in mine.
> Thine did proceed from sinful race,
> Mine from the heavenly dew of grace.
> Thine at their birth did pain thee bring,
> When mine are born, I sit and sing.
> Thine doth delight in nought but sin,
> My babes' work is, to praise heaven's King.
> Thine bring both sorrow, pain and fear,
> Mine banish from me dreadful care.
>
> (pp. 54-5)

Some of the later poems in *Eliza's Babes* describe the unavoidability of marriage, and work out a pattern whereby the poet can maintain her autonomy within it. Dutiful to her God and to the male hierarchy of the family, she finds herself 'given away' despite her own gift of her heart to God. The only solace offered in 'The Gift' is to continue to follow God's bidding.

> My Lord, hast thou given me away?
> Did I on earth, for a gift stay?
> Hath he by prayer of thee gained me,
> Who was so strictly knit to thee?
>
> To thee I only gave my heart,
> Wouldst thou my Lord from that gift part?
> I know thou wouldst deliver me
> To none, but one beloved by thee.
>
> But Lord my heart thou dost not give,
> Though here on earth, while I do live
> My body here he may retain,
> My heart in heaven, with thee must reign.
>
> Then as thy gift let him think me,
> Since I a donage am from thee.
> And let him know thou hast my heart,
> He only hath my earthly part.
>
> It was my glory I was free,
> And subject here to none but thee,
> And still that glory I shall hold
> If thou my spirit dost enfold.
>
> It is my bliss, I here serve thee,
> 'Tis my great joy; thou lovest me.
>
> (p. 42)

This fate, however, is exemplary. Making the married Eliza representative of women's rightful role in wedlock, the poet explains 'Not a husband, though never so excelling in goodness to us, must detain our desires from heaven' (p. 45). Even though the new spouse is kind—'with him I have no annoy' (p. 45)—this is unimportant in comparison with the spiritual freedom that a relationship with God gives her. Representative of all women, Eliza draws out the lesson that true religion frees the female sex from dependence on male approval or concern.

> For should our husband's love fixed be
> Upon some others, not on thee
> Heaven's Prince will never thee forsake,
> But still his darling will thee make.
> And should he of thee careless be,
> Heaven's Prince, He will more careful be.
> He from the earth will raise thy heart,
> That thou content mayst act that part.

Being married is merely playing a necessary role; her true identity is defined in relation to God.

Producing her 'babes', the fruit of her union with God, Eliza reflects that God must have 'something here remarkable for me to do, before I leave the earth' (p. 102). The relationship between woman and God that the poems represent and define makes her 'capable of as great a dignity as any mortal man'.

> Peace! Present now no more to me (to take my spirit from the height of felicity) that I am a creature of a weaker sex, a woman. For my God! If I must live after the example of thy blessed apostle, I must live by faith, and faith makes things to come, as present; and thou hast said by thy servant, that we shall be like thy blessed Son: then thou wilt make all thy people like kings and priests. Kings are men, and men are kings; and souls have no sex. The hidden man of the heart makes us capable of being kings; for I have heard it is that within makes the man. Then are we by election capable of as great a dignity as any mortal man.

It is through withdrawal from the world and in obedience solely to God, these 'virgin's offerings' demonstrate, that women can attain a measure of self-definition and control.

An Collins's *Divine Songs and Meditacions* appeared in 1653. The book, which is almost entirely in verse, is highly experimental in stanza form, and it is possible that some of the songs, at least, were intended to be set to music and performed. In the introductory address 'To the Reader', Collins explains that she has found writing 'so amiable, as that it inflamed my faculties, to put forth themselves in a practice so pleasing'. Writing is described, in other words, as a delightful and empowering activity for the author. Choice of subject-matter, however, was not free. She had found no satisfaction, she asserts, in writing 'profane history'. It was only when committing herself to the exposition of 'divine truth' that she found contentment. Composing poetry on such themes 'reduced my mind to a peaceful temper'. Her 'inflamed faculties', therefore, were at the same time 'peaceful'. The *Songs and Meditacions* proceed to promote tranquillity and contentment as qualities of the highest value, both for the state and for the individual. The author is portrayed in her poetry as a pattern for the reader, a Christian woman who has achieved satisfaction by following the rules promoted in the text.

If women's sphere, according to conventional wisdom and dominant practice, extended no further than the boundaries of her home, An Collins is shown as more especially confined within such limits. The long introductory poem 'The Preface' consists of a fascinating fusion of personal history, commentary on the contemporary religio-political conflicts and a brief history of Christianity, with a series of statements about the role of the author. Collins describes how her confinement to the house was necessitated by chronic ill-health, inactivity lulling her brain to sleep. Writing has revived her. In 'The Preamble' to her first meditation, she also describes writing as a release from crippling despair and misery.

> Amid the ocean of adversity,
> Near whelmed in the waves of sore vexation,
> Tormented with the floods of misery,
> And almost in the guise of desperation,
> Near destitute of comfort, full of woes,
> This was her case that did the same compose.[1]

Writing has empowered her, and it is particularly important that she is writing about divine truth. Since her subject matter is righteous, she is protected by a 'sovereign power' from the malice of her enemies who would wish her to remain silent. People have tried to hinder her, 'Yet this cannot prevail to hinder me / From publishing those truths I do intend' ('The Preface').

Firm in the duty to publish her truths, she makes no further apology for commenting on affairs of state. Her task is to give voice to God's truth, which entails a duty to pass on to her contemporaries and to future ages the need for moderation, peace and order. The people are

ON THE SUBJECT OF...

CATHERINE PARR (1512-1548)

The sixth wife of King Henry VIII, Parr was known in her day for her piety and learning as well her immensely popular devotional works. The volume she edited, *Prayers or Meditations* (1545), was one of the earliest Protestant devotional works, and her spiritual autobiography, *The Lamentation or Complaint of a Sinner* (1547), was one of the first Protestant confessionals and an especially unusual publication for a woman of her day. A devoted humanist, Parr worked tirelessly to make religious works available to the English reading public, and her works reveal her deep interest in promoting Protestantism and calling for reform. She also was a patron to a number of Reformist thinkers in her court circle and promoted the production of other Protestant religious works.

As a child Parr was encouraged to study by her mother, and became a notable scholar, fluent in Latin and capable in Greek and modern languages. When Henry VIII was away in France in 1544, Parr acted as regent in his absence. She was also said to have behaved kindly to his children, the future queens Mary and Elizabeth, encouraging them in their learning. Factions at court were envious of Parr's influence on Henry and sought to destroy her by linking her Protestant leanings with "heretical" religious reformers, and went so far as to accuse her of treason. In 1545 Henry signed a warrant for her imprisonment in the Tower of London, but Parr submitted to the king and did away with his suspicions.

Early in the twentieth century, scholars regarded Parr's writings as being of interest only as historical documents, but later feminist critics have emphasized Parr's effect on women's learning and religious life in the sixteenth century as well as the challenges she faced as a woman expressing her religious experiences.

'wrapped in fangles new', corrupted and confused by ill-doers ('Time past we understood by story'). Committed to the position that radical sectaries are merely producing 'new glosses' on 'old heresies' ('The Preface'), she argues for re-establishment of order and authority in church and state, and 'Another Song Exciting to Spiritual Mirth' proposes abandonment of concern over the outcome of human conflict.

> But those that are contented
> However things do fall,
> Much anguish is prevented,
> And they soon freed from all;
> They finish all their labours
> With much felicity.

If the author and reader become singleminded in the pursuit of wholly spiritual concerns, they will find happiness. Only by refusing rebellion and discord can the true Christian find happiness ('Another Song' "Having restrained discontent").

Quite clearly in such passages, the model Christian woman that the poet represents asserts that conflict and dissension are evils, the work of the devil, and so should be rejected in favour of social order and moderation. While calling for retreat from argument she is also, therefore, promoting a particular (and reactionary) political ideology. Arguing that state politics are unimportant, she makes a political statement, and holds up the contented poet persona as evidence that retirement from worldly concerns brings happiness. She looks to God to provide the only possible unity in the families of a nation torn apart by civil war.

> No knot of friendship long can hold
> Save that which grace hath tied,
> For other causes prove but cold
> When their effects are tried.
> For God who loveth unity
> Doth cause the only union
> Which makes them of one family
> Of one mind and communion.
> This is the cause of home debate,
> And much domestic woes,
> That one may find his household mates
> To be his greatest foes,
> That with the wolf the lamb may bide
> As free from molestation
> As Saints with sinners, who reside
> In the same habitation.
> ('A Song Declaring that a Christian May Find True Love only where True Grace Is')

The championing of withdrawal from the world indeed becomes particularly interesting when applied specifically to the question of family ties: a woman's duty of obedience to her father, and her subsequent absorption within her husband's identity were, after all, supposed to be of paramount importance. The retirement advocated in *Divine Songs and Meditacions,* therefore, is of particular advantage to women, and is certainly an important factor in the presentation of the poet's contentment. The good Christian of these *Songs* is not just singleminded, but also singlehearted. Her only spouse (like Eliza's) is Christ. She must withdraw from duties to men, as well as from conflicts of state.

> Then let them know, that would enjoy
> The firm fruition,
> Of his sweet presence, he will stay
> With single hearts alone,
> Who [but] their former mate,
> Do quite exterminate:
> With all things that defile.
> They that are Christ's truly,
> The flesh do crucify
> With its affections vile.
> The grounds of truth are sought
> New principles are wrought
> Of grace and holiness,
> Which plantings of the heart
> Will spring in every part,
> And so itself express.
> ('A Song Expressing Their Happiness who have Communion with Christ')

In this union with Christ, the female poet can justify her writing as proper feminine employment. 'The Preface' describes the *Songs* as offspring clad in homely dress—fitting products of a virtuous woman. She defends her writing

> Now touching that I hasten to express
> Concerning these, the offspring of my mind,
> Who though they here appear in homely dress
> And as they are my works, I do not find
> But ranked with others, they may go behind,
> Yet for their matter, I suppose they be
> Not worthless quite, whilst they with truth agree.

The fruit of this union with Christ is necessarily good.

> So sorrow served but as springing rain
> To ripen fruits, endowments of the mind,
> Who thereby did ability attain
> To send forth flowers, of so rare a kind,
> Which wither not by force of sun or wind:
> Retaining virtue in their operations,
> Which are the matter of those meditations.

The overriding assertion of the *Songs and Meditacions,* indeed, is that the poet, the Christian woman, having suffered greatly in the world from conflict and physical constraints, has found the wisdom to willingly abandon worldly concerns and fence herself into a narrow domain which allows, in practice, greater freedom. The final expression of this is the *Songs* themselves, 'flowers of so rare a kind, / Which wither not by force of sun or wind'. The most succinct statement of this conclusion appears in 'Another Song' "The winter of my infancy", which traces the poet's suffering and subsequent attainment of peace. The enclosing of her mind by the strictures of contentment and divine truth has brought with it safety, making it possible for her to write undisturbed and thus attain more than most women ever can. The cottage garden of her mind can grow rare fruits indeed.

> Yet as a garden is my mind enclosed fast
> Being to safety so confined from storm and blast
> Apt to produce a fruit most rare,
> That is not common with every woman
> That fruitful are.

Most women's 'fruitfulness' is shown in their ability to bear sons for their husbands. Her offspring were acquired, the text proclaims, through accepting the need for quiescence and withdrawal from worldly turmoil and family ties in a country split apart by civil war. This alone can bring happiness.

> For in our union with the Lord alone
> Consists our happiness.
> Certainly such who are with Christ at one
> He leaves not comfortless.
> ('A Song Expressing Their Happiness who have Communion with Christ')

In *Divine Songs and Meditacions* an apparently conventional restatement of a basic Christian tenet—that God alone is the source of secure joy—becomes a justification for female celibacy and a celebration of women's writing.

Elizabeth Major's *Honey on the Rod: Or a comfortable Contemplation for one in Affliction* appeared prefaced by a commendatory note by the censor Joseph Caryl in 1656. Caryl recommends the book to the reader as evidence that 'the Lord gives instruction with correction'. The author's own address to her readers is properly self-deprecating, while making the necessary claim that her writings are both godly and useful.

> If you please so far to descend, as to cast an eye upon these poor lines presented to you, you may behold in it a little (but a full) hive. I entreat thee not to be offended, if thou find in it more wax than honey, and more dross than either. The honey (the divine part) I commend to thee, and the wax (the mortal part) being clarified from the dross (that is, the faults and failings through weakness) is useful in its place.
>
> (sig. A3r-v)

That which is good in the book comes from the Lord, she asserts, or from the experience he has seen fit to give her (sig. A4). Since it is godly, her uneasiness about 'making it public' (sig. A6v) has been overcome: 'the subject will be the honour of it' (sig. A7v). Apologising for her 'lowly' achievements, she makes it clear that the book is all her own work (helped by the Lord), and that it is the best she can do. The book is her child.

> And now to you, O my friends, I present these poor and undressed lines, being as they came into the world, I not finding any hand to help me to put it into a better dress than what it brought with it . . . For though I was not ambitious of a beautiful babe, yet I confess I would gladly have had it appear comely; therefore where you find it harsh or uneven, know, it should not have come abroad so, had not my ignorance to find the fault been the cause of it.
>
> (sig. h3v)

As a godly text, *Honey on the Rod* is didactic. The author warns her reader to understand the 'comfortable contemplation' as exemplary, not just revealing the author's condition but also showing the sinner her/his own true, mortal state.

> Come, O come, I beseech you, whoever you are that read these lines, and behold yourselves and me in them, as objects of mortality, like dust before the wind or as stubble before a consuming fire; weak, and not able of ourselves to resist the least assault.
>
> (p. 9)

The recurrent simile of *Honey on the Rod* portrays the author as an erring child or poor scholar, God as the father and teacher. The author and reader together are led through a series of lessons in order to achieve their salvation.

The major part of the book—about three quarters of it—consists of a prose dialogue 'A Comfortable Contemplation for One in Affliction'. The main protagonists are 'Consolation' and 'Soul', who discuss how hope and salvation can be found in the midst of affliction. The soul, cast down and repentant, looks to language and specifically to writing as a way to find relief from despair.

> I could wish my tongue were as the pen of a ready writer, if there be hopes of ease by imparting; for my sighs are many, and my heart is heavy. I, I am she that hath seen affliction.
>
> (p. 2)

Honey on the Rod, then, acts as the site where affliction is made sense of, and a particular understanding and interpretation of suffering is given to the distressed author and reader. In the author's case, the suffering is not solely the conventional penitence of a believer seeking salvation and escape from the bondage of sin, but a particularly acute pain. Major explains to the reader that God 'was pleased in the prime of my years to take me, as it were, from a palace to a prison, from liberty to bondage, where I have served some apprenticeships' (sig. A4v). This 'prison' is physical confinement brought on by sudden and crippling illness.

> No help here is below; alas, I must, I must to prison here: where Lord, thou knowest, some apprenticeships I have close prisoner been: my strength thou were pleased to melt away by secret, unseen ways, leaving me almost as helpless, as when I first entered this vale of tears: and to my debility many other afflictions thy wisdom sees it needful here to add; for scarce doth the day break in upon me, before a new cause of sorrow hath made a breach.
>
> (p. 8)

Her weakness and consequent close confinement to the home are presented, however, as having a particular metaphorical significance. She reminds herself repeatedly that her disability is God's judgement on her as a sinner: 'because ye have sinned against the Lord, and have not obeyed his voice, therefore this thing is come upon you' (p. 14). She presents herself to the reader as a particularly clear exemplar of the state of sin; and, as the text proceeds, the sinner saved. Her illness and pain have given her the lesson that *Honey on the Rod* offers to the reader: we must withdraw from the world, and concern ourselves only with Christ who (like the author) suffered for the sake of our salvation.

The passive, chastened self can be useful, and so the sinner calls on God to humble and break her. In the context of constant references to real physical pain, such passages acquire poignancy. Passivity here is not a metaphorical state advocated by a man with real power and control in the world. It is an inescapable fate, based in female powerlessness and the author's chronic illness, which she is trying to present and interpret in a manner which gives it some purpose and her some stature.

> Lord, give an humble heart, that I may yield,
> O get the conquest ere thou quit the field:
> And melt it, Lord, by mercies, if that won't do,
> Break it in pieces, and then make it new.
> O frame it to thy will, to thee 'tis known,
> And not to me, O Lord, though 'tis mine own.
> O bring it to obedience, make't what thou wilt
> So thou wilt own it, help ere my soul be spilt.
>
> (p. 185)

The self torn apart and remade by God is one who has a right to write, and who can represent the sinner saved. The final section of the book includes several poems which do, quite literally represent (and re-present) the author in this exalted role. These poems use her name, Elizabeth Major, as a frame to lay out her qualities and aspirations, defining and constructing a self that is both saint and sinner, saved by suffering and God's grace. Elizabeth Major the author, as depicted in these verses, is a blessed and exemplary Saint. The most remarkable of these is 'The Author's Prayer'.

The Author's Prayer: O my blessed Lord and Saviour Jesus Christ, have mercy on thy poor hand-maid, Elizabeth Major.

Oh	gracious God, inhabiting	E ternity
My	blest redeemer, that hast	L ovingly
Blessed	me with hope, a kingdom to	I nherit,
Lord	of this mercy give an humble	S pirit,
And	grant I pray, I may my life	A mend:
Saviour	'tis thou that canst my soul	B efriend.
Jesus	with grace my guilty soul	E ndue
Christ	promised grace, and thou, O Lord art	T rue;
Have	care of me, deal out with thine own	H and
Mercy	to my poor soul, thou canst com-	M and
On	me a shower of grace, sin to	A void,
Thy	praise to sing, my tongue shall be	I mployed;
Poor,	Lord I am, with fear and care	O ppressed,
Handmaid	to thee I am, in thee I'll	R est.

The self thus defined and recommended to the reader is one with strictly limited freedoms. She must behave in acceptable, godly ways—something which would not usually involve writing, for a woman, necessitating her introductory justification of the act, and the didactic concern of the book. In order to explore the range of subject-matter relevant to a discussion of sinfulness, she also has to vindicate making reference to things 'that your blushing sex should want confidence to mention' (sig. h3). When writing 'On Immodesty', therefore, she inevitably reprimands women for not being sufficiently chaste and modest.

> For England sure doth Sodom pass in sins,
> O here's committed unseen, unheard of things
> To former ages, by my own sex are done,
> Things but to name, would taint a modest
> tongue:
> Therefore myself I'll silence, since tongue nor ear
> Of a chaste soul can it describe, nor hear:
> For certainly, 'tis scarce unknown to any.
> With grief I speak, ill's acted by too many.
>
> (p. 175)

She can only make the immodest step of writing and publishing by claiming to silence herself on certain matters, while warning other women against being overbold. Writing allows Major to create and inhabit a contradictory space, where she is both free to write as a sinner saved, and yet still tightly bound by rules of passivity and modesty. She constructs a new self, but a new self broken by suffering and made up only of permissible feminine elements.

> 'I could not see the need I had of my troubles, nor the end for which they were sent.'
>
> (Sarah Davy, *Heaven Realiz'd,* p. 5)

Women's published records of their spiritual lives have roots in the convention of spiritual self-examination recommended by Puritan divines. This practice served in part to replace the earlier Catholic pattern of confession to a priest to obtain absolution: each person had to examine their own soul's health to discover whether s/he would be numbered among the saved. Such a practice was particularly relevant when death seemed imminent, and it is thanks to the desire of the dying to recall evidence that they were included among God's chosen people that accounts survive of the lives of Elizabeth Moore, Mary Simpson[2] and Luce Perrot. The writings of all these women were published post-humously by men. None of them appeared as autonomous texts, but were reworked by their male editors to serve their own ends. Elizabeth Moore's *Evidences for Heaven,* for instance, appears in Calamy's *The Godly Man's Ark* as part of his argument in favour of patient forebearance. Luce Perrot's *Account* was divided into short sections, each one followed by far more lengthy interpretations and observations composed by her husband, Robert. In all three cases, the women's names only appear in print to be used to urge modesty and acceptance of duty.

It was not only when confronted by the fear of their own imminent demise, however, that Puritans assessed their chances of salvation. In the early 1650s, compilations of 'conversion experiences' were published by Henry Walker, Vavasor Power, Samuel Petto and John Rogers. These 'confessions', many of which were made by women, are professions of faith made by individuals seeking to join a specific Independent congregation. For an experience to be accepted as a genuine guarantee of salvation, it would have to fall within a specific pattern: otherwise the conversion might be a false one, and the sinner caught in the hypocrisy of a false confidence in their salvation. As Owen Watkins has demonstrated in *The Puritan Experience,* the conversion narrative rapidly established its own conventions, a particular pattern of false confidence, doubt, and renewed, true confidence coming to be seen as the necessary sequence in achieving genuine salvation, permitting admission to a gathering of Saints. This structure came to be so surely accepted as proof of true deliverance that Elizabeth Moore cited the fact that God had taken her through the same processes as those reported by other converts as evidence of her own Sainthood.[3] It was probably the same conviction of the inevitability of a specific pattern that led the editor of Sarah Davy's posthumous *Heaven Realiz'd* to divide it into sections, the headings of which trace a formal development that bears little relation to the actual content of the text.

The conventions of spiritual autobiography both provided an acceptable reason for women to write about their experiences, and established a framework through which they could order and make sense of disparate elements of their lives. On the whole, however, it was not possible for women themselves to publish their own accounts. These spiritual autobiographies were often published posthumously and they enter the public domain more carefully surrounded by a bevy of masculine praise, exhortation and interpretation than any other body of women's writing in the period. Anne Venn's *A Wise Virgins Lamp Burning,* for instance, although clearly written with a readership of Christians in mind, was not published until her parents found the manuscript in her closet after her death. It is prefaced by a recommendation from her congregation's minister, Thomas Weld, who hopes it will serve as an example of desirable female behaviour, even if 'to thy knowledge it should not add much'.[4]

The writings most excused and qualified by male approval include those by Sarah Wight, Jane Turner and Anne Venn. Sarah Wight had first entered the arena of public scrutiny in 1647 when, at the age of fifteen, she had fallen into a trance. She had arisen from this periodically to quote scripture or to converse with some of the crowds who came to observe her. Henry Jessey's best-selling description of this period of her life, *The Exceeding Riches of Grace,* includes a list of almost thirty ministers and over fifty 'persons of note' who came to visit her.[5] She was the ideal model of the divinely inspired woman, humbly submitting to being used as God's tool, and not presuming to speak on the issues of state politics that should lie beyond her scope. Unlike her fellow seer Anna Trapnel, she represented no threat to the civil authorities. It is consistent with this that her only publication should have found its way into print without her prior knowledge. (Perhaps the bookseller, Richard Moone, was hopeful that *A Wonderful Pleasant and Profitable Letter Written by Mrs Sarah Wight* would sell as well as Jessey's work about her had.) Although her *Letter* is of prodigious length—about fourteen thousand words—it shows no sign of having been written with any audience in mind other than the friend (minister Robert Bragg?) to whom it is addressed.[6] It records the stages of her conversion, and consists mainly of a detailed exposition of Christian doctrine, starting from the premise that 'A Christian's true happiness lies in being emptied of all self, self refined, as well as gross self; and being filled with a full God' (p. 5).

Jane Turner's *Choice Experiences* portray a woman far less hemmed in by male approbation, who nonetheless needs masculine endorsement for publication of her work. For her, a personal relationship with God engendered not passive submission but a new activity and responsibility for vigilance against backsliding. She explains

> In the work of conversion we are passive, I mean as to inward spiritual activity, we can do nothing being dead . . . But after conversion we are active, and therefore commanded to keep ourselves in the love of God.
>
> (p. 189)

Even her description of the 'passivity' of conversion itself is only a conventional acceptance of the tenet that it is God who calls the sinner, and decides who is to be saved. This quiescence does not mean that she should make no initial effort to find the truth. Her third 'Note of Experience' relates how she had read and rejected some unnamed book promoting the new theology. When her Presbyterian minister later preached against the text, however, and talked about it in terms which differed from her recollection of its contents, she went to considerable lengths to acquire another copy of this banned text. Finding that the minister had indeed misrepresented the book was a key element in her decision to change her religious allegiances (pp. 49-53).

It has frequently been noted that the ideas of the sects allowed women some measure of autonomy from their husbands. Quite what this could mean becomes apparent when we examine the writings of the women themselves. Jane Turner's husband, in fact, always enters the text as an afterthought. Only once she has pondered an issue and made her decision does it occur to her to discuss it with him. It is quite in accordance with this sense of separateness that she should have been writing her *Choice Experiences* without her husband's knowledge, and that his first sight of the book should have been when it was nearly finished (dedicatory epistle).

Jane Turner writes to be useful. Having found reading helpful in her own soul's growth, she wants the record of her experiences to profit others. Despite her disclaimer in her 'word from the author to the reader' that the thought of publication had never occurred to her, the text exhibits many signs that it was written with a public in mind. Details of her narrative are frequently omitted with the observation that it is fitting only to 'hint' at them, and a thorough attempt is made to order the story, referring the reader back and fore to other passages. This care for her work and attention to a reader's needs might even have extended to following it through the press, as more than one of these directions to the reader refers her/him to specific page numbers.

The lengthy prefaces to *Choice Experiences,* written by John Turner and two ministers, John Spilsbury and John Gardner, indicate the existence of a dispute within their church concerning the role of women. (Spilsbury's congregation were an offshoot of the Jacob group of churches in London. The group's membership ranged from the conservative Henry Jessey, who wrote the account of Sarah Wight's famous trance described above, to the radical Katherine Chidley, who was centrally involved in the pamphleteering by Leveller women in the 1640s.[7]) Jane Turner complains that her greatest discouragements have come from the Saints even while affirming her belief that 'such brethren only whose gifts are approved of by the church, may exercise their gifts publicly, and no other' (p. 7). She is determined that such approval should be given to her, and cautions her fellows 'to take heed of casting stumbling blocks in each other's way', and to leave the final selection of the Chosen to God (p. 8). It is only with the explicit backing of Spilsbury, and her husband's attesting to her modesty and his 'owning' of her work, that publication can be countenanced. The alternative would be to align herself with the more radical Quakers, whose advocacy of Inner Light she examines, and finally rejects as impermissible, in the course of her experiences (pp. 111-30). Having made her way into print, the conclusion of the text (which might well be the section written after her husband had seen and approved the work) contains a general reflection on the meaning of the concept of 'experience' and her recommendations on specific issues, such as the status of the church's younger members (pp. 193-207). Within the confines of her church, she gained the time to write carefully and at length about weighty matters, and was able to negotiate a route into print.

The pattern of the conversion experience could provide a framework to make sense of various crises in the course of a lifetime, and resulted in widely different reminiscences being written. In the case of these women writers, the experiences of falling in love, marrying and childbearing—events commonly regarded as key stages in female existence—were frequent matters of concern. The unifying factor of conversion allowed such issues to be understood and written about, and justified publication. Sarah Davy's reminiscences centre on the terror produced by her falling in love with a minister, another woman. Susannah Bell uses her text to work out the requirements of wifely duty, and Elizabeth White writes to produce a vision of marriage that discounts the relevance of romantic love. In Hannah Allen's account, finally, the usefulness of the written word itself, and of the conversion narrative framework in particular, are brought into doubt, though finally reaffirmed. Since almost all the texts under discussion here were published posthumously, the writers shared the problem that a third party had to be convinced, through the format of the conversion experience, of the potential interest of publishing a woman's work.[8]

Sarah Davy's 'precious relics', *Heaven Realiz'd,* were published by her minister Anthony Palmer, who recommends them as a model to be imitated by 'younger persons (especially young gentlewomen)', in the hope that they will help to stem the rise of atheism.[9]

Davy describes her early life as a period of great loneliness and isolation, during which time her mother and baby brother died and she passed through a crisis of faith. The turning point comes when she meets the person who effects her conversion to an Independent congregation. Her depiction of this, and of her subsequent heartache at being parted from her new-found friend, is in language which conjures up associations of romantic love. Release from misery arrives when she joins the Independent church her friend belonged to. God then addresses her directly, as recorded in one of her meditations.

> Did not I first love you? and therefore give you this new commandment, that as I have loved you so you should love one another, with a pure unbounded love . . . to love one another as I have loved you, or to love thy friend, as thou lovest thyself, most willingly to do that which may be for thy friend's good, although it be to some prejudice to thyself, this is love and by this you shall know that you are my disciples.
>
> (p. 37)

This divine command gives licence to love 'although it be to some prejudice to thyself', justifying to Davy and her reader a relationship which is taboo, since the friend who gave her so many 'sweet refreshments' (p. 21) was another woman. This female friend first enters *Heaven Realiz'd* in a passage which at first avoids assigning gender, dwelling on the religious significance of the encounter.

> One day the Lord was pleased by a strange providence to cast me into the company of one that I never saw before, but of a sweet and free disposition, and whose discourse savoured so much of the gospel, that I could not but at that instant bless God for his goodness in that providence. It pleased the Lord to carry out our hearts towards one another at that time, and a little while after, the Lord was pleased to bring us together again for the space of three days, in which time it pleased God by our much discourse together, to establish and confirm me more in the desires I had to join with the people of God in society, and enjoy communion with them according to the way of the gospel. She was of a society of the Congregational way called Independents . . . Then were our hearts firmly united, and I blessed the Lord from my soul for so glorious and visible an appearance of his love.
>
> (pp. 20-1)

Peace, the end of Davy's story, and the beginning of the possibility of writing about it, arrive when, having joined her friend's Independent church, she abandons this forbidden love and marries. She writes no meditations on wedded love.

The other longing that fills Davy's text is the desire to be useful in her life. She learns that this can be achieved by making herself the wholly passive instrument of God's will, and urges him to accept her converted soul: 'make me useful to thee in that way or any way thou shalt be pleased to choose' (p. 29). It is this submission to God's bidding that permits her both to be united with her friend, if only for a while, and to write the meditations which are finally published. By writing about the episode, she is able to make sense of it, and integrate it into an acceptable interpretation of the world. She had begun by puzzling over 'the need I had of my troubles' (p. 5). By accepting the logic of conversion she ends a Saint, a married woman and, once dead, a published author.

Susannah Bell's *Legacy of a Dying Mother* was also published by her church minister, the Independent Thomas Brooks.[10] Bell's account of her experiences was, Brooks tells us, written down by one of her sons as she spoke it on her deathbed. The 'Epistle Dedicatory' by Brooks which prefaces the story in fact fills two thirds of the book (pp. 1-43). He holds Bell up as a model of humility, who faithfully continued to justify the Lord during her suffering. Her acts of charity, earnest desires for the salvation of her friends and family, and loving behaviour to poor miscarrying Christians all gain a mention. She is presented as both virtuous and self-denying, the ideal woman.

The 'conversion experiences' which follow are as much concerned with Bell's conversion to the merits of wifely duty as they are with more mystical matters. She tells how when her husband had first wanted to go to New England she had resisted his will, as she had a small child and was heavily pregnant with another. The Lord reminds her of the command 'Wives submit yourselves unto your own husbands, as unto the Lord', and she submits. She has seen the error of her ways too late, however, and the second child dies. God tells her that this has happened as a punishment for her disobedience. She informs her husband of her decision to accompany him after all, and by the time they set out she is again 'big with child' (pp. 45-7). Most of the rest of the narrative is concerned with her life in New England, while her husband travels back and forth between the two countries. She has become a good wife and Christian, and is soon allowed to join the local church. She sees it as a reward for this godly behaviour that her family are not hurt by an earthquake, and that on their return to England they survive the Plague and the Great Fire (pp. 59-61). The only disturbance to this surface contentment comes during one of her husband's trips back to England. While he is there, war breaks out, and Susannah Bell's neighbours fear that he might have been killed. This, too, she accepts with cheerful resignation, telling them 'If God should take my husband out of the world, I should have a husband in heaven, which was best of all' (pp. 55-6).

The manuscript of Elizabeth White's *The Experiences of Gods Gracious Dealing* was found after her decease, as Anne Venn's had been, in her closet.[11] The reasons she gives for her writing are the same as those of the authors of meditations and conversion experiences: memory of God's goodness will support her in times of darkness, and prevent her forgetting its details. The text will remind her that 'he only hath wrought my works in me, for of myself I am not able to think a good thought, speak a good word, or do a good action' (pp. 21-2).

Her story follows the usual conversion narrative format of progress from ignorance and self-deception through spiritual torment to the acquisition of true confidence in her salvation. The experiences she describes, however, like those that Bell and Davy depict, are problems caused by love and childbearing. Her first crisis of faith occurs immediately before her marriage, the second about fifteen months later when she is expecting the birth of her first child. The wrongdoing which preoccupies her thoughts at both these times is the fact that she had spent so much time in her youth reading 'histories [i.e. romances], and other foolish books'.[12]

> I was a great lover of histories, and other foolish books, and did often spend my sleeping-time in reading of them, and sometimes I should think I did not do well in so doing, but I was so bewitched by them, that I could not forbear; and hearing of a friend of mine, which was esteemed a very holy woman, that did delight in histories, I then concluded it was no sin, and gave myself wholly then to this kind of folly, when I had any spare time, for two or three years. I had sometimes slight thoughts of repentance, but was loath to set about it.
>
> (p. 3)

Such reading might seem a venial enough sin, unless we reflect that the subject-matter of these romances which had so obsessed her was a glorification of the joys of love. Perhaps the reality had not matched up to her expectations. Certainly the thought that dominates as her confinement approaches is the fear that she will perish in childbed: 'I was much dejected, having a sense of my approaching danger' (p. 11). After giving birth, she has a vision and then a dream which confirm that she will die. While still convalescing from the birth, she finds release from fear by writing of 'God's Gracious Dealings' with her. As the title page informs the reader, she did then die in childbed, like many of her contemporaries (see Chapter Seven).

The introductory remarks to Hannah Allen's *Satan his Methods and Malice Baffled* seem to be written by a church minister and direct the reader to the expected interpretation of her story: melancholy is physical in its origins, but the devil can use this 'malady' to his own ends. Hannah Allen's experiences are to be understood as the tale of her overcoming, with God's help, Satan's temptations to despair and self-destruction. This interpretation of her story is remarkable in view of the fact that the problem the narrative centres on is the failure of this religious framework to explain or relieve Hannah Allen's state of mind.

Allen's story begins conventionally enough: she records being raised by religious parents, undergoing early doubts about her salvation, and finding relief and new hope when reading a book by Mr Bolton. After her marriage in 1655 or 1656 at the age of seventeen to a merchant, Hannibal Allen, she joined Edmund Calamy's church (pp. 1-6). Eight years later her husband died on one of his many foreign voyages, and she 'began to fall into a deep melancholy' (p. 7). She turned to the established routines of her religion to lift her depression, seeking evidence that she was one of the saved and could look forward to an eternity of bliss. Attempting to relieve her melancholy, Hannah Allen reread her diary, seeking proof that her writing had served some useful purpose and that her belief in her salvation was not 'hypocrisy'.

> Then I would repeat several promises to my condition, and read over my former experiences that I had writ down, as is hereafter expressed, and obligations that I had laid upon myself, in the presence of God, and would say, 'Aunt, I hope I write not these things in hypocrisy, I never intended any eye should see them; but the devil suggesteth dreadful things to me against God, and that I am an hypocrite'.
>
> (pp. 8-9)

Despite all the comforts her diary offered, her depression deepened. The Bible, too, failed to assuage her misery: 'When I had seen the Bible, I would say, "Oh that blessed book that I so delighted in once!"' (p. 9). Travelling between friends and relatives, and seeking spiritual counsel, she found no comfort and ceased bothering to keep her record of God's marks of favour to her, and began to despair. As she began to have dreams and visions confirming her doom, and found no relief in writing or in reading the Bible, she forbade her son to read and spurned the written word herself.

> Nor could I endure to be present at prayer, or any other part of God's worship, nor to hear the sound of reading, nor the sight of a book or paper; though it were but a letter, or an almanac . . . I would wish I had never seen book, or learned letter; I would say 'It had been happy for me if I had been born blind'; daily repeating my accustomed language, that I was a cursed reprobate, and the monster of the creation.
>
> (pp. 58, 59)

Throughout the time of her melancholy, which lasted about three years, she made a series of dramatic suicide attempts, smoking a pipeful of spiders (generally believed to be venomous) to poison herself (p. 33); trying to starve herself to death but losing courage (p. 36); cutting her arm so as to bleed to death (p. 44).

She gives no real explanation for the cessation of these efforts at self-destruction, or how her despair lifted. After about three years the melancholy began to leave her, she records,

> and then I changed much from my retiredness, and delighted to walk with friends abroad . . . And this spring it pleased God to provide a very suitable match for me, one Mr Charles Hatt, a widower living in Warwickshire; with whom I live very comfortably, both as to my inward and outward man, my husband being one that truly fears God.
>
> (p. 71)

Her religion had provided no explanation for the arrival of her melancholy at her first husband's death, and produced no reason for its leaving her at her remarriage. Nonetheless, with the problem gone the experience could be written about, and an attempt made to fit it into the accepted pattern of false confidence, doubt and new, true knowledge of salvation. The text ends by quoting a series of biblical passages selected to make sense of events in such a framework.

> Fear not: for I have redeemed thee, I have called thee by thy name; thou art mine. When thou passest through the water, I will be with thee; and through the rivers, they shall not overflow thee: when thou walkest through the fire, thou shalt not be burned; neither shall the flame kindle upon thee. Isaiah 43.1-2.
>
> Behold, we count them happy which endure. Ye have heard of the patience of Job, and have seen the end of the Lord: that the Lord is very pitiful and of tender mercy. James, 5.11.
>
> Ye are of God, little children, and have overcome them: because greater is he that is in you, than he that is in the world. 1 John, 4.4.

With the experience itself removed, the written word can be allowed once again to reinterpret its significance.

These books of religious poetry, meditations and conversion experiences indicate that even such apparently narrow and formulaic genres could be used by women to justify their writing. Also, it is clear that women were able to use the available formats to explore subject-matter that might be taboo, and that they wrote about love, marriage and their relationships with women and men in ways which challenge fundamentally the impressions of female existence that can be gleaned from male texts. The religious poetry, particularly, shows that women were not at all convinced that love and marriage were in their own best interests. Nonetheless, texts had to be publishable, and their female authors found it necessary to negotiate some acceptable way of existing within the constraints of the society in which they lived. The struggle to find a solution provides the dynamic of the texts themselves. Women daring to examine closely the limits of female behaviour are forced in their writing to reaffirm femininity, their texts becoming both an exploration of its constraints and an analysed self-policing which vindicates the fetters of feminine duty. The authorial personae that emerge in the process are model women, held up for admiration and emulation. The contradictions of this position are neatly expressed in *Eliza's Babes* in a couplet addressed by the author both to her God and to her poetry itself: 'My boundless spirits, bounded be in thee, / For bounded by no other can they be' (p. 36).

Notes

1. *Divine Songs and Meditacions* is unpaginated, and many of the poems are entitled simply 'Another Song'. I have therefore referred to such verses by quoting the first line as well as the title. A modern facsimile of part of Collins's book has been printed by the Augustan Reprint Society.
2. Mary Simpson's account is published with the sermon preached at her funeral by John Collings, in *Faith and Experience*. Sermons preached at women's funerals might prove a rich source of forgotten women's writings.
3. Edmund Calamy, *The Godly Man's Ark,* p. 203.
4. 'Dedicatory Epistle' by Thomas Weld. In this same year, Weld published a defence of his doctrines, after his refusal to baptise children had led him into trouble with other church officers. The Council of State removed his opponents. For details, see Michael Watts, *The Dissenters,* Oxford, 1978. Perhaps this incident encouraged Weld to publish Venn's writings and use them to promote his own theological position. She had died four years previously.
5. See Dorothy Ludlow, '"Arise and Be Doing": English "Preaching" Women, 1640-1660', unpublished PhD thesis, Indiana University, 1978; Murray Tolmie, *The Triumph of the Saints,* 1977; Watts, op. cit.
6. Ludlow, op. cit., p. 159.
7. Tolmie, op. cit.; H. N. Brailsford, *The Levellers and the English Revolution,* ed. Christopher Hill, 1961.
8. According to Owen Watkins, *The Puritan Experience: Studies in Spiritual Autobiography,* 1972, after 1670 almost all the printed conversion experiences written by men were also posthumous publications.
9. The prefatory remarks to Davy's text are signed 'A. P.'. A likely identity for this anonymous Baptist minister is Anthony Palmer of Pinners' Hall, London.
10. Brooks, along with Jessey, was one of the supporters of the 1647 *Declaration by Congregational Societies in and about London,* which 'solemnly repudiated polygamy, and community of property, and . . . defined liberty exclusively in terms of religious liberty' (Tolmie, op. cit., pp. 170-1).
11. Many diary manuscripts were discovered and printed in private editions in the nineteenth century. See, for instance, *The Priuate Diarie of Elizabeth, Vicountess Mordaunt.*
12. See also chapter 3 for a related discussion of Mary Rich.

WILLIAM J. SCHEICK (ESSAY DATE 1998)

SOURCE: Scheick, William J. "Captivity and Liberation." In *Authority and Female Authorship in Colonial America,* pp. 82-106. Lexington: The University Press of Kentucky, 1998.

In the following essay, Scheick analyzes two captivity narratives written by Elizabeth Hanson and Elizabeth Ashbridge.

The instances of logonomic conflict we have reviewed to this point occur in works written by Congregationalist and Presbyterian authors. As my discussion peripherally indicates, these women are by no means perfectly aligned in every aspect of their Reformed beliefs. Mary English and Anne Bradstreet do not share precisely the same cultural heritage or, perhaps, Congregationalist ideas, which were far from monolithic even at the start of the Puritan enterprise in England (Foster 1991). And compared with Bradstreet and English, Esther Edwards Burr reflects a more liberating exposure to both Presbyterian dogma and eighteenth-century thought, while at the same time in some important respects she also seems, in contrast to them, less able to accommodate the validation of secular interests. Nevertheless, whether conservative or liberal, these authors collectively share a Calvinistic reading of existence and a Puritan context for coming to terms with their identity as women. It is not surprising, therefore, that their writings should mutually reflect similar problems in self-expression and aesthetics despite some variation in authorial contexts.

We turn now to two Quaker women—Elizabeth Hanson (1684-1737) and Elizabeth Ashbridge (1713-55)—to consider whether they were more successful in negotiating the theocratic logonomic system in which they lived. It is reasonable to raise this possibility because in many important respects Quaker women, in comparison to their Congregationalist and Presbyterian peers, enjoyed a greater opportunity for enhancing their self-esteem (Edkins 1980). They found this opportunity within both the theological beliefs and the social structures of the Society of Friends.

Outside the Friends, of course, they were pariahs, as is attested by the well-known history of their persecution in many of the colonies. To their adversaries, Quaker women were whorish vagabonds, polluters of religious faith, and irrational opponents of both civil and ecclesiastical authority (Koehler 1980, 246-53). All of these charges readily converged in the handy suspicion that Quaker women routinely practiced witchcraft (288). Their adversaries often believed, in short, that male and female Quakers alike spoke in Satanic double-talk, not in Pentecostal tongues.

And speak they did, especially women, who found in Quakerism a communal legitimation of their voice. Similar to the early Christians, with whom the Quakers identified (Bowden 1850, 1:30), persecution from without strengthened communal bonding from within, even to the extent of encouraging the formation of a pantheon of Quaker martyrs. Within this community, Quaker women found an identity and voice unlike any offered by other colonial Christian sects. This greater liberation of female identity made Quakerism particularly attractive to women. For some women, it has been suggested (Koehler 1980, 258), Quakerism seems to have cured depression. More generally, however, it appealed to those who desired to breach some of the restraints placed upon their gender by the prevalent social structures of their day.

In fact, as was the case with Mary Fisher and Anne Austin (the first Quakers in the colonies, both jailed on the charge of witchcraft in 1656), Quaker women could serve as preachers, authorized to speak as men. During Oliver Cromwell's Protectorate, an apprehensive House of Commons affirmed that only officially ordained males may preach (Otten 1992, 358), but growing numbers of English Quaker women persisted in the practice and later even defended it in print. Such publications as Margaret Fell's *Womens Speaking Justified, Proved and Allowed of by the Scriptures* (1666, 1667), Anne Whitehead and Mary Elson's *An Epistle for True Love, Unity, and Order in the Church of Christ* (1680), and Mary Waite's *Epistle from the Women's Yearly Meeting at New York* (1688) anticipated the many eighteenth-century defenses of the practice that were to follow, all of which advanced the early case made by George Fox.

Fox, the first major proponent of Quaker beliefs, pointed to scriptural examples of female preachers. He understood Saint Paul's equation of the sexes in Galatians to refer to the quotidian, not only to the afterlife, as we saw Congregationalist minister Cotton Mather insist in *Ornaments for the Daughters of Zion*. Fox did acknowledge Saint Paul's comment that "women keep silence in the churches: for it is not permitted unto them to speak" (1 Cor. 14:34), but unlike Mather, who cited this same passage specifically against female Quakers, Fox unconventionally interpreted the Pauline admonishment to refer only to ignorant women (Sewel 1800, 2:1636), women who had not been illuminated by the Inward Light, "the true Light, which lighteth every man" (John 1:9).

Since female Quakers were, in theory if not always in custom (Berkin 1996, 91-97), thoroughly equal to men, should not their writings transcend the kind of authoritarian dissonance evident in documents by contemporary Congregational and Presbyterian women? Not necessarily, as we shall see in this chapter on Hanson's captivity narrative and Ashbridge's autobiography. Although some features change, especially assumptions pertaining to gender parity, logonomic conflict nonetheless oddly surfaces at critical junctures in both Hanson's oral report and Ashbridge's transcribed account.

Given their view of female evangelizing, the dwindling but still prominent notion that public expression, especially writing, was principally a male province was not likely a significant constituent of the conflictive negotiation of orthodox and personal authority in works by female Quakers as it was for Bradstreet and Burr. We might reasonably surmise, however, that part of what these women tried to surmount—particularly the prevalent colonial view of women as the weaker sex and the Reformed theocratic devaluation of human attachments in general—constituted a kind of authoritarian static within their more "emancipated" contemplation of the Quaker idea of woman.

Elizabeth Hanson's Captivity Narrative

Elizabeth Hanson's *God's Mercy Surmounting Man's Cruelty* (1728) is today not the most well-known colonial captivity narrative, but it was sufficiently popular before 1800 to go through thirteen editions at home and various reprints abroad (Derounian-Stodola and Levernier 1993, 14). In later editions, of which there also were many, it was variously modified by others for both propagandistic and marketing purposes (VanDerBeets 1984, 16, 25-26). Whereas the American versions bear the initials "E. H.," the English editions are said to have been "taken in substance from her own mouth" by Samuel Bownas, an English Quaker divine. Bownas's actual role is uncertain, however. More certain is the claim of the first American edition to be a transcription of an earlier account written by a friend to whom Hanson told her story. Hanson, by her own admission "not . . . capable of keeping a journal" (Vaughan and Clark 1981, 244), was one of the many colonial women who could not write in the early eighteenth century.

Although the first American edition claims to "differ . . . very little from the original copy, but is even almost in her own words" (231), the "almost" insists that the published version is in fact a revision of the amanuensis's written account of the oral report. To be borne in mind, as well, is the eighteenth-century Quaker practice of collective authorship, an editorial procedure that "refines" Quaker works, including John Woolman's journal (Fichtelberg 1989, 77-80), to reflect ideal communal values. (The assumption that Hanson was a Quaker is based not only on Bownas's editorial presence in the English edition but also on her husband's religion and her explicit attack on Puritan clergy [q.v. Vaughan and Clark 1981, 241].) Such cautionary considerations about the fidelity of the text to Hanson's intention are important to remember when basing any argument on her report in its published form.

In spite of these reservations, the first American edition conveys, in narrative terms at least, a sense of overall authenticity. It is not polished in any literary way, a fact that might make the work seem uninspired to latter-day readers. The manner of its expression and design is minimalist, but this very same lack of embellishment and grace imparts a sense of genuineness to the book. Moreover, even if one or more Quaker editors possibly oversaw even the American document, they would in all likelihood not have interfered with Hanson's scriptural allusions, save perhaps to make them accurate. Even the private journals and personal letters of colonial women indicate, we should recall here, an extensive use of biblical allusion, especially the scriptural loci they encountered by way of the pulpit, discussion groups, and books. Accordingly, the biblical allusions in *God's Mercy Surmounting Man's Cruelty* are altogether likely Hanson's selections. And that they become sites of logonomic conflict similar in effect to those of her Congregationalist female peers further testifies on behalf of their authenticity as her own choices.

After having witnessed the slaying of two of her young children, Elizabeth Hanson, her two teenage daughters, her six-year-old son, and her maid were taken captive in Dover Township in August 1724, and forced to journey to French Canada. During the ordeal of this trek, Hanson's family sustained a series of further divisions. First her eldest daughter Sarah was "carried to another part of the country far distant from" her; then the captors "divided again, taking [her] second daughter [Elizabeth] and servant maid from" her (234-35). Before long, her "daughter and servant were likewise parted" (235). She would have lost the child born to her during this captivity had not tribal women aided her in preventing its starvation.

Hanson and her two remaining children are ransomed by a Frenchman, whose civility surprises her (given traditional English vilification of the French). She is reunited with her husband, who also eventually "recovers" the younger daughter. And she finally witnesses the successfulness of her husband's refusal "to omit anything for [the] redemption" of "his dear daughter Sarah," who is on the verge of being married to a young Native American. However, as Hanson's family is painstakingly nearly reunited, it sustains one more substantial division. While seeking Sarah's liberation, her husband succumbs to an illness "in the wilderness" about "halfway between Albany and Canada" (243).

In short, the redemption of Hanson's family, its restoration to its wholeness prior to its traumatic rupture and subsequent divisions, never occurs. Two small children and a father are dead as a result of these events, and the remaining family members simply can never re-form the unit it once comprised. Hanson's family is, finally, at once reconstructed and fragmented, and this dichotomous condition henceforth defines the curious identity of her "redeemed" family.

Dichotomy likewise characterizes her overall response. On the surface, as the title of her little book indicates, she celebrates God's mercy in these providential events; below the surface, she unofficially registers an elegiac sense of loss akin to Bradstreet's in "Upon the Burning of Our House." The official, ventriloquized voice of praise observes, for example, that "though my own children's loss [of their father] is very great, yet I doubt not but his gain is much more" (243). Here the unauthorized, personal voice of mourning is evaded, consigned to the children (rather than herself) and to the anterior, the seemingly "left behind," portion of her figure of speech. In Hanson's use of *antithesis,* a neoclassical favorite for balancing one term against the other, proscribed sentiment appears to be prescriptively relinquished through the turn of a phrase. In a significant sense, of course, the ostensibly abandoned first part of this figure of speech (and its sentiment) lingers elegylike in the second part because the rhetorical play of the second part always depends on and points back to the first part for its effect and meaning.

A related interaction of public conviction and private sentiment can be detected more clearly when Hanson says at the end of her narrative that she "supplicat[es] the God and Father of all our mercies to be a father to [her] fatherless children" (243). To implore the Lord of mercy to serve as the father of the children, whom this same Lord mercilessly made fatherless, is an odd sentiment embodied here in a figure of speech (*ploce*) designed to negotiate Hanson's contrary feelings. The repetition of the word "father," commingling biblical and secular contexts, becomes a logonomic site subtly recording Hanson's resistant elegiac voice beneath the louder and more apparent expression of her acceptance of loss.

Sensitivity to this other voice here and in related instances in Hanson's book is stimulated by an indicative comment immediately preceding her unintentionally bivocal references to fatherhood: "I, therefore, desire and pray that the Lord will enable me patiently to submit to His will in all things" (243). Here her own sense of loss is not displaced, not attributed to her children. Here the conscious, official desire to submit counters an illegitimate desire to mourn. Hanson prays for patient acquiescence because by the end of her account she is apparently still unable to let go of the anterior, antithetical portion of her experience and narrative.

Earlier she had admitted her concern about "repining against God under [her] affliction"; at that time she "found it very hard to keep [her] mind as [she] ought under the resignation which is proper to be in under such afflictions and sore trials" (236). And this perfectly natural, if doctrinally illicit, response haunts the end of her tale when she speaks of needing divine empowerment if she is truly to resign herself to divine will. To grieve, after all, is not to submit to this will, for grieving is a form of resistance urged by unsanctioned sentiment. So at the close of her book the word "desire" becomes a site of conflict, a locus of an anxious negotiation of two opposite dispositions: resistant personal sorrow and submissive orthodox acceptance.

Hanson's desire for a sanctioned resignation she has yet to find not only calls attention to the experiential persistence of her grief but also erodes her narrational celebration of emancipation from coerced submission. In effect, her captivity narrative concludes in a mutually constitutive opposition: by praising God for liberating her from a captivity that separated her from her family; and, at the same time, by imploring God for a new captivity that would remove her from liberated, unlicensed feelings. If her family is not restored because all of its "divisions" cannot be temporally undone, if her precaptive state of mind is not restored because all of its dichotomous sentiments cannot be resolved, Hanson's captivity narrative likewise does not come full circle to restore her previous comfortable state of mind because it expresses a divided state of mind. Instead of restoration, in *God's Mercy Surmounting Man's Cruelty* one mode of bondage gives way to conditions that engender Hanson's earnest ache for another mode of captivity.

In this regard, Hanson's allusion to the Babylonian Captivity conveys more than she likely understood. During their wilderness trek, her daughter Sarah recites Psalm 137:1-3: "By the rivers of Babylon there we sat down, yea we wept when we remembered Zion; . . . there they that carried us away captives required of us a song" (233). Hope is communicated in this application of Scripture, hope to the effect that like the Jews under Cyrus (the conqueror of Babylon) the Hanson captives (likewise on the verge of "repining against God") will one day be freed from a "strange land" (Ps. 137:4) to return home and restore the temple of their previous confident faith. This is doubtless the analogy Hanson had in mind, although as we have seen at the end of her account, the comfort of both her home and her faith has not been fully recovered.

Indeed, it would seem—despite Hanson's probable ignorance of the detail—that the allusion aptly associates her final failure to escape the locus of her captivity (reinscribed through both an expressed concern with a lingering grief and a desire for a divinely imposed recapture) with those many Jews who never left Babylon after their emancipation. For them, as for the mourning part of Hanson's mind, the former theocratic home rather than the locality of captivity had become the strange land. The difference, of course, is that these Jews stayed voluntarily, whereas Hanson's continuing thralldom to grief in her life is as involuntary as is the persistent echo of Davidian lamentation throughout her narrative.

This issue of volition likewise emerges at a crucial moment of logonomic conflict in the final sentence of Hanson's book: "I have given a short but a true account of some of the remarkable trials and wonderful deliverances which I never purposed to expose but that I hope thereby the merciful kindness and goodness of God may be magnified, and the reader hereof provoked with more care and fear to serve Him in righteousness and humility, and then my designed end and purpose will be answered" (244). There is much here that is conventional, but of special interest is the allusion to Mary's canticle embracing her maternal role, replete with future sorrow, in the birth of Jesus: "My soul doth magnify the Lord" (Luke 1:46). This alignment with Mary, one far more comfortable for Hanson than it is for contemporaneous Congregationalist women, represents her conscious desire; at the same time, however, it peculiarly underscores a key difference between Elizabeth Hanson and Mary. Mary's submission is totally voluntary and achieved, whereas Elizabeth's is coerced and incomplete.

Hanson has not been given a choice as to whether or not she would play a role in a course of events that would result in the demise of her two children and her husband. She has, on the contrary, been given, and is expected to resign herself to, a providential fait accompli. As a result, the allusion to Mary's acquiescence to divine will is bivocal within the dual contexts of Hanson's narrative; it expresses Hanson's wish to conform to a licensed theocratic ideal of humility and voluntary submission, and it also inadvertently intimates another concurrent desire to align with an illicit personal sentiment of grief and its involuntary resistance to any renunciation of temporal loss.

It is, in fact, a curious feature of *God's Mercy Surmounting Man's Cruelty* that the language Hanson uses to describe her involuntary enslavement crosses over into the language she uses to describe her relationship with the deity. There is nothing typological or deliberate in this association; it is incidental and unwitting, albeit it possibly intimates Hanson's repressed personal sentiment. In response to her situation, Hanson fashions the following statements: "I must go or die. There was no resistance" (Vaughan and Clark 1981, 232); "This was a sore grief to us all. But we must submit" (234); "I dreaded the tragical design of my master" (237). These remarks refer to her Native American captors, but aside from their specific textual emplacement, these remarks are strikingly similar to her sense of both "having no other way but to cast [her] care upon God" and "the overruling power of Him in whose Providence [she] put [her] trust" (239). No wonder that at the end of her narrative she seeks a new form of captivity, seeks to be made "to submit to His will in all things"; for given the danger to the spiritual life of her soul occasioned by rebellious bitter feelings of resistant grief, once again she "must go or die. There was no resistance."

Hanson is doubtless straightforward when she openly declares her "designed end and purpose" as the stimulation of her reader's humble submission (like Mary's) to a God of "merciful deliverance[s]" (239). Nevertheless, the elegiac voice lingering throughout her account, and inadvertently countering the primary theme of God's "merciful kindness and goodness," implies a different "end and purpose." At moments of dichotomizing logonomic conflict, such as the allusion to Mary's voluntary willingness to magnify the Lord through submission, Hanson's bivocality includes another story altogether, a story she can barely articulate. This story concerns not the physical miseries she endured, but specifically the mental "afflictions [that] are not to be set forth in words to the extent of them" (236). They cannot be so "set forth" because the feelings they arouse surpass the capacity of language and, more important, are theocratically prohibited.

This illegitimate other story, as fatherless as Hanson's children, concerns lost sweetness and found bitterness. This underground version of her tale opposes the orthodox moral extracted from such an observation as "None knows what they can undergo till they are tried, for what I had thought in my own family not fit for food would here have been a dainty dish and sweet morsel" (238). The moral analogue for this passage surfaces earlier in Hanson's report when, apropos the captives being given pieces of old beaver skin to eat, she cites Proverbs 27:7: "to the hungry soul every bitter thing is sweet" (234). Contemplating the demise of her husband, she publicly asserts this sweetness—"his gain is much more"—while she privately husbands "the bitterness of death" (237). Before her captivity, she had not been hungry in either her physical or spiritual life. After her experiences in the wilderness, she indeed has become a hungry soul who laments the loss of her husband and who consequently requires divine force to make her accept "the bitterness of death." For Hanson, if we listen to her faint outlawed voice, the bitterness of dispossession in her life has hardly been translated into a gracious sweetness in her soul, even as the end of her captivity has hardly resulted in the "sweet" restoration of her family life or the "gracious" resolution of her narrative. Hanson may have wished to endorse the words that immediately follow Mary's express choice to magnify the Lord—"He hath filled the hungry with good things"

(Luke 1:46)—but certain embedded resistant features of her experience and her story insist otherwise.

Although Hanson is a Quaker, the effects we have reviewed in her book are similar to those in the well-known captivity narrative by Congregationalist Mary Rowlandson (c. 1635-post 1678). Rowlandson's *Sovereignty and Goodness of God* (1682) likewise evidences an undeclared tension between the experience of woe and its displacement through sanctioned moral representation (Breitwieser 1990, 10; Logan 1993). There are, as well, moments of logonomic conflict, especially when the Bible is cited. Such moments contain unidentified discrepancies between what actually happens and what is quoted by way of explanation. As a result, although Rowlandson (like Hanson) alludes to the Bible in an orthodox manner to analogize her situation, "her complicated use of Scripture reveals both a fear and an anger at a punishing God that must be transformed into an anger at herself, which nonetheless resurfaces as a paradoxically self-abnegating accusation of Him" (Toulouse 1992, 664). And similar to Hanson's manner, this complex effect is apparently not intentional: "The more mechanically Rowlandson acknowledges her submission in orthodox terms, the more she complicates the range of explanation offered to her by such orthodoxy"; "as hard as she might try to conceal it in her *Narrative,* the text reveals the impasse imposed upon her imagination by her own interrogation of the old models for establishing her sense of value" (669).

Hanson's oral report of her captivity is a work of less imagination than is Rowlandson's written document. Nevertheless, despite different religious orientations and slight editing by other hands, both works are equally rich in documenting certain problems with the authorization of personal sentiment and expression that were frequently experienced by female colonial authors, including Quakers.

Elizabeth Ashbridge's Autobiography

Some Account of the Fore Part of the Life of Elizabeth Ashbridge (written, c. 1753; 1st ed., 1774) is a far more complex Quaker testament than is *God's Mercy Surmounting Man's Cruelty.* Ashbridge's narrative, which we have only in others' transcriptions, recounts the numerous trials of a young woman who eloped at the age of fourteen and within months found herself widowed, exiled from her family home, and badly prepared to survive either in the world or in her mind. Her education, which had depended "mostly on [her] Mother," had primarily emphasized "the principles of virtue" (Shea 1990, 147); but in the world of economic exchange in which she now had become a bound servant, virtue seemed virtually valueless. Virtue's residual value, moreover, was readily bankruptable, even merely by calumnious words: "I began to think my Credit was gone (for they said many things of me which I blessed God were not True)" (153). Indentured physically and adrift emotionally, teenager Elizabeth is brought to the brink of suicide more than once during her tribulations in New York.

Ashbridge characterizes her experiences collectively as various forms of bondage. This metaphor pertains not only to her "becoming bound" through indentured "Servitude" (151), the abject conditions of which are similarly documented by Elizabeth Sprigs, Ashbridge's southern contemporary. The metaphor of bondage also represents Ashbridge's second marriage, of which she says, "I got released from one cruel Servitude & then not Contented got into another" (153-54). During this marriage, the itinerancy of her new husband was hardly the only "Disagreeable" matter to which she felt she "must submit" (155). Such experiences of servility, however, had an important antecedent, which Ashbridge seems reticent to declare openly but which her memoir associates with her later replications of thralldom: her constraining relationship with her father.

As was typical of early-eighteenth-century colonial daughters, Elizabeth was not free to decide much for herself, including her marriage. She explicitly admits that her courtship with the first young man she would marry was "without [her] Parents' consent," that her impetuous marriage to him was an act of "disobedience," and that her behavior had denied her parents the "right . . . to have disposed of [her] to their contents" (Shea 1990, 148). When she eloped with her first husband, she in effect dispossessed her parents, particularly her father, of the property of her body. Her act was a violation not only of filial respect but also of economic propriety concerning children, an issue as well in eighteenth-century representations of rape as a confiscation of patriarchal property (Williams 1993). Dispossessed of what was by custom rightfully his, Elizabeth's father "was so displeased," he "would not send for" her and "would do nothing for" her (148). Henceforth she was not only widowed but also orphaned. She was sheltered briefly by relatives and eventually turned loose in the world. Although some time later her father relented and apparently would have met the financial obligations of her indenture, Elizabeth "chose Bondage rather" than to return to his household (153), and she even desperately entertained the possibility of running off with an acting troupe.

Elizabeth presents her "Disobedience in marrying" (153), her tenuous rebellion against her father, as a kind of fall from grace. (The word "disobedience" is virtually a refrain in the first part, as the word "obedience" is in the second part of all versions of her account.) Insubordination serves as a primary determinant of the harrowing experiences that befall her in a harsh world where, subsequent to her postlapsarian expulsion from the security of her family home, widowed virtue can purchase little, if anything, and presumably can be forfeited by mere verbal deceit. As presented in all the versions of her narrative, her life in the world commences with and replicates this self-wounding insurrection against thralldom to her father. As best she is able, accordingly, she resists her inhumane master, who purchased her indenture; her stern father, who eventually relented and would permit her to return on his terms; and her domineering second husband, who "flew into a rage" and "Struck [her] with sore Blows" when she announced her willingness "to obey all his Lawfull Commands but where they Imposed upon [her] Conscience" (165-66). (Anticipating a prevalent custom today in marriage ceremonies, incidentally, Quaker women for some time have not agreed to obey their husbands [Frost 1973, 174].)

Ashbridge's coalescence of her original disobedience and her a posteriori acts of resistance to male authority include a significant revision of her stance toward the orthodox ministry. In her sheltered youth, she had looked upon the clergy as paragons of male empowerment in the world, so much so that she "sometimes wept with Sorrow, that [she] was not a boy [so] that [she] might have" become a minister (Shea 1990, 148). (This sentiment is expressed even more passionately, and hence possibly more authentically, in the variant report that she "sometimes grieved at . . . not being a boy" [Baym 1994, 602].) While adrift in the world, however, she becomes skeptical toward "that set of men," the "Very Religious" for whom "in [her] youth" she "had a Great Veneration" (152). Later still, she sees "beyond the Men made Ministers," those "Mercenary creatures" more devoted to "the Love of Money" than to "the regard of Souls" (163).

This repudiation of the traditional ministry amounts in effect to Ashbridge's ultimate defiance of male authority, a defiance she crowns by becoming a Quaker preacher. Ashbridge fulfills her youthful fantasy of becoming a minister by way of inversion. Far past the point of wishing she were a male so that she could join the traditional ministry, she now identifies with an unorthodox ministry in which women and men are equally "ordained" solely through their encounter with the Inward Light. And, Ashbridge's account further suggests, these Quaker preachers redeem the establishmentarian Christian ministry by displacing the male mercenary interest of such conformist clergy with a "female" alternative interest in the heretofore dispossessed principles of virtue (of the kind she learned from her mother).

This version of the plot of her autobiography reinforces a recent observation that Ashbridge records "the phenomenon of a woman speaking of her coming to speak" or, in other words, her progression from speechless listening to numerous voices to her proclamation of a "new identity . . . through the familiar Quaker usage of 'thee'" (Shea 1990, 132-33). But, as we shall observe, a specter-like question haunts this progress toward empowerment of voice, despite an authorizing belief in the Inward Light. This question challenges the "narrative restraint" that has been esteemed as "admirable" (Shea 1968, 37).

In fact, a key point in the loose structure of the autobiography provides an apt place to initiate an investigation of this instability in referential authority. . . .

At first, the trajectory of Ashbridge's experiences inclines downward. Unable to return home, she becomes a nearly powerless and voiceless indentured servant, a nondescript human whose beliefs (including her religious faith) are so unstable that she becomes despondent and suicidal. At the nadir of this downward turn lies a temptation, "another Snare," which "would Probably have been [her] Ruin." Here she is temporarily "Perswaded" to join a "Play house company then at New York" (153), indeed a temptation given the shared Congregationalist, Presbyterian, and Quaker association of theater productions and players with unchaste behavior and bad reputations, specifically in violation of the seventh commandment (Meserve 1977, 26-27).

The earliest contributors to these Reformed sects apparently did not construct the stage in these terms; in a work revered by these sects and commonly designated as *Book of the Martyrs* (English version, 1563), for instance, John Foxe associates "players, printers, [and] preachers" as allies "set up of God, as a triple bulwark" against the antiChrist (Foxe 1965, 6:57). But with the emergence of the new theater, the stage and the Reformed pulpit became antagonists in defining the nature of spirituality (Knapp 1993). By Ashbridge's time, Quakers spoke of the theater as the "floodgate of vice," especially "looseness and immorality," and they consequently influenced eighteenth-century laws against theatrical productions in Pennsylvania (Bowden 1854, 2:287-89).

As a naive teenager, Ashbridge is enticed by the theater, which evidently appealed to a number of other young women, most notably late in the eighteenth century, as a flagrant opportunity to invert the social paradigm of female impotence, invisibility, and silence (Dudden 1994). Ashbridge is attracted by the disingenuous promise that with membership in the troupe she would "Live Like a Lady" (153). Implied in this promise is the notion that the deception of on-stage representation could be transferred to the off-stage world, certainly an appealing proposition for such a luckless child as she was at that time. However, as suggested by the retrospective reference to her predictable "Ruin," many of young Elizabeth's adult contemporaries would have readily detected a shady nuance, an allusion to prostitution, in the euphemistic expression "Live Like a Lady." Ashbridge reads numerous plays in preparation for joining the troupe, but finally she resists this temptation after "Consider[ing] what [her] Father would say" now that he has "forgiven [her] Disobedience in marrying" (Shea 1990, 153).

Eventually Ashbridge remarries, which frees her from her indenture if not altogether from theatrical performances, for she has married a man who is attracted to her for her dancing (154) and who, in a demonstration of his hostility to her Quaker leanings, makes her "the Spectacle & discourse of [his] Company" in a tavern (162). If her marriage binds her in ways similar to her indenture—as she herself claims—it nonetheless results in encounters that collectively form the upward movement of her life. Ashbridge affirms that through the debilitating itinerancy of her husband "God [brought] unforeseen things to Pass, for by [her] going . . . [she] was brought to [the] Knowledge of [divine] Truth" (158). In terms of the structural scheme of her memoir, that is to say, she finds fulfillment in a new community where, as a Quaker preacher, she displaces corrupt father figures. Instead of participating in the false spectacle of voicing some humanly authored dramatic text and experiencing an illusory freedom under the controlling gaze of male spectators (akin to her later experience in a tavern), she now participates in the genuine drama of voicing a divinely authored providential text. Like other Quaker "Ministers . . . [likewise] dipt into all States, that thereby they might be able to Speak to all Conditions" (168), Ashbridge reconfigures theatricality so that the pulpit of her adult female ministry inverts/reconverts the stage demarcating the nadir of her youthful experiences.

Such an inversion, or reconversion, is meant to be as heuristic as are the official dichotomies (as opposed to the conflictive sentiments) of Hanson's captivity narrative. And on first encounter the redemptive message of inversion seems as definitively conclusive as Ashbridge apparently intended. On second thought, however, the trope of the stage steadfastly inheres within Ashbridge's implied reconstruction of it as the pulpit, just as mourning persists as a subversive undercurrent within Hanson's use of antithesis when speaking of her acceptance of divine will. (Ashbridge does not explicitly refer to a preacher's platform, which is not a usual feature of Quaker worship; but since the pulpit would likely be mentally imaged by most non-Quaker readers of her day whenever they encountered her references to preaching, it is an implicit contemporary metonymy for all the forums of her own ministry, including her memoir.) Ashbridge's oral and written preaching, like stage performances, are modes of theatricality, spectacles that cannot break free from what they once were culturally aligned with (as John Foxe suggested in 1563) and what they now invert or reconvert. Although in the autobiography the allegedly immoral stage may be superseded by the moral pulpit, the displaced stage persists as a palimpsest beneath this implicit pulpit. And, correspondingly, the practice of assuming and discarding various identities on the stage, including clever transgressions of gender boundaries, informs and latently destabilizes Ashbridge's depiction of her unconventional identity as a *female* preacher at the end of her memoir. How firm, and how firmly authorized, is such an identity if it is troped, however accidentally, in proscribed theatrical terms?

This is a literary not a religious query. But interestingly the semiotic equivocation suggested by Ashbridge's tacit reinscription of the metaphor of theatricality is also replicated in her management of her more overtly declared subject of disobedience. As we established earlier, Ashbridge coalesces her "fathering" act of disobedience and her subsequent acts of obedience to God through resistance to male authority, acts that collectively result in inversions of stage/pulpit theatricality and male/female ministry. As presented by Ashbridge, then, disobedience is bi-valent. It is, in other words, referentially unstable since it may produce good as well as bad effects. Left unasked, because the answer would become enmeshed in the vexatious issue of authority, is a key question: how is one—especially the *second* or *weaker* sex as defined in colonial times—to know when disobedience is appropriate?

This question of authorization is faintly inscribed, if finally unreadable, beneath the equivocal opening of the autobiography. In the very first sentence Ashbridge claims that some of the "uncommon Occurences" in her life were "through disobedience brought upon" herself, while "others . . . were for [her] Good" (147). Such a comment at once authorizes and deauthorizes disobedience, at least certain instances of disobedience. But which instances? The insubordination she directs at her master, at her second husband, and at mercenary ministers seems sufficiently clear, but it does not mask fully the prior defiance of her father, the oft confessed bad act that somehow leads to Ashbridge's salvation. Nor does the V-like symmetry of her plot—how the disobedience to her human father of the first part leads to her decline outside of her home and how the obedience to the divine father in the second part leads to her ascent to the pulpit—quite disguise the problem.

Indeed, an attempt to fashion from Ashbridge's memoir a moral map, as it were, based on her specific references to disobedience and obedience would result in a substantial confusion of vectoring. Obscured in the shadowy margins of this confusion is the issue of authority concerning how to recognize improper disobedience from proper disobedience, heuristic reproach from homiletic commemoration, especially when assessing one's own life. In this regard, at least, it is more of a mystification of the problem than a clarification to be told, as we previously heard, that "God brings unforeseen things to Pass," that "unforeseen things are brought to Pass, by a Providential hand" (158, 164).

The doctrine of the Inward Light, of interior divine revelation, is the official Quaker repository for negotiating this problem. Nevertheless, the *narrative* function of proper and improper disobedience in Ashbridge's account, from its ambiguous opening sentence onward, defies conclusive resort to such a closeting doctrinal rationale in this instance. History, moreover, attests to what complications can emerge from antinomian attempts to harken to an inner voice, and Ashbridge's document concurs. This memoir progresses from her youthful "giving way to a foolish passion" when she elopes (148), through inner promptings to hang herself (153), to receiving divine messages "as tho' [she] had heard a Distinct Voice" (167).

In narrative terms, as distinct from religious ones, a Bakhtinian heteroglossia (Holquist 1981, 428) lingers in the memoir, specifically a polyphony of competing inner provocations. In narrative terms, a confessional moment at midpoint in her account suggests the magnitude of this polyphony. There she admits how easy it is for her and others to mistake the voice of "the Subtile Serpent," when as an interior prompter he "hiddenly" interprets "the Texts of Scripture," as if his influence were "a timely Caution from a good Angel" (159). Although Ashbridge plots her story so that her youthful disobedience to her human father is redressed by "the fruits of [her adult] Obedience" to the divine father (167), she cannot repair the implicit confounding of authority that inheres in this very pattern, whereby improper disobedience leads to proper obedience. Contingently negotiating this crisis in authority, in short, Ashbridge's particular application of the disobedience/obedience equation is as "fatherless" as Hanson's particular application of the bitterness/sweetness equation.

The fragility of Ashbridge's construction of a plot in which proscribed disobedience is transformed into prescribed obedience, prohibited stage is transformed into the licensed pulpit, is likewise suggested by an incident reported near the conclusion of her autobiography. At this point she tells of "hearing a Woman relate a book she had read in which it was Asserted that Christ was not the son of God," merely "the Contrivance of men." Immediately "an horrour of Great Darkness fell upon [her], which Continued for three weeks" (167). Ashbridge's response is surprising given the advanced stage of her Quaker beliefs at this juncture. Could this woman's message, temporarily marring the heuristic plot of the narrative, inadvertently suggest a certain ambiguity in the design of Ashbridge's textualized life and theatrical memoir?

Consider that the opposition between this woman and Ashbridge is determined merely by inversion, the very same narrative device of Elizabeth's life and her autobiography as a whole. The two women are like opposite sides of the same coin. If Ashbridge's autobiography represents the assertion of self as authorized by its alignment with divine authority, the reading woman represents the supplanting of divine authority by the assertive self as the sole fashioner of the notion of divinity. Ashbridge's extensive incapacitation upon hearing this woman's views possibly indicates Ashbridge's unconscious acknowledgment of the ambiguity inherent in her personal reliance upon the precarious disobedience-obedience formula.

Such moments, I am inclined to believe, hint at Ashbridge's unwitting anxiety over the issue of authority; the failure of sanctioned obedience to displace altogether illicit disobedience and of the pulpit to displace altogether the stage in the autobiography corresponds to the failure of Ashbridge's attained voice (identity) to displace altogether her initial voicelessness. This observation indeed may seem very strange, especially in light of the trajectory of her life toward the pulpit. A closer consideration of her voice, however, suggests a distinctive complexity in this matter.

When Ashbridge disobeys in the first part of her memoir, she expresses herself through the authority of her passionate feelings for her first husband. But this self-expression, explicitly designated as illegitimate disobedience, is dispossessed of its authority and replaced by divinely inspired self-expression, explicitly designated as legitimate obedience: "[God] would require me to go forth & declare to others what he . . . had done for my Soul" (160). The latter is, however, a form of ventriloquism, as if on the world stage she were a player delivering lines from a divinely crafted script (Scripture). Her self-expression, in other words, is from her point of view authorized from an *inward* prompting determined by an *outward* divine force. In this sense, therefore, her speech is not, or at least not entirely, a form of self-expression. The voicelessness Ashbridge believes has been transformed into identity-giving voice has not at last been fully displaced. When she disqualifies her early personal feelings as unauthorized and credits her new beliefs as authorized, her voice is at once empowered on the basis of external license (God) and disempowered on the basis of internal license (sentiment). As a plot element, the conversion of viocelessness to voice remains, finally, as entangled in ambiguity as is the correspondent and implicated conversion of disobedience into obedience, stage into pulpit, male into female ministry.

This curiously equivocated sense of identity, particularly in terms of an inversion of gender roles, informs another key moment in Ashbridge's narrative. Here she reports one of her dreams, which combines several biblical allusions and provides a remarkable site of logonomic conflict:

> I had a Dream, & tho' some make a ridicule of Dreams, yet this seemed a significant one to me & therefore [I] shall mention it. I thought somebody knocked at the Door, by which when I had opened it there stood a Grave woman, holding in her right hand an oil lamp burning, who with a Solid Countenance fixed her Eyes upon me & said—"I am sent to tell thee that If thou'l return to the Lord thy God, who hath Created thee, he will have mercy on thee, & thy Lamp shall not be put out in obscure darkness;" upon which the Light flamed from the Lamp in an extraordinary Manner, & She left me and I awoke.
>
> [Shea 1990, 153]

This passage may be read, as it has been (131), as a prophecy of the narrator's eventual discovery of both "the Quaker Inner Light" and "an achieved identity." Also encoded in this dream, however, are conflictive elements concerning the nature and enablement of this identity.

The dream combines several biblical allusions. The last part of the prophecy echoes a scriptural admonition, that "the lamp of the wicked shall be put out," that "whoso curseth his father or his mother, his lamp shall be put out in obscure darkness" (Prov. 13:9 and 20:20). In terms of the latter passage, Ashbridge's vision evidently reassures her that she has been forgiven for her specific transgression against her parents—another clue, incidentally, to the problematic importance of her primary act of disobedience to the salvational outcome of her life. The dream as well alludes to those New Testament passages promising, for instance, that the followers of Jesus, as "the light of the world[,] . . . shall not walk in darkness, but shall have the light of life" (John 8:12).

Still more prominent in the dream is the scriptural text that advises Christians, "Let . . . your lights [be] burning" when the "Lord . . . cometh and knocketh" (Luke 12:35-36). In renderings of this scene—images of which Quakers would not have approved but which Ashbridge may have seen in books or while living abroad, especially among Roman Catholics—Christ holds a lamp in one hand while knocking on a door with the other.

Most interesting in the dream version of this scene is the transmutation of the gender of the light-bearing visitant at the door. This unacknowledged feature is far more significant than the acknowledged dubiety of dreams, the latter factor accommodated by Ashbridge's use of the equivocal word "seemed" in order to justify the inclusion of the vision in her account. The person in the dream is not Jesus or even John, who spoke of himself as a "witness of the Light, that all men through him might believe" (John 1:6). It is a woman with a grave countenance. In one sense, this figure usurps the male savior role, as a prominent colonial cultural feature, but unwittingly it also displaces John and Jesus as well. The figure *may* represent Ashbridge's attempt to awaken herself from her subjection to suicidal nonidentity as a commodity in a mercenary world controlled by men. Read as a projection of her later ministerial role as an ambassador of Christ, the woman in her dream seems a bold, even heretical, figuring of an achievable autonomous identity.

Beneath this fantasy of self-awakening, however, the woman in the dream derives her dramatic power by appearing in a scene and role given signification by someone prior to herself. In other words, the somber woman (like an actress in a theatrical performance) replays, but does not invent, a role in the dream. Her inversion/transformation of the role cannot break free from its antecedents anymore than can obedience from disobedience, the pulpit from the stage, or female from male ministry throughout Ashbridge's memoir. The grave woman's performance invokes the memory of and draws its own power from another, antecedent, and far more potent one: the image of Christ bearing the light of truth and knocking on our door. So, finally, if on first impression the scene seems an assertion of female selfhood that unwittingly displaces even Jesus, on second impression it is only a satellite reenactment of a biblical depiction. This biblical image inheres as an authorizing palimpsest beneath the more visible meanings of the dream, meanings always dependent on this submerged authority.

The reversal of gender is likewise equivocated in the dream. The female image of self-awakening (self-authorization) is also ultimately authorized from without by a male prototype. That is to say, female transgression (self-motivated disobedience) is also ultimately commissioned by conformity (obedience) to a male model, whether John's or Jesus'.

The logonomic conflict evident in this dream serves as an index to the dilemma Ashbridge faced as an mid-eighteenth-century woman seeking self-definition through personal expression. The paradox informing this dream is a microcosm of the entire pattern of her search for identity, founded on an illegitimate disobedience against her father, that culminates in her obedient arrogation of the male role of ministers and of the power they wield through spoken and written language. In the scheme of her story she tries to transform one thing into its opposite, an act that paradoxically unites and disunites contraries. She tries to warrant obedience to herself by means of obedience to God. But this equation is hardly equal in its parts, for as Ashbridge observes on another occasion, "if it be of God [you] can't over throw it, & if it be of your self it will soon fall" (167). In the dynamic of Ashbridge's implied equation, obedience to God necessarily overdetermines obedience to herself, and so they finally are not at all equitable.

Ashbridge achieves identity and voice, less from an internal authority than from an external authority. This means, despite her mystifying acknowledgment (like Hanson's) that God "Makest every bitter thing Sweet" (170), that *to some degree* the authority of her voice and identity remains firmly indentured. Ashbridge inadvertently reinscribes indenture in *Some Account,* just as Hanson reinscribes captivity in *God's Mercy Surmounting Man's Cruelty.* Their narratives dramatize, finally, an anxious, conflicted, and unresolved negotiation of authorization, expressed through the dynamic interplay of the dichotomous inversions and reconversions composing the mutual "plot" of their lives.

Works Cited

Akers, Charles W. 1975. "'Our Modern Egyptians': Phillis Wheatley and the Whig Campaign against Slavery in Revolutionary Boston." *Journal of Negro History* 60: 399-410.

Andrews, William D. 1970. "The Printed Funeral Sermons of Cotton Mather." *Early American Literature* 5: 24-44.

Bailyn, Bernard. 1960. *The Forming of American Society: Needs and Opportunities for Study.* Chapel Hill: Univ. of North Carolina Press.

Baker, Houston A., Jr. 1991. *Workings of the Spirit: The Poetics of Afro-American Women's Writing.* Chicago: Univ. of Chicago Press.

Ball, Kenneth R. 1973. "Puritan Humility in Anne Bradstreet's Poetry." *Cithara* 13: 29-41.

Baym, Nina. 1995. *American Women Writers and the Work of History, 1790- 1860.* New Brunswick, N.J.: Rutgers Univ. Press.

———. 1992. *Feminism and American Literary History.* New Brunswick, N.J.: Rutgers Univ. Press.

———, et al. 1994. *The Norton Anthology of American Literature: Fourth Edition, Volume 1.* New York: Norton.

Berkin, Carol. 1996. *First Generations: Women in Colonial America.* New York: Hill and Wang.

Berry, Philipa. 1989. *Of Chastity and Power: Elizabethan Literature and the Unmarried Queen.* London: Routledge.

Bosco, Ronald A., ed. 1989. *The Poems of Michael Wigglesworth.* Lanham, Md.: Univ. Press of America.

Bowden, John. 1850-54. *The History of the Society of Friends in America* 2 vols. London: W. and F. G. Cash.

Bowers, Bathsheba. 1709. *An Alarm Sounded to Prepare the Inhabitants of the World to Meet the Lord in the Way of His Judgment.* New York: [publisher uncertain].

Boyarin, Daniel. 1993. "Paul and the Genealogy of Gender." *Representations* 41: 1-33.

Boyer, Paul, and Stephen Nissenbaum. 1974. *Salem Possessed: The Social Origins of Witchcraft.* Cambridge: Harvard Univ. Press.

———, eds. 1977.*The Salem Witchcraft Papers.* New York: Da Capo Press.

Braude, Benjamin. 1997. "The Sons of Noah and the Construction of Ethnic and Geographical Identities in the Medieval and Early Modern Periods." *William and Mary Quarterly* 54: 103-42.

Breen, T. H. 1993. "Narrative and Commercial Life: Consumption, Ideology, and Community on the Eve of the American Revolution." *William and Mary Quarterly* 50: 471-501.

Breitwieser, Mitchell Robert. 1990. *American Puritanism and the Defense of Mourning: Religion, Grief, and Ethnology in Mary White Rowlandson's Captivity Narrative.* Madison: Univ. of Wisconsin Press.

Brewster, Martha. 1758. *Poems on Diverse Subjects.* Boston: Edes and Gill.

Brooke, Frances. [1769] 1961. *The History of Emily Montague.* Toronto: Mc-Clelland and Stewart.

Brown, Kathleen M. 1996. *Good Wives, Nasty Wenches, and Anxious Patriarchs: Gender, Race and Power in Colonial Virginia.* Chapel Hill: Univ. Of North Carolina Press.

Brown, William Hill. [1789] 1961. *The Power of Sympathy.* Ed. Herbert Brown. Boston: New Frontiers Press.

Bruce, Philip Alexander. 1910. *Institutional History of Virginia in the Seventeenth Century.* 2 vols. New York: Putnam's Sons.

Burke, Helen M. 1991. "The Rhetoric and Politics of Marginality: The Subject of Phillis Wheatley." *Tulsa Studies in Women's Literature* 10: 31-45.

Burroughs, Margaret G. 1974. "Do Birds of a Feather Flock Together?" *Jackson State Review* 6, 1: 61-73.

Calder, Isabel M., ed. 1935. *Colonial Captivities, Marches and Journeys.* New York: Macmillan.

Caldwell, Patricia. 1988. "Why Our First Poet was a Woman: Bradstreet and the Birth of an American Poetic Voice." *Prospects* 13: 1-35.

Carr, Lois Green, and Lorena S. Walsh. 1979. "The Planter's Wife: The Experience of White Women in Seventeenth-Century Maryland." In *A Heritage of Her Own: Toward a New Social History of American Women,* ed. Nancy F. Cott and Elizabeth H. Pleck, 25-27. New York: Simon and Schuster.

Cheever, George F. 1860. "Philip English—Part Second." *Historical Collections of the Essex Institute* 2: 237-48.

———. 1859. "A Sketch of Philip English" *Historical Collections of the Essex Institue* 1: 157-81.

Cole, David L. 1994. "Mistresses of the Household: Distaff Publishing in London, 1588-1700." *CEA Critic* 56, 2: 20-30.

Collins, Terrence. 1975. "Phillis Wheatley: The Dark Side of Poetry." *Phylon* 36, 1: 78-88.

Colman, Benjamin. 1735. *Reliquiae Turellae, et Lachrymae Paternae.* (Bound with *Memoirs of the Life and Death of the Pious and Ingenious Mrs. Jane Turell* by Ebenezer Turrell.) Boston: S. Kneeland and T. Green.

Cowell, Pattie. 1994. "Early New England Women Poets: Writing as Vocation." *Early American Literature* 29: 103-21.

———, ed. 1981. *Women Poets in Pre-Revolutionary America, 1650-1775: An Anthology.* Troy, N.Y.: Whitston.

Cremin, Lawrence A. 1970. *American Education: The Colonial Experience, 1607-1783.* New York: Harper.

Crèvecoeur, J. Hector St. John de. [1782; 1925] 1981. Letters from an American Farmer *and* Sketches of Eighteenth-Century America. Ed. Albert E. Stone. Harmondsworth, England: Penguin Books.

Cudworth, Ralph. [1678] 1845. *The True Intellectual System of the Universe.* 3 vols. London: Thomas Tegg.

Cugoano, Ottobah. [1787] 1969. *Thoughts and Sentiments on the Evil of Slavery.* London: Dawsons of Pall Mall.

Daly, Robert. 1978. *God's Alter: The World and the Flesh in Puritan Poetry.* Berkley: Univ. of California Press.

Davidson, Cathy N. 1986. *Revolution and the Word: The Rise of the Novel in America.* New York: Oxford Univ. Press.

Davis, Arthur P. 1953. "The Personal Elements in the Poetry of Phillis Wheatley" *Phylon* 12, 2: 191-98.

Davis, Natalie Zemon. 1995. *Women on the Margins: Three Seventeenth-Century Lives.* Cambridge: Harvard Univ. Press.

Davis, Richard Beale. 1978. *Intellectual Life in the Colonial South, 1585-1763.* 3 vols. Knoxville: Univ. of Tennessee Press.

Dayton, Cornelia Hughes. 1995. *Women before the Bar: Gender, Law, and Society in Connecticut, 1639-1789.* Chapel Hill: Univ. of North Carolina Press.

Derounian-Stodola, Kathryn Zabelle. 1990. "'The excellency of the inferior sex': The Commendatory Writings of Anne Bradstreet." *Studies in Puritan American Spirituality* 1: 129-47.

Derounian-Stodola, Kathryn Zabelle, and James Arthur Levernier. 1993. *The Indian Captivity Narrative, 1500-1900.* New York: Twayne.

Douglas, Ann. 1977. *The Feminization of American Culture.* New York: Knopf.

Dudden, Faye E. 1994. *Women in the American Theatre: Actresses and Audiences, 1790-1870.* New Haven, Yale Univ. Press

Eberwein, Jane Donahue. 1981. "'No rhet'ric we expect': Argumentation in Bradstreet's 'The Prologue.'" *Early American Literature* 16: 19-26.

Edkins, Carol. 1980. "Quest for Community: Spiritual Autobiographies of Eighteenth-Century Quaker and Puritan Women in America." In *Women's Autobiography: Critical essays,* ed. by Estelle C. Jelinek, 39-52. Bloomington: Univ. of Indiana Press.

Eldred, Janet Carey, and Peter Mortenson. 1993. "Gender and Writing Instruction in Early America: Lessons from Didactic Fiction" *Rhetoric Review* 12: 25-53.

Ellison, Julie. 1984. "The Sociology of 'Holy Indifference': Sarah Edwards' Narrative." *American Literature* 56: 479-95.

Erkkila, Betsy. 1993. "Phillis Wheatley and the Black American Revolution" In *A Mixed Race: Ethnicity in Early America,* ed. Frank Shuffelton, 225-40. New York: Oxford Univ. Press.

Felker, Christopher D. 1994. "'The Tongues of the learned are insufficient': Phillis Wheatley, Publishing Objectives, and Personal Liberty." *Resources for American Literary Study* 20: 149-79.

Fichtelberg, Joseph. 1989. *The Complex Image: Faith and Method in American Autobiography.* Philadelphia: Univ. of Pennsylvania Press.

Findlen, Paula. 1995. "Translating the New Science: Women and the Circulation of Knowledge in Enlightenment Italy." *Configurations* 3: 167-206.

Fiske, Sarah Symmes. 1704. *A Confession of Faith.* Boston: Benson Eliot.

Flanzbaum, Hilene. 1993. "Unprecedented Liberties: Re-Reading Phillis Wheatley." *MELUS* 18: 71-81.

Foster, Frances Smith. 1993. *Written by Herself: Literary Production of African American Women, 1746-1892.* Bloomington: Indiana Univ. Press.

Foster, Stephen. 1991. *The Long Argument: English Puritanism and the Shaping of New England Culture, 1570-1700.* Williamsburg, Va.: Institute of Early American History and Culture.

Foucault, Michel. 1977. *Language, Counter-Memory, Practice: Selected Essays and Interviews by Michel Foucault.* Ed. Donald F. Bouchard. Ithaca: Cornell Univ. Press.

Foxe, John. [1563] 1965. *The Acts and Monuments of These Latter and Perilous Days.* Ed. Stephen Cattley and George Townsend. 8 vols. New York: AMS Press.

Frost, William J. 1973. *The Quaker Family in Colonial America: A Portrait of the Society of Friends.* New York: St. Martin's Press.

Frye, Susan. 1993. *Elizabeth I: The Competition for Representation.* New York: Oxford Univ. Press.

Gallagher, Catherine. 1994. *Nobody's Story: The Vanishing Acts of Women Writers in the Marketplace, 1670-1820.* Berkeley: Univ. of California Press.

Gilman, Ernest B. 1986. *Iconoclasm and Poetry in the English Reformation: Down Went Dragon.* Chicago: Univ. of Chicago Press.

Godbeer, Richard. 1992. *The Devil's Dominion: Magic and Religion in Early New England.* Cambridge: Cambridge Univ. Press.

Goen, C. C., ed. 1972. *The Works of Jonathan Edwards, Volume 4: The Great Awakening.* New Haven: Yale Univ. Press.

Greenslade, S. L., ed. 1963. *The Cambridge History of the Bible.* 3 vols. Cambridge: Cambridge Univ. Press.

Hall, David H. 1989. *Worlds of Wonders, Days of Judgment: Popular Religious Belief in Early New England.* Cambridge: Cambridge Univ. Press.

Hamilton, Edith. 1940. *Mythology.* Boston: Little, Brown.

Hammond, Jeffrey A. 1993. *Sinful Self, Saintly Self: The Puritan Experience of Poetry.* Athens: Univ. of Georgia Press.

Harris, Sharon M. 1993. "Early American Women's Self-Creating Acts" *Resources for American Literary Study* 19: 223-45.

———, ed. 1996. *American Women Writers to 1800.* New York: Oxford Univ. Press.

Hastings, James. 1909. *Dictionary of the Bible.* New York: Charles Scribner's Sons.

Hayes, Kevin J. 1996. *A Colonial Woman's Bookshelf.* Knoxville: Univ. of Tennessee Press.

Hobby, Elaine. 1988. *Virtue of Necessity: English Women's Writing, 1649-88.* Ann Arbor: Univ. of Michigan Press.

Hodge, Robert. 1990. *Literature as Discourse: Textual Strategies in English and History.* Baltimore: Johns Hopkins Univ. Press.

Hodge, Robert, and Gunther Kress. 1988. *Social Semiotics.* Ithaca: Cornell Univ. Press.

Holmes, Thomas J. 1940. *Cotton Mather: A Bibliography of His Works.* 2 vols. Cambridge: Harvard Univ. Press.

Holquist, Michael, ed. 1981. *The Dialogic Imagination: Four Essays by M. M. Bakhtin.* Austin: Univ. of Texas Press.

Horn, James. 1994. *Adapting to a New World: English Society in the Seventeenth-Century Chesapeake.* Chapel Hill: Univ. of North Carolina Press.

Hubbard, Dolan. 1994. *The Sermon and the African American Literary Imagination.* Columbia: Univ. of Missouri Press.

Hudak, Leona M. 1978 *Early American Women Printers and Publishers, 1639-1820.* Metuchen, N.J.: Scarecrow Press.

Huddleston, Eugene L. 1971 "Matilda's 'On Reading the Poems of Phillis Wheatley, the African Poetess.'" *Early American Literature* 5: 57-67.

Hume, Sophia. 1747. *An Exhortation to the Inhabitants of the Province of South-Carolina.* Philadelphia: William Bradford.

Ingersoll, Thomas N. 1994. "'Releese us out of this Cruell Bondegg': An Appeal from Virginia in 1723." *William and Mary Quarterly* 51: 777-82.

Isani, Mukhtar Ali. 1979. "'Gambia on My Soul': Africa and the African in the Writings of Phillis Wheatley." *MELUS* 6, 1: 64-72.

———. 1982. "Phillis Wheatley and the Elegiac Mode." In *Critical Essays on Phillis Wheatley,* ed. William H. Robinson, 208-14. Boston: G. K. Hall.

Iser, Wolfgang. 1978. *The Act of Reading: A Theory of Aesthetic Response.* Baltimore: Johns Hopkins Univ. Press.

Jamison, Angelene. 1974, "Analysis of Selected Poetry of Phillis Wheatley." *Journal of Negro Education* 43, 3: 408-16.

Kamensky, Jane. 1992. "Words, Witches, and Woman Trouble: Witchcraft, Disorderly Speech, and Gender Boundaries in New England." *Essex Institute Historical Collections* 128: 286-307.

Karlsen, Carol F. and Laurie Crumpacker, eds. 1984. *The Journal of Esther Edwards Burr, 1754-1757.* New Haven: Yale Univ. Press.

Kelley, Mary. 1992. "'Vindicating the Equality of the Female Intellect': Women and Authority in the Early Republic." *Prospects* 17: 1-27.

Kendrick, Robert L. 1993. "Snatching a Laurel, Wearing a Mask: Phillis Wheatley's Literary Nationalism and the Problem of Style." *Style* 27: 222-51.

Kenyon, Olga. 1992. *800 Years of Women's Letters.* Phoenix Mill, England: Alan Sutton.

Kerber, Linda K. 1980. *Women of the Republic: Intellect and Ideology in Revolutionary America.* Chapel Hill: Univ. of North Carolina Press.

Kern, Louis J. 1993. "Eros, the Devil, and the Cunning Woman: Sexuality and the Supernatural in European Antecedents and in the Seventeenth-Century Salem Witchcraft Cases." *Essex Institute Historical* 34: 125-48.

Kibbey, Ann. 1982. "Mutations of the Supernatural: Witchcraft, Remarkable Providences, and the Power of Puritan Men." *American Quarterly* 129: 3-38.

Knapp, Jeffrey. 1993. "Preachers and Players in Shakespeare's England." *Representations* 44: 29-59.

Knight, Denise D., ed. 1989. *Cotton Mather's Verse in English* Newark: Univ. of Delaware Press.

Knight, Lucian Lamar, ed. 1910. *Biographical Dictionary.* Vol. 15 of *Library of Southern Literature,* ed. Edwin Anderson Alderman and Joel Chandler Harris. Atlanta: Martin and Hoyt Co.

Koehler, Lyle. 1980. *A Search for Power: The "Weaker Sex" in Seventeenth-Century New England.* Urbana: Univ, of Illinois.

Kristeva, Julia. 1980. *Desire in Language: A Semiotic Approach to Literature and Art.* Trans. Thomas Gora, Alice Jardin, and Leon Roudiez. New York: Columbia Univ. Press.

Lang, Amy Schrager. 1987. *Prophetic Women: Anne Hutchinson and the Problem of Dissent in the Literature of New England.* Berkeley and Los Angeles: Univ. of California Press.

Laughlin, Rosemary M. 1970. "Anne Bradstreet: Poet in Search of Form." *American Literature* 42: 1-17.

Levernier, James A. 1991. "Phillis Wheatley and the New England Clergy." *Early American Literature* 26: 21-38.

———. 1993. "Style as Protest in the Poetry of Phillis Wheatley." *Style* 27: 172-93.

———. 1981. "Wheatley's 'On Being Brought from Africa to America.'" *Explicator* 40, 1: 25-26.

Levernier, James A., and Douglas R. Wilmes, eds. 1983. *American Writers Before 1800.* 3 vols. Westport, Conn.: Greenwood Press.

Lewalski, Barbara Kiefer. 1993. *Writing Women in Jacobean England.* Cambridge: Harvard Univ. Press.

Lockridge, Kenneth A. 1974. *Literacy in Colonial New England.* New York: W. W. Norton.

Logan, Lisa. 1993. "Mary Rowlandson's Captivity and the 'Place' of the Female Subject." *Early American Literature* 28: 255-77.

Logan, Martha. 1772. *A Treatise on Gardening.* Charleston: [publisher uncertain].

Luxon, Thomas H. 1995. *Literal Figures: Puritan Allegory and the Reformation Crisis in Representation.* Chicago: Univ. of Chicago Press.

Main, Gloria. 1991. "An Inquiry into When and Why Women Learned to Write in Colonial New England." *Journal of Social History* 24: 579-89.

Margerum, Eileen. 1982. "Anne Bradstreet's Public Poetry and the Tradition of Humility." *Early American Literature* 17: 152-60.

Marshall, David. 1993. "Writing Masters and 'Masculine Exercises' in *The Female Quixote.*" *Eighteenth-Century Fiction* 5: 105-35.

Martin, Wendy. 1979. "Ann Bradstreet's Poetry: A Study of Subversive Piety." In *Shakespeare's Sisters: Feminist Essays on Women Poets,* ed. Sandra M. Gilbert and Susan Gubar, 19-31. Bloomington: Indiana Univ. Press.

Mason, Julian D, Jr., ed. 1989. *The Poems of Phillis Wheatley.* Chapel Hill: Univ. of North Carolina Press.

Mather, Cotton. [1741] 1978. *Ornaments for the Daughters of Zion.* Intro. Pattie Cowell. Delmar, N.Y.: Scholars Facsimiles and Prints.

Matson, R. Lynn. 1982. "Phillis Wheatley—Soul Sister?" In *Critical Essays on Phillis Wheatley,* ed. William H. Robinson, 113-22. Boston: G. K. Hall.

Mawer, Randall R. 1980. "Farewel Dear Babe': Bradstreet's Elegy for Elizabeth" *Early American Literature* 15: 29-41.

McElrath, Joseph R., Jr., and Allan P. Robb, eds. 1981. *The Complete Works of Anne Bradstreet.* Boston: Twayne.

McKay, Michele, and William J. Scheick. 1994. "The Other Song in Phillis Wheatley's 'On Imagination.'" *Studies in the Literary Imagination* 27: 71-84.

Meserve, Walter J. 1977. *An Emerging Entertainment: The Drama of the American People to 1828.* Bloomington: Univ. of Indiana Press.

Middlekauff, Robert. 1971. *The Mathers: Three Generations of Puritan Intellectuals, 1596-1728.* New York: Oxford Univ. Press.

Mignon, Charles W. 1968. "Edward Taylor's *Prepatory Meditations*: A Decorum of Imperfection." *Publication of the Modern Language Association* 83: 1423-28.

Miller, J. Hillis. 1989. "The Function of Literary Theory at the Present Time." In *The Future of Literary Theory,* ed. Ralph Cohen, 102-11. New York: Routledge.

Miller, Nancy K. 1986. "Changing the Subject: Authorship, Writing, and the Reader." In *Feminist Studies/Critical Studies,* ed. Teresa de Lauretis, 102-20. Bloomington: Indiana Univ. Press.

Monaghan, E. Jennifer. 1991. "Family Literacy in Early 18th-Century Boston: Cotton Mather and His Children." *Reading Research Quarterly* 26: 342-70.

———. 1989. "Literacy Instruction and Gender in Colonial New England." In *Reading in America: Literature and Social History,* ed. Cathy N. Davidson, 53-80. Baltimore: Johns Hopkins Univ. Press.

Moran, Gerald R., and Maris A. Vinkovskis. 1992. *Religion, Family, and the Life Course: Explorations in the Social History of America.* Ann Arbor: Univ. of Michigan Press.

Morgan, Edmund S. 1966. *The Puritan Family: Religion and Domestic Relations in Seventeenth-Century New England.* Rev. ed. New York: Harper and Row.

Mulford, Carla J., ed. 1995. *Only for the Eye of a Friend: The Poems of Ann Boudinot Stockton.* Charlottesville: Univ. Press of Virginia.

Newman, William R. 1994. *Gehennical Fire: The Lives of George Starkey, an American Alchemist in the Scientific Revolution.* Cambridge: Harvard Univ. Press.

Ogude, S. E. 1981. "Slavery in the African Imagination: A Critical Perspective." *World Literature Today* 55: 21-25.

O'Neale, Sondra. 1986. "A Slave's Subtle War: Phillis Wheatley's Use of Biblical Myth and Symbol." *Early American Literature* 21: 144-65.

Ong, Walter J. 1967. *In the Human Grain: Further Explorations of Contemporary Culture.* New York: Macmillan.

Otten, Charlotte F., ed. 1992. *English Women's Voices, 1540-1700.* Miami: Florida International Univ. Press.

Pettengill, Claire C. 1991. "Sisterhood in a Separate Sphere: Female Friendship in Hannah Webster Foster's *The Coquette* and *The Boarding School.*" *Early American Literature* 27: 185-203.

Pinckney, Elise, ed. 1972. *The Letterbook of Eliza Lucas Pinckney, 1739-1762.* Chapel Hill: Univ. of North Carolina Press.

Porterfield, Amanda. 1992. *Female Piety in Puritan England: The Emergence of Religious Humanism.* New York: Oxford Univ. Press.

———. 1980. *Female Spirituality in America from Sarah Edwards to Martha Graham.* Philadelphia: Temple Univ. Press.

Prarr, Mary Louise. 1992. *Imperial Eyes: Travel Writing and Transculturation.* London: Routledge.

Reid, J. K., ed. 1954. *Calvin: Theological Treatises.* Philadelphia: Westminster Press.

Richards, Phillip M. 1993. "Phillis Wheatley, Americanization, the Sublime, and the Romance of America." *Style* 27: 194-221.

———. 1992. "Phillis Wheatley and Literary Americanization." *American Quarterly* 44: 163-91.

Richmond, Merle A. 1974. *Bid the Vassal Soar: Interpretive Essays on the Life and Poetry of Phillis Wheatley and George Mason Horton.* Washington, D.C.: Howard Univ. Press.

———. 1982. "On 'The barter of her soul.'" In *Critical Essays on Phillis Wheatley,* ed. William H. Robinson, 123-27. Boston: G. K. Hall.

Robinson, William H., ed. 1982. *Critical Essays on Phillis Wheatley.* Boston: G. K. Hall.

———, ed. 1984. *Phillis Wheatley and Her Writings.* New York: Garland.

Rosenmeier, Rosamond. 1991. *Anne Bradstreet Revisited.* Boston: Twayne.

———. 1977. "Divine Translation: A Contribution to the Study of Anne Bradstreet's Method in Marriage Poems." *Early American Literature* 12: 121-35.

Rosenthal, Bernard. 1993. *Salem Story: Reading the Witch Trials of 1692.* Cambridge: Cambridge Univ. Press.

Rowson, Susanna Haswell. [1791;1828] 1991. *Charlotte Temple and Lucy Temple.* Ed. Ann Douglas. London: Penguin Books.

Rubin, Louis D. Jr., et al., eds. 1985. *The History of Southern Literature.* Baton Rouge: Louisiana State Univ. Press.

Scheick, William J. 1992. *Design in Puritan American Literature.* Lexington: Univ. Press of Kentucky.

———. 1974. *The Will and the Word: The Poetry of Edward Taylor.* Athens: Univ. of Georgia Press.

———, ed. [1960;1724] 1989. *Two Mather Biographies:* Life and Death *and* Parentator. Bethlehem, Pa.: Lehigh Univ. Press.

Schibanoff, Susan. 1994. "Botticelli's *Madonna del Masgnificat*: Constructing the Woman Writer in Early Humanist Italy." *Publications of the Modern Language Association* 109: 190-206.

Schweitzer, Ivy. 1988. "Ann Bradstreet Wrestles with the Renaissance." *Early American Literature* 23: 291-312.

———. 1991. *The Work of Self-Representation: Lyric Poetry in Colonial New England.* Chapel Hill: North Carolina Univ. Press.

Scruggs, Charles. 1981. "Phillis Wheatley and the Poetical Legacy of Eighteenth-Century England." *Studies in Eighteenth-Century Culture* 10: 279-95.

Sennett, Richard. 1980. *Authority.* New York: Knopf.

Sewel, William. 1800. *The History of the Rise, Increase, and Progress, of the Christian People Called Quakers.* 2 vols. London: J. Phillips.

Shea, Daniel B., Jr. 1968. *Spiritual Autobiography in Early America.* Princeton: Princeton Univ. Press.

———, ed. 1990. "Some Account of the Fore Part of the Life of Elizabeth Ashbridge." In *Journeys in New Worlds: Early American Women's Narratives,* ed. by William L. Andrews et al. 117-80. Madison: Univ. of Wisconsin Press.

Shields, John C. 1993. "Phillis Wheatley's Subversion of Classical Stylistics." *Style* 27: 252-70.

Silverman, Kenneth. 1984. *The Life and Times of Cotton Mather.* New York: Harper and Row.

Sistrunk, Albertha. 1982. "The Influence of Alexander Pope on the Writing Style of Phillis Wheatley." In *Critical Essays on Phillis Wheatley,* ed. William H. Robinson, 175-88. Boston: G. K. Hall.

Slemon, Stephen. 1990. "Unsettling the Empire: Resistance Theory for the Second World." *World Literature Written in English* 28: 30-41.

Smith, Theophus H. 1994. *Conjuring Culture: Biblical Formations of Black America.* New York: Oxford Univ. Press.

Smolinski, Reiner, ed. 1995. *The Threefold Paradise of Cotton Mather: An Edition of "Triparadisus"* Athens: Univ. of Georgia Press.

Smucker, Esther F. 1995. *Good Night, My Son.* Elverson, Pa.: Olde Springfield Shoppe.

Spruill, Julia Cherry. 1938. *Women's Life and Work in the Southern Colonies.* Chapel Hill: Univ. of North Carolina Press.

Stanford, Ann. 1966. "Anne Bradstreet: Dogmatist and Rebel." *New England Quarterly* 39: 373-89.

———. 1974. *Anne Bradstreet: The Worldly Puritan.* New York: Burt Franklin.

Stanford, Donald E., ed. 1960. *The Poems of Edward Taylor.* New Haven: Yale Univ. Press.

Starkey, Marion L. 1949. *The Devil in Massachusetts: A Modern Inquiry into the Salem Witch Trials* New York: Knopf.

Staten, Henry. 1993. "How the Spirit (Almost) Became Flesh: Gospel of John." *Representations* 41: 34-57.

Sweet, Timothy. 1988. "Gender, Genre, and Subjectivity in Anne Bradstreet's Early Elegies." *Early American Literature* 23: 152-74.

Thickstun, Margaret Olofson. 1988. *Fictions of the Feminine: Puritan Doctrine and the Representation of Women.* Ithaca: Cornell Univ. Press.

Tobin, Lad. 1990. "A Radically Different Voice: Gender and Language in the Trials of Anne Hutchison." *Early American Literature* 25: 253-70.

Toulouse, Teresa A. 1992. "My Own Credit': Strategies of (E)Valuation in Mary Rowlandson's Captivity Narrative." *American Literature* 64: 655-76.

Turell, Ebenezer. 1735 *Memoirs of the Life and Death of the Pious and Ingenious Mrs. Jane Turrell* (Bound with *Reliquiae Turellae, et Lachrymae Paternae* by Benjamin Colman.) Boston: S. Kneeland and T. Green.

Ulrich, Laurel Thatcher. 1982. *Good Wives: Image and Reality in the Lives of Women in Northern New England 1650-1750.* New York: Knopf.

VanDerBeets, Richard. 1984. *The Indian Captivity Narrative.* Lanham, Md.: Univ. Press of America.

Vaughan, Alden T., and Edward W. Clark, eds. 1981. *Puritans Among the Indians: Accounts of Captivity and Redemption, 1676-1724.* Cambridge: Harvard Univ. Press.

Vella, Michael W. 1993. "Theology, Genre, and Gender: The Precarious Place of Hannah Adams in American Literary History." *Early American Literature* 28: 21-41.

Waller, Jennifer R. 1974. "My Hand a Needle Better Fits': Anne Bradstreet and Women Poets in the Renaissance." *Dallhousie Review* 54: 436-50.

Watson, Marsha. 1996. "A Classic Case: Phillis Wheatley and Her Poetry." *Early American Literature* 31: 103-32.

Watson, Patricia Ann. 1991. *The Angelical Conjunction: The Preacher Physicians of Colonial New England.* Knoxville: Univ, Of Tennessee Press.

Watts, Emily Stipes. 1977. *The Poetry of American Women from 1632 to 1945.* Austin: Univ. of Texas Press.

Weber, Donald. 1988. *Rhetoric and History in Revolutionary New England.* New York: Oxford Univ. Press.

Weisman, Richard. 1984. *Witchcraft, Magic, and Religion in Seventeenth Century Massachusetts.* Amhest: Univ. of Massachusetts Press.

Wess, Robert C. 1976. "Religious Tensions in the Poetry of Anne Bradstreet." *Christianity and Literature* 25, 2: 30-36.

White, Elizabeth Wade. 1971. *Anne Bradstreet: The Tenth Muse.* New York: Oxford Univ. Press.

Whyte, Martin K. 1978. *The Status of Women in Preindustrial Societies.* Princeton: Princeton Univ. Press.

Wigger, John H. 1994. "Taking Heaven by Storm: Enthusiasm and Early American Methodism, 1770-1820." *Journal of the Early Republic* 14: 167-94.

Willard, Carla. 1995. "Wheatley's Turns of Praise: Heroic Entrapment and the Paradox of Revolution." *American Literature* 67: 233-56.

Williams, Daniel. 1993. "The Gratification of That Corrupt and Lawless Passion: Character Types and Themes in Early New England Rape Narratives." In *A Mixed Race: Ethnicity in Early America,* ed. Frank Shuffelton, 194-221. New York: Oxford Univ. Press.

Winship, Michael P. 1992. "Behold the Bridegroom cometh!: Marital Imagery in Massachusetts Preaching, 1630-1730." *Early American Literature* 27: 170-84.

———. 1990. "Cotton Mather, Astrologer." *New England Quarterly* 63: 308-14.

Winthrop, John. [1908] 1959. *John Winthrop's Journal: "History of New England," 1630-1649.* Ed. James Kendall Hosmer, 2 vols. New York: Knopf.

Wood, Forrest G. 1990. *The Arrogance of Faith: Christianity and Race in American from the Colonial Era to the Twentieth Century.* New York: Knopf.""-

Yates, Frances A. 1979. *The Occult Philosophy in the Elizabethan Age.* London: Routledge and Kegan Paul.

NORMAN K. RISJORD (ESSAY DATE 2001)

SOURCE: Risjord, Norman K. "Eliza Lucas Pinckney: The West Indies Connection." In *Representative Americans: The Colonists,* pp. 239-51. Lanham, Md.: Rowman & Littlefield Publishers, 2001.

In the following essay, Risjord describes the life and times of Pinckney.

Her words were oiled with affection and even deference, but there was no mistaking her firmness. The gentleman who desired her hand in marriage, she was telling her father, simply wouldn't do. "As I know tis my happiness you consult," she continued, "I must beg the favor of you to pay my thanks to the old gentleman for his generosity and favorable sentiments of me and let him know my thoughts on the affair in such civil terms as you know much better than any I can dictate; and beg leave to say to you that the riches of Peru and Chili if he had them put together could not purchase a sufficient esteem for him to make him my husband." In an age when marriages among the upper orders of society were often diplomatic and commercial alliances arranged by family heads, this was a remarkable statement of independence.

Eliza Lucas could afford to be independent. Her father was absent on military service in the West Indies; for some years she had been managing his South Carolina estates, making a good profit from the export of rice and naval stores. Small wonder that there was a line of suitors at her door. A wife with a business head was a prime asset for any planter. Far from being the giddy belles of the Cavalier myth, women in the colonial South played a vital role in the plantation economy. They managed the household and its servants, superintended the gardens and slaughtering pens that kept the plantation in daily fare, looked to the health of the labor force, and in some cases kept the business ledgers. The brisk self-confidence with which Eliza Lucas mastered all of these tasks bespoke a woman of uncommon wisdom and maturity. She had just turned seventeen.

From the Indies to Carolina

Eliza Lucas had, by the age of seventeen, already touched the three corners of Britain's Atlantic empire. She was born on Antigua in the West Indies, where her father, Lieutenant Colonel George Lucas, was stationed, but spent her youth in England acquiring the education and social graces thought suitable for ladies of her station in society. In 1738 Colonel Lucas moved his family to South Carolina, where he had inherited several plantations from his father. War loomed between Britain and Spain (the War of Jenkins' Ear), and Lucas apparently felt his family would be safer in South Carolina. (They were, as it turned out, due to the efforts of James Oglethorpe, although Eliza had small regard for his military capabilities.)

The family settled on a plantation overlooking Wappoo Creek, some six miles from Charleston by water. Within a year Colonel Lucas returned to Antigua to accept the post of governor, leaving his family in Carolina. Mrs. Lucas was in chronic ill health; George Lucas, Jr., was still in school in England. Management of Wappoo and its twenty slaves fell upon Eliza. In addition, she had to superintend the overseers on two other holdings, one an inland farm that produced tar and timber, the other a 3000-acre rice plantation on the Waccamaw River.

Eliza was happy with the arrangement; she had no desire to return to the Indies. Antigua was a low-lying, featureless island, sandy and dry, dependent on rainfall for fresh water. Its one asset was English Harbor, a deep, nearly landlocked roadstead large enough to accommodate the entire royal navy. Otherwise it was an unrelieved expanse of sugar plantations. South Carolina was also low-lying and level, but its landscape was broken by broad, smooth-flowing rivers and forests of live oak garbed in Spanish moss. "The country abounds with wild fowl," Eliza wrote her brother, "venison and fish, beef, veal, and mutton are here in much greater perfection than in the Islands, tho' not equal to that in England—but their pork exceeds any I ever tasted anywhere."

She also found the people "polite" and "genteel," as well she might, for most were of her own stock. South Carolina, alone among the mainland colonies, was populated principally from the West Indies. The spread of large-scale sugar planting on Jamaica and some of the Spanish islands (Cuba, Puerto Rico) undermined the economies of older, smaller, English islands (Barbados, Antigua, St. Kitts). Unable to compete, planters from these islands moved to the southernmost of the mainland colonies in the 1670s and '80s, taking their slaves with them. Because of this migration, blacks almost from the beginning of the colony outnumbered whites in low-country South Carolina.

Adapting to their new environment, the emigrants developed a flourishing trade in naval stores. The forests of long-leaf pine, which blanketed every well-drained slope in the colony, were nearly limitless sources of tar and pitch, the caulking compounds that kept wooden sailing ships afloat. And, like sugar, naval stores could be efficiently produced by gangs of semiskilled slaves. The profits from the export of naval stores, in turn, provided investment capital for the construction of rice plantations.

Rice, which was not grown in sizable quantities elsewhere in the British colonies, proved an enormously profitable crop. Parliament initially listed it among the "enumerated articles"—which meant that, like Virginia tobacco, it could be shipped only to the mother country—but after a few years, on the special plea of Carolina planters, that restriction was lifted. Able to ship their product directly to Spain, Portugal, and Italy, the planters made more profit than ever.

Wealth and the English gentlemanly ideal fostered the growth of an upper class, much as it had in Virginia, but the West Indian element gave the Carolina gentry a new dimension. There was no trace of a Puritan's conscience in South Carolina, not even a Virginian's spotty remorse. Whenever they could, Carolina planters turned their rice fields over to overseers and took their families into Charleston for a "season" of entertainment. The sprightliest town in America for its size, Charleston possessed both a music hall and a theater; its private clubs offered genteel diversions of every sort. Unlike Virginians, few Carolina planters developed any interest in politics and government. They preferred instead the dance hall and the racetrack.

This then was the environment that Eliza Lucas found so polite and genial. It was a blend of West Indian romance, English social custom, and New World riches—all resting on the sandy but momentarily stable foundation of slave labor. Nevertheless, she brought into this environment the personal work ethic of a Puritan. She arose each day at 5:00 A.M. and pursued a rigorous

ON THE SUBJECT OF...

ABIGAIL ADAMS (1744-1818)

That your Sex are Naturally Tyrannical is a Truth so thoroughly established as to admit of no dispute, but such of you as wish to be happy willingly give up the harsh title of Master for the more tender and endearing one of Friend. Why then, not put it out of the power of the vicious and the Lawless to use us with cruelty and indignity with impunity. Men of Sense in all Ages abhor those customs which treat us only as the vassals of your Sex. Regard us then as Beings placed by providence under your protection and in immitation of the Supreem Being make use of that power only for our happiness.

Abigail Adams, in an excerpt of a letter to her husband dated March 31, 1776.

Abigail Smith Adams is best known as the wife of John Adams, the second president of the United States, and as the mother of John Quincy Adams, the sixth president. The letters she wrote from the early 1760s until the end of her life reveal her efforts to fashion herself as a model woman according to the standards of the day: a capable and faithful wife, an effective household manager, a devoted mother and sister, and a discriminating reader and writer. Adams commented on the salient political issues of her time as well as voicing her concerns about religion, education, and child rearing. She noted details of everyday life, such as styles of dress and manners, and wrote of philosophy, science, and poetry. She appealed to her husband during the Revolutionary War to "remember the ladies" by providing them greater legal protection under the new government, and her correspondents included many of the great men of her time, such as her friend Thomas Jefferson. Abigail Adams's letters provide an invaluable view of the concerns of eighteenth-century women and their participation in a literary sphere that existed independently of the world of print, but was nonetheless culturally significant.

schedule of daily duties that included studying, supervising household servants, and providing instruction for her sister and some of the slave children. Whenever she had occasion to visit Charleston, she resisted its urbane temptations. She regretted "that giddy gayety and want of reflection which I contracted when in town." She consulted the psychological works of John Locke over and over to determine "if I was the very same self" in the city as when she was hard at work in the country.

The Business of Slaves, Rice, and Indigo

By 1739, South Carolina had not expanded much beyond the original settlements. Life still centered on the two rivers that joined at Charleston "to form the Atlantic ocean" (as Charlestonians would have it)—the Ashley and the Cooper. Both were broad, slow-moving streams, flanked by marshy flatlands ideal for rice culture. The Wappoo, where Eliza Lucas' main plantation was located, was a saltwater creek that connected the Ashley with the Stono River to the southwest of Charleston. Rice fields were laid out along the river and separated from it by a levee. The seed was broadcast over a dry field in the spring. Water was then let into the field through sluicegates. Tides helped back up the river to the level of the gates. In the autumn the field was drained for the harvest, taking advantage of a low tide. In the upper reaches of the rivers, especially on the Cooper (Goose Creek, Saint James Parish), spring floods helped flood the fields.

Rice was profitable, but it had some shortcomings, as Eliza Lucas quickly realized. The amount of land on any one plantation that could be devoted to it was sharply limited, and it required attention only in spring and fall. Slaves could be kept busy at other times of the year clearing land and repairing levees, but such tasks yielded no short-run profit. Carolina planters needed a market crop that could be grown on the uplands away from the river and one whose growth cycle varied from that of rice. The need was widely felt; a number of planters were experimenting with various seeds. George Lucas apparently brought some varieties with him from the West Indies, for as early as July, 1739, Eliza was writing her recently departed father about "the pains I had taken to bring the Indigo, Cotton, Lucern [alfalfa], and Cassada [cassava, a starchy root] to perfection, and had greater hopes from the Indigo—if I could have the seed earlier the next year from the [West] Indies—than any of the rest of the things I had tried."

Unlucky weather, stale seeds, and her own inexperience frustrated these early efforts, and Eliza turned her attention to making a profit from the crops she had. The following year she was again writing her father to thank him for sending "West India cucumber seed," and by the return vessel she shipped him two barrels of rice, two of corn, three of peas, some pickled pork, two kegs of oysters, and "one of eggs, by way of experiment, put up in salt." "My scheme," she added, "is to supply my father's [sugar] refining house in Antigua with eggs from Carolina."

Most of her rice, however, was consigned to agents in London, and from them she purchased the goods she needed, everything from a four-wheel chaise to medicine for her chronic headaches. She kept meticulous accounts of every transaction. One day a week, Thursday, was set aside for balancing ledgers, drafting instructions to overseers on the inland plantations, communicating with London, and summarizing her activities for her father. In early 1741 she wrote to a girlfriend in Charleston with evident enthusiasm, "I have planted a large fig orchard, with design to dry them and export them. I have reckoned my expense and the prophets [profits] to arise from those figs, but was I to tell you how great an estate I am to make this way, and how 'tis to be laid out, you would think me far gone in romance. Your good uncle [Charles Pinckney, Eliza's future husband] I know has long thought I have a fertile brain at scheming. I only confirm him in his opinion, but I own I love the vegitable [sic] world extreamly [sic]." By then, too, she had planted a grove of oak trees "for posterity," and her Charleston friends, the Pinckneys, were threatening to come for a visit so they could all sit and watch the oaks grow.

By 1744, indigo culture, for which she had always entertained high hopes, was showing true promise. Indigo was a broad-leafed weed, which produced a blue dye. The color blue, especially in its purple form, was in high demand in Europe because it was associated with royalty—and that perhaps because it was so scarce (red and yellow dyes abound in nature). Its preference for well-drained soils and its growth cycle (early spring to mid-summer) made it, from the planter's point of view, the perfect complement to rice. And the end product, a dry cake of blue, had relatively high value for its bulk and weight. Shipping charges, the difference often between profit and loss, were thus comparatively light, that is, compared to rice, cotton, or tobacco.

It was not an easy plant to grow or refine, however, and that is largely why Eliza Lucas took so long to develop it. Like corn, it does not compete well with other weeds; the soil must be carefully prepared and constantly tended. The leaves had to be cut at just the right moment—if too early the color was poor, if too late the leaves were juiceless. The leaves were placed in vats of water where they fermented and yielded their juice. The juice was then fermented further, while being stirred vigorously with paddles until it thickened. Lime was added to precipitate the dye and the excess water poured off. The precipitate was then dried into cakes and packed for shipment.

While it was fermenting the indigo juice had to be watched night and day, for the timing of each stage was critical. In the West Indies there were professional "indigo makers" who supervised this process. When Eliza produced her first crop in 1741, Governor Lucas sent out one of these experts from the island of Montserrat. To Eliza's dismay, however, the dye he produced was so poor as to be unsalable. The overseer blamed the climate, but Eliza, who had watched the process carefully, tried it herself and succeeded. She grilled the overseer, and he confessed that he had sabotaged the process by using too much lime. Mainland competition, he had come to fear, would ruin his home island. He may also have been uneasy about following the orders of a female.

Poor seed from the West Indies wasted the next two seasons, and it was not until 1744 that Eliza produced a marketable crop. A second overseer, employed by her father, produced seventeen pounds, and Eliza sent six of it to England for trial. Her agent gleefully reported: "I have shown your indigo to one of our most noted brokers . . . , who tried it against some of the best FRENCH, and in his opinion it is AS GOOD." Parliament, he suggested by way of further encouragement, might be persuaded to subsidize Carolina indigo because the drain on Britain for the purchase of French West Indian indigo amounted to £200,000 a year.

Eliza Lucas needed no such encouragement. Providence and patriotism had already induced her to save most of the 1744 crop for seed. What she herself could not use she gave away "in small quantities to a great number of people." Simultaneously she provoked interest in the crop by publishing the report of her London agent in *The South Carolina Gazette*. In the following year Eliza made £225 on her indigo shipment to London, and at the end of that harvest a half dozen planters were offering seed of their own for sale in columns of the *Gazette*. In 1747, parliament, true to form, placed a bounty on British indigo, and the crop became a major source of income until the bounty ended with the American Revolution. In good harvests South Carolina exported as much as a million pounds of blue cake—all the result of Eliza Lucas's love for the vegetable world and eye for profit.

Crops and profits were not her sole interests, despite her determination to be a success in business. To a Charleston friend who could not imagine what there was to do in the country she described her daily routine: "In general I rise at five o'clock in the morning, read till seven—then take a walk in the garden or fields, see that the servants are at their respective business, then to breakfast. The first hour after breakfast is spent in music, the next is constantly employed in recollecting something I have learned, least for the want of practice it should be quite lost, such as French and short hand." One day a week was set aside for business affairs, and she frequently checked on the overseers of her inland plantations. Her spare time in the afternoons was devoted to "little Polly and two black girls, who I teach to read." After dinner she practiced her music again, did needlework until twilight, and spent the evening writing letters. It was a routine not unlike that of the urbane William Byrd—except for the time devoted to the education of slaves.

That project was more than an idle pastime. Her purpose in tutoring the three girls was to make them "school mistresses for the rest of the Negro children," a project so daring that she took the trouble to secure the permission of her father. The sheriff, on the other hand, does not seem to have worried her, as well he might have, for the legislature made it illegal to teach slaves to read after the Stono River uprising of 1739. Perhaps she was given a subtle caution, for there is no further mention of the education project in her letters.

Her lack of reaction to the Stono uprising is itself mute testimony to her relations with her slaves. While the rest of South Carolina writhed in fear throughout 1739 and 1740 (unable even to send troops to Oglethorpe), Eliza Lucas ignored the event. There is not a whisper of it in her correspondence even though it took place a short distance from her plantation. The one mention of slave insurrection in her letters was in 1741 when a local religious fanatic predicted that slaves would destroy the low country "by fire and sword." Even then she was less alarmed at the prospect than amused by the antics of the enthusiast who tried to part the waters of a creek with a wand and, failing, wrote a letter of apology to the speaker of the assembly. Concluded Eliza: "I hope he will be a warning to all pious minds not to reject reason and revelation [i.e., Scripture] and set up in their stead their own wild notions." Hers was the voice of cool-headed Anglicanism, confident in its faith, secure in its environment.

It was, withal, a lonely environment, but she seems to have enjoyed being alone, though she could be garrulous enough in company. She took pains to keep herself intellectually alive. She borrowed books from the Pinckneys; she employed a music master to give her lessons every Monday. She must have devoured the weekly *South Carolina Gazette*, for she commented freely on politics and war. She had the Carolinian's contempt for Oglethorpe (without realizing that South Carolina's lack of support was the root of his difficulties); she had in general little use for war and warriors. "I wish all men were as great cowards as myself," she declared; "it would make them more peaceably inclined."

When a comet swept across the southern sky in the spring of 1743 she got up early every morning to watch it. A Charleston friend told her that some thought it was a reincarnation of a hero (others thought it heralded the Second Coming) and asked her to describe it. Eliza twitted her friend for being unable to get out of bed in time but described the phenomenon in great detail. And she had to admit that the tail did resemble human dress: "I could not see whether it had petticoats or not, but I am inclined to think by its modest appearance so early in the morning it won't permit every idle gazer to behold its splendor, a favor it will only grant to such as take pains for it—from hence I conclude if I could have discovered any clothing it would have been the female garb. Besides if it is any mortal transformed to this glorious luminary, why not a woman?"

Such warmth and wit must have early captured the attention of Colonel Charles Pinckney. The Pinckneys were acquaintances of George Lucas, and after the governor's departure for Antigua, Elizabeth Pinckney befriended Eliza. Whenever Eliza visited Charleston she stayed with the Pinckneys, and their niece, Mary Bartlett, became her closest friend. Eliza's relationship with Colonel Pinckney was an intellectual one. He lent her books, and her letters to him were extended, if somewhat simple discourses on Locke, Virgil, and the novels of Samuel Richardson.

Elizabeth Pinckney died in January, 1744, and a few weeks later Colonel Pinckney proposed to Eliza. Marriage, except in response to her father's efforts, rarely entered into her correspondence. She was a self-reliant woman with exacting standards. Men she met at Charleston festivities were too often, she found, full of "flashy nonsense." But Charles Pinckney was clearly different. The two were married in May, 1744. She moved to Belmont, the Pinckney plantation on the Cooper River, leaving her own farms in the hands of overseers, and began a new life.

From Carolina to England

Charles Pinckney's father Thomas had come to Carolina in 1692. Both he and his wife, Mary Cotesworth, were from the north country of England and evidently of prominent family. Thomas Pinckney styled himself "Gentleman" whenever he signed his name. He sent his sons to England for education. The eldest inherited his English estate; Charles, the second son, inherited the Carolina properties. Charles attended the Inns of Court, practiced law in South Carolina, and added considerably to his father's fortune. He had served as speaker of the house in the assembly and was a member of the Governor's council. He was forty-five years old when he married Eliza, just about double her age.

Belmont was an imposing brick mansion on a headland that commanded a view down the Cooper River to Charleston, five miles away. Eliza briskly took charge of the household and was soon planting trees. Oaks were her favorite because they had commercial value, but she also set out some magnolias for decoration. She corresponded frequently with a friend of her husband's, Dr. Alexander Garden, a Charleston physician with an interest in botany. Garden sent samples of American plants to the Swedish classifier Carolus Linneaus, who honored him by naming one luscious flower the gardenia. Linneaus, in turn, sent European specimens for trial in America, and Garden often sent them on to Eliza Pinckney. Her arboretum was the marvel of St. James Parish.

In February, 1745, she gave birth to a son, named, with due reverence for his pedigree, Charles Cotesworth Pinckney. Childbirth, always dangerous in that age, she sustained with her customary certitude, suffering "no disorder but weakness." Three months later she proudly informed Mary Bartlett that she could see "all his Papa's virtues already dawning in him." A month after that she wrote an English acquaintance to request the purchase of a special toy so her son could "play himself into learning . . . according to Mr. Locke's method." Her reference evidently was to John Locke's *Essay Concerning Human Understanding,* one of her husband's books that she had read "over and over." Locke rejected the ancient notion that people were born with "innate ideas." The mind, he said, is a blank tablet (*tabula rasa*) on which life experience writes. His "method" of education, then, must have been a matter of "learning by doing," an interesting anticipation of some twentieth-century pedagogical techniques. Eliza was delighted with the results. A year later, when her son was 22 months old, she reported that he "prattles very intelligibly," knew the alphabet, and was beginning to spell. What the son thought of all this was not recorded until his later years when he claimed he had been nearly ruined in his youth by being pushed too rapidly in his studies. In the next few years Eliza had two more children, Harriott and Thomas (a third died in infancy).

In between motherhood and household management she managed to wedge time for agricultural experiments. Silkmaking caught her attention in the late 1740s. There had been a number of efforts to make silk in the early days of the colony, but they had been abandoned in the rush to rice. The mulberry trees were still there, however, and Eliza Pinckney had only to procure some well-bred eggs. She also viewed it as a way of employing slaves who could do no other work, which eased her balance sheet. Children gathered the mulberry leaves and fed the worms; the elderly dried the cocoons and "reeled" the silk. No one in the colony could weave silk, apparently, for she took her raw silk with her when she went to England in 1753 and had it made into dresses there. One of these she presented to the Princess of Wales, daughter-in-law of the king.

The occasion for her return to the mother country was the assembly's appointment of Charles Pinckney to represent the colony in London. A secondary motive was the desire, shared by both parents, to give their children an English education. There was still something inferior in the name "colonial."

Luckily for Eliza, a poor sailor, the passage was a swift one, a mere twenty-five days. The south coast ports of Portsmouth and Southampton were ravaged by smallpox, so their vessel sailed up the channel to London. They took a house in Richmond, a short distance up the Thames from London, and put the whole family through inoculation. Eliza renewed old acquaintances and quickly settled into a routine of social visits and sightseeing. They traveled extensively through the midlands and north country (where Charles had lands) and spent the "season" at Bath. They thoroughly enjoyed themselves, but never forgot that they were "exiles," as Eliza put it. She disliked the idleness of the English upper class and especially "the perpetual card playing." Charles, even more restless, had "many yearnings after his native land." In describing to a Carolina friend a visit to the Princess of Wales, in which the princess had dealt quite informally with the Pinckney children, Eliza added: "This, you'll imagine must seem pretty extraordinary to an American." How lightly the phrase "an American" tripped from her pen, yet it revealed much about her developing sense of national identity.

The Pinckneys departed for home in May, 1758, having resided in Britain for five years. They left the two boys in London to finish their schooling and took nine-year-old Harriott home with them. The plantations had suffered much in their absence; overseers, as every planter knew, needed constant oversight. Charles Pinckney plunged into work, but soon contracted malaria. Swamp fever was not usually fatal, but Pinckney was advanced in years and perhaps weakened by the sea journey. He died within three weeks. Eliza resumed the solitary existence she had known before.

Founding Mother

Many months later she referred to it as a time when the "lethargy of stupidity" gripped her mind and she functioned barely enough to keep alive. For more than a year after Charles Pinckney's death her letters to friends bled with misery and lament. But time healed and duty pulled her back to life. She had not only her own lands but the vast Pinckney holdings to superintend. There were thousand-acre plantations on both the Ashley and Cooper rivers, five hundred acres on the Savannah River, a sea-island near Beaufort, and an elaborate town house in Charleston. Charles Pinckney had willed all this property to his sons; it was Eliza's duty to preserve and improve it until they came of age.

Belmont, after five years of neglect, had "gone back to woods again." She threw herself into work and soon found that it had its own therapeutic value. With the help of an overseer who was both efficient and honest (because of his rare talents he was in such demand that he could choose his own employer and chose to work only for widows and orphans), Belmont was soon restored to production. By the spring of 1760 Eliza was writing to her London agent that, but for an unforeseen drought she would have produced enough to clear all the Pinckney estate's British debts. And she resumed her tree-planting. By 1761 she had a nursery for magnolia and bay trees. Her experiment with the bay tree is especially interesting, for the leaves of this West Indian tree were used as both a spice and a medicine, and cinnamon was made from the bark. And she had devised a way of packing two-year-old seedlings for shipment to friends in England.

When the day's work was done, her children occupied her thoughts. The two boys, left in vice-ridden London without parental guidance, were a particular worry. She bombarded them with letters full of homiletic advice. Whether it was her concern, or native good sense, or a combination of the two, Charles and Thomas threaded their way through Oxford and the Middle Temple without recorded difficulty. Daughter Harriott was also a source of pride and comfort. At the age of nineteen she married Daniel Horry, a rice planter with large holdings on the Santee River and a comfortable house in Charleston. By that date (1768) Eliza herself had moved into Charleston; she occupied herself through her last active years rebuilding the Horrys' garden.

In 1769 her oldest son returned home (Thomas, five years younger, returned in 1774). After completing his legal studies and being admitted to the bar, Charles Cotesworth Pinckney had journeyed to France for study at the Royal Military College at Caen. It was almost as if he foresaw that there was a new nation being born in America and that it would need soldiers and statesmen. In any case, he returned a flaming patriot, whose fight against the Stamp Act and other parliamentary impositions on the colonies had earned him the sobriquet "The Little Rebel" among Americans in London.

Both Charles and Thomas rose to the rank of general in the American Revolution, and each played a prominent role in the politics of independence. Charles Cotesworth participated in the convention that drafted the federal Constitution, and Thomas, as governor of the state in 1787, submitted the Constitution to the assembly. Each served the Federalist administrations of George Washington and John Adams in a diplomatic capacity during the 1790s, and, at different times, each was a Federalist candidate for vice president. In 1808 Charles Cotesworth Pinckney ran unsuccessfully against James Madison for president.

Eliza spent her last years in the company of her daughter and husband, rotating with the seasons between Charleston and the Santee. When President Washington toured the southern states in 1791, he made a point of stopping at the

Horry plantation to visit Eliza Pinckney. An experimental farmer himself, Washington no doubt admired her as much for her agronomy as for her sons. Shortly thereafter she was stricken with cancer, a disease only recently identified and then not in all its forms. In the spring of 1793 she traveled to Philadelphia seeking treatment from a noted cancer specialist. She died there in May, 1793. At her funeral, in St. Peters Anglican Church, President Washington, at his own request, served as one of the pallbearers. In her youth she considered herself a transplanted Englishwoman; in maturity she knew herself to be an American.

Suggestions for Further Reading

Eliza Lucas Pinckney stands in need of a biographer. The only study currently available is by her great granddaughter, Harriet Horry Ravenal, *Eliza Pinckney* (1896). Pinckney's splendid letters, however, have been published by Elise Pinckney, ed., *The Letterbook of Eliza Lucas Pinckney* (1972). For the world in which she lived the following studies are recommended: M. Eugene Sirmans, *Colonial South Carolina, A Political History* (1966); Clarence L. Ver Steeg, *Origins of a Southern Mosaic: Studies of Early Carolina and Georgia* (1975); and George C. Rogers, *Charleston in the Age of the Pinckneys* (1969). Her agricultural experiments are put in context by Joyce E. Chaplin, *An Anxious Pursuit: Agricultural Innovation and Modernity in the Lower South, 1730-1815* (1993).

FURTHER READING

Altaba-Artal, Dolors. "Theology to Humanism: Aphra Behn's 'The Young King; or, The Mistake'." In *Aphra Behn's English Feminism: Wit and Satire,* pp. 26-45. Selinsgrove, Pa.: Susquehanna University Press, 1999.

Examines The Young King; or, The Mistake*'s debt to the work of Calderón de la Barca (1600-1681).*

Anthony, Katharine. *First Lady of the Revolution: The Life of Mercy Otis Warren.* Port Washington, N.Y.: Kennikat Press, 1972, 258 p.

Biography of Mercy Otis Warren, a prominent patriot, pamphleteer, historian, and woman of letters during the American revolutionary period.

Armstrong, Nancy. "Captivity and Cultural Capital in the English Novel." *Novel* 31, no. 3 (summer 1998): 373-98.

Contends that eighteenth century English novelists were heavily influenced by the Colonial captivity narrative.

Beckstrand, Lisa. "Olympe de Gouges: Feminine Sensibility and Political Posturing." *Intertexts* 6, no. 2 (2002): 185-202.

Examines how Olympe de Gouges's use of fictional autobiography enabled her to challenge gender restrictions.

Bohls, Elizabeth A. "Dorothy Wordsworth and the Cultural Politics of Scenic Tourism." In *Women Travel Writers and the Language of Aesthetics, 1716-1818,* pp. 170-208. Cambridge, England: Cambridge University Press, 1995.

Studies how Wordsworth disrupted mainstream aesthetic values by placing more emphasis on activity than on passivity.

Boland, Eavan. "Finding Anne Bradstreet." In *Green Thoughts, Green Shades: Essays by Contemporary Poets on the Early Modern Lyric,* edited by Jonathan F. S. Post, pp. 176-90. Berkeley: University of California Press, 2002.

Contemplates the impossibility of adequately grasping the world in which Anne Bradstreet wrote.

Boyer, H. Patsy. Introduction to *The Enchantments of Love: Amorous and Exemplary Novels,* by Maria de Zayas; edited by H. Patsy Boyer, pp. i-xl. Berkeley: University of California Press, 1990.

Overview of Maria de Zayas's life and works.

Crawford, Katherine. "Catherine de Médici and the Performance of Political Motherhood." *The Sixteenth Century Journal* 31, no. 3 (fall 2000): 643-73.

Follows Catherine's efforts at being a mother and wielding political power simultaneously.

Debby, Nirit Ben-Aryeh. "Vittoria Colonna and Titian's Pitti 'Magdalen'." *Woman's Art Journal* 24, no. 1 (spring/summer 2003): 29-33.

Examines the sensuality of a figure in a painting commissioned for Vittoria Colonna.

Fleming, Robert. "Supplemental Self: A Postcolonial Quest(ion) for (of) National Essence and Indigenous Form in Catharine Parr Traill's Canadian Crusoes." *Essays on Canadian Writing,* no. 56 (fall 1995): 198-223.

Discusses how the characters Catharine and Indiana challenged Victorian notions of proper female conduct.

Harvey, Tamara. "'Now Sisters . . . impart your usefulnesse, and force': Anne Bradstreet's Feminist Functionalism in 'The Tenth Muse' (1650)." *Early American Literature* 35, no. 1 (winter 2000): 5-28.

Contends that Anne Bradstreet was conscious of being a part of a debate tradition concerning the place of women in literature and society.

Hicks, Philip. "Catharine Macaulay's Civil War: Gender, History, and Republicanism in Georgian Britain." *Journal of British Studies* 41 (April 2002): 170-98.

Describes how Macaulay used her historical portraits of patriotic heroines to cast doubt on classical republican notions of masculinity.

Michaelsen, Scott. "Narrative and Class in a Culture of Consumption: The Significance of Stories in Sarah Kemble Knight's 'Journal'." *College Literature* 21, no. 2 (June 1994): 33-46.

Urges study of Kemble Knight's text to prepare for discussion of the "modern consumption community," which seeks to be entertained rather than edified.

Rosenmeier, Rosamond. *Anne Bradstreet Revisited.* Boston: Twayne Publishers, 1991, 174 p.

Attempts to integrate Anne Bradstreet's life and works.

Smith, William Raymond. "Mercy Otis Warren: New England Idealist." In *History as Argument: Three Patriot

Historians of the American Revolution, pp. 73-119. The Hague: Mouton & Co., 1966.

Investigates the interrelation of human nature, human history, divine nature, and divine history in Mercy Otis Warren's history of the American Revolution.

Stanford, Ann. *Anne Bradstreet: The Worldly Puritan.* New York: Burt Franklin & Co., 1974, 170 p.

Full-length study of Anne Bradstreet includes a chronology, a frequency list of images used in her poetry, and a list of books with which she was acquainted.

Tawil, Ezra F. "Domestic Frontier Romance, or, How the Sentimental Heroine Became White." *Novel* 32, no. 1 (fall 1998): 99-124.

Examines women's frontier romances in a study of relations between Anglo-Americans and Native Americans.

Ulrich, Laurel Thatcher. *Good Wives: Image and Reality in the Lives of Women in Northern New England 1650-1750.* New York: Vintage Books, 1991, 296 p.

Offers vignettes of the lives of common women.

Wahrman, Dror. "'Percy's' Prologue: From Gender Play to Gender Panic in Eighteenth-Century England." *Past & Present,* no. 159 (May 1998): 113-60.

Examines Hannah More's role in the cultural shift of attitudes concerning gender boundaries.

Wesley, Marilyn C. "Moving Targets: The Travel Text in 'A Narrative of the Captivity and Restauration of Mrs. Mary Rowlandson'." *Essays in Literature* 23, no. 1 (spring 1996): 42-57.

Emphasizes the travel narrative aspects of Mary Rowlandson's account.

Wiesner-Hanks, Merry. "Special Issue: Gender in Early Modern Europe." *The Sixteenth Century Journal* 31, no. 1 (spring 2000): 3-146.

Examines gender issues from the approaches of social history, art history, political history, religious history, and literature.

Wilcox, Helen. "'First Fruits of a Woman's Wit': Authorial Self-Construction of English Renaissance Women Poets." In *Write or Be Written: Early Modern Women Poets and Cultural Constraints,* edited by Barbara Smith and Ursula Appelt, pp. 199-215. Aldershot, England: Ashgate, 2001.

Discusses how several poets fashioned themselves in their prefaces.

Zimmerman, Sarah M. "Dorothy Wordsworth and the Liabilities of Literary Production." In *Romanticism, Lyricism, and History,* pp. 113-46. Albany: State University of New York Press, 1999.

Analyzes Dorothy Wordsworth's arguments against publication of her work.

CHRISTINE DE PIZAN

(1365 - c. 1431)

(Surname also transliterated as Pisan) French poet, prose writer, allegorist, epistler, and biographer.

Christine wrote poetry, military and political treatises, history, biography, and allegory first as a widow supporting her family, then, as her reputation as a gifted writer and thinker was established, as a strong political voice. Christine wrote with boldness and originality and, as her country sank deeper into turmoil and internal conflict, she was a consistent voice for peace. Her masterwork, *Le livre de la cité des dames* (1404-05; *The Book of the City of Ladies*), is among the first defenses of women written by a woman; it was translated into multiple European languages within years of her death and was widely read through the next several centuries as Christine's once-radical ideas about women gradually gained acceptance.

BIOGRAPHICAL INFORMATION

Christine was born in Venice, where her father, Tommaso da Pizzano, was a salaried counselor. When she was four she moved with her family to Paris, where her father served as an astrologer to Charles V. Pizzano was connected to the intellectuals of northern Italy, especially at the University of Bologna, and he shared his interest in education and knowledge with his daughter despite the contemporary belief that learning was dangerous for women. Christine moved in courtly intellectual circles and enjoyed access to the royal library. Her father's connections, position, and encouragement placed Christine in the midst of a growing intellectual movement that would later be known as classical humanism, characterized by a revived interest in Latin and Greek authors and the writings of Christian authors including St. Augustine and St. Thomas Aquinas, and by a new concern for the relationship between the individual and the society or state. Her own education was abbreviated by her marriage at age fifteen to a court notary, Etienne de Castel, who was appointed a secretary in the Royal Chancellery. The marriage was a happy one, resulting in three children (a daughter and two sons), but it lasted only ten years, ending with Etienne's unexpected death in 1390, possibly from a plague epidemic. The death of her husband left Christine and her children in difficult circumstances. Upon the death of Charles V in 1380, Pizzano lost his position at court, and died sometime after 1385. Responsible for supporting both her children and her mother, Christine attempted to secure her inheritance but was obstructed by lawyers who forced her to pay taxes on her father's land without giving her the titles to the property. She fought them for nearly fifteen years before prevailing, and her struggles influenced her later thoughts on women's household roles. She also attempted to support her family by writing, beginning with ballades inspired by her experiences, which she began circulating around 1395. Her first poetry collection appeared around 1399; it includes *Les cent balades,* a collection of ballads presenting a series of love affairs, first from a woman's, then from a man's perspective. Her courtly connections, particularly in the court of the king's brother, Louis of Orleans, assured an audience for her lyric poetry, but her fame increased considerably due to her *L'epistre au dieu d'amours* (1399; *The Letter of Cupid*), in which she attacked negative literary portrayals of women. In particular, she denounced the misogyny of Jean de Meun and his *Le roman de la rose* (c. 1269-78; *The Romance of the Rose*), launching a major cultural battle in which Christine's enemies contended that a woman could not understand the writings of an educated man. The *Querelle de la Rose* lasted three years and pushed Christine into the center of the French literary world. She then undertook extensive study of classical literature, culminating in *L'epistre d'Othéa* (c. 1400; *The Epistle of Othea to Hector*), a poem of moral instruction most likely written for her surviving son, Jean du Castel. As a result of Christine's growing literary reputation, Philip, Duke of Burgundy, commissioned her in 1404 to write a history of his brother, Charles V. Christine had by this point transferred her allegiance from Orleans to Burgundy when the latter helped find a place for her son Jean in his household. Drawing on her personal memories of life at court, she produced *Le livre des fais et bonnes meurs du sage roy Charles V* (1404; *The Book of the Wise Deeds and Good Conduct of the Wise King Charles V*). Philip's unusual choice of a female writer gave further endorsement to Christine's unique status as a major female literary figure in late medieval France. Christine then began to address contemporary moral, political, and educational issues in her writings. Among the most significant of these is *The Book of the City of Ladies,* in which she exposes and condemns the misogynistic society in which women suffered, defends the merits of women, and calls for their greater autonomy and freedom. She next wrote a practical companion to *The City of Ladies,* with advice for achieving true virtue and nobility: *Le livre des trois vertus* (1405; *The Book of the Three Virtues*), uniquely addressed to middle class women, became a successful conduct book as well as a defense of women. Also in 1405, Christine published the allegorical *L'avision-Christine* (*Christine's Vision*), a dream vision in which Christine talks of her life with figures including "Libera" (meaning "free woman"), "Opinion," and "Philosophie." Much of her work after 1405 is more explicitly political than her previous writings. In that year, she had also written an open letter to Queen Isabelle of France to reconcile a feud between the houses of Burgundy and Orléans, and in 1406 and 1407 she published *Le livre du corps de policie* (*The Body of Policye*), calling for universal justice and attention to the needs of common people. As a companion to *The Body of Policye,* Christine wrote *Le livre des faits d'armes et de chevalerie* (1410; *The Book of Fayttes of Armes and of Chyvalrye*), a history of the art of war. She wrote her last in this series of political texts for the Dauphin, Louis de Guyenne, France's teenage prince who would soon be struggling to achieve peace and order: *Le livre de la paix* (1413; *The Book of Peace*) aimed at educating and guiding Louis through the threat of civil war and foreign invasion. The situation in France worsened, however, beginning with the French loss to the English at Agincourt in 1415, an event which inspired Christine's *Epistre de la prison de vie humaine* (c. 1413-18; *Letter on the Prison of Human Life*), a poem of consolation to the widows of Agincourt. The increasing violence in Paris finally drove her from the city, and she relocated to Poissy Abbey, where her daughter was a nun, in 1418. While there she wrote little, except a poem likely in response to her son's death, entitled *Les heures de contemplation sur la passion de nostre Seigneur* (1425; *The Hours of Contemplation on the Passion of Our Lord*). Her last known work is a celebration of Joan of Arc's victories over the English, in *La ditié de Jeanne d'Arc* (1429; *The Tale of Joan of Arc*). Christine died at Poissy Abbey sometime between July 1429 and 1434, when court writings mention her in the past tense.

MAJOR WORKS

Christine's writings fall roughly into three thematic and stylistic groupings. Her early works are primarily poetry, especially love poetry; those from mid-career are mainly allegories in which Christine addresses broader social and philosophical concerns; and her later works could be generally characterized as political. Christine's writings reflect her concern with the reputation and status of women, and her vision for a more peaceful society for both women and men. Her early poetry followed the mode of the court of Orleans, where chivalry and romance were favored themes. Christine distinguished herself from earlier and contemporary models by writing about married love and loss in addition to the typical courtly *amours*. She presented a woman's perspective on chivalric conventions, as in the feminine half of *Les cent balades,* as well as the *Letter to Cupid,* the pastoral poem *Dit de la pastoure* (1403; *Tale of the Shepherdess*), and *Le débat de deux amans* (1400; *The Debate of Two Lovers*), in which an independent young woman rejects the chivalric notions of love presented by a knight and a squire. In Christine's allegorical works, *Le livre du chemin de long estude* (1400-3; *The Book of the Long Road of Learning*) and *Le livre de la mutacion de fortune* (1402-3; *The Book of the Mutation of Fortune*) she examines the ideals of world governance and the history of human affairs. *The City of Ladies* and *The Book of the Three Virtues* depict a city of noble women who claim their nobility not by birth but by virtue. These two allegories mark the apex of Christine's career as a defender of women, as she worked to dispel the myth that women were either inherently evil or divinely good. Christine's political prose works, written as the Burgundy-Orleans battles increased in severity and the English advanced their position within France, do not explicitly address women's issues, but are remarkable for their subject matter as well as the fact that they were highly-regarded among men despite their female authorship. Two of her last works, *The Epistle of the Prison of Human Life* and *The Hours of Contemplation of the Passion,* offer a unique perspective on war and politics, focusing on the consequences of war for the women left behind, both widows and mothers.

CRITICAL RECEPTION

Christine wrote with the imprimatur of the French royalty, an indication of the favorable reception her works received during her lifetime. She was, nevertheless, also negatively criticized; as her part in the *Quarrel of the Rose* suggests, several intellectuals of her day scorned her writing. Others, during her life and in subsequent centuries, argued that the quality of her work was beyond the capabilities of a woman and maintained that the texts signed by Christine de Pizan were actually written by a man. Her works enjoyed continued printings throughout the sixteenth century, and though interest in medieval authors waned during the seventeenth century, eighteenth-century scholars again included her among the major writers of medieval France. Commentary on her works increased, and as interest in women's rights became a part of the late eighteenth-century Enlightenment, Christine became known as an early feminist. French nationalism in the nineteenth century also stirred interest in her political writings, and by the end of that century a well-edited version of her collected works appeared. In addition to analyzing her political and social thought, modern scholars have studied her literary achievements, particularly as a poet. The accessibility of English versions of her works in the nineteenth and twentieth centuries, as well as increased emphasis on women's studies renewed and expanded interest in Christine's life and works. Christine's defense of women and her unique status as the first major woman author in France have compelled modern scholars to examine her linguistic and stylistic strategies, her connections to political figures of her era, and her influence on later writers, both male and female.

PRINCIPAL WORKS

Les cent balades [*One Hundred Ballads*] (poetry) 1399?

**L'Epistre au dieu d'amours* [*The Letter of Cupid*; translated by Thomas Hoccleve, 1721] (poetry) 1399

Le débat de deux amants [*The Debate of Two Lovers*] (poetry) c. 1400

L'epistre d'Othea [*The Epistle of Othea to Hector*] (poetry) c. 1400

Le livre de trois jugemens [*The Book of Three Judgments*] (poetry) 1402

Le livre de la mutacion de Fortune [*The Book of the Mutation of Fortune*] (allegory) 1400-1403

Le livre du chemin de long estude [*The Book of the Long Road of Learning*] (allegory) 1402-1403

Dit de la pastoure [*Tale of the Shepherdess*] (poetry) 1403

Le livre du duc des vrais amans [*The Book of the Duke of True Lovers*] (poetry) 1403-05

Le livre des fais et bonnes meurs du sage roy Charles V [*The Book of the Wise Deeds and Good Conduct of the Wise King Charles V*] (biography) 1404

Le livre de la cité des dames [*The Book of the City of Ladies*; translated by Earl Jeffrey Richards, 1982] (allegory) 1404-05

L'avision-Christine [*Christine's Vision*; translated by Glenda K. McLeod, 1993] (allegory) 1405

Epistre a Isabeau de Bavière, Reine de France [*An Epistle to the Queen of France*] (letter) 1405

†*Le livre des trois vertus* [*The Book of the Three Virtues*] (allegory) 1405

Le livre du corps de policie [*The Body of Polycy*; also translated as *The Book of the Body Politic*; translated by Kate Langdon Forhan, 1994] (prose) 1406-07

Le livre des faits d'armes et de chevalerie [*The Book of the Fayttes of Armes and Chyualrye*; translated by William Caxton, 1489] (prose) 1410

Le livre de la paix [*The Book of Peace*] (prose) 1412-13

Epistre de la prison de vie humaine [*The Epistle of the Prison of Human Life*; translated by Josette A. Wisman, 1984] (poetry) 1415-18

Les heures de contemplation sur la passion de nostre Seigneur [*The Hours of Contemplation on the Passion of Our Lord*] (poetry) 1425

Le ditié de Jehanne d'Arc [*The Tale of Joan of Arc*] (poetry) 1429

Oeuvres poétiques de Christine de Pisan [*Poetic Works of Christine de Pizan*] (poetry) 1886-96

The Writings of Christine de Pizan [edited by Charity Cannon Willard] (poetry, prose, allegory, and biography) 1994

The Selected Writings of Christine de Pizan [edited by Renate Blumenfeld-Kosinski] (poetry and prose) 1997

* Hoccleve's edition is a reorganized expansion, but not a literal translation, of *L'epistre au dieu d'amours*.

† Often referred to as *Le tresor de la cité des dames* (*The Treasure of the City of Ladies*).

PRIMARY SOURCES

CHRISTINE DE PIZAN (ESSAY DATE 1405)

SOURCE: Christine de Pizan. "Christine's Vision." In *The Writings of Christine de Pizan,* translated by Charity Cannon Willard, pp. 6-26. New York: Persea Books, 1994.

In the following excerpt from her autobiographical Vision, *first published in 1405, Christine relates the story of how she came to a life of study. In a complaint to the allegorical figure of Lady Philosophy, Christine explains that study and writing helped support her after the loss of family and friends, both financially and spiritually.*

Christine Continues Her Complaint

When, sweet mistress, you learn about those merry early days of my widowhood, you can well imagine how eager I was for romantic dalliance! Despite all that I had suffered at Fortune's hands, that faithless one, about whom I have already written one well-justified complaint, was not finished with me yet. For the pain in the tooth soon draws the tongue. I will continue, therefore, along the same lines, relating how Fortune continues to assail me even now.

During those trying days, as I have said, I was resolved to conceal my problems from others, for the reason that charity is rare, and a little of it can easily lead to servitude. But as it is indeed burdensome to contain one's sorrow entirely, Fortune could not assail me to the point of depriving me of the company of the poets' muses. Your banishment of poetry from Boethius notwithstanding (you had worthier fare in mind for him), I was moved to compose plaintive rhymes that lamented my dead husband and the days that had passed, as is clear in the early poems of my first collection of ***One Hundred Ballades.*** Then, in order to pass the time and also to cheer myself somewhat, I began writing gay love poems expressing others' feelings, as I state in one of my virelays.

Christine Relates How She Changed Her Way of Life

As my youth was already largely behind me, as were most of my outside obligations, I returned to the way of life that suited me best: seclusion and quiet. In my solitude, there came back to me some remnants of Latin and the beauteous sciences, along with sayings from the authors and rhetorical pieces I had heard my beloved father and husband recite but, in my frivolity, had remembered quite poorly. Despite the fact that my nature inclined me to learning from my earliest years, my duties as a married woman kept me otherwise occupied, as did the burden of frequent childbearing. In addition, youth, that tender enemy of good sense, will prevent even children with good minds from applying themselves to study, unless fear of punishment is brought to bear. And as this was not done in my case, the desire to play won out over intelligence and inclination, so that I could not be constant in the labor of learning.

Christine Complains of Youth

Oh flighty youth, so blind and capricious! You do not realize what is good for you; you take pleasure only in vain and worthless things, and pursue nothing else. Truly he who follows your way treads the path of perdition and stumbles in his own blindness. I should bear you great resentment, for when I was right beside those two founts of philosophy, so clear and pure, I was too young and foolish to drink my fill, even though those limpid streams pleased me greatly. Like the fool who sees the sun shining and does not give a thought to the rain, thinking he will always have sunlight, I paid no heed, believing I could recover what was slipping away. Ah, Fortune, what a treasure you took from me! My possibilities were greatly diminished when you did not let me keep those two until I had advanced in learning. You harmed the very character of my soul! For if I had the benefit of the clarity of their knowledge now, with my present desire not for vain activities and delights but for study only, I would fill myself so, that I would surpass all other women of this day and many generations preceding. Alas, when I had those learned masters beside me, I did not give much thought to study! And now I hunger in mind and spirit for that which I am no longer able to possess: the knowledge of you, sweet Philosophy! Ah, savory, honeyed treasure, sovereign above all others. Happy are those who delight in you fully! I nonetheless find small tastes of you in the subordinate branches of science. As I can reach no higher, I can only imagine the supreme delight of those who love and take relish in you completely. Oh, children and youths! If only you knew what good is to be found in the delight of knowledge, and the evil and ugliness in ignorance—if only you knew better, you would not complain about the labor of studying! Does not Aristotle say that the wise man naturally leads the ignorant, as the soul governs the body? What can be more beautiful than learning? And what uglier than ignorance, so ill-befitting human nature? One day, a man criticized my desire for knowledge, saying that it was inappropriate for a woman to be learned, as it was so rare, to which I replied that it was even less fitting for a man to be ignorant, as it was so common.

Christine Relates How She Turned to Study

Thus I arrived at the age when one naturally attains a certain level of knowledge, and looking back over my past life and ahead to the inevitable end, like a traveler who has just passed over a dangerous route and who, turning back in amazement, resolves never to go that way again but to find a better path, I came to the realization that the world is full of dangers and that there is only one good: the way of truth. So I turned to the path of study, towards which I was inclined by nature and constellation. I closed those gates that are the senses, which no longer wandered amongst external things, and took up those beautiful books with the intent of recovering part of what I had lost. I was not presumptuous enough to delve into the obscure sciences, whose language I could not understand, for as Cato says, "to read and fail to understand is not truly to read." But like a child who first learns the alphabet, I began with the ancient histories from the beginnings of the world, then the history of the Hebrews, the Assyrians, and the early kingdoms, proceeding from one to the other and coming to the Romans, the French, the Britons, and several other historians, and then to what scientific learning I was able to grasp in the time available for study.

Next, I took up the works of the poets, my knowledge increasing all the while. I was glad to find in them a style that seemed natural to me, and took pleasure in their subtle allegories and lovely material hidden beneath delightful moral fictions, as well as the beautiful forms of their verse and prose adorned with polished rhetoric, subtle language, and piquant proverbs. For this science of poetry, Nature rejoiced within me and directed: "Daughter, be glad when you have fulfilled the desire that I give you, studying all the while and understanding certain thoughts better and better." I felt then a certain dissatisfaction growing within me. Nature willed that from my studies and experience there be born new works, and commanded: "Take up your tools and hammer out on the anvil the material I shall give you, as lasting as iron and impervious to fire and everything else, and forge objects of delight. When your children were in your womb, you experienced great pain bringing them into the world. It is now my wish that new works be born from your memory in joy and delight, which will carry your name forever all over the world, and to future generations of princes. Just as the woman who has given birth forgets her suffering as soon as she hears her child cry, so too you will forget the toil of your labor once you have heard the voice of your writings."

Thus I began to write short pieces in a lighter vein, and like the workman who perfects his technique by practicing, I learned more and more new things through the study of diverse disciplines, and refined my style with greater subtleness and the use of nobler material. Between the year 1399, when I began writing, and the present, 1405, I have composed fifteen principal works, not counting some shorter ones, all of which fill seventy thick quires, as can easily be shown. I do not say this, Lord knows, to boast or seek praise, as my works are not remarkable for their subtlety, but recount it in the context of my good and bad fortunes.

The Pleasure That Christine Took in Study

Thus I had adopted a different way of life, but my fortunes did not improve. Misfortune, as though jealous of the comfort and peace of my solitary contemplation, persisted in her malevolence not only towards me but towards my friends as well, which I see as proof of her animosity towards me.

It is true that news of my studious way of life had already spread, contrary to my wishes, even among princes; but since this was so, I sent those nobles a number of my meager writings as gifts, thinking they might appeal by way of their novelty; and the gifts were accepted joyfully and with a graciousness befitting the nobles' rank. I attribute this reception not to the value of my works but rather to the fact that they had been written by a woman, a phenomenon not seen in quite some time. Thus, quite quickly, my writings became known and were read in many different lands.

At about that time, the daughter of the French king was given in marriage to King Richard of England, and a certain noble Count of Salisbury came to France for that reason. As this gentle knight loved poetry and indeed wrote beautiful poems himself, after seeing some of my works he had several nobles persuade me, despite my reluctance, to send back with him to England my elder son, a rather clever child of twelve with a gift for singing, so that he could serve as companion to a son of his of about the same age. Because the count was very generous with my child and promised even more for the future, I placed my confidence in him, and am certain that he would have kept his word, as he could well afford to do so.

Note, dearest mistress, the truth of my earlier statement that Fortune, by robbing me of my good friends, showed that she was enemy to my prosperity. Misfortune, who had visited so many ills upon me before, could not allow me to enjoy these friendships for long, and soon afterwards brought calamity down upon the said King Richard of England, as is well known. The good count remained loyal to his rightful lord and as a result was beheaded, which was an act of grave injustice. Thus my son's initial worldly good fortune was brought to an end, and since he was young and in a foreign land beset with such turmoil, he had good reason to be alarmed. What followed? King Henry, who seized power and still holds the throne, saw some of the many books and works I had sent for the count's pleasure, became aware of the situation, and took my son into his household, providing for him generously. Then he charged two of his kings of arms, Lancaster and Falcon, to invite me to come to England, promising a generous recompense. Under the circumstances, and as the prospect did not tempt me in the least, I feigned acquiescence in order to obtain my son's return. To get straight to the point, after laborious maneuvers on my part and the expedition of some of my works, my son received permission to come home so he could accompany me on a journey I have yet to make. Thus I rejected an opportunity for both of us, because I cannot believe that the faithless person can come to any good.

How happy I was to be reunited after those three years with my beloved child, whom Death had left my only son. My joy notwithstanding, his return added to my already burdensome expenses. I doubted, moreover, that he would be happy to come home after the grand way of life to which he had grown accustomed, for children, who have little discernment, are readily attracted to what appeals most to their eyes and their comfort. So I sought a situation for him in the household of a great and powerful lord; but as the talents of this young boy did not stand out among those of the many great men at this court, I remained responsible for his support myself, and reaped nothing from his service.

Thus had Fortune deprived me of one of my good friends and one of my best hopes. But since that time she has visited even worse upon me.

Christine Complains of Fortune, Who Took Her Good Friends from Her

As I related earlier, I had by this time achieved some fame, since many of my works had been given as gifts—not by myself but by others—to princes in foreign lands, and these were regarded as new works written from a woman's perspective. As the proverb says, novelty pleases; and I do not say it out of boasting, as that does not enter in. Thus, the first Duke of Milan in Lombardy heard of me, perhaps in a way more flattering than I deserve, and offered me a generous lifetime income if I would come live in his land. This can be verified by several nobles from that country who served as ambassadors in this regard. But

Fortune, true to her ways, would not suffer any improvement in my ruinous financial situation. So she took this benefactor away from me by death—not that I would have left France easily, even if to return to my native land. Nonetheless, she did me harm when she deprived me of this good friend, inflicting upon me no small loss, for as certain worthy individuals have told me, my books would have won his support even if I had decided to remain in France.

More on the Same Subject

There remains for me to relate the death of the prince who, after wise King Charles, represented the greatest loss for me. Now the most venerable and powerful Prince Philip, Duke of Burgundy, brother of Charles the Wise, had in his benevolence extended his affection to me after he became familiar with some of my works, which I had only recently sent him because I had considered them unworthy to be opened in his presence. In recognition of the constancy of my application rather than of any great subtlety found in what I wrote, he praised and remunerated me generously, and graciously took my son into his service. Moreover, he deigned to pay me the great honor of asking me in person to record as an example for all posterity the noble life and deeds of the said wise king. Was it not a sure sign of the heinous envy of my perverse enemy that soon afterwards she took him from me in death, just as his benevolence towards me was increasing? His death marked a renewal of my adversities, as well as a grave loss to the kingdom, as I sadly recount in the book he had commissioned, which was not yet finished at the time.

Christine Concludes Her Complaint

Thus, reverend mistress, have I related the causes of my past tribulations, but not all. For God knows that many other evils and trials assailed me at the same time; but the account of these would be too long and too tedious. And even today I do not see an end to my ills.

As for the present, I have had to make numerous entreaties to French princes still living because of the many losses suffered at Fortune's hands; and I have implored them to aid my little family and me far from my native land, not because of any merit of mine, but in memory of my father, who left his homeland to serve them, and did so with such devotion. I am not being either untruthful or ungrateful when I say that the value of the modest help I received from some of these noblemen has been somewhat diminished by the difficulties I encountered in obtaining it from their treasurers. What is your opinion in the matter, dearest Lady? What a trial it is for a woman like me, who is rather retiring by nature and little concerned with material possessions or money, to be forced by my financial responsibilities to seek out various officials, only to be tormented day after day by their smooth words! Such, honored Lady from whom nothing is hidden, is the plight of widows today. You know well how little interested I am in amassing riches or bettering my estate, for I wish only to maintain the one I inherited; although I am foolish to be concerned even with that, since I recognize that worldly goods are like the wind. As you know also that I have no desire for superfluous adornments or delicacies, I call upon you to witness that my sole concern is for my elderly mother, now totally dependent upon her only daughter, who has not forgotten all she has been given and desires to pay her debt, as is only just. I grow saddened and bewildered when Fortune thwarts my will and does not allow this noble and honorable lady to live in the manner that she deserves and to which she is accustomed. And add to this the burden of poor relatives for whom I must find suitable husbands, and other friends I must aid: nowhere do I see Fortune inclined in my favor.

Continuing in this vein, do you not think I consider myself unfortunate when I see other women living happily and comfortably with their brothers and families, and reflect that I am away from my friends in a foreign land? My two brothers, fine and worthy men both, had to return home to the estates inherited from my father because they were fortuneless here. And I who am tender by nature and open with my friends ask God why a mother has to live far from the sons she misses, and I far from my brothers. Thus you can see, dear mistress, that Fortune has served me contrary to my wishes and still perseveres in her evil doings.

And that I speak the truth, God, Who is You, and You who in fact are He, know full well. Thus I return to my earlier statement that Fortune has been my adversary in the past, and continues to assail me with burdens difficult for the heart of a woman to bear. What troubles me even more is the fact that my studies are interrupted by these many ills and worries, which so distract me that I cannot devote myself as I want to the delights of the mind.

GENERAL COMMENTARY

CHARITY CANNON WILLARD (ESSAY DATE 1984)

SOURCE: Willard, Charity Cannon. "The Quarrel of the Rose." In *Christine de Pizan: Her Life and Works,* pp. 73-89. New York: Persea Books, 1984.

In the following essay, Willard explores Christine's role in the famous literary quarrel over The Romance of the Rose, *questioning the popular assumption that Christine launched the dispute with the release of* A Letter to Cupid. *Willard discusses the importance of the quarrel to Christine's career in terms of both the woman-centered themes of her later writings and the prominence she achieved as an intellectual figure in France.*

No aspect of Christine's career has attracted more attention than her part in the first recorded literary quarrel in France. It has even been supposed that she instigated it with her ***Cupid's Letter,*** and that in this capacity she acted as the forerunner of all subsequent movements in behalf of women's rights. The truth of the matter is, however, somewhat less picturesque, although no less surprising when considered in the context of the times. Instead, it was Jean de Montreuil, one of the royal secretaries, who inspired the debate in the spring of 1401, which basically concerned the literary merits of Jean de Meun's part in *The Romance of the Rose.* The element of feminism was injected into the debate by Christine, who was prepared to admit some of the literary qualities of Jean de Meun's poem, but who had already deplored his attitude toward women and what she had called, in ***Cupid's Letter,*** written two years earlier, his bad influence on many contemporary men. It was this feministic aspect of the debate that caught popular attention, since to find a woman rising in defense of her sex against the sort of attack that was traditional throughout the Middle Ages was quite unheard of. Although other issues were involved in the quarrel, the attitude toward women continued to engender animus, not only in the fifteenth and sixteenth centuries, but right up to the present as well. Indeed, not long ago, a critic saw fit to attack Christine as an hysterical woman and a prude for her role in the affair.[1]

As far as Christine's literary development is concerned, it is more important to view her participation in the debate as marking a shift in her activities from purely courtly circles to broader contacts, notably with a group of intellectuals, some of them former colleagues of her husband's in the royal chancellery. In a certain sense, the debate over *The Romance of the Rose* was an outgrowth of the enthusiasm these Paris intellectuals were beginning to show for Italian humanism. At the end of the fourteenth century, a group of educated young men, primarily associated with the chancellery or the University of Paris, was filled with admiration for the writings of Petrarch and Boccaccio and also attempted to imitate their much-vaunted interest in the Latin classics. Some of these Frenchmen were in correspondence with such prominent Italians as Coluccio Salutati, their counterpart in the Florentine chancellery; or they were acquainted with the Italian merchants and bankers who had established themselves in Paris, in some cases seemingly purveying books as well as the silks frequently used for book bindings; or perhaps they had rubbed elbows with the duke of Milan's agents who arrived in Paris on diplomatic missions such as making arrangements for the marriage between the duke's daughter Valentina Visconti and Louis of Orleans in 1387. Among this last group was Ambrogio Migli, who remained in Paris to become the duke of Orleans's secretary and counselor.[2]

A number of manuscripts of the period bear witness to the interest of this group in what was going on in Italy. Frenchmen were inspired to translate Livy and Cicero and, eventually, Boccaccio, and also to write letters and verses in classical Latin. Jean de Montreuil was a prolific writer of Latin letters in which he, like his friends, aspired to cultivate a good classical style, despite the fact that Petrarch had already created a certain amount of bad feelings by referring to these French efforts as barbaric.[3]

One curious trait of the Italian humanists, who considered themselves talented orators as well as writers, was their enjoyment of debates on various subjects, such as comparisons of the moral qualities of Scipio and Caesar, the relative value of noble birth and personal merit in the conduct of life, or the virtues of law and medicine as professions.[4] In view of these Italian models, it is not surprising to find a literary debate attracting considerable attention in Paris shortly after 1400.

The Romance of the Rose was scarcely new. Written in the thirteenth century, it had enjoyed a success unmatched by any other work in the Middle Ages, and it continued to be read and to exercise an influence on its readers' minds and imaginations for nearly three centuries. The first 4,000 lines of the poem, written by Guillaume de Lorris around 1236, tells of a love affair conducted according to the best precepts of courtly love, but it is a psychological account, experienced in a dream world inhabited by allegorical characters. The poet, a young man of twenty, falls asleep on a

May morning and dreams that he discovers a walled garden. The gate is opened to him by a young woman named Idleness, a friend of the garden's owner, Pleasure. Another lady, Courtoisie, invites the young man to join a dance that is in progress. He then discovers a magic fountain that catches his attention by the reflection of a rose-bush, and he is attracted especially by one rose that he longs to pluck, although he is deterred by the thorns surrounding it. At that very moment, he is wounded by the golden arrows shot at him by the God of Love. He finds himself in Love's power and agrees to obey his commandments. These amount to a complete "Art of Love" as the poet has explained in the opening lines:

And if a man or maid shall ever ask
By what name I would christen the romance
Which now I start, I will this answer make:
"The Romance of the Rose it is, and it enfolds
Within its compass all the Art of Love."
The subject is both good and new. God grant
That she for whom I write with favor look
Upon my work, for she so worthy is
Of love that well she may be called the Rose.[5]

The rest of the first part of the poem recounts the poet's efforts to pluck the rose, assisted by such allies as Fair Welcome, Hope, and Friend, but deterred by Danger, Slander, Shame, and Fear. Venus offers some additional help that allows him to kiss the Rose, but Jealousy immediately builds a castle around it, shutting up Fair Welcome in a tower where he can no longer help the poet. At this point, the first part breaks off, apparently unfinished.

Jean de Meun's continuation of more than 17,000 additional verses was written some forty years later. A philosopher more than a poet, he belonged to another generation as well as to another social world. He was less interested in the actions of the characters than in their ideas, and they therefore show themselves to be rather argumentative, transforming the simple allegory of courtly love into social satire. Similarly, the garden of love turns into a forum for debate on many subjects only loosely related to the subject of love. Indeed, they often stand in the way of love. Reason, for instance, makes a long speech intended to turn the Lover against love, insisting that friendship is a more important human relationship. In the course of his discourse, he makes remarks about the human reproductive organs that the Lover finds offensive. To Reasons's insistence that God created these bodily parts, he replies that God did not create the words, which he finds offensive in polite conversation. Friend then advises opportunism in relations with women, who are seldom virtuous, debauchery being the least of their crimes. The fine clothes of women do not really enhance them, for a dung-heap covered with a silken cloth is still a dung-heap.

Persisting in his quest in spite of such advice, the Lover decides to accept the help of Deceit in attacking Jealousy's castle. Deceit lectures him at length on the prevalence of hyprocrisy in society,

FROM THE AUTHOR

CHRISTINE'S DEDICATORY LETTER TO A COLLECTION OF DOCUMENTS IN THE *QUARREL OF THE ROSE,* ASKING FOR THE SUPPORT OF THE QUEEN

Although I am very simple and ignorant among women, your humble chambermaid, subject to you, eager to serve you (if you consider me worthy), I am moved to send you the present letters. In these letters, my most awesome Lady, if you deign to honor me by listening to them, you can understand my diligence, desire, and wish to resist by true defenses, as far as my small power extends, some false opinions denigrating the honor and fair name of women, which many men—clerks and others—have striven to diminish by their writings. This is a thing not to be permitted, suffered, or supported. Although I am weak to lead the attack against such subtle masters, nonetheless my small wit has chosen and now chooses to employ itself in disputing those who attack and accuse women, for, being moved by the truth, I am firmly convinced that the feminine cause is worthy of defence. This I do here and have done in my other works. Thus, your worthy Highness, I petition humbly that you accept my argument, although I cannot express it in as fine a language as another might, and permit me to enlarge upon it, if, in the future, I am able to. May all this be done under your wise and benign correction.

Christine de Pizan. Christine's Dedicatory Letter to the Queen of France. From *La Querelle de la Rose: Letters and Documents.* Edited by Joseph L. Baird and John R. Kane. Chapel Hill: North Carolina Studies in the Romance Languages and Literatures, 1978, pp. 65-66.

FROM THE AUTHOR

CHRISTINE'S RESPONSE TO A LETTER FROM MASTER GONTIER COL, SECRETARY OF THE KING: COL HAD REQUESTED HER *LETTER OF CUPID* AND RETURNED HIS ANALYSIS OF HER WORK

And so in order to meet your wishes, I sent the letter requested. Whereupon, after you had read and thoroughly scrutinized my letter, wherein your error was punctured by truth, you wrote in a fit of impatience your second, more offensive letter, reproaching my feminine sex, which you describe as impassioned by nature. Thus you accuse me, a woman, of folly and presumption in daring to correct and reproach a teacher as exalted, well-qualified, and worthy as you claim the author of that book to be. Hence, you earnestly exhort me to recant and repent. Whereupon, you say, generous mercy will still be extended to me, but that, if not, I shall be treated as a publican, etc. Ha! man of ingenious understanding! Don't let your own wilfulness blunt the acuity of your mind! Look rightly according to the most sovereign theological way, and, far from condemning what I have written, you will ask yourself whether one ought to praise those particular passages I have condemned. And, furthermore, note everywhere carefully which things I condemn and which I do not. And if you despise my reasons so much because of the inadequacy of my faculties, which you criticize by your words, "a woman impassioned," etc., rest assured that I do not feel any sting in such criticism, thanks to the comfort I find in the knowledge that there are, and have been, vast numbers of excellent, praiseworthy women, schooled in all the virtues—whom *I* would rather resemble than to be enriched with all the goods of fortune.

Christine de Pizan. Letter to Gontier Col, October 1401. From *La Querelle de la Rose: Letters and Documents*. Edited by Joseph L. Baird and John R. Kane. Chapel Hill: North Carolina Studies in the Romance Languages and Literatures, 1978, pp. 62-63.

especially in religious matters. When the Old Woman who has been guarding Fair Welcome is captured, she freely offers her advice on love. Men are deceivers and unworthy of trust, so a woman's main objective should be to amass as much money as she can manage from her admirers. She also tells how to deceive a jealous husband.

Finally, a plan is devised for storming the castle where the Rose is imprisoned. The God of Love appeals to his mother, Venus, and to Nature, who works unceasingly at her forge to preserve the human race from extinction. Nature is assisted in her work by Genius, who also has views to express on the deceitful nature of women. But Nature agrees to help Venus seize the castle, so Genius carries the message for her to the God of Love, taking the opportunity to deliver a long speech on the necessity of continuing the species by whatever means necessary. So in the final assault on the castle, Venus shoots an arrow that sets the interior on fire, and the Lover, disguised as a pilgrim, is able to enter and pluck the Rose. In the final scene, Jean de Meun is not troubled by the stylized delicacy that marked Guillaume de Lorris's beginning; his purpose is to call attention to the artificiality and falseness of the whole system of courtly love.

Perhaps the aspect of the long poem that particularly intrigued its readers was precisely that it represented so effectively the complex mentality of a society evolving from the idealistic, chivalric spirit to a different one dominated by realism and logic. The fact that the work belonged to the tradition of Arts of Love that went back to Ovid had the effect of attracting both those who were devoted to idealistic concepts of love and also others, more intellectual, who were impressed by the classical tradition it represented.[6]

Jean de Meun was a graduate of the University of Paris with a scholarly turn of mind, and a great passion for teaching. His culture was quite evidently the product of the encyclopedic spirit that dominated certain universities of his day. He was also a member of the rising middle class who saw a need for revising the increasingly decadent aristocratic ideals of chivalry, courtesy, and asceticism expressed in the part of the poem written by Guillaume de Lorris.

In this respect, Jean de Meun's part is more a refutation than a continuation of the first part, and it is evident that he intends for the Lover to have the Rose in the end, by fair means or foul. Following the original plot in a desultory way, he invents a series of new allegories and replaces narrative with discourse in the long speeches by Reason, Nature, and Genius, all of whom advise the Lover in his quest but at the same time delay his approach to the Rose. These allegorical characters also give Jean de Meun scope to develop his ideas on a range of subjects, with the result that his part of the poem becomes a *summa* of the sort so popular in his day. It was this aspect of the poem that appealed greatly to Jean de Montreuil and his friends.

Until recently, almost all knowledge of the discussion of Jean de Meun's merits that took place between 1401 and 1403 was based on Christine's account of it. At the beginning of 1402, apparently with the aim of giving publicity to what had until then been a more or less private discussion, she gathered together a group of documents intended to support her own point of view and presented it to the French queen. In an introductory letter, she begged Isabeau of Bavaria for her support in the defense of women against so-called learned men who had been belittling them, as she puts it, "in a manner which it scarcely seems praiseworthy to permit or support."[7] She also addressed a second letter and copy of the documents to Guillaume de Tignonville, provost of Paris and one of the ministers of the Court of Love, which pretended to be devoted to honoring women. Tignonville was also known as the translator of the *Dicta Philosophorum* compiled a century earlier by John of Procida, a Sicilian doctor and statesman.[8] This *Dits Moraulx des Philosophes,* as Tignonville's translation was called, enjoyed considerable popularity. Christine herself had already used it as a source for her writings and obviously thought Tignonville's judgment was worth having. It is interesting to observe, furthermore, that she was appealing for support to both literary and official circles through Tignonville and the queen.

According to her account, the debate grew out of a conversation she had had with Jean de Montreuil, at which an unidentified third person was also present. When Jean de Montreuil lauded the exceptional merits of Jean de Meun's part in *The Romance of the Rose,* Christine had replied that, saving his grace, she did not agree that the poem was worthy of such extravagant praise. The tone of Christine's account is polite and moderate, and the scene described recalls the beginning of ***The Debate of Two Lovers***.[9]

More recently, further light has been thrown on the background of the debate by the publication of Jean de Montreuil's letters, including several referring to his part in the controversy.[10] It becomes evident that it was in April 1401 that Gontier Col, another royal secretary known for his humanistic interests, had persuaded his colleague to read *The Romance of the Rose.* (It is known that Gontier Col had been interested several years earlier in Jean de Meun's translation of the love letters exchanged by Abelard and Heloise, which could have led quite naturally to his interest in *The Romance of the Rose.)* Around the time that Col introduced his friend Montreuil to the poem, he was one of the diplomats involved in negotiations for the return of Isabelle of France to her father's court after the death of her husband, Richard II. During the same period, Christine was trying to arrange her own son's return from England, where the new king, Henry IV, would have been glad to retain him at his court. This combination of circumstances suggests that Christine and Gontier Col might have had some contact with each other with regard to the return of Christine's son to Paris.

In any case, the conversation between Christine and Jean de Montreuil, in the presence of someone who is referred to only as a "notable cleric" and who seems to have shared Christine's view of Jean de Meun, must have taken place in the late spring of 1401 because by the end of May Jean de Montreuil had sent both Christine and Gontier Col copies of his treatise, written in French, on the merits of Jean de Meun's poem. He also sent a copy of the treatise, with an accompanying letter in Latin, to his friend Pierre d'Ailly, the bishop of Cambrai, who may indeed have been the "notable cleric" in question.

Apparently, Christine replied to Jean de Montreuil before the middle of the summer. Her response was primarily concerned with expressing her support for the other person who had taken part in the original conversation, and she did this in a calm tone. Her tone changed only after others had entered the debate.

The most important of these other participants, from Christine's standpoint, was the chancellor of the University of Paris, Jean Gerson, another of the early French humanists. On August 25 he preached a sermon in which he seemed to be taking Jean de Montreuil to task for his views.[11] It was a custom for professors and students of the College of Navarre to meet together to celebrate the feast of Saint Louis and to hear a sermon delivered by one of their members. In 1401 it was Gerson who spoke, taking as a text "Consider the lilies of the field. . . ." In discussing the attributes necessary to a good teacher, he spoke of the matter of suitable language for such a person, making reference to his opinion about Jean de Meun's freedom of language in referring to physical and sexual matters. Perhaps this served as a warning to Jean de Montreuil, for he had nothing further to say to Christine on the subject, although he did continue the polemic with a lawyer of his acquaintance. It was Gontier Col who took up the discussion of Jean de Meun with Christine.

On his return to Paris in August, Col had learned of the affair from Jean de Montreuil, who wrote him a letter urging his support in the debate. So it was that Col wrote a letter to Christine on September 13, asking for a copy of her reply to Jean de Montreuil, which he had not been able to lay his hands on, and proposing an exchange of letters on the subject.[12] He expressed his astonishment that she should wish to detract from the reputation of such a learned man as Jean de Meun and suggested that she was merely the mouthpiece for others who did not dare to speak openly, adding that he was enclosing a copy of a short poem by Jean de Meun and promising to reply to whatever she wrote, no matter how busy he might be. The tone of Col's letter is noticeably arch, and there is a distinct suggestion that he is taking part in a literary game. It is true that the royal secretary was a great admirer of Jean de Meun, perhaps rather more because of the latter's translation of Boethius and his *Testament* than his part in *The Romance of the Rose,* for Col valued Jean de Meun as a link between French literature and the classical past, but, quite evidently, Col was also tempted by the idea of an exchange of letters, a debate in the style so favored by Italian humanists. His letter was signed in the presence of three other disciples of Jean de Meun, two counselors of Parliament and another royal secretary.

In Christine's first letter to Gontier Col, she enclosed a copy of her letter to Jean de Montreuil, which explains in detail her views on the poem. She insisted that her opinion of *The Romance of the Rose* was firm: she objected only to certain aspects of the poem and freely admitted certain merits.[13]

In common with Gerson, Christine had grave reservations about the propriety of some of the language of the poem, especially the naming in a literary work of private parts of the body, and through words put in the mouth of Reason, of all people. This point has led Christine's critics, both early and modern, to accuse her of attempting to exercise moral censorship.[14] A realistic consideration of her situation in life, however, makes it difficult to substantiate such an attack. She was a doctor's daughter and the mother of three children, neither of which circumstance is especially conducive to prudery; she was undoubtedly as well acquainted with the facts of life as the ordinary person of her day, and her references elsewhere to the accepted adulterous nature of so-called courtly love do not suggest any shrinking from reality. What she actually said was that words are neither good nor bad in themselves, but that the intention with which they are used makes them so. Jean de Meun had written, by way of an excuse:

> Sir lovers, I beseech, by Love's sweet game,
> That, if you find here words that seem unwise
> Or bawdy, whereof scandalmongering tongues
> Might make occasion to say slanderous things
> Of us because of what we have to tell,
> You'll courteously gainsay their criticism.
> And when you shall have stopped their calumny,
> Denied their charges, and reproved their speech,
> If still there shall remain some words of mine
> For which I rightfully should pardon beg,
> I pray that you will make excuse for them
> And make response to critics, as for me,
> That they are necessary to the tale,
> Which leads me to the words by its own traits.
> This is the reason why I use such words.[15]

Nevertheless, Christine suspected the motives of Jean de Meun, a sufficiently learned man to know that he was encouraging free love. Furthermore, she did not see why it was necessary to go to so much trouble to explain what comes all too naturally to most people, as she said:

> If you wish to excuse him by saying that it pleases him to make a pretty story of the culmination of love using such images, I reply that by doing so he neither tells nor explains anything new. Doesn't everyone know how men and women copulate naturally? If he were to tell us how bears or lions or birds or some other strange creatures mate, this might make amusing material for a fable, but would not tell us anything new.[16]

She suspected even more the motives of some of Jean de Meun's disciples, who appeared to her to be devising elaborate intellectual excuses for licentious behavior. Jean de Meun's poem had long been recognized as belonging to the Ovidian tradition of erotic literature in spite of its great show of erudition. Christine was not interested in discussing his use of allegory to reveal obvious truths; she was concerned about the influence of his ideas in contributing to the low estate of public morality that was evident around her—greed, slander, and promiscuity, of which the handsome duke of Orleans's multiple love affairs were perhaps the most notorious example. The festivals at the court were frequently accompanied by licentious pleasures, giving an Augustinian monk, Jacques Legrand, occasion to admonish the queen:

"Venus alone reigns at your court; drunkenness and debauchery follow in her train."[17] Froissart's account of the marriage festivities of Charles VI and Isabeau of Bavaria had already included references to the barely concealed innuendo that marked the lascivious attitude of the courtiers present. Eustache Deschamps's poem in celebration of the marriage of one of the duke of Burgundy's younger sons is even less restrained.[18] Yet these were the same circles that professed to honor the ideals of courtly love. Thus it is scarcely surprising that Jean de Meun's combination of the erotic central theme of the quest for the Rose with abstruse discussions of the fine points of lovemaking should have had a great appeal to them.

Christine had already called attention to the courtiers' hypocrisy in ***Cupid's Letter*** and denounced the deceit and insolence that characterized the attitude they displayed in real life. Later, in her reply to Jean de Montreuil's treatise, she also objected to Reason's advice that in the war of love it is better to deceive than to be deceived; she was horrified by the advice of the Old Woman; she saw no excuse for the meanderings of Jealousy; and, recalling examples of virtuous women, past and present, she found the unpleasant things Deceit had to say about feminine virtue especially distasteful. (In this last objection, it is possible to note the germ of a later work, ***The Book of the City of Ladies***.) She concludes by asserting that she sees no need to remind the human race of its shortcomings, the "leg on which it hobbles," and that there is no reason to attribute her attitude to the fact that she is a woman, for it is but a small matter for her to object to what a single man says, when he has felt free to blame, without exception, an entire sex.[19]

One may insist that Christine worked herself into considerable frenzy over this debate, yet the fact that Jean de Montreuil, a public official, was not eager to have his treatise read outside a select circle suggests that he may have spoken rather freely of his enjoyment of the poem. He seems to have feared that his words would make him appear frivolous and lascivious, although it is of course impossible to know what he really did say.

Gontier Col's second letter to Christine provided little to soothe her feelings. He said that although she was in error in her interpretation of such a learned doctor as Jean de Meun, if she would repent and confess her error, she would be forgiven and her opponents would take pity on her. Col's obviously patronizing tone infuriated Christine, who insisted stoutly that she would stick to her views. She retorted again that her position had nothing to do with her female nature, which he had seen fit to slander. At the end of her letter, she made reference once more to "the noble memory and continuing experiences of many valiant women who are worthy of praise and entirely virtuous," adding that she would rather resemble this company than be blessed by all of Fortune's riches.[20]

This is the end of the collection of documents that Christine publicized by sending it at the beginning of 1402 to the queen and to the provost of Paris. In her mind, at least, the principal issue had now become the unjust slander of women, more than the merits of Jean de Meun's poem. It is this insistence on respect for women who deserve it that identifies Christine most directly with feminists of later generations, and it was on this issue that she made her appeal to the queen.

Her gesture of publicizing the letters by circulating them in official circles brought to a close the second round of the debate. Christine, for her part, was busy with other matters. In February 1402, she wrote ***Le Dit de la Rose*** (***The Tale of the Rose***), which she dedicated to the duke of Orleans, and she was also gathering together her poetry for presentation in its first "edition" toward the end of June.[21] In the meantime, Jean de Montreuil continued to circulate his treatise among a group of humanist friends, soliciting their support in his defense of Jean de Meun.

Within a few months, the tone of the whole affair was modified once more. On May 18, 1402, Jean Gerson released a treatise against *The Romance of the Rose* on which he had very possibly been reflecting for some time. Making use, in his turn, of a dream, he imagines the High Court of Christianity, where the case of Chastity versus the Fool of Love is being tried.[22] Seven charges have been presented against this misguided lover, of which the first two are of particular interest here. Chastity's first complaint is that the Fool of Love tried to drive her from the land along with her bodyguards, Shame, Fear, and Danger. This was attempted with the assistance of the foolish Old Woman, worse than the devil himself, who has admonished young girls to sell their bodies as fast as they can and to the highest bidder, adding that they should not mind lying or deceiving in the process but should give themselves in haste while still young and beautiful to anyone who will have them, whoever he might be.

Chastity's second accusation is that the Fool of Love has made a jealous old man complain about the institution of marriage, saying that it is better to hang or drown oneself than to become involved in wedlock. The Fool of Love intends to make all men despise all women so that men will not want to marry.

The trial continues on other counts of a religious nature, but the high point occurs when the Fool of Love is called to account for a long series of misdeeds, including the fall of Troy, the exile of Tarquin from Rome, and civil disorders of all varieties. (It is interesting to note that in ***Cupid's Letter,*** Christine had already blamed human deceit for a good many of these same misfortunes.) And the prosecutor in Gerson's treatise continues:

> Who deceives by fraud and perjury honest girls?
> The Fool of Love.
> Who forgets God and the saints and paradise
> and his own end?
> The Fool of Love.
>
> Whence come robberies to maintain
> extravagances,
> bastardry or the suffocation of infants . . .
> the death of husbands, in short, all wickedness and all folly?
> The Fool of Love.
>
> But I can see that because of his name you will wish to excuse his follies, because one cannot cure folly in a fool.[23]

Gerson also makes reference to the obscenity of some of the numerous manuscripts that were in circulation. An idea of what he was talking about can be gleaned from one particularly handsome copy illustrated in Paris around this time. A highly suggestive portrayal of Venus in connection with the Fall of Man, which marked the end of the Golden Age, and the erotic overtones of an illustration of the final assault on the castle to take the Rose leave very little to the imagination.[24]

Gerson does not always do exact justice to what Jean de Meun had actually said, yet there is no question of the force of his eloquence. Although Christine and Gerson were not defending precisely the same things—Gerson was more concerned with the virtue of women than with their reputation in the world—together they formed a powerful opposition to the supporters of Jean de Meun.

The third and final round in the quarrel took on a sharper, more personal tone. It was opened by Gontier Col's brother Pierre, a canon in the chapter of Notre Dame of which Gerson was the presiding official. In a letter directed to Christine, he saw fit to expose his disagreements with Gerson as well as with her. His references to Gerson's treatise were unmistakable, although neither he nor Christine mention the chancellor by name.[25] Point by point, Col took up the charges both had made against Jean de Meun, quoting extensively from *The Romance of the Rose* itself and demonstrating a tiresome tendency to quibble.

He took Gerson to task for his accusations of the Fool of Love, insisting that he could scarcely have any knowledge of such love himself yet suggesting that he might still be its victim in the future. It is scarcely to be wondered that Gerson took offense at such an implication about his private life.

It is amusing, however, to find Col following the custom dear to his contemporaries of citing a list of heroes of antiquity to prove his point. His list of those who were educated yet fools of love included Pompey, Caesar, Scipio, and Cicero, among others. Then he added: "But I think that the author of that appeal is a cleric, a philosopher, and a theologian without being love's fool, so he thinks it must be so with others."[26]

With regard to Christine, his tone was patronizing and seemingly calculated to offend when, for instance, he said:

> O most foolish presumption! O word too soon issued and lightly spoken from the mouth of a woman to condemn a man of such high understanding [and] profound study who, after such great labor and mature deliberation, has written such a noble book as *The Romance of the Rose,* which surpasses all others ever written in the language in which he wrote his book. . . .[27]

Such extravagant claims are nonsense and can scarcely be taken as an objective reflection upon Christine's judgment, but he continued in a playful, but still more offensive, tone:

> So I beg of you, woman of great ingenuity, that you preserve the honor you have acquired for the extent of your understanding and your well-chosen language, and that if you have been praised because you have shot a bullet over the towers of Notre Dame, don't try to hit the moon for that reason with an oversized arrow; take care not to resemble the crow who, when his singing was praised, began to sing louder than usual and let the morsel he was holding fall from his mouth.[28]

Christine's reply to Pierre Col, dated October 2, 1402, shows increasing exasperation. She reproved him for his disrespectful remarks about Gerson, then replied to his points individually. Quite obviously, she felt that the affair had gone far enough, and she had ceased to be interested in going over the same ground again. In this second letter, she wrote:

> I beg you and those of your persuasion that you do not hold against me my writings and the present debate about the *Book of the Rose,* for the beginning of it came about through chance and not because of any desire of mine, whatever opinion I might have held, as you can know from a little treatise where I described the first theme and the final position of our debate. It would be most distressing to me to be subject to such servitude that I dared not speak the truth to someone else without its being held against me; for even a wiser person than I may be well advised to think about what he may not have considered for a long time because, as a common proverb says: It can happen that a fool can give counsel to a sage.[29]

Only a fragment of Pierre Col's second reply to Christine has survived, if indeed it was ever finished, for Gerson lost no time in writing him a letter in Latin giving full expression to his disapproval. Not only did Gerson reprove Col for the indiscreet implications about his own private life, but he also called attention to the fact that in his remarks about unrestrained language in children and their sinless state Col was skirting the religious heresy of certain groups like the Adamites who were condemned by the Catholic Church. He also reminded Col rather strongly that he, Gerson, defended virtue first of all because it was his professional duty to do so, and he recommended that the canon turn his thoughts to more serious and useful matters, for instance, to a reading of Saint Augustine's *Christian Doctrine.* Gerson ended with the pious admonition "Let us pray for our mutual salvation."[30]

In the face of such a pointed rebuke, Pierre Col could not continue to take issue with either Gerson or Christine. One final echo of the quarrel is to be found, however, in a series of sermons that Gerson preached during the month of December in the Church of St.-Germain-l'Auxerrois, not far from the Louvre. The general subject of this series was penitence, notably for two sins of the flesh, gluttony and lechery, and more especially the latter. In the sermon for December 24, Gerson undertook once more to reply to those fools of love who had tried to defend this sin. His allusion to the Quarrel of the Rose was unmistakable.[31]

By this time, however, the chancellor appears to have realized that his thundering against Jean de Meun's poem might be having exactly the opposite of the desired effect by calling too much attention to *The Romance of the Rose* and keeping public interest aroused. The discussion was finally closed.

From a careful examination of all the documents generated by the debate, several points become clear. The principal quarrel was not really between Christine and the two Col brothers, as their exchange of letters might suggest, but rather between Jean de Montreuil and Jean Gerson, who was supported by all those who felt that *The Romance of the Rose* was having a corrupting influence on public morality. The injection of the antifeminist issue was perhaps accidental, but it gave the discussion an unusual turn that would have important repercussions. This was also the aspect of the affair that caught popular attention, especially because a woman had dared to rise to the defense of her sex against traditional clerical attacks.

Christine's position has been frequently misinterpreted, yet the fact remains that throughout the exchange of letters with the Col brothers she insisted that she was not bent on attacking Jean de Meun's poem as a whole, but merely the excessive claims for its merits that she considered unfounded. Few of Christine's critics have called attention to the discourtesy of her opponents, nor have they wondered that she should have objected to being compared by Jean de Montreuil to "the Greek whore who dared to write against Theophrastus."[32] It was only after Pierre Col's thoroughly ungenerous attack that she began to sound, not hysterical, but exasperated. She continued to insist, however, that she spoke only *"de vrai science,"* which should be interpreted in this context as meaning out of her own personal experience of the world.

The basic issues of the debate may have remained unsettled, but Christine's role was of lasting importance: she removed theoretical discussions on women from intellectual circles and made it possible for a layperson, and a woman at that, to take part. Perhaps even more important for Christine herself was the encouragement she felt to continue writing in prose about one of her major concerns, the defense of women against what she considered unjust slander and against some of the hypocrisies of contemporary society. Finally, she had achieved a sort of fame that she could scarcely have gained so quickly in less dramatic circumstances.

Christine's interest in the situation of women in the society to which she belonged had been reflected in her early poetry and in ***Cupid's Letter.*** It also provided the principal theme for the ***One Hundred Ballades of a Lover and His Lady.*** What troubled her particularly, on practical as well as on moral grounds, was the veneer of nobility that served to disguise illicit love, all too frequently providing a snare for unsuspecting or inexperienced women. As for condemning all women for the sins of a few, Christine found the idea unjust as well as ridiculous. Her common-sense approach can be seen in a passage from one of her letters:

> As I said once before in a poem of mine called ***Cupid's Letter***: Where are the countries or the realms from which women are exiled for their great iniquities? Without prejudice, we would ask of what crimes even the worst of them, the most deceitful, can be accused? What can they do to you, how deceive you? If they beg you for money from your purse, if indeed they don't take it, you don't have to give it to them if you don't want to. And if you say that they make fools of you . . . do they go to your house to seek you out or take you by force? It would be interesting to know just how they deceive you.[33]

Christine would continue to develop this theme in two of her major works, ***The Book of the City of Ladies*** and ***The Book of the Three Virtues.*** The first grew directly out of the concern she expressed in one of her letters to Gontier Col. She returned to the praise of virtuous women, drawing examples from Boccaccio's *De Mulieribus Claris (Concerning Famous Women)* and citing parallel examples from French history. Thus she elaborated her earlier argument, undertaking to demonstrate that the achievements of certain women rendered them, as individuals if not as a whole sex, equal or superior to men. Special praise is reserved for the group of women who, inspired by conjugal love, risked or even sacrificed their lives for their husbands. Throughout her career, Christine consistently defended the institution of marriage and, as it has already been pointed out, this stand represented a more modern point of view than the ones held by her opponents in the debate, for while Jean de Montreuil and his friends were disparaging women, their Italian contemporary and admired friend Coluccio Salutati was composing a letter in praise of matrimony in terms that foreshadowed what Erasmus would have to say on the subject a century later.

It was, however, in ***The Book of the Three Virtues,*** which followed ***The Book of the City of Ladies*** and was sometimes called ***Le Trésor de la Cité des Dames,*** its "Treasury," that Christine gave her most definitive view of woman's vulnerability, dwelling on the bitter price that must almost inevitably be paid by a woman for any sort of illicit love. Her ideas are summarized in a long letter that she had already made use of in ***The Book of the Duke of True Lovers,*** but it would appear that Christine considered the points she had made there sufficiently important to bear repetition. The letter is no theoretical discussion of love but instead offers extremely practical advice for a young woman who is ready to throw away her good name for momentary happiness:

> And further, my very dear lady, it remains to speak of the perils and difficulties which accompany such love, which are without number. The first and greatest is that it angers God, and then, if the husband or kinfolk find out about it, the woman is ruined, or falls under such reproach that she never again has any happiness. But even if this should not come to pass, let us consider the disposition of the lovers, for though all were loyal (which they by no means are, since it is known that they are generally faithless, and in order to deceive say what they neither think nor would be willing to do), nevertheless it is certain that the heat of such love does not long endure, even with the most loyal. Ah, dear lady, be warned that you cannot possibly conceive of the trouble which dwells in her breast when this love comes to an end, and the lady, who has been blinded by the environment of foolish delight repents, as she thinks of the distractions and perils to which she has exposed herself, wishing that whatever the cost, this experience had never happened to her and that she would not be subject to reproach because of it.[34]

The letter, which continues at some length in this vein, is penned by an astute and rather bold woman who has had occasion to observe, with all illusions spent, the cruelty of the society around her.

It has been said that the results of this somewhat laughable debate were inconclusive or even insignificant, and it has been suggested more than once that Christine had the worst of it. But such a point of view overlooks the secondary results, which in the long run were far more important than the debate itself. Some of the same issues were evoked in a second debate, around 1424, by Alain Chartier's *La Belle Dame sans Merci* (*The Fair Lady without Mercy*).[35] The lady in question, who turned aside her lover's pleas, puts into practice just the sort of behavior Christine recommended. Her ideas were also echoed in Martin LeFranc's *Champion des Dames* (*The Champion of Ladies*) and in a whole series of rather artificial treatises for and against feminine honor that made up the debate in the sixteenth century known as the "*querelle des femmes.*" Some of the questions raised were argued around the middle of the sixteenth century in Marguerite de Navarre's *Heptameron,* making it evident that she was among Christine's readers.[36] Indeed, Christine can be considered a forerunner of certain ideas that became popular more than a century later when Baldissare Castiglione's *Book of the Courtier* became a model for social behavior throughout a good part of Europe.

Christine's letters in the debate over *The Romance of the Rose* represent only a small part of what she had to say about the position of women in society. But if these letters were relatively insignificant in her long effort to turn her contemporaries away from outworn concepts and traditions, they did have a certain value in publicizing her ideas and in bringing to public attention the issue of the right of half the human race to more consideration, a better chance for education, and a role beyond the domestic sphere.

Notes

1. D. W. Robertson, Jr., *A Preface to Chaucer in Medieval Perspectives* (Princeton, 1962), pp. 361-62; J. V. Fleming, "Hoccleve's 'Letter to Cupid' and the 'Quarrel' over the *Roman de la Rose," Medium Aevum,* 40 (1971), 21-40.

2. G. Ouy, "Paris, l'un des Principaux Foyers de l'Humanisme en Europe au Début du XVe Siécle," *Bulletin de la Société d'Histoire de Paris et de l'Ile de France,* (1967-1968) 71-98; M. Meiss, *French Painting . . . The Limbourgs,* pp. 19-23; L. Mirot, *Etudes Lucquoises* (Nogent-le-Routrou, 1930).

3. E. H. Wilkins, *Petrarch,* pp. 214-215; F. Simone, *Il Rinascimento Francese, Studi e Ricerche* (Turin, 1961), pp. 47-48; J. Huizinga, *The Waning of the Middle Ages* (New York, 1956), p. 325; J. Monfrin, "La Connaissance de l'Antiquité et le Problème de l'Humanisme en Langue Vulgaire dans la France du XVe Siècle," in *The Late Middle Ages and the Dawn of Humanism Outside Italy* (Louvain-The Hague, 1972), pp. 130-143.

4. On the popularity of humanistic debates, see P. O. Kristeller, *Renaissance Thought II* (New York, 1965), pp. 27-28; 54-56.

5. *The Romance of the Rose,* trans. H. W. Robbins (New York, 1962), pp. 3-4.

6. Recent studies of *The Romance of the Rose* and its importance include A. M. Gunn, *The Mirror of Love; A Reinterpretation of the Romance of the Rose* (Lubbock, Texas, 1952); J. V. Fleming, *The Roman de la Rose; A Study in Allegory and Iconography* (Princeton, 1967); D. Poirion, *Le Roman de la Rose* (Paris, 1973); C. Dahlberg, "Love and the *Roman de la Rose," Speculum* 44 (1969), 568-584; L. Friedman, "Jean de Meun's Antifeminism and Bourgeois Realism," *Modern Philology* 57 (1950), 13-23; J. V. Fleming, "The Moral Reputation of the *Roman de la Rose* before 1400," *Romance Philology* 8, (1964-1965), 430-435; Y. Badel, *Le Roman de la Rose au XIVe Siècle; Étude de la Réception de l'oeuvre,* (Geneva, 1980).

7. E. Hicks, ed., *Le Débat sur le Roman de la Rose* (Paris, 1977), p. 6.

8. R. Eder, "Tignonvillana Inédita," *Romanische Forschungen* 33 (1915), 815-1022.

9. Roy, Vol. 2, pp. 49ff.

10. J. de Montreuil, *Opera* vol. I: *Epistolario,* ed. E. Ornato. (Turin, 1963); E. Hicks and E. Ornato, "Jean de Montreuil et le Débat sur le *Roman de la Rose," Romania,* 98 (1977), 34-36; 186-219.

11. E. Hicks, *Le Débat sur le Roman de la Rose,* p. xlviii. Further references to the documents of the debate will be to this edition, which supercedes all others. See also M. Liberman, "Chronologie Gersonienne," *Romania* 83 (1962), 7-73.

12. E. Hicks, *Débat,* pp. 9-11.

13. E. Hicks, *Débat,* pp. 11-22.

14. E. Hicks, "The 'Querelle de la Rose' in the *Roman de la Rose," Les Bonnes Feuilles,* 3 (1974), 152-163.

15. *The Romance of the Rose,* p. 319.

16. E. Hicks, *Débat,* p. 20.

17. M. Laigle, *Le Livre des Trois Vertus et son milieu historique et littéraire* (Paris, 1912), p. 24; *Le Religieux de Saint-Denis,* Vol. III, pp. 268ff.

18. J. Huizinga, *The Waning of the Middle Ages* (New York, 1956), p. 109.

19. E. Hicks, *Débat,* p. 23.

20. E. Hicks, *Débat,* p. 25.

21. For the history of this "first edition," see F. Lecoy, *Mélanges . . . Robert Guiette,* pp. 107-114.

22. E. Hicks, *Débat,* pp. 59ff; E. Langlois, "Le Traité de Gerson contre *Le Roman de la Rose," Romania* 45 (1918), 23-48.

23. E. Hicks, *Débat,* p. 71.

24. E. Hicks, *Débat,* pp. 68 and 73 and the illustrations from the University of Valencia Ms. 387 reproduced in J. Fleming, *The Roman de la Rose,* figs. 26, 41 and 42. If, as F. Avril points out in "La Peinture Français au Temps de Jean de Berry," *Revue de l'Art,* 38 (1975), 50, the artist who illustrated this manuscript is the same who illustrated the copies of Christine's *Le Livre de Chemin de Long Estude* (1503), Christine's remarks take on particular significance. The *Rose* illustrations would have offended her.

25. E. Hicks, *Débat,* pp. 89-112.

26. E. Hicks, *Débat,* p. 97.

27. E. Hicks, *Débat,* p. 100.

28. E. Hicks, *Débat,* pp. 109-110.

29. E. Hicks, *Débat,* p. 149.

30. E. Hicks, *Débat,* pp. 173-175.

31. E. Hicks, *Débat,* pp. 180-181; L. Mourin, *Jean Gerson, Prédicateur Français* (Bruges, 1952), pp. 138-148.

32. E. Hicks, *Débat,* p. 43; J. de Montreuil, *Opera,* Vol. 1, p. 220.

33. E. Hicks, *Débat,* p. 54.

34. Roy, Vol. 3, pp. 168-169; the letter as a whole, pp. 162-171.

35. Poirion, *Le Poète et le Prince,* pp. 174 and 268; A. Piaget, "Alain Chartier, Chanoine de Notre-Dame de Paris," *Romania* 32 (1904), 393.

36. T. F. Crane, *Italian Social Customs of the Sixteenth Century,* (New Haven, 1920), pp. 118-19. This point of view is not strictly in agreement with that of E. Telle in *L'Oeuvre de Marguerite d'Angoulème, Reine de Navarre,*

et la Querelle des Femmes (Toulouse, 1937), although R. Marichal in his edition of *La Coche* has demonstrated that she imitated there Christine's *Le Livre du Dit de Poissy* and *Le Débat de Deux Amants* (Geneva-Paris, 1971), 3-21.

Bibliography

Modern Editions of the Works

Le Débat sur le Roman de la Rose. Critical edition, with introduction translations, and by Eric Hicks (Paris, 1977).

Oeuvres Poétiques. Ed. Maurice Roy. 3 vols. (Paris, 1886-1896).

Critical Studies

Avril, François. "La Peinture Française au Temps de Jean de Berry," *Revue de l'Art* 28 (1975), pp. 40-52.

Laigle, Mathilde. *Le Livre des Trois Vertus de Christine de Pisan et Son Milieu Historique et Littéraire* (Paris, 1912).

Lecoy, Félix, "Notes sur Quelques Ballades de Christine de Pisan." In *Fin du Moyen Age et Renaissance, Mélanges de Philologie Française offerts à Robert Guiette* (Antwerp, 1961), pp. 107-114.

Meiss, Millard. *French Painting in the Time of Jean de Berry: The Limbourgs and Their Contemporaries* (New York, 1974).

General Background

Badel, Pierre-Yves. *Le Roman de la Rose au XIVe Siècle; Étude de la réception de l'Oeuvre* (Geneva, 1980).

Crane, Thomas F. *Italian Social Customs of the Sixteenth Century* (New Haven, 1920).

Dahlberg, Charles. "Love and the *Roman de la Rose,*" *Speculum* 44 (1969), pp. 568-584.

Eder, Robert. "Tignonvillana inédita," *Romanische Forschungen* 33 (1915), pp. 851-1022.

Fleming, John V. "Hoccleve's 'Letter to Cupid' and the 'Quarrel' over the *Roman de la Rose,*" *Medium Aevum* 40 (1970), pp. 21-40.

———. *The Roman de la Rose: A Study in Allegory and Iconography* (Princeton, 1967).

Gunn, Alan M. *The Mirror of Love. A Reinterpretation of the Romance of the Rose* (Lubbock, Texas, 1952).

Kristeller, Paul O. *Renaissance Thought II; Papers on Humanism and the Arts* (New York, 1965).

Lieberman, Max. "Chronologie Gersonienne," *Romania* 83 (1962), pp. 71-73.

Montreuil, Jean de. *Opera.* Vol. 1, *Epistolario.* Ed. Ezio Ornato (Turin, 1963). Vol. 2, *L'Oeuvre Historique et Polémique.* Eds. Nicole Grévy et al. (Turin, 1975).

Mirot, Léon. *Etudes Lucquoises* (Paris, 1930).

Monfrin, Jacques. "La Connaissance de l'Antiquité et le Problème de l'Humanisme en Langue Vulgaire dans la France du XVe Siècle." In *The Late Middle Ages and the Dawn of Humanism Outside Italy,* M. C. Verbeber and J. Ijsewijn, eds. (Louvain-The Hague, 1972).

Mourin, Louis. *Jean Gerson, Prédicateur Français* (Bruges, 1952).

Poirion, Daniel. *Le Roman de la Rose* (Paris, 1973).

———. *Le Poète et Prince, l'Évolution du Lyrisme Courtois de Guillaume de Machaut à Charles d'Orléans* (Paris, 1965).

Robertson, D. W., Jr. *A Preface to Chaucer* (Princeton, 1962).

Simone, Franco. *Il Rinascimento Francese, Studi e Ricerche* (Turin, 1961).

Wilkins, Ernest H. *The Life of Petrarch* (Chicago, 1963).

Wilkins, Nigel. *One Hundred Ballades, Rondeaux and Virelais* (Cambridge, U. K., 1969).

TITLE COMMENTARY

Le livre de la cite des dames

MAUREEN QUILLIGAN (ESSAY DATE 1988)

SOURCE: Quilligan, Maureen. "Allegory and the Textual Body: Female Authority in Christine de Pizan's *Livre de la Cite des dames.*" *Romanic Review* 79, no. 1 (1988): 222-42.

In the following essay, Quilligan examines Christine's process of revising traditional texts as a strategy for creating her own authority.

In their massive study of the woman writer and the nineteenth-century literary imagination, Sandra Gilbert and Susan Gubar not only ask such impish questions as—if a pen is a metaphorical penis, with what metaphorical organ does a woman write?—they also revise Harold Bloom's influential thesis about the profound anxiety there is in all literary tradition and argue that for a woman writer the question is not so much an anxiety of influence as an "anxiety of authorship." For a woman to pick up a pen and write is laden, in the nineteenth century, with fears of madness and impropriety.[1]

To cite work by twentieth-century literary critics about nineteenth-century literature as a way of introducing the practice of a medieval woman's radical revision of her male precursors, may be allowed its own legitimacy—beyond the hint it provides that the question of authorial gender maintains a certain intractable (if metaphorical) physicality throughout all literary periods. Poststructuralist French feminist theorists, such as Hélène Cixous and Luce Irigaray, who ground their definition of "l'écriture féminine" in the female body—as well as the controversy such an "essentialist" position has caused in Anglo-

American feminist theory—may offer some more theoretically coherent terms in which to address the problem of the body in Christine's allegory.[2] However, Gilbert and Gubar's arguments about female authority in the nineteenth century, when novels by female authors have always been an accepted part of the popular and therefore "literary" canon, also usefully remind us that the legitimacy of any period in literary history depends upon the formation of a body of works deemed characteristic for that period. To argue for the insertion of a previously marginalized text into the canon necessarily destabilizes that canon and calls into question the means by which it was previously fixed.

If Christine de Pizan is herself a canonical 15th-century French author, because she remains taught in our curricula as a lyric poet, her prose is less well known. Although female, she was not completely marginalized by her society; rather she worked at the center of cultural production in her period, a privileged member of the French court.[3] However, as the first pro-woman polemic, the first female-authored history of women, the ***Livre de la Cité des Dames*** (1405) is not itself a canonical text, although it has been taken up as a possible starting point for a whole new canon of female writing.[4] As a marginal female author Christine takes a master discourse and makes it speak of her own concerns, explicitly commenting on her own process of rewriting her tradition. This is, of course, no more or less than the practice of medieval poetics in general with its assumptions about the necessity for the citation of *auctores*. Yet we cannot understand what Christine is doing without making some attempt to discover what her culture assumed her *auctores* were doing. By grounding our reading of Christine's revision of her precursors in the materiality of their manuscript texts—that is, by also looking at some illuminations—we may be in a better position to assess just how idiosyncratic Christine's rewrite of a masculine tradition of textuality may be.[5]

The text first mentioned in the reading scene generic to medieval allegorical narrative, with which Christine appropriately opens her ***Cité des Dames,*** is Mathéolus, a virulently misogynist tract. But Christine's real target, as she makes absolutely explicit, is Jean de Meun's far more authoritative *Roman de la Rose*.[6] In the "Querelle de la Rose," Christine had objected not only to Jean's misogyny, but to his vulgar language; in telling the story of Saturn's castration by Jupiter, Jean had made his Lady Reason use the slang term for testicles, "coilles."[7] This moment was a favorite one for illuminations of manuscripts of the *Rose,*

Manuscript page from *The Book of Ladies*.

and the illuminations are usually as explicit as Jean's very explicit language.[8] Christine's point was that the vulgar term for such a human body part derogated the sacred function of sexuality—and was furthermore most inappropriate to a character such as Lady Reason.

Christine's critique of Jean has drawn much criticism over the centuries, but her objection to the language of the castration story pinpoints her greatest move against Jean in the ***Cité de Dames***—as well as her remarkable swerve away from the authority of her second major *auctor* in the ***Cité,*** Boccaccio's *De Mulieribus Claris*. Her rewrite of her *auctores* goes straight to the heart of a castration anxiety which may be said to be the originary moment for the misogyny in the texts of both the *Rose* and the *De Claris*.[9] Reason's impolite language in Jean's text is the cause for which the lover dismisses Lady Reason as a figure of authority and rejects her kind of love: the lover specifically asks for "quelque cortaise parole," and thus Jean anticipates the kind of response readers like Christine would have and makes it part of his text. The rejection for the word, however, motivates the rest of the plot. In rejecting Reason, the lover turns to all the other dramatis personae of the poem. A number of other attempts are made in the *Rose* to explicate the story of Saturn's loss of his genitals; one may say, without much exaggeration, that Jean's text is slightly obsessed with getting the story and its implications of idolatry understood aright.[10]

The dismemberment of the male fathergod, through which erotic love is born, is not, of course, Jean's creation. But the myth and its crucial dismemberment of the male body underwrites the superficially polite but obscene tropes in which Jean describes—at epic length and in great (and hilarious) detail—a single act of sexual intercourse. Christine also appears to have understood the connection between the two, for she objected to the "unnaturalness" of such language with just as much vehemence as she argued against Jean's vulgarity.[11] And of course, Jean's images for this final, culminating act of sexual intercourse are all drawn from the euphemisms Lady Reason explains she *could* have used instead of "coilles" to refer to genitals (especially "reliques"—indicating the primary problem of idolatry).

There is no explicit dismemberment of the male body in the opening of Boccaccio's *De Mulieribus Claris*. However, the second story he tells (after the story of Eve) is of Semiramis. A glorious and ancient queen of the Assyrians, Semiramis, on the death of her husband Ninus, cross-dressed and masquerading as her young son, took over the rule of the realm and led the army on to great victories. After proving herself, she revealed her true identity, causing great wonder, Boccaccio says, that a mere woman could accomplish so much. In her own person she not only maintained her husband's empire, but added to it Ethiopia and India. She restored the city of Babylon and walled it with ramparts, Boccaccio stresses, of marvelous height. Boccaccio takes care to tell one particular incident when Semiramis, having her hair braided, was interrupted by the news that Babylon had rebelled. Vowing to wear her second braid undone until she had subdued the city, she soon vanquished it and brought it to good order. A bronze statue was erected in Babylon of a woman with her hair braided on one side and loose on another, a reminder of Semiramis' brave deed.[12] The usual illumination of the moment in manuscripts of the French translation of Boccaccio's text, however, emphasizes the infamous side of Semiramis' story. Not only was she a great warrior queen and city builder, she also practiced mother-son incest. Boccaccio makes clear the terrifying sexual ambiguity such an action causes.

> But with one wicked sin this woman stained all these accomplishments . . . which are not only praiseworthy for a woman but would be marvelous even for a vigorous man. It is believed that this unhappy woman, constantly burning with carnal desire, gave herself to many men. Among her lovers, and this is something more beastly than human, was her own son Ninus, a very handsome young man. As if he had changed his sex with his mother, Ninus rotted away idly in bed, while she sweated in arms against her enemies.[13]

A representative illumination of this aspect of Semiramis' story reveals the distinctly uncomfortable position in which his mother's martial power places the young son Ninus. Boccaccio's figurative sense of Ninus' exchange of sex with his mother implies an emasculation the illumination also hints at in Ninus' posture: the truncated hand, stuffed (protectively?) into the young boy's placket in the general area of the genitals all too clearly answers the menace of Semiramis' remarkably large sword. Doubtless the sword is meant to represent Semiramis' great martial courage and achievements; but juxtaposed with the figure of Ninus, it represents the young man's effeminization (his unworn armor hangs on a rack above him). That Semiramis' sword also bisects the head of one of the armed soldiers standing behind her to the left of the miniature may imply that her martial prowess menaces more than Ninus.

"Oh," Boccaccio laments, "what a wicked thing this is! For this pestilence flies about not only when things are quiet, but even among the fatiguing cares of kings and bloody battles, and, most monstrous, while one is in sorrow and exile. Making no distinction of time, it goes about, gradually seizes the minds of the unwary and drags them to the edge of the abyss." In order to cover her crime, Semiramis decreed "that notorious law" (legem . . . insignem) which allowed her subjects to do what they pleased in sexual matters. According to some, Semiramis invented chastity belts. According to others, her end was not good. "Either because he could not bear seeing his mother with many other lovers, or because he thought her dishonor brought him shame, or perhaps because he feared that children might be born to succeed to the throne, Ninus killed the wicked queen in anger." Ninus' distinctly overdetermined matricide opens up possible questions about the connection between the legend of Semiramis and the first story Boccaccio tells concerning Eve, the mother of us all. More importantly, Boccaccio's humanist uncertainty about Ninus' motives underscores the problematic nature of textual transmission. He offers many endings for Semiramis' story because the authorities conflict.[14]

Astonishingly, Christine makes Semiramis the first story Lady Reason tells in the building of her city of ladies. "Take the trowel of your pen and ready yourself to lay down bricks and labor diligently, for you can see here a great and large stone which I want to be the first placed as the foundation of your City" (p. 38; revised).[15] Christine's Semiramis is more of a city builder than Boccaccio's—the first empire was a dual achievement of the elder Ninus and Semiramis together, who no less than her husband campaigned in arms. Upon the husband's death, Semiramis does not cross-dress, but simply continues in her role of ruler and conqueror, adding Ethiopia, India, and fortifying Babylon. Christine retells the incident of the Babylonian rebellion, the braid left undone, and the statue, this time bronze richly gilt. Where Boccaccio begins his descant on incest, Christine acknowledges: "It is quite true that many people reproach her—and if she had lived under our law, rightfully so—because she took as husband a son she had had with Ninus her lord" (p. 40). Where Boccaccio spends time guessing as to Ninus' possible motives in killing his mother, Christine points out the reasons Semiramis may have had for taking her son as husband. First: she wanted no other crowned lady in the realm, and this would have happened if her son had married; and second, no other man was worthy to have her as a wife except her son. What troubles Christine most is that "de ceste erreur, que trop fu grande, ycelle noble dame fait aucunement a excuser" (II, 680); "But this error, which was very great, this noble lady did nothing at all to excuse" (p. 40). Why? Because "adonc n'estoit encore point de loy escripte"; "there was as yet no written law." Indeed then, Christine reasons, people lived according to the law of Nature, where all people were allowed to do whatever came into their hearts without sinning. Where Boccaccio's Semiramis decrees a law, Christine's lives before any such thing exists. That this law prior to which she lives is a *written* law, is, I think, significant. It subtly recalls all of the previous conversations between Christine and Reason about the written authorities of the misogynist tradition that Christine finds so daunting in the generic reading scene of this allegory. The only authority Christine has to oppose to the "grant foyson de autteurs," which are like a surging fountain and which have all denigrated women, is "moy meisme et mes meurs come femme naturelle"—my self and my conduct as a natural woman (II, 618).[16] That is, until the three crowned ladies appear and give her a lesson in allegorical reading.[17] Reason further undermines the authority of such texts when she wittily announces that any argument against women was not authorized by *her.* Such a tradition grows in part simply because "in order to show they have read many authors, men base their own writings on what they have found in books and repeat what other writers have said and cite different authors." This undermining of textual, written authority, makes Christine sound distinctly modern, much like Francis Bacon inveighing against the mindless quibblings of scholastic philosophy. A miniature from the late fifteenth-century Flemish translation of the *Cité* illuminates the moment when the detritus of misogynist opinion is cleared from the "field of letters" before the foundations for the city are dug. Christine's removal of such a written tradition is of a piece with her revision of Boccaccio's legal detail: by means of the speaking presence in the text of a visionary female figure of authority, who persistently says she speaks prophetically, and whose textual gender is made more literal by its coherence with the author's own, Christine appears to establish her specific, female authority on oral and prophetic grounds, different from a mere textual tradition. Christine suppresses Boccaccio's worry about textual transmission at the same time she suppresses Semiramis' ignoble end.

We do not need to invoke any anthropological argument (or authority) to see the priority granted oral experience in Christine's story of Semiramis—though it is intriguing that, for instance, Derrida's discussion of the violence of writing focuses on a scene that involves little girls divulging to Levi-Strauss the secret names of the tribe.[18] Christine's own authority in the ***Cité*** is, however, at the same time markedly scripted: Reason is constantly reminding Christine of what she has written in her own prior texts, so that Christine's own corpus forms part of the authorities to which Reason, Rectitude, and Justice appeal. Yet the ultimate claim of female authority is to a non-scripted, prophetic mode, grounded in a realm of discourse that is made to stand as far outside the textual as anything within a text can get.

In a sense, Christine's emphasis on a prior unscripted freedom which would authorize mother-son incest as being acceptable and even honorable is of a piece with her criticism of Jean de Meun's vulgar terms for body parts and also his euphemism in describing the act of sexual intercourse: the relations between language—written and oral—become most crucial in its relation to naming the body. If her two *auctores* founded their texts in stories that underscore the originary problem of castration anxiety, her objections—overt against Jean and silent against Boccaccio—react not only to their terms but to the fundamental importance of the problem. One does not need to invoke Freud to see the peculiar emotional burdens revealed by the manuscript illuminations of the two moments in Jean's and Boccaccio's texts. Christine's City is built with a foundation stone (the story of Semiramis) and written in the language of an allegory that refuses to recognize this peculiar terror as being first, or finally, very significant. The body upon which Christine focuses—both early and late—is, not surprisingly, the female body. And it is a body which also relentlessly—almost monotonously—refuses to be dismembered.

It is important to notice at the outset that the physical body which first bears mention in the text is Christine's own. The physicality of this body—and its essential femaleness—makes its appearance very subtly in the first paragraph of the text of the ***Cité.*** In the midst of the reading scene, just as Christine comes across the volume of Mathéolus while searching through the shelves for a volume of poetry, Christine's mother calls her to supper. (Imagine anyone calling any of the protagonists of allegorical dream visions to supper just after he has picked up the text which will be his authority in the subsequent journey.) That it is Christine's *mother* who calls her to supper is not only pertinent in terms of the continuum of female authorities Christine is going to supply in her text, it signals the humdrum domesticity of the scene. (Christine's mother did in fact live with her; one of the figures of authority in the ***Cité*** talks about this real, down-to-earth mother who had not wanted her daughter to get the education her father had given her.[19] Unlike Dante (or Chaucer, or the narrator of the *Rose,* Christine takes time out to eat and does not have a "dream"—such as most allegorical dream-visions insist. Rather, she has a waking vision, much like Dante's (whose authority in this she does follow—having explicitly preferred him to Jean de Meun in the Querelle de la Rose[20]). That next morning and most importantly, however, Christine's response to reading Mathéolus is revulsion against her own female body:

> Alas God, why did you not let me be born in the world as a man, so that all my inclinations would be to serve you better, and so that I would not stray in anything and would be as perfect as man is said to be? . . ." I spoke these words to God in my lament and a great deal more for a very long time in sad reflection, and in my folly I considered myself most unfortunate because God had made me inhabit a female body in this world.
>
> (Richards, p. 5)[21]

The vision begins with the arrival of the three ladies immediately after this lament; but Christine further specifies the exact physical position in which she sits in her chair.

> So occupied with these painful thoughts, my *head* bowed like someone shameful, my *eyes* filled with tears, holding my *hand* under my *cheek* with my *elbow* on the pommel of my chair, I suddenly saw a ray of light fall on my lap, as though it were the sun.
>
> (Richards, p. 6; revised)[22]

Given the fact that the description of the position follows directly upon Christine's lament about her "corps feminin," however, the specific mention of body parts is striking. In an earlier text, the ***Mutacion de Fortune,*** Christine had said that Fortune changed her into a man so she could take the helm of her foundering ship, but in the ***Cité,*** this gender-change is distinctly disallowed.[23] The three women arrive to chastise her for being like the fool in the story who was dressed in women's clothes while he slept; "because those who were making fun of him repeatedly told him he was a woman he believed their false testimony more readily than the certainty of his own identity" (Richards, p. 6). The woman who will later be identified as Reason, specifically by the mirror she holds—anyone who looks into it will achieve clear self-knowledge—specifically argues that all the misogynist argument which has so swayed Christine as to feel self-disgust for her femaleness, is like the fire which tries gold:

> Fair daughter, have you lost all sense? Have you forgotten that when fine gold is tested in the furnace, it does not change or vary in strength but becomes purer the more it is hammered and handled in different ways. Do you not know that the best things are the most debated and the most discussed? . . . Come back to yourself, recover your senses, and do not trouble yourself anymore over such absurdities.
>
> (Richards, pp. 7-8)

Such an insistence on the senses may simply be metonymic reference to the alternative authority of "experience" Reason wishes to stress against the scripted authority of misogynist tradition. The problematic relationship between the experience of the physical body and the bookish tradition may be seen in a miniature in the Flemish translation. [The] figure shows a despondent Christine, hand on cheek, elbow on chair, surrounded by books. The small detail of the knife on Christine's desk beneath her left hand, used for correcting scribal errors, itself pointing to the books to Christine's left, may suggest that the illuminator understood Christine's point quite well about the need to correct the written tradition.[24] (The same miniaturist painted the scene of digging as a representation of Reason's command to clear away misogynist opinion from the "field of letters"; the two pictures, then, make the same point.) Chaucer's Wife of Bath had announced her preference: "Experience though none auctoritee Were in this world is right enough for me." Chaucer's portrait of the anti-misogynist Wife also underscores a similar conflict. The Wife's deafness is caused when her fifth husband, the clerk Jankyn, hits her on the side of the head after she has ripped out some pages from his misogynist book. Does the deafness, one wonders, speak to the problematic orality of a female tradition that is necessarily opposed to the clerkly scripted tradition?

Of course, most of what gets said by the three figures of authority in the ***Cité des Dames*** comes out of books. The very building of the city is the writing of the *book* of the city of ladies. Christine cannot, nor as an allegorist would, escape textuality. As Jane Gallop has usefully reminded us, no writing can evade textuality, even that which would strain most resolutely to ground the difference between male and female writing in the biological differences between male and female bodies:

> At the very moment when she would proclaim the shift from metaphor to fact, the feminist critic cannot help but produce metaphors . . . this moment recurs in various texts . . . when, in reaching for some nonrhetorical body, some referential body to ground sexual difference outside of writing, the critic produces a rhetorical use of the body as metaphor for the nonrhetorical.[25]

It may be easier, however, to specify a distinctly female practice in writing that does not run into the contemporary modern dilemma of "essentialism" by focussing on a medieval female author's practice. Untouched by a biologism constructed by a modern "scientific" discourse, Christine's approach to the historical actuality of female bodies, translated into a transcendent textuality, is empowered by a long-lived ideology of fleshly sacrifice, which paradoxically insists upon the power of the word made flesh.[26] The very presence of the third section of the ***Cité,*** narrated by Justice, in which Christine provides an abbreviated female martyrology taken from Vincent of Beauvais, insists upon the centrality of the female body to her project. Of course, including a martyrology is also her greatest resistance to her *auctor* Boccaccio who had insisted that the stories of pagan and Christian women should be told together. Boccaccio rests his claim to humanist originality in the *De Claris* (and his own difference from Petrarch) on the distinction between the oft-told tales of saints' lives and the fact that the merits of pagan women "have not been published in any special work up to now and have not been set forth by anyone."[27] Christine is remarkably attentive to Boccaccio's representation of his own authority, as her inclusion of the martyrology attests. By including it, she aims to revise at the point where he bases his own greatest claim for originality. She further chooses to name him as her *auctor* for the first time when she retells his story of the Roman woman Proba, notable for having rewritten the stories of Scripture, from Genesis to the Epistles, in the verses of Virgil, "that is, . . . in one part she would take several entire verses unchanged and in another borrow small snatches of verse, and, through marvelous craftsmanship and conceptual subtlety" she was able to narrate the Bible in Virgil's poetry (p. 66). As David Anderson has very interestingly suggested, Boccaccio's praise of Proba's achievements indicates some of his own practice of imitation in rehearsing Statius' *Thebaid* in the *Teseide,* as well as, of course, his own use of sources in the *De Claris.*[28] Proba's practice proleptically stages the very problem the Renaissance would find so tricky to solve. Suffice it to say that at least one fifteenth-century reader noticed the significance of Boccaccio's story, if not for his practice, then for her own; Christine names him as her *auctor,* and quotes him verbatim with an acknowledgement for the first time. What Proba did to Vergil, so Christine does to Boccaccio.[29]

Christine's greatest difference from Boccaccio, however, is her three part structure and its allegorical frame, through which she analyzes and thematically organizes the materials she has taken from him. Through the allegorical frame she also stages her own authority, and, in effect, turns herself into her own figure of authority.[30] By positing herself ("moi mesme") as a "natural" woman at the center of her text, she literalizes the gender that has been implicit in all female figures of *auctoritas,* itself a feminine noun that would require a female figure for its personification. The famous illuminations of the ***Cité*** instructively indicate the nature of the wordplay on which Christine's allegorical metaphor rests: although the text of the ***Cité*** has been very little read, its illuminations are some of the best known in the history of art—

having been done by the hand which Millard Meiss has termed the "Cité des Dames Master."[31] They are important not merely for their artistic merit, however, but because of their close replication of authorial intention. In a brilliant study of the different political programs for two separate manuscripts of Christine's ***Epistre Othéa,*** Sandra L. Hindman has shown that Christine not only herself wrote the manuscript of the text that is presently collected in the volume known as Harley 4431 in the British Library, she also indicated in special rubrics in purple ink specific instructions for the illuminator to follow.[32] The illuminations of the ***Cité*** are from the same Harley two-volume collection of Christine's work. Although the text of the ***Cité*** does not bear the same authority as the text of the ***Othéa,*** its illuminations are so close to the copy which probably was overseen by Christine, that they will serve for our purposes.[33]

The first thing that strikes the eye about the incipit illumination to the ***Livre de la Cité des Dames*** is the femaleness of the enterprise. Christine's illuminator represents her as an author already; the text opens in Christine's book-filled study. The three crowned ladies holding their duly explained emblems are Reason, in the back, holding her mirror; Droiture, or Rectitude holding her ruler in the middle; and Justice in the foreground, holding her measuring vessel. To the right we see the actual construction of the city under way, with Reason handing Christine a building block, while Christine holds her trowel—or her pen. The coequal activity of the figure of authority and the author collapses their authority; it replicates the insistence in the text that the three ladies share with Christine the same opposition to the tradition against which she reacts. In an echo, I suspect, of Dante's cry that he was neither Aeneas or Paul to undertake such a journey, Christine complains that she is not Thomas the apostle to build in heaven a city for the king of India. When she complains that furthermore she has a weak female body, Reason tells her that she will carry materials on her own shoulders (much like father Virgil carries Dante over some difficult spots). Together they construct both a book and a city that will become a haven for women safe from further misogynist attack. Christine has the books—Reason provides the bricks. The two sides of the illumination are held together by a textual pun. Each of the three figures continually tell Christine that they will "livrerons" the material for her city: "Thus, fair daughter, to you is given the prerogative among women to make and build the City of Ladies. For the foundation and perfection of which, you will take and draw from us three living water as from clear fountains, and we will deliver (te livre-rons) enough material, strong and more durable than any marble with cement could be. So will your city be very beautiful without parallel, and of perpetual duration in the world" (Richards, p. 11, revised).[34] The "livre" and the "cité" are written and built simultaneously, with the delivery of the same "matiere."[35] Thus, every story narrated in the first section is another "pierre" laid in the walls of this edifying edifice.

The opening of the second section of the ***Cité*** is illuminated by another miniature. Droiture receives into the city the ten sybils, famous prophetesses whose authority is greater than all the Old Testament prophets; their stories begin the completion of the internal palaces.[36] In this section, Droiture tells the story of the Sybil Almathea; in her oral and prophetic authority, Droiture has more accurate knowledge than even the tradition of Virgil. Justice takes over for the third and final section of the ***Cité,*** shown welcoming Mary into the city as its queen. A later illumination rereads the figure of Mary, substituting a baby for the book. Such a book/baby translation is a legitimate reading of the corporeal textuality of the hagiography of the third section and one may say that this illuminator grants us a legitimate and interesting reading of the text. It is not merely a conventional substitution as the earlier, more careful count of ten sybils in the miniature for the second section attested. Before we consider how sensitively poised this body/book tension is in the last section, it will be useful to consider how the female body is represented in Boccaccio's text, at least as that text was read by Christine's contemporaries. There is a persistent vision of the display of violence against the female body throughout the illuminated manuscripts of the *Des Cleres Femmes;* such violence in Boccaccio's text may have provided another reason for Christine's inclusion of a martyrology in the ***Cité.*** A fairly representative miniature. [Shows] Nero having his mother Agrippina cut open so he may see the womb from which he was born.[37]

Christine's text incorporates and rewrites this violence against the female body by authorizing it as hagiography. In switching genres in her change of *auctors,* she not only moves against Boccaccio's decision not to write about martyred Christian women, she also selects a genre which insists upon a parity between male and female passion.[38] Both male and female saints are tortured and die in similar ways. Furthermore, the representations of such torture in the illuminations often insist upon the sexlessness of the saint's body. Two representative miniatures, one of Pope Urben, a male saint, and of Marcienne, a female saint, in a late 14th-century manuscript of Vincent of Beauvais *Miroir Historial* illustrate the gender-neutral body of the saint. The lack of genitals and the parallel musculature insist that in this moment of physical suffering the experience of martyrdom is sexless (in both senses of the term).

Christine, of course, in only telling of female saints' lives in the ***Cité,*** changes the pattern of parallelism. She further regenders the body and changes its social contexts by including a number of different details; her revisions of Vincent of Beauvais, her *auctor* for the last section, are thus similar to her subtle suppressions and corrections of Boccaccio. She also uses a similar maneuver to her well-timed naming of Boccaccio when she cites Vincent as her *auctor,* just before Justice recounts the story of St. Christine, Christine's own patron saint.

> If you want me to tell you all about the holy virgins who are in Heaven because of their constancy during martyrdom, it would require a long history, including Saint Cecilia, Saint Agnes, Saint Agatha, and countless others. If you want more examples, you need only look at the *Speculum historiale* of Vincent de Beauvais, and there you will find a great many. However, I will tell you about Saint Christine, both because she is your patron and because she is a virgin of great dignity. Let me tell you at greater length about her beautiful and pious life.
>
> (Richards, p. 234)

In naming Vincent just before she tells the story of her own patron saint, Christine distinguishes her own authority from his; she also implies that the story she tells will be necessarily different. One reads Vincent; we hear Justice speak.

The largest difference between Christine's and Vincent's versions of St. Christine's story is the ***Cité***'s treatment of the saint's parents. In the *Miroir,* it is both pagan parents who separately attempt to dissuade their headstrong daughter from refusing to sacrifice to their pagan gods. In Vincent's text, St. Christine's father has shut her up in a tower with some ladies in waiting so she may worship his gods.[39] When the young female companions tattle on her, and confess that she has not been worshiping the idols but rather looking out the window to pray to a single celestial god, he has her tortured. As soon as her mother finds out about this torture, she comes to visit her daughter to try to stop her from being so obstinate. Vincent's mother is a study in hysterical pathos:

> And then her mother, wife to Urben, hearing that her daughter had suffered so great pain, tore her clothes and put ashes on her head and went to the prison and threw herself at her daughter's feet and, crying, said, "My only daughter, have pity on me who nursed you at my breasts and make it clear why you worship a strange god."[40]

St. Christine harshly answers: "Why do you call me daughter; for you have no one in your lineage who is called a christian (crestiene). Do you not know that I have my name from Christ my savior? He is the one who tests me in celestial chivalry and has armed me to conquer those who do not understand." The mother, hearing this, returns to her house and denounces all to her husband.

In the ***Cité,*** St. Christine has no mother. Urben is sole parent, and it is to him, both father and first torturer, that Christine abjures her parentage.

> "Tyrant who should not be called my father but rather enemy of my happiness, you boldly torture the flesh which you engendered, for you can easily do this, but as for my soul created by my Father in Heaven, you have not power to touch it with the slightest temptation, for it is protected by my Savior, Jesus Christ."
>
> (Richards, pp. 235-36)

Such a suppression is of a piece with Christine's persistent emphasis on patriarchal control exercised by earthly fathers (as well as surrogate tyrant figures) in a number of other lives; it equally coheres with an emphasis on the generous and loving relations between earthly mothers and daughters.

In both texts, Urben has St. Christine stripped naked, beaten by twelve men, tied on a wheel over a fire, and rivers of boiling oil poured over her body. Angels break the wheel so that the virgin is delivered "healthy and whole," while in the meantime more than a thousand treacherous spectators who had been watching this torture without pity are killed. Urben decides to drown her; a great stone is tied around her neck and she is thrown into the sea, but angels save her and she walks on the water with them. Praying, she asks that the water be for her the holy sacrament of baptism which she has greatly desired, "whereupon Jesus Christ descended in His own person with a large company of angels and baptized her and named her Christine from His own name" (Richards, p. 236); "la baptisma et nomma de son nom Christine." However, in the *Miroir,* the waters are only a "signacle de beptesme," while a voice from heaven merely announces her prayer has been heard, as a cloud and a purple star descend on her head, representing the glory of Jesus Christ. While the notion of the name in the *Miroir* is the wedge between mother and daughter—and is present, if at all, only in a fairly unstressed use of the word "crestiene"—the granting of the baptismal name "Christine" from Christ's own name in the ***Cité*** is nowhere mentioned in the *Miroir*; neither is the baptism a literal sacrament in the *Miroir* as it is in the ***Cité,*** and Vincent also does not reiterate Christine's loyal suffering for Christ's "nom." Christine revises Vincent to make the baptism a literal event that underscores the naming of the saint by the divine son himself, with his own name. He is, of course, the baby who substituted for the book, the Logos who suffered a fleshly sacrifice. The baptism is one of two central events—both intricate conflations of verbal and physical issues—in the ***Cité***'s version of Christine's story; the other also concerns the physical fact of language.

Yet a third judge, named Julian, takes a different and very interesting tack in his torture. After having set some snakes upon her who merely nurse at her breasts, he decides to have them cut off (milk and blood issue forth). Then he commands that her tongue be cut out. In the ***Cité,*** Julian's decision is precisely motivated: "because she unceasingly pronounced the name of Jesus Christ," he decides to have her tongue cut out. She has already told him that he is blind—"if your eyes would see the virtues of God, you would believe in them." Her tongue is duly "coupee," but she goes on speaking more clearly than before of divine things. God speaks to her again, praising her for upholding the name of Christ. Hearing this voice, Julian charges the executioners to cut her tongue so short that she cannot speak to her Christ "whereupon they ripped out her tongue and cut it off at the root" (Richards, p. 239). Immediately thereafter:

> She spat this cut-off piece of her tongue into the tyrant's face, putting out one of his eyes. She then said to him, speaking as clearly as ever, "Tyrant, what does it profit you to have my tongue cut out so that it cannot bless God, when my soul will bless Him forever while yours languishes forever in eternal damnation. And because you did not hear my words, my tongue has blinded you, with good reason."
>
> (Richards, p. 239-40)

The French makes the witty connection between *langue* and *parole* more obvious: "Et pource que tu ne congnois ma parolle, c'est bien raison que ma langue t'ait aveugle." (II. 1009).[41] In the *Miroir,* the saint has a less witty if far more grisly denunciation:

> Je te condamne mengier en tenebras les members de mon corpse. Tu les avois destruez & tua trenchee ma langue qui beneissoit dieu. Et pource as tu droicturierment perdue sa veue.
>
> (f. 485)

> I condemn you to eat in hell the parts of my body. You have destroyed them and have cut off my tongue which blessed god. And therefore you have rightfully lost your sight.

In the ***Cité,*** this body is not accessible to a metaphorical infernal punishment. While in both texts, it is the physical, literal tongue which puts out the literal physical eye, only Christine calls attention to the metaphorical blindness that has been the problem all along.[42] One senses that the saint's curse in the *Miroir* has a literal, Dantesque character—a contrapasso punishment of the tyrant's eating the body parts of the saint he has so hideously dismembered. Christine de Pizan sacrifices this wittiness to stress her own sense of the relations between the power of the saint's fleshly, physical tongue to speak the truth in its continuing and miraculous confession of Christ's name and its power to make people see that truth—thousands have been converted by the saint's virtue. The dismembered tongue is capable of making a political intervention.

In the *Miroir* the story ends with the remark that "ung home de son lignage" writes the saint's legend. In the ***Cité,*** an ungendered "parent" takes "le saint corps et escript sa glorieuse legende" (II.1009). The body and its scripted legend are kept more closely connected, not consigned to an infernal region, but remaining a sainted flesh-form, apparently resurrected and still coextensive with the saint herself. Breaking into her own text for the only time, Christine directly addresses a prayer to St. Christine.

> O blessed Christine, worthy virgin favored of God, most elect and glorious martyr, in the holiness with which God has made you worthy, pray for me, a sinner, named with your name, and be my kind and merciful guardian. Behold my joy at being able to make use of your holy legend and to include it in my writings, which I have recorded here at such length out of reverence for you. May this be ever pleasing to you! Pray for all women, for whom your holy life may serve as an example for ending their lives well. Amen.
>
> (Richards, p. 240)

If the authorities of Reason, Rectitude, and Justice may be said to be merely allegorical representations of Christine's own female authority, this prayer stands finally outside the fiction of the text, in a "real" appeal to a functioning saint. St. Christine is one of the citizens who will dwell in the ***Cité***—but of course she already dwells in the *civitas dei,* transtemporally accessible to the author in this prayer. One could say that the details of the legend of Christine are exquisitely suited to representing a female anxiety of authorship. Christine did not make up the detail of the dismembered tongue; she does however save St. Christine's physical body in her text, against the witty authority of her *auctor.* The literal prayer, fully functional as active language, collapses distinctions between saint's legend, author's "escriptures," and the instrumental effect Christine hopes her text will have on her female readers in the political present of the French court in 1405 and in the future. Christine de Pizan remakes herself as her own figure of authority, punningly calling attention to the divine authority of her own name by dramatizing the naming of her patron saint.

Stephen G. Nichols has recently argued that hagiography is a mediated scripted genre controlled by the institution of the church, designed to marginalize unauthorized prophetic voices that would subvert central institutionalized authority, most specifically the voices of women. The only body that speaks in a hagiographical text is a dead body; it speaks, moreover, by having been turned into a text.[43] Christine's rewrite of Vincent's details, I have tried to suggest, reinvests the body with a living instrumentality, even as it is being dismembered. The mediated, interpreted events of St. Christine's legend in Vincent's rendition are made literal, present events in Christine's revision of her *auctor.* Mere signs become actual events. The prayer to St. Christine also functions to bring the possibilities of a present power into the text, which, while it remains a mere record, makes contact with a transtemporal and prophetic present. Christine's revisions of Vincent begin to turn hagiography into prophecy and connects the saints' legends of the last section of the ***Cité*** with the persistent emphasis on prophecy in the first two.

At the end of her life Christine de Pizan took to actual prophecy. After having retreated to a convent before the Burgundian invasion of Paris, and having remained silent for eleven years, Christine wrote the last poem of her life, the ***Ditié de Jehanne D'Arc,*** finishing it on July 31, 1429. It was the only poem to have been written about Joan during her lifetime. Christine nowhere mentions her own earlier texts in this poem; she does not call attention to her former persistent arguments about female virtue, her political treatises on peace, on the arts of war, or any of her other writings. She does, however, begin with her formulaic "Je, Christine," which may function as an authoritative sign for the existing corpus of texts.[44] It has always seemed like a peculiarly appropriate accident of history that Joan should appear on the scene of the hundred years' war in time for Christine to write about her and to welcome her as an (at that point) unambiguous sign of God's special love for the female sex: "Hee! quel honneur au feminin Sexe! Que Dieu l'ayme il appert" (265-66). As far as I know, no one has asked if there might not be a connection between the two unique occurrences, the presence of a prominent female author, the first professional woman of letters who made public and constant arguments for the virtue of women at the French court for over twenty years, and the acceptance by that court, a generation later, of a low-born female teenager as the martial savior of her country. To suggest a possible causal connection may be to do no more than to question whether or not the practice of a prominently placed author contributed to the "discursive possibilities" of a culture.[45] Criticism is now more comfortable with thinking of literature in its potential social instrumentality, how, in fact, the practice of an individual author may be seen as an "intervention" in the ideological constructs of a society. This was certainly Christine's stated intention in the ***Livre de la Cité des Dames,*** as well as in a number of her more overtly didactic manuals. With the ***Ditié***'s specific address of the king, the soldier, Joan herself, the city of Paris, and the nation at large, Christine certainly intended a prophetic and immediate intervention for this particular poem, as she apparently also assumed, from her first critique of the *Roman de la Rose,* that literature had real moral impact.

Her radical insertion of her gender-specific authority into a misogynist tradition proceeds in the case of her three different, explicitly named, *auctores,* in an almost text-book like demonstration of how it should be done. That she in the process creates an almost monolithically stable subjectivity in her persona as female author defies our current notions of the historical progress in the construction of the modern "subject." Her seeming modernity, predicated as I have tried to show, on the most "medieval" practice of authorial citation and revision, and her explicit and inexplicit scrutiny of a misogyny driven by what can be termed various oedipal anxieties, as well as her focus on the problematic relations between oral and written traditions of authority in the representation of the female body would seem to place her at the center of a number of late twentieth century critical concerns and therefore in a position somewhat anachronistic to her late medieval moment. However, her not entirely coincidental overlap with Joan of Arc negates such an ahistorical accounting for her career. Christine doubtless wrote the text of the ***Ditié*** with a simple pen, but she appears to have written it with a sense of the political instrumentality of literature that we are only now beginning to appreciate. If the laws decreeing the legitimacy of the middle ages do not at the moment account for her political practices, need it be said that they should perhaps be rewritten?

Notes

1. Sandra Gilbert and Susan Gubar, *The Madwoman in the Attic: The Woman Writer and the Nineteenth-Century Literary Imagination* (New Haven: Yale University Press, 1979).

2. A quick overview of the various positions taken by different French theorists may be found in Susan Suleiman, "(Re)Writing the Body: The Politics of Female Eroticism," in *The Female Body in Western Culture: Contemporary Perspectives,* ed. Susan Suleiman (Cambridge, Mass.: Harvard University Press, 1986), pp. 7-29.

3. For a recent study which places Christine in the context of the French court, see Sandra L. Hindman, *Christine de Pizan's "Epistre Othea": Painting and Politics at the Court of Charles VI* (Toronto: Pontifical Institute of Mediaeval Studies, 1986).

4. Although a modern edition of the French text by Monica Lange has been forthcoming since 1974, the *Cité* has yet to be printed. The more obviously conservative *Trésor de la Cité des Dames (Le Livre des Trois Vertus)* was published in three early printed editions in 1497, 1503, and 1536; the *Cité* remains the only major text by Christine never to have been printed. See Angus J. Kennedy, *Christine de Pizan: a Bibliographical Guide* (London: Grant and Cutler, Ltd., 1984).

5. Although a miniature can provide no sure check on textual interpretation, because visual evidence can be as easily misinterpreted as texts, the two were assumed to be coherently readable together. Early fifteenth-century understandings of the similar moral impact of both picture and text thus offer some historical legitimacy in taking pictures as evidence of possible interpretations. Jean Gerson, for instance, questions: "Mais qui plus art et enflemme ces ames que paroles dissolues et que luxuryeuses escriptures et paintures?" (But what burns and enflames these souls more than dissolute words and libidinous writings and paintings?) Eric Hicks, ed., *Le Débat sur Le Roman de la Rose* (Paris: Editions Honore Champion, 1977), p. 68.

6. "Et la vituperacion que dit, non mie seullement luy mais d'autres et messement le *Rommant de la Rose* ou plus grant foy est adjoustee pour cause de l'auctorite de l'auteur" (II. 624); "As for the attack . . . made not only by Mathéolus but also by others and even by the *Romance of the Rose* where greater credibility is averred because of the authority of its author." Citations are to "The 'Livre de la Cité des Dames' of Christine de Pisan: A Critical Edition," ed. Maureen Curnow (Ph.D. diss. Vanderbilt, 1975), 2 vols.: English translations are from *The Book of the City of Ladies,* trans. Earl Jeffrey Richards (New York: Persea Books, 1982).

7. Hicks, pp. 13-14, 117-118. For English translations of the documents see *"La Querelle de la Rose": Letters and Documents,* ed. J. L. Baird and K. R. Kane (Chapel Hill, N.C.: University of North Carolina Dept. of Romance Languages, 1978); Guillaume de Lorris and Jean de Meun, *Le Roman de la Rose,* ed. Felix Lecoy (Paris: Editions Honore Champion, 1965), 3 vols; I, line 5507.

8. The miniature is from Douce 195, Bodley Library, Oxford; it was done in the late fifteenth century for Louise of Savoy and the Count of Angouleme, parents of Francis I. For a peculiarly full illustration of the whole story, showing the birth of Venus from the dismembered genitals as well as the castrated body, see John V. Fleming, *The Roman de la Rose: A Study in Allegory and Iconography* (Princeton: Princeton University Press, 1969), Fig. 33. The Valencia MS Fleming prints may have been illuminated by one of the miniaturists Christine used, causing her—so Charity Canon Willard guesses—greater consternation about the vulgarity of the text. See Willard, *Christine de Pizan: Her Life and Works* (New York: Persea Books, 1984), pp. 229-30, n. 24.

9. When Lady Reason explains that Ovid turned to writing attacks on women only after he had been punished for his political and sexual transgressions by being "diffourmez de ses membres" (i.e. castrated), Christine would appear to point to this origin (*Cité,* II, 648; Richards, p. 21). The argument about Ovid was, of course, conventional, but in the context of the *Cité*'s rejection of the whole misogynist tradition, Christine would appear to anticipate a series of modern feminist critiques of Freudian theories about the oedipal complex and female sexuality. See, in particular, Hélène Cixous, "The Laugh of the Medusa," *Signs* 1 (1976), 875-93, and Luce Irigaray, *Speculum of the Other Woman,* Catherine Porter, trans. (Ithaca: Cornell University Press, 1986).

10. For further discussion of the perhaps defensible tactic Jean de Meun uses and his revision of his precursors, see my "Allegory, Allegoresis, and the Deallegorization of Language: the *Roman de la Rose,* the *De planctu naturae,* and the *Parlement of Foules,*" in *Allegory, Myth, and Symbol,* ed. Morton Bloomfield (Cambridge, Mass.: Harvard University Press, 1981), pp. 163-86.

11. Willard quotes Christine's basic argument: "If you wish to excuse him by saying that it pleases him to make a pretty story of the culmination of love using such images [figures], I reply that by doing so he neither tells nor explains anything new. Doesn't everyone know how men and women copulate naturally?" See Hicks, p. 20. Christine makes clear in a later document in the "Querelle" that her objections to the words are, in essence, political. Having argued that "the word does not make the thing shameful, but the thing makes the word dishonorable," Christine explains to Pierre Col that the "thing" in question is not precisely the physical body part (made by God, although polluted by the Fall), but the speaker's

"intention" in using the word: in contrast to Christine's own use of a polite term, for instance, whereby "la fin pour quoy j'en parleroye ne seroit pas deshonneste," a use of the proper name would be shameful because "la primere entencion de la chose a ja fait le non deshonneste" (Hicks, p. 117). Christine's ultimate objection to the *Rose* was to Jean's authorial misogyny: "lui, seul homme, osa entreprendre a diffamer et blasmer sans excepcion tout un sexe" (Hicks, p. 22). Her quarrel with his choice of words would appear to take aim at the bawdiness of a discursive practice which underwrote the overall misogyny. For a discussion of Christine's essentially political objections to the *Rose*, see Pierre-Yves Badel, *Le Roman de la Rose au XIVe siècle: Étude de la Réception de l'Œuvre* (Geneva: Librairie Droz, 1980), pp. 411-47, esp. p. 428.

12. The four-part incipit miniature in a manuscript of the French translation of the *De Claris*, the *De Cleres et Nobles Femmes,* probably done by Laurent de Primierfait in 1401, reveals the importance of Semiramis' story in the fourteenth-century French reading of the text. The episode of the messenger's arrival while Semiramis is having her hair braided is represented in the lower left quadrant, just beneath the author portrait in the upper left quadrant (British Library, London, MS Royal 20 C.V,f.1). The only text of the *Cité* to have any of its internal stories illustrated, the late fifth-century Flemish translation *De Lof der Wrouwen* (MS Add 20698 in the British Library) also illuminates this moment, for it is a signal event in Christine's version of the story as in Boccaccio's (f. 41).

13. Giovanni Boccaccio, *Concerning Famous Women,* trans. Guido A. Guarino (New Brunswick, N.J.: Rutgers University Press, 1963), p. 6. Ceterum hec omnia, nedum in femina, sed in quocunque viro strenuous, mirabilia atque laudabilia et perpetua memoria celebranda, una obscene mulier fedavit illecebra. Nam cum, inter ceteras, quasi assidua libidinis prurigine, ureretur infelix, plurium miscuisse se concubitui creditum est; et inter mechose, bestiale quid potius quam humanum, filius Ninias numeatur, unus prestantissime forme iuvenis, qui, uti mutasset com matre sexum, in thalamis marcebat ocio, ubi hec adversus hostes sudabat in armis. *De Mulieribus Claris,* ed. Vittorio Zaccaria, *Tutte Le Opere di Giovanni Boccaccio,* ed. Vittore Branca (Mondadori, 1967), 12 vols., XI, 36.

14. For a discussion of Christine's and Boccaccio's different relations to textual tradition, see Liliane Dulac, "Semiramis ou la Veuve heroique," *Mélanges de Philologie Romane offerts à Charles Camproux* (Montpellier: C.E.O. Montpellier, 1978), 315-43.

15. "Sy prens la truelle de ta plume et t'aprestes de fort maçonner et ouvrer par grant diligence. Car voycy une grande et large pierre que je veuil qui soit la premiere assise ou fondement de ta cite" (I, 676).

16. Susan Groag Bell, in "Christine de Pizan (1364-1430): Humanism and the Problem of a Studious Woman," *Feminist Studies* 3 (1976), 1 173-84, points out that whereas Boccaccio denigrates women's traditional pursuits, Christine ignores his deprecations in her rewrites of his stories. Bell also notices that in the sequel to the *Cité,* the *Trésor de la Cité des Dames* or *Le Livre des Trois Vertus,* Christine does not counsel women to study letters but rather gives practical advice on how to gain power in the current social conditions; Bell concludes that such a practice demonstrates Christine's assumption that "it was 'woman's work' that kept the fabric of society intact" (p. 181).

17. It is possible that Christine knew Alain de Lille's *De planctu naturae,* in which Lady Nature gives a long explanation of reading "per antiphrasim"; in the *Cité* Lady Reason explains that we are to read by "the grammatical figure of *antiphrasis*" (p. 7). In the debate over the *Rose,* Gerson had specifically taken Jean de Meun to task for plagiarizing Alain, pointing out however, that, after having reread Alain, he can state unequivocally that Alain never speaks as Jean does, but consistently condemns vices against nature (Hicks, p. 80).

18. For a discussion of this moment in Levi-Strauss' text, see Jacques Derrida, *Of Grammatology,* trans. Gayatri Spivak (Baltimore: Johns Hopkins University Press, 1976), pp. 101-40.

19. Motherhood is one of the more immediate stances for female authority; Christine was herself a mother of three children, and she uses this authoritative position in the *Ensignemens moraux* to address her son, Jean Castel, *Œuvres poétiques de Christine de Pisan,* ed. M. Roy (Paris: Firmin Didot), 3 vols: III, 27-44. The significant importance of her own mother, however, in the opening pages of the *Cité,* calls up large questions about the relation of real mothering to any female's identity as author or otherwise. Recent feminist discussions of female authors writing in later periods make interesting use of the object relations theory of mothering outlined by Nancy Chodorow in *The Reproduction of Mothering: Psychoanalysis and the Sociology of Gender* (Berkeley: University of California Press, 1978). At base, it is more difficult for a female to detach from the first love object, the mother, and to create a separate identity because of their shared gender (as well as their shared sociological role). The fact that Christine's mother is still feeding her (calling her to supper) also broaches notions of orality held over from infant attachments, and would need to be taken into account in a fuller discussion of the problematic relations of an oral, prophetic and specifically female tradition by which Christine in the *Cité* "corrects" a written male tradition.

20. Hicks, pp. 141-42; Dante's poem is a "hundred times better written"; there is "no comparison."

21. "Helas Dieux, pourquoy ne me faiz tu naistre au monde en masculin sexe, a celle fin que mes inclinacions fussent toutes a te mieulx servir et que je ne errasse en riens et fusse de si grant parfeccion come homme masle ce dit estre? . . ." Telz parolles et plus assez tres longuement en triste pensee disoye a Dieu en ma lamantacion, si comme celle qui par ma foulour me tenoye tres malcontent de ce qu'en corp femenin m'ot fait Dieus estre au monde. (II, 621)

22. "En celle dollente penssee ainsi que j'estoye, la *teste* baissiee comme personne honteuse, les *yeulx* plains de larmes, tenant ma *main* soubz ma *joe acoudee* sur le pommel de ma chayere, soubdainement sus mon giron vy descendre un ray de liumiere" (II, 621-22; emphasis added). Richards translates "joe" as "armrest" which is, of course, possible; however, I think the main burden of Christine's list of body parts in this description would tend to make the "joe" a human cheek rather than the side-part of an armchair. For "joe" as "joue," specifically as "cheek," see A. J. Greimas, *Dictionnaire de l'Ancien Francais* (Paris: Librairie Larousse, 1968). See also fig. 4.

23. Suzanne Solente, ed., *Le Livre de la Mutacion de Fortune* (Paris: Éditions A. & J. Picard, 1959), 2 vols; I, 9-12; lines 51-156. See Willard, p. 108, for a discussion of the transformation in the *Mutacion.*

24. I am indebted to Prof. Eugene Vance for this interesting reading of the detail of the knife.

25. Jane Gallop, "Writing and Sexual Difference: the Difference Within," in *Writing and Sexual Difference,* ed. Elizabeth Abel (Chicago: University of Chicago Press, 1980), p. 287.

26. Hélène Cixous, in *The Newly Born Woman,* co-authored with Catherine Clément, trans. Betsy Wing (Minneapolis: University of Minnesota Press, 1986), assumes a relationship between the female body and "writing" as she conceives it: "woman is body more than man is. Because he is invited to social success, to sublimation. More body hence more writing" (p. 95). Punning on the French word "voler," Cixous provides a double metaphor for a specifically female writing: "To fly/steal is woman's gesture, to steal into language to make it fly" (p. 96). Christine not only shares the wordplay with such a theorist, who assumes a continuity between writing and the body, she also would appear to have anticipated the anti-oedipal stance of such a theorist as Luce Irigaray, who bases her description of "écriture féminine" in a critique of Freud's too oedipally based sense of female sexuality. See in particular, "Psychoanalytic Theory: Another Look" in *This Sex Which is Not One,* trans. Catherine Porter with Carolyn Burke (Ithaca, New York: Cornell University Press, 1985) as well as the title essay.

27. "nullo in hoc editor volumine speciali . . . et a nemine demonstrata, describere, quasi aliquale redditur premium" (Zaccario, ed. p. 28).

28. David Anderson, unpublished manuscript.

29. See Richards' note for further corroboration, p. 262.

30. Sandra L. Hindman, *Christine de Pizan's "Epistre Othéa"* (Toronto: Pontifical Institute of Medieval Studies, 1986), p. 57, argues for a similar conflation of the authorities of Christine and the figure of Othea through the epistolary form. The *Cité* makes the conflation a part of the dramatic dialogue as the three figures dictate the stories to Christine as named author.

31. Millard Meiss, *French Painting in the Time of Jean de Berry: the late XIVth Century and the Patronage of the Duke* (London: Phaidon, 1967), 2 vols.

32. Hindman, pp. 75-89. Hindman also discusses Christine's naming of a female border-painter, pp. 69-70.

33. Paris, Bibliothèque Nationale, f. fr. 607; the MS was a presentation copy for the Duc de Berry.

34. "Ainsi, belle fille, t'est donne la prerogative entre les femmes de faire et bastir la Cite des Dames, pour laquelle fonder et parfaire, tu prendras et puiseras en nous trois eaue vive comme en fontaines cleres, et te livrerons assez matiere plus forte et plus durable que marbre. . . . Si sera ta cite tres belle sans pareille et de perpetuelle duree au monde" (II, 630).

35. Such wordplay is typical of allegory. See my *The Language of Allegory: Defining the Genre* (Ithaca: Cornell University Press, 1979), esp. pp. 58-79, for the function of puns in William Langland's *Piers Plowman.*

36. A later 15th century illumination counts their uncanonical number more carefully—Christine says there are ten rather than nine; Paris, B.N. f. fr. 1177, f. 45.

37. In a miniature illustrating even so chaste a story as that of Penelope, the violence of the suitors seems implicitly directed at the exemplary wife rather than at each other (Royal 20 CV, British Library, f. 6 1[vo)]).

38. The incipit illumination of Jean de Vignay's translation of Vincent of Beauvais' *Miroir Historial* (Paris, BN, f. fr. 313, f. 1) is split down the middle; on the left is a group of male saints standing before a monk seated in a high chair writing; on the right is a group of female saints standing before a monk seated in a slightly lower chair, also writing. While the difference in the size of the chairs, the placement of the figures (the floor of the males' side is higher than the floor for the females), and the use of a nimbus around one male saint's head but no corresponding haloes for the females, all suggest that the hierarchical nature of the gender division is observed, the miniatures are the same size and use the same format. The overall effect is of perfect parallelism.

39. The sexuality implicit in this miniature of the clothed St. Christine, opposed to the naked pagan idols, one white, one darker in color, strikes a contrast with the sexless nature of other martyrs' suffering, painted by the same hand. The idols are not nude, but naked, their shields covering genitals that must be present as a menace to the virgin saint. The color code of the pagan idols suggests that the threat of idolatry is both without and within, signed as a cultural other in the darker figure, but as the same in the lighter. Both of course, as male, represent idolatry as a sexual threat to the female saint, who bends away from them with hand gestures that cover her own genital areas (though this is, in fact, a typical placement for female hands even when there are no contextually present sexual implications).

40. Et donc sa mere femme Urben ouyante q' sa fille avoit suffert si grant peine derompit ses vestemens & mist cendres sus son chief & ala chartre et cheust aux pieds dicelle a pleur disant. Ma seule fille ayez pitie de moi qui alaictas mes mammelles qui ta len fait pour quoi tu aoures ung estrange dieu. (Paris, 1495, f. 483.)

41. Greimas notes that "langue" as meaning "langage parlé ou écrit" is "rare" in ancien français; however, if it ever slips into this meaning, it does so here.

42. The question of sightedness and blindness curiously recurs in a number of different father-daughter relations in other saints' lives. The stories of two cross-dressed saints, Euphrosine and Marine, both of whom become monks, are told in immediate sequence by both Christine and Vincent. However, Christine transfers the miraculous ability of St. Euphrosine's dead body to St. Marine's, whose dead body, when kissed by a monk who has lost the use of one eye, restores his sight. The signal difference between the two saints is that Euphrosine fled to the monastery to escape her father's attempt to marry her to an unwanted suitor, while Marine goes to the monastery, called there by her father who misses her too much after he has turned monk. Why Christine should suppress the power to restore eyesight in rebellious Euphrosine's case and to grant it to the dutiful daughter Marine is, to say the least, suspicious; what seems to be shifting about in this floating eyeball is a weird marker of Oedipal relations. Vincent's text allows the

initially hostile father of Euphrosine to "see" his daughter again before her death; she is—like the monk's eyesight—"restored" to him. Christine's text insists upon this father's further suffering, and his death. In Christine's text Euphrosine's dead body tenaciously holds the script that identifies it as female until the father can read it; this script-holding body does not restore sight.

43. Paper presented at the University of Pennsylvania, Spring 1987.

44. Christine de Pisan, *Ditié de Jehanne d'Arc,* ed. Angus J. Kennedy and Kenneth Varty (Oxford: Society for the Study of Mediaeval Languages and Literature, 1977), p. 28. The specification of the eleven years' of lamentation spent in an "abbaye close," since the time that Charles was forced to flee Paris, not only coordinates the present moment of the poem with contemporary history, but also establishes Christine's signature biography which marks the peculiarly specific authority of her texts. The poem is a part of history, but it is also a part of the writings of a speaker who persistently names herself.

45. There is doubtless some social coherence in the mistaken assumption that Jean Gerson, Christine's companion in arms during the Querelle de la Rose, was the author of a Latin tract defending Joan's transvestism, dated 14 May 1429, titled *De Mirabili Victoria Cujusdam Puellae,* as well as the *Breviarum Historiale* which describes the meeting at Chinon and compares Joan to Deborah, Esther and Penthesilea. The dauphin Charles who gave Joan further men of arms after their famous but rather mysterious meeting at Chinon, was the youngest son of Isabeau of Bavaria (if not of the mad king), for whom Christine had made the presentation edition of her works, the present Harley 4431. Marina Warner makes a very interesting argument about Joan of Arc's name having less to do immediately with the family name than with the subterranean Amazonian message it carries, the "arc" being the bow the famous warrior women carried; see *Joan of Arc: The Image of Female Heroism* (New York: Knopf, 1981), pp. 198-200. Christine was not the only writer to do so, but she was one who had discussed the Amazon kingdom at length. Christine devotes two huitains of her poem to a discussion of the process at Poitiers, at which clerks and learned men investigated Joan's "fait" before the battle of Orleans; but Christine also "proves" Joan's legitimacy by prophecy, including in the usual list of Bede and Merlin a "Sebile." Although Christine herself does not call La Pucelle an amazonian warrior, her presentation of Joan as authorized by sybilline prophecy connects her to the sybils prominent in the *Epistre Othéa* and the *Cité des Dames.*

ROSALIND BROWN-GRANT (ESSAY DATE 2000)

SOURCE: Brown-Grant, Rosalind. "Christine de Pizan: Feminist Linguist *Avant la Lettre?*" In *Christine de Pizan 2000: Studies on Christine de Pizan in Honour of Angus J. Kennedy,* edited by John Campbell and Nadia Margolis, pp. 65-76. Amsterdam: Rodopi, 2000.

In the following essay, Brown-Grant links Christine's language to her arguments, noting how she employed unique and innovative word choices to underscore her defense of women from earlier misogynist texts. Brown-Grant suggests that Christine changed the connotations of such words as dames *("ladies") and created a language for imagining women as philosophers and poets in the same class as men.*

As a fervent opponent of the misogyny which she saw as all-pervasive in the culture of her day, Christine de Pizan was well aware of the power of language not just to reflect but also actively to construct social reality.[1] Yet although much critical attention has been devoted to her texts in defence of women, particularly the ***Cité des dames,***[2] very few scholars have analysed how Christine's own linguistic practice was informed by her stand against misogyny.[3] Until recently, only Lucy Gay, Jan Gerard Bruins and Suzanne Solente have discussed her language in depth (Solente noting Christine's fondness for feminine diminutive forms), but none of them sought to link their analysis of her style to her pro-woman stance.[4] However, two major articles by Nadia Margolis have now begun to remedy this lack. In the first, Margolis develops Solente's comments and argues that Christine radically alters the significance of diminutive forms such as *seulette, pucelette* and *femmelette* (which were traditionally used to belittle women) in order to represent herself and other female figures such as Joan of Arc in a more favourable light.[5] In the second, Margolis shows how Christine, through her innovative use of suffixes (such as *-esse* in *clergesse*) and of sex-neutral or epicene words (such as *artiste*) by which to refer to female creativity, undertakes "[une] féminisation de la langue [qui] pourrait encourager les femmes de s'arroger, au moyen des signifiants de la sagesse et l'étude re-suffixés à leur genre, le droit d'être intelligentes, savantes, plus conscientes du monde réel et donc meilleures participantes au bien-être de leurs familles et de leur pays—au niveau correspondant à celui des hommes."[6]

This leaves certain questions open. Just how far did Christine's "feminisation" of the language actually go? What other linguistic strategies were available to her in her critique of misogyny?[7]

Building on Margolis's findings, I thus propose here to compare Christine's linguistic usage in the ***Cité des dames*** with that of the anonymous (and almost certainly male) author of her main source, *Des cleres et nobles femmes* (1401),[8] the French translation of Boccaccio's *De claris mulieribus.* A comparison between these two texts, which are of similar length, is particularly illuminating because, although they both belong to the "lives of famous women" genre, Christine makes her catalogue of heroines into a comprehensive defence of the female sex both past and present.[9] Unlike the author of the *Cleres femmes,* she was confronted not simply with the task of rewriting the history of women but also of finding a language which was adequate to express her defence of her sisters. Since Christine relied heavily on this French version of Boccaccio's text when writing the ***Cité des dames,***[10] any stylistic divergence from her source is thus likely to have been the result of conscious choice rather than mere accident.

This study, which is intended to be the first of two on Christine's use of language in her defence of women,[11] focuses exclusively on nouns, a key area since it raises important morphological and semantic issues related to gender. By examining feminine and generic nouns in turn, I shall demonstrate that Christine's usage differs markedly from that of the author of the *Cleres femmes.* However, perhaps less expectedly, her difference from her source arises as much from her desire to genericise the language by using sex-neutral forms so as to mark the common essence of male and female as from any wish to feminise language in order to represent women's experience fully within it.[12]

One of the most significant ways in which the author of the *Cleres femmes* and Christine diverge from each other is in their use of two of the commonest nouns which referred to women in Middle French: *femme(s)* and *dame(s).* In standard usage of the period, *femme(s)* designated the female sex as a whole, individual women, wives, and nonnoble women, whereas *dame(s)* was employed as a term of address, as an indicator of a woman's noble rank, to distinguish between a married, mature woman and a young, unmarried girl, and as the female equivalent of a *seigneur.*[13] The divergence in usage between the ***Cité des dames*** and the *Cleres femmes* is signalled by their very titles. Whilst the male author's text is concerned with the neutral *femmes*—women rather than ladies—whose distinction is indicated by the adjectives "cleres" and "nobles," Christine's work discusses *dames,* whose noble or high status is implicit in the noun itself. This difference in emphasis is mirrored not just in the titles but also in the body of their two works since the author of the *Cleres femmes* uses the less prestigious *femmes* even on those occasions where standard usage indicates that a high-ranking lady would normally have been referred to as a *dame,* as in the cases of the goddesses Ceres and Minerva (1:28-31 and 1:31-34), or the queens Semiramis or Penthesilea (1:19-24 and 1:101-13). It is only in the stories of Dido, Rhea Ilia, Gaia Cyrilla, Lucretia, Thamiris and Mariamme that he employs *dame* throughout, though it is not clear why he singles out these particular women in this way as they are not of higher status than any others in his catalogue (1:134-46, 1:150-53, 1:154-55, 1:158-61, 1:161-64, 2:109-12, respectively). In all, though, there are fewer than 40 examples of *dame(s)* in the *Cleres femmes* compared with 516 in the ***Cité des dames.*** Instead, to indicate a lady of high social standing, he prefers a different term altogether: *matrone(s),* meaning a respectable married woman, of which there are 25 examples.[14] Yet his use of this noun is highly selective as he employs it only to refer to Roman patrician women such as Veturia (2:7) or Virginia (2:36).

Moreover, following Boccaccio, the author of the *Cleres femmes* at times employs *femmes* as a derogatory term in order to insult men by referring to them as women. This is because, in the original text, Boccaccio deployed much of his invective to accuse his male contemporaries of effeminacy for having allowed themselves to be upstaged by mere pagan women who had shown much greater courage, strength or intelligence. For example, of Penthesilea and her followers the author of the *Cleres femmes* remarks: "ceste femme vierge et semblables a elle sont moult plus faites hommes en armes que ne soient ceulx que nature a fait masles et oiseveté et volupté ou delit charnel les tourne en femmes et lievres" (1:103). His use of *femme* as both a neutral and a pejorative term in preference to the noble *dame* and his parsimonious use of *matrone* only for certain types of women would thus seem to reflect much of Boccaccio's ambivalence towards the female examples in his catalogue, many of whom are chosen more for their personal notoriety than for the virtue of their deeds.[15]

In the ***Cité des dames,*** by contrast, Christine follows standard Middle French usage for both *dames* and *femmes.* Given that most of the women in her catalogue of heroines are of noble status, they are termed *dames,* whereas others of nonnoble origin, like the low-born widow who begged Jesus to save her child (88), are referred to as *femmes.* Yet Christine deviates from standard practice in the ***Cité des dames*** in one very important way when she extends the normal connotation of *dame* from being one of *noble birth* to that of *moral worth* irrespective of social origin. This is clearly seen at the end of her text when she addresses *all* the ladies in her catalogue as *dames* who have earned themselves a place in her city of the virtuous elect: "Mes tres redoubtees Dames, Dieux soit louez! Or est du tout achevee et parfaicte notre ***Cité des dames,*** en laquelle a grant honneur vous toutes, celles qui amez gloire, vertu et loz, povez estre hebergees, tant les passees dames, comme les presentes et celles a avenir, car pour toute dame honorable est faicte et fondee" (496). Likewise, Christine signals this shift in connotation when she describes high-ranking women of dubious morality, such as the evil queens Jezebel and Athaliah, as *femmes* and not *dames,* since she regards them as unworthy examples who should be shunned (344). Thus the way in which both the author of the *Cleres femmes* and Christine use *dames* as opposed to *femmes* is clearly dictated by each work's polemical agenda: whilst the former undermines the status of the vast majority of his examples by terming them simply *femmes,* Christine blurs the moral and social connotations of *dames* in order to upgrade all of her examples to the ranks of a meritorious élite.

In addition to exploiting or reinterpreting the meaning of well-established terms for women such as *dames* and *femmes,* both Christine and the author of the *Cleres femmes* were also concerned with feminising masculine noun forms for roles in which women had distinguished themselves. The main method at their disposal was to add suffixes such as *-esse* to the masculine noun (with *-eresse* as a variant corresponding to words ending in *-eur*). As Jean Batany observes, this suffix, which was brought into productive use in the twelfth century in the term *abbesse* (from the masculine form *abbé*) gained currency in the later Middle Ages as the most popular means of feminising masculine nouns, and was also used for feminine adjectival endings.[16] However, though our two authors both adopt this same method of morphological marking, their individual usage differs significantly, with important consequences for the status of the nouns themselves.

Discounting more familiar terms such as *princesse* and *baronesse,* which denote a woman's specific rank in society, both Christine and the male author employ the *-esse/-eresse* feminine suffix for a wide variety of roles. Surprisingly, perhaps, there are more of these suffixed terms in the *Cleres femmes* than in the ***Cité des dames***: 21 different ones as opposed to 12. Many of those found in the male author's text are extremely evocative terms: "batailleresses" (1:44) and "combateresses" (1:45)) in the military domain; "divineresse" (1:45), "prestresce" (1:53) and "enchanteresse" (1:120) in the spiritual realm; and "poeteresse" (1:150) and "painteresse" (2:13) in the artistic sphere. Others, which are more metaphorical than concrete terms, include "testamenteresse" (2:41), "trouverresse" (2:44) and "accroisseresse" (2:88). Indeed, the author of the *Cleres femmes* would appear to have been particularly innovative in this respect since neither Godefroy nor Tobler-Lommatsch list any prior instances of 5 of the 21 terms used: "batailleresses" (1:44), "divineresse" (1:45), "painteresse" (2:13), "quereresse" (2:44), and "rachateresse" (2:186) would all seem to be his coinages.

Given Christine's aim in the ***Cité des dames*** of celebrating the achievements of women in areas traditionally reserved for men, it might at first sight appear odd that there are fewer examples of these suffixed terms in her text than in the *Cleres femmes* and that she is less innovative than her source in coining new terms. Thus, whilst she employs "maistresse" (162), "clergece" (166) and "vainqueresse" (140) as concrete terms and "amministraresse" (58) and "defenderresse" (432) for women in more metaphorical roles, the only terms she herself appears to have created is "protectarresse" (432) (which is used to describe the Virgin Mary's chief role as Queen of the City of Ladies). However, Christine's decision not to borrow more of the large number of the *-esse/-eresse* suffixes from the author of the *Cleres femmes* becomes less surprising if we compare both the textual and grammatical circumstances in which such terms are used in each text. Firstly, Christine's choice of vocabulary was often dependent on the specific rhetorical point she was arguing. For example, in the case of the Amazon virgins Hippolyta and Menalippe, who brought down the Greek heroes Hercules and Theseus in combat, she makes great capital out of the fact that these two were mere "pucelles" and "damoiselles" fighting against two of the bravest and most fearsome "chevaliers" the world had ever seen (116-22). Elevating these two women into *batailleresses* or *combateresses* in this instance would actually have undermined the contrast Christine was drawing between their supposed physical inferiority and the knights' superior military prowess and experience. Secondly, there is a subtle but important grammatical difference between the way in which she and the author of the *Cleres femmes* use terms with the *-esse/-eresse* suffix within a sentence. In his text, their function is often to qualify a feminine noun: for example, "les filles combateresse" [*sic*] (1:45), "ceste femme enchanterresse et empoisonneresse Circés" (1:120), "ceste femme cruelle et procureresce de mort" (2:64), and "pucelles prestresses" (2:155). Used adjectivally, the force of such terms is lessened: they are reduced to indicating a quality of a person, rather than specifically designating that person themselves.[17]

FROM THE AUTHOR

CHRISTINE'S LAMENT TO GOD THAT OPENS HER *BOOK OF THE CITY OF LADIES*

"Oh, God, how can this be? For unless I stray from my faith, I must never doubt that Your infinite wisdom and most perfect goodness ever created anything which was not good. Did You yourself not create woman in a very special way and since that time did You not give her all those inclinations which it pleased You for her to have? And how could it be that You could go wrong in anything? Yet look at all these accusations which have been judged, decided, and concluded against women. I do not know how to understand this repugnance. If it is so, fair Lord God, that in fact so many abominations abound in the female sex, for You Yourself say that the testimony of two or three witnesses lends credence, why shall I not doubt that this is true? Alas, God, why did You not let me be born in the world as a man, so that all my inclinations would be to serve You better, and so that I would not stray in anything and would be as perfect as a man is said to be? But since Your kindness has not been extended to me, then forgive my negligence in Your service, most fair Lord God, and may it not displease You, for the servant who receives fewer gifts from his lord is less obliged in his service." I spoke these words to God in my lament and a great deal more for a very long time in sad reflection, and in my folly I considered myself most unfortunate because God had made me inhabit a female body in this world.

Christine de Pizan. Excerpt from *The Book of the City of Ladies.* Translated by Earl Jeffrey Richards. New York: Persea Books, 1982, p. 5.

For Christine, in comparison, these terms are almost always used as self-standing nouns, such as when she describes the inhabitants of the City as its "possessarresses" (250). Only in the one case of "femmelette pecharesse" (90) is the term in *-eresse* made adjectival. Thus, although there are fewer examples of such forms in Christine's text than in her source, where she does employ them they retain their full nominal value, particularly in those spheres of activity where she wants to highlight women's illustrious deeds.

However, where Christine and the author of the *Cleres femmes* differ most radically from each other is not in their suffixation of masculine nouns but in their use of epicene terms in order to refer to women. Being nouns which can take either a male or a female article, these terms designate roles that both men and women can potentially play without the need for any specific feminine morphological marking, particularly since such words already tend to end in silent *-e,*[18] as in the example of "disciple" which both Christine and her source employ (***Cité des dames,*** 190, and *Cleres femmes,* 2:27). Apart from this noun, there is only one other epicene in the male author's text ("hoir", 1:69), whereas Christine also uses "prophete" (228), "chef" (98, 432), "philosophe" (94, 158, 160), and "poete" (154, 156, 158). Though they may be few in number, these examples are extremely important for what they reveal about Christine's neologising practice. On the one hand, she seems to have revived the use of epicene *prophete,* which had been sex-neutral in Old French, whereas in Middle French the feminised forms *prophetesse* or *propheteresse* were employed instead to refer to a woman.[19] On the other hand, she was clearly innovative in her use of the terms *chef, philosophe* and *poete* as epicenes, given that they were traditionally deemed to be solely masculine roles, with *poeteresse* as the only feminised form of the three available at that time.[20] Christine therefore employs these epicene terms for the kind of high-status roles to which she herself aspired in her works, and which she deemed to be particularly important in her feminist agenda to put women firmly on the map of human creativity and achievement.[21] That she treats *prophete, philosophe* and *poete* as epicene is all the more significant given that she herself occasionally precedes *prophete* by the word *femme* (***Cité des dames,*** 288), but never seems to feminise it or any of these other terms with the suffix *-esse/-eresse.* The higher the status of the role concerned—and the greater the credit accruing to women for their achievement within it—the more likely Christine therefore was to genericise the role name to include the feminine rather than simply find a feminine equivalent of a masculine term, as the author of the *Cleres femmes* preferred to do.

Christine's use of epicene noun forms is, however, by no means an isolated example of her genericising practice. Her critique of sex-bias in language also extends to questioning the masculine term *hommes* which, when used as a generic noun, "absorbs" and thereby masks the feminine.[22] As Marina Yaguello puts it, through use of this term "l'homme a en quelque sorte 'confisqué' symboliquement la qualité d'être humain à son profit."[23] In the medieval context, the significance of *hommes* as an implicitly exclusive rather than inclusive generic term can be seen in the fact that many misogynist writers implied that women were somehow less human than men, being endowed with an inferior rationality, a voracious sexuality and a bestial nature.[24] Jean de Meun, for example, famously characterises woman as a "venimeuse beste" which seeks to destroy man.[25] Christine, in the ***Cité des dames,*** clearly rebuts this definition of women as a non-human race when she states, "les femmes sont aussi bien ou nombre du peuple de Dieu et de creature humaine que sont les hommes, et non mie une autre espece" (376-78).

Christine's art of refutation, here as elsewhere, must accomplish two seemingly conflicting goals: she must defeat a key point of misogynist doctrine by using the very language that underpins misogyny itself. In this instance, her challenge was to make the potentially exclusive noun *hommes* serve the feminist cause. The author of the *Cleres femmes* gives no indication that, for him, the noun *hommes* is in any way problematic. In his text, the term serves both to designate men, as for example, when he explains how the women of Lemnos freed themselves from male control, "la dominacion et servitute des hommes" (1:57), and to refer to people in general when he recounts how the pagans mistakenly regarded Opis, wife of Saturn, as a goddess: "ceste femme (. . .), selon l'erreur des hommes mortelz, est eue et reputee deesse et mere des dieulx" (1:24). Christine too, in the ***Cité des dames,*** uses *hommes* in a specific sense when she wants to distinguish between the male and the female sex, as in those passages in which Reason explains why some men slander women: "Ceulx a qui il est venu de leurs propres vices sont hommes qui ont usé leur jeunece en vie dissolue et abondé en plusieurs amours de diverses femmes" (70). However, though in a very few instances Christine clearly employs *hommes* in a generic sense, as when she states that "l'entencion—dist on—juge l'omme" (66), in many other cases, particularly those where Reason outlines all the benefits that women such as Ceres and Carmentis have brought into the world with their respective inventions of agriculture and the Latin alphabet, it is by no means as obvious whether *hommes* is being used specifically or generically. For example, in referring to Ceres's discoveries which rescued humankind from a primitive existence, Reason notes how "les engins des hommes vagues et pareceux, estans es cavernes d'ignorance, mua, attray et ramena a la haultece de contemplacion et excercitacions convenables, et ordena aucuns hommes es champs pour faire les labours par lesquieulx tant de villes et de citez furent remplies et ceulx soustenus qui font les autres oeuvres neccessaires a vivre" (182). Likewise, Reason explains that, thanks to Carmentis's achievement, "[en] infinis livres et volumes (. . .) sont mis et gardez en perpetuelle memoire les fais des hommes," and that "par elle, sont hommes, quoyque ilz ne le recongnoiscent, tirez hors de ignorence" (178-80). Unless one were translating these passages and needed to choose between reading *hommes* as meaning men in particular as opposed to humankind in general,[26] it is in fact possible, if not positively desirable, to read them as both being present simultaneously. This is because such semantic indeterminacy allows Christine to stress just how much the human race as a whole—but men especially—have benefitted from women's inventions, and to condemn the ingratitude of misogynist clerks and knights in calling women's intelligence into question when they themselves are the chief beneficiaries of women's gifts. Paradoxically then, whilst modern feminists have criticised the use of the term *hommes* as a generic precisely because it tends to mask the feminine in favour of the masculine, Christine turns this semantic ambiguity to her own rhetorical advantage, in order to criticise men, just as men had turned it to women's disadvantage in the past.

Yet though Christine often plays on the indeterminacy of *hommes* for her own ends, she is well aware of the need for a less ambiguous term when wanting to refer explicitly to both sexes at once. In the ***Cité des dames,*** the three unequivocally generic nouns which she employs as alternatives to *hommes* are *gens, creature* and *personne,* each of which, as we shall see, occurs with significantly greater frequency than in the *Cleres femmes.* Although all three words can take a male or a female referent, the last two are feminine nouns, whilst the first can be of either gender depending on its position and function in a sentence.[27] Thus, unlike the generic *hommes* with its grammatical and semantic masking of the feminine, none of these sex-neutral terms is more inclusive of one sex than the other. By using each term in a significant array of contexts, Christine appropriates them as important elements of her linguistic revisionism.

By far the most extensively used generic alternative to *hommes* in the ***Cité des dames*** is the term *gens* (with *gent* as a variant). Excluding other meanings of this word, such as an estate in society (e.g. "les gens de cheval et de pié," ***Cité des dames,*** 140), an army or followers (e.g. "Jason avec ses gens," *Cleres femmes,* 1:58), a race or nation (e.g. "les gens d'Egipte," ***Cité des dames,*** 176), *gens* in the sense of people in general occurs only 17 times in the *Cleres femmes* as against 34 in the ***Cité des dames.*** This compares with 27 instances of generic *hommes* in her source, as opposed to 22 in Christine's text (though we have already noted how difficult it is to identify many of these instances here as unquestionably generic). In both texts, *gens* can refer specifically to men or women, or can be used generically where the sex of the referent is left indefinite. In the *Cleres femmes,* for instance, "les corps de gens mors," which refers to the dead soldiers amongst whom Polynices' widow Argia searches for his corpse, are obviously male (1:92), as in the ***Cité des dames*** are the misogynists whom Reason condemns as "mauvaises gens dyaboliques" for claiming that women are childish (84). Conversely, Rectitude uses *gens* anaphorically to indicate women when she says that the City she and Christine are busy building must be "habitee toute de dames de grant excellence, car autres gens n'y voulons" (250). Finally, as an example where *gens* is used generically to mean people, male or female, Rectitude explains how Nero's destruction of Rome meant that "par ceste pestillence moururent moult de gens" (***Cité des dames,*** 340). However, where the term is clearly meant to refer to both men and women, Christine's usage in the ***Cité des dames*** diverges from that of the *Cleres femmes* in preferring *gens* to *hommes* and in employing it in a more inclusive way to indicate the equally human essence of both male and female. For instance, in order to counter the misogynist view that women are inherently less worthy than men, Reason replies that "la haulteur ou abbaissement des gens ne gist mie es corps selon le sexe mais en la perfection des meurs et des vertus" (80). In other words, virtue is not the prerogative of one sex to the exclusion of the other, a key point in Christine's defence of women.

Just as for *gens,* so the relative importance for Christine of the term *creature* is seen by the fact that it occurs only twice in the *Cleres femmes* as against 18 times in the ***Cité des dames.*** Unlike the word *homme,* whose meaning is largely determined in opposition to *femme, enfant* or *bête, creature* lays the emphasis on humans as part of God's creation; "(l'être humain) face à son créateur."[28] It can thus apply equally to a man or a woman.[29] Compared to the *Cleres femmes,* which uses *creature* solely in the neutral sense of "living creature" (1:17), Christine in the ***Cité des dames*** systematically exploits both its sex-neutrality and its stress on the human as part of the natural order of things. Applying it to women when Rectitude chides Christine for complaining about being a member of the female sex ("du sexe de tieulx creatures," 226), the text also uses the term to refer to men, describing Eve's creation from the rib of Adam as being from "la tres plus noble creature qui oncques eust esté creé" (78). Where the term really comes into its own in the ***Cité des dames*** is in Christine's bid to prove that God cherishes women as part of His creation, and has thus endowed them with the same capacity for rational thought and virtuous conduct as men possess. Reason uses *creature* in a particularly inclusive sense when discussing how both men and women alike can profit from gazing into her mirror and seeing their faults: "il n'est quelconques personne qui s'i mire, quelque la creature soit, qui clerement ne se congnoisce" (52). This emphasis on rationality is underscored when Christine couples *creature* with the adjective *raisonnable* on four separate occasions. For instance, Reason demonstrates women's aptitude for learning, given the opportunity to do so, exclaiming: "il n'est rien qui tant appreigne creature raisonnable que fait l'excercice et experience de plusieurs choses et diverses" (152). Christine even uses this term in a superlative sense when countering the misogynists' claim that women, in being more fickle in their emotions, are less virtuous than men. For example, in describing Artemisia's boundless grief at her husband's death as that of "si grant douleur que creature peut porter" (262), Christine does not just compare her suffering to that of other women but rather implies that Artemisia's heartfelt emotion is greater than anyone, woman *or* man, has ever had to bear.

If the noun *creature* allows Christine to stress the equality of the sexes in terms of their God-given rational essence, the generic *personne* enables her to highlight their common humanity. As Yaguello explains: "Le mot *homme* se trouve dans une relation d'opposition 'participative' avec le mot *femme*: le féminin est *inclus* dans le masculin. Le mot *personne,* lui, ne s'oppose à rien d'autre qu'à la non-personne (les animaux, les choses): il 'contient' à égalité le féminin et le masculin."[30] Setting aside examples where *personne* is used to mean "no-one" or "in person", which are not relevant to this discussion, there is once again a greater occurrence of this term in the ***Cité des dames*** than in the *Cleres femmes* (21 examples as against 16). More significantly, there is a noticeable difference in the way in which it is employed by the two writers. The male author largely uses *personne* to refer to unspecified individuals as in, for example, his account of how Agamemnon was killed "sans ce qu'il veist la personne qui ainsi faulcement et trayteusement le tua" (1:110), or in set phrases such as "par personne moyenne," which recurs three times (1:88, 2:116, and 2:143). Christine, on the other hand, capitalises fully on the implications of the term to include the two sexes, particularly when discussing women's intellectual and moral faculties. Thus Reason explains the conditions necessary for someone to act with good judgement as being "constance, noblece et vertu, sans lesquelles graces avoir ne peut estre en personne droite prudence" (202). Conversely, Christine exploits the non-exclusiveness of *personne* in order to deflect criticism away from women, thereby countering the misogynist habit of specifying certain sins and vices as exclusively feminine. For instance, on the question of inconstancy, Rectitude is careful to explain to Christine that this fault can be found in both sexes alike: "quant l'omme ou femme laisse vaincre a sensualité le regart de raison, c'est fragilité et inconstance. Et de tant que la personne chet en plus grant deffaulte ou pechié, de tant est en lui la fragilité plus grande, car elle est plus loing du regart de raison" (344). Rectitude similarly defends women against anti-feminist accusations of avariciousness by declaring that carefulness with money is indispensable when a person, implicitly either male or female, has little to play with: "qu'en peut povre personne se elle est escharce?" (416). This judicious use of generics such as *personne* is thus an integral part of Christine's project to show that neither vice nor virtue is the exclusive province of one particular sex.

Christine de Pizan is rightly famous for being the first female writer to plead the case for women against the misogynist culture of her day. However, for Christine, the challenge confronting her lay not just in changing *what* was said about women but *how* it was actually said. To this extent, then, she can truly be dubbed a feminist linguist *avant la lettre*. In the ***Cité des dames,*** her most forthright refutation of misogyny, she broke new ground in her use of both feminine and generic nouns. Far from simply feminising masculine forms in order to mark women's achievements, as the author of the *Cleres femmes* chose to do, Christine's innovations were more wide-ranging: employing *dames* as a marker of moral worth; making *chef, philosophe* and *poete* epicene indicators of women's prowess as intellectuals and leaders; and substituting sex-neutral terms such as *gens, creature* and *personne* for the more ambiguous *hommes*. To Christine's mind, therefore, it was only by universalising the human to encompass both sexes that her vision of the moral equality of men and women could properly be expressed in language.

Notes

1. Solterer 1995, 355-78.
2. For a detailed bibliography of studies of the *Cité des dames,* see items 392-400 in Kennedy 1984, and items 805-30 in Kennedy 1994.
3. One important exception is Curnow 1992, 157-72, who analyses her use of legalistic language in this text.
4. Gay 1908-9, 69-96; Bruins 1925; and Solente 1974/1969, 335-422.
5. Margolis 1992, 111-23.
6. Margolis 1996-97, 381-404, 396.
7. For a modern feminist linguist's view of feminisation, see Moreau 1999.
8. Boccaccio 1993-95; *Cité des dames,* ed. Richards.
9. McLeod 1992, 37-47.
10. *Cité des dames,* ed. Curnow, 1: 138-66; Dulac 1978, 315-43; Philippy 1986, 167-93; Bumgardner 1991, 37-52; Quilligan 1991; and Brown-Grant 1999, 128-74.
11. Christine's pronouns and adjectives relating to gender in the *Cité des dames* are treated in a paper given at the Fourth International Congress on Christine de Pizan, Glasgow, July 2000.
12. This usage is consistent with her practice in the *Epistre Othea*: see Brown-Grant 1999, 78-87.
13. Grisay 1969, 55-155; Andrieux-Reix 1987, 227-32.
14. Grisay 1969, 32-35, notes that this term was imported into the French language from Latin in the thirteenth century.
15. Jordan 1987, 25-47; McLeod 1991, 59-80.
16. Batany 1992, 191-19. See also Harrison 1989, 436-44.
17. See Batany 1992, 194: "l'adjectif réfère à une réalité inanimée, la qualité, tandis que le nom réfère plutôt à une personne (ou à une chose personnifiable)."
18. Yaguello 1987, 132; Gervais 1993, 130.
19. The epicene use of *prophete* in early texts such as *Dolopathos* is noted in Godefroy X, 433. The feminine form *propheteresse* is cited from the early fifteenth-century French translation of Boccaccio's *De casibus virorum illustrium* in Godefroy, 6: 436.

20. The use of *philosophesse* in the 1518 edition of *Le Rebours Matheolus* is noted in Godefroy 6: 138.
21. See Margolis 1996-97, 397, for Christine's similar use of *artiste* in this respect.
22. Spender 1980, 138-62; Cameron 1990.
23. Yaguello 1989, 88.
24. Lhoest 1991, 343-62; Blamires 1992 and 1997.
25. Guillaume de Lorris and Jean de Meun, ed. Lecoy, 2: 254.16577.
26. See my translator's note in *City of Ladies,* trans. Brown-Grant, xxxviii-xxxix.
27. Jokinen 1988, 114-40.
28. Yaguello 1989, 58.
29. Grisay 1969, 190-1.
30. Yaguello 1989, 89.

Abbreviations

Critical studies: frequently-cited volumes of essays devoted exclusively to Christine de Pizan are made in the following manner: editor(s) and date of publication. Below is a list of these abbreviated forms, followed by their full citations:

McLeod 1991 McLeod, Glenda, ed. *The Reception of Christine de Pizan from the Fifteenth through the Nineteenth Centuries: Visitors to the City.* Lewiston, NY: Edwin Mellen Press, 1991.

Richards, et al. 1992 Richards, Earl Jeffrey, with Joan Williamson, Nadia Margolis, and Christine Reno, eds. *Reinterpreting Christine de Pizan.* Athens, Ga.: University of Georgia Press, 1992.

General Bibliography

Primary Sources: Standard Editions and Translations of Christine's Works.

CITÉ DES DAMES:

Cité des dames, ed. Richards = *La Città delle Dame.* Introduction, original text, and translation by Patrizia Caraffi. Middle-French text edited by Earl Jeffrey Richards. Milan, Luni Editrice, 1997. Revised edition 1998.

"*Le Livre de la Cité des dames* of Christine de Pisan: A Critical Edition." Maureen Cheney Curnow. 2 vols. Ph.D. diss. Vanderbilt University, 1975.

Christine de Pizan. The Book of the City of Ladies. Translated by Rosalind Brown-Grant. Harmondsworth: Penguin, 1999.

MEUN, JEAN DE:

Guillaume de Lorris and Jean de Meun. *Le Roman de la rose.* Edited by Félix Lecoy. 3 vols. Classiques Français du Moyen Age, 92, 95, 98. Paris: Honoré Champion, 1966-76. Reprinted 1982.

Secondary Sources

A) BIBLIOGRAPHIES:

Kennedy, Angus J. *Christine de Pizan: A Bibliographical Guide.* Research Bibliographies & Checklists, no. 42. London: Grant & Cutler, 1984.

———. *Christine de Pizan: A Bibliographical Guide: Supplement I.* Research Bibliographies & Checklists, no. 42.1. London: Grant & Cutler, 1994.

B) CRITICAL AND HISTORICAL STUDIES:

Andrieux-Reix, Nelly. *Ancien Français: fiches de vocabulaire.* Paris: Presses Universitaires de France, 1987.

Batany, Jean. "Les 'Estats' au féminin: un problème de vocabulaire social du XIIe au XVe siècle." In *Approches langagières de la société médiévale,* 191-219. Caen: Paradigme, 1992.

Blamires, Alcuin. *The Case for Women in Medieval Culture.* Oxford: Clarendon Press, 1997.

———, ed. *Woman Defamed and Woman Defended: An Anthology of Medieval Texts.* Oxford: Clarendon Press, 1992.

Boccaccio, Giovanni. [*De claris mulieribus*] *Boccace "Des cleres et nobles femmes" Ms. B. N. 12420 (Chap. I-LII).* Edited by Jeanne Baroin and Josiane Haffen. 2 vols. Annales Littéraires de l'Université de Besançon 498, 556. Paris: Les Belles Lettres, 1993-95.

Brown-Grant, Rosalind. *Christine de Pizan and the Moral Defence of Women: Reading beyond Gender.* Cambridge: Cambridge University Press, 1999.

Bruins, Jan Gerard. *Observations sur la langue d'Eustache Deschamps et de Christine de Pisan.* Dordrecht: Dordrechtsche Drukkerrij, 1925.

Bumgardner, George H. "Christine de Pizan and the Atelier of the Master of the Coronation." In *Seconda Miscellanea di studi e ricerche sul Quattrocento francese,* edited by Jonathan Beck and Gianni Mombello, 37-52. Chambéry: Centre d'études franco-italiennes, 1981.

Cameron, Deborah. *The Feminist Critique of Language: A Reader.* London: Routledge, 1990.

Curnow, Maureen Cheney. "'La pioche d'inquisicion': Legal-judicial Content and Style in Christine de Pizan's *Livre de la cité des dames.*" In Richards, et al. 1992, 157-72.

———. "Un mythe didactique chez Christine de Pizan: Sémiramis ou la veuve héroïque (du *De Claris Mulieribus à la Cité des Dames*)." In *Mélanges de philologie romane offerts à Charles Camproux,* 315-43. Montpellier: Centre d'Etudes Occitanes de l'Université Paul Valéry, 1978.

Gay, Lucy M. "On the Language of Christine de Pizan." *Modern Philology* 6 (1908-09): 69-96.

Gervais, Marie-Marthe. "Gender and Language in French." In *French Today: Language in its Social Context,* edited by Carol Sanders, 121-38. Cambridge: Cambridge University Press, 1993.

Godefroy, Frédéric. *Dictionnaire de l'ancienne langue française . . . du XIe au XVe siècle . . .* 10 vols. Paris: F. Vieweg, 1881-92.

Grisay, A., G. Lavis, and M. Dubois-Stasse. *Les Dénominations de la femme dans les anciens textes littéraires français.* Gembloux: Duculot, 1969.

Harrison, Ann Tukey. "Fifteenth-Century French Women's Role Names." *French Review* 62 (1989): 436-44.

Jokinen, Ulla. "Le genre de gens en moyen français." *Studia Philologica Jyväskyläensia* 22 (1988): 114-40.

Jordan, Constance. "Boccaccio's In-famous Women: Gender and Civic Virtue in the *De Claris Mulieribus.*" In *Ambiguous Realities: Women in the Middle Ages and the Renaissance,* edited by Carole Levin and Jeanie Watson, 25-47. Detroit: Wayne State University Press, 1987.

Lhoest, Benoît. "Les dénominations de la femme en moyen français: approche lexicale et anthropologique." *Zeitschrift für Romanische Philologie* 107 (1991): 343-62.

Margolis, Nadia. "Elegant Closures: The Use of the Diminutive in Christine de Pizan and Jean de Meun." In Richards, et al. 1992, 111-23.

———. "Les Terminaisons dangereuses: lyrisme, féminisme et humanisme néologiques chez Christine de Pizan." In *Autour de Jacques Monfrin. Néologie et création verbale. Actes du Colloque international, Université McGill, Montréal, 7-8-9 octobre 1996,* edited by Giuseppe Di Stefano and Rose M. Bidler, 381-404. *Le Moyen Français* 39-40-41 (1996-97).

McLeod, Glenda K. "Poetics and Antimisogynist Polemics in Christine de Pizan's *Le Livre de la cité des dames.*" In Richards, et al. 1992, 37-47.

Moreau, Thérèse. *Le Nouveau Dictionnaire féminin-masculin des professions, des titres et des fonctions.* Geneva: Metropolis, 1999.

Phillippy, Patricia A. "Establishing Authority: Boccaccio's *De Claris Mulieribus* and Christine de Pizan's *Cité des Dames.*" *Romanic Review* 77 (1986): 167-93.

Quilligan, Maureen. *The Allegory of Female Authority: Christine de Pizan's "Cité des Dames."* Ithaca: Cornell University Press, 1991.

Solente, Suzanne. "Christine de Pisan." *Histoire littéraire de la France* 40 (1974): 335-422. Originally, as separate pre-print (Paris: Klincksieck, 1969).

Solterer, Helen. "Flaming Words: Verbal Violence and Gender in Premodern Paris." *Romanic Review* 86 (1995): 355-78.

———. *The Master and Minerva: Disputing Women in French Medieval Culture.* Berkeley: University of California Press, 1995.

Spender, Dale. *Man Made Language.* London: Routledge & Kegan Paul, 1980.

Yaguello, Marina. *Les Mots et les femmes.* Paris: Payot, 1987.

FURTHER READING

Bibliographies

Kennedy, Angus J. *Christine de Pizan: A Bibliographical Guide.* London: Grant and Cutler, 1984, 131 p.

Categorizes studies by individual works and major themes, with cross-referencing.

Willard, Charity Cannon. "Christine de Pizan." In *French Women Writers: A Bio-Bibliographical Source Book,* edited by Eva Martin Sartori and Dorothy Wynne Zimmerman, pp. 56-65. New York: Greenwood, 1991.

Surveys major themes and lists important editions and studies; includes many studies available only in French.

Yenal, Edith. *Christine de Pizan: A Bibliography, 2nd ed.* Metuchen, N.J.: Scarecrow Press, 1989, 185 p.

Updates Angus J. Kennedy's 1984 bibliography.

Biography

Willard, Charity Cannon. *Christine de Pizan: Her Life and Works.* New York: Persea Books, 1984, 266 p.

Addresses Christine's beliefs and ideals as reflected in her works and characterizes her as a dedicated scholar.

Criticism

Altman, Barbara K., and Deborah L. McGrady, eds. *Christine de Pizan: A Casebook.* New York: Routledge, 2003, 296 p.

Contains up-to-date original essays by important Christine scholars, including Earl Jeffrey Richards, Nadia Margolis, Marilyn Desmond, and Liliane Dulac.

Bell, Susan Groag. "Christine de Pizan (1364-1430): Humanism and the Problem of a Studious Woman." *Feminist Studies* 3 (spring-summer 1976): 173-84.

Relates Christine's personal life to her writings and addresses her awareness of the sacrifices she made to be a female scholar.

Davis, Natalie Zemon. "Gender and Genre: Women as Historical Writers, 1400-1820." In *Beyond Their Sex: Women of the European Past,* edited by Patricia H. Labalme, pp. 153-82. New York: New York University Press, 1980.

Briefly discusses Christine's roles as historical writer and defender of women's inherent abilities.

Delaney, Sheila. "Rewriting Woman Good: Gender and the Anxiety of Influence in Two Late-Medieval Texts." In *Chaucer in the Eighties,* edited by Julian N. Wasserman and Robert J. Blanch, pp. 75-92. Syracuse: Syracuse University Press, 1986.

Compares Chaucer's and Christine's literary attempts to portray women favorably.

Desmond, Marilyn, ed. *Christine de Pizan and the Categories of Difference.* Minneapolis: University of Minnesota Press, 1998, 287 p.

Includes essays on Christine's involvement in the production of her writings, the intertextuality of her works, and the context in which she wrote.

Enders, Jody. "The Feminist Mnemonics of Christine de Pizan." *Modern Language Quarterly* 55, no. 3 (September 1994): 231-49.

Interprets The Book of the City of Ladies *with a focus on both prose technique and gender issues.*

Forhan, Kate Langdon. *The Political Theory of Christine de Pizan.* Aldershot, Eng.: Ashgate, 2002, 187 p.

Focuses on Christine's political writings addressed to the French court and considers her defense of women in the context of her larger social vision.

Gabriel, Astrik L. "The Educational Ideas of Christine de Pizan." *Journal of the History of Ideas* 16, no. 1 (January 1955): 3-21.

Discusses Christine's educational philosophy for women, describing her as one of the great moralists in Christian literature.

Kelly, F. Douglas. "Reflections on the Role of Christine de Pisan as a Feminist Writer." *SubStance,* no. 3 (winter 1972): 63-71.

Considers how Christine came to be labeled a feminist, concluding that she was not a true feminist but instead a woman who improved the image of her sex by opposing antifeminist literature.

Margolis, Nadia. "Christine de Pizan: The Poetess as Historian." *Journal of the History of Ideas* 47, no. 3 (July-September 1986): 361-75.

Discusses Christine's feminist perspective in her works, comparing her writings with those of several male historians and philosophers.

Price, Paola Malpezzi. "Masculine and Feminine Personae in the Love Poetry of Christine de Pisan." In *Gender and Literary Voice,* edited by Janet Todd, pp. 37-53. New York: Holmes & Meier Publishers, 1980.

Compares Christine's love poetry to that of male writers, including those she used as models, and discusses her use of personae to introduce a feminine perspective.

Richards, Earl Jeffrey. "Rejecting Essentialism and Gendered Writing: The Case of Christine de Pizan." In *Gender and Text in the Later Middle Ages,* edited by Jane Chance, pp. 96-131. Gainesville: University Press of Florida, 1996.

Studies Christine's work in the context of gender and the question of a masculine or feminine mode of writing.

OTHER SOURCES FROM GALE:

Additional coverage of Christine de Pizan's life and career is contained in the following sources published by the Gale Group: *Dictionary of Literary Biography,* Vol. 208; *Literature Criticism 1400-1800,* Vol. 9; *Literature Resource Center;* and *Reference Guide to World Literature,* Eds. 2, 3.

SOR JUANA INÉS DE LA CRUZ

(1651 - 1695)

(Born Juana Ramírez de Asbaje) Mexican poet, playwright, and prose writer.

Sor Juana is widely considered one of the finest writers and greatest intellectuals of seventeenth-century Hispanic culture. She pursued knowledge with great fervor and evidenced such genius that, in spite of scant formal education, she had achieved renkown as a gifted writer and thinker by adolescence. Best known for her love lyrics and the long poem "El sueno," she was hailed as "the Tenth Muse of Mexico." Though she lived in a period when writing and scholarly pursuits were considered unseemly occupations for women, she was able to produce works that clearly established her as one of the best female poets, and possibly the best Hispanic poet, of the seventeenth century.

BIOGRAPHICAL INFORMATION

Born out of wedlock to a Spanish father and Creole mother, Sor Juana was raised in the village of her birth, San Miguel de Nepantla, near Mexico Cty. Exceptionally precocious, she began to learn to read at age three. She exhibited a passion for learning, asking her mother to dress her as a boy so she could attend the university in Mexico City. However, women at the time were barred admittance. She was tutored in Latin, the basics of which she quickly mastered. She acquired extensive knowledge in various fields during her teenage years by reading on her own, and began to write verse. She eventually attracted the attention of the viceroy, who brought her to court in Mexico City as a lady-in-waiting to the vicereine. Sor Juana was highly regarded at court for her beauty and talent, and was frequently asked to compose poems or dramatic pieces for various occasions; indeed, most of her total poetic canon consists of occasional pieces. Wishing to test her knowledge, the viceroy arranged to have forty of the city's scholars question Sor Juana, each in his own specialty. Proficient in moral and dogmatic theology, medicine, canon law, astronomy, advanced mathematics, and music, Sor Juana astonished them all; according to the viceroy, she defended herself "like a royal galleon assailed by small launches," greatly increasing her already lofty reputation. Not long afterward, in 1669, Sor Juana entered the convent of San Jerdnimo. The exact reason that Sor Juana took the veil is unknown and a matter of much speculation. What is clear is that she hoped the convent would prove a place where she could most completely give herself over to her studies. Still enjoying considerable renown, she continued to receive visitors and to write for both secular and church events. In time, though, Sor Juana became the focus of ecclesiastical disapproval. She was publicly chided for not paying enough attention to the study of Christ's teachings, and for preferring to study and write on secular subjects. After renouncing her studies, she begged forgiveness of the church and entered into public silence. Eventually she sold all the books in her large private library as well as her numerous musical and scientific instruments, giving the money she received for them to the poor. Sor Juana spent the last three years of her life engaged in her duties at the convent and in acts of charity for the poor of Mexico City. She died while ministering to the ill during an epidemic in 1695.

MAJOR WORKS

Although Sor Juana's poetry was influenced by both Luis de Góngora and Pedro Calderón de la Barca, it is generally considered to have transcended the ornamentation of her time. Critical interest has centered on very few poems, most particularly her longest poem, "El sueño" ("The Dream"), often called "Primero sueño" ("First Dream"). Her most celebrated work, "El sueño" describes through the form of a dream the soul's rising toward knowledge, employing extensively Sor Juana's knowledge of the sciences. The poem is very much in the baroque style, yet seems to foreshadow the Enlightenment in its scientifically oriented worldview. Interpretations of "El sueño"are diverse. It has been variously described as metaphysical, as a defense of the private viewpoint, and as a work that in outlook foreshadows modern Mexican nihilism. Regardless of interpretation, it is perhaps her most important piece, particularly because of her claim that it was the only work she composed on her own impulse rather than at the request of another.

Although she is usually remembered as a poet, Sor Juana wrote as much drama as she did poetry; her strength, in fact, is sometimes considered to lie in dramatic composition. She composed in numerous dramatic genres peculiar to Hispanic literature, writing mostly short pieces to function as introductions or interludes. But she also completed several longer dramas, modeling her work after the plays of Calderón. *El divino Narciso* (1690), partly based on the legend of Echo and Narcissus, is a sacramental play which, according to John Malone, "by a simple yet wonderful allegory [Sor Juana] weaves the fable of the pagan lover into a marvelous broidery of the life and passion of the Christ." Some critics consider *El divino Narciso* the height of Sor Juana's literary achievement. Another play, *Los empeños de una casa* (1683), is considered a fine example of baroque rhetoric in which Sor Juana successfully followed the formula of Spanish Golden Age comedy.

The facts surrounding the publication of Sor Juana's most-studied prose work, as well as the events that followed, are difficult to ascertain. In 1690 she was asked, perhaps by her friend the bishop of Puebla, to refute the points of a 1650 sermon by the Portuguese Jesuit Antonio de Vieyra. She did so, and her "respuesta," or "reply," was published, without her approval, along with a pseudonymous letter from the bishop (who signed himself "Sor Filotea de la Cruz") reproaching her for her habit of secular study. Sor Juana's largely autobiographical reply to this letter, entitled "Respuesta a Sor Filotea de la Cruz" (1692) defends her desire for knowledge and her course in life, arguing for the right of women to an education and the right of the individual to pursue a broad spectrum of knowledge. Though there are few extant prose pieces by Sor Juana, the "Respuesta" is widely viewed as exceptionally persuasive and well-written, and one of the finest essays produced in New Spain.

CRITICAL RECEPTION

Sor Juana attracted the adulation of her contemporaries in Mexico and Spain for both her writings and her intellect. Virtually ignored afterward, her work has elicited increasing interest and acclaim since the end of the nineteenth century. Critics have shown intense interest in Sor Juana's philosophical outlook and in her decisions concerning the course of her life. Her readers have wondered about her personal motivations for entering the convent when her fame was at its height and for her later renunciation of study. Sor Juana has often been viewed as a mystic since studies of her work were revived a century ago, while some critics consider her thought Cartesian in its emphasis on discursive reasoning. Gerard Flynn has dismissed both ideas, however, claiming that the autobiographical statements of the "Respuesta" dispel any notions of mysticism. He has noted that her method of thought is clearly in the tradition of Scholasticism, citing her distrust of intuition and her confidence in the senses as a means to knowledge. Interpretations of Sor Juana are quite varied, but her work is now universally praised and her poetry is held to be among the best of her era.

PRINCIPAL WORKS

Los empeños de una casa (drama) 1683

Amor es más laberinto [with Juan de Guevara] (drama) 1689

Inundacion castalida de la unica poetisa, musa decima (poetry and dramas) 1689

"Carta atenagórica" (letter) 1690

El divino Narciso (drama) 1690

"Respuesta a Sor Filotea de la Cruz" (letter) 1692

Segundo volumen de las obras (poetry, dramas, and prose) 1692

Fama y obras pósthumas del fenix de Mexico, dezima musa, poetisa americana (poetry, dramas, and prose) 1700

Obras completas. 4 vols. (poetry, dramas, and prose) 1951-57

The Pathless Grove (poetry) 1960

PRIMARY SOURCES

JUANA INÉS DE LA CRUZ (ESSAY DATE 1692)

SOURCE: Cruz, Juana Inés de la. *The Answer=La respuesta,* edited by Electa Arenal and Amanda Powell, pp. 77-87. New York: The Feminist Press, 1994.

In the following excerpt from her "Respuesta a Sor Filotea de la Cruz," written in 1692, Sor Juana argues for the importance of education for women. She cites several precedents for scholarly and wise women, then addresses the common claim that in his letters St. Paul forbade women to teach.

If studies, my Lady, be merits (for indeed I see them extolled as such in men), in me they are no such thing: I study because I must. If they be a failing, I believe for the same reason that the fault is none of mine. Yet withal, I live always so wary of myself that neither in this nor in anything else do I trust my own judgment. And so I entrust the decision to your supreme skill and straightway submit to whatever sentence you may pass, posing no objection or reluctance, for this has been no more than a simple account of my inclination to letters.

I confess also that, while in truth this inclination has been such that, as I said before, I had no need of exemplars, nevertheless the many books that I have read have not failed to help me, both in sacred as well as secular letters. For there I see a Deborah issuing laws, military as well as political, and governing the people among whom there were so many learned men. I see the exceedingly knowledgeable Queen of Sheba, so learned she dares to test the wisdom of the wisest of all wise men with riddles, without being rebuked for it; indeed, on this very account she is to become judge of the unbelievers. I see so many and such significant women: some adorned with the gift of prophecy, like an Abigail; others, of persuasion, like Esther; others, of piety, like Rahab; others, of perseverance, like Anna [Hannah] the mother of Samuel; and others, infinitely more, with other kinds of qualities and virtues.

If I consider the Gentiles, the first I meet are the Sibyls, chosen by God to prophesy the essential mysteries of our Faith in such learned and elegant verses that they stupefy the imagination. I see a woman such as Minerva, daughter of great Jupiter and mistress of all the wisdom of Athens, adored as goddess of the sciences. I see one Polla Argentaria, who helped Lucan, her husband, to write the *Battle of Pharsalia.* I see the daughter of the divine Tiresias, more learned still than her father. I see, too, such a woman as Zenobia, queen of the Palmyrians, as wise as she was courageous. Again, I see an Arete, daughter of Aristippus, most learned. A Nicostrata, inventor of Latin letters and most erudite in the Greek. An Aspasia Miletia, who taught philosophy and rhetoric and was the teacher of the philosopher Pericles. An Hypatia, who taught astrology and lectured for many years in Alexandria. A Leontium, who won over the philosopher Theophrastus and proved him wrong. A Julia, a Corinna, a Cornelia; and, in sum, the vast throng of women who merited titles and earned renown: now as Greeks, again as Muses, and yet again as Pythonesses. For what were they all but learned women, who were considered, celebrated, and indeed venerated as such in Antiquity? Without mentioning still others, of whom the books are full; for I see the Egyptian Catherine, lecturing and refuting all the learning of the most learned men of Egypt. I see a Gertrude read, write, and teach. And seeking no more examples far from home, I see my own most holy mother Paula, learned in the Hebrew, Greek, and Latin tongues and most expert in the interpretation of the Scriptures. What wonder then can it be that, though her chronicler was no less than the unequaled Jerome, the Saint found himself scarcely worthy of the task, for with that lively gravity and energetic effectiveness with which only he can express himself, he says: "If all the parts of my body were tongues, they would not suffice to proclaim the learning and virtues of Paula." Blessilla, a widow, earned the same praises, as did the luminous virgin Eustochium, both of them daughters of the Saint herself [Paula]; and indeed Eustochium was such that for her knowledge she was hailed as a World Prodigy. Fabiola, also a Roman, was another most learned in Holy Scripture. Proba Falconia, a Roman woman, wrote an elegant book of centos, joining together verses from Virgil, on the mysteries of our holy Faith. Our Queen Isabella, wife of Alfonso X, is known to have written on astrology—without mentioning others, whom I omit so as not merely to copy what others have said (which is a vice I have always detested). Well then, in our own day there thrive the great Christina Alexandra, Queen of Sweden, as learned as she is brave and generous; and too those most excellent ladies, the Duchess of Aveyro and the Countess of Villaumbrosa.

The venerable Dr. Arce (worthy professor of Scripture, known for his virtue and learning), in his *For the Scholar of the Bible,* raises this question: *"Is it permissible for women to apply themselves to the study, and indeed the interpretation, of the Holy Bible?"* And in opposition he presents the verdicts passed by many saints, particularly the words of [Paul] the Apostle: *"Let women keep silence in the churches: for it is not permitted them to speak,"* etc. Arce then presents differing verdicts, including this passage addressed to Titus, again spoken by the Apostle: *"The aged women, in like manner, in holy attire* [. . .] *teaching well";* and he gives other interpretations from the Fathers of the Church. Arce at last resolves, in his prudent way, that women are not allowed to lecture publicly in the universities or to preach from the pulpits, but that studying, writing, and teaching privately is not only permitted but most beneficial and useful to them. Clearly, of course, he does not mean by this that all women should do so, but only those whom God may have seen fit to endow with special virtue and prudence, and who are very mature and erudite and possess the necessary talents and requirements for such a sacred occupation. And so just is this distinction that not only women, who are held to be so incompetent, but also men, who simply because they are men think themselves wise, are to be prohibited from the interpretation of the Sacred Word, save when they are most learned, virtuous, of amenable intellect and inclined to the good. For when the reverse is true, I believe, numerous sectarians are produced, and this has given rise to numerous heresies. For there are many who study only to become ignorant, especially those of arrogant, restless, and prideful spirits, fond of innovations in the Law (the very thing that rejects all innovation). And so they are not content until, for the sake of saying what no one before them has said, they speak heresy. Of such men as these the Holy Spirit says: *"For wisdom will not enter into a malicious soul."* For them, more harm is worked by knowledge than by ignorance. A wit once observed that he who knows no Latin is not an utter fool, but he who does know it has met the prerequisites. And I might add that he is made a perfect fool (if foolishness can attain perfection) by having studied his bit of philosophy and theology and by knowing something of languages. For with that he can be foolish in several sciences and tongues; a great fool cannot be contained in his mother tongue alone.

To such men, I repeat, study does harm, because it is like putting a sword in the hands of a madman: though the sword be the noblest of instruments for defense, in his hands it becomes his own death and that of many others. This is what the Divine Letters became in the hands of that wicked Pelagius and of the perverse Arius, of that wicked Luther, and all the other heretics, like our own Dr. Cazalla (who was never either our own nor a doctor). Learning harmed them all, though it can be the best nourishment and life for the soul. For just as an infirm stomach, suffering from diminished heat, produces more bitter, putrid, and perverse humors the better the food that it is given, so too these evil persons give rise to worse opinions the more they study. Their understanding is obstructed by the very thing that should nourish it, and the fact is they study a great deal and digest very little, failing to measure their efforts to the narrow vessel of their understanding. In this regard the Apostle has said: *"For I say, by the grace that is given me, to all that are among you, not to be more wise than it behoveth to be wise, but to be wise unto sobriety, and according as God hath divided to every one the measure of faith."* And in truth the Apostle said this not to women but to men, and the *"Let [them] keep silence"* was meant not only for women, but for all those who are not very competent. If I wish to know as much as or more than Aristotle or St. Augustine, but I lack the ability of a St. Augustine or an Aristotle, then I may study more than both of them together, but I shall not only fail to reach my goal: I shall weaken and stupefy the workings of my feeble understanding with such a disproportionate aim.

Oh, that all men—and I, who am but an ignorant woman, first of all—might take the measure of our abilities before setting out to study and, what is worse, to write, in our jealous aspiration to equal and even surpass others. How little boldness would we summon, how many errors might we avoid, and how many distorted interpretations now noised abroad should be noised no further! And I place my own before all others, for if I knew all that I ought, I would not so much as write these words. Yet I protest that I do so only to obey you; and with such misgiving that you owe me more for taking up my pen with all this fear than you would owe me were I to present you with the most perfect works. But withal, it is well that this goes to meet with your correction: erase it, tear it up, and chastise me, for I shall value that more than all the vain applause others could give me. *"The just man shall correct me in mercy, and shall reprove me: but let not the oil of the sinner fatten my head."*

And returning to our own Arce, I observe that in support of his views he presents these words of my father St. Jerome (in the letter *To Leta, on the Education of Her Daughter*), where he says: *"[Her] childish tongue must be imbued with the sweet music of the Psalms.* [. . .] *The very words from which she will get into the way of forming sentences should not be taken at haphazard but be definitely chosen and arranged on purpose. For example, let her have the names of the prophets and the apostles, and the whole list of patriarchs from Adam downwards, as Matthew and Luke give it. She will then be doing two things at the same time, and will remember them afterwards.* [. . .] *Let her every day repeat to you a portion of the Scriptures as her fixed task."* Very well, if the Saint wished a little girl, scarcely beginning to speak, to be instructed thus, what must he desire for his nuns and spiritual daughters? We see this most clearly in the women already mentioned—Eustochium and Fabiola—and also in Marcella, the latter's sister; in Pacatula, and in other women whom the Saint honors in his epistles, urging them on in this holy exercise. This appears in the letter already cited, where I noted the words *"let her repeat to you . . ."* which serve to reclaim and confirm St. Paul's description, "teaching well." For the *"let her repeat the task to you"* of my great Father makes clear that the little girl's teacher must be Leta herself, the girl's mother.

Oh, how many abuses would be avoided in our land if the older women were as well instructed as Leta and knew how to teach as is commanded by St. Paul and my father St. Jerome! Instead, for lack of such learning and through the extreme feebleness in which they are determined to maintain our poor women, if any parents then wish to give their daughters more extensive Christian instruction than is usual, necessity and the lack of learned older women oblige them to employ men as instructors to teach reading and writing, numbers and music, and other skills. This leads to considerable harm, which occurs every day in doleful instances of these unsuitable associations. For the immediacy of such contact and the passage of time all too frequently allow what seemed impossible to be accomplished quite easily. For this reason, many parents prefer to let their daughters remain uncivilized and untutored, rather than risk exposing them to such notorious peril as this familiarity with men. Yet all this could be avoided if there were old women of sound education, as St. Paul desires, so that instruction could be passed from the old to the young just as is done with sewing and all the customary skills.

For what impropriety can there be if an older woman, learned in letters and holy conversation and customs, should have in her charge the education of young maids? Better so than to let these young girls go to perdition, either for lack of any Christian teaching or because one tries to impart it through such dangerous means as male teachers. For if there were no greater risk than the simple indecency of seating a completely unknown man at the side of a bashful woman (who blushes if her own father should look her straight in the face), allowing him to address her with household familiarity and to speak to her with intimate authority, even so the modesty demanded in interchange with men and in conversation with them gives sufficient cause to forbid this. Indeed, I do not see how the custom of men as teachers of women can be without its dangers, save only in the strict tribunal of the confessional, or the distant teachings of the pulpit, or the remote wisdom of books; but never in the repeated handling that occurs in such immediate and tarnishing contact. And everyone knows this to be true. Nevertheless, it is permitted for no better reason than the lack of learned older women; therefore, it does great harm not to have them. This point should be taken into account by those who, tied to the *"Let women keep silence in the churches,"* curse the idea that women should acquire knowledge and teach, as if it were not the Apostle himself who described them *"teaching well."* Furthermore, that prohibition applied to the case related by Eusebius: to wit, that in the early Church, women were set to teaching each other Christian doctrine in the temples. The murmur of their voices caused confusion when the apostles were preaching, and that is why they were told to be silent. Just so, we see today that when the preacher is preaching, no one prays aloud.

GENERAL COMMENTARY

DOROTHY SCHONES (ESSAY DATE NOVEMBER 1926)

SOURCE: Schones, Dorothy. "Some Obscure Points in the Life of Sor Juana Inés de la Cruz." *Modern Philology* 24, no. 2 (November 1926): 141-62.

In the following essay, Schones addresses some of the central questions about Sor Juana's life, including her motivation to join a religious order, her name and its bearing on her colonial loyalties, and her decision to stop writing after her "Respuesta."

I

The biography of Sor Juana Inés de la Cruz is yet to be written. Though much has appeared on the subject, many things still remain unexplained. Material of the period in which she lived is very limited. The fact that she was a nun made her figure less in the works of her contemporaries than would otherwise have been the case, and the period of literary stagnation following her death contributed still further to the oblivion in which she rested. When interest in Sor Juana finally revived in Mexico, it was already too late to preserve the documents that existed in the convent of St. Jerome and elsewhere. The laws of reform and the final closing of convents and monasteries scattered books of inestimable value. It is possible, however, even at this remote date to glean a few facts from the meager material that has come down to us. The present article is an attempt to answer in the light of contemporary books and manuscripts a few questions asked over and over again by her many biographers.

One question often raised is: Why did Sor Juana go into a convent? Why did she not remain in the world where she was admired for her beauty and her mental attainments? It will be remembered that Juana became lady-in-waiting to the Marchioness of Mancera, whose husband was the Viceroy of Mexico from 1664 to 1673. Endowed with a pleasing personality and gifted with unusual talents, she quickly attracted powerful friends at court, and met the outstanding people of her time. One would naturally expect that her life would here reach its climax in a blaze of glory. But in 1667, when not quite sixteen, she suddenly retired from the court and entered a convent. Why?

Some of her biographers believe that she must have taken this step because of an unfortunate love affair. Amado Nervo says:

> Dicen . . . que cierto caballero . . . se le adentró en el corazón, logrando inspirarle un gran afecto; añaden unos, que este gentilhombre estaba muy alto para que Juana, hidalga, pero pobre, pudiese ascender hasta él; otros, que se murió en flor cuando iba ya a posarse sobre sus manos unidas la bendición que ata para siempre. Juana de Asbaje, inconsolable, buscó alivio en el estudio y en el retiro.[1]

This romantic legend has long been connected with Juana's name. The story is based on nothing more substantial than the fact that her works contain a large number of love lyrics. This is insufficient evidence on which to build a case.

A few have accepted Juana's own explanation of the decisive change in her life and have declared that she entered a convent to find a place where she could devote herself to her intellectual interests. It must be remembered that she was one of the most unusual personalities developed in the New World, and is hardly to be judged by ordinary standards. José Vigil, one of the first to appreciate her remarkable personality, says:

> Muchos se han ocupado en conjeturar que la resolución de Sor Juana para haber adoptado la vida monástica, puede haber procedido de un amor desgraciado. . . . Yo creo, sin embargo, que tal opinión se apoya en un conocimiento imperfecto del carácter de la escritora mexicana.
>
> Yo veo en Sor Juana uno de esos espíritus superiores, . . . que son incapaces de sucumbir a debilidades vulgares.[2]

According to her own confession, she had been, from the age of three, a most enthusiastic devotee of learning. She had devoured any and every book that came within her reach. At the age of fifteen she had already established a reputation as the most learned woman in Mexico. That she sought refuge in her books because of a broken heart is impossible. It was because of her learning that she gained a position at the viceregal court. Her books were her first love, and they were probably one of the reasons that impelled her to seek the seclusion of a cloister.

One looks in vain for a religious motive underlying this important step in her life.[3] She even hesitated because she was afraid that convent life would interfere with her intellectual labors. She herself says that she did not wish any

> . . . ocupacion obligatoria, que embaraçasse la libertad de mi estudio, ni rumor de Comunidad, que impidiesse el sossegado silencio de mis Libros. Esto

me hizo vacilar algo en la determinacion, hasta que alumbrandome personas Doctas, de que era tentacion, la vencì con el favor Divino. . . .[4]

The biographer of her confessor testifies that she hesitated before taking the step.

Se sintió llamada de Dios al retiro . . . mas retardabale el parecerle cõdicion indispensable á las obligaciones de esse estado, aver de abandonar los libros, y estudios, en que desde sus primeros años tenia colocados todos sus cariños. Consultó su vocació, y temores con el Venerable Padre Antonio Nuñes. . . . Ya tenia el Padre noticia de las prendas, y dones singulares, que avia el cielo depositado en aquella niña . . . y . . . aprobò . . . la vocacion . . . animandola á sacrificar á Dios aquellas primeras flores de sus estudios, si conociesse, que le avian de ser estorvo à la perfeccion. . . .[5]

Juana knew that the religious state might interfere with her labors. In spite of this fact, however, she finally decided to become a nun. There must have been, then, another and a more powerful reason that caused her to take the veil. What was it?

Most of Juana's biographers have examined this point in her life with the eyes of the present instead of with the eyes of the past. To understand Juana's motives one must go back to the period in which she lived, and study the social conditions of her time. She lived in a most licentious age. A careful study of contemporary writers shows that moral conditions in Mexico were very bad. The presence of many races, of adventurers, of loose women and worse men brought about conditions that were possibly unequaled elsewhere in the world. How bad they were the following entry in a contemporary chronicle shows:

En 12 murió el Br. Antonio Calderón de Benavides, natural de Méjico, uno de los más singulares clérigos que ha tenido este arzobispado: sobre ser muy galán, de muy linda cara y muy rico, fué constante opinión que se conservó virgen.[6]

Had this not been an astonishing fact, the chronicler would not have taken the pains to record it. The male element of the population was under no restraint (even the priesthood was no exception) and roamed at will, preying on society. Not only immorality, but depravity and bestiality reigned. Things came to such a pass that the Inquisition brought the attention of the civil government to this state of affairs. In a letter written by the inquisitors in 1664 we read:

. . . veemos de tres ó cuatro años á esta parte en las causas que han ocurrido, principalmente de religiosos, que se halla comprehendido en este crimen mucho número de personas eclesiásticas y seculares . . . si á este cáncer no se pone remedio, . . . parece muy dificultoso que después lo pueda tenar . . . si el Santo Oficio no lo remedia, la justicia seglar no parece que ha de ser suficiente.[7]

The civil government, however, refused to interfere. The church was therefore forced to devise ways and means of combating this evil. If they could not fight it through the men, they could fight it through the women. By building convents and houses of refuge and putting women in them they hoped to improve matters somewhat, and protect women at the same time.

In all of this the attitude of the church toward women was medieval. They were looked upon as an ever present source of temptation to man. Ecclesiastics who did not wish to be tempted avoided them. The biographer of Francisco de Aguiar y Seixas, Archbishop of Mexico from 1682 to 1698, says:

. . . ponderaba [su Illma] quã necessario era para conservar la castidad el recato de la vista; encargaba que no se visitassen mugeres sin grave causa, y aun entonces, quando era necessaria la visita, no se les avia de mirar à la cara . . . le oymos decir algunas vezes, que si supiera avian entrado algunas mugeres en su casa, avia de mandar arrancar los ladrillos que ellas avian pisado. . . .

Y este genero de orror, y aversion a las mugeres fue cosa de toda su vida, predicando siempre contra sus visitas, y sus galas. . . . Tenia por beneficio grande de Dios el aver sido corto de vista.[8]

Juana's confessor, Antonio Núñez, was just as discreet. His biographer says that his motto was "Con las Señoras gran cautela en los ojos, no dexarme tocar, ni besar la mano, ni mirarlas al rostro, o trage, ni visitar a ninguna. . . ." And that he might not be tempted, he says: "Por las calles iba sipre con los ojos en el suelo, de la misma manera estaba en las visitas. . . . Por evitar qualquiera ocasion de que . . . le tocassen, ò besassen las manos . . . las llevaba siempre cubiertas con el manteo."[9] Many similar instances could be cited.

It was in such a world that Juana grew up. On the one hand, extreme license; on the other, extreme prudery. Out of such a state of society the famous *Redondillas* were born. Is it not this very attitude and these very conditions that she challenged so boldly in "Hombres necios, que acusáis a la mujer sin razón"? Is it not the terrible dissoluteness of the men of her time that she epitomizes with the words "Juntáis diablo, carne y mundo"?

To remedy this state of affairs, the church began to build *recogimientos*. Some of these were for *mujeres malas;* others for widows, orphans, and

FROM THE AUTHOR

SOR JUANA CELEBRATES THE TRIUMPH OF ENLIGHTENED WOMEN, WOMEN'S RIGHT TO STUDY, AND WOMEN'S RIGHT TO TEACH

• REFRAIN •

Victor! Victor! Catherine,
who with enlightenment divine
persuaded all the learned men,
she who with triumph overcame
—with knowledge truly sovereign—
the pride and arrogance profane
of those who challenged her, in vain
Victor! Victor! Victor!

• VERSES •

There in Egypt, all the sages
by a woman were convinced
that gender is not of the essence
in matters of intelligence.
Victor! Victor!

A victory, a miracle;
though more prodigious than the feat
of conquering, was surely that
the men themselves declared defeat.
Victor! Victor!

How wise they were, these Prudent Men,
acknowledging they were outdone,
for one conquers when one yields
to wisdom greater than one's own.
Victor! Victor!

Illumination shed by truth
will never by mere shouts be drowned;
persistently, its echo rings,
above all obstacles resounds.
Victor! Victor!

None of these Wise Men was ashamed
when he found himself convinced,
because, in being Wise, he knew
his knowledge was not infinite.
Victor! Victor!

It is of service to the Church
that women argue, tutor, learn,
for He Who granted women reason
would not have them uninformed.
Victor! Victor!

How haughtily they must have come,
the men that Maximin convened,
though at their advent arrogant,
they left with wonder and esteem.
Victor! Victor!

Persuaded, all of them, with her,
gave up their lives unto the knife:
how much good might have been lost,
were Catherine less erudite!
Victor! Victor!

No man, whatever his renown,
accomplished such a victory,
and we know that God, through her,
honored femininity.
Victor! Victor!

Too brief, the flowering of her years,
but ten and eight, the sun's rotations,
but when measuring her knowledge,
who could sum the countless ages?
Victor! Victor!

Now all her learned arguments
are lost to us (how great the grief).
But with her blood, if not with ink,
she wrote the lesson of her life.
Victor! Victor!

Tutelar and holy Patron,
Catherine, the Shrine of Arts;
long may she illumine Wise Men,
she who Wise to Saints converts.
Victor! Victor!

Sor Juana Inés de la Cruz. Villancico VI, from "Santa Catarina," 1691. In *Poems, Protest, and a Dream: Selected Writings*. Edited by Margaret Sayers Peden. New York: Penguin, 1997, p. 189. English translation reprinted from Sor Juana Inés de la Cruz: Poems. Bilingual Press/ Editorial bilingue, 1985.

single women. The Bishop of Puebla, Manuel Fernández de Santa Cruz, built a number of such *recogimientos* in his diocese, but they would not accommodate all the women clamoring for admission. His biographer writes:

> Franqueadas las puertas de su Palacio empezaron à entrar por ellas en busca de su Pastor . . . muchas mugeres que deseaban guardar intacta la Flor de la pureza, que hasta entonces habian conservado, . . . pero recelaban timidas perderla ò por ser muy pobres, ò por ser por hermosas, muy perseguidas.[10]

Of the Bishop's efforts on their behalf the same writer says:

> Compuesta ya en la forma dicha la Casa de las recogidas, determinò el Señor Don Manuel aplicar el remedio que le pedia la pureza de pobres nobles, y hermosas Doncellas para su resguardo; y aunque yà en la Ciudad avia un Collegio de Virgines, en que pudo assegurar algunas de las que reconocio en mayor peligro, assi por la corta capacidad de dicho Collegio, como por el numero de las pretendientes, tan crecido, que le viniera estrecho el mas espacioso Claustro, discurriò con su animo generoso, comprar la possession de cierto sitio, para ere-

gir a las Flores de la Virginidad un Collegio; pero como cada dia escuchaban sus atentos oydos mas y mas clamores de pobres Doncellas, se hallò obligado à formarles dos Collegios, ô cerrados Huertos, donde negadas à el examen de la ossadia, conservassen intactos los candòres de su virginal pureza.

De los dos dichos Collegios, como de floridos Huertos, salieron muchas Doncellas a florecer transplantadas en Monasterios religiosos, en que manteniendo el credito de la virtud, subieron cõ presurosos pasos à la cumbre de la perfecciõ; otras sugetandose à las coyundas de el Matrimonio desempeñaron bien la buena educacion. . . .[11]

This was the state of affairs in the diocese of Puebla. In Guadalaxara and other places conditions were the same. How about Mexico City? The biographer of Domingo Pérez de Barcía says:

No puede negarse la heroicad, y grandeza de la obra de enclaustrar mugeres, que voluntariamente se retiren, huyendo del Mundo, y sus peligros, para no caer en sus lazos, ni dàr en sus precipios, viendose expuestas, yá por la libertad en que viven, yà por la necessidad en que se hallan à vender su hermosura, à costa de su honestidad, valiendose de sus cuerpos para perdicion de sus almas. De la grandeza de esta obra se via privada esta Ciudad de Mexico, y tan necessitada de ella, quanto se atendia de mugeres mas abastecida, que no pudiendo todas entrar en Monasterios, se lloraban en el siglo en manifiestos peligros. . . .[12]

He goes on to say that various attempts were made to establish *recogimientos,* but lack of funds always prevented the realization of the project. A Jesuit, Luis de San Vitores, even wrote a book on the need of a *refugio,* and[13] finally, with the help of Father Xavier Vidal, a house big enough to accommodate six hundred women was built. But money was lacking for the maintenance of the place, and so Payo Henríquez de Ribera, Archbishop of Mexico from 1668 to 1680, was obliged to give the house to the Bethlemites for a hospital.[14]

During this time Juana was living at the viceregal court in *la publicidad del siglo*. She was the talk of the town because of her brilliant attainments. What her situation was she describes clearly in ***Los empeños de una casa:***

Era de mi patria toda
El Objecto venerado
De aquellas adoraciones,
Que forma el comun aplauso,

. . . . .

Llegò la supersticion
Popular à empeño tanto
Que ya adoraban Deydad
El Idolo que formaron.

. . . . .

Que aviendo sido al principio
Aquel culto voluntario,
Llegò despues la costumbre,
Favorecida de tantos,
A hazer como obligatorio,
El festejo cortesano,

. . . . .

Sin temor en los concursos
Defendia mi recato
Con peligro del peligro,
Y con el daño del daño.

. . . . .

Mis padres en mi mesura,
Vanamente assegurados,
Se descuidaron comigo:
Que dictamen tan errado.[15]

She was a curiosity, a veritable *monstruo de la naturaleza,* and must have been the object of persistent and in many cases unwelcome attentions. If ordinary women were in danger, the beautiful Juana Inés certainly was. To be sure, she had the protection of the Viceroy. But how long would the Marquis of Mancera retain that office? In a change of administration what would be her fate? Her family was poor, and besides, in her day the chimney-corner for the spinster member of the family had not yet been heard of. Moreover, she was a *criolla* living at a Spanish court. She was therefore at its mercy. That her position was not safe, we may gather from the biography of her confessor:

. . . el Padre Antonio . . . aviendo conocido . . . lo singular de su erudicion junto con no pequeña hermosura, atractivos todos á la curiosidad de muchos, que desearian conocerla, y tendrian por felicidad el cortejarla, solia decir, q no podia Dios embiar asote mayor a aqueste Reyno, que si permitiesse, que Juana Ines se quedara en la publicidad del siglo.[16]

He goes on to tell why she left the convent of St. Joseph and adds: ". . . le fue forçoso salir, y buscar otro puerto en donde atendiendo cõ menos peligros de enfermedad . . . se viesse libre de las muchas olas que la amenazaban."[17] Her biographer, Father Calleja, expresses the same idea. She realized, he says, that ". . . la buena cara de una muger pobre es una pared blanca donde no hay necio, que no quiera echar su borron: que aun la mesura de la honestidad sirve de riesgo, porque ay ojos, que en el yelo deslizan mas: . . ."[18] And she herself says of this step: ". . . con todo, para la total negacion que tenia al Matrimonio, era lo menos desproporcionado y lo mas decente, que podia elegir en materia de la seguridad . . . de mi salvacion."[19]

It was, undoubtedly, necessary for her to retire from public life at court. There was no *recogimiento* where she might live until she could decide definitely on her future occupation. She was, therefore, practically forced to choose convent life, or be at the mercy of the world. Juana Inés was, perhaps, even lucky to get into a convent, for there was not room for all who applied. With the powerful influence, however, of the Viceroy and of Father Núñez, a haven was found for her. The influence of the latter in this decisive step is not to be overlooked. He it was who finally persuaded her and hastened the ceremony lest the devil should tempt, meanwhile, his beloved Juana Inés.

We may safely conclude that the deep, underlying reason for Juana's retirement from the world is to be found in the social conditions of her time. She was persuaded to take the step, too, in the hope of being somewhat favorably situated for a continuation of her intellectual labors. And when she came under the influence of that powerful *norte de la Inquisición,* the pious Father Núñez, she accepted his advice and took the veil. That she tried convent life a second time shows what serious and what pressing reasons she had for taking the step.

II

Another question recently brought to the fore is whether Juana should properly be called Juana de Asbaje or Juana Ramírez. Amado Nervo, writing in 1910, called her Juana de Asbaje. Fernández del Castillo, writing in 1920,[20] calls her Juana Ramírez, and insists that this is correct, since she herself signed her name that way. He tries to prove that she was related to the Hernán Cortés family on her mother's side, her mother's name being Isabel Ramírez de Santillana. Speaking of her name, he says:

> Sor Juana, según el uso actual, debería de llevar el apellido Asvaje, que era el de su padre, . . . pero en aquella época cada hijo llevaba, diferente apellido, lo que origina no pocos trastornos en las investigaciones genealógicas; de suerte que, aun cuando le correspondía el apellido Asvaje, como ella firmaba Juana Ramírez, ese es el suyo verdadero, con el que se le debe mencionar, y así consta en su retrato que se conserva en el Museo Provincial de Toledo. . . .[21]

The inscription on the picture mentioned reads: "En el siglo fue conocida por D.ª Juana Ramirez (por ˜q assi firmaba)."[22] A careful study of this document shows that it is incorrect on two points. The author of the inscription goes on to say: "Tomo el Havito de Religiosa en el Conv^{to} dl Eximio Dr de la Iglesia S.ª Geronimo de esta Ciud. de Mex.^{co} 24 de Feb.^{o} de 1668 a.^{s} a los 17. de su edad. . . ." This is inaccurate as to her age, for she was only sixteen. Another error in the inscription is the following: ". . . haviendo vivido 44 años, 5 meses, 5 dias, y 5 horas." It should read: "43 años, 5 meses, etc." It seems possible, therefore, that the writer was also mistaken in regard to her signature. But Fernández del Castillo goes on to say:

> Se podría objetar que el retrato de la religiosa que se conserva en Toledo es muy posterior a la muerte de la poetisa, pero habiendo sido sacado según datos tomados del Convento de San Jerónimo en donde vivió, es claro que las religiosas sabrían cual era el verdadero nombre de Sor Juana.[23]

It is, in fact, more than likely that in the convent of St. Jerome she was always thought of as Juana Ramírez, rather than as Juana de Asbaje. It is a well-known fact that her mother was a *criolla* and her father a Spaniard (Basque). As Juana Ramírez she was a *criolla.* As Juana de Asbaje she was Spanish. It is also a well-known fact that in Mexico at that time the only avenues of preferment open to the *criollos* were the university and the church. In fact, so strong were the *criollos* becoming in the church during the seventeenth century that by the time of the Marquis of Mancera the Augustinians were demanding that all candidates for admission to the order be native born.[24] This caused constant bickering between the two factions. The convent of St. Jerome belonged to the Augustinian order. To enter it, therefore, one had to be a native of New Spain. That such was the case the following passage shows:

> Estaba yá para tomar el Avito cierta doncella, en el Convento de S. Geronimo, y no teniendo la dote para ello, entraba con nombramiento de algunos, que en dicho convento ay dotados; pero al fin, se advirtiò faltarle a esta doncella una de las condiciones, que la fundacion pedia; conviene, a saber, el que sean nacionales de Mexico, y esta no lo era; por lo qual huvosele de impedir su entrada. . . .[25]

When one considers that this was a foundation for *criollos,* that the hatred between the natives and the governing class was increasing, and that toward the end of the seventeenth century and the beginning of the eighteenth this hatred was becoming more and more open, one can well understand why the nuns of St. Jerome might have given out that Sor Juana was Juana Ramírez. To date, however, no such signature has been found.

There is evidence, on the other hand, that while she was at the viceregal court she went by the name of Asbaje. In 1668 Diego de Ribera published a poem by Doña Iuana Ynés de Asuage.[26] In November of the preceding year

Juana had left the convent of St. Joseph. If she was known as Juana de Asbaje in 1668 she must have been so called before she entered the convent in August, 1667. In other words, this was certainly her name at court. It was, undoubtedly, to her advantage to go by her Spanish name as lady-in-waiting to the Vicereine. Whether she had been known as Juana Ramírez before she went to court nobody knows. It is possible that the *criollos* knew her by that name. However, in the absence of more definite proof favoring the name Ramírez it seems preferable to continue to call her Asbaje since we know that she actually went by that name in 1668.

An easier question to answer is: Which name did she herself prefer? In the *Libro de Prophessiones* of the convent of St. Jerome she wrote: "Yo soror Ju^{a} ynes de la chruz hija legima de don p^{o} de asvaje y bargas machuca Y de isabel rramires, etc."[27] It will be noticed that she signs her father's name in full. This seems to indicate that at that time she preferred that name. Vargas Machuca is an honored name in the annals of Spanish arms, and the name Asbaje aligned her with the Basques, who must be credited with notable achievements in the New World. Was she a *criolla* or a Spaniard at heart? Her works show both tendencies. With their publication, however, she seems to have put herself definitely on the Spanish side. Her second volume, which appeared in Seville in 1692, was dedicated to Don Juan de Orue y Arbieto, a Basque. In that dedication she says: ". . . siendo, como soy Rama de Vizcaya, y Vm. de sus nobilissimas familias de *las Casas de Orue y Arbieto,* vuelvan los frutos à su tronco, y los arroyuelos de mis discursos tributen sus corrientes al Mar à qui reconocen su Orig." In some of her works she even used the Basque dialect. She was proud of her Basque ancestry. This, too, argues in favor of the name Asbaje.

III

Another question that has been discussed is: Why did Juana, when she was at the height of her fame, renounce fame? It seems impossible at first glance that Sor Juana, having made herself famous, having earned the title of *la décima musa,* and having published in Spain two volumes of poetry, should suddenly renounce her intellectual labors, her mathematical and musical instruments, her library of four thousand volumes, and everything that for her made life worth living to devote herself to a life of cilices and scourges, fasts and vigils. She had lived in the convent of St. Jerome a quarter of a century. She had lived on terms of intimacy with the most prominent people of the city. In Spain she had been the object of dozens of laudatory poems and articles. But for the second time in her life she suddenly retired from the world, and this time it was to lead the life of an ascetic, the life of a martyr. Why?

The blame for this strange renunciation has been generally laid at the door of the Bishop of Puebla, Manuel Fernández de Santa Cruz. A few attributed it to the Inquisition or to Father Núñez. Others have frankly declared it inexplicable. To understand the situation, let us go back and review briefly the preceding period in the life of Sor Juana.

In the year 1680 a new viceroy, the Count of Paredes, came to Mexico. The *cabildo* of the cathedral asked Juana to write a poem for one of the *arcos* erected in his honor. Placed thus in the limelight, it is not surprising that a friendship developed between Juana and the Count and Countess of Paredes. This was the beginning of a brilliant and happy period for the gifted nun. Her new patrons encouraged her in her literary ambitions. It was for them that she wrote some of her best works. During their residence in New Spain, Sor Juana devoted much more time than the church approved of to worldly things. The Viceroy and his wife were frequent visitors at the convent. The nun became very popular in court circles, and was the object of many attentions, of gifts, of letters, of poems. She was in constant contact with the world. She was in such demand socially that she could hardly find time for her literary work. In the spring of 1688, however, her patrons returned to Spain. With their departure Juana lost her most powerful protectors in New Spain. Though on friendly terms with the Conde de Galve, viceroy from 1688 to 1696, there was not the strong personal bond that bound her to his predecessor. It is to the Countess of Paredes that we owe the first volume of Juana's works.

The period just sketched had disastrous consequences for Sor Juana. Her worldly life brought down upon her the criticism of the more sinister, the more fanatical element in the church. Father Núñez broke off all relations with her. Oviedo says in this connection:

> Bien quisiera el Padre Antonio que tan singulares prendas se dedicassen solo á Dios, y que entendimiento tan sublime tuviesse solo por pasto las divinas perfecciones del Esposo que avia tomado. Y aunque se han engañado muchos, persuadidos, á que el Padre Antonio le prohibia â la Madre Iuana el exercicio decente de la Poesia sanctificado con los exemplos de grandes siervos, y siervas de Dios, estorvabale si quãto podia la publicidad, y

continuadas correspondencias de palabra, y por escrito con los de fuera; y temiendo que el affecto a los estudios por demasiado no declinasse al extremo de vicioso, y le robasse el tiempo que el estado santo de la Religion pide de derecho . . . le aconsejaba con las mejores razones que podia, á que agradecida al cielo por los dones conque la avia enriquecido olvidada del todo de la tierra pusiera sus pesamientos . . . en el mismo cielo.

Viendo pues el Padre Antonio, que no podia conseguir lo que desseaba, se retirò totalmente de la assistencia à la Madre Juana. . . .[28]

Father Núñez was one of the most powerful ecclesiastics in New Spain. Because of his learning he was popularly known as the "encyclopedia of the Jesuits." There is plenty of evidence to show that all important cases of the Inquisition passed through his hands. The break,[29] therefore, between him and Sor Juana was a most serious matter. The fact that Father Núñez disapproved of her conduct must have ranged against her some of the other intolerant churchmen of the time, such men as José Vidal and the Archbishop himself.

The latter was something of a fanatic. His character was very different from that of his predecessor, the much esteemed Fray Payo in whose honor Juana wrote several poems. Her relations with Aguiar y Seixas must have been quite different, for she never mentions him. If the biographer of the Archbishop is to be trusted, there was probably a good reason why he and Juana were not on intimate terms. He says:

Para remediar los pecados importa mucho el quitar las rayzes de ellos: en esto ponia el Señor Arçobispo mucho cuydado. Una causa muy principal de muchos pecados, suelen ser las comedias, y fiestas de toros; por lo qual aborrecia mucho su Il-l.ma estas, y otras semejantes fiestas, à que concurren muchos de todo genero de personas, hombres y mugeres. Predicaba con gran acrimonia contra estos toros, y comedias, y los estorvò siempre que pudo: quando andabamos en las visitas mandaba que en las solemnidades de los Santos, aunque fuessen titulares, no huviesse semejantes fiestas; . . .

Otro medio de que usaba el Señor Arçobispo para desterrar los vicios, y plãtar las virtudes, era el procurar acabar con los libros profanos de comedias, y otros; y repartir libros devotos. Quando venimos de España, truxo unos mil y quinientos libros, que se intitulan *Consuelo de pobres,* que tratan con especialidad de la limosna, para repartirlos entre los ricos, y trocarlos por otros libros malos; y assi lo hazia. Persuadia à los libreros, que no tomassen libros de comedias; y trocò con algunos de ellos todos quantos tenian por los dichos arriba de consuelo de pobres: y luego quemaba los de las comedias. . . .[30]

That Aguiar was a bitter enemy of the worldly life of the times is shown by the following extract from a contemporary:

Il Lunedi 27. dovea andare la Signora V. Regnia, con suo marito, in S. Agostino *de las Cuevas,* invitati dal Tesoriere della Casa della moneta; ma poi se n'astennero, per far cosa grata a Monsignor Arcivescovo, il quale biasimava quel passatempo, come scandaloso.[31]

Life in Mexico changed under his administration. It took on a gloomier aspect. Many festival days were abolished,[32] and an effort was made to reform the habits and customs of the people.

Under such an archbishop Juana passed the last days of her life. That Juana wrote *comedias* and even published them must have been a crime in his eyes. In Mexico during his administration no *comedias* and almost no secular verse were finding their way into print.[33] Conditions in Mexico were quite different from what they were in Spain, though even in Spain a movement which opposed the theater was gaining ground. Conditions in Spain, nevertheless, were liberal as compared with those that obtained in New Spain. What the difference was becomes plain when we consider that the books of Sor María de Jesús de Ágreda which were taken off the Index abroad (even the celebrated *Mística Ciudad de Dios* being cleared by the Pope)[34] were prohibited in Mexico by an edict of the Inquisition in 1690.[35] Moreover, the fact that Sor Juana's works appeared in Spain is significant. This was due to the strict censorship[36] on books that existed in New Spain, rather than to other difficulties of publication such as expense and scarcity of paper. The fact that of all her works the most popular one in Mexico was a religious work, the many times reprinted ***Ofrecimientos para un Rosario de quince Misterios,*** is also highly significant. One is forced to the conclusion that the publication of her collected works would have been impossible in Mexico. The fact that she published them in Spain must have widened the breach that was gradually establishing itself between her and the church. The first volume of her works appeared in Madrid in 1689. It contains a large number of secular poems: lyrics of love and friendship, satirical verse, and burlesque poems in the Italian manner. Whether the book came back to Mexico I do not know. But enough information about it must have traveled back to make things slightly uncomfortable for Juana.

At about this same time Sor Juana committed another crime in the eyes of the church. She wrote a refutation of a sermon preached in Lisbon by the brilliant Jesuit, Antonio de Vieyra. The latter had set up his own opinion in opposition to that of the Church Fathers, Aquinas, Augustine, and Chrysostom. Juana defended the Church Fathers with logic and erudition. Her refutation found its way into the hands of Manuel Fernández de Santa Cruz. He had it published late in 1690,[37] together with a letter, the famous letter signed Sor Philotea de la Cruz. In it he said in part:

> Para que V. md. se vea en este Papel de mejor letra, le he impresso, y para que reconozca los tesoros, que Dios depositò en su alma, y le sea, como mas entendida, mas agradecida . . . pocas criaturas deben a su Magestad mayores talentos en lo natural, con que executa al agradecimiento, para que si hasta aqui los ha empleado bien [illegible] en adelante sea mejor.
>
> No es mi juizio tan austèro Censor, que estè mal con los versos, en que V. md. se ha visto tan celebrada. . . .
>
> No pretendo, segun este dictamen, que V. md. mude el genio, renunciando los Libros; si no que le mejore, leyendo alguna vez el de Jesu-Christo. . . . Mucho tiempo ha gastado V. md. en el estudio de Filosofos, y Poetas; yà serà razon que se mejoren los Libros.[38]

This is the letter that has long been held responsible for Sor Juana's renunciation. It is quite clear from the letter that the Bishop did not really approve of her secular writings, but it is also clear that he did not ask her to give up her literary labors. All that he asked her to do was to devote herself to religious works. He was himself a lover of learning, and had during his youth written three books of commentary on the Scriptures. He is said to have bought many books for the Colegio de San Pablo in Pueblo. What gave the letter such force was the fact that it was printed along with the ***Crisis,*** and that in it he asked her to pay less attention to *las rateras noticias del dia*. It amounted to a public censure.[39]

Of the cause and effect of this letter, the biographer of the Bishop writes as follows:

> Era muy celebrada en esta Nueva España la Madre Sor Juana Ines de la Cruz, . . . assi por la grande capazidad, y soverano entendimiento de que Dios la havia dorado, como por la gracia de saber hazer y componer . . . versos: con esta ocasion era visitada de muchas personas, y de las de primera clase: corria la fama por todas partes . . . ; llegò la noticia à nuestro amantissimo Obispo . . . , y . . . condolido . . . de ´q un sujeto de tan relevantes prendas estubiera tan distraido, y combertido à las criaturas, . . . resolvio escrivirla la carta siguiente. . . .
>
> Tubo esta carta el deseado efecto. . . .[40]

More than two years were to elapse, however, before Juana's renunciation. It does not seem possible, then, that this letter was the cause of the step she took. It was another sign of the times, however, and a thorn in the flesh of the brilliant nun.

In March, 1691, Juana wrote an answer to the famous letter. Her letter is astonishingly frank. One wonders how she dared so reveal her innermost soul. Her answer could certainly have done nothing to mend matters.

Meanwhile, the ***Crisis*** was receiving wide publicity. In 1692 it was published in Mallorca. In the same year it was reprinted in the second volume of her works, and in the following year it appeared again in the second edition of that volume.[41] It was received with great enthusiasm in Spain. Why did it arouse a storm of criticism in Mexico? Was it heretical? It was so considered there. In her answer to the Bishop Juana wrote:

> Si el crimen està en la Carta Athenagorica, fue aquella mas que referir sencillamente mi sentir . . . ? . . . Llevar una opinion contraria de Vieyra, fue en mi atrevimiento, y no lo fue en su Paternidad, llevarla contra los tres Santos Padres de la Iglesia? . . . ni faltè al decoro, que à tanto varon se debe. . . . Ni toquè à la Sagrada Compañia en el pelo de la ropa; . . . Que si creyera se avia de publicar, no fuera con tanto desaliño como fue. Si es (como dize el Censor) Heretica, porquè no la delata?[42]

We gather from this that it was declared heretical. In Spain, however, Navarro Vélez, *Calificador del Santo Oficio,* declared that it contained nothing contrary to the faith.[43] That it was so strongly condemned in Mexico is due to the fact that conditions there were different. The Jesuits were all powerful. They were practically in control of the Inquisition. Father Vieyra was a Jesuit, and it was felt that the ***Crisis*** was an attack on that order. How Father Núñez felt about it one can easily guess. Juana had brought herself face to face with the Inquisition. At the time she wrote her reply she had not been brought to trial. No record has been found to show that she ever was. It is not likely that the Inquisition would have waited more than two years to do so. It does not seem possible, then, that it was directly responsible for her renunciation.

Did Juana, upon receiving the Bishop's letter, immediately stop writing about secular things? Not at all. Early in 1691 she wrote a *silva* celebrating a victory won by the *armada de Barlovento* against the French off the coast of Santo Domingo. This was published the same year by Carlos de Sigüenza y Góngora in his *Trofeo de la justicia española*. In 1692 she was still sending manuscripts

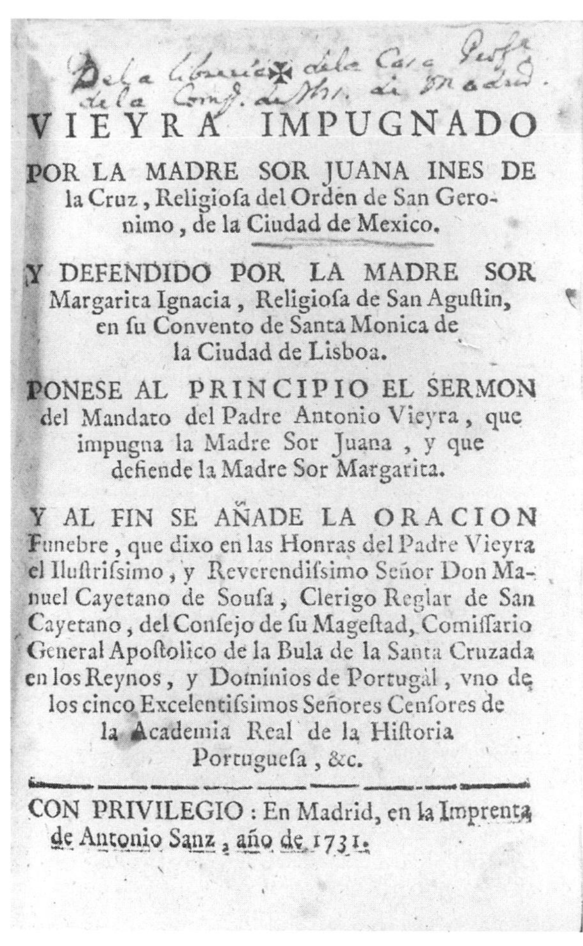

VIEYRA IMPUGNADO

POR LA MADRE SOR JUANA INES DE la Cruz, Religioſa del Orden de San Geronimo, de la Ciudad de Mexico.

Y DEFENDIDO POR LA MADRE SOR Margarita Ignacia, Religioſa de San Aguſtin, en ſu Convento de Santa Monica de la Ciudad de Lisboa.

PONESE AL PRINCIPIO EL SERMON del Mandato del Padre Antonio Vieyra, que impugna la Madre Sor Juana, y que defiende la Madre Sor Margarita.

Y AL FIN SE AÑADE LA ORACION Funebre, que dixo en las Honras del Padre Vieyra el Iluſtriſsimo, y Reverendiſsimo Señor Don Manuel Cayetano de Souſa, Clerigo Reglar de San Cayetano, del Conſejo de ſu Mageſtad, Comiſſario General Apoſtolico de la Bula de la Santa Cruzada en los Reynos, y Dominios de Portugàl, vno de los cinco Excelentiſsimos Señores Cenſores de la Academia Real de la Hiſtoria Portugueſa, &c.

CON PRIVILEGIO: En Madrid, en la Imprenta de Antonio Sanz, año de 1731.

Manuscript page from *Vieyra Impugnado* (1731), written by Sor Margarita Ignacia. This defense of Father Vieyra's sermon is said to have ended the "Crisis" for Sor Juana Inés De la Cruz.

abroad for the second edition[44] of the second volume of her works. It seems likely that early in 1692 she was still writing some poetry and collecting it for that volume. Sometime in 1692 or 1693 she also wrote a poem thanking her newly found friends in Spain for the laudatory poems and articles which appeared in her second volume. This poem was never finished, and is probably her last work.

Sor Juana's renunciation took place in 1693.[45] In March, 1691, when she wrote her answer to the Bishop, she was not yet ready for her great sacrifice. She still defended herself vigorously, claiming for herself the right to study. The letter is, in fact, a defense of the rights of women, a memorable document in the history of feminism. In the light of it, her renunciation is even more startling than it would be had the letter never been written. Yet in it she reveals, too, a struggle in which she was as a house divided against itself. What it was and how insidiously it undermined what a lifetime had built up, the following passage will make clear:

> Pues aun falta por referir lo mas arduo de las dificultades;—faltan los positivos [estorvos], que directamente han traido à estorvar, y prohibir el exercicio. Quien no creerà, viendo tan generales aplausos, que he navigado viento en popa, y mar en leche, sobre las palmas de las aclamaciones comunes? Pues Dios sabe, que no ha sido assi: porque entre las flores de essas mismas aclamaciones, se han levantado, y despertado tales aspides de emulaciones, y persecuciones, quantas no podrè contrar; y los que mas nocivos, y sensibles para mi han sido, no son aquellos, que con declarado odio, y malevolencia me han perseguido, sino los que amandome, y deseando mi bien . . . me han mortificado, y atormentado mas, que los otros, con aquel: *No conviene a la santa ignorancia, que deben este estudio; se ha de perder, se ha de desranecer en tanta altura con su mesma perspicacia, y agudeza.* Què me avrà costado resistir esto? Rara especie de martyrio, donde yo era el martyr, y me era el verdugo! . . . todo ha sido acercarme mas al fuego de la persecucion, al crisol del tormento: y ha sido con tal extremo, que han llegado a solicitar, que se me prohiba el estudio.
>
> . . . fuè tan vehemente, y podorosa la inclinacion à las Letras, que ni agenas reprehensiones (que he tenido muchas) ni propias reflexas (que he hecho no pocas) han bastado à que dexe de seguir este natural impulso, que Dios puso en mi: su Magestad sabe . . . que le he pedido, que apague la luz de mi entendimiento, dexando solo lo que baste para guardar su Ley, pues lo demàs sobra (segun algunos) en una muger; y aun hay quien diga, que daña.[46]

We gather from this that she was the object of constant persecution, and to such a degree that she began to ask herself if, after all, she was wrong. Should she give up her literary labors and devote herself to the *camino de perfección?* This was the struggle that was going on in her soul and that reached a climax in 1693. It had probably been going on a long time before it came out into the open with the publication of her works. She must have had many enemies. What she suffered we can but guess. Slowly but surely the criticisms of friends and enemies destroyed her peace of mind. Even so, it is doubtful if Sor Juana would ever have given up her books and studies had not events in Mexico so shaped themselves that she felt upon her an inward compulsion.

It now becomes necessary to take a look at what was happening in Mexico between 1691 and 1693. In the summer of 1691 rains and floods were beginning to cause terrible suffering. A contemporary writes:

> Lo q.^e se experimento de trabajos en Mexico en estos trece dias no es ponderable. Nadie entrava

en la Ciudad por no estar andables los caminos, y las calsadas. Faltò el carbon, la leña, la fruta, las hortalisas, las aves. . . . El pan no se sasonaba por la mucha agua . . . y nada se hallava de quanto hè dicho, sino à exsecivo precio. . . .

El crecimiento con q^e se hallava la Laguna de Tescuco à veinte y dos de Julio, dio motivo a los pusilamines para que dixesen à vozes *que se anega Mexico.*[47]

The crops were ruined and by the end of the year the city was in the grip of a famine. By the beginning of 1692 conditions were so bad that the Viceroy asked that secret prayers be said in convents and monasteries for the relief of the city. Many a day there was no bread. Moreover, the supply of grain in the *alhóndiga* was getting low. The populace began to threaten violence, blaming the Viceroy and his government for their sufferings. Finally, on the night of June 8, 1692, the Indians marched upon the viceregal palace and stormed it, setting fire to it and the surrounding buildings. The Viceroy and his wife took refuge in the monastery of St. Francis. Everybody sought monasteries and other places of security. The soldiers were helpless. Hordes of Indians pillaged the plaza and the surrounding neighborhood. Nothing could be done to stop the terrible riot. Bells rang all night. In the nunneries and monasteries prayers were said. Jesuits and Franciscans went in procession to the plaza in an effort to quiet the rioters, but they were hissed and their images were treated with disrespect. After days and nights of terror, during which the churches ceased to function, the civil government succeeded in restoring order. Weeks and months of *azotados* and *ahorcados* kept alive the memory of the tumult. Famine continued to take its toll, for there was no bread. Disease followed. Toward the end of the year the *peste* was general throughout the land. Those were dark days for Mexico. Why had this affliction visited the country? The consensus of opinion was that it was a punishment for the sin, the license and irreligiosity that had reigned in Mexico. Robles says:

Las causas de este estrago se discurren ser nuestras culpas que quiso Dios castigar, tomando por instrumento el mas debil y flaco, como es el de unos miserables indios, desprevenidos, como en otros tiempos lo ha hecho su Divina Magestad, como parece por historias divinas y humanas. . . . Dios nos mire con ojos de misericordia! Amen.[48]

Sigüenza y Góngora says, speaking of the floods: "Oyese por este tiempo una voz entre las . . . del bulgo q.^e atribuia à castigo de las pasadas fiestas la tempestad en el monte, el destroso en los Campos, y la inundacion de los arribales. . . ."[49] He says, furthermore: ". . . yo no dudo q.^e mis pecados y los de todos le motivaron [a Dios] à q.^e amenazandonos como Padre con azote de agua prosiguiese despues el castigo con hambre p.^a nuestra poca enmienda. . . ."[50] Another contemporary writes: ". . . hallándonos con un príncipe tan benigno por virey, . . . son tantos nuestros pecados, que no ha bastado su santidad y celo para que la justicia de Dios no nos castigue, como lo estamos esperimentando."[51]

The tragic events just narrated gave point to the remonstrances addressed to Juana on the score of her failure to walk in the *camino de perfección.* Where she had before stopped to reflect occasionally on her duty in the matter, now, with suffering and death on every hand, her own heart, her own conscience, must have taken a hand. It is not unlikely that she blamed herself somewhat for the sad state of affairs in Mexico. Death was everywhere. It took two of her lifelong friends, Juan de Guevara[52] and Diego de Ribera.[52] It laid a heavy hand on the convent of St. Jerome, where ten nuns died[53] between April 24, 1691, and August 5, 1692. And in September, 1692, news came from Spain of the death of her beloved patron, the Count of Paredes. Life was becoming stern. But it was not too late. She could yet make amends. It is something of this spirit that shines through the fanaticism of the last two years of her life. Stern religious counselors had turned her eyes inward upon herself. Could outward compulsion alone have worked such a change? Does it not bespeak inward conviction? Sor Juana had very much a mind of her own. The Inquisition could have made her give up her books, her instruments, her literary labors, but it could not make her *volar a la perfección.* Inner conviction was needed for that.

Does not Juana herself express this in the ***Peticion que en forma causidica presenta al Tribunal Divino la Madre Juana Ines de la Cruz, por impetrar perdon de sus culpas?*** In it she says:

. . . en el pleyto que se sigue en el Tribunal de nuestra Justicia contra mis graves, enormes, y sin igual pecados, de los quales me hallo convicta por todos los testigos del Cielo, y de la Tierra, y por lo alegado por parte del Fiscal del crim de mi propia consciencia, en que halla que debo ser condenada à muerte eterna, y que aun esto serà usando conmigo de clemencia, por no bastar infinitos Infiernos para mis inumerables crimenes y pecados: . . . reconozco no merezco perdon . . . con todo, conociendo vuestro infinito amor, è misericordia, y que mientras vivo, estoy en tiempo, y que no me han cerrado los terminos del poder apelar de la sentencia . . . con todo, por quanto sabeis vos que ha tantos años que yo vivo en Religion, no

> solo sin Religion, sino peor que pudiera un Pagano: . . . es mi voluntad bolver à tomar el Abito, y passar por el año de aprobacion. . . .[54]

Undoubtedly force of circumstances joining hands with many parallel influences had brought about a crisis in Juana's life; not one cause, but many, working toward a common end, gradually broke the strong spirit and made her accept the martyr's rôle.

How did Juana carry out her penitence, for such it was? Oviedo says, speaking of this and of Father Núñez' part in it:

> Quedose la Madre Iuana sola con su Esposo, y . . . el amor le daba alientos á su imitacion, procurando con empeño crucificar sus pasiones, y apetitos con tan ferveroso rigor en la penitencia, que necessitaba del prudente cuidado, y atencion del Padre Antonio para irle á la mano, porque no acabasse à manos de su fervor la vida. Y solia decir el Padre alabando à Dios, que Iuana Ines no corria sino que volaba á la perfeccion.[55]

Everything she had she sold for the relief of the poor. The same writer says:

> . . . se deshizo de la copiosa libreria que tenia, sin reservar para su uso sino unos pocos libritos espirituales que le ayudassen en sus santos intentos. Echô tambien de la celda todos los instrumentos musicos, y mathematicos singulares, y exquisitos que tenia, y quantas alhajas de valor, y estima la avia tributado la admiracion, y aplauso de los que celebraban sus prendas como prodigios; y reducido todo à reales, fuerõ bastantes á ser alivio, y socorro de muchissimos Pobres.[56]

This, too, confirms the theory that the suffering in Mexico had much to do with her renunciation. She was joined in her charitable enterprise by Aguiar y Seixas, who also sold his library for the relief of the poor.

Two years later her penitence reached the heights of the heroic when, during the plague that invaded the convent of St. Jerome, Juana labored night and day nursing the sick, comforting the dying, and laying out the dead. Her fragile spirit, broken by the storms that had beaten about her, gave up the unequal struggle, and she who once had been the object of hatred and jealousy died in the odor of sanctity, revered and loved by all.

Notes

1. *Juana de Asbaje* (Madrid, 1910), p. 78.
2. *Discurso pronunciado en la velada literaria que consagró el Liceo Hidalgo a la memoria de Sor Juana Inés de la Cruz* (Mexico, 1874), pp. 48-49.
3. For a discussion of this side of the question see Nemesio García Naranjo, "Biografía de Sor Juana Inés de la Cruz," *Anales del Museo Nacional de México, segunda época,* Vol. III, No. 1 (Mexico, 1906), pp. 567-68.
4. "Respuesta de la poetisa a la muy ilustre Sor Philotea de la Cruz," *Fama y obras posthumas* (Barcelona, 1701), p. 18. References hereafter will be to this edition.
5. Juan de Oviedo, *Vida y virtudes del Venerable Padre Antonio Nuñes de Miranda* (Mexico, 1702), p. 133.
6. Antonio de Robles, "Diario de sucesos notables," *Documentos para la historia de Méjico, primera serie,* Vol. III (Mexico, 1853), under date of July 12, 1668.
7. José Toribio Medina, *Historia del tribunal del Santo Oficio de la Inquisición de México* (Santiago de Chile, 1905), pp. 321-22. Part of this document is unprintable.
8. José Lezamis, *Breve relacion de la vida, y muerte del Doctor D. Francisco de Aguiar y Seyxas,* Mexico, 1699. Not paged. See chapter entitled: "De su castidad, mortificacion, y penitencia."
9. *Op. cit.,* pp. 153-54.
10. Miguel de Torres, *Dechado de principes eclesiasticos* (Puebla, 1716), p. 123.
11. *Op. cit.,* pp. 124-25, 150. Also see José Gómez de la Parra, *Panegyrico funeral de Manuel Fernandez de Santa Cruz* (Puebla, 1699), p. 64.
12. Julián Gutiérrez Dávila, *Vida y virtudes de Domingo Perez de Barcia* (Madrid, 1720), pp. 27-28.
13. *Op. cit.,* p. 30.
14. *Ibid.,* p. 31.
15. *Segundo tomo de las obras de Soror Juana Inez de la Cruz* (Sevilla, 1692), Act I.
16. Juan de Oviedo, *op. cit.,* p. 133.
17. *Ibid.,* pp. 134-35.
18. "Aprobación," *Fama y obras posthumas.*
19. *Fama y obras posthumas,* p. 18. As for matrimony, it is possible that the Viceroy had already selected a husband for her. This seems to have been the regular procedure, at any rate, and Juana had no reason to suppose that he would not select one in her case. Doña Oliva Merleti, a lady-in-waiting at the court, entered the Capuchin order in preference to marrying a man selected for her by the Marquis of Mancera. See Ignacio de Peña, *Trono mexicano en el convento de Capuchinas* (Madrid, 1726), p. 213.
20. Francisco Fernández del Castillo, *Doña Catalina Xuárez Marcayda* (Mexico, 1920).
21. *Op. cit.,* p. 83.
22. For a copy of this document see Amado Nervo, *op. cit.,* opp. p. 96.
23. *Loc. cit.*
24. Vicente Riva Palacio, *México a través de los siglos* (Mexico: Ballescá y Cía), II, 669.
25. Julián Gutiérrez Dávila, *op. cit.,* pp. 351-52.
26. This appeared in *Poetica descripcion de la pompa plausible que admiró esta Ciudad de Mexico en la Dedicacion de su Templo* (Mexico, 1668). This is cited by Medina, *La Imprenta en México* (8 vols.; Santiago de Chile, 1907-12), No. 1004. A copy of this work exists in the *Biblioteca Palafoxiana* in Puebla, Mexico.

27. This manuscript is now in my possession. González Obregón was the first to reproduce any part of it. See El Renaciminto, segunda época (Mexico, 1894), pp. 237-38.

28. *Op. cit.,* pp. 134, 136.

29. It is impossible to fix the exact date of this rupture. It must have taken place at some time during Juana's greatest worldly activity, i.e., between 1680 and 1690.

30. *Op. cit.,* chapter entitled: "De la oracion, contemplacion, amor de Dios y del proximo del Señor Arçobispo."

31. Gio. Francesco Gemelli Careri, *Giro del mondo, sesta parte* (Naples, 1700), p. 169. He visited Mexico in 1697.

32. Francisco Aguiar y Seixas, *Edicto pastoral sobre los días festivos,* Mexico, 1600.

33. Less than 25 per cent of the books printed in Mexico City were secular in character. These figures are based on tables developed from Medina, *La imprenta en México,* for the period between 1682 and 1698. From 1666 to 1682 about 32 per cent of the books were secular. These figures are only approximate since Medina is not complete, and besides, some of the material of the period has, undoubtedly, been lost. Of these secular works some were official documents, some were *gacetas,* and a few were scholarly works. There was very little of a purely literary character.

34. Emilia Pardo Bazán, "Prólogo," *Vida de la Virgen María según Sor María de Jesús de Agreda* (Barcelona, 1899), p. 7.

35. Antonio de Robles, *op. cit.,* under date of September 24, 1690.

36. The censorship in Mexico during the seventeenth century has not yet been studied. For methods used during the sixteenth see Francisco Fernández del Castillo, "Libros y libreros del siglo XVI," *Publicaciones del archivo general de la nación,* Vol. VI (Mexico, 1914).

37. Her refutation was reprinted under the title of "Crisis de un Sermón" in the second volume of her works.

38. *Fama y obras posthumas,* pp. 2-4.

39. The signature, Philotea de la Cruz, is pregnant with meaning. The name itself means "lover of God." The Bishop pretended that the letter was written by a nun of that name in the convent of the Holy Trinity. There may have been a nun of that name. But why did the Bishop choose that name? One of his predecessors in the bishopric of Puebla, the famous Juan de Palafox y Mendoza, published in Madrid in 1659 a book called *Peregrinacion de Philotea al santo templo y monte de la Cruz.* He says it was written in imitation of a "Philotea Francesa" because it had seemed to him "no inutil emulacion, sino espiritual y santa: que . . . otra Philotea Española instruyesse a las demas, con manifestarse humilde seguidora de la Cruz. . . ." The books of Palafox were very popular. It is probable that Fernández de Santa Cruz had this book in mind when he wrote Sor Juana. If so, the significance of the signature could not have been lost upon her.

40. *Op. cit.,* pp. 416, 421. The 1722 edition says that it was her *estudio de libros profanos* that called forth the letter.

41. The subject of the *Crisis* was kept alive until 1731, when a defense of Father Vieyra's sermon, written by Sor Margarita Ignacia, a Portuguese nun, was translated into Spanish by Iñigo Rosende in a volume entitled *Vieyra impugnado,* published in Madrid.

42. *Fama y obras posthumas,* pp. 50-51.

43. Juan Navarro Vélez, "Censura," *Segundo tomo de las obras de Soror Juana Ines de la Cruz,* Sevilla, 1692.

44. This edition, published in Barcelona in 1693, has on the title-page: "añadido en esta segunda impression por su autora." It also contains some *villancicos* dated 1691.

45. Both Oviedo and Calleja testify to this. The date can be established by the fact that in February and March, 1694, she signed her *Profesión de la fe* and the *Renovación de los votos religiosos.* To do this she must have served her year as novice. Her *Petición,* undated, says: ". . . es mi voluntad bolver a tomar el Abito, y passar por el año de aprobacion." This must have been written early in 1693.

46. *Fama y obras posthumas,* pp. 15, 26-27, 34-35.

47. *Copia de una Carta de don Carlos de Sigüenza y Góngora a don Andrés de Pez acerca de un tumulto acaecido en México* (MS), August 30, 1692.

48. *Op. cit.,* p. 97.

49. Letter cited.

50. *Ibid.*

51. "Copia de una carta escrita por un religioso grave," *Documentos para la historia de México, segunda serie,* III (Mexico, 1855), 311.

52. *Sucesos,* 1676-96 (MS), under date of April 11 and September 7, 1692.

53. *Libro de Prophessiones.*

54. *Fama y obras posthumas,* pp. 129-31.

55. *Op. cit.,* p. 137.

56. *Loc. cit.*

ELECTA ARENAL (ESSAY DATE 1983)

SOURCE: Arenal, Electa. "The Convent as Catalyst for Autonomy: Two Hispanic Nuns of the Seventeenth Century." In *Women in Hispanic Literature,* edited by Beth Kurti Miller, pp. 147-83. Berkeley: University of California Press, 1983.

In the following excerpt, Arenal offers a feminist reassessment of Sor Juana's life and work, discussing not only the "Respuesta" *but also portions of several poems and plays.*

Until recently, scholars have regarded Saint Teresa of Avila as an isolated instance of a woman of great energy and spirit, the epitome of the unique fusion of the real and the ideal in Spanish life and letters.[1] But the discovery of significant numbers of neglected manuscripts suggests that she was not alone, that around her and in her wake came other dynamic and contemplative women.[2] One of these was Venerable Madre Isabel de Jesús (1586-1648). She was an illiterate Castilian shepherdess and visionary, who struggled for twenty-five years to become a nun. Another, of quite different stamp, was Sor Juana Inés de la Cruz (1648-1695) of New Spain, who previewed the coming age of Enlightenment and defended the right of women to exercise and live by their minds. Without rivals in intellectual scope or artistic projection, the Mexican nun left poetry, plays, and prose, which were not compiled and edited until more than two hundred and fifty years after her death.[3]

Unlike Sor Juana, who was recognized in her own time as being among the greatest intellects and literary talents of the period, Madre Isabel lived in relative obscurity in a self-generated world of religious visions. Sor Juana wrote an autobiographical "letter" not as a literary endeavor but as the defense of an intellectual life in answer to attacks by her superiors; Madre Isabel dictated her life at the request of her superiors, again not as a literary endeavor but as a religious exercise. Sor Juana's autobiography is unique; Madre Isabel's resembles in effect hundreds of lives written in the sixteenth and seventeenth centuries in Spain and its colonies with the aim of inspiring emulation in the faithful.[4]

For centuries, most of the women who in Virginia Woolf's phrase had "a room of their own" found it in the cloister.[5] As Emily James Putnam stated in *The Lady: Studies of Certain Significant Phases of Her History,* "No institution in Europe has ever won for the lady the freedom of development that she enjoyed in the convent. . . . The impulse toward leadership which kept the men in the world sent the women out of it."[6] The cloister, which common opinion often represents as a refuge (or as a prison), was equally a place in which women could support each other and even cultivate a certain amount of independence. It provided women of greatly divergent personalities with a semiautonomous culture in which they could find sustenance, exert influence, and develop talents they never could have expressed as fully in the outside world. In that sense, the convent was a catalyst for autonomy. It is ironic that the greater inequality of women in Hispanic culture, a result in part of the strength and pervasiveness of the Church, made the very source of restrictions an outlet for freer expression. In effect, nuns found a way of being important in the world by choosing to live outside it.

Despite the rigor of convent life, there was room for variation, even eccentricity, as the lives of these two very different women illustrate. Madre Isabel, a poor shepherdess, worked as a domestic servant both in and out of the convent; Sor Juana, from a moderately wealthy land-holding family, was close to the most privileged ranks of society. Madre Isabel was uneducated; Sor Juana was an acknowledged prodigy. Peasant and aristocrat, poor and rich, illiterate and intellectual—the convent, echoing the outer world, held and maintained these contrasts in social status.

One of the aims of this chapter is to add a few threads to the reweaving of the tapestry of women's history and literature. Madre Isabel's recorded experience is part of the background against which Sor Juana's life and thought stands out in sharp relief. The juxtaposition of these two seventeenth-century lives provides us a more complete picture of the times and of the reactions of women within it. Many more women's lives resembled Madre Isabel's than Sor Juana's. In belief, religious ideas, and intellectual set, even the women of the upper classes were closer to the Spanish peasant mystic than to the Mexican preencyclopedist. The Spanish nun conforms to the climate of the times. Her road to exceptionality was a more allowable one; along the route of mysticism and of "holy ignorance," she reached the point of being able to exert influence. Sor Juana was a central figure in the cultural and intellectual life of the court of New Spain. She brilliantly refuted the concept of "holy ignorance" but was refused confession for this defiance—and ultimately capitulated or converted.

Because there is a tendency to regard those women who entered convents simply as nuns—as religious figures—they have been missed as people. Both Sor Juana and Isabel de Jesús felt guilt for taking time out to write (or dictate); both were clever and found ways of getting around obstacles such as the resentments or rulings of confessors and superiors. Although neither attained the political and economic power Putnam discusses (which medieval abbesses held), both struggled for self-realization. And this can be attributed to the fact that they were nuns. Since they were women outside of their sexual function in society—"disembodied" and seen more as spirit than as matter—they were free to deal with philosophical and spiritual issues.

Sor Juana presided as might a philosopher queen over a salon; in her own society, Madre Isabel, a kind of mystical madwoman, was called upon to give advice, make predictions, console those who mourned, and encourage those who wavered. Both held positions of respect within the convent, and both dedicated time to caring for their sisters. For Sor Juana the convent was the least of evils; for Isabel it was the last stop before heaven. For both of them it was essential, allowing them to consider themselves the equals, if not the superiors, of the men around them. Both explicitly claim such equality, Sor Juana by virtue of intellect, Isabel by virtue of spirit. . . .

The Life and Work of a Well-Known Poet

Sor Juana Inés de la Cruz, the great Mexican poet, playwright, and intellectual, last of the great seventeenth-century Hispanic Baroque writers, was born Juana Inés Ramírez y Asbaje, in the colony then called New Spain. She was known as a *gongorista,* after the Spanish mannerist poet, Góngora. Quevedo, Gracián, and Calderón were her contemporaries.

Juana Ramírez lived at the hub of New Spain's vice regal society, the most splendid and complex of the Spanish colonial empire. Five vice regal regimes succeeded each other during her lifetime. By education, she belongs to medieval scholasticism and Renaissance humanism; in her poetic and dramatic output to the Baroque or mannerist period; in her intellectual orientation to the dawning of the Age of Reason. But Sor Juana cannot be categorized because her genius and her womanhood prevented her from becoming part of a particular school or university tradition; the educational isolation which she at times lamented kept her in touch with herself.

Sor Juana, like most geniuses, was ahead of her time. Exceptionality, however, is treated differently in men than in women. What I want to suggest is not that we forget that Sor Juana was a woman but that we must reverse the manner in which we respond to that fact. Because Sor Juana Inés is one of the only two women who figure consistently and universally in the annals of Hispanic literary history before the nineteenth century, her position has an importance for women that it does not have for men.

The lives of Sor Juana and Saint Teresa are exceptions that prove the oppressive rule. Besides extraordinary talent and production, it took unusual circumstances and potent sources of support for both St. Teresa and Sor Juana to prevail. Could they have been the only women of such talent? Were they not perhaps the only ones with the cluster of requirements needed to break through the barriers against the success of women in the public world? Saint Teresa had the support of her mystical union with God, and of some prestigious earthly beings as well. Sor Juana was called by her contemporaries "the Tenth Muse,"[7] an epithet perpetuated by later scholars who have kept her ensconced on a literary pedestal.

Nancy Miller, in an essay on women's autobiography in France, advances one hypothesis in this regard. Observing that maleness and humanity are conflated by both male authors and most critic-consumers of autobiography, she introduces the notion of a gender-bound reading: "I would propose . . . a practice of the text that would recognize the status of the reader as differentiated subject; a reading subject named by gender and committed in a dialectics of identification to deciphering the inscription of a female subject."[8] Miller's proposed method will be kept in mind in this section.

Women—necessarily influenced by patriarchal culture and scholarship, but nevertheless, as women, reading differently—have contributed significantly to studies of Sor Juana. In bibliographies one of course finds many fewer works by women, and in the most widely distributed and popular anthologies even fewer.[9] Well-trained and first-rate or first-rated women critics are rare; the paternalistic and condescending underpinnings of university and publishing systems do little to encourage a change.

And yet women played an essential role in publicizing Sor Juana's work both during and after her lifetime. The marquise of Mancera, who doted on her, was a major affective support—if indeed a distraction—first in the court and later in the convent. She rescued Sor Juana from her first overly rigorous convent and visited her regularly in the second. A few years after the marquise's death, the countess of Paredes, wife of the new vice regent, occupied her place in Sor Juana's affections. A woman of culture who wrote poetry herself, she took Sor Juana's poems and plays to Spain to have them published. She shares responsibility for the solid grounding of Sor Juana's reputation in Spain and the colonies. Along with other figures of seventeenth-century literature, Sor Juana's fame waned in the eighteenth and nineteenth centuries.

Serrano y Sanz doesn't even mention the **"Respuesta a Sor Filotea de la Cruz"** (**"Reply to Sister Filotea de la Cruz"**) (1691) in summarizing Sor Juana's life and work in his bio-bibliography of women writers.[10] Pedro Henríquez Ureña and Manuel Toussaint began this century's rediscovery. And a North American scholar, Dorothy Schons

(1925), pioneered in finding documents, amplifying bibliography, investigating dates, and placing Sor Juana in her period. Her slim volumes and articles remain difficult to locate. Two other North American women scholars, Lota Spell (1947) and E. J. Gates (1939), also contributed to the research. Several Spanish and Spanish-American women scholars brought attention to Sor Juana.[11]

If one accepts the concept of gender-linked reading, there follows an understanding of the special sense of identification, sympathy, and consequently, the recognition evident in the work of women who have approached the work of Sor Juana. For example, Anita Arroyo responds, with a conviction based on her own female experience, to the sources of Sor Juana's torment and passion. Respecting Sor Juana's reticence, she argues that the absence of total confession does not detract from the essential meanings of Sor Juana's work. Arroyo also reviews briefly the contributions of women in a chapter on Sor Juana and the literary critics. Mirta Aguirre's short but excellent book, *Del encausto a la sangre: Sor Juana Inés de la Cruz* (From Imperial Red Ink to Blood), and Rachel Phillips's short essay "Sor Juana: Dream and Silence"[12] cut through mystifications and convolutions in tracing the probable chain of events—and Sor Juana's reaction to them—which led to her silence and finally her death. As women, they respond more to the seriousness and less to the "charm" of her work.

Like Saint Teresa and Madre Isabel, Sor Juana displayed self-effacement and humility, on the one hand, and, on the other, competitiveness, ambition, and a quality that some would call arrogance, others self-assertion and confidence. In speaking of her trials and tribulations, she compares herself to Saint Peter, Saint Jerome, and to Christ himself. She emphasizes her dedication to her chosen vocation of study and learning; natural ability was complemented by constant hard work and frequently by contention with the material being studied or created as well as with surrounding circumstances.

Sor Juana transcended the demands of gender and the limitations of what are to this day called in Hispanic countries "the tasks proper to her sex" because of an unusual combination of factors, among them her having been a child prodigy. Already too strong in intellectual development at the age when precocity in women is directly or subtly stifled, her life did not take the course usual for a woman of her class. It was her own idea in 1655, at the age of seven, to ask her mother to dress her in men's clothing and send her to the university in Mexico:

> Teniendo yo después como seis o siete años, y sabiendo ya leer y escribir, con todas las otras habilidades de labores y costuras que deprenden las mujeres, oí decir que había Universidad y Escuelas en que se estudiaban las ciencias, en Méjico; y apenas lo oí cuando empecé a matar a mi madre con instantes e importunos ruegos sobre que, mudándome el traje, me enviase a Méjico, en casa de unos deudos que tenía, para estudiar y cursar la Universidad.
>
> (IV, 445-46; p. 78)

> When I was about six or seven, having already learned to read and write, along with other skills such as embroidery and dressmaking which were considered appropriate for women, I heard that in Mexico City there was a university and schools where one could learn science. As soon as I heard that, I began to torture my mother with insistent and annoying pleas that she change my clothes and send me to live with relatives of hers in Mexico City so I could study at the university.

She had devoured the books in her maternal grandfather's library near the provincial town of Amecameca; they had provided her with an unsystematic but thorough education. All the autobiographical anecdotes and episodes offered by Sor Juana in the "**Respuesta**" refer to her precocity, her self-discipline, and her drive: in sum, to her education. She laments the lack of teachers and of the stimulation of student peers, and she underscores the sense of loneliness that hindered her intellectual development. When, in 1665, at the age of seventeen, she became a lady-in-waiting at the court of the Marquises of Mancera, despite the fact that she was nurtured by a close and loving relationship with them, the court treated her as a freak. One event organized by the viceroys recalls the tests found in old fairy tales: there gathered at the palace a group of the most learned men to examine Juana in their respective disciplines. She astonished them all. She was paraded, shown off, and expected to produce original poems and plays for all occasions. This episode was not recorded in the "**Respuesta**" but in the short essay of her first biographer, Diego Calleja, whom later commentators followed.[13] Sor Juana's own reactions passed into her drama and verse.

Sor Juana's switch from court to convent, which occurred when she was nineteen, was abrupt and remains partially unexplained. Nevertheless, in the "**Respuesta**" she says clearly:

> Para la total negación que tenía al matrimonio, era lo menos desproporcionado y lo más decente que podía elegir.
>
> (IV, 446; p. 78)

Given my complete opposition to the idea of marriage, it was the least shocking and most decent thing I could have chosen.

Her choice to stay in the world or to enter the convent she saw as fraught with difficulties for her main purpose in life, "de querer vivir sola; de no querer tener ocupación obligatoria que embarazase la libertad de mi estudio . . . el sosegado silencio de mis libros" (IV, 446; p. 79) (to live alone, to avoid any obligation which might disturb my freedom to study, the tranquil silence of my books). She chose religious life not because it was her true vocation but because it seemed the only way of attaining that purpose.

But Sor Juana's abode in the cloister was no ascetic cell; on the contrary, it came to be more like a salon. She was visited by people at the upper levels of the Church, the vice regal family, scholars, writers, and travelers from abroad. According to Padre Calleja, her private library held four thousand volumes.[14] She collected musical and scientific instruments. She became poet laureate, continuing to produce occasional poetry for lovers of the court, for birthdays, anniversaries, and deaths, and sacred poetry and plays for the celebrations of religious holidays at the great cathedrals of Mexico.

Writing played a major role in Sor Juana's life from her teens until her early forties when, shortly after composing the "**Respuesta a Sor Filotea,**" she signed away in blood—literally—her earthly pursuits and, in effect, her life. At this time, tremendous external economic and political crisis coincided with her own experience of censorship, persecution, isolation, and disillusionment. For more than twenty years she had flourished under difficult circumstances, in which, nevertheless, the balance had been weighted toward recognition and support of her work.

Sor Juana's tremendous drive helped her to cope with practical impediments and with her own emotional sensitivities. Convent routines and duties were demanding. And when there were moments for leisure, her sisters and the servants would often enlist her aid or attention, wishing mediation of quarrels, advice, conversation. Her description of her response to such demands is often quoted. She would give herself a period of ten days or so of solitude. Then her conscience would begin to prod her for neglecting her sisters, and she would put aside her own work and take up her social duties. A tone of muffled resentment characterizes her references to incursions on her time. One must recognize, on the other hand, the advantages that her privileged position offered her. Although it is perhaps true, as Sor Juana humorously claims, that Aristotle would have been a greater philosopher had he cooked, it is also certain that had *she* had to do more cooking—or sewing, or cleaning, or washing or ironing—she would not have produced the body of writing that she did.

In the "**Respuesta,**" Sor Juana describes her facility for writing as a double-edged gift. It encroached upon time she would have preferred to spend studying, and it provoked envy and resentment on the part of people of lesser talent. Reprimanded for her profane verse and rebuked for the theological trespass, as we shall see, she had good reason to describe herself as a writer only under duress.[15] Although she may have considered some of the assignments as encumbrances, she accomplished most of what she did with intensity and polish. She felt sensitive pride in being one of the two (with Carlos de Sigüenza y Góngora) official writers of the court.

Several studies have noted Sor Juana's hypersensitivity—how she became enraged by the attacks of enemies, upset by the criticism of friends, vain, exhibitionistic, and grudge-bearing, and sensitive to a fault.[16] But could it have been otherwise when she had been treated as an oddity from the beginning of her solitary childhood? In a sense her status as a "rare bird" gave her a perch for many years, though this same status was later to make her vulnerable to the attacks of those who resented her independence, her fame, and her exercise in scholastic discourse.

The ethical, philosophical, literary, and feminist implications of Sor Juana's autobiographical essay and of her entire legacy have yet to be fully explored or disseminated. Why they have not been is in part a feminist question since it is related to the fact that it was not until three hundred years after her birth that her ***Obras completas***—plays, poetry, and prose—were gathered together and published.[17] Her secular theater includes two comedies, two one-act intermezzos (*sainetes*), fourteen dramatic poems (*loas*), and one soiree (*sarao*). The longest speech in ***Los empeños de una casa*** (***The Trials of a [Noble] House***) is the female protagonist's narrative of her life, in which Sor Juana put much of herself—experience, feelings, reactions—telling of the zeal with which she studied and learned, the spread of her fame, and of a disappointment in love (IV, 36-43). For the Church she wrote three sacramental plays (*autos sacramentales*), three dramatic preludes (*loas*) to these plays, and another *loa* in praise of the Immaculate Conception (III, 3-278). ***El Divino Nar-***

ciso (***The Divine Narcissus***), one of the sacramental plays, and the *loa* written to precede it are considered her dramatic masterpieces. For Church celebrations she also wrote *villancicos,* sets of poems to be combined with prayers and masses, employing all the metric forms popular at the time. In the *villancicos* to Santa Catarina, Sor Juana identifies with this saint renowned for her wisdom:

De una Mujer se convencen
todos los Sabios de Egipto,
para prueba de que el sexo
no es esencia en lo entendido.

(II, 171)

By a Woman all the Sages
of Egypt are convinced,
as proof that one's sex
is not the essence of the mind.

Among these *villancicos* are poems in Nahuatl and Nahuatl and Spanish and several imitating the Spanish of the blacks, in which she expressed their resentment, resistance, and the urge for freedom.[18] The fifty love poems have been debated and dissected for their confessional meanings. The discussions sometimes seem to obscure the fact that Sor Juana wrote some of the most beautiful love poems in the Spanish language, poems characterized by uncanny insight into human psychology.

Sor Juana's most famous poem is the **"Sátira filosófica"** (**"Philosophical Satire"**), which begins, "Hombres necios, que acusáis" (I, 228-29) (Foolish men, who accuse). School children memorize it, but in the colleges it is not often enough seen in perspective as the culmination and refinement of a theme used and abused for several centuries, a masterful formal achievement, that sums up one of the debates between misogynists and philogynists so popular in that period. Sor Juana's protest against sexual abuse and her humor in showing that women are damned if they do and damned if they don't added a vibrancy to the poetic theme.[19] In Sor Juana's longest and perhaps her own favorite poem, **"Primero sueño"** (I, 335-59) (**"The First Dream"**), she casts herself as Phaëthon, who dared to steer his carriage toward the sun. Moving through the philosophical knowledge of her day, as she seeks to unravel the nature of the universe and of thought, she describes the stages of her own intellectual development, its difficulties, and her final sense of failure.[20] Courtly poems and philosophical, historical, and mythological sonnets complete Sor Juana's production in verse.

As is the case with most writers, there is autobiographical material throughout Sor Juana's work. In addition to Leonor's speech in ***Los empeños de una casa,*** the *villancicos* to Santa Catarina cited above, and the abstract yet significant **"Primero sueño"** there is the *romance,* **"Señor: para responderos"** (**"Sir, in response to you"**), in which Sor Juana answers "un caballero del Perú" (I, 136-39) (a gentleman from Peru) who had sent her verses suggesting that she turn into a man. Her rebuke seems relevant to modern ears accustomed to discussions of issues of masculinity and femininity and the search for androgyny:

porque acá Sálmacis falta,
en cuyos cristales dicen
que hay no sé qué virtud de
dar alientos varoniles.

Yo no entiendo de esas cosas;
sólo sé que aquí me vine
porque, si es que soy mujer,
ninguno lo verifique.

Y también sé que, en latín,
sólo a las casadas dicen
uxor, o mujer, y que
es común de dos lo Virgen.

Con que a mí no es bien mirado
que como a mujer me miren,
pues no soy mujer que a alguno
de mujer pueda servirle;

y sólo sé que mi cuerpo,
sin que a uno u otro se incline,
es nuestro, o abstracto, cuanto
sólo el Alma deposite.

(I, 138)

For Salmacis is not to be found here
in whose crystal ball they say
there is I know not what power to
endow one with manly spirit.

I am not acquainted with such things:
I know only that I came here
so that, if indeed I am a woman
no one might be led to prove it.

And I also know that in Latin
only married women are called
uxor, or woman, and that
virginity is expected of both.

So that it is not considered correct
that I be seen as a woman
for I am not a woman
who serves as anyone's woman;

and I know only that my body
without favoring one or another,
is neutral, or abstract, since
it houses only the Soul. . . .

Woman and wife are used synonymously in Spanish, which allows for the word play in the fourth stanza above. The most exaggerated analysis of these verses is to be found in Pfandl, who sees in them the declaration of her defective nature and her "psychic tragedy."[21]

Sor Juana's ***Respuesta a Sor Filotea*** is the major and most direct source of her autobiographical writing, and it is an essential document of seventeenth-century feminism.[22] As I indicated earlier, there exists an abundance of still unstudied autobiographical documents by women of this period; some may eventually prove exceptional, though it is doubtful that any will be comparable with Sor Juana's, which runs counter to the Counter-Reformation. No "holy ignorance" for her. The implication of all her writing is that she saw life as a loving labor in pursuit of knowledge. In the introduction to the second volume of her poems and plays, and again in the ***Respuesta,*** she uses a quotation from Saint Jerome that could stand as the epigraph to her work and as the epitaph on her tomb:

> Quid ibi laboris insumpserim, quid sustinuerim difficultatis, quoties desperaverim, quotiesque cessaverim et contentione discendi rursus inceperim; testis est conscientia.
>
> (IV, 451; p. 84)

> Of the effort I made, of the difficulties I suffered through, of how many times I despaired, and how many others I gave up and started again in my determination to learn, my conscience is the witness.

It is unlikely that Sor Juana would have written this autobiographical essay had she not been stunned by the reprimand and threat of damnation contained in the letter to which it was the reply. The year before, impressed by her theological reasoning in conversation, Don Manuel Fernández de Santa Cruz, bishop of Puebla, asked her to record for him her disagreement with a sermon written in 1650 by a famous but controversial Portuguese Jesuit, Antonio Vieyra. Without consulting her, the bishop had the essay printed as the ***Carta Atenagórica*** (Athenagoric Letter) (1690).[23] Don Manuel had long been one of Sor Juana's powerful friends, but he was involved in the internecine ecclesiastical warfare going on at the time. It is not clear whether or not he was innocent and acting alone in having Sor Juana's essay published. If her profane work had caused a stir (1689), the publication of her religious text caused her ultimate silence.[24]

Through an ironic twist of fate, her theological refutation came to be used as an "attack" on the liberal wing of the Jesuits and led to the marshaling of forces against Sor Juana that should have been in her favor. At the time of this crisis in her life, Sor Juana's relationship with members of the vice regal and Church establishment had changed. The vice regents who had befriended and supported her had died or returned to Spain. Further, the reaction set off by the publication of her poems in Spain and of her theological disputation in New Spain estranged her from her nearly life-long confessor, Antonio Nuñez de Miranda.

With the ***Carta Atenagórica,*** the bishop also published a preliminary letter to Sor Juana, criticizing her dedication to profane subjects, some of the arguments against Vieyra, and expressing worry about her salvation. He signed it with the pseudonym Sor Filotea.

If anything was typical of the seventeenth century it was that almost nothing was taken—or expressed—at face value. Neither life nor letters were approached simply and directly in that Baroque time. It is surprising that so many critics have understood both the letter from Sor Filotea and the answer to it as generous and almost ingenuous. But in view of attitudes about women, it is not surprising.[25] Smart women were seen as precocious children (*monjita, damita*). Women who wrote autobiographies were supposed to be making total confessions. Scholars such as Salceda, Cossio, Castro Leal, and Rivers claim that the ostensible reprimand for not applying her intelligence more to sacred and less to profane subject matter was really a friendly way of presenting Sor Juana with the opportunity of defending herself and of discoursing at length on her favorite subjects. In essence, it seems to have presented her with the need to make what she knew was a vain attempt at self-defense: it spurred her to write her intellectual and spiritual testament. The weight of Counter-Reformation ideology and of the personally devastating criticism she was trying to contest proved an overwhelming condemnation and turned Sor Juana ultimately to seek death and salvation in the manner eternally asked of women—self-sacrifice for the sick and dying. Within three months of receiving Sor Filotea's letter, she had replied with what she called a simple "narración de mi inclinación" (IV, 445; p. 78) (narrative regarding my inclination to letters), which is a not-so-simple *apologia pro vita sua.*

A demonstration of her mental virtuosity, a portrait of the origins and development of her intellectual passion and of the suffering it caused her, a defense of the education and intellectual life of women, the ***Respuesta*** is also a protest against ecclesiastic—and all kinds of—stupidity and repression.

At one point she was prohibited from reading, a prohibition which she treats with light and condescending humor:

> Una prelada muy santa y muy cándida que creyó que el estudio era cosa de Inquisición . . . me mandó que no estudiase. Yo la obedecí (unos tres meses que duró el poder ella mandar) en cuanto a no tomar libro, que en cuanto a no estudiar absolutamente, como no cae debajo de mi potestad, no lo pude hacer, porque aunque no estudiaba en los libros, estudiaba en todas las cosas que Dios crió, sirviéndome ellas de letras, y de libro toda esta máquina universal.
>
> (IV, 458; p. 90)

> A religious but simple-minded mother superior who thought that study was a matter for the Inquisition . . . ordered me not to study. I obeyed her (for the three months that she lasted in office) as far as not taking a book in hand. But as far as absolutely not studying, it wasn't in my power, I couldn't do it. For even though I wasn't studying in books, I studied in God's works, taking *them* as letters and the whole Creation as my book.

More is here than meets the eye. By ridiculing the "simple-minded" from a lofty position, Sor Juana is urging her reader to abjure the common attitudes and practices of the times. Would even a mother superior make such a prohibition without consulting her confessor? Was she the only one who thought that study was a matter for the Inquisition? Behind the prohibition stood surely confessor and other Church authorities who were gradually restricting her freedom.

The **"Respuesta"**'s full beauty and meaning become apparent only after more than one reading. It is full of Latin quotations (in most editions they are translated in footnotes). There is tight scholastic logic, classical aphorism, Renaissance harmonic play, and in a few instances familiar and popular expressions. Anger, defiance, challenge, humility, tenderness, and despair alternate as Sor Juana describes her childhood struggles to educate herself. As she affirms her love of study above all else, she defends the right of women to learn and to exercise the freedom to think and reflect and opine. She defends her right to refute the theological arguments of the famous Jesuit and to put forth her own. And she even speaks belligerently:

> ¿Llevar una opinión contraria de Vieyra fue en mi atrevimiento? . . . Mi entendimiento tal cual ¿no es tan libre como el suyo, pues viene de un solar?
>
> (IV, 468; p. 101)

> It was bold of me to oppose Vieyra? . . . My mind is not as free as his, though it derives from the same Source?

Time and again she refers to the inalienable freedom of the mind.

The most important source of support for her defense was one she herself had marshaled to her side in the course of a lifetime of reading: a long line of "tantas y tan insignes mujeres" (IV, 460-61; p. 93) (learned and powerful women of the past). For she buttresses her self-defense with more than forty-two examples of her female predecessors—names drawn from classical, mythological, biblical, and contemporary sources.[26] This company assured her that, despite the odds, she had a right to move in the world as she did, to follow her own bent.

The **"Respuesta"** itself is too rich and complex to be discussed in full here. But the essence of Sor Juana's convictions is present in the Latin quotations she employed in the essay. I have abstracted and examined seventy-eight such citations. Some must have occurred to her as she wrote; others she must have searched for in her effort to build her defense, which is also a challenge and a veiled announcement of her ultimate resolution. Seen thus, isolated, the quotations offer a sharp-focused and intensified version of the essay as a whole. They are not, as some critics have claimed, superfluous. The first quotation refers to the effect of *beneficio* ("favor"), "*Minorem spei* [*sic*], *maiorem benefacti* [*sic*] *gloriam pereunt* [*sic*]" (IV, 646; p. 73)[27] (Hopes produce less, favors produce more glory). The sentence immediately following is "In such a way that they silence the favored." By the last citation of the essay, she has come full circle back to the same concept. The implication is clear: she has been betrayed. The "favor" was the publication—with the flattering title (Athenagoric)—of ideas that she had expressed orally and in private and then upon request had written down, for private consumption only. Of those quotations she selects, both the first, from Quintilian, and the last, from Seneca, match the reference to the classically titled publication.

As is common in the work of the other great Baroque masters, there are frequently double edges and multiple meanings in the allusions, citations, and metaphors she employs. The first citation shows Sor Juana's understanding of her own and women's (let that stand for human) psychology. Real support does often give better results than promises. But in this case, of course, the support was a cruelty and an outrage. Lest the intent of the quotation be obscured by the most obvious meaning, she repeats it in the final statement—a bitter, regretful statement of her fate: "*Turpe est beneficiis vinci*" (IV, 663; p. 107) (What a humiliation [shame] to be vanquished by favors).

Other citations refer to justice, judgment, trials, accusations, and secrecy. They build her case and reveal her awareness that not only is Sor Filotea a disguise for her friend the bishop of Puebla but that behind him stand her confessor and other less friendly and more powerful forces. Both friends and enemies are defeating her, the first more painfully than the second.

It is notable that the quotation "*mulieres in Ecclesia taceant*" (Women are to be silent in church) is repeated three times. "*Mulier in silentio discat*" (Women are to learn in silence) and the universalizing "*Audi, Israel, et tace*" (Listen, Israel, and be silent) appear after the first two repetitions and before the third, adding impact to the theme (IV, 656, 660; pp. 94, 98, 100). It also associates the silencing of women—and of herself—with that of the wise, the innocent, the dominated.

The subtlety of Sor Juana's reasoning is evidenced throughout. For instance, in the citation of Martial on the very subject of understanding (closely related, through Gracián, whose writing she knew well, to ingenuity): "Rare is the one who will recognize the superior understanding of another." She has been discussing envy as a motivation for enmity and destruction, and the citation has a triple meaning in the context in which it is placed. On the first plane, it is a dismayed protest at the envy aroused by her intellectual superiority. On a second plane, it relates to her vying against her own human limitations—like Icarus and Phaëthon in whom she projected herself in her great poem, **"Primero sueño"**—for cosmic understanding. On a third and less apparent plane I detect an association with her own less glorious personal struggles with the emotion of envy.

The misogynistic, anti-intellectual,[28] "turgid atmosphere of uneasy orthodoxy,"[29] of New Spain is exemplified both affectively and symbolically through the citations. Misunderstanding of the Scriptures and of the interpretations of the Scriptures are highlighted. Not lack of faith but envy and stupidity are most to blame. It is Sor Juana's conviction that the road to God is paved by the process of learning and that women of rights must also travel that road. Beauty, understanding, and tireless effort to gain knowledge are what is truly holy; the holy is persecuted. Throughout the citations, a vivid sense of resentment, expressed with irony and bitterness, culminates in the final, disconsolate submission. In the Latin references she explains, defends, and clarifies: her disagreement with Vieyra was not an attack on him, nor on the Jesuits. She cites both according to what she might think her judges want to hear and to what she wants and needs to say.

Four of the citations refer to versifying, and they are presented with a tone of overt impatience with those who consider verse making sinful. From Cassiodorus she takes the statement that verse had its origin in the Holy Scriptures. From Ovid she draws a statement to support her tendency to say everything in verse, and, going further, she reminds the reader that Saint Paul associated verse with being itself.

Five Latin quotations are given in addition to the three already mentioned to substantiate women's right to learn and teach. From Quintilian, a citation that seems to espouse the cornerstone of modern philosophies of education—intellectual freedom and education through knowledge of the self: "*Noscat quisque, et non tantum ex alienis praeceptis sed ex natura sua capiat consilium*" (IV, 661; p. 101) (Let all learn and not from the precepts of others but rather from the teachings of their own nature). Having followed this advice, she claims herself formally unprepared to do even what is allowed to women in Church tradition—to teach by writing. By publishing what she wrote, the bishop had transformed it into what she had not intended it to be.

The need for guidance and independence but also the fear and sorrow attendant upon the acquisition of knowledge/understanding are the themes of citations that build toward a parallel with the greatest sufferer—Christ. The citations convey her sense of martyrdom to the cause. From Saint Jerome comes the description of the road toward knowledge as a Calvary (see p. 174). Another citation, from Saint Cyprian, hints at the dangers of writing, while ostensibly continuing the explanation of the dearth of religious subject matter in her works: "*Gravi consideratione indigent quae scribimus*" (IV, 660; p. 101) (That which we write requires careful [serious] consideration). Great consideration is being given to this **"Respuesta."**

Sor Juana fulfilled her purposes magnificently in this essay-letter: she excuses and explains her dedication to secular rather than religious letters. But she did much more. A superficially most ladylike defense exposes its author as a superb ironist. Claiming lack of adequate preparation, she displays her theological erudition; insisting on how little she knows, she shows how much less those who consider themselves sages know; apologizing for digressions, she creates cadenzas of wit; overly courteous, she unleashes her anger. The ***Respuesta*** can be and has been read also as a treatise on interdisciplinary study, a discussion of educational theory, a dissection of a society in which the excellent and the extraordinary were not only discouraged but not even tolerated. And yet in three hundred years we have not come so far. That no other Sor Juana has surfaced in the Hispanic literary world is surely in great part a result of the social circumstances that have kept women in "their place."

In spite of the fact that she was famous and her work well known, until quite recently the study of Sor Juana has been with few exceptions both limited and distorted.[30] Attitudes about morality, religion, and sexuality have charged Sor Juana criticism with bias and tendentiousness and have led to curious literary battles. Some critics have wanted to see her as a mystic, others as an atheist; some as a jilted or fallen woman, others as a tortured lesbian. For example, Ermilo Abreu Gómez calls Sor Juana's a viriloid nature;[31] Ezequiel Chávez describes her as a bird of paradise;[32] to Elias Rivers she is a "damita intelectual" (an intellectual little lady), a "monjita" (little nun), and "una ave tan rara" (such a strange bird).[33] Castro Leal calls her "un milagro" (a miracle) and "un ornamento de su siglo" (an ornament to her century)[34] and claims that her desire for knowledge did not detract from her femininity and charm. Pedro Salinas, affirming how advanced Sor Juana was for her time, envisions her as an American college girl riding a bike, wearing glasses, her hair blowing in the wind.[35] Américo Castro, pointing out her intellectual martyrdom, on the one hand, calls her "pobre monjita" (poor little nun), on the other.[36] (No one ever called Fray Luis de León or San Juan de la Cruz "poor little monk.") Sexist criteria continually obtrude in books and articles that otherwise contain much of value on Sor Juana's times, her life, and her work. Irving Leonard calls her "an ambivalent personality of feminine emotion and masculine intellectuality."[37] Pfandl, basing his Freudian analysis of her as a "classic psychoneurotic" on her urge to enjoy masculine intellectual pleasure, goes even further: "Her tragedy was this: that although she was born a woman, she should not have been."[38] These and similar labels and opinions, passed on from one critic to another and from critic to student or reader, have too long gone unquestioned.

Modification of sexist criteria can come only after the explosion of erroneous assumptions through intelligent and unrelenting insistence. Women in the field are going back to reckon with a giant who has so often been presented to us through the lens of diminution or condescension or deification. Those in other literatures, it is to be hoped, will soon include Sor Juana's work in seventeenth-century studies. The **"Respuesta a Sor Filotea"** deserves to take its place in the canon of basic feminist writings alongside the works of Christine de Pisan,[39] Flora Tristan,[40] Mary Wollstonecraft,[41] John Stuart Mill,[42] Virginia Woolf,[43] and Simone de Beauvoir.[44]

I have described some of the contrasts between Madre Isabel and Sor Juana Inés de la Cruz. Both women can be tied to earlier periods—the one to medieval mysticism, the other to the medieval abbesses of the Double Abbeys (those in the system of unified monasteries and convents), renowned for development and conservation of learning and the arts. If we can project them backward and place them in an earlier historical period, we can also project them forward and see them in relation to trends of more modern times. Madre Isabel might then remind us of the continuing relegation of women to beatitude and nonschooled culture, still the lot of millions of Hispanic women; Sor Juana is closer to the developments we associate with the age of Enlightenment (rational thinking, scientific inquiry, and experimentation), to the continuing increase in the numbers of women who participate in fields long the domain of men, and to the spreading movement of women's liberation.

Notes

1. See, for example, E. A. Peers, *Studies of the Spanish Mystics,* 3 vols. (New York: Macmillan, 1927-1930); H. Hatzfeld, *Estudios literarios sobre mística española,* 2nd ed. (Madrid: Gredos, 1965); D. Alonso, *Del siglo de oro a este siglo de siglas* (Madrid: Gredos, 1962).

2. The most important single reference source to works by women is Manuel Serrano y Sanz's *Apuntes para una biblioteca de escritoras españolas desde el año 1401 al 1833* (Madrid: Tipografía de la Revista de Archivos, 1903 and 1905; published in a facsimile edition in Madrid, 1975). I can mention two, Sor María de San José, a favorite of Saint Teresa's, and Juliana Morell, whose work I have traced to the Bibliothèque Calvet in Avignon. See Serrano y Sanz, II, 333-50 and 63-70 (incorrectly indexed). For the most part, however, works of this sort have been ignored. I traveled to Spain on a CUNY Faculty Grant in 1973 to do research at the Biblioteca Nacional and the Archivo Histórico Nacional, where documents by women, largely neglected, are plentiful. It was in the manuscript section of the Biblioteca Nacional that I discovered the *Life* of Madre Isabel, catalogued under the author's first

name, which is the only way such works are listed in that library. (At the Archivo Histórico Nacional they are listed by religious orders only.) Elsewhere in Spain, the archives of Simancas near Valladolid and of the convent of Las Huelgas in Burgos are also rich sources of manuscripts. Archives, convents, and libraries in many other cities—Seville, Avila, Barcelona—have more of such documents. But in many of these places, getting access to the manuscripts requires a great deal of perseverance.

3. Sor Juana Inés de la Cruz, *Obras completas* (Mexico: Fondo de Cultura Económica 1951-1957), Alfonso Méndez Plancarte, ed., vols. 1-3, Alberto Salceda, ed., vol. 4 (hereafter cited as *O.C.*). When citing the *Respuesta a Sor Filotea* (hereafter cited as *Respuesta*), I also provide page numbers from Elias L. Rivers' edition, Sor Juana Inés de la Cruz, *Antología* (Madrid: Anaya, 1965); I cite from this edition because it is readily available and reasonably priced.

4. These lives are mentioned, for example, in R. Trevor Davies' *The Golden Century of Spain (1501-1621)* (New York: Harper Torchbooks, 1961), p. 290; and Julio Caro Baroja, *Las formas complejas de la vida religiosa* (Madrid: Akal, 1978), pp. 81, 84, 87. See also Antonio Domíngues Ortíz, *Las clases privilegiadas en la España del Antiguo Régimen* (Madrid: Ediciones Istmo, 1973), p. 202.

5. Virginia Woolf, *A Room of One's Own* (1929; rpt. New York: Harcourt, Brace & World, 1957). Although Woolf's book is not directly related to the subject of this essay, it is essential reading for anyone interested in women writers.

6. Emily James Putnam, *The Lady: Studies of Certain Significant Phases of Her History* (1910; rpt. Chicago: University of Chicago Press, 1970), pp. 71, 78.

7. Such epithets were common in the seventeenth century. Applied to Sor Juana, it became part of the title of the first edition of her poems in Spain: *Inundación castálida de la única poetisa, musa dézima: Sor Juana Inés de la Cruz* (Madrid: Juan García Infanzón, 1689). The sexist nature of the carry-over into modern times of such epithets is what concerns us here.

8. Nancy K. Miller, "Women's Autobiography in France: For a Dialectics of Identification," in *Women and Language in Literature and Society*, ed. S. Connell-Ginet, R. Borker, and N. Furman (New York: Praeger, 1980), p. 267.

9. Of the relatively widely distributed popular paperback anthologies and presentations for students, Rivers lists 5 women among 45 entries; Xirau, 6 of 34; Veiravé, 1 of 24; Flynn, 3 of 23; and Monterde, 4 of 31. In Dorothy Schons's 1925 bibliography there are among "Articles and Studies" two that are anonymous, which must always be suspected, one with initials only, and 4 women's names out of 55. Pfandl (for 1873-1935) lists 3 women out of 35, and de la Maza (for 1936-1963) lists 31 of 213 (plus 3 that are doubtful). Anita Arroyo's bibliography of 179 entries contains 36 by women, 7 or so doubtful, and 2 anonymous. Of the authors participating in homages to Sor Juana, the one published in Mexico in 1951 presented no women critics among eleven authors; the one published in Colombia represented none among four.

10. Serrano y Sanz, *Apuntes*, I, 289-97.

11. Dorothy Schons's results are published as *Some Bibliographical Notes on Sor Juana Inés de la Cruz* (Austin: University of Texas Bulletin no. 2526, 1925); and "Some Obscure Points in the Life of Sor Juana Inés de la Cruz," *Modern Philology*, 24(2) (November 1926): 141-62. The work of Lota Spell and E. J. Gates is cited in Rivers, *Antología* (Madrid: Anaya, 1965), pp. 12, 15. From the review and citations given by Arroyo (*Razón y pasión*, pp. 163-66), I gather that a significant interpretation of Sor Juana and the Baroque—that Arroyo does not entirely agree with—was made by Jesusa Alfau de Solalinde, "El barroco en la vida de Sor Juana," *Humanidades* (Faculty of Philosophy and Letters of the University of Mexico) 1 (1943); I have not been able to locate this periodical.

12. Mirta Aguirre, *Del encausto a la sangre: Sor Juana Inés de la Cruz* (Havana: Casa de las Américas, 1975); Rachel Phillips, "Sor Juana: Dream and Silence," *Aphra*, 3(1) (Winter 1971-1972): 30-40.

13. Diego Calleja, "Aprobación del Reverendíssimo Padre Diego Calleja, de la Compañía de Jesús" in Sor Juana Inés de la Cruz, *Fama y obras posthumas del Fénix de México* (Madrid: Antonio G. de Reyes, 1714), unpaginated.

14. Dorothy Schons suggests four hundred volumes; see *O.C.*, I, lxi.

15. Dario Puccini, in his heavily footnoted study of Sor Juana, discusses this question and comes to a similar conclusion. See his *Sor Juana Inés de la Cruz: Studio d'una personalità del Barocco messicano* (Roma: Edizioni dell'Ateneo, 1967), pp. 91-96.

16. See Francisco de la Maza, "Sor Juana y Don Carlos: Explicación de dos sonetos hasta ahora confusos," *Cuadernos Americanos* 145 (2) (March-April 1966): 190-204.

17. For existing translations of Sor Juana, see: Margery Resnick and Isabelle de Cortivron, eds., *Women Writers in Translation: An Annotated Bibliography* (New York: Garland Press, 1981).

18. Mirta Aguirre (*Del encausto a la sangre*), mentioning the fact that Sor Juana had a slave among her servants, places the poems in a nonromanticized focus: "They are not insurrectional poems. . . . Sor Juana is not to be taken as an abolitionist. But slavery hurts her; one feels her sympathy . . ." (p. 84).

19. In Pilar de Oñate, *El feminismo en la literatura española* (Madrid: Espasa-Calpe, 1935), I found the texts of earlier rather mediocre poems on the same subject. Méndez Plancarte (*O.C.*, I, 488-92) also documented some poetic precursors and subsequent refutations in the notes to the poem.

20. Vicente Gaos, the Mexican philosopher, considers this poem in a class by itself, unequaled in the poetry of intellectual disillusionment; see his "El sueño de un sueño," *Historia de México*, 10(37) (July-August 1960): 70-71. Rachel Phillips ("Dream and Silence"), following Octavio Paz and agreeing with his estimation of it as one of the most complex poems in the Spanish language, gives a fine summation and claims that it "bears witness to human dignity" (p. 40). Alfonso Reyes called it, with the *Respuesta*, the front and back of the same fabric; see his *Letras de la Nueva España* in his *Obras completas*, vol. 12 (Mexico: Fondo de Cultura Económica, 1960), p. 371; English translation by Harriet de Onís in Alfonso Reyes, *The Position of America* (New York: Knopf, 1950), p. 126.

21. Pfandl, *La décima musa de México*, pp. 188-89.

22. Puccini (*Studio d'una personalità*) calls Sor Juana's feminism premature (p. 148). Salceda calls it "the Magna Carta of intellectual freedom of the women of America" (*O.C.*, IV, xliii). Arroyo (*Razón y pasión*) calls it the "first manifesto of women's spiritual liberation" (p. 126). Octavio Paz claims it is "one of the most important documents in the history of Spanish culture and in that of the intellectual emancipation of women," in *Anthology of Mexican Poetry*, trans. Samuel Beckett, compiled by O. Paz, preface C. M. Bowra (London: Thames & Hudson, 1958), p. 204.

23. The *Athenagoric Letter* (or *Letter Worthy of Athena*), then, was her refutation of Vieyra's "Maundy Thursday Sermon." (It was subsequently printed as *Crisis sobre un sermón;* see *O.C.*, IV, 631-32). One of his main theses is that God does human beings the great favor of putting the need to love one another above the need to love Him. In her refutation, Sor Juana's primary claim is that the greatest proof of God's favor is to go against His own nature, to refrain from doing us good, in order that we may learn. Although there is not the space here to discuss the subject further, it may interest readers in comparative literature and women's studies to know that the concept of God as a cause of pain (as well as of pleasure) and of the usefulness for learning of passing through pain and suffering was affirmed in a letter of 1693, written by the first English feminist, Mary Astell (1666-1731). It will be reprinted in a forthcoming book by the woman who has rediscovered her, Ruth Perry, of M.I.T. Letters between John Norris and Mary Astell were published in London in 1695.

24. See Puccini, *Studio d'una personalità,* pp. 34-49; Arroyo, *Razón y pasión,* Part 1, Chap. 3; Aguirre, *Del encausto a la sangre,* pp. 42-50.

25. See Margaret Adams, "The Compassion Trip," and other essays in *Woman in Sexist Society: Studies in Power and Powerlessness,* ed. Vivian Gornick and Barbara K. Moran (New York: Basic Books, 1971); Elise Boulding, *The Underside of History: A View of Women Through Time* (Boulder, Colo.: Westview Press, 1976); *Becoming Visible: Women in European History,* ed. Renate Bridenthal and Claudia Koonz (New York: Houghton Mifflin, 1977).

26. Some of the learned and powerful women she mentions are the mother of John the Baptist, Saint Paula, Saint Teresa, Deborah, the Queen of Sheba, Abigail, Esther, Rahab, Anna, the Sibyls, Minerva, Argentaria, Tiresias, Zenobia, Arete, Nicostrata, Aspasia Milesia, Hispasia, Leoncia, Jucia, Corina, Cornelia, Catherine, Gertrude, Paula Blesila, Eustoquio, Fabiola, Falconia, Queen Isabel, Christine Alexandra, the Duchess of Aveyro, the Countess of Villaumbrosa, Marcela, Pacatula, Leta, Bridgette, Salome, Mary the mother of Jacob, Sister Mary of Antigua, and Mary of Agreda. *O.C.*, IV, 460 et passim; Rivers ed., p. 93.

27. Medievalist Barbara Grant and Latin scholar Ellen Quackenbos have pointed out to me three errors in the citation: (1) *spei* should read *spes;* (2) *benefacti* should read *benefacta;* and (3) *pereunt* should read *pariunt.* I have checked the 1700, 1714, and 1725 editions. The errors appear in all three and were, therefore, probably either errors of Sor Juana's or misreadings by the Spanish printers of the original ms. They passed uncorrected into the *O.C.*

28. See Manuel Durán, "El drama intelectual de Sor Juana y el anti-intelectualismo hispánico," *Cuadernos Americanos,* 21(4) (July-August 1963): 238-53.

29. Phillips, "Dream and Silence," p. 30.

30. I do not wish to suggest that Sor Juana scholarship is lacking in value. I do, however, wish to point up and underline the limiting and distorting effects of sexist attitudes—which are both conscious and unconscious—inherent in the scholarship to which we are accustomed. See *Feminist Literary Criticism: Explorations in Theory,* ed. Josephine Donovan (Lexington: University of Kentucky Press, 1975). Octavio Paz, for instance, in a recently published article entitled "Juana Ramírez," *Vuelta* (Mexico), 2 (April 1978): 17-23, quotes, as lamentably still true, Dorothy Schons's comment, made in 1926: "Sor Juana's biography has yet to be written." He sets the record straight for a large reading public on the date of her birth, 1648, as established by Guillermo Ramírez España and Alberto G. Salceda, rather than 1651 as claimed by Calleja at the beginning of the eighteenth century and repeated in most subsequent studies. He reviews the history of her family and discusses the "illegitimacy" of Juana Ramírez, of her siblings, and of other relatives. But in summarizing and noting the virtues and failures of Pfandl's Freudian study of the poet, he seems to accept Freudian tenets himself without question. He points out that J. R. *had* to have become "masculinized" in order to accede to knowledge in a "masculine culture." A feminist examination of the question of intellect in a patriarchal culture would have a different focus. For example, why the label "masculine" for all outstanding intellectual products by women?

31. Ermilo Abreu Gómez, *Semblanza de Sor Juana* (Mexico: Ediciones Letras de México, 1938), p. 41.

32. Ezequiel Chávez, *Sor Juana Inés de la Cruz: Ensayo de psicología y de estimación del sentido de su obra* (Mexico: Editorial Porrúa, 1970), p. 36.

33. Sor Juana Inés de la Cruz, *Antología,* ed. Elias L. Rivers (Madrid: Anaya, 1965), p. 6.

34. Sor Juana Inés de la Cruz, *Poesía, Teatro y Prosa,* ed. Antonio Castro Leal (Mexico: Editorial Porrúa, 1968), p. vii.

35. "En busca de Juana de Asbaje," in Pedro Salinas, *Ensayos de literatura hispánica* (Madrid: Aguilar, 1958), p. 124.

36. Américo Castro, *De la edad conflictiva,* 2nd ed. (Madrid: Taurus, 1961), pp. 155, 157.

37. Irving Leonard, "The *encontradas correspondencias* of Sor Juana Inés: An Interpretation," *Hispanic Review,* 23 (January 1955): 33; this phrase is quoted in Gerard Flynn, *Sor Juana Inés de la Cruz* (New York: Twayne, 1971), p. 119.

38. Pfandl, *La décima musa de México,* p. 311; this is the passage selected for quotation in Sor Juana Inés de la Cruz, *Selección poética,* ed. Alfredo Veravé (Buenos Aires: Kapelusz, 1972), p. 162.

39. Christine de Pisan was a fifteenth-century French poet who wrote a treatise on women's education, protested against Ovid's *Ars Amatoria,* and participated in a controversy regarding *Le Roman de la Rose.* She was celebrated and attacked as a champion of her sex. See Eileen Power, *Medieval Women,* ed. M. M. Postan

(Cambridge: Cambridge University Press, 1975), pp. 12-13, 31-34, et passim; for bibliographic references, see note 2, p. 100.

40. Flora Tristan, a utopian socialist, best known as the grandmother of Gauguin, and a precursor of Marx, wrote in defense of the English and French working class, especially of the women of that class, in the third and fourth decades of the nineteenth century. See Dominique Desanti, ed., *Oeuvres et vie mêlées [par] Flora Tristan* (Paris: Union Générale d'Editions, 1973).

41. See Mary Wollstonecraft, "A Vindication of the Rights of Women," in *Feminism: The Essential Historical Writings,* ed. Miriam Schneir (1798; rpt. New York: Vintage, 1972).

42. See John Stuart Mill, *The Subjection of Women* (1869; rpt. Cambridge, Mass.: M.I.T. Press, 1970).

43. See Virginia Woolf, *A Room of One's Own* (1929; rpt. New York: Harcourt, Brace & World, 1957).

44. See Simone de Beauvoir, *The Second Sex* (French 1949; English 1955; rpt. New York: Bantam, 1970).

FROM THE AUTHOR

POEM 146

In my pursuit, World, why such diligence?
What my offense, when I am thus inclined,
insuring elegance affect my mind,
not that my mind affect an elegance?

I have no love of riches or finánce,
and thus do I most happily, I find,
expend finances to enrich my mind
and not mind expend upon finánce.

I worship beauty not, but vilify
that spoil of time that mocks eternity,
nor less, deceitful treasures glorify,

but hold foremost, with greatest constancy,
consuming all the vanity in life,
and not consuming life in vanity.

Sor Juana Inés de la Cruz. Poem 146. In *Poems, Protest, and a Dream: Selected Writings.* Edited by Margaret Sayers Peden, p. 171. New York: Penguin, 1997. English translation reprinted from *Sor Juana Inés de la Cruz: Poems.* Bilingual Press/Editorial bilingue, 1985.

TITLE COMMENTARY

"Respuesta a Sor Filotea de la Cruz"

OCTAVIO PAZ (ESSAY DATE 1982)

SOURCE: Paz, Octavio. "The Response." In *Sor Juana or, The Traps of Faith,* translated by Margaret Sayers Peden, pp. 411-24. Cambridge, Mass.: Belknap Press, 1988.

In the following excerpt, Paz examines the mixed messages of Sor Juana's **"Respuesta," or "Response,"** *observing that she often contradicts herself when discussing her education, her writing, and her vocation.*

Sor Juana and Fernández de Santa Cruz must have foreseen that the publication of the **"Carta atenagórica"** would provoke replies and commentaries. Their number, however, and the violence of some, must have amazed them both and slightly frightened Sor Juana. Only echoes from this polemic and a few actual documents have survived to our day; nevertheless, from what the **"Response"** tells us, we know that a number of clerics were involved and that some attacked Sor Juana furiously, despite the fact that she was a woman and a nun. The polemic reached across the sea, although there it lacked the acrimony and heat of the debate in Mexico.[1] From the beginning, through a kind of tacit agreement—there is nothing the Church detests more than scandal—there was an attempt to avoid publicity. This policy continued even after the death of the principal protagonists. In *Fame,* Castorena y Ursúa refers only in passing to the incident, although we know that he was one of Sor Juana's defenders; Calleja praises the critique of Vieyra's sermon in effusive terms but does not go to the heart of the matter; Oviedo is preoccupied with defending Núñez de Miranda and tries to show that Sor Juana did not return his affection; Torres, similarly, exalts and defends the memory of Santa Cruz; as for José de Lezamis, he does not even mention the affair. This silence is an attempt to conceal what actually happened.

Almost none of the commentaries were printed. Some were delivered from the pulpits of churches and in the lecture halls of schools and seminaries. Others circulated in manuscript. Sor Juana relates that her most rabid critic made and distributed copies of his comments. Dorothy Schons speaks of a "storm of criticism" and cites, among the works that circulated in manuscript, one written by a priest, Manuel Serrano de Pereda, and one by a friar, Francisco Ildefonso de Segura. But we need not dwell on this: Sor Juana always refers to her critics in the plural, calling them "impugners," "slanderers," and "persecutors." Among the documents discovered by Ermilo

Abreu Gómez was a pamphlet entitled "La fineza mayor" ("The Greatest Act of Love"), a sermon delivered on March 20, 1691, by the Valencian priest Francisco Xavier Palavicino Villarrasa in the convent of San Jerónimo itself. Sor Juana had sent off her **"Response to Sor Filotea de la Cruz"** barely ten days before. Palavicino's sermon holds special interest for us: it is an indication of the proportions the affair assumed in the months following the appearance of the **"Carta atenagórica."** Palavicino disagrees both with Vieyra's and Sor Juana's opinions: in his eyes, Christ's greatest *fineza* is to conceal Himself during the sacrament of the Eucharist. He begins his sermon with disproportionate praise of Vieyra: a Portuguese Demosthenes, a Jesuit Cicero, and "the Tertullian of our blessed age." He continues by praising Sor Juana, although he concludes with the familiar reservation: "The choicest intellect of this blessed century, Minerva of America, great talent limited by the handicap of her being a woman . . ." Probably the nuns of San Jerónimo, with the hope of calming high feelings, had invited the diplomatic Palavicino to intervene. What the Valencian priest wrote was vastly inferior both to Vieyra's sermon and to Sor Juana's critique, but at that moment the weight of the reasoning was less important than the personalities of the antagonists. It is revealing that the nuns of San Jerónimo thought it prudent to invite a homilist whose opinion on the *finezas* of Christ differed from those of Vieyra and Sor Juana, in this way demonstrating their detachment from the controversy. Sor Juana must have considered this a defection on the part of her sisters.

The reactions caused by the **"Carta"** were not exclusively negative. In spite of the "handicap of her being a woman" there were those who defended her, and in the **"Response"** she refers to their comments, although without naming the authors. She is particularly effusive in praising one of them, probably Castorena y Ursúa, to whom she also dedicated a poem of gratitude, in which she says gracefully: "you must let the light of your intellect / shine brightly in my defense." Castorena y Ursúa's defense, like most of the others, does not appear anywhere—still another indication that there was a concerted attempt to erase all traces of the scandal. This reticence, this silence and ambiguity, along with a fondness for pseudonyms and veiled allusions, is characteristic of all bureaucracies identified with an orthodoxy. This also explains the strangely ambiguous prologue by Sor Filotea de la Cruz. First, the pseudonym. The famed Juan de Palafox y Mendoza, Fernández de Santa Cruz's predecessor as the Bishop of Puebla, had in 1659 published "Peregrinación de Filotea al Santo templo y monte de la Cruz" ("Pilgrimage of Filotea to the Holy Temple and Hill of the Cross"), written in imitation of Francisco de Sales' "Filotea francesa" ("French Filotea"). As Filotea means "one who loves God," even the pseudonym chosen by the Bishop of Puebla was an invitation to leave secular letters and take up sacred subjects. The contrast between the first paragraph of the prologue and what follows is also remarkable. The text begins with extravagant praise of Sor Juana: in addition to Vieyra, she had surpassed another Portuguese preacher, Meneses, who had been Vieyra's teacher. Not without malice, Sor Filotea expresses amazement that a woman should have vanquished a great theologian. Following that statement, Sor Filotea agrees with the notion that women may study provided that study not make them arrogant. All this can be considered as a series of oblique thrusts against Aguiar. Then the author voices a reservation, one that is essential: what a pity that Sor Juana had devoted herself to secular and not sacred writing.

The Bishop of Puebla has been accused of intolerance. Rightly so, although it seems to me that this cautiously worded text has not been read with care. The paragraphs condemning Sor Juana's predisposition toward secular writing probably were intended to deflect any criticism that might arise from friends of the Archbishop of Mexico. I also believe that Fernández de Santa Cruz's reprimand, in addition to its tactical utility as a weapon of self-defense, accurately represented his point of view. Sor Juana's style of thinking and writing collided violently with his views. He believed that "any science that does not serve Christ is but ignorance and vanity." Sor Juana paid lip service to those ideas, but the attitude that ruled her life was radically different: her true passion was knowledge. Another source of conflict was the limits imposed on a woman's learning. Sor Juana wants them broadened, and in this she does not yield. Although her rebellion is undeclared, she does not give in: she advances with prudence, retreats, again advances. I emphasize the Bishop's ambivalence: he asks Sor Juana to write a critique of Vieyra; he publishes it, and does not hesitate to give it his imprimatur; he hides behind a pseudonym with ambiguous connotations and writes a no less ambiguous prologue in which he praises Sor Juana on the one hand and criticizes her on the other. If Sor Juana's enemies attack the Bishop, if they are startled that he published such a text, he can reply that he had already reprimanded the nun; at the same time, that reprimand offers her an opportunity to defend herself. José María de Cossío assumes that there was a prior agreement between Sor Juana and the Bishop: the prelate's letter was an invitation for her to present her case and defend herself. Possibly. But the Bishop could not have known what Sor Juana's response would be, nor could she have foreseen the prelate's cruel desertion. At the heart of their relationship there was something equivocal, something unstated; almost as soon as it came to light, the relationship dissolved. The Bishop's comments brought Sor Juana face to face with the problem of her vocation; that is, with the very meaning of her life. Christ's *finezas* and other theological points faded into the background.

Sor Juana was not long in replying; the "**Carta atenagórica**" appeared at the end of November of 1690, and the "**Response to Sor Filotea de la Cruz**" was dated March 1, 1691. It is a text written in different modes, ranging from that of a legal brief to autobiography to intellectual discourse. Certain passages—a mark of her time and her religious training—are pedantic and interlarded with Latin; others are simple, written in an admirable and fluid familiar prose. In spite of blemishes and lacunae, the "**Response**" is a unique document in the history of Hispanic literature, in which there are few confessions relating to the life of the mind, its illusions and disillusions. Reflection on the solitary adventures of the mind is a theme seldom explored by the great Spanish and Spanish American writers. In this, the "**Response**" departs from the prevailing tendencies of our culture and forms the complement to "**First Dream**": if the latter is the isolated monument of the mind in its hunger for learning, the "**Response**" is the account of the everyday labors of that same mind, told in a direct and familiar language.

The "**Response**" is more than a kind of prose version of "**First Dream**"; it is also, and first of all, a reply to the Bishop of Puebla. That reply, naturally, had to be a defense of secular letters. Sor Juana could not say that they were equal or superior to sacred writing—to say that would have led, ipso facto, to the Inquisition—but she used all her ingenuity to praise secular literature and to demonstrate its value and necessity. She was answering not just the Bishop but all her adversaries and critics. She realized that she was being attacked above all for being a woman, and thus her defense was immediately transformed into a defense of the female sex. To us, this is the part of her brief that is most vital and closest to present-day concerns. Finally, there is an invisible interlocutor with whom Sor Juana is in continual dialogue: herself. All her life she has lived in ambivalence: is she a nun or a writer? As she replies to the Bishop and others, she is writing to herself; she recounts the beginnings of her love of letters, and attempts to explain and justify that love to herself. The contradiction that pervades her life—she says it again and again—is born not of her nature but of circumstances imposed upon her: she was a nun because she had no other choice. But she always fulfilled her religious obligations, and more than twenty years after taking her vows she continued to believe in the compatibility of her two vocations. Any careful reader can perceive on reading those pages that if the "**Response**" was an examination of conscience, Sor Juana emerged from that examination unrepentant. Further, writing that text was a liberating experience that reconciled her with herself. Although its language is cautious and abounding in reservations and parentheses, the final impression is clear: she is not ashamed of what she is or has been. And this is what must have disturbed, pained, and offended men like Fernández de Santa Cruz and Núñez de Miranda.

Sor Juana begins her response with a long and ingenious preamble. She confesses that she was moved when she saw her "scribblings" published, and adds that "when the letter which you saw fit to call *atenagórica* reached my hands, in print, I burst into tears of confusion (although tears do not come easily to me)." The words are less than sincere: surely the Bishop would not have published her critique of Vieyra without her assent. Sor Juana prolongs the fiction by not disclosing the identity of the person to whom the "**Carta**" was addressed; she insists that she wrote it on the order of someone she cannot disobey, and reiterates that she had no hand in its publication. Neither is she sincere when she calls the Bishop's action a favor from God, who is thus chastising her for her ingratitude. She says she has not written much on theological matters, but the entire "**Response**" is specifically intended to explicate and justify that omission! The passage ends with a formal promise: she accepts Sor Filotea's admonition. Although "it comes in the guise of counsel," it will have for her "the force of a precept," and she will dedicate herself to the study of the Sacred Books (a promise not fulfilled, as we shall see). After this humble and conciliatory prelude, she takes up her defense.[2]

Why has she not written more on sacred subjects? The answer is disconcerting: she is not capable of penetrating the subtleties of theology. She invokes the authority of St. Jerome, who recalls that, among the Jews, those dedicated to the priesthood were forbidden to read the Song of Songs "until they have passed thirty years of age . . . in order that the sweetness of those epithalamia not prompt imprudent youth to translate their sentiment into desires of the flesh." Fear of misinterpreting the Holy Scripture often "has plucked my pen from my hand . . . , a scruple I did not find when it came to secular matters, for a heresy against art is punished not by the Holy Office but by the judicious with derision, and by critics with censure." The paragraph is ambiguous; it is clear that she did indeed have sufficient talent to deal with theological abstractions but, just as clearly, she preferred writing plays and sonnets. She affirms that she never wrote "except when compelled and constrained, and then only to give pleasure to others"—a surprising declaration if one recalls the effort she put into having her works published. Immediately, however, she modifies that statement: she says that this "repugnance" for writing refers specifically to sacred matters, and repeats, "I wish no quarrel with the Holy Office." Her true passion has been learning, not literature. The statement must be understood in its true sense: by *learning,* she means not only the sciences and philosophy but what in her time was called humane letters, with classical literature in the forefront.[3]

In the paragraphs that follow she defends not only her passionate dedication to literature but her womanhood:

> From the moment I was first illuminated by the light of reason, my inclination toward letters has been so vehement that not even the admonitions of others . . . nor my own meditations . . . have been sufficient to cause me to forswear this natural impulse that God placed in me; the Lord God knows why, and for what purpose. And he knows that I have prayed that he dim the light of my reason, leaving only that which is needed to keep his Law, for there are those who say that all else is unwanted in a woman.

The "those" referred to are the ones who according to the Bishop were guilty of ignobly "denying women the exercise of letters." Then she makes a remarkable confession, although again she blends the true with the false:

> I have sought to veil the light of my reason, along with my name, and to offer it up only to Him who bestowed it on me, and He knows that none other was the cause of my entering into religion, notwithstanding that the spiritual exercises and company of a community were repugnant to the freedom and quiet I desired for my studious endeavors.

A glaring contradiction: in the first part of the essay she says that in the convent she had wanted to veil not only her name but the light of her reason, which would have meant, specifically, renouncing her bent toward study; in the second part she says that she took the veil even though she knew that life in the convent would hinder her intention to study and read. Here, for the first time, we see a theme that will appear and reappear throughout the course of the "**Response**": the conflict between the vocation of a solitary scholar and the obligations of communal life in a convent.

Sor Juana's confessions do not entirely correspond to reality: she seems to forget how few roads were open to her in 1669. If not the road of the convent, what would her choice have been? A disastrous marriage, like those of her two sisters? Nonetheless, it is true that she entered San Jerónimo knowing that a convent was not the most propitious place for an intellectual like herself. That is why she had hesitated, and confessed her doubts to "only the one who should know," that is, her confessor, Núñez de Miranda. But he did not accept her uncertainty, "saying it was temptation: and so it would have been." A terrible admission that is also a veiled accusation: Núñez de Miranda had told her that it was temptation to want to bury her name and renown, along with her person, in the convent. He had urged her to take the veil, telling her that she could continue her studies without harm to her religious obligations. Surely Sor Juana is speaking the truth. For Núñez de Miranda, the first order of business was to get her into the convent. Later, gradually, he would persuade her to abandon poetry and secular letters and to consecrate herself to the religious life. It is clear that Núñez de Miranda changed during the course of his relationship with Sor Juana: at first he was kind; later, increasingly severe. He was a "fisher of souls," and in order to catch Sor Juana he minimized the conflict between religious life and dedication to study and letters. That is why, faced with her hesitation, he called it temptation. The Jesuit's transformation was the slow product of circumstances. During the long period in which Sor Juana was totally involved in literary affairs, Father Antonio did not overtly express his strong opposition; Sor Juana had become something akin to an official poet, linked to the palace by the double ties of commissions from the court and personal friendship. At the end of the paragraph, Sor Juana writes with true passion: "If it were in my power, my lady, to repay you in some part what I owe you, it might be done by telling you this thing which has never before passed my lips, except to be spoken to the one who should hear it [Núñez de Miranda]." These pained words reveal a private disagreement, until then kept secret, between her and her confessor.[4]

In the paragraphs that follow, she tells of her efforts: of having attended at the age of three "a school for girls we call the Amigas" in Nepantla (she lived in Panoayán, several kilometers away); of her voluntary abstention from eating cheese her favorite treat—because she had heard that it made one "slow of wits"; of her scheme to attend the university dressed as a man; of her readings in her grandfather's library; of having learned grammar, and the punishment she voluntarily inflicted on herself: cutting her hair four or six fingers' breadth and not letting it grow back until she had learned some lesson or other. I referred to these passages in Part Two, interpreting them there. A pity that they are so few, and that Sor Juana skimmed so rapidly over her childhood and youth. The account of her love of study leads again to her reason for having chosen the religious life. This is one of the themes that haunted her thoughts. She confesses that she had felt "a total antipathy to marriage," and that she had deemed life in a convent "the least unsuitable and most honorable I could elect." Hers is a case not of a call from God but of a rational choice: Sor Juana weighs her situation and with a clear head chooses San Jerónimo, in spite of "all the trivial aspects of my nature, such as wishing to live alone, and wishing to have no obligatory occupation that would inhibit the freedom of my studies, or the sounds of a community that would intrude upon the peaceful silence of my books." That is why, she repeats, she hesitated in taking her vows until "certain learned persons enlightened me, explaining that [my wishes] were temptation." Again the theme that she returns to throughout the **"Response"**: for her, although she was aware of the conflict between intellectual and convent life, entering the convent did not entail renouncing humane letters. This conflict was not one of substance but of regimen: the many obligations of the convent made studious concentration next to impossible. The result, naturally, was that her thirst for knowledge was not sated but, rather, intensified: "I brought with me my worst enemy, my inclination, which I do not know whether to consider a gift or a punishment from Heaven, for once dimmed and encumbered by the many activities common to religion, that inclination exploded in me like gunpowder, proving that *privatio est causa appetitus*."[5]

In the convent she continued the pursuit "of reading and more reading, of study and more study." There is bitterness in her account: it is difficult to study without a master. Although her studies were secular, her ultimate goal was to arrive at theology. This, again, sounds to me less than sincere. She herself confesses that if she dwelled so long on the preliminaries, it was "to flatter and applaud my own inclination, presenting its indulgence as an obligation." She explains then that one cannot understand "the style of the Queen of Sciences [theology] if one has not first come to know her servants." Without logic, rhetoric, music, arithmetic, geometry, history, law, languages, astrology, and even the mechanical arts, it is impossible to comprehend passages from Holy Scripture. Sor Juana's plan, aside from its intrinsic difficulty, was superfluous: the highly speculative nature of theology made unnecessary much of the knowledge she speaks of. With the exception of Albertus Magnus, his disciple St. Thomas, and one or two others, no theologian mastered all the sciences of his time. Besides, Sor Juana was too intelligent to believe what she was saying.

Her confidences continue; she tells us that she foundered in the variety of her studies, "having an inclination not toward any one thing in particular but toward all in general." Nevertheless, even in these apparently unstructured readings she held to a certain rhythm, moving from study to enjoyment. Sor Juana is severe with herself: "though I have studied many things I know nothing." This judgment on her method of acquiring knowledge, and its results, could perhaps justify José María de Cossío's opinion that she was a dilettante. Not so; her ideal was many-faceted knowledge. By that I mean that she wanted to be proficient in the themes and sciences central to the culture of her day, in the hope of discerning the links and connections that joined that disparate knowledge into a whole. This was an unattainable ideal in the New Spain of the end of the seventeenth century, although she probably did not know that. She was almost entirely ignorant of the great intellectual revolution that was transforming Europe. In view of that ignorance, her desire becomes even more poignant. Nevertheless, if her information was out-of-date and incomplete—especially in physics and astronomy—her concept of culture was singularly modern. It was the view not of the specialist but of the mind that attempts to discover the hidden links among disciplines. She would undoubtedly have been fascinated by the reasoning of a Lévi-Strauss, who finds hidden analogies between primitive thought and music; she would also have been excited by the ideas of modern linguistics, in which the phonemes and their components fulfill the same functions as elementary particles in physics and blocks of color in cubist painting. In spite of the fact that many of her notions were outdated, the view that modern science—from microbiology to astronomy—has given us of the universe as a vast system of communications would not have surprised her unduly.

After describing her experience with many and diverse disciplines in rather negative terms, in a sudden about-face—a common procedure in her writing—she says the opposite: familiarity with many matters is very advantageous, for "what I have not understood in an author in one branch of knowledge, I may understand in a second in a branch that seems remote from the first . . . And thus it is no apology, nor do I offer it as such, to say that I have studied many subjects, seeing that each augments the other." She invokes as a primary example "the chain the ancients believed issued from the mouth of Jupiter, from which were suspended all things linked one with another." Sor Juana attributes the image to Father Kircher. It comes, as we have noted, from Macrobius, who used it to illustrate the idea of the descending progression from the One to the Multiple: "From the Supreme God even to the fish in the depths of the sea there is one tie, binding at every link and never broken. This is the golden chain of Homer which God ordered to hang down from the sky to the Earth."[6] In the same paragraph, also as if it were taken from Kircher—"in his learned book *De magnete*"—she repeats her favorite maxim: God is at once center and circumference.[7]

When she reaches this point, she ponders her labors: not only has she lacked a teacher, she has had no fellow students. This comment reveals that during twenty years in the convent she has found no one interested in the sciences, letters, or arts. Instead, the nuns have hindered her with their incessant interruptions. The busy and empty life of the convent: unexpected visitors in her cell, constant gossip, songs and laughter from adjacent cells, the servants and their quarrels. A small world possessed by a fever for the trivial. But the difficulties of communal life—she calls them "inevitable and accidental obstacles"—were but a small part of the problems she experienced. In addition to her obligations as a nun, and the chatter and busyness of her sisters, she suffered the persecution of men and women who wanted to prevent her from studying and writing. Among them, the worst were

> not those who persecuted me with open hate and malice, but those who in loving me and desiring my well-being . . . have mortified and tormented me more than those others: "Such studies are not in conformity with sacred innocence; surely you will be lost; surely you will, by reason of your very perspicacity and acuity, grow heady at such exalted heights."

Among these pious persecutors was Núñez de Miranda. Sor Juana was also maligned for her "unfortunate facility in making verses, even if they are sacred verses." This entire passage is written with admirable subtlety. Imperceptibly, she moves from the defense of her hunger for learning to the defense of the art of writing poetry, whether sacred or secular. Thus she asserts, without stating it, her right to read and write on themes that were not religious.[8]

To read is a passive occupation; to write is the opposite of burying one's name in the obscurity of a nunnery: it is to emerge into public view. Eminence, however, always entails penalties: the rule of this vulgar world "is to abhor one who excels, because he deprives others of regard. And thus it happens, and thus it has always happened." The Pharisees' hatred of Christ was born of envy. They killed him "because that is the reward for one who excels." That is why, too, the ancients adorned the figure of Fame, placed on the highest point of their temples, with iron barbs: "the figure thus elevated cannot avoid being the target of barbs." Any superiority, "whether in dignity, nobility, riches, beauty, or knowledge, must suffer this punishment, but the eminence that undergoes the most severe attack is that of intelligence . . . for, as Gracián stated so eruditely, 'a man favored by intelligence is favored by nature.'" Sor Juana then launches into a disquisition on Christ as the victim of envy, although she notes that in her case she has been persecuted not "for my knowledge but merely for my love of learning." That love brought her "closer to the fire of persecution, to the crucible of torment, and to such straits that they have asked that study be forbidden to me." Who would "they" have been—Aguiar y Seijas? Núñez de Miranda? On one occasion they succeeded, and an abbess, "very saintly and ingenuous, who believed that study was a matter for the Inquisition . . . , commanded me not to study." The prohibition lasted three months. This incident illustrates another aspect of Sor Juana's character, one that separates her from her contemporaries and from Hispanic tradition: love of experimentation. Everyday objects, parallel shadows cast by a headboard, the tracings left on the floor by a spinning top—everything she saw and touched served as an excuse for posing questions and attempting to answer them. The kitchen was also her laboratory: "And what shall I tell you, lady, of the secrets of nature I have discovered while cooking . . . ?" And she asks, "What can we, as women, know if not the philosophies of the kitchen?" On the other hand, "had Aristotle prepared victuals, he would have written more." All these struggles, sleepless nights, hardships suffered for love of learning, were they merits? In the case of a man they would be, but not in a woman. No matter; she has been true to her inclination, she "cannot but study." She does not offer a judgment of herself; she leaves that to Sor Filotea.[9]

Although her love of letters was so great that she would not have needed examples to imitate, she always had in mind the names of women who had excelled in human and divine studies. Here begins a long and erudite enumeration embracing famous women of history—poets, philosophers, jurists, and others—from classical antiquity and the Bible to contemporaries such as the Duchess de Aveyro and Queen Christina of Sweden. Among the "learned women" she lists, many belong to pagan times, and to hear the name of some—such as Hypatia, "who taught astrology, and studied many years in Alexandria"—on the lips of a nun is somewhat startling. Hypatia of Alexandria, beautiful and intelligent, virtuous and wise, a Neoplatonic philosopher, was murdered in March of 415 by a band of Christian monks. Sor Juana must have known the circumstances of Hypatia's death, a martyr not to her professed faith but to philosophy. As when she mentions the wife of Simon Magus, the gnostic Ennoia, her admiration for these illustrious women was stronger than fear of going beyond the limits of orthodoxy. Two rival beliefs were at war within her: Christianity and feminism, her religious faith and her love of philosophy. Frequently, and not without risk, feminism and philosophy triumphed. Remarkable courage.[10]

The list of learned women offers her the opportunity to introduce a theme that obsesses her: can women teach and interpret Holy Scripture? It was St. Paul's opinion that they could not: "Let women keep silence in the churches; for it is not permitted them to speak." Basing her argument on the ideas of a Mexican theologian, Dr. Arce, on other authorities, and on her own wit, through a long, circuitous dialectic she reaches the conclusion that women *may* study, interpret, and teach Holy Scripture, with one limitation: they must do so not from the pulpit but in their homes and other private places. She proposes something akin to universal education for women, to be the responsibility of elderly educated women. She argues that women should also be taught the sciences and secular letters. She bases her idea in the reasoning she had expounded at the beginning: direct knowledge of the Scriptures is impossible without the study of history, law, arithmetic, logic, rhetoric, and music. The study of holy books "demands more learning than some believe, who, knowing only grammar . . . cling to that 'Let women keep silence in the churches.'" She scoffs at the idea, current in her day, that women are intellectually inferior. As stupidity is not confined to women, neither is intelligence an attribute only of men.[11]

The long passage on women brings her back to her own case. Why do they attack her? She does not teach or write theology. The **"Carta atenagórica"**? It was not a crime to write it. If the Church did not forbid it, why should others do so? Vieyra's opinions are not articles of faith. Furthermore, she writes with passion, "I maintained respect at all times . . . , and I did not touch a thread of the robes of the Society of Jesus." She complains that one of her critics has been lacking in decorum, and has labeled her letter rash and heretical—"why then does he not denounce it?" But the defense of the **"Carta"** is only one aspect of her brief; she is even more hurt by attacks on her "oft-chastised gift for making verses." She has searched for the harm that could result, and has not found it. She quotes the great poets and poetesses of the Bible and Catholic tradition to demonstrate that writing poetry is not at variance with the religious life. If so many holy women have cultivated poetry, why is what she has written evil? She states with assurance that "no verse of mine has been deemed indecent." (What about the burlesque sonnets and epigrams?) Immediately she falls back on the questionable argument she has repeated throughout the **"Response"**: "Furthermore, I have never written of my own will, but under the pleas and injunctions of others." This gives her the excuse to slip in the information that "the only piece I remember having written for my own pleasure was a little trifle they called **'El sueño'**." Although we have no reason to believe her literally—she surely must have been pleased with much of what she wrote—we can see why she would single out her spiritual autobiography.[12]

The end of the **"Response"** is more rambling: she repeats herself and skips about, as if she could not find a way to end. She persists in her statement that she wrote her critique at the request of someone she could not disobey, and that she had never thought it would be published. The blemishes and lacunae in the **"Carta"** are primarily due to the haste with which it had been composed: several arguments and proofs had been left in her inkwell. She does not venture to remit those "reasonings" directly to Sor Filotea, but "if they should wing your way (and they are of such little weight that they surely will), then you will command what I am to do." So it seems that Sor Juana sent the Bishop other "reasonings" that amplified and rounded out her critique of Vieyra's sermon. Fernández de Santa Cruz did not publish them, however, or even so much as mention them. How are we to judge this devious behavior? As for those who impugn her: others have responded for her; she has seen some of these replies and is sending one that is especially learned. Neither Fernández de Santa Cruz nor anyone else left any information concerning the content or the fate of those writings. Sor Juana continues: the attacks do not discourage her, as they are the price she has to pay for public notice: "calumny has often mortified me, but never harmed me." Having vented her feelings, without much logic, she repeats that she has never published anything of her own will, with the exception of two devotional compositions: **"Ejercicios de la Encarnación"** (**"Exercises for the Incarnation"**) and **"Ofrecimientos de los Dolores"** (**"Offerings for the Dolors"**), two folios that circulated unsigned among the nuns of the city.[13]

Before closing with the customary formulas of respect and gratitude, she makes the Bishop an offer: "If ever I write again, my scribbling will always find its way to the haven of your holy feet and the certainty of your correction." She is undoubtedly referring to theological writings or compositions; clearly she did not propose to send him poems on secular subjects.[14] Thus she ends this remarkable document. The form of her argument is that of a spiral; every advance is a withdrawal. The apparent complexity of her argument can be reduced to a few points: the conflict between religious life and secular study is not one of substance but of regimen; secular studies have always been, and are, steps toward higher and more difficult sacred subjects; the honest practice of poetry is not reprehensible; she claims for herself, and asks for women in general, the chance to be educated in secular as well as sacred literature and science; finally, none of this seems to her to be contrary to the laws of the Church. The **"Response to Sor Filotea de la Cruz"** is not only a confession but a defense of her intellectual bent; Manuel Fernández de Santa Cruz was seeking a retraction, but Sor Juana's answer was a refutation.

Notes

1. I stated earlier that an *Apologia a favor do R.P. Antonio Vieyra* was published in 1727, in Lisbon, signed by an Augustinian nun, Sister Margarita Ignacia. The author of this booklet was actually her brother Luis Gonçalves Pinheiro. Again, pseudonyms and sex changes—unusual symbolic "transvestism."

2. Lines 1-128. (I refer to the line numbers in volume 4 of the *Complete Works.*)

3. Lines 129-183.

4. Lines 184-215.

5. Lines 216-289.

6. Macrobius, chapter 14 of his *Commentary on the Dream of Scipio,* ed. William Harris Stahl. The image comes from the *Iliad* (VIII, 9). It also appears in Proclus.

7. Lines 290-440. Kircher did not write a book entitled *De magnete*. Sor Juana may be referring to *Magnes, sive de arte magnetica* (Rome, 1641), which is Kircher's most extensive study on magnetism. I previously pointed out the origin of the image of God as a circumference: Nicholas of Cusa. The frontispiece of *Magnes* contains, among other images, that of the chain descending from the heavens. This symbol appears in two additional books by Kircher: as a frontispiece in *Magneticum naturae regnum* (Rome, 1667) and in *Mundus subterraneus* (Amsterdam, 1678).

8. Lines 441-532.

9. Lines 533-844.

10. Between Hypatia and Sor Juana there are clear similarities of which she was undoubtedly aware. Beautiful, young, chaste, and learned, both were persecuted by intolerant prelates, although those who victimized the Alexandrian were incomparably more cruel and barbaric. Hypatia was the daughter and disciple of the Neoplatonic mathematician and philosopher Theon. She was perhaps the first woman to excel in the physical sciences: mathematics and astronomy. She lectured in the Platonic school of Alexandria, which rivaled that of Athens, and wrote several scientific treatises, now lost, commentaries on Diophantus, Apollonius of Perga, and Ptolemy. It is probable that, like all Neoplatonists of her day, she combined astronomy with astrology. She was the teacher and friend of Synesius

of Cyrene, Bishop *malgré lui* and author of a famous book on dream, *De insomniis,* which Sor Juana might have read, or known indirectly through quotations and commentaries. Hypatia, friend of another pagan, the prefect Orestes, a rival of the awesome patriarch of Alexandria, St. Cyril, a contentious and bloodthirsty theologian, was the target of the animosity of the groups of fanatic, patriarch-led monks who terrorized the city. One day in 415, during the Lenten season, these monks stopped her carriage, killed the coachman, stripped her of her clothes, and raped her. They then took her to the church, where they tore her body to pieces. Gibbon adds a horrible detail: "Her flesh was scraped from her bones with sharp oyster-shells." Her murder was the beginning of the end of Alexandria's position as the world center of learning. Her fate inspired the ancients. In one of his letters, Synesius speaks of her as "mother and sister, teacher and benefactress in everything and of everyone." A century later the poet Palladas dedicated a poem to her memory (*Palatine Anthology,* IX, 400). In modern times Hypatia has been memorialized by historians, philosophers, and scholars. Gibbon devoted a moving page to her, and the now-forgotten Charles Kingsley made her the heroine of his historical novel *Hypatia; or, New foes with an old face* (1853). Leconte de Lisle wrote two poems in her honor and, more recently, Charles Péguy delivered an exalted elegy of that soul "si parfaitemente accordée à l'âme platonicienne." On the subject of her relationship with Synesius, I cite the essay of H. I. Marrou in *The Conflict Between Paganism and Christianity in the Fourth Century,* ed. Arnoldo Momigliano (Oxford: Clarendon Press, 1963). As in the case of Sor Juana, all these writers speak of Hypatia's beauty and love of learning. Gibbon writes with his customary eloquence, "In the bloom of beauty and in the maturity of wisdom, the modest maid refused her lovers and instructed her disciples." She probably died a virgin, for in the poem Palladas dedicated to her, he sees her as one of the stars in the constellation of Virgo.

11. Lines 841-1150.

12. Lines 1150-1267.

13. They are interesting neither as literature nor as examples of ascetic or spiritual writing.

14. Lines 1267-1432.

FURTHER READING

Bibliography

Crossen, John F. "Sor Juana Ines de la Cruz." In *Catholic Women Writers: A Bio-Bibliographical Sourcebook,* edited by Mary R. Reichardt, pp. 181-86. New York: Greenwood Press, 2001.

Focuses on works emphasizing Sor Juana's theology.

Biography

Paz, Octavio. *Sor Juana or, The Traps of Faith,* translated by Margaret Sayers Peden. Cambridge, Mass.: Belknap Press, 1988, 547 p.

Examines Sor Juana's life and works in their cultural context.

Criticism

Arteaga, Alfred. "Tricks of Gender Xing." *Stanford Humanities Review* 3, no. 1 (winter 1993): 112-29.

Traces subversive elements in Sor Juana's writing style.

Feder, Elena. "Sor Juana Ines de la Cruz; or, The Snares of (Con) (tra) di (c) tion." In *Amerindian Images and the Legacy of Columbus,* edited by Rene Jara and Nicholas Spadaccini, pp. 473-529. Minneapolis: University of Minnesota Press, 1992.

Offers a gender-historical focus on Sor Juana's major works.

Flynn, Gerard. *Sor Juana Ines de la Cruz.* Boston: Twayne Publishers, 1971, 123 p.

Surveys Sor Juana's major works, with a brief biography and a discussion of her philosophy; the first book-length treatment of Sor Juana in English.

Friedman, Edward H. "Sor Juana Inés de la Cruz's *Los empeños de una casa*: Sign as Woman." *Romance Notes* 31, no. 3 (spring 1991): 197–203.

Studies Sor Juana's secular play The Determinations of a Noble House *as a revision of Spanish playwright Calederon's* Los empeños de una casa.

Graves, Robert. "Juana de Asbaje." In *The Crowning Privilege: The Clark Lectures 1954-1955,* pp. 166-75. London: Cassell & Company, 1955.

Presents Sor Juana in the tradition of a "desperate sisterhood" fated by their intelligence and beauty to a life of loneliness.

Henriquez-Urena, Pedro. "The Flowering of the Colonial World: 1600-1800." In *Literary Currents in Hispanic America,* pp. 58-93. Cambridge: Harvard University Press, 1946.

Presents portions of Sor Juana's poems as examples of her personal expression through verse.

Johnson, Julie Greer. "A Comical Lesson in Creativity from Sor Juana." *Hispania* 71, no. 2 (May 1988): 442-44.

Traces the ways Sor Juana adapts and employs conventional images of women and womanhood in her satirical poetry.

Kirk, Pamela. *Sor Juana Ines de la Cruz: Religion, Art, and Feminism.* New York: Continuum, 1998, 180 p.

Studies the intersection of religious belief and feminist beliefs in Sor Juana's work.

Luciani, Frederick. "Octavio Paz on Sor Juana Ines de la Cruz: The Metaphor Incarnate." *Latin American Literary Review* 15, no. 30 (July-December 1987): 6-25.

Critiques Paz's biography of Sor Juana, faulting his tendency to mythologize.

Merriam, Stephanie, ed. *Feminist Perspectives on Sor Juana Ines de la Cruz.* Detroit: Wayne State University Press, 1991.

Collects essays focusing on women's issues and feminist criticism as related to Sor Juana's life and writing.

Pallister, Janis L. "A Note on Sor Juana de la Cruz." *Women and Literature* 7, no. 2 (spring 1979): 42-46.

Promotes a critical rediscovery of Sor Juana's work.

Rabin, Lisa. "The *Blasón* of Sor Juana Ines de la Cruz: Politics and Petrarchism in Colonial Mexico." *Bulletin of Hispanic Studies* 72, no. 1 (January 1995): 28-39.

Discusses the literary and political implications of Sor Juana's use of the blazon in her poetry.

Scott, Nina M. "Sor Juana Ines de la Cruz: 'Let Your Women Keep Silence in the Churches'." *Women's Studies International Forum* 8, no. 5 (1985): 511-19.

Reviews Response to Sor Filotea de la Cruz *as a feminist treatise that reveals Sor Juana's passion for education and women's equality.*

Thurman, Judith. "Sister Juana: The Price of Genius." *Ms.* 1, no. 10 (April 1973): 14-16, 20-21.

Emphasizes the sacrifices made by Sor Juana in order to pursue an intellectual life in the male-centered culture of seventeenth-century New Spain.

Ward, Marilynn I. "The Feminist Crisis of Sor Juana Ines de la Cruz." *International Journal of Women's Studies* 1, no. 5 (September-October 1978): 478-81.

Discusses Sor Juana's life as a tragic instance of sexist repression.

OTHER SOURCES FROM GALE:

Additional coverage of Sor Juana's life and career is contained in the following sources published by the Gale Group: *Feminist Writers; Hispanic Literature Criticism Supplement,* Ed. 1; *Literature Criticism from 1400-1800,* Vol. 5; *Poetry Criticism,* Vol. 24; *Reference Guide to World Literature,* Eds. 2, 3; and *World Literature and Its Times,* Vol. 1.

MARGERY KEMPE

(1373 - 1440)

English autobiographer.

Credited with composing the first extant autobiography in English, Kempe was a self-proclaimed mystic who dictated an account of her spiritual experiences to two scribes in *The Book of Margery Kempe* (c. 1436). This work has been critically evaluated as an autobiography and as an example of medieval mystic literature.

BIOGRAPHICAL INFORMATION

The Book of Margery Kempe offers the only information available about Kempe's life. The work reveals that Kempe was born in King's Lynn (now known as Lynn), an important economic center in Norfolk, and that her father, John Brunham, served as mayor of the town. At age twenty, Margery wed John Kempe, a burgess of Lynn. Following the birth of the first of their fourteen children, Kempe fell ill and for eight months claimed to suffer from terrifying visions. Her cure, she asserted, came in the form of a vision of Christ. Increasingly drawn toward a religious life, Kempe avowed that she heard heavenly music and frequently conversed with Christ, the Virgin Mary, and various saints and angels, by whom she was instructed on a range of matters. Kempe's spirituality was often displayed through actions and observances that were viewed unfavorably by her contemporaries. One such practice was the uncontrollable weeping that possessed her whenever she approached the sacraments or contemplated the Passion of Christ. When she was approximately forty years old, Kempe convinced her husband (by promising to pay his debts for him) to join her in a vow of chastity, and she began a series of pilgrimages to the Holy Land and sacred palaces in Europe. Due to her behavior—including the fits of weeping, her habit of wearing white, and her insistence on the veracity of her visions and mystical conversations—Kempe was publicly ridiculed and tried on several occasions for heresy. She was always acquitted and found to be within the bounds of orthodoxy in her theology. The Archbishop of Canterbury proposed to Kempe that she write down her experiences and revelations, a suggestion that, Kempe claims, was mystically ratified by Christ. Since she was illiterate, in 1436 Kempe dictated her story to a scribe, but following his death, Kempe found that no one could decipher his handwriting. In 1438, a second scribe completed a new transcription based on the first compilation, which the second scribe was eventually able to comprehend.

MAJOR WORKS

For many years Kempe's only known writings were brief excerpts from *The Book of Margery Kempe* printed in the early sixteenth century, and it was assumed that only these fragments survived. In 1934, however, a complete manuscript dating from the mid-fifteenth century was discovered and identified. Although some critics have questioned the scribe's role in the *Book*'s composition and have doubted the authorial integrity of the work, many assert that the manuscript accurately records Kempe's own words. The narrative is told in the third person, an uncommon method of recording firsthand experiences in Kempe's time. The *Book* also differs from most medieval mystical writings in its broad scope. While such works typically focus exclusively on revelatory incidents, Kempe records reminiscences of her travels and daily life as well as her spiritual revelations. These spiritual revelations are, however, presented in the same manner of other religious mystics, such as Saint Bridget of Sweden and Julian of Norwich.

CRITICAL RECEPTION

As the first known autobiography in English, *The Book of Margery Kempe* met with responses that might be predictable for a work that did not fit into any categories then known to readers. The earliest editions of the book demonstrate the critical confusion: in one case, all chapters relating to Kempe's revelations were displaced and made into a separate appendix, and in another, the more mystical chapters were set in a smaller typeface in order to preserve the primacy of the narrative portion of the *Book*. Scholarly commentary has followed suit, with some critics interpreting the *Book* as a work of mysticism in the vein of other medieval mystical writings, and others as an autobiography. Kempe's earliest modern critics found her mysticism overwhelming, categorizing her as neurotic, self-deluded, even psychopathic. Others doubted the validity of her claim to authorship, suggesting that the scribe was truly the author of the book; in fact, the mix of oral and textual discourse in the *Book* has remained a central part of critical debate. Kempe's reliability as a narrator has also consistently been questioned: passionate in the extreme yet not possessed of the ability to pen her own story, Kempe has appeared to some critics as less an author than a character. Among these, Lynn Staley has gone so far as to approach the *Book* as a work of fiction, referring to "Margery" as the protagonist and "Kempe" as the author. Yet if scholars have doubted the veracity of her spiritual experiences as well as her self-presentation, many have nonetheless embraced *The Book of Margery Kempe* as a valuable social history, particularly as it documents the daily life of women in medieval England. Kempe's recent biographer Anthony Goodman (see Further Reading) has suggested that while the *Book* offers only highly selective evidence about the life of medieval women (and women of a particular social class at that), it gives some insight into what was considered acceptable and what was beyond the norm for women at that time, particularly within marriage relationships. Goodman assesses the *Book* as "one of our most valuable documents for English social history." *The Book of Margery Kempe* also reveals a slice of a particular moment in English religious history, and many critics have maintained that Kempe's writing is at its most powerful in this regard. Critics including Staley and Kathy Lavezzo have seen in Kempe's mysticism the potential for subverting patriarchal order, within the male-dominated ecclesiastical hierarchy, within private relationships between men and women, and in the public sphere in general. These scholars have reevaluated Kempe's apparent failings—irregular structures, confusing language, and intense emotionalism—as part of an effective strategy for expressing the disenfranchisement of women and the potential for a feminine subjectivity.

PRINCIPAL WORKS

**The Book of Margery Kempe* (autobiography) c. 1436

* Although this work was originally written c. 1436, it was not published until 1936, when it appeared in a modern English version by W. Butler-Bowden. The first Middle English version was published in 1940.

PRIMARY SOURCES

MARGERY KEMPE (ESSAY DATE C. 1436)

SOURCE: Kempe, Margery. *The Book of Margery Kempe*, translated by B. A. Windeatt, pp. 161-67. London: Penguin, 1985.

In the following excerpt from The Book of Margery Kempe, *written c. 1436, Kempe relates her examination by the archbishop. Kempe addresses the charge that she should refrain from sharing her revelations with others because she is a woman; she also upbraids the clerics who attack her for speaking out, causing many of them to change their minds about her.*

There was a monk who was going to preach in York, and who had heard much slander and much evil talk about the said creature. And when he was going to preach, there was a great crowd of people to hear him, and she present with them. And so when he was launched into his sermon, he repeated many matters so openly that people saw perfectly well it was on account of her, at which her friends who loved her were very sorry and upset because of it, and she was much the merrier, because she had something to try her patience and her charity, through which she trusted to please our Lord Christ Jesus.

When the sermon was over, a doctor of divinity who had great love for her, together with many other people as well, came to her and said, 'Margery, how have you got on today?'

'Sir,' she said, 'very well indeed, God be blessed. I have reason to be very happy and glad in my soul that I may suffer anything for his love, for he suffered much more for me.'

Shortly afterwards, a man who was also devoted to her came with his wife and other people, and escorted her seven miles from there to the Archbishop of York, and brought her into a fair chamber, where there came a good cleric, saying to the good man who had brought her there, 'Sir, why have you and your wife brought this woman here? She will steal away from you, and then she will have brought shame upon you.'

The good man said, 'I dare well say she will remain and answer for herself very willingly.'

On the next day she was brought into the Archbishop's chapel, and many of the Archbishop's household came there scorning her, calling her 'Lollard' and 'heretic', and swore many a horrible oath that she should be burned. And she, through the strength of Jesus, replied to them, 'Sirs, I fear you will be burned in hell without end, unless you correct yourselves of your swearing of oaths, for you do not keep the commandments of God. I would not swear as you do for all the money in this world.'

Then they went away, as if they were ashamed. She then, saying her prayers in her mind, asked for grace to behave that day as was most pleasure to God, and profit to her own soul, and good example to her fellow Christians. Our Lord, answering her, said that everything would go well.

At last the said Archbishop came into the chapel with his clerics, and he said to her abruptly, 'Why do you go about in white clothes? Are you a virgin?'

She, kneeling before him, said, 'No, sir, I am no virgin; I am a married woman.'

He ordered his household to fetch a pair of fetters and said she should be fettered, for she was a false heretic, and then she said, 'I am no heretic, nor shall you prove me one.'

The Archbishop went away and left her standing alone. Then for a long while she said her prayers to our Lord God Almighty to help her and succour her against all her enemies both spiritual and bodily, and her flesh trembled and quaked amazingly, so that she was glad to put her hands under her clothes so that it should not be noticed.

Afterwards the Archbishop came back into the chapel with many worthy clerics, amongst whom was the same doctor who had examined her before, and the monk who had preached against her a little while before in York. Some of the people asked whether she were a Christian woman or a Jew; some said she was a good woman, and some said not.

Then the Archbishop took his seat, and his clerics too, each according to his degree, many people being present. And during the time that people were gathering together and the Archbishop was taking his seat, the said creature stood at the back, saying her prayers for help and succour against her enemies with high devotion, and for so long that she melted all into tears. And at last she cried out loudly, so that the Archbishop, and his clerics, and many people, were all astonished at her, for they had not heard such crying before.

When her crying was passed, she came before the Archbishop and fell down on her knees, the Archbishop saying very roughly to her, 'Why do you weep so, woman?'

She answering said, 'Sir, you shall wish some day that you had wept as sorely as I.'

And then, after the Archbishop had put to her the Articles of our Faith—to which God gave her grace to answer well, truly and readily, without much having to stop and think, so that he could not criticize her—he said to the clerics, 'She knows her faith well enough. What shall I do with her?'

The clerics said, 'We know very well that she knows the Articles of the Faith, but we will not allow her to dwell among us, because the people have great faith in her talk, and perhaps she might lead some of them astray.' Then the Archbishop said to her: 'I am told very bad things about you. I hear it said that you are a very wicked woman.'

And she replied, 'Sir, I also hear it said that you are a wicked man. And if you are as wicked as people say, you will never get to heaven, unless you amend while you are here.'

Then he said very roughly, 'Why you! . . . What do people say about me?'

She answered, 'Other people, sir, can tell you well enough.'

Then a great cleric with a furred hood said, 'Quiet! You speak about yourself, and let him be.'

Afterwards the Archbishop said to her, 'Lay your hand on the book here before me, and swear that you will go out of my diocese as soon as you can.'

'No, sir,' she said, 'I pray you, give me permission to go back into York to take leave of my friends.'

Then he gave her permission for one or two days. She thought it was too short a time, and so she replied, 'Sir, I may not go out of this diocese so hastily, for I must stay and speak with good men before I go; and I must, sir, with your leave, go to Bridlington and speak with my confessor, a good man, who was the good Prior's confessor, who is now canonized.'

Then the Archbishop said to her, 'You shall swear that you will not teach people or call them to account in my diocese.'

'No, sir, I will not swear,' she said, 'for I shall speak of God and rebuke those who swear great oaths wherever I go, until such time that the Pope and Holy Church have ordained that nobody shall be so bold as to speak of God, for God Almighty does not forbid, sir, that we should speak of him. And also the Gospel mentions that, when the woman had heard our Lord preach, she came before him and said in a loud voice, "Blessed be the womb that bore you, and the teats that gave you suck." Then our Lord replied to her, "In truth, so are they blessed who hear the word of God and keep it." And therefore, sir, I think that the Gospel gives me leave to speak of God.'

'Ah, sir,' said the clerics, 'here we know that she has a devil in her, for she speaks of the Gospel.'

A great cleric quickly produced a book and quoted St Paul for his part against her, that no woman should preach. She, answering to this, said, 'I do not preach, sir; I do not go into any pulpit. I use only conversation and good words, and that I will do while I live.'

Then a doctor who had examined her before said, 'Sir, she told me the worst tale about priests that I ever heard.'

The Archbishop commanded her to tell that tale.

'Sir, by your reverence, I only spoke of one priest, by way of example, who, as I have learned it, went astray in a wood—through the sufferance of God, for the profit of his soul—until night came upon him. Lacking any shelter, he found a fair arbour in which he rested that night, which had a beautiful pear-tree in the middle, all covered in blossom, which he delighted to look at. To that place came a great rough bear, ugly to behold, that shook the pear-tree and caused the blossoms to fall. Greedily this horrible beast ate and devoured those fair flowers. And when he had eaten them, turning his tail towards the priest, he discharged them out again at his rear end.

'The priest, greatly revolted at that disgusting sight and becoming very depressed for fear of what it might mean, wandered off on his way all gloomy and pensive. He happened to meet a good-looking, aged man like a pilgrim, who asked the priest the reason for his sadness. The priest, repeating the matter written before, said he felt great fear and heaviness of heart when he beheld that revolting beast soil and devour such lovely flowers and blossoms, and afterwards discharge them so horribly at his rear end in the priest's presence—he did not understand what this might mean.

'Then the pilgrim, showing himself to be the messenger of God, thus addressed him, "Priest, you are yourself the pear-tree, somewhat flourishing and flowering through your saying of services and administering of sacraments, although you act without devotion, for you take very little heed how you say your matins and your service, so long as it is babbled to an end. Then you go to your mass without devotion, and you have very little contrition for your sin. You receive there the fruit of everlasting life, the sacrament of the altar, in a very feeble frame of mind. All day long afterwards, you spend your time amiss: you give yourself over to buying and selling, bartering and exchanging, just like a man of the world. You sit over your beer, giving yourself up to gluttony and excess, to the lust of your body, through lechery and impurity. You break the commandments of God through swearing, lying, detraction and backbiting gossip, and the practice of other such sins. Thus, through your misconduct, just like the loathsome bear, you devour and destroy the flowers and blossoms of virtuous living, to your own endless damnation and to the hindrance of many other people, unless you have grace for repentance and amending."'

Then the Archbishop liked the tale a lot and commended it, saying it was a good tale. And the cleric who had examined her before in the absence of the Archbishop, said, 'Sir, this tale cuts me to the heart.'

The said creature said to the cleric, 'Ah, worthy doctor, sir, in the place where I mostly live is a worthy cleric, a good preacher, who boldly speaks out against the misconduct of people and will flatter no one. He says many times in the pulpit: "If anyone is displeased by my preaching, note him well, for he is guilty." And just so, sir,' she said to the clerk, 'do you behave with me, God forgive you for it.'

The cleric did not know what he could say to her, and afterwards the same cleric came to her and begged her for forgiveness that he had been so against her. He also asked her specially to pray for him.

And then afterwards the Archbishop said, 'Where shall I get a man who could escort this woman from me?'

Many young men quickly jumped up, and everyone of them said, 'My lord, I will go with her.'

The Archbishop answered, 'You are too young: I will not have you.'

Then a good, sober man of the Archbishop's household asked his lord what he would give him if he would escort her. The Archbishop offered him five shillings, and the man asked for a noble. The Archbishop answering said, 'I will not spend so much on her body.'

'Yes, good sir,' said this creature, 'Our Lord shall reward you very well for it.'

Then the Archbishop said to the man, 'See, here is five shillings, and now escort her fast out of this area.'

She, kneeling down on her knees, asked his blessing. He, asking her to pray for him, blessed her and let her go.

Then she, going back again to York, was received by many people, and by very worthy clerics, who rejoiced in our Lord, who had given her—uneducated as she was—the wit and wisdom to answer so many learned men without shame or blame, thanks be to God.

ON THE SUBJECT OF...

JULIAN OF NORWICH

Margery Kempe is often compared to fellow female mystic Julian of Norwich, with whom she was acquainted. Both women were criticized for speaking about religion, a subject on which men claimed scripturally based authority. An excerpt from Julian's "Shewings" of 1373 appears below.

JULIAN OF NORWICH ON WOMEN SPEAKING OF GOD

For God is all that is good, and God has made all that is made, and God loves everything that He has made; and if any man or woman keeps his love from any of his fellow Christians, he does not love rightly, for he does not love all. And so, for that time, he is not safe, for he is not in peace; and he that loves his fellow Christians in general, he loves all that is. For in mankind that is to be saved is comprehended all, that is, all that is made and the maker of all; for God is in man, and so in man is all. And he that thus generally loves all his fellow Christians, he loves all; and he that so loves, he is saved. And thus I will love, and thus I do love, and thus I am safe. For I consider myself as in the person of my fellow Christians. And the more I love of this loving while I am here, the more I am akin to the bliss that I shall have in heaven without end—that is God, who of His endless love willed to become our brother and suffer for us. And I am sure that he that sees it thus, he shall be truly taught and mightily comforted, if he needs comfort.

But God forbid that you should say or take it that I am a teacher, for I do not mean that, no I never meant so. For I am a woman, ignorant, feeble, and frail. But know well, this that I saye; I have it of the showing of Him who is the sovereign teacher. But truly charity stirs me to tell you of it. For I would that God were known and my fellow Christians sped, as I would be myself, to hate sin more and love God more. Because I am a woman, should I therefore believe that I should not tell you the goodness of God, since I saw in that same time that it is His will that it be known? And that you shall see well in what follows, if it is well and truly understood. Then you shall soon forget me, a wretch; and do this so that I do not hamper you—and behold Jesus, who is the teacher of all.

Julian of Norwich. Excerpt from *The Shewings of Julian of Norwich*, pp. 207-08. Edited by Georgia Ronan Crampton. Kalamazoo, Mich.: Medieval Institute Publications for TEAMS, 1994.

MARGERY KEMPE (ESSAY DATE C. 1436)

SOURCE: Kempe, Margery. "Margery Kempe's visit to Julian of Norwich." In *The Shewings of Julian of Norwich,* edited by Georgia Ronan Crampton, pp. 211. Kalamazoo, Mich.: Medieval Publishing Institute, 1994.

In the following excerpt from her Book *Kempe describes her visit to fellow female mystic Julian of Norwich.*

And then she was bade by our Lord to go in the same city to an anchoress who is called Lady Julian. And so she did, and showed her the grace of compunction, contrition, sweetness and devotion, compassion with holy meditation and high contemplation that God had instilled in her soul, and many holy speeches and conversations that our Lord spoke to her soul; and she showed the anchoress many wonderful revelations in order to know if there were any deceit in them, for the anchoress was expert in such things and could give good counsel. The anchoress, hearing this marvelous goodness of our Lord, thanked God highly with all her heart for his visitation, counseling this creature to be obedient to the will of our Lord God and with all her might fulfill whatever he put in her soul, if it were not against the worship of God and welfare of her fellow Christians; for, if it were, then it would not be the moving of a good spirit but rather of an evil spirit. The Holy Ghost never moves anything against charity, and if he did, he would be contrary to his very being, for he is all charity. Also, he moves the soul to perfect chastity, for those living chastely are called the temple of the Holy Ghost. And the Holy Ghost makes a soul stable and steadfast in true faith and right belief. And a man double in soul is always unstable and unsteadfast in all his ways; he that is continually doubting is like the flood of the sea, which is moved and borne about by the wind, and that man is not likely to receive the gifts of God. That creature that has these tokens must steadfastly believe that the Holy Ghost dwells in his soul. And much more, when God visits a creature with tears of contrition, devotion, or compassion, he may and ought to believe that the Holy Ghost is in his soul. Saint Paul says that the Holy Ghost asks for us with mourning and weepings unspeakable, that is to say, he makes us to ask and pray with mournings and weepings so plenteously that the tears cannot be numbered. No evil spirit may give these tokens, for Jerome says that tears torment the devil more than do the pains of hell. God and the devil are forever contraries, and they shall never dwell together in one place. And the devil has no power in a man's soul. Holy Writ says that the soul of a righteous man is the seat of God. And so, I trust, sister, that you are. I pray that God grant you perseverance. Put all your trust in God and do not fear the language of the world, for the more spite, shame, and reproof that you have in the world, the more is your merit in the sight of God. Patience is necessary to you, for in that you shall keep your soul. Much was the holy talk that the anchoress and this creature had in the mutuality of their love of our Lord Jesus Christ the many days that they were together.

TITLE COMMENTARY

The Book of Margery Kempe

KATHARINE CHOLMELEY (ESSAY DATE 1947)

SOURCE: Cholmeley, Katharine. "The Character of Margery's Book." In *Margery Kempe, Genius and Mystic,* pp. 1-14. London: Longmans, Green and Co., 1947.

In the following essay, Cholmeley considers Kempe's Book *both as it represents the era in which Kempe lived and as it reflects the spiritual life of a devout mystic.*

Thirty years ago the name of Margery Kempe was known only to a few who were acquainted with the extracts from her ***Book*** that had been printed by Wynkyn de Worde in 1501. Now, by means of the discovery of the original narrative, she has become to many an intimate. So sincere is she, so frank in her self-revelation, that there can be little about her that we do not know. It is not easy for anyone to describe himself. He is so apt to conceal; to excuse; to seek subterfuge; to judge too hardly or too lightly; but this Norfolk woman, unself-conscious, simple and sincere, tells all she considers ought to be told, however unpalatable it may be.

For some four centuries the manuscript, once the property of the Carthusian Priory of Mountgrace, was in the hands of the Butler Bowden family. This, the only surviving copy of her ***Book,*** remained unread for generations. The small, crabbed script baffled the ordinary reader. Unknown it lay, with all its wealth of detail of everyday medieval life; unread was all it had to tell of the character of English anchorites, monks and friars; undreamed of, all it had to show of the meaning of the Church to the ordinary man and woman of Plantagenet days.

Now, suddenly, by means of it, a gate is opened; and we can walk the roads of Lancastrian England. So vivid, so keen, was Margery's experience of life that she makes us see the things that she saw, to hear the voices that she heard, and to breathe the air that she breathed.

Her narrative is the more remarkable because she herself could neither read nor write. Her ***Book*** was dictated. She could not read it over: ponder, check, and consider its effect; yet she is an unconscious stylist. She has much of the craft of the storyteller. She can in a few vivid words show us a character, give a life-like record of a conversation; or paint a scene. She has an unerring instinct for the thing that matters. She knows what to tell, and how to tell it. We are given a homely vignette such as that in which she describes herself and her husband coming from York, "in right hot weather," she with a bottle of beer in her hand, and he, with a cake in his bosom. We can see the glare, the dusty road, and the heated couple upon it. Her key phrase gives to us the feel of the sun, and the brilliance of the summer sky. She knows the art of description by implication; and her own memory quickens our imagination.

With the lightest touch and the greatest economy of language she can bring before us man, woman or child as a living individual.

A priest, at York, who took exception to the white clothing which she wore, pulled her by the collar of her gown, exclaiming:

"Thou wolf! What is this cloth that thou hast on?"

She stood silent, but some little boys from the monastery school, who overheard, piped up: "Sir, it is wool."

Across the centuries comes the sound of their high, half-laughing voices; we can see their roguish mouths and eyes.

It is difficult to condense or paraphrase her narrative, so excellent is her choice of words. The most moving, the most picturesque, the most telling phrases came to her apparently without effort, and instantaneously, moreover. She could not correct or revise her sentences like a deliberate writer. Who can better her description of the torrid Jordan valley when she tells us that she thought her feet would have burnt for the heat that she felt; who can make anything more pregnant than her statement: "She stood in the same place where Mary Magdalene stood, when Christ said to her, 'Woman, why weepest thou?'" Who, again, can write more poignant a passage than this incident of her sojourn in Rome:

"Another time, as she came to a poor woman's house, the poor woman called her into her house, and made her sit by her little fire, giving her wine to drink in a cup of stone. And she had a little man-child, which sucked a while on the mother's breast; another while, it ran to this creature, the mother sitting full of sorrow and sadness. Then this creature burst all into weeping, as if she had seen Our Lady and her Son at the time of His Passion, and had so many holy thoughts that she could never tell the half, but ever sat and wept plenteously a long time, so that the poor woman, having compassion on her weeping, prayed her to cease, not knowing why she wept.

"Then Our Lord Jesus Christ said to this creature. "'This place is holy.'"

Some singular gift was hers: a gift linked up with her vivid exactness of memory and her intensity of feeling. She who gathers into herself the tender medieval sorrow for the Passion is an invaluable exponent of the outward life of her time. Not everyone who is intent upon the inward is alive to the outer world also; but Margery's eyes were wide open upon them both.

She gives us the freedom of her world. We see the pilgrims setting forth for the Holy Land: sailing from Yarmouth to the Netherlands, journeying overland to Constance, and from thence to Venice, where they prudently bought each their own bedding, and brought the bales on board the great galley, all crisscrossed with rope, as was the way with medieval baggage. We hear the regrettable dispute between herself and a priest, when each laid claim to the self same sheet. We see the company arriving at Jerusalem, Margery riding on an ass, and praying God for His mercy that "as He had brought her to see His earthly city of Jerusalem He would grant her grace to see the blissful city of Jerusalem above, the city of Heaven." We see them following their guides, the Franciscans, the cross-bearer going before, each man and woman carrying a lighted candle, and listening to what the Friars related of Our Lord's suffering in each place.

The pulse of the age is in Margery's ***Book.*** We see old Bristol, with its fair churches and gabled houses; and the cobbled streets through which the Corpus Christi Procession wends its way with flickering candles borne in honour of That at Whose passing the people fall upon their knees. We see the Palm Sunday ceremonies of the time when the Host was carried into the churchyard for priest and people to bow down in adoration; and when the acolyte had knocked at the door with the cross-staff, all would follow in after Him who was hidden in form of bread. We see the unveiling of the crucifix which took place on that day. We gain, though in a heightened form, some notion of the effect of the ceremonial of the Church upon the unlettered, to whom she, in her wisdom, speaks thereby as eloquently as in her liturgy. When the cross-bearer "smote upon the door," and it opened to admit the priest bearing the Blessed Sacrament, Margery saw before her Christ at the gates of Limbo, denouncing the Devil, freeing from bondage the patient longing souls of the righteous.

Likely enough she had seen one of the Miracle Plays of the time, for much was always made of the intensely dramatic and appealing pageant of "The Harrowing of Hell." Satan, scurrilous, blasphemous, seething with hatred, was set over the serenity and majesty of the Redeemer. After a venomous speech to the fellow-devils from his throne, he was alarmed by a cry at the doors of Hell.

> "Attolite portas principes vestras. . . ."
> "Say, what is he, that King of Bliss?"

Swift come the answer:

> "The lord the which almighty is . . .
> For, man that sometime did amiss,
> To his bliss he will bring."

Christ, as Deliverer, then took Adam by the hand, calling him His darling. He blessed him and all the righteous with peace, and bid the Archangel Michael lead them all forth "to joy that lasteth ever."

The Miracle Plays must have had a profound effect upon all who saw them. The scenes of the Faith played out in their own streets must have been as keen and affecting as the experiences of life. The Gospel was not far away, and foreign. Everywhere it was portrayed in carving, painting, and sculpture. With the exception of such plays as *Robin Hood,* its drama was the only drama that the people knew. Margery Kempe, with her great power of love, was more profoundly stirred than most; but her mind is simply a mirror of the devout imagination of the time. The personal knowledge; the intimacy; the adoring sympathetic love of Jesus that show themselves in medieval art and literature, that belonged to the common man and woman, seep in a flood through her.

Margery tells us more of her time than do either Chaucer or Langland. That is to say, her picture is more complete than either of theirs. There is nothing in her ***Book*** equal to the character painting of the Introduction to the *Canterbury Tales.* She seldom gives any detail of dress; she does not call up before us an entire ugly countenance like that of the Miller, whose

> "beard as any sow or fox was red,
> and thereto broad as though it were a spade.
> Upon the cop right of his nose he had
> A wart, and thereon stood a tuft of hairs
> Red as the bristles of a sow's ears.
> His nostrils black were and wide"

and

> "His mouth as wide as was a furnace."

Nevertheless, she has a far wider range than that of Chaucer. We meet with a crowd of personages in her ***Book,*** both ecclesiastical and lay; and each one of the throng, by some deft stroke, by some unerring quality of right observation, stands forth as real as anyone of our acquaintance.

Chaucer, when all is said, is out chiefly to amuse and entertain. He writes chiefly for the folk of Court and manor whose pleasure lay much in somewhat artificial romance: in a dream world of woodland and garden. He is the child of the French poets; and the Roman de la Rose inspired much of his work. His English pilgrims are for the most part figures of comedy. They do not show us England. Chaucer is not giving us the spirit of his age; whereas Margery may with truth be said to do that.

Chaucer pokes fun at the Friar who is out to wheedle alms: the limitour who worked a district, whose "tippet was ay farsed full of knives, and pins, for to given fair wives"

> Of double worsted was his semi-cope,
> That round was as a bell out of the press
> Somewhat he lisped for his wantonness
> To make his English sweet upon his tongue.

That is inimitable in its cleverness, and its soft irony; but it need not be taken as proof that this Franciscan represents the sum total of the Minorites in England. Doubtless there were a fair number of Friars over-anxious to collect money. We can read of them elsewhere. Still, the curious fact remains that Margery, downright and outspoken as she is, does not concern herself with the avarice of the Friars. She tells us what good preachers they were, and how holy.

Again, she has a far wider range than Langland. The hammer of denunciation does not beat through her pages as it beats through those of Piers Plowman; certainly she could denounce when she deemed it necessary. With the bravery that was constantly characteristic of her, she rebuked even the Archbishop of Canterbury for the manner in which the servants of his household swore lightly by holy things. Yet to gaze upon evil; to rebuke evil, was but part of her task. She dwells upon the whole of her experiences, so that we see not only the sinfulness, but also the good, of the society of her day. We see what is perhaps the most important element of all: the ordinary folk: the good-hearted, kindly, wholesome-minded folk who are apt to be taken for granted, whom chronicle and document are apt to ignore because they do nothing extraordinary; who make life sound and sweet wherever they live.

She is chiefly acquainted with the townsfolk, rich and poor, with the middle class most of all. We know well what sort of neighbours were hers at Lynn; what kind of fellow-pilgrims; what manner of acquaintance she encountered on the road. Despite his homespun realism; despite his famous word-picture of the disreputable company at the Tavern, Langland has not Margery's gift for drawing us into the very place described. Despite all his passionate sympathy for the poor and oppressed, he is a little remote. But let Margery speak; and we are by her side in church, or house, or roadway. We do not merely see her world; we enter into it. Every detail that she gives is fascinating in its interest. We know that there can be no possibility of idealisation, of exaggeration or romancing. She tells of life as she knew it. Her outlook is matter-of-fact. The general effect of her narrative is to give to the early fifteenth century a character of soundness, of sanity, and cheerfulness.

There are some writers on the Middle Ages whose commentary makes one feel as though on a journey through a land of rayless gloom; but Margery, who lived at that period, takes one into a sunlit realm. We meet the unworthy priest and religious, it is true; but we are not filled with hopelessness at the sight thereof. There is the lecherous monk whom Margery reproved; who asked her prayers; and who later repented, becoming a worthy sub-prior of his monastery. There are careless clerics like those in the train of the Bishop of Worcester, who aped the silly extravagant dress of the Court dandies; but who, like many others, listened to Margery's reproaches with meekness. Beside the evil-living, the blasphemers, and the worldly, we meet the good and pious in plenty. Of these, some dwell in the cells of anchorites; some wear the religious habit; some are priests; many are simple, open-hearted lay folk.

Though Margery's fellow pilgrims took exception to her, and dubbed her a hypocrite; though she was frequently misunderstood and misjudged, nevertheless, they were not a few, who treated her with the greatest respect, because they held her holy. The society in which she moved was faulty; but it was not diseased. It was, on the whole, a civilised society. It was a Catholic society, one unmistakable mark of which, is the reverence for sanctity. It is not the politician, the money-maker, or even the King, who ranks highest in Catholic lands, but the man whose heart is set on God.

She has not much to say of farm labourers and bondsmen. She makes no reference to the Peasants' Revolt, though many of the aggrieved and embittered men had tramped out from Norfolk towards London. Except for one or two almost casual references, we would hardly know that there was a King in England. She says nothing of the murder of Richard II or of the bruit of Agincourt. We know nothing of her opinion of these things; or even if she deemed them of importance. Wars and politics apparently did not touch her. We hear nothing from her of trouble with the Scots, or of disturbances on the border of Wales. She does not even tell of the bridal journey of Henry IV's little daughter who was to wed the King of Denmark, though the ship set sail from Lynn; and the outfaring of the little Princess must have been a fireside tale for many a day.

She says nothing of the Council of Constance, though she was in that city in 1414; she seems not to be in the least concerned with the conflict between Pope and anti-Pope. To her, there is but the Pope for whom she prays. All else is ignored or held irrelevant.

She is like Langland, in so far, as she is primarily concerned with the relation between God and man. Man has sinned, and God is wronged; but even so, He is ready to pour out an abundance of mercy. This is exemplified in her own personal history. She thirsts after perfection; thirsts for sinners to repent; thirsts that God may be loved.

The specific object of her ***Book*** is to show the mercy of God: "the high and unspeakable mercy of our Sovereign Saviour Christ Jesus" who had drawn her careless irresolute soul to love Him, and had bestowed on her high graces of prayer. All that is written is to be to His honour. To her, her work is a spiritual treatise: a love-story. She had wronged her Love; and that she would make clear: she desires only to draw men to a realisation of His love-worthiness. Her realisation of the Passion was so intense that she saw it as clearly as any scene that came before her bodily eyes. The sorrow of it possessed her more than any sorrow of her own. Bitterly she wept for the pain and sorrow that were endured for unheeding Man's redemption.

The medieval mind, as we find it in the lyrics of Catholic England, had always gazed at the Passion as a thing present, known it as a personal grief. The poet will see the Rood amid the trees of the woodland; and while he looks upon the "wounds five," sing a song "of love-longing"; but in Margery this vision and this grief were intensified to an extraordinary degree.

She was as dominated by the love of Jesus as most of us are by the love of self. She hungered for the conversion of pagans, Jews and Saracens; for the conversion of sinners even unto the end of the world. In days when the doctrine of the mystical Body of Christ was not taught with the clarity of today, she saw Him continually in those about her. In children; in the poor; in the sick; in the wounded, and in the leprous. The Passion was in her very heart; the divine thirst for souls was in her soul.

In make-up, her ***Book*** is somewhat haphazard. There is nothing much by way of a climax. Part I ends somewhat abruptly. Another chapter might well be added. Part II is an account of the pilgrimage made in her old age to the Baltic States. It is even more sudden in its ending. She did not know how to round off her tale. There is little in the way of construction. She recounts incidents as they come into her mind: they are out of order, as she herself explains. It is impossible, at times, to perceive or guess what the right sequence should be. Nevertheless, the ***Book*** is an achievement. There is nothing like it before in English literature. She had no tradition upon which to draw. She has made a new thing.

By means of her own sincerity; her own shrewdness; her own clear-sightedness; she does what no one taught her to do. She makes a self-characterisation as vivid as any portrait by Titian or Rembrandt.

Despite a certain lack of plan, her story is masterly in its direct, straightforward narrative; its clear-cut pictures; its sureness of touch. It rings true in all that is told. She sees with sanity; she remembers with clarity; she describes with shrewd candour and homeliness. She judges without bitterness those who have done her wrong. As literature, it is remarkable for its balance; for its lack of verbiage; for its observation; for the sure eye; the sure speech; the steady judgement. As a spiritual work, it must rank among the highest. There is no strained or artificial language. It shows a soul utterly possessed by the love of Jesus: held by a close intimate love that is so strong that she is ready to suffer for Him the hardest of pain, which is humiliation.

LYNN STALEY (ESSAY DATE 1994)

SOURCE: Staley, Lynn. "The Image of Ecclesia." In *Margery Kempe's Dissenting Fictions,* pp. 83-126. University Park: Pennsylvania State University Press, 1994.

In the following excerpt, Staley focuses on Kempe's representations of women, authority, and church hierarchy, examining instances of Kempe superceding or transcending church authority and observing her emphasis on the inherent importance of women in Christian communities.

Kempe's account of Margery's experience in Rome suggests her appraisal of a Church that cannot recognize an embodiment of its own ideals. Margery is cast out of the congregation of the Hospital of Saint Thomas of Canterbury in Rome by the slander of an English priest "þat was holdyn an holy man in þe Hospital & also in oþer placys of Rome" (80). As Kempe implies, what passes for holy in Rome has less to do with spiritual insight than with worldly pomp. Though his malice deprives her of both a confessor and the eucharist, Kempe provides for Margery a new and compensatory series of relationships that are based upon spiritual understanding. Her account of the first of these relationships is especially curious. Upon being informed of her plight, the priest of a nearby congregation invites Margery to confess to him though he says he does not understand English. Kempe does not say whether or not Margery accepts the invitation; instead, she describes another sort of confession:

> Than owyr Lord sent Seynt Iohn þe Evangelyst to heryn hir confessyon, & sche seyd 'Benedicite.' & he seyd 'Dominus' verily in hir sowle þat sche saw hym & herd hym in hire gostly vndirstondyng as sche xuld a do an-oþer preste be hir bodily wittys. Than sche teld hym alle hir synnes & al hir heuynes wyth many swemful teerys, & he herd hir ful mekely & benyngly. & sythyn he enioyned hir penawns þat sche xuld do for hir trespas & asoyled hir of hir synnes wyth swet wordys & meke wordys, hyly strengthyng hir to trostyn in þe mercy of owyr Lord Ihesu Crist, & bad hir þat sche xulde receyuen þe Sacrament of þe Awter in þe name of Ihesu. & sithyn he passyd awey fro hir.
>
> (81)

Though the preceding description of the non-English-speaking priest implies that Margery is confessing to another human being, what Kempe, in fact, describes here is "priuy shrifte." Margery confesses to herself, or to her private vision of Saint John, is absolved by that same vision, and directed to the sacrament. Kempe's wording insists on the reality of what is a new, spiritual relationship. Margery sees and hears Saint John in her spiritual understanding as she would actually see and hear *another priest.* Kempe's nomination of Saint John as Margery's confessor may owe a debt to the *Revelations of St. Elizabeth of Hungary* where the Virgin presents the Evangelist to Elizabeth as a witness to the private charter between them. Signifying his obedience to the Virgin's spiritual authority as well as his own episcopal and literary authority, Saint John then writes the charter. The scene, however, is devoid of any social commentary or even of any social context. Kempe's use of Saint John links Margery to Elizabeth of Hungary, but it also suggests her ability to exploit incidents she found in the literature of the holy that served her complicated and intentionally ambiguous purposes.[1]

That Kempe is interested in the nature of the confessional relationship is clear from another incident that occurs during Margery's stay in Rome. Seeing a priest celebrate at the church of Saint John Lateran, she believes him to be a good and devout man. She wishes to speak with him, but he is German, and they cannot understand one another. However, they pray for thirteen days, and they are granted a sort of Pentecostal gift: they can understand one another though neither can actually speak the other's language. Bound by their love of Christ, they contract a new society. He forsakes his office to support her, taking her for his mother and his sister, and enduring a good deal of ill-will for Margery's sake. In exchange, Margery grants him her obedience, at his behest changing back into black clothing and serving an old woman for six weeks (see 82-86, 97). Where Margery directly challenges another English priest, who turns against her because she will not obey him, she meekly obeys the German priest because he is good (see 84-85). The relationship between penitent and confessor that Kempe describes is not described in the patriarchal language that defines a hierarchal unit. Instead, Margery is mother and sister to her priest; she is daughter only to Christ.

The subtle way in which Kempe substitutes God for male figures of spiritual authority reveals her awareness that, in describing Margery's life as a type of sexual revolution, she also provides a sharp look at the fundamental weaknesses of the ecclesiastical hierarchy. When Margery first feels the "fire of love" burning in her, God informs her that her private apprehension of him is more important than rituals signifying her conformity to accepted spiritual norms, such as fasting, wearing a hairshirt, saying many paternosters, or telling beads. By assuring her that "thynkyng, wepyng, & hy contemplacyon is þe best lyfe in erthe" (89) and by promising her that she will have more "merit" in heaven from "o ȝer of thynkyng in þi mende þan for an hundryd ȝer of preyng wyth þi mowth" (90), God (or Kempe) gives Margery the freedom of her feelings. God, both here and elsewhere, sounds suspiciously Wycliffite; compare the sentiments of the author of the important sermon "Of Mynstris in þe Chirche," which proclaims:

> For Crist nedude not hise apostlis to risen euermore at mydnyȝt, ne to faste as men don now, ne to be cloþud as þes newe ordris; but al þis is broȝt in by þe feend and fredom of Cristus ordre is left. For Crist wolde þat suche cerymonyes weron takon of hym by mennys fre wille aftur þat þei weron disposude to t[a]ke hem oþur more or lasse. But kepyng of Godus lawe, Crist wolde þat were grownd in his ordre. And Crist wolde teche as nede were chaunghyng of oure cerymonyes; for as God tolde Adam and Ioseph by luytul and luytul what þei schulden do, so Crist wolde telle men of his ordre how þei schulden worche and seruon hym.[2]

Just as the author of this sermon presents Christ as founding an order owing allegiance to no earthly figure, Kempe substitutes God for more conventional figures of spiritual authority. When one anchor bids Margery "be gouernyd" by him, she evades him, saying "sche xulde wete first ȝyf it wer þe wil of God er not" (103). Later, she sends the anchor word that God does not wish her to be so "governed." When Margery is despised by all for her weeping, God himself places the unsympathetic priest under heavenly interdict, "Dowtyr, ȝyf he be a preyste þat despisith the, knowyng wel wher-for þu wepist & cryist, he is a-cursyd" (155). When one such priest is won over to her, Kempe notes, "þus God sent hir good maystyrschep of þis worthy doctowr" (166). By using a term—*maysterschep*—that connotes sexual hierarchy (a term also beloved of the Wife of Bath), to describe the priest's change of heart, Kempe makes it clear that what is at issue here is the very nature of, or foundation of, spiritual authority. She therefore describes God as complicit in Margery's efforts to compensate for ecclesiastical strictures against her. He tells her "þer is no clerk in al þis world þat can, dowtyr, leryn þe bettyr þan I can do" (158). When the church limits her access to knowledge by forbidding Master Aleyn ("by vertu of obedience") to instruct her or to speak with her, God tells her that he is more worthy to her soul than the anchor and, since she now lacks spiritual conversation, he will speak more often with her (168-69). By offering her spiritual love and companionship, God provides Margery with a way around the strictly hierarchical relationship offered by the Church.

What Margery moves toward is a reliance on Christ that finally obviates the need for obedience to any representative of the earthly priesthood. This is nowhere more apparent than in the second part of the ***Book.*** Structurally, the second part seems designed to mirror the first: both parts open with scribal testimonials, recount conflicts rooted in gender roles and conventions, and finally outline the process by which Margery achieves a spiritual enfranchisement that liberates her from the constrictions society imposes on women. Thus, the first part of the ***Book*** ends with a picture of Margery as a fully empowered visionary and writer, a person whose power comes solely from her relationship to Christ. The image offers a sharp contrast to the initial portrait of Margery as a weak, maddened wife, dependent upon an inadequate priest as mediator between herself and God. Kempe begins the second part by pulling us back into the realm of the family and the community, describing Margery's concern for her son's lax living. Through her prayers, he is converted to a more regular life, marries a German woman, and settles down on the Continent. Later, when visiting England in the company of his wife, the son dies and a month later Margery's husband dies. A year and a half later, the son's wife wishes to return to her native Germany, and Margery begins to sense that she should accompany her. What might take another writer many pages to narrate, Kempe accomplishes in one and a half brief chapters. The point of these events is obviously not their effect on Margery, since Kempe never mentions grief and never describes any process of mourning. Kempe, for example, spends far more time describing Margery's fears for her son's spiritual condition than she does describing his death. Instead, the deaths of both son and husband provide the occasion for another type of story, whereby Margery as a sort of holy *pícaro* achieves a final and breathtaking dissociation from her community that places her beyond the reach of male authority.

Kempe begins her account of this last pilgrimage in Margery's church, specifically with a conflict between Christ and Margery's confessor. When Margery wonders whether she should take leave of her confessor and accompany her daughter-in-law home to Germany, Christ answers, "Dowtyr, I wote wel, yf I bode þe gon, þu woldist gon al redy. Þerfor I wyl þat þu speke no word to hym of þis mater" (225-26). Though Margery takes this to mean she will not have to contemplate another sea voyage at her age, she does ask for and receive permission from her confessor to take her daughter to Ipswich. When they are in route to Ipswich, Margery feels commanded to take her daughter all the way home to Germany. What Kempe then goes on to describe is the conflict Margery feels between Christ's command and her confessor's paternal care, "Lord, þu wost wel I haue no leue of my gostly fadyr, & I am bowndyn to obediens. Þerfor I may not do thus wyth-owtyn hys wil & hys consentyng" (227). Christ answers these objections by asserting the primacy of Margery's private feelings, "I bydde þe gon in my name, Ihesu, for I am a-bouyn thy gostly fadyr & I xal excusyn þe & ledyn þe & bryngyn þe a-geyn in safte" (227). That Kempe was aware of the force of these words is clear from the next incident, in which Margery recounts her feelings to a Franciscan she meets in Norwich. This "doctowr of diuinyte" has heard of her holy living and is well disposed to her; he counsels her to obey the voice of God, saying that he believes it is the Holy Spirit working in her. By having this man verify Margery's feelings as the stirrings of the Holy Spirit, Kempe maintains the fiction that Margery is an obedient daughter of Holy Church. But the incident nonetheless points up the difficulties of obeying someone if you do not believe he is right, and Kempe presents Margery as docile only when a priest's reading of a situation agrees with her own. With Christ and a doctor of divinity supporting the trip and only her confessor opposing it, Margery takes ship.

If Margery's final pilgrimage begins with hints of her disengagement from ecclesiastical authority, her return is even more potentially explosive. Kempe first describes Margery as enjoying a triumph in London. Not only does Margery face down her detractors; she also speaks out boldly against the worldly lifestyles of Londoners. Since her devotions make her an unwelcome communicant in the churches of London, she becomes a peripatetic worshiper and a figure of special holiness to the common people:

> . . . sche suffyrd ful mech slawndyr & repref, specyaly of þe curatys & preistys of þe chirchis in London. Þei wold not suffyr hir to abydyn in her chirchys, & þerfor sche went fro on chirch to anoþer þat sche xulde not ben tediows on-to hem.

> Mech of þe comown pepil magnifijd God in hir, hauyng good trost þat it was þe goodnes of God whech wrowt þat hy grace in hir sowle.
>
> (245)

Kempe follows up her account of Margery as a quasi-populist preacher, a potentially radical identity, by describing her as proceeding next to the Carthusian abbey of Shene, which had been founded by Henry V in 1415.[3] Not only was Shene a royal foundation; along with its sisterhouse, the Bridgettine abbey of Syon, Shene was a center for mystical piety during the later Middle Ages and was responsible for the dissemination of devotional texts like those Kempe evokes throughout her own ***Book.*** By locating Margery at Shene during Lammastide (see 245-46), Kempe appears to realign her with the Church and consequently with the spirit of obedience. First, as Kempe twice repeats, Margery goes to Shene to purchase her pardon on the day that was the "principal day of pardon." On Lammas Day, August 1, which was also one of the quarter days for rent-paying, loaves made from the new wheat were consecrated in English churches as signs of the congregation's thankfulness for harvest. On that day, which commemorated the settling of secular and spiritual debts, Margery goes as a devout daughter of the Church to purchase her own pardon. Kempe, however, neglects to detail this particular act of exchange, instead describing two events that focus our attention upon Margery's own assumption of authority: Margery's spiritual direction of a young man who observes her devotions in the church at Shene, and her successful negotiation of the final obstacle standing in her way back to Lynn. While she is in church to "purchase" this pardon, she sees the hermit who had led her and her daughter-in-law out of Lynn to Ipswich. She approaches him about leading her home and learns that her confessor has "forsaken" her because she went to Germany without telling him of her plans. Margery, the renegade penitent, nonetheless manages not only to persuade the hermit to accompany her back to Lynn but also to make peace again with her confessor. The end of the ***Book*** is worthy of Chaucer:

> Whan sche was come hom to Lynne, sche obeyd hir to hir confessowr. He ȝaf hir ful scharp wordys, for sche was hys obediencer & had tekyn vp-on hir swech a jurne wyth-owtyn hys wetyng. Þerfor he was meuyd þe mor a-geyn hir, but owr Lord halpe hir so þat sche had as good loue of hym & of oþer frendys aftyr as sche had be-forn, worschepyd be God. Amen.
>
> (247)

What Kempe describes is a female victory. Though she twice refers to obedience, even calling Margery her confessor's *obediencer,* denoting someone who has vowed obedience to a rule, such as a novice, the nature of that obedience is ambiguous.[4] Now that Margery has returned from her journey, every step of which she determined herself, and from a life as a sort of holy vagabond, preacher, and mystic, she obeys her confessor. Furthermore, as the passage suggests, her confessor is most annoyed because she went without his permission; in other words, because Margery contravened the terms of a relationship based upon hierarchy. Margery, like many an Eve before her, endures his wrath and soothes his ruffled pride. As Chaucer's Merchant gives May Persephone's help when old Januarie confronts her with marital infidelity, so Kempe gives Margery, who has broken her vows, the Lord's help, "so þat sche had as good loue of hym & oþer frendys as sche had be-forn." The "amen," repeated in red at the end of the chapter, helps to muffle the resonating irony of a scene that only appears to validate the authority vested in priests by women who feel compelled to go well beyond the boundaries those men have established for them.

The intercessory prayers with which the ***Book*** ends likewise image Margery as an obedient daughter of Holy Church, but they also suggest that her special relationship with Christ somehow allows her to transcend gender categories. Thus, along with sentences attesting to her charity and piety, there are those that hint at a new understanding of the nature of spiritual authority. Requests like "Lord, make my gostly fadirs for to dredyn þe in me" (249) or "for alle þo þat feithyn & trustyn er xul feithyn & trustyn in my prayerys in-to þe worldys ende, sweche grace as þei desiryn" (253-54) hint that Margery's power extends well beyond that of the churchmen who presume to direct her. What Kempe achieves through the conventional language of intercessory prayer is that same delicately poised ambiguity that characterizes her entire text. For Margery is at once a textbook exemplar of late medieval female piety and a reminder of the essential unruliness of the subjective, the feminine, and its fundamental urge to master those authorities who seek to contain what is, finally, uncontainable.

The comic irony inherent in the reversal of gender roles is, of course, designed to point up the folly of seeking to control the "feminine" with instruments inadequate to the task. If Jankyn will not, then his "book of wicked wives" cannot make order out of hierarchy, particularly when that hierarchy rests on foundations as shaky as the marriage of Jankyn and Alisoun. Through Margery and her comic insurrection, Kempe provides an image of the Church that underscores its inadequacies. Her point, however, is hardly satiric: through Margery she projects a community where harmony is a manifestation of true spiritual authority. Such authority rests on a literal and personal interpretation of the Gospel story, which Kempe presents to us through Margery whose visions and conversations with God mediate the central doctrines and events of Christianity.

What can be described as Kempe's "Passion sequence" (187-99) owes, as Gibson has pointed out, a genuine debt to Love's *Mirror of the Blessed Life of Jesus Christ*.[5] Both sequences heighten the pathos of the Gospel accounts of the Passion by dramatizing scenes of primarily human interest. Thus, the intricate courtroom scenes on which the medieval dramatists expended so much care are not included. Instead of depicting the ironies of law and empire that undergird such public scenes in the mystery plays, both Kempe and the *Mirror* describe extratextual scenes like Jesus' parting from his mother, Mary's terrible grief, the exhaustion and bewilderment of Holy Saturday, and Jesus' appearance to his mother very early on Easter morning. By concluding Margery's experience of the Passion with her apprehension of the Purification, Kempe suggests her awareness that, in privileging the affective piety of Mary and the early followers of Christ in her treatment of the Passion, she foregrounds the feminine. The feast of the Purification, or Candlemas, is, of course, a woman's feast, for it celebrates Mary's offering in the Temple as her thanksgiving for the safe delivery of a male child (see Luke 2:22-35).[6] Rather than the pair of doves required by the law and that Luke recounts Mary and Joseph as offering, Kempe describes Mary as offering only her son, thereby suggesting Mary's awareness that the baby in her arms needs no symbolic pair of doves; he himself will satisfy the law of sacrifice. Kempe then describes Margery as responding to a moment of female ritual: "Sche thowt in hir sowle þat sche saw owr Lady ben purifijd & had hy contemplacyon in þe beheldyng of *þe women* wheche comyn to offeryn wyth *þe women* þat weryn purifijd" (198; emphasis added). Margery weeps because the Passion sequence she has just seen is the denouement of that joyful presentation. Like Mary, she understands the significance of the one act in the light of the other.[7]

However, though Kempe appears at times simply to imitate the affective emphasis of works like the *Mirror,* she, like Julian of Norwich before her, subtly alters a reader's response to these scenes by locating authority in the female beholder.[8] The reader of the *Mirror* is directed by an authoritative male voice to imagine or "behold" these scenes, and is implicitly urged to use the Virgin as her point of reference. In empathizing and identifying with Mary, she participates in the Passion. In contrast to such a prescriptive narrative technique, Julian of Norwich presents herself as the visionary, telling the reader what she saw—how, for example, Christ's body appeared dried out after much time on the Cross in the "dry sharp wynd, wonder colde," of the day of the Crucifixion.[9] Julian thereby focuses our attention on the sight itself, on the pictures she passes on to us, that then demand the sort of highly intellectual analysis she provides for each of her visions. Thus, the picture she evokes of Christ's dried-up flesh is used as a means of understanding his words from the Cross, "I thirst," which as she comes to understand signify both a physical and a spiritual thirst. Julian offers the reader not only the images and scenes she has been privileged to behold, but also the picture of a mind thinking and guiding our understanding of those visions upon which she has spent so many years' efforts. In her presentation of the same scene of sacrifice, Kempe betrays her awareness that she who directs the reader's line of sight governs the reader's response to the act of viewing. The "scribe" describes for us what Margery "sees," using Margery herself as a key participant in the drama of the Passion. Instead of Mary, Margery becomes our focal point. Mary is Margery's point of reference; she empathizes with the Virgin's grief and love in the way the *Mirror* directs its female reader to respond to the pictures the narrator composes for her. But for the reader, the viewer, Margery is the active participant, our spiritual directress. Kempe uses the voice of the scribe in a particularly sophisticated way in such scenes: it appears to function as the narrator of the *Mirror* functions. In fact, however, that voice focuses the reader on Margery herself, whose authority is verified by the reality of vision.

Kempe also suggests the nature of Margery's authority by dramatizing her literal application of the Gospel to her own life. She seeks to imitate Christ's poverty, meekness, self-sacrifice, and charity. Moreover, when the Archbishop of York tries to order her not to "teach" or "challenge" (reprove) people in his diocese, she firmly replies,

> And also þe Gospel makyth mencyon þat, whan þe woman had herd owr Lord prechyd, sche cam be-forn hym wyth a lowde voys & seyd, "Blyssed be þe wombe þat þe bar & þe tetys þat ȝaf þe sowkyn." Þan owr Lord seyd a-ȝen to hir, "For-soþe so ar þei blissed þat heryn þe word of God and kepyn it." "And þerfor, sir, me thynkyth þat þe Gospel ȝeuyth me leue to spekyn of God."
>
> (126)

Though Margery goes on to defend herself against the charge that she preaches, her use of the Gospel as precedent for her actions underlines her increasing reliance on her own, in opposition to ecclesiastical, authority. In fact, her "translation" of the passage (Luke 11:27-28) suggests her presumption of authority, for she does not translate word for word, but "sense for sense." First, she heightens the effect of verse 27 ("sum womman of the cumpany reysinge hir vois") by saying the woman who had heard Jesus preach spoke with a *loud* voice. Second, she recounts Jesus as agreeing with, rather than differing from, the woman's words. Where Luke reads, "*Rathere* blessid ben thei, that heeren Goddis word, and kepen it," Margery uses *forsoþe so,* which implies agreement and not distinction.[10] Since Margery, like the Wife of Bath, seems to have no qualms about validating her own actions by quoting and (mis)translating Scripture, it seems fitting that one good wife should reply to one of Margery's prognostications by saying, "Now Gospel mote it ben in ȝowr mowth" (202).[11] Kempe's characterization of Margery as basing her actions upon a literalist reading of the Gospel would also have had Wycliffite associations for any astute fifteenth-century reader. She thus follows up Margery's audacious use of Scripture with the tale of the bear and the pear tree, a fable that it is unlikely any Lollard preacher would have used. Rather than tell tales, the Lollards, who described themselves as "Bible men," focused on Scripture; mendicants and other popular preachers were more likely to weave stories into their sermons. By inserting the fable into the scene with the Archbishop of York, Kempe contains the effect that Margery's words might well produce by focusing our attention on her faintly scatological tale about the bear whose defilement of a fair pear tree is intended to suggest the need for clerical purity. That the fable, as I have suggested, may have more than a surface relevance adds one more layer of irony to an already dense episode. Kempe could wish for no finer advocate for Margery than Henry Bowet, archbishop of York, whose zeal against the Lollards was well known; she therefore notes his liking of the tale as well as his judicious support for such a Bible-quoting woman. Kempe's strategy here follows a familiar pattern; she at once suggests Margery's own assumption of authority and her assimilation into the patriarchal hierarchy of the contemporary Church. Archbishop Bowet serves Kempe as an official stamp of approval for a protagonist whose words and actions actually indicate her break with all earthly fathers.

It is clear moreover that Margery's "Gospel" is not the Church's, that what Margery is, the Church is not. Margery, with her private visions of the life of Christ (which serve as a type of unauthorized translation), with her certainty that the Gospel provides a precedent for her own provocative life, and with her growing espousal of a literalist interpretation of that Gospel, presents a challenge to a Church whose authority rested on privilege, hierarchy, and the tradition of biblical exegesis and allegory that had defined patristic culture for a thousand years. Kempe characterizes the nature of that challenge by dramatizing the negative effect Margery's strictly regulated behavior has on contemporary churchmen. In particular, Margery's espousal of a doctrine of apostolic poverty would have been seen as a direct threat to a Church that, since the days of Richard II, had sought to defend its secular wealth and privilege from those who wished to see the Church divest itself of temporal goods that compromised its ability to function as a spiritual power.[12] The subject of poverty was also linked to the ongoing controversy about (and within) the mendicant orders, which had long since abandoned a literalist interpretation of Christ's injunction to genuine poverty.[13] It is therefore appropriate that Christ's command to become poor for his sake comes to Margery in Rome, the center of Christian power. Margery, now poor, must, like the original followers of Francis, depend upon the charity of others for her food, clothing, and shelter. As she discovers, not every churchman meets her poverty with goodwill. In losing the safety net her money gives her, Margery loses the nominal respect she is granted by virtue of her social status.

In exchange, however, Margery gains a new community, organized according to a system of relations defined in familial language. Kempe not only suggests the ineffectuality and the harshness of a male priesthood and, in Margery's visions, the male violence visited upon the body of Christ; she also presents Margery as a figure who nurtures

FROM THE AUTHOR

KEMPE DESCRIBES A REVELATION FROM GOD ADDRESSING FEMALE DISCIPLESHIP

At the time that this creature had revelations, our Lord said to her, 'Daughter, you are with child.'

She replied, 'Ah, Lord, what shall I do about looking after my child?'

Our Lord said, 'Daughter, don't be afraid, I shall arrange for it to be looked after.'

'Lord, I am not worthy to hear you speak, and still to make love with my husband, even though it is great pain and great distress to me.'

'Therefore it is no sin for you, daughter, because it is reward and merit instead for you, and you will not have any the less grace, for I wish you to bring me forth more fruit.'

Then the creature said, 'Lord Jesus, this manner of life belongs to your holy maidens.'

'Yes, daughter, but rest assured that I love wives also, and specially those wives who would live chaste if they might have their will, and do all they can to please me as you do. For though the state of maidenhood be more perfect and more holy than the state of widowhood, and the state of widowhood more perfect than the state of wedlock, yet I love you, daughter, as much as any maiden in the world. No man may prevent me from loving whom I wish and as much as I wish, for love, daughter, quenches all sin. And therefore ask of me the gifts of love. There is no gift so holy as is the gift of love, nor anything so much to be desired as love, for love may gain what it desires. And therefore, daughter, you may please God no better than to think continually on his love.'

Kempe, Margery. Excerpt from *The Book of Margery Kempe,* translated by B. A. Windeatt, pp. 84-85. London: Penguin, 1985.

her converts in ways the male-dominated church does not. She therefore describes Margery's male converts as her sons, even when many of these supporters are priests and supposedly have care for her soul. An English priest she meets in Rome who offers to relieve her physical want displays filial piety toward Margery, "mekely he cleped hir modyr, preying hir for charite to receyuen hym as hir sone" (96). When Margery suddenly decides to accompany her daughter-in-law to Germany and is therefore without provisions, the master of her ship provides for her needs and "was as tendyr to hir as sche had ben hys modyr" (231). The young man she encounters in the church at Shene asks her to counsel him in the Christ-like life, saying, "Schewith modirly & goodly ȝowr conceit vn-to me" (246).[14]

Kempe also offers a rather startling picture of the way in which that new community is constituted in a series of phrases intended to preface another incident. Kempe writes, "On þe Fryday aftyr, as þis creatur went to sportyn hir in þe felde & men of hir owyn nacyon wyth hir, þe whech sche informyd in þe lawys of God as wel as sche cowde—& scharply sche spak a-gayns hem for þei sworyn gret othys & brokyn þe comawndment of owr Lord God" (101). Kempe here images Margery as a Lollard preacher, poor for Christ's sake, speaking in the open air against swearing and the taking of oaths, as well as against breaking the laws of God. Thus one Wycliffite sermon notes that it is better to hear God's word and pray than to be encumbered by a wealthy and corrupt Church, going on "and þis is comunly beture doon in þe eyr vndur heuene; but often tyme, in reyny weder, chirchis don good on holy day."[15] As it turns out, rainy weather chases Margery and her group home to shelter, but Kempe nonetheless provides a glimpse of a fellowship that has formed around Margery, a community that is not circumscribed by parochial boundaries. The authority Margery claims for herself and is granted by her listeners derives from her private relationship with God. But the very terms of that private relationship inevitably point up the inadequacies of a Church whose buildings, ecclesiastical households, worldly power and wealth, and frequently self-interested interpretation of Christ's literal commands suggest the need for a new understanding of the nature of spiritual authority.

By using Margery as such a radical figure for charity and devotion, Kempe suggests the ways in which the Church might function as a transcendent (or transnational) community. Despite the fact that she speaks only English, Margery is able to communicate very well with a wide variety of people. Whereas her fellow English scorn her for her tears, the Saracens Margery encounters in the

Holy Land make much of Margery and lead her where she wants to go (75). In Rome, a Dame Margaret Florentyn communicates with Margery by "syngnys er tokenys & in fewe comown wordys" (93). She is invited into a poor woman's house where the sight of a little boy reminds Margery of the love Mary had for her son. Although Kempe records no actual conversation on this visit, Margery nonetheless leaves with Jesus' words in her ear, "Thys place is holy" (94). This gift of tongues is likewise verified in her relations with those foreign priests and confessors she meets in Rome, whose virtue, meekness, and holiness render them capable of communicating with Margery. Finally, Margery herself serves as a figure for translation; she translates into contemporary terms the Christ-like life, just as her private visions translate "her gospel" for the reader. Furthermore, in her handling of the Passion, where the women of Jerusalem step forward to offer Mary their sympathy and to acknowledge that "owr pepil han don hym so meche despite" (195), Kempe implicitly draws a distinction between the "cruel Iewys" (192) who crucify Christ and the women who align themselves with those who follow him, mourn him, and take care of him. Similarly, it is frequently women who come to Margery's aid, offering her food (79), wine in a stone cup (94), compassion for her spiritual sorrow (99), aid in prison (130), or safety when she is on the road. By linking gender to such works of mercy, Kempe adumbrates the character of a new Church that ministers to those in need. Just as Margery is drawn to devotion of the Christ child when she sees the women of Rome carrying male children, so many of the women in the ***Book*** remind us of the ways in which the Church might minister to a world increasingly ruled by economic relationships.

As the bride of Christ, Margery emerges as a figure for a new *ecclesia,* where love, vision, and purity of life are the criteria for authority. The multiplicity of roles that Kempe describes Christ as assigning to the private relations between himself and Margery early in her spiritual career, she elaborates on throughout the ***Book***:

> Þerfor I preue þat þow art a very dowtyr to me & a modyr also, a syster, a wyfe, and a spowse, wytnessyng þe Gospel wher owyr Lord seyth to hys dyscyples, "He þat doth þe wyl of my Fadyr in Heuyn he is bothyn modyr, broþyr, & syster vn-to me." Whan þow stodyst to plese me, þan art þu a very dowtyr; whan þu wepyst & mornyst for my peyn & for my Passyon, þan art þow a very modyr to haue compassyon of hyr chyld; whan þow wepyst for oþer mennys synnes and for aduersytes, þan art þow a very syster; and, whan thow sorwyst for þow art so long fro þe blysse of Heuyn, þan art þu a very spowse & a wyfe, for it longyth to þe wyfe to be wyth hir husbond & no very joy to han tyl sche come to hys presens.
>
> (31)

Kempe here glosses Christ's words about spiritual kinship (mother, brother, and sister) solely in terms of female roles—daughter, sister, mother, and wife—each of which she describes as directed by a special type of love. She goes even farther than some Lollard preachers, who made a point of underlining the centrality of women to the Gospel community. As one sermon notes in reference to this same scriptural passage, "And þus telleþ Crist a sutylte þat is of gostly breþren in God: for be it man, or be it wornman, þat seruep God trewly, he is on þes þre maners knyt to Crist in sybrede," going on to explain that we are Christ's brothers by soul, sisters by flesh, and mothers by both. The explanation ends with, "And þis is betture cosynage and more sotyl þan is of kynde."[16]

By describing Margery as substituting a network of spiritual kinship for a natural or fundamentally literal network, Kempe emphasizes the genuine freedom to be found in a fellowship of "gostly breþren." Where the kinship of "kynde" restricts Margery to roles and activities sanctioned by social hierarchies and expectations, her new and divinely ordained spiritual identity releases her into a new realm of meaning where those roles used to define the limits of womankind become signifiers of a different order. Thus the "mulier fortis" of Proverbs 31, whom the Wycliffite translator(s) renders as "strong woman," was conventionally identified with the Church.[17] Her activities are those writ large of womankind: she is a figure of fruitfulness and nurture, upholding her husband's honor, providing food, clothing, and livelihood for her family, and charity for the poor, blessed, in turn, by her many children. As Theresa Coletti has suggested, the *mulier fortis* may well underlie Chaucer's portrait of the Wife of Bath, whose real and metaphoric barrenness, rampant sexuality, and selfish mercantilism set her in opposition to the common good.[18] When translated, however, out of the realm of the actual, those very activities that delimit woman's sphere of activities in earthly relationships can be used to define the mission and thus the authority of the Church by reference to the feminine. The Wycliffite glosses upon the passage in Proverbs are especially illuminating:

> Cristen doctours expownen comynly this lettre, til to the ende, of hooly chirche, which bi figuratif speche is seid a strong womman; hir hosebonde is

> Crist, hir sones and dou3tris ben Cristen men and wymmen; and this is the literal vndurstonding, as thei seyen; and this exposicioun is resonable and set opinly in the comyn glos. But Rabi Salomon seith, that bi a strong womman is vndurstondun hooli Scripture; the hosebonde of this womman, is a studiouse techere in hooly Scripture, bothe men and wymmen; for in Jeroms tyme summe wymmen weren ful studiouse in hooly Scripture.[19]

The first part of this gloss echoes the conventional explanation for the passage that can be found in the *Glossa Ordinaria*.[20] The second part, which compares the woman to the sacred text, whose "housband" is its student and exegete subtly points up the Wycliffite challenge to conventional authority by stressing that this student may be either a man or a woman. For readers of Chaucer and Kempe, the passage resonates with additional ironies. Chaucer's Wife—the antitype of the *mulier fortis*—who defines herself as the physical text well and carnally "glossed" by Jankyn the clerk, or student, who is her fifth husband, situates herself in opposition to authorities like Saint Jerome, whom she sees as merely constricting the feminine. Kempe, perhaps echoing Chaucer and/or the gloss on Proverbs, likewise defines Margery as the text displayed for confessors and fellow townspeople, ultimately for the reader of her ***Book***.[21] Kempe presents Margery as her own best exegete, even slyly using Saint Jerome, whose reputation for antifeminism was notorious in the Middle Ages, to authorize Margery's assumption of spiritual authority (see 99).

Throughout the ***Book***, Kempe further extends the meaning and the range of female roles and thereby defines Ecclesia's role in contemporary life. Whereas Margery is constricted by her physical role as wife and mother, Kempe's emphasis upon her espousal to Christ and "mothering" of others is meant to underline Margery's translation into the freedom of the metaphoric. Her freedom of movement, her powers of communication and intercession, and her refusal to accept the limits of a hierarchical and conformist society proclaim the message of a radical gospel, a message the women who followed and ministered to Christ indeed bore to their skeptical and temporarily immobile brothers, who took the witness of women as madness (see Mark 16, Luke 24, John 20). As one Wycliffite exegete noted of John's account of the Resurrection, "While men gon awey, stronger loue haþ set þe womman in þe same place." He goes on to use a female figure, Mary Magdalene, as an example of the true preacher, "so must they that han office of preching, that if any sign of heuene is schewed to þem, bisily þey telle it to her nei3boris."[22] Through the transforming power of the Resurrection, female garrulity, or gossip, has become "busy telling," or the Gospel itself. Like other contemporary gospellers, Kempe develops a revolutionary rhetoric, imaging through Margery what she could, perhaps, only image through a woman. The challenge to existing hierarchies she dramatizes in Margery's life is based on cultural assumptions about gender categories, but gender is, finally, the means of expressing what are radical ideas about spiritual dominion.

Notes

1. Bokenham, like Kempe an East Anglian, includes Saint Elizabeth in his *Legendys of Hooly Wummen*; see lines 9607-24 for her devotion to Saint John.
2. *English Wycliffite Sermons*, ed. Hudson and Gradon, 3:362.
3. For a detailed account of the history of this abbey, see F. R. Johnson, "Syon Abbey," in Cockburn et al., *A History of the County of Middlesex*, 182-91; Meech, *The Book of Margery Kempe*, 348-49.
4. According to the *Middle English Dictionary*, *Obediencer* is a late medieval word.
5. Gibson, *Theater of Devotion*, 49.
6. In a paper delivered at the 1992 meeting of the Medieval Academy of America, Gail McMurray Gibson elaborated upon the communal ritual of Candlemas. For a "fictional" account of Mary's Purification that became canonical, see *The Golden Legend*.
7. The N-Town Purification pageant depicts Mary as first laying her son on the altar as a sign of her recognition of his role in human salvation history. It is a more literal-minded figure, the Chaplain, who reminds her that she still must make an offering, the pair of doves required by the Law. For a cogent discussion of the ways in which depictions of the experience of the Virgin are designed to link maternal joy with sorrow, see Gibson, *Theater of Devotion*, 155-66.
8. For work on the "gender-implications" of the gaze, see Stanbury, "Feminist Film Theory: Seeing Chrétien's *Enide*"; idem, "The Virgin's Gaze."
9. See Colledge and Walsh, eds., *The Showings*, the Long Text, chapter 8, 357-59. The quoted passage is on 358.
10. I quote from the *Wycliffite Bible*, ed. Forshall and Madden. Carruthers (*The Book of Memory*, 61) has suggested that such "mistranslations" reflect the medieval way of memorizing sense for sense and that what appear to us as lapses may, instead, suggest the techniques of "memoria ad res." If this is the case in the above passage, it highlights Kempe's internalization of the text as well as the close connection between translation and interpretation. For a discussion of this issue, see pages 133-35; Copeland, *Rhetoric, Hermeneutics, and Translation in the Middle Ages*, 91-95.
11. The prologue to the Wycliffite glossed gospel known as "Short Mark" (London B.L. Additional MS. 41175) defines "gospel" as "good telling." For a discussion of these manuscripts, see Hargreaves, "Popularizing Biblical Scholarship."

12. For a study of apostolic poverty as it relates to English ecclesiastical and political trends, see Aston, "Caim's Castles"; Hudson, *The Premature Reformation,* 114-15, 338-40. See also "The Clergy May Not Hold Property" in Matthews, ed., *The English Works of Wyclif;* "Of Mynystris in þe Chirche," in *English Wycliffite Sermons,* ed. Hudson and Gradon, 2:329-65.

13. See Leff, *Heresy in the Later Middle Ages,* chapter 7; Little, *Religious Poverty,* 177-78.

14. We can find a similar emphasis upon a differently configured "kinship" group in Wycliffite treatises, such as the sermon on Matthew 12 ("here is my mother and my brother") collected in *English Wycliffite Sermons,* ed. Hudson and Gradon, 2:280-81.

15. Ibid., 2:101. Oath-taking was, of course, inimical to the Lollards; see pages 147-50.

16. Ibid., 2:280-81. Atkinson (*Mystic and Pilgrim,* 133-34) also remarks on Kempe's wording, noting Saint Anselm's use of bisexual and multifunctional language.

17. The *mulier fortis* deserves a special note, for she has been translated in ways that adumbrate a history of the feminine. Thus, while the heirs to Wyclif, with a certain stake in privileging the feminine, offer her as a "strong" woman, the Renaissance translators who prepared the Geneva Bible present her as a "virtuous" woman, focusing our attention upon her womanly activities and underlining her obedience rather than her strength or her force as an allegorical figure. The translators of the Douai Old Testament equivocate and use "valiant."

18. Coletti, "Biblical Wisdom: Chaucer's *Shipman's Tale* and the *Mulier Fortis,*" 180-81.

19. Forshall and Madden, *The Wycliffite Bible,* v. Proverbs 31, p. 51.

20. See *PL* 113:1114-16.

21. For the fullest exposition of textual metaphors in relation to the *Book,* see Lochrie, *Margery Kempe and Translations of the Flesh,* especially chapter 3.

22. This passage is taken from the Wycliffite glossed gospel, known as "Short John," MS. Bodley 243.

Works Cited

Primary Texts

Bokenham, Osbern. *Legendys of Hooly Wummen.* Ed. Mary S. Serjeantson. EETS 206. London: Oxford University Press, 1938.

Colledge, Edmund, and James Walsh, eds. *A Book of Showings to the Anchoress Julian of Norwich.* 2 vols. Toronto: University of Toronto Press, 1978.

Forshall, Josiah, and Sir Frederic Madden, eds. *The Holy Bible containing the Old and New Testaments, with the Apocryphal Books in the Earliest English Versions made from the Latin Vulgate by John Wycliffe and his Followers.* 4 vols. Oxford: Oxford University Press, 1850; repr., AMS Press, 1982.

Hudson, Anne, and Pamela Gradon, eds. *English Wycliffite Sermons.* 3 vols. Oxford: Clarendon Press, 1988-90.

Matthews, F. D., ed. *The English Works of Wyclif hitherto unprinted.* EETS 74. London: Oxford University Press, 1880.

Meech, Sanford Brown, ed. *The Book of Margery Kempe.* EETS 212. London: Oxford University Press, 1940; repr., 1961.

Secondary Studies

Aston, Margaret. "'Caim's Castles': Poverty, Politics, and Disendowment." In *The Church, Politics, and Patronage in the Fifteenth Century,* ed. Barrie Dobson. New York: St. Martin's, 1984. 45-81.

Atkinson, Clarissa. *Mystic and Pilgrim: The Book and the World of Margery Kempe.* Ithaca: Cornell University Press, 1983.

Cockburn, J. S., H. P. F. King, and K. G. T. McDonnell. *A History of the County of Middlesex.* 3 vols. Oxford: Oxford University Press, 1969.

Coletti, Theresa. "Biblical Wisdom: Chaucer's *Shipman's Tale* and the *Mulier Fortis.*" In *Chaucer and Scriptural Tradition,* ed. David Lyle Jeffrey. Ottawa: University of Ottawa Press, 1984. 171-82.

Copeland, Rita. *Rhetoric, Hermeneutics, and Translation in the Middle Ages: Academic Traditions and Vernacular Texts.* Cambridge: Cambridge University Press, 1991.

Gibson, Gail McMurray. *The Theater of Devotion: East Anglian Drama and Society in the Late Middle Ages.* Chicago: University of Chicago Press, 1989.

Hargreaves, Henry. "Popularizing Biblical Scholarship: The Role of the Wycliffite *Glossed Gospels.*" In *The Bible and Medieval Culture,* ed. W. Lourdaux and D. Verhelst. Louvain: Louvain University Press, 1979. 171-89.

Hudson, Anne. *The Premature Reformation: Wycliffite Texts and Lollard History.* Oxford: Clarendon Press, 1988.

Leff, Gordon. *Heresy in the Later Middle Ages.* 2 vols. New York: Barnes and Noble, 1967.

Little, Lester K. *Religious Poverty and the Profit Economy in Medieval Europe.* Ithaca: Cornell University Press, 1978.

Lochrie, Karma. *Margery Kempe and Translations of the Flesh.* Philadelphia: University of Pennsylvania Press, 1991.

Stanbury, Sarah. "Feminist Film Theory: Seeing Chrétien's *Enide.*" *Literature and Psychology* 36 (1990): 47-66.

———. "The Virgin's Gaze: Spectacle and Transgression in Middle English Lyrics of the Passion." *PMLA* 106 (1991): 1083-93.

KATHY LAVEZZO (ESSAY DATE 1996)

SOURCE: Lavezzo, Kathy. "Sobs and Sighs Between Women: The Homoerotics of Compassion in *The Book of Margery Kempe.*" In *Premodern Sexualities,* edited by Louise Fradenburg and Carla Freccero, pp. 175-98. New York: Routledge, 1996.

In the following essay, Lavezzo draws on the insights of Freud, French feminist theorist Julia Kristeva, and feminist film theorist Laura Mulvey to explore Kempe's sexuality as depicted in her Book. *Lavezzo considers the tone of Kempe's narrative as a homoerotic and subversive expression of feminine authority, particularly as Kempe envisions predominantly female communities.*

"Don't be ashamed to weep for Jesus . . . Mary Magdalene wasn't ashamed." Mary said this in a breathy whisper and wavered in mild pervasive distortion when Margery visited her grave; she cupped Margery's breasts in her hands. She viewed Margery's nipples as an opportunity to multiply flavor, skin tasting like honey or sugar. . . . Mary was naked beneath the thin chemise of a bathhouse attendant. . . .

—(Gluck, 1994, 62)

After her arrest by the Mayor of Leicester as "a fals strumpet, a fals loller, & a fals deceyuer of þe pepyl" ("a false strumpet, a false Lollard, and a false deceiver of the people"; Kempe 1940, 112), Margery Kempe receives the kind of interrogation one might expect of such a suspect—an inquiry into both her religious and her marital propriety (115-16). But then, unexpectedly, Kempe's heretofore predictable examination takes a remarkable turn, as the mayor tells her "I trowe yow art comyn hedyr to han a-wey owr wyuys fro us & ledyn hem wyth ye" ("I believe you have come here to take our wives away from us and lead them with you"; 116). From querying her fidelity to God and husband, the mayor asserts an attraction between Margery and Leicester's wives. And the mayor is not the only man in ***The Book of Margery Kempe*** to express anxiety over Margery's capacity to draw women from their husbands. Later in the ***Book*** the suffragen to York's Archbishop claims that Margery—yet again apprehended as a heretic—"cownseledyst my Lady Greystokke to forsakyn hir husbonde" ("advised my Lady Greystoke to forsake her husband"; 133).[1] Both Leicester's mayor and York's suffragen bespeak a masculine anxiety over female desire: the likelihood, on the one hand, that behind this mystic's overt claim to love God "a-bouyn al thynge" ("above all things"; 115) lies a covert attachment to women and, on the other, that women find this female mystic appealing—more appealing, according to the Mayor's charge, than their own husbands (115).[2]

The concern these men display over Margery's relation to other women is well founded; behind this medieval woman's "proper" devotion to Christ stands the desire for a far-from-proper reward. The reward Margery seeks—and, indeed, attains—constitutes a powerful and disruptive form of female homoerotic bonding. This bonding emerges in the context of Margery's primary religious practice: her affective mourning for "owyr Lordys Passyon" ("our Lord's Passion"; 39). During her weeping—an activity triggered by any image, such as a crucifix, which recalls Christ's Passion—Margery registers not only her devotion to the suffering Christ, but also her mystical figuration of the most powerful woman in Christianity, the Virgin Mary; as Christ tells Margery in a vision, "I ȝeve þe gret cryis and roryngys for to makyn . . . þat my Modrys sorwe be knowyn by þe" ("I give you great cries and roarings in order that . . . my mother's sorrow may be known through you"; 183). Margery performs her Mary-identified lamentation in an extravagantly emotional fashion: through the "plentyows terys & boystows sobbyngys, wyth lowde cryingys and schille schrykyngys" ("plenteous tears and boisterous sobbings, with loud cryings and shrill shriekings"; 107) that distinguish her piety. Often such extremes provoke the censure of masculine authorities (Lochrie 1991, 186-87); indeed, it is Margery's very compulsion (after seeing a crucifix) to mourn that prompts her arrest by Leicester's mayor (111).

In itself, this medieval woman's compassion is unsurprising, given mourning's long-standing designation in Western culture as "woman's work" (Schiesari 1993, 210). As Louise Fradenburg (1990) and Juliana Schiesari (1993) have demonstrated, women's mourning has typically served patriarchal ends, where the female lamenter "piously" consents to death for the sake of a compensatory masculinist "good," such as a dead soldier's eternal fame, or the sake of the nation (cf. Marcuse 1959, 74-75). For premodern Christianity, such significations often hinged upon a stoic mourning style; for example, church fathers imagined the Virgin possessing a modest grief, bolstered by her faith in the Resurrection. Margery's excessive lamentation diverges from such devotional decorum. The always-emotional Margery challenges patristic theology by portraying Mary as an inconsolable witness to the Passion. But the transgressions that obtain through Margery's mourning consist of more than her failure to signify calmly the "principle of resurrection" (Kristeva 1987, 251); they display one way in which women may have refigured mourning as an erotic and potentially empowering form of female same-sex bonding in late medieval Europe.[3]

Margery was not alone in her somatic piety, as Christian devotion underwent a markedly emotional turn in the late Middle Ages—a transformation rooted significantly in the Franciscan meditative tradition, with its Marian affective piety and literal imagining of the crucified Christ (Gibson 1989, 1-18; Kieckhefer 1984, 106; see also Duffy 1992, 260; Bennett 1982, 59). Neither was Margery unique in provoking ecclesiastical censure, which criticized compassionate excess in art as well as life: "We . . . do not excuse those who portray in pictures or writings how the mother of God fainted upon the earth at the cross, overwhelmed and senseless from pain, similar to those women who, caught up in their sorrow . . . proclaim loudly their misery. . . ." (Hamburgh 1981, 47). As this sixteenth-century condemnation displays, anxiety over depictions of excessive compassion directed themselves not only at literature, but also at the visual arts, a medium epitomizing the late medieval devotional tendency toward vivid images. In speculating that the female homoeroticism represented in Margery's ***Book*** suggests a more general European phenomenon of the late Middle Ages, I will refer to visual representations of the Passion and Lamentation that complement the scenes of female-female bonding in Margery's text. Censure of depictions of an inconsolable Virgin and of actual female mourning practices may have been motivated by precisely the same anxiety over desire between women that lay behind the Mayor of Leicester's condemnation of Margery.[4] As Lochrie observes in her commentary on such attacks, the church criticized representations of an emotional Mary insofar as they "threatened to valorize not only female mourning practices but female mystical practices as well" (187). Even further, these depictions made available an emotional and even erotic vision of a woman, Mary, for consumption by the many women who made up a major component of the audience for Christian artifacts.

While Margery's compassion threatens to supplant the figure of Christ with that of a woman performing her figurative relation to an ever-powerful Virgin Mary, thus displaying a feminine version of the masculinist pleasures of historical identification discussed by Louise Fradenburg and Carla Freccero in this volume, this scenario is made doubly problematic by the extent to which these boisterous tears signify Margery's identification with not only Mary, but also all other Virgin-identified women. Margery's comparison with Bridget of Sweden, whose glorification of Mary bordered on the heretical (Graef 1963, 309), throughout the ***Book***—in which Margery even makes a pilgrimage to the Brigittine convent at Syon—offers just one instance of how Margery's attachment to Mary also implies her identification with other holy women.[5] A metonymic relation between the suffering Virgin Mother and a community of religious women may even have figured as a trope in medieval passion discourses; in a Harley lyric from the Sequence *Stabat iuxta Christi crucem,* Mary constructs a triangulated relation between herself, her son, and "all þo þat to [her] grede, maiden, wif, ant fol wymmon" ("all who call to [her], maidens, wives and foolish women"; Brook 1956; 57, lines 47-48; Stanbury 1991, 1088).

Just as Margery—like the Harley lyric's Virgin—may include a broadly defined female community in the circuitry of suffering between herself and Christ, her boisterous sobbings (40) render Margery herself an object of both female same-sex identification and homoerotic desire. In locating the operations of both identification and desire in the scenes of female affective mourning staged within the ***Book,*** I follow Diana Fuss in arguing for the "the collusion and collapsibility" of these two terms (Fuss 1993, 12). Dismantling the fundamental psychoanalytic law of their independence, Fuss argues for an imbricated relation between same-sex identifications and desires—where, for example, a woman's desire to *be* like another woman may slip into the desire to *have* that woman, or where desire may even underwrite an identification, and vice versa. Thus, by aligning Margery's affective piety with her longing to be Christ's mother, I am pointing to Margery's identification with, and also her desire for, Mary and all other women who share in the Virgin's sorrows. Margery renders herself, through this display of woman-identified sorrow, an object of identification and desire in her own right, available for consumption by other Christian women.

As the triangulated organization of Passion devotion displays, the circulation of identifications and desires between women in the ***Book*** depends on the presence (and frequently the exchange) of a masculine icon—Christ. The *imago Christi* serves in this structure of relations as the *medium* through which Margery enables both her imaginative and her actual bonding with the Virgin Mother and other Christian women. This "traffic in Christ"—to appropriate Gayle Rubin's phrase (1975)—suggests how an inverted version of the homosocial bonding so powerfully discussed by Eve Sedgwick (1985) may have been produced in the context of medieval compassion devotion. It displays how, as Terry Castle has argued, the linkage of two female terms around a single male term effects an "alternate structure" to that of the male-female-male erotic triad—"a female-male-female triangle" that redistributes power to the two female figures, while relegating the male to the passive position of mediator (1993, 72).[6]

It is in arguing for the representation of female homoeroticism in Margery's ***Book*** that I most clearly depart from the ***Book***'s other readings since its discovery in 1934. While some of the most sensitive readers of gender and the construction of the female subject in the ***Book*** discuss Margery's affective identification with Mary, these critics locate only heterosexual desires at work in this text.[7] Neglecting to trace the homoerotic valences of female-female identifications in such artifacts is by no means unusual in medieval scholarship. With a few notable exceptions, scholars have left unexamined the question of desire between women, especially in the context of female affective spirituality, in the Middle Ages.[8] The lack of analyses sensitive to female same-sex desire results, in part, from the fact that the concept of a "lesbian" identity was not articulated in medieval textual culture, and even on those rare occasions when the question of sex between women was addressed, its discussion was at best obscure (Brown 1986, 17; Traub 1992; 1993). The extreme difficulty of exploring female same-sex relations is, in part, an effect of the patriarchal bias of late medieval signifying practices, which aimed explicitly at pushing the female subject outside their discursive boundaries.[9] For example, Jean Gerson's fifteenth-century reference to female sodomy as a sin that "should not be named or written" displays his intention to hide "lesbian" desires from both the eyes and ears of his culture (Brown 1986, 19).

Because medieval heterosexist cultural authorities occluded manifestations of desire between women, my essay engages with a number of modern theories of sexuality—all of which are indebted to and revise psychoanalysis—in an effort to delineate late medieval structures of female same-sex desire. While my methodology risks charges of anachronism, I contend its necessity for a politically engaged feminist inquiry;[10] and I claim that applying modern theories of the sex/gender system to premodern cultural productions does not in fact constitute the strange imposition it may seem to be.[11] If we look to late medieval devotional practices, we find that, notwithstanding attempts by ecclesiastical authorities to deny a voice to same-sex desires, imbedded within medieval religious practices is a tendency for medieval "writers and artists to fuse or interchange . . . genders" that lends itself remarkably well to recent theories of sexuality (Bynum 1991, 114). The fluidity with which ostensibly male and female religious figures were imagined (where Christ could be likened to a mother and Mary to a priest), together with the prominent position cross-dressing and cross-identification played in devotion, suggest how, in the words of Caroline Walker Bynum, "the late Middle Ages found gender reversal at the heart of Christian art and Christian worship" (1991, 92).[12] The medieval Christian perception of gender as not an essential and fixed *category* but an ever-changing and contingent *role* appropriable through identificatory performance, not only stands in uneasy relation to disciplinary discourses such as Gerson's; it also bears considerable similarities to contemporary revisionary gender analyses.[13] If, as Bynum argues, religious thinkers "used gender imagery . . . fluidly" and "put men and women on a continuum," what, we might ask, is there to prevent "queer" identifications and desires from emerging in the context of Christian devotional practices such as Margery's?

While the gender fluidity that generally characterized medieval Christian piety offers us an identificatory field in which a number of "queer" positions could arise in any devotional context during the Middle Ages, the particular trends produced within Margery's East Anglian culture may have especially enabled female-female identifications and desires. Christian women had received an extraordinary amount of prestige in this region of England.[14] East Anglian Osborn Bokenham, for instance, wrote the first all-female hagiographic anthology, whose lives included those of popular local saints such as Margaret, Anne, and Katherine.[15] But above all other Christian holy women, East Anglians revered the Virgin Mary. While England's identification as "the dower of the Virgin" suggests Mary's prominence in the national imaginary, in East Anglia Mariology verged upon a Mariolatry in which Christ's mother may have figured more greatly than Christ himself (Gibson 1989, 138). From the local (and international) renown accorded the Marian shrine at Walsingham, to the preponderance of Marian guilds and confraternities in towns such as Norwich, to the Marian preoccupations of the "N-town" cycle, abundant evidence points to Mary's prominence in Norfolk and Suffolk cultures. The prestige East Anglians allotted Mary would have rendered her an easily accessible object for identification by the region's women,[16] who could identify with Mary not only as Christ's mother, but as an active subject of Christian history in her own right—as, for example, the N-town "Assumption" play attests (Gibson 1989, 168).

At the same time that Mary and other women saints may have served as attractive objects for identification by East Anglian women, the very potential for identification between Christian women was imaginatively accomplished by the female groupings portrayed in East Anglian Christian art and literature—such as the "whole galaxy" of virgin martyrs depicted with such frequency upon rood screens that they outnumber all other saintly groupings on these liturgical "stage sets" (Duffy 1992, 171).[17] The predominance of Mary, together with such portrayals of religious female groups, may very well have reflected as well as produced female-female identification in East Anglia. Figuring in homologous relation to these representations of powerful women and female groups in East Anglian discourses are the two alternative communities of lay women who lived together in fifteenth-century Norwich. While we know little about these *"sorores castitate dedicate"* ("sisters dedicated to chastity"; Tanner 1984, 65) their status as the only groups of their kind known in England suggests that the climate for women gathering together in nontraditional circumstances was especially evident in Margery Kempe's native region.[18] Perhaps, indeed, it was the fear that Margery would "han a-wey" their wives for the purpose of forming such a community that lay behind the Mayor of Leicester's accusation. We can only speculate on what the women in such a community did with each other; perhaps they took their cue from the four allegorical daughters of God represented in the N-town Mary play, whose heavenly parliament, mediating the narrative movement from Mary's Betrothal to her Annunciation, culminates in an exchange of kisses between these women, in which *"osculabunt pariter omnes"* ("all kiss each other"; Merideth 1987, 72).

The rich cultural context I have sketched out, a religious environment particularly conducive to the imagining and production of female communities, suggests how the bonds between women at stake in Margery's devotional practices may have developed out of her native region's spiritual preoccupations. Of course, however prominently women figured in East Anglia, this society was finally patriarchal in character; within this world, as Hope Weissman observes, "Margery's encounters with women authorities . . . occur as decided exceptions" (1982, 202). Yet despite the marginalized position her engagements with powerful women occupy in the ***Book*** with respect to her many encounters with male authorities, Margery's feminine interactions—homoerotic or otherwise—occur more frequently than many readings of the ***Book*** indicate. Moreover, the tearful *means* by which Margery attains both her visionary and actual female homoerotic attachments constitute, in fact, *the* dominant refrain in the text. In an otherwise uneven, nonchronological, and loosely organized "lytyl tretys" ("little treatise"; 1), the spectacular sobs and sighs woven throughout Margery's ***Book*** hold together the text's often confusing mix of worldly adventures, domestic duties, and mystical revelations. Thus Margery's affective mourning exerts a unifying effect that is twofold, binding together both the ***Book*** itself and, at times, the women represented in it. The frequency of her tears suggests, moreover, that while Margery may not consistently succeed in bonding with women in her ***Book,*** she is always—consciously or unconsciously—trying to.

Visual Pleasure and Liturgical Spectacle

As Margery herself puts it, her lamentations take place "specialy on Sundays" (84)—that is, during the Mass, the event in which most late medieval devotional practices occurred (Duffy 1992, 91-130). On the analogous occasion of the "sermownys [which] Duchemen & oþer men" ("sermons [which] German and other men"; 98) preach in Italy during Margery's pilgrimage to Rome and Jerusalem, a tearful outburst results from Margery's failure to comprehend these foreign men's words.[19] With a "mornyng cher for lak of vndirstondyng" ("a sorrowful expression at her lack of understanding"; 98), Margery complains to Christ, who agrees to "preche" and "teche" her personally. Not surprisingly, Christ's preaching constitutes a vision of his Passion, which leaves Margery inebriated with weeping:

> . . . sche turnyd hir fyrst on þe o syde & sithyn on þe oþer wyth gret sobbyng, vn-mythy to kepyn hir-selfe in stabilnes for þe vnqwenchabyl fyer of lofe whech brent ful sor in hir sowle. þan meche pepyl wonderyd up-on hir, askyng hir what sche eyled, to whom sche as a creatur al wowndyd wyth lofe & as reson had fayled, cryed wyth lowde voys, "þe passyon of Crist sleth me."
>
> . . . she turned herself first on one side and then on the other, with great sobbing, unable to keep herself stable because of the unquenchable fire of love burning in her soul. Then many people wondered at her, asking her what ailed her, to whom she, as a creature all wounded with love and as one whose reason had failed her, cried with a loud voice, "The Passion of Christ slays me".
>
> (98-99)

Significantly, while Margery may tell the onlookers that Christ's Passion lies behind her tearful gesticulations, her bodily gestures—as represented in Margery's ***Book***—seem to "say" something else. For while the Passion may stir the "fire of love" in Margery, the spectacle of her pleasure deflects attention away from, not only the "Duchemen" and other male preachers, but also away from Jesus himself to the writhing figure of Margery.

Margery's sobs recall the Virgin Mary's compassion. The affective logic of this moment in the ***Book*** also follows that of late medieval visual representations of the Virgin during the Crucifixion—where, despite Christ's central positioning, the display of a grieving Virgin Mother vies with that of her dead son for attention (figs. 1-3).[20] Just as these distracting images of Mary's sorrow threaten to upstage Christ's Passion narrative, when Margery's copious tears and sensuous tossings and turnings arise, they break the flow of the Mass (and here, the public sermons), calling the service to a halt, and replacing the Christ-centered drama with the spectacle of a woman overcome by the "fire of love."[21] Confronted by Margery's disruptive tears, men in the ***Book,*** such as the Mayor of Leicester, seek to punish Margery; alternately, others seek to rescue her, while still others fetishize her into a reassuring mother figure (see Mulvey 1992, 64). The particular passage cited above, however, specifies no masculine reaction to Margery, only a feminine response. And what this feminine reaction reveals is the attraction—indeed the love—that Margery's rhythmic and autoerotic wellings stir within women: "þe good women, hauyng compassyon of hir sorwe & gretly meruelyng of hir wepyn & hir crying, meche þe mor þei louyd hir" ("The good women, having compassion for her sorrow and greatly marveling at her weeping and crying, loved her much more"; 98). Indeed, the women love Margery so much that "þei, desiryng to make hir solas & comfort . . . preyid hir and in a maner compellyd hir to comyn hom to hem, willyng þat sche xulde not gon fro hem" ("they, desiring to console and comfort her . . . prayed her and in a way compelled her to come home with them, desiring that she should not go from them"; 99).

Just as Margery's affective mourning attracts feminine devotion in this episode, Mary—in the works of Van Ghent and Di Tommi—likewise draws the grieving, loving and even erotic attention of many, if not all, of the women represented in the visual works, each of which depicts the collapsed Virgin supported by two other women,[22] of whom one is grasping the Virgin's breast. The feminine display that so threatens to disrupt the ostensible Christic focus of these visual scenes thus involves not merely Mary's grief, but also the compassionate and potentially erotic attentions of the women about her. In these representations of individual women fondling Mary's breast, we might locate an emphasis on Mary's body and her sexuality akin to that which Leo Steinberg claims was placed upon Christ (1983). Of course, Mary's breasts here possess multiple iconographic significations—among them, her intercessory role, which Mary assumed by virtue of her breasts, which nursed Jesus (Lane 1984, 7). But alongside such theological meanings, I would argue, the representation of one woman caressing another's breast in these artifacts also carries with it a sexual referent—as representations of the body always at least potentially do—especially given the erotically charged source of much Marian breast iconography, the Song of Songs (Mundy 1981-1982).[23]

In the same way that her son's suffering presumably produced Mary's compassion in the Passion representations, Margery's mystical experience begins with a visionary communication with Christ. But the product of this mystical dalliance signifies a feminine self-reflexive pleasure or *jouissance* which triggers a narrative of "primary intensity"—a melodrama of sorts—between Margery and the women around her, a scene of feminine bonding akin to that which the Passion depictions dramatically visualize (Rich 1983, 192). These pleasurable sobs draw attention from the German preachers and even from Christ—the ostensible object of Margery's contemplation—to the homoerotic desires circulating between Margery herself and the women who love her.

Holy Babies, Phallic Mothers

While the Mass, with its emphasis upon the Passion, most frequently leads to Margery's tearful outbursts, another common stimulus for Margery's excessive weeping—any image of the baby Jesus—results from the connection medieval culture drew between Christ's passion and his infancy (Kieckhefer 1984, 106-107; Sinanoglou 1973). In the same way that the birth and death of Christ were linked, for example, by diptychs juxtaposing the Madonna with the Man of Sorrows and by spiritual writers such as St. Bridget of Sweden (Blunt 1973, 245), Margery swathes Jesus "wyth byttyr teerys of compassyon, hauyng mend of þe scharp deth þat he schuld suffer" ("with bitter tears of compassion, mindful of the painful death that he would suffer"; 19) during a vision in which she serves as both Mary's and her baby's handmaiden (Keickhefer 1984, 106-107; Kempe 1940, 265-66). To move Margery, the baby need not be Jesus himself: while witnessing a poor woman with "a lytel manchylde sowkyng on hir brest" ("a little baby boy sucking on her breast"; 94) Margery bursts "al in-to wepyng, as þei sche had seyn owr Lady and hir sone in tyme of hys Passyon" ("into weeping, as though she had seen our Lady and her son during the time of his Passion"; 94). Just as Margery's tears during the Mass episode described above evoke the loving attention of her female witnesses, her sobs before the impoverished nursing mother lead to "þe powr woman hauyng compassyon of hir wepyng" ("the poor woman having compassion over her weeping"; 94). A similar trajectory obtains in the extraordinary passage below, in which Margery encounters a number of women with a "child," who share her devotion to the baby Jesus. The suggestive moment occurs during Margery's travels from Jerusalem to Rome, via Venice and Assisi, with a fellow pilgrim, a woman possessing a curious devotional doll modeled "aftyr our Lord":

> þer came too Grey Frerys & a woman þat cam wyth hem fro Ierusalem, & sche had wyth hir an asse þe whech bar a chyst & an ymage þerin mad aftyr our Lord. . . . And þe woman the which had þe ymage in þe chist, whan þei comyn in good cityes, sche toke owt þe ymage owt of hir chist & sett it in worshepful wyfys lappys. & þei wold puttyn schirtys þerup-on & kyssyn it as þei it had ben God hym-selfe. &, whan þe creature sey þe worshep & þe reverens þat þei dedyn to þe ymage, sche was takyn wyth swet deuocyon & swet meditacyons þat sche wept wyth gret sobbyng & lowde crying.
>
> there came two Grey Friars and a woman that came with them from Jerusalem, and she had with her an ass which bore a chest and an image therein fashioned in the image of our Lord. . . . And the woman who had the image in the chest, when they arrived in great cities, took the image out of her chest and set it upon distinguished wives' laps. And the women would put shirts upon it and kiss it as though it were God himself. And, when the creature saw the worship and the reverence that they gave to the image, she was seized with such sweet devotion and sweet meditations that she wept with great sobbing and loud crying. (77-78)

As Bynum observes, practices such as these women's attentions to the Christ-child were not uncommon among both the medieval female laity and religious, who "acted out maternal . . . roles in the liturgy, decorating life-sized statues of the Christ child for the Christmas creche" (1991, 198; Schlegel 1970). According to Bynum, such behavior signifies one way medieval women "simply" took "ordinary nurturing roles over into their most profound religious experiences" (1991, 197). If we apply Bynum's understanding of these practices to the "worshepful wyfys" in Margery's ***Book,*** we might call them precisely what she calls the fifteenth-century "nuns and beguines" who engaged in decorating a cradle for the liturgy: "just little girls, playing with dolls!" (198).[24]

If the wives are in fact regressing to the role of girls "playing with dolls," what is it that little girls do when they play with dolls? According to what Margaret Homans has called "the social imperative to measure all women's activities by their suitability to motherhood" (1986, 27), the "proper" cultural interpretation of this activity presumably would be that, through their doll-playing, girls playfully foreshadow what their sexual identity as women inevitably will demand of them: marriage and child-rearing.[25] The women would then be using the Christ doll for the same reason that they supposedly have a baby—as a "penis substitute," the fantastic fulfillment of their desire "to appropriate for (themselves) the genital organ that has a cultural monopoly on value" (Irigaray 1985, 87). However, Freud himself stresses an important difference between little girls playing with dolls and women having babies. In his essays on femininity and feminine sexuality, Freud contends that, while playing with dolls is often viewed as an indication of the first stirrings of femininity within a child, this activity in fact has little to do with the "proper" passive role which distinguishes the female subject from her masculine counterpart (1963, 205). According to Freud, the very active attention little girls give their dolls—much like the caressings and dressings which the wives lavish on the Christ doll—is not directed toward any masculine object, but to the original feminine object of their affection: their mothers. That is, when little girls play with their dolls, they play with their mothers, albeit indirectly. On the question of a daughter's sexual aims regarding her original maternal object, Freud argues that, although part of a girl's libido passively enjoys being suckled, fed, and cleansed by her mother, another part of the child's energies actively mimics, in play, her sexually charged passive experiences (1963, 205). Thus, identification with and desire for the mother merge in the girl's doll-play, as the girl routes through the doll (in Freud's words) "the exclusiveness of her attachment to her mother, accompanied by a total neglect of her father-object" (1963, 206; see also Freud 1973, 128; Fuss 1993).

Applied to the episode from the ***Book,*** Freud's scenario shows how what may seem to be a locale for "worshep & . . . reverens" aimed at Christ makes a space for the representation of an attachment to a woman. The women are recalling a pre-Oedipal phallic sexuality, directing through the doll the original maternal object of their affection. But the doll here functions not solely as a conduit for the ladies' original maternal desires; it enables the condensation of a number of female same-sex fantasies. As the doll is not just any doll, but an image "mad after owyr Lord," it figures also as a means by which the wives, taking such good care of baby Jesus, perform their identification with and desire for *his* holy mother, the Virgin Mary.[26] Moreover, even as the doll enables the wives to perform their individual attachments to both their mothers and "owyr Lady," its fondling and passage from wifely lap to wifely lap additionally renders it a medium through which these women homosocially bond. In sharing the doll, the women perform a kind of traffic in Christ; endowing this Christic commodity with a symbolic exchange value through their feminine labor, their "worshep & . . . reverens," the wives refigure Christ as the bearer of feminine needs and desires.[27]

While the doll's function in the ***Book*** suggests how a passivized Christ could enable female homoeroticism, Margery herself speaks of no such possibility, telling the reader only that the women kiss the doll "as though it had been God himself." Registering only her identification with the ladies, she explains that:

> sche was meuyd in so mych þe mor as, while sche was in Inglond, sche had hy meditacyons in þe byrth & þe childhode of Crist, & sche thankyd God for-as-mech as sche saw þes creaturys han so gret feth in þat sche sey wyth hir bodily eye lych as sche had be-forn wyth hir gostly eye.
>
> she was moved so much the more since, while she was in England she had high meditations on the birth and the childhood of Christ, and she thanked God forasmuch as she saw these creatures had as much faith in what she saw with her bodily eye as she had before with her spiritual eye.
>
> (78)

Yet Margery's own somatic response to the women tells us something else—that she not only identifies with the ladies' maternal devotion to Christ, but may indeed also imagine *herself* as the object of the wives' attentions. Of course, the affectionate "worshep & . . . reverens" which the ladies lavish upon the Christ doll can effect no "response" from that inanimate object. But the wives' attentions do cause a proliferation of sweet tears in Margery, so that it seems that it is not the fetishized doll but the body of Margery herself that receives their caresses. Moreover, by means of her sobs, this fantasy is realized, literally, by Margery:

> Whan þes women seyn þis creatur wepyn, sobbyn & cryen so wondirfully & mythyly þat sche was nerhand ouyrcomyn þerwyth, þan þei ordeyned a good soft bed & leyd hir þerup-on & comfortyd hir as mech as þei myth for owyr Lordys lofe, blyssed mot he ben.
>
> When these good women saw this creature weeping, sobbing and crying so wonderfully and mightily that she was nearly overcome by it, they prepared a good soft bed and laid her upon it and comforted her as much as they could for our Lord's love, blessed may he be.
>
> (78)

Here Margery not only turns from spectator into spectacle, but also shifts from her position as an imagined recipient of feminine attention to its outright object. Through her sobs, Margery compels the women to abandon the doll, turn to her, put her to bed, and provocatively "[comfort] hir as mech as þei myth." We cannot know exactly how the ladies comfort Margery; yet the playful and affectionate prelude to this moment, as well as its bedroom setting, may suggest that the woman assuming the doll's position may have received from the wives kisses like those originally directed at the Christ-child.

While the Christ doll passage in Margery's ***Book*** illustrates one site in medieval culture for the playful production of roles both pious and proper, it also illustrates the capacity for the displacement, at that very same site, of these roles. Just as the Christ-child's presence legitimates the women's gathering, conferring a pious and proper motivation upon their congregation, its position as passive and commodified object for exchange allows for a homosocial relation among the women.[28] And the intrusion of Margery's tears adds a provocative twist to this situation, whereby attending to the image of the Christ-child ends in attending to another woman.[29]

Envisioned Compassions

Invariably, Margery's mystical revelations prompt her affective piety: it is earlier visions of Christ's infancy that amplify Margery's somatic response to the ladies' behavior in the Christ-child episode (78), and, similarly, it is Christ's voice "sownding in her sowle" ("sounding in her soul"; 98) that produces Margery's spectacular sobs during the Mass. While Margery's contemplations always constitute the hidden spiritual referent for the visible tears and cries that enable bonds between women, the Passion-centered world of Margery's visionary experience itself also serves as a mystical locale for feminine bonding. Margery offers the most extensive account of her visions of the Passion in chapters 78 to 81 of her ***Book,*** where she describes the "gostly syghtys" ("spiritual visions"; 190-91) that occur primarily during Lent. Margery's visions offer a detailed and often gory imagining of Christ's suffering that departs significantly from the Gospels, and instead realizes popular medieval meditations on the Passion, such as Nicholas Love's *Myrror of the Blessyd Lyf of Christ,* a translation of pseudo-Bonaventure's *Meditationes Vitae Christi* now ascribed to Giovanni de Caulibus (Sticca 1988, 196 n.13). Love's vernacular text, authorized by the Archbishop of Canterbury, Thomas Arundel, constituted part of the church's attempt to at once produce and control private devotion during a time of rising lay literacy. As Sarah Beckwith and Elizabeth Salter note, the "ideological function" of such vernacular works lay precisely in their capacity to mitigate the effects of Lollard heresies by textually "stage-manag[ing]" the reader to identify compassionately with a suffering Christ (Beckwith 1986, 45). To a certain extent, Margery's text seems to realize the aims of church authorities: for example, after having envisioned Christ's "betyng . . . & bofetyng" ("beating and buffeting"), Margery imagines him telling her "Dowtyr, þes sorwys & many mo suffyrd I for þi lofe, & diuers peynys . . . þu has great cawse to luyn me ryght wel" ("Daughter, these sorrows and many more I suffered for your love, and diverse pains . . . you have good reason to love me very much"; 190-91).

Yet, just as Margery's vision seems influenced by the *Myrror* in much the way authorities such as Arundel might have hoped, it also reflects and elaborates upon aspects of Love's text (and works like it) in ways that the church may not have desired. For Love "stage-manages" the spectator to identify not only with Christ, but also with other "characters in the drama" he outlines (Bennet 1982, 54). The dramatic direction which especially affects Margery is the appeal Love makes to his reader on the Sabbath following Christ's death: "And thou also by deuoute ymaginacioun, as thou were there bodily present, comfort our lady and that other felauschippe, prayenge hem to ete somwhat, for 3it they ben fastinge" ("And also by devout imagination, as if you were physically present there, comfort our Lady and that other fellowship, imploring them to eat something, for they are still fasting"; Love 1992, 256; cf. Kempe, 335 n. 195/7). In addition to carrying out literally Love's entreaty, making "for owr Lady a good cawdel" ("for our Lady a good hot drink of gruel and spiced wine"; Kempe 1940, 195), Margery extends Love's notion of comforting and identifying with Mary throughout her vision, in which Margery serves as the Virgin's handmaiden (190). Moreover, it is Mary with whom Margery most closely identifies in her Passion visions, which consistently balance images of Christ's suffering with the exchange of tears between the Virgin and Margery.

As we have seen, Margery's desire to be with Mary, to serve and to share sorrows with her, is not confined to this passage, but surfaces throughout the ***Book.*** And when this desire arises in Margery's visions, it almost always coincides with Christ's legitimating presence—as it does in the ***Book***'s eighty-sixth chapter, where Christ, enumerating the many things Margery has done to merit his gratitude, lists Margery's practice of keeping both him *and* his mother as bedfellows: "And also, dowtyr, I thank þe for all þe tymys þat þu hast herberwyd me & my blissyd Modyr in þi bed" ("And also, daughter, I thank you for all the times that you have harbored me and my blessed Mother in your bed"; 214).[30] Apparently, this line was a bit too provocative for one (presumably) Carthusian annotator of Margery's ***Book,*** who wrote beside it in the Butler Bowdon manuscript's margin the word "gostly" or spiritual (Kempe 1940, xxxvi). Significantly, Christ consistently figures in his triadic relation with Margery and Mary as a passive presence: as a helpless baby, a grown man suffering the Passion, or a lifeless body deposed from the Cross.[31] In Margery's vision of the Passion, for example, while she and the Virgin actively exchange sorrows, both women are repeatedly beholding a Christ who is both passivized and infantilized:

> & [he] went forth ful mekely a-forn hem al modyrnakyd as he was born to a peler of ston & spak no worde a-geyn hem but leet hem do & sey what þei wolde . . . & than hyr thowt owr Lady wept wondir sor. And þerfor þe sayd creatur must nedys wepyn & cryin whan sche sey swech gostly sy3tys in hir sowle as freschly & as verily as 3yf it had ben don in dede in hir bodily syght, and hir thowt þat owr Lady & sche wer al-wey to-gedyr to se owr Lordys peynys.
>
> And he went forth very meekly before them all mother-naked as he was born to a pillar of stone and spoke no words against them but allowed them to do and say what they wished . . . and then she thought our Lady wept wondrously sorely. And therefore the said creature had to necessarily weep and cry when she saw such spiritual sights in her soul as freshly and as truly as if they had actually happened before her physi-

> cal sight, and she thought that our Lady and she were always together to see our Lord's sufferings.
>
> (190)

Unrestrainedly weeping, the Mary depicted in Margery's vision conflicts with the stoic Virgin, unique to her sex, often emphasized by Marian scholarship (see Coletti 1993); rather, Mary signifies here as a woman with whom Margery identifies and homosocially shares sorrows over a suffering Christ. The women's inability to help Jesus gives rise to the exchange of grief between them: as Mary tells Margery, she "must nedys suffyr it for (her) Sonys lofe" ("must needs suffer it for [her] Son's love"; 189). Yet while the Passion ostensibly must be endured for the love of Jesus, it also—with the passivization and infantilization that accompany it in the ***Book***—becomes something that "must nedys" be so that Margery and Mary can get together, sighing and sobbing over the helpless body of Jesus.

Just as the Passion of an infantilized Christ, "al modyr-naked as he was born," enables Margery to mourn with the Virgin Mother, the Lamentation of Christ's lifeless body similarly occasions the embrace of loss among women. This emotionally charged scene focuses initially upon Mary, and then broadens to the women around her, whom the Virgin gives leave to fondle Christ's limp limbs, lavish them with kisses, wash them with tears:

> . . . And þan owr blisful Lady bowyd down to hir Sonys body & kyssyd hys mowth & wept so plentyuowsly ouyr hys blissyd face þat sche wesch a-wey þe blod of hys face wyth þe terys of hir eyne. An þan þe creatur thowt sche herd Mary Mawdelyn seyn to owr Lady, "I pray ȝow, Lady, ȝyf me leue to handelyn & kissyn hys feet, for at þes get I grace." Anon owr Lady ȝaf leue to hir & all þo þat wer þer-abowte to do what worschip & reverns þei wold to þat precyows body. And a-non Mary Mawdelyn toke owr Lordys feet & owr Ladijs sisterys toke hys handys, þe on syster on hand & þe oþer sister an-oþer hand, & wept ful sor in kissyng of þo handys & of þo precyows feet.
>
> . . . And then our blissful Lady bowed down to her Son's body and kissed his mouth and wept so plentifully over his blessed face that she washed away the blood upon his face with the tears from her eyes. And then the creature thought that she heard Mary Magdalene say to our Lady, "I pray you, Lady, give me leave to handle and kiss his feet, for I get grace from them." At once our Lady gave leave to her and all those who were there thereabout to perform what worship and reverence they desired to that precious body. And at once Mary Magdalene took our Lord's feet and our Lady's sisters took his hands, the one sister one hand and the other sister another hand, and wept very sorely in kissing those hands and those precious feet.
>
> (193-94)

Margery's vision of the Lamentation reflects the influence of the *Meditationes,* as it describes both Mary supporting Christ's head in her lap and Mary Magdalen holding "the feet at which she had formerly found so much grace" (1961, 342); a striking realization and extension of this dramatic scene occurs in Giotto's famous *Lamentation* (1305-1306; fig. 4). Depicting four women surrounding, handling and grieving over Christ's body, this visual piece, like Margery's ***Book,*** portrays women assuming an active mourning role.[32]

Like the Christ doll, the body of Christ in the Lamentation is passivized, constituted less by anything Christ actually does than by what is done to him. That is, the power the Christic object represents is not intrinsic to itself, but is, rather, conferred upon it by the women, whose tears, caresses, and kisses invest the Christ-doll as well as the dead Christ's body with meaning. Through this investment in a passivized Christ, the women resignify his body as object for their own desiring ends, crucially resisting, at least for the duration of their performance, subordination to masculine power structures.[33] Instead of demonstrating the exalted acceptance of Christ's sacrifice prescribed by patristic theology, the women around the dead Christ spectacularly and sensuously sob, exploiting the lack embodied by Christ as well as their own gendered relation to the dead (Kempe 1940, 74-75). In opposition to a serene consent to death, which would presumably generate symbolic capital in a patriarchal economy, the feminine erotic exhibition of tears in Margery's vision produces an alternate form of symbolic capital (or, to use Kathryn Bond Stockton's term, "anti-capital") in an alternate economy of feminine desire (Stockton 1992, 348). Now appropriated as a fetishized commodity exchanged among women, the Lord's lifeless body is passed to Mary, then offered by Mary to the Magdalen, and finally extended to Mary's two sisters, uniting all four women around their communal object of desire.

As I have argued in this essay, ***The Book of Margery Kempe*** suggests how we might rethink Christian women's mourning, as an active and empowering practice. Whether mediated by the figure of a passivized Christ, or dispensing with that third Christic term entirely, the female homoeroticism produced at the site of female lamentation constitutes a disruptive act in which the proper turns improper, and the pious strays into the perverse. Moreover, as a cultural artifact, Margery's ***Book*** offers us compelling grounds for resisting the kinds of theological hermeneutics which often dictate that medieval texts such as ***The Book of Margery Kempe*** must be interpreted only in terms of the extent to which the spiritual subjects they produce are heretical or holy.[34] We need instead a more flexible definition of medieval spirituality, where devout ends mingle with and possibly serve as a legitimizing cover for other, less decorous and patriarchal ends; where, to turn to one final example from ***The Book of Margery Kempe,*** a woman's imagining of heaven, as described by Christ, suggests a version of the afterlife that is predominantly female: "I xal take þe be þe on Hand in Hevyn & my modyr be þe oþer hand & so xalt þu dawnsyn in Hevyn wyth oþer holy maydens & virgynes. . . ." ("I shall take you by the one hand in Heaven and my mother by the other hand, and so shall you dance in Heaven with other holy maidens and virgins. . . ."; 53). Picturing the afterlife as a kind of alternate female community—as a group of women dancing, united through the medium of Christ—Margery suggests, yet again, that behind her Christic devotions lies the longing for a very feminine, and very pleasurable, reward.

Notes

1. Elizabeth, wife of John of Greystoke, was in the process of divorcing her husband (Kempe 1940, 317 n. 133).

2. Following Valerie Traub's use of the word in her analysis of early modern "lesbian" desires, I will refer to the female same-sex desires represented in *The Book of Margery Kempe* as "homoerotic," a term which usefully falls between the modern category of the lesbian and premodern masculinist interpellations of the sodomite (Traub 1993, 69).

   Although no women in the *Book* express the desire to renounce their spouses for Margery, some wish that Margery "not gon fro hem" (99). Other women, moreover, want Margery to perform as their children's godmother (94).

3. A contemporary parallel to this enabling form of mourning may be found in Douglas Crimp's work on AIDS (1988), which promotes an "active alternative to the personal, elegiac expressions that appeared to dominate the art-world response to AIDS" (15). For a summary of readers who reject Margery's mystical practices as empowering, see Harding (1993), who argues for the subversiveness of Margery's mysticism.

4. Cf. Sedgwick (1990, 136-41); Rambuss (1994); and Stockton (1992). We may also note here the Dresden Madonna's pivotal role in Freud's famous Dora case, before which Dora "remained two hours . . . rapt in silent admiration" (Freud 1974, 116; see Fuss 1993), as well as the possession of "two photographs of the Sistine Madonna" by Olive Chancellor and Verena Tarrant in Henry James's *The Bostonians* (1945, 301). My thanks go to Harry Stecopoulos for giving me this latter citation.

5. See Kempe (47 and lxi); on Syon, Gibson (1989, 20-21).

6. Christ's "commodification" as a medium for feminine homosocial bonding displays yet another way that, as Sheila Delany (1975) first noted, the precapitalist market organization of late medieval England—in which "small scale commodity production for exchange" predominated—informs Margery's structures of feeling (Aers 1988a, 14). Here we might consider how Margery's Passion devotion fantastically resolves the problems the market posed for her (a woman whose precapitalist ventures as a brewess and miller—always failed). For readings after Delaney on the market's influence on Margery's spiritual and secular endeavors, see Atkinson (1983); Beckwith (1986); Aers (1988a); and Ellis (1990).

7. In her fine study, Lochrie, while acknowledging that Margery "makes known the Virgin's sorrow," subordinates this Marian referent to "the text of (Mary's) sorrow"—Christ (1991, 193), and thus neglects to consider how such a reading may indeed rewrite the Passion drama in the way that I suggest. Two readers who do foreground Margery's Marian identifications in their important studies of the *Book,* David Aers and Hope Weissman, nevertheless interpret this association in terms of Margery's fantasy of at once regaining her virginal purity and playing the role of mother (Aers 1988a, 104-106; Weissman 1982, 211). While not specifically discussing identification with the Virgin in popular devotional literature, Sarah Beckwith notes that such texts encourage female readers such as Margery to play various domestic roles, including that of mother, in relation to Jesus (1986).

8. The exceptions include scholars such as Judith Brown (1986), E. Ann Matter (1986; 1989), and Bruce Holsinger (1993).

9. Just as androcentric culture forbids woman access to its figurative language, this very discourse is grounded upon her identification with that which is not figurative, that is, the literal; see Homans (1986, 1-39).

10. The endeavor to understand the late medieval period the way its authorities intended it to be understood, risks, as Fradenburg puts it, "confusing 'the Middle Ages' with the ways in which the Middle Ages (mis)represented itself to itself" (1989, 75).

11. Traub has played a groundbreaking role in displaying how "historically distant representations of female desire *can* be correlated, though not in any simple or linear fashion, to modern systems of intelligibility and political efficacy" (1993, 62; 1992).

12. My use of Bynum here is ironic, as her assertion forms part of an overall argument about how medieval and modern readers *differ*: "For all their application of male/female contrasts to organize life symbolically, medieval thinkers used gender imagery more fluidly and less literally than we do" (1991, 108). On Bynum and sexuality see Rambuss (1994) and Biddick (1993).

13. I am thinking here of the work of Butler, Sedgwick, and Fuss. See also Goldberg, who claims a similar gender/sexual fluidity in the Renaissance (1994a, 227).

14. See Hope Emily Allen's introduction to the Butler-Bodown manuscript (Kempe 1940).

15. "The Holy Matriarch" St. Anne enjoyed a strong cult following in Norfolk (Gibson 1989, 82-84; Duffy 1992, 181-83). On Bokenham see Delany (forthcoming).

16. I refer to women such as Anne Harling, who commissioned a series of stained-glass windows depicting Mary's Joys and Sorrows for an East Harling church in the 1460s. Harling's gift asserts both her identification with Mary as well as Harling's own power in determining the devotional imagery within her parish. As Gibson suggests, many of the windows' details suggest their intended consumption by a female audience (1989, 101).

17. The virgin martyrs depicted on the screens are enlisted for their powers by Margery herself (52; *cf.* Duffy 1992, 176).

18. Both communities were in Norwich: an unknown number of sisters lived for roughly fifteen years in St. Swithin's parish, while another group of two or three lived from 1442 to 1472 in St. Laurence's parish (Tanner 1984, 65). As the tenement in which the latter community dwelled was owned by a Low Countries' native—the center of Beguine movement—these East Anglian communities may have been affiliated with beguinages (Tanner 1984, 65).

19. On Margery's foreign influence, see Allen's preface to the *Book* (Kempe 1940, liii-lxii).

20. Among the details that draw the viewer's eye to Mary are her eye-level placement near the bottom of each work, as well as the inclination of Christ's head, directing the viewer's gaze down and to the left of the picture, where Mary is situated. See also the *Crucifixions* of Master Hans in Vienna and the Venetian School (Meiss 1951, Plate 92; Sticca 1988).

21. My reading of Margery here reflects and revises Mulvey's analysis of woman's visual presence in Hollywood narrative film (1992). I assume a broad and flexible understanding of the terms "drama" and "performance." In referring to the Mass as a "Christ-centered drama," I recall Hardison (1965, 78). The imbrication of liturgical drama with explicitly dramatic forms—such as Corpus Christi plays—that were themselves performed within or near the very churches in which the Mass took place suggests how a late medieval Christian such as Margery may well have viewed her church as a stagelike site for spectacular impersonation. See also Honorius of Autun, quoted in Hardison (1965, 39-40), and Duffy (1992, 19-22).

22. This arrangement presumably follows the Virgin and her sisters' (the two Mary's) traditional positioning to the left of the cross.

23. Commenting on this feminine version of the emphasis on Christ's sexual organ, which Steinberg himself notes (1983, 127-30; quoted in Bynum 1991, 330), Bynum writes, *contra* Steinberg: "[t]here is reason to think that medieval viewers saw bared breasts (at least in painting and sculpture) not primarily as sexual but as the food with which they were iconographically associated" (1991, 86). But in response to such claims I would ask, with Richard Rambuss, "why should we turn away from regarding the body as always at least potentially sexualized, as a truly polysemous surface where various significances and expressions—including a variety of erotic ones—compete and collude with each other in making the body meaningful?" (1994, 268).

24. Bynum is here describing what she thinks "anyone who has stood before the lovely beguine cradle on display in the Metropolitan Museum in New York . . . and realized that it is a liturgical object must have thought, at least for a moment" (1991, 198).

25. For example, Bynum writes that "devotional objects . . . came increasingly in the fourteenth and fifteenth centuries to reflect and sanctify women's domestic and biological experience" (1991, 198).

26. The devotion of the fourteenth-century Dominican nuns of Toess, who constructed during Advent a "kind of a doll house . . . [which] contained a bath tub in which to bathe a figure of the infant," similarly displays female identification with a woman (Mary) as mother (Berliner 1946, 268).

27. A visual analogue to the Christ child's mediatory function in the *Book* can be found in the Master of the Passion's *Entombment* (1380-1385; Barasche 1976, 85). Behind Christ's sarcophagus, one woman (presumably Mary) puts her face near Christ's own visage while another places one hand upon his crotch. But even more suggestive for my purposes are the two women crouching before his sarcophagus: as one woman holds Christ's arm, another, huddled beside her, half covers her eyes as she looks intently over Christ's limp limb into the eyes of the smiling woman near her. The dead Christ's arm's placement between the women's heads vividly demonstrates his body's positioning as a medium for female bonding. One thousand years before the *Entombment,* in a letter from Church Father Saint Augustine to his sister, there appears an ironic gloss for the structure of desire represented in the painting: "It is not by touch alone, but also by feeling and sight, that a woman desires and is desired. Do not claim to have chaste minds if you have unchaste eyes, because the unchaste eye is the messenger of the unchaste heart; and when unchaste hearts reveal themselves to each other by a mutual glance, even though the tongue is silent, . . . chastity flees from the character though the body remain untouched. . . ." (1956, 5: 45). If looking can express the lust between a man and a woman, what prevents the exchange of looks between two women from being interpreted similarly? Later in the letter, Augustine implicitly refers to "lesbian" love when he warns his sister, a nun, that "the love between you [nuns], however, ought not to be earthly but spiritual," at once opening the field of desire beyond the realm of genital contact and acknowledging the possibility that an "earthly" love between women could occur there (although, of course, he frames his acknowledgment of desires between women in prohibitive terms).

28. The role of censorship as that which both leads to and is outwitted in condensation, is displayed by the simultaneously enabling and legitimizing presence of Christ in the doll scene, as well as the other moments in the *Book* analyzed in this essay (*cf.* Freud 1960, 170-73).

29. Both episodes from the *Book* analyzed thus far take place in Italy during Margery's pilgrimage there and in Jerusalem. Other scenes of female-female bonding in the *Book* take place in England (where Margery is accused of luring wives from their husbands). See

especially ch. 53, 130-31. But as the two moments analyzed here are perhaps the most provocative, I would like to offer two reasons why this might be the case. Firstly, much of what contributed to Margery's devotional practice came from Italy—above all the enormously influential piety of the Franciscans. Secondly, pilgrimage's figuration in medieval Christianity could also explain why versions of the female homoerotics that occur in Margery's mystical visionary life are realized in the space of pilgrimage. Perceived as a center of devotion, where both miracles and a strengthening of faith occur, pilgrimage constitutes an exteriorized version of the interior journey of the mystic. Cf. Turner (1978, 6-7). Margery indicates this parallel relation herself in the Christ doll scene, where she links her meditations on the Infancy "in Inglond" with the Italian wives' actual attentions to the image of the baby Jesus (78). As Turner also argues, pilgrimage is "the mode of liminality for the laity," offering lay Christians such as Margery a place where normal social strictures are relaxed and social orderings—such as the male homosocial triad—are inverted. Could this perhaps be the reason why so many women engaged in pilgrimage—to the condemnation of authorities such as Boniface (*Ep.* XLVIII 169, cited in Sumption 1975, 347)?

30. As Allen notes (Kempe 1940), Christ is probably recalling here Margery's role as Mary's handmaiden and Jesus's nurse, mentioned earlier in the *Book.*

31. David Aers, noting the infantilization and passivization of Christ, speculates that "It enabled Margery to identify with the 'good' mother in a way that her experience in the earthly family denied," and that it "offers an image of one sphere in which the woman obviously controls males" (1988a, 104-107). See also Beckwith (1986, 48).

32. As she spent thirteen weeks in Venice, Margery may have seen Giotto's piece in Padua's Arena Chapel (Kempe 1940, 65). Like Giotto's painting, Niccoló di Tommaso's *Lamentation* in the Congregazione de la Caritá, Parma, depicts the dead Christ surrounded solely by female mourners (Meiss, plate 123).

33. *Cf.* Butler, who asserts that the essentially historical and thus contingent nature of patriarchal cultural signifiers allows for their disfiguration into unauthorized forms (see, for example, 1992, 162).

34. Readers who assess the *Book* in theological terms include Lochrie (1991), who describes the status of Margery's tears as signifiers of Margery's devout love for Jesus (see especially 167-202), Gibson 1989, who argues for Margery's successful assertion of "her own spiritual health" (65; see also 47-49); Hirsh (1989, 9); Dickman (1980); McEntire (1987). Alternately, Weissman provocatively argues that Margery "formally accept[s] conventional (theological) images while actually coopting them" (1982, 203).

Works Cited

Aers, David. 1988a. *Community, Gender and Individual Identity: English Writing 1360-1430.* London and New York: Routledge.

———. 1988b. "Rewriting the Middle Ages: Some Suggestions." *Journal of Medieval and Renaissance Studies* 18: 221-40.

Atkinson, Clarissa W. 1983. *Mystic and Pilgrim: The Book and World of Margery Kempe.* Ithaca: Cornell University Press.

Augustine. 1956. Letter 211. In *Letters,* trans. Sr. Wilfrid Parsons. 5 vols. New York: Fathers of the Church.

Bailey, Derrick Sherwin. 1975. *Homosexuality and the Western Christian Tradition.* Hamden, CT: Shoestring.

Barasche, Mosche. 1976. *Gestures of Despair in Medieval and Early Renaissance Art.* New York: New York University Press.

Beckwith, Sarah. 1986. "A Very Material Mysticism: The Medieval Mysticism of Margery Kempe," in *Medieval Literature: Criticism, Ideology & History,* ed. David Aers. Sussex: Harvester. 34-57.

Bennett, J. A. W. 1982. *Poetry of the Passion: Studies in Twelve Centuries of English Verse.* Oxford: Clarendon.

Berliner, R. 1946. "The Origins of the Creche." *Gazette des Beaux—Arts* 30: 249-78.

Biddick, Kathleen. 1993. "Genders, Bodies, Borders: Technologies of the Visible." *Speculum* 68.2: 389-418.

Blunt, John Henry, ed. 1973. *The Myroure of Oure Ladye.* EETS, e. s. 19. London: Oxford University Press.

Boswell, John. 1980. *Christianity, Social Tolerance and Homosexuality: Gay People in Western Europe from the Beginning of the Christian Era to the Fourteenth Century.* Chicago: University of Chicago Press.

Brook, G. L., ed. 1956. *The Harley Lyrics: The Middle English Lyrics of Ms. Harley 2253.* Manchester: Manchester University Press.

Brown, Judith. 1986. *Immodest Acts: The Life of a Lesbian Nun in Renaissance Italy.* New York & Oxford: Oxford University Press.

Butler, Judith. 1990. *Gender Trouble: Feminism and the Subversion of Identity.* London and New York: Routledge.

———. 1992. "The Lesbian Phallus and the Morphological Imaginary." *Differences* 4: 133-71.

Bynum, Caroline Walker. 1987. "Religious Women," in *Christian Spirituality: High Middle Ages and Reformation,* ed. Jill Raitt in collaboration with Bernard McGinn and John Meyendorff. New York: Crossroad. 121-39.

———. 1991. *Fragmentation and Redemption: Essays on Gender and the Human Body in Medieval Religion.* New York: Zone.

Castle, Terry. 1993. *The Apparitional Lesbian: Female Homosexuality and Modern Culture.* New York: Columbia University Press.

Coletti, Theresa. 1993. "Purity and Danger: The Paradox of Mary's Body and the En-gendering of the Infancy Narrative in the English Mystery Cycles," in Lomperis and Stanbury, *Feminist Approaches.* 65-95.

Crimp, Douglas, ed. 1988. *AIDS: Cultural Analysis, Cultural Activism.* Cambridge and London: MIT.

Delaney, Sheila. 1975. "Sexual Economics, Chaucer's Wife of Bath, and *The Book of Margery Kempe.*" *Minnesota Review* 5: 104-15.

———. *Patronage, Politics and Augustinian Poetics in Fifteenth-Century England* (forthcoming).

Dickman, Susan. 1980. "Margery Kempe and the English Devotional Tradition," in *The Medieval Mystical Tradition in England,* ed. Marion Glasscoe. Exeter: University of Exeter Press. 156-72.

Duffy, Eamon. 1992. *The Stripping of the Altars: Traditional Religion in England, c.1400-c.1580.* New Haven and London: Yale University Press.

Ellis, Deborah. 1990. "The Merchant's Wife's Tale: Language, Sex and Commerce in Margery Kempe and in Chaucer." *Exemplaria* 2: 595-626.

Ennen, Edith. 1984. *The Medieval Woman,* trans. Edmund Jephcott. Cambridge, MA: Basil Blackwell.

Fradenburg, Louise. 1989. "Criticism, Anti-Semitism and the *Prioress's Tale.*" *Exemplaria* 1: 69-115.

———. 1990. "Voice Memorial: Loss and Reparation in Chaucer's Poetry." *Exemplaria* 2: 169-202.

Freud, Sigmund. 1960. *Jokes and Their Relation to the Unconscious* (1905). *The Standard Edition of the Complete Works of Sigmund Freud,* trans. and ed. James Strachey. Vol. 8. London: Hogarth.

———. 1963. "Feminine Sexuality," in *Sexuality and the Psychology of Love,* intro. and ed. Philip Rieff. New York: Collier. 194-211.

———. 1973. "Femininity." *The Standard Edition of the Complete Works of Sigmund Freud* (1932-1936), trans. and ed. James Strachey. Vol. 22. London: Hogarth. 112-36.

———. 1974. *Dora: An Analysis of a Case of Hysteria,* ed. Philip Rieff. New York: Collier.

Fuss, Diana. 1992. "Fashion and the Homospectatorial Look." *Critical Inquiry* 18: 713-37.

———. 1993. "Freud's Fallen Women: Identification, Desire, and 'A Case of Homosexuality in a Woman'." *The Yale Journal of Criticism* 6: 1-24.

Gibson, Gail McMurray. 1989. *The Theater of Devotion: East Anglian Drama and Society in the Late Middle Ages.* Chicago and London: University of Chicago Press.

Gluck, Robert. 1994. *Margery Kempe.* New York and London: High Risk.

Goldberg, Jonathan. 1992. *Sodometries: Renaissance Texts, Modern Sexualities.* Stanford, CA: Stanford University Press.

———. 1994a. "Romeo's and Juliet's Open Rs," in Goldberg, *Queering.* 218-35.

———, ed. 1994a. *Queering the Renaissance.* Durham, NC and London: Duke University Press.

Graef, Hilda. 1963. *Mary: A History of Doctrine and Devotion.* Vol. 1. New York: Sheed and Ward. 2 Vols.

Hamburgh, Harvey E. 1981. "The Problem of *Lo Spasimo* of the Virgin in *Cinquecento* Paintings of the Descent from the Cross." *Sixteenth Century Journal* 12: 45-76.

Harding, Wendy. 1993. "Body into Text: *The Book of Margery Kempe,*" in Lomperis and Stanbury, *Feminist Approaches.* 168-87.

Hardison, O.B. 1965. *Christian Rite and Christian Drama in the Middle Ages: Essays in the Origin and Early History of Modern Drama.* Baltimore: Johns Hopkins University Press.

Hirsch, John C. 1975. "Author and Scribe in *The Book of Margery Kempe.*" *Medium Aevum* 44: 145-50.

———. 1989. *The Revelations of Margery Kempe.* New York: Brill.

Holsinger, Bruce Wood. 1993. "The Flesh of the Voice: Embodiment and the Homoerotics of Devotion in the Music of Hildegard of Bingen (1098-1179)." *Signs* 19: 92-125.

Homans, Margaret. 1986. *Bearing the Word: Language and Female Experience in Nineteenth-Century Women's Writing.* Chicago and London: University of Chicago Press.

Irigaray, Luce. 1985. *This Sex Which is Not One,* trans. Catherine Porter. Ithaca: Cornell University Press.

James, Henry. 1945. *The Bostonians,* intro. Philip Rahv. New York: Dial.

Johnson, Lynn Staley. 1991. "The Trope of the Scribe and the Question of Literary Authority in the works of Julian of Norwich and Margery Kempe." *Speculum* 66: 820-38.

Kempe, Margery. 1940. *The Book of Margery Kempe,* ed. Sanford Brown Meech and Hope Emily Allen. EETS 212. Oxford: Oxford University Press.

Kieckhefer, Richard. 1984. *Unquiet Souls: Fourteenth-Century Saints and Their Religious Milieu.* Chicago and London: University of Chicago Press.

Klapisch-Zuber, Christiane. 1985. *Women, Family, and Ritual in Renaissance Italy.* Chicago: University of Chicago Press.

Kristeva, Julia. 1987. *Tales of Love,* trans. Leon S. Roudiez. New York: Columbia University Press.

Lane, Barbara G. 1984. *The Altar and the Altarpiece: Sacramental Themes in Early Netherlandish Painting.* New York: Harper and Row.

Lochrie, Karma. 1991. *Margery Kempe and the Translations of the Flesh.* Philadelphia: University of Pennsylvania Press.

Lomperis, Linda and Sarah Stanbury, eds. 1993. *Feminist Approaches to the Body.* Philadelphia: University of Pennsylvania Press.

Love, Nicholas. 1992. *Mirror of the Blessed Life of Jesus Christ,* ed. Michael G. Sargent. New York & London: Garland.

Marcuse, Herbert. 1959. "The Ideology of Death," in *The Meaning of Death,* ed. Herman Feifel. New York: McGraw-Hill. 64-76.

Matter, E. Ann. 1986. "My Sister My Spouse: Women-identified Women in Medieval Christianity." *Journal of Feminist Studies in Religion* 2: 81-93.

———. 1989. "Discourses of Desire: Sexuality and Christian Women's Visionary Narratives." *Homosexuality and Religion* 18: 119-31.

McEntire, Sandra. 1987. "The Doctrine of Compunction From Bede to Margery Kempe," in *The Medieval Mystical Tradition in England. Exeter Symposium IV,* ed. Marion Glasscoe. Cambridge: D. S. Brewer. 77-90.

Meditations on the Life of Christ: An Illustrated Manuscript of the Fourteenth Century. 1961. Trans. Isa Ragusa, ed. Isa Ragusa and Rosalie B. Green. Princeton: Princeton University Press.

Meiss, Millard. 1951. *Painting in Florence and Siena After the Black Death.* Princeton: Princeton University Press.

Merideth, Peter. 1987. *The Mary Play From the N-town Manuscript.* London and New York: Longman.

Mueller, Janel M. 1986. "Autobiography of a New 'Creatur': Feminine Spirituality, Selfhood, and Authorship in *The Book of Margery Kempe,*" in *Women in the Middle Ages and Renaissance: Literary and Historical Perspectives,* ed. Mary Beth Rose. Syracuse: Syracuse University Press. 155-71.

Mulvey, Laura. 1992. "Visual Pleasure and Narrative Cinema," in *Film Theory and Criticism: Introductory Readings,* ed. Gerald Mast, Marshall Cohen, and Leo Braudy. New York and Oxford: Oxford University Press. 746-57.

Mundy, E. James. 1981-1982. "Gerard David's Rest on the Flight into Egypt: Further Additions to Grape Symbolism." *Simiolus: Netherlands Quarterly for the History of Art* 12.4: 211-22.

Rambuss, Richard. 1994. "Pleasure and Devotion: The Body of Jesus and Seventeenth-Century Religious Lyric," in Goldberg, *Queering.* 253-79.

Rich, Adrienne. 1983. "Compulsory Heterosexuality and Lesbian Existence," in *Powers of Desire: The Politics of Sexuality,* ed. Ann Snitow, Christine Stansell and Sharon Thompson. New York: Monthly Review. 177-205.

Roof, Judith. 1992. *A Lure of Knowledge: Lesbian Sexuality and Theory.* New York: Columbia University Press.

Rubin, Gayle. 1975. "The Traffic in Women: Notes Toward a Political Economy of Sex," in *Toward an Anthropology of Women,* ed. Rayna Reiter. New York: Monthly Review Press. 157-210.

Schiesari, Juliana. 1992. *The Gendering of Melancholia: Feminism, Psychoanalysis, and the Symbolics of Loss in Renaissance Literature.* Ithaca and London: Cornell University Press.

Schlegel, Ursula. 1970. "The Christchild as Devotional Image in Medieval Italian Sculpture: A Contribution to Ambrogio Lorenzetti Studies." *Art Bulletin* 52: 1-10.

Sedgwick, Eve Kosofky. 1985. *Between Men: English Literature and Male Homosocial Desire.* New York: Columbia University Press.

———. 1990. *Epistemology of the Closet.* Berkeley: University of California Press.

Sinanoglou, Leah. 1973. "The Christ Child as Sacrifice: A Medieval Tradition and the Corpus Christi Plays." *Speculum*: 491-509.

Stanbury, Sarah. 1991. "The Virgin's Gaze: Spectacle and Transgression in Middle English Lyrics of the Passion." *PMLA* 106: 1083-93.

Steinberg, Leo. 1983. *The Sexuality of Christ in Renaissance Art and in Modern Oblivion.* New York: Pantheon.

Sticca, Sandro. 1988. *The Planctus Mariae in the Dramatic Tradition of the Middle Ages,* trans. Joseph R. Berrigan. Athens, GA and London: University of Georgia Press.

Stockton, Kathryn Bond. 1992. "God Between Their Lips: Desire Between Women in Irigaray and Eliot." *Novel* 25: 348-59.

Sumption, Jonathan. 1975. *Pilgrimage: An Image of Mediaeval Religion.* London: Faber & Faber.

Tanner, Norman P. 1984. *The Church in Late Medieval Norwich 1370-1532.* Toronto: Pontifical Institute of Mediaeval Studies.

Traub, Valerie. 1992. *Desire and Anxiety: Circulations of Sexuality in Shakespearean Drama.* London and New York: Routledge.

———. 1993. "The (In)Significance of 'Lesbian' Desire in Early Modern England," in Goldberg, *Queering.* 62-83.

Turner, Victor and Edith Turner. 1978. *Image and Pilgrimage in Christian Culture: Anthropological Perspectives.* New York: Columbia University Press.

Weissman, Hope Phyllis. 1982. "Margery Kempe in Jerusalem: *Hysterica Compassio* in the Late Middle Ages," in *Acts of Interpretation: The Text in its Contexts 700-1600,* ed. Mary J. Carruthers and Elizabeth D. Kirk. Norman, OK: Pilgrim. 201-217.

Woolf, Rosemary. 1968. *The English Religious Lyric in the Middle Ages.* Oxford: Clarendon.

FURTHER READING

Biographies

Collis, Louise. *Memoirs of a Medieval Woman: The Life and Times of Margery Kempe.* New York: Crowell, 1964, 270 p.

Offers a novelistic and sometimes inaccurate biography of Kempe, though highly accessible.

Goodman, Anthony. "Margery and Urban Gender Roles." In *Margery Kempe and Her World.* New York: Longman, 2002, 274 p.

Provides a biography emphasizing the details Kempe provides about her life as a medieval Englishwoman.

Criticism

Allen, Hope Emily. Preface to *The Book of Margery Kempe,* Vol. 1, edited by Sanford Brown Meech, pp. i-v. Oxford: Oxford University Press, 1940.

Discusses various influences on Kempe's Book, *particularly the work of other medieval mystic writers.*

Atkinson, Clarissa W. *Mystic and Pilgrim: The Book and the World of Margery Kempe.* Ithaca: Cornell University Press, 1983, 241 p.

Examines Kempe's book as an autobiography with an emphasis on her role in the tradition of women in Christian history.

Beckwith, Sarah. "A Very Material Mysticism: The Medieval Mysticism of Margery Kempe." In *Gender and Text in the Later Middle Ages,* edited by Jane Chance, pp. 195-212. Gainesville: University Press of Florida, 1996.

Studies the issue of Kempe's female mysticism from the perspective of developing a feminine subjectivity.

Delaney, Sheila. "Sexual Economics, Chaucer's Wife of Bath, and *The Book of Margery Kempe.*" *Minnesota Review,* n.s., no. 1 (fall 1975): 104-15.

Characterizes Kempe's life as an attempt to escape from the social and sexual oppressions of her day.

Dickman, Susan. "Margery Kempe and the Continental Tradition of the Pious Woman." In *The Medieval Mystical Tradition in England: Papers Read at Dartington Hall, July 1984,* edited by Marion Glascoe, pp. 150-68. Cambridge: D. S. Brewer, 1984.

Views Kempe's life as "an identifiably medieval, bourgeois, English adaptation" of the role of a pious woman.

Harding, Wendy. "Body Into Text: *The Book of Margery Kempe.*" In *Feminist Approaches to the Body in Medieval Literature,* edited by Linda Lomperis and Sarah Stanbury, pp. 168-85. Philadelphia: University of Pennsylvania Press, 1993.

Contends that The Book of Margery Kempe *is a dialogue between Kempe's scribe as a representative of the literate, celibate, male clerical segment of society, and Kempe, as a representative of illiterate, married women who were not attached to a religious order; maintains that the* Book *disrupts these hierarchical oppositions.*

Holbrook, Sue Ellen. "'About Her': Margery Kempe's Book of Feeling and Working." In *The Idea of Medieval Literature: New Essays on Chaucer and Medieval Culture in Honor of Donald R. Howard,* edited by James M. Dean and Christian K. Zacher, pp. 265-84. Newark: University of Delaware Press, 1992.

Analyzes Kempe as a female writer, rather than as simply a storyteller or hysteric; emphasizes the significance to Kempe of creating a book of spiritual revelations, instead of receiving the revelations and sharing them with a select group.

Howes, Laura L. "On the Birth of Margery Kempe's Last Child." *Modern Philology* 90, no. 2 (November 1992): 220-25.

Discusses Kempe's pregnancy during a portion of her pilgrimage; suggests that the congruence of these events emphasizes the commingling of Kempe's physical and spiritual lives.

Knowles, David. "Margery Kempe." In *The English Mystical Tradition,* pp. 138-50. New York: Harper & Brothers, 1961.

Concludes that Kempe was not a mystic on the level of Richard Rolle or Julian of Norwich while acknowledging that her Book *is a valuable document for religious history.*

Lochrie, Karma. "*The Book of Margery Kempe*: The Marginal Woman's Quest for Literary Authority." *Journal of Medieval and Renaissance Studies* 16 (spring 1986): 33-55.

Observes strategies that Kempe used as a medieval woman author to legitimize her text.

———. "From Utterance to Text: Authorizing the Mystical Word." In *Margery Kempe and Translations of the Flesh,* pp. 97-134. Philadelphia: University of Pennsylvania Press, 1991.

Asserts that medieval mystical texts strive to "authorize the oral text within their written text"; examines Kempe's efforts to do so and the challenge presented by her illiteracy.

McAvoy, Liz Herbert. "'Aftyr Hyr Owyn Tunge': Body, Voice and Authority in *The Book of Margery Kempe.*" *Women's Writing* 9, no. 2 (2002): 159-76.

Connects the physical body to the authority of the female narrator in Kempe's Book.

Medcalf, Stephen. "Inner and Outer." In *The Later Middle Ages,* edited by Stephen Medcalf, pp. 108-71. New York: Holmes & Meier, 1981.

Discusses Kempe's religion in comparing the Roman Catholic emphasis on outer signs and realities with the Protestant emphasis on inner attitudes and faith.

Mueller, Janel M. "Autobiography of a New 'Createur': Female Spirituality, Selfhood, and Authorship in *The Book of Margery Kempe.*" In *Women in the Middle Ages and the Renaissance: Literary and Historical Perspectives,* edited by Mary Beth Rose, pp. 155-68. Syracuse: Syracuse University Press, 1986.

Analyzes Kempe's Book *as an autobiography exploring the issues of female spirituality and selfhood, focusing on narrative and thematic design.*

Shklar, Ruth. "Cobham's Daughter: *The Book of Margery Kempe* and the Power of Heterodox Thinking." *Modern Language Quarterly* 56, no. 3 (September 1995): 277-304.

Suggests that the Lollards—a sect of religious reformers under the leadership of John Wycliffe—offered a framework of discourse from which Kempe developed her own methods of dissent and sense of vernacular spirituality.

Stevenson, Barbara. "Autobiographical Firsts: *The Book of Margery Kempe* and *The Sarashina Diary.*" *Medieval Perspectives* 15, no. 2 (fall 2000): 81-93.

Compares early women's autobiographies across cultures, from England to Japan.

Thornton, Martin. *Margery Kempe: An Example in the English Pastoral Tradition.* London: S.P.C.K., 1960, 120 p.

Examines Kempe's work from a theological perspective, emphasizing her English outlook and considers her role in the history of English spirituality.

Weissman, Hope Phyllis. "Margery Kempe in Jerusalem: *Hysterica Compassio* in the Late Middle Ages." In *Acts of Interpretation: The Text in its Contexts, 700-1600,* edited by Mary J. Carruthers and Elizabeth D. Kirk, pp. 201-17. Norman, Okla.: Pilgrim Books, 1982.

Presents Kempe's Book *as an expression of the motivating forces in her "life journey"; interprets Kempe as trapped within the patriarchal and ecclesiastical system, yet triumphant in flouting that authority.*

OTHER SOURCES FROM GALE:

Additional coverage of Kempe's life and career is contained in the following sources published by the Gale Group: *Dictionary of Literary Biography,* Vol. 146; *Literature Criticism from 1400-1800,* Vols. 6, 56; *Literature Resource Center; Reference Guide to English Literature,* Ed. 2.

MARY WORTLEY MONTAGU

(1689 - 1762)

(Born Mary Pierrepont) English epistler, poet, essayist, translator, and playwright.

Montagu is celebrated as a consummate writer of intelligent, witty, and frequently scandalous letters. Spanning the years 1708 to 1762, Montagu's correspondence is addressed to a wide variety of recipients and is considered remarkable for its versatility and range. By turns philosophical, descriptive, eccentric, affectionate, worldly, thoughtful, and sarcastic, the letters share one common attribute: the forceful imprint of their author's personality.

BIOGRAPHICAL INFORMATION

Mary Pierrepont was born in London to an aristocratic family. She was known as Lady Mary after her father became the earl of Kingston in 1690. As a child devised for herself a rigorous academic program, that included writing poetry and teaching herself Latin. While she was still in her teens Lady Mary captured the attention of Edward Wortley Montagu (usually referred to simply as Wortley), a politician eleven years her senior. Wortley asked Lady Mary's father for permission to marry her, but the men could not agree on the financial conditions of the proposed marriage, and Wortley and Lady Mary eloped in 1712. Montagu spent the first few years of her marriage alone in the country while Wortley attended to business in London. Her letters from this period reflect her dissatisfaction with the arrangement and her husband's seeming indifference to her.

In 1715 Montagu joined Wortley in the capital, where his political career was flourishing. She moved with ease in prominent social and literary circles, counting among her many friends and admirers Alexander Pope. Wortley was appointed ambassador to Turkey the following year, and the couple, along with their young son, moved to Constantinople. There, displaying her customary curiosity and enthusiasm, Montagu studied Turkish life and language and wrote a number of letters detailing her observations and experiences to friends and acquaintances back in England. These missives later formed the basis of her famous *Turkish Embassy Letters* (originally published in 1763 under the title *Letters of the Right Honorable Lady M—y W—y M—e: Written, during her Travels in Europe, Asia and Africa, To Persons of Distinction, Men of Letters, & c. in Different Parts of Europe.* Her visit to Turkey is important from a medical as well as a literary standpoint: noting the success of the Turkish practice of smallpox inoculation, Montagu had the procedure performed on her son and, later, her daughter. Through this example and her anonymously published essay "A Plain Account of the Inoculating of the Small Pox by a Turkey Merchant" (1722), she promoted the practical merits of the procedure.

Montagu returned to London in 1718 and for the next two decades presided over high society, which celebrated her wit and flamboyant behavior. Beginning sometime around 1728 she and Pope engaged in a bitter public quarrel. Pope lampooned Montagu in *The Dunciad* and elsewhere, and she retaliated with *Verses Address'd to the Imitator of the First Satire of the Second Book of Horace* (1733). Between December 16, 1737 and February 21, 1738, Montagu anonymously wrote and published nine issues of the periodical *The Nonsense of Common-Sense,* offering articles of various sorts, including economic analysis, social commentary, and fiction. Having met and fallen in love with Francesco Algarotti, a young Italian count in 1736, Montagu left her husband, her children, and her country in 1738 to live with Algarotti in Italy; the count, however, apparently had a change of heart and failed to meet her in Venice. Nevertheless, for over twenty years Montagu remained abroad, mainly in Italy. She returned to England shortly before her death in 1762.

MAJOR WORKS

As a female aristocrat, Montagu abhorred the notion of writing for print, and circulated her works primarily in manuscript. A few were published in her lifetime, however, usually without her consent. In collaboration with Pope and poet John Gay she wrote *Six Town Eclogues,* satires of well-known society personalities. Montagu had no intention of publishing the work, but in 1716 three of the eclogues were pirated, with coy hints of their authorship, as *Court Poems*. The original grouping was later issued in *Six Town Eclogues. With Some Other Poems* (1747). Aside from the anonymously published pieces in *The Nonsense of Common-Sense* (1737-38) the only work Montagu intended for publication was *Turkish Embassy Letters*. The fifty-two letters in the collection are thought to be based in part on Montagu's real correspondence and in part on a journal she kept during her journey to and residence in Turkey. Due to popular demand, successive editions of *Turkish Embassy Letters* were augmented with Montagu's other, private, correspondence as it became available.

CRITICAL RECEPTION

Montagu's letters have maintained scholarly interest both because they offer intimate biographical details and because of Montagu's ability to write witty, engaging, and informative prose. Montagu told her sister in 1726, "The last pleasure that fell in my way was Madam Sevigny's Letters; very pretty they are, but I assert without the least vanity that mine will be full as entertaining 40 years hence." Montagu's work was described by nineteenth-century critics as masculine due to the confidence, intelligence, and honesty apparent in her writing. Critics described some passages as too coarse for a woman writer, and warned that young ladies should avoid reading them. Because the letters are often so personal, Montagu herself has been the object of criticism, even into the twentieth century. Especially in the earlier part of the century, critics found Montagu's witty social gossip malicious, and interpreted their formal character as cold and lacking in genuine emotion. Feminist critics have generally embraced Montagu's concern for women's issues, as evidenced especially in her *Turkish Embassy Letters*.

PRINCIPAL WORKS

Court Poems [with Alexander Pope and John Gay] (poetry) 1716

The Genuine Copy of a Letter Written from Constantinople by an English Lady . . . to a Venetian Nobleman (verse letter) 1719

"A Plain Account of the Inoculating of the Small Pox by a Turkey Merchant" (essay) 1722

Verses Address'd to the Imitator of the First Satire of the Second Book of Horace [possibly with John, Lord Hervey] (poetry) 1733

The Dean's Provocation for Writing the Lady's Dressing Room (poetry) 1734

The Nonsense of Common-Sense. 9 issues (periodical essays) 1737-38

**Six Town Eclogues. With Some Other Poems* [with Alexander Pope and John Gay] (poetry) 1747

†*Letters of the Right Honorable Lady M—y W—y M—e: Written, during her Travels in Europe, Asia and Africa, To Persons of Distinction, Men of Letters, & c. in Different Parts of Europe.* 3 vols. (letters) 1763

The Poetical Works of the Right Honorable Lady M—y W—y M—e (poetry) 1768

The Works of the Right Honorable Lady Mary Wortley Montagu. Including Her Correspondence, Poems, and Essays. 5 vols. (letters, poetry, essays) 1803

The Nonsense of Common-Sense, 1737-1738 [edited by Robert Halsband] (periodical essays) 1947

The Complete Letters of Lady Mary Wortley Montagu. 3 vols. [edited by Robert Halsband] (letters) 1965-67

Court Eclogs Written in the Year, 1716: Alexander Pope's Autograph Manuscript of Poems by Lady Mary Wortley Montagu [edited by Halsband] (poetry) 1977

Essays and Poems, with Simplicity, A Comedy [edited by Halsband and Isobel Grundy] (essays, poetry, and drama) 1977

Turkish Embassy Letters [edited by Malcolm Jack] (letters) 1993

* This work contains the earlier *Court Poems.*

† This work is commonly referred to as *Turkish Embassy Letters.*

PRIMARY SOURCES

MARY WORTLEY MONTAGU (LETTER DATE 1 APRIL 1717)

SOURCE: Montagu, Mary Wortley. "Letter to Lady Mar (1 April 1717)." In *The Complete Letters of Lady Mary Wortley Montagu, Vol. 1,* edited by Robert Halsband, pp. 325-30. Oxford: Clarendon Press, 1967.

In the following letter, Montagu writes to Lady Mar about her experiences in Turkey, telling her about the Turkish dress she adopts.

I wish to God (dear Sister) that you was as regular in letting me have the pleasure of knowing what passes on your side of the Globe as I am carefull in endeavouring to amuse you by the Account of all I see that I think you care to hear of. You content your selfe with telling me over and over that the Town is very dull. It may possibly be dull to you when every day does not present you with something new, but for me that am in arrear at least 2 months news, all that seems very stale with you would be fresh and sweet here; pray let me into more particulars. I will try to awaken your Gratitude by giving you a full and true Relation of the Noveltys of this Place, none of which would surprize you more than a sight of my person as I am now in my Turkish Habit, thô I believe you would be of my Opinion that 'tis admirably becoming. I intend to send you my Picture; in the mean time accept of it here.

The first piece of my dresse is a pair of drawers, very full, that reach to my shoes and conceal the legs more modestly than your Petticoats. They are of a thin rose colour damask brocaded with silver flowers, my shoes of white kid Leather embrodier'd with Gold. Over this hangs my Smock of a fine white silk Gause edg'd with Embrodiery. This smock has wide sleeves hanging halfe way down the Arm and is clos'd at the Neck with a diamond button, but the shape and colour of the bosom very well to be distinguish'd through it. The Antery is a wastcoat made close to the shape, of white and Gold Damask, with very long sleeves falling back and fring'd with deep Gold fringe, and should have Diamond or pearl Buttons. My Caftan of the same stuff with my Drawers is a robe exactly fited to my shape and reaching to my feet, with very long strait falling sleeves. Over this is the Girdle of about 4 fingers broad, which all that can afford have entirely of Diamonds or other precious stones. Those that will not be at that expence have it of exquisite Embrodiery on Satin, but it must be fasten'd before with a clasp of Di'monds. The Curdée is a loose Robe they throw off or put on according to the Weather, being of a rich Brocade (mine is green and Gold) either lin'd with Ermine or Sables; the sleeves reach very little below the Shoulders. The Headress is compos'd of a Cap call'd Talpock, which is in winter of fine velvet embrodier'd with pearls or Di'monds and in summer of a light shineing silver stuff. This is fix'd on one side of the Head, hanging a little way down with a Gold Tassel and bound on either with a circle of Di'monds (as I have seen several) or a rich embrodier'd Handkercheif. On the other side of the Head the Hair is laid flat, and here the Ladys are at Liberty to shew their fancys, some putting Flowers, others a plume of Heron's feathers, and, in short, what they please, but the most general fashion is a large Bouquet of Jewels made like natural flowers, that is, the buds of Pearl, the roses of different colour'd Rubys, the Jess'mines of Di'monds, Jonquils of Topazes, etc., so well set and enammell'd tis hard to imagine any thing of that kind so beautifull. The Hair hangs at its full length behind, divided into tresses braided with pearl or riband, which is allways in great Quantity.

I never saw in my Life so many fine heads of hair. I have counted 110 of these tresses of one Lady's, all natural; but it must be own'd that every Beauty is more common here than with us. 'Tis surprizing to see a young Woman that is not very handsome. They have naturally the most beautifull complexions in the World and generally large black Eyes. I can assure you with great Truth that the Court of England (thô I beleive it the fairest in Christendom) cannot shew so many Beautys as are under our Protection here. They generally shape their Eyebrows, and the Greeks and Turks have a custom of putting round their Eyes on the inside a black Tincture that, at a distance or by Candle-light, adds very much to the Blackness of them. I fancy many of our Ladys would be overjoy'd to know this Secret, but tis too visible by day. They dye their Nails rose colour; I own I cannot enough accustom my selfe to this fashion to find any Beauty in it.

As to their Morality or good Conduct, I can say like Arlequin, 'tis just as 'tis with you, and the Turkish Ladys don't commit one Sin the less for not being Christians. Now I am a little acquainted with their ways, I cannot forbear admiring either the exemplary discretion or extreme Stupidity of all the writers that have given accounts of 'em. Tis very easy to see they have more Liberty than we have, no Woman of what rank so ever being permitted to go in the streets without 2 muslins, one that covers her face all but her Eyes and another that hides the whole dress of her head and hangs halfe way down her back; and their Shapes are wholly conceal'd by a thing they call a Ferigée, which no Woman of any sort appears without. This has strait sleeves that reaches to their fingers ends and it laps all round 'em, not unlike a rideing hood. In Winter 'tis of Cloth, and in Summer, plain stuff or silk. You may guess how effectually this disguises them, that there is no distinguishing the great Lady from her Slave, and 'tis impossible for the most jealous Husband to know his Wife when he meets her, and no Man dare either touch or follow a Woman in the Street.

This perpetual Masquerade gives them entire Liberty of following their Inclinations without danger of Discovery. The most usual method of Intrigue is to send an Appointment to the Lover to meet the Lady at a Jew's shop, which are as notoriously convenient as our Indian Houses, and yet even those that don't make that use of 'em do not scruple to go to buy Pennorths and tumble over rich Goods, which are cheiffly to be found amongst that sort of people. The Great Ladys seldom let their Gallants know who they are, and 'tis so difficult to find it out that they can very seldom guess at her name they have corresponded with above halfe a year together. You may easily imagine the number of faithfull Wives very small in a country where they have nothing to fear from their Lovers' Indiscretion, since we see so many that have the courage to expose them selves to that in this World and all the threaten'd Punishment of the next, which is never preach'd to the Turkish Damsels. Neither have they much to apprehend from the resentment of their Husbands, those Ladys that are rich having all their money in their own hands, which they take with 'em upon a divorce with an addition which he is oblig'd to give 'em. Upon the Whole, I look upon the Turkish Women as the only free people in the Empire. The very Divan pays a respect to 'em, and the Grand Signor himselfe, when a Bassa is executed, never violates the priveleges of the Haram (or Women's apartment) which remains unsearch'd entire to the Widow. They are Queens of their slaves, which the Husband has no permission so much as to look upon, except it be an old Woman or 2 that his Lady chuses. 'Tis true their Law permits them 4 Wives, but there is no Instance of a Man of Quality that makes use of this Liberty, or of a Woman of Rank that would suffer it. When a Husband happens to be inconstant (as those things will happen) he keeps his mistrisse in a House apart and visits her as privately as he can, just as tis with you. Amongst all the great men here I only know the Tefterdar (i.e. Treasurer) that keeps a number of she slaves for his own use (that is, on his own side of the House, for a slave once given to serve a Lady is entirely at her disposal) and he is spoke of as a Libertine, or what we should call a Rake, and his Wife won't see him, thô she continues to live in his house.

Thus you see, dear Sister, the manners of Mankind doe not differ so widely as our voyage Writers would make us beleive. Perhaps it would be more entertaining to add a few surprizing customs of my own Invention, but nothing seems to me so agreable as truth, and I beleive nothing so acceptable to you. I conclude with repeating the great Truth of my being, Dear Sister, etc.

MARY WORTLEY MONTAGU (POEM DATE 1724)

SOURCE: Montagu, Mary Wortley. "Epistle from Mrs. Y[onge] to her Husband." In *Essays and Poems, with* Simplicity, *A Comedy,* edited by Robert Halsband and Isobel Grundy, pp. 230-32. Oxford: Oxford University Press, 1977.

In the following poem, written in 1724, Montagu adopts the voice of Mary Yonge, an heiress whose acrimonious divorce and financial settlement caused a stir in London society. Mr. Yonge was a well-known adulterer, and Mrs. Yonge separated from him prior to their divorce. During the separation, she also had an affair. Mr. Yonge sued for and won damages from her lover, totaling 1,500 pounds, and in the divorce he was awarded most of Mrs. Yonge's inheritance. Montagu's poem addresses the injustice of Mrs. Yonge's penalties.

Think not this Paper comes with vain pretence
To move your Pity, or to mourn th'offence.
Too well I know that hard Obdurate Heart;
No soft'ning mercy there will take my part,
Nor can a Woman's Arguments prevail,
When even your Patron's wise Example fails,
But this last privelege I still retain,
Th'Oppress'd and Injur'd allways may complain.
   Too, too severely Laws of Honour bind
The Weak Submissive Sex of Woman-kind.
If sighs have gain'd or force compell'd our Hand,
Deceiv'd by Art, or urg'd by stern Command,
What ever Motive binds the fatal Tye,
The Judging World expects our Constancy.
   Just Heaven! (for sure in Heaven does Justice
      reign
Thô Tricks below that sacred Name prophane)
To you appealing I submit my Cause
Nor fear a Judgment from Impartial Laws.
All Bargains but conditional are made,
The Purchase void, the Creditor unpaid,
Defrauded Servants are from Service free,
A wounded Slave regains his Liberty.
For Wives ill us'd no remedy remains,
To daily Racks condemn'd, and to eternal
      Chains.
   From whence is this unjust Distinction
      grown?
Are we not form'd with Passions like your own?
Nature with equal Fire our Souls endu'd,
Our Minds as Haughty, and as warm our blood,
O're the wide World your pleasures you persue,
The Change is justify'd by something new;
But we must sigh in Silence—and be true.
Our Sexes Weakness you expose and blame
(Of every Prattling Fop the common Theme),
Yet from this Weakness you suppose is due
Sublimer Virtu than your Cato knew.
Had Heaven design'd us Tryals so severe,
It would have form'd our Tempers then to bear.
   And I have born (o what have I not born!)
The pang of Jealousie, th'Insults of Scorn.
Weary'd at length, I from your sight remove,
And place my Future Hopes, in Secret Love.
In the gay Bloom of glowing Youth retir'd,
I quit the Woman's Joy to be admir'd,
With that small Pension your hard Heart allows,
Renounce your Fortune, and release your Vows.
To Custom (thô unjust) so much is due,
I hide my Frailty, from the Public view.
My Conscience clear, yet sensible of Shame,
My Life I hazard, to preserve my Fame.
And I prefer this low inglorious State,
To vile dependance on the Thing I hate—
—But you persue me to this last retreat.
Dragg'd into Light, my tender Crime is shown
And every Circumstance of Fondness known.
Beneath the Shelter of the Law you stand,
And urge my Ruin with a cruel Hand.
While to my Fault thus rigidly severe,
Tamely Submissive to the Man you fear.
   This wretched Out-cast, this abandonn'd Wife,
Has yet this Joy to sweeten shamefull Life,
By your mean Conduct, infamously loose,
You are at once m'Accuser, and Excuse.
Let me be damn'd by the Censorious Prude
(Stupidly Dull, or Spiritually Lewd),
My hapless Case will surely Pity find
From every Just and reasonable Mind,
When to the final Sentence I submit,
The Lips condemn me, but their Souls acquit.
   No more my Husband, to your Pleasures go,
The Sweets of your recover'd Freedom know,
Go; Court the brittle Freindship of the Great,
Smile at his Board, or at his Levée wait
And when dismiss'd to Madam's Toilet fly,
More than her Chambermaids, or Glasses, Lye,
Tell her how Young she looks, how heavenly fair,
Admire the Lillys, and the Roses, there,
Your high Ambition may be gratify'd,
Some Cousin of her own be made your Bride,
And you the Father of a Glorious Race
Endow'd with Ch———l's strength and Low——
      r's face.

MARY WORTLEY MONTAGU (ESSAY DATE 24 JANUARY 1738)

SOURCE: Montagu, Mary Wortley. "Number VI (Tuesday, January 24, 1738)." *The Nonsense of Common-Sense, 1737-1738,* edited by Robert Halsband, pp. 24-28. Evanston, Ill.: Northwestern University, 1947.

In the following essay, taken from Montagu's anonymous periodical The Nonsense of Common-Sense, *Montagu makes a characteristically witty attack on men who lampoon women as weak, irrational, and faithless.*

I have always, as I have already declared, professed myself a Friend, tho' I do not aspire to the Character of an Admirer of the Fair Sex; and as such, I am warmed with Indignation at the barbarous Treatment they have received from the ***Common-Sense*** of *January* 14, and the false Advice that he gives them.—He either knows them very little, or like an interested Quack, prescribes such Medicines as are likely to hurt their Constitutions.—It is very plain to me, from the extreme Partiality with which he speaks of *Operas,* and the Rage with which he attacks both *Tragedy* and *Comedy,* that the Author is a *Performer* in the *Opera*: And whoever reads his Paper with Attention, will be of my Opinion: Else no *Thing* alive would assert at the same Time the Innocence of an Entertainment contrived wholly to soften the Mind, and sooth the Sense, without any Pretence to a Moral, and so vehemently declaim against Plays, whose End is, to shew the fatal Consequence of Vice, to warn the Innocent against the Snares of a well-bred designing *Dorimant.* You see there to what Insults a Woman of Wit, Beauty, and Quality, is exposed, that has been seduced by the artificial Tenderness of a vain, agreeable Gallant;

and, I believe, that very Comedy has given more Checks to Ladies in Pursuit of present Pleasures, so closely attended with Shame and Sorrow, than all the Sermons they have ever heard in their Lives.—But this Author does not seem to think it possible to stop their Propensity to Gallantry, by Reason or Reflection: He only desires them to fill up their Time with all Sorts of Trifles: In short, he recommends to them Gossiping, Scandal, Lying, and a whole Troop of Follies, instead of it, as the only Preservatives for their Virtue.

I am for treating them with more Dignity, and as I profess myself a Protector of all the Oppressed, I shall look upon them as my peculiar Care. I expect to be told, this is downright *Quixotism,* and that I am venturing to engage the strongest Part of Mankind with a Paper Helmet upon my Head. I confess it is an Undertaking where I cannot foresee any considerable Success, and according to an Author I have read somewhere,

The World will still be rul'd by Knaves,
And Fools contending to be Slaves.

But however, I keep up to the Character of a Moralist, and shall use my Endeavours to relieve the Distressed, and defeat vulgar Prejudices, whatever the Event may be. Amongst the most universal Errors, I reckon that of treating the weaker Sex with a Contempt which has a very bad Influence on their Conduct. How many of them think it Excuse enough to say, they are Women, to indulge any Folly that comes into their Heads? This renders them useless Members of the Common-wealth, and only burdensome to their own Families, where the wise Husband thinks he lessens the Opinion of his own Understanding, if he at any Time condescends to consult his Wife's. Thus what Reason Nature has given them is thrown away, and a blind Obedience expected from them by all their ill-natured Masters; and on the other Side, as blind a Complaisance shewn by those that are Indulgent, who say often, that Women's Weakness must be complied with, and it is a vain troublesome Attempt to make them hear Reason.

I attribute a great Part of this Way of thinking, which is hardly ever controverted, either to the Ignorance of Authors, who are many of them heavy *Collegians,* that have never been admitted to politer Conversations than those of their *Bed-makers,* or to the Design of selling their Works, which is generally the only View of writing, without any regard to Truth, or the ill Consequences that attend the Propagation of wrong Notions. A Paper smartly wrote, tho' perhaps only some old Conceits dressed in new Words, either in Rhime or Prose: I say *Rhime,* for I have seen no *Verses* wrote of many Years. Such a Paper, either to ridicule or declaim against the Ladies, is very welcome to the Coffee-houses, where there is hardly one Man in ten but fancies he hath some Reason or other to curse some of the Sex most heartily.—Perhaps his Sister's Fortunes are to run away with the Money that would be better bestowed at the Groom-Porter's; or an old Mother, good for nothing, keeps a Jointure from a hopeful Son, that wants to make a Settlement on his Mistress; or a handsome young Fellow is plagued with a Wife, that will remain alive, to hinder his running away with a great Fortune, having two or three of them in love with him.—These are serious Misfortunes, that are sufficient to exasperate the mildest Tempers to a Contempt of the Sex; not to speak of lesser Inconveniences, which are very provoking at the Time they are felt.

How many pretty Gentlemen have been unmercifully jilted by pert Hussies, after having curtisied to them at *half a Dozen Operas*; nay permitted themselves to be led out *twice*: Yet after these Encouragements, which amount very near to an Engagement, have refused to read their *Billets-Doux,* and perhaps married other Men under their Noses.—How welcome is a Couplet or two in scorn of Womankind, to such a disappointed Lover; and with what Comfort he reads in many profound Authors, that they are never to be pleased but by *Coxcombs*? and consequently, he owes his ill Success to the Brightness of his Understanding, which is beyond Female Comprehension.—The Country 'Squire is confirmed, on the elegant Choice he has made, in preferring the Conversation of his Hounds to that of his Wife; and the kind Keepers, a numerous Sect, find themselves justified in throwing away their Time and Estates on a Parcel of Jilts, when they read, that neither Birth nor Education can make any of the Sex rational Creatures; and they can have no Value but what is to be seen in their Faces.

Hence springs the Applause, with which such Libels are read; but I would ask the Applauders, if these Notions, in their own Nature, are likely to produce any good Effect, towards reforming the *Vicious,* instructing the Weak, or guiding the Young?—I would not every Day tell my Footmen, if I kept any, that their whole Fraternity were a Pack of Scoundrels; that Lying and Stealing were such inseparable Qualities to their Cloth, that I should think myself very happy in them, if they confined themselves to innocent Lies, and would only steal Candles Ends. On the contrary, I would say in their Presence, that Birth and Money were

Accidents of Fortune, that no Man was to be seriously despised for wanting; that an honest faithful Servant was a Character of more Value than an insolent corrupt Lord; That the real Distinction between Man and Man lay in his Integrity, which in one Shape or other generally met with its Reward in the World, and could not fail of giving the highest Pleasure, by a Consciousness of Virtue, which every Man feels that is so happy to possess it.

With this Gentleness would I treat my Inferiors, with much greater Esteem would I speak to that beautiful half of Mankind, who are distinguished by *Petticoats*.—If I was a Divine, I would remember, that in their first Creation they were designed a Help for the other Sex, and nothing was ever made incapable of the End of its Creation. 'Tis true, the first Lady had so little Experience that she hearkened to the Persuasions of an impertinent Dangler; and if you mind, he succeeded by persuading her that she was not so wise as she should be.

Men that have not Sense enough to shew any Superiority in their Arguments, hope to be yielded to by a Faith, that, as they are Men, all the Reason that has been allotted to human Kind, has fallen to their Share.—I am seriously of another Opinion.—As much Greatness of Mind may be shewn in Submission as in Command; and some Women have suffered a Life of Hardships with as much Philosophy as *Cato* traversed the Desarts of *Africa,* and without that Support the View of Glory offered him, which is enough for the human Mind that is touched with it, to go through any Toil or Danger. But this is not the Situation of a Woman, whose Virtue must only shine to her own Recollection, and loses that Name when it is ostentatiously exposed to the World.—A Lady who has performed her Duty as a Daughter, a Wife, and a Mother, raises in me as much Veneration as *Socrates* or *Xenophon*; and much more than I would pay either to *Julius Cæsar* or *Cardinal Mazarine,* tho' the first was the most famous Enslaver of his Country, and the last the most successful Plunderer of his Master.

A Woman really virtuous, in the utmost Extent of this Expression, has Virtue of a purer Kind than any Philosopher has ever shewn; since she knows, if she has Sense, and without it there can be no Virtue, that Mankind is too much prejudiced against her Sex, to give her any Degree of that Fame which is so sharp a Spur to their greatest Actions.—I have some Thoughts of exhibiting a Set of Pictures of such meritorious Ladies, where I shall say nothing of the Fire of their Eyes, or the Pureness of their Complexions; but give them such Praises as befits a rational sensible Being: Virtues of Choice, and not Beauties of Accident. I beg they would not so far mistake me, as to think I am undervaluing their Charms: A beautiful Mind in a beautiful Body, is one of the finest Objects shewn us by Nature. I would not have them place so much Value on a Quality that can be only useful to One, as to neglect that which may be of Benefit to Thousands by Precept or by Example.—There will be no Occasion of amusing them with Trifles, when they consider themselves capable of not only making the most amiable but the most estimable Figures in Life.—Begin then Ladies, by paying those Authors with Scorn and Contempt, who, with a Sneer of affected Admiration, would throw you below the Dignity of the human Species.

GENERAL COMMENTARY

ISOBEL GRUNDY (ESSAY DATE SPRING 1982)

SOURCE: Grundy, Isobel. "The Politics of Female Authorship: Lady Mary Wortley Montagu's Reaction to the Printing of Her Poems." *The Book Collector* 31, no. 1 (spring 1982): 19-37.

In the following essay, Grundy reviews Montagu's personal annotations of Dodsley's Collection of Poems, *which included poems printed without her permission. In the marginalia, Montagu claims some poems and vehemently denies writing others, revealing her thoughts on the controversies of her publication. Grundy suggests that the annotations add to the portrait of Montagu as a reluctant writer, with mixed emotions about being published.*

In the stormy career of Lady Mary Wortley Montagu the ambition of authorship played a large but mostly secret part. One of the earliest controversies to involve her was Edmund Curll's illicit publication of three more or less scandalous poems which she had been quietly circulating in manuscript among her friends; one of the latest was the feud that developed between her and the British Resident and British Consul in Venice,[1] about which new information has recently come to light. Each episode brings out the period's feeling that it was not fitting for a well-born woman to publish verses except in circumstances of the most careful decorum and discretion. When Curll scooped the three eclogues which appeared as ***Court Poems,*** 1716, various aristocratic women had already published their poems; Lady Winchilsea had put her name on title-pages, though Lady Chudleigh had not. But in Curll's pamphlet the first poem satirized the Princess of Wales—and must have appeared, to those readers who failed to appreciate Lady Mary's irony, to satirize her a good deal more heavily than it in fact did—and the resulting furore was such that Pope felt justified in taking the emetic vengeance he described in *A Full and True Account of a Horrid and Barbarous Revenge by Poison, on the Body of Mr Edmund Curll, Bookseller,* and in *A Further Account of the Deplorable Condition of Mr Curll.*[2] By the time Lady Mary, now settled in Italy, encountered John Murray in the late 1750's, something of a revolution was occurring in England, with a flood of books, mostly novels, issuing from the pens of women. Lady Mary had already remarked that the Italians, unlike her own countrymen, respected literary or learned women; she had also received evidence of the revolution at home, in the boxes of books sent her by her daughter; but she probably felt as much differentiated by her class from the new ranks of writing Englishwomen as she felt by nationality from the female professor of mathematics at Bologna.[3] Among the English at Venice, to be known as an authoress was still a liability. So when she discovered, apparently for the first time, that an appreciable number of her poems had been for ten years in print in the century's most popular anthology, she does not seem to have been pleased. Her enmity with Murray and his satellites, though political in foundation, was exacerbated by the natural antipathy between a rake praised by Casanova as 'prodigieusement amateur de beau sexe' and as having always 'les plus jolies filles de Venise', and an old woman, one of the 'most despicable creatures alive', as she wrote bitterly during an early phase of the quarrel, whose penchant for writing provided the readiest handle for attack and derision.[4]

New information on these affairs, albeit rather sparse and dubious is contained in a set of Robert Dodsley's *A Collection of Poems . . . By Several Hands,* annotated by Lady Mary in Venice in 1758. Each of the six volumes, handsomely bound in contemporary vellum, bears the engraved bookplate of 'Joseph Smith British Consul at Venice'.[5] This is odd for two reasons. Firstly, Smith's then existing collection of books was bought *en bloc* by George III in 1765 and now 'form[s] an important part of the king's library in the British Museum', so that his set of Dodsley's *Collection* must somehow have separated itself from the rest, if only to join those books which Smith continued to amass after the King's purchase, and which were sold after his death.[6] Secondly Lady Mary had disliked Smith even during her first stay in Venice 1739-40, and disliked him more strongly since he had married in 1757 at past the age of eighty, the sister of John Murray the Resident.[7] She wrote satirically about the marriage in May 1758; she said nothing in her letters, then or later, about the *Collection.* Her motives for annotating volumes owned by Smith therefore remains matter for speculation. Whether he gave her the set while they were still on speaking terms, whether she borrowed it and never returned it as a consequence of their growing hostility, or whether some other person was responsible for Smith's loss of it, we cannot now know. Very many of Lady Mary's own books were scattered before her surviving library was offered for sale at Sotheby's on 1 August 1928, so the non-appearance of the set in the catalogue of that sale tells us nothing.

Dodsley's *Collection of Poems* had begun in three volumes published on 15 January 1748.[8] The third volume included twelve poems by 'L. M. W. M.', all except three of them from ***Six Town Eclogues. With some other Poems. By the Rt. Hon. L. M. W. M.,*** which Horace Walpole had printed without her permission the previous year. Walpole wrote in his set of the *Collection* that Dodsley had printed Lady Mary's poems (which he found 'too womanish') 'from my Copy', and another owner wrote in his that 'Dodsley affirms the Collection was pict out by Mr. Spence'.[9] Evidence of both these statements, insofar as the second refers to Lady Mary, is provided by a transcript, apparently made in Rome in 1741 from Lady Mary's own holograph album, in a scribal hand with corrections in that of Joseph Spence, who met Lady Mary at the same time as Walpole, and who recorded information about her both in his *Anecdotes* and in his letters, where his dazzlement with her comes through most engagingly.[10] The transcript of her poems which he had made is endorsed in a late 18th-century hand 'The Book of Ly M's Verses at Dodsley's?'[11] Lady Mary liked both Walpole and Spence, with a liking which she might well have modified if she had seen them as not only admirers but also potential publishers of her poems.

The success of Dodsley's *Collection* was such that he issued a 'Second Edition' in December of the same year, 1748.[12] Lady Mary's poems seem to have been associated with his success, since he transferred them in the second edition from volume III to volume I. Joseph Smith acquired his first three volumes of the *Collection* in their fourth edition, 1755, presumably together with the fourth volume, which came out that year. Volumes V and VI were published in March 1758,[13] the year that Lady Mary made her notes. Smith's copies of these last volumes contain no notes by her, and since letters seem to have taken anything from a month to four and a half months to make the journey from England to Venice, though 'all the Shops are full of English Merchandize',[14] it seems probable that the set which she annotated consisted of four volumes only.

When the *Collection* first appeared, Lady Mary had already been nine years resident abroad—if 'resident' is the word to describe her unsettled sojourns, first in Venice, then (after a year-long tour of Italy and a winter in Geneva and Chambéry) in Avignon, then in the remote village of Gottolengo near Brescia in North Italy. This last move cut her off, more than the War of the Austrian Succession had already done, from English travellers. She was not cut off, however, from all news from home. She had been exchanging increasingly brief and dull letters with her husband since her departure from England, letters—equally far from her best—with Lady Oxford since 1744, and was by 1748 well launched on the much livelier correspondence with her daughter, from whom as recently as 1740 she had been still estranged.[15] Lady Bute had moved from Scotland to London, where news was more readily available, in 1746; her husband began his rise to power not long afterwards, meeting the Prince of Wales in 1747 and becoming Lord of the Bedchamber to him on 30 September 1750.[16] It seems, however, that if Lady Mary's correspondents in England noticed the appearance of her poems, first in Walpole's publication and then in Dodsley's, they thought it better to keep silent. Lady Mary's first note in Consul Smith's set claims, implicitly, that she had remained ignorant of her appearance in print for ten years. Beside the title 'An Epistle from a Lady in England, to a Gentleman at Avignon' (I.63) she wrote 'I renounce and never saw till this year 1758.'[17] Apparently someone had spoken of this poem as hers. If the second part of her note is true, it follows that she had not seen either the anthology or her own verses until after her move, in 1756, back from Gottolengo to Venice and Padua.

It is another oddity that she did not know this 'Epistle'. It was in fact by Thomas Tickell, and in Dodsley's *Collection* firmly associated—as 'By the Same'—with other well-known poems of his, and quite separate from the poems identified by Lady Mary's initials. It had been published anonymously in 1717 (during another of Lady Mary's absences from England) and reached five editions that year.[18] Whoever accused her of writing it

FROM THE AUTHOR

MONTAGU DESCRIBES HER MEETINGS WITH TURKISH WOMEN

The Sultana Hafife is what one would naturally expect to find a Turkish Lady, willing to oblige, but not knowing how to go about it, and tis easy to see in her Manner that she has liv'd excluded from the World. But Fatima has all the politeness and good breeding of a court, with an air that inspires at once Respect and tenderness; and now I understand her Language, I find her Wit as engaging as her Beauty. She is very curious after the manners of other countrys and has not that partiality for her own, so common to little minds. A Greek that I carry'd with me who had never seen her before (nor could have been admitted now if she had not been in my Train) shew'd that Surprize at her Beauty and manner which is unavoidable at the first sight, and said to me in Italian: This is no Turkish Lady; she is certainly some Christian. Fatima guess'd she spoke of her, and ask'd what she said. I would not have told, thinking she would have been no better pleas'd with the Complement than one of our Court Beautys to be told she had the air of a Turk. But the Greek Lady told it her and she smil'd, saying: It is not the first time I have heard so. My Mother was a Poloneze taken at the Seige of Caminiec, and my father us'd to rally me, saying he beleiv'd his Christian Wife had found some Christian Gallant, for I had not the Air of a Turkish Girl. I assur'd her that if all the Turkish Ladys were like her, it was absolutely necessary to confine them from public view for the repose of Mankind, and proceeded to tell her what a noise such a face as hers would make in London or Paris. I can't beleive you (reply'd she agreably); if Beauty was so much valu'd in your Country as you say, they would never have suffer'd you to leave it.

Montagu, Mary Wortley. Letter to Lady Mar, 10 March 1718. From *The Collected Letters of Mary Wortley Montagu, Vol. 1,* edited by Robert Halsband, pp. 386-87. Oxford: Clarendon Press, 1967.

probably did so as a joke, perhaps a hurtful one; but they did so not without apparent evidence: that of a London and Dublin reprint, also 1717, of Tickell's epistle 'To which is added Court Poems. Part II. The second edition.'[19] So something which Curll's piracy had by implication attributed to Lady Mary had once appeared between the same covers as Tickell's poem.

Lady Mary's need to 'renounce' this poem shows how vulnerable she was to the campaign of Murray the Resident, now Smith's brother-in-law, to bring her into mockery and disrepute. Real political differences existed between them: William Pitt had formed a joint Ministry with Newcastle in October 1756 (another Minister in it was Holdernesse, the relation to whom Murray owed his position), and Lady Mary, though she compared the resulting coalition to 'Arlequin's Coat', looked on Pitt as the chief hope for peace and national renewal, while Murray was full of 'zeal for the contrary faction'.[20] But the real issues were overshadowed by exaggeration and fantasy. Lady Mary's attitude progressed rapidly from an affectation of amusement that she should be taken for a politician (in February 1758), through admission that Murray's 'political Airs' made her wish she had 'settled in some other part of the World' (in April), to writing of his contempt and low malice. Three years later she self-mockingly resolved to perish if necessary in maintaining her ground 'with the true spirit of old Whiggism'.[21] Murray almost immediately expanded his basic charge against her—that of] supporting Pitt—into the larger and vaguer one of being 'in the Interest of Popery and Slavery' because of the friendship which she struck up, on their arrival in Venice in May 1758, with Sir James and Lady Frances Steuart, exiles on account of Sir James's Jacobite politics whom Murray refused to receive. It was an intellectual friendship, with Lady Mary reading and discussing Sir James's works, including part of the important but as yet unpublished *Inquiry into the Principles of Political Economy.*[22] Her letters throw out many dark jesting hints that she was suspected of witchcraft—traditionally the accusation levelled at undocile old women—but this may have been chiefly because Sir James was interested in the supernatural.[23] To her daughter she shows a touching defensiveness: 'I am afraid you may think some imprudent behaviour of mine has occasion'd all this ridiculous persecution', and again

> Do not tell your father these foolish squabbles; it is the only thing I would keep from his knowledge. I am apprehensive he should imagine some misplac'd Railery or vivacity of mine has drawn on me these ridiculous Persecutions. 'Tis realy incredible they should be carry'd to such a height without the least provocation.[24]

The modern reader, instinctively sharing the 18th century's low opinion of old women, is likely to wonder at first how much Lady Mary is exaggerating. One answer is provided by Lord Bute's kinsman General Graeme: although a friend of Murray's, he nevertheless wrote 'I do think the resident ought to show some more respect than he has done of late to a woman of her birth and country.'[25] Her birth and country, precisely the things which forbade her to be a published female writer, were her only possible hope for enforcing respect in the face of sneers about her excessive reading and writing.[26]

In this atmosphere it would not be difficult to make an insinuation that would rankle about Tickell's poem, in which an imaginary lady laments her banished Jacobite lover with insurrectionist fervour which transforms itself gradually but not very convincingly to acceptance of the status quo and to the hope that her lover will after all follow her in submitting to prosperity-bringing 'Brunswick'. At about the time that she read it, Lady Mary was writing, 'It is very remarkable that after having suffer'd all the rage of that Party at Avignon for my attachment to the present reigning Family, I should be accus'd here of favoring Rebellion, when I hop'd all our Odious Divisions were forgotten.'[27] Though Tickell's poem voices Jacobite sentiments at its beginning, it is clear to the least literate reader that the author must be a Whig; nevertheless I think it likely that Lady Mary's indignant repudiation of it had something to do with the scandal given by her welcome to the Steuarts.

Lady Mary then came to her own poems. Beside the heading of the ***Six Town Eclogues***[28] she noted 'mine wrote at 17'. The first word of her note was a response to a long-standing controversy about their authorship. Curll, by prefixing to his piracy a quibbling identification of the writer either as 'a LADY of QUALITY', or as John Gay, or as given as the opinion of a thinly-disguised Addison—as Pope himself,[29] had drawn public attention to a recent and no doubt indiscreet literary friendship of the young Lady Mary. Gay reinforced his association with the eclogue series by including in his *Poems on Several Occasions,* 1720, a poem called 'The Toilette. A Town Eclogue', 106 lines long, of which 43 lines are precisely the same as in Lady Mary's **'Friday. The Toilette'** in her 78-line holograph copy.[30] His version makes something light, whimsical and wistful out of Lady

Mary's more embittered heroine. It is easy to appreciate the quality of Gay's additions but impossible to tell how much he contributed to the lines common to his and Lady Mary's copies, or indeed which of the two friends conceived the poem's original idea. Pope, who continued to believe **'Friday'** to be 'almost wholly Gay's', also kept among his own papers a manuscript copy of 'Thursday' which caused some later editors to ascribe this eclogue to him; and in the beautiful handwritten transcript of the 'Eclogs' which he made for Lady Mary[31] he gave the concluding lines of 'Wednesday' in an entirely different form from that of her own manuscript. No wonder, then, that the 67-year-old Lady Mary should wish to establish her authorship of all six eclogues, for any readers of Consul Smith's volumes, with 'mine'. Her 'wrote at 17' is harder to justify. The earliest eclogue, **'Monday'**, dates from 'the coming over of the Hanoverian family' in 1715; the last, **'Satturday'** describes Lady Mary's own recovery from smallpox, which was complete by January 1716. She was born on 26 May 1689. One can only hope that '17' (which it is not possible to misread) was a slip of the pen for '27' rather than a deliberate untruth.

Beside the first couplet of **'Epistle from Arthur Grey, the Footman after his Condemnation for attempting a Rape'**, printed as 'By the Same',[32] Lady Mary wrote 'I confess it'. She was indulging in a touch of self-dramatization, for there is little in this romantic, Ovidian poem that calls for confession, nothing to embarrass the victim of the assault, her erstwhile friend Mrs Griselda Murray (no relation)—except an erotic passage, which six years later Lady Mary's old flame Francesco Algarotti was to imitate in Italian in a poem of his own.[33] What Mrs Murray had indignantly charged upon Lady Mary thirty-six years before were 'vile ballads' on the same subject, and these Lady Mary had, by implication, denied writing, though one of them is almost certainly by her and has now been printed as such.[34] At this moment the scornful gossip about her 'sudden liking' for Sir James Steuart made it particularly unsuitable for her to be known as an erotic poet.

Dodsley printed Lady Mary's **'The Lover: A Ballad'** as **'To Mr. C———'**,[35] no doubt following Horace Walpole, who believed, with Spence, that this description of the ideal lover was addressed to Richard Chandler (1703?-69), with whom Lady Mary was supposed to have had an affair. The identification says more for Walpole's nose for gossip than for his ear for literature. The speaker of this poem explains, to a friend who has blamed her for 'stupid Indifference', that she is not kept back from love-affairs by 'Nature, [by] fear or [by] Shame'; she can imagine a combination of qualities that would win her love, but has not yet found it: and 'till this astonishing Creature I know / As I long have liv'd Chaste I will keep my selfe so.' The amorous advances of 'Lewd Rake' and 'dress'd Fopling', she says, push women into a metaphorical experience of Ovidian metamorphosis: 'We harden like Trees, and like Rivers are cold.' The whole tone of the poem (confidential complaint of the inadequacies of modern men as lovers) suggests, what the 'We' of the last line reinforces, that it is written by a woman to a woman, *about* a lover but *to* a friend. This impression is borne out by Lady Mary's holograph in her album, where the second line of the poem reads 'Molly'—the nickname of Maria Skerrett, mistress of the Prime Minister and a close friend of hers. In Consul Smith's copy Lady Mary altered 'C———' in the second line to read 'M', and expanded this in the margin to 'Molly'. The subtitle **'To Mr. C———'** she replaced with **'to a Lady, to the Tune of My Time O ye Muses'**—a ballad by John Byrom which had been printed in *Spectator* No. 603.

Next in order Lady Mary found a poem of hers which had first appeared in print in a newspaper (Aaron Hill's *The Plain Dealer*) on 27 April 1724 and was titled there **'The Lady's Resolve'.** Since she claimed in her album that it was 'Written ex tempore in Company in a Glass Window', it might have reached Hill by various routes. In any case the printed version substituted 'He comes too near, that comes to be deny'd' for Lady Mary's manuscript 'Too near he has approach'd who is deny'd.' All Lady Mary's subsequent editors followed Hill instead of her holograph, even W. Moy Thomas in 1861, though he noted 'that this very line occurs in Ben Johnson's conversation with Drummond'.[36] (It is actually in Sir Thomas Overbury's *A Wife, Now A Widowe,* 1614). In Smith's copy Lady Mary crossed out the Overburean line and wrote in her own, but did nothing about the other considerable textual corruptions of the printed version. She added to the printed title, 'wrote 2 months after my marriage'; her own album puts it 'the first year I was marry'd.' To an answer printed by Dodsley (and earlier by Hill) as 'The Gentleman's Resolve' she added the note 'Sir W.Y.'—a useful piece of information, since it has been attributed to Pope as well as to Sir William Yonge.[37]

Lady Mary claimed the next two poems, **'An Epistle to Lord B———t'** and **'An Epilogue To**

Mary, Queen of Scots', with 'mine' in the margin by each title.[38] In line 67 of the **'Epistle'** she altered 'the' to 'has'—a change bringing the printed text into line with her manuscript, which reads 'O how unlike has Heaven my Soul design'd!' Lady Mary was remarking how differently Heaven had designed her soul from Bathurst's—not, as Dodsley's reading suggests, that Bathurst was unlike some ideal of manhood which she had designed as her heaven. **'A Receipt to Cure the Vapours'** was Dodsley's (and earlier Spence's) title for the next poem, which Lady Mary's album calls simply **'Song'**.[39] We know from the letters of Lady Mary's friend Lady Irwin that the song was addressed to her impromptu: nevertheless Lady Mary (shunning publicity?) has here heavily obliterated the sub-title 'Written to Lady J——— n', as well as adding, 'to the Tune of, do not ask me charming Philis'. Perhaps it was to this tune that the verses, a witty argument against eternal constancy, were later (1781) sung at Ranelagh.

Having made some mark of annotation by each of her own poems in this volume, Lady Mary went on to comment on four poems which W. P. Courtney notes as all written by Lord Chesterfield to Lady Fanny Shirley.[40] Lady Mary annotated 'Advice to a Lady in Autumn' with 'To Lady F. Sh. by Chester', 'Verses written in a Lady's Sherlock upon Death' with 'Chesterfield to Lady Tankerville', and two 'Songs' (beginning respectively 'When Fanny blooming fair' and 'Whenever, Chloe, I begin') with 'The same to F. Shirly' and 'The same to Miss Poultney'. Lady Mary had written mockingly about Chesterfield in the 1720s but admired his essays.[41] She kept copies of the first of these poems by him, and another more risqué one to Lady Frances Shirley, in an album of miscellaneous verse.[42] Lady Frances (1706-78), with whom Bonamy Dobrée says Chesterfield had 'a romantic attachment which went on for some years', was a former neighbour of hers (and still of her husband's) at Twickenham, and had played an important part (though probably unknown to Lady Mary) in Lady Bute's reconciliation with her parents.[43] Of the other ladies to whom Lady Mary wished to reassign two of Chesterfield's verse tributes, one was Camilla (Colville) Bennet (1698-1775), Countess of Tankerville and Lady of the Bedchamber to Queen Caroline in 1737, whom Robert Walpole apparently described as 'a very safe fool' for the purpose of a possible affair with the King.[44] The other is harder to identify. In one of her albums of poetry Lady Mary obliterated six lines (those following line 56 of her epistle 'Miss Cooper to————')[45] with an odd hotchpotch of scribbled words and names: what she wrote over the last line was apparently 'Poultney to [?] Lord Chesterfield I am not'. Since at least one other scribble on these lines seems to refer to a love-affair, Lady Mary was very likely associating Chesterfield here with the same Miss Poultney, rather than with either of the political Pulteneys, Daniel or William. The poem in question dates from 1723, but the scribblings from some time later than that.

At the beginning of Dodsley's volume II Lady Mary added the writer's name, 'Ld Lyttleton', on the divisional title-page of his 'The Progress of Love. In Four Eclogues.' She had in the past disputed with George, later 1st Baron Lyttelton, on political subjects; he was now politically on the same side as her rising son-in-law. She seems not to have thought highly of his 'fine things wrote . . . for the good of Mankind', but she kept copies of his 'Jealousy. The Third Eclogue' and 'Advice to a Lady.'[46] The latter poem, which in Dodsley occupies five pages, she had summarized in a satirical couplet:

> Be plain in Dress and sober in your Diet;
> In short my Dearee, kiss me, and be quiet.[47]

Beside its title she noted 'to Mrs Pit'—that is, Anne Pitt (1721-81), sister of the Pitt whom Lady Mary admired. Lyttelton's instructions to Miss Pitt included the prohibition:

> Make not dang'rous Wit a vain pretence,
> But wisely rest content with modest Sense;
> For Wit, like wine, intoxicates the brain,
> Too strong for feeble woman to sustain.

Despite her naturally strong desire to protest against this, Lady Mary seems to have shared Lyttelton's opinion of Anne Pitt, whose promotion at Court in 1751 she deplored without fully stating her reasons 'She has Wit but———'.[48] Beside Lyttelton's song beginning 'Say Myra, why is gentle Love' (p. 57), she wrote 'To Lady Buck'. It is not easy to know who she meant. Possible candidates are the widow of Sir Charles Buck, Bt (Anne, *née* Sebright, *c.* 1701-64); the sister-in-law of George II's mistress Lady Suffolk, who was from 1746 Countess of Buckinghamshire (whose family house in Norfolk Lyttelton visited);[49] or even Mary Boughton, née Greville (d. 1786), who was however Mrs not Lady, and who is generally identified as Lyttelton's Delia, now Myra. Lady Mary made and kept a copy of this poem, labelled as by Lyttelton, in which she writes 'Delia' for 'Myra', so it is possible she knew the facts.

In volume iv Lady Mary found three more poems ascribed to 'Lady M. W. M.'.[50] In line 24 of her **'An Answer To a Love-Letter'** she altered 'love' to 'Truth', eliminating a repetition of the idea already conveyed in 'fondness', emphasising that a return of sincerity is what the writer seeks, and of course restoring her original text. **'In Answer to a Lady Who advised Retirement'** called from her the unimportant correction of 'court' for 'courts' in line 3. She also deleted 'my' in line 8, which read 'And wait for my dismission without fear', an insufficient change which left a halting line without restoring the way it should have read: 'And wait Dismission without painfull Fear'. She found nothing to change in **'Verses written in a Garden.'** Nor, disappointingly, did she make any comment on what Dodsley printed as 'Answer to the foregoing Lines. By the late Lord Hervey',[51] following 'Elegy to Miss Dashwood. In the Manner of Ovid' by James Hammond. Although Dodsley so confidently ascribed it to Hervey, it had already appeared in print as **'By a Lady, Author of the Verses to the Imitator of Horace'**. Since the balance of evidence tends to make Lady Mary chief author of the ***Verses Address'd to the Imitator of Horace,*** published the same month as this poem, March 1733,[52] and in view of the **'Answer'**'s pithy style and feminist approach to its subject, it is far more likely to be by Lady Mary than by Hervey. Her failure to claim it as her own in Consul Smith's Dodsley is disappointing, but can perhaps be accounted for by the general atmosphere of defensiveness in which she made her notes. It would not have helped her position to become known as the author of one more poem of feminine complaint against men and against society.

She made only one more comment in the set. On p. 227 of the fourth volume she noted that 'On Sir Robert Walpole's Birth-day' is 'by Dr Young'—although it is printed as 'By Mr. D——ton' and accepted by Courtney (p. 39, following the *DNB*) as by Bubb Dodington. She might have been misled by memory of Edward Young's several other poems extolling Walpole; but she must have been familiar with his works, since she had been his patron in the 1720s;[53] her attribution at least needs to be seriously considered.

I have already concluded from the lack of notes by Lady Mary in Smith's fifth and sixth volumes that these, published in March 1758, were probably not available to her at the time when she saw the others. One reason for thinking this is the presence in volume vi of another of her poems, printed in circumstances calculated to cause her extreme annoyance, and unlikely to have been passed over in silence.[54] A burlesque rejection of an older woman by a younger man, which she said she herself had written to put into the mouth of Lord William Hamilton, whom Lady Hertford was indecorously pursuing, appeared here as the work of the William Yonge mentioned above, and as a riposte on his part to advances from none other than 'Lady Mary W*****' herself. The misattribution was richly ironical. If Lady Mary's account of the story is true then she, so often a literary champion of her own sex in its dealings with the other, had for once permitted herself, in verse, the kind of tough-minded and brutal put-down of feminine foolishness which was not uncommon in her conversation.[55] She had attacked not only a woman, but a woman who was, like herself, subject to attack for intellectual interests; pure chance (presumably) not only put her at the receiving end of her own attack, but put at the delivering end a man who had particular cause to seek poetical revenge upon her. Yonge (*c.* 1693-1755), a man universally and it seems with good reason disliked by his contemporaries, had in 1724 divorced his wife for her adultery, notwithstanding his own notorious extramarital affairs, and had recovered costs and damages of £1500 from her lover and the bulk of her considerable fortune for himself. Lady Mary had on that occasion voiced her indignation in an **'Epistle From Mrs Y[onge] to her husband'.**[56] All this past history must have made more bitter the picture given in Dodsley's sixth volume of Yonge rejecting advances from herself. She wrote furiously to her daughter about this 'new story' in November 1758; it seems to have touched off further teasing from Murray's circle and more remarks about witchcraft.[57] The same incident probably provoked her to label the verses concerned, and some other questionable ones in her album which contained poems both by herself and others, with the possessive initials MWM, and to add more detail to some titles and ascriptions elsewhere in the album (Harrowby MS 255).

Lady Mary was not, at the time she discovered herself figuring in Dodsley's earlier volumes, a virgin muse. Her experience included reacting with indignation at Curll's ***Court Poems*** in 1716 and at Anthony Hammond's inclusion of her **'Constantinople, To——'** in *A New Miscellany,* 1720, and probably at various newspaper printings of single poems.[58] On her own account, however, she had contributed to the *Spectator* and published nine numbers of her own political journal, ***The Nonsense of Common-Sense,*** in 1737-38. She may at least have connived at the printing of her two outrageous lampoons, ***Verses to the Imitator of Horace,*** 1733, and ***The Dean's Provocation For Writing the Lady's Dressing-Room,*** 1734.[59] She must have known about her friend the Abbé Conti's inclusion of seven of her poems in Italian versions in his *Prose e Poesie,* 1756, though she probably did not know that the *London Magazine* had been printing poems by her, in ones and twos to the number of ten, in 1749, 1750 and 1754. Dodsley's was, however, the most considerable body of her verse that she had ever seen in print. It came to her notice at a time when her friendship with Sir James Steuart and her enmity with Murray made her especially conscious of her poetic ambitions and acutely aware of the way in which they made her vulnerable to mockery. To the Steuarts she recalled how her poem on Constantinople had been 'miserably printed', though in terms which suggest covert boasting; she repeatedly alluded to herself as a poet, but in a sinister manner: she is haunted 'by the Daemon of Poesie', or by those 'real Devils', the nine Muses. Even to the Steuarts she emphasizes that 'All my works are consecrated to the fire for fear of being put to more ignoble uses, as their betters have been before them'; she never refers to Dodsley but with contempt and disapprobation; and to her daughter she comments revealingly on Horace Walpole's inclusion of Queen Elizabeth I in his *Catalogue of Royal and Noble Authors.* If Walpole has treated the Queen's character with disrespect, she writes, 'all the Women should tear him to pieces for abusing the Glory of their Sex.' But even without intending disrespect it seems he has done the Queen an injury: 'Neither is it Just to put her in the list of Authors, having never publish'd any thing, thô we have Mr. Cambden's Authority that she wrote many valuable Pieces'.[60] Walpole wished to serve Queen Elizabeth's reputation, just as he, Spence, and Dodsley wished to serve that of Lady Mary; unhappily the battles in which she was involved as an old woman made her too insecure to accept willingly the role of *published* poet.

Notes

1. The Resident was John Murray (*c.* 1715-75); the Consul was Joseph Smith (*c.* 1675-1770), famous as a collector of art and of books.
2. See Robert Halsband, 'Pope, Lady Mary, and the *Court Poems*', *PMLA,* 68 (1953), pp. 237-50; and *The Life of Lady Mary Wortley Montagu,* 1956, pp. 53-4.
3. *Complete Letters,* ed. R. Halsband, 1965-7, iii. 39.
4. *Letters,* iii. 127 n.4, 189.
5. Each bears also the same note: '15s/6d: for six Volumes—C. Hurt jun: Winksworth: May 6-1830—'.
6. *DNB.* The *Bibliotheca Smithiana . . . ,* Venice, 1755, does not mention Dodsley's *Collection,* nor does it appear in the *Catalogue of the Remaining Part of the Curious and Valuable Library of Joseph Smith,* issued by James Robson in 1775. The set's most recent resting place was the Pforzheimer Library, New York
7. *Letters,* iii. 18, 146-7.
8. R. Strauss, *Robert Dodsley,* 1910, p. 334.
9. Walpole, *Correspondence,* ed. W. S. Lewis *et al,* xiii, 1948, p. 234; his copy of Dodsley, BL C.117, aa. 16; *Notes and Queries,* 2nd Series, i. 1856, p. 237.
10. Spence (1699-1768), *Observations, Anecdotes, and Characters of Books and Men,* ed. J. M. Osborn, 1966, i. 303-12; *Letters from the Grand Tour,* ed. S. Klima, 1975, pp. 356-62.
11. Cornell University Library, Ithaca, N.Y.: MS E6004.
12. Straus, p. 337.
13. *Gentleman's Magazine,* p. 134.
14. *Letters,* iii. 115.
15. Mary (Wortley Montagu) Stuart (1719-94), Countess of Bute. Lady Mary began writing to her in 1740, but only two letters survive from before 1748, and nine from that year (*Letters,* ii. 162-3, 200, xvi.)
16. *Letters,* ii. 369 nn., 397 n. 4, 470 and n.1.
17. In transcribing Lady Mary's hand I have expanded abbreviations and lowered raised letters. Her annotations have been printed, in their catalogue A1115, Autumn 1978, p. 9, by Blackwell's Rare Books, to whose staff I am indebted for much help and kindness.
18. W. P. Courtney, *Dodsley's Collection of Poetry, Its Contents and Contributors,* 1910, p. 8; David Foxon, *English Verse 1701-1750,* 1975.
19. Foxon, *English Verse,* T280.
20. *Letters,* iii. 113, 116, 137 and n.5, 140.
21. *Letters,* iii. 140, 142, 277.
22. *Letters,* iii. 145-6, 149, 181 and n.4.
23. *Letters,* iii. 157, 188-9.
24. *Letters,* iii. 151, 160.
25. *Letters,* iii. 206.
26. *Letters,* iii. 216-17.
27. *Letters,* iii. 146.
28. One for each day of the week except Sunday: Dodsley, i. 84-106; Lady Mary *Essays and Poems,* ed. R. Halsband and I. Grundy, 1977, pp. 182-204.
29. *Court Poems,* 1716, pp. i-ii.
30. Harrowby MSS Trust, Sandon Hall, Stafford, 256 ff. 35-7.

31. Reproduced in facsimile as *Court Eclogs Written in the Year, 1716,* ed. R. Halsband, 1977.

32. Dodsley, i. 107-11; *Essays and Poems,* pp. 221-5.

33. *Opere,* Leghorn, 1764-5, viii. 134.

34. *Essays and Poems,* pp. 216-21.

35. i. 111-13; *Essays and Poems,* pp. 234-6.

36. Lady Mary, *Letters and Works,* 3rd ed., ii. 431 note.

37. P. 114. For Yonge see further below.

38. Dodsley i. 114-19; *Essays and Poems,* pp. 242-4, 240-1.

39. Dodsley, i. 120-1; *Essays and Poems,* pp. 257-8.

40. Dodsley, i. 334-8; Courtney, pp. 15-16.

41. *Letters,* ii. 37-38, iii. 146.

42. Harrowby MS 255, [ff. 62-4].

43. Chesterfield, *Letters,* 1932, i. 76; Lady Mary, *Letters,* ii. 369 and n.2.

44. Lord Hervey, *Some Materials Towards Memoirs of the Reign of King George II,* ed. R. Sedgwick, 1931, ii. 490-1.

45. *Essays and Poems,* p. 229; Harrowby MS 81, f.42.

46. *Letters,* ii. 481, iii. 232; Harrowby MS 81, ff. 32-3, 210-13.

47. Dodsley, ii. 43-8; *Essays and Poems,* p. 264.

48. *Letters,* ii. 490.

49. Rose Mary Davis, *The Good Lord Lyttelton,* 1939, p. 179.

50. Dodsley, iv. 196-8; *Essays and Poems,* pp. 300-1, 244-6, 258-9. The hand which identified 'An Epistle from S. J. Esq' as by Soame Jenyns (iii. 125) was not hers.

51. Dodsley, iv. 79-82; *Essays and Poems,* pp. 270-2.

52. See I. Grundy, '*Verses Address'd to the Imitator of Horace*: A Skirmish between Pope and Some Persons of Rank and Fortune', *SB,* xxx, 1977.

53. *Letters,* ii. 34-6, 61.

54. 'Sir W***** Y*****'s Answer', vi. 230-1; *Essays and Poems,* p. 263.

55. E.g. Robert Halsband, *The Life of Lady Mary Wortley Montagu,* 1956, p. 119.

56. *Essays and Poems,* pp. 230-2. See also I. Grundy, 'Ovid and Eighteenth-Century Divorce: An Unpublished Poem by Lady Mary Wortley Montagu *RES,* n.s. xxiii, 1972, pp. 417-28.

57. *Letters,* iii. 186-91.

58. *The Plain Dealer,* 17 April 1724; *The Weekly Journal or Saturday's-Post,* 26 December 1724; *The Gentleman's Magazine,* June 1735, and others which were merely reprints.

59. *Essays and Poems,* pp. 69-74, 105-49, 265-70, 273-6.

60. *Letters,* iii. 169, 170, 183, 190, 191, 185.

TITLE COMMENTARY

Turkish Embassy Letters

INGE E. BOER (ESSAY DATE WINTER, 1995-96)

SOURCE: Boer, Inge E. "Despotism from under the Veil: Masculine and Feminine Readings of the Despot and the Harem." *Cultural Critique* 32 (winter, 1995-96): 43-73.

In the following excerpt, Boer examines Montagu's Turkish Embassy Letters *as a voice within a silenced subculture in a despotic society. Boer suggests that Montagu offers an alternate understanding of the power relationship between the watcher-subject (usually male), and the object being watched (usually female).*

Despotism figures as a persistently dominant concept in Western representations of the Orient.[1] Because of concepts commonly related to despotism, such as polygamy, the harem, and the presumed oppressed position of women under despotism, representations of Oriental women have been affected in particular.

Montesquieu's *De l'esprit des lois,* published in 1748, has been instrumental in establishing despotism as a basically *political* system.[2] Simultaneously, through the Greek *despotes,* meaning "master over slaves in a domestic space," despotism maintains a link with the domestic. This linkage between despotism and the domestic is present in various forms in *De l'esprit des lois.* Given the extraordinary influence of Montesquieu's work, the specific position despotism occupies in his analysis of different forms of government, and the reproduction of his ideas in representations of the Orient, the study of representations of Oriental women necessitates an analysis of Montesquieu's ideas on despotism. Montesquieu's seemingly inevitable logic of oppression operates on the Western representation of Oriental women, and thus they too become defined, through his definition of despotism.

The first part of this article, therefore, focuses on three different relations between despotism and domestic space in *De l'esprit des lois* in order to uncover the implicit inequalities of power in Montesquieu's system of ordering and to explore the way in which gender intersects with those relations. The three relations indicated are, first, that between the monarchy and the republic, on the one hand, and despotism, on the other; second, that between the despot and his subjects generally speaking; and third, that between the master and his slaves.

Pierre Bourdieu argues that Montesquieu is not by accident led to pose explicitly the question of the link between domestic rule and the political in *De l'esprit des lois,* because

> it is there in fact that, in addition to sexuality and politics, the threads of conscious reasons become knotted—where it is a matter of "domestic servitude" in the sense of "control over women"—with the hidden chain of unconscious socially organized phantasms—where it is a matter of control *exercised by* women (with the theme of *ruse,* the power of the weak) and of despotism as the only means left to men to escape from the control of women.
>
> (Bourdieu 235; original emphases)[3]

I want to take the domestic in a somewhat broader sense than Bourdieu so as to bring all the connotations of the domestic into play. The domestic, according to the *Oxford English Dictionary,* signifies that which pertains to the house(hold), that which pertains to a particular or to one's own country, and that which pertains to what is domesticated.

The second part of my analysis foregrounds the domestic space, the term mostly silenced in Montesquieu's investigations. My examination of *Lettres persanes* and of a recent analysis of the seraglio by Alain Grosrichard, *La structure du sérail,* is meant to show how the political and the domestic converge in the representations of the harem. Both texts hinge on a system of surveillance, which reproduces a dominant and dominating masculine perspective and whose forces work toward control of the women in the harem. The fear of a revolt by the women is countered by the regulation of their visibility. To render an account of but one aspect of the complex interaction in the harem—that is, by emphasizing the despot's point of view—maintains women as the object of surveillance.

Therefore, in the third section, I will juxtapose these two texts with the so-called ***Turkish Embassy Letters*** by Lady Mary Montagu. Her letters, although partaking in a dominant mode of representing Oriental women, provide critical instances that arrive at a partial difference in scopic regimes. From a perspective "within" the harem, achieved through the narratological conception of a first-person embedded discourse, the letters by Lady Montagu show how surveillance also provides possibilities for resistance. My reading of the ***Turkish Embassy Letters*** proposes alternative perspectives that draw attention to a system of communication among women that goes unnoticed and that also point out the potentially threatening character of women in the harem, where they confront the despot as a group. I aim at an analysis in which the monolithical and unidirectional character of relations among despotism, the domestic, and ensuing scopic regimes are subverted. A deconstructive and feminist critique of the hierarchical ranking inherently present in Western representations of the Orient, and of women in the Orient in particular, provides possibilities for women's empowerment and pleasure that have received very little attention until now. . . .

Reading from "within" the Harem

Montesquieu's *Lettres persanes* form a stark contrast with the letters from Constantinople by Lady Mary Wortley Montagu,[4] written during the years 1717-1718. The ***Turkish Embassy Letters,*** as they were called, were published for the first time in 1763, a year after her death. They immediately won high acclaim. In his complete edition of Lady Montagu's letters, Robert Halsband concludes that the ***Turkish Embassy Letters*** are not actual letters, but that "in the main Lady Mary compiled her Embassy letters from actual letters which she 'edited' by transposing sections and otherwise manipulating them to achieve a more artistic collection" (I: xvi). Therefore, I will analyze Lady Montagu's letters as representations and focus mainly on her attention for and description of the position of women in the Ottoman Empire.[5]

It is striking to see how Lady Montagu divides the subjects of her writing among her addressees. In the letters to Alexander Pope and the Abbé Conti, for example, she addresses questions related to the organization of the Ottoman Empire and Islam, and refutes the faulty representations given by earlier travellers. Her letters to women, especially those to her sister, Lady Mar, deal extensively with the position of women and her visits to women's quarters. The comparison of the position of English and Turkish women turns out favorably for the latter.

Contrary to travel accounts by previous writers, which kept repeating the by then familiar stereotypical tale of women's oppression in the Ottoman Empire, Lady Montagu emphasizes the liberty of Turkish women:

> Now that I am a little acquainted with their ways, I cannot forbear admiring either the exemplary discretion or extreme stupidity of all the writers that have given accounts of 'em [Turkish women, IB]. Tis very easy to see they have more liberty than we have, no Woman of what rank so ever being permitted to go in the street without 2 muslins. . . . You may guess how effectually this

ABOUT THE AUTHOR

MARY ASTELL'S PREFACE TO MONTAGU'S *TURKISH EMBASSY LETTERS* (1763)

I confess I am malicious enough to desire that the World shou'd see to how much better purpose the LADYS Travel than their LORDS, and that whilst it is surfeited with Male Travels, all in the same Tone and stuft with the same Trifles, a *Lady* has the skill to strike out a New Path and to embellish a worn-out Subject with variety of fresh and elegant Entertainment. For besides that Vivacity and Spirit which enliven every part and that inimitable Beauty which spreads thro the whole, besides that Purity of Style for which it may justly be accounted the Standard of the *English* Tongue, the Reader will find a more true and accurate Account of the Customs and Manners of the several Nations with whom the Lady Convers'd than he can in any other Author. But as her Ladyship's penetration discovers the inmost follys of the heart, so the candor of her Temper passes over them with an air of pity rather than reproach, treating with the politeness of a Court and gentleness of a Lady what the severity of her Judgment cannot but Condemn.

In short, let her own Sex at least do her Justice; Lay aside diabolical Envy and its Brother Malice with all their accursed Company, Sly Whispering, cruel backbiting, spiteful detraction, and the rest of that hideous crew, which I hope are very falsely said to attend the *Tea Table,* being more apt to think they haunt those Public Places where Virtuous Women never come. Let the Men malign one another, if they think fit, and strive to pul down Merit when they cannot equal it. Let us be better natur'd than to give way to any unkind or disrespectful thought of so bright an Ornament of our Sex, merely because she has better Sense. For I doubt not but our hearts will tell us that this is the Real and unpardonable Offence, whatever may be pretended. Let us be better Christians than to look upon her with an evil eye, only because the Giver of all good Gifts has entrusted and adorn'd her with the most excellent Talents. Rather let us freely own the Superiority of this Sublime Genius as I do in the sincerity of my Soul, pleas'd that a *Woman* Triumphs, and proud to follow in her Train. Let us offer her the *Palm* which is justly her due, and if we pretend to any Laurels, lay them willingly at her Feet.

Astell, Mary. Preface to the *Turkish Embassy Letters.* From *The Collected Letters of Mary Wortley Montagu, Vol. 1,* edited by Robert Halsband, p. 467 Oxford: Clarendon Press, 1967.

> disguises them, that there is no distinguishing the great lady from her Slave, and 'tis impossible for the most jealous Husband to know his Wife when he meets her, and no Man dare either touch or follow a Woman in the street.
>
> (Letter to Lady Mar, I: 328)

The liberty of Turkish women finds expression, ironically, in their dress. The very dress meant to keep the women from being looked at provides possibilities for masquerade and free movement. This point of view emphasized by Lady Montagu contrasts sharply with the current interpretation of women's dress as oppressive only. Another source for a certain freedom of action, Lady Montagu states, is the disposal Turkish women have over their dowries. "Neither have they much to apprehend from the resentment of their Husbands, those ladys that are rich having all their money in their own hands, which they take with 'em upon a divorce with an addition which he is oblig'd to give 'em" (I: 328). Taking the financial position of English women, or even worse, that of French women, into account, it must have impressed Lady Montagu that Turkish women enjoyed certain financial privileges.[6]

Lady Montagu is equally impressed by the availability of exclusively female spaces like baths, where women have the chance to meet. She perceives the baths as a women's coffee house, where the latest news and gossips are exchanged. Rank or standing are effaced: "all being in the state of nature, that is, in plain English, stark naked, without any Beauty or defect conceal'd, yet there was not the least wanton smile or immodest Gesture amongst 'em" (Letter to Lady Mar I: 313). Lady Montagu cannot, however, escape from the fact that she herself proved to be an incursion in this egalitarian female domain. As she watches the women, she is fully dressed in a riding dress that she doesn't want to take off despite the encouragement of the women present in the bath. Reluctantly, and only after repeated requests, she shows the women her stays, "which satisfy'd 'em very well, for I saw they believ'd I was so lock'd up in that Machine that it was not in my own power to open it, which contrivance they attributed to my husband" (I: 314).[7]

Although Lady Montagu takes great pains to show and subvert the presuppositions of her male predecessors, she nevertheless does not escape from common fantasies about Oriental women. No immodest gestures, she informs her addressee, were perceived by her. The fact that Lady Montagu explicitly mentions the absence of wanton smiles or immodest gestures implies that she did expect their occurrence. The fantasy that women, waiting in frustration for the attention of their master, would start sexual relations among themselves, was commonly referred to in seventeenth-century travel journals, and, as this detail suggests, it informs Lady Montagu's discourse as well.

On some occasions she has difficulty in warding off her attraction for the women she meets or the scenes unfolding before her eyes, as Lowe (*Critical Terrains* 47) also argues. Writing to her sister, who always receives the most intimate details of Lady Montagu's adventures, she relates her visit to the beautiful Fatima. She is dumbfounded with so much beauty:

> I was struck with admiration that I could not for sometime speak to her, *being wholly taken up in gazing.* That surprising Harmony of features! that charming result of the whole! that exact proportion of Body! that lovely bloom of her Smile! But her Eyes! large and black with all the soft languishment of the bleu! After my first surprize was over, I endeavor'd by nicely examining her face to find out some imperfection, without any fruit of my search but being clearly convinc'd of the Error of that vulgar notion, that a face perfectly regular would be agreable . . .
>
> (Letter to Lady Mar I: 350; my emphasis)

Lady Montagu excuses herself for speaking about beauty in terms of such enchantment, and phrases her appreciation in the form of a defense of divine creation versus human creation. She compares her description of Fatima with the way writers speak about statues or paintings.

> I think I have read somewhere that Women always speak in rapture when they speak of Beauty, but I can't imagine why they should not be allow'd to do so. I rather think it Virtue to be able to admire without any Mixture of desire or Envy. The Gravest Writers have spoke with great warmth of some celebrated Pictures or Statues. The Workmanship of Heaven certainly excells all our Weak Imitations, and I think has a much better claim to our Praise.
>
> (I: 351)

Lady Montagu's claim that human beauty exceeds artistic production is substantiated and reinforced by attributing to it a divine origin. The aesthetic value of pictures and sculptures is no more than a weak imitation and is therefore less to be admired. The admiration Lady Montagu projects onto Fatima is virtuous, because not tainted, as she claims, by desire or envy.

Yet Lady Montagu has to exert herself to show distance or disinterested praise while she is captured by the obvious appeal of Fatima. The rapture about Fatima is augmented by the dance her slaves perform.

> This Dance was very different from what I had seen before. Nothing could be more artfull or more proper to raise *certain Ideas,* the Tunes so soft, the motions so languishing, accompany'd with pauses and dying Eyes, halfe falling back and then recovering themselves in so artfull a Manner that *I am very positive the coldest and most rigid Prude upon Earth could not have look'd upon them without thinking of something not to be spoke of.*
>
> (I: 351; my emphases)

Lady Montagu's emphasis on the artful manner in which the dance was executed strives to include her audience, her sister, in the effects the dance has on Lady Montagu herself. The double-talk, alluding both to sexual desire and a tender melancholy, speaks of lack of control. The control that Lady Montagu was more or less able to sustain in her description of Fatima—a virtuous admiration without desire or envy—breaks down under the forceful impression that would have led any woman, even the coldest and most rigid prude, let alone herself, to sexually charged fantasies. But at the same time the male discourse she uses does not give her the means to talk of what she experiences. Lowe (*Critical Terrains* 47) phrases Lady Montagu's rapture in terms of homoeroticism and makes explicit what in my opinion is exactly what cannot be expressed.

Clearly, Lady Montagu perceives the places where she meets women as "women's own spaces." To argue that the harems or baths, for that matter, are utterly controlled spaces is to forget that they can also be seen as relatively "safe" spaces where women can be among themselves. Baths and harems, without doing away completely with the fact that women were kept under surveillance, serve equally as places for exchange of information and learning by and through women. The dominant masculine representation of women waiting in agony for the master, separated from each other by their desire for him, sustains the effort to divide and rule over women and leaves out this crucial understanding of a feminine space.

Therefore, I want to take up an argument made by Lowe and carry it further. Lowe (*Critical Terrains*) argues that

> the harem is not merely an orientalist voyeur's fantasy of imagined female sexuality; it is also a possibility of an erotic universe in which there are no men, a site of social and sexual practices that are not organized around the phallus or a central male authority.
>
> (48)

The practices Lowe refers to can take place in the absence of men, but that is not a necessary condition. The bonding between women might lie beyond or outside male perceptions and fantasies and might express itself in terms of female sexuality—sexuality understood in a broad sense—which is pleasurable and "autonomous."

Notes

1. The Orient has had different meanings in the course of time and could in its most extended form signify a region including the Middle East, the Indian subcontinent, and the Far East. My use of the term is limited to the Islamic/Arab world as it existed in the period 1750-1850.

2. The quotes in the text are taken from the English translation *The Spirit of Laws.* Book numbers (in Roman numbers) and chapter numbers (in Arabic numbers) will be given in the text. At times parts remained untranslated in this edition, in which cases I used for my own translation Charles-Louis de Secondat, Baron de Montesquieu, *De l'esprit des lois* (Paris: Librairie Garnier Frères, 1927).

3. All translations are mine unless otherwise indicated.

4. Lady Montagu's husband was sent to Constantinople as the English ambassador to the Ottoman Empire. He was credited with securing the English interests during negotiations taking place between Russia and the Ottoman Empire. The couple arrived in Constantinople in April 1717. In September of the same year, he was recalled from his duties by the king, and he and Lady Montagu left Constantinople in July 1718.

5. See also Billie Melman (77-98) for an analysis of Lady Montagu's letters.

6. A full account of Lady Montagu's own problems with her father about her dowry in relation to her suitor, Wortley, is given in the introduction by Dervla Murphy in *Embassy to Constantinople: The Travels of Lady Mary Wortley Montagu* (10-24). See also Robert Halsband (13-17) and Billie Melman (88).

7. For a reading of Lady Montagu's letters about her visits to Turkish bath-houses and the influence of those letters on Ingres' paintings, see Wendy Leeks (29-38). For an analysis of Lady Montagu's conception of liberty, see Melman (85-98).

Works Cited

Bourdieu, Pierre. "La rhétorique de la scientificité: contribution à une analyse de l'effet Montesquieu." *Ce que parler veut dire: l'économie des échanges linguistiques.* Paris: Fayard, 1982.

Grosrichard, Alain. *La structure du sérail: la fiction du despotisme asiatique dans l'Occident classique.* Paris: Seuil, 1979.

Halsband, Robert, ed. *The Complete Letters of Lady Mary Wortley Montagu.* 3 vols. Oxford: Clarendon P, 1965.

Leeks, Wendy. "Ingres Other-Wise." *The Oxford Art Journal* 9.1 (1989): 29-38.

Lowe, Lisa. *Critical Terrains: French and British Orientalisms.* Ithaca: Cornell UP, 1991.

Melman, Billie. *Women's Orients. English Women and the Middle East, 1718-1918: Sexuality, Religion and Work.* London: Macmillan, 1992.

Montesquieu, Charles de Secondat, Baron de. *De l'esprit des lois.* 1748. Paris: Garnier-Flammarion, 1979.

———. *Lettres persanes.* 1721. Paris: Garnier-Flammarion, 1964.

Pick, Christopher, ed. *Embassy to Constantinople: The Travels of Lady Mary Wortley Montagu.* London: Century, 1988.

KATHERINE S. H. TURNER (ESSAY DATE 1999)

SOURCE: Turner, Katherine S. H. "From Classical to Imperial: Changing Visions of Turkey in the Eighteenth Century." In *Travel Writing and Empire: Postcolonial Theory in Transit,* edited by Steve Clark, pp. 113-28. London: Zed, 1999.

In the following essay, Turner compares the correspondence of Montagu to that of Elizabeth Craven, a later letter-writer who argued that Montagu's Turkish letters were not authentic and were probably written by a man.

Lady Mary Wortley Montagu's Turkish ***Embassy Letters,*** written between 1716 and 1718 but published (posthumously) only in 1763, remains one of the best known of eighteenth-century travelogues, and Montagu herself was one of the most celebrated woman writers of her time. Born in 1689, she was an indefatigable and accomplished letter writer, corresponding with leading literary figures such as Alexander Pope as well as an extensive network of family and friends. She also wrote essays and poems (both romantic and satirical), and a play (collected in Montagu 1977);

her participation in a wide range of genres, including travel writing, indicates her ability to transcend gender-based literary categories. Fewer than twenty British women published travel narratives during the eighteenth century, and Montagu was a pioneer of this small but highly significant cluster of women, whose works provide a fascinating, often oblique, commentary on the cultural and political trends of their time.

The attractive vision of Turkey presented in the ***Embassy Letters*** typifies a particular version of English Enlightenment culture and aesthetics. Bernard Lewis sees in Montagu's account 'the new myth, still in its embryonic form, of the non-European as the embodiment of mystery and romance' (Lewis 1993: 83). In many ways, however, Montagu's ***Letters*** are uncharacteristic of the eighteenth century of which they are so often claimed to be paradigmatic. In 1789, Lady Elizabeth Craven, England's other great eighteenth-century woman traveller to Turkey, takes issue with many of Montagu's opinions in her own travelogue, *A Journey through the Crimea to Constantinople,* and pronounces indeed that Montagu 'never wrote a line of them' (Craven 1789: 105). In her later *Memoirs,* and in the enlarged edition of the *Journey,* published in 1814, Craven expands on this view, pronouncing that the ***Embassy Letters*** 'were most of them *male* compositions, pretending to female grace in the style, the facts mostly inventions' (Craven 1814: 289). There had in fact been a spurious 'fourth' volume of Montagu's ***Embassy Letters*** published in 1767, perhaps written by John Cleland; but by the 1780s its spuriousness, and the authenticity of the 1763 volumes were not in doubt.

Montagu's highly favourable impressions of abroad, especially of Turkey, and especially of Turkish women, are Craven's chief targets. Craven found an unexpected ally in the person of Lady Bute, Montagu's daughter, who, having failed to suppress the publication of the ***Embassy Letters*** in 1763, was later delighted to find support for her disowning of her mother's vulgar publishing activities. Ladies Craven and Bute later corresponded about the authorship of the ***Embassy Letters,*** Lady Bute agreeing heartily that most of the Letters were 'composed by men', and suggesting that Horace Walpole 'and two other wits' had written them (Craven 1826: II 116).

No one else seems to have taken these assertions seriously; yet, questions of personal grievance and arrogance aside, this curious episode suggests how uncongenial Montagu's account became to at least some later eighteenth-century readers. It therefore provides a point of entry into a wider discussion of changes in eighteenth-century perceptions of travel writing, of women travel writers, and (not least) of Turkey itself. It is worth noting here that Craven's critical observations on Turkey, which to a large extent are a reactionary engagement with Montagu's, were taken seriously by the influential reviews (the *Monthly,* the *Critical* and the *Analytical*), although they slyly mocked her style and arrogance. Moreover, the *Monthly Review* commended her liberal reflections, 'which do honour to the writer, both as a lover of her own country, and as a citizen of the world' (*Monthly Review* 80 [1789], 209).

There are two main reasons for the generally positive reception of Craven's text in 1789. First, little else in the way of original travel writing on Turkey had been published since Montagu's text in 1763: James Porter's *Observations on the Religion, Law, Government, and Manners, of the Turks* (1768) was a compilation of travellers' accounts, and the focus of Richard Chandler's *Travels in Asia Minor* (1775) was largely archaeological. Second, a woman travel writer was still something of a novelty in her own right, no doubt because the genre's roots in masculine erudition and experience—at least until the closing decades of the century—remained powerfully deterrent (see Turner 1995: 168-246). The *Analytical Review,* anticipating its readers' interest in Craven's travelogue, notes that 'The letters of this sprightly female will naturally excite curiosity' (*Analytical Review* 3 [1789], 176). Craven's personal notoriety—her private life was nothing if not colourful—is also hinted at here.

The Turkish aspect of Craven's account seems to have been its main source of marketable interest. The title of the travelogue places Constantinople as the climax of her journey, and the running head throughout the volume is 'Lady Craven's Journey to Constantinople'. In fact, only about 70 of the 327 pages of Craven's *Journey* deal with Turkey, as critics were quick to point out (e.g. *Monthly Review* 80 [1789], 200-1; *Critical Review* 67 [1789], 281; *Gentleman's Magazine* 59 [1789], 237); and the revised title of the 1814 edition duly read *Letters from the Right Honorable Lady Craven, to His Serene Highness the Margrave of Anspach, during her Travels through France, Germany, and Russia in 1785 and 1786.* In 1789, though, Craven was no doubt exploiting public interest in Turkey: not only did the harem still exert a powerful pull on the British reader's imagination, but recent political developments made the Turkish focus of the *Journey* topical. The increasingly aggressive behaviour of Russia and Austria towards the declining Ottoman Empire was becoming an alarming threat to British trading interests in the Levant. Craven's account was published during the Russian and Austrian war against Turkey, 1787-92 (though her journey was made earlier, 1785-86). Britain had formed the Triple Alliance with the United Provinces and Prussia *against* Austria in 1788; and by 1789 all parties were eager for peace between Turkey and its aggressors, not least because the Triple Alliance were anxious to direct their energies against the tide of the French Revolutionary army (Shaw 1976: i 258-60). With the turmoil, indeed even disintegration of European affairs, following a decade on from the loss of America, it seems likely that Britain was anxious to preserve trading links with a safely weak but *intact* Ottoman Empire, which might indeed offer itself as an arena ripe for colonial domination; by British rather than Russian or Austrian interests.

What follows is a comparison of Montagu's and Craven's accounts, which will illuminate crucial changes in representations of gender and empire, as mediated through the eyes of the woman travel writer in Turkey. An account of the publishing histories of the travelogues will lead—through the issue of gender and propriety—into an analysis of the conflicting visions of Turkish women offered by Montagu and Craven. The latter part of the chapter will probe the changing concepts of cultural politics and history which the texts illuminate. In particular, Craven's repudiation of Montagu is a significant contribution to an emergent colonial discourse, displacing Montagu's classical, tolerant and largely ahistorical stance. Craven's text exemplifies what Homi K. Bhabha has defined as 'the objective of colonial discourse', which is to construe the colonised as a 'population of degenerate types on the basis of racial origin, in order to justify conquest and to establish systems of administration and instruction' (Bhabha 1986: 154).

The mere existence of their narratives testifies to the privileged status of Montagu and Craven. Their rank made possible nor only their access to European and Turkish high society—'The Turks are very proud, and will not converse with a stranger they are not assured is considerable in his own country' (Montagu 1763: II 131-2)—but their very expeditions. Lady Mary, who travelled through Austria and Hungary to Constantinople, with 'thirty covered waggons for our baggage, and five coaches . . . for my women' (vol. II, p. 110), points out that:

> The journey we have made from Belgrade hither, cannot possibly be passed by any out of a public character. The desert woods of Serbia, are the common refuge of thieves, who rob, fifty in a company, so that we had need of all our guards to secure us; and the villages are so poor, that only force could extort from them necessary provisions.
>
> (Montagu 1763: II 2)

Elsewhere, she describes her distress at the 'insolencies' of their escorts 'in the poor villages through which we passed' (vol. I, p. 152). Craven travelled with a smaller entourage but rather less sensitivity. Her *Journey* (1789) is peppered with name-dropping, and pervaded by a strong sense of her own importance, as in this passage: 'At Soumi I conversed with a brother of Prince Kourakin's and a Mr. Lanskoy, both officers quartered there; and to whom I was indebted for a lodging: they obliged a Jew to give me up a new little house he was upon the point of inhabiting' (p. 154).

The *Critical Review* concludes its account of Craven with the waspish pronouncement that the 'rest of the journey affords little subject of remark, except that whatever accommodations rank and beauty could demand, and despotic power could procure, Lady Craven enjoyed' (*Critical Review* 67 [1789], 286).

The circumstances under which Montagu's and Craven's texts were published testify to the critical significance not only of their rank, but also of their gender, and illuminate changing concepts of private and public identity. The ***Embassy Letters*** emerged into the literary world like the elegant ghost of their recently deceased author, appearing in 1763 in three small octavo volumes. The first of these contained a preface written in 1724 by Mary Astell, confessing herself

> malicious enough to desire, that the world should see, to how much better purpose the Ladies travel than their Lords; and that, whilst it is surfeited with *Male-Travels,* all in the same tone, and stuff with the same trifles; a lady has the skill to strike out a new path, and to embellish a worn-out subject, with variety of fresh and elegant entertainment.
>
> (Montagu 1763: I viii)

Montagu is the eighteenth-century woman travel writer of whom it was most often and enthusiastically proclaimed that her gender qualified her to describe scenes 'not to be paralleled in the narrative of any *male* Traveller' (*Monthly Review* 28 [1763], 392): namely, the Turkish bath, the harem, and the lifestyles of aristocratic Turkish women. She was evidently proud of this privilege and of the distinction it guaranteed her within the corpus of travel literature; she concludes the letter describing the bath as follows: 'Adieu, Madam, I am sure I have now entertained you, with an account of such a sight as you never saw in your life, and what no book of travels could inform you of, as 'tis no less than death for a man to be found in one of these places' (Montagu 1763: I 164-5).

For all her contempt of authors who descended to the vulgar activity of publication (see for example Montagu 1965-67: III 37; 'it [is] not the busyness of a Man of Quality to turn Author'), Montagu was clearly anxious that the ***Embassy Letters*** eventually be published. She kept the manuscript with her wherever she travelled, and on her final journey home entrusted them to an English clergyman at Rotterdam, with instructions to publish them after her death. (See Halsband 1956: 278-9, 287-9, for an account of their journey into print.) It was her travel letters, rather than her poems or essays (some of which had been circulated in manuscript or even published anonymously during her lifetime), that Montagu was concerned to have preserved for posterity.

Astell's 'Preface' aside, the propriety of publishing is not an issue within Montagu's text, for all its prominence in her thought and activity elsewhere. Craven, however, engages vigorously with the issue. She seems to have had few qualms about the propriety of publishing; indeed, she somewhat showily published in a quarto volume illustrated with six engravings. Of the women travel writers who published in the eighteenth century, only Craven and Radcliffe (whose literary reputation was already well established) published in anything grander than octavo; and only Craven's book had plates. The *Gentleman's Magazine* is unimpressed, however, noting that 'What Lady C. here offers to the publick in a costly quarto might certainly have been very well compressed to the size of Lady Montague's Letters' (*Gentleman's Magazine,* 59 [1789], 237). The *Journey* is prefaced with a claim that Craven is publishing in order to satisfy friends' curiosity, and 'to show the world Where the real Lady Craven has been', her husband's mistress having for some years passed herself off as Lady Craven on *her* travels through France, Switzerland and England. The *Monthly Review* observes: 'the one great object in view, in publishing this correspondence, appears to be an effort to wipe away some unfavourable imputations at home, and to manifest the respect shewn to the writer abroad' (*Monthly Review* 80 [1789], 201).

The 'letters' which make up the *Journey* are written to the Margrave of Anspach, with whom Craven had developed 'a more than *sisterly* affection' on her travels in Europe following her scandalous separation from Lord Craven in 1781 (*Monthly Review* 53 [1789], 201). Unfortunately, his wife the Margravine was still alive, albeit in a sickly fashion, and it appears that Craven decided on a grand tour of exotic locations in order to remove the embarrassment to the Margrave created by her continued residence at Anspach, and to kill time until both the Margravine and Lord Craven had expired; he in fact held out until 1791, at which point she promptly married the Margrave. She and the Margrave then returned to England, but her long absence and widely publicised adultery had enabled Lord Craven to turn their children against her: all six refused to acknowledge her (J. Robinson 1990: 87). Moreover, she was no longer received at court, which must have been a serious blow to a woman of her pretensions. In 1814, Craven, now the Margravine of Anspach, reissued the *Journey* with minor alterations and additions. The new title blazons the name and rank of her correspondent, and celebrates their relationship: *Letters from the Right Honorable Lady Craven, to His Serene Highness the Margrave of Anspach* . . . Their relationship and Craven's virtue are indignantly defended in several additional letters, and in the new preface, where we are informed that she 'constantly refused estates and titles' offered by foreign potentates lest she be called suddenly home by her husband and children:

> my husband had all his [sic; for 'my'] fine property in his own power, and therefore I could not consent to take any duties on me, when I felt, that my first duty, that of a mother, must make me forsake those duties my gratitude and pride might have made me take elsewhere—my duty as a mother lay in England.
>
> (Craven 1814: v)

The 1814 edition also inserts references to her marital problems with Lord Craven and her deepening friendship with the Margrave; he is presented as a saintly refuge from the callous Lord Craven, who had prevented their children from writing to her, and whose appalling behaviour is clearly intended to exonerate her from any accusations of unwifely conduct. Craven casts herself in the role of restless exile, happy neither at home nor abroad, whose journeying is less a violation than a proof of propriety. The changes made to the 1814 edition engage with the increasingly severe moral climate of the late eighteenth century and early nineteenth, and negotiate the difficult no-man's-land between public propriety and private affairs which the earlier *Journey* had, perhaps naively, opened up for public inspection.

Craven capitalises (in both editions) not only on her personal notoriety but also on the increasingly autobiographical scope of travel writing in the later eighteenth century. While Montagu's reasons for travel and her personal affairs are largely absent from the ***Embassy Letters,*** Craven's private dramas provide, quite publicly, a moral justification for her travels, as well as an almost novelistic source of semi-scandalous interest. This expanding narrative scope within travel writing could create problems for women travel writers, for whom the acts of publication and indeed travel might appear morally questionable, and for whom autobiographical frankness might be problematic. Craven's text and apologetic signals her awareness of these issues, but her aristocratic self-importance permits her to rise above bourgeois anxiety. When it comes, however, to describing Turkish women, Craven's moral sensibility is closer, as we shall see, to the middle-class propriety of the 1780s and 1790s than to any aristocratic largesse. Moreover, the emphasis she increasingly places on her submissive married relationship (Montagu, by contrast, barely mentions her husband, although she does briefly describe her experiences of childbirth in Turkey) can be related to an emergent imperial sensibility, within which visible domestic affection in the Christian institution of marriage testifies to the moral superiority of the coloniser. Craven and Montagu present strikingly different accounts of Turkish women. Montagu's approach is poetic and aesthetic, Craven's moral and economic. Robert Halsband has observed that while in the courts of western Europe Montagu mingled with princes and diplomats, at the Ottoman court her sex deprived her of this privilege (Halsband 1956: 71). Craven is similarly excluded, but with chagrin; at one point she resorts to spying on the Sultan through a telescope. This exclusion partly explains the absence of political and diplomatic material in both women's accounts and their focus instead on the status of Turkish women. Both writers commend the respect and apparent liberty granted to Turkish women, but Montagu's account of their grace and beauty is vigorously contradicted by Craven. Montagu describes the women of the harem with admiration:

> They have naturally the most beautiful complexions in the world, and Generally large black eyes. They generally shape their eye-brows, and both Greeks and Turks have the custom of putting round their eyes a black tincture, that, at distance, or by candle-light, adds very much to the blackness of them. I fancy many of our ladies would be overjoyed to know this secret; but 'tis too visible by day.
>
> (Montagu 1763: II 31-2)

Craven is less favourably impressed:

> I have no doubt but that nature intended some of these women to be very handsome, but white and red ill applied, their eye-brows hid under one or two black lines—teeth black by smocking, and an universal stoop in the shoulders, made them appear rather disgusting than handsome . . . The frequent use of hot-baths destroys the solids, and these women at nineteen look older than I am at this moment.
>
> (Craven 1789: 225-6)

'Nature' here is implicitly associated with British standards of beauty; Craven frequently equates it with western, and usually British, behaviour. The *Critical Review* notes the prevalence of the adjective 'ugly' in her account (*Critical Review* 67 [1789], 282). More recently, Montagu has also been accused of forcing Turkish women into a western frame of reference, most notoriously in this famous description of the Turkish bath:

> They walked and moved with the same majestic grace, which Milton describes our General Mother with. There were many amongst them, as exactly proportioned as ever any goddess was drawn, by the pencil of a Guido or Titian,—And most of their skins shiningly white, only adorned by their beautiful hair, divided into many tresses, hanging on their shoulders, braided either with pearl or ribbon, perfectly representing the figures of the graces.
>
> (Montagu 1763: I 161-2)

Such aestheticising strategies, Isobel Grundy (1992) and Cynthia Lowenthal (1990) have argued, allow Montagu simultaneously to appreciate the exotic otherness of Turkish women and to evade the more problematic issues of freedom and happiness within the harsher realities of Turkish women's experience. Elizabeth Bohls (1995), however, has recently presented a more radical version of Montagu's aestheticising strategies, arguing that she presents herself, daringly, as an aesthetic subject (a privilege usually reserved for males) in order to neutralise orientalist stereotypes of women, and to re-present them as aesthetic rather than erotic objects: statues and paintings rather than the lascivious harpies of seventeenth- and eighteenth-century male-authored travels by the likes of Paul Rycaut and Aaron Hill.

Craven's strategy, by contrast, is simultaneously to de-aestheticise the oriental female, and to render her morally dubious once more. Where

Montagu celebrates the steamy beauty of the Turkish bath, Craven (1789) is appalled by the baths at Athens, 'full of naked fat women; a disgusting sight' (p. 264). Craven's account of a 'Turkish' bath in fact occurs in Athens. This displacement testifies not only to Craven's tendency to lump together Greeks, Turks, Tartars and Cossacks as eastern and primitive, regardless of politics or national identity—and indeed to use the term 'Turk' as a term of abuse for any objectionable eastern individual—but also to the distance which Craven strenuously constructs between herself and the eastern other, especially in Turkey and its dominions, where the pernicious influence of Islam is stressed. The *Critical Review* observes that Craven is interested not only in 'the stupidity and indolence of the Turks', but also in 'the effects of their despotism on the conquered Greeks' (*Critical Review* 67 [1789], 285).

Craven's horror at the Turkish bath is similar to her 'disgusted' reaction to a Cossack belly dancer, 'who never lifted her feet off the ground but once in four minutes, and then only one foot at a time, and every part of her person danced except her feet' (Craven 1789: 173). A description in Montagu's earlier account of a similar entertainment had, by contrast, employed the term 'proper' in an aesthetic sense devoid of moral implication, and envisaged a neutralising coalescence of art and eroticism which would cast the insensitive western prude as the villain of the piece:

> This dance was very different from what I had seen before. Nothing could be more artful, or more proper to raise *certain ideas*. The tunes so soft!—the motions so languishing!—Accompanied with pauses and dying eyes! half-falling back, and then recovering themselves in so artful a manner, that I am very positive, the coldest and most rigid prude upon earth, could not have looked upon them without thinking of something not to be spoke of.
>
> (Montagu 1763: II 89-90)

In the more proper climate of the 1780s, Montagu's aesthetic oriental women are re-becoming lascivious. Craven's reintroduction of moral judgement signals a germinating imperial ideology, as potent as had been previous moral assaults on Turkish sexuality (see Bohls 1995: 28-31 on the 'sexualised Orient' constructed by earlier male travel writers), but further bolstered, as we shall see, by a broader sense of Turkish cultural degeneracy. This new grounding permits Craven to claim what Norman Daniel (1966) has described as 'imperialism's perceived "moral right" to civilise any alien people which comes to replace the legal right that had characterised the Crusading impulse' (p. 67).

Craven treats with prurient disapproval what Montagu had appraised with amused tolerance in their respective accounts of Turkish women's 'liberty'. Both mention the freedoms offered by the anonymous garb of Turkish women, but Craven dwells repeatedly on its possibilities for intrigue and licentiousness, even imagining sexual assignations being conducted during services at Santa Sophia, by figures 'wrapped up like a mummy' (Craven 1789: 218). Montagu herself exploits the liberty which Turkish dress affords, wandering the streets of Constantinople 'every day, wrapped up in my *Feriae* and *Asmak*' (Montagu 1763: III 26). Craven would not countenance such assimilation:

> As to women, as many, if not more than men, are to be seen in the streets—but they look like walking mummies—A large loose robe of dark green cloth covers them from the neck to the ground, over that a large piece of muslin, which wraps the shoulders and the arms, another which goes over the head and eyes . . . If I was to walk about the streets here I would certainly wear the same dress, for the Turkish women call others names, when they meet them with their faces uncovered—When I go out I have the Ambassador's sedan-chair, which is like mine in London, only gilt and varnished like a French coach, and six Turks carry it; as they fancy it impossible that two or four men can carry one; two Janissaries walk before with high fur caps on—The Ambassadors here have all Janissaries as guards allowed them by the Porte—Thank Heaven I have but a little way to go in this pomp, and fearing every moment the Turks should fling me down they are so awkward.
>
> (Craven 1789: 205-6)

Montagu's experience of Turkey stands in opposition to the restrictive idea of gendered space which was becoming a fact of life in eighteenth-century England, and London especially (see Lew 1991: 445-6). The trappings of Turkish femininity offer unlimited access to public spaces (and Craven also notes that 'as many, if not more' women than men occupy the streets). Craven's text rewrites the concept of separate spheres so that space and activity are divided along racial lines. Her 'if I was to walk about the streets here' is purely rhetorical. The Englishwoman is resolutely opposed to the anonymity of Turkish feminine costume (perhaps here the developing discourse of English individuality and strong character is an influence). Consequently, her evident difference opens up perceptible hostility between the women of different races, which can only be contained, quite literally, within a sedan chair borne by Turkish males. And yet this too poses a threat, Craven 'fearing every moment the Turks should fling me down they are so awkward'. For her journey out of Turkey, Craven is given as an escort another threatening male, 'a Tchouadar, that is to say, a kind of upper servant, or rather creature of the Visir' (Craven 1789: 285). This 'yellow looking Turk' (p. 286) is a constant source of irritation to Craven, competing with her for the servants' attention and for the lion's share of the party's provisions. At one point she finds that he has used her kettle to make himself coffee:

> If any travellers were to meet us, they would certainly take him for some *Grand Seigneur,* and that I am of his suite, by the care taken of him, and the perfect indifference all, but my two companions and my servants, show for my ease and convenience . . . I thought it right to point to two most excellent little English pistols I wear at my girdle, and assure him they would be well employed against any offence I met with. And when the interpreter had done I could not help calling him a stupid disagreeable Turk, in English, which he took for a compliment, and bowed his head a little.
>
> (Craven 1789: 291)

Turkish degeneracy and luxury here emerge as *sexual* savagery, barely containable through the brandishing of English pistols worn in a highly defensive position, 'at my girdle' (and through the futile yet cathartic effect of English insults). The 'moral right' of the English over the Turk is again asserted.

In 1763, the *Monthly Review* praises the ***Embassy Letters*** in gendered terms: 'There is no affectation of female *delicatesse,* there are no *prettynesses,* no *Ladyisms* in these natural, easy familiar Epistles' (*Monthly Review* 28 [1763], 385). Paradoxically, Montagu is celebrated as a writer because she is not typical of her gender, even though it is her gender which makes possible her most novel observations (her descriptions of the harem). In 1789, by contrast, the *Critical Review* notes archly that Craven saw objects 'in the true female view' (*Critical Review* 67 [1789], 282). If this is true, then Craven is doing so partly in response to the increasing cultural and ideological separation of male and female fields and abilities. Similarly, her highly restrictive notions of sexual propriety are very much of her time. If we recall Craven's aspersions on the authorship of Montagu's text, moreover, it becomes clear that narrowing concepts of female activity colour Craven's reading of Montagu's text to the extent that the ***Embassy Letters***' tolerant view of Turkish manners evinces their spuriousness.

Montagu's broader cultural tolerance is if anything still more offensive to Craven than her views on women. Jill Campbell (1994) has described how Montagu imagines Turkish culture as 'outside history, as a place where past and present, the literary and the natural, coexist' (pp. 74-5). She relates this to the anthropological phenomenon observed by Johannes Fabian (in *Time and the Other*), by which western travellers deny the contemporaneity of different cultures, co-existing in the same historical moment, and instead imagine the alien cultures they encounter as inhabiting the distant past of their own culture's history or prehistory (p. 75).

A letter to Pope, written at Adrianople, shows Montagu adopting precisely this position:

> I read over your *Homer* here, with an infinite pleasure, and find several little passages explained, that I did not before entirely comprehend the beauty of: Many of the customs, and much of the dress then in fashion, being yet retained. I don't wonder to find more remains here, of an age so distant, than is to be found in any other country, the Turks not taking that pains to introduce their own manners, as has been generally practised by other nations, that imagine themselves more polite.
>
> (Montagu 1763: II 44)

This is to Pope, and about poetry, and is therefore consciously idealistic. This letter invokes a cultural continuity which dissolves national boundaries and represents difference as innocence from the ravages of civilisation: 'I never see half a dozen of old Bashaws (as I do very often) with their reverend beards, sitting basking in the sun, but I recollect good King *Priam* and his counsellors' (vol. II, p. 45). The ***Embassy Letters*** as a whole strives to articulate an innocence of history and politics, which are barely mentioned, and also of cultural judgement. Crucial to this project is the fragmentation of narrative identity which occurs within the ***Embassy Letters.*** Montagu's text differs markedly from Craven's in being addressed (rather unusually, in eighteenth-century travel literature) to a wide range of correspondents (fifteen in all, twelve of whom are women), ranging from her depressed sister, Lady Mar, to the Abbe Conti, to Alexander Pope, and including assorted female friends. All of Craven's letters, by contrast, are addressed to the Margrave (which may partly account for their celebration of her virtues and of the esteem in which she is held throughout Europe, Russia and Turkey). This formal difference makes for a greater stylistic variety within the ***Embassy Letters*** than in Craven's *Journey.* Montagu uses different literary and conversational registers for different correspondents, and deploys a range of descriptive topics. She addresses one letter to the Princess of Wales, writing as ambassadress for Christendom as well as Britain: 'I have now, Madam, finished a journey that has not been undertaken by any Christian, since the time of the Greek Emperors; and I shall not regret all the fatigues I have suffered in it, if it gives me an opportunity of amusing your R. H. by an account of places utterly unknown amongst us' (vol. I, p. 151).

To Lady Mar, Montagu writes anecdotal, humorous accounts of social and sexual customs and visits to exotic notables like the Grand Vizier's 'lady' and the Sultana Hafiten. With assorted Ladies, she is chatty and occasionally risqué. All her detailed (and celebrated) accounts of Turkish women, in harem or public bath or private audience, are addressed to women.

With the Abbe Conti and with Pope, not surprisingly, Montagu is most scholarly and philosophical. To the Abbe she writes 'of manners and religion' (vol. II, p. 1), government and welfare, antiquities and architecture, commerce, military parades, and Islam. To Pope she addresses witty and sometimes flirtatious letters, writing about poetry and pastoral; she resolutely denies Pope the almost erotic satisfaction which her letters to women friends offer, in accounts of her Turkish costume and luxurious lifestyle. One detects a distinctively plaintive note to Pope's declaration: 'I long for nothing so much as your Oriental Self. I expect to see your Soul as much thinner dresed as your Body' (Pope 1956: I 494). Through this dazzling variety of subjects and styles, Montagu refracts her narrative identity into a prismatic multiplicity. The ***Letters'*** observing self becomes, quite literally, an embodiment of Enlightenment pluralism. Their multifaceted narrator was no doubt an important factor in the enthusiastic reception of the *Critical Review* which itemises the narrator's separate attractions, declaring that the letters will display, 'as long as the English language endures, the sprightliness of her wit, the solidity of her judgement, the extent of her knowledge, the elegance of her taste, and the excellence of her *real* character' (*Critical Review* 15 [1763], 435).

The freedom of the ***Embassy Letters*** from opinion, judgement, or 'vulgar prejudice' (to use a frequent eighteenth-century criticism of travel writing) seems to have made them peculiarly attractive to the critical and reading public of the 1760s. Montagu must have seemed a true citizen of the world. The ***Embassy Letters*** were published in the year of the cessation of the Seven Years' War in Europe; the war had in some ways undermined the viability of Enlightened ideals and seen them compromised by political contingency and nationalistic feeling. Montagu's visions of a distant and not immediately threatening foreign world perhaps reassured the reading public that Enlightened tolerance was still, albeit remotely, alive and possible. Alternatively, the confidence-boosting territorial gains made at the Peace of Paris may have fostered a relaxed and culturally tolerant mood among the reading and critical public. Furthermore, remarks like 'Upon the whole, I look upon the Turkish women, as the only free people in the Empire' (Montagu 1763: II 35) must have offered a pleasurable alternative to the bitter resonances of 'liberty' in its domestic context in 1763. The ***Embassy Letters*** were published and reviewed in May of 1763; the anti-government *North Briton* edited by John Wilkes had published its incendiary issue 45 in April; and 'Wilkes and Liberty' was becoming a rallying cry.

For all the enlightened pluralism of the ***Embassy Letters,*** one might argue that there are letters in which Montagu's narrative persona is more emphatically English and where, correspondingly, things Turkish are presented in a more ambivalent light. The first is in a letter (her only) to the Princess of Wales, in which (as mentioned earlier) she writes as spokeswoman for Christendom. She describes her arrival in Turkish territory:

> The country from hence to Adrianople, is the finest in the world. Vines grow wild on all the hills, and the perpetual spring they enjoy, makes every thing gay and flourishing. But this climate, happy as it seems, can never be preferred to England, with all its frosts and snows, while we are blessed with an easy government, under a King, who makes his own happiness consist in the liberty of his people, and chooses rather to be looked upon, as their father than their master.
>
> (Montagu 1763: I 155)

This is a striking passage in Montagu's text; all the more so in that it sounds, almost parodically, like a great deal of other eighteenth-century travel writers who draw such comparisons so frequently as to make them at best a trope, at worst a cliché, of the genre. It is, however, hardly xenophobia; the same could *not* be said for a letter to Pope, describing Austro-Turkish atrocities in the battle for Belgrade, which contains a virulent diatribe against the Turks:

> You see here that I give you a very *handsome* return for your obliging letter. You entertain me with a most agreeable account of your amiable connexions with men of letters and taste, and of the deli-

> cious moments you pass in their society under the rural shade; and I exhibit to you in return, the barbarous spectacle of Turks and Germans cutting one another's throats. But what can you expect from such a country as this, from which the muses have fled, from which letters seem eternally banished, and in which you see, in private scenes, nothing pursued as happiness but the refinements of an indolent voluptuousness, and where those who act upon the public theatre live in uncertainty, suspicion, and terror.
>
> (Montagu 1767: 27-8)

This letter implicitly rejects the classical idealising of Turkey which dominates most of the ***Embassy Letters,*** and declares indeed: 'I long much to tread upon English ground, that I may see you and Mr. Congreve, who render that ground *classick ground*' (Montagu 1767: 32). These passages are almost worthy of Smollett's Smelfungus, and disrupt the tolerant pluralism of the other letters. Or, I should say, *would* disrupt; although a recent editor of Montagu (Clare Brant, Montagu 1992: 148-50) includes this letter, it did not in fact appear in the 1763 edition of ***Embassy Letters.*** It was first published in the spurious 'fourth volume', containing five fake letters and some genuine material (an essay, a letter, some verse), which appeared in 1767. Robert Halsband, in his definitive edition of Montagu's letters, has documented the inauthenticity of most of the 1767 volume (Montagu 1965-67: I xviii and I 371). Discredited by the time Craven was writing, this literary imposture had nevertheless 'deceived even . . . the critics' in 1767, as the *Monthly Review* (70 [1784], 575) ruefully admits. The 1767 volume is a fascinating hoax, and reveals the extent to which Montagu's pluralistic tolerance is already nostalgic, indeed outdated, by the later 1760s; or at least is co-existing somewhat uneasily with a more xenophobic, politically defensive sensibility. Revealingly, Lady Bute was convinced that the volume published in 1767 must be 'genuine' (Montagu 1965-67: I xviii). In the genuine volumes of the ***Embassy Letters,*** by contrast, Turkish indolence is invested with a complex philosophical value, embodying both classical (specifically, Elysian) tranquillity, and the possibility of a modern epicureanism:

> I am almost of opinion they [the Turks] have a right notion of life. They consume it in musick, gardens, wine and delicate eating, while we are tormenting our brains with some scheme of politicks, or studying some science to which we can never attain . . . Considering what short liv'd weak animals men are, is there any study so beneficial as the study of present pleasure? I dare not pursue this theme.
>
> (Montagu 1763: III 52-3)

Elsewhere, Montagu surrenders to the 'wicked suggestions of poetry', and observes 'the warmth of the climate, naturally inspiring a laziness and aversion to labour' (Montagu 1763: II 40-2). For Craven in the 1780s, however, indolence is anything but 'naturally' inspired: her 'nature' favours industry and (where such industry is not indigenous) colonisation. And her version of pastoral, as in this description of the valley of Baydar in Turkey, is decidedly imperial: 'a most enchanting and magnificent spot, intended by nature for some industrious and happy nation to enjoy in peace—A few Tartar villages lessen the wildness of the scene, but, in such a place, the meadow part should be covered with herds, and the mountainous with sheep' (Craven 1789: 190-1).

Craven's response to Turkish languor is one of prosaic disapproval: 'The quiet stupid Turk will sit a whole day by the side of the Canal, looking at flying kites or children's boats . . . How the business of the nation goes on at all I cannot guess' (p. 207). Her visions of commercial imperialism are couched in the language of emancipation and vision:

> Can any rational being, dear Sir, see nature, without the least assistance from art, in all her grace and beauty, stretching out her liberal hand to industry, and not wish to do her justice? Yes, I confess, I wish to see a colony of honest English families here; establishing manufactures, such as England produces, and returning the produce of this country to ours—establishing a fair and free trade from hence, and teaching industry and honesty to the insidious but oppressed Greeks, in their islands—waking the indolent Turk from his gilded slumbers, and carrying fair Liberty in her swelling sails . . . This is no visionary or poetical figure—it is the honest wish of one who considers all mankind as one family.
>
> (Craven 1789: 188-9)

This passage is especially commended by the *Monthly Review* for its 'liberal reflections, which do honour to the writer, both as a lover of her own country, and as a citizen of the world' (*Monthly Review* 80 [1789], 209). This judgement testifies to the ideological gulf not only between Montagu and Craven, but between the values of mid-century and those of later eighteenth-century culture, which looks forward to a new world of imperial expansion. The East is no longer merely an exotic playpen, but a land ripe for the type of colonial appropriation already well under way in India.

Although the reviews criticise Craven's arrogant style, her ideological stance is congenial, and she represents an important strand in travel literature (and much else) of the 1780s and 1790s. P. J. Marshall and Glyndwr Williams (1982: 67) have claimed that, despite continuing interest in the Near East, the growth of British influence in India was rapidly eclipsing Near Eastern concerns. Craven's account and its reception would suggest otherwise; or, indeed, might suggest that the Turkish experience was providing a paradigm for British attitudes towards India in the following century. As Norman Daniel puts it:

> It was in Turkey that the imperial attitude developed most rapidly, and not in India, where empire was further advanced. The mood of the conquerors of Bengal was as humble culturally as it was active, even aggressive, in war and commerce. Warren Hastings was a great patron of the study of Persian culture. The serious-minded servants of the Company contributed learned notes and translations and adaptations of Persian verse to specialised periodicals. The forms of the Mogul Empire were carried on, and diplomacy in India still used the Persian language. The significant change in the European attitude came in relations with the Ottoman Empire, a change that soon affected India.
>
> (Daniel 1966: 71)

The years separating Montagu and Craven show quite graphically the disappearance, as far as Turkey is concerned, of such cultural interest and humility. Montagu transcribes Turkish poetry, pronounces herself 'pretty far gone in Oriental learning' (Montagu 1763: II 46-56), and is enormously impressed by Turkish cultural traditions. Craven displays no such interest, and represents the Turks as barbaric philistines. Admittedly, she has some justification for this view, given that the Turks are bombarding Athens during her journey; however, her concern is less with the destruction of the Parthenon per se, and more with the British failure to get in on the act: 'ruins, that would adorn a virtuoso's cabinet, are daily burnt into lime by the Turks; and pieces of exquisite workmanship stuck into a wall or fountain' (Craven 1789: 221). She is particularly chagrined when the Turks forbid any of her party to remove any fragments of sculpture: 'alas, Sir, I cannot even have a little finger or a toe' (p. 256).

The sense of Turkey as a degenerating culture which is expressed only in the *spurious* letter from Montagu to Pope dominates Craven's account, and chimes with contemporary opinion, which was coming to view the Turks not only as 'idle and effete under the influence of despotism, but as worse than savages' (Burke, speech on 29 March 1791; cited Marshall and Williams 1982: 165). Montagu combines a respect for Turkish cultural history with a poetic imagining of Turkish culture as existing *outside* history and indeed politics; Craven constructs an alternative history, within which Turkish culture is erased, and the Turks are instead configured as almost pre-historic in their barbaric indolence. Craven's travelogue looks forwards, not back, to the assimilation of the East into British imperial history. And the forceful narrative personality projected by Craven's text foreshadows the emergence of the moral centre which the colonial woman is to provide for the colonial project.

Bibliography

1. Primary

Craven, Elizabeth, Lady (1789) *A Journey through the Crimea to Constantinople. In a Series of Letters from the Right Hon. Elizabeth Lady Craven, to his Serene Highness the Margrave of Brandebourg, Anspach, and Bareith. Written in the Year MDCCLXXXVI,* London: G. G. J. Robinson.

———Margravine of Anspach (1814) *Letters from the Right Honorable Lady Craven, to His Serene Highness the Margrave of Anspach, during her Travels through France, Germany, and Russia in 1785 and 1786,* London.

———(1826) *Memoirs of the Margravine of Anspach, Written by Herself,* 2 vols, London: Henry Colburn.

Montagu, Lady Mary Wortley (1763) *Letters of the Right Honourable Lady M——y W——y M———e: Written, during her Travels in Europe, Asia, and Africa, to Persons of Distinction, Men of Letters, & c. in different Parts of Europe. Which contain, among other curious Relations, Accounts of the Policy and Manners of the Turks; drawn from Sources that have been inaccessible to other Travellers,* 3 vols, London: T. A. Becket and P. A. de Hondt.

———[spurious] (1767) *An Additional Volume to the Letters Of the Right Honourable Lady M——y W——y M———e: Written, during her Travels in Europe, Asia and Africa, to Persons of Distinction, Men of Letters, & c. in different Parts of Europe,* London.

———(1965-67) *The Complete Letters of Lady Mary Wortley Montagu,* ed. Robert Halsband, 3 vols, Oxford: OUP.

———(1977) *Essays and Poems, and 'Simplicity, a Comedy',* ed. Robert Halsband and Isobel Grundy, Oxford: Clarendon Press.

———(1992) *Letters,* ed. Clare Brant, London: Dent.

Pope, Alexander (1956) *Correspondence of Alexander Pope,* ed. George Sherburn, 5 vols, Oxford: Clarendon Press.

2. Secondary

Bhabha, Homi K. (1986) 'The Other Question: Difference, Discrimination and the Discourse of Colonialism', in Francis Barker et al. (eds), *Literature, Politics and Theory: Papers from the Essex Conference 1976-84,* London: Methuen, 148-72.

Bohls, Elizabeth A. (1995) *Women Travel Writers and the Language of Aesthetics 1716-1818,* Cambridge: CUP.

Campbell, Jill (1994) 'Lady Mary Wortley Montagu and the Historical Machinery of Female Identity', in Beth Fowkes Tobin (ed.), *History, Gender and Eighteenth-Century Literature,* Athens: University of Georgia Press, 64-85.

Daniel, Norman (1966) *Islam, Europe and Empire,* Edinburgh: Edinburgh University Press.

Fabian, Johannes (1983) *Time and the Other: How Anthropology Makes its Object,* New York: Columbia University Press.

Halsband, Robert (1956) *The Life of Lady Mary Wortley Montagu,* Oxford: Clarendon Press.

Lew, Joseph W. (1991) 'Lady Mary's Portable Seraglio', *Eighteenth-Century Studies* 24: 432-50.

Lewis, Bernard (1993) *Islam and the West,* Oxford: OUP.

Lowenthal, Cynthia (1990) 'The Veil of Romance: Lady Mary's Embassy Letters', *Eighteenth-Century Life* 14: 66-82.

Marshall, P. J. and Glyndwr Williams (1982) *The Great Map of Mankind: British Perceptions of the World in the Age of Enlightenment,* London: Dent.

Robinson, Jane (1990) *Wayward Women: a Guide to Women Travellers,* Oxford: OUP.

Shaw, Stanford (1976) *History of the Ottoman Empire and Modern Turkey,* 2 vols, Cambridge: CUP.

Turner, Katherine S. H. (1995) 'The Politics of Narrative Singularity in British Travel Writing, 1750-1800', unpublished D Phil dissertation, University of Oxford.

FURTHER READING

Biographies

Grundy, Isobel. *Lady Mary Wortley Montagu.* New York: Oxford University Press, 1999, 680 p.

Considers Montagu's life as a series of struggles.

Halsband, Robert. *The Life of Lady Mary Wortley Montagu.* Oxford: Clarendon Press, 1956, 313 p.

Offers a modern scholarly biography of Montagu.

Criticism

Campbell, Jill. "Lady Mary Wortley Montagu and the Historical Machinery of Female Identity." In *History, Gender and Eighteenth-Century Literature,* edited by Beth Fowkes Tobin, pp. 64-85. Athens: University of Georgia Press, 1994.

Focuses on the Turkish Embassy Letters *as a demonstration of Montagu's use of cultural difference to discuss feminine pleasure and desire.*

Cooley, Emily. "Proto-Feminism and Ethnography in Lady Mary Wortley Montagu's Turkish Embassy Letters." *Publications of the Mississippi Philological Association* (2002): 8-15.

Critiques Montagu as an amateur anthropologist, including her attitude toward the otherness of foreign cultures.

Darby, Barbara. "Love, Chance, and the Arranged Marriage: Lady Mary Rewrites Marivaux." *Restoration and Eighteenth-Century Theatre Research* 9, no. 2 (winter 1994): 26-44.

Studies Montagu's comedy Simplicity *in terms of her revisions to the original French play and the attitudes towards women reflected in those revisions.*

Dobie, Madeleine. "Embodying Oriental Women: Representation and Voyeurism in Montesquieu, Montagu, and Ingres." *Cincinnati Romance Review* 13 (1994): 51-60.

Compares Montagu's depiction of Turkish women to Montesquieu's Lettres persanes *and the paintings of Jean-Auguste-Dominique Ingres.*

Fernea, Elizabeth Warnock. "An Early Ethnographer of Middle Eastern Women: Lady Mary Wortley Montagu (1689-1762)." *Journal of Near Eastern Studies* 40, no. 4 (October 1981): 329-38.

Discusses Montagu's role as an ethnographer of the status of women in Middle Eastern life in her letters from Turkey.

Halsband, Robert. "'Condemned to Petticoats': Lady Mary Wortley Montagu as Feminist and Writer." In *The Dress of Words: Essays on Restoration and Eighteenth-Century Literature in Honor of Richmond P. Bond,* edited by Robert B. White, Jr., pp. 35-52. Lawrence: University of Kansas Libraries, 1978.

Surveys a variety of Montagu's works in terms of her feminism, addressing topics including marriage and divorce, politics, and the propriety of women's writing.

Lew, Joseph W. "Lady Mary's Portable Seraglio." *Eighteenth-Century Studies* 24, no. 4 (summer 1991): 432-50.

Studies the Turkish Embassy Letters *as a critique of Ottoman and British culture, and as an anticipation of modern feminism.*

Looser, Devoney. "Scolding Lady Mary Wortley Montagu? The Problematics of Sisterhood in Feminist Criticism." In *Feminist Nightmares: Women at Odds: Feminism and the Problem of Sisterhood,* edited by Susan Ostrov Weisser and Jennifer Fleischner, pp. 44-61. New York: New York University Press, 1994.

Questions critical attempts to describe Montagu as a feminist and apply her concerns to modern feminist issues.

Lowenthal, Cynthia. "The 'Spectatress': Satire and the Aristocrats." In *Lady Mary Wortley Montagu and the Eighteenth-Century Familiar Letter,* pp. 114-52. Athens: University of Georgia Press, 1994.

Suggests that Montagu's letters explore the intersections of class and gender, and public and private, emphasizing her satirical writings on the aristocracy.

Sherman, Sandra. "Instructing the 'Empire of Beauty': Lady Mary Wortley Montagu and the Politics of Female Rationality." *South Atlantic Review* 60, no. 4 (November 1995): 1-26.

Discusses those works by Montagu that are potentially antifeminist, including "A Satyr."

Snyder, Elizabeth. "Female Heroism and Legal Discourse in Lady Mary Wortley Montagu's 'Epistle from Mrs. Y[onge] to Her Husband." *ELH* 34, no. 4 (June 1997): 10-22.

Argues that Montagu subverts the legal term submission *to create a powerful and authoritative female hero.*

Spacks, Patricia Meyer. "Female Rhetorics." In *The Private Self: Theory and Practice of Women's Autobiographical Writings,* edited by Shari Benstock, pp. 177-91. Chapel Hill: University of North Carolina Press, 1988.

Uses Montagu's correspondence as a basis for considering the conflict between the drive for self-expression and the social requirement for restraint.

OTHER SOURCES FROM GALE:

Additional coverage of Montagu's life and career is contained in the following sources published by the Gale Group: *Dictionary of Literary Biography,* Vols. 95, 101; *Literature Criticism from 1400-1800,* Vols. 9, 57; *Literature Resource Center; Poetry Criticism,* Vol. 16; and *Reference Guide to English Literature,* Ed. 2.

SAPPHO

Fl. 6th century B.C.

Greek poet.

Many critics consider Sappho the greatest female poet of the classical world and the most accomplished of an influential group of lyric poets who were active in Greece between 650 B.C. and 450 B.C.—a period often designated the Lyric Age of Greece. Though most of her work survives only in fragments, the imagery and phrasing of those fragments have been striking enough to inspire readers from her own time to the present day to deem her one of the greatest poets of all time. Many of her poems discuss the female speaker's feelings for another woman, making Sappho an important figure in homosexual literary history. (Sappho's homeland of Lesbos lent its name to the modern term "lesbian.") Moreover, as one of the first female authors of the West, Sappho has been embraced by many later authors as an icon of the feminine poetic voice.

BIOGRAPHICAL INFORMATION

Very few details of Sappho's biography are known, and even fewer can be considered trustworthy. Accounts of her life have become thoroughly interwoven with legend, myth, and rumor. The only standard—but unreliable—source of information about Sappho's life is the *Suidas,* a Greek lexicon compiled around the end of the tenth century. Based on earlier lexicons, scholarly commentaries, and excerpts from the works of historians, grammarians, and biographers, the *Suidas* records that Sappho was a native of Lesbos, an island in the Aegean, and that she was probably born in either Eresus or Mytilene. Her father's name is given as Scamandronymus, and her mother's as Cleis. Evidence also suggests that Sappho had three brothers and that her family belonged to the upper class. According to tradition, she lived briefly in Sicily around 600 B.C., when political strife on Lesbos forced her into exile. After returning, she probably married a wealthy man named Cercylas, had a daughter named Cleis, and apparently spent the rest of her life in the city of Mytilene. Most of her time there was occupied with organizing and running a *thiasos,* or an academy for unmarried young women. As was the custom of the age, wealthy families from Lesbos and from the neighboring states would send their daughters to live for a period of time in these informal institutions in order to be instructed in the proper social graces, as well as in composition, singing, and the recitation of poetry. Intended as a transition between their parents' homes and the homes of their future husbands, Sappho's *thiasos* ranked as one of the best and most prestigious in that part of Greece, and as its dedicated teacher and spiritual leader, she enjoyed great renown for having educated generations of young women for fulfilling their social and marital responsibilities. Some legends of Sappho's life indicate that she lived to old age, but others relate that she fell hopelessly in love with a young boatman, Phaon, and, disappointed by their failed love affair, leaped to her death from a high cliff—a story made famous by the Roman poet Ovid in his *Heroides,* but one which has been largely discredited by modern scholars.

MAJOR WORKS

The textual history of Sappho's poetry is as sketchy as her biography. According to the *Suidas,* her substantial body of work was collected into a standard nine-volume edition in the third century B.C.; the arrangement of these volumes was based on the type of meter she used—Sapphic, choriambic, Alcaic, and others—with a whole volume devoted to epithalamia, or marriage songs. Nothing is known about the way Sappho's poetry was transmitted or recorded from her lifetime until the printing of the uniform edition in the third century B.C. Until the nineteenth century, the only known texts of her poetry were miscellaneous fragments quoted in the works of several Alexandrian grammarians to illustrate the Lesbian-Aeolic dialect), and two poems: the ode to Aphrodite, reprinted by Dionysius of Halicarnassus in his treatise on style, and the poem which begins "Peer of the gods he seems to me," presented by Longinus in *On the Sublime* as an example of polished style. Though composed in approximately the first century B.C., the two treatises, and the two poems by Sappho, were not discovered until the Renaissance, when they came to the attention of Italian scholars. The chief importance of the two poems lay in the fact that they were believed to be preserved in their entirety and therefore constituted the most substantial remains of Sappho's to date. In 1898, scholars discovered third-century B.C. papyri containing additional verse fragments. Then, in 1914, archaeologists excavating cemeteries in Oxyrhynchus, Egypt, unearthed coffins made from papier-mâché composed of scraps of paper containing fragments of literary writings, including some by Sappho. These discoveries sparked new interest in Sappho and her poetry, inspiring new critical studies of the text. Though the first English translations of Sappho had appeared in the seventeenth century, it was not until the nineteenth century that translations and commentary on her work began to proliferate, with the first English scholarly edition appearing in 1885. Sappho wrote within the lyric tradition of poetry, influenced by the poets Terpander and Alcaeus, both from Mytilene, and Archilochus, a poet from the nearby island of Paros. Many lyrics, including Sappho's, were intended to be sung accompanied by the lyre and critics have noted the melody and cadence of her poetry. Much of Sappho's poetry was also occasional, or written to commemorate a particular event, but, too, she composed narrative poetry, religious hymns, and epithalamia, for which she was famous. Historians have recorded that Sappho was a frequent and sought-after guest at weddings, where she would sing a marriage song composed especially for the couple. Sappho's lyric verse was personal, emotional, and written in a simple, translucent style which contrasted with the epic poetry of Homer—the dominant mode of composition at the time she was writing. Sappho's poems use a vernacular language which is closer to natural speech and they address feelings of friendship, desire, jealousy, playfulness, and anger.

CRITICAL RECEPTION

Sappho's works have met with critical and popular praise since she first wrote them, and other poets in particular have praised her gift for imagery and portraying emotion. Plato called her the tenth muse and Catullus and Horace imitated her openly, as did the English Romantics including Alfred Lord Tennyson, Algernon Charles Swinburne, and Dante Gabriel Rossetti, who translated some of her fragments. She became an important poet during the rise of German nationalism and was a key influence on American and English Imagists, including Ezra Pound and Hilda Doolittle (known as H. D.). The literary relationship between H. D. and Sappho in particular has been a frequent subject of scholarly interest. Nevertheless, Sappho's personal reputation has often suffered in public discourse. Two or three centuries after her death, rumors began to circulate about her supposed immorality and licentiousness: she was said to be the lover of Alcaeus, an instructor of homosexual practices at her *thiasos,* and a seductress. Speculation about these and other rumors was for centuries the focus of writing on Sappho. Not until the early nineteenth century, when the German classicist Friedrich Gottlieb Welcker published the seminal essay "Sappho von einem herrschenden Vorurtheil befreit" ("Sappho freed from a common prejudice"), did critical focus begin to shift again to her poetry, although the issue of her sexual orientation continues to inform modern scholarship. Because Sappho's poems were intended for performance, the identity of the speaker and its relationship to the meaning of the poems has been a crucial question: several critics have pointed out that the "Sappho" in the poems does not necessarily speak for Sappho the woman. Judith Hallett contends that the poems do not reflect homosexual desire, but instead encourage the listeners—whom Hallett imagines as the young women of Sappho's school—toward heterosexual love. Although Hallett's interpretation has not been universally accepted, her notion of a non-autobiographical persona speaking in the poems continues to inform scholarship. Many critics have proposed that the speaker of the poems, whether or not she is Sappho, makes possible a feminine subjectivity, or a place from which a woman could speak in a culture and literary tradition dominated by men and a masculine perspective. One of the central twentieth-century scholars who advanced this view is Eva Stehle Stigers; in several essays on Sappho, Stigers demonstrates how Sappho's use of a speaking persona expands the possibilities of female identity. Another school of Sappho scholarship has focused on Sappho as a symbol for later women writers. This criticism acknowledges how the idea of Sappho, even more than her writings, was influential and inspirational for other women writing in male-centered cultures. As Susan Gubar asserts, even centuries after her death, Sappho as symbol has legitimized the efforts of women authors and has given them a place from which they can speak.

PRINCIPAL ENGLISH TRANSLATIONS

"Sapphic Fragments" in *Poems* [translated by Dante Gabriel Rossetti] (poetry) 1870

Sappho: Selected Renderings and a Literal Translation [translated by Henry Thornton Wharton] (poetry) 1885

The Poems of Sappho [translated by Edwin Marion Cox] (poetry) 1924

The Songs of Sappho [translated by Marion Mills Miller and David M. Robinson] (poetry) 1925

Sappho: The Poems and Fragments [translated by C. R. Haines] (poetry) 1926

Poetarum Lesbiorum Fragmenta [translated by Edgar Lobel and Denys Page] (poetry) 1955

Sappho: A New Translation [translated by Mary Barnard] (poetry) 1958

Sappho: Lyrics in the Original Greek with Translations [translated by Willis Barnstone] (poetry) 1965

Sappho: Poems and Fragments [translated by Guy Davenport] (poetry) 1965

Sappho: Love Songs [translated by Paul Roche] (poetry) 1966

The Poems of Sappho [translated by Suzy Q. Groden] (poetry) 1967

"Sappho" in *Archilochos, Sappho, Alkman: Three Lyric Poets of the Late Greek Bronze Age* [translated by Guy Davenport] (poetry) 1980

Greek Lyric Poetry: Including the Complete Poetry of Sappho [translated by Willis Barnstone] (poetry) 1987

Sappho's Lyre: Archaic Lyric and Women Poets of Ancient Greece [translated by Diane J. Raynor] (poetry) 1991

If Not, Winter: Fragments of Sappho [translated by Anne Carson] (poetry) 2002

PRIMARY SOURCES

SAPPHO (POEM DATE C. 600 B.C.)

SOURCE: Sappho. "Hymn to Aphrodite." In *The Sappho Companion,* edited by Margaret Reynolds, p. 29. London: Chatto and Windus, 2000.

In the following poem, one of her best known and most complete, Sappho displays her characteristic yearning. The translation is by John Addington Symonds (1883).

Star-throned incorruptible Aphrodite,
Child of Zeus, wile-weaving, I supplicate thee,
Tame not me with pangs of the heart, dread
    mistress,
  Nay, nor with anguish.

But come thou, if erst in the days departed
Thou didst lend thine ear to my lamentation,
And from far, the house of thy sire deserting,
    Camest with golden

Car yoked: thee thy beautiful sparrows hurried
Swift with multitudinous pinions fluttering
Round black earth, adown from the height of
    heaven
  Through middle ether:

Quickly journeyed they; and, O thou, blest Lady,
Smiling with those brows of undying lustre,
Asked me what new grief at my heart lay,
    wherefore
    Now I had called thee,

What I fain would have to assuage the torment
Of my frenzied soul; and whom now, to please
    thee,

Must persuasion lure to thy love, and who now,
Sappho, hath wronged thee?

Yea, for though she flies, she shall quickly chase
thee;
Yea, though gifts she spurns, she shall soon
bestow them;
Yea, though now she loves not, she soon shall
love thee,
Yea, though she will not!

Come, come now too! Come, and from heavy
heart-ache
Free my soul, and all that my longing yearns to
Have done, do thou; be thou for me thyself too
Help in the battle.

OVID (POEM DATE C. 43 B.C.-18 A.D.)

SOURCE: Ovid. "Sappho to Phaon." In *The Sappho Companion,* edited by Margaret Reynolds, pp. 77-78. London: Chatto and Windus, 2000.

In the following poem, the Roman poet Ovid speaks in the voice of Sappho, thereby commenting on Sappho's passion, her lyric mode of writing, her appearance, and her lasting reputation.

So, when you inspected this elegant letter
composed by my right hand
Did your eye know at once that this was
mine?
Or, if you hadn't read my signature, Sappho,
Would you not have known whence this brief
word came?
Perhaps you will ask why I resort to couplets
When I am better suited to the lyric mode?
Well, I must weep for my love—and elegy is the
weeping style . . .
I cannot make my lyre adjust to my tears.
I burn,—as fierce flames fanned by winds,
Scorch the fertile plains with their ardour.
The fields where Phaon lives are far away by Ty-
phoean Aetna
But my heat is like Aetna's and no less a fire
consumes me.
Nor am I capable of arranging a well-ordered
poem;
an empty head is the thing for poetry!
Neither the girls of Pyrrha or Methymna
Nor the Lesbian maids, nor all the rest arouse
me.
Vile is Anactoria, vile to me now is blonde Cy-
dro,
Atthis delights not my eyes as she once did,
Nor any of the other hundred that I loved
without crime.
Unworthy One! what the many once had, is
now yours alone.
Beauty is in you, your youth is apt for delight
and makes
A beauty which fascinates my eyes!
Take up the lyre and shine—then you are Apollo;
Grow horns on your head—behold, you are
Bacchus!
And Phoebus Apollo loved Daphne, and Bac-
chus, Ariadne of Knossis,
Yet neither the one nor the other knew the
lyric mode.
While, for me, the Muses, daughters of Pegasus,
dictate delightful verses,
So that my name is praised throughout the
world.
Not even Alcaeus, who shares my country and
career,
Has more praise, though he does sing more
grandly.
If, to me, nature was unkind and denied me
beauty
I am recompensed with genius.
If I am short, an illustrious name, known
throughout the world
Is mine; take the measure of me from my
fame.

GENERAL COMMENTARY

DAVID M. ROBINSON (ESSAY DATE 1924)

SOURCE: Robinson, David M. "The Writings of Sappho." In *Sappho and Her Influence,* pp. 47-100. Boston: Marshall Jones, 1924.

In the following excerpt, Robinson traces the theme of love throughout Sappho's poetry, emphasizing the beauty of her language and imagery.

The passion of love is the supreme subject of Sappho's songs, as shown by these first two and many a short fragment, as for example (E. 81) where Love is called for the first time in literature "sweet-bitter." Some scholars have credited it to the much later Posidippus, but he and Meleager took the word from Sappho, though it may not have been original even with her. Sappho's order of the compound word is generally reversed in translation, but Sir Edwin Arnold says "sweetly bitter, sadly dear," and Swinburne in *Tristram of Lyonesse* speaks of "Sweet Love, that are so bitter." Tennyson also has the same order in *Lancelot and Elaine* (pp. 205-206). To Sappho love is a second death, and in the second ode death itself seems not very far away. The Greek words for swooning are mostly metaphors from death, and so we are not surprised when we read that like death love relaxes every limb and sweeps one away in its giddy swirling, a sweet-bitter resistless wild beast. Here is Sir Sidney Colvin's translation (*John Keats,* 1917, p. 332): "Love the limb-loosener, the bitter-sweet torment, the wild beast there is no with-standing, never harried a more helpless victim." Another fragment (E. 54) also shows the power of love:

Love tossed my heart as the wind
That descends on the mountain oaks.

(Edmonds)

Sappho's range of subjects is much greater than the personal emotions of love, though very personal and individual feelings predominate. She touches almost every field of human experience, so that there is much in her scant fragments to bring her near to us. The wail against ingratitude comes home to those high-strung natures who do good to others but are sensitive to every wrong when they have the unfortunate experience of learning that one's friends are sometimes one's own worst enemies. "Those harm me most by whom I have done well" (Mackail). But she is not one of those who bear a grudge long, her heart is for peace. One of the few ethical fragments, as Mackail says, "is a speech of delicate self abasement, spoken with the effect of a catch in the voice and tears behind the eyes;" "No rancour in this breast runs wild, I have the heart of a child." Sappho's love of sermonizing is seen in her commandment: "when anger swells in the heart, restrain the idly barking tongue." From Aristotle's *Rhetoric* Edmonds (91) reconstructs another fragment:

Death is an ill; the Gods at least think so,
Or else themselves had perished long ago.

In another fragment of a different nature (E. 120) we read: "Stand up, look me in the face as friend to friend and unveil the charm that is in thy eyes." In other fragments we enter a Lesbian lady's home and see woman's love of dress,—no short skirt for her, for they "wrapped her all around with soft cambric" (E. 105). "A motley gown of fair Lydian work reached down to her feet" (E. 20), or, if we believe Pollux (VII. 93), it is the Greek love of fine shoes. No Lesbian butchery for her tender feet, but she must wear soft luxurious Lydian slippers: "A broidered strap of fair Lydian work covered her feet." Punning on the name of Timas (precious), another fragment, which perhaps refers to a statue of Aphrodite in Sappho's home, seems to dote on fancy handkerchiefs; "and hanging on either side thy face the purple handkerchief which Timas sent for thee from Phocaea, a precious gift from a precious giver" (E. 87).[1] The fragment (E. 21), "shot with a thousand hues," refers to dress rather than to the rainbow. The sight of beautiful gowns thrilled her: "Come you back, my rosebud Gongyla, in your milk-white gown." Again she says: "Many are the golden bracelets and the purple robes, aye and the fine smooth broideries, indeed a richly varied bride-gift; and without number also are the silver goblets and the ornaments of ivory" (E. 66). She coined new words for women; she calls the chest in which women keep their perfumes and like things a *grutė* or hutch (E. 180). Again she uses (E. 179) the word *Beudos* for a short diaphanous frock or blouse. She is the first to use the word *Chlamys,* where she speaks of Love as "coming from Heaven and throwing off his purple mantle" (E. 69). Blondes were much admired among the fair-haired Lesbians, though Sappho herself was a brunette, and so she herself mentions (E. 189) a kind of box-wood or scytharium-wood with which women dye their hair a golden color. She is fond of cassia and frankincense (E. 66), and she dotes on myrrh and royal perfumes (E. 83). She rebukes the foolish girl who prides herself on her ring.[2] With "a keen swift flicker of woman's jealousy," and well acquainted with the philosophy of clothes and with the new Ionic dresses introduced into Lesbus during her own lifetime at the beginning of the sixth century B.C. from Asia Minor, she jests about her rival Andromeda, the country girl who knows not how to manage the train of her new gown[3] (E. 98):

What rustic hoyden ever charmed the soul,
That round her ankles could not kilt her coats!
(THOMAS DAVIDSON in *Warner's Library of the World's Best Literature*)

There is an intimate love of the loveliness of nature in Sappho, as we should expect of one resident on an island under Ionian skies where, as Herodotus (I. 142) says, "the climate and seasons

FROM THE AUTHOR

TWO TRANSLATIONS OF SAPPHO'S "FRAGMENT 130," FROM JOHN ADDINGTON SYMONDS (1883) AND GUY DAVENPORT (1965)

Lo, Love once more, the limb-dissolving King,
The bitter-sweet impracticable thing,
Wild-beast-like rends me with fierce quivering.

John Addington Symonds, 1883

Percussion, salt and honey,
A quivering in the thighs;
He shakes me all over again,
Eros who cannot be thrown,
Who stalks on all fours
Like a beast.

Eros makes me shiver again
Strengthless in the knees,
Eros gall and honey,
Snake-sly, invincible.

Guy Davenport, 1965

Sappho. "Fragment 130." In *The Sappho Companion,* edited by Margaret Reynolds, p. 61. London: Chatto & Windus, 2000.

are the most beautiful of any cities in the world." "The many garlanded earth puts on her broidery" (E. 133). "Thus of old did the dainty feet of Cretan maidens dance pat to the music beside some lovely altar, pressing the soft smooth bloom of the grass (E. 114)." As Thomas Davidson has so well said: "every hour of the day comes to Sappho with a fresh surprise." We lie down for a noonday siesta in "a murmurous, blossomy June," as Stebbing puts it, in the orchard of the nymphs where (E. 4),

around
Through boughs of the apple
Cool waters sound.
From the rustling leaves
Drips sleep to the ground.

(Unpublished, RHYS CARPENTER)[4]

In the Greek, as Edwin Cox says, "the sound of the words, the repetition of long vowels particularly omega, the poetic imagery of the whole and the drowsy cadence of the last two words give this fragment a combination of qualities probably not surpassed in any language." The beautiful verses about the pippin on the topmost branch we shall quote below. In another fragment (E. 3) Sappho sees the stars in a way which Tennyson echoes when he writes: "As when in heaven the stars about the moon Look beautiful." Or again Sappho's love of nature appears in the line (E. 112): "the moon rose full and the maidens took their stand about the altar." In the new *Ode to Atthis* the moon is not silver (as in E. 3) but rosy-fingered: "after sunset the rosy-fingered moon beside the stars that are about her, when she spreads her light o'er briny sea and eke o'er flowery field, while the dew lies so fair on the ground and the roses revive and the dainty anthrysc and the melilot with all its blooms" (E. 86). Recently (1922) A. C. Benson in *The Reed of Pan* has combined fragment (E. 3) with the beautiful half stanza quoted above, under the title *Moonrise:*

The moon high-hung in the hollow night
Resistless pours her silver tide;
Swift, swift the stars withdraw their light,
And their diminished glories hide.

And where cool streams through reed-beds slip,
The breeze through the orchard alley stirs,
And slumber well-nigh seems to drip
From the dark arms of dusky firs.

In another fragment, which we quote below, Sappho pictures a spring midnight with almost astronomical exactness. She loves the sun: "I have loved daintiness [from childhood] and for me love possesses the brightness and beauty of the sun." William Stebbing in his *Minstrel of Love* expands the two verses into ten, the last "Dazzling my brain with gazing on the Sun." Sappho knows the golden-sandalled and queenly dawn (E. 19, 177). She wrote an ode to Hesperus, the Evening Star, of which we have only the tantalizing beginning, "fairest of all the stars that shine" (E. 32). Another graceful fragment quoted in antiquity to show the charm of repetition (E. 149)[5] on the Evening Star, which comes in Catullus too, has influenced not only Byron in *Don Juan* but Andrew Lang in *Helen of Troy* (II. 4) and especially Tennyson (see p. 206). "That Greek blockhead," as Sir Walter Scott was called, though he knew more Greek than most undergraduate students of Greek to-day, even if he didn't know the Sappho fragment, expresses the same idea in the *Doom of Dever Girl,* "All meet whom day and care divide."

Sappho is fond of birds, the dove, the lovely or heavenly swallow (E. 122), the nightingale. The doves drive Aphrodite's car in the first ode and in E. 16 "their heart grows light and they slacken the labor of their pinions." Ben Jonson took from Sappho (E. 138) his line in *The Sad Shepherd,* "the dear good angel of the spring, The nightingale," and Swinburne, "The tawny sweet-winged thing Whose cry was but of spring." A fragment published even since Edmonds' book speaks of the "clear-voiced nightingales." She knows exactly what crickets do at noon of a summer's day. Listen to their song (E. 94), rescued from Alcaeus, to whom Bergk had wrongly ascribed it:

And clear song from beneath her wings doth raise
When she shouts-down the perpendicular blaze
Of the outspread sunshine of noon.

(EDMONDS)[6]

We see the woman also in her love of flowers as well as of birds. Flowers are her favorites and she worships them with almost the modern reverence of the Japanese, whom I have sometimes seen saying their morning prayers to a beautiful bouquet. Take, for example, this simple but pretty flower-picture of Sappho's (E. 107):

I saw one day a-gathering flowers
The daintiest little maid.

(EDMONDS)

She sympathizes with the hyacinth (E. 151), which the shepherd tramples under foot on the mountain, and uses it in one of the most attractive flower-similes in all literature. Listen to this aubade which has been recently found and very tentatively restored (E. 82). It gives a delightful glimpse also of Sappho's ménage:

'Sappho, I swear if you come not forth I will love you no more. O rise and shine upon us and set free your beloved strength from the bed, and then like a pure lily beside the spring hold aloof your Chian robe and wash you in the water. And Cleïs shall bring down from your presses saffron smock and purple robe; and let a mantle be put over you and be crowned with a wreath of flowers tied about your head; and so come, sweet with all the beauty with which you make me mad. And do you, Praxinoa, roast us nuts, so that I may make the maidens a sweeter breakfast; for one of the Gods, child, has vouchsafed us a boon. This very day has Sappho the fairest of all women vowed that she will surely return unto Mytilene the dearest of all towns—return with us, the mother with her children.'

Dearest Atthis, can you then forget all this that happened in the old days? . . .

(EDMONDS)

Or take this other example of Sappho's love of flowers which Symonds has expanded into a sonnet too long to quote here. I give Tucker's new version:

Take springs of anise fair
With soft hands twined,
And round thy bonny hair
A chaplet bind;
The Muse with smiles will bless
Thy blossoms gay,
While from the garlandless
She turns away.

Sappho speaks of the golden pulses (E. 139):

[*It was summer when I found you*
In the meadow long ago,]
And the golden vetch was growing
By the shore.

(BLISS CARMAN)

Sappho knows the little and common flowers, the dainty anthrysc and melilot, the violets and the lilies (E. 86, 83, 82), but, like Pindar, she especially loves the rose. Meleager's garland of song assigned the rose to Sappho. She says in one of the new fragments (E. 83): "with many a garland of violets and sweet roses mingled, you have decked my flowing locks as I stood by your side, and with many a woven necklet made of a hundred blossoms you have adorned my dainty throat." Philostratus in his *Letters* (51) says: "Sappho loves the rose and always crowns it with a meed of praise, likening beautiful maidens to it; and she compares it to the bared fore-arms of the Graces." Fragment E. 68 says: "Hither pure rose-armed Graces, daughters of Zeus." Sappho's love of the rose has led earlier collectors of Sappho's fragments to include among her verses the famous song in praise of the rose quoted by Achilles Tatius in his love romance on *Clitophon and Leucippe,* which Elizabeth Barrett Browning has translated:

IF ZEUS *chose us a King of the Flowers in his mirth,*
He would call to the Rose and would royally crown it,
For the Rose, ho, the Rose, is the grace of the earth,
Is the light of the plants that are growing upon it.

For the Rose, ho, the Rose, is the eye of the flowers,
Is the blush of the meadows that feel themselves fair—
Is the lightning of beauty that strikes through the bowers
On pale lovers who sit in the glow unaware.

Ho, the Rose breathes of love! Ho, the Rose lifts the cup
To the red lips of Cypris invoked for a guest!
Ho, the Rose, having curled its sweet leaves for the world,
Takes delight in the motion its petals keep up,
As they laugh to the wind as it laughs from the west!

Sappho, however, does mention the roses of Pieria in the famous lines spoken with characteristic teacher's tone, almost in the manner of Mrs. Poyser. According to Plutarch, in one passage, the verses are addressed to a wealthy woman, in another passage,[7] to a woman of no refinement or learning; according to Stobaeus,[8] to a woman of no education; probably it was some rich but uncultured Lesbian girl, who would not go to the Lesbian Smith or Vassar or Bryn Mawr:

Thou shalt die and be laid low in the grave, hidden from mortal ken
Unremembered, and no song of the Muse wakens thy name again;
No Pierian rose brightens thy brow, lost in the nameless throng,
Thy dark spirit shall flit forth like a dream, bodiless ghosts among.

(SHOREY)

For another expanded version by Swinburne in his *Anactoria* I must refer to Wharton. Sappho had known and loved the wee wee maiden Atthis when she was an awkward school girl, but now in the bloom of beauty after a sad parting the fickle Atthis has flitted away to another woman's college and clean forgotten Sappho for a rival teacher, Andromeda; "I loved you, Atthis, long ago, when my own girlhood was still all flowers, and you—you seemed to me a small ungainly child" (E. 48).[9] "So you hate to think of me, Atthis; 'Tis all Andromeda now" (Edmonds).

Lesbus was a land of flowers, of the rose and the violet, "a land rich in corn and oil and wine, in figs and olives, in building-wood and tinted marble," as Tucker says. But this triangular island (about thirty-five by twenty-five miles) had mountains rising from two to three thousand feet at its corners and two deep fiords on its southern coast. From the northern coast Sappho must often have looked across the short seven miles of laughing sea upon Troyland and thought of the Homeric poems in which Lesbus played such an important rôle.[10] The air like that of Athens as described by Pindar, with a glamor wreathing such cities as Smyrna, was so translucent that in the northeast across the dividing sea many-fountained Ida could easily be seen. It is perhaps an accident that there is so little mention of mountain or sea in Sappho. But she was no "landlubber," as Professor Allinson would have us believe.[11] Pindar and the other lyric poets were acquainted with the sea and so must Sappho have known it, as she daily saw the ships fly in and out of their haven on white wings (cf. first stanza of poem on p. 82). In one of the new fragments (E. 86) we have a marvellous picture of the sea in the last stanza of a poem which otherwise, with its love of flowers, with the beautiful simile of the rosy-fingered moon, is one of the most perfect things in literature. The telepathic and telegraphic sympathy of Sappho startles us and the wireless message sent by night across the severing sea, whose sigh you can hear in the original Greek, anticipates the modern radio.[12] As this is a memory poem, and *Anactoria,* like Hallam, is "lost," for the time being at least, I have followed as a model Tennyson's *In Memoriam* in metre, stanza, and rhyming. The first line seems to be "remembered" in rhyme as it were after the interval during which the second and third lines have been made and rhymed.

SAPPHO'S GIRL FRIEND ACROSS THE SEA

Atthis, in Sardis far away
Anactoria dear to thee
And dear indeed alike to me
Now dwells, but hither often stray

Her thoughts sent usward by the power
That lives anew the life she loved
When thou her glorious goddess proved,—
Thy songs her joy at every hour.

You were her sun, now set too soon;
Among the Lydian dames she shines
As, after sunset, glow the lines
Of light the rosy-fingered moon

Throws on her retinue of stars
Spreading a far-flung lane of beams
That gleams the salt sea o'er and streams
Across the rocky shore that bars

In vain the light that floods its gloom,
And leaping landward bathes the fields
Where many a flower its beauty yields
With fragrant variegated bloom.

Full fair the dew springs forth and holds
The light, the roses lift their heads,
The dainty anthryscs quit their beds,
The clover, honey-rich, unfolds.

Through all this beauty, hard unrest
And longing crushing like a stone
Her tender heart, ofttimes alone
She wanders with a weighted breast.

She cannot calm her quivering lip
And through the balmy, scented dark
She cries aloud we must embark
And thither come on some swift ship.

Full clear her words to thee and me,
For night with all her many ears
Their ardent sound full gladly hears
And sends us o'er the severing sea.

(D. M. R.)

This ode alone marks Sappho as a great poetess. The reasons are: (1) the loving notice of little and common flowers, (2) the comparison of Anactoria when surrounded by other women to the moon in the midst of her surrounding stars, the bold personification of the moon secured by the use of the single figure "rosy-fingered," (3) sudden and masterful survey of land and sea, (4) the successful centering of attention upon Anactoria's homesickness even in the midst of such far-reaching beauty of land and sea, (5) the remarkably forceful portrayal of what in our day we call thought-transference as seen, for example, in Tennyson's *Aylmer's Field* or *Enoch Arden,* (6) and not least important, the simplicity and sharpness of outline displayed in the imagery. "Night" is a vague, widely diffused, mystic thing, but Sappho makes us see her a thing of many ears and one of them close to Anactoria's face. Night does not send a mystic intimation such as Tennyson's vibration of light might indicate. But she speaks right out in a clear voice that carries far enough to reach across the sea to Sappho. A seventh reason is the strange, hot emotion of love and sorrow and longing that throbs like a pulse in every line and makes the whole letter a living creature. Milton said and lovers of poetry have always agreed that poetry must be simple, sensuous, and passionate. By sensuous he of course meant expressed in images involving the use of the bodily senses. Is there anything in poetry, ancient or modern, that more exactly meets Milton's requirements than these few lines of Sappho's letter to her girl friend? Now if this is evident to the reader of an English translation, it is vastly more so to one who knowing the meaning of the words has read them in the Greek and then read them again because they were so sweet, and read them a third time and many times until the music haunts him like the face of a lover.

Notes

1. For such head-cloths cf. the Latin word *struppus* and the festival at Falerii, called *struppearia,* Dion. Hal., XI. 39 and Poulsen, *Etruscan Tomb Paintings,* p. 23. Edmonds' new reading is very uncertain; for his previous reading and poetical version cf. *Sappho in the Added Light of the New Fragments,* p. 28.

2. I keep Bergk's reading, "Foolish woman, pride not thyself on a ring." Edmonds changes the text and translates, "But come, be not so proud of a ring."

3. Cf. Poulsen, in *Jahrbuch,* XXI. 209 ff. (1906); *Die Bronzen von Olympia,* IV., pl. VII. 74.

4. There are many other poetical versions by Merivale, Symonds, F. Tennyson, Tucker, Cox, Edmonds, etc. For an absurd interpretation *Sappho in the Rain,* cf. *Wiener Studien,* XXXVIII. 176 ff. (1916).

5. Poetical translations by Merivale, Arnold, Appleton, F. Tennyson, Symonds, Edmonds, Miller, Percy Mackaye, etc.

6. *Sappho in the Added Light of the New Fragments,* p. 25, but in *Lyra Graeca,* I, p. 253, he changes his previous emendation and reads a text which I consider very uncertain, "and pours down a sweet shrill song from beneath his wings, when the Sun-god illumines the earth with his downshed flame outspread."

7. *Praec. Con.,* 48; *Qu. Conv.,* III. 1. 2.

8. *Flor.,* IV. 12.

9. For Swinburne's expansion cf. p. 210; cf. also Percy Mackaye in *Sappho and Phaon.* Bliss Carman has evolved the following from Sappho's one line:

   I loved thee, Atthis, in the long ago
   When the great oleanders were in flower
   In the broad herded meadows full of sun.
   And we would often at the fall of dusk
   Wander together by the silver stream,
   When the soft grass-heads were all wet with dew
   And purple misted in the fading light,
   And joy I knew and sorrow at thy voice,
   And the superb magnificence of love—
   The loneliness that saddens solitude,
   And the sweet speech that makes it durable,
   The bitter longing and the keen desire,
   The sweet companionship through quiet days
   In the slow ample beauty of the world
   And the unutterable glad release
   Within the temple of the holy night;
   O Atthis, how I loved thee long ago
   In that fair perished summer by the sea.

10. Cf. Miss Shields, "*Lesbos in the Trojan War,*" in *The Classical Jour.,* XIII. 670 ff. (1918); *The Cults of Lesbos* (Johns Hopkins University Diss.) 1917.

11. Cf. *Transactions and Proceedings of the American Philological Association,* LIII. xvi (1922).

12. For Mnesidice, Edmonds would now read Anactoria. There is a good metrical translation by G. M. Whicher in Manatt, *Aegean Days,* London, 1913, p. 286.

Selected Bibliography of Recent Books on Sappho

Aly, see Pauly-Wissowa.

Bascoul, J. M. F., *La chaste Sappho de Lesbos et le mouvement féministe à Athènes au IVe siècle av. J. C.* Paris. 1911.

Bascoul, J. M. F., *La chaste Sappho de Lesbos et Stésichore. Les prétendues amies de Sappho.* Paris, 1913.

Bergk, Th., *Poetae Lyrici Graeci.* Vol. III, Leipzig, 1914.

Bethe, E., *Griechische Lyrik.* Berlin, 1920.

Brandt, Lida R., *Social Aspects of Greek Life in the Sixth Century B.C.* Philadelphia, 1921.

Brandt, P., *Sappho, ein Lebensbild aus den Frühlingstagen altgriechischer Dichtung.* Leipzig, 1905.

Bunner, Anne, see Wharton.

Carman, Bliss, *Sappho, One Hundred Lyrics.* Boston, 1904.

Carroll, M., *Greek Women.* Philadelphia, 1907.

Christ, W.von-Schmid, W., *Geschichte der griechischen Litteratur.* Munich, 1912.

Cox, E. M., *Sappho and the Sapphic Metre in English.* London, 1916. *Poems of Sappho.* London, New York, 1924.

Cipollini, A., *Saffo.* Milan, 1890.

Croiset, A., *Histoire de la Litterature Grecque* (vol. II, pp. 226-244). Paris, 1898.

De Courten, Maria L. G., *Saffo* (Supplementi ad "Aegyptus"). Milan, 1921.

Diehl, E., *Supplementum lyricum*[3] (Kleine Texte, 33-34). Bonn, 1917.

Edmonds, J. M., *The New Fragments of Alcaeus, Sappho and Corinna.* Cambridge, 1909.

Edmonds, J. M., *Sappho in the Added Light of the New Fragments.* Cambridge, 1912. (Has some poetical translations.)

Edmonds, J. M., *Lyra Graeca,* I, in *The Loeb Classical Library.* New York, 1922. [Abbreviated as E.]

Edmonds, J. M., Various articles in *Classical Review, Classical Quarterly* and *Cambridge Philological Society's Proceedings,* from 1909 to 1922.

Farnell, G. S., *Greek Lyric Poetry.* London, 1891.

Glaser, R., *Sappho, die zehnte Muse* (Südwest-deutsche Monatsblätter). 1916.

Grenfell, B. P., and Hunt, A. S.,*The Oxyrhynchus Papyri.* Vols. I-XV, especially I, X, and XV. London, 1898. 1922.

Higginson, T. W., *Atlantic Essays.* Boston, 1871.

Latini, Giov., *Saffo, Mimnermo e Catullo* Viterbo, 1914.

Lavagnini, B., *I Lirici Greci.* Turin, 1923.

Lobel, E., *Sappho.* Oxford, 1925.

Mackail, J. W., *Lectures on Greek Poetry* (pp. 83-112). London and New York, 1911.

Meabe, T., *Saffo* (Spanish translation). Paris, 1913.

Merino, A. Fernandez, *Estudios de Literatura Griega. Safo ante la critica moderna.*[3] Madrid, 1884.

Meunier, M., *Sappho, Traduction nouvelle de tous les fragments.* (Has not recent fragments.) Paris, 1911.

Milburn, Lucy McD., *Lost Letters from Lesbos.* Chicago, 1902.

Miller, Marion Mills, and Robinson, D. M. *The Songs of Sappho* (Greek text of all Sappho, of all the epigrams about her, of Erinna, of the new papyrus biography of Sappho, etc., prepared and annotated and literally translated by D. M. Robinson. Introduction on *The Recovery and Restoration of the Egyptian Relics of Sappho* and a critical *Memoir of the Real Sappho* by D. M. Robinson. Introduction by M. M. Miller on the Sapphic Metre, and Poetical Adaptations of Sappho. New York, 1924.

MUSTARD, W. P., *Classical Echoes in Tennyson.* New York, 1904.

O'HARA, J. M., *The Poems of Sappho.* Portland, 1910.

OSBORN, PERCY, *Poems of Sappho.* London, 1909.

PASELLA, PIETRO, *I Frammenti di Alceo e di Saffo tradotti.* Rome, 1922.

PATRICK, MARY MILLS, *Sappho and the Island of Lesbos.* Boston, 1914. Reprinted, 1924.

PAULY-WISSOWA-KROLL-WITTE, *Real-Encyclopädie.* Exhaustive article on Sappho by Aly. Stuttgart, 1920.

PETERSEN, W., *The Lyric Songs of the Greeks. Translated into English Verse.* Boston, 1918.

REINACH, TH., *Pour mieux connaître Sappho* (*Académie des Inscriptions et Belles-Lettres*). Paris, 1911.

ROBINSON, D. M., *See* Miller-Robinson.

SCOLLARD, C. L.,-JONES, T. S., *Sapphics.* Clinton, N. Y., 1910.

SITZLER, J., *Bibliography on Sappho* in Bursian (Kroll) *Jahresbericht über die Fortschritte der klassischen Altertumswissenschaft.* CXXXIII, 1907, pp. 104 ff., pp. 176 ff., CLXXVIII, 1919, pp. 46 ff.

SMITH, J. S. EASBY-, *Songs of Sappho.* Washington, D. C., 1891.

SMYTH, H. W., *Greek Melic Poets.* London, 1900.

STACPOOLE, H. D. V., *Sappho, a new rendering.* London 1920.

STANLEY, ALBERT A., *Greek Themes in Modern Musical Settings.* (Includes, pp. 1-68, Music to Percy Mackaye's *Sappho and Phaon*). *University of Michigan Humanistic Studies,* XV, 1923.

STEBBING, W., *Greek and Latin Anthology thought into English Verse.* Part III, *Greek Epigrams and Sappho.* Adaptations and Expansions of Sappho. None of the new fragments included. London, 1923.

STEINER, B., *Sappho.* Jena, 1907.

STORER, EDWARD, *Sappho* (*Poets Translation Series*). London, 1916.

TUCKER, T. G., *Sappho.* Melbourne, Australia, 1914.

TUTIN, J. R., *Sappho, The Queen of Song.* London and Boston, 1914.

VIVIEN, RENÉE [pseudonym of an American lady, Pauline Tarn, 1877-1909, who lived in Paris], *Sappho, traduction nouvelle avec le texte grec.* Paris, 1903. Reprinted in the anonymous *Sappho et huit poetesses grecques. Texte et reduction.* Paris, 1909.

WAGNER, R., *Übersetzung der grösseren Bruchstücke Sapphos im Versmass des Originals nebst erläuternden Bemerkungen.* 1916.

SUSAN GUBAR (ESSAY DATE 1996)

SOURCE: Gubar, Susan. "Sapphistries." In *Re-Reading Sappho: Reception and Transmission,* edited by Ellen Greene, pp. 199-217. Berkeley: University of California Press, 1996.

In the following essay, Gubar discusses the influence of Sappho on later poets, particularly women and lesbian poets, and on modern feminist sensibility in general. Gubar focuses on H. D. and Renee Vivien, but also discusses the writings of Virginia Woolf, Willa Cather, Amy Lowell, and Marguerite Yourcenar. As Gubar notes, Sappho was important to these writers as a symbol and literary model—representing female communities in addition to being a classical precedent for women's writing.

From the poems by Katherine Philips, "The English Sappho," celebrating female friendship to the provocative blank page under the entry for Sappho in Monique Wittig and Sande Zeig's *Lesbian Peoples: Material for a Dictionary* (1979), from Elizabeth Barrett Browning's translations and Christina Rossetti's variations to recent publications like Sidney Abbott and Barbara Love's *Sappho Was a Right-On Woman* (1972) and Pat Califia's *Sapphistry* (1980), the person and poetics of Sappho have haunted the female imagination.[1] Since the late nineteenth century, of course, the words we use to describe female homosexuality derive from the poet of Lesbos, although the 1971 edition of the *Oxford English Dictionary* actually defines "Sapphism" as "unnatural sexual relations between women," and "Lesbian rule" as "a mason's rule made of lead. . . ." In a manner that might have surprised the lexicographers, however, doubtless because of a flood of male-authored classic scholarship and decadent poetry at the turn of the century, Sappho influenced women writing in the early decades of the twentieth century. Just when translators of Sappho were beginning to honor her choice of a female pronoun for her beloved and classicists were disputing the legends and facts about her life,[2] Sappho's status as a female precursor empowered a number of female modernists to collaborate in exuberant linguistic experiments.

Like "Michael Fields" (pen name of Katherine Bradley and Edith Cooper), whose volume of Sapphics were entitled *Long Ago,* Isadora Duncan viewed Sappho as a legendary survivor from a paradise lost long ago; while Edna St. Vincent Millay identified her as a lovelost suicide, Sara Teasdale idealized Sappho as a mother-poet crooning to her daughter Cleis, Elizabeth Robbins meditated on a Sappho who is "the nursing mother of intellectually free women," and Isak Dinesen associated her with prostitution.[3] Despite their differences, however, all evince the same desire to recover Sappho that impels Virginia Woolf's women's studies collective in her 1921 short story, "A Society." When the members of this Society of Outsiders evaluate the world of culture created by men, they discover one Professor Hobkin's edition of Sappho, which is primarily devoted to a defense of Sappho's chastity. As Jane

Marcus has shown, Hobkin's gynecological obsession with "some implement which looks remarkably like a hairpin" dramatizes Woolf's recognition that exceptional women like Sappho have been used not for but against the nurturing of a female literary tradition.[4] One year before writing "A Society," moreover, Woolf discerned in Desmond MacCarthy's newspaper article on the paucity of women's poetry precisely the sentence her society would read in the newspaper: "Since Sappho there has been no female of first rate." In a letter of rebuttal, Woolf claimed that "external restraints" have inhibited the growth of women's literary history after Sappho, for Sappho lived in a time that accorded "social and domestic freedom" to women who were "highly educated and accustomed to express their sentiments." The conditions that make possible the birth of Sappho are first, artistic predecessors; second, membership in a group where art is freely discussed and practices; and third, freedom of action and experience: "Perhaps in Lesbos," Woolf speculates, "but never since have these conditions been the lot of women."[5]

Significantly, however, some of Woolf's contemporaries were in the process of recovering the artistic freedom they, too, associated with this classical literary foremother who evaded masculine definitions and therefore freed them from the anxiety of authorship suffered by so many women writers.[6] As if to illustrate the problem creativity continued to pose for twentieth-century women artists, as late as 1944 Edith Sitwell complained that "women's poetry, with the exception of Sappho" and a few poems of Christina Rossetti and Emily Dickinson, "is *simply awful*—incompetent, floppy, whining, arch, trivial, self-pitying."[7] Whether the woman poet confronted no poetic tradition of her own or a tradition only of what Sitwell termed "ghastly wallowing," she suffered isolation and feelings of inferiority. Like so many women writers, both Woolf and Sitwell mulled over the inadequacy of their classical education, specifically the inadequacy of their knowledge of Greek, which made it difficult for them to be what Woolf called Sappho, "an inheritor as well as an originator."[8] Yet, in order to become originators inheriting Sappho's poetic genius, both Woolf and Sitwell would have certainly agreed with Willa Cather that, "If all of the lost riches we could have one master restored to us, . . . the choice of the world would be for the lost nine books of Sappho," for "those broken fragments have burned themselves into the consciousness of the world like fire."[9] To be sure, male writers from Catullus to Lawrence Durrell also turned to Sappho, thereby providing women artists with a prism through which to view their only classical precursor.[10] But, as Louise Bogan has explained, women readers search for the lost fragments of Sappho "less with the care and eagerness of the scholar looking for bits of shattered human art, than with the hungry eyes of the treasure hunter, looking for some last grain of a destroyed jewel."[11]

Sappho represents, then, all the lost women of genius in literary history, especially all the lesbian artists whose work has been destroyed, sanitized, or heterosexualized in an attempt to evade what Elaine Marks identifies as "lesbian intertextuality."[12] Antithetically, the effort to recover Sappho illustrates how twentieth-century women poets try to solve the problem of poetic isolation and imputed inferiority. For the woman poet who experiences herself as inadequate or inadequately nurtured by a nonexistent or degraded literary matrilineage, for the lesbian poet who looks in vain for a native lesbian poetic tradition, Sappho is a very special precursor. Precisely because so many of her original Greek texts were destroyed,

ABOUT THE AUTHOR

HILDA DOOLITTLE, BETTER KNOWN AS THE MODERNIST POET H. D., ON SAPPHO'S ARTISTIC LEGACY

Little—not little—but all, all roses! So at the last, we are forced to accept the often quoted tribute of Meleager, late Alexandrian, half Jew, half Grecian poet. Little but all roses! True, Sappho has become for us a name, an abstraction as well as a pseudonym for poignant human feeling, she is indeed rocks set in a blue sea, she is the sea itself, breaking and tortured and torturing, but never broken. She is the island of artistic perfection where the lover of ancient beauty (shipwrecked in the modern world) may yet find foothold and take breath and gain courage for new adventures and dream of yet unexplored continents and realms of future artistic achievement. She is the wise Sappho.

H. D. Excerpt from "The Wise Sappho." In *Notes on Thought and Vision,* edited by Anne Janowitz, p. 67. San Francisco: City Lights Books, 1982.

the modern woman poet could write "for" or "as" Sappho and thereby invent a classical inheritance of her own. In other words, such a writer is not infected by Sappho's stature with a Bloomian "anxiety of influence," because her ancient precursor is paradoxically in need of a contemporary collaborator,[13] or so the poetry of Renée Vivien and H. D. seems to suggest. What Sandra Gilbert would call a "fantasy precursor" or what I would term a "fantastic collaboration" simultaneously heals the anxiety of authorship and links these two women poets to an empowering literary history they could create in their own image.

Sappho's preeminence provides Vivien and H. D. with evidence that the woman who is a poet need not experience herself as a contradiction in terms, that the woman who achieves the confessional lyricism of Sappho will take her place apart from but also beside a poet like Homer. Through the dynamics of their collaboration with Sappho, feminist modernists like Renée Vivien and H. D. present themselves as breaking not only with patriarchal literary tradition, but also with nineteenth-century female literary history. Replacing the schizophrenic doubling Sandra Gilbert and I have traced throughout Victorian women's literature with euphoric coupling in which the other is bound to the self as a lover, such poets also offer divergent interpretations of what lesbianism means as an imaginative force. The fantastic collaborations Vivien and H. D. enact through their reinventions of Sappho's verse are not unrelated to the eroticized female relationships that quite literally empowered them to write. By recovering a female precursor of classical stature, moreover, Vivien and H. D. could mythologize the primacy of women's literary language. Whether the recovery of Sappho results in a decadent aesthetic, as it does for Vivien, or in a chiseled classicism, as for H. D., it holds out the promise of excavating a long-lost ecstatic lyricism that inscribes female desire as the ancient source of song. Only in the later work of writers like Amy Lowell and Marguerite Yourcenar would the liabilities of such a collaboration be uncovered.

Like Cather, who especially admired Sappho's creation of "the most wonderfully emotional meter in literature," Renée Vivien was fascinated with Sappho's resonant lines that, in Cather's words, "come in like a gasp when feeling flows too swift for speech."[14] But, unlike Cather, Vivien self-consciously dramatized her efforts to regain Sappho's erotic language specifically for lesbians. Curiously, in 1900, Vivien met the woman she would desire and resist all her life: at a theater, Natalie Barney was reading a letter from Liane de Pougy that would be published the next year in her *Idylle saphique*. And, as Elyse Blankely has shown, Sappho's legend continued to provide the scenic background for the stormy relationship Vivien and Barney pursued, as well as being the central symbol of their respective arts.[15] Motivated at least in part by her friendship with Pierre Louÿs, the famous author of *Chansons de Bilitis* (1894) and *Aphrodite* (1896), Natalie Barney published *Cinq petits dialogues grecs* in 1902. In 1906 she produced her *Acts d'entr'actes,* with Marguerite Moreno playing the leading role of a Sappho who dies not from love of the boatman Phaon, as the followers of Ovid claimed, but because of her desire for a girl promised in marriage.[16] During this same period, after teaching herself Greek, Vivien published *Sapho* (1903), a collection of translations and imitations of Greek fragments that the Anglo-American Vivien composed in French. In 1904, she and Natalie Barney traveled to Mytilene where Vivien eventually purchased a house of her own. In that same year, she published *Une femme m'apparut* (*A Woman Appeared to Me*), a roman à clef that focused on an androgynous avatar and disciple of the poet of Mytilene who argues not only that Phaon is the vulgar invention of low humorists but also that Sappho is the only woman poet of distinction because she did not deign to notice masculine existence, which is "the Unaesthetic par excellence."[17]

In both her poetry and her novel, Vivien appropriates the sadistic Sappho so prevalent in the late-nineteenth-century work of Baudelaire and Swinburne.[18] In a setting of voluptuous, "evil" flowers and narcissistic mirrors like those associated with Swinburne's vampire and suicidal heroine Lesbia Brandon, Vivien's Sappho morbidly sings, "I believe I take from you a bit of your fleeting life when I embrace you"; like Baudelaire, who portrays the sinful delights of Lesbos, Vivien identifies Sappho with Satan, the incarnation of cunning and the antagonist of both God and his poet, Homer.[19] This satanic Sappho is, of course, the same haunted figure Colette perceived in Vivien herself, living shrouded in the scented darkness of fin de siècle decadence, wasting away in a twilight of anorexic self-incarceration.[20] But while in her life Vivien clearly did suffer the consequences of such internalization, in her art she tapped the energy of the decadents' alienated lesbian. The unholy excess and implacable cruelty of lesbian desire in Vivien's fiction and poetry—the tormented hair, unappeased breasts, insatiable thighs, and ardent hands of the lovers described by Vivien—uncover the demonic power that drew Baudelaire and Swinburne to the lesbian femme fatale. Indeed, Vivien suggests that the "unnatural" longing of the decadents' Sappho turns the lesbian into a prototypical artist, for her obsession with a beauty that does not exist in nature is part of a satanically ambitious effort against nature to attain the aesthetic par excellence.

Vivien therefore implicitly reveals the centrality of the lesbian in decadent poetry to claim this image for herself. Like Proust, who had declared "Femmes damnées" the "most beautiful [long poem] that Baudelaire had written," Vivien must have been struck by what Proust called the "strange privilege" Baudelaire assigned himself in "Lesbos": "For Lesbos of all men on this earth elected me / To sing the secret of its flowering virgins / And as a child I was admitted to the dark mystery."[21] Swinburne, with less presumption, responded to a friend's critique of his Sapphopersona by explaining, "It is as near as I can come; and no man can come close to her."[22] As if diagnosing his and Baudelaire's efforts to "come close," the Sapphic androgyne of Vivien's novel explains the limits of such voyeuristic masculine fantasies of lesbianism: "Men see in the love of woman for woman only a spice that sharpens the flatness of their regular performance. But when they realize that this cult of grace and delicacy will permit no sharing, no ambiguity, they revolt against the purity of a passion which excludes and scorns them."[23] Vivien implies that Baudelaire, who originally gave the title *Les Lesbiennes* to *Les Fleurs du mal,* and Swinburne, who spoke to "Anactoria" in the accents of a passionately depraved Sappho, were themselves excluded from what she is elected to sing: the secrets, the dark mysteries of Mytilene. She subversively implies, moreover, that the lesbian is the epitome of the decadent and that decadence is fundamentally a lesbian literary tradition.

No wonder, then, that this Anglo-American girl christened Pauline Tarn seems to have renamed herself after the insinuating seductress Vivien of Arthurian legend: in Tennyson's *Idylls of the King* and Burne-Jones's *Beguiling of Merlin,* the enchantress Vivien literally steals Merlin's magical book, which contains a powerful charm to enthrall women to men.[24] Like the Arthurian Vivien, Renée Vivien appropriates the male-authored book of power to usurp male authority and to break what Gayle Rubin calls the male monopoly over women.[25] Of course, as critics like Sandia Belgrade and Pamela Annas have noted, when Pauline Tarn renamed herself Renée Vivien she was also effecting a transformation in which she was reborn (re-*née*), even as she was insisting on retaining her maiden name (*née*) and her maidenhood.[26] Like the sinister but sensuous figure in her poem "Viviane," who has "changed her name, her voice, her visage," Vivien is "born anew" ("elle renaît").[27] Just as the Arthurian Vivien casts Merlin in a lifeless spell, just as Vivien's "Viviane" weaves so that "you fall asleep in her eternal arms," Vivien is reborn a lesbian poet; thus she evades heterosexual consummation with *its* vampiric consumption of women, for in her view the penetration of women ensures the perpetuation of patriarchy.

In a number of poems, therefore, Vivien flouts heterosexual homophobia: "You will never know how to tarnish the devotion / Of my passion for the beauty of women"; in others, she praises female virginity as virility:

> I shall flee imprint
> And soiling stain.
> The grasp that strangles, the kiss that infects
> And wounds shall I shun.[28]

For Vivien, Sapphism, precisely because it is what the decadents called "barren," provides access not to the future of the human species but to the present of the female of the species. "Our love is greater than all loves," Vivien declares in "Sappho Lives Again,"for "we can, when the belt comes undone, / Be at once lovers and sisters."[29] Similarly, in "Union," Vivien begins, "Our heart is the same in our woman's breast," and she explains, "Our body is made the same"; "we are of the same race"; "I know exactly what pleases you"; "I am you."[30] Because the beloved feels so much like oneself, however, the realization of her separateness is tormenting. Vivien's feelings about Barney's promiscuity, to which Sappho's poems on the loss of Atthis could serve as utterance, underscore this sense of aloneness, allowing Vivien to privilege lesbianism as the preferred eroticism because it raises crucial issues of fusion and identity.[31]

By opening up the relationship of women to eroticism, Vivien admits an influx of jealousy and self-abasement as well as of consolation and pleasure. Sapphic desire implicates the lover in the beloved's abandonment and the rival's competition, both of which complicate the monolithic ideal of sisterhood that informed so much feminist rhetoric in her time: "For Andromeda," Vivien laments in one Sapphic meditation, "the lightning of your kiss," while she herself is left with only "the grave cadences" of Atthis's voice.[32] Even when the beloved is present to the lover, their lovemaking offers paradoxical intimations of their separateness: in "Chanson," for example, Vivien sees in her beloved a "form . . . that leaves me clutching emptiness" and a "smile . . . that one can never clasp."[33] The need to "evoke the fear, the pain and the torment" of such love repeatedly turns Vivien toward Sappho:

O perfume of Paphos! O Poet! O Priestess!
Teach us the secret of divine sorrow,
Teach us longing, the relentless embrace
Where pleasure weeps, faded among the flowers
O languors of Lesbos Charm of Mytilene
Teach us the golden verse stifled only by death,
  Of your harmonious breath,
  Inspire us, Sappho[34]

Vivien's dramatic poems—"La Mort de Psappha" ("The Death of Sappho"), "Atthis délaissée" ("Atthis Abandoned"), and "Dans un verger" ("In an Orchard")—are elegies mourning not only the death of the poet of fugitive desires but also the death of desire itself.[35] Paradoxically, however, "Sappho Lives Again" in these elegies, reborn as Vivien: "Some of us have preserved the rites / Of burning Lesbos gilded like an altar."[36] Prefaced with fragments of Sappho's, Vivien's French becomes an aspect of the other muted languages of languor in the poetry: the lexicon of scents, the syntax of flowers, the sign language of fingers on flesh, the intonation of swooning voices sighing in broken phrases. While Vivien's French aligns her poetry with the flagrant fragrance of Continental eroticism in the *belle époque* and thereby frees her to speak the unspoken, prefaced with Sapphic phrase, set off with ellipses, her most fragmentary translations seem to attest to a form of aphasia, symptomatic of an ontological or sexual expatriation, for Vivien's French is as foreign to her native English as her homosexuality is to the hegemonic heterosexual idiom. At a loss for words, Vivien signals her exile from Lesbos, her expatriation from a native language of desire.

Two of the finest of Vivien's original poems that equate the recovery of Sappho with the rediscovery of a distant but distinct female country and the translation of the poet carried across the seas and the centuries to this country are "En débarquant à Mytilène" ("While Landing at Mytilene") and "Vers Lesbos" ("Toward Lesbos").[37] In the first, the poet begins with an effort at return: "From the depths of my past, I turn back to you / Mytilene, across the disparate centuries." Similarly, in "Toward Lesbos," she speaks to a beloved on board a ship headed for Mytilene: "You will come," she tells her lover, "your eyes filled with evening and with yesterday." In both poems, fine fragrances fill the air: in the first, the poet brings her love "like a present of aromatics," and in the second, "our boat will be full of amber and spices." In both poems the trip to Greece involves dying into a new life; the poet discovers waves, trees, and vines, a place in which to "melt and dissolve." Or again the boat is "frail like a cradle," as the lovers, sleeping through the risks and rites of passage, wonder if they will be able to move to where "we will live tomorrow." Most important, in both poems the Greek island is a place of the female erotic imagination: in the first, Mytilene is quite simply a woman's body rising out of the sea, "golden-flanked Lesbos"; in the second, the lovers on board hear "mysterious songs," the intimation of "supreme music," as they approach "the illusionary island."

This utopian yearning for a visionary land and language of female primacy also impelled the American-born poet H. D. The Englishwoman Bryher saved H. D.'s life in 1919 by caring for her through influenza and a difficult childbirth when she had been abandoned both by her husband and by the father of her child; and in 1920 Bryher took H. D. to the Greek islands to recuperate.[38] H. D. describes the events that led to her recovery in the first section of her novel *Palimpsest:* her heroine, Hipparchia, is a translator of Moero, an ancient woman poet whose imagery resembles Sappho's, although Hipparchia has renounced the struggle to recapture Sappho "as savouring of sacrilege."[39] After she is visited by a girl who has memorized all her translations, Hipparchia embarks on the regenerative voyage which taught H. D. that "Greece is not lost" because "Greece is a spirit."[40] Two or three years after her trip with Bryher, H. D. may have visited Lesbos with her mother, an experience she apparently found overwhelming.[41] Yet, while Vivien and H. D. took imaginative and actual passage to Greece in a similar spirit, they excavate two quite different Sapphos: Vivien's Sappho is languorous and tormented, H. D.'s stark and fierce in her commitment to artistic perfection—a shift in attitude that doubtless reflects the translation history of Sappho's texts in this period. Also, unlike Vivien, who exclusively defines Sappho as a satanic lesbian, H. D. is strikingly reticent about the homosexual content of Sappho's verse. Instead, placing Sappho in a Greek context that extends from Homer to Euripides, H. D. explicitly adopts Sappho's texts as anachronistic literary models to remove herself from the contamination of contemporary sentimentality, even as she implicitly demonstrates that lesbianism furnishes her with a refuge from the pain of heterosexuality and with the courage necessary to articulate that pain.

H. D.'s first use of Sappho, "Fragment 113," is an original poem that presents itself as an exploration of Sappho's fragment "Neither honey nor bee for me."[42] Organized around a series of negatives, this poem refrains from assenting to an old desire. "Not honey," the poet reiterates three times in the first stanza, refusing thereby "the sweet / stain on the lips and teeth" as well as "the deep plunge of soft belly." The voluptuous plight of the plundering bee is associated with sweetness and softness. "Not so" would the poet desire, "though rapture blind my eyes, / and hunger crisp, dark and inert, my mouth." Refusing "old desire—old passion— / old forgetfulness—old pain—," H. D. speculates on a different desire:

> but if you turn again,
> seek strength of arm and throat
> touch as the god;
> neglect the lyre-note:
> knowing that you shall feel,
> about the frame,
> no trembling of the string,
> but heat, more passionate
> of bone and the white shell
> and fiery tempered steel.

Bone, not belly, shell, not lyre; fiery tempered steel instead of the stealings of the plundering bee: as in her essay on Sappho, H. D. finds in Sappho's poems "not heat in the ordinary sense, diffused, and comforting," but intensity "as if the brittle crescent-moon gave heat to us, or some splendid scintillating star turned warm suddenly in our hand like a jewel."[43]

Sappho's imagery—the storm-tossed rose, lily, and poppy; the wind-swept sea garden; the golden Aphrodite—dominates H. D.'s early poetry. The lyricism of both poets is characterized by a yearning intensity expressed through direct address and situated in a liminal landscape.[44] In her notes on Sappho, entitled "The Island," H. D. imagines Sappho as "the island of artistic perfection where the lover of ancient beauty (shipwrecked in the modern world) may yet find foothold and take breath and gain courage for new ventures and dream of yet unexplored continents and realms of future artistic achievement."[45] Certainly, from H. D.'s earliest imagist verse to her later, longer epics, the Greek island is a place of female artistry. Specifically, from her dramatization in "Callypso" of Odysseus fleeing Calypso's island, to her paradisal vision in *Trilogy* of "the circles and circles of islands / about the lost center-island, Atlantis," to the central section of *Helen in Egypt,* which is situated on Leuke, *l'île blanche,* H. D. affirms what she proclaims in her last volume, *Hermetic Definition,* that "the island is herself, is her."[46]

Susan Friedman has explained that "Sappho's influence on imagists no doubt helped to validate H. D.'s leadership role in the development of the modern lyric."[47] Just as important, Sappho's Greek fragments furnished H. D. a linguistic model for the poems that would define the imagist aesthetic. "Fragment 113" presents itself as a numbered remnant, a belated version of a mutilated vision, a translation of a lost original. As H. D. knew, Sappho's texts, excavated in 1898 from Egyptian debris, survived as narrow strips torn from mummy wrappings. Her own poems, narrow columns of print with not a few phrases broken off with dashes, meditate on a loss they mediate as the speaker's series of negatives, presumably a response to a prior sentence omitted from the poem, seems to imply that the text has been torn out of an unrecoverable narrative context. H. D.'s lifelong effort to recreate what has been "scattered in the shards / men tread upon"[48] is reflected in her early fascination with Sappho's poetry, as in her recurrent presentation of herself as a translator of unearthed texts that can never be fully restored or understood. Certainly, H. D. uses the runes of Sappho as the fragments she shores up against her own ruin.

"Fragment 113" was published in the volume *Hymen* in 1921. Significantly, in the title piece of this volume, H. D. begins to extend her short lyrics in the direction of narrative. A cluster of poems describes the bride's impending fate, the loss of her virginity, in terms of the plundering bee who "slips / Between the purple flower-lips."[49] In the context of Sappho's "Neither honey nor bee for me," H. D.'s image of the bee's penetration brings to the foreground the silence and isolation of the veiled, white figure of the bride. In addition, as Alicia Ostriker has pointed out, the very title, "Hymen," with its evocation both of female anatomy and of a male god, turns this celebratory sequence into a somber meditation on the predatory pattern of homosexuality,[50] a pattern explicitly associated with the simultaneity of the bride's marriage and her divorce from the female community. H. D. transforms Sappho's epithalamia into the choruses of girls, maidens, matrons, and priestesses accompanying the silent bride. The stage directions between the lyrics consist of descriptions of musical interludes (flute, harp), of costumes (tunics, baskets), and of the spatial arrangement of figures in their processionals before the temple of Hera. Linking the lyrics together into a liturgy, these italicized prose passages solve the poetic problem H. D. faced as she struggled to extend a minimalist form without losing the intensity she associated with the image. "Hymen" therefore epitomizes the way in which Sappho empowered H. D. to turn eventually toward a reinvention of Homeric epic in *Helen in Egypt,* where she perfected the interrelationships between individual lyrics and a prose gloss that contextualizes them.

Unlike her husband, Richard Aldington, who published a book of voluptuous Sapphic lyrics, *The Love of Myrrhine and Konales* (1926), and unlike Ezra Pound, whose elegiac point in *Lustra* (1917) was that Sappho's fragments could not be reconstituted, H. D. uses the other five meditations on Sapphic fragments that she wrote early in her career to address the contradiction for the woman poet between artistic vocation and female socialization.[51] Heightening this contradictory need for autonomy as a lyricist and dependence as a desiring woman is the sense she has of her own fragility and frigidity; two poems directly confront these complex emotions. In "Fragment Forty-one" (". . . thou flittest to Andromeda"), H. D. describes her beloved's betrayal while defending herself against his charges: "I was not asleep," she declares; or "I was not dull and dead." In "Fragment Forty" ("Love . . . bitter-sweet"), Sappho's bittersweet love becomes H. D.'s honey and salt, an unnerving blend of tastes that epitomize the grief of love's abandonment.[52] In these two poems, H. D. is "deserted," "outcast," "shattered," "sacrificed," "scorched," "rent," "cut apart," and "slashed open" by her love for a man who is absent or unfaithful. Paradoxically, however, it is precisely the torment of rupture that sparks the poetry of rapture associated by H. D. with Sappho's ecstasy, her ex stasis, her breaking out of the self into lyric song.[53] In "Fragment Forty-one," the poet discovers her strength in a supremely generous gift, namely, "the love of my lover / for his mistress." Similarly, at the close of "Fragment Forty," she admits that "to sing love, / love must first shatter us."

That Eros is "he" in "Fragment Forty" and that the poet's lover is in love with "his mistress" in "Fragment Forty-one" unmistakably and—in the Sapphic context—surprisingly mark desire as heterosexual. Why would H. D. invoke the celebrated poet of lesbianism to articulate what Rachel Blau DuPlessis has called her "romantic thralldom" to a series of male mentors?[54] While it is certainly true that H. D. writes obsessively about her desire for the mastery of such men as Pound, Aldington, and Lawrence, her poetry is motivated less by their presence than by their absence. Like her autobiographical prose, which frequently dramatizes her frigidity when she is with these men,[55] H. D.'s revisions of Sapphic fragments articulate her effort to accept the intensity of desire that, transcending the beloved and his inevitable desertion, compels the poet to translate erotic abandonment into poetic abandon. The very number of Sappho's beloveds—Atthis, Anactoria, Gyrinno, Eranna, Gorgo—implies that her confessional poetry is an occasion for experiencing and expressing "an island, a country, a continent, a planet, a world of emotion" that H. D. considers the "spirit of a song."[56] For H. D., then, inspiration and abandonment (by men) are inextricably intertwined. Both Sappho and lesbianism function as a refuge for her, a protective respite from heterosexual deprivation, not unlike the maternal deities she celebrates in her later epics.

While Sappho's lyrical evocation of Aphrodite triumphs over the pain and confusion of mortal love, H. D.'s lyrical invocation of Sappho testifies to her own artistic survival, which was in large measure due to the companion who took her to the Hellas she associated with Helen, her mother. Indeed, just as H. D. is empowered to find the strength and integrity to create poetry out of the pain of abandonment by turning to the intensity she associates with Sappho, in her life she survived male rejection by returning to Bryher, a woman who quite literally shared her visions: repeatedly, in the autobiographical prose, H. D. describes not only how Bryher encouraged her to maintain the heretical concentration necessary to sustain the mystical experiences that would inform H. D.'s poetic development but also how Bryher occasionally saw such visions "for" H. D.[57] While Bryher herself is perceived as a brother in a poem like "I Said,"[58] their joy—which cannot be spoken "in a dark land"—puts H. D. in touch with the prophetic wisdom she associates with Hellas (Helen). If, as Susan Friedman has argued, Adrienne Rich was drawn to H. D. because of Rich's "desire to recreate a strong mother-daughter bond through her reading,"[59] H. D. herself accomplished such a task through both Bryher and Sappho.

While the dynamic of collaboration impels the linguistic experimentation of both Renée Vivien and H. D., it is analyzed most consciously by Amy Lowell, a poet who used Sappho's images to celebrate her passionate response to her lifelong companion, Ada Russell.[60] In "The Sisters" (1926), a poem explicitly about literary matrilineage, Lowell explores not only the significance of Sappho as the first female lyricist, but also the problematic limitations of precisely the collaboration with Sappho that Vivien and H. D. attempted to sustain. Sappho is first "remembered" by the author of "The Sisters," as she is by Vivien and H. D., at the moment when she is wondering why there are so few women poets: "There's Sappho, now I wonder what was Sappho."[61] Imagining a conversation with Sappho, Lowell supposes that she could surprise Sappho's reticence by flinging her own to the wind in order to learn how this irrepressibly sensuous "sister" came at the "loveliness of [her] words." For Lowell, as for Vivien and H. D., Sappho (who is neither a "Miss" nor a "Mrs.") embodies the elemental grandeur of "a leaping fire" and of "sea cliffs," in direct opposition to a poet like Mrs. Browning who writes "closeshuttered" and "squeezed in stiff conventions." Unlike the Victorian poetess, who is shut up in the parlor of propriety, once again Sappho represents the physical release of wind, sea, and sun as well as the mental relief from reticence associated with the "tossing off of garments" and with female conversation. Yet, for all her attraction to Sappho, Lowell also implies that the gulf between the ancient tenth Muse and the modern woman poet may not be negotiable: Lowell does not actually talk with Sappho; she wishes that she could. Imagining what "One might accomplish" in a conversation with Sappho, speculating on Mrs. Browning speculating on Sappho, Lowell describes the first sister of her "strange, isolated little family" as "a burning birch-tree" who wrote like "a frozen blaze before it broke and fell."

Although both Vivien and H. D. reject Ovid's influential version of Sappho leaping suicidally from the Leucadian cliff because of her unrequited love for Phaon, both seem to agree with Lowell that the intensity of Sappho's passion presages a fall: Vivien literally starves and poisons herself, and H. D. writes a number of poems—most notably "Oread"[62]—asking to be obliterated on the shore by the oncoming waves. Both therefore illustrate what Lawrence Lipking has called the "poetics of abandonment."[63] Just as potentially destructive, Lowell implies, is the strangely isolated situation of a classical poet defined not as a powerful foremother but as a vulnerable sister. From this point of view, the hegemonic position of Sappho in female poetic history privileges personal sincerity and passionate ecstasy as the lyricism perceived to be appropriately "feminine." In the context of lesbian literature, moreover, Sappho's preeminence as a model paradoxically sets up a single standard for writers defining themselves by their sexual difference, a standard that personalizes experiences already painfully privatized. Writing colloquially and conversationally, Lowell concludes "The Sisters" by admitting to Sappho and her descendants, "I cannot write like you. . . ." Indeed, all of her older "sisters" leave her feeling "sad and selfdistrustful."

A number of contemporary women writers express this same distrust of Sappho. For every Rita Mae Brown, writing "Sappho's reply" to protect those "who have wept in direct sunlight" with Sappho's voice, which "rings down through thousands of years," there is a Muriel Rukeyser who, rejecting Sappho "with her drowned hair trailing along Greek waters," calls out, "Not Sappho, Sacco"; or an Ann Shockley who uncovers the implicit racism of elitist Sapphic cults in "A Meeting of the Sapphic Daughters."[64] Equally suspicious, for various reasons, are poets from Sylvia Plath to Robin Morgan: Plath begins her poem "Lesbos" with the satiric line, "Viciousness in the kitchen" while Carolyn Kizer begins "Pro Femina" by considering the poetic line, "From Sappho to myself," only to remind herself that it is still "unwomanly" to discuss this subject; Susan Griffin writes marginalia to her poems that condemn them as "too much an imitation of Sappho"; and Robin Morgan exclaims defiantly, "get off my back, Sappho. / I never liked that position, / anyway."[65] Perhaps May Sarton explains Lowell's resistance to Sappho best when, placing Sappho in the company of Emily Dickinson and Christina Rossetti, she claims, "Only in the extremity of spirit and the flesh / And in the renouncing passion did Sappho come to bless." She thus demonstrates that "something is lost, strained, unforgiven" in the woman poet.[66]

These writers may help to explain why Djuna Barnes, the historian of Natalie Barney's salon in Paris, and Gertrude Stein, the center of her own coterie, only refer to Sappho tangentially, even sardonically, although they were themselves in the process of creating what Lillian Faderman calls "Lesbos in Paris."[67] Like Lowell's, their swerve from Sappho seems less a fear of being obliterated by her power as literary foremother, as it would be if Bloom's "anxiety of influence" were in effect, than a fear that Sappho was herself enmeshed in contradictions that threatened to stunt their own creative development. But it is Marguerite Yourcenar's treatment of Sappho that directly engages Lowell's reservations in order to question the dynamic of collaboration with Sappho. Although Yourcenar does not situate herself in the lesbian literary tradition, she, like most of the writers discussed here, was to become an expatriate. Her

Bronze bust of Sappho.

prose poem, "Sappho, or Suicide," concludes *Fires,* a work she wrote in French in 1935, four years before her departure for America with Grace Frick, and some four decades before she became the first woman to be elected to the French Academy. Reversing the immigration pattern of her predecessors, Yourcenar dramatizes the tragic demise of the dream of a separate sphere for women and thereby engages the tradition we have been tracing here—as she would, too, in her first translation work, of Virginia Woolf's *The Waves.*

"Just as in ancient times she was a poetess," Yourcenar's Sappho is an impoverished, graying acrobat, a "star" in the circus, a "magnetic creature, too winged for the ground, too corporal for the sky."[68] Because she cannot hold her lovers' bodies very long in "this abstract, space bordered on all sides by trapeze bars" (117) and because she is fated to worship in her female lovers "what she has not been" (118), she loses Attys, only to fall in love with a Phaon who seems like a "bronze and golden god" (125). Just at this point of thralldom, she begins to neglect "the discipline of her demanding profession" (125) and, after seeing Phaon dressed up to impersonate Attys, she discovers that he "is nothing more than a stand-in for the beautiful nymph" (126). Sappho's final act can only be to search above the spotlight in the highest reaches of the arena's canopy for "a place to fall." Climbing the rope of her "celestial scaffold" (127) high above what Sylvia Plath would call in "Lady Lazarus" the "peanut-crunching crowd,"[69] Yourcenar's Sappho must make her art itself a form of suicide: unable to lose her balance, "no matter how she tries" (128), she dives, "arms spread as if to grasp half of infinity" (129). Yet "those failing at life run the risk of missing their suicide," and she is ultimately pulled from the mesh nets "streaming with sweat like a drowning woman pulled from the sea" (129).

While such a summary hardly catches the subtle brilliance of Yourcenar's lyrical meditation, it does illustrate how she insists on the lonely isolation of the woman artist who can neither break nor keep "the pact that binds us to the earth" (116). For Yourcenar, clearly, this aerial artist, this light princess with a heavy heart, is a divided creature. Finally, then, Sappho falls not only from lesbianism into heterosexuality, but from the fluid and supple women who were her "sky companion[s]" (117) to the unfortunate girl to whom she can only offer a maternal and tender "form of despair" (121) and ultimately to the "weight of her own sex" (126) when she knows herself to be captivated by a man who infiltrates the image of Attys. As it does so often, the revision of Sappho's story here provides a vision of lesbianism. Like Djuna Barnes in *Nightwood* (1936), Yourcenar sets her fable in the "international world of pleasure-seekers between the wars" (xii) to explore the disintegration of the lesbian community, implying that lesbianism can degenerate when it replicates the hierarchy implicit in heterosexual relationships. Her title, "Sappho, or Suicide"—with its ambiguous "or"—seems to assume on the one hand that the woman writer must choose either suicide or a lifeline to Sappho, her personal "sky companion," who is destined to be revived and retrieved over and over again; on the other hand, Sappho's second name may be suicide, for the writer who invokes Sappho's fame may be collaborating with the enemy; she may be destined to associate the grace and daring of her art with the anguish of a fated, if not fatal, eroticism. In either case, by the 1930s, the dream of recovering Mytilene had degenerated for Yourcenar into a circus act. She sees lesbianism as an artful and courageous but doomed effort to defy the laws of gravity.

Yet in *Fires,* Yourcenar describes that effort in a mode that preserves the utopian grandeur of the lesbian aesthetic project in the modernist period. For, like her soaring acrobatic Sappho, the writers in this tradition were clearly attempting a radical redefinition of the barren grounds of heterosexual culture in general and of a male-dominated literary history in particular. Their two forms of collaboration—writing "for" the admired precursor and/or writing "for" the beloved other—challenge assumptions about the autonomy/authority of the author and the singularity of the subject: to use the language of Gertrude Stein, the writer who analyzed most fully the mechanisms of her own collaboration with Alice B. Toklas, to be "one" is to know oneself as "two."[70] The act of writing cannot be said to originate from a single source, these writers seem to suggest—as Amy Lowell does, too, when she entitles her sequence of Sapphic poems "Two Speak Together."[71]

Early-twentieth-century lesbian poets had to reach back into antiquity to find a literary foremother, whose texts had been falsified by classical legends and partially obliterated by patristic injunctions. Clearly, they were empowered to do so by the formation of autonomous female communities that the friendships of nineteenth-century women poets could only adumbrate. It is a striking biographical contrast, the shift from the seclusion of Emily Dickinson or the familial sisterhood of Christina Rossetti or the married life of Elizabeth Barrett Browning to the bonding between women that we find in the erotic unions and female friendships of Vivien, H. D., Lowell, and Yourcenar, and also of Cather, Sitwell, Woolf, and Barnes. In other words, even as it situates itself on the margins, at the edge, of patriarchal culture, the lesbian tradition may serve as a paradigmatic solution to the problem creativity posed to nineteenth-century women artists.

Finally, then, the sapphistries of Vivien, H. D., Lowell, and Yourcenar demonstrate how feminist modernists found—if only fleetingly—what Woolf had thought lost in Lesbos; artistic predecessors, membership in a group where art is freely discussed and practiced, and freedom of action and experience. Living, all but one of them, *ex patria,* outside of their fathers' country, they represent their exile as a privileged marginalization that paradoxically exposes the homogeneity of heterosexual culture, the heterogeneity of homosexual coupling. Together, they draw on the strength of collaboration in much the way Sappho had prayed for an empowering union with Aphrodite:

> Come, then, loose me from cruelties.
> Give my tethered heart its full desire.
> Fulfill, and come, lock your shield with mine.
> Throughout the siege.[72]

Notes

1. The indispensable background for the lesbian tradition in literature is Faderman, *Surpassing the Love of Men;* see esp. 69-71 on Katherine Philips (see Philips, "To My Most, Excellent Lucasia: On Our Friendship"). Significantly, Barrett Browning's only mention of a female precursor in "A Vision of Poets" is Sappho (see ll. 11. 318-21), and Rossetti's "Sappho" (1846) and "What Sappho Would Have Said Had Her Leap Cured Instead of Killing Her" (1848) were excised from her collected work by William Michael Rossetti (see Hatton, "Unpublished Poems of Christina Rossetti").
2. The poet Anne Winters, of Berkeley, Calif., describes the shift from T. W. Higginson's male pronouns (1871) to J. A. Symonds's female pronouns (1873) in an unpublished paper.
3. [Bradley and Cooper], *Long Ago;* Duncan, *My Life* 58, 116-22; Millay, "Sappho Crosses the Dark River into Hades"; Teasdale, "To Cleis (The Daughter of Sappho)"; Elizabeth Robbins, *Ancilla's Share* 125; Dinesen, *Out of Africa* 316. Robinson discusses Teasdale's "Phaon and the Leucadian Leap" in *Sappho and Her Influence* 227-28. Watts, *The Poetry of American Women* 75-82, analyzes the use of Sappho in nineteenth-century American poetry by women.
4. Marcus, "Liberty, Sorority, Misogyny" 87.
5. See "Affable Hawk's" review of Arnold Bennett's *Our Women* and Otto Weininger's *Sex and Character* in *The New Statesman* (2 October 1920) 704, and Woolf's exchange with him (9 October 1920) 15-16; (16 October 1920) 45-46. The quotations are taken from the second letter.
6. Sandra M. Gilbert and I analyze the anxiety of authorship in *The Madwoman in the Attic* 45-92.
7. Sitwell, *Selected Letters* 116.
8. Woolf, *A Room of One's Own* 113.
9. Cather, "Three Women Poets," in *The World and the Parish.*
10. Lipking in "Sappho Descending" examines how male and female poets interpret Sappho's "Second Ode."
11. Bogan, *A Poet's Alphabet* 429.
12. Marks, "Lesbian Intertextuality" 353-77.
13. Bloom, *The Anxiety of Influence.*
14. Cather, "Three Women Poets" 147.
15. Blankely, "Returning to Mytilene"; Wickes, *The Amazon of Letters;* Chalon, *Portrait of a Seductress;* and Rogers, *Ladies Bountiful.*
16. Foster, *Sex Variant Women in Literature* 154-73. Also see Harris, "The More Profound Nationality of Their Lesbianism."
17. Vivien, *A Woman Appeared to Me* 34.
18. Praz discusses the lesbian female fatale in *The Romantic Agony* 236-40, 260-61, as does Faderman, *Surpassing the Love of Men* 269-75. See also Foster, *Sex Variant Women* 76-80, 104, 114.
19. A recitation of San Giovanni, Sappho's avatar in *A Woman Appeared to Me* 17; see Rubin's introduction, viii.

20. Colette, *The Pure and the Impure* 71.

21. Baudelaire, *Flowers of Evil* 106-7. I have departed somewhat from this translation. Also see Proust, "A propos of Baudelaire" 125-26.

22. Swinburne, *Selected Poetry and Prose* 328-29. Klaich, *Woman Plus Woman* 143, sees Vivien as victimized by Swinburnean decadence.

23. Vivien, *A Woman Appeared to Me* 36.

24. Both of these popular Victorian works of art would have been familiar to Vivien. I am indebted to Elliot Gilbert for my understanding of Tennyson's *Idylls of the King*. Sandra M. Gilbert and I place Vivien's pseudonym in the context of other feminist modernist names of power in "Ceremonies of the Alphabet."

25. Gayle Rubin's brilliant introduction to *A Woman Appeared to Me* provides an indispensable introduction to Vivien (iii-xx). Auerbach, *Woman and the Demon* 74-81, 104-6, discusses the relationship between the female and the demonic in Pre-Raphaelite painting and in Swinburne's poetry.

26. Belgrade, introduction to *At the Sweet Hour of Hand in Hand* xv; Annas, "Drunk with Chastity."

27. "Viviane" is translated in *At the Sweet Hour* 47-49. Unless otherwise indicated, I am using the Naiad Press translations of Vivien's poetry because they are a pioneering achievement that makes possible the teaching and study of Vivien in this country. For those who wish to see the original, a collected *Poèmes de Renée Vivien* has been reprinted in facsimile by Arno Press.

28. Vivien, "The Disdain of Sappho" and "I shall be always a virgin" in *The Muse of the Violets* 46, 44.

29. Vivien, "Sappho Lives Again," in *At the Sweet Hour* 2-4.

30. Vivien, "Union," in *Muse of the Violets* 73.

31. The best analysis of Sappho's poetry in terms of the "illusion of perfect union, the inevitability of parting," is Stehle [Stigers], "Romantic Sensuality, Poetic Sense" (quotation on 467). Adrienne Rich addresses the issue of privileging lesbianism as the preferred eroticism in "Compulsory Heterosexuality and Lesbian Existence."

32. Vivien, "For Andromeda, she has a beautiful recompense," in *Muse of the Violets* 36.

33. Vivien, "Chanson," in *Muse of the Violets* 24; thanks to a gift from Elin Diamond, I have taken the original, "Sonnet," from *Études et preludes* 24.

34. Vivien, "Invocation," in *Muse of the Violets* 59. The original appears in *Cendres et poussiers* 2-4.

35. Although Vivien's verse dramas have not yet been translated into English, they are available in French in *Poèmes de Renée Vivien.*

36. Vivien, "Sappho Lives Again," in *At the Sweet Hour* 2; but I have departed from this translation here with the help of Star Howlett.

37. Vivien, "While Landing at Mytilene" and "Toward Lesbos," in *At the Sweet Hour* 25-26, 64-65.

38. The most recent biography of H. D. is Barbara Guest's *Herself Defined;* see 118-20, 123-26. Also see H. D., *Tribute to Freud* 49.

39. H. D., *Palimpsest* 129.

40. Ibid., 131.

41. Wolle's account of H. D.'s life records such a visit (*A Moravian Heritage* 58). However, Guest argues that there is no other evidence of such a trip (*Herself Defined* 167).

42. H. D., "Fragment 113," in *Collected Poems* 131-32.

43. See H. D.'s "The Wise Sappho" 57-58.

44. See the excellent discussion of Sappho's poetry in Friedrich, *The Meaning of Aphrodite* 107-28.

45. H. D., "The Wise Sappho" 67. The heading, a section title, is found in the manuscript "Notes on Euripides, Pausanias, and Greek Lyric Poets" (1920), Beinecke Library, Yale University.

46. H. D., "Callypso," in *Collected Poems* 388-96; *Trilogy* 15; *Helen in Egypt* 109; *Hermetic Definition* 29.

47. Friedman, *Psyche Reborn* 10. Adalaide Morris has noted that the existence of women poets like Sappho, Nossis, and Telesilla illuminates H. D.'s attraction to classical literature ("Prospectus for Gender and Genre Session on H.D"). Kenner describes Pound's use of Sappho in "The Muse in Tatters."

48. H. D., *Trilogy* 36.

49. H. D., "Fragment 113," in *Collected Poems* 109.

50. Ostriker, "The Poet as Heroine."

51. This point is made by both Swann, *The Classical World of H. D.* 109-21, and Quinn, *Hilda Doolittle* 43-46.

52. H. D., "Fragment Forty-one" and "Fragment Forty," in *Collected Poems* 181-84, 173-75.

53. Barnstone, *The Poetics of Ecstasy* 29-41, discusses Sappho's poetry.

54. DuPlessis, "Romantic Thralldom in H. D."

55. H. D., *HERmione* 73; *Bid Me to Live* 51, 55, 160; *Tribute to Freud* 16. D. H. Lawrence captures this "frozen" quality in two of his fictionalized portraits of H. D., the priestess of Isis in *The Man Who Died* and Julia in *Aaron's Rod.*

56. H. D., "The Wise Sappho" 58-59.

57. Rich has written about the collaborative vision H. D. shared with Bryher on Corfu in her introduction to *Working It Out.* See also H. D., *The Gift* 142, and *Tribute to Freud* 56, 130; and the discussion of female friendship in Bernikow, *Among Women* 163-92.

58. H. D., "I Said," in *Collected Poems* 22-25.

59. Friedman, "'I go where I love,'" esp. 229.

60. In *Tendencies in Modern American Poetry,* Lowell defended H. D.'s poetry, which she also published in three imagist anthologies. See poems like "A Decade" and "Opal" in Lowell's *Complete Poetical Works* 217, 214.

61. Lowell, *Complete Poetical Works* 459.

62. H. D., "Oread," in *Collected Poems* 55.

63. Lipking, "Aristotle's Sister," esp. 75.

64. R. M. Brown, "Sappho's Reply"; Rukeyser, "Poem out of Childhood"; Shockley, "A Meeting of the Sapphic Daughters."

65. Plath, "Lesbos," in *Collected Poems* 227; Kizer, "Pro Femina"; Griffin, "Thoughts on Writing" 115; Morgan, *Monster* 73.

66. Sarton, "My Sisters, O My Sisters."

67. Faderman, *Surpassing the Love of Men* 70-72. Barnes, in her *Ladies Almanack* 71-72, invokes "a peep of No-Doubting Sappho, blinked from the Stews of Secret Greek Broth, and some Rennet of Lesbos" in one of its potent potions.

68. Yourcenar, *Fires* 116. Further citations will be given in parentheses in the text.

69. Plath, "Lady Lazarus," in *Collected Poems* 245.

70. The anxiety of becoming the other is dramatized in Stein's depression after the popularity of *The Autobiography of Alice B. Toklas* (1933), her fear that the public was more interested in her personality than in her work; on the other hand, in works like "Ada" and "Lifting Belly," she articulates the pleasure and merriment of speaking for and with the one who is the lover.

71. Lowell, *Complete Poetical Works* 209-18.

72. Sappho's "Ode to Aphrodite," in Davenport, *Archilochos, Sappho, Alkman* 121.

Bibliography

Annas, Pamela. "Drunk with Chastity: The Poetry of Renée Vivien." *Women's Studies* 13 (1986) 11-22.

Auerbach, Nina. *Woman and the Demon.* Cambridge: Harvard University Press, 1982.

Barnes, Djuna. *Ladies Almanack.* 1928. Reprint, New York: Harper and Row, 1972.

Barnstone, Willis. *The Poetics of Ecstasy: From Sappho to Borges.* New York: Holmes and Meier, 1983.

Baudelaire, Charles. *The Flowers of Evil/Les Fleurs du mal,* edited by Wallace Fowlie. New York: Bantam, 1964.

Bernikow, Louise. *Among Women.* New York: Crown, 1980.

Blankely, Elyse. "Returning to Mytilene: Renée Vivien and the City of Women." In *Women Writers and the City: Essays in Feminist Literary Criticism,* edited by Susan Squier, 45-67. Knoxville: University of Tennessee Press, 1984.

Bloom, Harold. *The Anxiety of Influence.* New York: Oxford University Press, 1973.

Bogan, Louise. *A Poet's Alphabet: Reflections on the Literary Art and Vocation,* edited by Robert Phelps and Ruth Limmer. New York: McGraw-Hill, 1970.

Bradley, Katherine, and Edith Cooper. *Long Ago.* London: G. Bell and Sons, 1889.

Brown, Rita Mae. "Sappho's Reply." In *Lesbian Poetry,* edited by Elly Bulkin and Joan Larkin, 163. Watertown, Mass.: Persephone Press, 1981.

Cather, Willa. *The World and the Parish: Willa Cather's Articles and Reviews,* 1883-1902, edited by William M. Curtin. Lincoln: University of Nebraska Press, 1970.

Colette. *The Pure and the Impure,* translated by Herma Briffault. 1932. Reprint, New York: Penguin, 1971.

Davenport, Guy, trans. *Archilochos, Sappho, Alkman: Three Lyric Poets of the Late Greek Bronze Age.* Berkeley: University of California Press, 1980.

Dinesen, Isak. *Out of Africa.* 1936. Reprint, New York: Random House, 1965.

Duncan, Isadora. *My Life.* New York: Liveright, 1955.

DuPlessis, Rachel Blau. "Romantic Thralldom in H. D." *Contemporary Literature* 20 (1979) 178-203.

Faderman, Lillian. *Surpassing the Love of Men: Romantic Friendship and Love Between Women from the Renaissance to the Present.* New York: William Morrow, 1981.

Foster, Jeanette. *Sex Variant Women in Literature.* 1956. Reprint, Baltimore: Diana Press, 1975.

Friedman, Susan. "'I go where I love': An Intertextual Study of H. D. and Adrienne Rich." *Signs* 9 (1983) 228-45.

———. *Psyche Reborn: The Emergence of H. D.* Bloomington: Indiana University Press, 1981.

Friedrich, Paul. *The Meaning of Aphrodite.* Chicago: University of Chicago Press, 1978.

Gilbert, Sandra M., and Susan Gubar. "Ceremonies of the Alphabet." In *The Female Autograph,* edited by Domna Stanton, 23-52. New York: New York Literary Forum, 1984.

———. *The Madwoman in the Attic: The Woman Writer and the Nineteenth-Century Literary Imagination.* New Haven: Yale University Press, 1979.

Griffin, Susan. "Thoughts on Writing: A Diary." In *The Writer on Her Work,* edited by Janet Sternburg, 107-20. New York: Norton, 1980.

Guest, Barbara. *Herself Defined: The Poet H. D. and Her World.* New York: Doubleday, 1984.

H. D. *Bid Me to Live (A Madrigal).* New York: Grove Press, 1960.

———. *Collected Poems,* 1912-1944, edited by Louis L. Martz. New York: New Directions, 1983.

———. *The Gift.* New York: New Directions, 1982.

———. *Helen in Egypt.* 1961. Reprint, New York: New Directions, 1974.

———. *Hermetic Definition.* New York: New Directions, 1972.

———. *HERmione.* New York: New Directions, 1981.

———. *Palimpsest.* 1926. Reprint, Carbondale: Southern Illinois University Press, 1968.

———. *Tribute to Freud* (1944-46). New York: McGraw-Hill, 1974.

———. *Trilogy.* 1944-46. New York: New Directions, 1973.

———. "The Wise Sappho." In *Notes on Thought and Vision and The Wise Sappho,* 57-69. San Francisco: City Lights Books, 1982.

Harris, Bertha. "The More Profound Nationality of Their Lesbianism: Lesbian Society in Paris in the 1920s." In *Amazon Expedition: A Lesbian Feminist Anthology,* edited by Phyllis Birkby, 77-88. Washington, N.J.: Times Change Press, 1973.

Hatton, Gwynneth. "Edition of the Unpublished Poems of Christina Rossetti." Master's thesis, Oxford University, 1955.

Kenner, Hugh. "The Muse in Tatters." In *The Pound Era*, 54-75. Berkeley: University of California Press, 1971.

Kizer, Carolyn. "Pro Femina." In *Psyche*, edited by Barbara Segnitz and Carol Rainey, 131. New York: Dell, 1973.

Klaich, Dolores. *Woman Plus Woman*. New York: Simon and Schuster, 1974.

Lipking, Lawrence. "Aristotle's Sister: A Poetics of Abandonment." *Critical Inquiry* 11 (1983) 61-81.

———. "Sappho Descending: Abandonment through the Ages."In *Abandoned Women and Poetic Tradition*, 57-96. Chicago: University of Chicago Press, 1988.

Lowell, Amy. *The Complete Poetical Works of Amy Lowell*. Boston: Houghton Mifflin, 1955.

———. *Tendencies in Modern American Poetry*. New York: Macmillan, 1917.

Marcus, Jane. "Liberty, Sorority, Misogyny." In *The Representation of Women in Fiction*, edited by Carolyn B. Heilbrun and Margaret R. Higonnet, 60-97. Baltimore: John Hopkins University Press, 1983.

Marks, Elaine. "Lesbian Intertextuality." In *Homosexualities and French Literature*, edited by George Stambolian and Elaine Marks, 353-78. Ithaca: Cornell University Press, 1978.

Millay, Edna St. Vincent. "Sappho Crosses the Dark River into Hades." In *Collected Lyrics*, 293-94. New York: Harper and Brothers, 1939.

Morgan, Robin. *Monster*. New York: Vintage, 1972.

Morris, Adelaide. "Prospectus for Gender and Genre Session on H. D." Paper presented at the Modern Language Association convention, Los Angeles, December 1982.

Ostriker, Alicia. "The Poet as Heroine: Learning to Read H. D." In *Writing Like a Woman*, 7-41. Ann Arbor: University of Michigan Press, 1983.

Plath, Sylvia. *The Collected Poems*, edited by Ted Hughes. New York: Harper and Row, 1981.

Praz, Mario. *The Romantic Agony*, translated by Angus Davidson. Oxford: Oxford University Press, 1970.

Quinn, Vincent. *Hilda Doolittle*. New York: Twayne, 1967.

Rich, Adrienne. Foreword to *Working It Out: Twenty-three Women Writers, Artists, Scientists, and Scholars Talk about Their Lives and Work*, edited by Sara Ruddick and Pamela Daniels, xiv-xxiv. New York: Pantheon, 1977.

———. "Compulsory Heterosexuality and Lesbian Existence." *Signs* 5 (1980) 631-60.

Robbins, Elizabeth. *Ancilla's Share*. 1924. Reprint, Westport, Conn.: Hyperion, 1976.

Robbins, Emmet. "'Every Time I Look at You . . .': Sappho Thirty-One." *Transactions of the American Philological Association* 110 (1980) 255-61.

Roberts, W. Rhys, ed. *Longinus On the Sublime*. 2nd ed. Cambridge: Cambridge University Press, 1907.

Robinson, David M. *Sappho and Her Influence*. Boston: Marshall Jones, 1924.

Rukeyser, Muriel. "Poem out of Childhood." In *The Collected Poems of Muriel Rukeyser*, 3. New York: McGraw-Hill, 1982.

Sarton, May. "My Sisters, O My Sisters." In *Selected Poems of May Sarton*, 192-93. New York: Norton, 1978.

Shockley, Ann Allen. "A Meeting of the Sapphic Daughters." *Sinister Wisdom* 9 (1979) 54-59.

Sitwell, Dame Edith. *Selected Letters, 1919-1964*, edited by John Lehmann and Derek Parker. New York: Vanguard, 1979.

Stehle [Stigers], Eva. "Romantic Sensuality, Poetic Sense: A Response to Hallett on Sappho." *Signs* 4 (1979) 465-71.

Stein, Gertrude. *The Autobiography of Alice B. Toklas*. 1933. Reprint, New York: Modern Library, 1969.

Swann, Thomas Burnett. *The Classical World of H. D.* Lincoln: University of Nebraska Press, 1962.

Swinburne, Algernon Charles. *Selected Poetry and Prose*, edited by John D. Rosenberg. New York: Modern Library, 1968.

Teasdale, Sara. "To Cleis (The Daughter of Sappho)." In *Helen of Troy and Other Poems*, 88-89. New York: Macmillan, 1928.

Vivien, Renée. *The Muse of the Violets*, translated by Margaret Porter and Catherine Kroger. Tallahassee, Fla.: Naiad Press, 1977.

———. *Poèmes de Renée Vivien*. 2 vols. 1923-24. Reprint, New York: Arno, 1975.

———. *A Woman Appeared to Me* (1904), translated by Jeanette H. Foster. Tallahassee, Fla.: Naiad Press, 1979.

Watts, Emily Stipes. *The Poetry of American Women from 1632 to 1945*. Austin: University of Texas Press, 1977.

Wolle, Francis. *A Moravian Heritage*. Boulder, Colo.: Empire Reproductions, 1972.

Woolf, Virginia. *A Room of One's Own*. 1929. Reprint, New York: Harcourt, Brace and World, 1957.

Yourcenar, Marguerite. *Fires* (1963), translated by Dori Katz. New York: Farrar Straus Giroux, 1981.

EVA STEHLE (ESSAY DATE 1997)

SOURCE: Stehle, Eva. "Sappho's Circle." In *Performance and Gender in Ancient Greece: Nondramatic Poetry in Its Setting*, pp. 262-318. Princeton: Princeton University Press, 1997.

In the following excerpt, Stehle reads Sappho's poetry through the lens of performance, distinguishing the narrator and poet from the performer to examine how Sappho creates various possibilities for feminine identity and subjectivity.

Love among women was an area of women's interest, so one would expect that Sappho's love poetry was performed to her circle.[1] But Sappho's love poetry does not support the analogy with the symposium poets; the major poems and fragments are antithetical to the creation of collective bonhomie. It is not just that they intimately address one person but that they implicitly reject the circle. Given their disinterest in striving for the psychological efficacy of renewing the group,

I think that these poems had another function. To demonstrate my reason for thinking that the circle was not their primary setting, I begin by examining 31 *V*, then I propose a setting for it that makes more sense of its communicative strategy.

Here is the poem, one over which there has been much dispute:[2]

φαίὑεταί μοι χῆνοσ ἴσοσ θέοισιυ
ἔμμευ' ὤνηρ, ὅττισ ἐυάτιόσ τοι
ἰσδάνει χαὶ πλάσιου αδυ φωνεὶσασ ὑπαχούει

. . . . .

χαι γελαίσασ ἰμέροευ, τὸ μ' ἦάυ
χαρδίαυ ἐυ στήθεσιυ ἐπιοαισευ
ὠσ γάρ ἔσ σ' ἴδω βροχέ' ὥσ με φώυησ' οὖδἔυ ἔτ'
εἴχει,[3]

. . . . .

ἀλλὰ †χαμ† μὲυ γλῶσσα †ἔαγε†, λέπτου
δ' αὔτιχα χρῶ πυρ ὑπαδεδρῶμαχευ,
ὤππᾶτεσσι οὐδὲυ ᾦρημ, ἐπιβρώμεισι δ' ᾶχουαι,

. . . . .

†ἐχαδε† μ'ἴδρωσ χαχχέεται, τρῶμοσ δὲ
παισαυ ᾶγρει, χλωροτέα δὲ ποίασ
ἔμμι, τεθυάχηυ δ'ὀλὶγω 'πιδεῦησ φαίυομ' ἦμ'
αὔτ[αι.

. . . . .

ᾶλλᾷ πὰυ τολματου, ἐπεὶ †χαι πένητα†ε

He appears to me to be equal to the gods, that man who sits facing you and listens to you sweetly speaking right near him and laughing enchantingly—a thing that truly makes the heart in my breast cower. For as I look at you fleetingly I can no longer utter a thing, but my tongue is shattered (?), instantly light fire runs through my flesh, I see nothing with my eyes but my ears resound, sweat flows down me and a shiver seizes me whole, I am a fresher green than grass, and I seem to myself to lack little of death. But all is bearable, since even a poor man (?) . . .

The song puts the speaker into a fictional situation: she is looking at a man and woman conversing. She also addresses the woman in this scene ("you" in lines 2 and 7), who by the logic of the setting cannot hear her. The singer must be speaking to herself.[4] The audience must overhear her since her imaginary situation means that she is not speaking to it. The singer shifts her attention to her own state in the second stanza, and thereafter she is speaking about herself to herself. After describing the symptoms of emotional distress that afflict her each time she looks at the woman, Sappho reasserts emotional control at line 17, at the moment of near fainting. Her recovery is reflected in the few remaining words of that line: "all is bearable."[5] The tight inward focus of "I seem to myself" in line 16, followed by her recall of some mitigating idea, further denies the audience its obvious role as sympathetic substitute for the woman who affects Sappho. Far from striving to affirm her membership in a circle of friends, the singer of 31 *V* does not allow room for the listeners' presence in her fiction or insinuate that the group has any function in relation to her.[6]

I have characterized this poem as "overheard," but the image is not adequate to describe the communicative situation that the poem establishes. The singer's visible and audible control as she sings, the beauty of the highly organized words, mean that the listeners must suppose a radical disjunction between outer poise and inner turmoil. More than that, the singer describes herself immediately as unable to speak.[7] What then are we hearing as we hear the poem performed? In the fourth stanza the singer adds that she is *looking* distressed—sweating, trembling, and pale. The singer in the here and now is not the same as the speaker constituted by the text of the poem.[8] A split between the physically present performer (the singer) and the poem's first-person self-representation (the speaker) has opened up.[9]

The separation of singer and speaker combined with the fictional situation described and the soliloquizing creates a fictional character within the poem whose inner emotional state is laid open to secret observers—a remarkable configuration for archaic lyric. To see the difference from symposium poetry, we can recall several of the poems discussed in Chapter 5. Symposium poets address absent figures: Archilochos, for instance, accosting Lykambes in 172 *W*. But his speech is meant to be public, as public as possible, for Archilochos is engaged in shaming Lykambes. The address therefore renders Lykambes imaginatively present so that the symposium group can share in denigration of him. Anakreon addresses a boy who, he says, cannot hear him (360 *PMG*). However, he does not establish a fictional situation for himself, so the remark is not overheard; rather, the boy's failure to "hear" marks the boy as absent or uncomprehending. Anakreon's poem therefore functions both as an admission of love and as a comment to the audience about the paradox of desirable innocence. Ibykos, by contrast, exploits the disjunct between singer's control and inner chaos to express his very being as love-torn, but his poems have no addressee or fictional setting. They are presented as confessions to the actual audience.

The symposium poets also create fictions in their poetry. Alkaios' poem from exile (130B *V*)—the closest parallel—posits a fictional situation for the speaker but does not inhibit identification of speaker and singer. He therefore threatens his audience by portraying his assumed isolation, while Sappho's poem takes it as a given. Alkaios' poem has an addressee, Agesilaidas, whose identity is unknown. He is a sympathetic figure, for the singer complains to him. He is probably a member of the group or someone who could be imagined as a participant, in which case the address to him represents communication to the group. Conceivably Agesilaidas' identity was such that speaking to him precluded speaking to the *hetaireia*. Barring the latter possibility, utterance is still communication from actual singer to actual audience, even though it must be thought of as traversing a distance. Hipponax too offers a partial parallel with Sappho, though with utterly different effect, but despite the lively fictional accounts of lowlife doings, usually told in the past tense, his short and broken fragments do not appear to split singer and speaker. The poems that are narratives are directed to their actual audience and the prayers are a humorous form of self-staging as rogue.[10]

The various aspects, therefore, of Sappho's technique are found in symposium poetry. But no extant symposium poem uses all of Sappho's devices together: the fictional situation, the unreachable addressee, the inward focus, the coherent exposition of psychosomatic devastation; nor does any symposium poem push them so far. In its creation of fantasy scene and inner monologue, Sappho's poem actually denies the situation of performance by detaching the speaker from the actual setting, singer, and collected audience. This is certainly not a poem for a group like a symposium group, one that used performance to reinforce a sense of collectivity. How then can we understand the poem as performance?

To one who would study it as performed communication, the poem presents two choices. One can pursue the idea that the poem was performed to a group of a different sort, a group within which it was appropriate for the singer to make a point of her distance and detachment from the audience in her self-presentation. Or else one can look for an altogether different performance context for it. The first is Anne Burnett's approach. Burnett notes Sappho's detachment (which she finds in the content and tone of the poetry, not in performance dynamics). She also accepts an informal version of the initiation theory and sees the audience as a circle of *parthenoi* preparing for marriage.[11] She therefore takes Sappho's aloofness as a didactic stance. Thus in this poem Sappho uses herself as a model to demonstrate a method of recovering self-possession: the poem begins with a statement that "smilingly" compliments the addressee (to sit near you is the highest happiness) and articulates an extreme sense of the difference between the speaker's position and the man's; but it ends by redefining the difference in mundane terms (poor versus rich) that might easily change—a hopeful idea that revives the speaker.[12] Love, says the poem, is both immortalizing and ephemeral. Overall Burnett finds Sappho's lesson in the need to transmute desire into appreciation of beauty.[13] In sum, Sappho's strategy is to demonstrate her ultimate detachment from any erotic involvement and to bring detachment within the circle as an ideal, promoting an aesthetic sensuality in response to the ineluctable problem of women's being separated by their families' command.

But would 31 *V* be heard that way? If Sappho in person sang the poem to a group of *parthenoi* who knew her, they would inevitably take it as an expression of her attitude toward them. If they thought that she had a specific person in mind, the rest would feel emotionally left out, for the contrast between Sappho's intense reaction to one and her disregard for all the others present would be evident. If they thought that she had no one in mind, her description of her symptoms would seem mocking. It seems to me that as a didactic piece the poem would fail because an impersonal attitude projected within a small group will be read as rejection of friendship with other members of the group.

Let us make the other choice and think further about a performance context for the poem. The only way 31 can be heard without appearing to ignore or spoof the emotions of its audience is for each auditor to take it as meant for herself alone. As a result, the poem gains immediacy as each listener loses consciousness of any rival auditor.[14] But members of a group with established relationships, affections, and jealousies could not banish each other from mind. The poem would achieve its greatest emotional impact, therefore, if a woman sang it to herself. Instead of hoping that Sappho envisioned her, she would envision Sappho. The separation of speaker and singer effected by the poem means that a woman who sang the poem could simultaneously hear it as another's voice. The fictional setting invites her to imagine herself in that situation, feeling "Sappho's" eyes on her and hearing "Sappho's" thoughts. She could easily picture "Sappho," since the latter gives such full description of herself. To be its focus makes the poem thrilling to any auditor.

From the singer/addressee's point of view, the poem has two powerful effects. First, the poem creates an illusion of communication with "Sappho." Within the framework of the fictional setting, "Sappho's" speech is telepathic, for the addressee becomes cognizant of it as she speaks to the man. Nor does "Sappho" withdraw: since the poem does not begin as a soliloquy for the addressee (as it does for other listeners), she would take lines 8 and following as the continuation of "Sappho's" address to her.[15] The result is two-way interchange: since "Sappho" describes herself, the addressee knows what "Sappho" feels and sees "Sappho" along with "Sappho" seeing her and seeing herself. From the recipient's point of view, each woman is seeing herself and the other; she also hears "Sappho"—and can imagine "Sappho" hearing her thoughts. The poem actually invites her participation in a secret conversation.

Dependent on the first effect is the second: the addressee would have to imagine herself as desirable to others, for she would find both "Sappho" and the man beside her in thrall to her, and the reactions of both would guide the representation of herself that she projects into the picture.[16] And how unconventionally Sappho goes about signaling her attractiveness! To feel the full impact of the scene of the addressee's speaking to the man, we must compare it to one of Greek culture's most prevalent narratives of female beauty, the rape. The loveliness of a young woman in myth is routinely represented by her ability to attract a god or hero, who seizes the opportunity for an act of intercourse and then is off. Examples are mentioned in Chapter 2. In Sappho's poem, by contrast, the man seems "like a god" but sits immobilized. Instead of acting, he listens to "you" talking and laughing. Since she is thus the one who defines the situation rather than the object of his wilful desire, she finds herself represented as a speaking subject in the mirror of the poem. Even if the addressee does not construe the man as important, his behavior reflects on the image of herself that she is invited to create.

With respect to "Sappho," the revisionist image granted the addressee is even stronger: "Sappho" both listens and sees her but does not objectify her, since "Sappho's" perception leads to an overwhelming sense of her very being. The addressee accordingly perceives herself not as a body caught in "Sappho's" gaze, but as a presence for others.[17] Her subjectivity and desirability are inseparable in the phrases "sweetly speaking" and "laughing enchantingly." Thus the poem provides its addressee with an ideal image of herself in terms that resist the culture's objectification of women, just as Sappho reversed the dominant construction of the female in her own self-presentation.

We can see that when we explore its effects from the position of a unique recipient the poem comes most to life as communication and appears to have the greatest psychological efficacy; that is, it has the power to influence the auditor positively in ways that one can imagine Sappho wanted. It creates more impression of interchange, paradoxically, than if Sappho were to sing it to a group as an illustration of her feelings. The earlier analysis of the disjunct between speaker and singer has already shown that the poem is not a libretto for self-presentation: the fictional speaker cannot be realized by the singer but must rely on the auditor's imagination. Let us take these two aspects of the poem together: they suggest that the poem was created as *text,* as Sappho's projection of herself into a form that would be independent of her presence. I propose, therefore, that Sappho composed this poem as a gift for a woman from whom she expected to be cut off for some reason. Poems 16, 94, and 96 *V* show that separation was a painful reality for women. The poem then has as its function to keep a sense of contact alive over time and distance. In blurring subject-object distinctions as she does, Sappho tries not only to foster the fantasy of continued intimacy but to reproduce the sense of mutual affirmation that women must have gotten from Sappho or in her circle. We can add that the telepathic communication implied within 31 mirrors its actual mode of communication, writing, which is silent and able to traverse distance. The repeatability of the scene (the man sits in the continuative present and Sappho collapses every time she looks) reflects the reiterability of the written statement. If I am right, then Sappho was one of the first major poets to exploit the textual possibilities of writing, with its ability to project an implied speaker independent of the physical mode of transmission. I return to this issue at the end of the chapter.

How, then, should we think about gendered speech in this poem? Since it is not a poem designed for a singer's self-presentation to a circle of friends, we should look at the en-gendering of the singer/addressee who creates an image of herself for herself as she performs it. I have already pointed out that she can perceive the force of her presence by its effect on the other figures in the poem. Yet more subtly, the poem forces the recipient to define her own desire by construing the scene. The extant lines never name "Sappho's" emotion, only its symptoms, so the singer/addressee can decide what "Sappho" feels, depending on what she wants from "Sappho." The man might or might not be important, depending on her inflection of the scene. He might function for an addressee simply to indicate a setting in which "Sappho" cannot approach, or she might find the idea of proximity to a man or the implication of marriage exciting. Nor must the man be a future husband; a listener could think of him as an alternative to her present husband, for imagination is free. The poem provides a field in which the recipient can arrange a variety of relationships centered on herself, while she must act as subject in positioning the other figures emotionally.

In singing the poem, the addressee speaks of herself through the mouth of another whom she creates in imagination. Within the poem she sees and hears herself through the others' eyes and ears. She therefore conceives herself as a split subject, finding herself in another's consciousness of her; but because she creates the other whose voice she uses to represent herself, hers is a self-conscious split subjectivity. Her performance therefore counteracts women's gendered public self-presentation as unaware objects for others. The significance of Sappho's poem must be seen in light of the stance assigned to women speakers as we uncovered it in Chapter 2: in public performance women dramatized their dissociation from their bodies and voices. None of the poems examined there comes from Lesbos, but, as the wedding poetry shows, the same assumptions about male and female seem to have been prevalent on Lesbos. When juxtaposed with Alkman's *partheneia,* 31 *V* seems subversive: it elicits the singer/recipient's awareness of herself as desiring and desirable in addition to fabricating a female speaker who speaks of her own desire.[18]

If 31 *V* had no specific performance context because it was written for a woman to sing to herself, we have no hope of identifying the age of the recipient or her actual relationship to Sappho. Sappho may have given 31 to a *parthenos* whom she had trained for performance but would not expect to see again. She may have composed it for a companion from her circle. The separation would not necessarily result from one woman's departure from Lesbos, for the shifts of political alignment alone probably barred women from seeing one another at times. Sappho may in fact have been a lover of the one she begifted, but her poems do not reveal actual relationships. They use the expression or intimation of desire to bridge the distance and keep contact with her emotionally alive. It is a striking fact that Sappho's declarations and descriptions of love and desire are always mediated by distance, the inaccessibility of one even to the other's speech by normal channels.[19] Desire in Sappho's poetry, then, is a form of and metaphor for contact despite separation.

In 1 *V* Sappho achieves similar effects by another route. Sappho begins by calling on Aphrodite not to tame her with pains but to come as she has come before in her sparrow-drawn chariot. I quote the latter part of the poem (13-28):

αἶψα δ' ἐξίℵοντο· σsgr;ὺ δ', ὦ μάℵαιϐα,
μειδιαίσsgr;αισ' ἀθανάτωι πϐοσώπωι
ἤϐε' ὄττι δηὖτε πέπονθα ℵὤττι
δηὖτε ℵάλημμι

. . . . .

ℵὤττι μοι μάλιστα θέλω γένεσθαι
μαινόλαι θύμωι· τίνα δηὖτε πείθω
]σάγην ἐς σὰν φιλότατα;[20] τίς σ', ὦ
ψαπφ', ἀδίℵησι;

. . . . .

ℵαὶ γὰϐ αἰ φεύγει, ταχέως διώξει,
αἰ δὲ δῶϐα μὴ δέℵετ', ἀλλὰ δώσει,
αἰ δὲ μὴ φίλει, ταχέως φιλήσει
ℵωὐℵ ἐθέλοισα.

. . . . .

ἔλθε μοι ℵαὶ νῦν, χαλέπαν δὲ λῦσον
ἐℵ μεϐίμναν, ὄσσα δέ μοι τέλεσσαι
θῦμος ἰμέϐϐει, τέλεσον, σὺ δ' αὔτα
σύμμαχος ἔσσο.

. . . swiftly they arrived; and you, blessed one, with a smile on your immortal face, asked what again I suffer and why again I call and what I most wish in my mad heart to have happen; whom again should I persuade to [ ] into your affection (*or* lead you back into her affection)? Who does you injustice, Sappho? For even if she flees, soon she will chase, and if she does not accept presents, she will nevertheless give them, and if she does not love, soon she will love, even if unwilling. Come to me now also, free me from harsh cares, bring to fulfillment all that my heart yearns to accomplish, and you yourself be my ally.

In the poem the address to Aphrodite becomes a recalled conversation, which switches from indirect into direct discourse, blurring the time difference. The past appears to be now, the divinity there in "Sappho's" presence. A collective audience would be reduced to the status of ignored observers as the narration of a past event turns into a dramatic projection in the present. This poem, like 31 *V,* does not present its singer to the audience as one among them or constitute its auditors as a group.

The dramatic situation is further displaced from the actual context of performance by the treatment of the first person. The whole poem is an address to Aphrodite, but within that address the singer narrates to Aphrodite a previous epiphany of the goddess's. This narration begins in mediated form: "you" remains Aphrodite from the opening address through the first part of the narration, while "I" is the singer. Then in mid-stanza (line 18) the construction switches to direct discourse and "I" becomes Aphrodite.[21] Two successive first-person verbs (θέλω and πείθω) have different referents. Just after the moment when the singer's voice becomes Aphrodite's, "Aphrodite" addresses "Sappho" by name. The effect of this transfer is to detach the character "Sappho" from the singer and make her a figure in the imagination of the listener.

The poem withholds even knowledge from a collective audience: the woman who causes "Sappho's" pain is not named, and the listeners would be left in the dark. Nor do I think that her identity would be known to the audience from real life, given that the poem would seem gloating if the woman had (re)turned to Sappho and risky if she had not: if the woman did not soon reconcile with Sappho, Sappho's influence with Aphrodite would appear to have faded. And the poem makes a rather remarkable claim: Aphrodite once told Sappho that she would coerce *whomever* Sappho wanted (back?) (18-24). How many current intimates, ex-lovers, or rivals for others' affection would want to hear that?

Like 31, the poem is textual; it presents a fictional "Sappho" to be created in imagination by a singer/recipient who identifies herself as the "she" of whom "Sappho" speaks. She would overhear "Sappho's" determination to gain (or recover) intimacy (φιλότας) with her.[22] She would hear herself described by Aphrodite as bound to become an active pursuer, an agent of her own desire. The second of the two effects treated above, portrayal of the other woman as at once desiring and desirable, seems to operate in this poem too. On the other hand, this poem sounds very different in tone and attitude from 31. Aphrodite's speech has an aggressive edge, which "Sappho" seconds with her military metaphor in the last line. Aphrodite's repeated "again" makes it clear that she has been summoned before. These features are reminiscent of 130 and 71 *V*, discussed above as poems about women who appear to be transferring their loyalty to new friendships. The beauty of the other woman is not mentioned, and the problem is not unbridgeable distance but the other woman's refusal to close the distance. I would therefore hazard a guess that 1 *V* offers a singer who identifies with "she" the motivation to come (or return) to Sappho's circle. She hears that Aphrodite is likely to compel her despite her own resistance, just as Aphrodite has brought others (back). Aphrodite moreover thinks that she is committing "injustice" by staying away. If the singer/recipient is torn between the impulse to come and advice from others not to come, this poem will give her both precedent and justification for yielding to impulse. Sappho's unparalleled use of legal and military language, as well as her unique request that Aphrodite take practical steps to bring a woman (back), indicate that Sappho seeks a different effect from that of 31 *V*. Like the poems discussed in the last section, this may be a political poem veiled in the language of personal need. The term φιλότας can mean either "love" or "friendship," so would be well-suited to link Sappho's fictional self-presentation as desiring to her actual meaning of seeking political intimacy within a circle.[23]

The textuality that we discovered, put to use in 31 *V* to counteract the effects of separation, is deployed here to undo separation. If Sappho sent the poem to the woman she meant, the woman could always renew and justify her attachment to Sappho through the imagery of erotic compulsion. She might notice the veiled threat as well, contained simply in the lack of a specifying pronoun in lines 23-24: Aphrodite does not say whether the other woman will pursue "you" (i.e., "Sappho") or will pursue some other (and learn what it is to be disdained).[24] Sappho clearly seeks reciprocity of attachment, so if the woman was inclined to return to Sappho she could supply "you" without making anything of its absence.[25] But if she resisted the idea of joining Sappho, she might hear Aphrodite's promise as a threat to make her pursue others.

Some will object that I have demoted 1 *V* from a love poem to a political poem. I do not think that any of the love poems are a candid cry of emotion or even a taming of ardor by controlled expression. They are rather the vehicle for expenditure of emotion: Sappho lent her body and desire to others in order to sustain them with the energy of her response to them. We, who cannot pretend to know her personally and are not engaged by her political life, must approach her power by creating a biography of loves, but the desire we feel to know her desire attests to her power to draw women to her, even absent an expectation of becoming lovers. Poem 1 *V* may be both a love poem and a political protreptic, but at the least its vocabulary gives it an additional field of reference missing in the other love poems.

For her project in 1 *V*, Sappho uses a bold technique: she portrays herself in conversation with a god. Interchange with divinity is another method by which Sappho creates a fictional textual character separate from the singer, for such privilege belongs to mythical and heroic figures.[26] Like a hero the speaker calls on her favoring deity; the full stanza it takes Aphrodite to arrive is a measure of the distance the speaker's voice can reach. Like a hero she can endure the undisguised presence of a god. The listener who creates a fictional Sappho can either take the epiphany as "real" and imagine Sappho in quasi-mythical terms or can take it as imagined by the fictional Sappho, who becomes a figure of intense inward emotions.[27]

This method has a further dimension that the portrayal of psychosomatic chaos in 31 *V* lacks: it lends authority to the speaker. She is like a bard as well as a hero, for she can also "see" Aphrodite leave Olympus and can make her visible to the audience. On the other hand, Sappho uses bardic authorizing techniques in counterpoint to bards' practice: Aphrodite validates her speaking, not Zeus; she chooses as her "ally" in this poem the god whom Athena mocked in the *Iliad* as a useless adjuvant in war (21.423-33).[28] Sappho's authority is antipatriarchal, and she gains thereby an alternative source of "truth."

In other fragments as well, the speaker portrays herself in conversation with a god. In fragment 95 *V* Sappho appears to report a conversation with a god; her interlocutor this time may be Hermes.[29] She repeats a speech she made to him in which she expressed longing to die and see "the lotusy, dewy banks of Acheron" (8-13). Images of loss of consciousness and renewal interact in the description.[30] Of the addressee or the dramatic context for the reported speech, almost nothing is preserved: the name Gongyla and the word *sign* are almost the only other words of significance that can be read. We cannot tell, then, how Sappho used the figure she created as speaker in this poem, but perhaps she again revealed intense longing for another woman.

Other small fragments hint at Sappho's habit of fictionalizing herself by revealing her interaction with divinities. In 96.21-23, which may open a new poem, the speaker says, "It is not easy for us (?) to equal the goddesses in lovely shape . . ." In the following two stanzas, something is said about Aphrodite, who "poured nectar from golden [pitchers?]" (26-28). The speaker's idea about whether mortal women resemble the gods gains weight from her personal vision of Aphrodite. A line is quoted by Maximus of Tyre with the explanation that Aphrodite is speaking to Sappho (159 *V*):

οὖ τε χἄηοσ θερᾶλωυ Ερoσ

You and my attendant Eros

The goddess addresses Sappho, as she does in 1 *V*, with the added distinction that Sappho is paired with the daimonic Eros; we can see how this poem might have detached the speaker from the singer and created a mythicized figure of "Sappho." Another quotation (134 *V*) seems to say, "I narrated a dream to (?) Aphrodite," and yet another, garbled passage is reported as spoken to Aphrodite (101 *V*). Sappho must have used the technique frequently.

Poem 96 *V* is somewhat different from 31 and 1. Though the opening is lost, it appears to have been addressed to Atthis, to judge from the name in the genitive in line 16. The extant part, beginning with scraps of what may well be the first stanza, evokes a woman who is now in Lydia; she may have been named as well:

] σαϐδ[
πόλ]λαℵι τυίδε [ ]ων ἔχοισα
. . . . .
ὡσπ[ ]ώομεν, [
σε †θεασιℵελαν ἀϐι-
γνωτα†, σᾶι δὲ μάλιστ' ἔχαιϐε μόλπαιἐ·
. . . . .
νῦν δὲ Λύδαισιν ἐμπϐέπεται γυναί-
ℵεσσιν ὤς ποτ' ἀελίω
δύντος ἀ βϐοδοδάℵτυλος ‹σελάννα›
. . . . .
πάντα πεϐ‹ϐ›έχοισ' ἄστϐα· φάος δ' ἐπί-
σχει θάλασσαν ἐπ' ἀλμύϐαν
ἴσως ℵαὶ πολυανθέμοις ἀϐούϐαις·
. . . . .
ἀ δ' ‹ἐ›έϐσα ℵάλα ℵέχυται, τεθά-
λαισι δὲ βϐόδα ℵἄπαλ' ἄν-
θϐυσℵα ℵαὶ μελίλωτος ἀνθεμώδης·
. . . . .
πόλλα δὲ ζαφοίταισ' ἀγάνας ἐπι-
μνάσθεισ' ῎Ατθιδος ἰμέϐωι
λέπταν ποι φϐένα ℵ[]ϐ[ ] βόϐηται·
. . . . .
ℵῆθι δ' ἔλθην ἀμμ[ ]ισα τόδ' οὐ
νωντα[ ]υστọνυεṃ[ ] πόλυς
γαϐύεị [ ]αλοụ[ ]τọ μέσσον·

. . . Sardis (?) [ ] often turning her [mind] in this direction [ ], [she honored?] you like a manifest goddess (?),[31] and she delighted most in your song and dance, but now she stands out among the Lydian women as sometimes, when the sun has set, the rosy-rayed moon outshines all the stars; its light reaches equally over the briny sea and the flower-filled fields; and the beautiful dew settles and the roses and tender chervil and fragrant clover are in bloom. Often pacing up and down, remembering gentle Atthis with longing, she is consumed [ ] in her delicate heart (?).[32] But for us to go there [ ] this (is) not [possible?] much [ ] sounds [ ] middle.

The poem does not detach its speaker from the singer. Instead its speaker pronounces with an air of oracular authority about the thoughts and feelings of the woman in Lydia, offering no explicit self-presentation at all. It too concentrates on one addressee and allows the audience no way to participate, so I take this poem also as one intended for the addressee to perform for herself. The addressee is not described as distant from the speaker, but through the poem she can recall a woman who is gone. We could say that "Sappho" portrays the woman in Lydia as playing the same role toward Atthis that "Sappho" herself fills for the addressee in 31 and 1, with the same two effects. On one hand, the woman in Lydia attests to Atthis' desirability and subjectivity in that she used to compare Atthis to a goddess and loved her singing. On the other, her longing allows Atthis to think of the intimacy as continuing across the distance that separates them. "Sappho" speaks for the absent woman; in her name she offers magnificent praise of Atthis, for the phrase "manifest goddess" (4-5) recalls a passage from the *Odyssey* in which Nausicaa is compared to Artemis (6.107-9).[33] "Sappho" also reveals her to Atthis, pacing and yearning. Poem 96 therefore confirms the intent of 31 by showing us the same mystic communication, arranged by the speaker now but affecting two others. In what was perhaps the last stanza (18-20), as in 31 *V*, the speaker acknowledges separation—unless line 21 is not the opening of a new poem, in which case the speaker goes on to suggest that Atthis looks like a goddess, compensation proffered for the other woman's absence.

Since it involves three figures, 96 *V* has even more of a polymorphous quality than does 31 *V*. Atthis could sing the poem to herself and feel "Sappho's" urgency, as well as the longing of the woman in Lydia. The woman's beauty like the moon, an image that seems to overflow the simile and drench the poem in its light, would call forth Atthis' own desire for the absent woman—and perhaps for Sappho too as the producer of such sensuous imagery. "Sappho's" sentiment for Atthis is unspecific, if heartfelt: is she comforting or seductive?[34] Perhaps she wishes to draw Atthis to herself. Atthis could construct the scene as she wished. The woman in Lydia could also sing it to herself and hear herself described in terms of beauty and sexual subjectivity together, the latter as the one who praises Atthis. The poem implies by its existence that Atthis longs for her. She could also imagine that "Sappho," who extols her beauty, desires her. The power of "Sappho's" feeling for Atthis, or for the woman in Lydia, or both, gives her recreation of their intimacy its force, as though they both draw from her their energy of desire for one another. The poem thus creates a play of intersubjectivity in which each woman who sings and puts herself into the song is desirer and desired. For each woman it offers, in the course of creating a fiction of continued communication, the possibility of mutual interchange in escape from the subject-object division encoded in hegemonic culture.

Fragment 22 *V* shows us another dimension of Sappho's project. I quote the best-preserved section (9-17) from Campbell:[35]

[ϰ]έλομαι σ' α[είδην
Γο]γγύλαα ["Αβ]ανθι λάβοισαν ἀ[
πᾶ]ϰτιν, ασ σε δηυτε πόθος τ[
ἀμφιπόταται

. . . . .

τὰν ϰάλαν· ἀ γ]ὰϱ ϰατάγωγις αὔτα[ς σ'
ἐπτόαισ' ἴδοισαν, ἔγω δὲ χαίϱω·
ϰαὶ γὰϱ αὔτα δήπο̣[τ'] ἐμέμφ[ετ' ἄγνα
Κ]υπϱογέν[ηα,

. . . . .

ως ἄϱαμα[ι
τοῦτο τωπος
β]όλλομα[ι

[ ] I order you [to sing of Gongyla, Abanthis?] taking [ ] lyre [ ] while desire yet again [ ] flies around you, the lovely one. For her (?) garment overwhelmed [you?] when you (?) saw it, and I rejoice, for even the [holy?] Cyprian herself (= Aphrodite), no less, once rebuked (me) on the grounds that I pray [ ] this word (?) [ ] I want [

The papyrus does not show whether line 9 is the opening of a new poem, but it looks as though it could be, and I will assume that it is. As in 96, there may have been specific names, although the restorations in line 10, Gongyla and Abanthis, are uncertain. Edgar Lobel does not think that "Gongyla" fits the trace of a letter at the edge of the papyrus.[36] The name Abanthis is borrowed from an unattributed fragment of Aeolic lyric.[37] Other completions of the visible letters are possible, and the whole restoration is tentative; it is not implausible, however, so with that caveat I will adopt it.[38]

"Sappho" speaks to one woman about another, recreating a past moment of attraction. The fragment does not reveal whether Gongyla is now absent, but the parallel with 96 *V* suggests that she is. If so, Sappho is again the link between the two women by her observation and memory of what once transpired. Sappho also fictionalizes herself through conversation with Aphrodite as in 1 *V* and more overtly than in 96. Since the poem shows the same features as these two poems, I analyze it too from the recipient's perspective.

From this angle one can see that Sappho devises a new mode of fostering another woman's subjectivity. The speaker asserts Abanthis' desire and desirability, as we have seen in other poems, but does not create the illusion of continued communication between Abanthis and Gongyla. She does not evoke Gongyla in the present for Abanthis or convey her thoughts like a seer. Instead she orders Abanthis to compose and sing for herself. We should therefore examine the effect on the recipient more closely.

The speaker opens by telling one woman, Abanthis, to sing about another for whom she feels longing. At the same time she (the speaker) attests to Abanthis' beauty, for τὰν ϝάλαν (the lovely one) should refer to the nearer accusative (σε in 11). But the adjective does not simply stay put: because it stands at the beginning of the line and has the same metrical shape as Γογγύλαν two lines above, it could be heard as applying to Gongyla also and epitomizing what Abanthis should sing about her. What the speaker says about Abanthis, Abanthis should say about Gongyla. Then too the phrase "desire . . . flies around you" must refer to the longing that Abanthis feels, but in its vivid unspecificity it suggests the longing that Abanthis causes as well. Like Erotes fluttering about a bride or beautiful woman in later Greek vase-painting, longing flying around Abanthis hints at a double movement of desire between her and another who also finds her desirable.

The next sentence specified that one woman's dress made the other lose her breath, but because of the ambiguity, or rather two-way nature, of the relationship between the two women, we cannot decide between two possible restorations, αὔτας σ' or αὔταν, at the end of line 13.[39] The first yields the statement "her dress overwhelmed you when you saw it," and the second the reverse, "your dress overwhelmed her when she saw it." The second creates mutual attraction, for Gongyla responds to Abanthis as well. Even if the original line was the first (as given above), the double movement of desire from and to Abanthis would not be canceled, for Abanthis is the "lovely one" and the focus of the poem. The dress itself is an object onto which desire is deflected to generalize it.[40] Abanthis would surely hear confirmation of her desire and desirability in the poem.

"Sappho" shifts attention to herself in line 14, describing her own reaction to the moment just mentioned: she "rejoices" at the sight of one woman overwhelming the other. Her delight must mean that she sees in Abanthis assailed by desire another like herself, and therein lies her reason for commanding Abanthis to sing. Abanthis, who is like "Sappho" in the intensity of her emotions, should become like her also in articulating her acute responsiveness to another and presenting herself as the subject of her sexuality.

On the other hand Aphrodite reproves "Sappho" for wanting [ ]. "Sappho," for her part, seems to refuse to give up the fervor of her own desire despite the criticism. One who not only converses with a god but insists on her own perspective makes herself a subject in the face of powerful authority. Because Abanthis should imitate her, "Sappho" provides a paradigm for the addressee to follow by expressing her self-knowledge in spite of others' disfavor. Abanthis therefore should compose and sing songs herself, whatever those around her make of her passion. Like 1 *V*, this is a poem of resistance: it establishes a counterweight to other pressures in the recipient's immediate life. It is more vital to understanding Sappho's overall endeavor than 1 *V*, however, because it does not seek to produce a specific action but to make the recipient more autonomous in expressing her own emotional states.

Yet two problems must be addressed if I am to include this poem with those a recipient sings to herself. First, because the speaker's communication with Abanthis in the fragment appears to be direct and unhindered, the poem seems to be one that Sappho could sing to Abanthis among other women in the circle of friends. Second, the verb "I order" in line 9 (which I take to be the first line of the poem) seems odd in a poem urging another to speak autonomously about her desire. In fact, the two problems cancel each other out. If Sappho were to sing this poem to Abanthis, she would impose herself, with her "I order you" and her interchange with Aphrodite, as superior in power (even if playfully). The poem would then be contradictory in its effect, for Abanthis' singing would not be an expression of her own desire to speak and therefore not a sign of her desire. The impossibility of the verb "I order" in this poem if Sappho meant to sing it to Abanthis shows that the poem must be treated otherwise. If Abanthis, however, were to sing the poem, she would issue the command to herself, and by projecting it onto a mythicized figure whom she creates in imagination she would gain the authority (in her own eyes) to speak about herself as a sexual subject. Claiming divine or mythic validation was of course a normal form of authorizing one's speech or actions in Greek culture. Thus, the split subjectivity Abanthis creates by uttering another's command to her is the springboard to her own freedom to speak.

Fragment 95 *V*, discussed earlier, could be classed with 22 *V* as offering a model for speaking. As in 22 *V* "Sappho" uses her account of interaction with divinity to emphasize her human difference, for she asks not for immortality or gratification but for death. She appears to speak as soon as Hermes arrives: ι ευπον (I said) is positioned at the beginning of the stanza (8), highlighting her act of speech. Poem 1 *V* likewise shows Sappho speaking, compelling Aphrodite's response despite the latter's smile. As remarked earlier, "that man" in 31 can stand in for the whole social system in separating "Sappho" and the addressee. Persistence in subjectivity in spite of lack of power in fact describes all of Sappho's love poetry, composed in the face of the dominant culture, but 22 manifestly propels another to take up Sappho's resistance to the cultural definition of women.

One more poem, 94 *V*, combines all these functions and shows Sappho urging the role of speaker on another. It is made difficult by the loss of at least one line from the beginning. The text follows:

. . . . .

τεθνάκην δ' ἀδόλως θέλω·
ἄ με ψισδομένα κατελίμπανεν

. . . . .

πόλλα καὶ τόδ' ἔειπι [μοι·
ὤιμ' ὡς δεῖνα πεπ[όνθ]αμεν,
ψάπφ', ἦ μάν σ' ἀέκοισ' ἀπυλιμπάνω.

. . . . .

τὰν δ' ἔγω τάδ' ἀμειβόμαν·
χαίροισ' ἔρχεο κἄμεθεν
μῖμναισ', ορσθα γὰρ ὤς ‹σ›ε πεδήπομεν·

. . . . .

αἰ δὲ μή, ἀλλά σ' ἔγω θέλω
ὄμναισαι [ ]έαι
οο[ ] καὶ κάλ' ἐπάσχομεν·

. . . . .

πο[λλοις γὰρ στεφάν]οις ἴων
καὶ βρ[όδων]κίων τ' ὔμοι
κα[ ] πὰρ ἔμοι π‹ε›ρεθήκα‹ο›

. . . . .

καὶ πέλλαις ὐπαθύμιδας
πλέκταις ἀμφ' ἀπάλαι δέραι
ἀνθέων ἐ[ ] πεποημέναις.

. . . . .

καὶ π[ ] μύρωι
βρενθείωι [ ]ἐυ[ ]ν
ἐξαλ‹ε›ίψαο κρ[ὶ βασ]υληίωι

. . . . .

καὶ στρώμν[αν ἐ]πὶ μολθάκαν
ἀπάλαν παὲ[ ]ọτων
ἐξίης πόθọ[ν]νίδων

. . . . .

κωὔτε τις [οὔ]ιε τι
ἶρον οὐδ' ὐ[
ἔπλετ' ὄπ[ποθεν ἄμ]μες ἀπέσκομεν,

. . . . .

οὔκ ἄλσος [

I truly want to die. She left me weeping much and said this [to me]: "oh! how terribly we are suffering; Sappho, in truth I leave you unwillingly." I answered her thus: "Go in joy and remember me, for you know how we sought you out. Or if you don't, then I want to remind you [ ] and we 'suffered' lovely things. For many wreaths of violets and roses and [crocuses?] together and [ ] you put around yourself, beside me, and many plaited garlands made of flowers [you put?] around your tender neck and [ ] with much (?) fragrant myrrh [ ] you anointed yourself and with royal (perfume), and on a soft bed, tender [ ] you satisfied longing for [ ], and no [ ] and no shrine [ ] was there from which we stayed away, no grove [

One must decide to whom to attribute the first extant line, the speaker of the poem or the woman who is departing. Anne Burnett argues for the view that it was spoken by the leave-taker. Her "Sappho" expresses no sentiment, which allows her to take the poem as a straightforwardly didactic one.[41] Burnett assumes that the girl addressed is one whom Sappho loved. Sappho's lesson for her, repeated for the others, is that she must accept the fact that the circle will continue without her and that Sappho will have other loves; in the dreamlike sensuousness of perfume and flowers she is to give up the specificity of her experience.[42] On the other hand, no parallel offers itself among the fragments for a quoted speech begun, interrupted, and taken up again, as we must assume if the other woman speaks the line.[43]

Emmet Robbins makes a persuasive case for giving the line to "Sappho."[44] In that case, as often noticed, "Sappho" confesses that she cannot take her own advice to remember the past without pain.[45] This is a more ironic but conceptually almost as simple a poem: pain leads to rehearsal of now-lost pleasures, which must lead to fresh access of pain (or to some consoling thought).[46] The didactic version of the poem actually gives the later stanzas more point, but the confessional one more typically superimposes present and past and is rhetorically the more likely.

In either version the audience is irrelevant to the speaker. Either "Sappho" could calmly lose all of her auditors or else no one can distract her from the loss of one. Or if Sappho were to sing "I truly want to die" one day and appear cheerful the next, her protestations of emotion would seem overblown. Unless it is grandstanding, the statement is too extreme to serve as a singer's self-presentation among a group of those with whom she has close ties.

Let us instead read the poem as I have been doing, as a text that another woman could sing to herself, taking the first extant line as "Sappho's."[47] The singer/recipient would hear "Sappho's" confession that she misses the leave-taker and discover that "Sappho" now reviews the (perhaps fictional) final conversation with emotions different from those she conveyed then. She could interpret "Sappho's" intense but unspecific expression of emotion as she wished—as erotic desire or more diffuse sense of emotional loss. There follows, embedded in the first-level narrative, a reported conversation that takes over as the envisioned scene, just as in 1 *V*. The recipient speaks first in the interchange, so in singing the song she repeats her (alleged) words, addressing "Sappho" by name. Thus the direct discourse returns the recipient in fantasy to communication with "Sappho." "Sappho's" response, sung by the recipient, allows her to hear Sappho again and carries the scene presented to her mind still farther back, to the time when she was a member of a group around Sappho. Thus she can soothe her sense of loss and fulfil "Sappho's" admonition to remember.

At the same time, in "Sappho's" embedded speech she would find mirrored her own enjoyment of herself, her ways of enhancing her sensuousness. Two of the verbs are middle voice ("you put around yourself" in 14 and "you anointed yourself" in 20), focusing attention back on the addressee's own body.[48] Sappho's desire for her is a possible subtext within the embedded recollection, for "beside me" in line 14 gives license to it. And even as she sees herself through "Sappho's" eyes, the woman also finds reminders of her interaction with a whole group. This second theme appears with the verb πεδήπομεν (8, "we sought out"), which does not mean "we cherished," as it is often translated.[49] Some take it as Sappho's reminder of her own love for the addressee, but they must overtranslate and deny any weight to the plural.[50] In line 23 also, the noun expressing the persons or things for whom the addressee satisfied desire is plural.[51] The poem recalls for the singer a broader set of affirmative relationships within the imaginatively restored communication with "Sappho."

Still, "Sappho" appears to undermine her own advice by her confession, "I simply wish to die." Is this inconsistency more than ironic? Logically, "Sappho" contrasts her despair now with the advice she gave then to enjoy the memory. But as the poem moves, the memory replaces despair. Or, as Ellen Greene puts it, narrative gives way to reciprocal apostrophes, which give way to "a detemporalized mode of discourse."[52] Thus the recipient can indulge both in the pleasure of believing that Sappho misses her and in positive recollection of her participation in a group. In portraying herself as devastated, Sappho lends her erotic energy to the catalogue of mutual pleasures that follows, vivifying it and enabling the addressee to revive her memories without the torment of feeling forgotten by those she leaves behind.

Furthermore, "Sappho's" confession is contained in a poem that must be performed with discipline and harmony, so the move that she recommends, to forge self-defining speech from painful experience, she herself has already made. From this perspective "Sappho's" admission of current pain is essential to her point. As the recipient sang the song, she too would replace weeping with poetry that is at the same time remembering—she would remember Sappho, other times, and the poem itself. Sappho's song sets itself in implicit contrast with weeping and shows the recipient the difference. The poem also seduces the recipient into extending the poem's mode of speaking about the past. "Sappho's" list of pleasures is not individualized to specific events, yet it would induce memories of particular days. The addressee's remembering would leap beyond these generic activities and impel her to continue the recitation, to extend her speech about the past and thus become the speaker that "Sappho" urges her to be. In light of 22 *V* we can interpret this poem as an inspiration to the recipient to transcend the split subjectivity created by singing Sappho's songs and compose her own.

If this is a poem for an addressee to sing to herself, it sets up the same interplay between two figures who are separated but still in communication as we found in the other poems. We can now return to the problem of the opening. Most scholars think (or hope) that there is only one missing line. But Sappho does not usually begin so abruptly as this poem appears to, so perhaps a full stanza plus a line is gone.[53] The first stanza could have framed the poem as a report to a god;

Illustration of Sappho performing before an audience.

then it would be imagined by its singer/recipient as a confession she overhears, like 1 and perhaps 95 *V.* "Sappho's" self-presentation as despairing (a fictionalizing technique like that of 31) would be contained within another framework that displaced the song from the context of performance, making the fictionality of the speaker even clearer.

The poem, like the others, represents resistance to emotional passivity. It also confirms my reading of the other poems in that it shows "Sappho" creating a discourse for the addressee to adopt that will maintain (or create) both a living sense of intimacy with Sappho and an erotic subjectivity. That is to say, it shows us the genesis of poems like 1, 31, 96 *V* in which the recipient is invited to imagine her own emotional state in response to the speaker's longing. Like 22 *V* it also commands the addressee to shape her own speech in song. Poem 94, therefore, is the most revealing of the extant poems about the role Sappho envisioned for her poetry. It provides the addressee with a model speaker as well as a friend or lover for whom she continues to be a presence and who bears witness to her desire/desirability.

Poems for performance in a women's group, poems that commented on political life and celebrated common activities but that used the language of eros to characterize Sappho, are distinguishable from poems that detach themselves from performer and context. The latter appear within the category of love poetry that Dioskourides identified and can be characterized as poems that require a speaker constructed in the imagination and gain psychological efficacy when sung by one who identifies herself as the subject or addressee. These poems vary in the circumstances and relationships they imply, but they have a common theme in soliciting women's sense of subjectivity. Desirable, according to "Sappho," the recipient is also portrayed as desiring and invited to articulate her desire, even when making a song of it may be her only possible form of expression.

Sappho's poetry for others to perform relies on the kind of self-representation possible in writing. The heightened, mythicized speaker, whose emotion is at an absolute pitch and who consorts with the gods, is a figure created in a text. No singer performing as herself could claim to be the person who speaks from these poems of Sappho's. It is through this fictional character that Sappho can dramatize her unyielding energy of desire and convey it to other women as what they should recollect about her and take as a model for themselves. Yet Sappho wrote for those who knew her, and she must have wanted them to dress the textual speaker in their mental picture of her physical self. "Sappho" is not only a fiction but the woman raised to full power. That she speaks with such immediacy, surviving the fragmentation of Sappho's poetry, is an effect of oral style fleshed out (to speak in paradox) by the representation of the speaker included in the text to stand in for Sappho when others perform her poems.

Notes

1. See Saake 1972: 13-36 for a history of scholarship to circa 1963 and 1971 for bibliography on problems connected with the major fragments. Gerber 1976: 105-15 and 1987: 132-44 gives annotated bibliographies.
2. For bibliography on the question whether this was a wedding poem and how to take the man in the first

line, see Saake 1971: 19-22; Burnett 1983: 232-34 notes. For a history of scholarship on the poem, see Bonelli 1977: 463-85.

3. For a recent discussion of the text of these two lines, see Lidov 1993. I do not accept his emendation because I do not think that Sappho describes a single occasion but something that will always happen. Cf. Latacz 1985: 85-86 on the indicative. As to βρόχε', which Lidov says does not mean "briefly" at this time, it is already metaphorical in *Iliad* 10.226, which he cites (514), so it could easily be applied to time.

4. Cf. Johnson 1982: 1-23 on meditative verse compared with address to an audience; I do not think that this is meditative verse (see below). Latacz 1985: 80-81 points out the fictionality of the address but denies that it is inner monologue; he pictures Sappho performing in the presence of the young woman and projecting a scene that will soon take place (86-87). McEvilley 1978 thinks that Sappho is recreating for her circle of *parthenoi* the feelings she had while offering praise to a bride. Rösler 1990b: 282-83 points out that the verb *appear* in 1 and 16 marks the intervening section as fantasy, and Burnett 1983: 230 takes it as inner monologue. For the latter three scholars the poem is essentially meditative. For the views of Rösler and Burnett on the conditions of performance, see below.

5. The following words, "even a poor man," may be corrupt.

6. Rösler 1990b: 277-78 thinks the poem could not have been performed in the presence of the girl about whom it speaks because Sappho's self-consolation at the end has nothing to do with her. Burnett 1983: 241-43 (who believes that the poem is about approaching a new love, not about departure) thinks that the consolation consists of gaining the confidence to seek out the woman the speaker desires. Neither scholar allows a role for the audience.

7. O'Higgins 1990: 158-59 describes the threat that nonspeaking poses to oral poetry; it means the end of poetic creation. Cf. 164: silence assails Sappho repeatedly, and the act of creating poetry resists it.

8. Rösler 1990b: 282 also notes this: "Sappho" becomes part of the imaginary picture within the poem; the "Sappho" who glances is a different person from the one who sings.

9. It is standard new-critical procedure to distinguish the biographical subject (the poet) from first-person speaker in a poem. Kirkwood 1974: 112, for instance, distinguishes Sappho the woman from Sappho the speaker in the poems. Note that I am distinguishing the speaker in the poem from the *performer.*

10. E.g., 79 and 92 *W* (narratives), 34 *W* (prayer). See the translations in West 1993: 116-23 for the flavor.

11. Burnett 1983: 209n.2: "It is the assumption of the present study that the group met in daily intimacy and informality, and that most of Sappho's songs were first performed before this assembly of pupils who were also friends and temporary wards."

12. Burnett 1983: 241-42, accepting the final two words as part of the poem. West 1970a: 312-13 proposes by analogy with Theognis 657-64 that Sappho said, "All is bearable, since god suddenly makes even the poor man rich."

13. Burnett 1983: 277-312, esp. 309-12. Burnett's approach reveals that the very effort to locate the poems in a group context exposes their lack of engagement with the audience.

14. West 1970a: 310, commenting on the lack of names in several of Sappho's poems, suggests that like Theognis' songs, Sappho's could be resung. On 315 he describes her songs as freed from their context.

15. Contrast O'Higgins 1990: 164, who reads the effect psychologically: the act of making a poem replaces passion.

16. Hallett 1979 argues that Sappho's poetry has the function of awakening young women's sexuality.

17. See Stehle 1990: 107-8; Greene 1994: 42-43. Sara Lindheim reminds me of the importance of stressing this.

18. In this 31 *V* is like 16 *V.* In Stehle 1990: 109-12 I analyze 16, a description of Helen acting on her desire in going to Troy, as a validation of women's subjectivity in a cultural world defined by men. Poem 16 has a different rhetorical structure; it has no addressee but makes a general proposition, so performance in the circle would suit it.

19. Carson 1986: 17 and passim refers to this effect as "triangulation."

20. A papyrus fragment appears to give ψ as the second letter in this line. One could therefore restore ἄψ σ' ἄγην ἐς σὰν φιλότατα (to lead you back into her friendship), which Campbell 1982 prints. There are details that do not seem to accord with this reading, so it remains tentative. See Page 1955 *ad loc.;* Voigt *ad loc.*

21. See Führer 1967: 3-4 for other examples of the switch from indirect to direct discourse in lyric; none is a switch between first and second person. Cf. also his p. 60.

22. Wilamowitz-Moellendorff 1913: 48 has a biographical version of this point: the poem might have made the girl aware that she was the one meant and inspired love in her in turn.

23. Page 1955 *ad loc.* discusses the meanings of the word in Sappho.

24. Page 1955: 14-15 remarks that διώκω means "pursue someone who flees." This is not always true, but Sappho's use of the verb may carry overtones. For Giacomelli [Carson] 1980 the justice of Aphrodite consists of making the one who spurns someone's love fall hopelessly in love with another.

25. As Greene 1994: 50-55 argues.

26. See Marry 1979 for Sappho's implicit equation of herself with a Homeric warrior in 1 *V.*

27. Earlier commentators (e.g., Page 1955: 18) considered whether Sappho had actually experienced the epiphany of Aphrodite. If the poem is taken as a straightforward self-presentation, then the question is a legitimate one.

28. See Skinner 1991a on Sappho's calling on Aphrodite (rather than the Muses) for poetic inspiration. Greene 1994: 53 discusses Sappho's reconfiguration of military language in this poem.

29. Ἔρ]μας is a possible restoration of the end of line 6 (Voigt *ad loc.*)

30. Boedeker 1979 makes this point; she also reviews earlier literature on the fragment, in which a biographical approach predominates.

31. Accepting in the translation -σε θέα‹ι› δ' ἰ‹κ›έλαν ἀριγνώτα‹ι› (where -σε is the end of the verb), which Page 1955 prints. See his note *ad loc.*

32. This line has not been reconstructed in a satisfactory way. See Burnett 1983: 309-10n.92 for attempts; Bonanno 1990: 119-21.

33. Marzullo 1952: 90-92. The text is uncertain; some think that ἀριγνώτα is the name of the woman in Lydia. Marzullo gives arguments *contra.* Voigt's preference (*ad loc.*) is to take the word as a name in the vocative; then four women would be implicated: the speaker, the Lydian woman, Arignota, and Atthis.

34. For Hague 1984 Sappho is comforting; for Schadewaldt 1950: 123 Sappho expresses her own desire for Atthis while disguising it as that of the woman in Lydia; Saake 1972: 81 sees Sappho's attitude as seductive.

35. 22 Campbell 1982. The restored text, although speculative, gives a better idea of possibilities than Voigt's. See also Di Benedetto 1986: 21-25 on the text.

36. See *LP* ad loc.; Voigt *ad loc.* and *ad* 95.4.

37. *Incert. auct.* 35 *V;* cf. n. 87 above. Di Benedetto 1986: 22 thinks that it is not long enough to fill the lacuna but that a name did stand there. Alternatively, the word could be an imperative.

38. Cf. λάβοισα and ἄεισον in 21.11-12 *V.*

39. The accusative is restored in Page 1955: 135 although not in his edition of the same year; see also Voigt *ad loc.* Campbell 1982 prints αὔτα[ς σ' from West 1970a: 319. Di Benedetto 1986: 23-24 disputes West, preferring αὔτα[ν.

40. Cf. the eroticized landscape in 96 *V;* Snyder 1994.

41. Burnett 1983: 293-95. Her reason is that the rhetorical intensifier *truly* is indicative of an attempt to persuade, appropriate to the other speaker. Greene 1994: 47 concurs. Howie 1979: 302-5 discusses various proposed interpretations of the first line.

42. Burnett 1983: 296-300.

43. McEvilley 1971: 4-5n. 7 prefers to assign it to "Sappho" on the grounds that Sappho's poems typically begin in the present and move to the past. As Burnett 1983: 293 points out, however, we do not know that this is the first stanza of the poem.

44. Robbins 1990: 114-18, who bases his argument on a subtle rhetorical analysis.

45. The disparity between the first line, if it is attributed to "Sappho," and the tone of the reported speech is noted, e.g., by Schadewaldt 1950: 116-18; Saake 1971: 189-204.

46. Some see in the poem the implication that the addressee has now forgotten Sappho. Caduff 1972 defends this reading, earlier proposed by Wilamowitz-Moellendorff, but rejected by most commentators since.

47. Burnett 1983: 292 points out that the poem could be sung later by any of the girls in order to reinforce their memories of delight after they in turn had left.

48. McEvilley 1971: 9-11 reads the poem in psychological terms as the creation of an imaginary world, a world empty of anyone but the speaker and the beloved. Howie 1979: 310-29 analyzes it as consolation. Though his approach is very different, his conclusions complement mine.

49. The verb does not normally refer to an emotional state. *LSJ* s.v. creates a special category just for this instance, but it gets special treatment only because the poem is taken to be a love poem.

50. Burnett 1983: 296 notes the plural: "The lover who begins by saying 'Remember me' in an instant offers to revive the girl's knowledge of how the whole group had gathered adoringly about her."

51. The supplement νε]ανίδων (young women) in line 23 has been suggested but cannot be taken as probable. Page 1955 *ad loc.* says that, whatever the first visible letter was, it was not α. Burnett 1983: 298n.56 takes the genitive that stood there as subjective, "the desire that girls feel" (accepting the supplement), thus avoiding the idea that the recipient was involved with someone other than Sappho.

52. Greene 1994: 48.

53. In 31 and 95 *V* she describes the scene before speaking of her own state. Poem 31 begins with her speech, and so in this poem also she could open with an address to the divinity.

Bibliography

Editions

Campbell, D. A. 1982. *Greek Lyric.* Vol. 1: *Sappho and Alcaeus.* Cambridge, MA.

Page, D. L. 1955. *Sappho and Alcaeus.* Oxford.

West, M. L. 1993. *Greek Lyric Poetry: The Poems and Fragments of the Greek Iambic, Elegiac, and Melic Poets (Excluding Pindar and Bacchylides) Down to 450* BC, *Translated with Introduction and Notes.* Oxford.

Studies, Commentaries, Dictionaries

Boedeker, D. D. 1979. "Sappho and Acheron." In Bowersock et al. 1979: 40-52.

Bonelli, G. 1977. "Saffo, 2 Diehl = 31 Lobel-Page." *L'Antiquité Classique* 46: 453-94.

Burnett, A. P. 1983. *Three Archaic Poets: Archilochus, Alcaeus, Sappho.* Cambridge, MA.

Caduff, G. 1972. "Zu Sappho Fragment 94 LP. (= 96 D.)." *Serta Philologica Aenipontana II.* Ed. R. Muth. Innsbruck. 9-12.

Carson, A. 1986. *Eros the Bittersweet: An Essay.* Princeton.

Di Benedetto, V. 1986. "Integrazioni al *P. Oxy.* 1231 di Saffo (frr. 27 e 22 V.)." *QUCC* n.s. 24: 19-25.

Gerber, D. E. 1976. "Studies in Greek Lyric Poetry: 1967-1975." *CW* 70.2: *Special Survey Issue.*

Giacomelli [Carson], A. 1980. "The Justice of Aphrodite in Sappho Fr. 1." *TAPA* 110: 135-42.

Greene, E. 1994. "Apostrophe and Women's Erotics in the Poetry of Sappho." *TAPA* 124: 41-56.

Hague, R. 1984. "Sappho's Consolation for Atthis, fr. 96 LP." *AJP* 105: 29-36.

Hallett, J. P. 1979. "Sappho and Her Social Context: Sense and Sensuality." *Signs* 4: 447-64.

Howie, J. G. 1979. "Sappho *Fr.* 94 (LP): Farewell, Consolation and Help in a New Life." *Papers of the Liverpool Latin Seminar* 2: 299-342.

Johnson, W. R. 1982. *The Idea of Lyric: Lyric Modes in Ancient and Modern Poetry.* Berkeley.

Kirkwood, G. M. 1974. *Early Greek Monody: The History of a Poetic Type.* Ithaca.

Latacz, J. 1985. "Realität und Imagination. Eine neue Lyrik-Theorie und Sapphos φαίνεταί μοι κῆνος-Lied." *Museum Helveticum* 42: 67-94.

Lidov, J. 1993. "The Second Stanza of Sappho 31: Another Look." *AJP* 114: 503-35.

Marry, J. D. 1979. "Sappho and the Heroic Ideal: ἔρωτος ἀρετή." *Arethusa* 12: 71-92.

Marzullo, B. 1952. "Arignota l'Amica di Saffo." *Maia* 5: 85-92.

McEvilley, T. 1971. "Sappho, Fragment Ninety-Four." *Phoenix* 25: 1-11.

———. 1978. "Sappho, Fragment Thirty One: The Face Behind the Mask." *Phoenix* 32: 1-18.

O'Higgins, D. 1990. "Sappho's Splintered Tongue: Silence in Sappho 31 and Catullus 51." *AJP* 111: 156-67.

Robbins, E. 1990. "Who's Dying in Sappho Fr. 94?" *Phoenix* 44: 111-21.

Rösler, W. 1990b. "Realitätsbezug und Imagination in Sapphos Gedicht ΦΑΙΝΕΤΑΙ ΜΟΙ ΚΗΝΟσ." In Kullmann and Reichel 1990: 271-87.

Saake, H. 1971. *Zur Kunst Sapphos: Motiv-Analytische und Kompositions-technische Interpretationen.* Munich.

———. 1972. *Sapphostudien: Forschungsgeschichtliche, biographische und literarästhetische Untersuchungen.* Munich.

Schadewaldt, W. 1942. *Legende von Homer dem Fahrenden Sänger: Ein altgriechisches Volksbuch.* Leipzig.

———. 1950. *Sappho. Welt und Dichtung: Dasein in der Liebe.* Potsdam.

Snyder, J. 1994. "The Configuration of Desire in Sappho Fr. 22 L-P." *Helios* 21: 3-8.

Stehle, E. 1990. "Sappho's Gaze: Fantasies of a Goddess and Young Man." In Konstan and Nussbaum 1990: 88-125.

West, M. L. 1970a. "Burning Sappho." *Maia* 22: 307-30.

Wilamowitz-Moellendorff, U. von. 1913. *Sappho und Simonides.* Berlin.

SUSAN C. JARRATT (ESSAY DATE WINTER 2002)

SOURCE: Jarratt, Susan C. "Sappho's Memory." *Rhetoric Society Quarterly* 32, no. 1 (winter 2002): 11-43.

In the following excerpt, Jarratt examines Sappho's writings on memory in the context of gender differences. Placing Greek lyric poetry in the context of the rise of democracy in Athens, Jarratt finds that the language of absence and forgetting in Sappho's poetry reflects women's exclusion from the public sphere—the site of political activity in a democratic society.

Emotions are the matrix of memory impressions, and so—of course—desire moves intellect, as all learning is based in remembering.

Mary Carruthers, *The Book of Memory*

To lack memory is to be a slave of time, confined to space; to have memory is to use space as an instrument in the control of time and language.

Dominick LaCapra, *History and Memory after Auschwitz*

Feminist historiography in rhetoric has flourished over the last decade and a half. Women rhetors are now counted more regularly and numerously among canonical figures (Bizzell and Herzberg), and the works of both male and female rhetors are being held under a lens of gender analysis (e.g., Brody). These two approaches—recovery of female rhetors and gendered analysis of both traditional and newly rediscovered sources—are by no means exhausted and will no doubt continue to attract scholarly energies. As a gradual outcome of these processes, historians of every stripe are led to reconceive traditional rhetorical categories, and along with them, the relationships between past and present. The three proofs, the five canons, topoi, tropes and figures, situation, audience—any and all of these rhetorical materials are subject to transformation via the work of feminist historians (see Ede, Glenn, and Lunsford). In this process, feminism in historical rhetoric opens doors to a wide range of methodologies (including those employed by political theorists, anthropologists, and psychoanalytic critics, to mention a few) which may, in turn, be enriched through cross-fertilization with the rhetorical tradition.

I offer the following reading of memory in the works of Sappho as an example of the way our understanding and appreciation of a traditional canon of ancient rhetoric may change dramatically as a result of feminist historiographical research.[1] Sappho stands as the first and preeminent woman writer in the ancient Mediterranean, and as such, a powerful lure for a student of classical rhetoric interested in gender difference. Among the dozen well-known lyric poets of the Archaic era, Sappho was the one woman who created a body of text read, respected, and (to some extent) preserved by those who produced classical rhetoric and by many others, primarily for its beauties of style and poetic meter.[2] An almost unbelievably happy accident of history preserves the writings of a male poet of almost equal stature, Alcaeus, living in the same time and at the same place: an ideal situation for exploring gender difference. For some traditional historians of rhetoric, such an inquiry would pose the problem of rhetoric's official origins and naming: Sappho and Alcaeus lived during the sixth century B.C.E. in Mytilene on the island of Lesbos, one hundred and fifty years before—and several hundred miles across the Aegean from—the official founding of rhetoric in fourth-century Athens (Schiappa). But the case can be made for a broader definition of "rhetoric" and what counts as "rhetorical practice." Indeed, Jeffrey Walker has made this case convincingly in *Rhetoric and Poetics in Antiquity*. Lyric, he claims, is "the nearest relation to, and indeed the precursor for . . . the later 'rhetorical' tradition"; it functioned as "culturally and politically significant civic discourse" (140). Numerous feminist historians of rhetoric have argued for the necessity of identifying rhetorical practices outside the boundaries of the named tradition. In her study of Sappho, Page duBois identifies ancient rhetoric as a contested field with no stable point of origin (167-76). She terms the self-referential texts of the rhetorical tradition "metarhetoric," freeing up "rhetoric" for wider use (167). Krista Ratcliffe redefines the writings of Anglo-American feminists as implicit rhetorical theory. Molly Wertheimer collects essays on the "rhetorical activities" of women; Cheryl Glenn discusses the "protorhetoric" of Sappho; and, Joy Ritchie and Kate Ronald characterize women's rhetorical theories and practices in terms of "available means." Not only feminist rhetoricians hold this view. According to Oswyn Murray, in cities of the Archaic era, "the poet's role was still central; and so satisfactory for public expression were the varied poetic forms that they may well have delayed the appearance of a prose literature" (25). Because Sappho and Alcaeus were public poets in an era when lyric served as an instrument of persuasion (Podlecki xii; Walker), their texts become valuable sources of reflection on the rhetorical tradition.

A careful reading of all Sappho's fragments brought to my attention repeated references to memory. Could these references be related in any way to the techniques of memorizing speeches which become a mainstay of classical rhetoric? And what role might gender difference play in this process? Isolating memory and considering it in the context of the life of an elite woman in an Archaic era Greek colony suggested a broader context for this mental act, particularly in the light of historical research on memory broadly conceived and of contemporary theories of memory. Studies by scholars such as Frances A. Yates and Mary Carruthers treat memory in Western European intellectual history as a phenomenon of deep cultural significance. Further, recent studies in sexual abuse, racism, and the Holocaust have argued for memory as a powerful force in the interplay between psychic experiences and social structures of exclusion, discrimination, and violence (e.g., LaCapra, Cheng).

These studies concern people reconstructing their own memories of events they experienced. In such circumstances, one can query one's own memory processes. One can also reflect on the

FROM THE AUTHOR

SAPPHO'S "FRAGMENT 10," COMPARING FEMININITY AND LOVE POETRY TO THE MASCULINE EPIC POETRY POPULAR IN HER TIME

Some think the fairest thing in all creation
  To be of horse or foot an armèd host;
For battle-ships some have most admiration,
  But I my heart's beloved do cherish most.

And 'tis not hard to follow me for any;
  For queenly Helen, fairest of the fair,
Although surveying mortal beauties many,
  Did most of all for her famed lover care.

Forgetting her dear parents and her daughter,
  She followed him who glorious Troy destroyed.
Far from her friends and native land he brought
  her,
  By vanity and passionate love decoyed.

For easily is woman tempted ever
  When lightly she considers what is near.
E'en so, my Anactoria, you never
  Remember her who still today is here.

But I her lovely foot-fall hear more gladly,
  Prefer the brightness of her gleaming eye
To all the din of chariots rushing madly,
  To Lydian armoured foot-men's battle-cry.

I know to men the best cannot be granted:
  'Tis better far to ask a share of that
Which once was shared, to be with this contented,
  Than, vainly reaching higher, to forget.

Sappho. "Fragment 10." In *The Lyric Songs of the Greeks: The Extant Fragment of Sappho, Alcaeus, Anacreon, and the Minor Greek Monodists*, translated by Walter Peterson, pp. 22–23. Boston: Gorham Press, 1918.

memory practices of a group. Houston A. Baker, Jr., for example, exhorts African Americans to practice "critical memory" as opposed to nostalgia in reconstructions of Martin Luther King, Jr. The case of a historian reconstructing a distant past does not involve the historian's own memory but rather entails an examination of the processes of memory, insofar as they are revealed in textual records. Histories are lived and created by people with memories, thus public processes of representing the past are intimately connected with the workings of memory. Dominick LaCapra formulates this link powerfully: "critically tested memory may appear as the necessary starting point for all symbolic activity" (182). Ancient rhetoric—both narrowly and broadly defined—offers a detailed record of such operations.

Were there differently gendered needs for memory in the sixth century? Both men and (a few) women composed (probably in writing) and then orally delivered memorized text in the pre-classical period. The attention paid to rhetorical techniques for memorizing speeches beginning in the classical era provides us with a rich resource for exploring the more profound psychic function of memory in recording experiences of exclusion and loss—experiences inscribed within the rhetorical record in various ways. This exploration requires conceptualizing a link between memory and space. Classical rhetoric takes place in a public space inhabited jointly by speaker and listeners, but this space—as has been well documented—was occupied by only a small fragment of all the people who existed in the world of the ancient Mediterranean. Working back and away from the all-male, democratic setting of fifth-century Athens, we may imagine people who must articulate communal goals in the absence of others and in spaces less central and generally accessible than the Athenian assembly and courts. It is under such circumstances that memory becomes crucial. To construct the significance of memory on these terms, then, is to explore space.[3]

Difference and Space

The dominant mental image of the classical (i.e. fifth-century Athenian) rhetoric is a space of agonistic rhetorical practice: *polis* as public sphere, rhetoric as public spear. Jürgen Habermas's early work contributes to this image, sketching classical public in a dramatic chiaroscuro: the *agora* was a space of pure visibility and freedom, defined against the darkness of the *oikos,* the household, where women and slaves invisibly dealt with the necessities of material existence (*Structural Transformation* 1-5):

> Only in the light of the public sphere did that which existed become revealed, did everything become visible to all. In the discussion among citizens issues were made topical and took on shape. In the competition among equals the best excelled and gained their essence—the immortality of fame. Just as the wants of life and the procurement of its necessities were shamefully hidden inside the *oikos,* so the *polis* provided an open field for honorable distinction. . . .
>
> (4)

This heroic and binary image may accurately represent certain features of fifth-century *polis*-life, but a danger lies in transposing that classical map onto the Archaic world of a hundred and more years earlier. Scholarship suggests that it would be a mistake to jump to the conclusion that the spaces occupied by women in Archaic Greek-speaking cities were as confining as those of elite Athenian women during the democracy. Despite the similarity of domestic architecture across the centuries, women in the earlier era had more freedom: "they could move freely without escorts, discuss on equal terms with their husbands, and might even be present at the banquets in the great hall" (Murray 44). To the extent that we can speculate about the life of a woman who is represented in the fragments of poetry marked with Sappho's name (duBois 3), we get a picture of someone who occupied many, varied spaces: she moved and performed in mixed groups, traveled—by choice and in political exile, but may also have been married and a mother, was interested in beautiful clothing and grooming, and spent much time and energy in all-woman groups in composing, singing, and practicing cult religions. Before the status of male citizenship was fixed in the classical, Athenian democracy, who were the subjects of communal life in the ancient Greek city, what spaces did they inhabit, and how did they use language to reflect on and mediate their relations? Determining the nature of the actual spaces within which Sappho wrote in relation to her representations of them generates a complexly layered blueprint of public and private. In the interest of dispelling phantasms of both *agora* and *oikos,* we begin with the latter—its ideological legacies and archaeological remnants—references to which are almost completely absent in Sappho's fragments.

The House

> Life begins well, it begins enclosed, protected, all warm in the bosom of the house . . . In this remote region, memory and imagination remain associated, each one working for their mutual

> deepening . . . Through dreams the various dwelling-places in our lives co-penetrate and retain the treasures of former days. . . .
>
> Gaston Bachelard, *Poetics of Space*

Bachelard's idealized image sketches a thoroughly masculinized view of the house as safe and womb-like nest. Memories are treasures, stored and retrieved through dreams. Though appearing in this brief passage as a timeless form, Bachelard's house distills historically specific elements of the private, domestic space of eighteenth-century European bourgeois culture (Habermas 43-56). Like the middle-class wife and mother, the house itself becomes a maternal bosom, site of love and intimacy, and repository of memory. Contemporary feminist historians must guard against uncritically reproducing this appealing scene of femininity in readings of women writers from earlier cultures. We must look closely at specific features of place and gender, and seek to uncover the ideologies determining their meanings. Where we find familiar elements—separate or intimate spaces, cultivation of the person, emotional intensity, interest in natural beauty—we should ask a number of questions: are they exclusive to a feminine world in a particular time and place, or do they also appear in texts authored by men or in articulations of masculine culture and value? what material conditions support them? what social and political functions do they perform? Asking such questions of archaic Greek culture reveals complex answers.

In some accounts of domestic space and economy of archaic Greece, women occupy a place similar to that of other possessions: "The physical shape of the noble's house provides the key to the relationship between production of wealth and its use to establish the social status of the *basileus* [warrior king]. . . . [I]t consists essentially of a courtyard, stables, perhaps a porch where guests might sleep, *private* chambers for storing wealth and weapons and for women's quarters, and a great hall . . . (Murray 47-48, emphasis added). This is the house of Odysseus or Agamemnon—the heroes of the epics. As in many later descriptions, women are seen as cloistered in gender-segregated, "private" parts of the Greek house. But in a recent study of domestic space across several eras of ancient Greek life, archaeologist Michael Jameson offers a different perspective. There is no way to determine, he claims, which parts of the house were specifically designated for women (172). Most women's work—food preparation, child care, and weaving—went on in the central courtyard, he contends. The one room specially marked as "masculine," the *andrôn,* was probably not as exclusive nor as large and elegantly appointed as the symposium spaces typically represented on vases and in literature. Nor was it kept at a distance from "women's quarters." The point of his analysis is that, given the minimal physical evidence for clear division of gendered spaces in the Greek house, the work of gender separation is much more heavily a conceptual or ideological task (see also Vernant). Domestic archaeology reveals a "concept of the economic and social independence and privacy of the *oikos*" as "the household formed around a nuclear family" (195), but the "private" house of the nuclear family was not the private of a purely feminized domestic space. Nor is the house itself clearly divided into male- and female-inhabited spaces. Note the difference in this conception from the equation Habermas offers: public = *agora* = male; private = *oikos* = female. Reading the fragments of Sappho in relation to this altered conception of the "private" rather than exclusively in terms of gender segregation across a public/private axis gives a slightly different angle of vision. Although the textual space of a journal article prohibits me from treating this question with the thoroughness it deserves, we can sketch some outlines of the representation of space in Sappho's lyrics.[4]

The setting for her discourses is not domestic. In all but a few cases, the lyrics are set outdoors. Capturing the sense of these external spaces requires care. The natural settings of Sappho's fragments are neither highly cultivated nor are they completely wild. They evoke ritual practices and the sites marked out for such, but none of the fragments is generically "religious," nor are rituals described with specificity; they are only alluded to obliquely. Setting her lyrics outside the *polis* draws attention to the fact that women were not included in civic deliberations. Furthermore, a substantial number of the poems thematize presence and absence—women's coming and going—within spaces of women's habitual congregating, thus calling forth a gendered operation of memory.

Outdoors[5]

The lush beauty of natural spaces in Sappho's fragments tempts the contemporary reader into a divided frame of reference: her feminine world of natural beauty and peace—the private garden, in John Winkler's phrase[6]—vs. Alcaeus's busy masculine world of war, politics, and strife. Again we must be on guard against reading more current ideologies, in particular the bourgeois formulas so familiar to us, onto a much earlier and different era. The case of the garden is much like that of the house. We have inherited conceptions of the garden both from eighteenth-century English attitudes toward ownership and cultivation of land and from a Romantic reaction to those attitudes.[7]

Several significant words for places appearing in the fragments of Sappho are drawn from nature and from ancient Greek religious practices conducted outdoors, but the "nature" in these poems is neither wilderness nor precisely the domestic "garden." Michael Jameson suggests that in older Greek towns—with haphazard organization along routes leading to fields, shore, heights, and sanctuaries—as well as in the newer orthogonal settlements (i.e., those laid out in a rectilinear grid), the houses were so tightly packed that there would have been little space between them for gardens (177). Agricultural land (*chôra*) constituted, with the house, part of the "private" realm, but we know from Sappho's scornful reference (Fr. 57) to the couturial ignorance of a "country girl" (*agroiôtis*) in her "country garb" (*agroiôtin stolan*) that she has no love for farm or field. What then are we to make of the relation between the spaces created in these writings so as to imagine Sappho neither as a figure in an eighteenth-century landscape painting, proprietress of a cultivated garden, nor yet entirely confined within a house in the city? Recent archaeological work offers insight into this problem, shifting attention from Bronze Age palaces and classical-era monuments to the temporal and geographical spaces in between (Murray and Price). François de Polignac gives us a picture of newly emerging cities during the Archaic period:

> In the Greco-Aegean world of the eighth century, 'towns' often consisted of loose groups of villages or clusters of houses that the first elements of urbanization were, at the end of the century, just beginning to pull together in an organic fashion (above all by creating spaces reserved for public use), just as they were expanding as a result of demographic growth.
>
> (21)

One of the developments of the seventh and sixth centuries—crucial for the formation of the *polis*—was the establishment of cults and the building of temples. Polignac catalogues sites for religious practices in three different relations to the city: first the acropolis, a high central temple around which the city organizes itself; the second, what Polignac calls "suburban or periurban," located on the margins of the town or just a little way off. The most interesting of Polignac's findings involves a third category: the "extraurban" sanctuary, situated at a distance from the city so as to be out of the daily routine but close enough to be fairly accessible. He observes that "many of the Greek world's most famous sanctuaries fall into the nonurban category" (23) and that the formation of such extraurban sanctuaries was a significant accompaniment to the development of the *polis*. The organization of sacred spaces over the period of the eighth century involved the addition of features such as an altar, a temple (housing statues and offerings), and walls marking out the sacred area (16-17). These changes occurred unevenly across various sites (17-21), but "the appearance of sanctuaries implies a definite change in people's perception of space" (20). Polignac's work helps us to imagine that Sappho might have been physically present in extraurban sanctuaries. He notes the presence of one such sanctuary on Lesbos, situated at the center of the island, equidistant from its four cities (38; see also Walker 223-24, 227-28).

This data gives us a historical frame of reference for the ways Sappho describes outdoor space, and Fr. 2 offers the fullest and most suggestive picture of an extraurban sanctuary:

>] summit of the
> mountain descending,
> come to me from Crete to the sacred recess
> of this temple: here you will find a grove of
> apple trees to charm you, and on the altars
> frankincense fuming.
>
> Here ice water babbles among the apple
> branches and musk roses have overshadowed
> all the ground; here down from the leaves'
> bright flickering
> entrancement settles.
>
> There are meadows, too, where the horses
> graze knee
> deep in flowers, yes, and the breezes blow
> here
> honey sweet and softer [
> [ ]
>
> Here now you, my goddess [ ]
> Cypris
> in these golden wineglasses gracefully mix
> nectar with the gladness of our festivities
> and greet this libation.
>
> (trans. Jim Powell)[8]

I chose this translation in part because it preserves the incomplete line before the first full stanza, giving the picture of this grove not at an indeterminate distance out in the wilds but between mountain and city. This dreamlike poem contains many of the significant place terms Polignac associates with the extraurban sanctuary. The poet appeals to the goddess Aphrodite (associated with Crete) to come to a "recess" (*naûon,* l. 1). Translated by some as "temple," the term is less suggestive of a built monument than of a place outdoors which naturally lends itself to worship. Likewise, "grove" (*alsos,* l. 2) seems to be a natural site, but it has been furnished with altars (*bômoi,* l. 3). There are signs of cultivation—apple trees and roses—but also of wild vegetation. The place word *chôros* (translated as "all in the ground" in l. 7)[9] carries associations of land or country, but can also refer more generically to place or space; Liddell and Scott's first definition is "space to hold a thing," and its related word *chôra* suggests belonging—to be in one's place or take one's place (793-94).

Given those associations, this fragment's most striking aspect, noted by several commentators, is the eerie absence of people. Thomas McEvilley, for example, describes the grove as a "general image of a relationship of desire and withholding, of emptiness and fullness" (332). We have gone out of the city with the poet—perhaps along a processional path marked out from city to sanctuary, along which the whole community would have walked on another occasion: ending in a place where women would have enjoyed the rituals of the cult of Aphrodite—"private" in their separation from the rest of the group, but public in the sense of engaging in religious practices sanctioned by and in service of the *polis.* But instead of being accompanied by others, in Sappho's poem the listener is placed in this imagined space alone. More powerfully than the publicly sanctioned space of worship, the fragment represents the absence of women.

In another fragment (94), women are present together, facing imminent separation. The speaker here expresses a wish to die because she must leave a group of other women against her will. She describes this experience, what she has "undergone" (*pep[onth]amen*), as "fearful" (*deina*). The respondent, "Sappho," then consoles her, redefining the experience as a good one (*kal' epaschomen*), and corrects her memory: "and remember me, for you know how we have stood by you. Perhaps you don't—so I will remind you . . . and we have undergone beautiful things" (trans. John Winkler).[10] She goes on to remind the girl of wearing wreaths of flowers, being anointed with perfumed oil, lying on a soft bed and satisfying her longing. The verbs in both cases are forms of *paschô,* to undergo. This is an active voice verb but has something of a passive sense to it: to undergo something demands less agency than to do something. The poem combines the idea of a forced departure from the pleasure of a group of women in the ritual space of Aphrodite's sanctuary with the shaping of memory in the face of that departure, the reminder which is actually a changed impression of what was "undergone." The words for remembering—the imperative *memnais'* (*kamethen memnais'* - "remember me") and *omnaisai* (an infinitive in the phrase *egô thelô omnaisai* - "I want to remind you") are derived from *Mnemosune,* the name of the mother of Muses.[11] The rhetoric of the verse delicately reconstructs of a memory of pleasurable erotic and sensual experience to be carried into the new life (Burnett 290-300). The Sapphic speaker corrects the departing woman's memory in order to sustain her in a future in which she would perhaps be cut off from the richness of experience with the speaker and others who have shared those experiences, those who have "taken care of" the leaving woman. Similar uses of memory occur in other poems. Fr. 16, for example, uses the story of Helen in a speculation on a philosophical question: what is most beautiful? At the end of the existing fragment, the speaker says the mythic Helen has reminded her (*o]nemnai-s'*) of "Anactoria who is not here" and goes on to mention "her lovely walk and the bright sparkle of her face" (Campbell 67).[12] Fr. 24, of which no complete line remains intact, recreates the tone of Fr. 94: "remember (*emnasesth'*) . . . for we too did these things in our . . . youth: many lovely . . . we . . . the city . . . us . . . sharp" (Campbell 75). The speaker remembers (*epimnastheis'*) "Gentle Atthis" in Fr. 96, another verse filled with natural beauties: moon and stars, salt seas and flowery fields, dew, roses, chervil (Campbell 121).

Converting Desire to Memory: A Rhetorical Process

In these references to memory in Sappho's works lies an impulse related to rhetoric's desire to shape the ideas, feelings, and practices of those it reaches.[13] The motifs of memory in Sappho's poems do not offer an organized *technê* for memorizing speeches (cf. Burnett 277-313). But they arouse yearning (*pothos*), and it is because one can feel desire, can yearn for a different future, a just response to a past act, a fair valuation of a leader, that one can persuade and be persuaded.[14] Although Freud argues that civilization takes shape through the suppression of individual desire (*Civilization*), one might use Sappho's verse, particularly through references to the goddess Peitho, to make the opposite case: that the articulation of the most compelling of human desires—desire for another person—is related in some way to the capacity to articulate communal desires.[15]

Consciousness of others, present or absent, is necessary at that juncture.

Sappho's references to Peitho, the goddess of Persuasion, and the role of this figure in Archaic culture support such an interpretation. In the *Palatine Anthology,* a cumulative collection over ten centuries of thousands of Greek epigrams, the second-century B.C.E. poet Antipater of Sidon links persuasion and lyric in his praise of Sappho:

> Aeolian earth, you cover Sappho, who among the immortal Muses is celebrated as the mortal Muse, whom Cypris and Eros together reared, with whom Persuasion wove the undying wreath of song, a joy to Hellas and a glory to you. You Fates twirling the triple thread on your spindle, why did you not spin an everlasting life for the singer who devised the deathless gifts of the Muses of Helicon?[16]
>
> (Campbell 27-29)

Peitho is here connected with Aphrodite and her son Eros, figures for desire and yearning. In Sappho's Fr. 1 (the only complete poem among the remains of Sappho's verse), we see this association enacted when the speaker (called "Sappho") calls on Aphrodite to persuade a lover to submit to the speaker's desire for her. Although Peitho is not named as a goddess, her name would sound and thus her force be felt in the verb "to persuade" (l. 18, Campbell 54). Her assistance to Aphrodite often involves tricks or deception, later strongly associated with rhetorical persuasion. According to Burnett's analysis of the poem, "[Aphrodite's] magic, after all, is a heightened form of persuasion (as Sappho slyly reminds us) and it will be used in the interest of a special erotic justice which Aphrodite, like a little sister to Athena, here defends" (255-56).

In a more general observation, Anne Carson marks the power of the association between desire and persuasion in a primarily oral culture:

> The breath of desire is Eros. . . . Wings and breath transport Eros as wings and breath convey words: an ancient analogy between language and love is here apparent. The same irresistible sensual charm, called *peitho* in Greek, is the mechanism of seduction in love and of persuasion in words; the same goddess (Peitho) attends upon seducer and poet. It is an analogy that makes perfect sense in the context of oral poetics, where Eros and the Muses clearly share an apparatus of sensual assault.
>
> (49-50)

Peitho became one of Aphrodite's cult names (Burnett 256n.73), probably during Sappho's time. In a second-century C.E. papyrus commentary, Sappho refers to Peitho as a daughter of Aphrodite (Campbell 115). In Fr. 96 mentioned above, the words "Aphrodite" and "Peitho" appear in the final stanzas.

But Peitho's realm is not purely that of persuasion as personal, erotic seduction; she also has associations with the public life of communities. Her power is necessary for the establishment of civilization and democracy. One of the reports of the founding of her cult illustrates this dual association. Pausanias, the travel guide of the ancient Mediterranean, tells of a temple in Athens to Aphrodite Pandemos ("of all the people") and Peitho. Later, archaeologists find coins with Athena on one side and Aphrodite Pandemos and Peitho on the other. According to Walter Burkert, venerable authority on Greek religion, Aphrodite Pandemos was responsible for vulgar sexuality and prostitution, but the sources he cites here are later Athenian figures: Solon, Plato, and Xenophon (409n34). The older meaning of "Pandemos" he gives is "literally the one who embraces the whole people as the common bond and fellow-feeling necessary for the existence of any state" (155). Another story told by Pausanias speaks of the political power of Peitho. A local myth of Sicyon, an ancient city on the Peloponnesian peninsula, tells of the coming of Apollo and Artemis. The twin deities were ejected from a place called Phobos (Fear), an act that precipitated a plague in ancient Sicyon. Young suppliants from the city went to a river and persuaded the gods to return to Peitho's sanctuary in their town, thereby dispelling the plague. Polignac interprets this story as the banishing of Fear by Persuasion, giving "perfect expression to the ideal of relations within the city, where *philia* guarantees the cohesion of the community" (71).

Within this mix of sources, we find threads of persuasion cultivating desire or feeling in service at times of personal passion but at other times of forging group bonds. The rhetorical impulse in Sappho's fragments might be described as the cultivation of such feelings among women, particularly in service of a kind of memory useful to a woman separated from pleasurable contact with other women.[17]

Anne Pippin Burnett describes Sapphic memory training as a "discipline" with some rigor:

> . . . there is nothing sentimental or backward-looking about the Sapphic doctrine of memory, and its practitioners are not to be thought of as listlessly fingering old souvenirs. What Sappho taught was a disciplined mental process which, by reconstructing past actions in a certain way, kept one fit for the best that the present might propose.
>
> (290)

Burnett goes on to propose that the memory Sappho cultivates is an "organising and classifying one, and it must be accompanied by a complementary process of forgetting, as particular moments are dissociated from their particular contexts and rearranged with others of their kind" (300). Perhaps "doctrine" (295) is too strong a term, for Sappho lived in a world prior to discursive systematization—to the differentiation of types of discourse into philosophical, rhetorical, scientific, and aesthetic which began in earnest with Aristotle in the fourth century but would be fully enacted only with modernity. But the *technê* of Sappho's rhetorical lyric is no less artful, self-conscious, and serviceable for the needs of the culture. The question of whether or not this memory work forms a system is less compelling than that of its nature and ends.

The most prevalent references to memory throughout ancient Greek tradition concern a person's *kleos,* or fame. For warrior, politician, or poet, the ideal is to be remembered for great acts which garnered *kleos.*[18] Sappho's fragments include two examples of this kind of memory, notable because they present positive and negative poles. Fr. 147, preserved in the *Discourses* of Dio Chrysostom, promises "Someone, I say, will remember (*mnasesthai*) us in the future" (Campbell 159). The emphatic structure, along with the reference to the future, seems to suggest an assertion of *kleos* for the speaker and her companions. On the other hand, Fr. 55 puts a curse on someone who has failed to live up to speaker's artistic standards, or refused to participate in the world of poetry and pleasure: "But when you die you will lie there, and afterwards there will never be any recollection (*mnamosuna*) of you or any longing for you since you have no share in the roses of Pieria; unseen in the house of Hades also, flown from our midst, you will go to and fro among the shadowy corpses" (Campbell 99). Even in the imagined hell of the banished poet, woman is still in motion, going to and fro.

Treatments of memory specific to the Archaic period are outlined by Gregory Nagy, who notes the significance of memory in relationship to forgetting (*lêthê*) (46-47).[19] Characterizing lyric poetic practice in terms of a visual figure, Nagy observes that things are remembered because of the light cast on them by poetry and also through the active task of forgetting, or obscuring, other things: "Such a concept of *mnemosune* can only be achieved through an ever-present awareness of its opposite, *lêthê.* Without the obliteration of what need not be remembered, there cannot be memory" (46). There are two references to such forgetting in Sappho's fragments. In 44A—a poem concerning Artemis's birth, her pledge to remain a virgin, and her inaccessibility to Eros—appears an admonition "not to forget the anger" (*orgos mê 'pilathe,* Campbell 91-93). The temptation to supply a context for this enigmatic phrase is strong. Could it have to do with a woman's anger in a male-dominated culture? Perhaps it could be linked to Sappho's banishment under the tyrant Pittacus. There simply isn't enough information to support an interpretation. A more famous and fruitful reference to "forgetting," one that will bring us to a consideration of the distinctive functions of memory in Sappho's verse, occurs in the brief fragment about apple-picking, 105(a):

> As the sweet-apple reddens on the bough-top, on the top of the topmost bough; the apple-gatherers have forgotten it—no they have not forgotten it entirely, but they could not reach it.
>
> (Campbell 131)

Winkler interprets this verse as a commentary on female sexuality. The (male) apple-gatherers have "forgotten" the sweet apple reddening: i.e., they have ignored or neglected women's clitoral sexuality. But in the next line we find that, no, they haven't exactly "forgotten" it; they couldn't reach it. Forgetting becomes reinterpreted as a form of incapacity, or a combination of inattention and ineptitude. This subtle dramatizing of "forgetting" takes place in a different associational realm than the casting or withholding of light Nagy describes. Here, the obverse of forgetting requires a kind of physical attentiveness, a sensing of the physical presence of another, along with the capacity to "reach" the other—to respond in a way that suits the features, the state, the ripeness of the other. This kind of remembering is not available to everyone; it is out of reach of some. There is a "hidden-in-plain-sight" quality to it that couldn't be achieved by the switch-like action of turning on or off a light. In a true obverse of such forgetting, the scenarios of remembering created within Sappho's fragments often have more to do with the subtle interplay of relations—the dispositions—among those present than with the shining of a bright light of attention onto a heroic performer.

The memory cultivated in Sappho's verse employs rhetorical powers of lyric in service of the needs of a group. In the creation of an intersubjective space, Sappho disposes her listeners toward habits of mind and action that would help them to thrive within the constraints of their world.[20] In Sappho's lyrics, the others present (listeners) do not become the object of a gaze (Stehle), nor are they represented as fixed in space. In fact, people in the poems are often not represented at all but rather addressed or remembered. Particularly in the creation of the monody—the single person singing to a group—we have an adumbration of the "primal scene" of classical rhetoric.[21] Monody is like but unlike the bardic performance in that the text is new, unknown, "personal" to the singer, but it is presented by a single person to a group. But rather than slotting this genre into the category of "private," we need to remember that the archaic monodist had an important civic function. In the description of space as something to be in rather than look at (Shauf), Sappho's verse disposes her listeners in an attentive relationship toward each other—attuned to their movements in and out of a shared space, their desires, and the ways of remembering that will contribute to their well being. . . .

Conclusion

The linkage between loss, grief, memory, and the visual occurs repeatedly throughout public moments in history, and has been taken up recently by critical theorists interested in historical trauma and the personal damage wrought by racism, sexism, and homophobia. The experience of being excluded from spaces where others exercise power to determine collective actions that shape one's life must always entail some kind of pain: whether it takes the form of the incremental "strain trauma" of a daily life of subordination and silencing, as experienced by women and by queers of many races and classes across history, or more dramatic events of displacement (of American Indians from their ancestral lands), enslavement (of Africans), or genocide (of Jews under Hitler's regime). The project of reimagining public spaces in ways to include and empower such groups must involve the mobilization of memory; vital, multiple publics will engage in "forms of social action requiring the ability to remember in a desirable way" (LaCapra 6). Memory demands (and allows) a kind of agency essential for participation in the public: "Memory is a technology for gaining freedom of movement in and mastery over the subjective temporality of consciousness and the objective temporality of discursive performance" (LaCapra 194). In the passage offered as an epigraph for this essay, LaCapra relates this technique of memory to space.

Memory suggests a history made accountable to the lives of persons. But this is not to suggest the kind of memory contained in a family photo album, constructed by the powerfully normative frame of "the happy family" (Coward). Critical public memory takes its place between sculpted monuments, so familiar that they have become part of a neutral landscape, and a private collection whose names and faces are meaningful only to a handful of intimates. Such a memory will counter the tendency Fredric Jameson sees in our postmodern era: a "weakening of historicity, both in our relationship to public History and in the new forms of our private temporality" (6). Memory here refers to a practice: "a public, intersubjective practice, a collective recollection of a social past" (Mitchell 193). These rhetorical reflections help us to ask, How is it possible to keep reworking the past to make the present comprehensible?[22]

History and memory have an intricate relation to one another, particularly when we speak of those left along the side of the grand road of historical progress. Before (after and around) the technical memory systems formulated within the rhetorical tradition, Sappho inscribed a different practice of memory, one we might attempt to recognize and revitalize even today: "history . . . can provide us the experience of difference, a productive memory of latent fragments of human being" (duBois ix). Classical rhetoric has been remembered—memorialized—by some as a site of lost glory and unquestioned accomplishment: a monumental history, in Nietzsche's term. Placing Sappho in the narrative gives us the rhetorical means to mourn—a way of remembering that returns us again and again to the loss of countless others who have come and gone, and urges us to seek persistently their traces.

Notes

1. I wish to thank the faculty of Miami University's English department, Peter W. Rose, and especially Laura Mandell for their comments on an early draft of this article.

2. References to Sappho appear in the works of numerous Greek and Roman authors including Plato, Aristotle, Hermogenes, Demetrius, Menander, Himerius, Cicero, Catullus, Seneca, Strabo, Dionysus of Halicarnassus, Plutarch, Philostratus, Athenaeus, and others. Her poems were collected into nine volumes by a scholar of the Alexandrian era. The most important contemporary translators of and commentators on Sappho are Denys Page and David A. Campbell. I rely here on Campbell's collection, numbering, and translations (unless otherwise indicated) of ancient writings by and about Sappho and Alcaeus. See Snyder on other women writers in Greek and Roman antiquity.

3. The bibliography on gender and space is vast. For a thoughtful overview focusing on feminist scholarship

in U.S. history and literature, see Kerber. For a perspective from feminist geography, see Pratt and Hanson.

4. This article is based on a chapter of a book-in-progress, *Dispositions: Rhetoric, Difference, and Public Space.*

5. Jeffrey Walker titles his richly nuanced chapter on the poetry of Sappho and Alcaeus "Argument Indoors," referring to the "symposiumlike gatherings" which may have been the settings for the performance of works of both figures. Walker is less concerned with physical space than with the conditions of argument: the question he grapples with is the extent to which these poets spoke to a homogeneous audience before whom they would need "little more than a rhetoric of recapitulation" in order to solidify shared attitudes and identity (249). His answer is admirably qualified: the image of this closed system does not quite hold in either case.

6. In Winkler's elegant interpretation of Sappho's erotic verse, "garden" becomes less a natural space than a metaphor for female sexuality.

7. Tom Stoppard's drama *Arcadia* offers a delightful enactment of the landscape debates. See also Williams.

8. Brackets indicate missing words. Williamson offers an interesting account of the kinds of materials on which Sappho's texts have been preserved and stories of their discovery.

9. The Greek word *chôros* appears in l. 6 of the Greek text (Campbell 56).

10. Several interpreters of this fragment are interested in the problem of attributing the first line: is it spoken by the woman who is leaving, quoted clearly in the following lines, or is it the voice of "Sappho"? On this decision rests the degree of desperation one of the speakers feels at the prospect of separation. There is something of a power struggle involved in the decision: if it is Sappho who wishes to die, she has less power in the relationship than the woman who leaves. Or, vice versa. The "Sappho" speaker seems, in the balance of the fragment, to have more control over the situation—to have an interest in evoking emotional memories that will sustain the departing woman in the absence of the speaker. Thus, the contextually logical interpretation argues for the departing woman speaking first, expressing her wish to die.

11. The Greek lexicon explains the etymology of memory in the Muses: ". . . before the invention of writing memory was the Poet's chief gift" (Liddell and Scott 449).

12. This fragment takes the form of a priamel: a list of parallel items, evaluated on some common criterion, ending in a pointed closing—i.e., what is the best, the sweetest, the first, the strongest X? DuBois interprets this poem as an early form of philosophical logic (chapter five). Burnett discusses the uses of the priamel in the lyric tradition and ultimately reads the function of memory in this poem as an effort to have the listener shift attention from the transience of sensual beauty to the permanence of poetic vision: "the vision to which memory can lead is reflected in an image of changeless luminosity" (277; see also Walker 238-42).

13. Walker makes a compelling case for Sappho as a "protosophist" (249), both performing and arguing for "the persuasive power in the woman's act of speaking" (see especially 208-10, 236-37).

14. Kenneth Burke posits a similar connection between pathos and knowledge in his discussion of the "dialectic of tragedy" (38-41).

15. Laura Mandell remarks that "It's as if, for Sappho's culture and gender, the homosexual/homosocial continuum were visible *as* a continuum, making the sexual and social 'bedfellows' rather than opposites (as in the more homophobic/male suppression of the continuum: civilization *as* discontent, as suppression of desire)" (personal communication).

16. Greek epigrams, unlike the pithy sayings we associated with someone like Oscar Wilde, are occasional poems, inclusive of many subjects and eclectic in their scope. Antipater wrote a series of epigrams in praise of earlier poets: in addition to Sappho, he praised Homer, Orpheus, Anacreon, and Erinna (another of the few female poets in Greek antiquity) (Peter 16ff.)

17. Walker speculates that women's groups during this period would have an unstable quality, commenting that "Sappho's circle was not so much held together as continually reconstituted" (230-31). He imagines that women of the period, in addition to seeking consolation for this condition, might be expressing in its representation a desire for the agency that allows men to wander of their own volition (242).

18. See Jesper Svenbro's study of reading in ancient Greece for discussion of the concept of *kleos* as derived from the sound of poetry read aloud and of Sappho's fragments in terms of speech, writing, and personae.

19. Many will recognize in this root the name of the river over which the dead pass on their way to the underworld. When the prefix "a" is added (a "privative" or negating morpheme), the resulting words create another way to talk about remembering: i.e., as not forgetting. Truth, *aletheia,* refers to that which is not forgotten. The root also contributes to the English word "lethargy," suggesting the link between a neurotic forgetting of painful memories associated with depression and the lassitude often accompanying this mental state. Its cure produces not necessarily happiness but vitality.

20. On intersubjectivity, see Benjamin; Mohanty.

21. I borrow this term from Mitchell (who, of course, borrows it from Freud). Mitchell writes of the primal scene of a conversation, meaning two people talking face to face. My reference is to the single speaker delivering an oration before a group.

22. I wish to thank Laura Mandell for the form of this question and for excellent advice on the whole of this chapter, especially on the subjects of mourning and melancholy.

Works Cited

Baker, Houston A., Jr., "Critical Memory and the Black Public Sphere." Black Public Sphere Collective, eds. *The Black Public Sphere. A Public Culture Book.* Chicago: University of Chicago Press, 1995. 7-37.

Bachelard, Gaston. *The Poetics of Space.* Trans. Maria Jolas. New York: Orion, 1964.

Benjamin, Jessica. *The Bonds of Love: Psychoanalysis, Feminism, and the Problem of Domination.* New York: Pantheon Books, 1988.

Bizzell, Patricia, and Bruce Herzberg, eds. *The Rhetorical Tradition: Readings from Classical Times to the Present.* 2nd ed. Boston: Bedford/St. Martin's, 2001.

Brody, Miriam. *Manly Writing: Gender, Rhetoric, and the Rise of Composition.* Carbondale: Southern Illinois University Press, 1993.

Burke, Kenneth. *A Grammar of Motives.* Berkeley: University of California Press, 1945.

Burnett, Anne Pippin. *Three Archaic Poets: Archilochus, Alcaeus, Sappho.* Cambridge: Harvard University Press, 1983.

Campbell, David A., trans. *Sappho and Alcaeus.* Loeb Classical Library. Cambridge: Harvard University Press, 1982.

Carruthers, Mary. *The Book of Memory: A Study of Memory in Medieval Culture.* Cambridge: Cambridge University Press, 1990.

Carson, Anne. *Eros the Bittersweet: An Essay.* Princeton: Princeton University Press, 1986.

De Polignac, François. *Cults, Territory, and the Origins of the Greek City-State.* Trans. Janet Lloyd. Chicago: University of Chicago Press, 1995.

duBois, Page. *Sappho is Burning.* Chicago: University of Chicago Press, 1995.

Ede, Lisa, Cheryl Glenn, and Andrea Lunsford. "Border Crossings: Intersections of Rhetoric and Feminism." *Rhetorica* 13 (Autumn 1995): 401-41.

Freud, Sigmund. *Civilization and Its Discontents.* Trans. James Strachey. New York: Norton, 1961.

Glenn, Cheryl. *Rhetoric Retold: Regendering the Tradition from Antiquity Through the Renaissance.* Carbondale: Southern Illinois University Press, 1997.

Habermas, Jürgen. *The Structural Transformation of the Public Sphere: An Inquiry into a Category of Bourgeois Society.* Trans. Thomas Burger. Cambridge: Massachussetts Institute of Technology Press, 1991.

Jameson, Fredric. *Postmodernism or, The Cultural Logic of Late Capitalism.* Durham: Duke University Press, 1991.

Jameson, Michael. "Private Space and the Greek City." Murray and Price 175-90.

Kerber, Linda K. "Separate Spheres, Female Worlds, Woman's Place: The Rhetoric of Women's History." *The Journal of American History* 75.1 (1988): 9-39.

LaCapra, Dominick. *History and Memory after Auschwitz.* Ithaca: Cornell University Press, 1998.

Liddell and Scott. *A Lexicon.* Abridged from Liddell and Scott's Greek-English Lexicon. Oxford: Clarendon Press, 1871.

McEvilley, Thomas. "Sappho, Fragment 2." *Phoenix* 26 (1972): 323-33.

Mitchell, W. J. T. *Picture Theory: Essays on Verbal and Visual Representation.* Chicago: University of Chicago Press, 1994.

Mohanty, Satya P. "Us and Them: On the Philosophical Bases of Political Criticism." *Critical Conditions: Regarding the Historical Moment.* Ed. Michael Hays. Minneapolis: University of Minnesota Press, 1992. 115-45.

Murray, Oswyn. *Early Greece.* Stanford: Stanford University Press, 1980.

Murray, Oswyn, and Simon Price, eds. *The Greek City from Homer to Alexander.* Oxford: Clarendon Press, 1990.

Nagy, Gregory. "The Crisis of Performance." *The Ends of Rhetoric: History, Theory, and Practice.* Eds. John Bender and David E. Wellbery. Stanford: Stanford University Press, 1990. 43-59.

Page, Denys. *Sappho and Alcaeus: An Introduction to the Study of Ancient Lesbian Poetry.* London: Oxford University Press, 1955.

Peter, Jay, ed. *The Greek Anthology and Other Ancient Greek Epigrams.* London: Allen Lane, 1973.

Podlecki, Anthony J. *The Early Greek Poets and Their Times.* Vancouver: University of British Columbia Press, 1984.

Powell, Jim. *Sappho. A Garland. The Poems and Fragments of Sappho.* New York: Farrar, Straus, Giroux, 1993.

Pratt, Geraldine, and Susan Hanson. "Geography and the Construction of Difference." *Gender, Place and Culture* 1.1 (1994): 5-29.

Ratcliffe, Krista. *Anglo-American Feminist Challenges to the Rhetorical Traditions: Virginia Woolf, Mary Daly, Adrienne Rich.* Carbondale: Southern Illinois University Press, 1996.

Ritchie, Joy, and Kate Ronald, eds. *Available Means: Women in the Rhetorical Tradition.* Pittsburgh: University of Pittsburgh Press, 2001.

Sappho and Alcaeus. Trans. David A. Campbell. Loeb Classical Library. Cambridge: Harvard University Press, 1982.

Schiappa, Edward. "*Rhetorikê:* What's in a Name? Toward a Revised History of Early Greek Rhetorical Theory." *Quarterly Journal of Speech* 78 (1992): 1-15.

Shauf, Michèle S. *Memory Media.* CD-ROM Dissertation. University of Delaware, 1997.

Snyder, Jane McIntosh. *The Woman and the Lyre: Women Writers in Classical Greece and Rome.* Carbondale: Southern Illinois University Press, 1989.

Stehle, Eva. *Performance and Gender in Ancient Greece: Nondramatic Poetry in Its Setting.* Princeton: Princeton University Press, 1997.

Stoppard, Tom. *Arcadia.* London: Faber and Faber, 1993.

Svenbro, Jesper. *Phrasikleia: An Anthropology of Reading in Ancient Greece.* Trans. Janet Lloyd. Ithaca: Cornell University Press, 1993.

Vernant, Jean Pierre. *Myth and Thought among the Greeks.* Trans. of *Mythe et pensée chez les Grecs* (1965). London: Routledge and Kegan Paul, 1983.

Walker, Jeffrey. *Rhetoric and Poetics in Antiquity.* New York: Oxford University Press, 2000.

Wertheimer, Molly Meijer, ed. *Listening to Their Voices: The Rhetorical Activities of Historical Women.* Columbia: University of South Carolina Press, 1997.

Winkler, John. "Gardens of Nymphs: Public and Private in Sappho's Lyrics." *Reflections of Women in Antiquity.* Ed. Helene P. Foley. New York: Gordon and Breach Science Publishers, 1981. 63-89.

Yates, Frances A. *The Art of Memory.* Chicago: University of Chicago, 1966.

FURTHER READING

Criticism

Arnold, Edwin. "Sappho." In *The Poets of Greece,* pp. 105-18. London: Cassell, Petter, and Galpin, 1869.

Praises Sappho as an artist and counters her critics by asserting that she remained "true to her womanhood."

Bergmann, Emilie L. "Fictions of Sor Juana/Fictions of Sappho." *Confluencia: Revista Hispanica de Cultura y Literatura* 9, no. 2 (spring 1994): 9-15.

Compares Sappho's poetry to the work of the seventeenth-century Mexican nun Sor Juana Ines de la Cruz, focusing on sexuality and authorial personae.

Bonnard, Andre. "Sappho of Lesbos: Tenth of the Muses." In *Greek Civilization: From the Iliad to the Parthenon,* translated by A. Lytton Sells, pp. 86-100. New York: Macmillan, 1957.

Observes Sappho's movement in poetry between the outer natural world and the inner world of feeling; argues that in doing so she anticipates modern poetry.

Bowra, C. M. "Sappho." In *Greek Lyric Poetry: From Alcman to Simonides,* pp. 186-247. Oxford: Clarendon Press, 1936.

Analyzes the social and religious themes and the imagery of Sappho's work, calling her "the most gifted woman who has ever written poetry."

Brandt, Lida Roberts. "The Status of Women." In *Social Aspects of Greek Life in the Sixth Century B.C.,* pp. 44-72. Philadelphia: T. C. Davis & Sons, 1921.

Discusses the position of women in ancient Greece in the context of sixth-century B.C. society, religion, and domestic life; points out that the liberal spirit that characterized Lesbos facilitated Sappho's artistic development.

Burnett, Anne Pippin. "Sappho." In *Three Archaic Poets: Archilochus, Alcaeus, Sappho,* pp. 207-313. Cambridge: Harvard University Press, 1983.

Examines Sappho's major poems as representatives of the lyric genre.

DeJean, Joan. "Fictions of Sappho." *Critical Inquiry* 13, no. 4 (summer 1987): 787-805.

Explores the way male literary critics throughout history have interpreted Sappho's life and her poetry.

Douka-Kabitoglou, E. "Sappho of Lesbos and Diotima of Mantinea: The Maternal Subtext of Culture." In *Women, Creators of Culture,* edited by Ekaterini Georgoudaki and Domna Pastourmatzi, pp. 217-44. Thessaloniki, Greece: Hellenic Association of American Studies, 1997.

Interprets the works of Sappho and Diotima through the feminist literary theory of Luce Irigary; focusing on themes of motherhood.

duBois, Page. *Sappho Is Burning.* Chicago: University of Chicago, 1996, 206 p.

Argues that a rereading of Sappho offers a counterpoint to received histories of poetry, philosophy, and sexuality; uses Sappho to counter the work of Foucault and to reexamine Western conceptions of Asia.

Freedman, Nancy. *Sappho: The Tenth Muse.* New York: St. Martin's Press, 1998, 336 p.

A fictional autobiography of Sappho, using Sappho's poetic fragments as a guide.

Grahn, Judy. *The Highest Apple: Sappho and the Lesbian Poetic Tradition.* San Francisco: Spinsters, Ink., 1985, 159 p.

Discusses the theme of female relationships in Sappho's work and Sappho's influence in later writing; Grahn is a leading critic in the field of gay-lesbian studies.

Greene, Ellen, ed. *Reading Sappho: Contemporary Approaches.* Berkeley: University of California Press, 1996, 303 p.

Collects essays on the themes of language and literary context, Homer and oral tradition, ritual and social context, and women's erotics; the first anthology of Sappho scholarship.

Hallett, Judith P. "Sappho and Her Social Context: Sense and Sensuality." *Signs* 4, no. 3 (spring 1979): 447-64.

Suggests that the emphasis on the homoerotics of Sappho's poetry has been overstated; proposes instead that the intent of the persona created by the poet was to point young women toward sexuality within a heterosexual marriage.

Lefkowitz, Mary R. "Critical Stereotypes and the Poetry of Sappho." *Greek, Roman, and Byzantine Studies* 14, no. 2 (summer 1973): 113-23.

Argues that Sappho's poetry has been misinterpreted throughout history by critics who have judged her by special criteria reserved for female writers.

Patrick, Mary Mills. *Sappho and the Island of Lesbos.* New York: Methuen, 1912, 180 p.

Surveys Sappho's poetry, emphasizing the philosophical in addition to the erotic; praises the poet's intelligence, learning, and delicacy.

Rexroth, Kenneth. "Sappho, *Poems.*" In *Classics Revisited,* pp. 28-32. San Francisco: New Directions, 1986.

Briefly summarizes Sappho's literary accomplishments, adding that she provides a window into the hidden world of ancient Greek women.

Robinson, David Moore. "The Real Sappho: A Critical Memoir." In *The Songs of Sappho, Including the Recent Egyptian Discoveries,* edited and translated by Marion Mills Miller and David Moore Robinson, pp. 49-85. New York: Frank-Maurice, 1925.

Compares Sappho to Socrates and Shakespeare on the basis of their expansive minds and their passion for fellow men and women.

Snyder, Jane McIntosh. "Sappho of Lesbos." In *The Woman and the Lyre: Women Writers in Classical Greece and Rome,* pp. 1-37. Carbondale: Southern Illinois University Press, 1989.

Gives an overview of Sappho's life and work; in the context of early women's writing, briefly discusses Sappho's image and artistic representations of her in later literature.

———. *Lesbian Desire in the Lyrics of Sappho.* New York: Columbia University Press, 1997, 261 p.

Interprets lesbian themes in Sappho's poetry through close readings of the fragments; a significant modern updating of the topic of lesbian desire in the works of Sappho.

Stehle, Eva. "Romantic Sensuality, Poetic Sense: A Response to Hallett on Sappho." *Signs* 4, no. 3 (spring 1979): 465-71.

Asserts that Sappho's depictions of lesbian relationships create a world where feminine experience and desire can be explored apart from the dominant male views on love and sexuality.

Stigers, Eva S. "Sappho's Private World." In *Reflections of Women in Antiquity,* edited by Helene P. Foley, pp. 45-61. New York: Gordon and Breach Science Publications, 1981.

Discusses Sappho's place in the tradition of Greek love poetry; asserts that homosexual desire in Sappho's poetry was a way of presenting a female erotic subject.

Winkler, Jack. "Gardens of Nymphs." In *Reflections of Women in Antiquity,* edited by Helene P. Foley, pp. 63-90. New York: Gordon and Breach Science Publications, 1981.

Analyzes Sappho's reaction to Homer as emblematic of male Greek culture and her sexual relations in a female world.

OTHER SOURCES FROM GALE:

Additional coverage of Sappho's life and career is contained in the following sources published by the Gale Group: *Classical and Medieval Literature Criticism,* Vols. 3, 67; *Concise Dictionary of World Literary Biography,* Vol. 1; *Dictionary of Literary Biography,* Vol. 176; *DISCovering Authors Modules: Poets; DISCovering Authors 3.0; Poetry Criticism,* Vol. 5; *Reference Guide to World Literature,* Eds. 2, 3; *World Poets.*

PHILLIS WHEATLEY

(1753 - 1784)

(Also known as Phillis Peters) American poet.

Wheatley is the first black woman known to have published a book in the United States. Her *Poems on Various Subjects, Religious and Moral* (1773) was used as an example of the power of education by proponents of egalitarian and abolitionist aims, who emphasized Wheatley's command of Western literature and classical mythology as well as the religious expression strongly evident in her poetry. Wheatley's talent came to the attention of political and cultural leaders on both sides of the Atlantic, and she once corresponded with George Washington. Although her reputation as a poet has sometimes been disparaged and her literary skills challenged, most modern assessments recognize Wheatley's accomplishments as typical of the best poetry of her age.

BIOGRAPHICAL INFORMATION

Believed to have been born in West Africa circa 1753 (possibly in present-day Senegal or Gambia), Wheatley was purchased when she was about seven years old at a slave auction in 1761 by the wife of a wealthy Boston merchant, Susannah Wheatley. Bought to be a personal maid for her mistress, she was renamed by her owner and given the family's surname. She displayed a curiosity and aptitude for learning that led the Wheatleys to educate her, primarily through Bible study. Wheatley was taught to read and write English and studied classical and contemporary poetry as well as French, Latin, and Greek literature. She began writing poetry around the age of thirteen. She was given the unusual privilege of a private room with a lamp and writing materials in order to encourage her writing, but she was forbidden to associate with other slaves. Wheatley's first published poem, an elegy commemorating the death of the well-known abolitionist minister George Whitefield, was printed locally in 1770; however, she soon gained national and international attention when this poem was reprinted in newspapers throughout the colonies and in England. As a palliative for her asthma, she traveled to England in 1773 with the Wheatleys' son and was treated as a celebrity, especially among English abolitionists. Among them was the antislavery activist Selina Hastings, Countess of Huntington, who secured publication in London of Wheatley's collection *Poems on Various Subjects*. The work was first published with the signed testimonies of John Hancock and Reverend Samuel Mather affirming its authenticity as the work of a slave girl. Wheatley was granted an audience with King George III but missed the meeting in order to return to Boston to attend Mrs. Wheatley on her deathbed.

Wheatley was freed in 1774, about four months before Mrs. Wheatley's death. Wheatley married John Peters in 1778, a free black man who worked as a lawyer and a grocer, and they had three children, all of whom died in infancy. Her attempts to publish another volume of poetry were unsuccessful; she could not find enough subscribers to make publication financially possible, despite the praise of men including Voltaire, George Washington, and John Paul Jones. The family eventually fell into financial difficulties, and Peters was jailed in a debtor's prison. Wheatley spent her last years in poverty, working as a maid in boardinghouses until her death on December 5, 1784.

MAJOR WORKS

Wheatley was primarily an occasional poet, writing elegies and honorific works to commemorate the lives of friends and famous contemporaries and poems to celebrate important events, such as Washington's appointment as commander-in-chief of the revolutionary forces ("To His Excellency George Washington"). Her poems follow the then-widely imitated diction, meter, and rhyme patterns established by Alexander Pope and his school of neoclassical poetry, but Wheatley's technical skill sets her work apart from that of many of her contemporaries. *Poems on Various Subjects* contains thirty-nine poems which form the majority of her extant work and range in subject matter from very personal and philosophical musings, such as "An Hymn to Morning" and "An Hymn to Evening," to more conventional neoclassical subjects, as in "On Recollection." Many of the poems combine Christian imagery or scriptural interpretation with classical influences, particularly Homeric allusions. Her poems reflect an attention to the major political events of her day as well as more mundane occurrences among her acquaintances. Of the extant poems not contained in *Poems on Various Subjects,* many are variants of earlier poems, but these also include the poems in praise of George Washington and General Lee.

CRITICAL RECEPTION

Early reviews of the *Poems on Various Subjects* focus on the novelty of an educated, literate female slave more than the work itself, which was dismissed as merely average or simply imitative, though a few of Wheatley's defenders maintained that her poetry could hold its own with that of contemporary white poets. Twentieth-century African American critics scrutinized Wheatley's verse for evidence of racial pride or defiance of bondage, and some faulted her for what they perceived as a lack of either sentiment. More recent critics of the late twentieth century have argued that in using neoclassical and traditionally white modes of discourse, Wheatley subverted the language of her oppressors and used it for her own purposes. Some critics have contended that Wheatley's subjects must be judged within the context of the poetic models and social influences in her restricted surroundings, noting the irony of her position as a pampered favorite of Boston's privileged class and of her enforced isolation from other slaves. Despite much supposition concerning her poetic gifts and potential under different circumstances, Wheatley's poetry is considered a point of departure for the study of African American literature. Many commentators assess her poetry superior to that typical of her era, and cite instances of individuality that acquit her of the common charge of being a mere imitator. James Weldon Johnson has explained that when Wheatley's work is judged by the standards of her time, rather than those of a "later day," Wheatley "stands out as one of the important characters in the making of American literature, without any allowances for her sex or her antecedents."

PRINCIPAL WORKS

An Elegiac Poem, on the Death of that Celebrated Divine, and Eminent Servant of Jesus Christ, the Reverend and Learned George Whitefield (poetry) 1770

Poems on Various Subjects, Religious and Moral. By Phillis Wheatley, Negro Servant to Mr. John Wheatley of Boston (poetry) 1773

An Elegy, Sacred to the Memory of that Great Divine, The Reverend and Learned Dr. Samuel Cooper (poetry) 1784

Liberty and Peace, A Poem (poetry) 1784

Memoirs and Poems of Phillis Wheatley, a Native African and a Slave (memoir and poetry) 1838

Letters of Phillis Wheatley, the Negro-Slave Poet of Boston (letters) 1864

Phillis Wheatley (Phillis Peters), Poems and Letters (poetry and letters) 1915

Life and Works of Phillis Wheatley. Containing Her Complete Poetical Works, Numerous Letters and a Complete Biography of This Famous Poet of a Century and a Half Ago (poetry and letters) 1916

The Poems of Phillis Wheatley (poetry) 1966

The Collected Works of Phillis Wheatley (poetry, letters) 1988

PRIMARY SOURCES

PHILLIS WHEATLEY (LETTER DATE 1773)

SOURCE: Wheatley, Phillis. "Letter to John Thornton." In *Phillis Wheatley and Her Writings,* edited by William H. Robinson, pp. 327-28. New York: Garland Publishing, 1984.

In the following letter written in 1773, Wheatley informs John Thornton, a merchant she met with in London, that she has returned safely to her mistress in America.

Hon'd sir

It is with great satisfaction, I acquaint you with my experience of the / goodness of God in safely conducting my passage over the mighty waters, and returning / me in safety to my American Friends. I presume you will join with them and me / in praise to God for so distinguishing a favour, it was amazing Mercy, altogether / unmerited by me: and if possible it is augmented by the consideration of the bitter re- / verse, which is the deserved wages of my evil doings. The Apostle Paul, tells us / that the wages of sin is death. I don't imagine he excepted any sin whatsoever, / being equally hateful in its nature in the sight of God, who is essential Purity.

Should we not sink hon'd sir, under this sentence of Death, pronounced / on every sin, from the comparatively least to the greatest, were not this blessed Con- / trast annexed to it, "But the Gift of God is eternal Life, through Jesus Christ / our Lord?["] It is his Gift. O let us be thankful for it! What a load is taken from / the sinner's shoulder, when he thinks, that Jesus has done that work for him / which he could never have done, and suffer'd, that punishment of his imputed / Rebellions, for which a long Eternity of Torments could not have made suffici- / ent expiation. O that I could meditate continually on this work of wonder / ous Deity itself. This, which Kings & Prophets have desir'd to see, & have not seen[.] / This, which Angels are continually exploring, yet are not equal to the search,— / Millions of Ages shall roll away, and they may try in vain to find out to / perfection, the sublime mysteries of Christ's Incarnation. Nor will this desire / to look into the deep things of God, cease, in the Breasts of glorified saints & Ang- / els. It's duration will be coeval with Eternity. This Eternity how dreadful, / how delightful! Delightful to those who have an interest in the Crucified / Saviour, who has dignified our Nature, by seating it at the Right Hand of / the divine Majesty. They alone who are thus interested, have cause to rejoice / even on the brink of that Bottomless Profound: and I doubt not (without the / least Adulation) that you are one of that happy number. O pray that I may / be one also, who shall join with you in songs of praise at the Throne of him, who / is no respecter of Persons, being equally the great Maker of all:— Therefore disdain / not to be called the Father of Humble Africans and Indians; though despis'd / on earth on account of our colour, we have this Consolation, if he enables us to / deserve it. "That God dwells in the humble & contrite heart." O that I were / more & more possess'd of this inestimable blessing; to be directed by the imme / diate influence of the divine spirit in my daily walk & Conversation.

Do you, my hon'd sir, who have abundant Reason to be thankful for / the great share you possess of it, be always mindful in your Closet, of those / who want it, of me in particular.

When I first arriv'd at home my mistress was so bad as not to be expec- / ted to live above two or three days, but through the goodness of God, she is / still alive but remains in a very weak & languishing Condition. She begs / a continued interest in your most earnest prayers, that she may be daily / prepar'd for that great Change which she is likely soon to undergo; She in- / treats you, as her son is still in England, that you would take all opportuni - / ties to advise & counsel him. [She says she is going to leave him & desires you'd be a spiritual Father to him.] She will take it very kind. *She thanks you / heartily for the kind notice you took of me while in England.* please / to give my best Respects to M^rs^ & miss Thornton, and masters Henry / and Robert who held with me a long conversation on many subjects / which Mrs Drinkwater knows very well. I hope she is in better Health / than when I left her. Please to remember me to your whole family & I thank / them for their kindness to me, begging still an interest in your best hours / I am Hon'd sir / most respectfully your Humble serv[t]

Phillis Wheatley

PHILLIS WHEATLEY (LETTER DATE 1774)

SOURCE: Wheatley, Phillis. "Letter to Samson Occom." In *Phillis Wheatley and Her Writings,* edited by William H. Robinson, p. 332. New York: Garland Publishing, 1984.

In the following letter written in 1774, Wheatley directly addresses the injustice of slavery in a way that she does not in her poetry. This letter was written shortly after the death of her mistress, when she had been freed for four months. Her recipient, Samson Occom, was a Native American preacher who, like Wheatley, was introduced in England as a Christian prodigy.

Reverend and honoured Sir,

I have this Day received your obliging kind Epistle, and am greatly satisfied with your Reasons respecting the negroes, and think highly reasonable what you offer in Vindication of their natural Rights: Those that invade them cannot be insensible that the divine Light is insensibly chasing away the thick Darkness which broods over the Land of Africa; and the Chaos which has reigned so long is converting into beautiful Order, and reveals more and more clearly the glorious Dispensation of civil and religious Liberty, which are so inseparably united, that there is little or no Enjoyment of one without the other: Otherwise, perhaps the Israelites had been less solicitous for their Freedom from Egyptian slavery; I do not say they would have been contented without it, by no means, for in every human Breast, God has implanted a Principle, which we call Love of Freedom; it is impatient of oppression, and pants for Deliverance—and by the Leave of our modern Egyptians I will assert that the same principle lives in us. God grant Deliverance in his own Way and Time, and get him honour upon all those whose Avaraice impels them to countenance and help forward the Calamities of their fellow Creatures. This I desire not for their Hurt, but to convince them of the strange Absurdity of their Conduct whose Words and Actions are so diametrically opposite. How well the Cry for Liberty, and the reverse Disposition for the exercise of oppressive power over others agree I humbly think it does not require the penetration of a Philosopher to determine.

GENERAL COMMENTARY

M. A. RICHMOND (ESSAY DATE 1974)

SOURCE: Richmond, M. A. "The Critics." In *Bid the Vassal Soar: Interpretive Essays on the Life and Poetry of Phillis Wheatley (ca. 1753-1784) and George Moses Horton (ca. 1797-1883),* pp. 53-66. Washington, D.C.: Howard University Press, 1974.

In the following essay, Richmond surveys the critical response to Wheatley's work, including questions about her authenticity as a black author.

Most illustrious of Phillis Wheatley's contemporary critics was Thomas Jefferson, part revolutionary and part Virginia patrician, offering his judgment of the poet in his latter guise.

"Religion indeed has produced a Phyllis Whately [*sic*]; but it could not produce a poet," Jefferson wrote in his *Notes on the State of Virginia* (1781-82). "The compositions published under her name are below the dignity of criticism." (Note the gratuitous skepticism even about the authenticity of her authorship in the phrase "published under her name.")

One reply to Jefferson came from Samuel Stanhope Smith, president of the College of New Jersey and a member of the American Philosophical Society. In "An Essay on the Causes of the Variety of Complexion and Figure in the Human Species" (1810), Dr. Smith wrote: "The poems of Phillis Whately, a poor African slave, taught to read by the indulgent piety of her master are spoken of with infinite contempt. But I will demand of Mr. Jefferson, or of any other man who is acquainted with American planters, how many of those masters could have written poems equal to those of Phillis Whately?"

In one sense, Dr. Smith's challenge begs the question. To say that Phillis Wheatley wrote better verse than American planters is not yet to say she was a poet. It is on the anthropological or sociological plane, rather than the literary, that Dr. Smith scores a point in contesting Jefferson's belief in the inherent inferiority of blacks.

A similar thrust came from a distinguished French contemporary, Henri Grégoire, prominent abbé in the French Revolutionary era and later a bishop. Among Grégoire's labors was a pioneer treatise, *De la Littérature des Nègres* (1808), in which he reproaches the American President. "Jefferson," he wrote, "appears unwilling to acknowledge the talents of Negroes, even those of Phillis Wheatley. . . ." To refute this prejudice, Grégoire cites the public response to the Wheatley volume of

1773 and offers selections from that volume. Among the first French responses to the volume of 1773 was one from Voltaire, who on occasion expressed no high regard for blacks. But in 1774 he wrote to Baron Constant de Rebecq: "Fontenelle was wrong in saying that there were never any poets among the Negroes; there is in fact one Negress who writes very good English verse."

As in the United States and France, so in the Germanic states there was a dissent from Jefferson's judgment among his scholarly contemporaries. Johann Friedrich Blumenbach often referred to as the father of anthropology and an original investigator of ethnic categories, described the Wheatley volume as "a collection which scarcely anyone who has any taste for poetry could read without pleasure" (*Anthropological Treatises,* 1865).

In Britain, where her volume was comprehensively reviewed in major periodicals upon its publication in 1773 and where she was, at the time, the best known Colonial poet, the tide of opinion was stronger and more widespread. Not that there was an excessive praise for the poems (they "display no astonishing powers of genius," said one review, and another found them "merely imitative"), but sufficient merit was discerned in them to arouse concern "that this ingenious young woman is yet a slave."

Later, in 1788, Thomas Clarkson, a tireless antislavery agitator and leader in the successful campaign to halt British participation in the slave trade, protested, "if the authoress *was designed for slavery* . . . the greater part of the inhabitants of Britain must lose their claim to freedom."

This again is Abolitionist argument rather than literary criticism, but only a mindless literary purist would exclude it from an ultimate assessment of Phillis Wheatley. It was no small achievement for the African child to have become a modest standard in the conflict that dominated the first nine decades of this country's history and in a different form continues to this day. She did not aspire to become an Abolitionist symbol, but the role was thrust upon her just the same because she absorbed the New England culture so swiftly and so well as to be the peer of any white contemporary in its poetic expression.

The poetic world of Phillis Wheatley was circumscribed by rigid boundaries: by the decasyllabic line in the heroic couplet, by the ornate diction of neoclassicism and the ritualistic obeisances it prescribed. Within these boundaries of meter and language other narrowing constrictions defined the thoughts and emotions that inhabited her poetic world.

FROM THE AUTHOR

WHEATLEY'S POEM "ON BEING BROUGHT FROM AFRICA TO AMERICA"

'Twas mercy brought me from my *Pagan* land,
Taught my benighted soul to understand
That there's a God, that there's a *Saviour* too:
Once I redemption neither sought nor knew.
Some view our sable race with scornful eye,
"Their colour is a diabolic die."
Remember, *Christians, Negros,* black as *Cain,*
May be refin'd, and join th' angelic train.

Wheatley, Phillis. "On being brought from Africa to America." In *Poems on Various Subjects, Religious and Moral,* p. 18. London: A. Bell, 1773.

Conforming to neoclassical ritual, she constantly addressed the Muses, singly or collectively, in such terms as these: Celestial Muse, heavenly Muse, Muse divine, sacred Nine, indulgent Muse, gentle Muse, tuneful Nine, tuneful goddess, sacred choir, blooming graces.

Among representative invocations to the Muses were these: inspire my song; aid my high design . . . assist my strains . . . my arduous flight sustain—raise my mind to a seraphic strain . . . assist my labors—my strains refine . . . inspire—fill my bosom with celestial fire . . . lend thine aid, nor let me sue in vain.

In the effulgent imagery of neoclassicism the sky became ethereal space, ethereal train, starry train, heavenly plains, Phoebe's realms, orient realms, azure plain, empyreal skies. The earth appeared as this vast machine, rolling globe, dusty plain, dark, terrestrial ball.

The verse is peopled with figures from the Greek and Roman classics, literary and mythological; Homer and Virgil and Terence are here, as are gods and goddesses in profusion, and such place names as Helicon, Olympus, and Parnassus. Niobe appears much more often than any other figure from the Greco-Roman classics. Indeed, the tragedy of Niobe, as taken from Ovid's *Metamorphoses,* inspired her longest poem, running to 224 lines. Only one other is so ambitious, containing 2 lines less, and it, too, is derivative, transmuting into heroic couplets the biblical narrative of David and Goliath. These choices, Ovid and Samuel, attest to the primacy of the classics and the Bible in forming her poetical mind. The coincident and related influence of Puritanism probably accounts for a suggestive omission in her recital of David's conquest. She discreetly ignores the two biblical references to Goliath as an "uncircumcised Philistine."

Something of her style may be gleaned by juxtaposing a biblical passage and her rendition of it.

> And David spake to the men that stood by him, saying, What shall be done to the man that killeth this Philistine, and taketh away the reproach from Israel? for who *is* this uncircumcised Philistine that he should defy the armies of the living God?
>
> —I Samuel, 17:26

> Then Jesse's youngest hope:—"My brethern, say,
> "What shall be done for him who takes away
> "Reproach from Jacob, who destroys the chief,
> "And puts a period to his country's grief?
> "He vaunts the honours of his arms abroad,
> "And scorns the armies of the living God."
>
> —Phillis Wheatley

The biblical prose gains nothing in felicity or clarity by this rearrangement into neat columns, each line dressed, as it were, to the rhyming word on the right, and each marching to the beat of ten syllables. Only on rare occasions, as in the poems to her mistress, did she depart from this rigid form. In discussing Pope, the master of the form, George Saintsbury remarked that "artificiality . . . is the curse of the couplet," but in the same sentence he reiterated an admission that the curse "can be vanquished." Such conquest of artificiality depends not only upon prosodic skills in fashioning the mold, but even more upon the poetic sensibility that is poured into it. The more limited the sensibility, the more protrudent the artificiality. Phillis Wheatley's sensibility was indeed limited (although, as has often been repeated, hers was at least as fine as that of any Colonial poet). She was totally incapable, for example, of the playful sophistication in Pope's celebrated couplet:

> Nature and Nature's Laws, lay hid in Night:
> GOD said, *Let Newton be!* and all was Light.

More is contained here, however, than playful sophistication; there is not only an awareness of Newton but also a conception of his junior partnership with God. In some critical analysis, the decasyllabic couplet, which attained its apogee with Pope, is perceived as an appropriate reflection of a harmonious confluence between science and religion in the early eighteenth century. Newton's discovery of natural laws, the argument goes, was greeted by contemporaries as illumination of God's inflnite wisdom in designing the universe; thus, scientific discernment of order in the apparent chaos of nature reinforced the faith in divine order. In turn, the mathematical precision of Pope's couplets was attuned to the discipline of science and the vision of a larger divine order to which it bore witness.[1]

Whatever the merit of such interpretive speculation in relationship to Pope, its applicability to Phillis Wheatley is somewhat vitiated because she was imitative. Certainly her own work does not reflect a comparable familiarity with the science of the age. Yet imitation also involves an element of choice. That she chose Pope as her model is readily explicable by his fashionable pre-eminence at the time and the Colonial cultural dependence on England, but the New England ambience must also enter into the explanation. There was a manifest affinity between the Puritan culture, with its admixture of practicality and faith, and the conception of a universal order, created by God and corroborated by science.

Wheatley's vision of the universe was etched most explicitly in **"Thoughts on the Works of Providence"**:

> ARISE, my soul; on wings enraptured, rise,
> To praise the Monarch of the earth and skies,
> Whose goodness and beneficence appear,
> As round its centre moves the rolling year . . .
>
> Adored forever be the God unseen,
> Which round the sun revolves this vast
> machine . . .
>
> Almighty, in these wondrous works of
> thine,
> What Power, what Wisdom, and what
> Goodness shine!
> And are thy wonders, Lord, by men explored,
> And yet creating glory unadored?

In Wheatley's verse there is, indeed, a harmony between the symmetrical pattern and the apprehension of a well-ordered universe. There is a third part in this harmony: the human condition. In her view, despite the oh-so-slight reproach in the final lines cited above, there is no serious discord between man and the divinely enacted laws of nature. Nor is there much concern with the contradictions in man. She definitely does not imitate Pope's notorious flights into misogyny, and for her man was not, as he was for Pope, "The glory, jest, and riddle of the world . . . Born but to die, and reas'ning but to err . . . Created half to rise, and half to fall." With her benign disposition she does not divide man into such equal parts; her emphasis is on human redemption, not on wickedness and folly.

Even in her rare venture into polemic, the adolescent **"Address to the Atheist,"** sin and its wages are couched in the gentlest terms:

> Muse! where shall I begin the spacious field
> To tell what curses unbelief doth yield?
>
> If there's no heav'n, ah! whither wilt thou go
> Make thy Ilysium in the shades below?

There are scattered references in her work to divine wrath, and in her rendition of verses from Isaiah these lines appear:

> Great God, what lightning flashes from
> thine eyes!
> What power withstands if thou indignant rise?

But those are rare exceptions. She heralded God's wisdom and benevolence, not his vengeance. She was more prone to commend the human capacity for virtue than to scorn human susceptibility to vice. In the most personal testament to this credo, **"On Being Brought from Africa to America,"** she wrote:

> 'TWAS mercy brought me from my pagan
> land,
> Taught my benighted soul to understand
> That there's a God—that there's a Saviour too:
> Once I redemption neither sought nor knew.
> Some view our sable race with scornful eye—
> 'Their color is a diabolic dye.'
> Remember, Christians, Negroes black as Cain
> May be refined, and join the angelic train.

In this striking illustration of the suffusive religiosity in her work, slavery is incidental to salvation, and there is only the mild admonition to Christians that blackness is no bar to the angelic train. In a sense, this is her own adaptation of Pope's ultimate truth: "Whatever is, is right." Given her time and place and her conditioning, there is not much good in reproaching her for an insufficiency of mind and spirit to transcend Pope's dictum.

Nor is there much point in belaboring the contradiction between the depiction of a well-ordered universe in well-ordered verse and the overturn of the established order by revolutionary upheaval. True, the American Revolution was much less convulsive than the French one that followed, but even for the American an approximation of the carmagnole would have been more appropriate than the minuet. That the cadence of her verse more closely resembled the latter, even when she attempted to respond to the times, as in the ode to Washington, is also an explicable fault. Art, and most especially the forms in which it is rendered, often lags behind history, and there is no reason why Wheatley should have been less laggard than others.

So her poetry did not rise to the greatness that truly expresses the spirit of an age, but such poetry is rare, and there was none of it in Colonial times.

Summarizing the initial debate about her more than a century later (1915), Arthur Schomburg, who was devoted to the appreciation and preservation of black culture, offered his own judgment. "There was no great American poetry in the 18th century," Schomburg wrote, "and Phillis Wheatley's poetry was as good as the best American poetry of her age."

There is a depressing element in the literary argument to the degree that it hinges on whether she was a nonpoet or a mediocre one. To be sure, it is relevant to determine what was par for the course in a given time and place, but if this establishes her as the peer of her contemporaries, it also defines a less flattering place in the longer span of literary history. In purely literary terms, viewing her as a poet in the abstract, criticism cannot break out of such narrow confines. But she was a *black* poet, and it is not enough to say that the quality of her verse was as good as that of her best white contemporaries. She also has to be assessed in terms of her own identity.

Not until recently has black scholarship attempted to assess her in explicitly black terms. The more traditional view among black scholars was presented by James Weldon Johnson, who wrote:

> Phillis Wheatley has never been given her rightful place in American literature. By some sort of conspiracy she is kept out of most of the books, especially the text-books on literature used in schools. Of course, she is not a *great* American poet—and in her day there were no great American poets—but she is an important American poet. Her importance, if for no other reason, rests on the fact that, save one, she is the first in order of time of all the women poets of America. And she is among the first of all American poets to issue a volume.

Johnson concluded:

> . . . her work must not be judged by the work and standards of a later day, but by the work and standards of her own day and her own contemporaries. By this method of criticism she stands out as one of the important characters in the making

> of American literature, without any allowances for her sex or her antecedents.

This does not differ in substance from what has been said in sympathetic white criticism. It is not a matter of making allowances for her antecedents (that is, for her blackness and her slavery), but of taking them properly into account. This is attempted explicitly by the black critic J. Saunders Redding and in a curiously inverse way by the black novelist Richard Wright.

In his lecture on "The Literature of the Negro in the United States," Wright read passages from the works of Alexander Pushkin and Alexandre Dumas and made the obvious point that nothing in those passages suggested they were written by Negroes. "The writings I've just read to you," he went on, "were the work of men who were emotionally integrated with their country's culture; no matter what the color of their skins, they were not really Negroes. One was a Russian, the other a Frenchman."

Then he posed the question: has any American Negro ever written like the Russian poet and the French novelist? And he replied that one, only one, had done so—Phillis Wheatley. "Before the webs of slavery had so tightened as to snare nearly all Negroes in our land," he elaborated, "one was freed by accident to give in clear, bell-like, limpid cadence the hope of freedom in the New World."

Wright sketched an idyllic picture of her condition—she "was accepted into the Wheatley home as one of the family, enjoying all the rights of the other Wheatley children. . . . she got the kind of education that the white girls of her time received." As a consequence of her integration, he argued, she was able to articulate a "universal note" that was in total harmony with the Colonial culture. Only later on, he said, did a distinct "Negro literature" take form as "a reservoir of bitterness and despair and infrequent hope . . . a welter of crude patterns of surging hate and rebellion." This literature was the product of slavery, of its oppressions, lacerations, and humiliations, but since Wheatley did not experience these, and indeed antedated them, she "was at one with her colonial New England culture," just as Pushkin and Dumas were with theirs.

But was she? Is the comparison with Pushkin and Dumas valid? She was born an African; the two men were born Russian and French. She entered her incarnation as Phillis Wheatley a naked child, a slave, forcibly abducted and cruelly transported. They were born into social status and moderate means. Pushkin, the son of landed gentry and a reluctant attendant at the czar's court, was three generations removed from the black slave who was his maternal grandfather. Dumas, the son of a French general, traced his lineage to a black grandmother and a wealthy French colonist in Haiti. Such genealogical traces of blackness in the Russian and the Frenchman had no real bearing on their lives or social status, although Pushkin expressed his awareness of it with a narrative about his great-grandfather. For Wheatley blackness was an ever-present reality that made its heavy imprint on her life.

Wright could say about Pushkin that "he went to the schools of his choice; he served in an army that was not Jim Crow; he worked where he wanted to; he lived where he wanted to. . . ." One may quibble that this last is not altogether true; Pushkin certainly did not live or work where he wanted to during his forced exile because he had displeased the czar but it is sufficiently true to underscore the contrast with Wheatley. (For that matter, Pushkin was punished, not for his great-grandfather's blackness, but for political and literary unorthodoxies that, in a sense, reinforced his oneness with the emergent Russian literature of the early nineteenth century.) Wheatley did not serve in any army, but she did serve a church where she was consigned, according to all the circumstantial evidence, to a "Nigger Pew" or "Nigger Heaven." She did not live or work where she wanted to, not even when she was free. The black lodging house was not her choice, and its designation as black indicates it was not simply a matter of means. Black ghettoes—situated near the docks or riverfronts or in alleys—had already sprouted in the New England of Wheatley's time.

A distinction may be drawn between Wright's general thesis and its specific application to Wheatley. The works of Dumas and Pushkin are impressive evidence to support his general argument that Negro literature is not rooted in some anthropological or biological mystique but is a socially and historically conditioned response to slavery and its legacies. This thesis is stated succinctly in a reference to George Moses Horton's poetry: it "does not stem from racial feeling, but from a social situation." Applying this analysis to Wheatley, the issue is, did Wright accurately comprehend the social situation that enveloped her, and the degree to which her poetic reflection of that situation was artificial or authentic?

Wright's sketch of Wheatley's condition is much too idyllic, and in spots careless. (For example, referring to her trip to England, he adds, "This was, of course, after the Revolutionary

War.") To be sure, she was favored by kind and considerate masters, but the question still remains whether benign slavery, with its subtle discriminations, is the same as the freedom that Dumas and Pushkin enjoyed. It isn't, and the distinction makes dubious the identity that Wright discerned. It may be said that in Pushkin and Dumas, the oneness with the respective national culture was a natural extension of their social being. They wrote as a Russian or a Frenchman because this is, in fact, what they were. With respect to Wheatley, there is a nagging sense of contradiction between her cultural assimilation and her social situation, which was, despite its unique, individual features, also related to the general black condition.

It is to this contradiction that critic Redding addresses himself, arriving at a judgment that is the opposite of Wright's. What Wright hails as Wheatley's triumph, Redding deplores as her failure.

"There is no question but that Miss Wheatley considered herself a Negro poet: the question is to what degree she felt the full significance of such a designation," Redding wrote. "Certainly she was not a *slave poet* in any sense in which the term can be applied to many who followed her. She stands far outside the institution that was responsible for her. . . . Not once . . . did she express in either word or action a thought on the enslavement of her race; not once did she utter a straightforward word for the freedom of the Negro."

Redding quotes the lines from the poem to the Earl of Dartmouth:

> I, young in life, by seeming cruel fate
> Was snatched from Afric's fancied happy seat.

and comments:

> "Seeming cruel" and "fancied happy" give her away as not believing either in the cruelty of the fate that had dragged thousands of her race into bondage in America nor in the happiness of their former freedom in Africa. How different the spirit of her work, and how unracial (not to say unnatural) are the stimuli that release her wan creative energies. How different are these from the work of George Horton who twenty-five years [*sic*] later could cry out with bitterness, without cavil or fear:
>
> "Alas! and am I born for this,
> To wear this slavish chain?"
>
> It is this negative, bloodless, unracial quality in Phillis Wheatley that makes her seem superficial, especially to members of her own race. . . . She is chilly. . . . First and last, she was the fragile product of three related forces—the age, the Wheatley household, and New England America. Her work lacks spontaneity because of the first, enthusiasm because of the second, and because of the third it lacks an unselfish purpose that drives to some ultimate goal of expression.

Harsh as it is, Redding's judgment points to obvious truths, which are insufficient for their very obviousness. It is easy enough to characterize the quality of personality mirrored in the poetry—negative, bloodless, unracial, chilly. The difficult question is what made her so. Redding replies that "she was the fragile product of . . . the age, the Wheatley household, and New England America." This is not enough, for if you change the name of the household, you can say the same about any *white* product of middle-class or upper-middle-class New England. But Phillis Wheatley was *black* and this is the difference and also the contradiction: the contradiction between her blackness, which she recognized and never was permitted to forget by a thousand humiliations, and white, mercantile New England, whose world was never truly hers but whose values she seemed to accept. The same contradiction is suggested in Redding's remark that "she stands far outside the institution [of slavery] that was responsible for her. . . ." It would be more apt to say she was in the slave world but not truly of it. This is the contradictory reality that shaped the subjective raw material which was processed by the three forces Redding lists—the age, the Wheatley household, New England America. The vital element missing from his critical assessment is just what was fed into the triple-gear machine he specifies.

For this we must revert once more to the frail, near-naked girl of seven displayed for sale on a Boston dock. At that age the native African culture and values are not firmly imbedded, certainly not with the depth and strength needed to withstand the powerful assimilative impact of the new culture into which she is thrust. She has no defenses against Puritan certitude and self-righteousness, no resources for *critical* assimilation. To begin with she does not have a chance, and then two specific factors reinforce the process that is better described as inundation than assimilation.

One is her precocity, and the Wheatley's appreciation and cultivation of it. She is encouraged with patronizing kindness. Privileges and material rewards are compensation for piety and for poetry that respects the prevailing conventions in theme and style. It does no good to reproach an adolescent child for yielding to these attractive influences, especially when within herself there is no strong residue of any other influence or tradition. These are her formative years, and the subsequent years are so disordered and, as it turns out, so brief that they do not modify the initial mold.

This first factor is complemented by the second, her isolation from the society of slaves and its subculture. In this respect, Redding astutely notes the difference between her and George Moses Horton, who came a generation later. Unlike Wheatley, Horton was born a slave on a Southern plantation and there never was any ambiguity about his status or identity. Knowing clearly what he was, it was easier for him to determine what he ought to be.

From suckling infancy he absorbed the slave world subculture and its two interwoven strains: the African origins and the realities of slavery, of the master-slave relationship. Most of the original African slaves were, of course, older than Phillis Wheatley was at the time of her abduction, old enough to retain much of African culture and customs, and this retention, although diffused by time and diluted by the flow of strong stimuli from the immediate environment, remained a pervasive influence, handed down through the generations that shaped the Afro-American community. The more proximate influence was the master-slave relationship with its constant tensions, often bursting into open conflict, along with the contradictory accommodations of expediency. To survive as a human being in the context of slavery is no simple art, one not mastered without some training and without the folk wisdom born of community experience. Horton had such sustenance; Wheatley did not.

Further, as the first significant black writer in North America she faced a problem that her successors were to face. She wrote for a white audience, this being the audience created by the economics of publication and the realities of a market shaped by the affluence to buy and the literacy to consume. For the most part, her successors—even to this day—write for a white audience, but with the consciousness that on the sidelines and behind them black contemporaries are readers and critics. Removed as she was from black society, and possibly also because black reader-critics were so few then, no such critical restraints seemed to affect her.

"There is no question," Redding says, "but that Miss Wheatley considered herself a Negro poet: the question is to what degree she felt the full significance of such a designation." The answer is that all circumstances conspired to diminish, in her own perception, the significance of what she was. Therefore, she was diminished as a poet—and as a human being. For one reading her verse almost two centuries later, the almost reflex reaction is to scorn it and its creator. This response is misconceived and misaddressed. Anger would be more appropriate, and it ought to be addressed against the institution of slavery.

Perhaps the first significance of Phillis Wheatley is as a laboratory, test-tube exemplar of what was done to black identity, to black pride and self-awareness, by the institution of slavery with all its accessories of custom, culture, and ideological rationales. She was, after all, a first-generation African brought to these shores, and because she was articulate and had the opportunity to cultivate this gift, she left a singular record of this initial encounter between slave and master, between black and white, and its consequence in a setting of unusual circumstances.

She experienced this encounter under supposedly ideal conditions—a kind and understanding mistress, physical comforts, an opportunity to develop her talents—and this gives the experience its test-tube quality. It is not the typical experience of the mass of first-generation slaves, destined for hard, menial labor, for physical deprivation and a more oppressive regime. Such lacerations she was spared as long as she remained in her privileged sanctuary, placing in bolder relief the more refined inflictions she was not spared. What emerges most starkly from her poetry and her private correspondence is the near surgical, lobotomy-like excision of a human personality with warmth and blood and the self-assertiveness that is grounded in an awareness of one's self and relationship of this self to contemporary society. The religious moralisms that lard her letters to Obour Tanner are a poor form of sublimation, a substitute for the expression of emotional response to personal experience. The poems are vicarious in theme and imitative in style. In the circumstances it hardly could have been different. She was permitted to cultivate her intelligence, to develop her feeling for language and her facility in its use, but one thing she was not permitted to develop: the sense of her own distinct identity as a black poet. And without this there could be no personal distinction in style or the choice of themes that make for greater poetry. The barter of her soul, as it were, was no conscious contract. Enclosed by a cloying embrace of slavery at a tender age, alternatives did not at first intrude, and later, when she might have chosen one, she was drained of the will and perception to do so.

Involved here is not a condemnation of Puritanism as such, or of its general influence upon

American thought and behavior. Such a judgment, sorting and weighing all the sins and virtues, belongs elsewhere. The concern here is more particular: it is the imposition of Puritanism upon a young African whose color and bondage placed her outside of those premises and compensations to which Puritanism appealed for its validity. Property and its acquisition, the temporal rewards of thrift and abstinence, were not for slaves (and this was true despite the rare and paradoxical exceptions in New England's relatively lenient slave regime). Even the restricted personal range of moral and social choice open to white Puritans was foreclosed to blacks. The full measure of self-reliance was a paradox in the essential dependency of slavery. What blacks were offered was the theology, disembodied from its temporal matrix. It is this that makes Phillis Wheatley's piety seem so empty and repellent, so classical an instance of glorifying celestial promise to tolerate terrestrial misery. For her Puritanism entailed a substitution of simulation for reality as in the most ironic of master-servant cliches, "We treated her like a member of the family. . . ." In sum, whatever Puritanism might have done for its white believers, it was grotesque imposition, amputating and mutilating, upon the black poet.

It may be idle to speculate about her true potential, but surely, given the evidence of her intelligence and talent, it is a permissible assumption that it was far greater than the one realized with the oppressive restrictions imposed upon the flowering of her own personality as a black poet. One school of American literary criticism dwells on the aptitude of American society to frustrate its writers and truncate their growth. If this is a great American tradition, then few, if any, writers were so warped by it as was Phillis Wheatley.

In her case, the primary warping influence was slavery. It mutilated her. Having inflicted spiritual mutilation, its aftermath went on to achieve her physical destruction. Sketchy as it is, the preserved record of her final years—the cold neglect, the poverty, the drudgery, the infant deaths, and finally the circumstances of her own death at age thirty-one—is a searing indictment of slavery, of the cruel nexus of the white-black relationship in the evolution of American society.

Phillis Wheatley is not a great figure in American literary history, but she is a tragic one. It is the tragedy rather than the poetry of Phillis Wheatley that has the more enduring relevance for American life. Elements of the tragedy have far more contemporary urgency than is evoked by the echoes of her poetry. To those in the present black generations, who are involved in the assertion and definition of black identity, in the rekindling of black pride, she can represent, with rare purity, the initial deprivation of that which they seek to regain.

To the contemporary black militant, the poetry will indeed seem "superficial" and "chilly," assuming he reads it at all, and there is little reason to believe he will. The tragedy should be more germane. If this is so, then it is conceivable that in striking some militant blow for freedom, in a spirit of retribution and poetic justice, he might say, "This one is for you, baby."

Note

1. Of the many lines by Pope that celebrate the synthesis of nature and God the following may be cited:

   All are but parts of one stupendous whole,
   Whose body Nature is, and God the soul;

   All Nature is but Art, unknown to thee;
   All Chance, Direction which thou canst not see;
   All Discord, Harmony not understood;
   All partial Evil, universal Good.

   All of this is encompassed in a climactic line:
   One truth is clear, WHATEVER IS, IS RIGHT.

The Critics

James Weldon Johnson quotes Jefferson as saying "her poems are beneath contempt" (*American Negro Poetry,* [New York: Harcourt Brace & Co., 1922] p. xxiii). Though not so gentlemanly in expression, Johnson's phrase is no doubt much closer to what Jefferson actually felt than what he wrote.

The remarks of Jefferson, Samuel Stanhope Smith, Henri Grégoire, Johann Friedrich Blumenbach, and Thomas Clarkson are referred to by Arthur A. Schomburg (introduction, "Appreciation," [Charles Frederick] Heartman, *Wheatley, Poems and Letters* [New York, n.d.], pp. 14-15). Edward D. Seeber quotes Voltaire's remark ("Phillis Wheatley," *Journal of Negro History,* Vol. 24, no. 3, July, 1939, pp. 259-262); see also [Julian] Mason ([*The Poems of Phillis Wheatley* (Chapel Hill: University of North Carolina Press, 1966)] pp. xlvi-xlvii).

Mason is the source for the reviews of her poems in English periodicals (ibid., pp. xxxvi-xxxvii).

Thomas Clarkson's remark is in *An Essay on the Slavery and Commerce of the Human Species* (Philadelphia: Cruikshank, 1786), p. 122; see also Mason (*Poems,* p. xlvi).

George Saintsbury's discussion of Pope and the heroic couplet is to be found in *English Prosody,* 2:454.

There is an interesting presentation of the relation between science and poetry in *Science and English Poetry, A Historical Sketch, 1590-1950,* by Douglas Bush (New York: Oxford University Press, 1950).

The two lines on Newton are quoted from Pope's "Epitaph Intended for Sir Isaac Newton." The quotations from Pope contained in the footnote on page 56 [see note 1 below] are from his *Essay on Man,* Epistle I, lines 267-268, 289-294. The subsequent quotations from Pope are in his *Essay on Man,* Epistle II, lines (variously) 10-17.

James Weldon Johnson's assessment of her poetry is contained in his *American Negro Poetry* (pp. xxii-xxiv). His estimation of the time span between Anne Bradstreet and Phillis Wheatley ("Anne Bradstreet preceded Phillis Wheatley by a little over twenty years. She published her volume of poems, 'The Tenth Muse,' in 1750" [ibid., p. xxiii] is off by about a century. Bradstreet's collected works were first published in England in 1650; the second edition was published in 1678, and the third in 1758, the latter two in Boston (see Elizabeth Wade White, *Anne Bradstreet* [*The Tenth Muse* (New York: Oxford University Press, 1971)]). The critical comparison of Bradstreet and Wheatley made by Johnson appears on page xxiii. The quote from Arthur Schomburg is in his introduction to *Poems and Letters* by Phillis Wheatley (Phillis Peters) (New York: C. F. Heartman's Historical Series #8).

Richard Wright's discussion of Phillis Wheatley is in *White Man, Listen* (New York: Doubleday & Co., 1964), pp. 74-79.

For Redding's quotation see *To Make a Poet Black,* pp. 8-11. (He is the victim of either a mathematical or typographical error when he says that twenty-five years after Phillis Wheatley's poem to the Earl of Dartmouth [1772], Horton wrote the lines he quotes. The year of Horton's birth is usually estimated as 1797.) Loggins also advances the theme Redding develops, that ". . . she neglected almost entirely her own state of slavery and the miserable oppression of thousands of her race." He finds that "In all of her writings she only once referred in strong terms to the wrongs of the Negro in America." That once is her poem addressed to Lord Dartmouth [Vernon Loggins, *The Negro Author: His Development in America to 1900* (New York: Columbia University Press, 1931, 1959)], pp. 24-25).

BETSY ERKKILA (ESSAY DATE FALL 1987)

SOURCE: Erkkila, Betsy. "Revolutionary Women." *Tulsa Studies in Women's Literature* 6, no. 2 (fall 1987): 189-223.

In the following excerpt, Erkkila discusses Wheatley's life and work along with the correspondence of Abigail Adams, wife of the early American leader John Adams. Erkkila suggests that the writings of these women, a white colonist and a black slave, reveal the full extent of the force of the revolution. In their challenges to men of power, Erkkila contends, they attempted to link the fight for American freedom to the liberation of women, white and black.

In a letter written to John Adams during the Revolutionary war, Abigail Adams described the appearance of a new phenomenon in America: the female mob. Angry at "an eminent, wealthy, stingy Merchant," who was hoarding coffee and refusing to sell at a reasonable price, "a Number of Females some say a hundred, some say more assembled with a cart and trucks, marchd down to the Ware House and demanded the keys, which he refused to deliver, upon which one of them seazd him by his Neck and tossd him into the cart. Upon his finding no Quarter he deliverd the keys, when they tipd up the cart and discharged him, then opend the Warehouse, Hoisted out the Coffe themselves, put it into the trucks and drove off." The incident is remarkable both in its display of female physical force and violence and the seeming abandon with which the women break bounds and overturn traditional orders of masculine authority. Abigail Adams tells the story with obvious relish, noting in conclusion that "A large concourse of Men stood amazd silent Spectators of the whole transaction."[1] As told by Adams to her husband John, who was at that very moment at the Continental Congress constituting a new form of government that would exclude women, the female uprising has the quality of a cautionary tale: frustrated by an economy of injustice and deprivation, the female rioters take the law into their own hands as the men stand by in mute horror, gazing upon the scene of revolutionary destruction.

The rioting women of Boston were not unique. During the severe inflation of the war years, there were a number of instances in which "a corps of female infantry" attacked merchants as a form of what Joan Hoff Wilson has called "popular price control."[2] These female uprisings were legitimized both by the anti-authoritarian rhetoric of the revolutionary years and the many instances of mob action—most notably the "Boston Tea Party"—engaged in and abetted by the Sons of Liberty. The female mobs in Boston and elsewhere illustrate almost paradigmatically the radicalizing effect revolutionary rhetoric and action had on traditional female behaviors. For the founding fathers, the American Revolution became a kind of Pandora's box, releasing potentially violent and disruptive female energies that would not and could not be controlled once the war was over. Despite the attempt to silence and disembody women politically by depriving them of citizenship and legal rights under the terms of the Articles of Confederation and the Constitution of the United States signed by the Congress in 1787, a revolutionary female presence would continue to haunt and spook the political and cultural production of the new republic.

In his important essay "The Transforming Radicalism of the American Revolution," Bernard Bailyn traces the changes in the concepts of representation and consent, constitutions and rights, as well as the challenge to the institution of slavery, the religious establishment, and traditional social orders brought by the American Revolution. While the American Revolution was not intended to be a social revolution, he argues, society was changed not as a result of the economic displacements brought by the war, but because of "changes in the realm of belief and attitude." "For a decade or more," says Bailyn, "defiance to the highest constituted powers poured from the colonial presses and was hurled from half the pulpits of the land. . . . Defiance to constituted authority leaped like a spark from one flammable area to another, growing in heat as it went."[3]

It is perhaps a sign of the invisibility of women in the historical record that in tracing "the Democracy Unleashed" by the American Revolution, Bailyn says nothing of its transforming effect on the lives of women. In this essay, I shall argue that it is precisely in mounting a challenge to the constituted authority of patriarchy and to traditional constitutions of male and female nature that we find the American Revolution at its most radically transforming. I shall begin by tracing the effects that revolutionary rhetoric and action had on American women, focusing in particular on the lives and writings of Abigail Adams and Phillis Wheatley. I will then look at the ways the political constitution and cultural productions of the postwar period seek to restore a loose, "manly," and potentially dangerous daughter of liberty to her traditional familial role as wife and mother under the law of the father. I shall conclude by suggesting the long-term "flammable" effects of the American Revolution in giving women the education, the moral ground, and perhaps most of all the language and metaphors with which to renew their assault on the constituted orders of masculine authority in the nineteenth and twentieth centuries.

At the height of the agitation for independence from Britain, the Virginia clergyman Jonathan Boucher preached a sermon titled "On Civil Liberty, Passive Obedience, and Nonresistance" (1775) in which he defended the divine right of kings and the notion of "authority, settled subordinations, subjection, and obedience." "The first father was the first king," he argued, enjoining a policy of obedience and nonresistance in the relationship between America and England: "from the obedience due to parents, wisely derives the congenial duty of *honoring the king and all that are put in authority under him.*" The concepts of *equality* and *consent* were in Boucher's view "particularly loose and dangerous" notions. Recognizing and indeed advocating the close relationship between the orders of father and king, family and state, Boucher feared the potentially far-reaching social consequences of revolutionary rhetoric: "you are encouraged to resist not only all authority over us as it now exists, but any and all that it is possible to constitute."[4]

Those who advocated a break with England did so in the language of two primary social tropes: the family and slavery. The position of America was figuratively represented as the natural right of the son or daughter to revolt against a tyrannical parent and the natural right of a slave to revolt against a master. Through a masterful deployment of these parent/child and master/slave tropes in *Common Sense,* which was published in January 1776, Tom Paine galvanized popular support for the formal break with England that would occur six months later. In his attempt to "divest" the king and monarchy of its traditional authority, Paine represented the king as a slave master seeking to deprive Americans of their natural liberties: "When the republican virtue fails, slavery ensues. Why is the Constitution of England sickly, but because monarchy has poisoned the Republic; the crown has engrossed the Commons?" Pleading the cause of "final separation" from Britain in the language of the "violated unmeaning names of parent and child," Paine says: "No man was a warmer wisher for a reconciliation than myself, before the fatal nineteenth of April 1775 [Battle of Lexington], but the moment the event of that day was made well known, I rejected the hardened, sullen-tempered Pharoah of England for ever; and disdain the wretch that with the pretended title of FATHER OF HIS PEOPLE can unfeelingly hear of their slaughter, and composedly sleep with their blood upon his soul."[5]

In a political economy where the rights of women were absorbed and legally "covered" by the constituted authority of the male and where blacks were held as property under the institution of slavery, the widespread rhetorical representation of America as child of liberty or enchained slave oppressed by the tyranny of father/master had a particularly potent social appeal. This appeal was heightened by the violent and bloody visual iconography that accompanied the written representation of the American cause.

In the newspaper cartoon "Britannia Mutilated" (1774), for example, Britain appears as a naked female figure, enchained, amputated, and deprived of her former power by the aggressive Colonial policies of King and Parliament. In "The able Doctor, or America Swallowing the Bitter Draught" (1774), America is figured as a half-clad Indian woman who is violated by a number of male figures who force her to submit to the "bitter draught" of the Boston Port Bill and other British policies while Britannia turns away in distress. In the etching "Liberty Conquers Tyranny" (1775), Liberty leans on a pillar with her foot on the neck of a man whose crown and chain represent the oppressions of Britain as monarch and enslaver. The old world order of the patriarch is represented as a barren landscape of war and violence in which a female appears to be at the mercy of an aggressive male figure. The new world order of female liberty is represented as a pastoral landscape of abundance, fertility, and peace where male and female dance in apparent harmony. In "Columbia Trading With all the World," Columbia as a figure of the United States takes her sovereign place among the four sister continents: America, Africa, Asia, and Europe. Liberated from the oppressions of patriarch and slave master, she freely engages in commerce and exchange with the entire world.

The radicalizing effect that revolutionary rhetoric and iconography could have on women's self-conceptions and the traditional relations between male and female is particularly evident in the correspondence between Abigail and John Adams during the revolutionary years. Abigail Adams was one of the first to note and draw out the revolutionary implications of the analogy between the political position of America and the position of the female within a masculine economy. "I long to hear that you have declared an independancy," she wrote John on March 31, 1776; "and by the way in the new Code of Laws which I suppose it will be necessary for you to make I desire you would Remember the Ladies, and be more generous and favourable to them than your ancestors. Do not put such unlimited power into the hands of the Husbands. Remember all Men would be tyrants if they could. If perticuliar care and attention is not paid to the Laidies we are determined to foment a Rebelion, and will not hold ourselves bound by any Laws in which we have no voice, or Representation" (*AFC* [*Adams Family Correspondence*] I, 370). In this justifiably famous passage Adams not only challenges traditional orders of masculine authority in family and in state; her masterful deployment of the rhetoric of representation and consent, desire and power, self-sovereignty and natural law also illustrates the importance of the American Revolution in giving women the language and metaphors to "foment" further rebellion in their struggle for citizenship, suffrage, and full human rights.

Whereas John Adams and the founding fathers wanted a change of regime, Abigail Adams was asking for a change of world. Like such male satirists as Alexander Pope in England and John Trumbull in America, John Adams seeks to diffuse the logic and power of Abigail Adams's revolutionary appeal through humor. "As to your extraordinary Code of Laws, I cannot but laugh. We have been told that our Struggle has loosened the bands of Government every where. That Children and Apprentices were disobedient—that schools and Colledges were grown turbulent—that Indians slighted their Guardians and Negroes grew insolent to their Masters. But your Letter was the first Intimation that another Tribe more numerous and powerfull than all the rest were grown discontented." Recognizing the dangerous loosening of traditional bonds of rank and subordination brought by the revolutionary situation, John reasserts the absolute authority of patriarchy: "Depend upon it, We know better than to repeal our Masculine systems" (*AFC,* I, 382). His bantering tone does not disguise the fact of his self-contradiction. While he was advocating the right of rebellion in the political sphere, asserting that "the people have a right to revoke the authority that they themselves have deputed and to constitute abler and better agents, attorneys, and trustees," he was attempting to suppress the rebellion in his own household by maintaining the absolute authority of a "Masculine" system that was hereditary, divinely sanctioned, and beyond repeal.[6]

Abigail Adams refused to be silenced. She pointed out the contradiction between the anti-authoritarian rhetoric of the revolution and her husband's insistence on maintaining the divine right of the father as king. "I can not say that I think you very generous to the Ladies," she wrote; "for whilst you are proclaiming peace and good will to Men, Emancipating all Nations, you insist upon retaining an absolute power over Wives. But you must remember that Arbitary power is like most other things which are very hard, very liable to be broken" (*AFC,* I, 402).

Like other revolutionary women, Abigail Adams took advantage of the revolutionary moment to press for widespread political reform both within and outside of marriage. Alarmed by a "conspiracy of the Negroes" in Boston, who had agreed to fight on the side of the royalist Governor in return for arms and liberation, she expressed her essential sympathy with the slaves' demand for liberation: "I wish most sincerely there was not a Slave in the province," she wrote John in 1774, pointing out the contradiction between the rhetoric of liberty and the fact of slavery in America. "It allways appeard a most iniquitious Scheme to me—fight ourselfs for what we are daily robbing and plundering from those who have as good a right to freedom as we have. You know my mind upon this Subject" (*AFC,* I, 162).

Only a few weeks after the revolt against England was formalized in the Declaration of Independence, she complained of the "deficiency of Education" in America. "The poorer sort of children are wholly neglected, and left to range the Streets without Schools, without Buisness, given up to all Evil. . . . If you complain of neglect of Education in sons, What shall I say with regard to daughters, who every day experience the want of it." In making her case, Adams mounted a defense of female education that would become public policy for the next one hundred years. "If we mean to have Heroes, Statesmen and Philosophers, we should have learned women," she said (*AFC,* II, 94). But while Adams grounded her argument for female education in the political importance of women as wives and mothers of the future sons of the republic, like Mary Wollstonecraft and Judith Sargent Murray later in the century, she insisted on the essential equality of male and female mental capacities. Reflecting on the "difference of Education between the male and female Sex" in a letter to her cousin John Thaxter, she observed: "Pardon me sir if I cannot help sometimes suspecting that this Neglect arises in some measure from an ungenerous jealosy of rivals near the Throne—but I quit the Subject or it will run away with my pen" (*AFC,* II, 391-92).

During the revolutionary years, Adams's pen frequently ran away with its female "Subject," leading her to warlike fantasies of violence not only against Britain but against patriarchy itself as she imagined a larger field of action for women in the political constitution of the nation. "My pen is always freer than my tongue," she wrote to her sister Mary Cranch. For Adams in her letters as for Benjamin Franklin in his *Autobiography,* writing became a means not only of ordering and constituting the new republic, but a form of self-creation, self-enlargement, and self-display at a time when traditional social roles and relations were being eroded.

While John Adams served as delegate to the Continental Congress and later as ambassador to France, he relied on Abigail Adams's letters as a primary source of information about political happenings in America. He shared her correspondence with other delegates and even cited one of her letters in a speech to Congress.[7] "I think you shine as a Stateswoman," he wrote. "Pray where do you get your Maxims of State, they are very apropos" (*AFC,* I, 420). Comparing her with the British historian Catharine Macaulay and the French classical scholar Anne Dacier, he came to see her letters as a kind of history of the war (*AFC,* III, 122).

Abigail Adams was conscious of the pen as a form of political power. "What a politician you have made me," she wrote John of the elections under the new Massachusetts Constitution in 1780. "If I cannot be a voter upon this occasion, I will be a writer of votes" (*AFC,* III, 372). Reflecting the contemporary interest in the "epistle" as a form of literary and political discourse, Adams's correspondence enabled her to become, in effect, a woman of letters, trespassing on traditionally masculine terrain as she wielded the pen as weapon and power in the world. At a time when the writing woman was still an anomaly, Adams's self-consciously literary correspondence represented an affirmation of female literacy and an assertion of female agency in the process of cultural and national creation. Along with the many selves she invented and lived during the war, Adams's letters became a means at once of describing and writing herself into history.

After John Adams departed for the Continental Congress in 1774 and during the period when Boston was occupied by British troops, Abigail Adams began signing her letters with the name Portia, whose husband Brutus had famously opposed the tyranny of Julius Caesar in the Roman republic. Her assumption of the identity of Portia was not only a means of asserting the continuity of the American struggle with the republican struggles of the past; it was also a means of scripting herself into a starring role in the political drama of the nation. The figure of Portia enabled Adams to imagine herself historically as a rational, educated, independent, virtuous, and politically minded citizen of a new republican country.

The discourse of republicanism—which stressed political citizenship as the highest form of existence and sacrifice for the *patria* as the highest form of virtue—placed both John and Abigail Adams in an anomalous position. The overarching irony of their relationship during the revolutionary years is that while they played at being the ideal republican family, the republican ethos of civic virtue led them to spend much of their married life apart. In the ideal republican household, the father was, in effect, absent serving the country, while the mother assumed traditionally male functions as a form of self-sacrificial service to the state.

The revolutionary situation gave Abigail Adams a chance to play the man she had always in some sense wanted to be. "Had nature formed me of the other Sex," she wrote her cousin Isaac Smith when he departed for England in 1771, "I should certainly have been a rover" (*AFC,* I, 76). While John served as a delegate to the Continental Congress between 1774 and 1778, Abigail Adams assumed full management of the household and became a model republican farmer. "I find myself dear Marcia . . . doubled in Wedlock," she wrote Mercy Otis Warren in April 1776, referring to her assumption of both masculine and feminine roles in the Adams' household. "I find it necessary not only to pay attention to my own in door domestick affairs, but to every thing without, about our little farm &c." In the absence of male support, she begins to (re)imagine herself in the commanding role of a ship captain: "Frugality, Industery and ecconomy are the Lessons of the day—at least they must be so for me or my small Boat will suffer shipwreck" (*AFC,* I, 377).

When John departed for France in 1778, Abigail Adams rented their farm to tenants and started a private import business, first through John's mediation, and ultimately by corresponding directly with the French "House of Joseph Guardoqui and Sons." As a female merchant, she traded various goods—tea, china dishes, fabric, handkerchiefs, ribbon, shoe binding, thread—with townspeople, and she engaged her friends, including Mercy Otis Warren, to serve as agents for her business. For all her emphasis on rural virtue and republican self-sacrifice, Abigail Adams was in fact an ambitious and successful entrepreneur.

Recognizing the value of property and hard money during the inflationary war years, Adams also invested in real estate and engaged in land speculation with property that she could not legally possess as a woman under Massachusetts law. When John objected to her buying land in Vermont with the idea of eventually "retiring" to farm there, she bought the land anyway. "Nothing venture nothing have," she quipped in a letter to him once the deal was closed (*AFC,* IV, 345).

A little over a month after the Declaration of Independence and the outbreak of hostilities, Adams began to dream of a revolutionary free space in which she would have the liberty to write, to think, to choose alone. "I do not covet my Neighbours Goods," she wrote John from her Aunt's study in Boston, "but . . . I always had a fancy for a closet with a window which I could more peculiarly call my own" (*AFC,* II, 112). Throughout the war years there was a growing gap between her rhetoric of domesticity and dependence and the fact of her actual transgressions of traditional female bounds. "Whilst you are engaged in the Senate your own domestick affairs require your presence at Home, and . . . your wife and children are in Danger of wanting Bread," she wrote John in September 1776; but she concluded the same letter with an Amazonian dream of power in a female land: "We are no ways dispiritted here, we possess a Spirit that will not be conquerd. If our Men are all drawn of[f] and we should be attacked, you would find a Race of Amazons in America" (*AFC,* II, 128-29).

Even before the war, Abigail Adams expressed anxiety about constituting a new form of government in America. "I am more and more convinced that Man is a dangerous creature," she wrote John in November 1775, "and that power whether vested in many or a few is ever grasping" (*AFC,* I, 329). Toward the close of the war she suffered from "a dejection of Spirits" as she took note of the new breed of moneyed and self-interested men who were eroding the republican ethos of virtue and self-sacrifice for the public good. "You are loosing all opportunities for helping yourself," she wrote John, "for those who are daily becomeing more and more unworthy of your Labours and who will neither care for you or your family when their own turn is served—so selfish are mankind. I know this is a language you are unwilling to hear. I wish it was not a truth which I daily experience" (*AFC,* IV, 296). Ambiguously positioned between the "truth" of her "daily experience" of the American marketplace and the republican language that John wanted her to speak, Abigail Adams marked the growing gap between the self-sacrificial rhetoric of the founding fathers and the fact of an increasingly self-interested market economy.

But the anxiety and depression that Adams suffered toward the close of the war was at least in part provoked by her discovery of similarly "grasping" impulses in herself. There were times when she seemed to want to give up the language of republicanism and the mask of public virtue and take what she could get. "Desire and Sorrow were denounced upon our Sex; as a punishment for the transgression of Eve," she wrote John in 1782; "I never wonderd at the philosopher who thanked

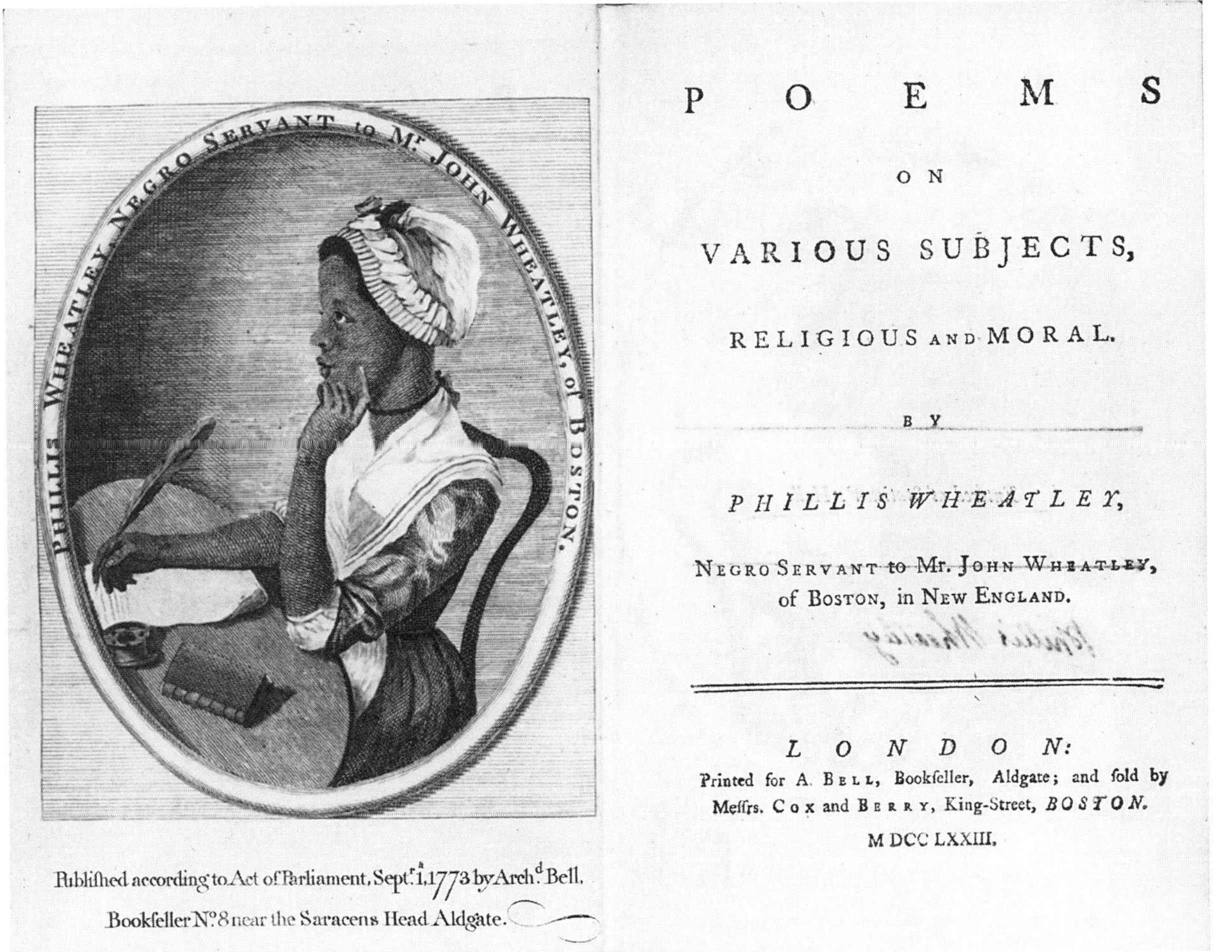

POEMS

ON

VARIOUS SUBJECTS,

RELIGIOUS AND MORAL.

BY

PHILLIS WHEATLEY,

NEGRO SERVANT to Mr. JOHN WHEATLEY,
of BOSTON, in NEW ENGLAND.

LONDON:

Printed for A. BELL, Bookſeller, Aldgate; and ſold by
Meſſrs. COX and BERRY, King-Street, *BOSTON.*

M DCC LXXIII.

Title page of *Poems on Various Subjects, Religious and Moral* (1773).

the Gods that he was created a Man rather than a Woman" (*AFC*, IV, 306). Adams's depression about the prospects of the American republic were linked with her uncertainty about the putative virtue of the republican mother upon whom the health of the new nation was said to depend. The new breed of men she saw in the external landscape of the republic were in fact uneasy reminders of the ambitious and transgressive new being she had discovered in herself during the war years.

* * *

During the American Revolution, the challenge to constituted authority came not only from privileged and high-born women like Abigail Adams, but, as John Adams had grudgingly noted, from Apprentices, Indians, and Negroes who "grew insolent to their Masters." The potential danger of this challenge is evident in the life and work of the black poet Phillis Wheatley, who was abducted from Africa and sold as a slave in Boston in 1761. Whereas Abigail Adams compared the condition of women in America to "Egyptian bondage," for Wheatley, drawing upon the same Old Testament image to describe the captivity of her people to "our Modern Egyptians," the language of bondage and freedom was no longer metaphoric but real. Knowing the truth of slavery as part of her daily experience as the slave of a prosperous Boston merchant, she, too, pointed out the contradiction between rhetoric and reality in America. In a letter to the Mohegan preacher Samuel Occom, which was printed in the *Boston Post-Boy* and the *Boston News-Letter* in 1774, she noted ironically "the strange Absurdity of their Conduct whose Words and Actions are so diametrically opposite. How well the Cry for Liberty, and the reverse Disposition for Exercise of oppressive Power over others agree,—I humbly think it does not require the Penetration of a Philosopher to determine."[8] Positioning herself in the breach between trope and truth, between the rhetoric of republican liberty and her felt experience of black

African enslavement, Wheatley transformed the revolutionary discourse on liberty, natural rights, and human nature into a subtle critique of the color code and the oppressive racial structures of republican America.

It is no coincidence that Wheatley's ***Poems on Various Subjects Religious and Moral*** (1773), which was the first book published by an Afro-American, appeared during the revolutionary period. According to her "Master" John Wheatley, "Phillis was brought from *Africa* to *America,* in the Year 1761, between Seven and Eight Years of Age. Without any Assistance from School Education, and by only what she was taught in the Family, she, in sixteen Months Time from her Arrival, attained the English Language."[9] By age twelve she was reading and translating Ovid, at age fifteen she published her first poem, and she was twenty when ***Poems*** was published. Wheatley and her book were, in effect, a revolutionary phenomenon.

Her volume of ***Poems*** was accompanied by the authenticating documents—a picture and a "Notice to the Public" signed by several local authorities—that would frame and mark later Afro-American writing. Wheatley's complex position as black woman slave in revolutionary America is suggested by the fact that the signatures of the royalist Governor Thomas Hutchinson and the leader of Boston resistance John Hancock were joined for a brief moment over the body of her ***Poems.*** But while Wheatley was the "property" of John Wheatley and the authenticating male figures who "notice" her text, she was possessed by the insurrectionary "Goddess of Liberty" who stalks her poems as she was at that very moment stalking the landscape of revolutionary America.

In *Home* Leroi Jones criticizes what he calls Wheatley's "ludicrous departures from the huge black voices that splintered southern nights."[10] But his criticism misses the point. Within the discourse of racial inequality in the eighteenth century, the fact of a black woman reading, writing, and publishing poems was in itself enough to splinter the categories of white and black and explode a social order grounded in notions of racial difference. The potential danger of her enterprise is underscored by the doubleness of the authenticating picture that represents her in the revolutionary figure of a black woman reading, thinking, and writing at the same time that it enchains her in the inscription: "Phillis Wheatley, Negro Servant to Mr. John Wheatley of Boston".

Even before Wheatley's book was published, the Philadelphia physician and antislavery advocate Benjamin Rush cited her poetry as a sign at once of black humanity and the sameness of human nature. In his anti-slavery tract, *An Address to the Inhabitants of the British Settlements in America Upon Slave Keeping* (1773), he wrote: "There is now in the town of Boston a Free Negro Girl, about 18 years of age, who has been but 9 years in the country, whose singular genius and accomplishments are such as not only do honor to her sex, but to human nature. Several of her poems have been printed, and read with pleasure by the public."[11]

Within the context of revolutionary America, loyalist and patriot alike laid claim to Wheatley's voice: for the loyalists she might serve as a means of garnering slave support for the cause of Britain in America; and for the patriots she represented a sign of human progress rather than degeneration in America. But while Wheatley seemed to utter the ideals of her time in the ordered and allusive heroic couplets of Pope and the neoclassical writers, she also knew how to manipulate language, image, and phrase in a manner that destabilized while it appeared to reinforce the categories of the dominant culture. As the poet Naomi Long Madgett says in a recent tribute to "Phillis," she "learned to sing / a dual song":

> *"Show to the world the face the world would see;*
> *Be slave, be pet, conceal your Self—but be."*
>
> Lurking behind the docile Christian lamb,
> Unconquered lioness asserts: "I am!"[12]

Within the revolutionary matrix of eighteenth-century America, Phillis Wheatley learned the power of speaking doubly as African American.

From the dedication to the Countess of Huntington that opens her ***Poems*** to her tribute **"To the Right Honorable William, Earl of Dartmouth"** enclosed within, Wheatley's book is enmeshed in a web of revolutionary associations. Margaret Burroughs exaggerates only slightly when she says: "If the Continental Congress had possessed an intelligent counter-intelligence service, Phillis Wheatley might have been interned for the duration as a security risk, on the principle of guilt by association."[13] The Countess of Huntington was a well-known supporter of both the evangelical and the antislavery movement in England. Her friend and associate, the Earl of Dartmouth, supported the British policy of inciting slaves to revolt against rebel masters when he served as Secretary of State for North America between 1772 and 1775.

As a book of poems by a woman slave celebrating the cause of American liberty, Wheatley's ***Poems*** is loaded with the irony of a cause and a country at odds with itself. While Wheatley was in London in 1773, where she met several supporters including the Earl of Dartmouth and Benjamin Franklin, no less than five petitions for freedom were presented to the Massachusetts General Council by Boston slaves: "We have no Property. We have no Wives! No Children! We have no City! No Country!" one exclaimed. In February 1774 an article in the *Massachusetts Spy* signed by an "African" patriot invoked the rhetoric of natural right and consent to point out the analogy between America's defiance of Britain and the slaves' defiance of their masters in America: "Are not your hearts also hard, when you hold them in slavery who are intitled to liberty, by the law of nature, equal as yourselves? If it be so, pray, Sir, pull the beam out of thine eye" (Akers, p. 404). At the time Wheatley's ***Poems*** was published, there was widespread fear of slave revolt; Abigail Adams's September 1774 letter to John on the conspiracy of Boston Negroes is only one of a number of signs that fear of slave insurrection was spreading from the south to New England. Perhaps because of this growing fear of blacks, whether free or enslaved, Wheatley's book, having failed to receive an adequate subscription in America, was sponsored and published in England.

Like others who have lived and written in a dangerous social environment, Phillis Wheatley knew the art and necessity of speaking with a double tongue. In her poetry, she makes subtle use of ambiguity and irony, double meaning and symbolic nuance to speak what was otherwise unspeakable from her position as an African woman slave in revolutionary America. Wheatley's ***Poems*** opens with an address **"To Maecenas,"** the patron of Horace and Virgil, who appears to represent her image of an ideal patron and audience for her poems. Wheatley enters the literary community by invoking the classical tradition of Homer and Virgil, but she ends with an invocation to Terence, the Roman slave of African descent who was able to use his literary talent to attain freedom:

> The happier *Terence* all the choir inspir'd,
> His soul replenish'd, and his bosom fir'd;
> But say, ye *Muses,* why this partial grace,
> To one alone of *Afric's* sable race;
> From age to age transmitting thus his name
> With the first glory in the rolls of fame?
>
> (p. 4)

Self-consciously placing herself and her poems within a specifically African tradition, Wheatley registers her own ambitious desire to share—or perhaps transcend—the "first glory" of her African forbearer in a poetics of ascent "That fain would mount, and ride upon the wind" (p. 3).

Wheatley's most anthologized poem, **"On Being Brought from Africa to America,"** is formally split, like the title, between Africa and America, embodying the poet's own split consciousness as Afro-American. In the opening quatrain, the poet speaks as an American, representing slavery as a paradoxical Christian deliverance, a necessary stage in the black person's advance toward redemption and civilization; in the second quatrain, the poet speaks as an African, turning the terms of Christian orthodoxy into a critique of white hypocrisy and oppressive racial codes.

> 'Twas mercy brought me from my *Pagan* land,
> Taught my benighted soul to understand
> That there's a God, that there's a *Saviour* too:
> Once I redemption neither sought nor knew.
> Some view our sable race with scornful eye,
> "Their colour is a diabolic die."
> Remember, *Christians, Negroes,* black as *Cain,*
> May be refin'd, and join th' angelic train.
>
> (p. 7)

As in **"To the University of Cambridge,"** Wheatley's "redemption" becomes the source of her moral authority, signalling her transformation from being passively "brought" and "taught" by God's Providence to being the active black subject who speaks and instructs as a kind of female preacher in the second quatrain of the poem.

The poem operates on what Maya Angelou has called the "Principle of Reverse": "Anything that works for you can also work against you."[14] Speaking as a black woman slave, Wheatley turns the racial codes of the dominant culture back upon themselves, giving them an ironic inflection. What appears to be repetition is in fact a form of *mimesis* that mimics and mocks in the act of repeating. This process is particularly evident in the final lines of the poem where Wheatley challenges and destabilizes the white discourse of racial difference by placing this discourse in quotation marks—"Their color is a diabolic die." As the racially conscious voice of her people, Wheatley literally "mimics" the white view of "our sable race" in a manner that recasts the discourse of racial difference in an ironic mode.

Within the context of the poem, the use of italicization has a similarly destabilizing effect: the italicized terms *Pagan, Christians, Negroes,* and *Cain* are simultaneously underscored and marked for interrogation. The slipperiness of these terms is evidenced in the final lines of the poem, where through punctuation and italicization the phrase "Remember, *Christians, Negroes,* black as *Cain*" might be read doubly as an address to Christians about black humanity and an address to Christians *and* Negroes that links them both in the figurative image "black as *Cain.*" Both readings undermine the color code by emphasizing the equality of spiritual condition shared by whites and blacks alike as sinful descendants of Adam and potentially "redeemed" heirs of Christ.

Wheatley's most overt criticism of the institution of slavery occurs in **"To the Right Honourable William, Earl of Dartmouth, His Majesty's Principal Secretary of State for North-America, &C."** Here again the poet speaks doubly as American patriot and African slave, celebrating "Fair Freedom" as the cause of New England patriots and "the *Goddess* long desir'd" by enslaved blacks. She associates the 1772 appointment of Dartmouth as Secretary of State for North-America with the return of *Freedom,* "long lost to realms beneath the northern skies":

> Elate with hope her race no longer mourns,
> Each soul expands, each grateful bosom burns,
> While in thine hand with pleasure we behold
> The silken reins, and *Freedom's* charms unfold.
> (p. 33)

When one remembers that as Secretary of State for the Colonies and President of the Board of Trade and Foreign Plantations between 1772 and 1775, the Earl of Dartmouth became engaged in the British policy of inciting American slaves to revolt against their patriot masters, the poet's "hope" of freedom for "her race" takes on a particularly insurrectionary cast.

Wheatley draws upon the revolutionary rhetoric of tyranny and enslavement to promote the cause of America, but as the language of an American slave her words bear specific reference to the cause of black liberation:

> No more, *America,* in mournful strain
> Of wrongs, and grievance unredress'd complain,
> No longer shalt thou dread the iron chain,
> Which wanton *Tyranny* with lawless hand
> Had made, and with it meant t' enslave the land.
> (p. 34)

Wheatley further literalizes the slave metaphor by calling attention to her own condition as an American slave:

> Should you, my lord, while you peruse my song,
> Wonder from whence my love of *Freedom* sprung,
> Whence flow these wishes for the common good,
> By feeling hearts alone best understood,
> I, young in life, by seeming cruel fate
> Was snatch'd from *Afric's* fancy'd happy seat:
> What pangs excruciating must molest,
> What sorrows labour in my parent's breast?
> Steel'd was that soul and by no misery mov'd
> That from a father seiz'd his babe belov'd:
> Such, such my case. And can I then but pray
> Others may never feel tyrannic sway?
> (p. 34)

Transforming the revolutionary trope of enslavement into the thing itself, Wheatley becomes self-authenticating, authorizing her voice as the poet of freedom in her historic experience as an American slave. Her most direct personal statement about her African past becomes as well her most direct protest against the reality of slavery as the true *Tyranny* in America.

Wheatley's reference to her "seeming cruel fate" might be read as a sign of the mutilating influence of slavery, the mark of the black poet's capitulation to the codes of the dominant culture.[15] But her words are self-protectively ambiguous. Read within the context of Wheatley's ardent Christian faith, her words also suggest a moving attempt to make sense of the fate of herself and her people as slaves within a "seeming cruel" providential order. The poet is not "brought" but "seiz'd" and "snatch'd from *Afric's* fancy'd happy seat," a phrasing that represents her enslavement as a kidnapping and Africa as a site not of illusory but of *still* imagined happiness. Bearing witness to slavery and the slave trade as a cold-blooded violation of the fundamental social unit—the familial bond between father and child—Wheatley turns her personal history into an emotionally charged "case" against the institution of slavery. Her prayer that "Others may never feel tyrannic sway" is a prayer that encompasses not only American patriots but the "Others" of her own African race.

According to her nineteenth-century biographer Margaretta Matilda Odell, Wheatley's only memory of her African homeland was the daily sunrise ritual of her mother, who "poured out water before the sun at his rising."[16] In Wheatley's writings, the memory of African sun worship merges with the language of evangelical Christianity and the language of revolutionary freedom to produce a poetics of ascent and liberation. In this poetics the sun/son is the central figure of a constellation of images that moves from dark to light, white to black, sin to redemption, bondage to deliverance.

The intersection of these languages is particularly evident in **"On Imagination,"** where Wheatley imagines herself mounting on the "silken pinions" of *Fancy* toward the sun, toward God, and toward liberation:

> Soaring through air to find the bright abode,
> Th' empyreal palace of the thund'ring God,
> We on thy pinions can surpass the wind,
> And leave the rolling universe behind:
> From star to star the mental optics rove,
> Measure the skies, and range the realms above.
> There in one view we grasp the mighty whole,
> Or with new worlds amaze th' unbounded soul.
>
> (p. 30)

Like Memory (*Mneme*) in **"On Recollection"** and Liberty ("the goddess") in **"To His Excellency General Washington"** and **"Liberty and Peace, A Poem,"** Wheatley's *Imagination* is a potent female figure, an "imperial queen" whose wings carry the poet into "new worlds" of the "unbounded soul." These "new worlds" are at once the heavenly other world of biblical Revelation and the poet's own "raptur'd" vision of an alternative earthly economy. In the last stanza of the poem the "rising fire" of Wheatley's poetic aspiration fuses with the language of revelation and revolution and her memory of the African sunrise, leading her to an insurrectionary vision of deliverance out of the "iron bands" of an oppressive white order—figured in the poem as the "frozen deeps" of *Winter*—into the "radiant gold" of a new dawn on earth. The poet's voice and vision "cease" in the final lines of the poem: "*Winter* austere forbids me to aspire, / And northern tempests damp the rising fire; / They chill the tides of *Fancy's* flowing sea" (p. 31). But the poet's closing images of herself as a "rising fire" and "flowing sea" suggest that she will continue to sing against and beyond the chill of white Northern oppression.

The visionary language of evangelical Protestantism gave Wheatley the means of engaging in the revolutionary struggle for black freedom without losing her devout Christian faith. Commenting on the "natural Rights" of Negroes in her 1774 letter to the Indian activist Samuel Occom, Wheatley envisions the black struggle against American slavery as a "type" of the Old Testament struggle of Israel "for their Freedom from Egyptian Slavery." "In every human Breast," says Wheatley, "God has implanted a Principle, which we call Love of Freedom; it is impatient of Oppression, and pants for Deliverance; and by the Leave of our Modern Egyptians I will assert, that the same Principle lives in us. God grant Deliverance in his own way and Time, and get him honor upon all those whose Avarice impels them to countenance and help forward the Calamities of their Fellow Creatures" (Akers, p. 406). Wheatley was the first in a long line of Afro-American writers to merge the revolutionary language of liberty and natural rights with the biblical language of bondage and deliverance in a visionary poetics that imagines the deliverance of her people not as a religious translation only but as a revolutionary change of world.

A few months after the publication of her ***Poems*** and at the urging of her English supporters and her mistress Susannah Wheatley, Phillis Wheatley was freed by John Wheatley. In a letter to Colonel David Wooster on the sale of her book in Connecticut she wrote: "I am now upon my own footing and whatever I get by this is entirely mine. It is the Chief I have to depend upon."[17] Both literally and figuratively, Wheatley's poems—like those of her forbearer, Terence—became a means of writing herself into freedom; and through them she continued to act, both directly and indirectly, toward the deliverance of her race.

On October 26, 1775, Phillis Wheatley sent a poem **"To His Excellency General Washington."** Inspired by "the goddess" Freedom and impelled by the "wild uproar" of Freedom's warriors, the poem is a subtle attempt to enlist Washington as a freedom fighter for real as well as for metaphoric slaves. "We demand," the poet says:

> The grace and glory of thy martial band.
> Fam'd for thy valour, for thy virtues more,
> Hear every tongue thy guardian aid implore!
>
> (pp. 89-90)

Like the addresses to Washington written by other revolutionary poets, including Joel Barlow and Philip Freneau, the poem suggests the potential power of writing at a time when poets as well as politicians were engaged in the process of creating a nation. As in Wheatley's addresses to other figures of cultural power, including the Earl of Dartmouth, the preacher George Whitefield, and the Lieutenant-Governor of Massachusetts, Andrew Oliver, the poem also suggests a certain openness and indeterminacy in black/white relations during the revolutionary years—an openness that would begin to close and rigidify once the war was over and slaves were written into the constitution as three-fifths human.

In 1784, only a year after the close of the war, Phillis Wheatley died and was buried in an unmarked grave. In the same year, Thomas Jefferson set very distinct limits on the revolutionary discourse of freedom, equality, and "self-evident" truth, when in *Notes on the State of Virginia* (1784)

ABOUT THE AUTHOR

LETTER FROM GEORGE WASHINGTON TO WHEATLEY IN RESPONSE TO A POEM WRITTEN FOR AND SENT TO WASHINGTON

To Miss Phillis Wheatley.
Cambridge, 28 February, 1776.
Miss Phillis,

Your favor of the 26th of October did not reach my hands till the middle of December. Time enough, you will say, to have given an answer ere this. Granted. But a variety of important occurrences, continually interposing to distract the mind and withdraw the attention, I hope will apologize for the delay, and plead my excuse for the seeming but not real neglect. I thank you most sincerely for your polite notice of me, in the elegant lines you enclosed; and however undeserving I may be of such encomium and panegyric, the style and manner exhibit a striking proof of your poetical talents; in honor of which, and as a tribute justly due to you, I would have published the poem, had I not been apprehensive, that, while I only meant to give the world this new instance of your genius, I might have incurred the imputation of vanity. This, and nothing else, determined me not to give it place in the public prints.

If you should ever come to Cambridge, or near head-quarters, I shall be happy to see a person so favored by the Muses, and to whom nature has been so liberal and beneficent in her dispensations. I am, with great respect, your obedient humble servant.

Washington, George. *The Writings of George Washington; Being his Correspondence, Addresses, Messages, and Other Papers, Official and Private, Selected and published from the Original Manuscripts; with a life of the Author, Notes and Illustrations,* edited by Jared Sparks, pp. 38-9. Boston: Little, Brown, 1855.

he advanced it "as a suspicion only, that blacks, whether originally a distinct race, or made distinct by time and circumstances, are inferior to the whites in the endowments of both mind and body." The potential danger of Wheatley's ***Poems*** as proof against Jefferson's "suspicion" of racial inequality is suggested by the fact that in advancing his argument, he singles out her work for criticism. In one of the earliest instances of the politics of canon formation in postrevolutionary America, he not only dismisses her work from serious literary consideration; he also, and perhaps intentionally, transmutes her name from "wheat" to "what": "Religion indeed has produced a Phyllis Whately [sic]; but it could not produce a poet. The compositions published under her name are below the dignity of criticism. The heroes of the Dunciad are to her, as Hercules to the author of that poem."[18] At a time when the "loose and dangerous" notions of equality and consent were threatening to subvert traditional orders of masculine authority, subordination, and subjection, Jefferson's comment on the issue of race represents one of the first attempts of the founding fathers to counter the revolutionary discourse of equality with the postrevolutionary discourse of racial and sexual difference.

Notes

1. *Adams Family Correspondence,* ed. L. H. Butterfield (Cambridge: Harvard University Press, 1963), II, 295. In this and other quotations from the letters, Abigail Adams's unorthodox spelling and punctuation have been preserved. Subsequent references will be cited in the text as *AFC.*
2. Joan Hoff Wilson, "The Illusion of Change: Women and the American Revolution," in *The American Revolution: Explorations in the History of American Radicalism,* ed. Alfred F. Young (Dekalb, Illinois: Northern Illinois University Press, 1976), p. 423.
3. Bernard Bailyn, "The Transforming Radicalism of the American Revolution," in *Pamphlets of the American Revolution* (Cambridge: Harvard University Press, 1965), pp. 191-92.
4. Jonathan Boucher, *A View of the Causes and Consequences of the American Revolution* (London: G. G. & J. Robinson, 1797), pp. 552-53.
5. *The Complete Writings of Thomas Paine,* ed. Philip S. Foner (New York: Citadel Press, 1945), pp. 16, 23, 25.
6. *The Political Writings of John Adams,* ed. George A. Peek (New York: Liberal Arts Press, 1954), p. 13.
7. Lynne Withey, *Dearest Friend: A Life of Abigail Adams* (New York: Free Press, 1981), p. 73.
8. *Boston Post-Boy,* 21 March 1774, p. 3. Cited in Charles W. Akers, "'Our Modern Egyptians': Phillis Wheatley And the Whig Campaign Against Slavery in Revolutionary Boston," *Journal of Negro History,* 60 (July 1975), 406-07. Subsequent references to this important essay on the historic context of Wheatley's work will be cited in the text.
9. *The Poems of Phillis Wheatley,* ed. Julian Mason, Jr. (Chapel Hill: North Carolina University Press, 1966), Part 1, p. 1. Subsequent references will be cited in the text.
10. Leroi Jones, *Home* (New York: William B. Morrow, 1966), p. 106.
11. Benjamin Rush, *An Address to the Inhabitants of the British Settlements in America Upon Slave Keeping* (Philadelphia: John Dunlap, 1773), in *Critical Essays,*

William H. Robinson, Jr., ed. (Boston: G. K. Hall, 1982), p. 24. For a review of the debate on the nature of the Negro that surrounded the publication of Wheatley's *Poems,* see Henry Louis Gates's excellent article, "Phillis Wheatley and the Nature of the Negro," in *Critical Essays,* pp. 213-33.

12. Naomi Long Madgett, "Phillis," in *Critical Essays,* p. 207.
13. Margaret G. Burroughs, "Do Birds of a Feather Flock Together?," in *Critical Essays,* p. 145.
14. Maya Angelou, *I Know Why the Caged Bird Sings* (New York: Random House, 1969), p. 215.
15. In *Bid the Vassal Soar* (Cambridge: Harvard University Press, 1974), Merle A. Richard comments on the "warping influence" of slavery on Phillis Wheatley. "It mutilated her," he says (p. 66). For others who have commented on Wheatley's internalization of racist attitudes, see Vernon Loggins, *The Negro Author* (New York: Columbia University Press, 1931), p. 24; and Terrence Collins, "Phillis Wheatley: The Dark Side of Poetry," *Phylon,* 36 (March 1975), 78-88.
16. Margaretta Matilda Odell, *Memoir and Poems of Phillis Wheatley* (Boston: George W. Light, 1834), pp. 10-11.
17. Cited in William H. Robinson, Jr., "On Being Young, Gifted, and Black," *Critical Essays,* p. 4.
18. *Notes on the State of Virginia,* ed. William Peden (New York: W. W. Norton, 1954), pp. 143, 140.

WALT NOTT (ESSAY DATE FALL 1993)

SOURCE: Nott, Walt. "From 'uncultivated Barbarian' to 'Poetical Genius': The Public Presence of Phillis Wheatley." *MELUS* 18, no. 3 (fall 1993): 21-32.

In the following essay, Nott surveys the public response to Wheatley's poetry.

The first edition of Phillis Wheatley's ***Poems on Various Subjects, Religious and Moral*** (1773) included an attestation that the volume was the work of its purported author. "To the PUBLICK" was signed by Massachusetts's royal governor Thomas Hutchinson, lieutenant governor Andrew Oliver, and sixteen other Bay Colony notables, including John Hancock and John Wheatley, "her Master." The signatories assured the volume's readers that ***Poems on Various Subjects*** was indeed "written by Phillis, a young Negro Girl, who was but a few years since, brought an uncultivated Barbarian from Africa, and has ever since been, and now is, under the Disadvantage of serving as a Slave in a Family in this Town" (Wheatley 48). When Wheatley landed in Boston upon her return from England in September 1773, the *Boston Gazette,* the newspaper of revolutionary Massachusetts, hailed the young slave woman as "the extraordinary Poetical Genius" ("Boston" 2). The two poles of public identity represented by "To the PUBLICK" and the *Gazette* notice—"uncultivated Barbarian" and "Poetical Genius"—suggest the possibilities open to Wheatley in eighteenth-century Anglo-American culture. However, the two identities also make it apparent that between arriving in America the first time from Africa on board the slaver Phillis and re-arriving from London on board the London Packet, shortly before the appearance of her book in the colonies, Wheatley's public presence had undergone a significant transformation. Construed as an "uncultivated Barbarian," Wheatley was just another slave among thousands, and therefore hardly worth notice. Yet recognized as a "Poetical Genius," Wheatley's comings and goings became worthy of public report. In a very real sense, upon her re-arrival in America, Wheatley had begun to exist. We might simply dismiss Wheatley's authorial metamorphosis as the "natural" result of the interconnected racial and intellectual presumptions of Anglo-American culture. However, seen from a more critical perspective, Wheatley's symbolic transformation in the eyes of contemporary white Anglo-American culture from "Barbarian" to "Genius" suggests her successful crafting of a public persona, her subsequent participation in the public discourse of her time, and, most important, her acquisition of a power such public participation entailed.

In part due to the aesthetics of the eighteenth-century public discourse in which her poetry participated, Wheatley's place in American literature has been problematic. In "Phillis Wheatley and the New England Clergy," James A. Levernier notes the peculiar literary destiny of the young slave woman who authored ***Poems on Various Subjects, Religious and Moral***: "in contrast to most major American writers, scholarship on Phillis Wheatley has tended to emphasize less what she accomplished than what she might have accomplished" (21). For example, Merle A. Richmond's assessment of the effect of slavery upon Wheatley's literary sensibility would seem to grow out of this "might have" tradition: "What emerges most starkly from her poetry is the near surgical, lobotomy-like excision of a human personality with warmth and blood and the self-assertiveness that is grounded in an awareness of one's self and the relationship of this self to contemporary society" (65). However, as Levernier notes, a number of scholars have since come to understand the impressive achievement Wheatley's poetry actually represents, and in the work of "William

H. Robinson, Jr., John C. Shields, Mukhtar Ali Isani, and Sondra O'Neale, among others" (21), we can trace a greater appreciation of the intricacies and implications of Wheatley's poetic practice.

As study of Wheatley's work has continued, critics have come to recognize the significance of Wheatley's discursive strategies, particularly as deployed within her cultural context, as key to understanding her literary contribution. Russell J. Reising sees Wheatley employing an intricate rhetorical negotiation that rendered her verse "virtually unreadable for a public with certain racial, political, theological, and cultural assumptions" and at the same time "eminently readable . . . within the discursive practices of her culture" (259). For Reising this seemingly contradictory discursive strategy is central to Wheatley's work: "What is crucial is that we cease processing her rhetoric as transparent and selfevident and that we begin to read her rhetoric as rhetoric—strategic, subtle, and veiled" (258). Similarly, Betsy Erkkila argues for Wheatley's powerful "challenge" to the "constituted authority" of her time, and she points to the transformative and frankly political impact of Wheatley's poetry: ". . . Wheatley transformed the revolutionary discourse on liberty, natural rights, and human nature into a subtle critique of the color code and the oppressive racial structures of republican America" (201). As both Reising and Erkkila show, Wheatley's poetry suggests anything but a lack, surgical or otherwise; instead, Wheatley's poetry manifests itself as a powerful public presence.

However, no study has yet discussed the mechanism by which the public authorial persona we know as Phillis Wheatley came into existence, or the literary, historical, and political means through which Wheatley's poetry called the racial assumptions of the dominant culture into question. The purpose of this essay is to provide a theoretical and historical construct within which Wheatley's poetry, especially ***Poems on Various Subjects, Religious and Moral,*** can be seen for the radical and incisive act it was. Wheatley's book represents her conspicuous participation in the "public sphere"—the eighteenth-century network of rational discourse whose formation and operation aimed at the acquisition of political power through the control of an emerging public opinion. The transformation symbolized in the movement from "uncivilized Barbarian" to "Poetical Genius" represents Wheatley's creation of a public presence and her participation within the eighteenth-century discursive network of the public sphere. Seen within this context, Wheatley's book becomes the manifestation of her power to call into question the conceptual assumptions that both formed the foundation of the public sphere and justified the American/European enslavement of Africans.

The London publication of ***Poems on Various Subjects, Religious and Moral*** in September 1773 was a significant literary event for several reasons. First, as Julian Mason has pointed out, the book was "probably the first book—and certainly the first book of poetry—published by a black American" (13). This accomplishment in itself would seem to make Wheatley's book noteworthy. However, simply being first barely begins to point to the true import of ***Poems on Various Subjects.***

For example, the conditions of the book's composition and subsequent publication are as significant as the historical timing of the publication itself. As Sondra O'Neale argues in "A Slave's Subtle War," any understanding of Wheatley's poetry must begin with the condition of her slavery: "Wheatley was one of only three Americans who were able to publish poetry and prose while still in bondage. (The other two were Jupiter Hammon [1711-1797] and George Moses Horton [1797-1883].)" (144). For a slave, the very act of publishing was, in O'Neale's words, "a monumental task" (144). The fact that only two others accomplished the task in itself suggests the achievement that Wheatley's poetry, and especially ***Poems on Various Subjects,*** represents. As O'Neale additionally notes, to "speak out against one's owners or the society which either condoned or ignored the owners' action" necessitated great risk and required guile and courage. Yet in spite of the significance of Wheatley's enslavement, very few critics have made Wheatley's publication out of slavery central to their readings of her work and the work's literary place (O'Neale 144).

The most important aspect of the publication of Wheatley's book involves the public presence the work creates. Nowhere is this presence more evident than in the portrait of Wheatley printed opposite the title page of the first edition of ***Poems.***[1] Rendered by Scipio Moorhead, a black artist and slave (Robinson, Phillis Wheatley 31), the engraving shows Wheatley seated at a table, left hand on her chin, looking into the distance, obviously lost in poetic contemplation. In her right hand she holds a quill pen poised above a page of paper on which she has already written two lines. A book rests just to the right of the paper. An inscription is printed around the oval border of the portrait: "Phillis Wheatley Negro Servant to

Mr. John Wheatley, of Boston." Two lines detailing publishing information are printed below the portrait; below them is Wheatley's signature.

The significance of the book's frontpiece has been noted by several critics. Betsy Erkkila refers to this portrait as the emblem of "Wheatley's complex position as a black woman slave in revolutionary America":

> Within the discourse of racial inequality in the eighteenth century, the fact of a black woman reading, writing, and publishing was in itself enough to splinter the categories of white and black, and explode a social order grounded in notions of racial difference.
>
> (202)

Erkkila emphasizes the "potential danger" this emblematic portrait embodies: the portrait is "enchain[ed]" by an inscription of slavery (202). David Grimsted has called the portrait "an icon of the dignified, respectable, literary, and especially thoughtful black" (396). The poet's printed visage, according to Grimsted, "is a quiet refutation, like most of the poems, of the tacit prejudice that a few men . . . were soon to make explicit in the justification of slavery: that blacks were incapable of being fully intelligent and respectable human beings" (396-97).

Therefore, in Wheatley's portrait the inherent power of her public poetic enterprise becomes evident. For here on the printed page in public view, the reader is confronted with a palpable presence—a face, a signature, an act. The picture portrays a black woman, a slave, engaged in literary work rather than menial labor—within a public context. And this portrait constitutes the graphic representation of Wheatley's public presence and the power it produces. In short, the portrait is the emblem of the book as a whole and is the public manifestation of her participation in the discursive sphere itself.

To discern the importance of Wheatley's public presence and the cultural opposition her book represented, we need to look more closely at what Erkkila calls "the discourse of racial inequality in the eighteenth century" (202). And we further need to recognize that the debate concerning race took place within a larger discursive structure. In particular, Terry Eagleton's discussion of Habermas's formulation of the eighteenth-century phenomenon known as the "public sphere" offers a useful theoretical and historical construct to describe the public context in which Wheatley's public presence made itself felt.

In *The Function of Criticism,* Eagleton defines the public sphere as "a distinct discursive space, one of rational judgement and enlightened critique . . . poised between the state and civil society." Comprised of clubs, coffee houses, and literary publications, the public sphere, according to Eagleton, presented an opportunity for individuals to engage in a "free, equal interchange of reasonable discourse." Formed in a complex historical process that produced an emergent middle class and a declining monarchy and aristocracy, the effect of this discourse network was to create a "polite, informal public opinion"—a consensus which "pit[ted] itself against the arbitrary diktats of autocracy . . . and weld[ed itself] into a relatively cohesive body whose deliberations . . . assume[d] the form of a powerful political force" (9). The result of "this ceaseless circulation of polite discourse among rational subjects" was, as Eagleton argues, "the cementing of a new power bloc at the level of the sign" (14). Wheatley's book appeared within this political and cultural discursive context.

A number of aspects of the public sphere are important to our discussion of Wheatley's work. First, this discursive network was public—open, available—and intensely political. Through her book, Wheatley gained access to this public network and the political power it made available. As has been noted, few slaves, if any, had access to this power.

Second, the public sphere was, as Eagleton argues, consensual in nature.

> Within the translucent space of the public sphere it is supposedly no longer social power, privilege and tradition which confer upon the individual the title to speak and judge, but the degree to which they are constituted as discoursing subjects by sharing in a consensus of universal reason.
>
> (9-10)

The ability to engage in reasonable discourse, as judged by the "normative regulations" applied by critics (Eagleton 15), became the primary criterion for admittance to the public sphere. Through the publication of her book and her ability to negotiate the requirements of "reasonable" discourse in her poetry, Wheatley participated in this politically and culturally powerful arena. Seen within this context, Wheatley's apparently conventional verse appears less an aesthetic and ethnic "treason" than as a deliberate strategy to power.

The third and final characteristic of the public sphere concerns the socio-economic underpinning of its reasonable and consensual character. What is assumed or inherent in the dynamic of the public sphere is the propertied basis for this reasonable discourse. According to Eagleton, the public sphere assumed that only those with property—in other words, those with an "interest" in the social and economic constitution—were capable of engaging in the public discourse. Property, therefore, created the "interest"—the part, the stake, the share in the public constitution that in turn bred the "reason" and "common sense" and "disinterest" that made discursive participation possible (Eagleton 15-16). Owning property and having an "interested disinterest" made possible the sitting, reading, writing, and thinking that comprised the discursive production and consumption of the public sphere. Within this complex network of reason, property, class, and power, Wheatley's public presence made its inherent critical demand felt.

The British publication of a major artistic work such as Wheatley's ***Poems on Various Subjects*** threatened the assumptions of the public sphere at a number of points. In "Phillis Wheatley and the 'Nature of the Negro,'" Henry Louis Gates indicates one area in which Wheatley's public presence affected the dominant culture's aesthetic and racial assumptions. According to Gates, the presence of Wheatley's poetry served to complicate the Enlightenment debate of human nature and human rights.[2] In particular, her poetry influenced discussion of the "humanity" of slaves and the role of their writing within logocentric EuroAmerican culture. Within the debate, Wheatley was often presented as "a living refutation of the charge of innate Negro inferiority" (68), and her poetry thereby called into question "commonly repeated assumptions about the nature of the Negro" (72). For a cultural context in which the deployment of language, "reasonable" discourse, was paramount, Wheatley's book presented itself as a significant challenge to the assumption of African inferiority based on a supposed lack of artistic and rhetorical ability and the pro-slavery position such assumptions upheld.

The impact Wheatley's poetry had upon the human rights debate is evident from the comments of two American participants in the debate. First, Benjamin Rush, physician and anti-slavery activist, cites Wheatley as evidence of African "humanity" in a footnote to *An Address to the Inhabitants of the British Settlements in America Upon Slave Keeping* (Philadelphia, 1773):

> There is now in the town of Boston a Free Negro Girl, about 18 years of age, who has been but 9 years in the country, whose singular genius and accomplishments are such as not only do honor to her sex, but to human nature. Several of her poems have been printed, and read with pleasure by the public.
>
> (qtd. in Gates 68; Robinson, *Critical Essays* 24; Erkkila 202)

Wheatley's impact on the human rights debate is obvious here: her public presence stands as a powerfully concrete example of the slave's inherent "humanity." One need only reasonably refer to the public text—Wheatley's public presence—for refutation of any number of pro-slavery arguments based on African cultural and intellectual inferiority.

The power of Wheatley's presence becomes even more evident in an attack penned by Thomas Jefferson in *Notes on the State of Virginia* (London, 1787), years after her death:

> Misery is often the parent of the most affecting touches in poetry. Among blacks is misery enough, God knows, but no poetry. . . . Religion, indeed, has produced Phillis Whately [sic]; but it could not produce a poet. The compositions published under her name are below the dignity of criticism. The heroes of the Dunciad are to her, as Hercules to the author of that poem. . . .
>
> (qtd. in Robinson, *Critical Essays* 42-3; Gates 5-6)

Jefferson's need to debase Wheatley's presence is evident throughout this excerpt. Since his library contained a copy of ***Poems on Various Subjects*** (Robinson, *Critical Essays* 43n), we might be tempted to assume that he deliberately misspelled her name in a childish attempt at denigration, but there is no proof for this interpretation. However, the charge that Wheatley was a product of "Religion" was particularly condemning coming from Jefferson the rationalist, since it implied a lack of reason and suggested the influence of superstition. Further, Jefferson specifically called into question Wheatley's authorship of the book "published under her name" and thereby anticipated a charge often to be leveled against nineteenth-century slave narratives by pro-slavery commentators. However, the fact that Wheatley elicited such a vehement attack from Jefferson almost fifteen years after her last major publication and three years after her death testifies to the strong public presence she exerted within the discourse of the time.[3] Specifically, Jefferson's attack suggests how strong an argument against African enslavement her presence represented, since as Erkkila notes, "he singles out her work for criticism" (210). However, in the years following her death, as Jefferson was writing his critique,

Wheatley had no "presence" except that as constituted by the public sphere and her discursive participation.

To these interconnected issues of reason, language, and slavery are related the propertied assumptions of the public sphere's discourse. For not only did Wheatley's public presence call into question the public sphere's assumptions about reason and a "common sense," it also stood as a discursive challenge to the assumptions of "interest" inherent in the discourse itself. When Thomas Hutchinson, John Hancock, John Wheatley, and their colleagues attested to Wheatley's authorship of ***Poems on Various Subjects,*** they were doing more than testifying to her genius. Inadvertently, they themselves were calling into question the propertied assumptions of a "reasonable" discourse. For if the ownership of property was prior to the interest necessary to participate in the public sphere, Wheatley's participation as property directly contradicted this assumption. If a person who owned not even an "interest" in herself could produce a competent literary creation and have it favorably received by the public, then the propertied basis for reasonable discourse was itself questionable, if not invalid. As we shall see, when ***Poems on Various Subjects, Religious and Moral*** appeared, the British critics approved.

In "The British Reception of Wheatley's *Poems on Various Subjects,"* Mukhtar Ali Isani details the reviews Wheatley's book received. In the four months following the publication of ***Poems on Various Subjects,*** notes Isani, "nine British periodicals reviewed the work, usually contributing space in generous amounts. . . . All [the] reviews were favorable" (145). Most of the reviews included a representative poem, and in a few cases more than one. In particular, two features of this critical reception are important to our discussion of Wheatley's presence and participation in the public sphere.

The first feature of Wheatley's critical reception is the right of participation a favorable judgement entailed. Eagleton observes that the role of the critic in the public sphere was that of cultural arbiter. In the view of the public sphere, "the truly free market is that of cultural discourse itself, within of course, certain normative regulations; the role of the critic is to administer those norms, in a double refusal of absolutism and anarchy" (15). This administration of the public sphere's norms is important because of the character of discourse within the sphere:

> What is said derives its legitimacy neither from itself as message nor from the social [or racial] character of the utterer, but from its conformity as a statement within a certain paradigm of reason. . . . One's title as speaker is derived from the formal character of one's discourse rather than the authority of that discourse derived from one's title. Discursive identities are not pre-given, but constructed by the very act of participation in polite conversation . . . for what counts as rationality is precisely the capacity to articulate within its constraints; the rational are those capable of a certain mode of discourse. . . .
>
> (15)

The critic, therefore, administered this judgement of capacity, and the positive response of the British critics to Wheatley's book indicated her successful negotiation of the forms of discourse and her participation in the power such discourse conferred.

The second feature of Wheatley's critical reception addresses the nature of the power her public presence created. Consider the following portion of a review printed in both *Gentleman's Magazine* and *Scots Magazine* (both September 1773):

> A testimony in favor of the poems as genuine productions of this young person, is signed by the Governor, the Lieutenant Governor, seven clergymen, and others eminent for station and literature, and also by her master: and in this it is said, disgraceful as it may be to all that have signed it, that "this poor girl was brought an uncultivated barbarian from Africa, and has ever since been, and now is—A SLAVE!"
>
> (qtd. in Isani 146 and 148; emphasis in original review)

The power available to Wheatley to bring into discussion both the reality of her own bondage, and by implication the reality of all in bondage, is clearly evident here. The testimony of authenticity, made necessary by the very nature of her enslaved condition, served to bring to the fore the actuality of her slavery and the moral issues her enslaved condition assumed. The foregrounding of this condition additionally brought into play questions concerning interest and the nature of property and its connection with reason and humanity. Here in this one review we can see the public presence of Phillis Wheatley in operation: the critic, artist, "master," slave, property, and literary form were joined in a complex and destabilizing network of discourse. All assumed relations and assumptions were brought into question. Until this time, no black American, slave or free, had been able to exert this kind of pressure.

Phillis Wheatley returned to Boston on 16 September 1773, her trip to England cut short by the illness of Susanna Wheatley, so the poet was not in London when her book, her public presence, emerged from the press of Archibald Bell. But her return was not without its moment of recognition. Four days after she disembarked in Boston, the 20 September 1773 number of the *Boston Gazette* noted her return: "In Capt. Calef came Passengers, Capt. Hillhouse and Lady, Mr. Alleing; also Phillis Wheatley, the extraordinary Poetical Genius, Negro Servant to Mr. John Wheatley" ("Boston" 2). There was some irony in this reception. After all, the citizens of Boston had the year before declined subscription to the very volume of poetry that was eliciting favorable British reviews at the time its author was setting foot on the Boston dock.

Beyond a brief moment of recognition, Wheatley's seemingly inconsequential mention in the *Gazette* serves to remind us of the intense political activity of the times in general and the public sphere in particular, especially as this activity was embodied in this particular newspaper. Frank Luther Mott characterizes the *Boston Gazette* as "one of the most Patriotic newspapers of the Revolution" (15). Royal Governor Bernard gave the paper a similar review—though from a different angle when in 1770 he called the *Gazette* "an infamous weekly paper which has swarmed with Libells of the most atrocious kind." Unfortunately for British interests, as the governor further complained, "seven eighths of the people read none but this infamous paper," (qtd. in Mott 75). The writers for the *Gazette* were drawn primarily from the membership of the Caucus Club: "a small and purposely obscure organization designed to control political action" (Mott 76). Additionally, the club claimed some of the most important political figures of the Massachusetts struggle against Great Britain: John and Samuel Adams, Samuel Cooper, Thomas Cushing, John Hancock, James Otis, Josiah Quincy, and Joseph Warren (Mott 76). At least two members of the club—Cooper and Hancock—signed the authenticating preface to Wheatley's book.

Edited by Boston printers Benjamin Edes and John Gill, the *Boston Gazette* was an important focus for political action against the crown. Edes later wrote that the leaders of the Boston resistance "constantly assembled within the confines of the *Gazette* office" (qtd. in Mott 76). John Adams described the political activity centering around the newspaper in his diary entry for Sunday, 3 September 1769: "The evening spent in preparing for the next day's newspaper,—a curious employment, cooking up paragraphs, articles, occurrences, etc., working the political engine!" (Adams 2:229). However, the *Gazette*'s role in the struggle for American independence went beyond cooking up the odd article or paragraph. Mott notes that according to tradition the members of the Boston Tea Party dressed for the occasion in the newspaper's offices (76). Writing and politics were joined in the *Gazette* offices.

The *Boston Gazette* provides a concrete example of the public sphere in operation. As Adams notes, the paper's purpose was frankly political and directed toward controlling public opinion. Within this context, rhetoric and writing went beyond simple personal expression. And the seemingly casual mention of Wheatley suggests just how close she was to this intense political activity. Boston was a small town. Wheatley knew many of the prominent political and religious figures, and they knew her. Not only had patriot, preacher, educator, and Caucus Club member Samuel Cooper attested to Wheatley's poetic abilities, he had baptized the poet in 1771 (Mason 10). The *Gazette* notice of Wheatley's return suggests that her public presence was very much a political presence.

However, the most significant consequence of Wheatley's public sphere participation—her public presence—is to be found on the front page of the same number of the *Boston Gazette* that announced her return from England:

> TO BE SOLD
>
> A very likely Molatto Boy, about 7 or 8 Years of Age, is very active, and can be well recommended for his many Qualities; he speaks good French, etc.
>
> Inquire of Edes and Gill.
>
> ("To Be Sold" 1)

History does not tell us the name of the linguistically talented young man offered for sale through the good offices of the *Gazette*'s publishers. His presence is confined to this brief mention. Yet the *Gazette*'s pages are filled with similar offerings: the concrete records of the colonial trade in human beings. Interwoven with these notices and the articles calling for American liberty and freedom is the public presence of a young black woman who thought and wrote, and whose very presence called the trade into question.

Notes

1. A facsimile reprint of the 1773 edition of *Poems on Various Subjects, Religious and Moral* appears in William Robinson, *Phillis Wheatley and Her Writing,* 141-275, with the portrait reprinted on page 142. Robinson briefly discusses the transformations Wheatley's picto-

rial representation has undergone on pages 78-81. Erkkila also reproduces the portrait on page 203 of her essay.

2. Gates is not alone in recognizing Wheatley's effect upon the human rights discussion. Erkkila discusses the debate (201-10), and David Grimsted offers a detailed analysis of it (394-436).

3. In fact, as Grimsted notes, Wheatley's presence served as such a potent refutation that subsequent pro-slavery advocates who adopted Jefferson's inferiority argument nevertheless ignored Wheatley as an example: "It was hard to read her poetry and conclude the mental incompetence or notable inferiority of blacks. It was impossible even to look at the frontpiece and complacently to tie human 'dignity and beauty' to racist denigration. She was obviously thinking, not asleep" (434).

Works Cited

Adams, John. *The Works of John Adams.* Ed. Charles Francis Adams. 1850-56. 10 vols. Freeport, NY: Books for Libraries P, 1969.

"Boston." *Boston Gazette and Country Journal.* 20 September 1773: 2.

Eagleton, Terry. *The Function of Criticism: From The Spectator to Post-Structuralism.* London: Verso, 1984.

Erkkila, Betsy. "Revolutionary Women." *Tulsa Studies in Women's Literature* 6 (1987): 189-223.

Gates, Henry Louis. "Phillis Wheatley and the 'Nature of the Negro.'" *Figures in Black: Words, Signs, and the "Racial" Self.* New York: Oxford U P, 1989. 215-33.

Grimsted, David. "Anglo-American Racism and Phillis Wheatley's 'Sable Veil,' 'Length'ned Chain,' and 'Knitted Heart.'" *Women in the Age of the American Revolution.* Ed. Ronald Hoffman and Peter J. Albert. Charlottesville, VA: U P of Virginia, 1989. 338-444.

Isani, Mukhtar Ali. "The British Reception of Wheatley's Poems on Various Subjects." *Journal of Negro History* 66 (1981): 144-49.

Levernier, James A. "Phillis Wheatley and the New England Clergy." *Early American Literature* 26 (1991): 21-38.

Mason, Julian D., Jr. Introduction. Wheatley 1-22.

Mott, Frank Luther. *American Journalism: A History, 1690-1960.* 3rd ed. New York: Macmillan, 1962.

O'Neale, Sondra. "A Slave's Subtle War: Phillis Wheatley's Use of Biblical Myth and Symbol." *Early American Literature* 21 (1986): 144-65.

Reising, Russell J. "Trafficking in White: Phillis Wheatley's Semiotics of Racial Representation." *Genre* 22 (1989): 231-61.

Richmond, Merle A. *Bid the Vassal Soar.* Washington, DC: Howard U P, 1974.

Robinson, William H., ed. *Critical Essays on Phillis Wheatley.* Boston: G.K. Hall, 1982.

———. *Phillis Wheatley and Her Writings.* New York: Garland, 1984.

"To Be Sold." *Boston Gazette and Country Journal.* 20 September 1773: 1.

Wheatley, Phillis. *The Poems of Phillis Wheatley.* Ed. Julian D. Mason, Jr. Rev. and enl. ed. Chapel Hill: U of North Carolina P, 1989.

TITLE COMMENTARY

Poems on Various Subjects, Religious and Moral

KATHERINE CLAY BASSARD (ESSAY DATE 1999)

SOURCE: Bassard, Katherine Clay. "Diaspora Subjectivity and Transatlantic Crossings: Phillis Wheatley's Poetics of Recovery." In *Spiritual Interrogations: Culture, Gender, and Community in Early African American Women's Writing,* pp. 28-57. Princeton: Princeton University Press, 1999.

In the following excerpt, Bassard focuses on Wheatley's "On Being Brought From Africa to America" as an instance of Wheatley's African American poetics.

Diaspora Subjectivity

In *Between Slavery and Freedom,* Bill E. Lawson writes of the "functional lexical gap" evidenced by the lack of an appropriate collective nomenclature for descendants of Africans enslaved in the Americas. Noting that "the language we use to frame a group's political and social status can have an impact on the public policy regarding that group," Lawson concludes that "our moral/political vocabulary is morally unsatisfactory and inadequate for characterizing the plight of present-day black Americans" (McGary and Lawson 72). Lawson's important observation about collective designation has its beginnings in the ritual misnamings of African peoples that characterized the transatlantic slave trade. Further, this "conceptual" and "lexical" gap (77) has had a direct impact on the perception and reception of Phillis Wheatley as an enslaved African woman and a poet. As June Jordan posed it in "The Difficult Miracle," "How could there be black poets in America? It was not natural and she was the first" (23).

While Jordan's appeal to "nature" might be off-putting to those concerned with de-essentializing "race," her question expresses the problematic of African American authorship as it is based on a subjectivity of displacement. Part of the difficulty arises from the discourse of American Africanism, which Morrison links to the beginnings of an "American" national identity: "the formation of the nation necessitated coded language and purposeful restriction to deal with the racial disingenuousness and moral frailty at its heart" (6). It is thus that terms like "black," "poet," and "America" become coded and conceptually shackled as part of a discourse which seeks to jettison "black" from the equation. Henry Louis Gates, Jr., has demonstrated how Wheatley's poetry became embroiled in prevailing discourses of black intellectual inferiority. He and others have discussed the presence of the "authenticating documents" at the beginning of ***Poems on Various Subjects Religious and Moral,*** including the frontispiece portrait of Wheatley by Scipio Moorhead, as evidence of the discourse of racial inferiority. What remains to be examined is the matrix of gender and culture in which this discourse of race and racialization occurs.

Questions of social, cultural, and racial positionality and origins have plagued the discourse surrounding Phillis Wheatley almost from the initial publication of ***Poems on Various Subjects Religious and Moral*** in 1773, an event that assured Wheatley, as the first African and only the second woman in America to publish a book of poems, a lasting place in American and African American literary history. Wheatley's "originary" position, however, has often attracted more critical commentary than her poetry. M. A. Richmond's conclusion, "it is the tragedy rather than the poetry of Phillis Wheatley that has the more enduring relevance for American life" (66), is exemplary of the type of dismissal Wheatley's work has suffered. While more recent critics have taken a variety of historical, anthropological, and discursive approaches to Wheatley's work, the emphasis remains on her "tragic" life rather than the poems themselves. June Jordan and Alice Walker, offering a black feminist corrective to the customary elision of Wheatley's gender, have revisioned Wheatley's life not as "tragedy" but as "miracle," yet the focus of their analyses is on her originary or "foremother" status rather than her poetry.[1]

The confusion over the cultural, racial, and social trajectories of identity and discourse becomes complicated even further by the problem of psychical processes and poetic production, memory and poetic utterance. Such a knot of discourses appears in the very first biography of Phillis Wheatley, published in 1834, a half-century after the poet's death, by Margaretta Matilda Odell, a self-styled "collateral descendant" of the Wheatleys.[2] The text appeared anonymously under the title *Memoir and Poems of Phillis Wheatley. A Native African and a Slave,* a title that creates the expectation of a relationship between life and work, identity and language, that the anecdotal, gap-ridden biographical narrative continually frustrates. Odell's central "thesis" is that Wheatley's "literary efforts were altogether the natural workings of her own mind" (18), a gesture of "authentication" that situates the African woman writer in America within discourses of black and female intellectual inferiority.[3] The *Memoir* inscribes, ultimately, one writer's memory of another writer's memories, as a significant portion of the text is devoted to a quasi-scientific explanation of what Odell supposes to be a defect of Wheatley's mind:

> [Phillis] does not seem to have preserved any remembrance of the place of her nativity, or of her parents, excepting the simple circumstance that her mother *poured out water before the sun at his rising*—in reference, no doubt, to an ancient African custom. The memories of most children reach back to a much earlier period than their seventh year; but there are some circumstances . . . which would induce us to suppose, that in the case of Phillis, this faculty did not equal the other powers of her mind.
>
> (12-13)

I will return to the issue of Odell's misreading of what are probably ritual libations for the ancestors as some form of "ancient" sun worship. My concern here is with the assumption that Wheatley's ability to learn English and Latin, to master literature, the Bible, geography, and astronomy well enough in nine short years to publish a book-length volume of poetry displaced a "normal" capacity for early childhood memories.[4] Odell's memory of Wheatley's lack of (certain) memories constructs the notion of a "life" that the title (*Memoir*) promises, even as the subtitle, *A Native African and a Slave* portrays Wheatley as a "Native African" with virtually no remembrance of Africa, a "Slave" whose very poems are used to underscore the fact of this erasure.

While many of the "facts" of Odell's *Memoir* have subsequently been proven false, the portrait of Wheatley's near-amnesia about her African past has since become cliché, used by scholars to prove everything from the wretchedness of enslavement to the much-held view of the total "whitewashing" of Wheatley resulting, the theory goes, in a body of poetry with no racial consciousness. The image remains of a Phillis Wheatley completely passive and powerless, if not oblivious, to the forces around her, rather than a young black woman with a "standpoint"[5] on her own oppression.

Morrison's analysis in *Playing in the Dark* helps put to rest the notion of a "raceless" Phillis Wheatley when she notes that "for both black and white writers, in a wholly racialized society, there is no escape from racially inflected language, and the work writers do to unhobble the imagination from the demands of that language is complicated, interesting, and definitive" (12-13). Here the debate becomes not whether Wheatley was African/black enough in her poems but what kind of Africanity (what theories of blackness) her work enacts and enables. And for me the answer is similar to Morrison's own description of her Africanist Americanist work: "The kind of work I have always wanted to do requires me to learn how to maneuver ways to free up the language from its sometimes sinister, frequently lazy, almost always predictable employment of racially informed and determined chains" (xi).

THE LANGUAGE OF SURVIVORSHIP

The slippage in the Wheatley discourse blurring the binaries memory/psyche, slave/social position, African/cultural evidences a crisis around the word "race" that deconstruction and de-essentialization have failed adequately to address. If, in the eighteenth century, the concept of race resulted from what Ali Mazrui calls "the dis-Africanisation of the diaspora,"[6] then the racialization of African peoples involved not only a dis-Africanizing but an un-Americanizing as well,[7] all of which bears directly on Wheatley's situation in Boston on the eve of the American Revolution. That Wheatley consistently refers to herself as "Afric[an]" or "Ethiop[ian]" in her poetry rather than "slave," "black," or, indeed "American" represents an act of self-naming that transgresses the racialized boundaries which sought to constrict African American subjectivity.[8] Thus Wheatley's self-designations keep ever in view "the crucial marker of difference in a US Real—the vital sign of 'Africanity'" (Spillers, "Who Cuts the Border?" 11).

Second, while Sondra O'Neale urges in "A Slave's Subtle Civil War" that "any evaluation of Phillis Wheatley must consider her status as a slave" (14), I propose to go beyond the nominative "slave," which denotes a racialized status or condition based on the notion of inherent (and inheritable) African inferiority, to refigure Wheatley as a Middle Passage survivor.[9] The weeks-to-months-long voyage across the Atlantic from the West African coast, often to the West Indies, and finally to North America, inscribes the condition of diaspora subjectivity as geocultural displacement. In the European-American scheme of things, Africans were positioned in a no-win situation (individually and collectively) between enslavement and death. Thus the survival of African peoples who crossed on the Middle Passage, a survival mandated by the enslavers, became not an "event" to be celebrated but, in the dialectic imposed by this discourse, yet another mark of African inferiority and thus "proof" of their enslavability. In the Iberian colonies, early attempts to enslave indigenous peoples had failed owing to harsh labor demands and lack of immunity to European diseases. The transfer of their labor functions to imported and enslaved Africans led to European beliefs that "the work output of one African was equal to four to eight Indians" (Reynolds 60).

The belief that Africans were physically and thus genetically fit for slavery recast their physical survival of the harsh conditions of the Middle Passage as a sign of mental, moral, and cultural weakness and docility. Indeed, their physical survival was mandated by the captors, as the captives were regularly forced to eat, exercise, and so forth. The only sign of "honor" recognized by the Europeans, suicide, meant self-annihilation. An English traveler in 1746 wrote of an African-born slave: "If he must be broke, either from Obstinacy, or, which I am more apt to suppose, from *Greatness of Soul,* will require . . . hard Discipline . . . you would really be surprized at their Perseverance; . . . they oft die before they can be conquer'd" (qtd. in Blassingame 12). Companies that insured slavers against accident and mishap counted as "natural death" disease and "also when the captive destroys himself through despair, which often happens" (qtd. in Reynolds 50).

A language of African survivorship calls to mind the survival of Africanity and African structures within New World spaces.[10] As Ngugi Wa Thiong'o writes, "you can destroy a people's culture completely only by destroying a people themselves" (45). Survivorship also signals generational survival, as one is survived by one's descendants. The issue of ancestors and remembrance will become crucial to an understanding of Wheatley's embracing of the elegiac genre. Finally, it points to the survival of black texts despite centuries of neglect and hostility. This is especially important in Wheatley studies, as drafts and variants of her poetry are still being recovered.[11] Connotations of survivorship—black bodies, African cultures, and black texts—converge in the figure and poetics of Phillis Wheatley.

Wheatley appears on the auction block in Boston in 1761 at a kind of crisis point of the transatlantic slave trade. Not only does her lifespan (1752?-84) encompass the peak years of the trade, but her presence in New England serves as a reminder that in the eighteenth century, the New England colonies were "the greatest slave-trading section of America" (Greene 24). As Philip D. Curtin's seminal study *The Atlantic Slave Trade: A Census* shows, an estimated 9,566,100 Africans landed in the Americas between 1502 and the mid-nineteenth century, 399,000 of them in British mainland North America. Moreover, the trade peaked in the eighteenth century (1741-1810) with 80 percent landed in the century and a half between 1701 and 1850. As sensational as these numbers appear, "the cost of the slave trade in human life was many times the number of slaves landed in America" (Curtin 275).[12]

In "Mama's Baby, Papa's Maybe" Hortense Spillers meditates on the instability of African categories of identity in "the socio-political order of the New World": "That order, with its human sequence written in blood, *represents* for its African and indigenous peoples a scene of *actual* mutilation, dismemberment, and exile. First of all, their New World, diasporic plight marked a *theft of the body*—a willful and violent (and unimaginable from this distance) severing of the captive body from its motive will, its active desire" (67). The horror of this description of bodily theft is only magnified when we consider the African Sacred Cosmos, whose worldview theorizes subjectivity in terms of not individual and nuclear family units but extended family, community, and land/environment.[13] Theologian Dwight Hopkins describes this "theological anthropology" as follows: "To be human meant to stand in connection with the larger community of the invisible ancestors and God and, of course, the visible community and family" (18). Thus with her transportation to America, Wheatley's very (black female) body marks her as a truncated part of a whole community and kin network. While the specifics of that community are unrecoverable, what we do recover is her own critical and interpretive displacements in which Wheatley writes/rewrites the Middle Passage in her poems.

Writing the Middle Passage

THE LANGUAGE OF DISPLACEMENT

The Middle Passage as the scene of psychic and communal fracture reinscribes black women's subjectivity at the metalevel of the utterance, as diaspora subjectivity authorizes a "claiming residence" in language (Holloway 63), a "making [one's] self at home" within the space of the text (June Jordan 26). Dispossessed as black women writers are of memory, culture, and history, their "possession of the *word*" is, fundamentally, "a cultural and gendered legacy" (Holloway 27). Thus we can reread Wheatley's memory of her mother's morning libations as a "(cultural) mooring" that initiates a series of African American female "(spiritual) metaphors" (Holloway 1). Moreover, insofar as this is a religious memory, Wheatley's own religiosity—enacted in her conversion to Christianity—repeats, however unconsciously, her mother's spiritual ritual, inadvertently, perhaps, laying claim to a legacy at once African and female. True to the displacements signaled by diaspora subjectivity, Wheatley's poetics of recovery will lead us simultaneously backward, to the African community from which she was prematurely severed, and forward, to the community of black women writers prefigured by her correspondence with Obour Tanner, a fellow female slave, one of the few black women of her era as Christian and as literate as she.[14] It is through this poetics of recovery that Wheatley challenges and revises the American Africanist notions inhering in the colonial discourse which surrounds her. Far from "assimilating" this discourse,[15] Wheatley both perceives its ideological form and configuration within the domain of sociopolitical relations of power and challenges its premises by displaying its constructedness as ideology. In Morrison's phrasing, she sees the "fishbowl" within which the oceanic discourse of African enslavement is contained, and through her bold poetics, she invents a discursive strategy for breaking the glass.

Significantly, Holloway writes that "spiritual and psychic fracture" is represented textually by the black woman writer's manipulation of "alternative spaces" (117), a moving "between worlds" (114) that stages the displacement of the diaspora subject. No reading of the poetry of Phillis Wheatley would be complete that did not account for her most famous and oft-anthologized poem, **"On Being Brought From Africa to America."** In this poem, Wheatley establishes the parameters for her own self-naming and self-positioning as poet, African American woman, diaspora subject. I quote the poem in its entirety:

> 'Twas mercy brought me from my *Pagan* land,
> Taught my benighted soul to understand
> That there's a God, that there's a *Saviour* too:
> Once I redemption neither sought nor knew.
> Some view our sable race with scornful eye,
> "Their colour is a diabolic die."
> Remember, *Christians, Negroes,* black as *Cain,*
> May be refin'd and join th'angelic train.

A terse, eight-line poem in a single stanza, **"On Being Brought"** appears to be a seamless whole even as its surface-level meaning is presented as a rational and unified argument ("'Twas mercy brought me from my *Pagan* land"). However, line 4—"Once I redemption neither sought nor knew"—creates a rupture that structurally breaks the poem in two.

From this structural fracture, a poem emerges that is *about* spiritual and cultural fracturing. As June Jordan observes, the single word "once" suggests that "[o]nce I existed beyond and without these terms under consideration. *Once I existed on other than your terms*" (26). If the "once" brings to consciousness some primal memory, some originary moment and place, then its positioning at the end of the "conversion narrative" part of the poem represents a critical realignment of the terms of narrativity.[16] The narrative frame "on being brought *from* Africa *to* America" is temporally displaced as the first half of the poem ends, as it were, at the beginning.

The "once" signifies not only another time but another place, representing a realignment of space as well. In the context of this utterance, the realignment of the place of originary memory forms a hinge; it provides a transition to the second quatrain, which brings the poem from the individual and psychical to the social and cultural. In the second half of the poem, the autobiographical "I" becomes renegotiated in what Julia Kristeva calls "the metamorphoses of the 'we'" (220). That is, it "reproduces itself" (Henriques et al. 227) within a social/cultural matrix that multiplies the very terms of its subjectivity. The "I" of the first half of the poem joins communally with its socially copositioned others to become "our sable race" (line 5). Even more dizzying is Wheatley's appropriation of the "gaze" of the Other(s)[17] and the voicing of the Other's racializing discourse ("'Their colour is a diabolic die,'" line 6). What emerges from this new position (as "other" of an utterance represented within the frame of her own poem) is what Mae Henderson refers to as the distinguishing feature of black women's writing: "the privileging (rather than repressing) of 'the other in ourselves'" (19).

These critical shifts renegotiate space as (past, present, and future) community. Yet owing to the dictates of diaspora subjectivity, space/community is multiple rather than singular, as the "I" is inscribed within three interlocking communal structures. First, following from the "once" in line 4, the "I" is embedded within the ancestral space of "My *Pagan* land," complete with the possessive pronoun. This "cultural mooring" will become significant in the later discussion of this poem's critique of American Africanist ideology. Second, it is repositioned within "our sable race," constructed as a community of "others" via the white gaze that perceives black skin as "a diabolic die." Finally, the "I" is located once again with the bi(non)racial "angelic train" that ends the poem. This multiple communal structure effaces both present *time*—as the poem moves from the originary "once" to the eschatological "angelic train"—and present *space*: "America," the designated point of arrival in the poem's title, which is refigured as a mere way station along the poet's real journey from Africa to Heaven. Heaven as "alternative space" (Holloway) marks the very dispersal of the diaspora subject, as it is specifically not Africa and, more important in Wheatley's context, *not America.*

ARRIVAL/DEPARTURE

In order fully to appreciate the achievement of this poem's African Americanist theorizing, we must compare it to four lines from **"To the University of Cambridge in New-England."** Following a conventional two-line invocation to the Muses, Wheatley writes:

> 'Twas not long since I left my native shore
> The Land of errors and *Egyptian* gloom:
> Father of mercy, 'twas thy gracious hand
> Brought me in safety from those dark abodes.
> (Lines 3-6)

This passage establishes the context of **"On Being Brought,"** which revises—in the sense of "repetition and difference" (Gates, *Signifying Monkey* 64)—this passage from **"Cambridge"** in terms of their relative placements in the narrative line of ***Poems.*** The narrativity of the volume is especially important to the reading of the elegies. Of importance now is the fact that **"On Being Brought"** appears to be a revision of an earlier poem identified in Wheatley's book proposal of February 29, 1772, as "Thoughts on being brought from Africa to America" and scheduled to appear tenth in the originally proposed volume.[18] The version of **"Cambridge"** printed in the 1773 ***Poems*** also underwent substantial revision from an earlier draft subtitled "Wrote in 1767" (when Wheatley was just fourteen) whose variant is extant. Scheduled to be placed fourth in the original proposal, the poem that was finally printed must have been composed between April 1772 and August 6, 1773,[19] when ***Poems*** was printed in London. Owing to the recovery of manuscript drafts and other variants of Wheatley's poetry, we now have a sense of her revision practices.[20] Thus it is reasonable to assume that the poem listed in the proposal as "Thoughts on being brought from Africa to America" underwent revisions by the time it appeared in ***Poems*** as **"On Being Brought."**

What all this establishes is that Wheatley was a meticulous reviser of her own work. Not only do **"Cambridge"** and **"On Being Brought"** repre-

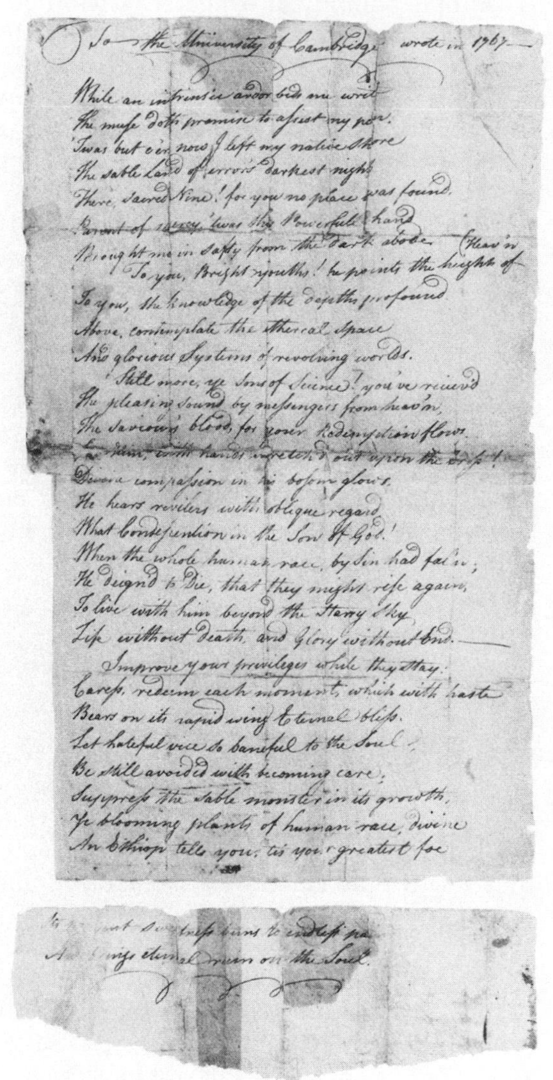
To the University of Cambridge wrote in 1767—

While an intrinsic ardor bids me write
The muse doth promise to assist my pen.
'Twas but e'en now I left my native Shore
The sable Land of error's darkest night
There, sacred Nine! for you no place was found.
Parent of mercy, 'twas thy Powerfull hand
Brought me in safty from the dark abode. (Heav'n
To you, Bright youths! he points the heights of
To you, the knowledge of the depths profound
Above, contemplate the ethereal Space
And glorious Systems of revolving worlds.
Still more, ye Sons of Science! you've receiv'd
The pleasing Sound by messengers from heav'n,
The saviour's blood, for your Redemption flows.
[illegible] him, with hands outstretch'd upon the [illegible]!
Divine compassion in his bosom glows.
He hears revilers with oblique regard
What Condescention in the Son of God!
When the whole human race, by Sin had fal'n;
He deign'd to Die, that they might rise again,
To live with him beyond the Starry Sky
Life without death, and Glory without End.—
Improve your privileges while they stay:
Caress, redeem each moment, which with haste
Bears on its rapid wing Eternal bliss.
Let hateful vice so baneful to the Soul,
Be still avoided with becoming care;
Suppress the sable monster in its growth,
Ye blooming plants of human race, divine
An Ethiop tells you, tis your greatest foe
[illegible] sweetness turns to endless pain
And brings eternal ruin on the Soul.

Autographed manuscript of the poem "To the University of Cambridge."

sent, in their final published forms, the development of Wheatley's thinking about her captivity and enslavement, the order in which they appear in ***Poems*** makes **"On Being Brought"** a "revision" of **"Cambridge"** within the context of the volume. To chart the development of Wheatley's thought on her own displacement to America, I will compare the 1767 variant of **"Cambridge"** to the 1773 version in ***Poems*** and demonstrate how the four lines about her transport from Africa were revised. Then I will return to the important relationship between them as they appear in ***Poems*** to construct a complete narrative of captivity, Middle Passage, and enslavement.

In the 1767 version, the relevant lines are:

> 'Twas but e'en now I left my native shore
> The sable Land of error's darkest night
> There, sacred Nine! for you no place was found.
> Parent of mercy, 'twas thy Powerful hand
> Brought me in safety from the dark abode.
>
> (Lines 3-7; Shields 196)

It is important to keep in mind that Wheatley was about fourteen when this poem was composed.[21] Shields claims that "Wheatley made few major alterations" between this version and the 1773 final version. I disagree. What appear to be "minor" revisions in the later version of **"Cambridge"** reveal a sharpening and development of Wheatley's thought on her experience of the Middle Passage.[22] The change from "'Twas but e'en now" to "'Twas not long since," for example, represents the advance of six years. The most obvious change is the omission of the line about the Muses, which appears as line 5 of the 1767 version. Indeed, it is an omission of a line about Africa's lack ("There, sacred Nine! for you no place was found"). It is chiefly through this line that Africa is cast in a negative light as lacking the inspiration for poetry. When the line is contrasted with the poem's first two lines, "While an intrinsic ardor bids me write / the muse doth promise to assist my pen,"[23] an important contradiction emerges that favors the poet's present location (in literate America) as the location for poetic expression and sensibility. Its omission in the 1773 poem suggests a change in Wheatley's visioning of Africa and her poetic heritage.

The next line of the 1767 **"Cambridge"** describes the poet's "native shore" as "the sable Land of error's darkest night." This line and the reference to the poet's gratefulness at being rescued from "the dark abode" have been taken to mean that Wheatley sees Africa as the stereotypical "dark continent" of American Africanism and thus to evince self-hatred and self-denial. Yet Wheatley here capitalizes "Land" and in describing it as "sable" is not necessarily invoking a discourse of inferiority. Wheatley's use of "sable" as an adjective for land and people ("our sable race") can be understood apart from American Africanist racialized proscriptions. It is only through the gaze of the White Other who racializes black peoples under the sign of inferiority ("'Their colour is a diabolic die'") that "sable race" is transformed into a socially constructed negativity. Recall Morrison: "Neither blackness nor 'people of color' stimulates in me notions of excessive, limitless love, anarchy, or routine dread" (x).

I am not arguing for the absence of a discourse of African inferiority in the 1767 **"Cambridge."** Indeed, such a discourse exists; it is not to be found, however, in the fact of "blackness," but in what Wheatley calls "error." In line 4 of the 1767 version, "error's" is a possessive. In the 1773 version, the entire line is rewritten as "the land of errors, and *Egyptian* gloom" (line 4). Addressed to Harvard divinity students, "**Cambridge**" is, after all, about sin and redemption. Wheatley exhorts the divinity students to "let sin . . . / By you be shunn'd" (lines 23-24). But what, exactly, is the sin she refers to and for which Africa, her "native shore," serves as a particular kind of "stage"?

I want to make an argument here that the "sin" is slavery, conceived of by Wheatley (because she probably experienced it as such) as a global system of captivity and forced labor.[24] I base this argument first on the rewriting of "The sable Land of error's darkest night" to "The land of errors, and *Egyptian* gloom." The vagueness of the first version's notion of "error's" is specified in the final version by the phrase "*Egyptian* gloom." That is, in the final version, Wheatley means to signal the reader as to exactly what she means by "the land of errors." Whatever the impetus behind the choice of the adjective "sable," Wheatley's substitution of "*Egyptian*" is probably a response to her growing awareness of the racialization of the society around her, a factor that would definitely affect her (white) readers' response.

This point can be glossed by a famous passage in Wheatley's letter to the Native American Reverend Samson Occom dated February 11, 1774:

> Reverend and Honoured Sir,
>
> I have this Day received your obliging kind Epistle, and am greatly satisfied with your Reasons respecting the Negroes, and think highly reasonable what you offer in Vindication of their natural Rights: those that invade them cannot be insensible that the divine light is chasing away the thick Darkness which broods over the Land of Africa; and the Chaos which has reigned so long, is converting into beautiful Order, and reveals more and more clearly, that glorious Dispensation of civil and religious Liberty, which are so inseparably united, that there is little or no enjoyment of one without the other: Otherwise, perhaps, the Israelites had been less solicitous for their Freedom from Egyptian slavery; I do not say they would have been contented without it by no Means, for in every human breast, God has implanted a Principle, which we call Love of Freedom; it is impatient of Oppression, and pants for Deliverance; and by Leave of our Modern Egyptians I will assert, that the same Principle lives in us.
>
> (Shields 176-77)

In keeping with colonial New England's relish for the epistolary genre, this letter was published in ten New England newspapers between March and April of 1774. The fact that it was intended as a public utterance helps explain the carefully worked out rhetorical structure that informs the letter. This passage follows the classic Wheatley pattern of beginning with statements straight out of the discourse of American Africanism only to *convert* that discourse to antislavery argument. By linking the story of African capture and enslavement to the Old Testament Israelites, she forces a link (one that transgresses "racial" and geographical boundaries) between white Anglo-Americans and the enslaving Egyptians.[25] Thus in using the phrase "*Egyptian* gloom" in "**Cambridge,**" Wheatley is signifying the slaveholding tendency of Egypt, not its "blackness" or "Africanness." When I talk of georacial transgressions, I mean that Wheatley understands slavery as a *global* system, encompassing Africa, Europe, the Caribbean, and North America. It is also quite possible that her original captors were black.[26] What we get, then, is a discourse that cuts across the racial divide imposed by American Africanism. "Modern Egyptians" can be of any race or nationality, according to Wheatley. Similarly, "Love of Freedom" becomes the great equalizer in a world structured on "Enlightenment" hierarchies of the "Great Chain of Being." Her overall project is to unwrite, if you will, the discourse of blackness/Africanity as a discourse of difference. As she states in her poem "**America,**" "Sometimes by Simile, a victory's won."

Following a mild exhortation about sin to "Let hateful vice so baneful to the Soul, / Be still avoided" (lines 26-27), the conclusion of the 1767 "**Cambridge**" reads:

> Suppress the sable monster in its growth,
> Ye blooming plants of human race, divine
> An Ethiop tells you, tis your greatest foe
> Its transient sweetness turns to endless pain,
> And brings eternal ruin on the Soul.
>
> (Lines 28-32)

In the 1773 revision, following a stronger imperative to "shun" sin and evil, we find these lines:

> Suppress the deadly serpent in its egg.
> Ye blooming plants of human race divine,
> An *Ethiop* tells you 'tis your greatest foe;
> Its transient sweetness turns to endless pain,
> And in immense perdition sinks the soul.
>
> (Lines 26-30)

By changing "sable monster" to "deadly serpent," Wheatley raises the "error" of slavery to the theological status of Original Sin. The reference to the Fall in line 17 is thus emphasized, as the serpent recalls the Garden of Eden. In this way,

Africa, the poet's "native shore," becomes the scene of man's Fall into "error" via slavery.

It could be argued that "sable monster" is a more precise designation for the slave trade than "deadly serpent," which connotes a more abstract notion of sin and temptation. Wheatley's use of the more abstract term in the final version supports my view that she would have felt "*Egyptian* gloom" to be specific enough to carry the antislavery message home, especially to a Bible-reading New England public. There is, however, another reference that would have signified the transatlantic slave trade to that audience: the mention of sin as "transient sweetness" that "turns to endless pain." In the eighteenth century the intended readers would have understood this as a reference to the "sweet" industries of sugar, rum, and molasses, which specifically connected New England to the slave trade. The New England distilleries, in fact, were among the most dependent on the traffic in African bodies: "Most of the so-called 'middle passages' terminated in the Caribbean, where the slaves were exchanged for specie, bills, and return cargoes of sugar or molasses."[27] Wheatley had experienced firsthand the brutalities of a system that literally traded human beings for the sugar and molasses so vital to the rum industry.

Finally, the matter of the "dark abodes," a phrase that appears to be a mere repetition of American Africanist discourse. First, it is singular ("dark abode") in the 1767 version and plural in the final draft. Second, in the final version "land" is singular while "abodes" is plural; thus the "dark abodes" cannot signify Africa (as it does in the first version). The entire couplet reads: "Father of mercy, 'twas thy gracious hand / Brought me in safety from those dark abodes" (lines 5-6). The key words here are "in safety." Wheatley is offering a prayer of thanksgiving (a direct address to God the "Father" as opposed to the third-person reference "'Twas mercy brought me . . ." of **"On Being Brought"**) for her survival of the hazardous journey of the Middle Passage. She is not, as some have assumed, thankful for slavery, but for her safety. Here, the "dark abodes" could signify nothing but the hateful and unsanitary ship's holds where the majority of enslaved Africans spent the bulk of their time during their crossing, chained together, deprived of light, air, decent food, and water. Scholars whose interest in the slave trade is medical and historical report that "at least one in three Africans died between the time they were removed from their homeland and the time they were unloaded in the West Indies of the Americas."[28] Not only would Wheatley have witnessed an incredible amount of suffering and death, but "in most cases, the seamen were allowed to have sexual intercourse with the females. Officers were always permitted access to the women" (Reynolds 50-51). The age of the victim would have been little protection against possible assault. By the time Phillis Wheatley stood on the auction block in Boston, she was wearing only a tattered piece of carpet over her frail body. In supplying these details, I am trying to include what had to be excluded from Wheatley's poems. By carefully placing a few key signifiers ("dark abodes," "transient sweetness," etc.), Wheatley is able to write her experience of the Middle Passage in the only way she could.

RACE, POWER/KNOWLEDGE

All of this serves as the context for the first line of **"On Being Brought From Africa to America"**—"'Twas mercy brought me from my *Pagan* land." My argument has been based on the observation that what appear to be "minor" revisions in the later version of **"Cambridge"** reveal a sharpening and development in Wheatley's thinking about the meaning of her experience of slavery and Middle Passage over the six intervening years. In this sense, **"On Being Brought"** represents her highest poetic achievement, especially if we appreciate it as a continuation of the narrative developed in the initial four lines of **"Cambridge."** For the **"Cambridge"** lines end precisely where **"On Being Brought"** begins. "Father of mercy, 'twas they gracious hand / Brought me in safety from those dark abodes" becomes "'Twas mercy brought me from my *Pagan* land." If, as I have argued, the appeal to "safety" and "dark abodes" calls up the weeks-to-months-long horror of the Middle Passage, **"On Being Brought"** picks up where the Middle Passage ends, that is, at the point of arrival. It is the task of its eight lines, then, to chronicle the remaining part of Wheatley's "journey": specifically, the twin processes of racialization and acculturation.

Crucially, if ironically, during the six years between the first draft of **"Cambridge"** and the publication of ***Poems,*** which contains both the final draft of that poem and **"On Being Brought From Africa to America,"** Wheatley was baptized in the Old South Meeting House of Boston (1771). This accounts for the changes in **"Cambridge"** from "Parent of mercy, 'twas thy powerful hand" (line 6, 1767 version) to "Father of mercy, 'twas thy gracious hand" (line 5, 1773 version). The more personal (and patriarchal) epithet "Father" is associated with "grace" rather than "power," a clear indication of a Judeo-Christian orientation toward divinity. Her baptism would also explain why Wheatley's critique of slavery as sin gains theological coherence in the final version. Yet—and here is the great irony—her reading of Africa is less pejorative in the second **"Cambridge"** than in the first. In other words, it is *after* Wheatley becomes converted to Christianity, a religion often associated with the theological justification for enslavement of African peoples as well as a major component of American Africanism, that her views about Africa and her own Africanness become more empathic. She moves, then, *through* the discourse of Christianity, from a repetition of American Africanism to its critique.

"On Being Brought" presents Wheatley with a new set of issues beyond the apparent presence/absence of the Muses in Africa and thankfulness for having been spared on the Middle Passage. By abandoning the personalized "Father of mercy 'twas thy gracious hand" in favor of the more abstract "'Twas mercy brought me," Wheatley opens the way to subject the "doctrine of merciful enslavement" to a more intense interrogation. To thank God for one's physical safety is one thing; to appear grateful for one's captivity and enslavement is quite another. God and Mercy, which are equated in **"Cambridge,"** must be read as two separate and distinct entities or forces in **"On Being Brought."** If a Judeo-Christian conceptualization of God as "Saviour" retains the personal connections witnessed (and witnessed to) in the thanksgiving prayer of **"Cambridge,"** "Mercy" in Wheatley's poetics cannot be conceived of apart from what Foucault calls the "power/knowledge axis."[29] That "mercy" *teaches*—"*Taught* my benighted soul to *understand*"; "Once I redemption neither sought *nor knew*"—foregrounds issues of epistemology within a terrain of global relations of power.

Structural shifts, multiple positionings, and temporal/spatial displacements discussed above serve to underscore the passive construction of the poem's title: "on *being brought*." The signifier "mercy" as the real subject (the agent of the passive voice) emerges as a site of interrogation and contestation. "Mercy" as it signifies in a Western discourse that sanctions the commercial exploitation of black bodies as a means of saving souls can only be a positive agent within the ideological construction of Enlightenment rationale. The conflation of conversion and enslavement is thus posited as an ideological discourse whose signifying power is problematized by the very terms of its othering. Ironically, it is the very apparatus of the slave trade, the transporting of black bodies from Africa, that most threatens the balance of power created and maintained by European hegemony. However much white slave owners insist on seeing black skin as "a *diabolic* die," the transportation of slaves from Africa assures that "Negros, black as Cain / May be refin'd and join th'angelic train" (lines 7-8).[30]

What **"On Being Brought"** ultimately encodes is the system of racialization in progress. With the displacement of African bodies from their homelands and the meanings and definitions associated with their land came the transformation of Africans into "Negros." Wheatley encodes this process of racialization in the tension created from the first four lines to the last four lines of this poem. If the trajectory of subjectivity, the "I" emerging as "Our"/"'their,'" creates a sense of continuity between the two sections, the issue of Africans' becoming "Negros" is more complicated.

Notes

1. See Gates, *Figures in Black,* and Baker, *The Journey Back.* See also June Jordan and Alice Walker.
2. Margarita Matilda Odell, *Memoir and Poems of Phillis Wheatley. A Native of Africa and a Slave. Dedicated to the Friends of the African* (Boston: George W. Light, 1834). Wheatley died in abject poverty and near-obscurity in 1784 at the approximate age of thirty-one.
3. For a comprehensive treatment of the use of Phillis Wheatley's image and poems in debates over black inferiority, see Gates, *Figures in Black.*
4. A related "deficiency," according to Odell, was Wheatley's habit of "forgetting" her own poems, a problem said "to have affected her own thoughts only, and not the impressions made upon her mind by the thoughts of others, communicated by books or conversation" (*Memoir* 19).
5. Patricia Hill Collins argues that "Black women have a self-defined standpoint on their own oppression" (32).
6. Mazrui writes, "So much of the history of the slave experience in the Western hemisphere amounted to the following command addressed to the captives, 'Forget you are African, remember you are Black!'" (110).
7. Toni Morrison refers to displaced Africans as "the not-Americans" (48).
8. Wheatley's references to herself as "Afric" and "Ethiop" can be found in the following poems: "To Maecenas" (line 40), "To the University of Cambridge" (line 28), "On Recollection" (line 62), "An Hymn to Humanity" (line 31), and "To His Honour the Lieutenant-Governor on the Death of His Lady" (line 28). Houston Baker discusses these references as "sign-vehicles" (after Eco) and reads "the complex mappings" of the terms as moving "in the direction of an extended African consciousness" (*The Journey Back* 12).
9. In using the term "survivor" I mean to connect Wheatley and other first-generation Africans in the Americas to such celebrated communities as Jewish

survivors of the Nazi Holocaust as well as to the various discourses of survivorship of individual "holocausts" like rape and incest that have historically characterized black women's lives.

10. On African "survivals," the classic debate has been between anthropologist Melville J. Herskovits (*The Myth of the Negro Past* [1924]) and sociologist E. Franklin Frazier (*The Negro Church in America* [1964]). See also Karla F. C. Holloway, ed., *Africanisms in American Culture* (Bloomington: Indiana University Press, 1990); Sobel; Mintz and Price; and Thompson. Americanist literary scholars are also beginning to apply the concept of "cultural syncretism" with respect to American and African American literature and culture. See Shelly Fisher Fishkin, *Was Huck Black?: Mark Twain and African American Voices* (New York: Oxford University Press, 1993); and Eric Sundquist, *To Wake the Nations: Race in the Making of American Literature* (Cambridge: Harvard University Press, 1993).

11. Mukhtar Ali Isani, "'An Elegy on Leaving———': A New Poem by Phillis Wheatley," *American Literature* 58, no. 4 (December 1986): 609-13. See also Shields.

12. In addition to Curtin, see Edward Reynolds, *Stand the Storm: A History of the Atlantic Slave Trade* (Chicago: Ivan R. Dee, 1985), which provides an analysis in terms of African, European, and American life and culture. See also the essays in Inikori and Engerman.

13. In *African Religions and Philosophy,* John S. Mbiti writes of the interconnectedness of African ontology as comprising God, Spirits, Man, Animals, and Plants, and "[p]henomena and objects without biological life" (15-16). Moreover, he writes that Africans are particularly tied to the land, as they conceive of subjectivity within the matrix of space: "The land provides them with the roots of existence, as well as binding them mystically to their departed. . . . To remove Africans by force from their land is an act of such great injustice that no foreigner can fathom it" (26). On African Sacred Cosmos, see also Sobel and Hopkins.

14. I discuss the correspondence between Obour Tanner and Wheatley more fully in chapter 1.

15. Phillip Richards argues that Wheatley "assimilates" Anglo-American discourse in her poetry, in "Phillis Wheatley and Literary Americanization," [*American Quarterly* 44 (1992): 163-91].

16. The first four lines of "On Being Brought" form a versified "conversion narrative," prefiguring black women's appropriation of a genre that will come to be dominated by Jarena Lee, Zilpha Elaw, Rebecca Cox Jackson, Julia A. J. Foote, Amanda Berry Smith, and others, in the nineteenth century. The conversion narratives of Lee, Elaw, and Foote are collected in Andrews, *Sisters of the Spirit.* Jackson's writings appear in Humez, *Gifts of Power.* Amanda Berry Smith's *Autobiography* appears in its entirety as part of the Schomburg Library of Nineteenth-Century Black Women Writers (New York: Oxford University Press, 1988). See also Houchins.

17. Mae Henderson, "Response to Baker," in Baker and Redmond 160.

18. The advertised proposal ran in the *Boston Censor* on February 29, March 14, and April 18, 1772. There were no local (American) publishers willing to publish a book of poems by an African slave, which necessitated their being published in England (August 6, 1773). Wheatley, who had sailed to London in May of 1773, was on hand to oversee the publication and printing of the volume. "Cambridge" and "On Being Brought" were repositioned to third and fifth, respectively, in the final volume.

19. The subtitle "Wrote in 1767" appeared in the 1772 proposal.

20. John Shields points out that most of the "editorial tampering" with Wheatley's verse was done in poems published after her death in 1784. The evidence confirms that during her lifetime, Wheatley displayed an astonishing amount of editorial control over her poetry.

21. Wheatley published her first poem, "On Messrs. Hussey and Coffin," on December 21, 1767, in the *Newport Mercury* also at the age of fourteen.

22. Here I also disagree with Russell Reising, who views Wheatley's poetics within a dialectic of "accommodation" and "resistance." If Wheatley's popularity depended on the "opacity" of her antislavery message to New England readers, then revisions should show an increase in the veiling of her language from earlier drafts to those published in *Poems.* Instead, Wheatley actually revised poems in order to make the antislavery message more clear. This is, to me, evidence that with the passing years, Wheatley became not more "domesticated" but more overtly abolitionist. See Reising, "Trafficking in White" [*Genre* 22 (Fall 1989): 231-61].

23. The final version of these lines reads: "While an intrinsic ardor prompts to write, / The muses promise to assist my pen."

24. The conceptualization of slavery as "sin" would have been available to Wheatley's eighteenth-century audience. Diaries of slave traders making this connection abound. See also Samuel Sewall's *The Selling of Joseph: A Memorial* (1703), ed. Sidney Kaplan (Amherst: University of Massachusetts Press, 1969), perhaps the earliest text specifically equating European slavery with biblical wrongdoing.

25. On African Americans' use of the biblical account in Exodus, see Theophus Smith's recent cultural history, *Conjuring Culture* 55-80. See also Hopkins 23-24.

26. See Olaudah Equiano, *The Interesting Narrative of Olaudah Equiano or Gustavus Vassa, the African,* in Gates, *Classic Slave Narratives.* See Reynolds, *Stand the Storm.*

27. Ronald Bailey, "The Slave(ry) Trade and the Development of Captialism in the United States: The Textile Industry in New England," in Inikori and Engerman 205-6.

28. Thomas W. Wilson and Clarence E. Grim, "The Possible Relationship between the Transatlantic Slave Trade and Hypertension in Blacks Today," in Inikori and Engerman 339-60. Several medical historical studies have been conducted in recent years to explore the possibility that black Americans' propensity to hypertension may be linked not only to diet and heredity but also possibly to the harsh physical conditions of the Middle Passage. While I find this interesting, I do not believe the Middle Passage constituted an "evolutionary gateway" that would have altered African physiology to as great a degree as some researchers think. See also Kenneth F. Kiple and Brian T. Higgins, "Mortality Caused by Dehydration during the Middle Passage," in Inikori and Engerman 321-38.

29. Foucault, *Power/Knowledge*. See also Henriques et al.

30. Russell Reising offers an extensive reading of the word "refin'd" (line 8) in its biological, theological, and cultural senses. See "Trafficking in White" 243-45.

Selected Bibliography

Andrews, William L., ed. *Sisters of the Spirit: Three Black Women's Autobiographies of the Nineteenth Century.* Bloomington: Indiana University Press, 1986.

Baker, Houston A. *The Journey Back: Issues in Black Literature and Criticism.* Chicago: University of Chicago Press, 1980.

Baker, Houston A., and Patricia Redmond, eds. *Afro-American Literary Study in the 1990's.* Chicago: University of Chicago Press, 1989.

Collins, Patricia Hill. *Black Feminist Thought: Knowledge, Consciousness, and the Politics of Empowerment.* New York: Routledge, 1991.

Curtin, Philip D. *The Atlantic Slave Trade: A Census.* Madison: University of Wisconsin Press, 1969.

Foucault, Michel. *Power/Knowledge: Selected Interviews and Other Writings, 1972-1977.* Translated by Colin Gordon, Leo Marshall, John Mepham, and Kate Soper. New York: Pantheon Books, 1980.

Frazier, E. Franklin. *The Negro Church in America.* New York: Schocken Books, 1974.

Gates, Henry Louis, Jr. *Figures in Black: Words, Signs, and the "Racial" Self.* New York: Oxford University Press, 1987.

Gates, Henry Louis, Jr., ed. *The Classic Slave Narratives.* New York: New American Library, 1987.

Henriques, Julian, Wendy Hollway, Cathy Urwin, Couze Venn, and Valerie Walkerdine. *Changing the Subject: Psychology, Social Regulation, and Subjectivity.* London: Methuen, 1984.

Herskovits, Melville J. *The Myth of the Negro Past.* Boston: Beacon Press, 1990.

Hopkins, Dwight N. *Shoes That Fit Our Feet: Sources for a Constructive Black Theology.* Maryknoll, NY: Orbis Books, 1993.

Houchins, Susan, ed. *Spiritual Narratives.* The Schomburg Library of Nineteenth-Century Black Women Writers. New York: Oxford University Press, 1988.

Humez, Jean McMahon, ed. *Gifts of Power: The Writings of Rebecca Cox Jackson, Black Visionary, Shaker Eldress.* Amherst: University of Massachusetts Press, 1981.

Inikori, Joseph E., and Stanley L. Engerman, eds. *The Atlantic Slave Trade: Effects on Economies, Societies, and Peoples in Africa, the Americas, and Europe.* Durham: Duke University Press, 1992.

Jordan, June. "The Difficult Miracle of Black Poetry in America; or, Something Like a Sonnet for Phillis Wheatley." In *Wildwomen in the Whirlwind: Afra-American Culture and the Contemporary Literary Renaissance,* edited by Joanne M. Braxton and Andree Nicola McLaughlin, 22-34. New Brunswick, NJ: Rutgers University Press, 1990.

Mazrui, Ali. *The Africans: A Triple Heritage.* Boston: Little Brown, 1986.

Mbiti, John S. *African Religions and Philosophy.* Oxford: Heinemann, 1990.

Morrison, Toni. *Playing in the Dark: Whiteness and the Literary Imagination.* Cambridge: Harvard University Press, 1992.

Shields, John, ed. *The Collected Works of Phillis Wheatley.* Schomburg Library of Nineteenth-Century Black Women Writers. New York: Oxford University Press, 1988.

Smith, Cynthia. "'To Maecenas': Phillis Wheatley's Invocation of an Idealized Reader." *Black American Literature Forum* 23, no. 3 (Fall 1989): 579-92.

Smith, Theophus H. *Conjuring Culture: Biblical Formations of Black America.* New York: Oxford University Press, 1994.

Sobel, Mechal. *Trabelin' On: The Slave Journey to an Afro-Baptist Faith.* Westport, CT: Greenwood Press, 1979.

Walker, Alice. *In Search of Our Mothers' Gardens.* San Diego: Harcourt, Brace, Jovanovich, 1983.

MARY MCALEER BALKUN (ESSAY DATE 2002)

SOURCE: Balkun, Mary McAleer. "Phillis Wheatley's Construction of Otherness and the Rhetoric of Performed Ideology." *African American Review* 36, no. 1 (2002): 121-35.

In the following essay, Balkun asserts that Wheatley wrote Poems on Various Subjects, *particularly the poems "To the University of Cambridge" and "On Being Brought from Africa to America," with a specific, moralistic audience in mind.*

Sometime in 1772, a young African girl walked demurely into a room in Boston to undergo an oral examination, the results of which would determine the direction of her life and work. Perhaps she was shocked upon entering the appointed room.

For there, perhaps gathered in a semicircle, sat eighteen of Boston's most notable citizens. Among them were John Erving, a prominent Boston merchant; the Reverend Charles Chauncy, pastor of he Tenth Congregational Church; and John Hancock, who would later gain fame for his signature on the Declaration of Independence. At the center of this group was His Excellency, Thomas Hutchinson, governor of Massachusetts, with Andrew Oliver, his lieutenant governor, close by his side.

Why had this august group been assembled? Why had it seen fit to summon this young African girl, scarcely eighteen years old, before it? This group of "the most respectable Characters in Boston," as it would later define itself, had assembled to question closely the African adolescent on the slender sheaf of poems that she claimed to have "written by herself." We can only speculate on the nature of the questions posed to this fledgling poet. . . . We do know, however, that the African poet's responses were more than sufficient to prompt the eighteen august gentlemen to compose, sign,

ABOUT THE AUTHOR

AN EXCERPT FROM JUPITER HAMMON'S POEM *AN ADDRESS TO MISS PHILLIS WHEATLEY*

I

O come you pious youth! adore
The wisdom of thy God,
In bringing thee from distant shore,
To learn His holy word.

II

Thou mightst been left behind
Amidst a dark abode;
God's tender mercy still combin'd,
Thou hast the holy word.

III

Fair wisdom's ways are paths of peace,
And they that walk therein,
Shall reap the joys that never cease,
And Christ shall be their king.

IV

God's tender mercy brought thee here;
Tost o'er the raging main;
In Christian faith thou hast a share,
Worth all the gold of Spain.

V

While thousands tossed by the sea,
And others settled down,
God's tender mercy set thee free,
From dangers that come down.

VI

That thou a pattern still might be,
To youth of Boston town,
The blessed Jesus set thee free,
From every sinful wound.

VII

The blessed Jesus, who came down,
Unvail'd his sacred face,
To cleanse the soul of every wound,
And give repenting grace.

VIII

That we poor sinners may obtain,
The pardon of our sin;
Dear blessed Jesus now constrain,
And bring us flocking in.

IX

Come you, Phillis, now aspire,
And seek the living God,
So step by step thou mayst go higher,
Till perfect in the word.

X

While thousands mov'd to distant shore,
And others left behind,
The blessed Jesus still adore,
Implant this in thy mind.

XI

Thou hast left the heathen shore;
Thro' mercy of the Lord,
Among the heathen live no more,
Come magnify thy God.

XII

I pray the living God may be,
The shepherd of thy soul;
His tender mercies still are free,
His mysteries to unfold.

XIII

Thou, Phillis, when thou hunger hast,
Or pantest for thy God;
Jesus Christ is thy relief,
Thou hast the holy word.

XIV

The bounteous mercies of the Lord,
Are hid beyond the sky,
And holy souls that love His word,
Shall taste them when they die.

Jupiter Hammon. Excerpt from "An Address to Miss Phillis Wheatley." In *The Complete Works of Jupiter Hammon of Long Island,* edited by Stanley Austin Ransom Jr., pp. 49-51. Port Washington, N.Y.: Kennikat Press, 1970.

and publish a two-paragraph "Attestation," an open letter "To the Publick" that prefaces Phillis Wheatley's book. . . .

(Gates vii-viii)

In his forward to ***The Collected Works of Phillis Wheatley,*** "In Her Own Write," Henry Louis Gates, Jr., describes the scene he imagines having preceded the validation of Wheatley's authorship by eighteen prominent Bostonians, during which the poet was questioned in order to ascertain her ability to have written the works ascribed to her. While there may be no historical evidence to support his recreation, as Kirstin Wilcox asserts (10), Gates does manage to capture some of the important elements in Wheatley's life as a poet in his imaginative recreation.[1] In particular, the scenario Gates recounts indicates an awareness of Wheatley's dominant audience as well as the unique historical moment in which she wrote.

While Wheatley's was clearly a bifurcated audience, there can be little doubt that the eighteen men who signed for her represented a major constituency for her poetry, among those who read the broadsides and newspapers in which she published and who had the public ear.[2] She knew these men because they had visited the Wheatley home, because she had heard them preach, or because they had established public reputations in Boston. These were also men for whom she had actually written poems, either to celebrate personal accomplishment or to mourn the passing of a loved one. In addition, they were men whose experience would not have included a Phillis Wheatley, and who might well have wondered whether the young author was a "serious" poet or a front for abolitionists. For, as previous critics have pointed out, Wheatley's poetry is not devoid of racial awareness, as had long been suggested. Antonio T. Bly asserts that Wheatley used her poems not simply to "denounce the hypocrisy practiced by white Christians, but also [to] express a strong sense of black pride to her fellow slaves, who were often read her poetry by slave masters who thought that her writings were harmless" (205-06). A number of the poems can be seen as direct appeals to her black counterparts to accept the Christian God as a means of salvation, if not in this world then certainly in the next. However, critics have yet to consider fully the possibility that Wheatley might have crafted her poems to work specifically upon the white audience that would have constituted her main readership, aside from overt pleas to accept the possibility of black Christians.

A close examination of two poems in particular, **"To the University of Cambridge, in New-England"** and **"On Being Brought from Africa to America,"** suggests that they were designed to manipulate this audience in very specific ways.[3] In effect, Wheatley's strategy casts the audience into the unfolding drama of the poem: She sets the stage, introduces the hypocritical stance that allows so-called Christians to accept and even promote slavery, and then lays the groundwork for a spiritual dilemma—either join with Wheatley, the black, female *Christian* in her critique of the existing power structure or accept the very position of "other" that she and all black Americans were expected to occupy. Read this way, these two poems, both included in Wheatley's only book of poetry, ***Poems on Various Subjects, Religious and Moral,*** turn out to be not so much about Wheatley herself or her created persona, as has been argued, as they are about her perceived audience.[4] It was an audience familiar with particular language and rhetorical devices—the jeremiad, the plea to the rising generation, the rhetoric of Revolution, to name a few—and one being increasingly exposed to the idea of black equality and liberation. It was also an audience used to active participation in rhetorical acts, especially in their forms of worship, and this awareness was crucial to whatever influence Wheatley might have hoped to exert. Irony, doubling, internal stress patterns, and puns, all of which have been identified as elements of the poet's technique, now emerge as among the devices she enlisted. Her strategy takes the audience from a position of initial confidence and agreement, to confusion and uncertainty, to a new ideological position at the conclusion of each poem.

This method of structuring a text with an eye toward the audience as participants in the ideological drama being enacted, what Steven Mailloux has referred to as "the rhetoric of performed ideology" (107), is fundamental for an understanding of these poems.[5] Wheatley casts the audience as critical of the prevailing ideology, expecting its members "to perform increasingly more challenging [rhetorical] tasks" (Mailloux 115). They must eventually accept a new form of authority, that of the black, female author, but in order to do so, they must be actively engaged in the "ideological performance" the poem enacts. It is a strategy that not only suggests the kind of response Wheatley may have been struggling to provoke in her reader but also implies a greater awareness of audience than she has been credited with to date. Her approach is calculated to make several complementary points: Christians who support, practice, or even tolerate slavery are guilty of the basest hypocrisy; it is possible for Africans to be redeemed and become Christians; and, most importantly, the inability to accept these arguments reflects an inherent moral failing in the reader.

Before proceeding to an analysis of the poems, it is necessary to establish the parameters of the audience for whom Wheatley conceivably wrote. This is not to suggest that there was a single, unified audience for these texts, but rather that we can identify at least one specific group they were intended to influence, a group that included the eighteen men who corroborated Wheatley's authorship.[6] In addition to those already named, the signers included Samuel Cooper, Joseph Green, and Mather Byles, amateur poets and, in the case of Cooper and Byles, mentors for Wheatley in her literary pursuits (Shields, ***Collected*** 275). John Wheatley, her master, was a signer of the attestation as well. Additional supporters not listed but among Wheatley's readers and professed admirers were men like Dr. Benjamin Rush of Philadelphia, signer of the Declaration of Independence and a member of the Continental Congress, and the Marquis de Barbe-Marbois, who served as Secretary to the French Legation during the American Revolution (Robinson 24). Many of these men, William H. Robinson reminds us, either owned slaves or were engaged in the slave trade (24), putting them in a strategic position for Wheatley's rhetorical project. They were also men with power within the community and with specific connections to Wheatley herself.

A number of these individuals can be identified as specific objects of Wheatley's poetic gifts. She wrote elegies for Samuel Cooper and John Moorhead, poems upon the deaths of Andrew Oliver's wife and Thomas Hubbard's daughter, and a poetic response to a rebus by James Bowdoin.[7] All five of these men signed the attestation. Wheatley wrote poems about other prominent citizens as well, such as Rev. Joseph Sewall, Rev. George Whitefield, and Dr. Samuel Marshall, and surely it would have been reasonable for her to assume that they, as well as their friends and families, would constitute her readership. Robinson points out that Wheatley "composed verses *only* for people who meant much to her in a practical way" (Robinson 29), but that might also mean those who could help her bring about change.

Although Wheatley has long been criticized for her inattention to public matters, especially slavery and racial issues, recent scholarship has demonstrated that she was indeed a socially aware poet, writing for an audience she knew and understood. Comparing ***Poems on Various Subjects*** as it was eventually published in London to the original proposal for Boston publication, Kirstin Wilcox observes that the Boston proposal clearly presents Wheatley as a local and public poet, one involved in the life of her community. As Wilcox puts it, the list of poems for that volume "reads less like a table of contents than a log of recent significant events in Boston, particularly in the city's mercantile and Methodist circles. . . . Wheatley not only knows the same people and has been present at the same events but she also has a real existence that can be changed by the actions of her readers" (14-15).[8] Wheatley gradually learns to exploit this connection to a community of readers, although not necessarily, as Wilcox asserts, to affect her own condition. Instead, her objective seems to have been to alter the perceptions of her audience as a preparation for future change.

Wheatley, who started publishing in her teens with the encouragement of her mistress, Susannah Wheatley, knew from the start exactly for whom she was writing and why.[9] Working from the two premises established thus far—that the signers of the attestation represent a significant segment of her audience, one she knew very well as a result of personal association, correspondence, or having heard them preach; and that her poetry in general implies a larger audience of Boston's elite that included these men—we can begin to draw some conclusions about the way the rhetorical strategies underlying certain of Wheatley's poems may have been intended to manipulate this audience toward very specific conclusions. And while it is true, as some might argue, that ***Poems*** was itself first published in England, the primary audience was clearly a colonial one; the first proposal was for a Boston publication, and many of the poems were originally published there, including **"To the University of Cambridge"** and **"On Being Brought From Africa to America."**[10]

While the specified audience for **"To the University of Cambridge,"** written in 1767, is a group of Harvard students, they are merely representatives of a larger group and Wheatley's actual audience: the fathers of these selfsame students, those who held positions of power and social influence.[11] Situating the speaker of the poem as a concerned member of the general citizenry, she attempts to forge a link between that speaker and the audience through the Puritan tradition of the experienced adult "preaching to the 'rising generation'" (Richards 169). Wheatley was also working from within another Puritan tradition, one that privileged the linguistic aspect of the redemption experience, "the power of words" (Kibbey 7). Ann Kibbey observes that, for the Puritans, "not only did speech generate conversion. The hearer's religious experience was itself a linguistic event." The Puritans expected the words of the preacher "to change the hearer's system of reference and thereby alter the hearer's perception" (7). This appears to have been Wheatley's strategy as well. Working at the level of the word, carefully setting up allusions and images with the ring of familiarity, the poem is structured in such a way as to alter her audience's system of reference and, as a result, its perceptions. Striving to gain sympathy and put the audience at ease, Wheatley begins with a justification of her activity as a writer: "While an intrinsic ardor prompts to write / The muses promise to assist my pen" (1-2). These lines are immediately followed by an ambiguous reference to her enslaved condition:

> 'Twas not long since I left my native shore
> The land of errors, and *Egyptian* gloom:
> Father of mercy, 'twas thy gracious hand
> Brought me in safety from those dark abodes.
>
> (3-6)

The ambiguity lies in Wheatley's use of *left,* as opposed to a more pointed word, to describe her removal from her homeland. This semantic decision signals Wheatley's determination not to apportion guilt, at least not in an overt way, since to do so would have put the audience on the defensive at the outset. But her choice of words also has the effect of undermining any assumed power others may believe they have over her and all slaves, a reading borne out by the next two lines: "Father of mercy, 'twas thy gracious hand / Brought me in safety from those dark abodes" (5-6). According to her interpretation of these events, Wheatley's removal from Africa was an act of God, as was her subsequent salvation. Simultaneously, she suggests that to deny this salvation is to question His will. Ultimately, since God himself was responsible for her redemption, she must be of the "elect," and, conversely, those who do not concede this point can only be nonelect and therefore damned or "other." As Paula Bennett astutely concludes, "Wheatley redeems her oppression by making it the source of her religious response to God and by making God . . . the power that liberates her speech" (66). The result is language that has been vouchsafed by God, as has the authority of its speaker.

Yet Wheatley's recollection of this early event is not devoid of criticism: The final line of the first stanza can also be read as a reference to the dangers of the Middle Passage and the fact that she did not perish along the way. The overall rhetorical effect for which she strives is one of gracious acceptance of God's will, at least as concerns her immediate condition. In the spirit of "errare humanum est," Wheatley aligns herself with the Divine by forgiving those who enslaved her, with the ironic consequence of then aligning them *against* the Divine for their own involvement, whether active or passive, in the slave trade.

This is a theme she develops more explicitly in the second stanza when she cites the great compassion of Christ toward sinners: "He hears revilers, nor resents their scorn: / What matchless mercy in the Son of God!" (15-16). The implication is that, while she bears no grudge toward her revilers, surely Christ will not look kindly upon those who fail to emulate Him in this way. Such a statement also begs the question: Should one then prefer to be the reviler or the reviled, especially if one must eventually answer to the Son of God for one's choice? The refusal to publicly criticize her masters or those involved in the slave trade reinforces Wheatley's authority as a spokesperson for Christianity. It is the reader, who might be tempted to reject the speaker on any of three grounds—as black, as woman, as slave—who is in danger of being situated in the position of "reviler." Should this not be enough to encourage the development of a more Christian attitude toward others, however, Wheatley continues with a statement that can leave no doubt about the true relation between black and white Christians. She observes that "the whole human race by sin has fall'n," and Jesus died "that they might rise again" (17, 18), meaning, of course, *all* humankind, not just whites. The shift in her use of pronouns, from "How *Jesus'* blood for *your* redemption flows" to "He deigned to die that *they* might rise again" (12, 18; my emphasis on the pronouns), broadens the application of her argument, as does the fact that it is "the *whole* human race" which "by sin has fall'n" (17; my emphasis). Wheatley's unwillingness to cast herself overtly as one of the saved—her use of *they* rather than *we*—underscores the subtlety of the mind at work in these lines and its awareness of the audience to which it is appealing. It also underscores her personal lesson of Christian humility and generosity.[12]

The treatment of Africa deserves careful attention in any discussion of Wheatley's rhetorical strategies. In this case, her homeland is designated as "the land of errors," thereby emphasizing a lack of knowledge on the part of the inhabitants rather than innate sinfulness. She could well have expected her intended audience to make certain inferences and connections based on the description of Africa as the land of "*Egyptian* gloom," among them the association of black slaves with God's chosen people, who were delivered from slavery in Egypt and led into Canaan. This is an association that also recalls the Puritan settlers, who cast themselves as the "New Israelites" and their destination as the "New Canaan." Thus, while Wheatley's image resonates with one of the classic archetypes of American ideology, the

Puritans as God's Chosen People, it also establishes a clear connection to this group, whose members saw themselves as maligned and persecuted, virtually enslaved, for their religious convictions. It was also a group that had already become central to the very notion of what it meant to be American.

In the second stanza, Wheatley adopts the narrative stance that informs the rest of the poem, that of the preacher exhorting her flock. It was during the eighteenth century that the jeremiad became a popular form in America, one that Larzer Ziff describes as striving "for a strong psychological reaction at the very time of the sermon's being preached," certainly a reaction Wheatley might have hoped for in the reader of her poems (35). In fact, this is strikingly similar to the effect the poems' rhetorical performance was calibrated to produce. While several critics have already noted the parallels between Wheatley's poem and the jeremiad, none has previously considered the ways this might have helped the poem work upon its audience. Instead, Wheatley's use of this genre is usually discussed in terms of her attempt to authorize herself as writer. This is certainly one effect, but it is also clear that Wheatley used the jeremiad to exploit the associations it would have produced in readers such as those described above.

As Sacvan Bercovitch has pointed out, the jeremiad as practiced in America "was a ritual designed to join social criticism to spiritual renewal, public to private identity, the shifting 'signs of the times' to certain traditional metaphors, themes and symbols" (xi). It was also a much more optimistic form as practiced in colonial America, one that stressed conversion as opposed to simple obedience and relied upon the same sense of errand and divine destiny that the early Puritans had espoused. To use a specific example, in "Sinners in the Hands of An Angry God," one of the best-known Puritan jeremiads, Jonathan Edwards uses a strategy very similar to Wheatley's. He addresses a group of auditors who see themselves as "elect" and therefore "saved" and gradually leads them into an awareness of themselves as "requiring salvation." Edwards' audience is advised that death can come at any moment, that the person each is sitting next to may be doomed to hell (and, of course, everyone is sitting next to someone), and that they must actively pursue redemption. Both Edwards' sermon and Wheatley's poem are marked by a measured and solemn tone, and both have conversion as their ultimate goal. However, Wheatley's goal is the conversion of her audience to an awareness of the evils being done on earth, slavery in particular, and her own authority as a Christian to speak to these matters.

In this role as preacher of temporal duty, Wheatley enjoins the students to turn their attention back to earth, where it belongs, a goal that is mirrored in the imagery she uses. She describes the students first as those who "scan the heights" and "traverse the ethereal space" (7-8), then as "sons of science" (10), and finally as "blooming plants," the last suggesting flowers turned to the sun but with their roots yet in the earth. However, it should be noted that they are "blooming plants of human race *divine*" (27; my emphasis), raising the question of whether the race is divine or whether she is flattering this particular group of representatives. This strategy reverses the usual conversion experience, where the unregenerate obey the call to turn *away* from worldly concerns and toward heaven and God. Wheatley understands the desire of these "sons of science" to study the heavens and "mark the systems of revolving worlds" (10, 9), but it is vital that, as future leaders of the colonies, they be concerned with the things of this earth if anything is to change. It is her mission to make sure they understand this duty. To this end, she threatens them with the possible loss of what they now possess, warning them to "Improve your privileges while they stay" (21). Her implication is that they will not be among the privileged forever, whether on earth or in heaven. Wheatley plays on her audience's fears of eternal damnation and suffering, as well as their awareness of the transience of all earthly things. Her vague use of the word *sin,* which includes the sin of the reviler in the previous stanza, allows the audience to participate in the poem by filling in that gap with specific sins. That she follows this with another reference to her position as an African, "An *Ethiop* tells you 'tis your greatest foe" (28), cannot help but suggest the exact form of sin to which she is alluding.[13]

Slavery frames the poem in a way that is unavoidable. But while the speaker begins the poem as a slave, grateful to have survived her ordeal and/or to have been saved at all, by the final lines she has metamorphosed into an "Ethiop," one with experience and knowledge beyond that of her audience. Wheatley's manipulation of tone, imagery, and literary form has resulted in her speaker's gradual "rise." No longer a victim of Egyptian gloom, she now has the confidence and authority to give advice to the sons of the elect because she has already been redeemed. This reference also conveys a vision of the "self" that extends beyond the label of "slave." It is a reference that elevates her in stature and announces that, if she is to be "other," it will be an "other" of her own choosing.

The general audience for this poem would certainly have had concerns similar to Wheatley's about the future of the colonies and the need for young men to be reminded of their duty in this regard. While these readers might initially have rejected any opinion offered by a black slave calling herself a Christian, the rhetorical strategy of the poem leaves them but one alternative: to *disagree* with the speaker's contention that the students have a responsibility to use their time at school wisely and well and be ever vigilant against sin. To reject Wheatley's position is to reject not only common sense but Christian doctrine as well, since she builds her case upon doctrinal evidence: the sinful nature of man, the generous and loving nature of Christ, and the transience of this world. Christ is invoked throughout the poem as the measure of truly Christian behavior, a measure the reader must acknowledge as well as the student. The same fate awaits all who are "saved" just as a certain fate awaits those who are not; black or white, they will not know "Life with death, and glory without end" (20). The alternative is only too well-known to her audience, and Wheatley capitalizes on this fear of eternal damnation.

By the final line the audience has become an active participant in the ideological drama of the poem through a variety of rhetorical ploys, not least of which are the rather general references to "students" (7) and "pupils" (22) that Wheatley plays upon. While appropriate to the audience within the poem, such terms also suggest the position of congregation to preacher or Christian to God. In this capacity as student/pupil in relation to wiser leader, the audience has been reminded, however gently, of the responsibilities that come with unearned good fortune, of the tenuous nature of existence, and of the mercy of Christ through whom all are redeemed. Wheatley invokes two of the three "parts" of God to make her case: the Father of the Old Testament, who punishes and scorns, and the Son of the New Testament, who redeemed all through his own suffering and death. These are related to the dual positions of the speaker. On the one hand, she conjures up images of "endless pain" and "immense perdition" (29, 30) in the traditional jeremiad style, positing a group of willing sinners far different from those living in the "land of errors" from which she originated. On the other hand, she is a disciple, concerned not with races but with the "human race" and the salvation of all God's children. To take one's place in the ranks of the saved, members of the audience must accept Wheatley in these dual roles, and this can only happen by an understanding of and active engagement in the rhetoric of the poem.

A number of cultural and social developments made the later eighteenth century an opportune time for the brand of literary activism Wheatley exhibits in **"To the University of Cambridge."** The most important was the gradual rise of a climate in New England in which anti-slavery sentiments were becoming more acceptable. In *White Over Black: American Attitudes Toward the Negro, 1550-1812,* Winthrop Jordan describes a number of trends that help explain this change. He paints a picture of a society and culture in flux, one in which a variety of forces were combining to produce a moment in which a woman of Wheatley's talent and race could emerge and be heard. For instance, it was in the 1760s and 1770s that the idea of prejudice as a reason for the treatment of blacks was popularized, especially the fact of skin color as a reason for such prejudice. There was a growing awareness that color/appearance played a major role in the subjugation of blacks, that in effect it was "the rock upon which slavery was founded" (Jordan 278-79). The very term *prejudice* as a way to describe the feeling of whites with regard to blacks and Native Americans emerged in these years (Jordan 276). In addition, the most outspoken group in the anti-slavery movement in the eighteenth century were ministers, so it should come as no surprise that condemnations of the institution contained an additional element: the appeal to religious sentiment, particularly claims that slavery was a sin for which all would eventually pay. Yet, as Jordan observes, "More important than this atavistic, generalized sense of slavery as a communal sin and of impending punishment was the way in which the clergy wove the sin of slaveholding into the fabric of the Revolutionary crisis" (298).[14]

A number of studies have considered Wheatley's relationship to the clergy. James A. Levernier points out that Wheatley "maintained an extensive network of connections with several prominent members of the New England clerical establishment" (23), men such as George Whitefield, Joseph Sewall (son of Samuel Sewall), John Lathrop (son-in-law of the Wheatleys), Timothy Pitkin (a guest in the Wheatley home), Eleazer Wheelock and Nathaniel Whitaker (founders of Dartmouth), and Samuel Hopkins (the abolitionist), in addition to the previously mentioned Samuel Cooper. In addition to Hopkins, many of these men were either "sympathetic with or outright involved in the Whig crusade for the abolition of slavery in New England" (Levernier 24). Levernier makes a strong case for an environment in which "Wheatley would have been surrounded by discussions of personal freedom and human rights, and, predictably, these subjects constituted much of the period's pulpit oratory" (25). She would have seen these ideas given respectful attention by audiences who were used to getting their lessons in sermon form. With such examples before her, it would have been an easy task for Wheatley—who learned to read and write English in sixteen months—to absorb what she needed in order to influence an audience of her own. Besides sermonic techniques, she would have learned what was and was not acceptable as material for her prospective audience and how her strategies might be used to greatest effect. In essence, Wheatley co-opted elements of several rhetorical trends—the language of equality and revolution in particular—combined them with the rhetoric of the pulpit, and gradually developed her rhetorical project.

Wheatley's central concern in this project may have been to expose and counteract the hypocritical ideological position held by many members of her perceived audience; however, as others have pointed out, her situation within that culture precluded her from an open attack on slavery.[15] Betsy Erkkila observes in "Phillis Wheatley and the Black American Revolution" that, when Wheatley's book was published, "there was widespread fear of slave revolt; Abigail Adams's September 1774 letter to John on the conspiracy of Boston Negroes is only one of a number of signs that fear of slave insurrection was spreading from the South to New England" (231).[16] To engage in a critique of slavery, Wheatley needed to find a strategy that made allies of her readers rather than critics. To this end, she used the genres and forms familiar to them—the sermon, the verse epistle, and the Bible—to establish a common ground from which to launch her attack. This is not to suggest that Wheatley expected the members of her intended audience suddenly to change their positions on slavery. But it does suggest that she was a keen observer of her culture, an evaluation that has been a long time coming.

Wheatley's cultural awareness is even more evident in the poem **"On Being Brought From Africa to America,"** written the year after the Harvard poem in 1768. The later poem exhibits an even greater level of complexity and authorial control, with Wheatley manipulating her audience by even more covert means. Rather than a direct appeal to a specific group, one with which the audience is asked to identify, this short poem is a meditation on being black and Christian in colonial America. As did **"To the University of Cambridge,"** this poem begins with the sentiment that the speaker's removal from Africa was an act of "mercy," but in this context it becomes Wheatley's version of the "fortunate fall"; the speaker's removal to the colonies, despite the circumstances, is perceived as a blessing. She does not, however, stipulate exactly whose act of mercy it was that saved her, God's or man's. One result is that, from the outset, Wheatley allows the audience to be positioned in the role of benefactor as opposed to oppressor, creating an avenue for the ideological reversal the poem enacts. Hers is a seemingly conservative statement that becomes highly ambiguous upon analysis, transgressive rather than compliant.[17]

While the use of italics for "*Pagan*" and "*Savior*" may have been a printer's decision rather than Wheatley's, the words are also connected through their position in their respective lines and through metric emphasis. (Thus, anyone hearing the poem read aloud would also have been aware of the implied connection.) In lieu of an open declaration connecting the Savior of all men and the African American population, one which might cause an adverse reaction in the yet-to-be-persuaded, Wheatley relies on indirection and the principle of association. This strategy is also evident in her use of the word *benighted* to describe the state of her soul (2). While it suggests the darkness of her African skin, it also resonates with the state of all those living in sin, including her audience. To be "benighted" is to be in moral or spiritual darkness as a result of ignorance or lack of enlightenment, certainly a description with which many of Wheatley's audience would have agreed. But, in addition, the word sets up the ideological enlightenment that Wheatley hopes will occur in the second stanza, when the speaker turns the tables on the audience. The idea that the speaker was brought to America by some force beyond her power to fight it (a sentiment reiterated from **"To the University of Cambridge"**) once more puts her in an authoritative position. She is both in America and actively seeking redemption because God himself has willed it. Chosen by Him, the speaker is again thrust into the role of preacher, one with a mission to save others. Like them (the line seems to suggest),

"Once *I* redemption neither sought nor knew" (4; my emphasis). However, in the speaker's case, the reason for this failure was a simple lack of awareness. In the case of her readers, such failure is more likely the result of the erroneous belief that they have been saved already. On this note, the speaker segues into the second stanza, having laid out her ("Christian") position and established the source of her rhetorical authority.

She now offers readers an opportunity to participate in their own salvation:

> Some view our sable race with scornful eye,
> "Their colour is a diabolic die."
> Remember, *Christians, Negroes*, black as *Cain*,
> May be refin'd, and join th' angelic train.
>
> (5-8)

The speaker, carefully aligning herself with those readers who will understand the subtlety of her allusions and references, creates a space wherein she and they are joined against a common antagonist: the "some" who "view our sable race with scornful eye" (5). The members of this group are not only guilty of the sin of reviling others (which Wheatley addressed in the Harvard poem) but also guilty for failing to acknowledge God's work in saving "Negroes." The result is that those who would cast black Christians as other have now been placed in a like position. The audience must therefore make a decision: Be part of the group that acknowledges the Christianity of blacks, including the speaker of the poem, or be part of the anonymous "some" who refuse to acknowledge a portion of God's creation. The word *Some* also introduces a more critical tone on the part of the speaker, as does the word *Remember,* which becomes an admonition to those who call themselves "Christians" but do not act as such. Adding insult to injury, Wheatley co-opts the rhetoric of this group—those who say of blacks that "'Their colour is a diabolic die'" (6)—using their own words against them. Betsy Erkkila describes this strategy as "a form of *mimesis* that mimics and mocks in the act of repeating" ("Revolutionary" 206). The effect is to place the "some" in a degraded position, one they have created for themselves through their un-Christian hypocrisy.

Suddenly, the audience is given an opportunity to view racism from a new perspective, and to either accept or reject this new ideological position. Further, because the membership of the "some" is not specified (aside from their common attitude), the audience is not automatically classified as belonging with them. Nor does Wheatley construct this group as specifically white, so that once again she resists antagonizing her white readers. Her refusal to assign blame, while it has often led critics to describe her as uncritical of slavery, is an important element in Wheatley's rhetorical strategy and certainly one of the reasons her poetry was published in the first place. Hers is an inclusionary rhetoric, reinforcing the similarities between the audience and the speaker of the poem, indeed all "Christians," in an effort to expand the parameters of that word in the minds of her readers. Rather than creating distinctions, the speaker actually collapses those which the "some" have worked so hard to create and maintain, the source of their dwindling authority (at least within the precincts of the poem).

Wheatley's shift from first to third person in the first and second stanzas is part of this approach. Although her intended audience is not black, she still refers to "our sable race." Her choice of pronoun might be a subtle allusion to ownership of black slaves by whites, but it also implies "ownership" in a more communal and spiritual sense. This phrase can be read as Wheatley's effort to have her privileged white audience understand for just a moment what it is like to be singled out as "diabolic." When the un-Christian speak of "'their color,'" they might just as easily be pointing to the white members of the audience who have accepted the invitation into Wheatley's circle. Her rhetoric has the effect of merging the female with the male, the white with the black, the Christian with the Pagan. The very distinctions that the "some" have created now work against them. They have become, within the parameters of the poem at least, what they once abhorred—benighted, ignorant, lost in moral darkness, unenlightened—because they are unable to accept the redemption of Africans. It is the racist posing as a Christian who has become diabolical.

The reversal of inside and outside, black and white has further significance because the unredeemed have also become the enslaved, although they are slaves to sin rather than to an earthly master. Wheatley continues her stratagem by reminding the audience of more universal truths than those uttered by the "some." For example, while the word *die* is clearly meant to refer to skin pigmentation, it also suggests the ultimate fate that awaits all people, regardless of color or race.[18] It is no accident that what follows in the final lines is a warning about the rewards for the redeemed after death when they "join th' angelic train" (8). In addition, Wheatley's language consistently emphasizes the worth of black Christians. For instance, the use of the word *sable* to describe the skin color of her race imparts a suggestion of rarity and richness that also makes affiliation with the group of which she is a part something to be desired and even sought after. The multiple meanings of the line "Remember, *Christians, Negroes* black as *Cain*" (7), with its ambiguous punctuation and double entendres, have become a critical commonplace in analyses of the poem. It has been variously read as a direct address to Christians, Wheatley's declaration that both the supposed Christians in her audience and the Negroes are as "black as Cain," and her way of indicating that the terms *Christians* and *Negroes* are synonymous. In fact, all three readings operate simultaneously to support Wheatley's argument. Following her previous rhetorical clues, the only ones who can accept the title of "Christian" are those who have made the decision not to be part of the "some" and to admit that "*Negroes* . . . / May be refin'd and join th' angelic train" (7-8). They must also accede to the equality of black Christians and their own sinful nature.

Once again, Wheatley co-opts the rhetoric of the other. In this instance, however, she uses the very argument that has been used to justify the existence of black slavery to argue against it: the connection between Africans and Cain, the murderer of Abel. The line in which the reference appears also conflates Christians and Negroes, making the mark of Cain a reference to any who are unredeemed.[19] Thus, in order to participate fully in the meaning of the poem, the audience must reject the false authority of the "some," an authority now associated with racism and hypocrisy, and accept instead the authority that the speaker represents, an authority based on the tenets of Christianity. The speaker's declared salvation and the righteous anger that seems barely contained in her "reprimand" in the penultimate line are reminiscent of the rhetoric of revivalist preachers.

In the event that what is at stake has not been made evident enough, Wheatley becomes most explicit in the concluding lines. While ostensibly about the fate of those black Christians who see the light and are saved, the final line in **"On Being Brought From Africa to America"** is also a reminder to the members of her audience about their own fate should they choose unwisely. It is not only "*Negroes*" who "may" get to join "th' angelic train" (7-8), but also those who truly deserve the label *Christian* as demonstrated by their behavior toward all of God's creatures. "*May* be refined" can be read either as synonymous for 'can' or as a warning: No one, neither Christians nor Negroes, should take salvation for granted. To the extent that the audience responds affirmatively to the statements and situations Wheatley has set forth in the poem, that is the extent to which they are authorized to use the classification "Christian." Ironically, this authorization occurs through the agency of a black female slave.

Starting deliberately from the position of the "other," Wheatley manages to alter the very terms of otherness, creating a new space for herself as both poet and African American Christian. The final and highly ironic demonstration of otherness, of course, would be one's failure to understand the very poem that enacts this strategy. Through her rhetoric of performed ideology, Wheatley revises the implied meaning of the word *Christian* to include African Americans. Her strategy relies on images, references, and a narrative position that would have been strikingly familiar to her audience. The "authentic" Christian is the one who "gets" the puns and double entendres and ironies, the one who is able to participate fully in Wheatley's rhetorical performance. In effect, both poems serve as litmus tests for true Christianity while purporting to affirm her redemption. For the unenlightened reader, the poems may well seem to be hackneyed and pedestrian pleas for acceptance; for the true Christian, they become a validation of one's status as a member of the elect, regardless of race.

It is no secret that Wheatley's poems drew a variety of readers, whether the Countess of Huntingdon, the plantation masters who ostensibly read the poems aloud to their slaves for the purposes of evangelization (O'Neale 145), or former slaves with access to her work, and that hers was a bifurcated audience. However, there was one specific group whose members had influence and power and were thus in a position to effect social change as well as personal change for Wheatley herself. It was for this audience that poems such as **"To the University of Cambridge, in New-England"** and **"On Being Brought from Africa to America"** were designed. In both poems, Wheatley manipulates language and genre in order to appeal to this particular audience in a way it would have found familiar, while simultaneously preserving her tenuous position as a public voice; she was writing in order to influence, enlighten, and perhaps even spur to action. It was an audience from whom she could anticipate certain reactions, and one she had good reason to believe would be responsive to the complex rhetorical performance these poems enact. A number of trends in the later-eighteenth century, including revivalism and the growing awareness of racism, had resulted in an audience more accustomed to a popularized and democratized relationship between speaker and audience than previously (Heimert 119), one on which Wheatley capitalized.

While two poems cannot be considered representative of an entire body of work, they suggest a complexity of thought and racial awareness that Wheatley exhibited more frequently and overtly over time, especially after she was given her freedom. In some ways these poems are more typical than otherwise. Poems such as **"To the University of Cambridge, in New-England"** and **"On Being Brought from Africa to America"** provide early evidence of a woman not only aware of her race but also increasingly adept at manipulating the system that enslaved her because of it. As the years passed, Wheatley became even more outspoken about the evils of slavery (Gilmore 605). For example, she added her most open condemnation of slavery, **"To the Right Honourable William, Earl of Dartmouth,"** to the London edition of ***Poems.*** In addition, her frequently quoted letter to the Rev. Samson Occom, written and published in 1774 after her manumission, contains a strong, albeit diplomatic, denunciation of slavery.[20]

Although this discussion focuses on just two poems in Wheatley's œuvre, a number of other poems would bear analysis that focuses on this poet's rhetorical techniques and awareness of audience. The Dartmouth poem, **"On Atheism,"** and **"An Address to the Deist"** are three that suggest themselves as apt texts for such a reading. As Hilene Flanzbaum and others have argued, despite the advances made to date, much still needs to be said about the language of Wheatley's poetic compositions. This type of analysis, which acknowledges her craftsmanship and complex racial consciousness, seems like the next logical step in Wheatley scholarship. The results can only be a deeper and more critical appreciation of this founding mother of African American literature.

Notes

1. Wilcox points out that there is no factual basis for the scene Gates imagines: "No one knows exactly how these signees came by their knowledge of Wheatley and her poetry. There is no evidence for the courtroom-like scene of judgement that Henry Louis Gates Jr. and Karla Holloway imagine. William H. Robinson envisions a more likely scenario: a series of drawing room performances before Susannah Wheatley's ever widening circle of influential friends, perhaps extending back before the attestation was deemed necessary. In either event, Wheatley's print persona was predicated on face-to-face encounters with prominent North American figures" (10). All references in this essay are to the edition first cited and are noted parenthetically in the text.
2. The attestation appeared in advertisements for the 1773 London edition of *Poems on Various Subjects, Religious and Moral,* Wheatley's only published volume of poetry, and as part of the front matter in all editions after the first.
3. In "'The Tongues of the Learned are Insufficient': Phillis Wheatley, Publishing Objectives, and Personal Liberty," Christopher D. Felker notes that Wheatley's book was originally marketed "as literature for 'extensive' reading and sold principally in the urban port cities (most notably Boston)" and "intended for a fashion-minded clientele prepared to buy the book on impulse" (159). Wheatley was clearly writing for a complex audience—her poetry was also known to fellow African Americans, such as the poet Jupiter Hammon and her lifelong friend Obour Tanner—but in this paper I am primarily interested in how the poems may have been intended to sway a segment of that audience with the power to end slavery.
4. Wheatley's poetic accomplishment has become more clearly understood and better appreciated in the last fifteen years due in large part to criticism that has focused on the structure and imagery of the poems as opposed to their biographical elements. The most promising analyses have focused either on her rhetorical strategies or the cultural work her poetry may have performed in Revolutionary America. See O'Neale, Reising, Richards, and Grimsted. Each treats the poems as complex rhetorical constructions that engage in what O'Neale refers to as Wheatley's "subtle war" against slavery.
5. While Mailloux's discussion focuses on *Adventures of Huckleberry Finn,* a text separated from Wheatley's poems by time, gender, and geography, among other things, the basic tenets of his theory are, I believe, still applicable.
6. As Brian Richardson has observed, there are always a number of audiences represented by any given text: those being addressed, those being excluded or ignored, and those under attack (46). My argument focuses specifically on the audience being addressed by Wheatley.
7. According to John C. Shields, "Both Mason and Robinson suggest that 'I. B.' is James Bowdoin, founder of Bowdoin College, governor of Massachusetts, founder of the American Academy of Arts and Sciences, and a signer of the attestation authenticating Wheatley's authorship of her 1773 *Poems*" (*Collected* 296).
8. Wilcox cites the statement near the end of the Boston call for subscribers (for which she credits Susannah Wheatley) which suggests that the publication of the poems might lead to Wheatley's freedom: "'It is hoped Encouragement will be given to this Publication, as a reward to a very uncommon Genius, *at present a slave*'" (15; my emphasis).
9. A number of recent studies, in addition to those already mentioned, have examined Wheatley's "sense of an intensely public poetic vocation" (Richards 171). Phillip M. Richards refers to the work of Muhktar Ali Isani and Cynthia Smith as integral in this regard, but his own analysis also focuses on Wheatley's attempts to legitimate herself in the eyes of her readers as a

"public poet," in particular an "evangelical or political poet" (174). Yet there remain those who question the intentionality of the effects she produced, Wheatley's artistry as opposed to her mere imitativeness. No previous study has considered whether Wheatley, like many writers, had a specific audience in mind as she wrote and how that might have influenced the construction of the poems. There has also been little examination of how the poems manifest this awareness of audience.

10. The very notion of a specific "reader" of a text, especially the "ideal reader" posited in the 1980s, has come under attack on a number of fronts, and for good reason. In an effort to distinguish between these terms, Stephen Railton has suggested that "we use the term 'reader' for anyone who at any time opens a book and begins processing a text. 'Audience,' on the other hand, could be reserved to designate the specific group, the contemporary reading public, to whom an author originally addresses the text. . . . Thus, the readers of *The Scarlet Letter* have all come into existence after the novel was written. The novel's audience, though, was there before Hawthorne sat down to write it" (138). Railton contends that "only the 'audience' . . . can play a role in the creation of the work itself. The reader responds to the text, but first, in the very act of literary conception, there is the response of the text to its audience; the way the text is shaped by the author's ambitions and anxieties about *performing* for a particular group" (138-39). The word *performing* is also significant in terms of my argument.

11. This poem was published by Wheatley prior to its inclusion in *Poems* in a slightly different version. However, as John C. Shields observes, she "made few major alterations" in the revision (*Collected* 281).

12. I am indebted to Angela Weisl for her observation about Wheatley's pronoun use in this instance. I am also deeply grateful for her careful readings of this manuscript in its several incarnations.

13. Sondra O'Neale discusses two possible effects of Wheatley's reference to herself as an "Ethiopian": It "might compel eighteenth-century Christians to consider that they had enslaved the heirs of biblical patriarchs," and it provided her "contemporary African-American readers [with] a sense of ethnicity related to Israel and antiquity that Europeans could not have" (153-54). Also addressing this reference, Robert Daly suggests that it is intended to evoke a line from Psalms 68:31: "Ethiopia shall soon stretch out her hands unto God" (18), especially in association with the line of the poem in which the persona "urges the students of Harvard to see Christ 'with hands outstretcht upon the cross'" (5).

14. Jordan elaborates upon these connections: "By the time of the Revolution the concept of natural rights was still suffused with religious feeling and, in its most common form, with explicitly religious ideas. The right to liberty was normally spoken of as God's gratuitous gift to mankind, as an endowment of the Creator. More important, all men partook of 'natural' rights because, as Thomas Paine wrote in the preamble to Pennsylvania's abolition law of 1780, 'all are the work of the Almighty Hand'" (294). Jordan also remarks on the similarity between anti-slavery writing at this time and the earlier jeremiads. The purveyors of this reasoning tended to be "men rooted in or deriving from a specifically *Puritan* tradition. . . . Thus it was Presbyterians, Congregationalists, and to a lesser degree Quakers who spoke in this fashion, and the more explicit denunciations came from men whose intellectual backgrounds were not explicitly Calvinist, men like Samuel Hopkins and Benjamin Colman" (300). It should be noted that, of the eighteen signers of Wheatley's attestation, seven were ministers.

15. David Grimsted maintains that "Wheatley knew herself and society with such clarity that she almost automatically asserted self while causing minimal irritation in others" (352). See also Levernier, "Phillis," and Burke. Levernier describes the poet as "encoding hidden messages" in her poems, a result of realizing "early in her poetic career . . . that a seemingly subservient voice was likely to be published while a more strident political voice was likely to be suppressed, if not punished" (25), while Burke argues that the poet had to find ways to work for justice from within the culture which confined her.

16. Erkkila also argues that this fear resulted in the failure of Wheatley's book to receive enough subscriptions to be published in Boston ("Phillis" 231).

17. Levernier's observation is useful here: "Wheatley, it should be remembered, was 'Brought from Africa to America' through the triangular trade, and as she was fully aware, economic gain rather than concern for the welfare of her soul was the real reason why Yankee slave traders had abducted her, against her will, from her native Africa" ("Wheatley's 'On Being'" 26).

18. Referring to her puns on dye and sugar cane, Levernier notes that "true Christians boycotted these products. At the very time when Wheatley was writing, for example, the Quaker evangelist John Woolman refused to use dye or sugar products on the grounds that they were obtained through 'the labours of poor oppressed Negroes'" ("Wheatley's 'On Being'" 26).

19. Watson observes that, "according to European Christian tradition, Cain was sinful, but was not black. If 'Negroes' are as 'black as *Cain*,' then they are not 'black' at all, or to be more precise, they're Semitic. To be as 'black as *Cain*' is to be part of the same family as Abel, descendants of Eve and Adam" (124).

20. Wheatley's 1774 letter to the Mohegan minister Samson Occom amply demonstrates her awareness of this paradox. She writes, as she puts it, "not for their Hurt, but to convince them of the strange Absurdity of their Conduct whose Words and Actions are so diametrically opposite. How well the Cry for Liberty, and the reverse Disposition for the Exercise of oppressive Power over others agree,—I humbly think it does not require the Penetration of a Philosopher to determine" (176-77). Not only does the letter provide evidence of Wheatley's race consciousness, but it contains many of the same allusions and images evident in the poems to be discussed: the redemption of Africans as God's work, the inherent relationship between words and actions, and the connection between African slavery and Jewish slavery under the Egyptians.

Works Cited

Bennett, Paula. "Phillis Wheatley's Vocation and the Paradox of the 'Afric Muse.'" *PMLA* 113.1 (1998): 64-76.

Bercovitch, Sacvan. *The American Jeremiad*. Madison: U of Wisconsin P, 1978.

Bly, Antonio T. "Wheatley's 'To the University of Cambridge in New England.'" *Explicator* 55.4 (1997): 205-08.

Burke, Helen M. "The Rhetoric and Politics of Marginality: The Subject of Phillis Wheatley." *Tulsa Studies in Women's Literature* 10.1 (1991): 31-45.

Daly, Robert. "Powers of Humility and the Presence of Readers in Anne Bradstreet and Phillis Wheatley." *Studies in Puritan American Spirituality* 4 (Dec. 1993): 1-23.

Erkkila, Betsy. "Phillis Wheatley and the Black American Revolution." *A Mixed Race: Ethnicity in Early America.* Ed. Frank Shuffleton. New York: Oxford UP, 1993. 225-40.

———. "Revolutionary Women." *Tulsa Studies in Women's Literature* 6 (1987): 189-223.

Flanzbaum, Hilene. "Unprecedented Liberties: Re-reading Phillis Wheatley." *MELUS* 18.3 (1993): 71-81.

Gates, Henry Louis, Jr. "In Her Own Write." Shields, *Collected* vii-xxii.

Grimsted, David. "Anglo-American Racism and Phillis Wheatley's 'Sable Veil,' 'Lengthened Chain,' and 'Knitted Heart.'" *Women in the Age of the American Revolution.* Ed. Ronald Hoffman and Peter J. Albert. Charlottesville: UP of Virginia, 1989. 333-444.

Heimert, Alan. "Jonathan Edwards, Charles Chauncey, and the Great Awakening." *The Columbia Literary History of the United States.* Ed. Emory Elliott, et al. New York: Columbia UP, 1988. 113-35.

Jordan, Winthrop D. *White Over Black: American Attitudes Toward the Negro, 1550-1812.* New York: Norton, 1968.

Kibbey, Ann. *The Interpretation of Material Shapes in Puritanism: A Study of Rhetoric, Prejudice, and Violence.* Cambridge: Cambridge UP, 1986.

Levernier, James A. "Phillis Wheatley." *Legacy* 13.1 (1996): 65-75.

———. "Wheatley's 'On Being Brought From Africa to America.'" *Explicator* 40.1 (1981): 25-26.

Mailloux, Steven. "Reading *Huckleberry Finn:* The Rhetoric of Performed Ideology." *New Essays on Huck Finn.* Ed. Louis J. Budd. Cambridge: Cambridge UP, 1985. 107-33.

O'Neale, Sondra. "A Slave's Subtle War: Phillis Wheatley's Use of Biblical Myth and Symbol." *Early American Literature* 21 (Fall 1986): 144-65.

Railton, Stephen. *Authorship and Audience: Literary Performance and the American Renaissance.* Princeton: Princeton UP, 1991.

Reising, Russell J. "Trafficking in White: Phillis Wheatley's Semiotics of Racial Representation." *Genre* 22 (Fall 1989): 231-61.

Richards, Phillip M. "Phillis Wheatley and Literary Americanization." *American Quarterly* 44.2 (1992): 163-90.

Richardson, Brian. "The Other Reader's Response: On Multiple, Divided, and Oppositional Audiences." *Criticism* 39.1 (1997): 31-53.

Robinson, William H. *Phillis Wheatley in the Black American Beginnings.* Detroit: Broadside P, 1975.

Shields, John C., ed. *The Collected Works of Phillis Wheatley.* New York: Oxford UP, 1988.

———. "Phillis Wheatley's Subversive Pastoral." *Eighteenth Century Studies* 27.4 (1994): 631-47.

Watson, Marsha. "A Classic Case: Phillis Wheatley and Her Poetry." *Early American Literature* 31.2 (1996): 103-32.

Wheatley, Phillis. *The Collected Works of Phillis Wheatley.* Ed. John C. Shields. New York: Oxford UP, 1988.

Wilcox, Kirstin. "The Body into Print: Marketing Phillis Wheatley." *American Literature* 71.1 (1999): 1-29.

Ziff, Larzer. "Literary Culture in Colonial America." *American Literature to 1900.* Ed. Marcus Cunliffe. London: Sphere, 1973. 23-52.

FURTHER READING

Bibliographies

Choucair, Mona M. "Phillis Wheatley." In *African American Authors, 1745-1945: A Bio-Bibliographical Critical Sourcebook,* edited by Emmanuel S. Nelson, pp. 463-68. Westport, Conn.: Greenwood, 2000.

Surveys Wheatley's major works and the most important pieces of criticism and biography on Wheatley from the eighteenth through the twentieth century.

Robinson, William H. *Phillis Wheatley: A Bio-Bibliography.* Boston: G. K. Hall, 1981, 166 p.

Provides a bibliography of criticism and writing on Wheatley, with a short biography.

Biography

DuBois, Shirley Graham. *The Story of Phillis Wheatley.* New York: J. Messner, 1949, 176 p.

Offers a biography of Wheatley written by African-American playwright and wife of W. E. B. DuBois.

Criticism

Brawley, Benjamin. "Phillis Wheatley." In *The Negro in Literature and Art in the United States,* 3rd ed., pp. 15-37. New York: AMS Press, 1971.

Critiques Wheatley's poetry, noting the detrimental influence of neoclassical English poets, and asserts her importance to American literary history.

Burke, Helen. "Problematizing American Dissent: The Subject of Phillis Wheatley." In *Cohesion and Dissent in America,* edited by Carol Colatrella and Joseph Alkana, pp. 193-209. Albany: State University of New York Press, 1994.

Challenges the idea that Wheatley's success as a poet reflects her escape from the oppressive situation of slavery.

Collins, Terence. "Phillis Wheatley: The Dark Side of Poetry." *PHYLON* 36, no. 1 (March 1975): 78-88.

Examines Wheatley's poetry as an expression of self-hatred engendered by the poet's submission to the dominant culture in a slave-holding society.

Erkkila, Betsy. "Phillis Wheatley and the Black American Revolution." In *A Mixed Race: Ethnicity in Early America,* edited by Frank Shuffleton, pp. 225-40. New York: Oxford University Press, 1993.

Emphasizes the revolutionary power of Wheatley's use of republican and religious figurations of enslavement and redemption.

Gates, Henry Louis, Jr. "Phillis Wheatley and the Nature of the Negro." In *Figures in Black: Words, Signs, and the 'Racial' Self,* pp. 61-79. Oxford: Oxford University Press, 1987.

Discusses the early reception of Wheatley's poetry and suggests that criticism of Wheatley set the pattern for centuries of literary criticism on African American authors.

———. "Phillis Wheatley On Trial." *New Yorker* (20 January 2003): 82-7.

Connects the public trial Wheatley faced to prove she was the author of her poems to the criticisms her poetry endured from twentieth-century black literary critics.

———. *The Trials of Phillis Wheatley: America's First Black Poet and Her Encounters with the Founding Fathers.* New York: Basic Civitas Books, 2003, 166 p.

Explores Wheatley's role in the development of the black literary tradition.

Grimstead, David. "Anglo-American Racism and Phillis Wheatley's 'Sable Veil,' 'Length'ned Chain,' and 'Knitted Heart.'" In *Women in the Age of the American Revolution,* edited by Ronald Hoffman and Peter J. Albert, pp. 338-445. Charlottesville: University Press of Virginia, 1989.

Disputes characterizations of Wheatley as lacking in self- and race-consciousness.

Hull, Gloria T. "Afro-American Women Poets: A Bio-Critical Survey." In *Shakespeare's Sisters: Feminist Essays on Women Poets,* edited by Sandra M. Gilbert and Susan Gubar, pp. 165-82. Bloomington: Indiana University Press, 1979.

Suggests that sexism may have influenced critical assessments of Wheatley's poetry and argues that Wheatley was more self-aware than other critics have allowed.

Johnson, James Weldon. "Preface to Original Edition." In *The Book of American Negro Poetry,* edited by James Weldon Johnson, pp. 9-48. New York: Harcourt Brace Jovanovich, 1931.

Surveys Wheatley's career and criticizes Wheatley's poetry.

Matson, R. Lynn. "Phillis Wheatley—Soul Sister?" *PHYLON* 33, no. 3 (fall 1972): 222-30.

Defends Wheatley from charges of abandoning her race and assimilating into white society; notes the importance of Wheatley's discovery of Christianity to understanding her writings.

O'Neale, Sondra. "A Slave's Subtle War: Phillis Wheatley's Use of Biblical Myth and Symbol." *Early American Literature* 21, no. 2 (fall 1986): 144-65.

Contends that Wheatley used the tropes of Anglo-American culture in a new and subversive way to define an abolitionist moral stance.

Robinson, William H. *Phillis Wheatley in the Black American Beginnings.* Detroit: Broadside Press, 1975, 95 p.

Attempts a modern reassessment of Wheatley's life and works; examines the themes of race, politics, and religion in her poetry.

OTHER SOURCES FROM GALE:

Additional coverage of Wheatley's life and career is contained in the following sources published by the Gale Group: *African-American Writers,* Eds. 1, 2; *Black Literature Criticism,* Ed. 3; *Concise Dictionary of American Literary Biography, 1640-1865; Dictionary of Literary Biography,* Vols. 31, 50; *DISCovering Authors; DISCovering Authors: Canadian Edition; DISCovering Authors Modules: Most-studied Authors, Multicultural Authors,* and *Poets; DISCovering Authors 3.0; Exploring Poetry; Literature Criticism from 1400-1800,* Vols. 3, 50; *Literature Resource Center; Poetry Criticism,* Vol. 3; *Poetry for Students,* Vol. 13; *Reference Guide to American Literature,* Ed. 4; and *World Literature Criticism.*

MARY WOLLSTONECRAFT

(1759 - 1797)

English essayist and novelist.

Wollstonecraft has been labelled by several scholars as one of the founders of modern feminism. Resembling other progressive figures of the eighteenth-century Enlightenment era, Wollstonecraft supported both political and social freedom in her polemic prose, calling for greater social justice and individual autonomy. She additionally emphasized the natural rights and reason of men and women as the foundation of personal liberty. An accomplished essayist and novelist, Wollstonecraft was influenced by such Enlightenment figures as Thomas Paine and Jean-Jacques Rousseau, but unlike most thinkers of the period, she extended the radical doctrine of the rights of man to include the rights of women. In support of Wollstonecraft's own claim that she was "the first of a new genus" of female advocates, many academics now consider her controversial manifesto *A Vindication of the Rights of Woman* (1792) the first modern feminist tract.

BIOGRAPHICAL INFORMATION

Born in London on April 27, 1759, Wollstonecraft was the daughter of a would-be gentleman farmer and his wife—her father having abandoned the prosperous family trade of weaving in order to pursue farming. The Wollstonecraft family relocated frequently during Mary's childhood, living at various times in London, Yorkshire, and Wales, but nowhere did Edward John Wollstonecraft succeed in his chosen career. The domestic life of the Wollstonecrafts progressively worsened as Mary's father succumbed to alcoholism. Wollstonecraft was frequently a witness to her father's physical abuse of her mother, who meekly suffered her husband's violence. Wollstonecraft also failed to receive emotional support from her mother, who openly preferred and indulged Mary's brother, Edward. Resolved to become independent, Wollstonecraft left home against her parents' wishes in 1778 to accept the position of paid companion to a widow in Bath. She was obliged to return to her family in London two years later to care for her dying mother, but upon the latter's death, she immediately left again, this time living with the family of her close friend Frances ("Fanny") Blood. Wollstonecraft remained with Fanny Blood and her parents for several years, contributing with her needlework to the family's meager income. In 1783 Wollstonecraft's sister Eliza suffered a mental breakdown following the birth of a daughter. Believing that her brother-in-law was the cause of his wife's distress, Wollstonecraft arranged to remove Eliza from his house and later obtained a legal separation. Having undertaken responsibility for her sister, and faced with the necessity of earning a living, Wollstonecraft opened a school at Newington Green, near London, with Fanny Blood, Eliza, and her other sister, Everina. The enterprise was a success, but the partnership dissolved in 1785 when Blood married a longtime suitor and traveled with him to Portugal. Some months later, Wollstonecraft also journeyed to Portugal in order to visit her pregnant and ailing friend but arrived only to witness Fanny's death in childbirth. Upon her return to England, Wollstonecraft was forced to close the school due to financial difficulties. Soon afterward she wrote her first essay, *Thoughts on the Education of Daughters: With Reflections on Female Conduct, in the More Important Duties of Life* (1787), and made the acquaintance of the liberal-minded publisher Joseph Johnson, who agreed to issue it. However, conscious of a pressing need for money, Wollstonecraft left England for Ireland, where she took a post as a governess to Lord Kingsborough's children. During her employment in Ireland, she wrote her first novel *Mary, A Fiction* (1788). In 1787 Wollstonecraft was dismissed from her duties by Lady Kingsborough and subsequently settled in London, determined to support herself by writing. Johnson became her mentor in this new venture, introducing her to London's literary and political worlds and charging her to undertake translations and reviews for the *Analytical Review,* a politically liberal periodical that he and Thomas Carlisle had recently founded.

With the publication of her *A Vindication of the Rights of Men, in a Letter to the Right Honourable Edmund Burke* in 1790 and *A Vindication of the Rights of Woman* in 1792, Wollstonecraft fully established herself as an equal in a circle of radical thinkers that included Thomas Paine, William Blake, William Godwin, and the painter Henry Fuseli. Wollstonecraft fell in love with Fuseli, but the feeling was not reciprocated. When her proposal to join the Fuseli household was firmly rejected by the artist's wife, Wollstonecraft journeyed alone to Paris to recover from her disappointment. Paris in 1792 was in the midst of the chaotic violence of the French Revolution, and while Wollstonecraft, like other liberal English intellectuals, wholeheartedly supported the revolution, she was nonetheless appalled and to some degree endangered by the excess of the Reign of Terror. Her thoughts and the conclusions she drew during this time are recorded in her *An Historical and Moral View of the Origin and Progress of the French Revolution; and the Effect It Has Produced in Europe* (1794). In Paris Wollstonecraft met Gilbert Imlay, an American author and businessman. They became lovers and, the following year, Wollstonecraft's daughter Fanny was born. Imlay soon lost interest in Wollstonecraft, but as he was unable or unwilling to admit this, the dissolution of their affair was both painful and protracted. Following a brief reunion in London in 1795, Wollstonecraft became so despondent upon learning of Imlay's involvement with another woman that she attempted suicide. Little is known of the circumstances of the attempt—it is thought that she took laudanum—but Imlay prevented its success and persuaded Wollstonecraft to undertake business of his in Scandinavia. Wollstonecraft accordingly embarked with Fanny and her nurse for an extended tour of Scandinavia, which resulted in her *Letters Written during a Short Residence in Sweden, Norway, and Denmark* (1796). When she returned to England, Wollstonecraft again despaired of a reunion with Imlay and attempted suicide a second time: she jumped off a bridge into the River Thames but was rescued by passing boatmen. Wollstonecraft recovered and eventually resumed writing, contributing material to the *Analytical Review.* She also renewed her acquaintance with William Godwin, now famous as the author of *An Enquiry Concerning the Principles of Political Justice, and Its Influence on General Virtue and Happiness* (1793), an essay much acclaimed in radical circles. Godwin and Wollstonecraft eventually became lovers and, after Wollstonecraft became pregnant, they married. The couple did, however, maintain separate residences as a means of retaining independence and keeping their relationship fresh. Within days of giving birth to a daughter, Mary (the future Mary Shelley), Wollstonecraft died of postpartum complications on September 10, 1797.

MAJOR WORKS

The tenor of Wollstonecraft's prose is intimately related to the time in which she lived, during which reason, empiricism, and individualism were beginning to supersede the long-established reliance on faith, prescription, and authority. Such Enlightenment ideals are integral to Wollstonecraft's work and form the basis of her argument in her most famous and controversial essay, *A Vindication of the Rights of Woman. A Vindication* is considered an important milestone in the development of modern thought and of modern feminism. In the essay, Wollstonecraft contends that the great majority of women are intellectually and ethically inferior to men not because of a lack of native ability or potential but rather due to inferior education and insidious social conditioning. Wollstonecraft argues that women are as rational and independent as men and as such are entitled to the same rights and responsibilities. *A Vindication* combines Wollstonecraft's pragmatic suggestions for ameliorating the status of women with elements of theoretical social philosophy. Many of the practical aspects of *A Vindication of the Rights of Woman* are an expansion of the ideas expressed in Wollstonecraft's earlier *Thoughts on the Education of Daughters*. *Thoughts* promotes educational theories similar to the system proposed in Rousseau's *Émile*, but Wollstonecraft's text envisions an academic utopia that is also coeducational. The philosophical perspective of *A Vindication of the Rights of Woman* is prefigured in *A Vindication of the Rights of Men,* which was Wollstonecraft's response to Edmund Burke's *Reflections on the Revolution in France, on the Proceedings of Certain Societies in London Relative to that Event.* Burke denounced the tactics of the French Revolution and warned England against similar democratic schemes, a position Wollstonecraft considered unacceptable to human liberty and demeaning to the human spirit. *A Vindication of the Rights of Men* highlights how Wollstonecraft's opposition to the oppression of women is further demonstrated in her attacks against class and economic barriers. *A Vindication of the Rights of Men* additionally shows how the author's feminism coexists with her broader advocacy for the worth of the individual and the natural right of humanity to govern itself. Wollstonecraft's other work on the French Revolution, the *Historical and Moral View,* mixes the author's personal observations of the Revolution's events with a philosophical and political treatise on natural rights and the consequences of violating those rights. Though Wollstonecraft's major feminist writings are contained in her essays, her fiction presents an equally passionate and notably more personal argument for the rights and education of women. *Mary, A Fiction* and *Maria; or, The Wrongs of Woman* (1799) both focus on a young heroine trapped by both an unhappy marriage with an unfeeling husband and restrictive social mores. The novels are largely autobiographical, particularly *Mary,* which details the misery of the young heroine's childhood and the fervor of her attachment to a friend who dies young. The melodramatic tone of her fiction is in keeping with her reportedly tempestuous personality as well as the notoriously dark style of English Romanticism.

CRITICAL RECEPTION

Initial response to Wollstonecraft's work focused on her political and social ideas and was predictably polarized. Her immediate circle of peers was one of like-minded progressive intellectuals who admired her candor and boldness as a champion of human rights. Conservative critics were especially disapproving of her feminism and her audacity as a publishing woman author: Horace Walpole famously called her a "hyena in petticoats." Like several other women who dared to publish in a male-dominated world, criticism of Wollstonecraft's work was colored by charges of promiscuity and depravity—charges that were fueled by Wollstonecraft's notorious difficult personality and her unusual romantic arrangements. By the end of the nineteenth century, however, Wollstonecraft was inarguably on the winning side of the Enlightenment war of ideas, and her position on natural rights eventually reflected political reality, though her popularity waxed and waned along with the fluctuations of feminism in society. Studies of Wollstonecraft from the early twentieth century, such as G. R. Stirling Taylor's *Mary Wollstonecraft: A Study in Economics and Romance,* celebrated her ideas and vision as the movement for women's suffrage gained power. A few decades later, critics were more likely to emphasize Wollstonecraft's character failings and minimize her contribution to political thought; in fact, Wollstonecraft's personal life has never ceased to be a central issue in Wollstonecraft scholarship, even in the twenty-first century. Accordingly, she has inspired an unusual number of biographies, many of which have been openly critical of her volatile nature and complicated personal relationships. Among these are two works written as the modern feminist movement peaked—Eleanor Flexner's *Mary Wollstonecraft: A Biography* and Claire Tomalin's *The Life and Death of Mary Wollstonecraft.* Some scholars, however, have sought to reexamine Wollstonecraft's extremes of temperament to provide a better understanding of her work. A feminist interpretation of "sensibility"—an eighteenth-century term that could be expressed in modern times as a strong sensitivity, both physical and emotional—contends that Wollstonecraft's language of feeling is a feminine mode of expression that is often devalued by men but remains empowering and inspirational to women. Cora Kaplan, Mitzi Meyers, Claudia L. Johnson, and Julie Ellison are among those critics who have attempted to revise traditional readings of sentiment in Wollstonecraft's work, transforming what was once seen as feminine weakness into a staunch battle against oppression. Even Wollstonecraft's novels, which were long dismissed as excessively sentimental and mediocre in style, have begun to appear in this light as extensions of her theoretical essays. Although Wollstonecraft's general premises of the rights of women no longer generate controversy, many feminists suggest that her writings continue to be influential. Recent models for literary analysis have generated new appreciation for the lessons Wollstonecraft has to teach men and women of the twenty-first century. In particular, Wollstonecraft's treatment of motherhood as an aspect of women's identity has attracted the attention of writers seeking to expand the possibilities of feminine and feminist identity, including Shawn Lisa Maurer, Miriam Brody, Angela Keane, and Cora Kaplan. Keane and Kaplan have each suggested that Wollstonecraft's inclusion of women's physical nature—and not just mental capacity—as part of their subjectivity maintains transformative potential for modern feminist political thought. Virginia Woolf once claimed of Wollstonecraft's *Vindications* that they "are so true that they now seem to contain nothing new in them—their originality has become our commonplace." A number of academics mirror Woolf's remarks, and assert that Wollstonecraft's radical critique of the position of women in society continues to offer challenges and inspiration to modern feminist theorists.

PRINCIPAL WORKS

Thoughts on the Education of Daughters: With Reflections on Female Conduct, in the More Important Duties of Life (essay) 1787

Mary, A Fiction (novel) 1788

Original Stories from Real Life; with Conversations, Calculated to Regulate the Affections, and Form the Mind to Truth and Goodness (juvenilia) 1788

The Female Reader; or, Miscellaneous-Pieces, in Prose and Verse, Selected from the Best Writers, and Disposed Under Proper Heads; for the Improvement of Young Women [editor] (poetry and essays) 1789

A Vindication of the Rights of Men, in a Letter to the Right Honourable Edmund Burke; Occasioned by His Reflections on the Revolution in France (essay) 1790

A Vindication of the Rights of Woman: with Strictures on Political and Moral Subjects (essay) 1792

An Historical and Moral View of the Origin and Progress of the French Revolution; and the Effect It Has Produced in Europe (essays) 1794

Letters Written During a Short Residence in Sweden, Norway, and Denmark (letters) 1796

**Posthumous Works of the Author of the Vindication of the Rights of Woman.* 4 vols. (essays, letters, and prose) 1798

Maria; or, The Wrongs of Woman: A Posthumous Fragment (unfinished novel) 1799

Godwin and Mary: Letters of William Godwin and Mary Wollstonecraft (letters) 1966

A Wollstonecraft Anthology (essays, letters, and prose) 1977

The Collected Letters of Mary Wollstonecraft (letters) 1979

The Collected Works of Mary Wollstonecraft. 7 vols. (essays, letters, and prose) 1989

* Includes *Maria; or, The Wrongs of Woman: a Posthumous Fragment.*

PRIMARY SOURCES

MARY WOLLSTONECRAFT (ESSAY DATE 1787)

SOURCE: Wollstonecraft, Mary. "Unfortunate Situation of Females, Fashionably Educated, and Left Without a Fortune." In *Works of Mary Wollstonecraft.* Vol. 4, edited by Janet Todd and Marilyn Butler, pp. 25-7. New York: New York University Press, 1989.

In the following essay, from her 1787 publication Thoughts on the Education of Daughters, *Wollstonecraft discusses the plight of single women without an independent fortune. Too many young women, Wollstonecraft argues, receive only a token education and are therefore left unable to provide for themselves.*

I have hitherto only spoken of those females, who will have a provision made for them by their parents. But many who have been well, or at least fashionably educated, are left without a fortune, and if they are not entirely devoid of delicacy, they must frequently remain single.

Few are the modes of earning a subsistence, and those very humiliating. Perhaps to be an humble companion to some rich old cousin, or what is still/worse, to live with strangers, who are so intolerably tyrannical, that none of their own relations can bear to live with them, though they should even expect a fortune in reversion. It is impossible to enumerate the many hours of anguish such a person must spend. Above the servants, yet considered by them as a spy, and ever reminded of her inferiority when in conversation with the superiors. If she cannot condescend to mean flattery, she has not a chance of being a favorite; and should any of the visitors take notice of her, and she for a moment forget her subordinate state, she is sure to be reminded of it./

Painfully sensible of unkindness, she is alive to every thing, and many sarcasms reach her, which were perhaps directed another way. She is alone, shut out from equality and confidence, and the concealed anxiety impairs her constitution; for she must wear a cheerful face, or be dismissed. The being dependant on the caprice of a fellow creature, though certainly very necessary in this state of discipline, is yet a very bitter corrective, which we would fain shrink from.

A teacher at a school is only a kind of upper servant, who has more work than the menial ones./

A governess to young ladies is equally disagreeable. It is ten to one if they meet with a reasonable mother; and if she is not so, she will be continually finding fault to prove she is not ignorant, and be displeased if her pupils do not improve, but angry if the proper methods are taken to make them do so. The children treat them with disrespect, and often with insolence. In the mean time life glides away, and the spirits with it; 'and when youth and genial years are flown,' they have nothing to subsist on; or, perhaps, on some extraordinary occasion, some small allowance may be made for them, which is thought a great charity./

The few trades which are left, are now gradually falling into the hands of the men, and certainly they are not very respectable.

It is hard for a person who has a relish for polished society, to herd with the vulgar, or to condescend to mix with her former equals when she is considered in a different light. What unwelcome heart-breaking knowledge is then poured in on her! I mean a view of the selfishness and depravity of the world; for every other acquirement is a source of pleasure, though they may occasion temporary inconveniences. How cutting is the contempt / she meets with!—A young mind looks round for love and friendship; but love and friendship fly from poverty: expect them not if you are poor! The mind must then sink into meanness, and accommodate itself to its new state, or dare to be unhappy. Yet I think no reflecting person would give up the experience and improvement they have gained, to have avoided the misfortunes; on the contrary, they are thankfully ranked amongst the choicest blessings of life, when we are not under their immediate pressure.

How earnestly does a mind full of sensibility look for disinterested friendship, / and long to meet with good unalloyed. When fortune smiles they hug the dear delusion; but dream not that it is one. The painted cloud disappears suddenly, the scene is changed, and what an aching void is left in the heart! a void which only religion can fill up—and how few seek this internal comfort!

A woman, who has beauty without sentiment, is in great danger of being seduced; and if she has any, cannot guard herself from painful mortifications. It is very disagreeable to keep up a continual reserve with men she has been formerly familiar with; yet / if she places confidence, it is ten to one but she is deceived. Few men seriously think of marrying an inferior; and if they have honor enough not to take advantage of the artless tenderness of a woman who loves, and thinks not of the difference of rank, they do not undeceive her until she has anticipated happiness, which, contrasted with her dependant situation, appears delightful. The disappointment is severe; and the heart receives a wound which does not easily admit of a compleat cure, as the good that is missed is not valued according to its real worth: for fancy drew the picture, and grief delights to create food to feed on./

If what I have written should be read by parents, who are now going on in thoughtless extravagance, and anxious only that their daughters may be *genteelly educated,* let them consider to what sorrows they expose them; for I have not over-coloured the picture.

Though I warn parents to guard against leaving their daughters to encounter so much misery; yet if a young woman falls into it, she ought not to be discontented. Good must ultimately arise from every thing, to those who look beyond this infancy of their being; and here the comfort of a good conscience is our only stable support. The main business of our lives is to / learn to be virtuous; and He who is training us up for immortal bliss, knows best what trials will contribute to make us so; and our resignation and improvement will render us respectable to ourselves, and to that Being, whose approbation is of more value than life itself. It is true, tribulation produces anguish, and we would fain avoid the bitter cup, though convinced its effects would be the most salutary. The Almighty is then the kind parent, who chastens and educates, and indulges us not when it would tend to our hurt. He is compassion itself, and never wounds but to heal, when the ends of correction are answered.

MARY WOLLSTONECRAFT (ESSAY DATE 1792)

SOURCE: Wollstonecraft, Mary. Introduction to *A Vindication of the Rights of Woman.* 1792. Reprint, pp. 6-10. Mineola, N.Y.: Dover, 1996.

In the following introduction to the 1792 edition, Wollstonecraft delineates the purpose of her Vindication of the Rights of Woman.

After Considering the historic page, and viewing the living world with anxious solicitude, the most melancholy emotions of sorrowful indignation have depressed my spirits, and I have sighed when obliged to confess, that either nature has made a great difference between man and man, or that the civilization which has hitherto taken place in the world has been very partial. I have turned over various books written on the subject of education, and patiently observed the conduct of parents and the management of schools; but what has been the result?—a profound conviction that the neglected education of my fellow-creatures is the grand source of the misery I deplore; and that women, in particular, are rendered weak and wretched by a variety of concurring causes, originating from one hasty conclusion. The conduct and manners of women, in fact, evidently prove that their minds are not in a healthy state; for, like the flowers which are planted in too rich a soil, strength and usefulness are sacrificed to beauty; and the flaunting leaves, after having pleased a fastidious eye, fade, disregarded on the stalk, long before the season when they ought to have arrived at maturity.—One cause of this barren blooming I attribute to a false system of education, gathered from the books written on this subject by men who, considering females rather as women than human creatures, have been more anxious to make them alluring mistresses than affectionate wives and rational mothers; and the understanding of the sex has been so bubbled by this specious homage, that the civilized women of the present century, with a few exceptions, are only anxious to inspire love, when they ought to cherish a nobler ambition, and by their abilities and virtues exact respect.

In a treatise, therefore, on female rights and manners, the works which have been particularly written for their improvement must not be overlooked; especially when it is asserted, in direct terms, that the minds of women are enfeebled by false refinement; that the books of instruction, written by men of genius, have had the same tendency as more frivolous productions; and that, in the true style of Mahometanism, they are treated as a kind of subordinate beings, and not as a part of the human species, when improveable reason is allowed to be the dignified distinction which raises men above the brute creation, and puts a natural sceptre in a feeble hand.

Yet, because I am a woman, I would not lead my readers to suppose that I mean violently to agitate the contested question respecting the equality or inferiority of the sex; but as the subject lies in my way, and I cannot pass it over without subjecting the main tendency of my reasoning to misconstruction, I shall stop a moment to deliver, in a few words, my opinion.—In the government of the physical world it is observable that the female in point of strength is, in general, inferior to the male. This is the law of nature; and it does not appear to be suspended or abrogated in favour of woman. A degree of physical superiority cannot, therefore, be denied—and it is a noble prerogative! But not content with this natural pre-eminence, men endeavour to sink us still lower, merely to render us alluring objects for a moment; and women, intoxicated by the adoration which men, under the influence of their senses, pay them, do not seek to obtain a durable interest in their hearts, or to become the friends of the fellow creatures who find amusement in their society.

I am aware of an obvious inference:—from every quarter have I heard exclamations against masculine women; but where are they to be found? If by this appellation men mean to inveigh against their ardour in hunting, shooting, and gaming, I shall most cordially join in the cry; but if it be against the imitation of manly virtues, or, more properly speaking, the attainment of those talents and virtues, the exercise of which ennobles the human character, and which raise females in the scale of animal being, when they are comprehensively termed mankind;—all those who view them with a philosophic eye must, I should think, wish with me, that they may every day grow more and more masculine.

This discussion naturally divides the subject. I shall first consider women in the grand light of human creatures, who, in common with men, are placed on this earth to unfold their faculties; and afterwards I shall more particularly point out their peculiar designation.

I wish also to steer clear of an error which many respectable writers have fallen into; for the instruction which has hitherto been addressed to women, has rather been applicable to *ladies,* if the little indirect advice, that is scattered through Sandford and Merton, be excepted; but, addressing my sex in a firmer tone, I pay particular attention to those in the middle class, because they appear to be in the most natural state. Perhaps the seeds of false refinement, immorality, and vanity, have ever been shed by the great. Weak, artificial beings, raised above the common wants and affections of their race, in a premature unnatural manner, undermine the very foundation of virtue, and spread corruption through the whole mass of society! As a class of mankind they have the strongest claim to pity; the education of the rich tends to render them vain and helpless, and the unfolding mind is not strengthened by the practice of those duties which dignify the human character.—They only live to amuse themselves, and by the same law which in nature invariably produces certain effects, they soon only afford barren amusement.

But as I purpose taking a separate view of the different ranks of society, and of the moral character of women, in each, this hint is, for the present, sufficient; and I have only alluded to the subject, because it appears to me to be the very essence of an introduction to give a cursory account of the contents of the work it introduces.

My own sex, I hope, will excuse me, if I treat them like rational creatures, instead of flattering their *fascinating* graces, and viewing them as if they were in a state of perpetual childhood, unable to stand alone. I earnestly wish to point out in what true dignity and human happiness consists—I wish to persuade women to endeavour to acquire strength, both of mind and body, and to convince them that the soft phrases, susceptibility of heart, delicacy of sentiment, and refinement of taste, are almost synonymous with epithets of weakness, and that those beings who are only the objects of pity and that kind of love, which has been termed its sister, will soon become objects of contempt.

Dismissing then those pretty feminine phrases, which the men condescendingly use to soften our slavish dependence, and despising that weak elegancy of mind, exquisite sensibility, and sweet docility of manners, supposed to be the sexual characteristics of the weaker vessel, I wish to shew that elegance is inferior to virtue, that the first object of laudable ambition is to obtain a character as a human being, regardless of the distinction of sex; and that secondary views should be brought to this simple touchstone.

This is a rough sketch of my plan; and should I express my conviction with the energetic emotions that I feel whenever I think of the subject, the dictates of experience and reflection will be felt by some of my readers. Animated by this important object, I shall disdain to cull my phrases or polish my style;—I aim at being useful, and sincerity will render me unaffected; for, wishing rather to persuade by the force of my arguments, than dazzle by the elegance of my language, I shall not waste my time in rounding periods, or in fabricating the turgid bombast of artificial feelings, which, coming from the head, never reach the heart.—I shall be employed about things, not words!—and, anxious to render my sex more respectable members of society, I shall try to avoid that flowery diction which has slided from essays into novels, and from novels into familiar letters and conversation.

These pretty superlatives, dropping glibly from the tongue, vitiate the taste, and create a kind of sickly delicacy that turns away from simple unadorned truth; and a deluge of false sentiments and overstretched feelings, stifling the natural emotions of the heart, render the domestic pleasures inspid, that ought to sweeten the exercise of those severe duties, which educate a rational and immortal being for a nobler field of action.

The education of women has, of late, been more attended to than formerly; yet they are still reckoned a frivolous sex, and ridiculed or pitied by the writers who endeavour by satire or instruction to improve them. It is acknowledged that they spend many of the first years of their lives in acquiring a smattering of accomplishments; meanwhile strength of body and mind are sacrificed to libertine notions of beauty, to the desire of establishing themselves,—the only way women can rise in the world,—by marriage. And this desire making mere animals of them, when they marry they act as such children may be expected to act:—they dress; they paint, and nickname God's creatures.—Surely these weak beings are only fit for a seraglio!—Can they be expected to govern a family with judgment, or take care of the poor babes whom they bring into the world?

If then it can be fairly deduced from the present conduct of the sex, from the prevalent fondness for pleasure which takes place of ambition and those nobler passions that open and enlarge the soul; that the instruction which women have hitherto received has only tended, with the constitution of civil society, to render them insignificant objects of desire—mere propagators of fools!—if it can be proved that in aiming

FROM THE AUTHOR

EXCERPT FROM WOLLSTONECRAFT'S DEDICATION TO M. TALLEYRAND-PÉRIGORD, A FRENCH DIPLOMAT WHOSE REPORT ON PUBLIC EDUCATION EXCLUDED INFORMATION ON THE EDUCATION OF WOMEN

Contending for the rights of woman, my main argument is built on this simple principle, that if she be not prepared by education to become the companion of man, she will stop the progress of knowledge and virtue; for truth must be common to all, or it will be inefficacious with respect to its influence on general practice. And how can woman be expected to co-operate unless she know why she ought to be virtuous? unless freedom strengthen her reason till she comprehend her duty, and see in what manner it is connected with her real good? If children are to be educated to understand the true principle of patriotism, their mother must be a patriot; and the love of mankind, from which an orderly train of virtues spring, can only be produced by considering the moral and civil interest of mankind; but the education and situation of woman, at present, shuts her out from such investigations.

Wollstonecraft, Mary. Excerpt from "To M. Talleyrand-Périgord." In *A Vindication of the Rights of Woman*. London: J. Johnson, 1792.

to accomplish them, without cultivating their understandings, they are taken out of their sphere of duties, and made ridiculous and useless when the short-lived bloom of beauty is over,[1] I presume that *rational* men will excuse me for endeavouring to persuade them to become more masculine and respectable.

Indeed the word masculine is only a bugbear: there is little reason to fear that women will acquire too much courage or fortitude; for their apparent inferiority with respect to bodily strength, must render them, in some degree, dependent on men in the various relations of life; but why should it be increased by prejudices that give a sex to virtue, and confound simple truths with sensual reveries?

Women are, in fact, so much degraded by mistaken notions of female excellence, that I do not mean to add a paradox when I assert, that this artificial weakness produces a propensity to tyrannize, and gives birth to cunning, the natural opponent of strength, which leads them to play off those contemptible infantine airs that undermine esteem even whilst they excite desire. Let men become more chaste and modest, and if women do not grow wiser in the same ratio, it will be clear that they have weaker understandings. It seems scarcely necessary to say, that I now speak of the sex in general. Many individuals have more sense than their male relatives; and, as nothing preponderates where there is a constant struggle for an equilibrium, without it has naturally more gravity, some women govern their husbands without degrading themselves, because intellect will always govern.

Note

1. A lively writer, I cannot recollect his name, asks what business women turned of forty have to do in the world?

MARY WOLLSTONECRAFT (LETTER DATE 4 SEPTEMBER 1796)

SOURCE: Wollstonecraft, Mary. "Letter from Mary to Godwin, September 4, 1796." In *Godwin and Mary: Letters of William Godwin and Mary Wollstonecraft,* edited by Ralph M. Wardle, pp. 27-9. Lawrence: University of Kansas Press, 1966.

In the following letter, Wollstonecraft responds to Godwin's critique of her writing by describing the passion she feels for her writing and the importance of her work.

Labouring all the morning, in vain, to overcome an oppression of spirits, which some things you uttered yesterday, produced; I will try if I can shake it off by describing to you the nature of the feelings you excited.

I allude to what you remarked, relative to my manner of writing—that there was a radical defect in it—a worm in the bud—& c What is to be done, I must either disregard your opinion, think it unjust, or throw down my pen in despair; and that would be tantamount to resigning existence; for at fifteen I resolved never to marry for interested motives, or to endure a life of dependence. You know not how painfully my sensibility, call it false if you will, has been wounded by some of the steps I have been obliged to take for others. I have even now plans at heart, which depend on my exertions; and my entire confidence in Mr. Imlay plunged me into some difficulties, since we parted, that I could scarcely away with. I know that many of my cares have been the natural consequence of what, nine out of ten would [have] termed folly—yet I cannot coincide in the opinion, without feeling a contempt for mankind. In short, I must reckon on doing some good, and getting the money I want, by my writings, or go to sleep for ever. I shall not be content merely to keep body and soul together—By what I have already written Johnson, I am sure, has been a gainer. And, for I would wish you to see my heart and mind just as it appears to myself, without drawing any veil of affected humility over it, though this whole letter is a proof of painful diffidence, I am compelled to think that there is some thing in my writings more valuable, than in the productions of some people on whom you bestow warm elogiums—I mean more mind—denominate it as you will—more of the observations of my own senses, more of the combining of my own imagination—the effusions of my own feelings and passions than the cold workings of the brain on the materials procured by the senses and imagination of other writers—

I am more out of patience with myself than you can form any idea of, when I tell you that I have scarcely written a line to please myself (and very little with respect to quantity) since you saw my M.S. I have been endeavouring all this morning; and with such dissatisfied sensations I am almost afraid to go into company—But these are idle complaints to which I ought not to give utterance, even to you—I must then have done—

Mary

GENERAL COMMENTARY

GARY KELLY (ESSAY DATE 1997)

SOURCE: Kelly, Gary. "(Female) Philosophy in the Bedroom: Mary Wollstonecraft and Female Sexuality." *Women's Writing* 4, no. 2 (1997): 143-54.

In the following essay, Kelly examines Wollstonecraft's personal life as well as her writings and argues that Wollstonecraft was a forerunner in reimagining women's sexuality outside of traditional marriage structures. In doing so, Kelly also defends Wollstonecraft from criticism of her relationships with men and her seemingly extreme behavior.

At a certain point in Sade's *La Philosophie dans le boudoir* (1795), the relentless pedagogical exercises in the Sadean grammar of sexuality are suspended by, or perhaps culminate in, the reading of a revolutionary polemical tract. Despite the apparently revolutionary sexual and textual articulations in Sade's novel, the pupils are female, the instructors male, and the novel could be claimed to reproduce a gender hierarchy inherent in the courtly *ancien régime.* This was just what Mary Wollstonecraft claimed about an earlier proposal for ostensibly revolutionary pedagogy. In *her* polemical tract, ***A Vindication of the Rights of Woman,*** she attacked Talleyrand's scheme for national education in France because it assigned a subordinate place to women and thus ran the risk of reproducing the *ancien régime*'s subordination of women, thereby wrecking the revolutionary project itself. As Sade and Wollstonecraft both recognised, however, female sexuality, its construction and emancipation, was central in both courtly and revolutionary regimes. In this essay I will describe Wollstonecraft's articulation of that issue, partly in her writings, but also in her personal life, and the key terms I use are those in my essay's title.

By *Mary Wollstonecraft* I mean an archive and an agent. The archive is a set of texts ranging from manuscript letters and documents, through published works and the testimony of others about *Mary Wollstonecraft,* to the initials M. W. marked on the stays worn by an unidentified female, later recognised as Wollstonecraft's daughter Frances, at the time the latter committed suicide (Wardle, p. 335). These texts have material form, however, as works wrought by an agent addressing others in a socially and historically specific discursive situation, and, though that situation cannot be fully or finally known to us, it is not ours.

By *female* here I mean not just the usual modern sense of those persons so classified according to the discourse of biology. Wollstonecraft and her contemporaries such as Mary Hays would use the term to include what we would now consider the feminine, that is, subjective, cultural, and social practices learned as part of a historically and socially particular "language" of gender, as distinct from sex. The sense of "female" used here is, then, based on what is often referred to as "social constructionism" (Berger & Luckmann).

By *philosophy* I mean the term as used in Wollstonecraft's day, that is, a certain politicised intellectual critique of unreason, principally the court system of the *ancien régime,* with the "prejudice" and "custom" that sustained it and the "ignorance" and "superstition" that enabled it to perdure. Philosophy as such was gendered masculine in Wollstonecraft's day and, in the opinion of many people, females, like children and the common people, were excluded by nature or education from mastery of analytical and theoretical discourses. Accordingly, these social groups were widely considered to be naturally or all too easily the dupes of "prejudices" and "custom", "ignorance" and "superstition". Thus these groups were seen as both characteristic of unmodernised society and culture and reproducers of it. Not surprisingly, then, many in Wollstonecraft's day would have considered the phrase "female philosopher" to be an oxymoron.

These conventional attitudes were precisely what Wollstonecraft and other feminists of her time challenged, pointing out that if women, like children and plebeians, were excluded from philosophy as analytical discourse and from philosophy's revolutionary programme, they would hinder or even prevent the realisation of that programme. For Wollstonecraft, female philosophy meant not just access to philosophy for women or a distinct and desirable supplement to philosophy as conventionally and historically practised by men. To them, female philosophy was an urgently necessary reformation of male philosophy by "feminine" elements, in order to effect philosophy's potential for revolutionary transformation. Inevitably, revolutionised philosophy would have to enter the bedroom because the sexualisation of women to the exclusion of other attributes was, in the view of a broad range of late eighteenth-century writers, the cause of the courtisation and thus the degradation of women—their exclusion from the broad middle-class revolutionary project.

More particularly, feminists such as Wollstonecraft understood philosophy in practical terms to be the analytical method and discursive practice required by men in order to be successful in the professions (Wollstonecraft, 1792, ch. 2). To call for women, especially of the middle classes (Wollstonecraft's declared subject and audience), to become female philosophers was to call for the professionalisation of women of those classes. Wollstonecraft argues that, if women of the middle classes are not professionalised, or given appropriate knowledge, intellectual training (which she calls "reason"), and moral self-discipline ("virtue"), they will remain the subjects of undisciplined desire ("custom", "prejudice", "superstition", etc.) and thus liable to courtisation, as they had been for centuries. Such women could only impede and would probably wreck the middle-class revolution that was in train in Wollstonecraft's day, not only in France but, in various ways and to varying degrees, throughout the Western world.

By *sexuality* I mean subjective and somatic practices that are designated erotic and amorous by a particular society and culture. Such practices have long been represented as "natural" to or inherent in individuals in ways that are extra-social and extra-cultural, arising from deep, perhaps prelinguistic or extra-linguistic structures in subjectivity, or from "human nature". In this sense, sexuality seems authentic. A contrastingly different representation of sexuality is as performance (Butler), and therefore as no more authentic than any other kind of practice. In general, post-modernism questions any attribute as "naturally" or essentially human, and this questioning would include sexuality. Another strong approach to sexuality has been through psychoanalytic theory. Here my interest, however, is in sexuality as socially constructed, historically and socially specific, and yet a form of personal agency. Thus sexuality pertains to gender rather than to biological sex. The question of the conjunction of the sexuality of deep psychological structures and that which is socially constructed and historically particular remains unresolved here.

In addition, by defining sexuality as I do, I am not presenting sexuality as a form of discipline or policing, a compulsory regime scripted by society and merely enacted or performed by individuals (Foucault). I am more interested here in sexuality as being like a language, or rather sociolect and idiolect, one that individuals learn and employ for particular personal and social aims or reasons. Here I am using Roy Harris's model of language as a social practice. Thus I am not considering sexuality as a psychic, biological, or physiological imperative but rather as a psychic, biological, and physiological potential realised in culture and society, or a historically particular culture and society. Inasmuch as society and culture are political, or inevitably differentiated by relations of power, sexuality is also always political. As Cora Kaplan has pointed out, this relationship is central for feminist criticism, and Wollstonecraft and her writings form an exemplary case of it (Kaplan, pp. 32-54, 121-125, 155-160).

Similarly, by *the bedroom* I mean not a particular chamber but the politically, socially, and culturally designated and sanctioned scene for such practice of sexuality, though of course any place, indoors or out, could and can serve as a temporary site for it. More particularly, I mean the bedroom as *boudoir,* a private if not secret domestic space historically assigned to women as a site for conducting their private, including sexual, relationships. It is, of course, interesting in itself that this particular sense of "bedroom" is covered in English by a word appropriated from French, the language of Sade, and the sense used by Sade, suggesting that what transpires in the "boudoir" may not have been considered to be fully or properly "English" or "British". It is additionally interesting that a "boudoir" was originally a private room into which a woman could retire in order to sulk (*bouder*), presumably as a result of some rebuff or neglect in the public social sphere. Later the term came to mean a room in which a woman could receive her intimate acquaintances, and this is the sense that was appropriated into English, though "boudoir" retains the sense of a scene of sexual practice.

This leaves the words *in* and *and*—though small, they are important for articulating an argument. By female philosophy *in* the bedroom I mean a complex relationship. Philosophy and the bedroom could be distinct if not opposing discursive sites and practices. Philosophy and the bedroom could also be seen in hierarchical relationship, with philosophy able to account for the bedroom, but not the other way around. Here philosophy masters the bedroom, or even forestalls it. Yet the bedroom could be seen as the site of a practice more "authentic", more practical, more "real" than philosophy. In this view the bedroom is not just a place where philosophers (too) can be off duty, can be themselves, but the bedroom triumphs over philosophy by exposing its impractical, abstract, dehumanising character. All of these possible relationships were current in Wollstonecraft's day, seen in Wollstonecraft's texts and those of her fellow English Jacobins and their French contemporaries such as Laclos and Sade.

For example, the bedroom could be the recreation and refuge of the man—less often the woman—weary of the practice of philosophy as contestation and critique, as in Sade. Philosophy could also extend its critique to the bedroom, analysing sexual practices as necessary products or symptoms of one kind of political regime or another, as in Sade and Wollstonecraft. Here philosophy could also imagine the bedroom and sexuality otherwise, as a site among others for avant-garde or revolutionary political practice. The bedroom could also be the site of philosophy's failure, its lapse into courtly sexuality, thus exposing avant-garde, revolutionary philosophy's impracticality or hypocrisy, as in the Anti-Jacobin counter-revolutionary critique of Wollstonecraft. It was particularly in the aftermath of the Jacobin Terror, during the early Directory period of the Revolution, that sexuality of a particular kind came to seem intrinsic to the Revolution and, in the eyes of many in Britain, to reveal the Revolution's "true" character as at once a broad programme of license and transgression, including sexual, and a return of decadent courtliness. It was during the Directory period of the mid-1790s that the Revolution became associated, for many British observers, with excess of all kinds, including sexual excess. Wollstonecraft's public reputation was to be ruined by this association.

For those, like Wollstonecraft, who had determined to apply philosophy even to sexuality, however, philosophy had to be applied in the bedroom or the Revolutionary project would fail, would lapse back into the vitiated and vitiating gender relations of the *ancien régime*. Furthermore, the principles of revolutionary philosophy required enactment of this critique in the philosopher's own sexual practice in the bedroom and its surrounding domestic space and culture. That the personal is political and vice versa was a common understanding in the age of Mary Wollstonecraft, as an examination of the "paper war" over the Revolution amply illustrates. Though this commonplace was pursued with particular energy in the Revolution debate, it did not originate in revolutionary culture. It was partly a residue of court culture under the *ancien régime* and partly a recreation of the culture of Sensibility that was designed to oppose and supersede court culture.

Court government had long been represented by its (largely middle-class and puritan) critics and opponents as a system of intertwined political and sexual intrigue, of favourites and mistresses manipulating the top of a patronage system that in turn controlled the social, economic, cultural, and political life of the country and largely determined social and domestic relations and personal characters of individuals. This was the system that Wollstonecraft attacked in ***A Vindication of the Rights of Woman*** and elsewhere as the cause of the courtisation of women, or their intellectual and moral trivialisation for erotic subordination. It was the system that Wollstonecraft thought the first wave of Revolutionaries had unthinkingly subsumed in their state constitution by excluding women from the full process of state education. This exclusion, Wollstonecraft argued, denied women the civil consciousness and roles they must have if they were not to continue to be courtly coquettes undermining the Revolution at home, and subverting the public and political sphere for private and personal ends, as the court system forced them to do.

Before the Revolution, writers of Sensibility reformulated the relation of the personal and political as a comprehensive oppositional culture constructed in the interests and image of the self-idealised professional middle class (see Brissenden, Barker-Benfield). According to the politics of Sensibility, the illegitimate personality politics of court government were to be supplanted by a politics of merit, or the disciplined moral and intellectual subject that was the idealised image of the professional man of the time. The court system was routinely figured as a regime of the father, or interconnected systems of patronage, paternalism, and patriarchy. Thus Sensibility, as an oppositional culture, tended to figure its idealised self as female and feminine after a bourgeois rather than courtly model of woman. Sensibility was feminised in a historically and socially specific way, though in fact it was available to both men and women of the subaltern middle classes, addressing men in the first instance, and addressing men and women differently. It was this culture that enabled Wollstonecraft to theorise her own experience of sexuality as a mediation of gender and class difference within the revolutionary politics of the professional middle class in her time.

In order to explicate the *and* in "Wollstonecraft and female sexuality", I turn now to a narrative of Wollstonecraft's encounter with and attempt to revolutionise, as a *female* philosopher, female sexuality for the larger revolutionary project of philosophy.

Her early letters, written while a girl living with her family in Yorkshire, show her grappling uncertainly and ambivalently with the courtisation of women of her class (Wollstonecraft, 1979). Within her family and early circle of friends she experienced and observed the degrading and brutalising effect of the courtly code of gender relations filtered down into the margins of the gentry and middle classes in which she grew up. Her mother was beaten and possibly raped by a drunken, over-ambitious father. Wollstonecraft and her siblings were deprived of proper education and reasonable expectations in order to fund the social advancement of her oldest brother. Her sister Eliza married and was probably rushed into motherhood and thus driven into mental and marital breakdown. Her friend Frances Blood was kept dangling by the self-interested family of her fiancé and, once married, unwisely became pregnant and removed to Portugal, where she died after childbirth. Blood's sister Caroline became a prostitute and workhouse inmate. While living in Windsor as a lady's companion Wollstonecraft was amused and irritated at the flutter caused by the notoriously gallant Prince of Wales, a figure to whom she would return in ***The Wrongs of Woman.*** In Ireland, as governess in the family of the titled and wealthy Kingsboroughs, she rejected courtisation in the education of her young female charges and observed with amusement and contempt the coquetting manipulativeness of Lady Kingsborough.

It was at this point that the literature of Sensibility, with its basis in Enlightenment philosophy, spoke so forcibly to Wollstonecraft in her social no man's land as professional and intellectual woman, as it did to many other men and women in similar situations in Western societies of the time. The relevance of Sensibility for her was focused in Jean-Jacques Rousseau as self-feminised male and her model for self-reconstruction as female philosopher. Rousseau's writings made clear the conflict between the political and the personal, including sexuality and private life. By the late 1780s Wollstonecraft was increasingly critical of the subjection of women by the gentry property system, expressed in the English tradition of female conduct literature with its pessimistic and repressive view of female sexuality. Yet she also knew how easily women could be seduced by courtly ideology. At this point, then, both conventional marriage and unconventional sexual conduct would, it seemed to her, vitiate her project of self-construction as a "female philosopher", or avant-garde exemplar of female emancipation within the horizon of possibilities offered by late eighteenth-century society.

In the face of this impasse Wollstonecraft struggled to find an acceptable practice of sexuality. One way was through intense female friendship of the kind she had with Frances Blood. Such relationships could of course have an erotic dimension, as implied by conduct-books' anxiety about them. Blood's death put an end to this experiment in female sexuality, but the intensity of Wollstonecraft's feeling about it may be taken to indicate a lesbian or potentially lesbian relationship. Such homosocial intensity was and is not uncommon, was licensed to a degree by social convention at that time, and was indeed encouraged in the culture of Sensibility. Adopting lesbian sexuality and way of life was a possible though highly risky political gesture, and if Wollstonecraft did so she didn't make the relationship into such a gesture. Later, in ***A Vindication of the Rights of Woman,*** she regards girls' boarding schools as morally dangerous in part because by their nature they encourage masturbation and lesbianism (Wollstonecraft, 1792, p. 164). In short, whatever personal satisfactions lesbianism may have offered, its political usefulness in Wollstonecraft's day, if openly avowed, was not what it may be today.

A different field for personal and political construction of female sexuality was offered by religious Dissent. As a marginalised urban and commercial middle-class community, Dissent defined itself largely by rejecting hegemonic culture, including courtly sexuality. At that time, such rejection was not necessarily repressively puritanical but could liberate men and women from the codes and roles of courtly sexuality. Partly for this reason intellectual women such as Wollstonecraft found Dissent a congenial environment in many ways. Furthermore, as an oppositional culture Dissent also embraced feminisation and facilitated useful and safe relationships of male-female intellectual equality or mentorship, such as that enjoyed by Wollstonecraft with several clergymen, including Richard Price (whom she would later defend in her ***Vindication of the Rights of Men***). A more dangerous relationship of a similar kind involved George Ogle, one of Lady Kingsborough's circle, who turned out, in Wollstonecraft's view, to conceal courtly amorousness beneath Rousseauist feminisation.

Wollstonecraft's most important relationship with a feminised man, however, would be with her publisher. Joseph Johnson was a Dissenter, a bachelor, the leading publisher of the English Dissenting Enlightenment, and had close friendships with creative, feminised men such as William Roscoe and Henry Fuseli, who also became Wollstonecraft's friends. She not only earned a living thanks to Johnson, but, as a member Johnson's circle of progressive writers, intellectuals, and artists, she could ignore courtly femininity and sexuality to create an identity as a female philosopher, discussing subjects conventionally closed to women or barred from mixed company, such as science, politics, and sexuality itself. Like many men and women in her situation she welcomed the French Revolution, and even identified with it by becoming a "philosophical sloven", or adopting the style of dress, comportment, and domestic life affected by Parisian women who had thrown off courtly femininity and sexuality for an openly revolutionary counter-culture.

By this point she was reinventing her female sexuality in a relationship with the expatriate Swiss artist and critic Henry Fuseli. His presence in her intellectual and personal life facilitated her emergence as a public character, first with ***A Vindication of the Rights of Men*** (1790), and then ***with A Vindication of the Rights of Woman*** (1792). In the latter, Wollstonecraft consistently casts the expression of female sexuality in a negative light. For example, in chapter 4, significantly entitled, "Observations on the State of Degradation to which Woman is Reduced by Various Causes", she states:

> *Love, considered as an animal appetite, cannot long feed on itself without expiring. And this extinction in its own flame, may be termed the violent death of love. But the wife who has been thus rendered licentious, will probably endeavour to fill the void left by her husband's attentions . . .*
>
> *Personal attachment is a very happy foundation for friendship; yet, when even two virtuous people marry, it would, perhaps, be happy if some circumstances checked their passion . . . In that case they would look beyond the present moment, and try to render the whole of life respectable, by forming a plan to regulate a friendship which only death ought to dissolve.*
>
> (*Wollstonecraft, 1792, p. 73*)

Here Wollstonecraft seems to repeat the commonplace warning of female conduct-books against expression of female sexual desire. The dim view of conjugal sexuality is also found in her letters of the late 1780s and early 1790s, and there is her own observation of the disorienting effect of sexual desire in her younger sister, Fanny Blood, and other women. Wollstonecraft's concern here, however, is that women be able to resist courtisation in marriage, given the prevalence of such pressures in society and culture at large. It is not so much female sexuality that she denies as its distortion by the dominant ideology and culture—a distortion that works to subordinate and oppress women.

Between the two ***Vindications*** Wollstonecraft also reflected on a new model, the "bluestocking" and notorious female philosopher of an earlier generation, Catharine Macaulay Graham. Macaulay Graham was a second generation bluestocking writer and intellectual who had transgressed the gendered boundary of discourse by writing full-scale and frankly political historiography—otherwise a masculine discourse. Macaulay Graham also breached conventional femininity by openly advocating classical republicanism. More seriously damaging was her decision, once widowed, to marry a man younger and from a lower social class, thereby advertising, in the eyes of many, that she was marrying for sexual pleasure. She was satirised accordingly. Significantly, Wollstonecraft decided to memorialise Macaulay Graham in ***A Vindication of the Rights of***

Woman. While writing the book, she also abandoned her avant-garde Parisian and Revolutionary-style coarse attire and appearance and adopted a more "bluestocking" style of dress, conduct, and life.

This transformation has been interpreted as an attempt to please Fuseli and to formalise her relationship with him. Yet it is clear from her letters and actions that she had no intention of giving up her ideal of avant-garde revolutionary intellectual companionship or betraying the anti-courtly sexual politics she had advocated in ***A Vindication of the Rights of Woman.*** She did, finally, propose joining the Fuseli household as his intellectual partner, while Fuseli's wife Sophia, a former model who may have been illiterate, was to remain his sexual partner and housekeeper. Such an arrangement would obviously have been problematic, however, since it could too easily have been seen to subsume the interrelated class and gender differences of court culture; in any case the proposal was rejected.

By this time, Wollstonecraft must already have heard of the avant-garde conjugality being practised in Girondin Revolutionary coteries and expatriate British circles at Paris, including the salon of Marie Roland and the society around Johnson's partner, Thomas Christie. Here amorous and conjugal relationships were formed without marriage, which was rejected as an institution of gentry property and court government. Among women Wollstonecraft knew who were involved in such relationships were Helen Maria Williams, Marie Roland, and Thomas Christie's wife Rebecca. Wollstonecraft went to Paris to pursue both her writing career and the kind of relationship she had failed to achieve with Fuseli. She soon found with Gilbert Imlay a way to practise female philosophy in the bedroom.

What we know of this relationship, especially from Wollstonecraft's letters, suggests that it was intensely intimate yet open, allowed much independence to both partners, and was obstructed and thus probably intensified by the actual political and economic situation of France at the time. Under the Jacobin Terror, and with a state of war existing between Britain and France, Wollstonecraft as a British subject was in a dangerous position. She had herself registered as Imlay's wife with the American embassy, though they did not marry, and had to live outside Paris for some time; Imlay, as an American with commercial experience, could engage in business, especially blockade running, for the French government. To Wollstonecraft's irritation, this work seemed to require long absences from Wollstonecraft and their daughter, who was born in the spring of 1794. Wollstonecraft was also irritated by the Jacobin regime's negative attitude to female philosophers and politicians and their exhortations to women to stay at home to raise good citizens with literal and metaphorical "lait républicain".

Nevertheless, her letters, especially to Imlay, show a determined endeavour to practise her new-found revolutionary conjugality as both female and philosopher. In this endeavour, she strove over some period to keep her sexual needs and desires in balance and relationship with what she believed to be a reflective, "philosophical" self-awareness, and with an economy of mutuality and equality in desire as in all aspects of their relationship. Eventually, his loss of sexual feeling for her proved overwhelmingly disappointing in terms of her politics of sexuality and conjugality. Imlay became involved with another woman and the relationship with Wollstonecraft broke down, though whether Imlay's involvement with the other woman was the symptom or cause cannot be known. In fact, we have on record only one side of their relationship and the available evidence is open to conflicting interpretations. The letters show that Wollstonecraft tried to keep the relationship going and was prepared to overlook Imlay's infidelities up to a point. When this failed she threatened or attempted suicide, but then agreed to be his agent in recovering money he was using to purchase embargoed goods for the French government. On her return she found Imlay with a new partner and again attempted suicide. After some months she accepted that the relationship was over, though she remained fearful of being betrayed again.

The prevailing view has been that Wollstonecraft made a fool of herself over Imlay, that he was probably not worthy of her, and that as a feminist she ought to have been stronger and more decisive in dealing with him. My reading is that she saw in Imlay and her relationship with him the sexual, domestic, and conjugal realisation of her female philosophy and the personal basis for sustaining her public and political dissemination of that philosophy. That she may have been mistaken in the circumstances cannot be known and should not be to her discredit. Besides, during and from this personal and public-political crisis she produced, in ***An Historical and Moral View of the French Revolution*** (1794), a feminisation of historiography and the Revolution in the style of Catharine Macaulay Graham, and, in ***Letters from Sweden*** (1796) and ***The Wrongs of Woman*** (1798), a textualisation of female philosophy both in the bedroom and at large in society of pre-Revolutionary and post-Revolutionary Europe. In this text, as I have argued elsewhere (Kelly), she created, in the figure of the author-in-the-text, an exemplary avant-garde consciousness for a new revolutionary cadre at a moment when revolutionary hope seemed about to be extinguished. It is not coincidental that this avant-garde consciousness is represented repeatedly as a female philosopher in the bedroom, as a subjective yet embodied site of lost and remembered revolutionary sexuality and of post-Revolutionary reflection and self-reconstruction.

If Imlay turned out to be not enough of a philosopher to sustain a relationship with her, Wollstonecraft's next partner, William Godwin, was the most famous and infamous philosopher in Britain. Their relationship is well documented through their letters and notes and Godwin's journal. They intended from the outset to practise an avant-garde sexuality and conjugality called for and validated by their philosophy. As with Imlay, Wollstonecraft's relationship with Godwin was to be part of a revolutionary subculture implicitly criticising and proleptically replacing hegemonic relations between the sexes. Significantly, in their bedroom they alternated avant-garde philosophy and sexuality, giving up the latter for the former whenever Wollstonecraft might have become pregnant. Again, however, this relationship was hindered by repressive political and social values and also by financial pressures. Opposition to such personal-political subcultures was less obviously dangerous and more diffused than in Jacobin France, but Wollstonecraft and Godwin had to protect their livelihoods and their political usefulness in an atmosphere of increasing political repression, social surveillance, and moral policing, especially after Wollstonecraft became pregnant, against her wishes. Therefore they legalised their relationship, though this was in effect a public admission that Wollstonecraft had not been married to Imlay.

Her unexpected death from complications of childbirth was not, of course, the end of the story. Godwin chose to publish work she left unfinished at her death, with a candid memoir of her and what are evidently selections from her letters to Imlay and Johnson (he would have included letters to Fuseli but the latter refused access to them). These texts enabled counter-revolutionary journalists to pillory Wollstonecraft as an example of the commonplace Anti-Jacobin argument that reformers and revolutionaries were merely using a political programme to advance their ambitions and gratify their appetites, including sexual appetite. These journalists made common practice of discrediting reformist and revolutionary programmes by showing how their proponents betrayed their own principles, theories, and arguments. Feminism was but one reform cause of many successfully smeared and marginalised or suppressed in this way. In the intense ideological and armed struggle of the later 1790s and early 1800s there were many who believed the smear and many others who thought such means were justified for the end of national survival against resurgent Revolutionary France under Napoleon. The social, political, and economic crises of the post-war years, up to the reform movements of the 1830s, again deferred any useful opportunity to reinsert Wollstonecraft and her work into the public political sphere, though there were opportunities to do so, and it was attempted in early socialist circles (as Barbara Taylor has shown) and attempted obliquely or covertly in the work of Mary Shelley, Lady Caroline Lamb, and other women writers of the 1820s and 1830s.

A politicised female sexuality such as Wollstonecraft enacted and represented in her work was diverted into and continued to be part of avant-garde and "bohemian" practice. Counter-revolutionary propaganda successfully disabled it, however, as an important element in transgressive and reformative practice in the public political sphere, except within socialist, feminist and other reform movements. In the meantime, Wollstonecraft's views about and practice of sexuality remained a problem. Answers to this problem, unfortunately, comprise a history of the sexual double standard and middle-class moralising. The counter-revolutionary condemnation formed after the appearance of Godwin's memorialising texts continued to have a strong influence, even with feminists. The commonest and longest-lived view has been that Wollstonecraft preached female independence but practised dependence, that she betrayed her feminist principles or at best could not live up to them, that her sexuality let her feminism down, that the female philosopher was defeated in the bedroom. Since the 1970s, when female sexuality became a central issue in feminist discourse, some commentators have also criticised Wollstonecraft's apparent denial of female sexuality in ***A Vindication of the Rights of Woman.***

In re-presenting Mary Wollstonecraft as the (female) philosopher in the bedroom, I have aimed to re-place Wollstonecraft in her time in order to represent her as a philosopher with much to tell us about the discourse of sexuality and whatever comes into it, in any time and place. In doing so I have approached sexuality as socially and historically particular, and, like other social and cultural discourse, one way that human agents express and negotiate social difference and relations of power in particular circumstances. Like language as theorised by Roy Harris, sexuality may be treated as a field of creative communication within a particular horizon of possibility. In order to understand Wollstonecraft's exercise of such agency, and thus illuminate our own, it is necessary to understand her horizon of possibility, which was not ours. Such an approach may not produce Wollstonecraft as the female philosopher in the bedroom who is what Angela Carter calls the "Sadeian woman", and there are, of course, other ways of treating sexuality than that used here; each has its limits, as does this one. Certainly, readings of Wollstonecraft based on gender-only or transhistorical assumptions about sexuality often seem to produce her as victim, hypocrite, bourgeois liberal, or all of these. Historicising her and the discourse(s) of sexuality in her time perhaps produces a more interesting Wollstonecraft, for some of us; and, at the risk of indulging in celebratory criticism, such a reading also produces a Wollstonecraft who is admirable, exemplary, and instructive, even now.

References

Brissenden, R. F., *Virtue in Distress: Studies in the Novel of Sensibility from Richardson to Sade* (London, 1974).

Barker-Benfield, G. J., *The Culture of Sensibility: Sex and Society in Eighteenth-Century Britain* (Chicago: University of Chicago Press, 1992).

Berger, P. L. & Luckman, T., *The Social Construction of Reality: A Treatise in the Sociology of Knowledge (1966)* (Harmondsworth: Penguin Books, 1971).

Butler, J., *Bodies that Matter: On the Discursive Limits of "Sex"* (New York: Routledge, 1993).

Butler, M. (Ed.) *Burke, Paine, Godwin, and the Revolution Controversy* (Cambridge: Cambridge University Press, 1984).

Cobban, A. (Ed.) *The Debate on the French Revolution, 1789-1800,* second edition (London: Adam & Charles Black, 1960).

Foucault, M., *The History of Sexuality,* 3 volumes (London: Lane, 1979).

Harris, R., *The Language Myth* (London: Duckworth, 1981).

Kaplan, C., *Sea Changes: Essays on Culture and Feminism* (London: Verso, 1986).

Kelly, G., *Revolutionary Feminism: The Mind and Career of Mary Wollstonecraft* (London: Macmillan; New York: St Martin's, 1992).

Taylor, B., *Eve and the New Jerusalem: Socialism and Feminism in the Nineteenth Century* (London: Virago, 1983).

Wardle, R. M., *Mary Wollstonecraft: A Critical Biography* (Lincoln: University of Nebraska Press, 1951).

Wollstonecraft, M. (1792) *A Vindication of the Rights of Woman,* edited by Carol Poston, second edition (New York: W. W. Norton & Co., 1988).

Wollstonecraft, M. (1976) *Letters Written During a Short Residence in Sweden, Norway, and Denmark,* edited by Carole H. Poston (Lincoln: University of Nebraska Press).

Wollstonecraft, M. (1979) *The Collected Letters of Mary Wollstonecraft,* edited by Ralph M. Wardle (Ithaca: Cornell University Press).

WENDY GUNTHER-CANADA (ESSAY DATE 2001)

SOURCE: Gunther-Canada, Wendy. "A Voice From the Void." In *Rebel Writer: Mary Wollstonecraft and Enlightenment Politics,* pp. 40-70. DeKalb: Northern Illinois University Press, 2001.

In the following excerpt, Gunther-Canada examines Wollstonecraft's early work in order to better understand how Wollstonecraft developed her politics and her writing. Considering Wollstonecraft's early letters, her Thoughts on the Education of Daughters, *and her first novel,* Mary, A Fiction, *Gunther-Canada suggests that Wollstonecraft's focus on girls represented a new voice in the history of women.*

> Before I go on will you pause—and if after deliberating you will promise not to mention to anyone what you know of my designs (though you may think my requesting you to conceal them unreasonable) I will trust to your honor—and proceed. Mr. Johnson whose uncommon kindness, I believe, has saved me from despair, and vexations I shrink back from—and feared to encounter; assures me that if I exert my talents by writing I may support myself in a comfortable way. I am then going to become the first of a new genus.
>
> —Mary Wollstonecraft to her sister Everina, November 7, 1787

Mary Wollstonecraft mused that she would be the first of a new genus when she chose to live as an author. Yet in the autumn of 1787, it must have seemed highly unlikely that she would leave any mark at all upon posterity. The vast majority of the women of her generation were married and were the mothers of children. The facts of Wollstonecraft's life were very different. At twenty-eight and unmarried she had already exhausted most forms of respectable employment for a middle-class woman of the late eighteenth century. She had earned her bread for over a decade as lady's companion, seamstress, teacher, and governess. When Mary Wollstonecraft claimed the authority to write, and (more significant) to write about political rights, she broke with her personal past and created a wave in the history of political thought that had not been seen since Socrates discussed women's capacity to be Guardians in the *Republic.* The political intent of her writing was nothing less than the complete subversion of the traditional philosophical plot in which she claimed women were born only to "propagate and rot."[1]

Wollstonecraft's political theory, born of a feminist consciousness, has been largely ignored by mainstream political theorists, the descendants of the canonical tradition. Her work has been considered illegitimate because she refused to acknowledge the patriarchy of the canonized forefathers. As Carole Pateman has noted, the genesis of political theory is singularly masculine:

> Only men—who can create political life—can take part in the original pact, yet the political fictions speak to women, too, through the language of the "individual." A curious message is sent to women, who represent everything that the individual is not, but the message must continually be conveyed because the meaning of the individual and the social contract depend on women and the sexual contract. Women must acknowledge the political fiction and speak the language even as the terms of the original pact exclude them from the fraternal conversation.[2]

Historically, only men have had the generative capacity to bring political theory to life in dialogues, tracts, and treatises. Wollstonecraft's criticism of the canonical tradition directly confronted the sexual politics of gender and generation and created a new form of feminist political analysis that made it possible to theorize women's lives.

Yet a mere ten years after she proposed her brave plan to live as an author, in what was surely one of the tragic ironies of history, Mary Wollstonecraft died from complications of childbirth. Today she has been reborn in the works of many scholars who have used her writings to construct a political history for women. The name of the woman author whose own authority was constantly under attack has become a basis for legitimating the work of a new generation of feminist writers. She has been read as a humanist, who in arguing for women's rights embraced the Enlightenment ideals of reason and self-government. She has also been read as a feminist, who recognized in her analysis of the situation of women the false universalism of Enlightenment humanism. However, while illuminating important aspects of Wollstonecraft's feminist theory, these readings fail to examine the complex ways in which her writing focuses our attention on the sexual politics of authority.

ABOUT THE AUTHOR

AN ANONYMOUS DEFENSE OF MARY WOLLSTONECRAFT, DISCUSSING HER DEATH DURING CHILDBIRTH

It is not very improbable that, if we possessed the means of knowledge equal to a full investigation, the cause of the fatal issue, which closed the light of this world upon one of its most brilliant ornaments; that robbed rational liberty of one of its most able and determined advocates, and that deprived your sex in particular of their firmest champion, might be traced to the violent agitations and anxieties that she had formerly sustained. Though her mind, in consequence of its native elasticity, had relaxed but little, if any thing, of its former vigour; yet the mere animal frame, it is not improbable, had received so rude a shock, as materially to affect the delicacy of its internal organization.—If so; we can be at no loss to determine to whose account Humanity will ascribe the being deprived of one of her most intelligent and determined friends.

In good truth, my dear Madam, my decided and unequivocal opinion of Mary Wollstonecraft Godwin is, that *the world was not worthy of her;*—for its absurdities, its prejudices, its vices, and its vanities, she was much too intelligent, too independent, too good, and too great.

Anonymous. Excerpt from *A Defense of the Character and Conduct of the Late Mary Wollstonecraft Godwin,* pp. 147-48. London, 1803.

To read Mary Wollstonecraft is to ask how a woman is authorized to write political theory. The history of political thought has often been represented as a conversation that invites everyone to take their place at the theoretical table. Feminist theorists, beginning with Wollstonecraft, argue that women have been excluded from the canonical conversation.[3] Wollstonecraft's writing, unauthorized by the canonical tradition, interrupts the fraternal conversation of political thought. Her work, from first page to last paragraph, represents a voice from the void. She invites to the theoretical table subjects that had not been represented within the writings of the fathers of the canon, foremost among them being the girl. The canon of political thought does not discuss female development or chart a developmental course for women as citizens. Mary Wollstonecraft gave voice to the girl and made her presence felt in the eighteenth-century debates about a woman's place. In speaking of the girl in her early works, and in letting the girl speak throughout her writings, Wollstonecraft articulated what had not been said within the canonical conversation. Indeed, the girl gives voice to the conflicts of gender and generation unacknowledged within the history of political thought. More important, by focusing on the girl we are better able to understand the gender politics of the infantilization of women.

Wollstonecraft's close attention to female development, from girlhood to womanhood, empowered her to attack the subject position of women within canonical political theory. Her critical focus on the girl enabled her to fully visualize women as autonomous subjects and responsible citizens. In her first published works, an educational text and a didactic novel, she began to develop the arguments that form the basis of her twin political tracts, the two vindications. In this manner Wollstonecraft's early writings on the girl anticipated some of the most pressing concerns of contemporary feminist theorists, who from Carol Gilligan to Luce Irigaray have claimed that until we acknowledge the voice of the girl we will not be able to articulate a truly feminist theory.[4]

In this chapter I examine Mary Wollstonecraft's earliest writings. We first encounter the girl in Wollstonecraft's own adolescent letters, where we meet the feminist as a fourteen year old who dreamed of independence. In Wollstonecraft herself we may see an eighteenth-century predecessor of Gilligan's "female resister."[5] This girl was also present in her early publications as she wrote of the duties of daughters and the conflicts of coming of age in a sexist society. Paradoxically, the appearance of the girl in Wollstonecraft's writings has gone relatively unnoticed by many scholars who have dismissed these works as juvenilia. ***Thoughts on the Education of Daughters*** provides a thoughtful analysis of the effects of social prejudice on female education and economic dependence on women's situation. ***Mary, a Fiction*** displays a new approach to female friendship and marriage. ***Original Stories*** offers an original look at the relationship between adults and children. Read alone, these works may seem unremarkable; but if we read them together and place them within their historical context we become aware of how the voice of the girl in Wollstonecraft's writing matured into a distinctive feminist language with which to speak of self. I believe it is here in these early writings that we find an outline of Mary Wollstonecraft's most famous arguments, and it is also here that she found the inspiration and the authority to articulate a theory of women's rights.

The Voice of the Girl

> According to my promise I sit down to write to you.
>
> —Mary Wollstonecraft to Jane Arden, May 1773

Remarkably, we have a great deal of evidence about Mary Wollstonecraft's own girlhood. Even more fortuitous is the fact that the majority of this information comes from Wollstonecraft herself. Her biographer Ralph Wardle collected and edited her personal letters, which begin with correspondence to a childhood friend at the age of fourteen. Wollstonecraft frequently returned to her own youth in her writing and it is here that we first hear the voice of the girl. Her earliest correspondence, with a clergyman's daughter named Jane Arden, reveals a girl's struggle to find the time to read and write. These letters, filled with poetry, country gossip, and demands for a quick and affectionate response, usually ended with her mother's call or the cries of her younger siblings. "I have a hundred things to add, but can't get time for Mama is calling me, so shall reserve them for another letter."[6]

The young Mary was concerned that her letters to the older and better-educated Jane would reveal her grammatical errors as well as her personal faults. "I have glanced over this letter and find it so ill written that I fear you cannot make out one line of this last page, but—you know, my dear, I have not the advantage of a Master as you have, and it is with great difficulty to get my brother to mend my pens." Stuck in what she termed a "dilemma," without "one pen that will make a stroke," she signed her name.[7] Ned, the oldest son, had both books and pens as he was destined for a career at the bar. Mary, the oldest daughter, was destined for marriage and she expended her energy in the tug-of-war of caring for their younger sisters and brothers. These constant battles pitted self-improvement against familial obligations and taught lessons that took a toll on her spirit as well as on her handwriting.

Even at this young age Mary Wollstonecraft dreamed of independence. But her daydreams reveal a very practical account of the necessary exchange of money for liberty, an exchange in which eighteenth-century English women, considered by law as property themselves, were at a decided disadvantage. In a subsequent letter the fourteen-year-old girl details the settlement of a "great fortune" of three hundred pounds on the Miss N———s, noting that "a woman of any oeconomy may live very genteelly on 150 pounds a year." These wild speculations aside, the letter concludes, "I am afraid you cannot read this as all the children are plaguing me."[8] Just a few years later, beset by financial problems as she struggled to support herself and her sisters without a legacy, Wollstonecraft wrote another letter in which she figured that three young women working at embroidery and watercolor landscapes could manage to scrape by on their collective earnings of a pound a week.[9]

However, at fourteen Mary's desire for a singular friendship, rather than the endless needs of child care, put an end to this first and formative correspondence. Jane Arden, the daughter of a preacher and self-styled philosopher, had a wider circle of acquaintances than Mary, daughter of a father whose dissipated ways would soon cost him the title of both gentleman and farmer. Even in a country town like Beverly in the northern county of Yorkshire, everyone had their place in the social hierarchy. On a visit to the Ardens, Mary believed herself to be displaced by a new arrival. She quickly picked up her pen. "Before I begin I beg pardon for the freedom of my style.—If I did not love you I would not write so;—I have a heart that scorns disguise, and a countenance which will not dissemble: I have formed romantic notions of friendship."[10]

Indeed, in this letter the young Wollstonecraft drew a vivid portrait of herself in ink that flowed with jealousy and was blotted by an awareness of hurt pride. "I am a little singular in my thoughts of love and friendship; I must have the first place or none.—I own your behavior is more according to the opinions of the world, but I would break from such narrow bounds." In the great chain of being, even a child at play must know her place. But in girlhood Wollstonecraft refused to play by the rules of the social game. She argued that she had been intentionally snubbed by Mrs. Arden. "When I have been at your house with Miss J———the greatest respect has been paid to her; every thing handed to her first;—in short, as if she were a superior being.—Your Mama too behaved with more politeness to her."[11] Wollstonecraft's words speak to a self-consciousness of position as well as her knowledge of the social conventions that afforded the newcomer primacy of place. This awareness of women's situation and class position was a theme that would distinguish her writing throughout her career. Wollstonecraft's desire "to have first place or none" would lead her repeatedly to break the "narrow bounds" of the world of opinion.

Six years later, at the age of twenty, Mary Wollstonecraft resumed her correspondence with her girlhood friend Jane Arden. Neither woman had married and each of them had left their families to make their own way in the world. She wrote, "I often recollect with pleasure the many agreeable days we spent together when we eagerly told every girlish secret of our hearts—Those were peaceful days; your's since that period may have been as tranquil, but mine have been far from otherwise."[12] In these letters Wollstonecraft, now employed as a companion to an elderly woman in Bath, tried to bring their friendship up to date, giving an account of herself to Arden who was living in Norfolk as a governess. Her letters from Bath are a sad corrective for anyone who has read Jane Austen's fiction. Under different circumstances a young lady in this spa town would have enjoyed many entertaining diversions, but Wollstonecraft as a working woman had little experience of these pleasures, even though for two years she had lived within walking distance of the Pump Room, the Promenade, and the Assembly Rooms. She wrote to Arden, "Bath is remarkably full at present, and nothing is going forward but Balls and plays without end or number.—I seldom go into public;—I have been but twice to the rooms." The social season in full swing, Wollstonecraft sat on the sidelines while the choreography of marriage twirled ceaselessly around her.

> I am quite a piece of still life, not but that I am a friend to mirth and cheerfulness; but I would move in a small circle;—I am fond of domestic pleasures and have not spirit sufficient to bustle about. . . . There is no prospect of my quitting this place in a hurry, necessity not choice ties me to it (not but that I receive the greatest civility from this family)—yet, I am detained here only by prudential motives, if I was to follow the bent of my inclination, I shod [*sic*] haste away. You will not wonder at this,—when you consider that I am among Strangers, far from all my former connections:—The more I see of the world, the more anxious I am to preserve my old friends, for I am now slower than ever in forming friendships;—I would wish to cherish a universal love to all mankind, but the principal part of my heart must be occupied by those who have for years had a place there.

Her half-hearted assertions to the contrary, she concluded, "I wish I could write any thing that would entertain you, but I mix so little with the world, that I am at a loss for news."[13]

To the sympathetic reader Mary Wollstonecraft seems to have lost her sense of self. Certainly there is something new about these letters. It is her concern about boundaries; her adult world suddenly appears to be so much smaller than the Yorkshire countryside of her childhood. Perhaps in the quiet, monotonous hours of her enforced seclusion she began to develop her theory that men's superior ability to reason as well as their physical strength were not the products of nature but of the social conventions that allowed men the freedom to interact with the world. Wollstonecraft was drawn inward to explore a mental landscape that may have been familiar to many women in her situation. "My wishes and expectations are very moderate.—I don't know which is the worst—to think too little or too much.—'tis a difficulty to draw the line, and keep clear of melancholy and thoughtlessness."[14] What had happened to the young girl whose knowledge of her own heart enabled her to so powerfully speak her mind?

Wollstonecraft's letters demonstrate that her resignation to her predicament gradually turned to resentment, and ultimately to resistance. It seems she was painfully aware of how her marginalized position as a woman in service placed her at the edge of social life and restricted her participation in the wider world:

> To say the truth, I am very indifferent to the opinion of the world in general;—I wish to retire as much from it as possible,—I am particularly sick of genteel life, as it is called;—the unmeaning civilities that I see every day practiced don't agree with my temper;—I long for a little sincerity, and look forward with pleasure to the time when I shall lay aside all restraint. . . . This is the gayest of all gay places; nothing but dress and amusements are going forward;—I am only a spectator—I have lost all my relish for them:—early in life, before misfortune had broken my spirits, I had not the power of partaking of them, and now I am both from habit and inclination averse to them.

At this point in her life the weight of dependence and the isolation of a life in service had broken the spirit of the girl who had "formed romantic notions of friendship" and who wanted "first place or none."

> I beseech you; struggle with any obstacles rather than go into a state of dependence:—I speak feelingly.—I have felt the weight, and would have you by all means avoid it. . . . Your employment tho a troublesome one, is very necessary, and you have the opportunity of doing much good, by instilling good principles into the young and ignorant, and at the close of life you'll have the pleasure to think that you have not lived in vain, and, believe me, this reflection is worth a life of care.[15]

If we look closely at this correspondence, we find Mary Wollstonecraft writing about the extravagance of the court of George III at Windsor, composing her letter on top of a chest of drawers that she used as her desk. The author of ***A Vindication of the Rights of Woman*** sometimes appears within these letters only to vanish into the page, the strength of her argument diluted like the watered-down ink she used to save a few pence. "I have put so much water in my ink, I am afraid you will not be able to read my faint characters, and besides my candle gives such a dreadful light."[16] Short on time, candles, and money she yearned to be her own mistress. It was in a letter from this period that Wollstonecraft learned of the Arden sisters' plan to live together, earning their keep by running that peculiar eighteenth-century institution, the dame school.

Soon after, Wollstonecraft determined to follow a similar course and set up a household with Fanny Blood, a young woman who had been her constant friend since their introduction by the Reverend Clare five years earlier when the Wollstonecraft family lived in Hoxton outside of London.

> I know this resolution may appear a little extraordinary, but in forming it I follow the dictates of reason as well as the bent of my inclination; for tho' I am willing to do what good I can in my generation, yet on many accounts I am averse to any matrimonial tie . . . To my great satisfaction, I found Miss Blood in better health than I expected from accounts I had of her.—She received me as she ever has done in the most friendly manner, and we passed a comfortable week together, which knew no other alloy than what arose from the thoughts of parting so soon.—The next time we meet, it will be for a longer continuance, and to that period I look, as to the most important one of my life: this connection must give the color to my future days, for I have now given up every expectation and dependence that wod [*sic*] interfere with my determination of spending my time with her.[17]

Thus, we find evidence of one of the keynotes of Wollstonecraft's feminism as she repeatedly claimed in these early letters that she would never marry. The force of her aversion to an institution she would later liken to prostitution, slavery, and imprisonment was displayed in an angry letter to Jane in acknowledgment of the marriage of

Arden's sister. Just four weeks after the wedding, Wollstonecraft was not sure that her well wishes would still be appropriate:

> I was just going to desire you to wish her joy (to use the common phrase) but I am afraid my good wishes might be unseasonable, as I find by the date of your letter that the honey moon, and the next moon too must be almost over—The joy, and all that, [here she has crossed out "sort of thing" but it is still legible to the reader] is certainly over by this time, and all the raptures have subsided, and the dear hurry of visiting and figuring away as a bride, and all the rest of the delights of matrimony are past and gone and have left no traces behind them except disgust:—I hope I am mistaken, but this is the fate of most married pairs.[18]

She followed this outburst by misquoting Ecclesiastes as the wisdom of Solomon and ended the letter by reiterating her own commitment to live free or die: "'there is nothing new under the sun' for which reason I will not marry, for I dont want to be tied to this nasty world, and old maids are of so little consequence—that 'let them live or die, nobody will laugh or cry.'"

Here, Wollstonecraft, a self-styled old maid who had survived the social disaster of having a younger sister marry before she herself made the trip to the altar, made a resolution of much consequence: *"It is a happy thing to be a mere blank, and to be able to pursue one's own whims, where they lead, without having a husband and half a hundred children at hand to teaze and controul a poor woman who wishes to be free."*[19] Better indeed to be a blank than to follow the scripted lines of womanhood filling the role of biblical helpmate and domestic drudge. Better still for a woman to avoid the perils of the marriage plot entirely by supporting herself. Mary Wollstonecraft knew well that few couples lived happily ever after. As her parents' daughter she had witnessed firsthand the death and destruction that often sealed the marriage contract. Her younger sister Eliza Wollstonecraft Bishop had suffered postpartum depression after giving birth to her first child. Mary, called to care for her sister, watched as she sobbed uncontrollably and ranted about the abuse she received at the hands of her husband. In time Mary became convinced that Eliza was sinking into madness and that she would never recover as long as she remained within her husband's house. So she helped her sister run for her life, leaving behind her infant daughter, to seek refuge in a boardinghouse while Meredith Bishop scoured London for his fugitive wife. In this desperate situation it was up to Mary to devise a new story for herself and her sister.

The harsh realities of poverty and legal limbo that Mary confronted as she and Eliza began to plot a different chapter in their lives would become the basis of the realism that marks her books. Mary and Eliza enlisted the aid of their younger sister, Everina, and the help of Fanny Blood to open a dame school. First in Islington and later at Newington Green, the four women worked to teach their students and earn a living. Just as their independence seemed secure, however, Fanny Blood announced that she would marry and follow her husband, Hugh Skeys, to Portugal. Once again the marriage plot seemed to twist the life out of a young woman, as Fanny, already weakened by consumption, sickened under the weight of her first pregnancy. Mary borrowed money from her Newington Green neighbor, the widow of the preacher James Burgh, to travel to Lisbon and attend her friend during her confinement. She arrived at Fanny's bedside only to see her die and to help Hugh Skeys bury his wife and infant son.

Burdened and embittered by her experiences of marriage and childbearing, Mary Wollstonecraft would rework these events over and over again in her didactic novels and polemical tracts. Maybe then it is not surprising that her words to Jane Arden resonated with a hard-won wisdom. It is here that she began to write her own "book of woman" as she asserted her birthright to a better life. "Some may follow St. Paul's advice 'in doing well,' but I, like a true born Englishwoman, will endeavour to do better."[20] In the following years, what had begun as a dream of negative liberty, freedom from the familial obligations of gender and the womanly duty of generation, was transformed with age and experience into a dream of positive liberty, freedom to become a new type of being. But what would that new being be? Wollstonecraft was determined not to marry or bear children. Her determination was the product of her own experience of the darker side of the marriage plot. Regardless of the risks, she asserted her independence as a freeborn Englishwoman. Freed from the constraints of gender and generation that were the lot of many of her sisters in England, she resolved to become the "first of a new genus." She continues, "I tremble at the attempt yet if I fail—I *only* suffer—and should I succeed my dear Girls will ever in sickness have a home—and a refuge where for a few months in the year, they may forget the cares that disturb the rest."[21] Mary Wollstonecraft had decided to create herself anew as a woman author.

Verbalizing The Void

> In the following pages I have endeavoured to point out some important things with respect to female education. It is true, many treatises have been already written; yet it occurred to me, that much still remained to be said.
>
> —Mary Wollstonecraft, ***Thoughts on the Education of Daughters***

What could a young woman with little formal instruction of her own add to the eighteenth-century discourse on education? Mary Wollstonecraft brought her observations of the relationship between the inferior education of the girl and the limited opportunities available to the woman. In her first published work she analyzed her own situation and reflected on the position of women within late-eighteenth-century English society. Her resolve to live free of the marriage bond and the ties of motherhood had required her to earn her own subsistence. She had made a meager living by trying her hand at the various forms of respectable employment available to a woman of the middling classes. Wollstonecraft believed that her experience as a working woman, combined with the lessons she had learned as a schoolmistress in the dissenting community of Newington Green, gave her the authority to enter the debate about female education.

Wollstonecraft knew ***Thoughts on the Education of Daughters*** would be compared to other popular tracts such as Dr. Gregory's *Father's Legacy to Daughters* and Dr. Fordyce's *Sermons for Young Ladies*. She would deal with the inadequacies of these texts later in ***A Vindication of the Rights of Woman.*** But for now she prefaced her book with the statement that, from her perspective as a woman and a daughter, there appeared "much that still needed to be said." Her audience consisted of parents like her own who had not given much thought to the education of their female children. Wollstonecraft's formal education had consisted of nothing more than a few years in the village school when her family lived in Beverly in Yorkshire. From an early age she believed that this education had not prepared her for the struggles of life. To supplement her knowledge of the world and support herself in the trials she faced, Wollstonecraft had engaged in a program of reading and self-improvement. She hoped her book would reach an audience of female readers similarly employed in a program of self-help, so that they might find comfort and counsel in her words. Emboldened by her project Wollstonecraft refused in her preface to apologize for her efforts, as was the literary custom of many of her contemporaries who, as Mary Poovey has noted, made a rhetorical ritual of begging the public's pardon for daring to put their ideas on paper. "I will not swell these sheets by writing apologies for my attempt." Instead she claimed that her writing would not be in vain if it might "prove useful to one fellow-creature, and beguile any hours, which sorrow has made heavy."[22]

Wollstonecraft's first published work, ***Thoughts on the Education of Daughters,*** displays her search for an authoritative voice with which to address her audience. There is a tension within this text; conventional advice for modifying girls' behavior similar to that found within other eighteenth-century conduct books often mingles on the same page with radical calls for girlhood freedom. For example, she wrote, "I must own, I am quite charmed when I see a sweet young creature, shrinking as it were from observation, and listening rather than talking." But in the following paragraph she indicated a contradictory desire for the girl to actively engage in the pleasurable pursuit of ideas. "Above all, try to teach them to combine their ideas. It is of more use than can be conceived, for a child to learn to compare things that are similar in some respects, and different in others. *I wish them to be taught to think*—thinking, indeed, is a severe exercise, and exercise of either mind or body will not at first be entered on, but with a view to pleasure" (11; my emphasis).

A few pages later the shrinking girl has lost her charm. The author who claimed that there was still much to be said on the subject of female education disregarded the customary edict that children are better seen and not heard. She argued, "Children should be permitted to enter into conversation; but it requires great discernment to find out such subjects as will gradually improve them." She suggests that stories about animals are a proper object of children's attention, providing lessons that "form the temper and cultivate the good dispositions of the heart." She recommends a series of books for children including Dorothy Kilner's *The Life and Perambulations of a Mouse* and Anna Laetitia Barbauld's *Hymns in Prose for Children.* Her own contribution to this literature, ***Original Stories From Real Life,*** contains a number of tales that teach children to treat animals humanely (10). Later, in the preface to ***Original Stories,*** she protested she would have had no reason to write her book if parents would just talk with their children.

Her wish that the girl be taught to think materialized in her argument that girls be given the cognitive tools to develop independent thought. "It may be observed, that I recommend the mind's being put into a proper train, and then left to itself" (21). Throughout her letters of this period, she made frequent mention of the idea that a mind of genius would educate itself. Perhaps this maxim brought resolution to her conflicted thoughts about the inadequacy of her own education. She argued that freedom of expression and action were necessary for independent thinking.

> Fixed rules cannot be given, it must depend on the nature and strength of the understanding; and those who observe it can best tell what kind of cultivation will improve it. The mind is not, cannot be created by the teacher, though it may be cultivated, and its real powers found out. . . . I would have everyone try to form an opinion of an author themselves, though modesty may restrain them from mentioning it. Many are so anxious to have the reputation of taste, that they praise authors whose merit is indisputable. I am sick of hearing of the sublimity of Milton, the elegance and harmony of Pope, and the original untaught genius of Shakespeare.
>
> (21)

The role of the teacher was to cultivate the girl's understanding, not to impose an artificial order on a young mind that would restrict the free flow of ideas. Wollstonecraft claimed that a girl's potential for wisdom was determined by her own "nature and strength," not by the social markers of birth and rank. Thus, in her scheme for female education, the "real power" is vested in the girl. Indeed, she was concerned about the potential dangers of the teacher/student relationship, a concern that prefigures her argument in ***A Vindication of the Rights of Woman.*** Wollstonecraft read Rousseau's *La Nouvelle Heloise* as a dangerous depiction of the evils of trusting the moral education of an innocent girl to a man with a world of experience.

Wollstonecraft's ***Thoughts on the Education of Daughters*** is an important text because it displays her attempts to differentiate the girl from the woman. It is here that she first created the continuum of female development from childhood to adulthood that forms the foundation of her later theoretical writings. *The aim of her pedagogy, teaching a girl to think for herself, is also the first principle of her political theory, namely, that rational women have the right to govern themselves.* For Wollstonecraft, it was education, not marriage, that determined female maturity. Her analysis of the situation of her sex began in the intimacy of the nursery and concluded with a chapter concerning women in public places. In tracing this path she carefully distinguished the girl from the woman, using the capacity for rational thought rather than social customs of courtship and marriage to differentiate the seasons of a female life.

One of the most interesting components of her analysis of girlhood education and womanly maturation is her treatment of beauty, a discussion that would have serious implications for her response to Edmund Burke's *Reflections on the Revolution in France.* Wollstonecraft quickly dismissed the social conventions of female beauty, which pitted the exercise of the mind against the development of the body, conventions that for centuries had been used to justify keeping women in the bondage of ignorance. Throughout her argument she contrasted the glow of youthful beauty to the "mind illumined face" of the mature woman. "The lively thoughtlessness of youth makes every young creature agreeable for the time; but when those years are flown, and sense is not substituted in the stead of vivacity, the follies of youth are acted over, and they never consider, that things which please in their proper season, disgust out of it. It is very absurd to see a woman, whose brow time has marked with wrinkles, aping the manners of a girl in her teens" (12-13). The woman who "apes the girl" and mimics the happy "thoughtlessness" of youth robs herself of the humanity of her wrinkles. Wollstonecraft was concerned that women act their age and proudly display the markings of their maturity. She suggested that society should focus its attention on the benefits bestowed by the careful actions of the thinking woman rather than applaud the frivolous attributes of the pretty girl.

Following the form of other books within the genre, Wollstonecraft devoted sections of her text to such items of female protocol as dress, artificial manners, card playing, and temper. Yet she deviated from the path taken by male authors by including a chapter entitled "Unfortunate Situation of Females, Fashionably Educated, and Left Without a Fortune." It is here that Wollstonecraft first speaks directly in print about the void in women's lives created by the sexual politics of gender and generation. This chapter is unique within the context of eighteenth-century conduct books in that it considers how patriarchal privilege encoded in the customs of primogeniture and coverture limited the life choices of educated women in England. In this short chapter Wollstonecraft pointed out much of what remained to be said concerning the education of daughters. She began with a disclaimer, "I have hitherto only spoken to females, who will have a provision made for them by their parents. But many who have been well, or at least fashionably educated, are left without a fortune, and if they are not entirely devoid of delicacy, they must frequently remain single" (25).

Educated daughters of once wealthy families were not likely to attract eligible bachelors of the appropriate class. Mary Poovey argues that the marriage of daughters became an increasingly expensive burden upon families during the eighteenth century in England. The sons of the landed aristocracy were attracted to the daughters of the mercantile elite by the offer of large endowments. Finances were not the only obstacle to matrimony. Poovey writes, "The disproportionate number of socially and economically suitable bachelors also meant that a woman had less choice as to her future husband; the complaisance of male suitors, who took their success for granted, is a commonplace of eighteenth-century novels, as is the sad circumstance of uncourted daughters."[23] As Wollstonecraft herself had learned, a young woman's entrance into the world was mediated by money. Without a large settlement to entice the interest of a beau, the accomplished woman might be excluded from the mating rituals of courtship and later exiled from polite society by her poverty.

Wollstonecraft's letters attest that she was well acquainted with the hardships confronted by daughters of families in financial decline. Speaking for herself, she wrote, "It is hard for a person who has a relish for polished society, to herd with the vulgar, or to condescend to mix with her former equals when she is considered in a different light. What unwelcome heart-breaking knowledge is then poured in on her." This knowledge darkens the colors in the landscape of a woman's life. "The painted cloud disappears suddenly, the scene is changed, and what an aching void is left in the heart!" (26). The intimate nature of Wollstonecraft's comments in this text led Claire Tomalin to remark:

> A striking omission from her book, as from her letters, was any mention of her pupils. There were plenty of personal references, but they were almost all to herself. She never could write without inserting more or less veiled remarks about her own emotional state, and though they read a little curiously in the middle of an educational manual, they make it abundantly clear that she was far more interested in the state of her own life and the prospects that lay ahead of young women than in their years at school.[24]

At this stage in her own intellectual development Wollstonecraft suggested that her sisters in woe, the "unfortunate, fashionably educated women," turn to religion to fill the void in life that was traditionally filled by marriage and child rearing (25). Subsequently, in ***Mary, a Fiction,*** she would modify her view that women should look to the afterlife, imagining a heaven without marriage or marrying. Even in this first book we see her emphasis on futurity to make right present wrongs. Her own experience of hardship would quickly lead her to replace an attitude of religious resignation with the spirit of political revolution.

In the remaining chapters of ***Thoughts on the Education of Daughters,*** Wollstonecraft examined the conventional roles of women. Her analysis of marriage provides her definitive statement that education differentiates girls from women. Early marriages are particularly harmful in that they interrupt or restrict the rational development of females. Wollstonecraft foreshadowed the arguments of modern feminist political theorists concerning female "vulnerability in marriage" by asserting that girls and women "forced to act before they have had time to think" were at a decided disadvantage upon entering the marriage contract.[25]

> Early marriages are, in my opinion, a stop to improvement. If we were born only "to draw nutrition, propagate and rot," the sooner the end of creation was answered the better; but as women are here allowed to have souls, the soul ought to be attended to. In youth a woman endeavors to please the other sex, in order, generally speaking, to get married, and this endeavor calls forth all her powers. If she has a tolerable education, the foundation only is laid, for the mind does not soon arrive at maturity, and should not be engrossed by domestic cares before any habits are fixed. The passions also have too much influence over the judgment to suffer it to direct her in this most important affair; and many women, I am persuaded, marry a man before they are twenty, whom they would have rejected some years after. Very frequently, when education has been neglected, the mind improves itself, if it has the leisure for reflection, and experience to reflect on; but how can this happen when they are forced to act before they have had time to think, or find that they are unhappily married?
>
> (31)

By defining female maturity by education, not marriage, Wollstonecraft inverts the order of other models like Locke's *Some Thoughts Concerning Education* and Rousseau's *Emile.* Although both these works moved past the politics of generation to focus on childhood neither Locke nor Rousseau, both famous tutors, could get beyond the politics of gender to educate the girl. Wollstonecraft argued that the education of the girl was first and foremost for her own benefit. "Reason must often be called in to fill up the vacuums of life; but too many of our sex suffer theirs to lie dormant" (32).

For women, reason could supplement religion as they tried to fill the empty spaces of traditional femininity. Wollstonecraft bitterly attacked early marriages because she believed that they carried a girl away from her lessons to become a prisoner of the hearth and possibly the companion of the wrong man.

> When a woman's mind has gained some strength, she will in all probability pay more attention to her actions than a girl can be expected to; and if she thinks seriously, she will chuse for a companion a man of principle; and this perhaps young people do not sufficiently attend to, or see the necessity of doing. . . . Many are but just returned from a boarding school, when they are placed at the head of a family, and how fit they are to manage it, I leave the judicious to judge. Can they improve a child's understanding, when they are scarcely out of the state of childhood themselves? (31)

Marriage limited the sphere of a woman's actions and further restricted the exercise of her reason. "Women are said to be the weaker vessel, and many are the miseries which this weakness brings on them. Men have in some respects very much the advantage. If they have a tolerable understanding, it has a chance to be cultivated. . . . Nothing, I am sure, calls forth the faculties so much as being obliged to struggle with the world; and this is not woman's province in a married state" (32). Wollstonecraft argued that, if indeed woman was the "weaker vessel," much of this weakness was the result of institutions and conventions that inhibit or stunt the cognitive growth of the girl into the thinking woman.

Her final chapter details the position of women in "Public Places." Wollstonecraft concludes her thoughts on female education by again redirecting our vision. We are asked to observe the funeral of the "fine lady," an uneducated woman who like a child is of "so little use" to society. "In the fine Lady how few traits do we observe of those affections which dignify human nature! If she has maternal tenderness, it is of a childish kind. We cannot be too careful not to verge on this character; though she lives many years she is still a child in understanding, and of so little use to society, that her death would scarcely be observed" (48). Her warning to girls is clear: get an education or else. Females, if raised to please males, would remain children all their lives without the rational education needed to mature as human beings. Only thinking women have the ability to govern themselves and the hope of escaping the female void of dependence by the reasonable management of their households and their substantive contributions to society.

In ***Thoughts on the Education of Daughters*** Wollstonecraft presents many portraits of women who have been buried alive, suffocated by their situation as women in a society in which they are economically powerless and civilly dead. In writing this educational text she articulated the connection between the obstacles that restrict the education of girls and the social and political impediments to female autonomy. She identified marriage as the primary institution that denied women the opportunity to explore the meaning of their own lives by restricting their access to and their vision of the world into which each one was born. Her own place in the world was uncertain following the failure of her school in Newington Green. This first book focused her thoughts on her experience as a teacher. She wrote that "a teacher at a school is only a kind of upper servant, who has more work than menial ones." In the next sentence she commented that the role of a governess was "equally disagreeable" (25).

Thoughts on the Education of Daughters may have made Wollstonecraft an author, but it gave her little authority with her numerous creditors. Instead of settling her debts, she used the money she received for her book from Joseph Johnson to settle Fanny Blood's family in Ireland. She would soon follow them across the Irish Sea. Given her own "unfortunate situation," a penniless Wollstonecraft accepted the position of governess on the Kingsborough estate for the sum of forty pounds a year.

The Mind of a Thinking Woman is Displayed

> In delineating the Heroine of this Fiction, the Author attempts to develop a character different from those generally portrayed. This woman is neither a Clarissa, a Lady G———, or a Sophie.
>
> —Mary Wollstonecraft, ***Mary, a Fiction***

In the advertisement to ***Mary, a Fiction,*** Wollstonecraft promised her reader that in this "artless tale, without episodes, the mind of a woman, who has thinking powers is displayed." She observed that both popular opinion and historical experience seemed to confirm the belief that "female organs have been thought too weak for this arduous employment." But she countered that, "Without arguing physically about *possibilities*—in a fiction, such a being may be allowed to exist, whose grandeur is derived from the operations of its own faculties, not subjugated to opinion; but drawn by the individual from the original source."[26] The "original source" from which Mary Wollstonecraft drew the generative power to create her heroine were her reflections on her own life. The semi-autobiographical ***Mary, a Fiction*** traced the development of a woman of mind from her infancy and childhood to her marriage and rebellion against her husband and the opinions of a world that deny women their own thoughts and restrict their actions. Wollstonecraft, who had argued in ***Thoughts on the Education of Daughters*** that most parents neglect the education of their female children, resolved this pedagogical dilemma in a new way in ***Mary.*** She wrote to her sister Everina as well as her friend the Reverend Henry Gabell that the novel served to demonstrate an idea she had drawn from her reading of *Emile,* that "a genius will educate itself."

Most literary critics have found little evidence of genius in ***Mary.*** Wollstonecraft wrote a few months before her death that she thought the novel a "crude production," and that she would rather not share it with "people whose good opinion, as a writer, I wish for."[27] Yet it was in writing this novel that Wollstonecraft began to see herself as the "first of a new genus." Here she further developed the central idea of her earlier educational tract, that a woman needed her own mental resources in order to survive the "warfare of life." In this manner ***Mary*** fulfilled Wollstonecraft's pledge to show the intricate workings of the mind of a woman with thinking powers. But the novel accomplished far more, by demonstrating the continuity of Wollstonecraft's own thoughts about women's situation and expanding her critique of women as property in marriage relations. Ultimately, the novel represents her first attempt to pose the larger philosophical question of the existence of a thinking woman at the end of the Enlightenment.

Mary, a Fiction is an alternative tale of a woman's situation that differs in dramatic detail from the stories of Clarissa, Lady Grandison, or Sophie. The plot revolves around the coming of age of a young woman, fashionably educated and left *with* a fortune. Here Wollstonecraft continues her discussion of female development begun in ***Thoughts on the Education of Daughters,*** yet unlike the dispossessed daughters of her educational tract, the Mary of fiction inherits the family fortune when her older brother dies of a "violent fever" at boarding school. The death of the brother gives new life to the sister. Her position within the family has changed. "She was now an heiress, and her mother began to think of her of consequence, and did not call her the child" (18). From society's perspective this transfer of wealth transformed the inconsequential girl into a woman of substance.

Marriage is the consequence of her inheritance, and her father gives the fictional Mary away as a bride to settle a patrimony dispute. But the marriage portrayed here is macabre in every aspect. Instead of the literary conventions of a church ceremony, the heroine is wed at her mother's deathbed to fulfill her parent's last wish. "The clergyman came in to read the service for the sick, and afterwards the marriage ceremony was performed. Mary stood like a statue of Despair, and pronounced the awful vow without thinking of it; and then ran to support her mother, who expired the same night in her arms" (20). This morbid scene juxtaposes the marriage and quest plots in gothic style as the daughter is symbolically wed over the dying body of the mother. "Her husband set off for the continent the same day, with a tutor, to finish his studies at one of the foreign universities" (20). Mary is schooled in the double standards of patriarchy while the young husband completes his education with his tutor and the grand tour of Europe. "As her mind expanded, her marriage appeared a dreadful misfortune; she was sometimes reminded of the heavy yoke, and bitter was the recollection" (22). The woman of thinking powers, in a moment of grief, unthinkingly becomes a wife. The remaining chapters of the novel detail the fictional Mary's struggle with this contradiction.

A revolutionary female emerges from this conflict of womanhood as the unthinking wife is transformed into the thinking woman who scorns her wedding vows. Mary establishes a household with a female friend, travels to Lisbon when her friend becomes ill, and after the friend's death turns her intellectual attention and sentimental affections toward an older man who is not her husband. Unwilling to dismiss her unconventional ideas or repress her feelings she exclaims, "With these notions can I conform to the maxims of worldly wisdom?" (47). Certainly ***Mary, a Fiction*** did not conform to the model of the feminine novel of the late eighteenth century. Mary "gave her hand" to her husband only in the last two pages of the novel with the wish "that earth would open and swallow her" (72). Wollstonecraft concludes the book with one last journey into the mind of the thinking woman: "in moments of solitary sadness, a gleam of joy would dart across her mind—She thought she was hastening to that world where there is neither marrying, nor giving in marriage" (73). The fictional Mary, like the author herself, had not yet discovered a world in which women were free to pursue their intellectual interests as well as their erotic desires.

At the end of the eighteenth century the novel as a literary genre allowed the woman writer in general to explore the boundaries of convention and to challenge the ideological borders that separated men from women and adults from children. It offered Wollstonecraft a literary public space, an entry into the debates about power and membership in a radical community that was attempting to redefine and revolutionize discourse. It also served as a popular literary form for politic polemic. Before Jean-Jacques Rousseau wrote *The Social Contract,* he was the author of *La Nouvelle Heloise*; William Godwin followed *Political Justice* with *Caleb Williams.* J. M. S. Tompkins's remarks on this novel still hold true today:

> Conspicuous as the male philosophers are, it was the women in the revolutionary circle who focused the horrified attention of the public. The ethics of the woman's novel, that established harmony of submission, delicacy and self-control, were rudely shaken. Mary Wollstonecraft in her ***Vindication of the Rights of Woman*** (1792) had said that independence was the soil of every virtue, and had based delicacy on candor instead of concealment. She had written ***Mary, A Fiction*** (1788) in which "the mind of a woman, who has thinking powers, is displayed," and had exhibited the development of these powers as consequent of the most unconventional behavior. She had spoken freely of passion and saw it as an educative force.[28]

Mary Wollstonecraft was first able to speak freely within the context of the novel. ***Mary, a Fiction*** represents her early theoretical attempts to analyze and respond to the powerlessness of women within the home and civil society. It was here that she began to equate women's condition as wives with slavery (55). Modern readers will recognize that this is not the type of story that has yet been told within the history of political thought. Rather, ***Mary*** is an experimental novel, displaying the conflict between a thinking women who would make her own way in the world and the obstacles she encounters from the world of opinion. It is also a cautionary tale that has not received sufficient attention from Wollstonecraft scholars; it depicts an existential crisis of a girl becoming a woman. Her argument raises the question of how traditional political theory, which blurs the boundaries between the child and the adult, serves the purposes of fathers and husbands when the property in dispute is female. Wollstonecraft develops the power of the mind of her fictional heroine. But could this woman with thinking powers overcome the body of literature that conditioned men to treat girls as women and women as perpetual children?

Notes

1. Wollstonecraft, *Rights of Woman,* 132.
2. Pateman, *Sexual Contract,* 221.
3. See Susan Moller Okin, *Women in Western Political Thought* (Princeton: Princeton University Press, 1979); Martin, *Reclaiming the Conversation*; Pateman, *Sexual Contract*; Coole, *Women in Political Theory.*
4. See Carol Gilligan, Nona Lyons, and Trudy Hammer, eds., *Making Connections: The Relational Worlds of Adolescent Girls at the Emma Willard School* (Cambridge: Harvard University Press, 1990); Luce Irigaray, *This Sex Which Is Not One,* trans. Catherine Porter (Ithaca: Cornell University Press, 1985); Jill McLean Taylor, Carol Gilligan, and Amy Sullivan, eds., *Between Voice and Silence: Women and Girls, Race, and Relationship* (Cambridge: Harvard University Press, 1995).
5. Carol Gilligan, "Teaching Shakespeare's Sisters: Notes from the Underground of Female Adolescence," in Gilligan, Lyons, and Hammer, *Making Connections,* 25.
6. "I should likewise beg pardon for not beginning sooner so agreeable a correspondence as that I promise myself yours will prove, but from a lady of your singular good nature I promise myself indulgence." Mary Wollstonecraft to Jane Arden, May 1-20, 1773, *Collected Letters,* 51-52.
7. Wollstonecraft to Arden, June 4-July 31, 1773. Ibid., 56.
8. Ibid., 57.
9. Wollstonecraft to Everina Wollstonecraft, January 1784. Ibid., 86.
10. Wollstonecraft to Arden, June 4, 1773-November 16, 1774. Ibid., 60.
11. Ibid., 60-61.
12. Wollstonecraft to Arden, May-June 1779. Ibid., 64.
13. Wollstonecraft to Arden, December 10, 1779-January 5, 1780. Ibid., 70-71.
14. Wollstonecraft to Arden, April-June 1780. Ibid., 72.
15. Ibid., 71-72.
16. Wollstonecraft to Arden, June-August 1780. Ibid., 75.
17. Wollstonecraft to Arden, April-June 1780. Ibid., 73.
18. Wollstonecraft to Arden, October 20, 1782-August 10, 1783. Ibid., 79.
19. Ibid. (my emphasis).
20. Ibid.
21. Wollstonecraft to her sister Everina, November 7, 1787. Ibid., 164.
22. Mary Wollstonecraft, *Thoughts on the Education of Daughters,* in *Works,* 4:5, 7. Page references will be given parenthetically in the text. See also Mary Poovey, *The Proper Lady and the Woman Writer* (Chicago: University of Chicago Press, 1984), 14.

23. Poovey, *Proper Lady*, 13.

24. Tomalin, *Life and Death*, 39.

25. See "Vulnerability by Marriage," in Susan Moller Okin, *Justice, Gender, and the Family* (New York: Basic Books, 1989).

26. Wollstonecraft, *Mary, a Fiction*, 5 (original emphasis). Page references will be given parenthetically in the text.

27. Wollstonecraft to Everina Wollstonecraft, March 22, 1797, *Collected Letters*, 385.

28. J. M. S. Tompkins, *The Popular Novel in England, 1770-1800* (Lincoln: University of Nebraska Press, 1961), 314.

Bibliography

Burke, Edmund. [1790] 1989. *Reflections on the Revolution in France*. Edited by John Pocock. Indianapolis: Hackett Publishers.

Coole, Diane. 1993. *Women in Political Theory*. Boulder: Lynne Reinner Publishers.

Fordyce, James. 1809. *Sermons to Young Women*. Philadelphia: Carey and Riley of New York.

Gregory, John. 1788. *A Father's Legacy to His Daughters*. Edinburgh: A. Strahan and T. Cadell.

Martin, Jane Roland. 1985. *Reclaiming the Conversation: The Ideal of the Educated Woman*. New Haven: Yale University Press.

Pateman, Carole. 1988. *The Sexual Contract*. Stanford: Stanford University Press.

Rousseau, Jean-Jacques. [1761] 1987. *La Nouvelle Heloise*. Edited and translated by Judith McDowell. University Park: Pennsylvania State University Press.

———. [1762] 1979. *Emile, or On Education*. Edited and translated by Allan Bloom. New York: Basic Books.

———. [1762] 1978. *The Social Contract*. Edited by Roger Masters, translated by Judith Masters. New York: St. Martin's Press.

Tomalin, Claire. 1974. *The Life and Death of Mary Wollstonecraft*. New York: New American Library.

Wollstonecraft, Mary. [1787] 1989. *Thoughts on the Education of Daughters*. In *The Works of Mary Wollstonecraft*, vol. 4, ed. Marilyn Butler and Janet Todd. New York: New York University Press.

———. [1788] 1989. *Mary, a Fiction*. In *The Works of Mary Wollstonecraft*, vol. 1, ed. Marilyn Butler and Janet Todd. New York: New York University Press.

———. [1792] 1989. *A Vindication of the Rights of Woman*. In *The Works of Mary Wollstonecraft*, vol. 5, ed. Marilyn Butler and Janet Todd. New York: New York University Press.

———. 1979. *The Collected Letters of Mary Wollstonecraft*. Edited by Ralph Wardle. Ithaca: Cornell University Press.

TITLE COMMENTARY

A Vindication of the Rights of Woman

CORA KAPLAN (ESSAY DATE 1985)

SOURCE: Kaplan, Cora. "Pandora's Box: Subjectivity, Class and Sexuality in Socialist Feminist Criticism." In *Making a Difference: Feminist Literary Criticism*, edited by Gayle Greene and Coppelia Kahn, pp. 146-76. London: Methuen, 1985.

In the following excerpt, Kaplan considers Wollstonecraft as an early feminist author whose conceptions of female subjectivity and potential continue to have currency in modern discussions of women as mothers, lovers, and political actors. Kaplan examines A Vindication of the Rights of Woman *and contends that Wollstonecraft's writing—despite its still-limited sense of women's potential—is central to formulating a modern socialist feminism that also accepts women as maternal, erotic, or simply feeling beings.*

> Feminist criticism, as its name implies, is criticism with a Cause, engaged criticism. But the critical model presented to us so far is merely engaged to be married. It is about to contract what can only be a *mésalliance* with bourgeois modes of thought and the critical categories they inform. To be effective, feminist criticism cannot become simply bourgeois criticism in drag. It must be ideological and moral criticism; it must be revolutionary.
> (Lillian Robinson, 'Dwelling in Decencies' (1978))

> The 'Marriage' of marxism and feminism has been like the marriage of husband and wife depicted in English common law: marxism and feminism are one, and that is marxism . . . we need a healthier marriage or we need a divorce.
> (Heidi Hartmann, 'The Unhappy Marriage of Marxism and Feminism' (1981))

I

In spite of the attraction of matrimonial metaphor, reports of feminist nuptials with either mild-mannered bourgeois criticism or macho mustachioed Marxism have been greatly exaggerated. Neither liberal feminist criticism decorously draped in traditional humanism, nor her red-ragged rebellious sister, socialist feminist criticism, has yet found a place within androcentric literary criticism, which wishes to embrace feminism through a legitimate public alliance. Nor can feminist criticism today be plausibly evoked as a young deb looking for protection or, even more problematically, as a male 'mole' in transvestite masquerade. Feminist criticism now marks out a broad area of literary studies, eclectic, original and provocative. Independent still, through a combination of choice and default, it has come of age without giving up its name. Yet Lillian Robinson's astute pessimistic prediction is worth remembering. With maturity, the most visible, well-defined and extensive tendency within feminist criticism has undoubtedly bought into the white, middle-class, heterosexist values of traditional literary criticism, and threatens to settle down on her own in its cultural suburbs. For, as I see it, the present danger is not that feminist criticism will enter an unequal dependent alliance with any of the varieties of male-centred criticism. It does not need to, for it has produced an all too persuasive autonomous analysis which is in many ways radical in its discussion of gender, but implicitly conservative in its assumptions about social hierarchy and female subjectivity, the Pandora's box for all feminist theory.

This reactionary effect must be interrogated and resisted from within feminism and in relation to the wider socialist feminist project. For, without the class and race perspectives which socialist feminist critics bring to the analysis both of the literary texts and of their conditions of production, liberal feminist criticism, with its emphasis on the unified female subject, will unintentionally reproduce the ideological values of mass-market romance. In that fictional landscape the other structuring relations of society fade and disappear, leaving us with the naked drama of sexual difference as the only scenario that matters. Mass-market romance tends to represent sexual difference as natural and fixed—a constant, transhistorical femininity in libidinized struggle with an equally 'given' universal masculinity. Even where class difference divides lovers, it is there as narrative backdrop or minor stumbling-block to the inevitable heterosexual resolution. Without overstraining the comparison, a feminist literary criticism which privileges gender in isolation from other forms of social determination offers us a similarly partial reading of the role played by sexual difference in literary discourse, a reading bled dry of its most troubling and contradictory meanings.

The appropriation of modern critical theory—semiotic with an emphasis on the psychoanalytic—can be of great use in arguing against concepts of natural, essential and unified identity: against a static femininity and masculinity. But these theories about the production of meaning in culture must engage fully with the effects of other systems of difference than the sexual, or they too will produce no more than an anti-humanist avant-garde version of romance. Masculinity and femininity do not appear in cultural discourse, any more than they do in mental life, as pure binary forms at play. They are always, already, ordered and broken up through other social and cultural terms, other categories of difference. Our fantasies of sexual transgression as much as our obedience to sexual regulation are expressed through these structuring hierarchies. Class and race ideologies are, conversely, steeped in and spoken through the language of sexual differentiation. Class and race meanings are not metaphors for the sexual, or vice versa. It is better, though not exact, to see them as reciprocally constituting each other through a kind of narrative invocation, a set of associative terms in a chain of meaning. To understand how gender and class—to take two categories only—are articulated together transforms our analysis of each of them.

The literary text too often figures in feminist criticism as a gripping spectacle in which sexual difference appears somewhat abstracted from the muddy social world in which it is elsewhere embedded. Yet novels, poetry and drama are, on the contrary, peculiarly rich discourses in which the fused languages of class, race and gender are both produced and re-represented through the incorporation of other discourses. The focus of feminist analysis ought to be on that heterogeneity within the literary, on the intimate relation there expressed between all the categories that order social and psychic meaning. This does not imply an attention to content only or primarily, but also entails a consideration of the linguistic processes of the text as they construct and position subjectivity within these terms.

For without doubt literary texts do centre the individual as object and subject of their discourse. Literature has been a traditional space for the exploration of gender relations and sexual difference, and one in which women themselves have been formidably present. The problem for socialist feminists is not the focus on the individual that is special to the literary, but rather the romantic theory of the subject so firmly entrenched within the discourse. Humanist feminist criticism does not object to the idea of an immanent, transcendent subject but only to the exclusion of women from these definitions which it takes as an accurate account of subjectivity rather than as a historically constructed ideology. The repair and reconstitution of female subjectivity through a rereading of literature becomes, therefore, a major part, often unacknowledged, of its critical project. Psychoanalytic and semiotically oriented feminist

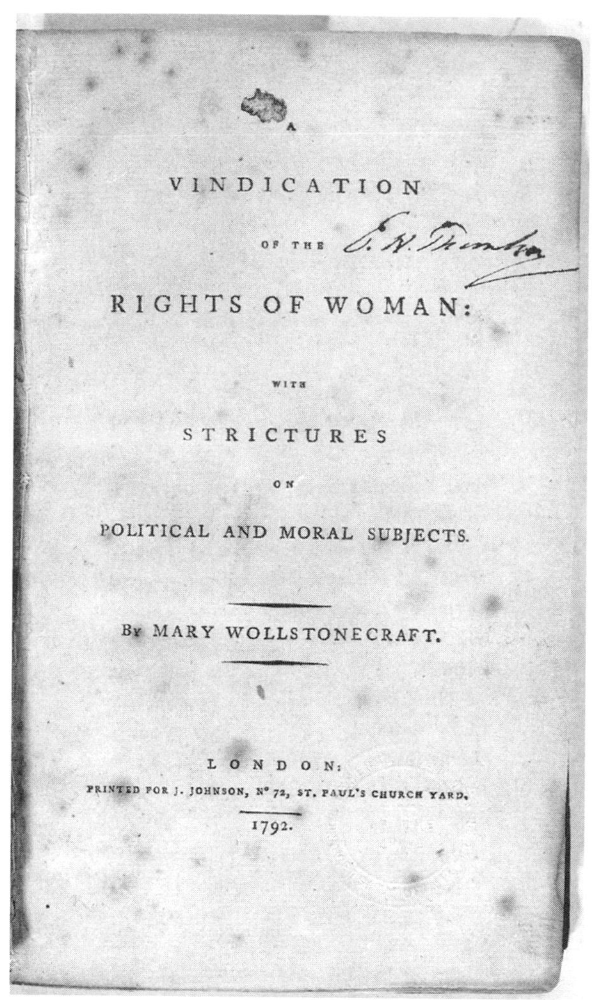

A

VINDICATION

OF THE

RIGHTS OF WOMAN:

WITH

STRICTURES

ON

POLITICAL AND MORAL SUBJECTS.

BY MARY WOLLSTONECRAFT.

LONDON:

PRINTED FOR J. JOHNSON, N° 72, ST. PAUL'S CHURCH YARD.

1792.

Title page of *A Vindication of the Rights of Woman: With Strictures on Political and Moral Subjects* (1792).

criticism has argued well against this aspect of feminist humanism, emphasizing the important structural relation between writing and sexuality in the construction of the subject. But both tendencies have been correctly criticized from a socialist feminist position for the neglect of class and race as factors in their analysis. If feminist criticism is to make a central contribution to the understanding of sexual difference, instead of serving as a conservative refuge from its more disturbing social and psychic implications, the inclusion of class and race must transform its terms and objectives.

II

The critique of feminist humanism needs more historical explication than it has so far received. Its sources are complex, and are rooted in that moment almost 200 years ago when modern feminism and Romantic cultural theory emerged as separate but linked responses to the transforming events of the French Revolution. In the heat and light of the revolutionary decade 1790-1800, social, political and aesthetic ideas already maturing underwent a kind of forced ripening. As the progressive British intelligentsia contemplated the immediate possibility of social change, their thoughts turned urgently to the present capacity of subjects to exercise republican freedoms—to rule themselves as well as each other if the corrupt structures of aristocratic privilege were to be suddenly razed. Both feminism as set out in its most influential text, Mary Wollstonecraft's ***A Vindication of the Rights of Woman*** (1792), and Romanticism as argued most forcefully in Wordsworth's introduction to *Lyrical Ballads* (1800) stood in intimate, dynamic and contradictory relationship to democratic politics. In all three discourses the social and psychic character of the individual was centred and elaborated. The public and private implications of sexual difference as well as of the imagination and its products were both strongly linked to the optimistic, speculative construction of a virtuous citizen subject for a brave new egalitarian world. Theories of reading and writing—Wollstonecraft's and Jane Austen's as well as those of male Romantic authors—were explicitly related to contemporary politics as expressed in debate by such figures as Tom Paine, Edmund Burke and William Godwin.

The new categories of independent subjectivity, however, were marked from the beginning by exclusions of gender, race and class. Jean-Jacques Rousseau, writing in the 1750s, specifically exempted women from his definition; Thomas Jefferson, some twenty years later, excluded blacks. Far from being invisible ideological aspects of the new subject, these exclusions occasioned debate and polemic on both sides of the Atlantic. The autonomy of inner life, the dynamic psyche whose moral triumph was to be the foundation of republican government, was considered absolutely essential as an element of progressive political thought.

However, as the concept of the inner self and the moral psyche was used to denigrate whole classes, races and genders, late nineteenth-century socialism began to de-emphasize the political importance of the psychic self, and redefine political morality and the adequate citizen subject in primarily social terms. Because of this shift in emphasis, a collective moralism has developed in socialist thought which, instead of criticizing the reactionary interpretation of psychic life, stigmatizes sensibility itself, interpreting the excess of feeling as regressive, bourgeois and non-political.

Needless to say, this strand of socialist thought poses a problem for feminism, which has favoured three main strategies to deal with it. In the first, women's psychic life is seen as being essentially identical to men's, but distorted through vicious and systematic patriarchal inscription. In this view, which is effectively Wollstonecraft's, social reform would prevent women from becoming regressively obsessed with sexuality and feeling. The second strategy wholly vindicates women's psyche, but sees it as quite separate from men's, often in direct opposition. This is frequently the terrain on which radical feminism defends female sexuality as independent and virtuous between women, but degrading in a heterosexual context. It is certainly a radical reworking of essentialist sexual ideology, shifting the ground from glib assertions of gender complementarity to the logic of separatism. The third strategy has been to refuse the issue's relevance altogether—to see any focus on psychic difference as itself an ideological one.

Instead of choosing any one of these options, socialist feminist criticism must come to grips with the relationship between female subjectivity and class identity. This project, even in its present early stages, poses major problems for the tendency. While socialist feminists have been deeply concerned with the social construction of femininity and sexual difference, they have been uneasy about integrating social and political determinations with an analysis of the psychic ordering of gender. Within socialist feminism, a fierce and unresolved debate continues about the value of using psychoanalytic theory, because of the supposedly ahistorical character of its paradigms. For those who are hostile to psychoanalysis, the meaning of mental life, fantasy and desire—those obsessive themes of the novel and poetry for the last two centuries—seems particularly intractable to interpretation. They are reluctant to grant much autonomy to the psychic level, and often most attentive to feeling expressed in the work of non-bourgeois writers, which can more easily be read as political statement. Socialist feminism still finds unlocated, unsocialized psychic expression in women's writing hard to discuss in non-moralizing terms.

On the other hand, for liberal humanism, feminist versions included, the possibility of a unified self and an integrated consciousness that can transcend material circumstance is represented as the fulfilment of desire, the happy closure at the end of the story. The psychic fragmentation expressed through female characters in women's writing is seen as the most important sign of their sexual subordination, more interesting and ultimately more meaningful than their social oppression. As a result, the struggle for an integrated female subjectivity in nineteenth-century texts is never interrogated as ideology or fantasy, but seen as a demand that can actually be met, if not in 1848, then later.

In contrast, socialist feminist criticism tends to foreground the social and economic elements of the narrative and socialize what it can of its psychic portions. Women's anger and anguish, it is assumed, should be amenable to repair through social change. A positive emphasis on the psychic level is viewed as a valorization of the anarchic and regressive, a way of returning women to their subordinate ideological place within the dominant culture, as unreasoning social beings. Psychoanalytic theory, which is by and large morally neutral about the desires expressed by the psyche, is criticized as a confirmation and justification of them.

Thus semiotic or psychoanalytic perspectives have yet to be integrated with social, economic and political analysis. Critics tend to privilege one element or the other, even when they acknowledge the importance of both and the need to relate them. A comparison of two admirable recent essays on Charlotte Brontë's *Villette,* one by Mary Jacobus and the other by Judith Lowder Newton, both informed by socialist feminist concerns, can illustrate this difficulty.

Jacobus uses the psychoanalytic and linguistic theory of Jacques Lacan to explore the split representations of subjectivity that haunt *Villette,* and calls attention to its anti-realist gothic elements. She relates Brontë's feminized defence of the imagination, and the novel's unreliable narrator-heroine, to the tension between femininity and feminism that reaches back to the eighteenth-century debates of Rousseau and Wollstonecraft. Reading the ruptures and gaps of the text as a psychic narrative, she also places it historically in relationship to nineteenth-century social and political ideas. Yet the social meanings of *Villette* fade and all but disappear before 'the powerful presence of fantasy', which 'energizes *Villette* and satisfies that part of the reader which also desires constantly to reject reality for the sake of an obedient, controllable, narcissistically pleasurable image of self and its relation to the world' (Jacobus 1979, p. 51). In Jacobus's interpretation, the psyche, desire and fantasy stand for repressed, largely positive elements of a forgotten feminism, while the social stands for a daytime world of Victorian social regulation. These social meanings are referred to rather than explored in the essay, a strategy which renders them both static and unproblematically unified. It is as if, in order to examine how *Villette* represents psychic reality, the dynamism of social discourses of gender and identity must be repressed, forming the text's new 'unconscious'.

Judith Lowder Newton's chapter on *Villette* in her impressive study of nineteenth-century British fiction, *Women, Power, and Subversion* (1981), is also concerned with conflicts between the novel's feminism and its evocation of female desire. Her interpretation privileges the social meanings of the novel, its search for a possible *détente* between the dominant ideologies of bourgeois femininity and progressive definitions of female autonomy. For Newton, 'the internalized ideology of women's sphere' includes sexual and romantic longings—which for Jacobus are potentially radical and disruptive of mid-Victorian gender ideologies. The psychic level as Newton describes it is mainly the repository for the worst and most regressive elements of female subjectivity: longing for love, dependency, the material and emotional comfort of fixed class identity. These desires which have 'got inside' are predictably in conflict with the rebellious, autonomy-seeking feminist impulses, whose source is a rational understanding of class and gender subordination. Her reading centres on the realist text, locating meaning in its critique of class society and the constraints of bourgeois femininity.

The quotations and narrative elements cited and explored by Jacobus and Newton are so different that even a reader familiar with *Villette* may find it hard to believe that each critic is reading the same text. The psychic level exists in Newton's interpretation, to be sure, but as a negative discourse, the dead weight of ideology on the mind. For her, the words 'hidden', 'private' and 'longing' are stigmatized, just as they are celebrated by Jacobus. For both critics, female subjectivity is the site where the opposing forces of femininity and feminism clash by night, but they locate these elements in different parts of the text's divided selves. Neither Newton nor Jacobus argues for the utopian possibility of a unified subjectivity. But the *longing* to close the splits that characterize femininity—splits between reason and desire, autonomy and dependent security, psychic and social identity—is evident in the way each critic denies the opposing element.

III

My comments on the difficulties of reading *Villette* from a materialist feminist stance are meant to suggest that there is more at issue in the polarization of social and psychic explanation than the problem of articulating two different forms of explanation. Moral and political questions specific to feminism are at stake as well. In order to understand why female subjectivity is so fraught with *Angst* and difficulty for feminism, we must go back to the first full discussion of the psychological expression of femininity, in Mary Wollstonecraft's ***A Vindication of the Rights of Woman.*** The briefest look will show that an interest in the psychic life of women as a crucial element in their subordination and liberation is not a modern, post-Freudian preoccupation. On the contrary, its long and fascinating history in 'left' feminist writing starts with Wollstonecraft, who set the terms for a debate that is still in progress. Her writing is central for socialist feminism today, because she based her interest in the emancipation of women as individuals in revolutionary politics.

Like so many eighteenth-century revolutionaries, she saw her own class, the rising bourgeoise, as the vanguard of the revolution, and it was to the women of her own class that she directed her arguments. Her explicit focus on the middle class, and her concentration on the nature of female subjectivity, speaks directly to the source of anxiety within socialist feminism today. For it is at the point when women are released from profound social and economic oppression into greater autonomy and potential political choice that their social and psychic expression becomes an issue, and their literary texts become sites of ambivalence. In their pages, for the last 200 years and more, women characters seemingly more confined by social regulation than women readers today speak as desiring subjects. These texts express the politically 'retrogade' desires for comfort, dependence and love as well as more acceptable demands for autonomy and independence.

It is Mary Wollstonecraft who first offered women this fateful choice between the opposed and moralized bastions of reason and feeling, which continues to determine much feminist thinking. The structures through which she developed her ideas, however, were set for her by her mentor Jean-Jacques Rousseau, whose writing influenced the political and social perspectives of many eighteenth-century English radicals. His ideas were fundamental to her thinking about gender as well as about revolutionary politics. In 1792, that highly charged moment of romantic political optimism between the fall of the Bastille and the Terror when ***A Vindication*** was written, it must have seemed crucial that Rousseau's crippling judgement of female nature be refuted. How else could women freely and equally participate in the new world being made across the Channel? Rousseau's ideas about subjectivity were already immanent in Wollstonecraft's earlier book ***Mary: A Fiction*** (1788). Now she set out to challenge directly his offensive description of sexual difference which would leave women in post-revolutionary society exactly where they were in unreformed Britain, 'immured in their families, groping in the dark' (Wollstonecraft 1975a, p. 5).

Rousseau had set the terms of the debate in his *Emile* (1762), which describes the growth and education of the new man, progressive and bourgeois, who would be capable of exercising the republican freedoms of a reformed society. In Book V, Rousseau invents 'Sophie' as a mate for his eponymous hero, and here he outlines his theory of sexual asymmetry as it occurs in nature. In all human beings passion was natural and necessary, but in women it was not controlled by reason, an attribute of the male sex only. Women, therefore,

> must be subject all their lives, to the most constant and severe restraint, which is that of decorum; it is therefore necessary to accustom them early to such confinement that it may not afterwards cost them too dear . . . we should teach them above all things to lay a due restraint on themselves.
>
> (Rousseau 1974, p. 332)

To justify this restraint, Rousseau allowed enormous symbolic power to the supposed anarchic, destructive force of untrammelled female desire. As objects of desire Rousseau made women alone responsible for male 'suffering'. If they were free agents of desire, there would be no end to the 'evils' they could cause. Therefore the family, and women's maternal role within it, were, he said, basic to the structure of the new society. Betrayal of the family was thus as subversive as betrayal of the state; adultery in *Emile* is literally equated with treason. Furthermore, in Rousseau's regime of regulation and restraint for bourgeois women, their 'decorum'—the social expression of modesty—would act as an additional safeguard against unbridled, excessive male lust, should its natural guardian, reason, fail. In proscribing the free exercise of female desire, Rousseau disarms a supposed serious threat to the new political as well as social order. To read the fate of a class through the sexual behaviour of its women was not a new political strategy. What is modern in Rousseau's formulation is the harnessing of these sexual ideologies to the fate of a new progressive bourgeoisie, whose individual male members were endowed with radical, autonomous identity.

In many ways, Mary Wollstonecraft, writing thirty years after *Emile,* shared with many others the political vision of her master. Her immediate contemporary Thomas Paine thought Rousseau's work expressed 'a loveliness of sentiment in favour of liberty', and it is in the spirit of Rousseau's celebration of liberty that Wollstonecraft wrote ***A Vindication.*** Her strategy was to accept Rousseau's description of adult women as suffused in sensuality, but to ascribe this unhappy state of things to culture rather than nature. It was, she thought, the vicious and damaging result of Rousseau's punitive theories of sexual difference and female education when put into practice. Excessive sensuality was for Wollstonecraft, in 1792 at least, as dangerous if not more so than Rousseau had suggested, but she saw the damage and danger first of all to women themselves, whose potential and independence were initially stifled and broken by an apprenticeship to pleasure, which induced psychic and social dependency. Because Wollstonecraft saw pre-pubescent children in their natural state as mentally and emotionally unsexed as well as untainted by corrupting desire, she bitterly refuted Rousseau's description of innate infantile female sexuality. Rather, the debased femininity she describes is constructed through a set of social practices which by constant reinforcement become internalized parts of the self. Her description of this process is acute:

> Every thing they see or hear serves to fix impressions, call forth emotions, and associate ideas, that give a sexual character to the mind. . . . This cruel association of ideas, which every thing conspires to twist into all their habits of thinking, or, to speak with more precision of feeling, receives new force when they begin to act a little for themselves.
>
> (Wollstonecraft 1975a, p. 177)

For Wollstonecraft, female desire was a contagion caught from the projection of male lust, an ensnaring and enslaving infection that made women into dependent and degenerate creatures, who nevertheless had the illusion that they acted independently. An education which changed women from potentially rational autonomous beings into 'insignificant objects of desire' was, moreover, rarely reversible. Once a corrupt subjectivity was constructed, only a most extraordinary individual could transform it, for 'so ductile is the understanding and yet so stubborn, that the association which depends on adventitious circumstances, during the period that the body takes to arrive at maturity, can seldom be disentangled by reason' (p. 116).

What is disturbingly peculiar to ***A Vindication*** is the undifferentiated and central place that sexuality as passion plays in the corruption and degradation of the female self. The overlapping Enlightenment and Romantic discourses on psychic economy all posed a major division between the rational and the irrational, between sense and sensibility. But they hold sensibility *in men* to be only in part an antisocial sexual drive. Lust for power and the propensity to physical violence were also, for men, negative components of all that lay on the other side of reason. Thus sensibility in men included a strong positive element too, for the power of the imagination depended on it, and in the 1790s the Romantic aesthetic and the political imagination were closely allied. Sexual passion controlled and mediated by reason, Wordsworth's 'emotion recollected in tranquility', could also be put to productive use in art—by men. The appropriate egalitarian subjects of Wordsworth's art were 'moral sentiments and animal sensations' as they appeared in everyday life (Wordsworth and Coleridge 1971, p. 261). No woman of the time could offer such an artistic manifesto. In women the irrational, the sensible, even the imaginative are all drenched in an overpowering and subordinating sexuality. And in Wollstonecraft's writing, especially in her last, unfinished novel ***Maria, or the Wrongs of Woman*** (1798), which is considerably less punitive about women's sexuality in general than ***A Vindication,*** only maternal feeling survives as a positively realized element of the passionate side of the psyche. By defending women against Rousseau's denial of their reason, Wollstonecraft unwittingly assents to his negative, eroticized sketch of their emotional lives. At various points in ***A Vindication*** she interjects a wish that 'after some future revolution in time' women might be able to live out a less narcissistic and harmful sexuality. Until then they must demand an education whose central task is to cultivate their neglected 'understanding'.

It is interesting and somewhat tragic that Wollstonecraft's paradigm of women's psychic economy still profoundly shapes modern feminist consciousness. How often are the maternal, romantic-sexual and intellectual capacity of women presented by feminism as in competition for a fixed psychic space. Men seem to have a roomier and more accommodating psychic home, one which can, as Wordsworth and other Romantics insisted, situate all the varieties of passion and reason in creative tension. This gendered eighteenth-century psychic economy has been out of date for a long time, but its ideological inscription still shadows feminist attitudes towards the mental life of women.

The implications of eighteenth-century theories of subjectivity were important for early feminist ideas about women as readers and writers. In the final pages of ***A Vindication,*** decrying female sentimentality as one more effect of women's psychic degradation, Wollstonecraft criticizes the sentimental fictions increasingly written by and for women, which were often their only education. 'Novels' encouraged in their mainly young, mainly female audience 'a romantic twist of the mind'. Readers would 'only be taught to look for happiness in love, refine on sensual feelings and adopt metaphysical notions respecting that passion'. At their very worst the 'stale tales' and 'meretricious scenes' would by degrees induce more than passive fantasy. The captive, addicted reader might, while the balance of her mind was disturbed by these erotic evocations, turn fiction into fact and 'plump into actual vice' (p. 183). A reciprocal relationship between the patriarchal socialization of women and the literature that supports and incites them to become 'rakes at heart' is developed in this passage. While Wollstonecraft adds that she would rather women read novels than nothing at all, she sets up a peculiarly gendered and sexualized interaction between women and the narrative imaginative text, one in which women become the ultimately receptive reader easily moved into amoral activity by the fictional representation of sexual intrigue.

The political resonance of these questions about reader response was, at the time, highly charged. An enormous expansion of literacy in general, and of the middle-class reading public in particular, swelled by literate women, made the act of reading in the last quarter of the eighteenth century an important practice through which the common sense and innate virtue of a society of autonomous subject-citizens could be reached and moulded. An uncensored press, cheap and available reading matter and a reading public free to engage with the flood of popular literature, from political broadsheets to sensational fiction, was part of the agenda and strategy of British republicanism. 'It is dangerous', Tom Paine warned the government in the mid-1790s after his own writing had been politically censored, 'to tell a whole people that they shall not read.' Reading was a civil right that supported and illustrated the radical vision of personal independence. Political and sexual conservatives, Jane Austen and Hannah More, as well as the republican and feminist left, saw reading as an active, not a passive function of the self, a critical link between the psychic play of reason and passion and its social expression. New social categories of readers, women of all classes, skilled and unskilled working-class males, are described in this period by contemporaries. Depending on their political sympathies, observers saw these actively literate groups as an optimistic symptom of social and intellectual progress or a dire warning of imminent social decay and threatened rebellion.

Wollstonecraft saw sentiment and the sensual as reinforcing an already dominant, approved and enslaving sexual norm, which led women to choose a subordinate social and subjective place in culture. The damage done by 'vice' and 'adultery', to which sentimental fiction was an incitement, was a blow to women first and to society second. Slavish legitimate sexuality was almost as bad for women in Wollstonecraft's view as unlicensed behaviour. A more liberal regime for women was both the goal and the cure of sentimental and erotic malaise. In ***A Vindication*** women's subjection is repeatedly compared to all illegitimate hierarchies of power, but especially to existing aristocratic hegemony. At every possible point in her text, Wollstonecraft links the liberation of women from the sensual into the rational literally and symbolically to the egalitarian transformation of the whole society.

'Passionlessness', as Nancy Cott has suggested (Cott 1978), was a strategy adopted both by feminists and by social conservatives. Through the assertion that women were not innately or excessively sexual, that on the contrary their 'feelings' were largely filial and maternal, the imputation of a degraded subjectivity could be resisted. This alternative psychic organization was represented as both strength and weakness in nineteenth-century debates about sexual difference. In these debates, which were conducted across a wide range of public discourses, the absence of an independent, self-generating female sexuality is used by some men and women to argue for women's right to participate equally in an undifferentiated public sphere. It is used by others to argue for the power and value of the separate sphere allotted to women. And it is used more nakedly to support cruder justifications of patriarchal right. The idea of passionlessness as either a natural or a cultural effect acquires no simple ascendancy in Victorian sexual ideology, even as applied to the ruling bourgeoisie.

As either conservative or radical sexual ideology, asexual femininity was a fragile, unstable concept. It was constructed through a permanently threatened transgression, which fictional narrative obsessively documented and punished. It is a gross historical error to infer from the regulatory sexual discourses in the novel the actual 'fate' of Victorian adulteresses, for novels operated through a set of highly punitive conventions in relation to female sexuality that almost certainly did not correspond to lived social relations. However, novels do call attention to the difficulty of fixing such a sexual ideology, precisely because they construct a world in which there is no alternative to it.

References

Alexander, Sally (1984) 'Women, Class and Sexual Difference', *History Workshop,* 17, pp. 125-49.

Bakhtin, M. M. (1981) *The Dialogic Imagination: Four Essays,* ed. Michael Holquist. Austin, Texas: University of Texas Press.

Brontë, Charlotte (1976) *Jane Eyre* (1847) ed. Margaret Smith. London: Oxford University Press.

Cott, Nancy F. (1978) 'Passionlessness: An Interpretation of Victorian Sexual Ideology, 1790-1850', *Signs,* 2, 2, pp. 219-33.

Hartmann, Heidi (1981) 'The Unhappy Marriage of Marxism and Feminism: Towards a More Progressive Union'. In Lydia Sargent (ed.), *The Unhappy Marriage of Marxism and Feminism: A Debate on Class and Patriarchy,* pp. 1-42. London: Pluto Press.

Jacobus, Mary (1979) 'The Buried Letter: Feminism and Romanticism in *Villette*'. In Mary Jacobus (ed.), *Women Writing and Writing about Women,* pp. 42-60. London: Croom Helm.

Marxist-Feminist Literature Collective (1978) 'Women's Writing: *Jane Eyre, Shirley, Villette, Aurora Leigh*'. In *1848: The Sociology of Literature,* proceedings of the Essex conference on the Sociology of Literature (July 1977), pp. 185-206.

Newton, Judith Lowder (1981) *Women, Power, and Subversion: Social Strategies in British Fiction 1778-1860.* Athens, Ga.: University of Georgia Press.

Radcliffe, Ann (1966) *The Mysteries of Udolpho* (1794). London: Oxford University Press.

Robinson, Lillian S. (1978) 'Dwelling in Decencies: Radical Criticism and the Feminist Perspective'. In *Sex, Class and Culture,* pp. 3-21. Bloomington, Ind.: Indiana University Press.

Rousseau, Jean-Jacques (1974) *Emile* (1762). London: Dent.

Said, Edward W. (1978) *Orientalism.* London: Routledge & Kegan Paul.

Stedman Jones, Gareth (1983) *Languages of Class: Studies in English Working Class History 1832-1982.* Cambridge: Cambridge University Press.

ABOUT THE AUTHOR

WOLLSTONECRAFT'S HUSBAND WILLIAM GODWIN ON HER *VINDICATION OF THE RIGHTS OF WOMAN*, FROM 1798

Never did any author enter into a cause, with a more ardent desire to be found, not a flourishing and empty declaimer, but an effectual champion. She considered herself as standing forth in defence of one half of the human species, labouring under a yoke which, through all the records of time, had degraded them from the station of rational beings, and almost sunk them to the level of the brutes. She saw indeed, that they were often attempted to be held in silken fetters, and bribed into the love of slavery; but the disguise and the treachery served only the more fully to confirm her opposition. She regarded her sex, in the language of Calista, as

"In every state of life the slaves of man:"

the rich as alternately under the despotism of a father, a brother, and a husband; and the middling and the poorer classes shut out from the acquisition of bread with independence, when they are not shut out from the very means of an industrious subsistence. Such were the views she entertained of the subject; and such were the feelings with which she warmed her mind.

Godwin, William. Excerpt from *Memoirs of Mary Wollstonecraft*, 1927. Reprint, edited by W. Clark Durant, pp. 53-4. New York: Haskell House, 1969.

Wollstonecraft, Mary (1975a) *A Vindication of the Rights of Woman* (1792). New York: Norton.

Wollstonecraft, Mary (1975b) *Maria, or The Wrongs of Woman* (1798). New York: Norton.

Woolf, Virginia (1973) *A Room of One's Own* (1929). Harmondsworth: Penguin.

Woolf, Virginia (1979) 'Women and Fiction'. In Michèle Barrett (ed.), *Women and Writing*, pp. 44-52. London: Women's Press.

Wordsworth, William, and Coleridge, Samuel Taylor (1971) *Lyrical Ballads* (1798, 1800), ed. R. L. Brett and A. R. Jones. London: Methuen.

SUSAN GUBAR (ESSAY DATE 1995)

SOURCE: Gubar, Susan. "Feminist Misogyny: Mary Wollstonecraft and the Paradox of 'It Takes One to Know One.'" In *Feminism Beside Itself*, edited by Diane Elam and Robyn Wiegman, pp. 133-54. New York: Routledge, 1995.

In the following essay, Gubar examines the anti-woman aspects of Wollstonecraft's feminist writings, and places her work in the context of a long history of so-called "feminist misogyny." Reading A Vindication of the Rights of Woman, *Gubar finds Wollstonecraft frequently describing women in highly negative terms and taking pains to dissociate herself from women even as she attempts to assert their value. According to the critic, Wollstonecraft's paradoxical stance prefigures the attitude of many modern feminists, including Olive Schreiner, Kate Millett, and Andrea Dworkin, among others.*

In a self-reflexive essay representative of current feminist thinking, Ann Snitow recalls a memory of the early seventies, a moment when a friend "sympathetic to the [woman's] movement but not active [in it] asked what motivated" Snitow's fervor:

> I tried to explain the excitement I felt at the idea that I didn't have to be a woman. She was shocked, confused. *This* was the motor of my activism? She asked, "How can someone who doesn't like being a woman be a feminist?" To which I could only answer, "Why would anyone who likes being a woman *need* to be a feminist?"
>
> Quite properly my colleague feared woman-hating. . . . Was this, as [she] thought, just a new kind of misogyny?

Though Snitow eventually finds "woman-hating—or loving—. . . beside the point," she admits that she "wouldn't dare say self-hatred played no part in what I wanted from feminism," a remark that takes on added resonance in terms of her first reaction to consciousness raising: "'Woman' is my slave name," she felt back then; "feminism will give me freedom to seek some other identity altogether."[1]

"'Woman' is my slave name; feminism will give me freedom to seek some other identity altogether": Snitow's formulation dramatizes a curious contradiction that feminism exhibits from its very inception to present times. The oxymoronic title of this essay—feminist misogyny—risks political incorrectness and implicitly asks us to pause, to consider the efficacy of the appellations "feminism" and "misogyny," not to derail our commitment to social justice but to make it more savvy, more supple. When put to the test in the "Can you really tell?" game, current conceptualizations may not always help us distinguish feminist from misogynist claims.

On the one hand, can you judge the sexual politics of the thinker who wrote the sentence

"There is a pleasure, . . . an enjoyment of the body, which is . . . *beyond the phallus*?" What does it mean that this apparently liberated sentiment comes from Jacques Lacan (the same Lacan who boasted, "[women] don't know what they're saying, that's all the difference between them and me")?[2] On the other hand, can you surmise the ideology of the writer who declared that "woman is body more than man is" or of the theorist who stated that "*woman has sex organs more or less everywhere*?"[3] What does it mean that these two quotations, authored by feminist theorists Héléne Cixous and Luce Irigaray, eerily reiterate a proposition made by masculinist writers from Rousseau to Ambrose Bierce, so as to deny women equal educational opportunities, specifically the idea that "to men a man is but a mind. . . . But woman's body is the woman"?[4]

Pursuing the same inquiry, we might ask why Denise Riley recently chose the allusive title "*Am I That Name*?" (1988) for a book advocating a post-structural approach to feminism, when the line (originally spoken in the femicidal atmosphere of Shakespeare's *Othello*) conflates the "name" woman with the name-calling that demotes woman to whore?[5] Finally, who would guess that this critique of Adrienne Rich—"The feminist dream of a common language . . . is a totalizing and imperialist one"—issues not from Lacan or some modern-day Iago but from the women's studies scholar Donna Haraway?[6] If the histories of feminism and misogyny have been (sometimes shockingly) dialogic, as I will try to suggest, what impact should that have on the ways in which we understand the once and future state of feminist theory?

The subtitle of my meditation may seem just as incongruous as its title because we generally view Mary Wollstonecraft as a pioneer whose feminist efforts were tragically misunderstood by the misogynist society in which she lived. And, of course, as the aesthetic foremother of feminist expository prose, Wollstonecraft established a polemical tradition mined by such literary descendants as Olive Schreiner, Emma Goldman, and Virginia Woolf as well as by contemporary thinkers from Simone de Beauvoir to Kate Millett and, yes, Cixous and Riley. Indubitably, all of these theorists profited from and extended Wollstonecraft's insistence on righting the wrongs done to women. Paradoxically, however, they also inherited what I am calling her feminist misogyny. Indeed, the very troubling tenacity of this strain in feminist expository prose calls out for further thought.

That Wollstonecraft did, in fact, function as an effective advocate for women is probably self-evident, especially to anyone familiar with the political and literary culture into which she interjected her views. Though I will be examining a pervasive contradiction in her life and work, in no way do I mean to diminish or disparage her achievements. Quite rightly regarded as the founding feminist text in English, ***A Vindication of the Rights of Woman*** (1792) links the radical insurrection of the French revolution to the equally radical insubordination of the feminist project. Nor do I think we should judge Wollstonecraft by late twentieth-century definitions of feminism and find her wanting, "as if"—to quote Frances Ferguson—"Wollstonecraft would have turned out better work if she had had a word processor or a microwave oven."[7]

Although she has been faulted for adhering to a suspect faith in reason as an innate human characteristic,[8] Wollstonecraft exploited enlightenment language to claim that—at least theoretically—men and women were alike in being endowed with reason, a divine faculty that only needed to be cultivated so as to perfect the human species. Many of the thinkers of her time emphasized the differences between the sexes, with the influential Rousseau demanding that women's education "should be always relative to the men. To please, to be useful to [men,] . . . to advise, to console us, to render our lives easy and agreeable: these are the duties of women at all times."[9] But Wollstonecraft believed that because both sexes shared an equal capacity for reason, women—considered as *human,* not as sexual, beings—should benefit from the educational programs historically only afforded men. In addition, Wollstonecraft's commitment to rationality made her especially sensitive to representations of female irrationality that enslaved women's hearts and minds.

From her meditations on the Bible and Milton's *Paradise Lost* to her interpretations of Pope's, Dr. Gregory's, and Rousseau's treatises, Wollstonecraft's analyses of debilitating female images assume that we are what we read, and therefore these passages in ***A Vindication of the Rights of Woman*** constitute one of the earliest instances we have of feminist criticism. According to Wollstonecraft, female readers necessarily internalize male-authored and manifestly false impressions of who they are and what they should aspire to be, impressions that weaken rather than strengthen women's self-image. Confronting the socialization process effected by reading as well as by other childrearing practices, Wollstonecraft used her expository prose and her two novels to theorize about the psychological and cultural engendering of femininity. None of her contemporaries devised as sophisticated a model for understanding the social construction of womanhood, speculations that laid the groundwork for Simone de Beauvoir's famous claim that "one is not born a woman, but rather becomes one."[10] Yet it is in this area—Wollstonecraft's analysis of the feminine—that we will find most striking evidence of the contradiction in her thinking that I am terming "feminist misogyny."

What image of woman emerges from the pages of ***A Vindication of the Rights of Woman***? Repeatedly and disconcertingly, Wollstonecraft associates the feminine with weakness, childishness, deceitfulness, cunning, superficiality, an overvaluation of love, frivolity, dilettantism, irrationality, flattery, servility, prostitution, coquetry, sentimentality, ignorance, indolence, intolerance, slavish conformity, fickle passion, despotism, bigotry, and a "spaniel-like affection."[11] The feminine principle, so defined, threatens—like a virus—to contaminate and destroy men and their culture. For, as Wollstonecraft explains, "Weak, artificial beings, raised above the common wants and affections of their race, in a premature unnatural manner, undermine the very foundation of virtue, and spread corruption through the whole mass of society."[12]

Here in ***A Vindication,*** as in the next sentences I quote, femininity feels like a malady:

> [Women's] senses are *inflamed,* and their understandings neglected, consequently they become the *prey* of their senses, delicately termed sensibility, and are *blown about* by every momentary *gust* of feeling. Civilized women are, therefore, . . . *weakened* by false refinement. . . . Ever *restless* and *anxious,* their *over exercised* sensibility not only renders them *uncomfortable* themselves, but *troublesome* . . . to others. . . . [T]heir conduct is *unstable,* and their opinions are *wavering.* . . . By *fits and starts* they are *warm* in many pursuits; yet this *warmth,* never concentrated into perseverance, soon *exhausts* itself. . . . *Miserable,* indeed, must be that being whose cultivation of mind has only tended to *inflame* its passions! (emphases mine)[13]

According to this passage, civilized women suffer from an illness, a veritable fever of femininity, that reduces them to "unstable" and "uncomfortable," "miserable," exhausted, invalids. Wollstonecraft's description of women's restlessness, of the "warm gusts" of inflammation they suffer, sounds like nothing less than contemporary complaints about hot flashes and menopausal mood swings, as if the long disease of femininity has itself become a critical "change of life." At the close of the paragraph in which these words appear, Wollstonecraft takes to its logical conclusion the implications of women's "fits and starts": when "passions" are "pampered, whilst the judgement is left unformed," she asks, "what can be expected to ensue?" and she promptly answers, "Undoubtedly, a mixture of madness and folly!"

Elsewhere in a related series of metaphors, women operate like "gangrene, which the vices engendered by oppression have produced," and the mortal damage they inflict "is not confined to the morbid part, but pervades society at large."[14] Even if she is not noxious, the female is obnoxious, a diminished thing that has dwindled, dehumanized, into something like a doll, providing merely an aimless leisure pastime for men: "She was created," Wollstonecraft claims, "to be the toy of man, his rattle, and it must jingle in his ears whenever, dismissing reason, he chooses to be amused."[15] Like a virus spreading corruption; like an illness condemning its victim to madness; like gangrene contaminating the healthy; like a jingling toy distracting irrational pleasure-seekers: because femininity figures as, at best, frivolity and, at worst, fatality, the principle character emerging from the pages of ***The Vindication of the Rights of Woman*** is the femme fatale.

Wollstonecraft's derogations of the feminine, to be sure, are framed in terms of her breakthrough analysis of the social construction of gender. The above quotations, for instance, insist that women's "senses are inflamed" because "their understandings [are] neglected"; that women are artificially "raised" above the race; that the gangrene of their vices is "engendered" by oppression; and that they are "created" to be toys. Thus, her thesis—that a false system of education has "rendered [women] weak and wretched"—emphasizes the powerful impact of culture on subjectivity, the capacity of the psyche to internalize societal norms.[16] Indeed, Wollstonecraft stands at an originatory point in feminist thought precisely because she envisioned a time when the female of the species could shed herself of an enfeebling acculturation or feminization. Yet although (or perhaps because) ***A Vindication*** sets out to liberate society from a hated subject constructed to be subservient and called "woman," it illuminates how such animosity can spill over into antipathy of those human beings most constrained by that construction.

Laying the groundwork for the first and second wave of the women's movement, ***A Vindication of the Rights of Woman*** implies that

"'Woman' is my slave name; feminism will give me freedom to seek some other identity altogether." About the "few women [who] have emancipated themselves from the galling yoke of sovereign man," therefore, Wollstonecraft speculates that they are virtually transsexuals. Just as Newton "was probably a being of superior order accidentally caged in a human body," she imagines that "the few extraordinary women" in history "were *male* spirits, confined by mistake in female frames."[17] No wonder that, as Mary Poovey has pointed out, Wollstonecraft often speaks of herself "as a philosopher," "as a moralist," even "as [a] man with man," concluding her work with a plea to "ye men of understanding."[18] Rarely, in other words, does she present herself as a woman speaking to women.

Curiously, then, Wollstonecraft's radical stance nevertheless ends up aligning her with women's most fervent adversaries, as she herself admits: "after surveying the history of woman," she concedes, "I cannot help, agreeing with the severest satirist, considering the sex as the weakest as well as the most oppressed half of the species."[19] And several passages in ***A Vindication*** do seem to agree with "the severest satirist[s]" of women. While analyzing the "sexual weakness that makes woman depend upon man," for example, Wollstonecraft scorns "a kind of cattish affection which leads a wife to purr about her husband as she would about any man who fed and caressed her."[20] If the female looks subhuman in her cattiness here, elsewhere she appears sinful in her cunning trickery. To castigate those made "inferior by ignorance and low desires," Wollstonecraft describes "the serpentine wrigglings of cunning" that enable women to "mount the tree of knowledge, and only acquire sufficient to lead men astray."[21] Like their foremother, Eve, women bear the responsibility for the fall of man and they do so because of their misuse of knowledge. Predictably, one of Wollstonecraft's favorite Greek allusions is to Eve's prototype, Pandora.

And a number of other passages in ***A Vindication of the Rights of Woman*** concur with the severest satirists of the weaker sex, whom Wollstonecraft actually echoes. Take, for example, the following attack on the institution of marriage as a commodities market:

> It is acknowledged that [women] spend many of the first years of their lives in acquiring a smattering of accomplishments; meanwhile strength of body and mind are sacrificed to libertine notions of beauty, to the desire of establishing themselves—the only way women can rise in the world—by marriage. And this desire making mere animals of them, when they marry they act as such children may be expected to act—they dress; they paint, and nickname God's creatures—Surely these weak beings are only fit for a seraglio![22]

Not only does Wollstonecraft paraphrase Hamlet's angry speech to Ophelia—"You jig, you amble, and you lisp; you nickname God's creatures and make your wantonness your ignorance"; by relegating the feminine woman to a seraglio, she also glosses his refrain—"get thee to a nunnery": both nunnery and seraglio were common euphemisms for whorehouse. But the word "seraglio"—a Turkish or Eastern lodging for the secluded harem of Islamic noblemen—captures Wollstonecraft's disdain for a feminine lassitude so degenerate, so threatening to Western Civilization that it must be marked as what Edward Said would call a kind of "Orientalism."[23]

If we compare Wollstonecraft's portrait of the feminine here with the notoriously severe eighteenth-century satirists of the weaker sex, it becomes clear that she shares with them Hamlet's revulsion. Judge Wollstonecraft's emphasis on libertine notions of beauty, for example, in terms of Pope's famous lines in his "Epistle to a Lady"—"ev'ry Woman is at heart a Rake" and "Most women have no characters at all"—as well as his insistence that the best woman is "a contradiction" in terms, "a softer man." Consider her picture of female animality and dilettantism in relation to Swift's monstrous Goddess of Criticism in *The Tale of the Tub,* a symbol of ignorance portrayed as part cat, part ass. Compare Wollstonecraft's vision of feminine hypocrisy and prostitution to Swift's attacks in his mock pastorals on dressing and painting, debased arts that conceal syphilitic whores; or place her indictment that unaccomplished women "nickname God's creatures" up against Dr. Johnson's comparison between a woman preaching and a dog dancing. Finally, examine Wollstonecraft's childish wives in terms of the Earl of Chesterfield's definition of women as "children of a larger growth."[24]

Why does Wollstonecraft's text so eerily echo those composed by masculinist satirists?[25] A number of critics have noted problems, tensions, and repressions in the *oeuvre* produced by Wollstonecraft.[26] In particular, these scholars claim that, by appropriating an enlightenment rhetoric of reason, Wollstonecraft alienated herself and other women from female sexual desire. While it is certainly the case that throughout ***A Vindication of the Rights of Woman,*** Wollstonecraft elevates friendship between the sexes over romantic and erotic entanglements (which she condemns as ephemeral or destructive), I would view this motif not merely as a repression of sexuality but more inclusively as a symptom of the paradoxical feminist misogyny that pervades her work, only one sign of the ways in which Wollstonecraft's feminism operates vis-à-vis feminization and by no means an eccentric fault of her philosophizing. For, as Cora Kaplan has insightfully remarked, "There is no feminism that can stand wholly outside femininity as it is posed in a given historical moment. All feminisms give some ideological hostage to femininities and are constructed through the gender sexuality of their day as well as standing in opposition to them."[27]

If feminist expository prose necessarily situates itself in opposition to self-demeaning modes of feminization even as it is shaped by them, what Moira Ferguson describes as Wollstonecraft's propensity "to find women culpable of their vanity, their acceptance of an inferior education, their emphasis on feeling," her tendency to "locate herself outside what she deem[ed] self-demeaning behavior," takes on not only personal but also political and philosophical import.[28] Indeed, the tensions at work in Wollstonecraft's text dramatize, on the one hand, the ways in which "feminisms give some ideological hostage to femininities," as Kaplan puts it, and on the other hand, the ironies embedded in the stage of patrilineal affiliation that Sandra Gilbert and I have examined in the aesthetic paradigm we call "the female affiliation complex."[29]

To take the first subject first, is it possible to view Wollstonecraft's description of the fever of femininity in ***A Vindication of the Rights of Woman*** as a portrait of any middle-class woman of her age, indeed as a *self*-portrait? Could the disgust at fallen, fated, or fatal females be *self*-disgust? In the words of Emma Goldman, the "sexually starved" Wollstonecraft was "doomed to become the prey of more than one infatuation" and her "insatiable hunger for love" led not only to a tragic desire for the married painter Fuseli but also to the two suicide attempts resulting from her tempestuous involvement with the philanderer Gilbert Imlay.[30] Wollstonecraft was so overcome by passion for Fusseli that she had suggested a *ménage à trois* to his shocked wife; after discovering Gilbert Imlay's actress-mistress, she soaked her skirts so as to sink into the water after she threw herself from Putney Bridge. Did anyone better understand slavish passions, the overvaluation of love, fickle irrationality, weak dependency, the sense of personal irrelevance, and anxiety about personal attractiveness than Wollstonecraft herself?

Thus, Virginia Woolf, considering the various ways in which Wollstonecraft "could not understand . . . her own feelings," believed that the eighteenth-century polemicist made theories every day, "theories by which life should be lived," but "Every day too—for she was no pedant, no cold-blooded theorist—something was born in her that thrust aside her theories and forced her to model them afresh."[31] From the perspective of Goldman's and Woolf's essays, therefore, the misogyny of ***A Vindication*** dramatizes the self-revulsion of a woman who knew *herself* to be constructed as feminine and thus it exhibits a kind of "anti-narcissism."[32] Indeed, what both Goldman and Woolf implicitly ask us to confront is the disparity between the feminist feats of ***A Vindication of the Rights of Woman*** and the gothic fates inflicted on Wollstonecraft's fictional heroines in ***Mary, a Fiction*** (1788) and ***Maria*** (1798).

Of course the subtitle of ***Maria—The Wrongs of Woman***—establishes it as a counterpart or extension of ***A Vindication of the Rights of Woman,*** as does the gloomy insight of its heroine when she asks, "Was not the world a vast prison, and women born slaves?"[33] Curiously, however, both novels negate or traverse the argument of ***A Vindication*** which, after all, condemns precisely the conventions of sentimental fiction ***Mary*** and ***Maria*** exploit. For the enflamed, volatile emotions Wollstonecraft castigates as weakness, folly, and madness in ***A Vindication*** infuse, motivate, and elevate the heroines of both novels. After weeping, fainting, and bemoaning her love for a dead friend and a dead lover, the admirable paragon of sensibility who is the central character of ***Mary*** exclaims, "I cannot live without loving—and love leads to madness."[34] Just as rapturous and tearful, the heroine of ***Maria*** exhibits the passion denounced throughout ***A Vindication*** in a narrative that at moments seems not to caution against romance so much as to consecrate it: "So much of heaven" do the lovers of ***Maria*** enjoy together "that paradise bloomed around them. . . . Love, the grand enchanter, 'lapt them in Elysium,' and every sense was harmonized to joy and social extasy."[35]

But the startling slippages in Wollstonecraft's thinking about heterosexuality are accompanied by equally dramatic strains in her meditations on the bonds between women. Though historians of homosexuality have been led by Wollstonecraft's emotional relationships with Jane Arden and Fanny Blood to argue that the female intimacies celebrated in ***Mary*** should be situated on what Adrienne Rich calls a "lesbian continuum," several passages in ***A Vindication of the Rights of Woman*** inveigh against the "grossly familiar" relationships spawned in female communities.[36] Women "shut up together in nurseries, schools, or convents" engage in "nasty customs," share "secrets" (on subjects "where silence ought to reign"), and indulge in "jokes and hoiden tricks."[37] Wollstonecraft the novelist valorizes the nurturing comfort and intensity of female intimacies; however, Wollstonecraft the philosopher hints at the obscene debaucheries of such contacts.

The odd juxtapositions between the ***Vindication*** and the novels imply that the misogynist portrait of the feminine penned by the feminist may, in fact, represent Wollstonecraft's efforts to negotiate the distance between desire and dread, what she thought she should have been and what she feared herself to be. In other words, ***A Vindication of the Rights of Woman*** presents a narrative voice of the feminist-philosopher and a fictive profile of femininity that interact to illuminate a dialogue between self and soul, the culturally induced schizophrenia of an anti-narcissist. And in some part of herself, Wollstonecraft seemed to have understood this very well. In October 1791, after she had begun composing ***A Vindication of the Rights of Woman*** and while she was sitting for a portrait a friend had commissioned, she wrote that friend the following lines: "I do not imagine that [the painting] will be a very striking likeness; but, if you do not find me in it, I will send you a more faithful sketch—a book that I am now writing, in which I myself . . . shall certainly appear, head and heart."[38]

Just this dialectic—between head and heart, between a hortatory philosophic voice and a debased self-portrait of femininity—characterizes the feminist misogyny Wollstonecraft bequeathed to her literary descendants, including feminist polemicists writing today. Partially, it was informed by Wollstonecraft's inexorable entrapment inside a patrilineal literary inheritance. In *The War of the Words,* Sandra Gilbert and I argued that women writers before the late nineteenth century necessarily affiliated themselves with an alien and alienating aesthetic patrilineage. But this is even more true for the author of feminist expository prose than it is for the woman poet or novelist who, like Elizabeth Barrett Browning, "look[ed] everywhere for [literary] grandmothers and [found] none" because, instead of looking for aesthetic grandmothers, Wollstonecraft set out to debate the most powerfully paternal influences on her own culture: Moses and St. John, Milton and Rousseau, Pope and the authors of conduct and etiquette books.[39]

As a genre, feminist expository prose inevitably embeds itself in the misogynist tradition it seeks to address and redress. Representing the masculinist voice in order to controvert its messages, one chapter of ***A Vindication***—brilliantly analyzed by Patricia Yaeger—proceeds by lengthily quoting Rousseau's portrait of womanhood "in his own words, interspersing [Wollstonecraft's] comments and reflections."[40] Thus, another dialectic emerges beyond the one between the individual author's head and heart, specifically in ***A Vindication*** the conversation between Wollstonecraft and Rousseau and more generally in the expository prose of her descendants the dialogic relationship between the histories of feminism and misogyny.

"It Takes One to Know One": the "One" in my subtitle is meant to indicate that it takes a feminist to know a misogynist, and vice versa. The terms of their engagement—as they bob and weave, feint and jab, thrust and parry in their philosophical fencing match or boxing ring—are particularly important to understand because, although feminism historically has not been the condition for misogyny's emergence, the pervasive threat of misogyny brought into being feminist discourse. To the extent that there can be (need be) no feminism without misogyny, the sparring of this odd couple—the feminist, the misogynist—takes on a ritualized, stylized quality as they stroll through the corridors of history, reflecting upon each other and upon their slam dancing. A full description of the choreography of their steps remains beyond the scope of this paper; however, a brief study of the eccentric dips and swirls executed by these curiously ambivalent partners at the beginning and end of this century can begin the task Judith Butler sets feminist critique, namely understanding "how the category of 'woman,' the subject of feminism, is produced and restrained by the very structures of power through which emancipation is sought."[41]

Like Mary Wollstonecraft's, Olive Schreiner's feminist prose stands in a vexed relationship to her fiction: specifically her polemical *Woman and Labour* (1911)—calling for "New Women" and "New Men" to enter "a new earth"—contrasts with a novel that obsesses over the self-pitying masochism of those who dream of altered sexual arrangements, just as it broods with nauseated fascination on the horrible tenacity of traditional women.[42] The would-be author of an introduction to ***A Vindication,*** Schreiner formulated her demands for female liberation as an attack not on men but on women, and specifically on what she called "the human female parasite—the most deadly microbe . . . on the surface of any social organism."[43] In *Woman and Labour,* which functioned as "the Bible" for first wave feminists, the idle, consuming "parasite woman on her couch" signals "the death-bed of human evolution."[44] Strangely, too, Schreiner seems to blame the limits of evolution on female anatomy when she speculates that the size of the human brain could only increase "if in the course of ages the *os cervix* of women should itself slowly expand."[45]

Just as discomforting as the thought of an os cervix having to extend so as to produce larger human heads may be the less biologistic but comparable woman-blaming in Schreiner's second-wave descendants. Perhaps Ann Douglas's *The Feminization of American Culture* (1977) furnishes the best case among the pioneers in women's studies. For here, nineteenth-century women's "debased religiosity, their sentimental peddling of Christian belief for its nostalgic value," and their "fakery" manage to "gut Calvinist orthodoxy" of its rigorous intellectual vitality.[46] So aware was Douglas herself about faulting women for the fall (the "feminization") of American culture that she used her introduction to defend herself against the charge that she had "Sid[ed] with the enemy." Though Douglas claimed to be motivated by a "respect" for "toughness," this (implicitly male) toughness seems entwined with self-hatred: "I expected to find my fathers and my mothers," she explains about her investigations into the past; "instead I discovered my fathers and my sisters" because "The problems of the women correspond to mine with a frightening accuracy that seems to set us outside the processes of history."[47]

About the immersion of Douglas's contemporaries in the literary history of the fathers, we might ask, what does it mean that a generation of readers was introduced to the works of Henry Miller and Norman Mailer through the long quotations that appeared in Kate Millett's important text, *Sexual Politics* (1969)? In this respect, her work typifies a paradox that persists in a branch of feminist criticism which, following in the wake of ***A Vindication,*** tackles the problematics of patriarchy by examining sexist authors (from Milton to Mailer) or by exploring male-dominated genres (pornography, the Western, adventure tales, men's magazines, film noir). No matter how radical the critique, it frequently falls into the representational quandary of ***A Vindication of the Rights of Woman***: replication or even recuperation. Throughout the feminist expository prose of the 1970s, the predominant images of women constellate around the female victim: foot-binding and suttee, cliterodectomy and witch-burning appear with startling frequency; the characters of the madwoman, the hysteric, the abused whore, the freak, and the female eunuch abound.

From *The Troublesome Helpmate* (1966), Katharine Roger's ground-breaking history of misogyny in literature, to my own work with Sandra Gilbert, moreover, feminist literary criticism has demonstrated that the most deeply disturbing male-authored depictions of women reveal with exceptional clarity the cultural dynamics of gender asymmetries. Thus, although Sandra and I usually focus on the female tradition, it seems striking that our most extended meditations on male authors center on such infamous masculinists as Milton, Rider Haggard, Freud, D. H. Lawrence, and T. S. Eliot, rather than, say, John Stuart Mill, George Meredith, or George Bernard Shaw, all self-defined friends of the women's movement. When questioned about our reliance on Freud, Sandra and I tend to respond by emphasizing how we have sought to disentangle the *de*scriptive powers of his insights into the sex/gender system from the *pre*scriptive overlay contained in the values he assigns aspects or stages of that system.

Perhaps this speculation tells us as much about the masculinist tradition as it does about the intervention of feminism. Can we extend it by proposing that misogynist texts often elaborate upon feminist insights, but within structures of address or rhetorical frames that—in different ways, to different degrees—vilify, diminish, or dismiss them? To return to *Hamlet* or, for that matter, *Othello* and *King Lear,* can it be that Shakespeare's portraits of femicidal heroes lay bare the causes and dynamics of woman-hating, albeit in plots that equivocate about the value placed upon such an emotion? To return to Freud, didn't his description of psychosexual development in Western culture make possible the radical revisions of a host of feminist theorists, ranging from Joan Riviere and Karen Horney to Shulamith Firestone, Juliet Mitchell, Gayle Rubin, Nancy Chodorow, and Adrienne Rich? In other words, if Wollstonecraft's ***Vindication*** embeds within it a misogynist text, do Shakespeare's *Hamlet,* Milton's

Paradise Lost, Rousseau's *Confessions,* and Freud's "Female Sexuality" contain antithetical feminist subscripts?[48]

The idea of feminist misogyny might thereby explain a host of critical controversies over the ideological designs of individual authors or texts. For at the current time probably every "major" writer in the canon, possibly every touchstone work, has been claimed by one scholar or another as prototypically feminist and quintessentially masculinist. Nor is this surprising, given that each individual's "language," according to the foremost theorist of this issue, "lies on the borderline between oneself and the other." As Bakhtin's most evocative description of the "overpopulation" of language explains,

> The word in language is half someone else's . . . it exists in other people's mouths, in other people's contexts, serving other people's intentions; it is from there that one must take the word, and make it one's own.[49]

"[E]xpropriating" language from the purposes or designs of others, "forcing it to submit to one's own intentions and accents": this is the "complicated process" in which feminists and misogynists necessarily engage so their discourses inevitably intersect in numerous ways, undercutting or supplementing each other over time, contesting what amounts to a complex nexus of ideas, values, perspectives, and norms, a cultural "heteroglossia" of gender ideologies and power asymmetries. Like the concept of black self-hatred and Jewish anti-Semitism, feminist misogyny might bring to critical attention the interlocutionary nature of representation; that is, the crucially different effects of the sentence "I am this" and "You are that."[50]

Inevitably, as the interaction between "I am this" and "You are that" implies, feminist consciousness today still bears the marks of its having come into being through interactions with a masculinism that has been shaped, in turn, by women's independence movements, a phenomenon that explains a number of anomalies: that Mary Daly, not Norman Mailer, entitled a volume *Pure Lust* (1984) and coined the phrase "fembot," for instance; that Norman Mailer, not Kate Millett, wrote *The Prisoner of Sex* (1971); that after Kate Millett's *Sexual Politics*—an analysis of masculine domination, feminine subordination—she published *The Basement* (1979), a gothic meditation on the sexual subordination and ultimate annihilation of a young girl by a power-crazed, sadistic *woman.*[51] Similarly, feminist misogyny amplifies the eerie reverberations set in motion by Germaine Greer's decision to follow *The Female Eunuch* (1970) with *Sex and Destiny* (1984). The former sprinkles quotations from ***A Vindication*** throughout a plea for a "revolution" in consciousness that requires that women refuse to bow down to "the Holy Family," reject the desexualization of their bodies, and protest against the manifold ways "our mothers blackmailed us with self-sacrifice."[52] However, the latter champions the family as the best social organization for women and children; touts chastity, coitus interruptus, and the rhythm method as optimal birth control methods; and nostalgically hymns the praises of the nurturance provided in so-called primitive cultures, specifically lauding "Mediterranean mothers [who] took their boy babies' penises in their mouths to stop their crying."[53]

Feminist misogyny in Mary Wollstonecraft's *oeuvre* may also help us understand why Andrea Dworkin has supplemented her anti-pornography expository prose with a gothic novel that could be said to be pornographic: *Ice and Fire* (1986) stands in as vexed a relation to *Intercourse* (1987) as ***Mary*** and ***Maria*** do to ***A Vindication.*** Dworkin the anti-pornography polemicist condemns sexual intercourse in our culture as "an act of invasion and ownership undertaken in a mode of predation: colonializing, forceful (manly) or nearly violent."[54] However, her novel *Ice and Fire* includes two types of sexually explicit scenes that contravene this definition, one in which "a girl James Dean" uses men to invade or colonize herself:

> When a man fucks me, she says, I am with him, fucking me. The men ride her like maniacs. Her eyes roll back but stay open and she grins. She is always them fucking her, no matter how intensely they ride.

In the second, the female narrator takes on the office of instructing her male lover on how to invade or colonize her:

> I teach him disrespect, systematically. I teach him how to tie knots, how to use rope, scarves, how to bite breasts: I teach him not to be afraid: of causing pain.[55]

To be sure, when the masochistic speaker here explains about her abusive lover "Reader, I married him" and when "Reader, he got hard" metamorphoses into "he got hard: he beat me until I couldn't even crawl," we are meant to understand that Dworkin is returning to the romance tradition of Charlotte Brontë's *Jane Eyre* ("Reader, I married him") so as to uncover its abusive sexual politics.[56] Nevertheless, the question remains, if the anti-pornography ordinance Dworkin framed with Catherine McKinnon were deemed constitutional, would she be able to publish this kind of fiction? How can it be that her heroines resemble the actresses in the snuff films she seeks to outlaw, women bent on finding sexual fulfillment in their own destruction?

More generally, the feminist misogyny that pervades Dworkin's work typifies the uncanny mirror dancing that repeatedly links feminist polemicists to their rivals and antagonists. In 1975, the feminist-linguist Robin Lakoff published her ground-breaking *Language and Woman's Place,* a description of the genderlect she called "women's language": euphemism, modesty, hedging, polite forms of address, weak expletives, tag questions, empty adjectives and intensives, and hypercorrect grammar were said to characterize women's speech. Curiously, her findings accorded with those of Otto Jesperson, whose 1922 study *Language: Its Nature, Development and Origin* proved that women were timid, conservative, even prudish language-users and thus incapable of linguistic inventiveness. As I intimated earlier, another odd coupling could be said to exist between Jacques Lacan, who viewed women as inexorably exiled from culture, and the French feminists Luce Irigaray and Hélène Cixous, who valorize female fluidity, multiplicity, sensuality, and libidinal *jouissance.* Are all these feminists dancing with wolves?

"Feminism," Nancy Cott reminds us in much less heated or metaphorical terms, "is nothing if not paradoxical":

> It aims for individual freedoms by mobilizing sex solidarity. It acknowledges diversity among women while positing that women recognize their unity. It requires gender consciousness for its basis, yet calls for the elimination of prescribed gender roles.[57]

Just as aware of internal differences, Jane Gallop locates tensions within the psychology of feminism that explain the questions with which I began, the query of Ann Snitow's friend ("how can someone who doesn't like being a woman be a feminist?") as well as Snitow's response ("Why would anyone who likes being a woman need to be a feminist?"): "The feminist," according to Gallop, "identifies with other women but also struggles to rise above the lot of women. Feminism both desires superior women and celebrates the common woman."[58]

Over the past two decades, the stresses described by Cott and Gallop, along with professional competition inside the academy and social setbacks outside it, have given rise to internecine schisms in women's studies, divisions widened by feminists faulting other feminists as politically retrograde or even misogynist: activists and empiricists denounced theorists and vice versa; lesbian separatists castigated integrationists; "pro-sex" and anti-pornography advocates clashed; class and race divided feminists, as did competing methodologies based on sexual difference or sexual equality, as did contested definitions of womanhood arising from cultural or poststructuralist thinkers.[59] In-fighting reached a kind of apex in literary criticism as various histories began to appear, some featuring feminist critiques of feminism which served intentions not always hospitable to academic women. Here the Toril Moi of *Sexual/Textual Politics* (1985) can officiate over feminist woman-bashing: Moi dismisses American women's studies scholars as "patriarchal" because of their naive faith in the authority of the female subject and the unity of the work of art while she touts as her heroine Julia Kristeva, who "refuses to define 'woman'" and judges the belief that one "is a woman" to be "absurd."[60]

This atmosphere in which women need to beware women is probably what has led me to see feminist misogyny now and not, say, back in the seventies. As "constructionists" like Moi continue to vilify "essentialists," both groups segue into defensive and offensive steps that recall nothing so much as the rhythms of competing nationalities satirized in Sheldon Harnick's song "Merry Little Minuet":

> The whole world is festering with unhappy souls.
> The French hate the Germans, the Germans hate the Poles,
> Italians hate Yugoslavs, South Africans hate the Dutch,
> And I don't like anybody very much.[61]

Does the price of institutionalization—of women's studies' inclusion in the academy—consist of our reduction to a plethora of jostling fields or approaches in which unhappy souls war for precedence with even more ferocity than they do in longer established areas or departments?

Have we attained our maturity in an age of ethnic purges and nationalistic frays that in our own domain take the form of battle dances that cause us to lose sight of our common aim to expropriate not only language but also society of overpopulated intentions hostile to women's health and welfare? When strutting our stuff with each other, among ourselves (and who, after all, are "we," given our institutional, generational, ethnic, and methodological differences?), have we lost sight of the ways in which unsympathetic outsiders or hostile institutions can appropriate or co-opt our internal debates, transforming self-critiques into assaults against our larger project? The recent brouhaha over Katie Roiphe's book epitomizes such difficulties. When in *The Morning After: Sex, Fear, and Feminism on Campus* Roiphe—a self-defined feminist—attacked *Take Back the Night,* anti-pornography, and sexual harassment activists for re-enforcing Victorian stereotypes of predatory men and victimized women, it seemed eerily appropriate that she aligned herself with Ishmael Reed by entitling one of her chapters "Reckless Eyeballing": just as Reed's masculinist novel *Reckless Eyeballing* lambastes Alice Walker for promoting a knee-jerk, racist suspicion about the criminality of African-American men (and in the process illuminates the culturally diverse constructions of the feminist-misogynist dialogue), Roiphe's chapter presents contemporary feminists as retrograde zealot-puritans who would criminalize all men and indeed all forms of heterosexuality.[62]

Questioning another feminist critique of other feminists, namely constructionists' wholesale dismissal of essentialists, Diana Fuss has recently argued that "the political investments of the sign 'essence' are predicated on the subject's complex positioning in a particular social field, and . . . the appraisal of this investment depends not on any interior values intrinsic to the sign itself but rather on the shifting and determinative discursive relations which produced it."[63] Similarly, about feminist misogyny I think that—instead of furnishing us with yet another label to brand each other—it should make us sensitive to the proliferation of sexual ideologies, to the significance of who is deploying these ideologies and with what political effect, even as it breeds a healthy self-skepticism born of an awareness of our own inexorable embeddedness in history. Because we cannot escape how culture makes us know ourselves, we need to understand that even as our own theorizing engages with the social relations of femininity and masculinity, it is fashioned by them. Ultimately, then, the game of "Can you really tell?" reminds us that claims and counterclaims in the feminist-misogynist dialogue cannot be appraised without some consideration of the complex social identities, rhetorical frameworks, and historical contexts upon which they are predicated.

To adopt Gallop's words once again, "I am as desirous of resolving contradictions as the next girl, but I find myself drawing us back to them, refusing the separations that allow us to avoid but not resolve contradiction."[64] On the list of paradoxes she and other thinkers have enumerated, I would write the one so telling and compelling in the work of Mary Wollstonecraft. For the contradiction-in-terms that her life and letters dramatizes continues to fashion the discourses through which many have struggled to vindicate the rights of men and women. As I think this, I seem to see them lining up for a succession of *pas de deux*; or is it a Virginia Reel? a dos-e-doe? a last tango? a merry little minuet?—Rousseau and Wollstonecraft, Havelock Ellis and Olive Schreiner, Freud and Woolf, Sartre and Beauvoir, Mailer and Millett or Dworkin, Lacan and Irigaray or Cixous, Reed and Walker.

But out of whose mouth does a voice issue to save the waltz by declaring, "Your turn to curtsy, my turn to bow"? And who takes the lead, if (when?) we turn to tap-dance or shuffle along with one another?

Notes

1. Ann Snitow, "A Gender Diary," *Conflicts in Feminism,* ed. Marianne Hirsch and Evelyn Fox Keller (New York: Routledge, 1990), p. 33, p. 9.
2. Both Lacan passages are discussed by Jane Gallop, *The Daughter's Seduction: Feminism and Psychoanalysis* (Ithaca: Cornell University Press, 1983), p. 34, p. 45.
3. Hélène Cixous in Cixous and Catherine Clement, *The Newly Born Woman,* tr. Betsy Wing (Minneapolis: University of Minnesota Press, 1986), p. 95; Luce Irigaray, *This Sex Which Is Not One,* tr. Catherine Porter with Carolyn Burke (Ithaca: Cornell University Press, 1985), p. 28.
4. Ambrose Bierce, in "Know Your Enemy: A Sampling of Sexist Quotes," *Sisterhood Is Powerful; an anthology of writings from the women's liberation movement,* ed. Robin Morgan (New York: Random House, 1970), p. 34. Throughout this paragraph, I am grateful to Henry Louis Gates, Jr., who questions the efficacy of the "Can you really tell?" test with reference primarily to the ethnicity of the author in "'Authenticity,' or the Lesson of *Little Tree,*" *New York Times Book Review* 24 (November 1991), p. 1.
5. Denise Riley, *"Am I That Name?": Feminism and the Category of 'Women' in History* (Minneapolis: University of Minnesota Press, 1988). Tania Modleski cogently argues about this and other so-called "postfeminist" theorists that "for many 'women' the very term arouses a visceral, even phobic reaction" (*Feminism Without Women: Culture and Criticism in a 'Postfeminist' Age* [New York: Routledge, 1991], p. 16).
6. Donna Harraway, "A Manifesto for Cyborgs: Science, Technology and Socialist Feminism in the 1980s," *Socialist Review* 80, 15, 2, (March-April 1985), p. 92.
7. Frances Ferguson, "Wollstonecraft Our Contemporary," *Gender and Theory: Dialogues on Feminist Criticism,* ed. Linda Kauffman (Oxford: Basil Blackwell, 1989), pp. 60-61.
8. See Timothy J. Reiss, "Revolution in Bounds: Wollstonecraft, Women, and Reason," *Gender and Theory,* pp. 11-50.

9. Rousseau's infamous remark appears in Mary Wollstonecraft, *A Vindication of the Rights of Woman,* ed. Carol H. Poston (1792; rpt. New York: Norton Critical Edition, 1988), p. 79.

10. Sandra M. Gilbert and I have examined the seeming eccentricity of the literary women of Wollstonecraft's generation and the problem they pose to conventional definitions of the period in "'But Oh! That Deep Romantic Chasm: The Engendering of Periodization,'" *Kenyon Review* 13, 3 (1991), pp. 74-81. For an interesting discussion of Beauvoir's much quoted point, as well as Monique Wittig's revisionary response to it, see Judith Butler, *Gender Trouble: Feminism and the Subversion of Identity* (New York: Routledge, 1990), pp. 111-12.

11. Wollstonecraft, *Vindication,* p. 34.

12. Wollstonecraft, *Vindication,* p. 9.

13. Wollstonecraft, *Vindication,* pp. 60-61.

14. Wollstonecraft, *Vindication,* p. 178.

15. Wollstonecraft, *Vindication,* p. 34.

16. Wollstonecraft, *Vindication,* p. 7.

17. Wollstonecraft, *Vindication,* p. 35. Equally telling, as Elissa S. Guralnick points out, Wollstonecraft couples the term "woman" with bashaws, despots, kings, emperors, soldiers, and courtiers, all of whom exercize "illegitimate power" and thus "enjoy the degradation of the exalted": Wollstonecraft, *Vindication,* p. 21 and Guralnick, "Radical Politics in Mary Wollstonecraft's *A Vindication of the Rights of Woman,*" Wollstonecraft, *Vindication,* pp. 308-16.

18. Mary Poovey, *The Proper Lady and the Woman Writer: Ideology as Style in the Works of Mary Wollstonecraft, Mary Shelley, and Jane Austen* (Chicago: University of Chicago Press, 1984), pp. 79-80. Along similar lines, Joan B. Landes argues that Wollstonecraft subscribes to an ideology of republican motherhood that views women's civic role as one performed inside the home, ascribes to men unbridled physical appetites, sets up a model of female duty, and displays an adherence toward male linguistic control that aligns her with the male philosophers of her day: see *Women and the Public Sphere in the Age of the French Revolution* (Ithaca: Cornell University Press, 1988), pp. 129-38.

19. Wollstonecraft, *Vindication,* p. 35.

20. Wollstonecraft, *Vindication,* p. 175.

21. Wollstonecraft, *Vindication,* p. 173.

22. Wollstonecraft, *Vindication,* p. 10.

23. Edward Said, *Orientalism* (New York: Pantheon, 1978).

24. For a general discussion of the misogyny in these eighteenth-century texts, see my "The Female Monster in August Satire," *Signs* 3 (1977), pp. 380-94.

25. Ironically, then tragically, Wollstonecraft's detractors exploited precisely the images she shared with her philosophical opponents. She was depicted as one of the "philosophizing serpents in our bosom," a "hyena in petticoats," lampooned in *The Unsex'd Females: A Poem* as a "Poor maniac," ridiculed in a review in the *European Magazine* as a "philosophical wanton," and mocked in *The Shade of Alexander Pope on the Banks of the Thames* as "passion's slave." Similarly, her *Memoirs and Posthumous Works* was judged to be "A Convenient Manual of speculative debauchery" and in 1801 the author of "The Vision of Liberty" intoned, "Lucky the maid that on her volume pores / A scripture, archly fram'd, for propagating w———s": see Ralph M. Wardle, *Mary Wollstonecraft: A Critical Biography* (Lawrence: University of Kansas Press, 1951), p. 318, p. 321, p. 322 as well as Janet Todd, "Introduction," in *A Wollstonecraft Anthology,* ed. Janet Todd (New York: Columbia University Press, 1990), pp. 16-19.

26. Besides Poovey's and Landes's studies, see Mary Jacobus, "The Difference of View," *Women Writing and Writing about Women,* ed. Mary Jacobus (London: Croom Helm, 1979), pp. 16-17, as well as Cora Kaplan, "Pandora's Box: Subjectivity, Class and Sexuality in Socialist Feminist Criticism," *Making a Difference: Feminist Literary Criticism,* ed. Gayle Greene and Coppélia Kahn (London: Methuen, 1985), pp. 157-60. Janet Todd reviews all these critics in *Feminist Literary History* (New York: Routledge, 1988), pp. 103-10. On Wollstonecraft's making "genius a machismo male," see also Christine Battersby, *Gender and Genius: Towards a Feminist Aesthetics* (London: Women's Press, 1989), p. 98.

27. Cora Kaplan, "Wild Nights: Pleasure/Sexuality/Feminism," *Formations of Pleasure* (London: Routledge, 1983), p. 29.

28. Moira Ferguson, "Mary Wollstonecraft and the Problematic of Slavery," *Feminist Review* 42 (1992), p. 97.

29. Sandra M. Gilbert and Susan Gubar, *The War of the Words,* vol. 1 of *No Man's Land: The Place of the Woman Writer in the Twentieth Century* (New Haven: Yale University Press, 1988), chpt. 4.

30. Emma Goldman, "Mary Wollstonecraft: Her Tragic Life and Her Passionate Struggle for Freedom," Wollstonecraft, *Vindication,* pp. 254-55.

31. Virginia Woolf, "Mary Wollstonecraft," in Wollstonecraft, *Vindication,* pp. 269-70.

32. I am relying here on a term proposed by Hélène Cixous in "The Laugh of the Medusa," tr. Keith Cohen and Paula Cohen, *Signs* 1 (1976), p. 878.

33. Mary Wollstonecraft, *Maria: or, The Wrongs of Women* (1798; rpt. New York: Norton, 1975), p. 27.

34. Mary Wollstonecraft, *Mary, A Fiction* (1788; rpt. New York: Schocken, 1977), p. 102.

35. Wollstonecraft, *Maria,* p. 51.

36. Adrienne Rich, "Compulsory Heterosexuality and Lesbian Existence," *Women: Sex and Sexuality,* ed. Catharine R. Stimpson and Ethel Spector Person (Chicago: University of Chicago Press, 1980), pp. 60-91. On Wollstonecraft, see Jeannette Foster, *Sex Variant Women in Literature* (1956; rpt. Baltimore: Diana Press, 1976), pp. 56-60 and Lillian Faderman, "Who Hid Lesbian History?," *Lesbian Studies: Present and Future,* ed. Margaret Cruikshank (Old Westbury, N.Y.: Feminist Press, 1982), p. 117. Interesting in this regard is the misogyny in lesbian literature that can be traced back to Radclyffe Hall's portraits of "feminine" women in *The Well of Loneliness;* many of whom strike her mannish Stephen Gordon as manipulative, materialistic, and frivolous ("Grossly familiar": Wollstonecraft, *Vindication,* p. 127).

37. Wollstonecraft, *Vindication,* p. 128.

38. Mary Wollstonecraft, *Collected Letters of Mary Wollstonecraft,* ed. Ralph M. Wardle (Ithaca: Cornell University Press, 1979), pp. 202-3.

39. Elizabeth Barrett Browning, *The Letters of Elizabeth Barrett Browning,* ed. Frederic G. Kenyon, 2 vols (New York: Macmillan, 1897), 1, pp. 231-32. In *The War of the Words,* Sandra Gilbert and I discuss the woman writer's "turn toward the father": pp. 171-81. The two female precursors Wollstonecraft admires are Hester Mulso Chapone and Catharine Sawbridge Macaulay Graham, both discussed quite briefly in *A Vindication,* pp. 105-6, p. 137.

40. Patricia Yaeger, "Writing as Action: *A Vindication of the Rights of Woman,*" *Minnesota Review* 29 (1987), pp. 74-75; and Wollstonecraft, *Vindication,* p. 77.

41. Judith Butler, *Gender Trouble,* p. 2.

42. Olive Schreiner, *Woman and Labour* (1911; rpt. London: Virago, 1978), p. 272, p. 282. The long, slow death of the New Womanly Lyndall in *The Story of an African Farm* (1883) contrasts throughout the novel with the obesity, stupidity, voracity, racism, and cruelty of the traditional woman Tant' Sannie. Like Wollstonecraft, too, Schreiner publicly protested against female dependency on men but suffered repeated thralldom to men in her private life.

43. Schreiner, *Woman and Labour,* p. 82.

44. On Schreiner's plans to produce an introduction to *A Vindication* and on *Woman and Labour* as a "Bible," see Joyce Avrech Berkman, *Olive Schreiner: Feminism on the Frontier* (St. Alban's, Vt.: Eden Women's Publications, 1979), p. 7, p. 10, and p. 2. Schreiner's discussion of the "parasite woman on her couch" appears in *Woman and Labour,* pp. 132-33.

45. Schreiner, *Woman and Labour,* pp. 129-30.

46. Ann Douglas, *The Feminization of American Culture* (New York: Knopf, 1977), p. 6, p. 12, and p. 8.

47. Douglas, *The Feminization of American Culture,* p. 11.

48. In a recent essay, Sandra M. Gilbert explains her own attraction to D. H. Lawrence's works and that of women readers from Katherine Mansfield and H. D. to Anais Nin by envisioning Lawrence as "a proto French feminist" (Gilbert, *Acts of Attention: The Poems of D. H. Lawrence* [2nd ed., rpt. Ithaca: Cornell University Press, 1990), p. xix]. It is interesting in this regard that Rachel Blau DuPlessis' often reprinted essay "For the Etruscans" evokes D. H. Lawrence's *Etruscan Places* (*The Pink Guitar: Writing as Feminist Practice* [New York: Routledge, 1990], pp. 1-19).

49. M. M. Bakhtin, "Discourse in the Novel," *The Dialogic Imagination,* tr. Caryl Emerson and Michael Holquist, ed. Michael Holquist (Austin: University of Texas Press, 1981), pp. 293-94.

50. According to Barbara Johnson, in a subtle analysis of the impact of racial stereotypes on racial identity, "questions of difference and identity are always a function of a specific interlocutionary situation—and the answers a matter of strategy rather than truth" ("Thresholds of Difference: Structures of Address in Zora Neale Hurston," *Critical Inquiry* 12 [1985]), p. 285.

51. On "fembot," see Mary Daly, *Pure Lust: Elemental Feminist Philosophy* (Boston: Beacon Press, 1984), p. 93.

52. Germaine Greer, *The Female Eunuch* (New York: Bantam, 1971), p. 335, p. 12, and p. 157.

53. Germaine Greer, *Sex and Destiny: The Politics of Human Fertility* (New York: Harper and Row, 1984), p. 248.

54. Andrea Dworkin, *Intercourse* (New York: Free Press, 1987), p. 63.

55. Andrea Dworkin, *Ice and Fire* (New York: Weidenfeld and Nicolson, 1986), p. 72, pp. 54-55, and p. 101.

56. Dworkin, *Ice and Fire,* p. 101 and pp. 104-5.

57. Nancy Cott, "Feminist Theory and Feminist Movements: The Past Before Us," *What Is Feminism?,* ed. Juliet Mitchell and Ann Oakley (New York: Pantheon, 1986), p. 49.

58. Jane Gallop, *Around 1981: Academic Feminist Literary Theory* (New York: Routledge, 1992), p. 138.

59. For background on such debates, see Joan Scott, "Deconstructing Equality-Versus-Difference" and Theresa de Lauretis, "Upping the Anti (sic) in Feminist Theory," both in Marianne Hirsch and Evelyn Fox Keller ed., *Conflicts in Feminism,* pp. 134-48 and pp. 255-70.

60. Toril Moi, *Sexual/Textual Politics: Feminist Literary Theory* (London: Methuen, 1985), pp. 62-63 and p. 163. Later, Moi stated that her book was "written from a feminist perspective, or, in other words, from a perspective of political solidarity with the feminist aims of the critics and theorists I write about." In addition, she claimed that after "the reactionary backlash of the eighties," she found it "far more difficult to be sanguine about one's feminist position" and "would now emphasize much more the risks of being a feminist": see Moi, *Feminist Theory and Simone de Beauvoir* (Oxford: Basil Blackwell, 1990), p. 95 and p. 102.

61. Quoted in *Songs of Peace, Freedom, and Protest,* ed. Tom Glazer (New York: McKay Press, 1970), pp. 217-18. Here, as always and elsewhere, I am grateful for the help of Marah Gubar.

62. Katie Roiphe, *The Morning After: Sex, Fear, and Feminism on Campus* (Boston: Little, Brown and Company, 1993), p. 85. Significantly, Roiphe also aligns herself with John Irving and David Mamet: p. 35 and p. 107. Yet in the opening of the book, she describes her own brand of feminism which she inherited from her mother. On *Reckless Eyeballing* and Alice Walker, see Ishmael Reed, "Steven Spielberg Plays Howard Beach," *Writin' Is Fightin'* (New York: Atheneum, 1988), pp. 145-60.

63. Diana Fuss, *Essentially Speaking: Feminism, Nature and Difference* (New York: Routledge, 1989), p. 20. See also Claire Goldberg Moses, "'Equality' and 'Difference' in Historical Perspective: A Comparative Examination of the Feminisms of French Revolutionaries and Utopian Socialists," *Rebel Daughters: Women and the French Revolution,* ed. Sara E. Meltzer and Leslie W. Rabine (New York: Oxford University Press, 1992), p. 248, in which Goldberg Moses points out that "The argument that feminist discourses of 'equality' and 'difference' are neither right nor wrong but relate to historically specific concerns or opportunities is further strengthened by noting the instability of these categories."

64. Jane Gallop, *Around 1981,* p. 139.

FURTHER READING

Bibliographies

Todd, Janet M. *Mary Wollstonecraft: An Annotated Bibliography.* New York: Garland Publishers, 1976, 124 p.

Surveys criticism on Wollstonecraft from her contemporaries through the mid-1970s.

Windle, John. *Mary Wollstonecraft Godwin, 1759-1797: A Bibliography of the First and Early Editions, with Briefer Notes on Later Editions and Translations.* New Castle, Del.: Oak Knoll Press, 2000, 71 p.

Contains entries covering the publishing history of Wollstonecraft's major and minor works.

Biographies

Flexner, Eleanor. *Mary Wollstonecraft: A Biography.* New York: Coward, McCann & Geoghegan, Inc., 1972, 307 p.

Emphasizes the role of Wollstonecraft's early life in the development of her ideas, but is somewhat critical of Wollstonecraft's behavior; updates and corrects Ralph Wardle's 1951 biography.

Jacobs, Diane. *Her Own Woman: The Life of Mary Wollstonecraft.* New York: Simon & Schuster, 2001, 333 p.

Uses new letters and sources to update Wollstonecraft's biography; also discusses the lives and work of her daughters and the scope of her influence in women's history.

Jump, Harriet Devine. *Mary Wollstonecraft, Writer.* New York: Harvester Wheatsheaf, 1994, 172 p.

Stresses the development of Wollstonecraft's feminist thought in the context of the political atmosphere of her times, especially the growth of radicalism; also offers a complete overview of Wollstonecraft's life as an author.

Rauschenbusch-Clough, Emma. *A Study of Mary Wollstonecraft and the Rights of Woman.* New York: Longmans, Green, 1898, 234 p.

Links Wollstonecraft to the emerging thought of her time as well as the socialist writers who followed her; the first full-length study of Wollstonecraft.

Todd, Janet. *Mary Wollstonecraft: A Revolutionary Life.* London: Weidenfeld & Nicolson, 2000, 516 p.

A scholarly but engaging biography from an important scholar of eighteenth-century women's writing; details Wollstonecraft's difficult family relationships, drawing primarily from Wollstonecraft's letters.

Tomalin, Claire. *The Life and Death of Mary Wollstonecraft.* New York: Harcourt Brace Jovanovich, 1974, 316 p.

Narrative biography recounting Wollstonecraft's many personal quirks and failings as well as her drive and intellectual achievements; Tomalin is the author of several popular biographies of major writers including Jane Austen, Katherine Mansfield, and Samuel Pepys.

Wardle, Ralph. *Mary Wollstonecraft: A Critical Biography.* Lincoln: University of Nebraska Press, 1951, 366 p.

Relies heavily on letters to tell the story of Wollstonecraft's life, noting the course of her intellectual development; considered a milestone in twentieth-century scholarship on Wollstonecraft.

Criticism

Badowska, Ewa. "The Anorexic Body of Liberal Feminism: Mary Wollstonecraft's *A Vindication of the Rights of Woman.*" *Tulsa Studies in Women's Literature* 17, no. 2 (fall 1998): 283-303.

Focuses on the intersection of the female body and political discourse as sites for constructing feminine identity in Wollstonecraft's A Vindication of the Rights of Woman.

Barlowe, Jamie. "Daring to Dialogue: Mary Wollstonecraft's Rhetoric of Feminist Dialogics." In *Reclaiming Rhetorica: Women in the Rhetorical Tradition,* edited by Andrea A. Lunsford, pp. 117-36. Pittsburgh: University of Pittsburgh Press, 1995.

Examines Wollstonecraft's use of different genres as an effort to engage in dialogue with the male-dominated intellectual tradition in the larger service of achieving the practical social ends of feminism.

Blakemore, Steven. "Rebellious Reading: The Doubleness of Wollstonecraft's Subversion of *Paradise Lost.*" *Texas Studies in Language and Literature* 34, no. 4 (winter 1992): 451-80.

Claims that Wollstonecraft subverted the ideology of Paradise Lost *by creating a picture of Eve that both sustains and undermines Wollstonecraft's feminist myth.*

Brody, Miriam. "Mary Wollstonecraft: Sexuality and Women's Rights." In *Feminist Theorists: Three Centuries of Key Women Thinkers,* edited by Dale Spender, pp. 40-59. New York: Pantheon Books, 1983.

Considers Wollstonecraft's view of sexuality and its implications for her feminist argument in A Vindication of the Rights of Woman.

———. "The Vindication of the Writes of Women: Mary Wollstonecraft and Enlightenment Rhetoric." In *Feminist Interpretations of Mary Wollstonecraft,* edited by Maria J. Falco, pp. 105-23. University Park: Pennsylvania State University Press, 1996.

Contends that A Vindication of the Rights of Woman *asserts women's right to write polemically.*

Cole, Lucinda. "(Anti)Feminist Sympathies: The Politics of Relationship in Smith, Wollstonecraft, and More." *ELH* 58, no. 1 (spring 1991): 107-40.

Discusses the language of sympathy in Wollstonecraft's works as compared with Adam Smith's The Theory of Moral Sentiments *and the works of Hannah More.*

Conger, Syndy M. *Mary Wollstonecraft and the Language of Sensibility.* Rutherford, N.J.: Fairleigh Dickinson University Press, 1994, 214 p.

Addresses the apparent paradox of Wollstonecraft's strong faith in reason and her intense emotionalism, applying modern critical insight from diverse fields including linguistics, psychology, and feminist theory.

D'Arcy, Chantal Cornut-Gentille. "Mary Wollstonecraft's *A Vindication of the Rights of Woman* as Generator of Differing Feminist Traditions." *Links and Letters* 2 (1995): 47-61.

Relates Wollstonecraft's A Vindication of the Rights of Woman *to the development of modern feminist literary theory in its various aspects.*

Ellison, Julie. "Redoubled Feeling: Politics, Sentiment, and the Sublime in Williams and Wollstonecraft." *Studies in Eighteenth-Century Culture* 20 (1990): 197-215.

Compares Helen Maria Williams's Letters from France *to Wollstonecraft's* A Vindication of the Rights of Woman, *noting the relationship between politics and the language of feeling.*

Gunther-Canada, Wendy. "Mary Wollstonecraft's 'Wild wish': Confounding Sex in the Discourse on Political Rights." In *Feminist Interpretations of Mary Wollstonecraft,* edited by Maria J. Falco, pp. 61-84. University Park: Pennsylvania State University Press, 1996.

Demonstrates how Wollstonecraft disputed the gender distinctions that excluded women from the discourse of political rights; examines both A Vindication of the Rights of Woman *and her* Vindication of the Rights of Men.

Guralnick, Elissa S. "Radical Politics in Mary Wollstonecraft's *A Vindication of the Rights of Woman." Studies in Burke and His Times* 18, no. 3 (autumn 1977): 155-66.

Argues that A Vindication of the Rights of Woman *carries implications beyond feminism in that it is a "radical political tract" on the order of, though surpassing,* A Vindication of the Rights of Men.

Harasym, S. D. "Ideology and Self: A Theoretical Discussion of the 'Self' in Mary Wollstonecraft's Fiction." *English Studies in Canada* 12, no. 2 (June 1986): 163-77.

Examines the novel Maria; or, The Wrongs of Woman, *contending that Wollstonecraft's identification of herself with her protagonist complicated her portrayal of a utopian feminist ideology.*

Homans, Margaret. "Feminist Fictions and Feminist Theories of Narrative." *Narrative* 2, no. 1 (January 1994): 3-16.

Compares the ways in which Wollstonecraft's Maria; or, The Wrongs of Woman *and Zora Neale Hurston's* Their Eyes Were Watching God *comment on the narrative structures available to women.*

Johnson, Claudia L. "Mary Wollstonecraft." In *Equivocal Beings: Politics, Gender, and Sentimentality in the 1790s: Wollstonecraft, Radcliffe, Burney, Austen,* p. 239. Chicago: University of Chicago Press, 1995.

Considers the language of sentiment, particularly "excessive" feminine feeling, as a site of feminist struggle in Wollstonecraft's writing.

———, ed. *The Cambridge Companion to Mary Wollstonecraft.* Cambridge: Cambridge University Press, 2002, 284 p.

Collects several essays addressing Wollstonecraft's views on women, education, and religion; contributors include Wollstonecraft scholars Janet Todd, Mitzi Myers, Vivien Jones, Anne K. Mellor, Cora Kaplan, and others.

Jones, Vivien. "Femininity, Nationalism, and Romanticism: The Politics of Gender in the Revolution Controversy." *History of European Ideas* 16, nos. 1-3 (1993): 299-305.

Compares Helen Maria William's Letters From France *and Wollstonecraft's* Historical and Moral View of the Origin and Progress of the French Revolution *in terms of the construction of national, sexual, and literary identities.*

Keane, Angela. "Mary Wollstonecraft's Imperious Sympathies: Population, Maternity, and Romantic Individualism." In *Body Matters: Feminism, Textuality, Corporeality,* edited by Avril Horner and Angela Keane, pp. 29-42. Manchester, England: Manchester University Press, 2000.

Views Wollstonecraft's feminism as a critique of capitalism as it enforced a mind-body split in women; focuses on images of motherhood in Wollstonecraft's writing.

Mackenzie, Catriona. "Reason and Sensibility: The Ideal of Women's Self-Governance in the Writings of Mary Wollstonecraft." *Hypatia* 8, no. 4 (fall 1993): 35-55.

Examines the language of feeling and sentiment in Wollstonecraft's writings as applied to women and the capacity for individual authority.

Maurer, Shawn Lisa. "The Female (As) Reader: Sex Sensibility, and the Maternal in Wollstonecraft's Fictions." *Essays in Literature* 19, no. 1 (spring 1992): 36-54.

Contends that Wollstonecraft attempted to develop an active subjectivity for women constituted in relation to a woman's role as mother.

Myers, Mitzi. "Pedagogy as Self-Expression in Mary Wollstonecraft: Exorcising the Past, Finding a Voice." In *The Private Self: Theory and Practice of Women's Autobiographical Writings,* edited by Shari Benstock, pp. 192-210. Chapel Hill: University of North Carolina Press, 1988.

Applies a feminist approach and theory of autobiography to reading Wollstonecraft's autobiographical writings as well as her fiction; addresses the female struggle to craft an identity in writing.

———. "Sensibility and the 'Walk of Reason': Mary Wollstonecraft's Literary Reviews as Cultural Critique." In *Sensibility in Transformation: Creative Resistance to Sentiment from the Augustans to the Romantics; Essays in Honor of Jean H. Hagstrum,* edited by Syndy McMillen Conger, pp. 120-44. Rutherford, N.J.: Fairleigh Dickinson University Press, 1990.

Examines Wollstonecraft's writings for the Analytical Review *as attempts to develop her unique voice as a theorist of gender, particularly as she attempts to combine sensibility and reason into a broader humanism.*

Paulson, Ronald. "Burke, Paine, and Wollstonecraft: The Sublime and the Beautiful." In *Representations of Revolution (1789-1820),* pp. 57-87. New Haven: Yale University Press, 1983.

Examines Wollstonecraft's Rights of Men *as an answer to Burke, focusing on Wollstonecraft's critique of feminine beauty as a tyrannical concept.*

Poovey, Mary. "Mary Wollstonecraft: The Gender of Genres in Eighteenth-Century England." *Novel* 15, no. 2 (winter 1982): 111-26.

Delineates Wollstonecraft's central ambivalence in Maria; or, The Wrongs of Woman.

———. "Man's Discourse, Woman's Heart: Mary Wollstonecraft's Two *Vindications.*" In *The Proper Lady and the Woman Writer: Ideology and Style in the Works of Mary Wollstonecraft, Mary Shelley, and Jane Austen,* pp. 48-81. Chicago: Chicago University Press, 1984.

Posits that Wollstonecraft's life and work indicate an unresolved conflict between the author's belief in female autonomy and her continuing adherence to traditional bourgeois cultural roles.

Robinson, Daniel. "Theodicy versus Feminist Strategy in Mary Wollstonecraft's Fiction." *Eighteenth-Century Fiction* 9, no. 2 (January 1997): 183-202.

Contrasts the ways in which Wollstonecraft attempts to reconcile her feminism and her religious faith in Mary, A Fiction *and* Maria; or, The Wrongs of Woman.

Sapiro, Virginia. *A Vindication of Political Virtue: The Political Theory of Mary Wollstonecraft.* Chicago: University of Chicago Press, 1992, 366 p.

Describes Wollstonecraft's views on women as part of a fully developed political philosophy; links Wollstonecraft's thought to modern debates on liberal democracy.

Shanley, Mary Lyndon. "Mary Wollstonecraft on Sensibility, Women's Rights, and Patriarchal Power." In *Women Writers and the Early Modern British Political Tradition,* edited by Hilda L. Smith, pp. 148-67. Cambridge: Cambridge University Press, 1998.

Explores Wollstonecraft's discussion of the relationship between domestic and political patriarchy; focuses on A Vindication of the Rights of Woman *and the novel* Maria; or, The Wrongs of Woman.

Taylor, G. R. Stirling. *Mary Wollstonecraft: A Study in Economics and Romance.* John Lane, 1911, 210 p.

A very admiring early study of Wollstonecraft's work and thought, with attention to the condition of women in Wollstonecraft's time and the ongoing need for improvement in women's rights.

Wilson, Anna. "Mary Wollstonecraft and the Search for the Radical Woman." *Genders* 6 (November 1989): 88-101.

Compares Wollstonecraft's A Vindication of the Rights of Woman *to Thomas Paine's* The Rights of Man, *emphasizing the treatment of radicalism.*

Woolf, Virginia. "Four Figures." In *Collected Essays.* Vol. III, pp. 181-206. New York: Harcourt Brace Jovanovich, 1967.

Characterizes Wollstonecraft's life, work, and influence, focusing on the writer's passion and originality.

Yeo, Eileen James, ed. *Mary Wollstonecraft and 200 Years of Feminisms.* London: Rivers Oram Press, 1997, 276 p.

Contains essays addressing Wollstonecraft's influence on modern feminism and surveying the history of Wollstonecraft's reputation and critical interpretations of her work.

OTHER SOURCES FROM GALE:

Additional coverage of Wollstonecraft's life and career is contained in the following sources published by the Gale Group: *British Writers Supplement,* Vol. 3; *Concise Dictionary of British Literary Biography, 1789-1832; Dictionary of Literary Biography,* Vols. 39, 104, 158, 252; *Feminist Writers; Literature and Its Times,* Vol. 1; *Literature Criticism from 1400-1800,* Vols. 5, 50, 90; *Literature Resource Center; Reference Guide to English Literature,* Ed. 2; *Twayne's English Authors*; and *World Literature and Its Times,* Vol. 3.

INDEXES

The main reference

Austen, Jane 1775-1817 **1:** 122, 125, 220; **2:** 104, 196, **333-384**

lists the featured author's entry in volumes 1, 2, 3, 5, or 6 of Feminism in Literature; *it also lists commentary on the featured author in other volumes of the set, which include topics associated with* Feminism in Literature. *Page references to substantial discussions of the author appear in boldface.*

The cross-references

See also AAYA 19; BRW 4; BRWC 1; BRWR 2; BYA 3; CD-BLB 1789-1832; DA; DA3; DAB; DAC; DAM MST, NOV; DLB 116; EXPN; LAIT 2; LATS 1; LMFS 1; NCLC 1, 13, 19, 33, 51, 81, 95, 119; NFS 1, 14, 18; TEA; WLC; WLIT 3; WYAS 1

list entries on the author in the following Gale biographical and literary sources:

AAL: Asian American Literature
AAYA: Authors & Artists for Young Adults
AFAW: African American Writers
AFW: African Writers
AITN: Authors in the News
AMW: American Writers
AMWR: American Writers Retrospective Supplement
AMWS: American Writers Supplement
ANW: American Nature Writers
AW: Ancient Writers
BEST: Bestsellers (quarterly, citations appear as Year: Issue number)
BG: The Beat Generation: A Gale Critical Companion
BLC: Black Literature Criticism
BLCS: Black Literature Criticism Supplement
BPFB: Beacham's Encyclopedia of Popular Fiction: Biography and Resources
BRW: British Writers
BRWS: British Writers Supplement
BW: Black Writers
BYA: Beacham's Guide to Literature for Young Adults
CA: Contemporary Authors
CAAS: Contemporary Authors Autobiography Series
CABS: Contemporary Authors Bibliographical Series
CAD: Contemporary American Dramatists
CANR: Contemporary Authors New Revision Series
CAP: Contemporary Authors Permanent Series
CBD: Contemporary British Dramatists
CCA: Contemporary Canadian Authors
CD: Contemporary Dramatists
CDALB: Concise Dictionary of American Literary Biography
CDALBS: Concise Dictionary of American Literary Biography Supplement
CDBLB: Concise Dictionary of British Literary Biography
CLC: Contemporary Literary Criticism
CLR: Children's Literature Review
CMLC: Classical and Medieval Literature Criticism
CMW: St. James Guide to Crime & Mystery Writers
CN: Contemporary Novelists
CP: Contemporary Poets
CPW: Contemporary Popular Writers
CSW: Contemporary Southern Writers
CWD: Contemporary Women Dramatists
CWP: Contemporary Women Poets
CWRI: St. James Guide to Children's Writers
CWW: Contemporary World Writers
DA: DISCovering Authors
DA3: DISCovering Authors 3.0
DAB: DISCovering Authors: British Edition
DAC: DISCovering Authors: Canadian Edition
DAM: DISCovering Authors: Modules
DRAM: Dramatists Module; *MST:* Most-Studied Authors Module;
MULT: Multicultural Authors Module; *NOV:* Novelists Module;
POET: Poets Module; *POP:* Popular Fiction and Genre Authors Module
DC: Drama Criticism
DFS: Drama for Students
DLB: Dictionary of Literary Biography
DLBD: Dictionary of Literary Biography Documentary Series
DLBY: Dictionary of Literary Biography Yearbook
DNFS: Literature of Developing Nations for Students
EFS: Epics for Students
EXPN: Exploring Novels
EXPP: Exploring Poetry
EXPS: Exploring Short Stories
EW: European Writers
FANT: St. James Guide to Fantasy Writers
FW: Feminist Writers

GFL: Guide to French Literature, Beginnings to 1789, 1798 to the Present
GLL: Gay and Lesbian Literature
HGG: St. James Guide to Horror, Ghost & Gothic Writers
HLC: Hispanic Literature Criticism
HLCS: Hispanic Literature Criticism Supplement
HR: Harlem Renaissance: A Gale Critical Companion
HW: Hispanic Writers
IDFW: International Dictionary of Films and Filmmakers: Writers and Production Artists
IDTP: International Dictionary of Theatre: Playwrights
LAIT: Literature and Its Times
LAW: Latin American Writers
JRDA: Junior DISCovering Authors
LC: Literature Criticism from 1400 to 1800
MAICYA: Major Authors and Illustrators for Children and Young Adults
MAICYA: Major Authors and Illustrators for Children and Young Adults Supplement
MAWW: Modern American Women Writers
MJW: Modern Japanese Writers
MTCW: Major 20th-Century Writers
NCFS: Nonfiction Classics for Students
NCLC: Nineteenth-Century Literature Criticism
NFS: Novels for Students
NNAL: Native North American Literature
PAB: Poets: American and British
PC: Poetry Criticism
PFS: Poetry for Students
RGAL: Reference Guide to American Literature
RGEL: Reference Guide to English Literature
RGSF: Reference Guide to Short Fiction
RGWL: Reference Guide to World Literature
RHW: Twentieth-Century Romance and Historical Writers
SAAS: Something about the Author Autobiography Series
SATA: Something about the Author
SFW: St. James Guide to Science Fiction Writers
SSC: Short Story Criticism
SSFS: Short Stories for Students
TCLC: Twentieth-Century Literary Criticism
TCWW: Twentieth-Century Western Writers
WCH: Writers for Children
WLC: World Literature Criticism, 1500 to the Present
WLCS: World Literature Criticism Supplement
WLIT: World Literature and Its Times
WP: World Poets
YABC: Yesterday's Authors of Books for Children
YAW: St. James Guide to Young Adult Writers

AUTHOR INDEX

The Author Index lists all of the authors featured in the Feminism in Literature *set. It includes references to the main author entries in volumes 1, 2, 3, 5, and 6; it also lists commentary on the featured author in other author entries and in other volumes of the set, which include topics associated with* Feminism in Literature. *Page references to author entries appear in boldface. The Author Index also includes birth and death dates, cross references between pseudonyms or name variants and actual names, and cross references to other Gale series in which the authors have appeared. A complete list of these sources is found facing the first page of the Author Index.*

A

Akhmatova, Anna 1888-1966 **5: 1–38**
See also CA 19-20; 25-28R; CANR 35; CAP 1; CLC 11, 25, 64, 126; DA3; DAM POET; DLB 295; EW 10; EWL 3; MTCW 1, 2; PC 2, 55; RGWL 2, 3

Alcott, Louisa May 1832-1888 **2:** 78, 147, **297–332**
See also AAYA 20; AMWS 1; BPFB 1; BYA 2; CDALB 1865-1917; CLR 1, 38; DA; DA3; DAB; DAC; DAM MST, NOV; DLB 1, 42, 79, 223, 239, 242; DLBD 14; FW; JRDA; LAIT 2; MAICYA 1, 2; NCLC 6, 58, 83; NFS 12; RGAL 4; SATA 100; SSC 27; TUS; WCH; WLCWYA; YABC 1; YAW

Allende, Isabel 1942- **5: 39–64**
See also AAYA 18; CA 125; 130; CANR 51, 74, 129; CDWLB 3; CLC 39, 57, 97, 170; CWW 2; DA3; DAM MULT, NOV; DLB 145; DNFS 1; EWL 3; FW; HLC 1; HW 1, 2; INT CA-130; LAIT 5; LAWS 1; LMFS 2; MTCW 1, 2; NCFS 1; NFS 6, 18; RGSF 2; RGWL 3; SSC 65; SSFS 11, 16; WLCS; WLIT 1

Angelou, Maya 1928- **5: 65–92**
See also AAYA 7, 20; AMWS 4; BLC 1; BPFB 1; BW 2, 3; BYA 2; CA 65-68; CANR 19, 42, 65, 111; CDALBS; CLC 12, 35, 64, 77, 155; CLR 53; CP 7; CPW; CSW; CWP; DA; DA3; DAB; DAC; DAM MST, MULT, POET, POP; DLB 38; EWL 3; EXPN; EXPP; LAIT 4; MAICYA 2; MAICYAS 1; MAWW; MTCW 1, 2; NCFS 2; NFS 2; PC 32; PFS 2, 3; RGAL 4; SATA 49, 136; WLCS; WYA; YAW

Atwood, Margaret (Eleanor) 1939- **5: 93–124**
See also AAYA 12, 47; AMWS 13; BEST 89:2; BPFB 1; CA 49-52; CANR 3, 24, 33, 59, 95; CLC 2, 3, 4, 8, 13, 15, 25, 44, 84, 135; CN 7; CP 7; CPW; CWP; DA; DA3; DAB; DAC; DAM MST, NOV, POET; DLB 53, 251; EWL 3; EXPN; FW; INT CANR-24; LAIT 5; MTCW 1, 2; NFS 4, 12, 13, 14; PC 8; PFS 7; RGSF 2; SATA 50; SSC 2, 46; SSFS 3, 13; TWA; WLC; WWE 1; YAW

Austen, Jane 1775-1817 **1:** 122, 125, 220; **2:** 104, 196, **333–384**
See also AAYA 19; BRW 4; BRWC 1; BRWR 2; BYA 3; CDBLB 1789-1832; DA; DA3; DAB; DAC; DAM MST, NOV; DLB 116; EXPN; LAIT 2; LATS 1; LMFS 1; NCLC 1, 13, 19, 33, 51, 81, 95, 119; NFS 1, 14, 18; TEA; WLC; WLIT 3; WYAS 1

B

Beauvoir, Simone (Lucie Ernestine Marie Bertrand) de 1908-1986 **5: 125–174**
See also BPFB 1; CA 9-12R; 118; CANR 28, 61; CLC 1, 2, 4, 8,

14, 31, 44, 50, 71, 124; DA; DA3; DAB; DAC; DAM MST, NOV; DLB 72; DLBY 1986; EW 12; EWL 3; FW; GFL 1789 to the Present; LMFS 2; MTCW 1, 2; RGSF 2; RGWL 2, 3; SSC 35; TWA; WLC

Brontë, Charlotte 1816-1855 **1:** 553; **2:** 17, 100, 133, 135, 177, 183–185, 198–202, **385–428**
See also AAYA 17; BRW 5; BRWC 2; BRWR 1; BYA 2; CDBLB 1832-1890; DA; DA3; DAB; DAC; DAM MST, NOV; DLB 21, 159, 199; EXPN; LAIT 2; NCLC 3, 8, 33, 58, 105; NFS 4; TEA; WLC; WLIT 4

Brontë, Emily (Jane) 1818-1848 **2: 429–466**
See also AAYA 17; BPFB 1; BRW 5; BRWC 1; BRWR 1; BYA 3; CDBLB 1832-1890; DA; DA3; DAB; DAC; DAM MST, NOV, POET; DLB 21, 32, 199; EXPN; LAIT 1; NCLC 16, 35; PC 8; TEA; WLC; WLIT 3

Brooks, Gwendolyn (Elizabeth) 1917-2000 **4:** 287–289; **5: 175–210**
See also AAYA 20; AFAW 1, 2; AITN 1; AMWS 3; BLC 1; BW 2, 3; CA 1-4R; 190; CANR 1, 27, 52, 75; CDALB 1941-1968; CLC 1, 2, 4, 5, 15, 49, 125; CLR 27; CP 7; CWP; DA; DA3; DAC; DAM MST, MULT, POET; DLB 5, 76, 165; EWL 3; EXPP; MAWW; MTCW 1, 2; PC 7; PFS 1, 2, 4, 6; RGAL 4; SATA 6; SATA-Obit 123; TUS; WLC; WP

Browning, Elizabeth Barrett 1806-1861 **1:** 429, 432, 439; **2: 467–502**
See also BRW 4; CDBLB 1832-1890; DA; DA3; DAB; DAC; DAM MST, POET; DLB 32, 199; EXPP; NCLC 1, 16, 61, 66; PAB; PC 6; PFS 2, 16; TEA; WLC; WLIT 4; WP

Burney, Fanny 1752-1840 **1:** 115–116, 122, 219, 224; **2: 503–539**
See also BRWS 3; DLB 39; NCLC 12, 54, 107; NFS 16; RGEL 2; TEA

C

Cather, Willa (Sibert) 1873-1947 **5: 211–252**
See also AAYA 24; AMW; AMWC 1; AMWR 1; BPFB 1; CA 104; 128; CDALB 1865-1917; DA; DA3; DAB; DAC; DAM MST, NOV; DLB 9, 54, 78, 256; DLBD 1; EWL 3; EXPN; EXPS; LAIT 3; LATS 1; MAWW; MTCW 1, 2; NFS 2; RGAL 4; RGSF 2; RHW; SATA 30; SSC 2, 50; SSFS 2, 7, 16; TCLC 1, 11, 31, 99, 132; TCWW 2; TUS; WLC

Chopin, Kate 1851-1904 **3: 1–46**
See also AAYA 33; AMWR 2; AMWS 1; BYA 11, 15; CA 104; 122; CDALB 1865-1917; DA; DAB; DA3; DAC; DAM MST, NOV; DLB 12, 78; EXPN; EXPS; FW; LAIT 3; MAWW; NFS 3; RGAL 4; RGSF 2; SSC 8, 68; SSFS 17; TCLC 127; TUS; WLCS

Christine de Pizan 1365(?)-1431(?) **1:** 39–40, 66–68, 84, 86, **281–320**
See also DLB 208; LC 9; RGWL 2, 3

Cisneros, Sandra 1954- **5: 253–284**
See also AAYA 9, 53; AMWS 7; CA 131; CANR 64, 118; CLC 69, 118; CWP; DA3; DAM MULT; DLB 122, 152; EWL 3; EXPN; FW; HLC 1; HW 1, 2; LAIT 5; LATS 1; LLW 1; MAICYA 2; MTCW 2; NFS 2; PC 52; PFS 19; RGAL 4; RGSF 2; SSC 32; SSFS 3, 13; WLIT 1; YAW

Cixous, Hélène 1937- **5: 285–312**
See also CA 126; CANR 55, 123; CLC 92; CWW 2; DLB 83, 242; EWL 3; FW; GLL 2; MTCW 1, 2; TWA

D

Dickinson, Emily (Elizabeth) 1830-1886 **2:** 408, 412; **3: 47–92**
See also AAYA 22; AMW; AMWR 1; CDALB 1865-1917; DA; DA3; DAB; DAC; DAM MST, POET; DLB 1, 243; EXPP; MAWW; NCLC 21, 77; PAB; PC 1; PFS 1, 2, 3, 4, 5, 6, 8, 10, 11, 13, 16; RGAL 4; SATA 29; TUS; WLC; WP; WYA

Doolittle, Hilda (H. D.) 1886-1961 **4:** 271–272, 287, 292–293; **5: 313–358**
See also AMWS 1; CA 97-100; CANR 35; CLC 3, 8, 14, 31, 34, 73; DA; DAC; DAM MST, POET; DLB 4, 45; EWL 3; FW; GLL 1; LMFS 2; MAWW; MTCW 1, 2; PC 5; PFS 6; RGAL 4; WLC

Duras, Marguerite 1914-1996 **5: 359–404**
See Donnadieu, Marguerite
See also BPFB 1; CA 25-28R; 151; CANR 50; CLC 3, 6, 11, 20, 34, 40, 68, 100; CWW 2; DLB 83; EWL 3; GFL 1789 to the Present; IDFW 4; MTCW 1, 2; RGWL 2, 3; SSC 40; TWA

Dworkin, Andrea 1946- **5: 405–416**
See also CA 77-80; CAAS 21; CANR 16, 39, 76, 96; CLC 43, 123; FW; GLL 1; INT CANR-16; MTCW 1, 2

E

Edgeworth, Maria 1768-1849 **3: 93–128**
See also BRWS 3; DLB 116, 159, 163; FW; NCLC 1, 51; RGEL 2; SATA 21; TEA; WLIT 3

Eliot, George 1819-1880 **2:** 100–108, 130, 133, 135–136, 138–139, 177–179, 182–186, 194–203, 398–399, 426; **3: 129–166**
See also BRW 5; BRWC 1, 2; BRWR 2; CDBLB 1832-1890; CN 7; CPW; DA; DA3; DAB; DAC; DAM MST, NOV; DLB 21, 35, 55; LATS 1; LMFS 1; NCLC 4, 13, 23, 41, 49, 89, 118; NFS 17; PC 20; RGEL 2; RGSF 2; SSFS 8; TEA; WLC; WLIT 3

Emecheta, (Florence Onye) Buchi 1944- **5: 417–432**
See also AFW; BLC 2; BW 2, 3; CA 81-84; CANR 27, 81, 126; CDWLB 3; CLC 14, 48, 128; CN 7; CWRI 5; DA3; DAM MULT; DLB 117; EWL 3; FW; MTCW 1, 2; NFS 12, 14; SATA 66; WLIT 2

Erdrich, Louise 1954- **5: 433–468**
See also AAYA 10, 47; AMWS 4; BEST 89:1; BPFB 1; CA 114; CANR 41, 62, 118; CDALBS; CLC 39, 54, 120, 176; CN 7; CP 7; CPW; CWP; DA3; DAM MULT, NOV, POP; DLB 152, 175, 206; EWL 3; EXPP; LAIT 5; LATS 1; MTCW 1; NFS 5; NNAL; PC 52; PFS 14; RGAL 4; SATA 94, 141; SSFS 14; TCWW 2

F

French, Marilyn 1929- **5: 469–484**
See also BPFB 1; CA 69-72; CANR 3, 31; CLC 10, 18, 60, 177; CN 7; CPW; DAM DRAM, NOV, POP; FW; INT CANR-31; MTCW 1, 2

Fuller, Margaret 1810-1850 **3: 167–198**
See also AMWS 2; CDALB 1640-1865; DLB 1, 59, 73, 183, 223, 239; FW; LMFS 1; NCLC 5, 50; SATA 25

G

Gilman, Charlotte (Anna) Perkins (Stetson) 1860-1935 **1:** 3–5, 314, 325, 462–463; **5: 485–528**
See also AMWS 11; BYA 11; CA 106; 150; DLB 221; EXPS; FW; HGG; LAIT 2; MAWW; MTCW 1; RGAL 4; RGSF 2; SFW 4; SSC 13, 62; SSFS 1, 18; TCLC 9, 37, 117

H

Hansberry, Lorraine (Vivian) 1930-1965 **6: 1–30**
See also AAYA 25; AFAW 1, 2; AMWS 4; BLC 2; BW 1, 3; CA 109; 25-28R; CABS 3; CAD; CANR 58; CDALB 1941-1968; CLC 17, 62; CWD; DA; DA3; DAB; DAC; DAM DRAM, MST, MULT; DC 2; DFS 2; DLB 7, 38; EWL 3; FW; LAIT 4; MTCW 1, 2; RGAL 4; TUS

Head, Bessie 1937-1986 **6: 31–62**
See also AFW; BLC 2; BW 2, 3; CA 29-32R; 119; CANR 25, 82; CDWLB 3; CLC 25, 67; DA3; DAM MULT; DLB 117, 225; EWL 3; EXPS; FW; MTCW 1, 2; RGSF 2; SSC 52; SSFS 5, 13; WLIT 2; WWE 1

Hellman, Lillian (Florence) 1906-1984 **6: 63–88**
See also AAYA 47; AITN 1, 2; AMWS 1; CA 13-16R; 112; CAD; CANR 33; CLC 2, 4, 8, 14, 18, 34, 44, 52; CWD; DA3; DAM DRAM; DC 1; DFS 1, 3, 14; DLB 7, 228; DLBY 1984; EWL 3; FW; LAIT 3; MAWW; MTCW 1, 2; RGAL 4; TCLC 119; TUS

Holley, Marietta 1836(?)-1926 **3: 199–220**
See also CA 118; DLB 11; TCLC 99

Hurston, Zora Neale 1891-1960 **4:** 31–32, 249–251, 485–492; **6: 89–126**
See also AAYA 15; AFAW 1, 2; AMWS 6; BLC 2; BW 1, 3; BYA 12; CA 85-88; CANR 61; CDALBS; CLC 7, 30, 61; DA; DA3; DAC; DAM MST, MULT, NOV; DC 12; DFS 6; DLB 51, 86; EWL 3; EXPN; EXPS; FW; HR 2; LAIT 3; LATS 1; LMFS 2; MAWW; MTCW 1, 2; NFS 3; RGAL 4; RGSF 2; SSC 4; SSFS 1, 6, 11, 19; TCLC 121, 131; TUS; WLCS; YAW

J

Jacobs, Harriet A(nn) 1813(?)-1897 **3: 221–242**
See also AFAW 1, 2; DLB 239; FW; LAIT 2; NCLC 67; RGAL 4

Jewett, (Theodora) Sarah Orne 1849-1909 **3: 243–274**
See also AMW; AMWC 2; AMWR 2; CA 108; 127; CANR 71; DLB 12, 74, 221; EXPS; FW; MAWW; NFS 15; RGAL 4; RGSF 2; SATA 15; SSC 6, 44; SSFS 4; TCLC 1, 22

Juana Inés de la Cruz, Sor 1651(?)-1695 **1: 321–358**
See also FW; HLCS 1; LAW; LC 5; PC 24; RGWL 2, 3; WLIT 1

K

Kempe, Margery 1373(?)-1440(?) **1:** 87, 193, 222, **359–392**
See also DLB 146; LC 6, 56; RGEL 2

Kingston, Maxine (Ting Ting) Hong 1940- **4:** 493–496; **6: 127–150**
See also AAL; AAYA 8, 55; AMWS 5; BPFB 2; CA 69-72; CANR 13, 38, 74, 87, 128; CDALBS; CLC 12, 19, 58, 121; CN 7; DA3; DAM MULT, NOV; DLB 173, 212; DLBY 1980; EWL 3; FW; INT CANR-13; LAIT 5; MAWW; MTCW 1, 2; NFS 6; RGAL 4; SATA 53; SSFS 3; WLCS

L

Lessing, Doris (May) 1919- **4:** 272, 291, 294, 299; **6: 151–178**
See also AFW; BRWS 1; CA 9-12R; CAAS 14; CANR 33, 54, 76, 122; CD 5; CDBLB 1960 to Present; CLC 1, 2, 3, 6, 10, 15, 22, 40, 94, 170; CN 7; DA; DA3; DAB; DAC; DAM MST, NOV; DLB 15, 139; DLBY 1985; EWL 3; EXPS; FW; LAIT 4; MTCW 1, 2; RGEL 2; RGSF 2; SFW 4; SSC 6, 61; SSFS 1, 12; TEA; WLCS; WLIT 2, 4

M

Millay, Edna St. Vincent 1892-1950 **4:** 245, 259; **6: 179–200**
See also AMW; CA 104; 130; CDALB 1917-1929; DA; DA3; DAB; DAC; DAM MST, POET; DLB 45, 249; EWL 3; EXPP; MAWW; MTCW 1, 2; PAB; PC 6; PFS 3, 17; RGAL 4; TCLC 4, 49; TUS; WLCS; WP

Montagu, Mary (Pierrepont) Wortley 1689-1762 **1:** 116, 118–119, 122, 193, 219–220, 225–226, **393–422; 2:** 504, 506
See also DLB 95, 101; LC 9, 57; PC 16; RGEL 2

Moore, Marianne (Craig) 1887-1972 **4:** 244; **6: 201–232**
See also AMW; CA 1-4R; 33-36R; CANR 3, 61; CDALB 1929-1941; CLC 1, 2, 4, 8, 10, 13, 19, 47; DA; DA3; DAB; DAC; DAM MST, POET; DLB 45; DLBD 7; EWL 3; EXPP; MAWW; MTCW 1, 2; PAB; PC 4, 49; PFS 14, 17; RGAL 4; SATA 20; TUS; WLCS; WP

Morrison, Toni 1931- **4:** 349–353; **6: 233–266**
See also AAYA 1, 22; AFAW 1, 2; AMWC 1; AMWS 3; BLC 3; BPFB 2; BW 2, 3; CA 29-32R; CANR 27, 42, 67, 113, 124; CDALB 1968-1988; CLC 4, 10, 22, 55, 81, 87, 173; CN 7; CPW; DA; DA3; DAB; DAC; DAM MST, MULT, NOV, POP; DLB 6, 33, 143; DLBY 1981; EWL 3; EXPN; FW; LAIT 2, 4; LATS 1; LMFS 2; MAWW; MTCW 1, 2; NFS 1, 6, 8, 14; RGAL 4; RHW; SATA 57, 144; SSFS 5; TUS; YAW

O

Oates, Joyce Carol 1938- **6: 267–292**
See also AAYA 15, 52; AITN 1; AMWS 2; BEST 89:2; BPFB 2; BYA 11; CA 5-8R; CANR 25, 45, 74, 113, 129; CDALB 1968-1988; CLC 1, 2, 3, 6, 9, 11, 15, 19, 33, 52, 108, 134; CN 7; CP 7; CPW; CWP; DA; DA3; DAB; DAC; DAM MST, NOV, POP; DLB 2, 5, 130; DLBY 1981; EWL 3; EXPS; FW; HGG; INT CANR-25; LAIT 4; MAWW; MTCW 1, 2; NFS 8; RGAL 4; RGSF 2; SSC 6, 70; SSFS 17; SUFW 2; TUS; WLC

P

Plath, Sylvia 1932-1963 **4:** 297, 463, 466; **6: 293–328**
See also AAYA 13; AMWR 2; AMWS 1; BPFB 3; CA 19-20; CANR 34, 101; CAP 2; CDALB 1941-1968; CLC 1, 2, 3, 5, 9, 11, 14, 17, 50, 51, 62, 111; DA; DA3; DAB; DAC; DAM MST, POET; DLB 5, 6, 152; EWL 3; EXPN; EXPP; FW; LAIT 4; MAWW; MTCW 1, 2; NFS 1; PAB; PC 1, 37; PFS 1, 15; RGAL 4; SATA 96; TUS; WLC; WP; YAW

R

Rich, Adrienne (Cecile) 1929- **4:** 385, 387, 511–521, 524–533; **6: 329–350**
See also AMWR 2; AMWS 1; CA 9-12R; CANR 20, 53, 74, 128; CDALBS; CLC 3, 6, 7, 11, 18, 36, 73, 76, 125; CP 7; CSW; CWP; DA3; DAM POET; DLB 5, 67; EWL 3; EXPP; FW; MAWW; MTCW 1, 2; PAB; PC 5; PFS 15; RGAL 4; WP

Rossetti, Christina (Georgina) 1830-1894 **2:** 136–139; **3: 275–298**
See also AAYA 51; BRW 5; BYA 4; DA; DA3; DAB; DAC; DAM MST, POET; DLB 35, 163, 240; EXPP; LATS 1; MAICYA 1, 2; NCLC 2, 50, 66; PC 7; PFS 10, 14; RGEL 2; SATA 20; TEA; WCH; WLC

S

Sand, George 1804-1876 **3: 299–332**
See also DA; DA3; DAB; DAC; DAM MST, NOV; DLB 119, 192; EW 6; FW; GFL 1789 to the Present; NCLC 2, 42, 57; RGWL 2, 3; TWA; WLC

Sappho fl. 6th cent. B.C. **1: 423–470; 4:** 243, 254, 258, 512; **5:** 334–341; **6:** 538
See also CDWLB 1; CMLC 3, 67; DA3; DAM POET; DLB 176; PC 5; RGWL 2, 3; WP

Sedgwick, Catharine Maria 1789-1867 **2:** 163–165; **3: 333–362**
See also DLB 1, 74, 183, 239, 243, 254; NCLC 19, 98; RGAL 4

Sexton, Anne (Harvey) 1928-1974 **6: 351–388**
See also AMWS 2; CA 1-4R; 53-56; CABS 2; CANR 3, 36; CDALB 1941-1968; CLC 2, 4, 6, 8, 10, 15, 53, 123; DA; DA3; DAB; DAC; DAM MST, POET; DLB 5, 169; EWL 3; EXPP; FW; MAWW; MTCW 1, 2; PAB; PC 2; PFS 4, 14; RGAL 4; SATA 10; TUS; WLC

Shelley, Mary Wollstonecraft (Godwin) 1797-1851 **3: 363–402**
See also AAYA 20; BPFB 3; BRW 3; BRWC 2; BRWS 3; BYA 5; CDBLB 1789-1832; DA; DA3; DAB; DAC; DAM MST, NOV; DLB 110, 116, 159, 178; EXPN; HGG; LAIT 1; LMFS 1, 2; NCLC 14, 59, 103; NFS 1; RGEL 2; SATA 29; SCFW; SFW 4; TEA; WLC; WLIT 3

Staël, Germaine de 1766-1817 **3: 403–426**
See also DLB 119, 192; EW 5; FW; GFL 1789 to the Present; NCLC 3, 91; RGWL 2, 3; TWA

Stanton, Elizabeth Cady 1815-1902 **2:** 7, 59–65, 207–209, 211, 228–229, 231, 233, 235, 237–238, 240, 249–255, 259, 263, 269, 285, 287–290, 292–293; **3: 427–454**
See also CA 171; DLB 79; FW; TCLC 73

Stein, Gertrude 1874-1946 **4:** 272, 278; **6: 389–432**
See also AMW; AMWC 2; CA 104; 132; CANR 108; CDALB 1917-1929; DA; DA3; DAB; DAC; DAM MST, NOV, POET; DC 19; DLB 4, 54, 86, 228; DLBD 15; EWL 3; EXPS; GLL 1; MAWW; MTCW 1, 2; NCFS 4; PC 18; RGAL 4; RGSF 2; SSC 42; SSFS 5; TCLC 1, 6, 28, 48; TUS; WLC; WP

Stowe, Harriet (Elizabeth) Beecher 1811-1896 **2:** 74–75, 127, 147–150, 154–157, 159–165; **3: 455–491**
See also AAYA 53; AMWS 1; CDALB 1865-1917; DA; DA3; DAB; DAC; DAM MST, NOV; DLB 1, 12, 42, 74, 189, 239, 243; EXPN; JRDA; LAIT 2; MAICYA 1, 2; NCLC 3, 50, 133; NFS 6; RGAL 4; TUS; WLC; YABC 1

T

Tan, Amy (Ruth) 1952- **4:** 493–497; **6: 433–464**
See also AAL; AAYA 9, 48; AMWS 10; BEST 89:3; BPFB 3; CA 136; CANR 54, 105; CDALBS; CLC 59, 120, 151; CN 7; CPW 1; DA3; DAM MULT, NOV, POP; DLB 173; EXPN; FW; LAIT 3, 5; MTCW 2; NFS 1, 13, 16; RGAL 4; SATA 75; SSFS 9; YAW

W

Walker, Alice (Malsenior) 1944- **6: 465–494**
See also AAYA 3, 33; AFAW 1, 2; AMWS 3; BEST 89:4; BLC 3; BPFB 3; BW 2, 3; CA 37-40R; CANR 9, 27, 49, 66, 82; CDALB 1968-1988; CLC 5, 6, 9, 19, 27, 46, 58, 103, 167; CN 7; CPW; CSW; DA; DA3; DAB; DAC; DAM MST, MULT, NOV, POET, POP; DLB 6, 33, 143; EWL 3; EXPN; EXPS; FW; INT CANR-27; LAIT 3; MAWW; MTCW 1, 2; NFS 5; PC 30; RGAL 4; RGSF 2; SATA 31; SSC 5; SSFS 2, 11; TUS; WLCS; YAW

Wharton, Edith (Newbold Jones) 1862-1937 **6: 495–534**
See also AAYA 25; AMW; AMWC 2; AMWR 1; BPFB 3; CA 104; 132; CDALB 1865-1917; DA; DA3; DAB; DAC; DAM MST, NOV; DLB 4, 9, 12, 78, 189; DLBD 13; EWL 3; EXPS; HGG; LAIT 2, 3; LATS 1; MAWW;

TITLE INDEX

The Title Index alphabetically lists the titles of works written by the authors featured in volumes 1, 2, 3, 5, and 6 of Feminism in Literature *and provides page numbers or page ranges where commentary on these titles can be found. English translations of foreign titles and variations of titles are cross referenced to the title under which a work was originally published. Titles of novels, dramas, nonfiction books, and poetry, short story, or essay collections are printed in italics; individual poems, short stories, and essays are printed in body type within quotation marks; page references to illustrations appear in italic.*

A

C

D

E

F

G

H

I

M

N

O

P

Q

R

T

U

V

W

Y

Z

SUBJECT INDEX

The Subject Index includes the authors and titles that appear in the Author Index and the Title Index as well as the names of other authors and figures that are discussed in the Feminism in Literature *set. The Subject Index also lists literary terms and topics covered in the criticism, as well as in sidebars. The index provides page numbers or page ranges where subjects are discussed and is fully cross referenced. Page references to significant discussions of authors, titles, or subjects appear in boldface; page references to illustrations appear in italic.*

A

B

SUBJECT INDEX

SUBJECT INDEX

D

SUBJECT INDEX

E

SUBJECT INDEX

G

SUBJECT INDEX

H

I

J

K

SUBJECT INDEX

SUBJECT INDEX

P

SUBJECT INDEX

Q

R

S

T

U

SUBJECT INDEX

X

Y

Z